The Wow Factor

SECOND EDITION

HOW SOCCER EVOLVED . . .
. . . WITHIN THE SOCIAL WEB

By John Blythe Smart

First Edition published in 2003
Second Edition published by Blythe Smart Publications in 2005

A CIP catalogue record for this book is available from the British Library

ISBN 0 - 9545017 - 2 - 1

Typesetters: Originate Design, PO Box 171, Heathfield TN21 8XW
Printers: Short Run Press Limited

Note 1 - The facts and information contained in the book are perceived as correct at the time of printing however this does not preclude any later adjustment in the light of further research. Such alterations would not affect the essence and intention of the work.

Note 2 - There are a number of births, marriages and deaths contained in the book that were obtained from records of Civil Registration. In several instances the quarter date has been used so, for example, June 1865 covers the period April to June 1865.

Blythe Smart Publications
Bay Road, Freshwater, Isle of Wight

CONTENTS

Section II - **The Grounds**

About the Author

John Smart was born at Farnborough in Kent in 1960 and educated at Alleyn's School in south London and then Nottingham University, where he obtained a degree in Historical Geography and History of Architecture. He worked in various jobs including Trading Standards, Accountancy and even apple picking before entering into the world of writing and publishing. Colin Blythe (1879-1917), his great uncle, was a slow bowler for Kent and England and he is also related to Edward Gibbon Blythe and Edmund Henry Niemann who were both 19th century artists - the latter family exhibited at the Royal Academy. More recently his cousin John Spellar was M.P. for Northfield and Warley West near Birmingham. His family supported Millwall F.C. from the 1920s and he began following them in 1970, thus his football experience over the last 35 years provided the initial inspiration for the book. He has also done work as a genealogist in the last 30 years and has been involved in a number of historical projects. He began by writing a book on football grounds entitled *Football Nostalgia* in 1999 and became interested in the lives of the founders of soccer and thus published *The Wow Factor* in 2003. This was followed with a fiction book *The Wizards of Wight* later the same year. It soon became apparent that the first edition of the book had much scope for improvement and after considerable new research the second edition of *The Wow Factor* was published in 2005. The author has travelled widely in England and visited 150 football grounds whilst much of the archive work was done in the various record offices in London. The research for the book also involved travel to Scotland, Gibraltar, Chamonix France, Malta, Norway, New York U.S.A. and New Zealand. The name of *The Wow Factor* is self-explanatory.

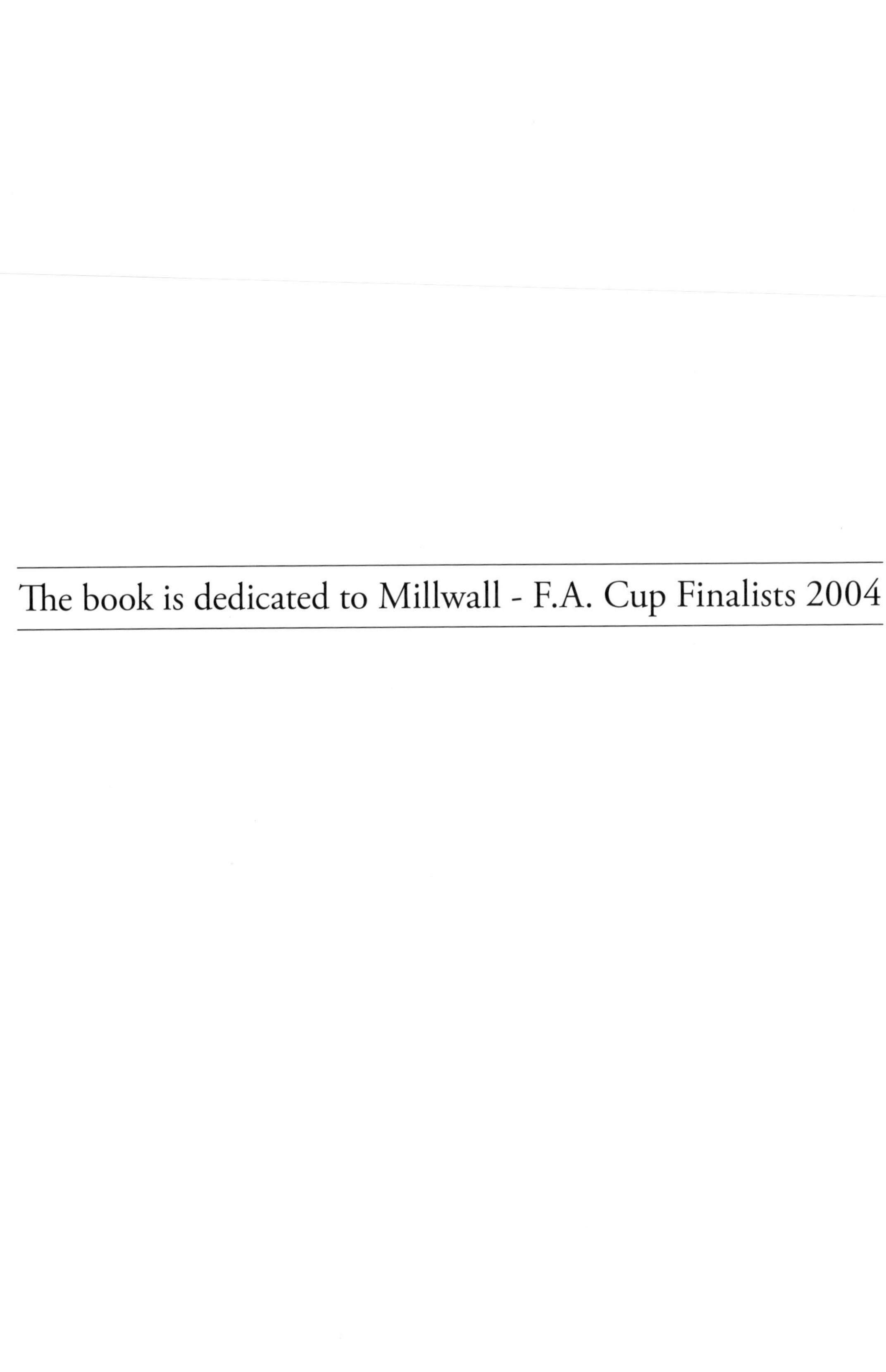

The book is dedicated to Millwall - F.A. Cup Finalists 2004

Quotes of a Historical Nature

A people without history is like wind on the buffalo grass
Sioux proverb

What is past is prologue
William Shakespeare (1564-1616) - playwright

History with all her volumes vast, hath but one page
George Gordon Noel Byron, Lord Byron (1788-1824) - poet

The whole past is the procession of the present
Thomas Carlyle (1795-1881) - Scottish historian and essayist

We learn from history that we learn nothing from history
George Bernard Shaw (1856-1950) - Irish playwright and critic

Human history becomes more and more a race between education and catastrophe - it is in essence a history of ideas
Herbert George Wells (1866-1946) - science fiction writer

The farther backward you can look,
the farther forward you are likely to see
Sir Winston Leonard Spencer-Churchill (1874-1965) - politician

A generation which ignores history has no past and no future
Robert Anson Heinlein (1907-88) - science fiction writer

Football is the opiate of the modern masses
- Anonymous

Acknowledgements

Special thanks go to my wife Glenys Smart who was involved in every stage of the research and editing over several years and many hundreds of hours. Thanks go to - my friend Derek Blow for his football 'chats' and suggestion of the name The 'Wow' Factor, my friend Kevin Scullin for his advice on various historical and literary matters, Chris Ambler for his encouragement and advice on Bradford history and Keith Warsop (author of *The Early F.A. Cup Finals and the Southern Amateurs*) for his explanation of soccer formations and other facts regarding the amateur players. Lastly thanks must go to the many archives, libraries, local record offices and their staff, at home and abroad, that gave valuable assistance in finding the information.

Introspection

The new stands are going up bigger and better than ever before and League football grounds have arrived in the 21st century. Around the country there are an increasing number of impressive new stadiums and visitors to Manchester United and Newcastle United are struck in awe with the sheer scale of the grounds. There has been an opportunity for architects to shine, hence the advanced design at Bolton and Huddersfield. The new grounds provide a modern football experience far removed from that of the past, their striking design and composition being comparable to other architectural wonders. Historically, football grounds grew in response to the local surroundings and the dictates of financial constraints hence the modern venues have a uniformity not seen in the past and lack the quirks of yesteryear. Despite this the new grounds do grow on one and have been discussed in many books on the subject. The aim here is to show the variety of historical grounds, some extraordinary characters in the early game and amazing facts regarding soccer's history.

The busy High Streets are crowded with shoppers and nearby cars hurry to their destinations. There is a distinct lack of fun in these situations, however in the distance there is a glimpse of a floodlight pylon or stand and a movement in that direction thus it seems you are on the right track. The crowd builds in number, the corner is turned, and there is the awesome sight of the football ground. The excitement and anticipation mounts as you push your way through the turnstiles and relief comes as you are in the ground. The steps up to the terrace beckon and the noise of the arena resounds around you, the green of the pitch breaks before your eyes and a 'roar' goes up as the players run out. There are many people in the crowd, mostly unknown, but in the football throng you are at home.

These common sentiments come from around the country, yet there was a time when you attended your first football match and were thrilled by the atmosphere. In some cases you were struck by the vibrant green of the pitch when television and newspapers 'said' football pitches were grey. The national sport was now truly Technicolor. Football seldom disappoints and such sensations and excitement have been repeated through the years and the American saying of 'I just love this sport' can be applied to soccer, however football was once in its infancy and the early history of the game is a fascinating story. Many people and factors had an influence and most of these are explored in the following chapters under six main areas: the early history, the officials, the amateur players, the Football League and grounds, the building of grounds and unusual names-venues. The research of all these subjects provided many new facts and posed some interesting questions:

Who had a religious conversion in 1787 and helped produce the impetus behind the F.A? What role did the Inner Temple have during the early days? What part did upholstery and shipbuilding play in the F.A. Cup? What was the mystery of William Wall of Wormley? Which member of the F.A. provided the inspiration for Sherlock Holmes? Who stood on their head at a Cup Final and supported the Submarine Miners? Which F.A. official was related to Princess Diana? Where do Barclays and Coutts Bank fit in? Which football ground designer learnt his trade at sea? Where was Etruria House and how were the Wedgwoods connected? Who was dubbed the "Prince of Dribblers"? How do Whitbreads and Watneys fit into the football picture? What was the role of the British Empire and India in early football history? How is the principal of dephlogisticated air connected to the story? Who played in the Cup Final and then went up the Zhob Valley? The answers to all of these questions and more are revealed in the following pages, plus their connection to the history of soccer.

THE EARLY DAYS

The origins of soccer can be traced to Shrovetide football played traditionally in English villages on Shrove Tuesday. There was an unmarked pitch that included streams, ponds, roads and cottages and a primitive ball that was carried or kicked between two goals. There were no proper rules and no restriction on the number of participants thus the game provided an opportunity to work out frustrations with your neighbours. This was indeed a very rough pastime and was played in villages throughout the country - the most famous location being Ashbourne in Derbyshire where such a tradition is claimed from 217 A.D. Hopefully the native Britons were already showing the Italians how to play! There is also a yearly re-enactment at Alnwick, Northumberland where the kick-off involves releasing the ball from the castle walls, and other such traditions at Atherstone, Chester, Corfe and Sedgefield. These early players restricted their exploits to Shrove Tuesday and presumably spent the rest of the year growing crops and attending to their animals. There were limited prospects for the game's development in such an arena thus the early history is centred on the sporting activities at England's public schools.

Many of them played football especially Charterhouse, Eton, Harrow, Shrewsbury, Westminster and Winchester although each had different rules. The game was played at Westminster as early as 1710 and the school had to stop boys from wasting time - they were found playing in the cloisters! These games could go on for two-three days (like cricket) and numbers were often unrestricted - the 'Dowling' game at Shrewsbury was 50-a side. The most famous 'primitive' form of soccer was the Eton Wall Game and was played against a wall built in 1717. This took place as early as 1766 and was traditionally played between the *Collegers* and *Oppidans* on St. Andrew's Day (30 November). The first record of these opponents was in 1844 and the rules were formalised in 1849. The game was contested on a pitch 120 yards long, but only six yards wide, next to a wall bordering the college playing fields and was like a long drawn-out rugby scrum. No hands could be used in the play however a 'shy' was scored when the ball was touched against the wall at each end. The team scored 1 point and had a throw at goal (a door and a tree) and if converted they received a further 9 points. The last 'goal' was in 1909 and indeed the tradition is maintained up until today.

The variation of rules at these schools in the mid-19th century meant it was difficult for them to play one another, and the two most controversial issues centred on attitudes towards handling of the ball and rough practices like hacking. There was a famous moment at Rugby School in 1823 when William Webb Ellis (1806-72) picked up the ball and ran with it. Indeed the game of 'rugby' was first played at the school in 1841 and the rules formalised in 1845 and many favoured this code of play rather than that of the Association game (or soccer). Schools such as Eton, however, with their Wall and Field game forbade the use of the hand, whilst Charterhouse and Westminster developed the skill of 'dribbling' to gain possession of the ball (rather than a scrum). The emphasis in the public schools was on the physical aspect and the skills encouraged included mauling, shinning and tagging thus it was not for the feint hearted! Many believed kicking the opponent's legs to obtain the ball was an integral part of the game and a test of resilience and courage. Such practices were connected with other character building ideas at these public schools.

Cambridge University was a centre for the early game and their players attempted to unify the code of play as early as 1846. The students John Charles Thring and Henry De Winton arranged a meeting at Trinity College and compiled the Cambridge Rules in October 1848. They were tried out on Parker's Piece - a flat area of land east of the town centre and surrounded by Georgian and Victorian housing. This swath of soccer history still remains today, being little changed, and there are plans to erect a monument to the Cambridge Rules on the green. John Charles the son of John Gale Dalton Thring rector of Alford, Somerset and Sarah Jenkyns was baptized at Alford on 11 August 1824 - grandfather John was a banker of 'Alford House', Warminster. He matriculated at St. John's, Cambridge in Michaelmas 1843 gaining a B.A. in 1848 and was a curate in 1848-55. His elder brother Edward (1822) gained a B.A. at Cambridge in 1845 and was a curate and private tutor then Headmaster of Uppingham School in 1853-87.

When he arrived the school had 25 boys and two masters in mean premises, but he raised it to a foremost position amongst public schools with 11 boarding houses, 30 masters and 320 boys. He married

Parker's Piece, Cambridge. The Cambridge Rules were tested here in 1848.

Marie L. Koch from Bonn, Rhine in Prussia a naturalised British subject. John joined his brother at the school and was assistant master in 1859-69, then continued his interest in soccer and developed the Uppingham Rules (1862). He was curate of Alford in 1870-74 and of Bradford on Avon in 1875-91 and lived at Chantry House, Bradford in 1881 - he died 2 October 1909. Henry De Winton the son of Walter clerk of Hay Castle and vicar of Llanigen, Brecons was born at Hay-on-Wye in 1822. He matriculated at Trinity, Cambridge in Michaelmas 1842 gaining a B.A. in 1846 and became a deacon in 1848. He was rector of Boughrood, Radnors in 1849-81 and lived at the Rectory with his six children, a governess and four servants in 1881. He was the Archdeacon of Brecon from 1875 and died on 7 April 1895.

The 11 Cambridge Rules were designed for all players and had a number of precepts including a goal scored 'under' the tape, throw-ins from the side and an offside rule (with three players) however this was still unlike modern soccer and permitted the free catch followed by a 'kick' forward. There was much to decide in the early days one important issue being goal size, and (as stated) Eton had a door at one end and a tree at the other. At Harrow the posts were a difficult 12 feet apart and this presented too much of a challenge to some thus if a replay was required the goal size was increased to 24 feet. The Cambridge Rules set a width of 15 feet and the F.A. set the present width of 24 feet in the 1860s, whilst early goals had two uprights with tape across the top (at a height of 8 feet) - so keep the ball down!

Freemasons Tavern, Great Queen Street, Holborn.
The first F.A. meetings took place here in 1863.

The introduction of the Cambridge Rules in 1848 was only the first step and there was a movement to establish the game on a firmer footing in the 1860s. J.C. Thring developed ten rules at Uppingham School (1862) and these were based on his time at Cambridge. No tripping was allowed and Rule III stated: "Kicks must be aimed only at the ball," however there was still a free catch and a player was 'out of play' if in front of the ball. The main developments took place in London and Ebenezer Cobb Morley (1831-1924) the football pioneer led the way. He formed Barnes F.C. at Limes Field in Mortlake, Surrey in 1862 near the old railway bridge (built 1846-49). By a strange coincidence this was next to White Hart Lane and today the truncated Limes Field Road 'witnesses' this historic venue. Under Morley's guidance the Football Association was formed at the Freemasons Tavern, Great Queen Street, London near Lincoln's Inn in 1863 and 12 clubs were at the first meeting: Barnes, Blackheath, Blackheath Proprietary School, Charterhouse School, Crusaders, Crystal Palace, Forest (Leytonstone), Kensington School, No Names Club of Kilburn, Percival House (Blackheath), Surbiton and the War Office Club. The first officials were appointed and 13 rules adopted based on those of Cambridge (1848) and Uppingham (1862). The F.A. rules included the fair catch and did not allow hacking or a forward pass, however a goal was scored when the ball went between the posts (at whatever height).

Barnes played Richmond in the first game under these laws already being old opponents, and were an important club in the early days, since in addition to E.C. Morley (captain) they fielded R.W. Willis and R.G. Graham who were the first three secretaries of the F.A. There was great debate about the rules, which were based on those in Cambridge and the southern game, and the issues of hacking and handling were hotly contested. This dispute threatened to break-up the organisation but eventually both were banned (for outfield players) and this led to the departure of clubs such as Blackheath and Richmond who helped develop rugby. Of course some players still try such antics but these result in an instant caution. Football, meanwhile, also developed in the north and Sheffield F.C. (1857) are the oldest surviving club in the world, whilst Cray Wanderers F.C. (1860) who play at Bromley are the second oldest and Notts County

(1862) the oldest League club. This northern focus resulted in the 'Sheffield Association' who established 11 Rules in 1857. These were different to those in London and allowed charging at the kicker, pushing with the hands and use of the hand to knock the ball on, but running with the ball was strictly forbidden. The first competitive club match is said to be the game between Sheffield and Hallam at the County Cricket Ground, Bramall Lane on 29 December 1862 (see Ch. 1).

THE CUP COMPETITION

The Harrow game involved a knockout competition between the 'Houses' of the school thus Charles Alcock a pupil at Harrow and early member of the F.A., realised such a contest would work for the Association clubs and it was used as the basis for the F.A. Cup. There was a meeting at the Sportsman Newspaper, Ludgate Hill to establish the competition on 20 July 1871 and it was called the F.A. Challenge Cup or simply 'The Cup'. The first contest took place in 1871-72 but only 15 clubs entered from the 50 members, since the gentlemen feared such games would lead to excessive rivalry - the passion the Cup invokes suggests they were quite correct. The first fifteen participants came mainly from London and the south east viz. Barnes, Civil Service, Clapham Rovers, Crystal Palace, Donington Grammar, Hampstead Heathens, Harrow Chequers, Hitchin, Maidenhead, Marlow, Queen's Park (Scotland), Reigate Priory, Royal Engineers, Upton Park and the Wanderers (Forest Club). Donington Grammar School was one exception being located between Boston and Spalding whilst only Maidenhead and Marlow have entered the Cup every year since it started.

These were, however, the formative years of the Cup and it was not run on the basis that it is today. The first competition included Queen's Park, a Scottish club, who were unable to find adequate opposition north of the border and thus entered the English contest. In the first round Donington and Queen's Park received a bye thus they met in the second but the Scottish side had a walk over and indeed the school never entered again. Queen's Park received another bye in the third round and reached the semi-final without kicking a ball. They travelled to the Oval to play the game (0-0 draw) but could not afford another journey to London and withdrew, thus their opponents the Wanderers went through with a walk over.

The first Cup Final was contested between the Wanderers and the Royal Engineers at the Oval in front of 2,000 spectators and Morton Peto Betts of the Wanderers scored the only goal, although one player disputed this (discussed later). Betts played the game under the name A.H. Chequer a synonym for A Harrow Chequer - the team he had begun the tournament with. He was a member of the F.A. Committee and helped organise the Cup however all was legal since the Harrow Chequers withdrew from the contest in the first round - needless to say players can no longer swap teams and are also Cup-tied. Indeed the 1872-73 Cup was even more extraordinary and the Wanderers received a bye all the way to the Final. Their opponents Oxford University had a more strenuous task and beat Crystal Palace 3-2, Clapham Rovers 3-0, Royal Engineers 1-0, Maidenhead 4-0 and had a walk over against Queen's Park. The Final was played at Lillie Bridge near Fulham in front of 3,000 with a morning kick-off so the players could watch the Boat Race in the afternoon, however Oxford were exhausted by their efforts and lost the game 2-0.

This was a time when the amateur players went on to manage the F.A. and this could have led to accusations of impropriety, however the early problems were mainly administrative since the concept of the Cup was ground breaking at the time. There were several unusual entrants in the Cup in 1872-73 including the 1st Surrey Rifles, South Norwood and Windsor Home Park and the pattern continued in 1873-74 with teams such as Brondesbury, Farningham and Uxbridge as well as the Swifts and Sheffield F.C. The rules of the Football Association (and the southern clubs) were combined with those of the northern game, in 1877, to form the basis of the modern Association game and this hastened the arrival of northern clubs in the Cup (1878-79). Only a few teams were prepared to make the long journey south namely Darwen, Notts County and Nottingham Forest and the latter two met in the first round Forest winning 3-1 (in extra time). Darwen reached the quarter final in 1879 but there was consternation at the F.A. over their use of paid Scottish players, whilst Reading also played in the competition. The big guns Aston Villa, Blackburn Rovers and an early Birmingham side arrived in 1879-80 and Forest again played County this time beating them 4-0. Indeed the dominance of the amateur clubs in the competition was soon to end.

THE OLD BOY NETWORK

In addition to Barnes a number of amateur clubs made their mark viz. Wanderers, Royal Engineers, Old Carthusians, Old Etonians, Clapham Rovers, Oxford University and Queen's Park. All these played a significant role in the formative years of the game and their brief history follows below. The original Wanderers were formed as Forest F.C. at Snaresbrook, Epping Forest in 1859 and played in the 'attractive' orange, violet and black, whilst the club's founders were Old Harrovians (see Alcock Ch. 2). They changed their name to the Wanderers and moved to the attractive location of Battersea Park, south London in 1864 and a player Vidal said he preferred it to any other venue. The Wanderers moved to the Oval in 1870 and won the F.A. Cup a remarkable five times in the first seven years (1872, 1873, 1876, 1877 and 1878) winning it outright after three victories, but being gentlemen returned it to the F.A. They had a double *University Challenge* in 1877 beating Cambridge 1-0 in the semi-final and Oxford 2-1 in the Final. They fielded Alfred Kinnaird, C.H.R. Wollaston (who took part in all the Cup Finals) and A.G. Guillemard the founder of Rugby Union, however the team dispersed in c.1881 and their players moved to various old boys teams. Barnes had a similar fate and played their last Cup tournament in 1886-87.

The Royal Engineers were an army football team at Chatham in Kent although all their players were officers who were educated at public school (see later). The Engineers appeared in four Cup Finals from 1872-78 however their only success was in 1875 when they beat Marlow 3-0, Cambridge University 5-0, Clapham Rovers 3-2 and Oxford University 1-0 (after 1-1). Some of these games became epic struggles against old foes and in the Final the Engineers beat the Old Etonians 2-0 after a 1-1 draw (with extra time). The most notable player with the Royal Engineers was Major Francis Arthur Marindin their captain who was elected F.A. President in 1874, whilst later success included winning the Amateur Cup in 1908.

Charterhouse was established in what was once a Carthusian monastery and their old boys formed the Old Carthusians soccer team. They won the F.A. Cup in 1881 beating Darwen 4-1 in the semi-final and the Old Etonians 3-0 in the Final and won the Amateur Cup in 1894/97. They had four international players and Charles Wreford Brown who was born Clifton (then Gloucester-shire) in 1867, played for England in 1889, and was credited with the invention of the word 'soccer'. Alfred Kinnaird was founder and captain of their rivals the Old Etonians who were formed at Cambridge University in 1867. He was one of the best amateur players later becoming F.A. President (1890-1923). They went on to dominate English football and appeared in six Cup Finals from 1875-83 winning against Clapham Rovers in 1879 (1-0) and the mighty Blackburn Rovers in 1882 (1-0).

Clapham Rovers, a gentlemen's club, reached the semi-final in 1874 and were runners-up in 1879. They also reached the Final in 1880 and on the way defeated Romford 7-0, South Norwood 4-1, Pilgrims 7-0, Hendon 2-0, Old Etonians 1-0, and had a bye in the semi-final (Romford and Hendon being earlier incarnations of the present day clubs). Rovers were victorious in the Final and beat Oxford University 1-0 in front of 6,000 spectators - a crowd that reveals the game's growth. Charles Alcock explains that C.C. Dacre of Clapham Rovers took the dribbling game to New Zealand although the country was a stronghold of rugby in 1894. Charles Craven Dacre was born in Sydney in 1848 but went to Auckland in 1859 and was then educated at Clapham Grammar School. He was found to be an excellent 'dribbler' and played for his school and for Clapham Rovers. He returned to Auckland in c.1870 and started a soccer team plus an inter-provincial contest between Auckland, Wellington, Canterbury and Otago.

Oxford University took part in four Cup Finals from 1873-80 and like the Old Etonians included players from the Wanderers side. They lost to the Wanderers in the 1873 Final despite having beaten the Engineers in an earlier round then met the Royal Engineers in the 1874 Final itself. The army team was the strongest side at the time and their strikers were free scoring beating Brondesbury 5-0, Uxbridge 2-1, Maidenhead 7-0 and Swifts 2-0 (neutral ground) however Oxford won the Final at the Oval 2-0 - a result that showed the strength of the university side. Queen's Park, Scotland's oldest club, were formed in 1867 and provided the basis of the early Scottish team being strongest in the 1880s. They reached two Finals but lost both to Blackburn Rovers (1884, 2-1 and 1885, 2-0) and were most unhappy when Major Marindin the referee disallowed two goals in 1884. They believed they would have won but for these decisions and the Cup would have gone to Scotland. Queen's Park was the last of the amateur clubs to appear in a Cup Final but they continued to be important and developed Hampden Park from 1903.

Football always had some fascinating characters and this was true during the early years when the founders had interests of a multifarious nature viz. Ebenezer Cobb Morley the 'Father of Football' had a prominent role in rowing and athletics, established the first set of laws for soccer and was F.A. Secretary (1863-66) and President (1867-74). Many amateur players, however, made their mark at the F.A. and Charles Alcock, Major Marindin and Alfred Kinnaird were three of the most prominent. Each had a different background but all of them were far from ordinary. Charles Alcock started Forest F.C. with his brother John Forster (not James as in some sources) and came to the fore through his association with the

Wanderers. He was F.A. Secretary in 1870-95 and as Secretary of Surrey County Cricket Club played a role in bringing football to the Oval, whilst his career as a journalist gave the game publicity through papers such as 'The Sportsman'.

Major Francis Arthur Marindin was captain and full back of the Royal Engineers and played for them in the Cup Finals of 1872 and 1874. He was also goalkeeper for the Old Etonians and it is often noted how he had a problem when the sides met in the 1875 Final. He promptly withdrew from the game to avoid causing offence to either party and was commended for putting honour before his own personal gain, however, it seems likely this event did not happen and K. Warsop explains that Marindin was in fact away at Harwich at the time. Indeed such romantic versions of soccer are debated throughout the book and Marindin himself would want the truth, without undue credit. He was a referee at nine F.A. Cup Finals (1880, 1884-90 - replay 1886) and also for the international at the Oval on 6 March 1875. He was described as "one of the very few referees who really know all the rules," and there have been many games since where supporters might have wished he was in charge. He was F.A. President from 1874-90 but being a staunch promoter of the amateur game resigned after the arrival of the professionalism.

These were gay days at the F.A. and no character was more remarkable than 'Alfred' Kinnaird or to give him his full title Lord Arthur Fitzgerald Kinnaird. He was a tall bearded sportsman who took part in nine F.A. Cup Finals (but not the first) and won five winners medals with the Wanderers and Old Etonians. He played for the latter when they beat Blackburn Rovers 1-0 in the 1882 Final and was remembered for his exuberant celebrations, then became 11th Lord Kinnaird in 1887 and was F.A. President from 1890-1923. His playing career also involved appearances for the Scottish national side, his family coming from Perth, whilst he was a gentleman involved in many activities (see Ch. 5). His contribution was honoured when he was presented with the second F.A. Cup trophy in 1911 (then replaced by the third).

The English F.A. became the blueprint for similar organisations around the world and the Scottish F.A. was formed in 1873 and the Welsh in 1876. The Scottish Cup began in 1874 and 16 clubs entered whilst Queen's Park won the first three competitions without conceding a goal - 1874 Clydesdale 2-0, 1875 Renton 3-0 and 1876 Third Lanark 2-0. They let in their first goal in the 1876-77 Cup semi-final when they lost to Vale of Leven. A Scottish League was formed in 1890 and the 11 original members were: Abercorn, Cambuslang, Celtic, Cowlairs, Dumbarton, Heart of Midlothian, Rangers, Renton, St. Mirren, Third Lanark and Vale of Leven. The contest in 1890-91 was not settled conclusively hence Dumbarton were the first League champions in 1891-92. The club played at Boghead Park from 1879 and this later became the oldest Scottish ground (in continuous use), whilst Queen's Park retained their amateur status and only joined the League in 1900.

THE PROFESSIONAL GAME

There were some major changes in England after the arrival of northern clubs in the Cup in 1878, and this caused quite a stir, thus the debate regarding paid players soon dominated soccer. The F.A. and others feared that money in the game would lead to a decline in the ethics of play, which in turn would compromise the founders' high ideals. The most significant game regarding this matter was the Cup quarter final between Darwen and the Old Etonians in 1879. The Lancashire club had attracted Scottish players Jimmy Love and Fergie Suter with financial incentives and the game turned into a lengthy struggle settled over three meetings at the Oval. The inhabitants of Darwen, a relatively poor community, were gripped by 'Cup Fever' and undeterred by the costs made public collections to fund the trips. In fact the expense of sending the team to London, three times, was huge and was more than a fare to the other side of the world. The northern side had a disadvantage since the games should have been played at club venues but all took place at the Oval. The first game was a 5-5 draw (with four goals in the last 15 minutes) and the second a 2-2 draw (after extra time) however Darwen were exhausted with all the travelling and the Old Etonians won the last game by a comfortable 6-2 score line.

The victors defeated Nottingham Forest and Clapham Rovers to win the Cup however Darwen were accused of playing a 'professional' game and trouble was in the air. Forest reached the semi-final again in 1880 and Darwen in 1881 whilst other Scottish players came to the northern clubs therefore the F.A. formed a sub-Committee to investigate the 'problem' in 1882. Blackburn Rovers were one of the first teams found guilty of paying players and this was followed by the expulsion of Accrington from the Cup in 1883, whilst the contest between Upton Park and Preston North End brought further accusations of professional play in 1884. Preston openly defied the F.A. and "Major" William Sudell their manager admitted to paying players, saying he had to do it to maintain the club's status. The F.A. initially banned

Preston from the Cup but there was mounting pressure from the northern clubs.

William McGregor (1846-1911). He established the Football League in 1888.

The F.A. wanted to maintain the amateur game and the high ideals of the founders, but also realised the amateur clubs could no longer beat the northern professional outfits. New names then appeared on the F.A. Cup trophy and the first break-through was in 1882 with Blackburn Rovers runners-up to the Old Etonians. Their rivals Blackburn Olympic formed in 1878 and reached the Final in 1883 beating Accrington 6-3, Lower Darwen 8-1, Darwen Ramblers 8-0, Church 2-0, Druids 4-1 and Old Carthusians 4-0 (at the Oval) although most of these games were against local teams. The side consisted of plumbers and weavers trained by halfback Jack Hunter who took them to Blackpool to prepare for the Final against the Old Etonians. The game was at the Oval in front of 8,000 spectators and the amateurs took the lead in the first half and would have gone two up but Kinnaird had a goal disallowed (scored direct from a free kick). Olympic scored twice, once in extra time, and won the game taking the Cup 'up north' for the first time. The amateur days were over and the F.A. was forced to concede hence the professional game was sanctioned at Anderton's Hotel, Fleet Street in London on 20 July 1885.

Blackburn Rovers emerged as the premier team in the town (and the country) winning the F.A. Cup in 1884, 1885 and 1886 since it was then legal to run a club on a professional basis. The controversy continued, however, and Major Marindin a leading advocate of the amateur game resigned as F.A. President over the issue in 1890 whilst a temporary split occurred between the amateur and professional game in 1906. There were further arguments regarding the penalty kick, which was opposed by amateur clubs who believed it questioned their sportsmanship. The Corinthians, in particularly, were peeved by the rule and their goalkeeper would stand defiantly by the goalpost while the spot kick was taken. The first ever penalty was scored by J. Heath of Wolves against Accrington on 14 September 1891.

The Football League came into existence due to the efforts of William McGregor in 1888 and was a separate organisation from the start. Gregor McGregor tailor married Jean McNicol at Muthill, Perth on 5 June 1825 and a son William was born there on 27 January 1846 - the youngest of nine children. He also became a tailor and left Perth in his twenties to open a drapers shop in Birmingham. William McGregor of Albert Road, Aston married Jessie Scrimgeour from Moneydie, Perth at St Peters and St Paul's, Aston on 13 January 1876. Indeed the church overlooked the Lower Aston Grounds where Villa began playing in 1875. He was a busy man being an umpire, district organiser and charity worker and was described as, "A bearded Scotsman of liberal beliefs with considerable energy and humour." He was interested in local football at the Lower Aston Grounds and joined the Aston Villa F.C. Committee, the club moving to Wellington Road, Perry Barr not far from his home in 1876. He was a supporter of the Cup but not a football player like his counterparts in the south and had a questionable constitution stating: "I've never taken part in active football. I tried it once when young and had to take to bed for a week."

William and his brother Peter McGregor (1836), linen drapers, traded at 131 Gooch Street and 306-307 Summer Lane in 1880 whilst John McGregor, linen draper, was at 112 Gerrard Street, Birmingham (possibly related). William a draper employing five assistants resided at 301 Summer Lane, Birmingham in 1881 with wife Jessie and children William Gregor and Jessie Murray. It was from this background that he promoted the formation of a Football League. McGregor believed a contest was needed like that operating for cricket (since 1873) and only under these conditions would it develop and prosper, whilst he took further inspiration from the American Baseball League. He sent a letter to Aston Villa, Blackburn Rovers, Bolton Wanderers, Preston North End and West Bromwich Albion on 2 March 1888 stating: "I beg to tender the following suggestion.... that ten or twelve of the most prominent clubs in England combine to arrange home and away fixtures each season...."

There was a meeting of interested parties at Anderton's Hotel, Fleet Street on 23 March 1888 - the Cup Final being played the next day between Preston North End and West Bromwich Albion. Initially it was to be called "The Association Football Union" but this was replaced by the "Football League" and a second meeting took place at the Royal Hotel, Piccadilly, Manchester on 17 April 1888, as no southern club expressed any interest at all. After a study of Cup fixtures, and the like, it was found there were 22 free days in the season and 12 out of 15 applicants were admitted: Accrington, Aston Villa, Blackburn Rovers, Bolton Wanderers, Burnley, Derby County, Everton, Notts County, Preston North End, Stoke, West Bromwich Albion & Wolverhampton Wanderers. Major Sudell manager of Preston gave them the grand title: "The Founder Members of the Football League" whilst the teams that lost out were Halliwell, Nottingham Forest and the Wednesday. The League kicked off under the guidance of William McGregor on 8 September 1888 and his vision was soon a great success, whilst new impetus came to the F.A. Cup and the Final of 1889 had the first attendance of over 20,000.

The southern clubs continued to play on an amateur basis however the Royal Arsenal turned professional in 1891 followed by Millwall (1893) and Southampton (1894). The F.A. Cup had grown rapidly from its beginnings and a crowd of 32,810 were at the Oval in 1892, far too many for the cricket ground, thus the Final moved to a purpose built venue at the Crystal Palace in 1895. The crowds continued to increase and 114,815 watched the Final between Tottenham and Sheffield United in 1901. The game was replayed at Burnden Park, Bolton and Tottenham won 3-1 to become the only non-League winners of the Cup in the 20th century. There was a crowd of 101,117 in 1905 to see Aston Villa beat Newcastle United 2-0. William McGregor watched the League flourish with many new grounds and his own team Aston Villa were champions in 1894, 1896, 1897, 1899, 1900 and 1910. He lived at Summer Lane, Birmingham in 1904 and was a 'Life Member' of the Football League but died at 70 Newhall Street on 20 December 1911 aged 65. He was then a retired draper of 8 Salisbury Road, Birchfields, Handsworth and lived with his son in law Ernest Hinchley, the husband of daughter Jessie.

The game continued to grow after his death and a world record crowd of 121,919 saw Aston Villa beat rivals Sunderland 1-0 in the 1913 Cup Final. These were the teams of the moment and soon after Sunderland won the League just 4 points ahead of Villa however the ultimate crowd came when the Final moved to Wembley in 1923. There was an official attendance of 126,047 (close to the capacity) but it was estimated that about 250,000 descended upon the ground. Bolton Wanderers beat West Ham United 2-0 however with such a crowd it was a miracle the game went ahead and the ball bounced back into play off a wall of spectators. As a result of these problems the Wembley Finals were made all ticket affairs and never again exceeded 100,000 and were reduced to around 79,000 in the 1990s.

THE INTERNATIONAL GAME

So was there anything about early football that didn't begin in England? Indeed, the answer was no, and international football started at the Oval with an unofficial game between England and Scotland in 1870. Charles Alcock and England won the contest 1-0 whilst Alfred Kinnaird captained the Scottish side. The first full international was played between England and Scotland at the West of Scotland Cricket Ground, Hamilton Crescent, Glasgow, on 30 November 1872 and was a 0-0 draw. Queen's Park F.C. organised the fixture and the Scottish side was composed entirely of their players - England and Scotland are the oldest such sides in the world. These contests were keenly fought with large crowds especially in Scotland, and the Corinthians F.C. was formed in 1882 with the express aim of developing a 'club' side to challenge Scotland. The first games between England, Scotland, Wales and Ireland were 'friendly' but the British Championships or Home Internationals began in 1884 (England's 20th game) and England beat Ireland 8-1 in Belfast, lost to Scotland 1-0 at Cathkin Park and beat Wales 4-0 at the Racecourse Ground, Wrexham.

England was the most successful of the home countries in the 1890s and superior to continental opposition during occasional foreign tours until the 1920s. The first 'true' international was at the Cricketer Platz, Wien (Vienna) on 6 June 1908 and England defeated Osterreich (Austria) 6-1 in front of 3,500 spectators. This historic game was played during the first official foreign tour to the Austro-Hungarian Empire. There was a return match in Vienna on 8 June, a game against Hungary in Budapest on 10 June and finally a game in Prague on 13 June (the city was in Bohemia and part of the Austro-Hungarian Empire until 1919 - Czech capital). There was also a foreign tour in 1909 with games in Budapest on 29 and 31 May and a final game in Vienna on 1 June but these were the only England internationals on the Continent before the First War.

Some unusual venues were used for early internationals and quite often these were the grounds of newly emerging clubs. The West of Scotland Cricket Ground was used in 1872, 1874 and 1876, the 1st Hampden Park in 1878, 1880 and 1882 and Cathkin Park in 1884. Queen's Park developed the latter as the 2nd Hampden Park in October 1884 and it was used for further internationals in 1886, 1888 and 1890 (attendance of 26,379). The Racecourse Ground Wrexham was used 12 times from 1880 to 1912 and all these statistics relate to games against England, whilst the Oval was used 10 times from 1873-90. Other venues used before 1890 were Alexandra Meadows Blackburn (1881), Bramall Lane (1883/87), Leamington Street Blackburn (1885/87), Nantwich Road Crewe (1888), Victoria Ground Stoke (1889) and Anfield Road (1889) whilst further choices were Aigburth Cricket Ground south Liverpool (1883) and Whalley Range Manchester (1885). In later years, however, two international venues really stand out these being Richmond Athletic Ground used in 1893 (see Alcock Ch. 3) and Queen's Club at West Kensington used in 1895. The Corinthians played at the latter and fielded the full England side in 1894 and 1895, which explains this choice whilst the Oxford v Cambridge varsity match was at the Oval in 1873-87 and then at the Queen's Club until at least 1903.

An unofficial soccer tournament was played at the Olympics after they re-started in Athens in 1896 and amateur club Upton Park who played in the first F.A. Cup represented Britain and won at Athens in 1896 and at Paris in 1900, whilst Galt F.C. (Canada) won at St. Louis, Missouri in 1904. According to Charles Alcock: "The game of football was well established in Canada and had even reached the western shores of that great continent." Mount Vesuvius had erupted in 1906 causing chaos in Italy thus Rome declined to hold the 1908 Olympics and they were transferred to London. Soccer was then an official sport in the Olympic games and Great Britain beat Denmark 2-0 at the White City Stadium, London to win gold in 1908 - the bronze going to the Netherlands. The games were a success but there was controversy when the marathon distance was changed from 24.8 miles to 26 miles (the distance to Windsor) - 385 yards were then added to reach the Royal box! Great Britain beat Denmark 4-2 at Stockholm to win the gold again in 1912 with the bronze to the Netherlands. There were three more soccer contests at the Olympics, the medals:

1920 Antwerp	Belgium by forfeit, Spain, Netherlands
1924 Paris	Uruguay 3-0, Switzerland, Sweden
1928 Amsterdam	Uruguay 1-1, 2-1, Argentina, Italy

F.I.F.A. the organisation of international football was formed in 1904 and the first meeting took place in Paris with Belgium, Denmark, France, Netherlands, Spain, Sweden and Switzerland represented. England lagged behind in Europe as usual and only joined in 1906 but then proceeded to have a prominent role in its affairs. A World Cup was discussed by F.I.F.A. as early as 1904 however only began when Uruguay agreed to host the contest in 1930, clearly after their Olympic success. The English F.A. had several disputes with F.I.F.A. in Zurich and as a consequence withdrew from 1918-22 and again in 1928. As a result England did not play in any World Cup Finals until 1950 and the supposed invincibility of the national side was never properly tested.

After the Second War there was a 'golden era' for English clubs however the national team was under scrutiny. The U.S.A. was not regarded as a football nation but reached the semi-final of the 1930 World Cup. Tom Finney, Wilf Mannion, Stan Mortensen and Billy Wright all played for England and took on the U.S.A. in the 1950 contest the result being considered a foregone conclusion, however the U.S.A. won the game 1-0 and England's chance in the competition ended. The problem was compounded with home defeats against Ireland in 1949 (2-0) and the notorious thrashing by Hungary in 1953 (6-3). England was no longer the undisputed champion of the world but of course this was all put right in 1966. The country continued to have a prominent role in world affairs and Sir Stanley Rous was F.A. Secretary in 1934-61 and F.I.F.A. President in 1961-74 whilst the World Cup trophy was named after the President, Jules Rimet.

The F.A. Cup, Football League and international games were established however there was more to soccer than teams and promoters. The emerging clubs had to find grounds at which to play these fixtures and many were unusual to say the least. There was seldom enough land available and clubs had to settle for what was on offer; factors and constraints that dictated ground development for years to come and fashioned many familiar grounds. In fact the majority of League clubs had a number of early grounds often with basic facilities and would soon outgrow their venues. They would move to a more suitable site or at least to something they could afford and development was on a piece-meal basis, unlike the purpose built stadiums of the modern era. Money was the main factor and new stands were often built after selling a top player or a good Cup run thus, like individuals, these grounds developed a number of idiosyncrasies. These 'strange but true' features are highlighted later and include: the first twelve grounds, Cup venues, London grounds, the Kop grounds, the Leitch grounds, shared cricket venues and remarkable stands.

The period since the 1980s was one of great change and many old grounds and terraces were consigned to history, although some remain. Today the majority of grounds are just for football, however the idea of the multi-purpose stadium began early and many of the first grounds were combined with other sports. They often had a running and cycle track around them and shared with athletics, cricket and cycling although early conflicts with rugby meant these sports seldom shared venues. If no flat site was available a man-made excavation was used and many a famous club began life in a quarry or on a vegetable patch. Football's growth was phenomenal a fact shown by Cup Final attendances. In the 1870s there were no more than 5,000 spectators however the figures had reached 20,000 plus by 1889 and 40,000 plus by 1893. The growth was exponential and there were over 65,000 in 1897 and nearly 115,000 in 1901.

The attendance figures at club level were equally amazing and even in the 19th century there could be large crowds, however the early grounds were basic and as a result struggled to cope with these attendances. Many of the records in the 20th century were set in Manchester and Maine Road, opened in 1923, had an estimated capacity of 80-90,000 making it the largest English club ground. The record club attendance of 84,569 took place there on 3 March 1934 during a Cup-tie between Manchester City and Stoke whilst the record for a League game of 83,260 occurred there on 17 January 1948 during a Division One game between Manchester United and Arsenal (Old Trafford had to be repaired after war damage). The club record in London of 82,905 was at Stamford Bridge on 12 October 1935 during a Division One game between Chelsea and Arsenal.

All football clubs have record attendances but none is more remarkable than that for Doncaster Rovers. Their ground Belle Vue Stadium was developed with extensive banking on three sides and had a record attendance of 37,149 in October 1948 during a Division Three (North) game v Hull City. The Doncaster side finished third that season with 50 points whilst Hull were champions with 65 points and Doncaster also played in Division Two in the 1950s. The club and ground, however, then went into a decline and the earth banking was redundant in the 1990s hence the capacity was reduced to around 6,500. There are other similar records and Mr. A.E. Jones wrote a letter to the *Halifax Evening Courier* on 20 April 1911 leading to a public meeting at the Saddle Hotel on 23 May, thus Halifax Town were formed. The Shay was developed in a natural hollow on the site of a former Council rubbish tip, the name coming from the local area Shay Syke, and the club moved there in 1921 when they were founders of Division Three (North). There was banked terracing at the ends and on the Skircoat Road Side, the latter covered with a stand taken from Hyde Road, Manchester in 1923, whilst the shape was determined by speedway introduced in 1948-51 (and after 1965). The club played Tottenham there in the fifth round of the Cup on 15 February 1953 in front of 36,885, which must have been quite a squeeze on the earth-banked terraces.

Crystal Palace and Millwall set the Fourth Division record of 37,774 at Selhurst Park on 31 March 1961 (Good Friday) - a record that can never be beaten. At the other end of the scale were little known League club Thames F.C. who played at West Ham Greyhound Stadium just to the south of Upton Park. A crowd of just 469 turned up there in 1930 for a Division Three (South) game against Luton Town and this stands as the lowest League crowd ever seen on a Saturday afternoon. Indeed soccer history contains many extraordinary facts regarding the founders of the game and the grounds where they played - these are explored in detail in the following chapters.

SECTION I

The Players

CHAPTER 1

The Barnes Football Association

The previous section provides a brief summary of the history of our national game and the facts mentioned can be read in most books on the subject. The games founders were ordinary people with diverse personalities and had much to commend them however they were clearly far from perfect. Despite this, official publications give a biased view of these gentlemen players with a 'glow' around them and are often limited in their extent. The following chapters aim to investigate the true story behind these people since there was far more to them than meets the eye, thus the true driving force behind soccer can finally be revealed. The following accounts are of a genealogical nature and give real substance to the lives of notable people, whilst most facts have not seen the light of day for 100 years and are truly illuminating. These ten chapters re-write football history and discuss the F.A. Officials, the Wanderers, the Royal Engineers and the first Cup Final. The book focuses on the early period thus the debate is limited to the first five secretaries and presidents of the F.A. These men shaped football during its development and growth (1863-1937) hence the 'modern era' is after the Second War.

EBENEZER COBB MORLEY

All football histories begin with Ebenezer Cobb Morley and this is a basic fact that cannot be changed however we can ask a few searching questions about him. What was it that set him apart? What gave him his sporting drive and ambition? Why was he the leading force behind the growth of soccer? The following history will show that the answer is clear and that his sense of purpose came from a religious background and in particular nonconformist Christianity. Indeed the Victorians had strong values and drives and much has been written of their ambiguous moral values. In the middle of the 19th century there was a concept going around called "Muscular Christianity" that had clear objectives although slightly patronising overtones. It was thought that sporting activity was good for body and soul and would keep people away from more dubious activities and vices - clearly in the public school tradition of 'we'll make a man of you!' The Victorians were clearly on the right lines and in modern times the benefits of sporting activity have been proven. Indeed much has been written about the high ideals of the founders who aimed to develop a game for gentlemen and many of them were dashing sportsmen, however not all were convinced about soccer and the following statement was made: "Rugby is a game of hooligans played by gentlemen, soccer is a game of gentlemen played by hooligans."

Ebenezer Cobb Morley was no hooligan and his ancestry is traced to grandfather John Morley who was born in London on 27 September 1770 and became a preacher in the Congregational Church. John Morley, son of John and Margaret, was baptized at St. James' Garlickhithe, London on 15 April 1770 and this may have been him since no others fitted however the dates question the accuracy. The Congregational Year Book (1864) gives a good account of his life and begins with his baptism (although this may have been an adult one): "It was carried out by Andrew Kinsman a coadjutor of Whitefield in the Tabernacle House." George Whitefield (1714-70) was involved in the growth of 'Calvinistic' Methodism and as an evangelical Christian believed in, "A religion of the feelings in a period of rationalist enlightenment." Charles and John Wesley had religious conversions in 1738 however their 'Arminian' Methodism was strictly a rival to Whitefield's faith.

The Tabernacle was built in Tabernacle Street near Finsbury Square, north London in the 1740s whilst Wesley's Chapel was built 40 years later between Tabernacle Street and City Road - a fact that leads to some confusion. Whitefield's Tabernacle was later part of the Central Foundation School at the junction of Tabernacle and Leonard Streets whilst Wesley's Chapel remains on City Road. The Tabernacle registers start on 16 May 1768 and George Whitefield carried out the first two baptisms whilst Andrew Kinsman performed five baptisms in 1776-86 but that of John Morley is not recorded. George Whitefield died on 30 September 1770 three days after Morley's birth and for those believing in re-incarnation he could be considered his spiritual successor.

John Morley wrote that his parents intended him for a career in business but at 17 he experienced salvation and recorded that: "The thunder rolled tremendously loud and the lightnings flashed vividly; there was an earthquake in my conscience and I feared the earth would open and swallow me up." He then found himself in a dark place until in his own words: "My mind was set at happy liberty under a sermon preached in the Tabernacle by the Rev. Edward Parsons of Leeds from Acts 13th, 38 and 39 verses." His relief of mind was at hand and he said: "The reading of the text melted me into tears and every sentence in the sermon came with holy unction to my spirit." The whole direction of his life was altered and he shortly came into connection with the fellowship of Spa Fields Chapel at the junction of Spa Field Street and Exmouth Street (Market), Clerkenwell. The chapel was a devotee of the Countess of Huntingdon's Connexion - a denomination that followed the same Calvinistic Methodism as Whitefield.

The children of George and Jane Morley were baptized at Spa Fields Chapel in 1786-89 and it is likely these were his relatives. Meanwhile he gained his early training at Spa Fields and then entered his public ministry in November 1793. He was ordained pastor of the Independent Church at Alford in Lincolnshire, which was also under the patronage of the Countess of Huntingdon's Connexion and remained there from 1793-1800. He was then invited to preach at Thorngumbald near Hull, a small chapel being erected in the village at the time under benefactor Sir S. Handidge of Hull Corporation. It should be noted that these were very different days and England was sparsely populated with slow journey times from London to Hull by coach.

John Morley married Mary Elizabeth at this time and his son Ebenezer was born at Thorngumbald on 20 April 1801, however he had connections at the Providence Chapel, Hope Street, Hull and his son was christened there on 27 May 1801 (the entry was added to the register at a later date on a slip of paper). John Morley replaced Rev. Samuel Barnard as minister at Hope Street on 26 October 1801, an association that lasted nearly 50 years, and then adopted the precepts of the Congregational Union. The Providence Chapel was erected off Paragon Street, Hull in 1797 and took the place of the former Ebenezer Chapel (a good name for a child), whilst the street gave the name for Hull's Paragon Station. The couple had a daughter Mary Elizabeth christened at Hope Street on 8 October 1802 and then resided at West Street in Hull however the mother Mary died soon after the event. John Morley then married Hannah Maria daughter of Christopher and Amelia Atkinson at Sculcoates on 11 October 1804. His second wife was baptized in Hull on 12 November 1780 and her parents were members of the Fish Street Calvinistic Chapel in Hull. The second union brought forth two children Salome (1805) and Josephus (1806) and Rev. Morley lived at Anlaby Road, Hull in 1821 near to the future home of Hull City F.C.

Kingston upon Hull was a medium sized town on the River Hull in 1834, with many chapels and Anglican churches and a central area encircled by the Humber, Junction and Old Docks. John Morley lived north of the centre at 24 George Street in 1842 and retired as the minister of Hope Street on 7 July 1850. He was a widower living with daughter Salome (housekeeper) at 1 Caroline Place in 1851 and preached his final sermon at the Sailors' Institute, Hull on 11 October 1857, aged 87. Salome nursed him through the last years of his life and she lived with him at 23 Caughey Street, Hull in 1861. His son Ebenezer died on 8 August 1862 reminding him of life's temporary nature thus he made his last will on 20 August 1862. He left his worldly goods to the widows and children of Protestant ministers and to Salome his daughter. He died in Hull on 24 October 1863 aged 93 and she proved his will at York on 2 April 1864 his effects under £450.

His sons took completely different paths in life and Josephus Morley married Sarah Bromby at Holy Trinity, Hull on 2 April 1829 and had children Sarah Ann (1830), Salome (1832), Elizabeth (1834), John Septimus (1836) and William B. (1839) the first four being baptized at Providence Chapel. Josephus remained in Hull and was a brewer at 20 Waterhouse Lane in 1835 and a coal merchant at Trundle Street but residing Edwards Place, Cogan Street in 1842. He was a widower and grocer visiting his son William, ale and porter merchant, at 22 Wilberforce Street, Hull in 1881 and died June that year age 74. Ebenezer Morley, however, followed his father into the Congregational church and discussed life after his mother died stating: "He was left under the care and guidance of his pious father and enjoyed the advantages of a religious education and training." He began as a collector for the London Missionary Society and was a devoted Sunday school teacher and was a member of the Providence Chapel in 1817. He worked as an itinerant preacher and went to Cheshunt College (Hertford) in 1819 however formed an association with Zion Independent Chapel, Bridlington and was ordained there on 19 November 1823. He had great energy and zeal and held three services every Sunday and preached at surrounding villages in the week!

William Cobb married Mary Watson at Walkington near Hull on 22 March 1794 and had children William (1795), Mary (1797), Hannah (20 January 1799), Betty (1800) and Elizabeth Ann (1803) all baptized at St. Mary's, Hull - he was a wharfinger of 3 Salthouse Lane, Hull in 1821. Ebenezer Morley did not spend all his time in Bridlington and married Hannah Cobb at St. Mary's, Hull on 26 April 1826. They did not marry in the Congregational church due to the legislation at the time and in fact only Anglican churches could perform marriages in 1754-1837. Elizabeth Ann Cobb married Thomas McBride at St. Mary's on 3 April 1827 and had children William Peter (1828), Elizabeth Mary (1830), Janet Agnew (1831), Thomas Agnew (1833) and Elizabeth Ann (1835) all baptized Providence Chapel. Ebenezer's marriage was to be most fortuitous and he soon received valuable assistance from his father-in-law. Indeed, William Cobb was a successful ship-owner and merchant who had a business at 21 High Street and lived at Holborn Street, Holderness Road near Hull in 1835.

Ebenezer continued to preach at Zion Independent Chapel in Bridlington and his son William John was baptized there on 10 April 1829. He was laid low with illness and exhaustion in 1830, however he was blessed during his time of confinement and his father-in-law built him a new chapel in Holborn Street, Sutton in the east of Hull. Ebenezer and his family left Bridlington and he recommenced his ministry at Holborn Street on 1 December 1830 and stayed there 27 years. A most significant event regarding this discourse then took place and son Ebenezer Cobb Morley was born on 16 August 1831 and baptized at Holborn Street on 11 September. The couple then had three more children viz. Hannah Mary (1833), George Henry (1836) and Elizabeth Lucy (1838) however the eldest son William John died in December 1838. Ebenezer Morley dissenting minister lived at Pemberton Street, Sutton next to Holborn Street in 1841 with wife Hannah, children Ebenezer, Hannah, George and Elizabeth, and one servant. Their last child Selina Ann was born in September 1841 but there was further family grief when son George Henry died in March 1848.

Ebenezer Morley an "Independent minister of Holborn Street Chapel" lived at 2 Holborn Place, Witham, Sutton near to Hull in 1851 with wife Hannah, children Ebenezer, Hannah, Elizabeth and Selina and two servants. At this time Ebenezer Cobb Morley was aged 19 and was described as a solicitor's articled clerk. The family then moved to London and Rev. Morley began work at the Albany Chapel, Brentford on 13 July 1853 describing the church as "that desolate sanctuary." He became Secretary to the *Bible Association* at this time and was much engaged in open air preaching and stayed at Brentford for five years. He wrote his last will on 6 June 1857 and left his household and personal effects to his wife Hannah these to be divided equally amongst his children after her decease. He then added: "I give devise and bequeath all that my chapel situate in Holborn Street in the parish of Sutton, Hull and the dwelling house yard and other outbuildings and appurtenances thereunto belonging and used therewith, unto and to the use of my said wife Hannah Morley and my son Ebenezer Cobb Morley…." He requested that they dispose of the chapel in the most befitting way and the residue of his estate was left in trust to Hannah and Ebenezer to be divided equally amongst his children. He lived at Brentford when the will was written however it was witnessed at Messrs. Phillips & Copeman solicitors, Hull.

The Morley family then moved to West Brompton, London and Ebenezer managed to erect a temporary chapel it being opened for worship on 26 February 1858. Despite his age he worked with untiring zeal and stated: "He had never enjoyed his ministry more than in that place." Rev. Morley lived with wife Hannah, daughters Hannah, Elizabeth and Selina, niece Elizabeth A. McBride and one servant at 12 Victoria Grove, Chelsea in 1861. The house was situated just off Fulham Road and still remains although is a shadow of its genteel past and is renamed Netherton Grove. Ebenezer Morley had to give up his ministry in July 1862 and died at 12 Victoria Grove on 8 August 1862 being buried in Abney Park Cemetery at Stoke Newington (now a nature reserve). Hannah Morley widow and Ebenezer Cobb Morley a gentleman of 3 King's Bench Walk, Temple (son) obtained his probate on 13 October - he was rich spiritually but his effects were under £200.

During this period there were further developments 'up north'. James Boden a Congregational minister married Mary Frances Thornton at Sculcoates on 4 February 1819. He was an itinerant preacher at Chapel Gate in East Retford, Lairgate in Beverley and Queen Street in Sheffield. He had several children including Mary Ann (1828) born Sheffield, and William Henry (1833) and James (1837) born Beverley. William Henry Boden, merchant, married Hannah Mary Morley at Hove Church on 11 September 1862 the witnesses including Lucy Morley. Their only daughter Lucy Helena was born in Hull in 1864 and the family lived at 3 Richelieu Crescent, The Boulevard, Hull, in 1881 with one servant - the father a timber merchant. William and Hannah Boden lived at Hornsea in 1901 and he died at Skirlaugh in

June 1907 and she at Ecclesall in March 1928 (aged 94). Matthew Henry H. Habershon (1856) was born Rotherham and married Lucy Helena Boden at Sculcoates in June 1890 - he was a mining engineer (coal) and they lived in Sheffield in 1901. James Boden married Elizabeth Ann McBride at Sculcoates in September 1862. They had at least three sons and lived at Anlaby Road next to the female penitentiary and convent in 1881 with two servants - he was also a timber merchant. James Boden insurance agent lived with his wife and two sons in Hull in 1901 and he died there in March 1922 and she in December 1925. Mary Ann Boden had a daughter Lucy born in Hull in September 1866, the father William Peter McBride. Indeed Mary Ann Boden (53) and Lucy McBride (14) were lodgers at 60 Morpeth Street, West Sculcoates in 1881.

Ebenezer Cobb Morley was born near Holborn Street, Hull on 16 August 1831 and was to have a long life, longevity being a characteristic of the family. He spent his formative years in a religious environment at Holborn Street and inherited qualities from his father (and grandfather) including a determination to succeed, commitment to a cause and managerial skills, but most of all passion. He was a solicitor's articled clerk in Hull in 1851 possibly with Messrs. Phillips & Copeman then moved with his father to Brentford on 13 July 1853, and was admitted to the Law Society and registered as a London solicitor in 1854. He stayed with his father in Brentford however across the Thames the town of Barnes was a popular abode for "legal" families. In fact three barristers and a solicitor lived at The Terrace, Barnes in 1851.

Charles Ireland Shirreff was born at St. Anne's, Soho in 1793 and married Mary Cuff at St. Martin in the Fields on 25 July 1822. He had children at St. Martin's (1823-29) and St. Giles in the Fields but moved to Barnes in c.1845. Charles a solicitor aged 58 lived at 27 The Terrace, Barnes in 1851 with wife Mary, son William (18) and five other children, and they remained there at least 30 years. This was a substantial brick property with picture windows and balconies that looked out on the Thames. William Moore Shirreff, his son, was born at St. Giles in 1833 and was admitted to the Law Society in 1854 but more significantly was first Honorary Secretary of the Barnes and Mortlake Regatta in 1858. Ebenezer became a member of the London Rowing Club at the time and the White Hart Inn at the west end of Barnes Terrace was a meeting place for leading oarsmen. He then had business and sporting contacts in the area and moved to Barnes in 1858 when his father went to West Brompton. Initially, he did not buy a house, but resided at the White Hart Inn and boarded there with Christopher Willcox local innkeeper and family in 1861. The present White Hart Inn was rebuilt on the site in 1899.

Ebenezer purchased 26 The Terrace, Barnes, in c.1862 (next door to Shirreff) and this notable property was his home for 60 years. Richard Alfred Goodman was born as a nonconformist at Market Harborough on 7 October 1804 and was admitted to the Law Society in 1835. He married Martha and had children at St. Pancras in 1841-50 and was baptized there as an adult on 6 January 1845. Richard then formed a partnership with Ebenezer and was senior partner in the firm of Goodman and Morley at 3 King's Bench Walk, Inner Temple in 1862, and was counsel for indictments on the Oxford Circuit that year. Ebenezer then had a sound professional base but was also influenced by the religious zeal of his forbears and became inspired by the growing sports movement. He had a tumultuous time in the 1860s and coped by sinking his energies into the formation of the F.A. His father died on 8 August 1862 and he then turned his attentions to soccer.

He played some games with his friends on Barnes Green after moving there and helped to form Barnes F.C. at Limes Field, Mortlake (west of White Hart Lane) in late 1862. Indeed this was just a short walk from his home at 26 The Terrace and near to the White Hart Inn. The club soon played some important games and although just formed were said to be, "A live proposition boasting a big membership." In particular they had early contests against Richmond F.C. and first met at Barn Elms Park towards Putney by the Thames in November 1862. A large number of spectators gathered for the game including many of the fairer 'sex' and it was arranged that the winning team was the first to score two goals. Barnes managed this in just 20 minutes and left as victors. The game predates that of Sheffield v Hallam on 29 December that year thus Barn Elms Park was the venue for the first ever 'club' football match. A return game was played at Richmond Green in December 1862 but due to heavy rain the pitch became extremely muddy and 400-500 spectators were greatly amused as the players failed to keep their feet. Barnes won this fixture by a single goal however the game was neither soccer nor rugby. Mr. Gregory scored the goal and it was described thus: "He made a neat catch about 15 yards exactly in front of the Richmond base and after making his mark scored with a drop kick." The gentlemen of the two clubs later dined at the Talbot Hotel.

Richmond Green. Barnes played Richmond here in December 1862 but the paths restricted play.

Ebenezer was a founder of the Barnes and Mortlake Regatta and succeeded William M. Shirreff as Secretary in 1862, and also became honorary solicitor for the London Rowing Club. The Boat Race itself began at Henley in 1829 and moved to Putney in 1845 thus the area was a centre for rowing, and the owner of Barn Elms Estate liked to entertain the Boat Race crews. Ebenezer continued to play football although the lack of established rules meant teams played in their own style and this led to disputes. The Barnes Club played Forest F.C. in March 1863 and *Bell's Life* noted that, "Mr. Morley was a pretty and most effective dribbler," the art of dribbling being a skill much admired at the time. The paper went on to record a further tribute and stated, "We cannot abstain from saying that the play of Mr. Morley of Barnes and Mr. C. Alcock of the Forest Club elicited great applause from the spectators of whom there were a large number present."

With the above problems in mind Ebenezer, captain of Barnes, sent a letter to *Bell's Life* suggesting the rules for football should be established on similar lines to those of the M.C.C. for cricket. He was determined with others to form "an association of football clubs" that would enable contests to be established and a common code of rules formulated. He wrote to the public schools however there was little interest and Charterhouse, Harrow and Westminster replied without enthusiasm whilst Eton, Rugby and Winchester did not reply at all. Despite such setbacks he was undeterred and convened a meeting of interested parties at the Freemasons Tavern, Great Queen Street, Holborn on 26 October 1863 - those present included Arthur Pember of the No Names Club, Kilburn and John Forster Alcock of the Forest Club. The location might have been pre-destined from his time in Holborn Street however the meeting was a success and the Football Association was formed. He started the F.A. two days after the death of his grandfather (24 October 1863) and news of this may have reached him just before the meeting. It was the start of a new era for football and on a personal level however all was not plain sailing and the rules were much debated (see Ch. 4).

The development of the game is quite complex but it is a book of rugby history that clarifies matters: "Richmond F.C. 1861 to 1925 by E.J. Ereaut (a member of the club)." The latter were formed in 1861 and the founder Edwin H. Ash worked at a military college in Richmond and was Secretary for a number of years. Indeed the first players came from the college (and public school) and Edwin Ash chose Richmond Green to play on and promptly erected posts and started a game - although he did not check if it was legal. The Green was at the rear of the 'Old' Royal Palace in Richmond and was used for recreation since mediaeval times but in fact the only games allowed were cricket and bowls! The game that Richmond played was similar to that of Harrow School and was quite unlike modern rugby or soccer. There are few records of their games in 1861-62 and since the club was not properly constituted were absent when the F.A. formed on 26 October 1863. Despite this they supported early Association football and played two games against Forest F.C. in November 1863, one at Richmond Green and the other at Leytonstone

(Snaresbrook). Forest won 5-0 at home with Charles Alcock a goal scorer and also won away whilst a third game was drawn in December 1863. The first F.A. rules were debated at this time and were based on those at Cambridge (1848) and Uppingham School (1862).

Ebenezer prepared the first 13 rules at 26 The Terrace, Barnes and presented them for approval at the fifth meeting of the F.A. on 1 December 1863. Richmond F.C. were properly constituted for the 1863-64 season and Edwin Ash represented them at the meeting. He apologised for the club's earlier absence adding that Richmond would adopt the rules if they were ready for winter however, as stated, the issues of handling and hacking were hotly debated and three rules in particular were important: Rule VIII - "If a player makes a fair catch he shall be entitled to a free kick providing he claims it by making a mark with his heel at once." Rule IX - "No player shall carry the ball." Rule X - "Neither tripping nor hacking shall be allowed." This was a stormy meeting as the rules forbidding handling and hacking had been added without universal approval whilst Rule IV stated that - "A goal is scored by kicking the ball over the space between the goal-posts (at whatever height)." The rules were accepted at the time but the "fair catch" was later abolished and Rule IV changed so that a goal was scored ".... between the posts under the tape."

Ebenezer Cobb Morley (1831-1924)
"The Father of Football."

Richmond F.C. initially accepted this form of the game and met Barnes at Limes Field on 19 December 1863. The game was in fact fifteen a side however the rules were easy to understand and no disputes arose. Barnes had six "tries at goal" however they failed to score once and the game was drawn after one and a half hours - not the best of test matches. Richmond played a few Association games but they were soon drawn to the rules of Rugby School as several of their members were old boys and preferred a game where they carried the ball - thus soccer and rugby went separate ways. Richmond played rugby against Blackheath on 2 January 1864 whilst Edwin Ash was instrumental in the formation of the Rugby Union in January 1871. Richmond Green, meanwhile, proved to be an impractical venue and the *Sportsman* reported on the ground in December 1871 noting that the pitch narrowed at one end due to a number of paths crossing the site. The club remained there until 1873 and then removed to the Richmond Athletic Ground, which is shown as Richmond Town Cricket Ground on late 19th century maps. They still play there today and the pitch is located in front of the historic pavilion and beside a modern grandstand. The club must not be confused with non-League Hampton & Richmond - formerly Hampton F.C.

The Football Association Rules established by Morley and Co. in December 1863 had a number of differences from the modern game viz. kicking between the posts at whatever height and an 'offside' rule that allowed no forward pass. This meant that the skill of "dribbling" was most important and the tactic used was to have a player, or players, running behind the man in possession so they could pick up the ball if he lost it ('backing-up'). Ebenezer was first F.A. Secretary in 1863-66 and also continued with his other sporting activities and stroked for the London Rowing Club eight in the Grand Challenge Cup at Henley in 1864. Further to this Barnes F.C. had their first athletics meeting at Limes Field on the day of the Boat Race in 1864 (the latter ending just near his home). Ebenezer gave his full support to these meetings, which went on for many years and attracted the top athletes of the day. His partner Richard Alfred Goodman died at 245 Camden Road, Middlesex on 24 October 1865 and Ebenezer practiced alone at 3 King's Bench Walk, Temple until at least 1868. These red brick chambers were erected after the 'fire of London' in 1668-78 and were across a paved-cobbled walkway and are present today.

The F.A. wanted their Rules to extend to the whole country and sent a letter to Sheffield F.C. who had joined the Association. There was a meeting of club captains in the chambers at 3 King's Bench Walk in early 1866 and the reply from W.J. Chesterman Secretary of Sheffield F.C. was read out. Indeed these chambers could be considered a spiritual home of football since in addition to Morley three other 'soccer families' practiced there - Meysey-Thompson, Welch and Merriman (see later). **Note** The F.A. also met at Great Queen Street, the Oval, the Sportsman Newspaper, Boy Court and the Cricket Press, 6 Pilgrim Street off Ludgate Hill but took permanent offices in 1881. R.W. Willis then arranged a game between a representative London side and Sheffield at Battersea (home of the Wanderers) on 31 March 1866. This was to be played under F.A. Laws and the following were to apply:

1. The teams to be eleven a side.
2. The ground to be 120 yards long by 80 wide.
3. London dress is white jersey or flannel shirt and white trousers.
4. The ball to be Lillywhite's No.5.
5. The play to commence 3 p.m. and terminate at half-past four.
6. Notice of the match to be sent to *The Field, Bell's Life, Sporting Life* and *The Sportsman.*

Morley and Willis of Barnes, C. Alcock and Kinnaird of the Wanderers, Pember (captain), C.M. Tebbut and A. Baker of the No Names Club played for London whilst W.J. Chesterman was the captain of Sheffield. During the game both sides delivered a number of hard knocks and Morley was credited with scoring the first ever goal in representative soccer and Alcock had the first offside called against him. The game was played under the F.A. Rules and London won by 2 goals and 4 touchdowns to nothing (source *History of the Football Association* 1953). This was an unusual statement since the rules of both teams stated a goal 'must' be kicked, and this was possibly a romantic version, since the differences between soccer and rugby were then well defined. The occasion was rounded off in the evening with "a splendid dinner for the contestants at the Albion Hotel." There was a return game against Sheffield under the Sheffield Rules later that year and the contest became a 'fixture' for many years. Ebenezer then relinquished the position of Secretary and was a Committee member in 1866-67 but was appointed F.A. President in 1867-74. He was most active in Barnes and with his friend 'Bob' Willis built and equipped a small gymnasium opposite the White Hart Inn in 1867. The work was carried out by members of the Barnes team as well as rowing men and was used for five or six years, but was then home to the Bardowie Skittle Club.

The original Cambridge Rules stipulated that a ball passed to a player could not be touched unless three of the opposition were before him however the Association Rules stated that **any** player forward of the ball was offside. The latter was restrictive and the F.A. tried to gain greater appeal in 1867 and amended the offside rule to coincide with that at Charterhouse and Westminster. Once the new offside rule was introduced the tactics of play were changed and the skill of "middling" became important, although in many schools the old rules persisted and it took some time for players to adjust to these changes. The F.A. then announced in the press: "The rules shall be tested in a county match, Middlesex v Kent and Surrey, and the game will be played on Saturday November 2nd, 1867 at Beaufort House." The location was the headquarters and rifle ground of the South Middlesex Volunteers and consisted of a path or track around a pitch, as well as a rifle range, and backed on to Lillie Bridge Cricket Ground - venue of the 1873 Cup Final. A large crowd assembled for this inaugural game however Lord Ranelagh and the Secretary of the Amateur Athletic Club had a disagreement, and the players and spectators had to seek refuge in the 'wilds' of Battersea Park.

Middlesex included Charles Alcock whilst Kent-Surrey had R.G. Graham and R.W. Willis of Barnes although some of the players were quite young. Charles E.B. Nepean was born London c.1850 and attended Charterhouse and played for Middlesex - he was vicar of Lenham in Kent in 1881. Charles C. Dacre was born in Sydney in 1848 (already discussed) and represented Clapham Grammar School in the Kent-Surrey side. Both these players were noted dribblers whilst an injury to C.C. Dacre on Clapham Common hastened the rules forbidding hacking. *Bell's Life* stated the game was a goalless draw and a success in terms of its aims but "the ground was in a most objectionable state and totally unfit for football purposes and the grass, which was several inches long and extremely thick, effectually prevented all attempts at dribbling or any exhibition of play which we might have expected from the reputation of many of the players engaged in this contest." There was a second game between Kent and Surrey at the West London Running Grounds, Brompton or Lillie Bridge on 25 January 1868. The Kent side included A. Kinnaird (captain) of Trinity Cambridge and E. Lubbock of West Kent F.C. whilst Surrey had Morley, Willis and Graham (captain) of Barnes and A. Thompson of the Wanderers. All these people, though unfamiliar today, had an important role in soccer's history and are discussed later. This second game had twelve players and also ended in a goalless draw however it was seen as a success and the press stated: "The Rules now meet with universal approval."

Ebenezer Cobb Morley an attorney-at-law from Barnes married Frances Bidgood of 304 Camden Road at Christchurch in St. Pancras on 14 October 1869 - the witnesses W.E.A. Bidgood and E.L. Morley (sister). Alexander Masters Bidgood son of John and Elizabeth was baptized at Clyst Hydon, Devon on 1 January 1800. He came to London as a woollen merchant and with wife Mary had children: Charles Henry (1825) Mary Anne (1826), Emily (1828) and Frederick (1830). These children were born in St. James's and baptized at Robert Street, Grosvenor Square - independent chapel. Their daughter Frances (c.1837) may have been born in 'Brixton' and the couple no doubt met through his partner's family (also Camden Road). Indeed they resided at 26 The Terrace in 1871 with two servants and a visitor Charles Herbert Goodman (23). They did not have children and Ebenezer used his energies in other directions. The F.A. Committee had a Secretary, President, Treasurer and four other members in 1863 but this was increased to 10 members in 1869 and they were poised to make a most important decision.

A meeting took place at the Sportsman Office, Ludgate Hill on 20 July 1871 those present: E.C. Morley (President), C.W. Alcock (Secretary), Captain F.A. Marindin (Royal Engineers), M.P. Betts (Harrow), Alfred Stair (Treasurer, Upton Park Club and Cup Final referee), C.W. Stephenson (Westminster), J.H. Giffard (Civil Service) and D. Allport (C. Palace). They were unanimous and agreed that: "It is desirable that a Challenge Cup should be established, in connection with the association, for which all clubs belonging to the association should be invited to compete...." The F.A. Cup was thus started in 1871-72 and the saying 'from small acorns come great oaks' clearly applies. Ebenezer also had a role in international soccer and after an informal game at the Oval in 1870 the first full international took place at Glasgow on 30 November 1872. Other developments included the introduction of the corner kick in 1873.

So what of his personal life? Ebenezer then practiced as a commissioner for oaths in Chancery and was senior partner in Morley and Shirreff by 1871. His other partner was his neighbour and rowing associate William Moore Shirreff and their chambers were at 59 Mark Lane, City of London. He then stepped down as F.A. President in 1874 and left the running of the organisation to Alcock and Marindin. He was engaged in other pursuits and was involved in the conservation of Barnes Common and, being a keen rider, kept a pack of beagles and hunted with Surrey Union Foxhounds (from the 1870s). Ebenezer and Frances Morley lived at 26 The Terrace with his sister Elizabeth L. and two servants in 1881. The other 'players' lived as follows: (1) Charles C. Shirreff wine merchant and family (incl. Langford) at 27 The Terrace. Langford Shirreff was admitted to the Law Society in 1876 and joined the partnership. (2) W.M. Shirreff his partner and wife Sophia at 42 Belsize Park, London. (3) Frederick Bidgood, wife Marian and four children at 35 Finchley Road - he was a woollen merchant at 6 Vigo Street. (4) William James, wife Emily (née Bidgood) and son Dudley W.H. age 8 at 87 Finchley Road - the father a woollen merchant and hotel proprietor. They also had a daughter Elizabeth Hilda born at Hampstead in 1864.

26 The Terrace, Barnes. E.C. Morley lived on the left from 1862 until his death.

Morley and Shirreff had offices at 13 Palmerston Buildings and 53 Gresham House, Old Broad Street by 1882 and business was going well. Ebenezer, meanwhile, was Secretary of the Barnes and Mortlake Regatta until 1880 and the event continued until 1888. Limes Field was present on a map dated 1885 however Barnes F.C. played in their last Cup tournament in 1886-87 and First and Second Avenue covered the site by 1895. Ebenezer Morley a solicitor lived at 26 The Terrace in 1901 with his wife Frances and sister Elizabeth L., whilst his wife's family had some notable associations. Elizabeth Hilda James, his niece, married Dr. Malcolm Mackintosh at Hampstead in March 1890 and they resided at Battersea in 1901. *Morley's Hotel* was built at 25 Cockspur Street in 1831 and was on the east side of Trafalgar Square next to St. Martin in the Fields. Dudley W.H. James was born at Hampstead in 1873 and was a hotel proprietor at St. Martin's in 1901 and may have inherited *Morley's Hotel* from his father. South Africa House replaced the hotel (in 1935) although the end elevation was similar to that of Canada House opposite. Ebenezer tried to revive the Regatta in 1908 and in subsequent years but was eventually forced to concede defeat. He had varied activities and was President of *Barnes Artizan's Club*, a local J.P and represented Barnes on Surrey County Council in 1903-19. He continued to hunt as a member of the Devon and Somerset Staghounds from 1902 and his wife Frances died at the *Imperial Hotel*, Taw Vale Parade, Barnstaple, on 15 August 1911 - she was buried at Barnes. The F.A. recognized his contribution at their jubilee in 1913 whilst his sister Elizabeth L. Morley died at Wharfedale in March 1916 (aged 77).

26 The Terrace was in a quiet suburb beside the Thames and in a time untainted by motor traffic he could ride past the house. This was a plain fronted property with a conservatory on the east side and only survives by chance - the neighbouring houses were demolished when Elm Bank Gardens West was built and it is now on a corner. One can imagine Ebenezer looking out at the river and watching the Boat Race in some comfort in later years. Indeed this was a desirable location and his neighbours included Gustav Holst composer 10 The Terrace (1908-13) and Archibald Leitch ground designer Lonsdale Road (1915-22), whilst the Ranelagh Club, Barn Elms was a fashionable centre for sport in 1884-1939.

Ebenezer Cobb Morley made his last will on 29 October 1918 and gave his address as 53 Gresham House, Old Broad Street and Barnes. He had no children or surviving brothers thus he left his estate in trust for a number of relatives and left bequests and legacies for local charitable causes and his employees. Dudley William Henry James of *Morley's Hotel* and Frank Oliver Hart of 33 Bedford Row, solicitor were his executors and he first left eight legacies including - £500 to niece Lucy Helena Habershon widow of Matthew, £500 to Lucy Boden daughter of cousin William Peter McBride, £5,000 in trust for his sister Hannah Mary Boden and daughter Lucy Helena Habershon, £1,500 to Elizabeth Hilda Mackintosh widow of Doctor Malcolm Mackintosh and £50 to his clerks at Morley and Shirreff - if twelve years of service. There were also charitable legacies to Mortlake Police Court Poor Box £10, Children's Convalescent Home Bognor £200, and Hospital for Consumption & Chest Disease Fulham Road £200. He then left £1,000 to coachman Charles Frost and £200 to gardener Joe Leppard and paid back a mortgage of £250, which was granted to him by Moses Snook of the Artizan's Club, Barnes.

The remainder of his real and personal estate was distributed equally amongst the nieces and nephews of his wife Frances, namely the children of sister-in-law Emily James and those of brother-in-law Frederick Bidgood but the bequests excluded a mortgage he held on "The Bungalows", Mortlake (see below). He lastly discussed the legal implications of the will and then made several changes in four codicils - he was a solicitor! He appointed Elizabeth Hilda Mackintosh as a further executor on 5 February 1920, and confirmed the legacies of £500 and £5,000 being worried the original will was not clear on 26 April 1921. Dudley W.H. James died at Wycombe in early 1922 (aged 48) thus he made niece Lucy Helena Habershon an executrix on 22 February 1921. He cancelled all previous trustees and appointed Elizabeth Hilda Mackintosh and Lucy Helena Habershon (d. of sister Lucy Elizabeth Boden sic.) on 13 September 1922.

Ebenezer Cobb Morley was a remarkable man of great energy and died at 26 The Terrace, Barnes on 20 November 1924 aged 93 years the informant being R.D. Mackintosh of The Bungalow, Mortlake. The churchyard of St. Mary's, Barnes was overcrowded in the mid-19th century thus the Dean and Chapter of St. Paul's (who held it from Athelstan c.925) permitted two acres of Barnes Common to be enclosed for a new cemetery in 1854. This was located just south of Barn Elms Park, off Rocks Lane with Putney Cemetery immediately behind and had a central path and chapel with memorial

Memorial to E.C. Morley. Located in Barnes Old Cemetery, but now neglected.

to the Hedgeman family at one end. His funeral took place at Barnes Church and he was buried in Barnes Old Cemetery not far from where he played the first football game in 1862. Those at the service included: Mrs. Habershon and Mrs. Mackintosh (nieces), Mr. James, Dr. R.D. Mackintosh, G.S. Steel and G.T. Maudling partners in Morley, Shirreff & Co., members of Barnes Council, members of the Artizan's Club and family and friends. His memorial was a plain cover of grey granite stating: "Frances Morley 15th August 1911, Ebenezer Cobb Morley 20th November 1924 aged 93." Details of his life were recorded in two local papers the *Herald* and the *Richmond & Twickenham Times* that same month.

His will was proved on 3 February 1925 and probate granted to Frank Oliver Hart of 33 Bedford Row, Elizabeth Hilda Mackintosh of 82 West Side Clapham Common, and Lucy Helena Habershon of Ivydene, St. Mark's Crescent, Sheffield his estate being valued at £48,994 10s 9d. Meanwhile, Barnes Old Cemetery was closed in the mid-1950s and the local Borough Council removed the perimeter railings planning to make it a lawn cemetery, however it came under the jurisdiction of Richmond Borough in 1965 and little was done hence it was recently designated a nature reserve. It is now completely overgrown although Morley's grave survives and can be found by virtue of being the last in the southeast corner. His house 26 The Terrace also remains and has recently been restored however there is nothing to commemorate his life or achievements and this is a theme seen throughout the book. This is not the case with other sports and there is a blue plaque at 33 St. George's Square, Pimlico stating: "Major Walter Clopton Wingfield (1833-1912) the Father of Lawn Tennis."

ROBERT WATSON WILLIS

The next two secretaries of the F.A. also came from the ranks of Barnes F.C. and were Robert Watson Willis (1866-68) and Robert George Graham (1868-70). Both were local residents and young gentlemen who lived near to Mr. Morley in Barnes and since he was also on the Committee, at this time, the club had a monopoly at the F.A. The Willis family are traced to Leith in Edinburgh and the grandfather Robert Willis was born at South Leith in c.1771 and married Agnes, daughter of John Hay, at either Canongate, Edinburgh on 3 December 1795 or at South Leith, Midlothian on 4 December. The couple had four children namely Agnes (1796), Robert (1799), Elizabeth (1802) and Ann (1804) whilst the father was a spirit dealer at the *Pipes* in 1801. Two of his daughters were married at St. Cuthbert's, Edinburgh: Agnes Willis to William Mason on 24 May 1817 and Eliza Willis to Colin Mackenzie Fraser on 4 September 1827, whilst Anne Willis married James Syme in Edinburgh parish on 22 October 1829.

Robert Willis was born Leith on 13 February 1799 and baptized at South Leith on 1 March following. He trained as a physician and qualified as an M.D. in Edinburgh being a fellow of the Royal College of Surgeons Edinburgh (F.R.C.S.E.) and a licentiate of the Royal College of Physicians Edinburgh. He moved to London, however, in the 1820s and initially became a general practitioner at Westminster. David Watson, meanwhile, married Ann Mary Underwood (minor) of St. Luke's with her father's consent at St. Margaret's, Westminster on 22 July 1793. David established a business that same year as upholsterer at 14 Bridge Street, Westminster and advertised at this address until 1810. He also traded with his brother Henry Watson at 51 Parliament Street. The couple had four children baptized at St. Margaret's Church next to Westminster Abbey namely Ann Isabella (1798), Frances Jane (1799), Henry (1801) and Eleanor (born 2 June 1804) whilst the father appeared in St. Margaret's rate books in 1808-10. His property was in Parliament Street and had an annual poor rate value of £150 and a charge of £9 7s 6d whilst for the watch rate the figures were £200 and £1 17s 6d.

David Watson of Whitehall made his last will on 2 November 1810 and left 3/10 of the annual produce of his property to wife Ann Mary but to be replaced by £80 p.a. if she remarried. In that case or at her decease the 3/10 was to be divided amongst his children for their support and education. He also left his executors £20 each for mourning and requested rings be given to his sisters Mrs. Walter, Mrs. Woodreston, Mrs. Henry Watson, brother Mr. Henry Watson and John Watson Esq. of Torryburn (see Marindin Ch. 5). His executors were wife Ann, John Kershaw Esq. of 31 Walcot Place Lambeth and William Walter Esq. of 7 James Street Covent Garden and his household goods were left to his family. He died soon after and his executors proved his will in London on 9 January 1811 whilst William Bownas replaced him in the rate books at Parliament Street. His widow Ann Mary Watson moved to a smaller property located at Princes Court, Westminster, this being a small street of 12 houses at the end of Great George Street next to Storey's Gate (entrance to St. James's Park). She was listed in the rate books there from 1812-30 and the property had an annual value of £30/40 and later £36. **Note** Princes Court was demolished for road widening and the Institute of Mechanical Engineers, 1 Birdcage Walk is on the site.

Henry Watson, his brother, was then sole proprietor of the upholstery business and traded at 14 Bridge Street, Westminster next to the Houses of Parliament from 1811-26. He wrote his last will on 11 November 1826 and was a gentleman of 31 Parliament Street (south end of Whitehall). He was unmarried and left his freehold in Bridge Street occupied by William Walter (brother-in-law), to the said, and also to William Walter nephew and William Francis Abrams ironmonger of Parliament Street, in trust, the rents to go to Mary Maria wife of Baron de Berenger de Beautain. His two properties in Parliament Street where he lived, likewise, went to Mary Maria for her use under an indenture of 15 April 1822 and he asked for his personal property to be sold. He left some annuities as follows: £90 p.a. to Mary Clipson under an indenture to her and William Walter dated January 1816, £20 p.a. to servant Bessey Cobley under a bond dated 25 June 1821 and Government annuities to Mary Fethers (600), Louisa Philpot (200) and Maria Walter (250). He also left several other amounts, in particular to John Hunter now or late of Torryburn and the widow of John's late brother - this link indicates that the Watson family came from the Edinburgh region. Henry finally left his furniture etc. at 31 Parliament Street to Mary Maria except his books of work and the residue was divided into three portions viz. children of sister Margaret Walter, sister Rebecca Woodreston, children of late brother David and his widow. Henry Watson of Parliament Street was buried at St. Margaret's on 17 March 1830 aged 69 and his will proved in London on 2 April.

There were two weddings during this period at St. Margaret's, Westminster - John Sedgwick Esq. (of Wimbledon) married Anne Isabella Watson on 1 June 1822 witnesses D. Watson, F. Watson and E. Watson; Robert Willis M.D. married Eleanor Watson (of St. Martin in the Fields) on 31 March 1831 witnesses D. Watson, Frances Jane Watson, H. McDougall and John Henry Watson. The second couple moved to Princes Court and Robert Willis replaced Ann Watson in the rate books at an annual value of £36 in 1831 and then at £40 in 1832-34. Robert and Eleanor had three children at Princes Court and baptized at St. Margaret's Church namely Eleanor (1832), Anne Mary (1833) and Agnes Aders (1836) the father being described as a physician. Indeed Dr. Robert Willis had a good number of patients and the family moved to a more affluent property at 25 Dover Street, Piccadilly in 1837. The couple had two more daughters there and both were baptized at St. George's Hanover Square: Frances La Touche (1839) and Mary Watson (1841). Robert Willis physician resided at 25 Dover Street in 1841 and the household included his wife Eleanor, five daughters, lodger Robert Mason (20) an engineer from Scotland, two students in medicine and five servants. The property was a four-storey Georgian town house with a plain but narrow front, and is still present today.

St. Margaret's, Westminster. Robert Willis married Eleanor Watson here in 1831.

The couple had one son Robert Watson Willis who was born at 25 Dover Street on 26 January 1843 and baptized at St. George's Hanover Square on 4 September that year, his father a physician. This was the church of the rich and famous and the children of H.M. Queen Victoria and H.R.H. Prince Albert of Buckingham Palace were baptized there - Victoria Adelaide Mary Louisa on 10 February 1841 and Alice Maud Mary on 2 June 1843. Dr. Robert Willis stayed at 25 Dover Street until 1846 and then moved his practice to Barnes, Surrey. The family had a comfortable country lifestyle and lived in a notable property Rose Cottage on the edge of Barnes Common. This was situated side-on to Church Road between Nassau Road and Grange Road that were built later (but

Rose Cottage, Barnes. The home of Robert Willis M.D. (demolished in 1911).

opposite them). The cottage had a good-sized garden with wicker fence and was surrounded by the common whilst the façade had a colonial appearance and a veranda supported by tree trunks. Robert Willis M.D. Edinburgh and G.P. (in Middlesex and Surrey) lived at Rose Cottage, Barnes with his wife Eleanor, six children all 'scholars at home' and three servants in 1851.

Agnes Aders Willis married Henry Edward Vernet at Barnes Church, just down the road, on 10 May 1859. He was born in Geneva, Switzerland in 1833 and was the son of Charles Andrew Vernet gentleman, whilst Robert and Eleanor Willis and Charles Vernet were the witnesses. Robert Willis physician and surgeon M.D. Edinburgh lived at Rose Cottage in 1861 with wife Eleanor, four daughters, Robert (18) a merchant's clerk and two servants. The latter was attracted to the local fascination with football and joined Barnes F.C. at its formation in 1862 and was soon involved in the games development. The family's happiness, however, did not last long and wife Eleanor Willis died at Barnes on 24 March 1863 and was buried in the newly opened cemetery. Robert Willis M.D. of Barnes esq. made his last will on 21 July 1864 and left his personal estate to son Robert or his eldest or only unmarried daughter. It was to be converted to money and invested in stocks and shares of the British-Indian Government, railway, dock, canal, harbour companies, or public works, and the income to be paid to his unmarried children in equal shares. If all were married or aged 21 or deceased then the money to be used for their children and advancement in life as tenants-in-common. Robert W. Willis and his eldest surviving daughter were executors and his house and other possessions were to be used as they deemed fit. Charles Francis Hore of 52 Lincoln's Inn Fields solicitor and Rose Newell of Barnes were witnesses. Anne Isabella Sedgwick widow died at 31 George Street near Hanover Square on 6 January 1865 the informant Frances L. Willis and was also buried at Barnes. There were two weddings at Barnes Church and Henry Melville (rector 1863-70) performed the ceremonies: (1) William Marshall M.D. of Mortlake married Anne Mary Willis on 29 July 1865 wit. Robert Willis, Eleanor Willis (sister) and (Wm) Marshall. He was born in St. Thomas, West Indies in 1840 the son of John a merchant. (2) Mark Dewsnap widower and barrister of Barnes married Frances La Touche Willis on 19 August 1865 wit. Robert Willis, Eleanor Willis and R.G. Graham. His date of birth is uncertain but he was the son of Mark Dewsnap a surgeon.

'Bob' Willis was a prominent member of Barnes F.C. and was clearly a friend of E.C. Morley and R.G. Graham. He became Secretary of the F.A. in 1866 aged only 23 years and played for the London side in the test match against Sheffield on 31 March 1866 (with Morley) and, as stated, helped build a gymnasium near the White Hart Inn in 1867. His social life revolved around his football activities, and possibly rowing, thus there was a happy event later that year. Robert Watson Willis married Helen Eliza Graham (sister of Robert George) at Barnes Church on 28 August 1867 and Rev. Henry Melville B.A. Canon of St. Paul's Cathedral and rector performed the ceremony assisted by Rev. John Graham (brother). The witnesses were Robert Willis, Robert George Graham and Emily Sophia Graham (sister) and the event was reported in the Times on Thursday 29 August. Robert also appeared for the Kent-Surrey side on 2 November 1867 (with Graham) and the Surrey side on 25 January 1868 (with Morley and Graham) thus he took part in some important games in terms of football's evolution. He stepped down as Secretary in 1868 and was then on the F.A. Committee in 1869-71.

Robert and Helen Willis resided at 5 Beverley Villas, Barnes after their marriage in 1867, which was a new property at the time. Beverley Villas consisted of six semi-detached houses on the edge of Barnes Common near the station and next to Clyde Road (later Beverley Road). They were later numbered 106-116 Station Road, whilst 118 'Prospect House' on the corner of Scarth Road was dated 1878. No. 5 (now 114) was an elegant three-storey house with white stone at the ground floor and around the windows,

5 Beverley Villas, Barnes. R.W. Willis lived here in 1867-72 after his marriage.

and grey-yellow brickwork above but only a small garden. The couple had children Robert Graham (June 1868) and Mabel Helen (September 1869) hence Robert W. Willis, wine merchant, lived at 5 Beverley Villas in 1871 with wife Helen, his two children and four servants. Indeed the property was near to Barnes Green and his father Robert Willis M.D. G.P. resided at Rose Cottage, Church Road in 1871 with his daughters Eleanor and Mary W., grand children Augusta, Florence and Hugh Dewsnap, a visitor May Dewsnap and three servants.

Henry Frederick Aladro Willis was born at 5 Beverley Villas on 14 May 1871 and his initials were Henry F.A. Willis. This choice of name took group loyalty to a new level or perhaps it was a coincidence? Robert finished his connection with the F.A. and left Barnes in 1872 and moved a short distance to "Hinxton House" near Upper Richmond Road in East Sheen - the significance of the name is revealed shortly. The couple had three children there, namely Norman Edward Ommanney (October 1872), Enid Alice Graham (May 1876) and Vere Mary (July 1879) who were all baptized at East Sheen Parish Church. During this period Robert W. Willis was a Spanish merchant or wine merchant at 25 Crutched Friars in the City of London. There were many such merchants in this area, however he was not in trade under his own name and he no doubt worked for a company. Robert Willis M.D. died at Rose Cottage, Barnes on 21 September 1878 and was buried with his wife in Barnes Cemetery. Robert Watson Willis of 25 Crutched Friars, London City, merchant and Eleanor Willis spinster obtained his probate at the Principal Registry on 10 October 1878 and his estate was valued at under £3,000 but re-sworn in January 1879 at under £5,000.

The 'Misses' Willis or Eleanor and Mary lived at Rose Cottage in 1879 however they soon left the property and went travelling. Eleanor Willis late of Barnes died at Florence in Italy on 15 November 1881 and news of her death arrived by telegraph and there was a brief obituary in the Times on 17 November. Robert Watson Willis of 25 Crutched Friars merchant proved her will in London on 21 January 1882 and her personal estate was £3,496 0s 9d but re-sworn in March 1883 at £1,177 0s 3d. Rose Cottage then had several residents but due to its position near Church Road its days were numbered. Rev. Walter Harry Rammell M.A. curate of Barnes lived there in 1884, C. Tonge in 1887-88 and Richard W. Nunn from 1895-1911. Rose Cottage was purchased from Mrs. Attwell and others on 29 September 1911 and the last tenant was Mrs. Nunn - it was demolished for road widening on 3 October 1911.

The Willis and Graham families were linked by marriage and a series of inter-connections would determine their future. Robert W. Willis, Spanish merchant, lived at Hinxton House, East Sheen in 1881 with wife Helen E. and children Mabel, Harry, Norman, Enid and Vere, one visitor, a governess and six servants. The property was near to Sheen Lodge and Richmond Park and next door was Henry Edward and Agnes Aders Vernet at the Grange (see below) - indeed the stables of Hinxton and the Grange were adjacent to one another. His son Robert Graham Willis died on 1 July 1889 aged 21 years and was buried at the 'Old' Mortlake Burial Ground in Avenue Gardens - a cross with stone base was erected. Robert W. Willis merchant and employer lived at Hinxton House in 1891 with wife Helen E. children Mabel, Harry F.A. (merchant's clerk), Norman (clerk in the Crown Agents' office), Enid and Vere, and five servants with one from Switzerland. His brother-in-law Henry Edward Vernet and sister still lived at the Grange however the situation was soon to change.

Joseph Napier (1804-82) of Merrion Square was M.P. for Dublin University in 1848-58, Attorney General in 1852, Lord Chancellor in 1858, and became a baronet on 9 April 1867. His son Joseph Napier was born in 1841, married Maria Octavia Mortimer, then spent time in Canada and died 13 November 1884. The grandson William Lennox Napier was born in Montreal on 12 October 1867 and was a pupil at Park House School, Tilehurst in 1881. The school was situated in Prospect Park House near Reading and Arthur C. Bartholomew was the Headmaster of the school (see Wollaston Ch. 6). He completed his education at Uppingham and Jesus College, Cambridge and thus established a connection with Graham and Forster of Hinxton (near Cambridge), and joined the Sussex Artillery Volunteers in 1888. William Lennox Napier married Mabel Edith Geraldine Forster at Hinxton, Linton district in September 1890. Her father Charles T. Forster was vicar of the parish (after John Graham) and her family are discussed in the next section. The links with the Graham family meant that William L. Napier, student at law, lived at 1 Temple Sheen, Mortlake in 1891 with wife Mabel E.G., brothers-in-law Arthur E.T. Forster (stockbroker's clerk), Leopold H.V. Forster (16) and two servants both from Hinxton. This was a large Victorian house in its own grounds and faced northward down Derby Road at the junction with Temple Sheen Road, and was near both Hinxton House and the Grange. Indeed there can be some confusion on present day maps since there is also Temple Sheen and West Temple Sheen. The family, however, soon departed for London and their friends from Hinxton moved in.

Robert Watson Willis was to have a short life and after a long illness died at 1 Temple Sheen, East Sheen on 16 January 1892 aged just 48 years. A local paper *The Herald* dated January 22, 1892 stated: "It is with great regret we have to record the death of Mr. Robert Watson Willis of Temple Sheen, which took place at his residence on Saturday last after a long illness. He was greatly respected in the parish, hence it was that yesterday (Thursday) a large number of parishioners collected at Mortlake Cemetery to pay a last tribute of respect to his memory and many carriages belonging to local gentry followed the coffin, which was hidden due to the great number of wreaths sent by relatives and friends. The vicar Rev A.S. Shute rendered an impressive service and much sympathy is felt in the parish for the relatives." There was a brief mention in the *Richmond and Twickenham Times* dated 23 January 1892 ".... at his residence Temple Sheen Robert Watson Willis only son of the late Robert Willis M.D. age 48 years." Helen Eliza Willis widow and Mabel Helen Willis spinster, his executors, were granted probate in London on 29 February 1892 the effects being valued at £12,357 11s 11d. He was buried next to his son Robert Graham and a large cross was erected on a three-step stone base, the inscription stating: "In loving memory of Robert Watson Willis of Hinxton House East Sheen who died January 16th 1892 aged 48 years deeply mourned." Sadly the respect and esteem given at the time was not continued in later years and the memorial is now up-turned and desecrated although can still be read. Obviously this was done with no knowledge that he was one of the founders of football.

William Lennox Napier became a barrister of the Inner Temple in 1894 and a territorial force officer of the 7th Battalion Royal Welsh Fusiliers. He was a barrister and baronet living at 26 Argyll Road, Kensington in 1901 with wife Mabel E.G. and his children Marjorie (6) born East Sheen, Joseph, Charles, Vivien and Gwendolyn born Kensington and five servants. He was admitted to the Law Society as a solicitor in 1902 and lived at 9 Bramham Gardens, S. Kensington and had an address Mowbray House, Norfolk Street, Strand. He retired from the Fusiliers in 1912 but offered his services at the outbreak of war in August 1914 and was a major in the 4th South Wales Borderers on 24 September. He was promoted to lieutenant colonel but died from a sniper's bullet at Gallipoli on 13 August 1915 and there is correspondence from Mabel E.G. Napier (relating to the death) at Leeds University Library dated 1915-18. Joseph William Lennox Napier (1 August 1895) then succeeded him as baronet, and his wife died in 1955 and son in 1986. The 24th Regiment became the South Wales Borderers (in 1881) and had their main depot at Brecon, thus the 14th-century Harvard Chapel in Brecon Cathedral was dedicated to them. Six of their officers including William Lennox Napier are commemorated beneath the regimental crest.

Helen E. Willis of independent means lived at 1 Temple Sheen in 1901 with children Mabel, Harry F.A. (Bank of England clerk), Norman (clerk in Crown Agents for the colonies), Enid and Vere, and three servants. Indeed the whole family stayed close together and Richard W. Cory (46) a barrister born Bloomsbury was at 2 Temple Sheen (see next section) and Henry and Agnes Vernet and their family were at 3-4 Temple Sheen (in 1901). Helen Eliza Willis (née Graham) still lived at 1 Temple Sheen in 1906, but moved to "Sheen House", Portsmouth Road in Esher from 1910-30 and was then titled Mrs. R.W. Willis. There is a notable 8-foot high circular milestone at the junction of Portsmouth Road and Esher Station Road and several old houses and cottages are on the north side with Sandown Park Racecourse behind. The 'Old' Tudor church in Esher was used until 1854 and was replaced with Christchurch, which has a memorial to Chetwynd-Talbot Governor of Boston, Massachusetts (there is no memorial to Willis). Helen Eliza Willis died at "Sheen House" on 24 March 1930 and her probate was granted to Harry F.A. Willis and Norman E.O. Willis, her effects valued at £5,290 18s 10d. It is worth noting that Esher is not far from Hampton, north of the Thames, and this connection is seen in the following section on Graham.

William Marshall M.D. G.P. lived at Mortlake after his marriage in 1865 until at least 1875 and may have moved to Barnes upon the death of Robert Willis M.D. in 1878. He resided at Torrieburn, Barnes in 1881 with his wife Ann Mary, children William H.W., Eleanor M., Violet A., Arthur Von Helm and Wilfred Robert all born Mortlake and two servants. The house was next to Nassau Gardens and opposite Rose Cottage on Barnes Green and the name may have been related to the Watson family viz. Torryburn near Dunfermline. William Marshall M.D. and surgeon lived at Torrieburn, Church Road, Barnes in 1901 with wife Annie M. daughter Violet A. and two servants, whilst Miriam and Philip Nunn lived next door (presumably at Rose Cottage). Anne Mary Marshall of Torrieburn, Barnes died on 5 January 1910 aged 76 and her daughter Violet Annie Marshall obtained her probate at £3,667 10s 9d. Her name was recorded with her parents and aunt on the stone at Barnes Cemetery and the Barnes and Mortlake Historical Society recorded this in 1981 but it has since become very hard to read. William Marshall of Torrieburn, Church Road died on 17 March 1917 and William Hamilton Willis Marshall clerk obtained his probate, the amount being £1,178 6s 7d.

Henry Edward Vernet lived at Wandsworth after his marriage in 1859 and was there until at least 1874. He had several children but his son Cosmo John was born at Barnes in March 1875 and died on 16 February 1879 - he was buried with the Willis family at Barnes Cemetery. Henry Vernet, agent and Consul General for Switzerland (merchant and banker), lived at the Grange, Mortlake in 1881 with wife Agnes, children Adelaide, Louisa, Agnes C. and Arthur J. all born Wandsworth and five servants. He remained at the same property as a merchant and banker in 1891 with wife Agnes, children Eleanor C., Adelaide F., Henry A. (American merchant), Robert (stockbroker), Arthur J. and Agnes C., Louisa M.A. Ross and her daughter Angela C.M. Ross and Ernest W.C. Squirl, visitor, a captain in the Suffolk Militia and six servants. Henry Vernet banker and employer lived at 3-4 Temple Sheen in 1901 with wife Agnes A., children Adelaide F. (teacher of music), Robert (stockbroker), Agnes C., daughter Louisa M. Ross and her daughter Angela C.M. Ross and five servants. His work, however, was abroad thus Henry Edward Vernet of 25 Old Broad Street died at Geneva, Switzerland on 4 May 1908. Agnes Aders Vernet widow, Henry Augustus Vernet merchant and Robert Vernet stockbroker obtained his probate in London on 30 June and his estate was worth £15,297 12s 1d but re-sworn at £16,232 12s 1d. Arthur James Vernet of Temple Sheen died at Beri Beri Camp, Jebba, Northern Rhodesia on 30 October 1908 and Agnes Clara Vernet of Temple Sheen died at 33 Belgrave Square on 11 February 1915. Agnes Aders Vernet of 10 Sheffield Terrace, Kensington died on 6 January 1930 and Henry Augustus Vernet banker and Robert Vernet a member of Stock Exchange obtained her probate at £11,742 3s 5d.

Mark Dewsnap Esq. barrister a widower was married in 1865 and lived at Barnes Common in 1867. There was a relative May Dewsnap born at Barnes in 1862 however he had three children with Frances at Barnes viz. Augusta (1867), Florence (1868) and Hugh J. (1870). Mark Dewsnap aged 81 died at Kensington in March 1874 and this may have been him (but was possibly his father). Frances La T. Dewsnap a widow lived on income from dividends at London Road, Bushey, Herts in 1881 with daughters Augusta and Florence and one servant. She continued on her own means at 41 Rowan Road, Hammersmith in 1901 still with her two daughters and one servant. Frances La Touche Dewsnap died at 26 Pembroke Road, Kensington on 23 December 1935 and Florence Powles widow obtained probate at £4,648 14s 2d.

ROBERT GEORGE GRAHAM

The F.A. kept it in the family at this stage consequently the third Secretary was Robert George Graham the brother-in-law. His ancestry is traced to his grandparents who came from Wetheral in Cumberland, this being a small village east of Carlisle in the shadow of Corby Castle. William Graham married Mary Robinson at Wetheral Church on 19 September 1789 and had a daughter Ann Graham baptized there on 10 October 1789. These dates suggest that it was something of a shotgun wedding. Their son John Graham was baptized at Wetheral Church on 8 July 1792 but was destined to leave the land of his ancestors and trained in the ministry. He matriculated at St. John's College, Cambridge with its impressive Tudor gateway and 16th century courtyards in 1811 and must have found it a great contrast to Wetheral. He gained his B.A. in 1815 and was appointed curate of Wardley, Rutland that year and of Swaffham Bulbeck, Cambridge-shire in 1816. He liked the academic life and gained his M.A. in 1818 and was a fellow of St. John's, Cambridge in 1819. This was followed with a Bachelor of Divinity in 1825 and he was made a fellow of Jesus College in 1828.

He left the university and was appointed vicar of Comberton near Cambridge in 1830-33 and then of Hinxton a village on the River Cam, 10 miles south of Cambridge, in 1833. He was also appointed vicar of Swavesey a church of some substance north west of Cambridge in 1833. He did not reside there and his curate presumably ran the latter parish although he would have received income from both livings. Hinxton Hall was the main property in the village and Trinity College, Cambridge, held some of the land. Several coach services went to Hinxton after 1832 and there were plans for a railway in 1834 but this was not built until 1845. St. Mary and St. John's Parish Church was at the centre of the village on Church Green whilst the 'old' vicarage was beside the church. It remains an attractive village with several half-timbered houses exhibiting examples of pargeting (plaster decoration).

John Graham took the coach to Hinxton in 1833 however may have had a warm welcome upon his arrival, since there was a riot in the village during that year. There was much hardship at the time and 150 agricultural labourers gathered in the High Street to protest about exploitation by the local landowners. They received only a small sum of money for their efforts consequently they attacked their employers outside the local public house. The main protagonists of the disturbance then appeared in court and were sentenced to one month's hard labour. The new vicar clearly had important work to do there. William Gillson married Sarah Hall at Risley, Derbyshire on 29 December 1794 and then had fourteen children at Greetham in Rutland from 1795-1809. Their daughter Frances Maria was baptized there on 20 May 1804 and the parish was just north of Exton Hall home of the Noel family (see Kinnaird Ch. 5). John Graham married Frances Maria Gillson at Claybrook in Leicestershire on 28 May 1834 and as well as being vicar had the life of a country gentleman. He proceeded to live in the village for many years and had seven children baptized at the church: Fanny Maria (1835) *infant*, William (1838), Charles James (1839), John (1841), Mary Frances (1843), Robert George (1845) and Helen Eliza (1846).

A country vicar had an important position in the community and this meant he occasionally appeared in local records, and indeed Rev. Graham was soon involved in a heated dispute. Some repair work had been done on a number of local cottages at the request of the church however there was an argument over who should pay. Northfield Reynolds wanted 42 guineas for his labour but was left out of pocket thus he could not pay his uncle William Reynolds. The latter took Rev. Graham to court in 1846 to try and recover his money from the third party. There was much legal wrangling regarding the issue however William Reynolds won the case in the end. This was not the only dispute and on another occasion a young couple arrived at the church to be married. They failed to produce a licence and John Graham sent them away thus they were forced to marry later at Saffron Walden. The vicar then had a last daughter Emily Sophia born at Lutterworth, Leicestershire in 1848.

A certain amount of land, meanwhile, came with the living at Hinxton and the farming thereon made for good local news. There was a report regarding Rev. Graham's sick cow in 1854 and the *Cambridge Independent Press* noted on 2 August 1856: "the getting in of some forward oats the property of Rev. J. Graham." Such was the news of interest at this time and no wonder his son helped to start soccer! John Graham vicar of Hinxton was living at the Vicarage in 1861 with his wife Frances Maria, children William (student of Inner Temple), Mary Frances, Helen Eliza and Emily Sophia - the other three sons were at school and university. The household was completed with two visitors: one from Dieppe and a student of Emmanuel, Cambridge, and three servants (one of them also from Dieppe). The family's life, however, was soon to change and this occurred with the Rev. Graham's untimely death on 8 July 1862. He was buried in Hinxton churchyard and his memorial states: "Sacred to the memory of John Graham late fellow of St. John's and Jesus College Cambridge 29 years vicar of this parish and the parish of Swavesey and a magistrate for the county. Died July 8th 1862 aged 70 years. Also of Frances Maria his wife died August 5th 1889 in her 86th year whose body rests at Mortlake Surrey." This is situated to the immediate left of the church porch and parallel to the main path and is a flat limestone slab, weathered, with moss in the lettering. Grass surrounds the stone and often covers it making it hard to find. Frances Maria Graham widow, William Graham and John Graham Esq. proved his will on 8 August 1862 the effects being under £4,000.

John Graham was the incumbent of Hinxton for 29 years and was followed by two other long-term vicars, namely Rev. Charles Thornton Forster (1865-91) and Rev. Richard Twells (1892-1926) - the latter the longest serving vicar at 33 years. There is now a brief digression that helps to explain some Willis links above and introduces some important literary connections with regard to the Graham family. Henry Thornton a banker lived at Battersea Rise near Clapham Common and married Marianne Sykes and had children baptized at Holy Trinity, Clapham viz. Marianne (18 April 1797), Lucy Jane (1801), Watson Joseph (1802), Isabel (1804), Sophia (1806), Henrietta (1807) and Laura (23 September 1808). Henry Thornton was a Southwark M.P and a leading member of the Clapham Sect thus the group met in his house. They were evangelists and reformers, many being in Parliament, and their main aim was the abolition of slavery although they also tackled other social evils (prison reform, bear baiting, the lottery). William Wilberforce was the most famous member and in his youth was a nominal Christian but became aware of this whilst travelling on the Continent and was inspired by John Newton's hymn *Amazing Grace*. The group met from 1790-1830 and also included Zachary Macaulay an estate manager who had seen slavery in Jamaica (father of Thomas Babington Macaulay), John Venn vicar of Holy Trinity in 1793-1813, Henry Venn, James Stephen, Hannah More, Granville Sharp a lawyer, John Shore Lord Teignmouth Governor General of India, and Charles Grant of the East Indies Council. They were the most important reforming group at the time and achievements included the Church Missionary Society (1799), British and Foreign Bible Society (1804), abolition of the slave trade (1807), publication of the Christian Observer (1823) and the abolition of slavery in the Empire (1833).

Charles Forster a Welsh clergyman born c. 1812 married Laura Thornton at Holy Trinity, Clapham on 31 August 1833 and their children included two notable sons. Charles Thornton Forster was born at Ash in Kent in 1836 and married Lucy Selina Geraldine (1841) born in Rome. He became vicar of Hinxton after the death of John Graham in 1865 and had six children in the village: Arthur E.T. (1867), Ethel L.C. (1868), Mabel Edith Geraldine (1870), Charles H.T. (1872), Henry Leopold V. (1874) and Maud W.D. (1878). The family resided at Hinxton Vicarage in 1881 with three visitors Eugene Mainwaring, Irine and Dora Calliphronas, and four servants. The daughter Mabel E.G. Forster married William Lennox Napier in 1890 and lived at 1 Temple Sheen with brothers Arthur and Leopold in 1891 - no doubt they moved there due to an ongoing link with the Graham family. Charles Thornton Forster died at Bakewell in December 1891 aged 55 years.

Edward Morgan Llewellyn Forster was born in 1848 and trained as an architect and married Alice Clara Whichelo at Wandsworth in March 1877 - she was born in Lambeth in March 1855. Their son Edward Morgan Forster otherwise E.M. Forster was born in Marylebone on 1 January 1879 and was destined to be a famous writer. He was the cousin of the Forsters of Hinxton and also of Mabel Napier who lived at 1 Temple Sheen. His father Edward Morgan L. Forster died at Christchurch in December 1880 aged 32 years and he was brought up by his mother 'Lily' and had assistance from his great aunt Marianne Thornton. Indeed Alice C. Forster (26), widow and gentlewoman, lived at 6 Melcombe Place next to Marylebone Station in 1881 with son Edward M. (2), a visitor Mary Ann Lynnot (42) born in the East Indies and two servants. Marianne Thornton (1797) continued her father's work in Clapham and was an evangelist and reformer as well as writer. She became friends with Thomas Babington Macaulay (1800-59) through the Clapham Sect, whilst he wrote the famous *History of England from James II* that became a bestseller. Indeed only Sir Walter Scott and Charles Dickens could match him in terms of sales. Marianne Thornton age 84, unmarried, lived at the Sweep, Clapham in 1881 with nieces Henrietta Lynnot (40), Emily Sykes (42) the wife of Cam, son Ernest Ruthven Sykes (13) and five servants. She was a benefactor of her great nephew E.M. Forster and left him £8,000 in trust when she died in 1887.

This improved the family's prospects and his mother moved to Rooksnest, Stevenage in 1883-93 and then to Tonbridge in 1893. He was educated at Tonbridge School and then attended King's College, Cambridge in 1897-1901 and after graduating travelled with his mother to Italy and Greece. This experience gave him some notable inspiration and he began to write and published A Room with a View (1908), Howards End (1910) and A Passage to India (1924). He then had further good fortune and inherited a house Abinger Harvest in 1924 and then gave the Clark Lectures at Trinity, Cambridge on his book *Aspects of the Novel* (1927). This contained just 7 chapters on the composition of writing and during the lectures made reference to *The Craft of Fiction* (1921). Percy Lubbock the author of the latter was born the same year and it is thought they were acquainted (see Ch. 7). E.M. Forster was also loosely associated with the likes of Virginia Woolf and the Bloomsbury Group. Alice C. Forster his mother died at Surrey S.E. in March 1945 aged 89 and he wrote a biography of his great aunt Marianne Thornton (1956) and died in 1970. His books give an evocative depiction of Victorian and Edwardian days and the Merchant Ivory Company made many of them into films.

Robert George Graham was born at Hinxton on 2 January 1845 and baptized in the parish church on 2 February that year. He spent his childhood living at the Vicarage with his family and was educated at Cheltenham College in 1861-62. He was there at the same time as H.W. Renny-Tailyour but before G.W. Addison although he was older than both. His education, however, came to an end at his father's decease in July 1862 and he then went into business. The family moved to Barnes in Surrey although the reason for this is uncertain and Robert, having played football at school, then joined Barnes F.C. soon after it was formed. Mrs. Graham lived at 2 Lonsdale Villas, Lonsdale Road, in 1865-67 near to Hammersmith Bridge and the house is still there today. The Wedgwood family lived next door at 4 Park Villas, Lonsdale Road and also at 11 Castelnau Villas (see Ch. 16). Helen Eliza Graham was born at Hinxton on 25 October 1846 and baptized on 20 December that year and moved with her family to Barnes. She met Robert Watson Willis through her brother and, as stated, married there on 28 August 1867. Those present included Rev. John Graham junior, Robert George and Emily Sophia Graham.

Robert was on the F.A. Committee in 1867-68 thus he played for Kent-Surrey on 2 November 1867 and for Surrey on 25 January 1868. He took part in both games with R.W. Willis who was his colleague, friend and relative and on the second occasion was captain of the Surrey team. He was elected Secretary of the F.A. from 1868-70 as well as F.A. Treasurer in 1869-70 and was only 23 years old when he took on the position of Secretary. John Hackblock gentleman and his wife Matilda lived at Denmark Hill, Camberwell and had children John (4 May 1844) baptized 2 September at St. Giles, William H. (1846), Arthur (June 1847), Emma (June 1848) and Alice (March 1851) but moved to East Sheen by the 1860s. Robert George Graham stockbroker of Barnes married Alice Hackblock (18) by licence at Christchurch, East Sheen on 15 September 1869. Edward Gillson performed the ceremony (born Greetham in 1799) and Norman Trouson, J. Hackblock and Emma Hackblock were the witnesses. Indeed the church and village of East Sheen are still present today but are concealed in suburban developments. Emma Hackblock (sister) married Duncan McKenzie (1842) solicitor at East Sheen on 12 April 1871 and Matilda her mother died at Kensington in March 1873 aged 66 whilst Duncan McKenzie lived at 8 Trebovir Road, Earl's Court in 1881 with wife Emma and daughters Margaret, Madeline and Lillias. William H. Hackblock barrister not practicing lived at Mousehold House, Thorpe near Norwich in 1881 with wife Matilda, children Emily born Barnes, May born Caterham and Arthur and Herbert C. born Mulbarton. He was a company director and barrister living at Coltishall in 1901 with Herbert a brewer's manager and Emily.

Meanwhile Robert a member of the Stock Exchange lived at "Lyndhurst", Barnes in 1871 with wife Alice, cousin Florence J. Ingle (18) from Plymouth, a visitor Mary E.A. Stephens (28) from Barnstaple and three servants. The house was situated on Upper Richmond Road two doors away from Thomas Merriman at the Manor House (see Ch. 10). The remainder of his story is treated below and his family are now considered. His mother Frances Maria Graham, independent, lived at St. Margaret's Cottage, 23 The Terrace in 1871 with daughter Emily Sophia (22) and two servants. She was at 24 The Terrace, however, in 1872-78 and both properties were near the home of E.C. Morley at no. 26 - unlike the latter they are no longer present and flats cover the site. Sir Francis Molyneux Ommanney M.P. and Navy agent was married to Georgiana Frances Hawkes and their son Octavius was baptized at Mortlake on 19 January 1817 and married Helen Gream at Rotherfield, Sussex on 2 September 1841. The latter's son Frederick Gream Ommanney was born on 11 December 1847 and married Emily Sophia Graham at Barnes in June 1871.

Robert George Graham (1845-1922). He was F.A. Secretary in 1868-70 and lived in Barnes.

The couple had four children: Constance Helen Graham (June 1872) born in Mortlake, Douglas Gream (18 May 1874) baptized Mortlake, Margaret Frederica Graham (14 April 1878) baptized at East Sheen and Gwendolen Ethel Graham (June 1884) born in Walmer, Eastry district in Kent. Indeed the family then resided at Sheen House, Upper Walmer although Octavius and Helen Ommanney moved to Bloxham, Oxford with their children Robert Nelson (lieutenant R.N.), Octavia Manston and Erasmus (retired commander R.N.). The story had one more twist and that is now considered and in the words of Sir Walter Scott "Oh what a tangled web we weave…." Thomas Kenyon of Pradoe in Salop married Charlotte Louisa Lloyd at Oswestry on 21 April 1803. Their son John Robert Kenyon of Pradoe was born on 13 January 1807 (died 1880) and had issue Robert Lloyd (1848-1931) and Edward Ranulph (3 November 1854-1937) who was a major general R.E. The latter's son Herbert Edward Kenyon was born on 2 December 1881 and educated at Winchester then went to the R.M.A. Woolwich and became a lieutenant colonel R.A. He was first cousin once removed of William Slaney Kenyon-Slaney (see Ch. 6) and married Gwendolen E.G. Ommanney on 16 July 1907. He fought with honour in the First War and was mentioned in despatches four times and received the D.S.O. and French and Belgian Croix de Guerre. He was later a governor of Oswestry Grammar School.

Frances Maria Graham left The Terrace, Barnes after 1878 and was a funded proprietor at "Wetheral", Keswick Road, Putney, in 1881 with a visitor and two servants. The names "Wetheral" and "Hinxton" reflected the family's connections however the former no longer exists and Keswick Road has few traces of Victorian times. Frances died at "Wetheral" on 5 August 1889 and was buried in Mortlake Cemetery next to Robert Watson Willis and his son Robert Graham Willis. Indeed all three graves are in the form of a cross with stepped bases and have a single border around them. The former memorial states: "Fanny M. Graham widow of the Rev. John Graham vicar of Hinxton and Swavesey, Cambs who died August 5 1889 aged 85 years." William Graham her son and barrister of 2 Temple Gardens, Temple proved her will on 1 March 1890 the effects being £1,113 1s 4d.

William Graham was born at Hinxton on 3 March 1838 and was baptized in the church on 9 March. He was educated at Sedbergh a famous public school and the choice may have resulted from family connections in the area. Sedbergh was east of Kendal at the northern extremity of Yorkshire (West Riding) and in fact Wakefield the county town was 70 miles away. It was only with local government re-organisation in 1974 that it became part of Cumbria. He matriculated at Emmanuel College, Cambridge in 1856 and entered the Inner Temple on 3 May 1859, then lived at Hinxton in 1861 and became a barrister on 27 January 1862. William Graham married Sarah Anne Orford at St. Matthew's, Ipswich on 24 August 1867 - she was born in the town on 20 June 1834 the daughter of John Orford and Hannah Giles. The couple resided at Notting Hill from 1869-75 but then moved to the Barnes area and William Graham, barrister, lived at Fairfield House, Upper Richmond Road in 1881 with his wife Sarah A., children Ethel, Gerard, Annie E., Norah, Marmaduke W. a nurse and four servants. He had chambers at 1 New Court, Temple and 2 Temple Gardens and practiced on the Midland Circuit and was a special pleader. He became a bencher in 1885 and spoke on the matter of Parnell in 1888 - the latter obstructed Parliament in the 1880s over the question of Irish "home rule". He was standing counsel for the Times and a J.P. for Berks. Sarah A. Graham (married) lived at 41 Upper Richmond Road in 1891 with children William J., Ann E. and Norah, a visitor and two servants, however the son William John attended Cambridge University in 1890-92 and died on 12 September 1893 aged 22. Sarah Ann Graham died on 4 May 1898 aged 63 and William Graham died at 41 Upper Richmond Road, Putney on 5 November 1899 aged 61 - all were buried at Mortlake Cemetery with Frances M. Graham. Near the three graves is a memorial to Charles Dickens *younger* 1837-96 eldest son of Charles Dickens.

Charles James Graham was born at Hinxton on 27 October 1839 and baptized at the church on 15 December. He was initially educated under Edward Thring at Uppingham but then went to Bury St. Edmunds from 1855-58. He matriculated at Peterhouse, Cambridge in Michaelmas 1858 and gained his B.A. in 1862. He then took a different direction and became a sheep farmer in Australia and was a member of the Queensland Government. He came back to London for a time but on his return to the antipodes died at Albany, Southern Australia in March 1886. John Graham was born at Leckhampton near Cheltenham on 3 July 1841 but was baptized at Hinxton on 31 October. He attended Bury (1855-56) and Oakham (1856-59) and matriculated at Jesus College, Cambridge in Michaelmas 1859, gaining his B.A. in 1863. He was ordained a deacon at Ripon in 1867 and became a priest in 1868. He then held a series of curacies viz. Chapelthorpe, Yorks (1867-68), Holy Trinity Hoxton (1869-73), Wells by the Sea (1873-76), St. Clement Danes (1876-79) and Carshalton (1880-85). Indeed John Graham, unmarried, a lodger lived with Mary Grace Baines a widow and her two young sons at Loughborough Terrace, West Street, Carshalton in 1881. He was curate of St. John's, Deptford (1885) and Buckhurst Hill, Essex (1888-90) and rector of Asterby with Goulceby, Lincolnshire from 1890. He stayed at the latter 25 years and died on 22 April 1915, his obituary appearing in the Times on 28 April.

Robert and Alice Graham initially remained in Barnes and had just two daughters from their marriage, which was unusual at this time of large families. Robert was a stockbroker from at least 1869 and as stated lived at "Lyndhurst" in 1871 beside Barnes Common near to Upper Richmond Road (towards Roehampton). Alice Evelyn Manners was born at "Lyndhurst" in December 1871 however her sister Matilda Winifred Muriel was born at 12 Bolton Gardens, South Kensington on 21 April 1873. The house was on the east side and one of three semi-detached properties nos. 10-15. There was an iron-gate and mosaic path with a white stucco ground floor and yellow sandstone brick on the upper two floors. The road then turned by 90° and nos. 16-46 Bolton Gardens were on the south side, with nos. 16-23 being of a similar style with columned porches whilst the houses beyond had red brick on all three floors. Bolton Gardens was south of Barkston Gardens (see Leitch Ch. 17) and north of The Boltons (see Bonsor Ch. 6), and Beatrix Potter lived around the corner in Old Brompton Road from 1866-1913. The latter spent much time at the local museums and wrote the Peter Rabbit stories at the house, before marrying in 1913 and moving to the Lake District (died in 1943). Indeed the literary associations in this chapter such as Thornton, Macaulay, Forster, Dickens and Potter soon provided further inspiration.

The father Robert was a stockbroker with Glyn & Co. from 1876-78 and would have been familiar with the Pembers who are discussed in Ch. 4. He continued to live at "Lyndhurst" until at least 1878 but then moved to a large house called St. Alban's on the banks of the River Thames at Hampton. This was a plain four-storey property in red brick east of the parish church on Thames Street (now Hampton Court Road). The house was of an unusual design due to the constraints of site and was long and narrow, backing right onto the road. There was a lawn in front going down to the river and a boathouse with a horse chestnut to one side, the gardens stretched away to the east and at the far end there were a series of stepped terraces. There was a narrow lodge beside the house and behind was Bushy Park, whilst the property Garrick's House was just to the west. A short distance further on the opposite side of the road was Garrick's Villa and this now has a plaque stating: "David Garrick 1717-79 actor lived here." Nearby in gardens beside the river was Garrick's Temple an octagonal building with Classical portico. The actor had it built in 1756 as a tribute to Shakespeare and Capability Brown was the designer. It stands in attractive gardens and was restored in 1999, whilst St. Mary's Church was just beyond. The house was in an attractive location with extensive grounds and had views of the several islands punctuating the Thames at this point. It would have been a peaceful place before the age of the car and was to be the scene of much creativity.

Robert G. Graham a member of the Stock Exchange lived at St. Alban's Bank in 1881 with wife Alice, daughters Alice and Matilda both scholars, a governess, three house servants, a coachman and a horse trainer. This was the principal property on Thames Street other than Garrick's Villa, the Vicarage and two inns, whilst gardeners, a coachman, the parish schoolmaster and the park-keeper for Bushy Park lived nearby. Indeed the Graham family were to live there for eighty years. Teddington purchased its first fire engine in 1830 but there were few facilities in Hampton and a serious fire occurred at Rose Villa in Station Road in November 1867. The engine that attended could not find sufficient water and the hose was too short - the house stood on the Beveree now the home of Hampton & Richmond F.C. There were similar problems in 1870 and a volunteer fire brigade was established at Hampton Hill in June 1876. There were still no such facilities in the village itself hence there was a vestry meeting in 1885, and the parish asked someone to take the initiative. Several men came forward to form a volunteer fire brigade and Robert Graham consented to act as their captain. He was to be a considerable influence on the brigade and was associated with it until his death.

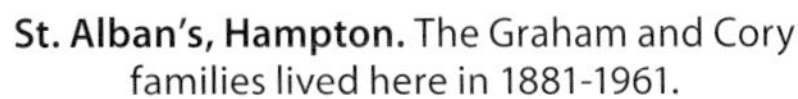

St. Alban's, Hampton. The Graham and Cory families lived here in 1881-1961.

Robert George Graham, company director and employer, lived at St. Alban's Bank, Hampton Court Road in 1891 with wife Alice, daughters Alice Evelyn and Matilda Winifred, visitor Maxwell S. Kerving stockbroker's clerk and three servants. It was at this time that William and Mabel Napier lived at 1 Temple Sheen with the brother-in-law Arthur E.T. Forster also a stockbroker's clerk. The latter lived near the sister Helen E. Willis at "Hinxton House" and may have worked for Robert at the Stock Exchange. A serious fire destroyed the Bell Hotel in 1892 not due to a lack of water but too few hands to pump it. This high-lighted the need for a steam pump thus the Urban District Council obtained premises for a new fire station in Thames Street in 1895. There was then a merger with Hampton Hill and the fire station opened in February 1898. Today, the Southwark and Vauxhall Water Company, Riverdale Works and clock tower (1897) are in Thames Street opposite the 'old' fire station with its red brick and bright-red doors, now used as a photographers. The first steam powered engine arrived at Hampton fire station in 1900 and clearly such matters took time to organize - fire or no fire. The area was changing and trams came down Church Street and past St. Alban's in the 20th century.

John Hubert Grogan was born in Ireland in 1866 and married Alice Evelyn M. Graham at Kensington in September 1895 and went to live in Worthing. Their son Hubert was born there in 1897 whilst Robert was born in Ireland in 1900. The family were living at Worthing in 1901 with his mother Elizabeth Grogan (61) from Upper Clapton. Robert G. Graham a retired member of the Stock Exchange lived at St. Alban's Bank in 1901 with his wife Alice, daughter Winifred Graham (27) and three servants. Literary skills pervaded the corridors of St. Alban's and the daughter became a writer of some distinction. Her aunt Helen E. Willis then lived at 1 Temple Sheen and Richard W. Cory (46) a barrister was next door at no. 2, which may have resulted in a liaison. Richard Cory was born Bideford in 1830 and married Emily Vivian at Gwinear near Redruth in Cornwall in September 1854. He was a colliery proprietor at Oscar House, Newport Road - St. John's, Cardiff in 1881 with wife Emily, children Saxton Campbell (25) merchant, Mabel (10) and Theodore John Cory (6) - born Cardiff June 1874. Richard Cory a retired coal merchant lived at Cardiff in 1901 and his son Theodore John (26) was a law student living at the Inner Temple, London. It seems likely he met the Grahams through relatives at Temple Sheen and Richard was probably his brother.

Theodore John Cory married Matilda Winifred M. Graham at Kensington in September 1906 and he followed a career in the law whilst she was a prolific writer. The family must have spent pleasant days together in the garden by the river, however Robert George Graham died at St. Alban's on 6 April 1922 aged 77. His probate was granted to Alice Graham on 31 May 1922 and his effects were valued at £892 15s 4d. Theodore and Winifred Cory may have come to live at the house after his decease. His widow Alice died at St. Alban's on 17 November 1938 and her probate went to Alice Evelyn Mạnners Grogan and Matilda Winifred M. Cory. The daughters erected a notable alabaster tablet to their memory above the vestry door in the south aisle of St. Mary's viz. "To the glory of God and the dear memory of Robert George Graham Esq. of St Albans Hampton chairman of the National Fire Brigade widows and orphans fund, for 26 years the beloved chief of the Hampton Volunteer Fire Brigade. He passed into the fullness of life April 26th 1922 aged 77 (verse). Also of Alice his beloved wife who re-joined him November 17th 1938 aged 87." Hampton Church was established in 1342 by monks from Takeley Priory, Essex and included a place of worship and grammar school. An impressive grey-stone church with two side galleries and tower replaced the old structure in 1831 and the most important monuments were moved there.

That of most significance is next to the Grahams' memorial in the south aisle and states: "Mrs Susannah Thomas sole daughter and heiress of Sir Dalby Thomas knight governor of all the African companies settlements and of Dame Dorothy daughter of John Chettle of St. Mary Blandford 4 April 1731. Descended from an antient family in Wales." The architect Thomas Archer designed the tomb and Sir Henry William Powell carried out the work. It was a notable piece of funerary architecture with Ionic columns on each side, a 'broken' pediment above, and a marble sculpture showing two reposing figures - it soon came to people's attention. Jerome Klapka Jerome was born at Walsall in 1859 and grew up in poverty and was educated in London. He worked as a railway clerk, actor, reporter, teacher and editor and his most famous book was "Three Men in a Boat" published 1889. It was a comic work about exploits on the Thames and since Jerome married a local Hampton girl it featured the church. He wrote as follows: "Harris wanted to get out at Hampton Church to go

Memorial to R.G. Graham. Located in St. Mary's Church, Hampton.

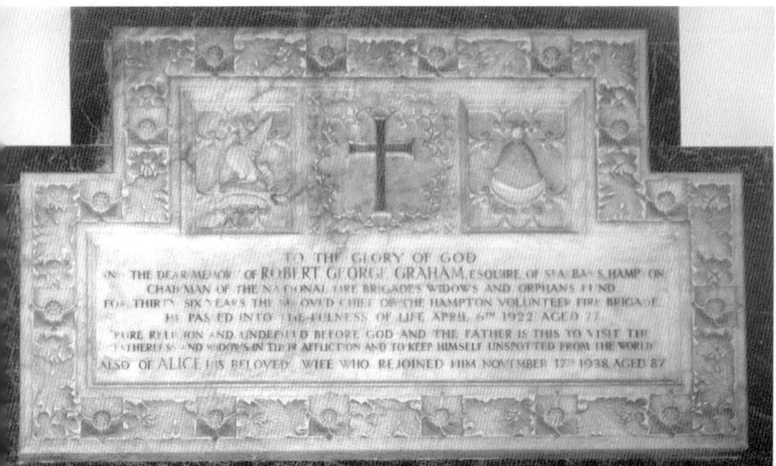

and see Mrs. Thomas's tomb. 'Who is Mrs Thomas?' I asked. 'How should I know?' replied Harris. 'She's a lady that's got a funny tomb and I want to see it'." Jerome also wrote "I like work, it fascinates me, I can sit and look at it for hours." He died in 1927.

Winifred Graham (1873) spent much of her life at St. Alban's in Hampton and it was there that she wrote most of her 88 books. She may have known E.M. Forster a friend of the family from the Hinxton days and thus received inspiration. She was educated at home and began to write at an early age and became a prolific writer of popular novels. These were dramatic and sentimental fictions in an easy and flowing, critical style, although they were not very exacting. She succeeded to carry off situations that the more sophisticated reader might have found unbelievable. She wrote short stories for the Strand Magazine and Red Magazine, and others, including a series entitled The Idylls of Suburbia, all in 1898-1912 (held at the British Library). After her marriage she became anti-Mormon and campaigned against the religion writing 'Ezra the Mormon' (1908) and 'The Mormons - a popular history from earliest times to the present day' *Hurst and Blackett* (1913). On a more positive note she was author of 'The Highway of God' London (1923) notes on 24 lessons for adolescents by a Sunday school teacher at the Sunday School Institute. She maintained a busy social life but after her mother's death became increasingly retrospective and had a great interest in psychic phenomena (like Conan Doyle - see Ch. 4). She published, 'My letters from heaven being messages from the unseen world given in automatic writing to Winifred Graham from her father Robert George Graham' *Rider* (1940) reprint 1943. Her final work was a trilogy and the three books formed her autobiography: 'Observations Casual and Intimate' (1945) and 'I introduce Winifred Graham' that included stories of nice people and pleasant memories and her association with Aleister Crowley a literary friend in Torquay (*Express Dec 1947 Ch 8*). Her 87th book was 'That Reminds Me' (1949) and included, "All those varied experiences which might be of interest to my public." Skeffington & Son Ltd. published these later works.

Matilda Winifred Muriel Cory died at St. Alban's, Hampton Court Road on Sunday 5 February 1950 and her obituary was in the Times the following day. Her probate went to her husband on 27 April her effects £53,600 13s. Theodore John Cory continued to live at St. Alban's however he died at Ashford Hospital, Stanwell on 21 September 1961. Robert Wilberforce Cory and Edward James Howson solicitor obtained his probate on 6 November next his effects being £74,189 11s. There was then an entry in the Times on Wednesday November 15, 1961 stating: "He left his house St Alban's (and St Alban's Lodge after the determination of tenancy trusts) to the Borough of Twickenham to be maintained in perpetuity for the purposes of a museum for the benefit of the inhabitants of Hampton on Thames." Indeed Theodore had high hopes of preserving the house, which had been the family home and source of creative writing for over half a century. He also made a gift of a stained glass window to St. Mary's, Hampton in memory of his wife. Eric Fraser designed the window and Victor Drury & Co. carried out the work (as well as others there) both being members of the church. The tracery windows depicted the four winged archangels Gabriel, Michael, Uriel and Raphael - the latter a traveller with traditional fish in a sling, staff and pouch, and standing above an open book signifying the work of Winifred Graham with a background of St. Alban's, Garrick's Temple and St. Mary's Church. The window is extremely beautiful and is on the south wall next to the Graham memorial and Mrs. Thomas's tomb - it was dedicated on 22 September 1963.

The plans for a local museum came to very little and St. Alban's passed to Richmond Council during re-organisation in 1965. This event signalled the end and after what some considered under-hand dealings the house was demolished in 1972. Today there is only a mound beside a cedar and horse chestnut tree where the house once stood. The grounds, however, have been preserved and provide a walk beside the river whilst the garden terraces at the eastern end still survive. There is an old brick wall from the Grahams' day backing on to St. Alban's Lodge, and the gatepost of the latter displays a coat of arms. There is a plaque in St. Alban's Gardens that states: "These gardens mainly comprise the former property of 'St. Albans' which was given to the local authority by the late Mr. T.J. Cory for the benefit of the inhabitants of Hampton as a memorial to the authoress - Winifred Graham his wife." The churchyard of St. Mary's, Hampton was closed in 1883 however there is a memorial beside the old wall of 1798 that states: "In loving memory of Winifred Graham authoress beloved wife of Theodore John Cory born 21 April 1874 died 5 February 1950. Gently her pen is laid aside but the love, light and joy it gave lives on. Theodore John Cory died 21 September 1961 and his brother Robert W. Cory 12 February 1972, 95." This is a fitting tribute and is in the form of an open book resting on a plinth, with a cord bookmark at the centre. The first 10 years of the F.A. were greatly influenced by the people of Barnes and the fresh air and open spaces no doubt contributed to this fact, however football was soon played on a wider stage and hence the reins passed to Messrs. Alcock and Marindin.

CHAPTER 2

From Sunderland to Snaresbrook

When the Football Association started in 1863 it was a regional organisation and only gained national significance with the arrival of the professional clubs in the late 1870s and 1880s. Ebenezer Morley and his friends had done a great job in getting things started however the F.A. now needed a new kind of official - in particular, someone who could organise its affairs and take them forward over a number of years. The ideal man for the job soon came forward in the form of Charles William Alcock and he held the position of Secretary from 1870-95. Indeed this seemed to be a hard act to follow however the F.A. was soon doubly blessed and Frederick Joseph Wall held the post from 1895-1934. These two most able dignitaries are discussed in the next two chapters.

ALCOCK IN SUNDERLAND

C.W. Alcock was a great organizer and excellent sportsman who played football at the highest level. He had notable antecedents and a privileged education that instilled in him some excellent qualities, which he applied to the developing sports of cricket and football. The Alcock family are mainly traced to Bishopwearmouth in the town of Sunderland however the earliest records show them to be in Newcastle. His great grandfather Samuel Alcock married Barbara Hopper daughter of John and Alice at St. Nicholas's, Newcastle on 29 December 1770 - she being born in Sunderland in 1737. The couple had seven children baptized at St. Nicholas's namely Ann (1772), John (7 November 1773), William (1775), Samuel (1777), Thomas (1778), Ralph (1780) and Mary (1782) *infant*. The father Samuel Alcock was proprietor of *Cannon* P.H. and a Hackney horse-keeper at the Fleshmarket, Newcastle in 1778 however had moved to the *Fun* P.H at East End Close in 1790, and died in 1791. His younger sons remained in Newcastle as brush makers and grocers however it is with his eldest son John that the story really begins.

John Alcock first went south to London and married Elizabeth Preston at St. George's Hanover Square on 4 March 1797 the witnesses being James Cragg and Frances Sarah Woolley. The church was near to Regent Street and he may have had family or business connections in London but he soon returned to the north and lived at Bishopwearmouth east of Sunderland. This was an historic area and Benedict Biscop founded the Saxon church of St. Peter's in A.D. 674, which became Monkwearmouth parish north of the River Wear - he also founded a monastery at Jarrow in A.D. 682 and the two churches were home to 600 monks. The area south of the river was in the jurisdiction of the Bishop of Durham - hence Bishopwearmouth. This was an important centre for shipbuilding that attracted mariners and allied trades, whilst coastal vessels travelled to London especially regarding the coal industry and Sunderland was a separate parish in the early 19th century. Every town has its High Street however in Sunderland one of the main arteries was Low Street, which was close to the River Wear and its docks. Indeed there were over 400 shipyards beside the river but most of these went bankrupt or were taken over in the late 19th century.

Bishopwearmouth was closely connected to Sunderland being the area of the town between the railway and the North Sea. The Alcock family lived at the former for at least 100 years and they became prominent and successful in the town, but did maintain some links with Newcastle. John Alcock had established himself in Bishopwearmouth by 1798 and traded in two areas, firstly as upholsterer and secondly as ship owner and shipbuilder - the two businesses were not so different since both involved wooden construction and fitting out. John and Elizabeth Alcock had seven children born in the town: Samuel (1798), John Thomas (1799), William (1801) *infant*, Henry (1803), Thomas Cape (1804) *infant*, Charles (1806) and Elizabeth (1809). The four surviving brothers entered the family business or traded in their own right and were notable people in Sunderland in the mid-19th century. Further to this Samuel Alcock (1777) the brother married Sarah Henderson at Bishopwearmouth in 1809 - probably worked in the business.

Charles Dickens (1812-70) was born at Landport, Hants and his father was then a clerk in the Navy pay office, but they moved to London and Chatham after 1814. He had a limited education and had to work in a blacking factory in Hungerford Market in 1824 as his father was in the Marshalsea debtors prison. There was then an improvement and he attended Wellington House Academy in 1824-27. He was a law office clerk and legal reporter at Doctors' Commons in 1828 and all these experiences influenced his later writings. He first wrote for magazines and then published some of the most important books regarding Victorian social history. *Hard Times* was published in 1854 and Dickens exposed the poverty of northern industrial towns with his character Thomas Gradgrind a heartless industrialist and the fictional Coketown. These were *Hard Times* indeed and Elizabeth Alcock died in c.1810 leaving John Alcock a widower with five children under twelve years.

Thomas Crawhall married Ann Bownas at Allendale west of Newcastle on 21 November 1771 and their daughter Hannah was baptized in the local chapel on 28 November 1776. John Alcock then married Hannah Crawhall at St. Nicholas's, Newcastle on 1 October 1811 and had four children in Bishopwearmouth viz. Ann (1813), Barbara (1814), Hannah (1817) and Thomas Crawhall (1818) - the latter was the fifth son of John and like his brothers went into business. John Alcock continued to be successful but was seriously ill when he made his last will on 3 January 1838 and died five days later. He was described as ship owner and his executors were Hannah Alcock wife, John Robinson (ship owner and late upholsterer) and Joseph Crawhall of St. Anne's House, Newcastle (rope manufacturer). He left his personal estate, household goods, reading books, pheaton carriage, horse and haystack to his wife Hannah, his mode of transport being much prized. The property that he left showed he was a wealthy man - most was near to Sunderland Station and Wearmouth Bridge:

1. Copyhold, messuage or dwelling house situated in Tatham Street called *Tavistock House* with garden, coach house and appurtenances.

2. Warerooms, workshops and yard in the back street between Sunniside and Nile Street (see below re. Sunniside).

3. Copyhold dwelling house in Cross Street at the back of Nile Street, opposite my workshops - occupied by Mr. Fotheringham.

4. House and shop in Charles Street - occupied by Mary Hall.

5. 3/5 Freehold of two shops in the Blose, Newcastle.

John then bequeathed his share and interest in the business of upholsterer and cabinet-maker to son Samuel Alcock (who was already a partner) and left, "his ships, vessels, monies and other personal estate," in trust, the rents etc. to be paid to his wife Hannah while she remained his widow, then after she died or remarried they were to be sold and the money paid to his children as tenants-in-common. Thomas Crawhall, Ann and Hannah Alcock could purchase *Tavistock House* and the Tatham Street premises at a value of £1,200 whilst unmarried. He asked his executors to invest any monies, "and to carry on the business of upholsterer and cabinet-makers, navigate his ships and vessels and arrange for the required insurances.... and to sell his ships at their discretion," the proceeds for his widow Hannah. His estate was to be divided equally amongst his children with the proviso of "hotchpot". They had to 'repay' money given to them to enable an equal division and the following sums applied: Samuel £400, John Thomas £325, Charles £325, Henry £325, Thomas Crawhall £225, Elizabeth £280 and Barbara £200 (sons and two married daughters) - William Snowball a solicitor and Hannah Hudspith were the witnesses. John Alcock a ship owner of Tavistock Place died of 'cause unknown' at Norfolk Street on 8 January 1838 age 65 the informant his son Samuel also of Norfolk Street. He was buried at Bishopwearmouth Church on 12 January 1838 and his executors (and trustees) proved his will in Durham on 27 March 1839 the effects under £6,000. Life however had to go on and his five sons took different paths.

Samuel Alcock (1798) married Elizabeth Wright in c.1827 and had five children - John Wright (1828), William Charles (1831), Samuel (1835), Margaret Wright (1840) and Elizabeth (1842). He continued to run the business of cabinet-maker and upholsterer and placed an advert in the *Sunderland Herald* in 1838 stating: "Owing to the recent death of Mr. J. Alcock his son Samuel will carry on the business, cash sale etc...." He lived at 24 Norfolk Street, Bishopwearmouth in 1841 and 1851 and appeared in the local directory in 1847, whilst Alcock and Sons also had premises at 64 Nile Street and he was described as a ship owner in 1851. He was a notable character in the town being an alderman and magistrate (J.P.) for Sunderland and was the Mayor in 1853 and moved to Ashmore House, Stockton Road by 1855. He was also Mayor in 1859/60 and died at Ashmore House on 1 November 1879 when his personal estate was under £30,000. John Wright Alcock was involved in the family business and was a councillor and Town Clerk whilst Samuel Alcock junior was a solicitor and attorney with premises at 4 East Sunniside. The latter married the niece of William Snowball (Town Clerk) and was a councillor and Deputy Town Clerk but had housing problems in 1880 and was bankrupt in 1885 (see below). There was a court case regarding the misuse of funds and Samuel absconded to America for a time although other sources suggest the Isle of Wight.

THE TIMES

TUESDAY, MAY 2, 1882

The Mayor of Sunderland v Alcock

The question raised in this case was as to the right of a corporation to recover expenses incurred under the Public Health Act from persons who had become owners of the property after the works were completed. In the year 1877 the Corporation of Sunderland, after giving the proper notices under the Public Health Act of 1875 (38 and 39 Vic, chap. 55), executed certain sanitary works in Ward Street, Sunderland, and apportioned the cost on the houses in the street. The corporation did not proceed to recover the money in the summary manner provided by the Act, but in August, 1880, they brought this action against the defendant, Samuel Alcock, who was not the owner at the time the works were executed, but had bought the houses in 1879, claiming that the sums apportioned might be declared a charge on the houses, under the 257th section of the Act, and might be raised accordingly. The section alluded to provided that where any local authority had incurred expenses, for the repayment whereof the owner of the premises for the time being was liable, such expenses might be recovered, with interest at 5 per cent, from any person who was the owner of such premises when the works were completed for which such expenses had been incurred, and until the recovery thereof the same should be a charge on the premises in respect of which they were incurred.

Mr. Higgins Q.C. and Mr. H. Humphreys appeared for the corporation. Mr. Rigby Q.C. and Mr. Warmington, for the defendant, contended that the person liable was the owner of the houses when the works were done, not a subsequent purchaser.

Mr. Justice Kay said there was no doubt that the corporation might have recovered the money from the owner at the time the works were executed by summary process. The time for that had now expired, and on the construction of the Act his Lordship was of opinion that a charge on the property was created, and that the mere negligence of the corporation did not deprive them of the right to a charge. Nor was there any hardship in holding this view, as the defendant was aware of the state of things when he purchased. The plaintiffs were, therefore, entitled to recover, and the defendant must pay the costs.

Henry Alcock (1803) was the third son of John and there was no mention of him in the 1851 directory but he was a ship owner in 1855 and a widower and ship owner at 1 Cumberland Terrace, Bishopwearmouth in 1861. He died at Dunstan in the Low Team district of Gateshead on 1 March 1872 and his estate was under £300. Thomas Crawhall Alcock (1818) only son from the second marriage remained at *Tavistock House*, 78 Tatham Street with his mother and sisters after his father's decease in 1838, but the situation did not last and mother Hannah died on 25 April 1845 and sisters Ann on 2 November 1851 and Hannah on 15 May 1854 (spinsters). Thomas stayed at *Tavistock House* but took a different route to his brothers and was a solicitor at 1/9 Nile Street, just around the corner, and a ship owner and agent for the Scottish Union Fire and Life Insurance Co. He married Ellen Horsfall in c.1854 and then had five children at *Tavistock House*: Ellen (1855), Thomas Horsfall (1856), Alfred (1859), Francis Crawhall (1860) and Beatrice (1863). Thomas a gentleman died on 3 August 1864 and his widow Ellen obtained his probate on 3 September his effects under £6,000. William Farrar a chemist and druggist of West Hartlepool (nephew) administered his sisters' effects in 1865 whilst his estate was re-sworn at under £5,000 in July 1867.

The most important characters in the story, however, are John Thomas Alcock (1799) and Charles Alcock (1806) who entered the ship building industry in a big way and established a shipyard in 1835-42. This was located at the western end of Low Street in an area called Pann's Bank and a plaque states: "This was the commercial heart of old Sunderland since the 16th century and was used by a succession of industries until the shipyard closures of the 1960s." The Alcock shipyard began as a partnership and the company first built ships from 200-300 tons - 4 in 1835, 2 in 1836, 4 in 1837 and 2 in 1838 and roughly one vessel a year after generally of a larger tonnage. The partnership was dissolved in 1842 and

Charles Alcock went into ship brokerage whilst John Thomas Alcock continued as a ship builder. The latter married Margaret Bolton in c.1837 and had seven children: John (1838), Grace (1839), Elizabeth (1841), Jane Bolton (1842), Lucy (1844), George Henry (1845) and Margaret Florence Dora (1855).

He ran the shipyard at 1 Low Street from 1842-65 and it was described as: "A building yard, patent slipway and hard in Low Street" in 1852. He was an original member of the Shipbuilders Association in 1853 serving on the Committee and the Court of Arbitration and lived at "North Grange", 7 Stockton Road in 1847-55 then moved to Grindon Hall, Silksworth by 1859. He was "a shipbuilder employing 60 men and 40 boys" in 1861 and was also a ship owner. Indeed the company constructed large vessels and the scale increased with time viz. snow of 205 tons in 1847, barque of 421 tons in 1852 and ship of 561 tons in 1853 - the "Lobelia" their largest ship was built in 1855 and weighed 823-840 tons (owned by the Alcock family). They built further vessels in 1857-65 and these were described as snow, brig, barque and ship whilst the tonnage varied from 166-623 tons and most had names of flowers. Their last construction the "Prudhoe" a barque of 576 tons was built in 1865. Some vessels were sold, however John Thomas Alcock owned many of them and had 17 in his own name with a further 8 where the company purchased the finished hull, whilst his family owned others - for instance:

1835 - Allendale 256 tons, John and Henry Alcock

1835 - Water Witch 220 tons, selves, upholsterers

1845 - Stagshaw 258 tons, selves - lost 1850

1851 - Eos barque 348 tons, Thomas C. Alcock - lost 1862

1852 - Acacia barque 353 tons, Charles Alcock

1859 - Melita barque 324 tons, Forster

1859 - Harkaway ship 615 tons, Alcock, London (later Malta)

1859 - Laurel ship 638 tons, 1873 Willis, London (R.W. Willis)

The shipyard was sold by 1870 and John Thomas Alcock lived at 9 Percy Terrace, Jesmond near Newcastle in 1881 and died there on 24 May 1884 - his estate worth just £259 10s 8d. This was a surprising figure as the company was most prolific and the bulk of the wealth was distributed before his decease - the Scotia Engine Works were built on the shipyard in 1895. Charles Alcock was born in Bishopwearmouth on 21 May 1806 and lived his early life in the town being the fifth ship-owning brother. He helped to establish the shipyard in 1835 then married Elizabeth Frances (1816) daughter of John Forster ship owner at Bishopwearmouth on 19 December 1839. Charles Alcock wrote his last will soon after the marriage on 2 April 1841 and gave some useful details - indeed it was written forty years before his death: "This is the last will and testament of me Charles Alcock of Bishopwearmouth in the County of Durham, shipbuilder. I give devise and bequeath all my part share and interest in the shipbuilding yard and premises in Sunderland near the sea, in the County of Durham, adjoining and near the River Wear, now in the occupation of myself and brother John Alcock.... and all my real and personal estate.... unto my dear wife Elizabeth Alcock." He left any trust property to his executors namely his wife, Robert Fairfield ship owner and William Snowball gentleman and his will was witnessed by clerks of the latter. This confirmed his role in the shipyard however there were two unusual elements (i) he never wrote another will (ii) he left the shipyard soon after. He made the will with a forthcoming birth in mind and the couple lived at 10 Norfolk Street and had two sons there: John Forster Alcock (14 April 1841) and Charles Alcock (2 December 1842) - both were to have an important role in the evolution of soccer.

Druries House at Harrow. The building was extended in 1865 after the Alcocks left.

The couple lived at 10 Fawcett Street in 1847 and had children Edward (1844), William (1846), Arthur (1848) and Horatio

Robert (1850) *infant.* Charles Alcock ship owner and broker lived at 17 John Street in 1851 with his wife Elizabeth, five sons and three servants and stayed at this address until at least 1855. He had daughters Anne Elizabeth (1853) and Ada Mary Eugenie (1856) and was a shipbroker and merchant at 54 Sans Street in 1847-55: Alcock & Smith secretaries to the Albion Premium Insurance Association were also at this address. The family were affluent and two sons went to Harrow School: John Forster (1855-57) and Charles (1855-59) the latter arriving there soon after his brother. They lodged in "Druries" house at the junction of Church Hill and the High Street, this being a notable building below the original School House (1615) at the centre of the complex. The house remains today and the date 1865 is inscribed on it although some parts are far older. Sport was an important part of the curriculum in the 19th century and this included cricket and football however the rules of the latter were most unusual (see later). The playing of soccer is recorded in the street names and Football Lane leads downhill to the playing fields. The Alcocks then left Sunderland and followed the two brothers south to the "Great Wen".

ALCOCK IN THE SOUTH

Charles Alcock senior was described as a shipbuilder of Ayres Quay in 1859. This was an area to the west of Sunderland and opposite the Stadium of Light however it was apparently just a business address since he moved south about 1855-57 and he lived at "Sunnyside", Chingford, Essex by 1857. Indeed it seems that his sons' presence at Harrow brought this about and he soon had the life of a country gentleman. Chingford was originally a rural village on the edge of Epping Forest however it became a fashionable area for London gents in the 18th and 19th centuries and a number of country houses were built, although the main changes occurred when the railway arrived in 1873. "Sunnyside" house may have been built for him and was located to the west of Chingford Green and overlooked the valley towards Edmonton. It was just behind the historic Kings Head Inn and had extensive grounds with a tree lined avenue leading up to it, and a lodge at the entrance on Kings Head Hill. This was a rural location and the whole property looked out over the fields - the name was derived from the Sunniside area of Sunderland.

William Alcock the son died of heart disease at Chingford soon after their arrival on 20 April 1858 aged just 11 - a family tragedy and significant event regarding this discourse. This was clearly a great loss that affected brother Charles and he took the middle name William in memory of his brother - he was born as 'Charles' but was called 'Charles William' by the time of his marriage. The other event of importance was the education of the two younger sons at Forest School near Snaresbrook and this had a material effect on soccer history. Edward Alcock was sent to Bramham College, Yorkshire in c.1855 but went to Forest School when his family moved south and was there from 1857-59 - he then went to sea. His brother Arthur Alcock attended the school in 1859 and stayed until Christmas 1862 when he left to go into business. Charles Alcock, ship owner, lived at "Sunnyside" in 1861 with his wife Elizabeth, John F. (19), Charles (17) both shipbrokers, Arthur (11) scholar, Anne E., Ada M. and a servant and nurse. John Forster and Charles Alcock left Harrow by 1859 then had to make their way in the world. Charles William Alcock became an author, journalist and publisher and produced *The "Oval" Series of Games* in 1894. It was a joint publication detailing the history of the Rugby Union and Association Game and provides a valuable insight into early soccer history. It was from his perspective and is most illuminating however, as shall be shown, it was biased in some areas and the truth altered to 'paint' a certain picture.

Sunnyside Lodge, Chingford. This was at the entrance to the Alcocks' estate in 1857-90.

He begins by describing the early development of soccer in the public schools and at several clubs and states: "There was little progress in the sport before 1859 however there were some developments in Sheffield whilst the Crusaders played games against Charterhouse and Westminster Schools in London." He says that these schools provided the inspiration for the F.A. code and their rules were most in accord with the Association game. The contests were at Charterhouse Square north of the City and at Vincent Square near Westminster

Abbey - both are present today. Charterhouse removed from Aldersgate to Godalming in 1872 but the buildings remain beside the square. The tree-lined green is small and there is barely room for a game of soccer, and it appears they actually played on the hard school quadrangle. Westminster School began as a school for clerks in mediaeval times in Little Dean's Yard as part of the Benedictine Abbey of Westminster. It continued after the dissolution of the monasteries in 1540 and was re-formed by Elizabeth I in 1560. It has historic buildings dated 1090-1100 however was always restricted being entirely within the Abbey precincts. Notable pupils include Sir Christopher Wren and Charles Wesley and the school had 570 pupils in 1980 including 70 girls. The Westminster School Playing Fields are still at Vincent Square near Pimlico and these are quite extensive with an old pavilion and two lodges at the northern end. There is room for three football pitches and one can imagine the early players kicking a ball there.

Charles Alcock suggests the game developed at these schools due to their proximity to London - it being easy for old boys and others to play there after leaving jobs in the City. This gave soccer some much-needed support however he was less complimentary about some other schools. He said that the 'purest' game was at Eton where no hands were allowed and there was an offside rule, whilst Winchester played a similar sport to the Eton Wall Game and Harrow surprisingly came in for the most criticism! He says that they had heavy ground there with, 'a peculiar species of football,' that prevailed as late as 1894. He noted that the goal was referred to as a base and they used the extraordinary 'Three Yard Rule' where a player could catch the ball, shout out "Three Yards", and jump through the goal posts to score in three strides. This clearly agitated Alcock even though it was at Harrow that he came to love football, and this brings us to the point where a half-truth was told.

Alcock mentioned some centres where early football developed including Barnes, Richmond Green, Thames Valley and a group at Mincing Lane in London. The sport, however, had opposition from some quarters and especially from *The Lancet* medical magazine, who believed it was most dangerous and they jumped on every accident of the most trivial kind - to prove their point. The movement, meanwhile, was growing deep in Epping Forest and Alcock provided the following commentary: "It was the winter of 1859-60, that really saw the first game of the great football revival. Great things it is said, from trivial causes spring. The trivial cause in this instance was the humble desire of a few Old Harrovians, who had just left school, to keep up the practice at all events of the game, at which they had some considerable aptitude." Under the shadow of the Merchant Seamen's Orphan Asylum at Snaresbrook 'sprang the Forest F.C.' and they played using the Harrow School code but omitted giving a catch to a player running behind (rugby). The club became 'a resplendent butterfly' when Forest was renamed Wanderers F.C. in 1864.

Charles Alcock clearly deserves much credit for the creation of the famous Wanderers side however he has tried to take it all. There are two important questions that come to mind in relation to this: Firstly, why were they called Forest F.C.? Secondly, why did they play at Snaresbrook, Leytonstone? The club was formed in 1859 and played games on land near the Forest School and in the words of Alcock: "In the shadow of the Merchant Seamen's Orphan Asylum." The simple answer might be that his brothers' connection with Forest School took the club there, however the details are more complex. The first area of interest is the orphan asylum and one can ask - was there a connection to C. Alcock senior and the shipping industry? The original orphan asylum was established at St. George's in the East near Stepney in 1817 but had outgrown these facilities by 1859, thus a new seven acre site was purchased from Lord Mornington of Wanstead Hall for the sum of £1,686 19s 6d.

Garrett Wesley (1735-81) 1st Earl of Mornington was an Irish politician and his sons included: Richard Colley Wellesley (1760-1842) Marquis and 2nd Earl, William Wellesley-Pole (1763-1845) 3rd Earl and Arthur Wellesley (1769-1852) the Duke of Wellington - 1814. William was heir to the estates of cousin William Pole in 1778 and became Earl of Mornington in 1842 upon the death of his brother Marquis Wellesley - he died in 1845 and the Earldom passed to his son. The 4th Earl of Mornington was born in 1788 and had a notable and notorious life, and married Catherine sister and co-heiress of Sir James Tylney-Long Bart who had a large personality and estates to match in Essex and Hampshire worth over a million p.a. He took the names Tylney Long upon marriage in 1812 and became William Pole Tylney Long-Wellesley. He was an infamous character commemorated in a famous line of verse: "Bless every man possess'd of aught to give, long may Long Tylney Wellesley Long Pole live." His wife died in 1825 and he was generally charged with using up her fortune, but he could not do this as he only had a life interest. He married his mistress Helena Bligh widow of Captain Thomas Bligh of the Coldstream Guards in 1828. The 4th Earl of Mornington led a dissipated life and was deprived of the custody of his children in the Chancery Court and committed to Fleet Prison for contempt in July 1831. Despite these flaws he spent time as a Tory in Parliament and helped defeat the Wellington ministry in 1830 - indeed he stood against his uncle who was Prime Minister (and a staunch Tory). To add insult to injury the 4th Earl spent the rest of his life living off the bounty of his uncle and died in 1857 and was succeeded by William Richard Arthur his son. The 5th Earl of Mornington lived from 1813-63 and inherited his mother's estates in Essex. It was he who provided the land for the orphan asylum thus the Alcock family appears to have no direct link to the orphanage, despite their maritime associations.

The Merchant Seamen's Orphan Asylum is of some note and well worth a mention being erected beside the Chigwell Road in 1861-62, on a section later known as Hermon Hill. G.C. Clarke designed the building in the Venetian Gothic style and Albert 'Prince Consort' laid the foundation stone. The structure was of truly Gothic proportions and provided places for 300 orphans of British merchant seamen. It was built on three storeys with a large tower at the front and an extensive wing to the rear, and had red brick with black banding and ogee window arches at the first floor. No expense was spared in the construction and there was elaborate stonework around the window lintels and ornate detail on the roof pediment. Prince Albert who had backed the Crystal Palace Exhibition was no doubt impressed. There was a monumental columned entrance with a frieze above the door that had shipping scenes - the Victorians did their best but the irony was that they depicted shipwrecks! The entrance had black, red and white stone with a niche and clock tower above, whilst three more friezes of shipping scenes were at the north side, and there was a detached chapel. The orphans needed this for prayer after seeing the intimidating nature of the building and must have felt like a child in Dickens, however the patrons probably felt they had done well by these orphans. This was a strange backdrop for the emergence of soccer and the club played there until 1864 when they moved to Battersea Park (as the Wanderers).

This was an unusual location for such a large building since Snaresbrook was a small hamlet with just a few houses. The only other buildings were Eagle Inn on Woodford High Road, Eagle Pond and an 18th century country house, whilst the orphanage was located beyond the Woodford to Loughton branch line. The building became "The Convent of the Good Shepherd" in 1919 a fact witnessed by the addition of a girls' entrance on the north side. It had Draconian Victorian attitudes and was described as: "A home for girls in need of care or correction and readjustment of morals" - they worked in the laundry and on needlework. Essex C.C. purchased the building in 1937 and planned to demolish it and build a new hospital on the site, but the war intervened and the original orphanage became Wanstead Hospital. The building was then listed and transformed into private housing in 1996.

John and Charles Alcock, meanwhile, were only interested in football and would not have thought of living there and resided at Chingford after leaving Harrow School. They both played for the Forest F.C. and John Alcock became the captain, so why would they choose to play at Snaresbrook when their Chingford home was four miles to the north? Clearly their brother Arthur was at the Forest School in 1859-62 and this was significant, however there is strong evidence that the Harrovians were not the sole founders of the club. This statement goes contrary to the official records and the claims of Charles Alcock, and the evidence is as follows. The Forest F.C. team photograph of 1863 (*Official F.A. History, Bryon Butler*) lists the players as J. Pardoe, F.E. Adams, R. Edmonds, C. Bigland, J.F. Alcock, C.W. Alcock, C.D. Jackson, C.M. Tebbut, W.B. Standidge, A.M. Tebbut and A.L. Cutbill. It appeared wise to investigate the history of these players to check out the statement of Charles Alcock - was it really Old Harrovians who started the Forest F.C? The initial step was to look at the Harrow records but this was the first surprise since only three of these players went to Harrow School viz. John/Charles Alcock and John Pardoe. This problem immediately put a question mark against the statement of Charles Alcock and posed the question - were other people involved in the formation of the Forest F.C.? Indeed the Old Harrovians and the Harrow Chequers (who were connected to the school) also played soccer hence it seems likely that other factors had an influence. It was not possible to trace all the players however the results obtained were most valuable.

John Pardoe was a member of a long-established Leyton family and his ancestor John Pardoe was a director of the Honourable East India Company (John Co.) and had a son John who was born in 1760. The latter was educated at Hackney School and Trinity College, Cambridge and married Jane Oliver in 1786, she being from "The Great House", Leyton and they had a son John Pardoe in 1787. He went to Emmanuel College, Cambridge and married Charlotte Jane Allix of Swaffham, Cambs in 1808 and held lands in Hertfordshire but resided at Leyton Manor in Essex. This couple had a son John Pardoe who was born at Ayott St. Peter's in Hertfordshire on 31 August 1813 and was educated at Eton and St. John's,

Cambridge and became the curate of Leyton in 1838 and vicar from 1848-75. John Pardoe senior was patron of Leyton Church and his son vicar and both lived at Capworth Street, Leyton in 1861 - one at the Manor House and the other at the Vicarage. The latter married Frances daughter of George Thornhill M.P. on 24 April 1838 and their son John Pardoe was born at Leyton on 1 April 1839.

He was educated at Harrow in April 1853-58 and was there at the same time as the Alcock brothers. He went to Trinity College, Cambridge in 1858 and gained his B.A. in 1861/62 but was living with his father at Leyton Vicarage in 1851 and 1861. He became a man of the cloth and was curate of Hitchin (1864-66), St Ippolyts (1866-73) and Graveley (1873-79) and rector of Graveley (1879-92) but died there on 23 April 1892. His family lived at Leyton Manor House and may have known Lord Mornington of Wanstead, and it was possibly John Pardoe who arranged the pitch at Snaresbrook then started the team with the Alcocks. He lived two miles from Snaresbrook at the time and his brother Charles William Pardoe (1849) was a solicitor with chambers at 6 King's Bench Walk, Temple near those of E.C. Morley. John may have joined the side when he came down from Cambridge but this is half the story as the Forest team had other connections.

Charles Tebbut (1793-1871) was born at Limehouse in London's dockland and married Marian Augusta Mansfield at West London (city) in September 1838 - she was born at St. Andrew's, Holborn in 1818. Charles Tebbut was a ship builder in the firm Tebbut, Stoneman and Spence who traded at Limekiln Dock, Limehouse East and New Crane Dock, Wapping Wall, Shadwell from 1841-71. He had five children including sons Charles Mansfield (Dec 1839) who was a shipbuilder and Arthur Marshall (Mar 1841) who was a captain of the reserve forces. They lived at Cedars House, High Road, Leytonstone in 1841/51 and met the Alcocks through shipbuilding or school sport then moved to Whips Cross, Walthamstow in 1859-61. This was a mile from Snaresbrook and the brothers no doubt played a part in the formation of the Forest F.C. being sportsmen of some note. The family moved to Hampstead by 1866 and resided at 31 Alexandra Road in 1871 and 92 Belsize Road in 1881. Charles M. Tebbut joined the No Names Club when his family moved there thus he knew Arthur Pember, the F.A. President - indeed he played for London v Sheffield in 1866 as a member of the No Names Club and died at Hampstead in September 1898 aged 58.

The real question, however, surrounds the Forest School near Leytonstone since the natural assumption is that members of the school formed the "Forest F.C". Some sources suggest the club played near the school and not 'under the shadow of the orphan asylum,' the latter being 15-minutes away by foot. The Forest School archives state there was no direct connection with the club, but some of their pupils did play for them, whilst the school XI played against the Forest F.C. - Arthur Alcock may have been in the school side against his brothers. In addition the *History of Association Football* by William Pickford (F.A. President 1937-38) states that Forest School and the Wanderers were members of the F.A in 1868 - there must be a connection with so many links.

The Forest School was formed as a 'private' or proprietary grammar school near Snaresbrook Road in Epping Forest on 1 October 1834, and the school buildings were situated in a house on the edge of the open common. The school remains today and the original buildings form the centre viz. five ivy-clad Georgian houses of two-three storeys with modern buildings and a games field at the rear. Rev. John Gilderdale D.D. was Headmaster in 1848 and changed the foundation to that of a public school and played an important role in its development. The religious aspect had priority and four senior masters were "Reverends" in 1863 including John Gilderdale and his son J.S. Gilderdale. The school encouraged sport in the tradition of "Muscular Christianity" hence football was an important part of the curriculum. It was played on the notorious common just in front of the school gates, which was a games field with an uneven surface upon which many a boy came to grief. The common was used until 1865 and at this time playing fields were laid out at the rear of the school, after an area of Epping Forest was cleared. There were inter-school contests at the time and they would have played Harrow (and Forest F.C.)

The Cutbill family originated in Hackney hence their sons went to Forest School in the 1840-60s and had contact with the Alcocks through the school connection and thus had a prominent role in the formation of the Forest F.C. Thomas and Sarah Cutbill had six children baptized at Christchurch, Spitalfields in 1805-26 including Thomas Samuel (7 April 1805) and Alfred Richard (24 January 1810). The latter married Lucy and was a commercial manager who resided at Dartmouth Hill House, Blackheath in 1861 and had a business at 6 Lothbury. His son Alfred was born at London Fields, Hackney in 1836 and was educated at Forest School under Rev. Gilderdale being a pupil there on the 1851 census. He matriculated at Trinity, Cambridge in 1854 and gained a B.A. in 1858 and M.A. in 1862. He was admitted to the

Inner Temple in 1856 and was a barrister in 1860 with chambers at 3 Tanfield Court, Temple (1862) and 7 King's Bench Walk (1868-71). He lived at Lawrie House, Dartmouth Hill, Lewisham, in 1871 but died at Hastings on 5 December 1877 aged just 41 years - there are links to John Pardoe in terms of Trinity, Cambridge and King's Bench Walk.

Meanwhile Thomas Samuel Cutbill married Elizabeth Newton at St. Leonard's, Shoreditch on 12 April 1834 and the couple had eight children in 1835-49. They resided at Hackney in 1835-37, Maidstone in 1839-45 and Hackney again in 1846-49 - the father being described as railway secretary and then a merchant. They lived at 8 Shacklewell Lane near Dalston in 1851 and two of their children were important. Walter John Charles Cutbill (Jun 1843) was educated at Forest School from 1857-60 and became an accountant and merchant and died at Lewisham on 27 January 1915. Arthur Lockett Cutbill (Mar 1847) was educated at Forest School from 1858-64 and died at Epsom on 24 February 1929 (his 82nd birthday). The school records state both of them played for Forest F.C. The family resided at Southwood Lodge, Lawrie Park, Upper Sydenham in 1861 and the household included Walter John (18) Arthur L. (14) and cousin Alfred Cutbill (25). The photograph of Forest F.C. shows A.L. Cutbill as a moustached gentleman but he was only 15-16 years old at the time and still at school - perhaps it was his brother Walter or cousin Alfred (these mistakes are made). Indeed Walter J.C. Cutbill was a member of the Crystal Palace club in 1864, the team playing half a mile from his home in Sydenham and was a member of the F.A. Committee from 1864-70. He represented Crystal Palace at both the County matches in 1867-68 playing for Surrey-Kent in 1867 and for Kent in 1868. The family's contribution must not be under estimated and they almost certainly had a role in the formation of Forest F.C. (being at school with the Alcocks) and may have suggested the name. It is inconceivable that the school was not connected when the team played so near, and took its name.

There is, however, one more person connected with the story. William Standidge married Harriet Burford at Chigwell, Essex on 26 January 1830 and had seven children in 1830-45, living at St. Pancras in 1830-34, Westminster in 1836-41 and Hackney in 1844-45. Their two most notable sons were born at St. Pancras: William John Burford (27 August 1831) and Charles Watson (18 March 1834) and they lived at Lansdowne House, Hackney and for a time at Camberwell. The established Church started King's College and its associated school on 14 August 1829 as an answer to the Godless foundation of University College, London. The Duke of Wellington was a patron however stormy debates ensued regarding these religious issues and the tension nearly led to disaster - the Duke fought a duel against Lord Winchelsea at Battersea Fields in 1829 and the affair made the headlines. King's College could not confer degrees and thus established a 'school' in the Strand to help provide students. There were eleven feeder schools by 1836, including Forest School, however King's College School removed to Wimbledon at the end of the 19th century, and of these only the Forest School survives.

The Standidge family were in business and this paid for a good education hence William J.B. attended King's College School in 1838 (3rd term) and his brother Charles W. went to Winchester College in 1848. The family traded as, "William Standidge & Co., Lithographers and Artists to H.M. Stationery Office, 36 Old Jewry, London," in 1851 but William Standidge died at St. Pancras in March that year. His widow Harriet and the family lived at Debden Green, Loughton, Essex, in 1861 and son William was a lieutenant of the militia. Their home was not far from the Alcocks at Chingford and William Standidge was the oldest member of the Forest F.C. in 1863 and this clearly shows in the team photograph. Harriet and son Charles Watson continued the business of lithographer at 36 Old Jewry and employed 140 men and boys in 1871 whilst the family lived at George Lane, Wanstead in 1871-81. The house was next to George Green (now covered by the A12) and was a ¼-mile from the Orphan Asylum at Snaresbrook, which could be clearly seen on Hermon Hill. William and his sisters were all unmarried in 1881 and "of independent means," whilst he died at Wanstead in March 1901 aged 69.

John Pardoe, Charles and Arthur Tebbut and William Standidge all lived near to Snaresbrook and the Cutbills were pupils at the Forest School yet the Alcocks (despite their connections with the school) lived four miles away at Chingford. It can be assumed that a number of people helped form the Forest F.C. after playing football at their schools but not all of them came from Harrow. This contradicts Charles Alcock's statement and is a conclusion that differs from the official history, whilst the presence of Arthur and Edward Alcock at Forest School is clearly significant. Further to this there were strong links between the club and the school and this was no doubt the source of the name. Forest F.C. had important fixtures against Barnes and Richmond in 1859-64 and although the origins can be debated, it was John and Charles Alcock who took the club forward as the Wanderers in 1864.

CHAPTER 3

The Movers and Shakers

In terms of business the Alcock family continued in the same line of work as in Sunderland, and were trading as Charles Alcock & Co. (ship and insurance brokers) at Colonial House, 155 Fenchurch Street, City of London, in 1861. Charles and Elizabeth Alcock lived at "Sunnyside", Chingford with their sons John, Charles and Arthur and daughters Anne and Ada however there was soon a late addition to the family and Edith Marion was born in December 1862 - the birth was registered in Sunderland. The F.A. was formed in 1863 and John Forster and Charles William Alcock had an important role to play. It was initially elder brother John who led the way; he represented the Forest F.C. at the first meeting on 26 October 1863 and was on the F.A. Committee in 1863-65 but soon stepped aside and made way for his brother Charles. The football team became the Wanderers and moved to Battersea in 1864, whilst the two brothers left Chingford upon their respective marriages viz. Charles (1864) and John (1867) and moved to London, however Arthur remained in Chingford and owned three cottages there in the 1871 rate books. Charles and his sons John and Arthur continued to run the business of shipbrokers at 42-43 Ethelburga House, 70-71 Bishopsgate Street (within) near the mediaeval church of St. Ethelburga's in 1871.

The Alcocks were very successful and had a desirable London residence in addition to their home in Chingford. Charles Alcock a magistrate lived at 14 Park Square East, Marylebone in 1871 with wife Elizabeth, son Edward (a sailor) and three servants (including a lady's maid) - Admiral Burton lived next door. This town house was located off Marylebone Road and had a good view across Regent's Park and was near the notable Park Crescent. There were several columns at ground floor level, a wrought iron balcony, large round-headed windows (with shutters) on the first floor and a pediment at second floor level. The house was part of a Classical terrace with uniform stucco façade and had the appearance of one large property - with central and end features, whilst Regent's Park Chapel was just behind (see Peto Ch. 6). Indeed the house remains today and "The Prince's Trust" is nearby at 18 Park Square East, thus showing the status of the area. The Alcock family still owned the Chingford house at this time although it was vacated and there was a farmer residing on the estate. The son Edward, a sailor, married Catherine C. (born 1856 Quebec) in Liverpool in December 1876 and had children Annie E.R. and Charles W. soon after - they lived at 18 Shallot Street, Toxteth Park, Liverpool, in 1881 and Edward was then a master mariner.

14 Park Square East, Marylebone. Charles Alcock senior lived here near Regent's Park in 1871.

Charles Alcock senior was a prominent gentleman in Chingford being a local magistrate (J.P) however he died at "Sunnyside" on 23 February 1881 and the event was recorded in the *Sunderland Post* two days later. He was buried high on the hill at All Saints Church, Old Church Road, Chingford, in the direction of Walthamstow and had a simple inscription:

"Charles Alcock J.P. for Essex born 1806 died 1881…." His will was written way back in 1841 and the section regarding the shipyard no longer applied, however he left everything to his widow Elizabeth and she proved the will in London on 24 March 1881, with William Snowball the other surviving executor - the estate worth £16,000. Elizabeth Alcock widow lived at "Sunnyside" in 1881 with son Arthur (civil engineer), daughters Anne and Ada and two servants. The son John Forster Alcock then took control of the business and was a shipbroker at 98 Bishopsgate Street (within) in 1881. The death of Charles brought a great change to the family and presumably some insecurity thus his two eldest daughters were married soon after - indeed the marriages may have been arranged.

Ada Mary Eugenie Alcock (26) married Henry Blois Turner (74) widower at All Saints, Chingford on 12 October 1882 - the church being a mile away from "Sunnyside" on "Old Church Road", and the witnesses included Elizabeth Alcock and Arthur Alcock. The groom resided at 131 Harley Street in 1881/82 and was the son of Thomas Turner a physician, however he was born at Bloomsbury in 1808 and joined the Bombay Engineers as a first lieutenant in 1825. He served in the expedition against Kolapore in 1827 and spent his life in the army, rising through the ranks to become a major general in 1865 and retired by 1870. The Bombay Engineers were then a part of the Royal Engineers and the Alcocks were apparently not bothered that he was a rival on the football field! The couple had an age difference of nearly 50 years and this might have been of more concern, however this was a common practice at the time (see Hooman Ch. 6) and indeed the marriage lasted some years - Henry Blois Turner died at Marylebone in March 1897. Meanwhile John Francis Taylor was born at Wisbech in 1854, the son of John Taylor a gentleman, and later lived in London but was visiting Thomas L. Palmer a farmer of 318 acres at North Moore, Banham, Norfolk in 1881. Anne Elizabeth Alcock (of Chingford) married John Francis Taylor a gentleman of 4 Raymond's Buildings, Gray's Inn at St. Andrew's, Holborn on 9 October 1883. Henry Blois Turner was a witness whilst the curate of All Souls', Langham Place performed the ceremony.

The links to Chingford, however, were soon to end and Elizabeth Alcock died at "Sunnyside" on 28 December 1890 and was buried at the historic All Saints Church. This has a nave and tower in white stone with unusual gable windows in the roof and there is an ancient red brick porch - held together with tie beams. The Alcock memorial is at the rear of the churchyard and remembers the following: William (1858), Horatio Robert (infant), Charles (1881) and Elizabeth (1890). The church soon fell into decay and was closed and a new church St. Peters & St. Paul's was erected on Chingford Green in 1904, but with a growing population All Saints was rededicated in 1930. "Sunnyside" was sold and demolished in the 1930s to make way for suburban housing and the original drive up to the house became Woodberry Way, whilst a side road was named Sunnyside Drive. The only building that survives is "Sunnyside Lodge" which was at the entrance to the estate - this is an attractive red brick cottage with a slate roof and some later additions. Meanwhile, Arthur Alcock (civil engineer) continued in the family business and was a shipbroker at 21 Great St. Helen's, City of London in 1890 (with his brother John). The family had dispersed in 1901 and Edward Alcock retired master mariner lived at Canton in Cardiff; John Francis Taylor a private secretary and his wife Annie lived at Paddington as did Edith Alcock who lived on her own means. Indeed the family were often colourful and Arthur Alcock died at Tetuan, Morocco on 17 April 1902. It is uncertain why he was there however there were clearly shades of "Casablanca", and he left no will thus J.F. Alcock administered his estate in England - his effects being £33 6s 8d. The most colourful character, however, was John Forster Alcock and his story is now discussed in detail.

JOHN FORSTER ALCOCK

The elder brother stepped down from the F.A. in 1865-66 however he should have stuck to football since he entered into a tumultuous marriage and the solicitors had a field day. Charles Rowse (1808) son of Vincent and Catherine was born at Ottery St. Mary, Devon and married Ann Saville (1809) from Clare in Suffolk. They lived at Marylebone and had children: Mary Ann (1838), Alice (1839), Susan (1844), Henry Saville (1845), Catherine Ruth (1847) and Amelia (1850). The father Charles was a coffeehouse keeper at 85 Crawford Street, Marylebone and his daughter Catherine Ruth Rowse was born there on 22 May 1847 - he also had rooms at 4 Macclesfield Street South, City Road. The family resided at 55 Crawford Street in 1851 and as well as selling coffee they had eight lodgers, five of them policemen - they were soon going to be needed! The coffee house was located with various shops but was also near St. Mary's, Bryanston Square and its Regency housing - indeed the Rowse family improved their situation and moved to Pimlico. John Forster Alcock (26) ship agent of Chingford married Catherine Ruth Rowse (20) of 5 Sutherland Place by licence at St. Gabriel's, Pimlico on 27 August 1867 and there were no family witnesses, it being likely they did not approve. The couple could have met over a cup of coffee but this was certainly not the case and the *Times* newspaper gave a vivid description of events (see below).

John and Catherine Alcock began married life with the in-laws and lived with the Rowses at 5 Sutherland Place, Pimlico for about a year, but then set up home at 2 Albert Villas, Amyand Park Road, Twickenham, in about October 1868. This was a country town on the banks of the River Thames and had long been a retreat from London for the rich and famous, having several large houses viz. Richmond House, Fortescue House, Lancaster Lodge (see Welch Ch. 7), York House, Orleans House and Marble Hill House - built by George II for his mistress Henrietta Howard in 1728. The road from Richmond was only a lane and wound into the town through Church Street and carriages would have seen Lancaster Lodge in front and York House to the left. There was a small street called Oak Lane on the right, opposite to York House, and a visitor could have walked up the lane in 1868 and seen 2 Albert Villas at the far end. Indeed this junction was like a small village and Grove Cottage (later Devoncroft House) was on one corner and Amyand House, which became St. John's Hospital in 1879, on the other. There were a number of properties on the north side of Amyand Park Road and these included Albert Villas, Magdala Villas and St. Stephen's Villas. Four houses made up Albert Villas and these were located on the corner with Beauchamp Road and its line of terraced houses, which were visible to the rear. The Windsor Branch of the Western Railway was behind the house and its arrival resulted in the development of Twickenham whilst the coal depot and goods yard had a cobbled entrance in Amyand Park Road. The scene is little changed today although there are maisonettes nearby and a development called Candler Mews in the goods yard.

2 Albert Villas, the second house, was semi-detached and was a small but comfortable Victorian dwelling of grey-yellow brick. The arched doorway was at the centre above a flight of stairs and there was a large living room to the right, with two main floors. The door and window frames had white plaster surround (with moulding) and the house is little altered today, even having some old slate roof tiles. The property may have been sound however the marriage was bad from the start hence the couple soon ended up in the divorce court (he thought he could change her). There were lengthy deliberations and the solicitors made a fortune since the claims and counter claims were complex, however the basic story was as follows. Catherine considered she was the aggrieved party and had far more to say than John did! Her main accusations included various acts of cruelty and desertion and she listed a number of incidents that took place at 2 Albert Villas, Twickenham. He assaulted her without provocation and called her a prostitute on 18 October 1868 just a year after their marriage. Indeed the couple lived in the house with servant Kate Corbett in 1871 - a 14 year old domestic from Ireland. Who knows what she heard or saw but had to keep secret?

The trouble continued and Alcock assaulted his wife and knocked her down in 1872 and knocked her down again in the back kitchen and bashed her head on the ground in early 1873. There were further incidents of misconduct in streets around Twickenham, Richmond and Kingston in 1871, 1872 and 1873, which were most humiliating to her. On one occasion he threw a dustpan and cut his cheek and he also hit her with a poker and threw bricks. He once broke down the door into her bedroom and was often absent from home in 1871 and 1872, being away for 3 months in the winter of 1872. He would sleep alone and blocked the door to his bedroom with the bedstead, had no conversation for months at a time, denied her conjugal rights and finally deserted her on 10 May 1873. He told her he would not return on 23 May 1873 and wrote the following letter to his wife in August 1873: "To Mrs J.F. Alcock, I enclose a postal order of £1 for your allowance due today. I have received your letter dated the 29th July, and I repeat viz. my determination not to live with you is final. Yours truly J. Forster Alcock." The problems had remained behind closed doors until now but the whole matter soon became public and Catherine filed a petition on 22 November 1873 claiming cruelty and desertion and asked the court for the restoration of conjugal rights as her pride was sorely wounded. This however was only the beginning and matters soon got worse.

Alcock employed an auctioneer on 28-29 December 1873 and sent 7 or 8 men to 2 Albert Villas and they removed all the furniture including the bedding. Indeed his wife only procured some sheets and blankets after a loan from the neighbours and she claimed the men assaulted her and grossly insulted her calling her, "a divorced wife," and left her without fire or candle - this was clearly most painful to her. Alcock filed a petition for divorce on 18 February 1874 and requested the dissolution of the marriage. This was a cross suit and followed the previous petition from his wife, although he made just one accusation against her this being the crime of adultery, however he clearly had other issues that he did not mention.

His main claim was that she committed adultery at Bloomsbury Street, Bloomsbury on 12 February 1874 but there was more to come. Catherine left Albert Villas and went to live at 69 New Compton Street, Soho in March 1874 however John continued his accusations and a common jury passed a verdict on 26 May 1874 - they set alimony of £3 per week on 15 June (backdated to 18 February). **Note** This was a male dominated society and the law was strongly against her.

An affidavit was sworn on 12 November 1874 and Ann Rowse, the mother, was appointed guardian of Catherine whilst the petitioner (Alcock) was given leave to renew his application to prove his wife's insanity. The appointment of Ann Rowse was confirmed on 26 January 1875 and Alcock had to pay £55 costs on 2 February 1875. A further affidavit was sworn on 6 February 1875 and this stated that Catherine should be brought to London to be placed in an asylum, her mother and solicitor to have access. There was a trial on 21 July 1875 and the respondent (Alcock) was ordered to pay sums of £3 to the Peckham House Asylum, the money to be paid to Catherine but at the discretion of the superintendent (of the asylum). Despite these arrangements she did not stay there long and was residing with Mr. and Mrs. Wynne at 7 Nassau Street, Marylebone in August 1875 in a lodging next to Middlesex Hospital. An affidavit was lodged on 9 October 1875 with statements from both Ellen Wynne and John Forster Alcock citing further cases of adultery and they were given leave to proceed without the name of a co-respondent. It was like a conspiracy! Alcock filed a further petition on 18 October 1875 and indeed his solicitor served this on Catherine as she walked along the pavement in Cannon Street. It stated: "I have been informed, and verily believe, that in August 1875 my wife lodged with Mr. and Mrs. Wynne at 7 Nassau Street. On two occasions a man was with her in her room and she committed adultery on the 19th and 25th August with a man unknown. There is no way of ascertaining, who the man or men are. I was informed of this by my solicitor on the 6th October and there has been no collusion with the respondent."

A High Court Divorce Case took place at Westminster on 27 November 1875 in open court with a common jury (all male) and the presiding judge was the Right Honourable Sir James Hannen. The jury arrived at three verdicts: (1) adultery was committed (2) there was no connivance between the two parties (3) there was no act of cruelty - the decree absolute would be in 6 months and the petitioner was asked to pay 10s a week to the court for the respondent. There was a bond between John Alcock and Henry Saville Rowse on 9 February 1876 he being the brother and trustee of Catherine. There was no end to the injustice and John Alcock paid the court costs of his wife but received them back on 11 June 1876 and the decree absolute was on 13 June 1876, no evidence to the contrary being provided, and the marriage was dissolved. The matter was finally over after nearly nine years however the emotional scars were to last much longer. It is not clear how much truth there was in all these accusations, however this is clearly a damning story, in a time when the rights of women came secondary to those of men. The episode was reported in the *Times* however the paper had a different story:

THE TIMES

MONDAY, NOVEMBER 29, 1875

PROBATE, DIVORCE AND ADMIRALTY DIVISION

PROBATE AND DIVORCE CAUSES

Alcock v Alcock

Mr. Inderwick Q.C & Mr. Searle appeared for the petitioner, Dr. Spinks Q.C & Mr. H. Kisch for the respondent.

In 1866 the petitioner, a shipbroker in business in the City, made the acquaintance of the respondent, who was at the time leading an immoral life. He became attached to her and married her on the 27th August 1867, after which he took a house at Twickenham, where they lived happily for a few years. The respondent then complained of the monotony of their life, and taking to drink, was guilty of repeated acts of violence towards the petitioner, the result being a final separation between them in 1873. Shortly after their separation the petitioner discovered that his wife, whom he had allowed to remain in occupation of the residence at Twickenham, and for whose maintenance he had otherwise made suitable provision, had sold off the greater part of the furniture, and, coming to London, had resumed her old life of prostitution. He then filed a petition for divorce on

> the ground of her adultery. The respondent answered, denying the charge and also pleading cruelty and connivance, but pending the suit she became afflicted with mental disorder, the consequence of her intemperance, and had to be placed under restraint. In July last she was discharged from the asylum as cured, but she no sooner regained her liberty, it was stated, than she relapsed into her old vicious ways. In opening the case counsel for the petitioner intimated that he was unwilling that she should be left wholly destitute, and that he was prepared, with the sanction of the Court, to make a small provision for her support.
>
> Dr. Spinks admitted that he could not contest the charges in the petition or support the pleas filed by his client, and, a verdict having been found for the petitioner, the Court pronounced a decree nisi.

John Forster Alcock was a shipbroker in the City throughout these proceedings and worked with his father, until the latter's decease in February 1881. He then picked up the pieces of his life and resided at 20 Tyndale Place, Islington in 1881 with his "wife" Alice (aged 25) who was born Dalston and three servants. He was not married to this young woman and, indeed, was probably in no hurry to marry again. Today, divorce is commonplace, but it was rare in the 19th century with only 150-200 cases per year and some cases were only judicial separations. His house was located at the north end of Upper Street at its junction with Canonbury Road whilst he continued to work in the City and, as stated, was a shipbroker at 98 Bishopsgate Street (within) in 1881. The Victorians built several large hospitals around London to deal with mental health and Middlesex had asylums at Banstead, Friern Barnet and Wandsworth. Catherine's condition did not improve in the eyes of the authorities and C.R.A. (33) 'married', occupation none, was a patient at Banstead County Lunatic Asylum in 1881. This was the other side of Victorian 'success' and large numbers of people denoted only by initials appear in lunatic asylums, poor houses and prisons on the census returns - the forgotten people of the history books. Her mother Ann Rowse a widow was living with daughter Alice Haines at London Road, Hillingdon in 1881. Alcock, however, clearly had a penchant for young ladies and soon took the plunge again - but there were further complications.

Augusta Lackland White was born at Middleton Cottages, Pelham Street in Brompton on 4 November 1867 near to South Kensington Station. Her mother Sarah White of the same address registered the birth and gave the father's name as Edward Lackland however this was soon erased. Meanwhile, Nathaniel Bancroft (1653) was born in Windsor, Connecticut and his family settled in Massachusetts. His descendant Edward Bancroft (1744-45) was born at Westfield, Hampden (Mass.) and was introduced to Paul Wentworth, a Tory, who sent him to a plantation in Guiana. He travelled to London in 1766 and qualified as an M.D. (F.R.C.P.) and was a fellow of the Royal Society. He married Penelope Fellows and had two children in London: Edward Nathaniel (1772) *Marylebone* and Samuel Forrester (1775) *Downing Street*. He was a friend of Benjamin Franklin who considered him a patriot of America and employed him as an agent and spy, however Bancroft was mainly interested in the money. Silas Deane the American representative in France hired Bancroft in 1776 and he then commuted between London and Paris and gave the Americans details of naval operations - these were passed to George Washington however were basically false. Bancroft also worked as an agent for Paul Wentworth and his superior William Eden (Lord Auckland) and gave them details of the Americans and in fact the English paid more. He had four children born at Chaillôt near Paris: Maria Françoise (1777), Julia Louisa (1779), John Paul (1780) and Catherine Penelope (1781) whilst his role as an agent came to an end with American Independence in 1783. He was a spy for France (in Ireland) at the time of the Revolution but retired to England and was then involved in scientific research. He died at Margate on 7 September 1821 and was buried at Iden in Kent.

Rev. George Augustus Lamb D.D. was born c.1774 and married Julia Louisa Bancroft at St. Marylebone on 25 June 1806 and had children: William Pitt (1809), Julia Louisa (1812), Edward Augustus (1813) at Iden, and Thomas Adam (1815) at Marylebone. George Augustus Lamb was involved in politics however there is no evidence he was related to William Lamb, Lord Melbourne P.M. (see Kinnaird Ch. 5). There was a petition in the House of Commons on 12 March 1830 regarding illegal voting and elections at Rye in Sussex. Philip Pusey Esq. was elected to Parliament and defeated De Lacy Evans Esq. a lieutenant colonel. The latter with some friends brought a petition stating the election was illegal and that Mayor, Nathaniel Proctor, had stopped some of the votes. They also stated that Rev. George Augustus Lamb of Mountsfield Lodge, Rye with no cure in the town but rector of Iden, Playden and Guldeford (some distance away) had for many years past, exercised illegal and unconstitutional control over the election of M.P.'s in the town, and for 20 years with his brothers and immediate connections held the post of Mayor. There was a petition

"Exhims", Northchurch. J.F. Alcock lived here in 1891-1910, his conservatory to the left.

on 16 July 1830, in response to these charges, and Rev. Lamb explained the complex rules behind the appointment of freemen in the 'ancient' town of Rye - it was these that debarred the petitioners from voting and he stated the election was quite legal and should stand. The family stayed in Iden and Julia Louisa died at the parsonage in 1851 and George in Rye in December 1864.

Edward Augustus Lamb (1813) was a London barrister and had lodgings at 29 Brook Green Road, Hammersmith in 1881 and was unmarried. He was the reputed father of Augusta L. White and died at Chelsea in September 1882 aged 69. John Forster Alcock (45) a "bachelor" and merchant of Kensington married Augusta Lackland White (18) of Hampstead by licence at St. Stephen's, Hampstead on 21 April 1886. The church was on Haverstock Hill and the witnesses were James A. Davies a lodging-house keeper of 12 Well Walk and Maggie A. McGilchrist. The couple had a son Frank Alcock in London in c.1886 but there is no record of the birth under Alcock and he was possibly an illegitimate child Frank White - indeed it is unclear if John was the father. The marriage, however, was to be a success and the couple moved to Egerton Terrace, High Street, Berkhamsted and their daughter Augusta Theodora was born there in December 1888. John F. Alcock, ship-owner shipbroker and employer, lived at High Street, Berkhamsted in 1891 with his wife, two children and three servants whilst the brokerage business was at 21 Great St. Helen's, City of London near Bishopsgate Street (with brother Arthur). **Note** Clementine Hozier (1885) wife of Sir Winston Churchill lived at an early 19th century terrace in the town - possibly Egerton Terrace. There was a great contrast in the lives of J.F. Alcock Esq. and his unfortunate first wife and there was soon some sad news. Catherine Ruth Alcock wife of 'Alcock' (rank, profession and address unknown) died of heart disease and bronchitis at Middlesex County Lunatic Asylum, Wandsworth on 28 March 1891 aged 43. The informant was H. Gardiner Hill (superintendent) and it appears she remained in these institutions from the divorce until her death.

The Alcock family moved to "Exhims", High Road, Northchurch in late 1891 just north of Berkhamsted, next to Northchurch House and almost opposite St. Mary's Church. Thomas Exham owned the two-storey red brick property, in 1616, and it had five windows across the front and a main doorway near to the road. The roof was tiled and there was a large brick chimney whilst the coach-house and stables were to the rear. A conservatory with three round arches was built in the 19th century on the south side. The ivy clad house remains today with courtyard and conservatory, but modern buildings and a car park diverted Darr's Lane on the north side. J.F. Alcock & Co. traded as shipbrokers at 21 Great St. Helen's until 1894 in an area of London that was a centre for shipping activity. Indeed the African Steam Ship Co. and Dawson Bros (ship and insurance brokers) were also at 21 Great St. Helen's whilst nearby buildings housed: ship and insurance brokers, shipping agents, ship owners, naval architects, merchants, marine surveyors, steamship

A view from Skjørsvik towards Kragerø.
The ice was shipped to London from the quayside.

agents, the Steamship Share Exchange Agency and the Mutual Shipping Investment Association Ltd. The company, however, then made further contacts and the business was developed in a new direction.

The Kragerø skerries or archipelago with its 495 islands and reefs was in Telemark County, Norway - 90 miles south west of Oslo. The region included Sannidal to the west, the town of Kragerø and the islands and coastal area of Skåtøy (archaic Skaatø). In maritime terms it rose to prominence in the 19th century and Kragerø became the sixth largest sailing-ship port in Norway with the main industries being the export of timber and ice. The island of Skåtøy had the third largest wooden church in Norway and was at the centre of the archipelago, whilst Jomfruland was five miles long and ½-mile wide and gave the area shelter (formed from a terminal moraine). Ships reached Kragerø along a fjord or channel between Skåtøy Island and the district of Løvdalen - a headland connected to the mainland in the west. The latter was settled at an early date and Løvdalen Farm was present in 1600 and the estate included two smaller farms at Bjelkevik and Skjørsvik on the coast. The second of these outlying farms was above a horseshoe bay and ships would often moor there to find shelter from a storm. Skjørsvik Farm was built in c.1650 and had many owners and was mainly a home for farm workers. It was operated from Løvdalen in the 18th century and the situation only changed after J.C. Barth purchased the farm in 1792. He was a wealthy ship owner and postmaster for Kragerø and added a large wooden extension on the western side of the old farmhouse. The new building had two storeys, wooden porch entrance, balcony and many rooms, and faced across the bay towards Kragerø - there were few roads at the time and the principal access was by boat.

The area became important for the export of timber whilst William Leftwich sailed there in 1822. He was the first English ice merchant in Norway and did business with Thomas I. Wiborg a member of a prominent local family. J.C. Barth owned Skjørsvik until at least 1838 and Barthebrygge in Kragerø was named after him, which was an affluent waterside street with four large wooden houses belonging to merchants. Indeed two of the houses had wooden window pediments and Classical cornice details as in Belgravia! The farm had a number of owners and Nils Thorbjornsen was renting it to Lars and Anne Nilsen in the years up to 1865. There was only a small amount of land thus the couple had a subsistence living with 2 horses, 10 cows, 6 sheep and corn and potatoes in the fields (amongst the woods). There were then further owners and occupiers until more dramatic changes took place in the 1890s. The Thorsdals Iskompani or ice business purchased Skjørsvik and stone dams were built in the woods above the farm thus creating two large lakes. The main one of these was a long lake known as Blåbær-Tjenna or blueberry 'little' lake and in winter would freeze to a considerable depth. Local men were employed to saw out blocks of ice, which were moved through the trees then lowered down the rocks to the bay on wooden tracks. The ice was insulated using sawdust (a by-product of the timber industry) and shipped to England. A further lake was formed in the trees above the farm where a small dam was used to flood a field.

J.F. Alcock had contact with the area through his shipping links and became an ice merchant at 21 Great St. Helen's in 1895. He then purchased Skjørsvik from Thorsdals Iskompani as a base for his business although the owner was listed as Augusta Lackland Alcock (for tax purposes). He worked with Thorsdals and during the winter months ice was shipped to London and supplied to large homes in areas such as Belgravia and also to the country estates with their 'ice-houses'. John Forster Alcock ship owner of

Skjørsvik Farm. J.F. Alcock owned the property in c.1895-1910.

Blåbær-Tjenna. Thorsdals ice company worked here with Alcock.

21 Great St. Helen's made his last will on 24 November 1895 and left his estate to his 'dear wife' Augusta Lackland Alcock his executrix, and Jane Garner and Mark Wade of Northchurch were witnesses. The couple clearly had some mutual respect and they had a son John Forster who was born at "Exhims" in March 1896. The father put his turbulent past behind him, and entered fully into local affairs. He joined the Parish Council at its inception in 1898 and soon replaced Rev. A.F. Birch as Chairman and held the post nearly ten years, and helped the aged poor of the parish and assisted both the church and local school. He was a London ice merchant living at "Exhims" in 1901 with his wife, children Augusta and John, and three servants whilst Frank was a scholar at Tavistock in Devon (now born Berkhamsted).

The family had a comfortable lifestyle in Northchurch and it seems likely they visited the large house at Skjørsvik during the summer months. This was an attractive coastal area with many pine-covered islands amongst granite rock outcrops, and made a perfect holiday retreat. There are stories that an Englishman came there and 'built' the house but he probably just made some improvements. Augusta Lackland Alcock owned Skjørsvik on a tax return for the Skaatø area in 1905 and had two areas of land - the farm near the bay and the flooded field above it. The other landowners in Løvdalen were Erik Pedersen and S. Wiborg at Løvdalen, Konsul N. Wiborg at Vandret and Tomt og vandfeld (land and waterfall), Thorsdals Iskompani at Skjørsvik isforetn (ice-business) and Fyrvæsenet at Strømtangen - the latter being the 'Admiralty' and lighthouse. Indeed Nicolay Wiborg was a very rich ship owner in Kragerø and also had an ice-business - as did many along the coast. He built a large two-storey house in Barthebrygge with a view of Skjørsvik to the right of Øya Island. It was entered at first floor level and had seven windows along the front and a roof cornice with Classical design.

John F. Alcock continued to support local interests at home and was involved in a dispute regarding Berkhamsted School. He also vigorously contested the County Council elections for Northchurch-Aldbury in 1907 and lost out to Mr. H. Craufurd who was re-elected, but had no bitterness and actually proposed Mr. Craufurd for the same post just before he died. Was this really the same man who had wielded pokers and thrown bricks? He clearly had a spiritual experience and the most enduring image sees him growing orchids in his attractive conservatory (for which he was noted). John Forster Alcock died at "Exhims" on 13 March 1910 and his obituary was in the *Berkhamsted Times* and other local papers on 19 March: "Mr. Alcock was Chairman of the Parish Council for practically the whole of its existence and had shown how thoroughly he had the welfare of the parish at heart in all he did. Though they had not always agreed there was no doubt that he did his very best for the parish at large. It was moved that a letter of sympathy and condolence be sent to Mrs. Alcock." Augusta his widow obtained his probate on 1 April that year and his estate was worth £11,509 16s 7d.

J.F. Alcock was listed as an ice merchant at 21 Great St. Helen's in 1910-11 however Skjørsvik Farm was sold soon after his death to Nicolay Wiborg. The latter did not keep the farm long and sold it to Erik Pedersen alias Løvdalen (1872-1938) in the year 1911. He was a local gentleman born at Bjelkevik who resided at Løvdalen in 1905 and his descendants the Sandvik family still live at Skjørsvik today. Indeed the property is little changed from Alcock's time and the Blåbær-Tjenna where much of the ice business took place is now an attractive lake amongst the Norwegian woods, although a large barn was demolished and the field above the house drained. Kragerø became popular with writers whilst Edvard Munch the painter lived there in 1909 and described it as "the pearl of the coastal resorts." It remains an attractive town with brightly coloured wooden buildings on the hillside and ferries sail to the many pine clad islands with their granite outcrops. The drama in Alcock's early life was but a distant memory and Augusta outlived him by 46 years and died at Worthing, Sussex in December 1956.

CHARLES WILLIAM ALCOCK

There was no such scandal in the life of C.W. Alcock and he soon overtook his brother and played a significant role in the growth of soccer. He left Harrow School in 1859 and lived at "Sunnyside", Chingford with his family, spending his leisure time playing soccer with Forest F.C. at Snaresbrook. He worked as a shipbroker with his father in the City for a number of years however he had greater ambitions that he intended to fulfil. With his brother John he helped transform Forest F.C. into the Wanderers in 1864 and saw them move to Battersea Park and change was in the air. Charles William Alcock a shipbroker of 33 Sherborne Street near Islington married Eliza Caroline Ovenden at St. Phillip the Evangelist, Islington on 19 December 1864, she being the daughter of Francis Webb Ovenden, an artist, and born Kentish Town in March 1841 and baptized at St. Pancras on 27 April 1841. Charles remained in Islington with his wife and worked as a (insurance) broker, and his son William Edward Forster was born there on 26 October 1865. He continued to play for the Wanderers and met the likes of Alfred Kinnaird at this time and joined the F.A. Committee in 1866, in place of John. He was involved in the rule changes and played for London v Sheffield at Battersea in March 1866, for Middlesex v Kent-Surrey in November 1867 and for the Wanderers v the No Names Club of Kilburn in 1867. In terms of cricket he did not appear for the Harrow "eleven" but later played for the Harrow Wanderers, Gentlemen of Essex and Incogniti Club and once captained France v Germany in Hamburg - the reason for this is unknown. The history of Surrey C.C.C. states: "He was a steady bat, a fair change fast bowler, and an excellent long stop or long field."

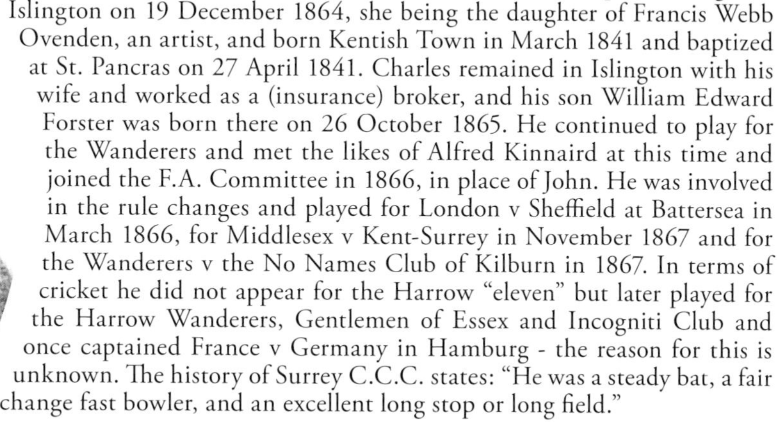

Charles William Alcock (1842-1907). He was F.A. Secretary in 1870-95 and began the F.A. Cup in 1871.

He was deeply involved in the growth of soccer (and cricket) and began to write on the subject and published his first *Football Annual* in 1868, and when his daughter Elizabeth Maud was born at Islington on 21 September 1869 he called himself a reporter. He was on the F.A. Committee 'til 1869-70 but replaced R.G. Graham as Secretary in 1870, whilst the Wanderers left Battersea for the Oval at the same time. He moved to "Grassendale", Rosendale Road, West Dulwich that year and daughter Florence Caroline was born there on 20 October 1870. Charles W. Alcock a journalist lived at "Grassendale House" in 1871 with his wife, three children and two servants from Limerick and Bavaria. He developed his career as a writer and reporter and was involved in journalism and publishing and produced his football magazine annually (until 1905). He wrote several books, contributed to the *Sportsman* and the *Field* and published a cricket calendar and annual from the 1870s. His publishing connections helped promote both soccer and cricket and F.A. meetings were then held at the Oval, the Sportsman Newspaper Office, Boy Court and the Cricket Press Office, 6 Pilgrim Street (both in Ludgate Hill) up until 1881. N.B. The Sportsman Office was at 139-140 Fleet Street in 1892, the Cricket Press Office at 17 Paternoster Square in 1882 and the Cricket Reporting Agency at 112 Fleet Street in 1892.

The F.A. Committee met at the Sportsman Office on 20 July 1871 and took up Alcock's suggestion for a knockout competition and the F.A. Cup started in 1871-72. Billy Burrup, Secretary of the Surrey C.C.C. arranged for Alcock and the Wanderers to play at the Oval in 1870 and agreed to stage the Cup semi-finals and the Final in 1872 (although Alcock usually receives the credit). The Cup contest was a success and the Wanderers, with Alcock as captain, won the Final at the Oval on 16 March 1872. Indeed he was already well involved and replaced Burrup as Secretary of Surrey County Cricket Club on 6 April 1872, whilst his daughter Charlotte Mabel was born at Dulwich on 15 April - just 9 days later. He then had a dual role (as well as being F.A. Treasurer in 1872-77) and this had a substantial affect on football's evolution thus it is worth considering the story of the Oval cricket ground. The History of Surrey C.C.C. by David Lemmon states that the Montpelier Club was formed at Walworth in 1796 and played in an area now covered by Lorrimore Square and Chapter Road (not far from Kennington Park). Their pitch was built upon in 1844 and they needed a new home and looked at some land called the Oval in 'Kings Town', or Kennington, owned by the Duchy of Cornwall. The Otter family had been granted a 99-year lease on this piece of land on 27 January 1834 and it was described as, "a nursery and garden ground in extent about 10 acres called the Oval with buildings thereon." William Baker, Treasurer of the Montpelier Club, negotiated a lease to play cricket there on 10 March 1845 and they became Surrey C.C.C. on 22 August that year.

William Dennison was the first Secretary in 1845 but was followed by John Burrup in 1848 and the club owed much to the efforts of the latter and also to Albert the Prince Consort. Despite a good start there was a financial crisis in 1855 and twin-brother William Burrup took over as Secretary. The brothers were sons of John Burrup and Mary Maynard and were baptized at Stockwell New Chapel (Ind.) on 22 September 1820, although some years later William said he was born in Southwark and John gave his birthplace as Blackfriars! These were on opposite sides of the Thames and he possibly meant Blackfriars Road. Indeed both John and William were employed as stationers and printers and may have met Alcock in a professional capacity. William Burrup built the pavilion at the Oval in 1858 and handed over to Charles Alcock at a committee meeting at the Bridge House Hotel near London Bridge in 1872. William remained involved and negotiated a new lease with the Otter family in 1873 and they then dealt directly with the Duchy of Cornwall - this secured the club's future and provided a stage for Alcock. The cricket club experienced a fall in membership in the early 1870s and the arrival of soccer was a partial remedy to the resulting financial problems. It was under Charles Alcock that football stayed at the Oval and he also had a major role in cricket's development. Indeed William Burrup resided at 113 Vassall Road not far from the Oval in 1881.

Alcock helped to start international football against Scotland and played in the unofficial game at the Oval (in 1870) and ran the line at the West of Scotland Cricket Ground on 30 November 1872 and again at the Oval on 8 March 1873. He then appeared in an official capacity and was less prominent on the pitch, whilst the Oval hosted further internationals and several representative matches: North v South, London v Sheffield and Oxford v Cambridge University. The F.A. Cup Final was played at the Oval in 1872 and 1874-92 and the Rugby Union also played there from 1872-78, thus it was a true sporting 'Mecca'. Meanwhile in his private life this was a time when people often rented property and moved from house to house, and it was certainly true of Alcock. He moved to Jersey Lodge, Norwood Road, Tulse Hill and had a son Charles Ernest on 16 September 1873 but he died as an infant on 13 February 1874 and the family purchased a plot in West Norwood Cemetery. He published his first book *Football our Winter Game* ('Field' London) in 1874 and had two daughters born at Jersey Lodge: Helen Mary (11 October 1874) and Marion Frances (7 August 1875),

Alcock was soon extremely busy and captained England against Scotland on 6 March 1875 in a game that ended 2-2, indeed Alcock scored the goal to make it 2-1 (he was the second earliest born international player). He was referee for the Cup Final and replay on 13 March 1875, when old rivals the Royal Engineers won the Cup - of course both games were at the Oval. His family remained at Jersey Lodge in 1876, however his last daughter Violet May was born at Stoke Newington on 14 May 1878 and was to follow in her father's footsteps (see below). He also refereed the Cup Final between the Old Etonians and Clapham Rovers in 1879. Charles Alcock was a man of great energy being responsible for many innovations in both cricket and soccer, and arranged the first test match v Australia in 1880 and was managing official at the first Ashes game in 1882. His contribution to sport was endless however the 'wandering' continued and Charles W. Alcock, publisher and journalist employing 3 men, lived at 36 Somerleyton Road, Brixton in 1880-81 with wife Eliza, six children (not Charlotte) and two servants - the area is now greatly changed with no trace of the house. The family then returned to the Rosendale Road area and lived at "Lulworth House", Carson Road, West Dulwich, in 1884 and the road is little changed today with the oldest Victorian houses at the northern end.

He worked with Major Marindin at the F.A. (after 1874) and they were now faced with the arrival of professional teams in the F.A. Cup. There was much debate about this issue (as with the rules in 1863)

and several of the northern clubs were brought to account however the professional game was finally sanctioned at Fleet Street on 20 July 1885. This change affected Charles Alcock and he was the first paid Secretary in 1887 whilst the F.A. took permanent offices at 28 Paternoster Row (1881-85) and at 51 Holborn Viaduct (1885-92). His son William Edward Forster worked with his father as a clerk at the F.A. however he died on 16 March 1887 and was buried at West Norwood. The family lived briefly at 16 Stanthorpe Road, Streatham in 1887 whilst Alcock published the Association Games (G. Bell & Sons) in 1890 revised 1906. He moved to a more permanent home at "Heathlands", 212 Kew Road in Richmond in 1891-97. This was a large property on the corner with Eversfield Road facing Kew Gardens and its temperate house and pagoda, and Thornycroft Lodge and 'St. Johns' were next door (then the Avenue). The modern Paxton Close covers the site and only the boundary wall remains, with Thornycroft Court adjacent. Charles W. Alcock journalist, author and employer lived at "Heathlands" in 1891 with wife Eliza, daughters Elizabeth, Florence, Charlotte and Helen and three servants, and followed in his father's footsteps and became a J.P. for Richmond. He presided over the phenomenal growth of the F.A. Cup and the 15 entrants in 1872 had risen to 163 in 1892 whilst crowds had grown exponentially, and he took the Final to Fallowfield in 1893 and to Goodison in 1894. A good opportunity occurred whilst at "Heathlands" and he arranged an England international at the nearby Richmond Athletic Ground in 1893, the referee being J.C. Clegg later F.A. President.

He was a prolific writer at Richmond and edited *The 'Oval' Series of Games* in 1894 the publishers being George Routledge and Son Ltd., Broadway, Ludgate Hill (with offices in Manchester and New York). The book, as stated, had a section on Rugby Union by Charles J.B. Marriott and another on The Association Game by C.W. Alcock. In the book he discussed the rules and history of soccer and the arrival of the professional game when they aimed for, "the protection of the genuine amateur by the legalization of professionalism." Like Major Marindin, however, he did not approve of this change and added, "It was under conditions which certainly must be described as onerous, rather than otherwise." Despite this he was proud of his contribution to football and noted how the game had spread throughout the Empire as far as Western Canada, the hot climates of India, Australia and New Zealand. The book was published in 1893-1920 and his other work included: Famous cricketers and cricket grounds (Hudson & Kearns) 1895, Management of a club: cricket etc 1900 and Surrey cricket its history and associations (Longmans & Co. London) 1902. He was still producing football annuals and his other periodicals were Famous Footballers and Athletes with G. Rowland Hill 1895-96 (see Creswell Ch. 9) and F.H. Smirks handbook of northern Rugby Union matches 1895-96 etc - all held at the British Library.

Ennerdale Road, Kew. The Alcock family lived here from 1901-30.

The F.A had offices at 61 Chancery Lane (1892-1902) and Charles Alcock's last act was to take the Cup Final to the Crystal Palace in early 1895 but he stepped down as F.A. Secretary in August 1895 and was made Vice-President in 1896. He held the latter post and that of Secretary of Surrey C.C.C. up until his death and continued to work within cricket and gave a contact address the Oval in 1898-99 and York Mansions, Battersea Park in 1899-1900. Charles Alcock a J.P. for Surrey and journalist "on his own account" lived at 16 Ennerdale Road, Richmond in 1901 with his wife Eliza, daughters Florence, Helen and Violet and two servants - in fact Violet was also a journalist and author (see below). He was listed thus in 1901-06 and the house was around the corner from "Heathlands" at the other end of Eversfield Road. This was a substantial two-storey red brick building with central gable, and ornate wooden porch with tiled roof. The property was hard to identify due to some unusual numbers on the west side viz. 2,4,6, *Holmesdale Road,* 8,10,

Branstone Road, 12, *Hatherley Road*, *The Avenue*, 14, 16, *Eversfield Road* then fields; whereas the East Side was from 1-57. A large white property was on the corner of Ennerdale Road but this was one of two houses on the north side of Eversfield Road (now no. 8) and must not be confused (*source* Richmond Archives). The main problem regarding this is modern flats in Ennerdale Road and Alcock's house is now no. 68.

Memorial to C.W. Alcock. Located in West Norwood Cemetery.

Charles Alcock may have rented the house out after 1906 hence he died at 7 Arundel Road, Brighton on 26 February 1907 and was buried with his young son at West Norwood Cemetery (he acquired the latter in 1903). His obituary was in the Times the next day and stated that he was one of the 'real' founders of soccer. He did not leave a will and his wife Eliza administered his effects in London on 22 March 1907, the amount being £3,186 1s 2d. His widow and daughters lived at "Hazelwood", 16 Ennerdale Road for many years although Charlotte was not found and Marion died in 1922. They remained at "Hazelwood" until 1930 but Florence and Violet moved to the coast in 1932 and Eliza Caroline Alcock died at "Newick", 70 Richmond Road, Worthing, on 30 January 1937. Her probate was granted to her daughter Florence and it seems likely they had contact with Augusta L. Alcock. The daughters never married and died soon after viz. Elizabeth (1937), Florence (1938) and Helen (1946).

The youngest Violet May Alcock was born on 14 May 1878 and had a career of note and established herself as a journalist and author. She may have worked with her father and was 'at home' in Ennerdale Road in 1901, but almost certainly had her own career and was involved in women's emancipation. A number of women belonged to the Writers Club in London in 1902, including Constance Smedley and her friends Christina Gowans Whyte, Elsa Hahn, Violet Alcock and Jessie Trimble an American. The five wanted to start a club for women (like those for men) and Constance approached the Writers Club Committee but was turned down. She had support from her father W.T. Smedley (film producer) who believed women should have "a professional life and full freedom of development." They were undeterred and established the club with 1,000 members in March 1903 - at first for writers and illustrators but 'academics' and wives and daughters of prominent men were soon added. This was named the "Lyceum Club" (after Athens) at the suggestion of Jessie Trimble and the first clubhouse was opened at Piccadilly in 1904. Lady Frances Balfour (sister-in-law of the P.M.) was Chairman for fifteen years and as planned the club soon became international. Violet May Alcock received the M.B.E. and died at 70 Richmond Road, Worthing on 20 February 1952.

Charles W. Alcock had less worldly success than his brother John in terms of their probate however it seems likely he had the more satisfying life. His contribution to cricket and soccer was of great importance and he played for the Wanderers from 1859-72 (at least), established the F.A. Cup in 1871, worked for the F.A. from 1866-1907 and was Secretary of Surrey C.C.C. from 1872-1907. He edited important publications that helped the sport grow, in particular the *Football Annual* (1868-1905) and *The Association Game* (1894) and made the Oval a centre for sport and has a room named after him there. His family have a memorial at West Norwood Cemetery - this is up the hill and reached by turning right at the monument to James William Gilbert F.R.S. London & Westminster Bank (1794-1863) - "he was engaged in the science of banking." The family names recorded are as follows: Charles (1907), William E.F. (1887), Charles Ernest (1874), Eliza Caroline (1937) and Marion Frances (1922). The marble gravestone was restored by the F.A., Surrey C.C.C. and friends of West Norwood Cemetery in 1999 and has an image of the F.A Cup on it - providing a fitting epitaph: "C.W. Alcock an inspiring secretary of the F.A. 1870-95 and of Surrey C.C.C. 1872-1907."

SIR FREDERICK JOSEPH WALL

A vacuum was left at the Football Association after the departure of Charles Alcock in August 1895 and one asked - who could possibly fill his shoes and make an equally telling contribution? Whether it was by luck or good judgement a worthy successor was found and the unlikely man was Frederick Joseph Wall who took the F.A to new heights and was, without doubt, a secretary as good as Alcock. This was a time of great change in football and in the world in general however F.J. Wall was up to these challenges and being a skilful administrator led the F.A. bravely into the new century. The most interesting feature of his story is the description of his father as "William Wall of Wormley" however this was a fallacy and there was no such person, at least not together. This was not a slip up on the part of the historians but was in fact an attempt to conceal the truth. Frederick Wall came from quite humble origins but mixed with the rich and famous at the F.A. and later received a knighthood, and was clearly uncomfortable with his antecedents thus he slightly altered the facts - this was not a reflection on him but more on a Victorian society of 'class' that made such demands. He led the F.A. and had to have the respect of his colleagues such as Lord Kinnaird and there might have been problems if his background was an issue, although in terms of football he was clearly judged on his merits. With this in mind his history can be considered in depth.

John Wall, born c.1792, was a labourer at Rainham in Essex and married Ann in c.1812 and had seven children there: Sarah (1813), Eliza (1817), George (1824), Jane Amy (1826), Mary Ann (1828), William (1830) and James (1833). John Wall, agricultural labourer, lived at Rainham in 1841 with his wife Ann, George (15) a labourer, Mary (12) and William (10) - they had no servants but shared the house with two other labourers. George Wall married Mary from Hornchurch in c.1844 and lived at Upminster Road, Rainham in 1851 with children Sarah, Eleanor, Elizabeth and Louisa - George was still described as an agricultural labourer. William Wall was baptized at Rainham on 22 August 1830 and grew up in humble surrounds however "William Wall of Rainham" was soon to take a more lucrative path. Indeed his father John Wall became a grocer and may have moved the family to London to find work. William Mansfield, meanwhile, was born at Wormley, Hertfordshire a small village north of Waltham Abbey in 1783 and married Frances in c. 1810 and had eight children there: William (1811), Mary (1813), Susan (1815), John (1816), Sarah (1820), Elizabeth (26 April 1821), Joseph (1823) and Esther (1831). The last three children were baptized together at Wormley on 27 March 1831 and William Mansfield, journeyman shoemaker, lived at the High Street, Wormley in 1841 with wife Frances and children Joseph (15) and Esther (10) although Elizabeth was not at home. William Mansfield a widower and son Joseph remained at Wormley in 1851 and both were shoemakers although it seems likely some of the family had gone to London. In fact there is no record of any person surnamed Wall in the village of Wormley.

William Wall, servant, married Elizabeth Mansfield at St. Botolph's, Bishopsgate on 13 May 1850 and the witnesses included Joseph Mansfield. The couple gave their address as 12 Bishopsgate Street - a bustling-artery leading north to Shoreditch, whilst St. Botolph's was near to the City and the Great Eastern Railway had a terminus at Bishopsgate Station. Victorian commuters considered this the worst station in London and Liverpool Street replaced it in the 1860s. William and Elizabeth, however, moved to Stratford in East London and two sons were born there - William George (December 1852) and Arthur Alfred (6 November 1856). The father then secured a position as coachman south of the River and Frederick Joseph was born at St. John's Road, Battersea on 14 April 1858 near Lavendar Hill and Clapham Junction Station. He was baptized with his brother Arthur at St. Mary's, Battersea (by the Thames) on 26 December 1858. In fact William Wall, coachman domestic, lived at 2 St. John's Road in 1861 with wife Elizabeth, three sons, niece Eleanor Wall (daughter of brother George) and two lodgers.

The family had limited circumstances however their son Frederick Joseph Wall was educated at St. Mark's College, Chelsea. In an age of poor education there were those who sought to improve matters and the National Society wanted to establish colleges for teachers and purchased the historic Stanley House at Little Chelsea in 1839. The property dated back to the 16th century and Sir Robert Stanley the Earl of Derby's second son 'lived in a great house here' in 1623, whilst the Society developed Stanley House as St. Mark's Training College (for schoolmasters). Further to this a school was started in a house next to the Royal Military Asylum, Chelsea in 1760 and the Society purchased this in 1842 and it became Whiteland's College (for women teachers). Rev. Derwent Coleridge, son of Samuel Taylor Coleridge the poet, was an early principal at St. Mark's and proposed the addition of a school so that his student teachers could gain experience. The latter was soon built and was an eight-sided octagon next to St. Mark's College Chapel on Fulham Road, and had places for 260 children. It is still present beside the chapel and at first glance must have been a 'squeeze' for all the pupils although further classrooms were added behind. The college merged with St. John's Battersea in 1923 and later moved to Plymouth, whilst King's College used the site until the 1980s when the octagon became a private school for junior students. The college buildings are now refurbished as part of a development called Kings Chelsea - located between King's Road and Fulham Road near Stamford Bridge, whilst St. Mark's College Chapel and the octagon are still present. F.J. Wall received a good education there and soon went on to great things.

The family had a long association with Battersea and Clapham and William Wall, coachman domestic, resided at 3 Shelgate Road off Northcote Road in 1871 with wife Elizabeth, three sons and Caroline Lynch (12) servant - Frederick was a scholar aged 12. The son William George Wall married Annie M. of Piddletrenthide (1846) at Dorchester in September 1876 and initially lived at Grove Cottage, Bolingbroke Grove, Battersea - their daughter Winifred G. was born there (1879). Indeed William Wall his father was still at 3 Shelgate Road in 1878 however it was then called "Clifton House". Today, this is a vibrant area with a busy Saturday market (as in the 1870s) and most of the old houses in Shelgate Road remain, however numbers 1-3 have been replaced. The family had moved to "Clifton Villa", 118 Northcote Road by 1880 and it seems likely this was a new house since the road only went as far as Belleville Road (at the time). 108-118 Northcote Road was a terrace of 'identical' houses between Wakehurst Road and Belleville Road and near to a Baptist church - all being quite substantial and gentrified. Each had grey brickwork, an ornate band of plaster and flower detail (at both floors) and a moulded plaster entrance with columns and facial design, however the rear was like a normal red brick terrace. 118 Northcote Road had an additional rear extension along Belleville Road - with a back door at ground level and three sets of windows at the first floor. These houses are still present today and are impressive, but 118 had a desirable corner location thus it became an estate agents.

William Wall and his sons managed to cross the Victorian social boundaries even though the family remained in the Battersea area. Frederick Joseph Wall a solicitor's clerk of "Clifton Villa", Northcote Road married Marie Louise White daughter of Charles a gentleman from Clapham at St. Mary's, Battersea on 2 September 1880. She was born at Passy near Paris in 1859 and a British subject whilst his brother William George Wall was a witness - the couple then moved to Temperley Road, Balham (see below). William Wall, coachman domestic, lived at "Clifton Villa" in 1881 with wife Elizabeth and son Alfred A. a shorthand solicitor's clerk - the latter was then married at Wandsworth in September 1881. William George Wall the eldest son a clerk in the tobacco trade lived at 13 Lancroft Terrace, Lancroft Road, East Dulwich, in 1881 with wife Annie, daughter Winifred and young son Francis (1 month). He then returned to his roots and lived at "Gothic Villa", 4 St. John's Road, Battersea, in 1887. The name may have offended 'Jane Austen' and probably referred to the age of the buildings since they were rebuilt as shops in 1889 and William (junior) moved to 33 St. John's Hill Grove by 1891-93.

The façade of the Wall family home suggested a degree of success however there were hidden problems and the mother Elizabeth Wall died at 118 Northcote Road on 22 March 1890 - the cause of death was chronic alcoholism lasting three years, compounded by severe physical problems during the last 14 days. This was a difficult period for the Wall family since the problem was little understood at the time and was believed to be a moral weakness - this was long before organisations like Alcoholics Anonymous and the modern treatments and twelve step programmes. The family were left to suffer and grieve alone although, strangely, this coincided with a change in circumstances. William Wall, cab proprietor and employer, lived at 118 Northcote Road in 1891 with Frederick W. Weaver groom and boarder (in his employ), Annie Weaver wife and housekeeper, and Eliza Taylor (13) servant. Clearly William had moved up in the world but he was not a gentleman of Wormley! His son William G. Wall, a mercantile clerk, lived at 33 St. John's Hill Grove, Battersea in 1891 with his wife and two children, and the four remained in Battersea in 1901. The younger son Arthur A. Wall lived in Wandsworth at the latter date and was then a clerk in the Church of England. William Wall "of independent means" died of heart disease and bronchitis at 5 Harbert Road, Battersea on 10 January 1901 - near St. John's Hill Grove. Arthur A. Wall of 29 Beechcroft Road, Wandsworth was the informant and William was buried in Wandsworth Cemetery with his wife Elizabeth - there is a flat grey marble memorial.

The London, Brighton and South Coast Railway arrived in Balham in the 1850s and the area became a separate parish in 1855 thus Balham Road (High Road) was developed and some large Victorian houses were built. Despite this growth it remained a 'rural' area in 1872 with fields behind Balham Road, whilst the opulent Clapham Park Estate was to the east. Indeed Temperley Road and Ramsden Road were laid out in 1872 - although no houses had been built. Frederick may have played soccer at St. Mark's College and joined the local team known as Rangers F.C. in 1875, when aged 17 (he lived with his father at

Shelgate Road). This was a little known club who played at Balham Cricket Ground in Bedford Hill Road near to Balham High Road. This venue was extremely difficult to find and the cricket ground and football pitch was situated on the right under the railway bridge (going south). The cricket ground was absent in 1872 however an ancient field boundary covered the site and there was an old gravel pit in the southwest corner. This was presumably less fertile land and the pit was filled in and the field turned into a sports venue by 1875 - the club were formed at this time. Frederick played in defence for Rangers F.C. and was a stout halfback and a notable goalkeeper - in keeping with his personality, however the club failed to make much progress (unlike their Scottish rivals). Frederick continued to play for them after his marriage on 2 September 1880 and indeed the ground was only a ½-mile walk from Temperley Road - no doubt with his boots hanging over his shoulder.

The club entered the F.A. Cup in 1880-81 and had the Wanderers in the first round however their opponents withdrew from the contest and they received a walkover. Rangers (London) received a bye in the second however they played the Royal Engineers in the third and lost 6-0 (this was their only Cup game). Frederick was 22 at the time and may have played in goal or on the pitch but it is significant that he was an F.A. Cup player - like his counterparts. Frederick Wall, solicitor's clerk, lived at 19 Temperley Road in 1881 with wife Marie however they had no servants and strangely the entry was recorded in the surname *Hall* (see below), whilst his son Frederick Mansfield Hastings was born at Balham in September 1881. His house was in walking distance of his father at Northcote Road whilst his mother-in-law Mary Ann White, dressmaker and widow, was a visitor at 21 Formosa Street, Paddington in 1881 (born Hungerford, Berks in 1829). Frederick was not a famous player his main talent being on the administration side and he was made Honorary Secretary of Rangers F.C., and elected to the Council of the London F.A. in 1881 - indeed he kept goal for the latter. His club entered the Cup again in 1881-82 and drew an "old" Romford side however they dropped out of the contest. Frederick had time for other pursuits and was in the 7th Surrey Rifle Volunteers and rose to the rank of colour sergeant. He was one of the first cyclists, enjoyed cricket and often spent his leisure time rowing on the river. He resided at 16 Temperley Road, Balham near the junction with Ramsden Road in 1885 this being a small terraced house, although today there are modern additions at the side. He had three children there: Arthur (December 1883) *infant*, Ethel Marie (March 1887) and Herbert William (September 1889).

Balham Cricket Ground is shown on a map dated 1886 however the outline of a new road is superimposed and its days were clearly numbered, thus it was built over by 1888. Rangers F.C. and the ground had a very short life span (that coincided) whilst Frederick Wall was a member of the club from 1875-88. Larch Road, Balham then covered the site and its houses and gardens followed the exact boundary of the sports field, however the Victorian houses were also demolished and the modern development of Larch Close replaced them. Indeed the boundary of the old field can still be seen. How many people know that this was once a football venue and that teams such as the Royal Engineers played there? Frederick was then elected to the Council of the Middlesex County Association in 1888 and became their Honorary Secretary and Treasurer in 1890, and was kept very busy being Vice-President as well.

Frederick J. Wall, solicitor's managing clerk, lived at 148 Ramsden Road, Balham in 1891 with his wife Marie, children Frederick, Ethel and Herbert, and one servant. This was a larger property around the corner from his old house with elaborate front door, white columns, moulded plaster lintels and large bay window to the left. The roofline was recently altered but no. 146 shows how it would have looked. He was on the way up and represented Middlesex on the Council of the F.A. from 1891-95 and became Vice-President of the London F.A in 1892. He also became Secretary of the Amateur Cup when it started in 1892 and his last child May was born at Balham that year. He almost had his foot in the F.A. door and had considerable credentials and experience thus he was appointed Secretary, in place of Alcock, in August 1895. His

Balham O.S. Map 1872. Rangers F.C. played at Balham Cricket Ground in 1875-88.

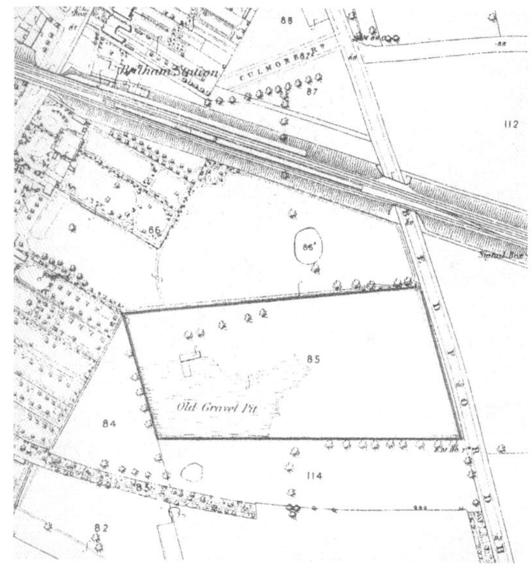

predecessor shared his F.A. duties with cricket and journalism however the position was now far more demanding (being paid since 1887) hence Frederick took it on as a full time job. The previous secretaries such as Morley and Alcock had led from the front however Frederick was different since he had risen through the ranks. The official records describe him as a lawyer but he was basically a company secretary and became a fellow of the Chartered Institute of Secretaries (F.C.I.S.).

His promotion to the Football Association was the signal for him to change house and his family left their roots in Balham and moved a short distance to 15 Cavendish Villas, St. Julian's Farm Road, West Norwood in 1895 - not far from Alcock's old home. The property is little changed from Wall's day and has moulded window lintels and a tiled mosaic path. He was recorded at 54 St. Julian's Farm Road in 1898 and this was the same property, since there are twenty identical semi-detached houses on the south side of the road (the 15th being no. 54). This was, however, a modest property for the F.A. Secretary and he had his eye on something a bit more prominent, hence he moved down the road to "Casewick House", 1 Casewick Road, West Norwood by 1901 and then lived there for twenty years - despite a change of circumstance. This was a two-storey semi-detached house on the corner of St. Julian's Farm Road and had a double front and arched doorway. The construction was of yellow sandstone brick however there was red brick 'detail' in the walls and a slate roof (with red ridge tiles). The whole aspect must have been pleasing to him although the garden was small.

Frederick J. Wall, "Secretary to the Football Association", lived at "Casewick House" in 1901 with his wife Marie, children Frederick (articled to electrical engineer), Ethel, Herbert and May, Mary Ann Churchman (mother-in-law and widow), a visitor and one servant. Frederick Wall senior was then very active at the F.A. and worked at their offices at 104 High Holborn from 1902-10. He was instrumental in securing and establishing the rights of referees being involved in the Referees Association and was first President of the Society of Referees in 1902. He was Secretary of the F.A. when the Cup Final was played at the Crystal Palace and this was most convenient for him, his house being less than a mile from the venue. He cut a dashing figure at the Cup Finals and other important matches and indeed there was once a dispute about the dress code of F.A. officials that prompted Sir Charles Clegg to state, "I would remind you that Sir Frederick Wall went to matches in a top hat and frock coat," however in later years he was best known for his bowler hat and extensive moustache. His duties at the F.A. increased rapidly but he took this in his stride and showed infinite patience, wisdom and courtesy. He constantly travelled to committee meetings or to make inquiries in all parts of the country, and attended representative and international matches, as well as being a regular at games on a Saturday afternoon. The British Olympic Association was formed at the House of Commons on 24 May 1905 and Lord Desborough was the first Chairman - Sir Theodore Cook and Frederick Wall were also founders. They hosted the Olympic games in 1908 and 1948, whilst only Australia, France, Great Britain, Greece and Switzerland have taken part in all games since 1896.

There were soon great changes and Marie Louise Wall died of influenza and pneumonia at "Casewick House", West Norwood on 15 February 1913. Frederick was then a widower and had to face the First War on his own. His son Frederick became a Civil Servant and may have been in a reserved profession, but his other son Herbert fought in the war as an army captain in 1914-17 and was awarded the Military Cross and the O.B.E. Britain and the world had changed dramatically after the First War (1914-18) and the whole social fabric and class structure was altered throughout the country and Empire. In some ways the F.A. was unchanged however in other ways it went forward. The F.A. offices moved to 42 Russell Square, Bloomsbury in 1910 - a plain fronted brick town house built in the 18th century and just behind the British Museum. This was his work place during the war years but he probably had little to do as the Football League and the F.A. Cup were suspended in 1915 and did not recommence until 1919. Despite this he spent some of his time socialising.

Sir Frederick Joseph Wall (1858-1944). He was F.A. Secretary from 1895-1934.

Frederick Joseph Wall (60), secretary to a limited company, of "Casewick House" married Agnes Frances Hall (32) of 26 Janson Road, Stratford at West Ham Register Office on 12 June 1918 - the surnames must have caused some confusion and they no doubt had a laugh about it! The wedding was a real family affair and three of the Halls were witnesses whilst Alfred Hall was Superintendent Registrar. The bride was born at Stratford in March 1886 and was the daughter of Alfred Henry Hall - engineer. Frederick had a complex character that was sometimes overstated and at other times played down. His father William was in truth a servant, coachman and cab proprietor but was called a 'farmer' on the marriage certificate of 1918 - he had been raised to a landed proprietor! Inaccuracies are not uncommon in old records and this may have been an error however it seems likely this was a further addition to the story of 'William Wall of Wormley'. The idea his father was a gentleman had become almost real in his mind, or at least necessary in his position. On the other hand he described himself as a private company secretary in 1913 and secretary to a limited company in 1918, this being the Football Association Ltd. It seems he was prepared to reveal this fact for the census but not at a private family event and was, indeed, modest about his status. There was soon more sadness and daughter Ethel Marie died at Winnipeg, Canada on 17 February 1920.

Football recommenced in 1919 and the F.A. was confronted with a serious but familiar problem - where should they play the F.A. Cup Final? The initial solution was to use Stamford Bridge however this was only a short-term answer and the search was on for a national stadium. Frederick Wall took part in some important negotiations and is credited with taking the F.A. Cup to Wembley in 1923 and securing the famous site for many decades to come. He must be commended for this magnificent arena since English football was then played on a superior stage. Frederick Wall was now in his sixties however he continued his role with the aid of his wife and in fact Agnes Frances Wall was hostess of the F.A for 17 years. The couple lived initially at "Casewick House", West Norwood but had left this address by 1921 and may have resided at 42 Russell Square in the 1920s, although there is no record of Frederick Wall in the directories which state: "The Football Association Ltd., 42 Russell Square, Bloomsbury." England played major games in the 1920s against Belgium, France, Sweden, Luxembourg and Spain and several of these were played abroad. Sir Charles Clegg presented Wall with a cheque for £1,000 on his 70th birthday in April 1928, and the Prince of Wales and the Lord Mayor were patrons of a national presentation in 1929.

22 Lancaster Gate, Hyde Park. F.J. Wall lived here in the 1930s - home of the F.A. 1929-72.

Mrs. Jane Gloyne was proprietor of a private hotel at 22 Lancaster Gate in 1922-27 and the F.A. moved their offices there in 1929. This was the second house after Lancaster Gate "square" and although part of a terrace was individual in style with a strict Classical design. It had a columned porch entrance, pilaster and pediment features and a white stucco façade, but was plain brick at the rear and backed onto some mews. Frederick and Agnes entertained in style at 22 Lancaster Gate and were ambassadors for the F.A. at home and abroad, whilst Frederick Wall received a knighthood on 6 March 1930 for services to football. The real test came, however, when England played Germany at the Deutches Stadion, Berlin-Grunewald on 10 May 1930. The game was a 3-3 draw in front of a 50,000 crowd and the goal scorers for England were Joseph Bradford of Birmingham (8, 30) and David B.N. Jack of Arsenal (78). Later records state that Frederick and Agnes formed part of the F.A. contingent and had the dubious pleasure of meeting Adolf Hitler - there is a discrepancy in this fact since he was not in power (until 1933). There were then further away games against Austria, France and Belgium before another stern test against Italy at the Stadio Nazionale del Partito Nazionale Fascista, Roma on 13 May 1933. The game was a 1-1 draw in front of another 50,000 crowd and the England goal scorer was Cliff Bastin of Arsenal (24), whilst Frederick and Agnes were present and on this occasion met Mussolini.

22 Lancaster Gate had two occupants in 1933-34, the first being the F.A. and the second Sir Frederick Wall. He resided above the ground floor offices and his wife probably told him not to bring his work home! The *Hotel Omba* was at 16 Lancaster Gate in 1933-34 and the F.A. offices moved there and to no. 17 in 1972 (although more recently went to 25 Soho Square). The three properties can still be seen at Lancaster Gate - in all their splendour. There were further internationals against Switzerland, Hungary, the Czechs, Holland, Finland, Sweden, Norway and Romania in the 1930s, however Sir Frederick Wall retired from the F.A. in 1934 since he felt that at 76 years, he was too old to rule the game of soccer. In these latter days he was an associate of Sir Charles Clegg, John McKenna and W. Pickford. He had seen great changes in the game and the F.A. had 1,000 members when he became Secretary but ¾ million when he left. He was of humble origin but was described as a true gentleman and one of the most dignified men in football, thus the F.A. gave him a cheque for £10,000 when he retired. To put this in perspective a semi-detached suburban house cost about £1,000 in 1934 and this was not the whole story. A Sutton newspaper stated this was a gift from the F.A. to show appreciation but this was a very large sum of money and it seems likely it was a payment to him for the property at 22 Lancaster Gate. He became a director of Arsenal Football Club from his retirement in 1934.

Frederick then moved to "Kinsale", 37 Langley Park Road, Sutton, in 1935 this being a large Victorian red brick house with double front and pilaster detail around the windows - it is still present but is now the *Kinsale Hotel* (no.57). He then received some bad news and his daughter May Wall died at Bulawayo, South Rhodesia on 16 August 1935. He was not happy in the property and moved next door to 35 Langley Park Road in 1936 and renamed it "Weetwood" - it was previously "Rotorua" but he presumably had no connection to New Zealand. The latter property is no longer present and was replaced with a building in the Victorian style, however it was an affluent area and some properties still retain their coach house. The lower end of the road had terraced properties and H.G. Wells lived at no. 25 in 1893-94. Sir Frederick Wall spent his retirement in Sutton where he was a familiar character, regarded with affection and respect. He was keen to share his football experience and published *Fifty Years of Football* in 1935 and wife Lady Agnes Wall was involved in the Women's Citizen's Association and Conservative Association. They no doubt continued to follow soccer and there was a game against Germany at the Olympiastadion, Berlin on 14 May 1938. England won 6-3 in front of a 100,000 crowd and Stanley Matthews scored the fourth goal, however the politics of war overshadowed the game. England also played Italy at the Stadio Calcistico di San Siro in Milan on 13 May 1939 and the score was 2-2 in front a 60,000 crowd.

Memorial to Sir F.J. Wall. Located in Wandsworth Cemetery.

Sir Frederick became an invalid in c.1940 and was then nursed by Lady Wall and wrote his last will on 24 December 1942. He made suitable provision for his wife and left his property and estate in trust for Frederick M.H. Wall and Captain Herbert William Wall - his sons. The most interesting section was clause 3 which stated: "I bequeath to my said son Frederick Mansfield Hastings Wall all my presentation cups and vases and medals." His rise to prominence was confirmed when he had an entry in Kelly's Titled, Landed and Official Classes in 1943: "Sir Frederick Wall son of the late *William Wall of Wormley* and Secretary of the Football Association 1895-1934." Sir Frederick Wall died at "Weetwood", 35 Langley Park Road, Sutton, on 25 March 1944 and his funeral was at Wandsworth Cemetery. His obituary appeared in the Sutton and Cheam Advertiser and Sutton Times and he was described as a great sportsman with the headline: "Football World loses Grand Old Man." An account of his life was in the Times on Monday 27 March 1944 and further details appeared in the paper on 28 March and 31 March: Mr. H.J. Huband and Mr. S.F. Rous represented the F.A. at his funeral. His will was proved by Frederick junior on 16 June 1944 and his estate was valued at £17,000 0s 4d. There is a memorial to the Wall family in Wandsworth Cemetery on the right past the two chapels - unlike Alcock's it is not restored and has a headstone and base (with flat cross) with red marble and grey stone surround viz. Arthur (1886), Marie Louise (1913), Ethel Marie (1920), May (1935) and Sir Frederick Wall 1858-1944.

Lady Agnes Wall continued to live at 35 Langley Park Road and indeed there was a large movement of people at the end of the war thus the house accommodated many lodgers in 1945-47 (and these included ex-servicemen). Lady Agnes left 35 Langley Park Road in 1947 dropping out of sight and her last entry in Kelly's Gentry was that year. She died at Hove in Sussex in March 1964. The passing of Sir Frederick was the end of an era for soccer and a time of great change for the world in general, however he left the country with the legacy of Wembley and laid the foundations for the "glory days" of the 1950s. This was not the end of the story as for every secretary there was a president, and these notable gentlemen are discussed in detail in the next two chapters.

Table 1: **SECRETARIES OF THE F.A.**

1863 - 66	Ebenezer Cobb Morley
1866 - 68	Robert Watson Willis
1868 - 70	Robert George Graham
1870 - 95	Charles William Alcock
1895 - 1934	Sir Frederick Joseph Wall

CHAPTER 4

Beware of the Boot

The F.A. Secretary dealt with the day-to-day business whilst the President would preside over the numerous meetings and was the figurehead, thus important and influential characters were chosen for the position. The first President was appointed during the meeting at the Freemasons Tavern, Great Queen Street on 26 October 1863 - the New Connaught Assembly Rooms now cover the site. The first action taken by the F.A. was to appoint the Chairman and President and it was proposed by Mr. Morley and seconded by Mr. Mackenzie (and carried), "that Mr. Pember do take the Chair." The first eleven clubs included the No Names club of Kilburn represented by their captain, Arthur Pember. The origin of the name is uncertain although it may have a connection to "Lloyd's Names" by way of a quip and, indeed, other early clubs came from institutions like the Civil Service and War Office. The official records state little is known of Arthur Pember except that he was a London solicitor and concentrated on the administration side, however he was a gentleman from an illustrious family with a fascinating history to boot. He was difficult to trace and could be known as "the elusive" Arthur Pember.

THE PEMBER FAMILY

The family are traced to the period just after the 'Restoration' of Charles II in 1660 and lived in Herefordshire near the border with Wales. They were entitled to bear a coat of arms after a *Herald's Visitation* to the county in 1683 and this consisted of a shield of three pheasants with azure and argent mantling, crowned with a crest of a single pheasant (feeding on a stalk of wheat). The motto at the base was "Cave Calcem" and the College of Arms in London gave the best possible explanation and stated that cave means beware, whilst calcem comes from calx. The latter has a number of meanings viz. lime or chalk, a goal marked by a chalk line, an end as oppose to a start, a heel and a kick. The Biblical explanation comes from Acts IX verse 5 and states, "it is hard for you to kick against the pricks," and in this context the word pricks refers to a goad for oxen, whilst the literal translation is "Beware the kick" or "Watch out for the boot". The soccer connotations are clear and this archaic motto was to be most prophetic. Henry and Ann Pember lived at Kenchester (*Magnis*) next to Credenhill, five miles west of Hereford, and had three children baptized there: Ann (1666), John (29 January 1669/70) and Richard (1673) - at least these are the probable ancestors. It is more certain that John Pember (22) bachelor of *King's Caple* married Katherine Hodges (23) of Credenhill by licence at Lugwardine on 17 May 1692 - William Pember, glover, bondsman. John and Katherine had five children baptized at Credenhill namely Elizabeth (1693), Mary (1695), John (1698), Katherine (1701) and Ann (1703) - there was also a son Thomas and it is possible the entry for John was a clerical error. John Pember a yeoman had a busy life and Katherine died in September 1705 and he married Margaret Hunt at Credenhill on 20 May 1706 (died January 1708). He married Anne at Hereford Cathedral in May 1709 who died in November 1729, and lastly married fourth wife Margaret Meredith a widow.

Beware of the Boot. The family motto was an omen regarding hacking.

His son Thomas Pember moved to the market town of Ledbury, 10 miles east of Hereford, and married Esther Chamberlain on 5 February 1721 and had three children baptized there namely Ann (1725), John (16 July 1727) and Thomas (1730). Ledbury is an attractive town with a 17th century market hall (supported on pillars of chestnut), and several half-timbered houses lead up to a parish church that has gunshot holes in the door - poets Browning and Wordsworth liked the town. To confuse matters a 'cousin' Thomas Pember married sister Elizabeth Pember (1693) at All Saints, Hereford on 20 October 1716 - a deed between Thomas Pember glover of Credenhill, his wife Elizabeth and Thomas Pember tailor of Ledbury is dated 1 May 1733. The latter would have traded in the market hall but died in December 1749 and was buried at Credenhill, whilst a deed dated 20 January 1753 states: "John Pember of Ledbury tailor son of Thomas Pember of same tailor (deceased) and grandson of John Pember of Credenhill yeoman…." The latter died at Credenhill in January 1756 aged 86 and left property to his grandson Thomas Pember of Ledbury who was executor with his widow Margaret (she died March 1762).

Meanwhile John Pember tailor married Mary Parker at Ledbury on 26 October 1758 and had five children baptized there namely Mary (1759), John (1761) *infant*, Edward (c.1764), Esther (1767) and Saint John (30 June 1769). Mary Pember of Ledbury widow and relict of John Pember tailor made her last will on 27 April 1791 and left her children, upon trust, a messuage, tenement and orchard land conveyed to Edmund Taylor and William Mutlow by an indenture of settlement dated 17 January 1769. She also left lands and tenements in Much Marcle held by Nathaniel Bundy (tenant) to daughter Mary Pember and sons Edward and Saint John Pember - the residue to her three children, the executors. It is not clear how the unusual name of the last child was chosen but he soon followed in the footsteps of Dick Whittington and headed for the gold-paved streets of London. Saint John Pember of Clapham married Mary Carless of St. Anne's, Blackfriars, City of London, by licence from the Archbishop of Canterbury at Holy Trinity, Clapham on 29 January 1801. The church was on the north side of the Common and had a plain Classical façade with white colonnade and clock tower but a 'city style' nave of brown brick. William Wilberforce and the 'Clapham Sect' worshipped at Holy Trinity in the late 18th and early 19th century and started an important social movement - indeed Henry and John Venn the curate and rector were part of the 'sect'. They placed pressure on Parliament and the slave trade was abolished in 1807 although the freedom of slaves throughout the Empire was not secured until 1833 - a few weeks after the death of Wilberforce.

Saint John and Mary Pember lived at Vauxhall Terrace in the neighbouring parish of Lambeth but had further premises at Crescent Place, Blackfriars (possibly their business). They soon had five children viz. John Edward Ross (20 September 1801), Mary Jane (c.1803), Edward Henry (1804) died 1806, Elizabeth (c.1806) and Helen Edwardena (1807) although only three were baptized at St. Mary's, Lambeth - the other two in London. A sixth child Jane Woodhouse was born on 11 August 1808 but the father Saint John then travelled back to Ledbury and his mother Mary signed a codicil on 28 October 1808. She noted that her will was deposited in the hands of Messrs. Webb bankers of Ledbury and stated that, "My daughter Mary is married to a man whose situation in life often calls him out of the Kingdom…. Mr. L'Hermitte is to have no authority under my will to intermeddle or interest him-self in any way whatsoever." She clearly had strong feelings in this matter and the codicil was signed in front of Saint John Pember and James Gibbs. The son returned to London and daughter Jane Woodhouse was baptized at St. Mary's, Lambeth on 12 January 1809 however the will of his mother Mary was proved on 6 October 1809 at the P.C.C. - probate went to Edward Pember and a like grant to Mary L'Hermitte however Saint John renounced the same.

The family remained at Vauxhall Terrace south of St. Mary's Church and Lambeth Palace and had four more children: Anne Hester (1810), Henry James Hartley (1811), Frederick (c.1813) and Kate (c.1814) died 1815, although only two were baptized at St. Mary's - the others in London. The outskirts of the metropolis were a hard place to live in the early 19th century and there was always the risk of illness and disease, thus the Pember family suffered hard times. The daughter Anne (Hester) died at Vauxhall Terrace in July 1820 age 10, whilst Jane Woodhouse died at Vauxhall Walk in April 1824 age 15 - they were buried at St. Mary's, Lambeth with their brother and sister. Mary Pember the mother died at Vauxhall Walk and was buried at St. Mary's, Lambeth on 1 February 1825 age 48. The father and some of the six surviving children left Lambeth and lived at his other property Crescent Place, New Bridge Street in St. Anne's, Blackfriars.

John Edward Ross (otherwise John Edward) Pember was a very successful businessman who made a fortune at the Stock Exchange and resided in the high prestige Clapham Park. He first lived in Stockwell and married Elizabeth Devey with her parents consent at St. Matthew's, Brixton on 9 August 1825 the witnesses being William Devey and John Pember. In fact St. Matthew's was first consecrated in 1825 and this was only the tenth ceremony to take place there. The bride was born at 5 Harp Alley, St. Bride's, London, on 30 October 1809 the daughter of Roger Chamberlain Devey (brass founder) and wife Elizabeth and later lived at Shoe Lane - near Crescent Place. John Edward Pember, a gentleman, then resided at Stockwell, South Lambeth and had a son John Child who was baptized at Brixton on 2 August 1826 but buried at St. Mary's, Lambeth on 22 February 1827 - the mother Elizabeth died soon after and he was left a widower. Meanwhile his sister Helen Edwardena died at St. Anne's, Blackfriars and was buried at St. Mary's, Lambeth on 20 March 1829 age 21, whilst Elizabeth Pember married John Joseph Starie ironmonger of Kennington in c.1830. The couple had a daughter Elizabeth Jane baptized at St. Mark's, Kennington on 9 December 1831 and also Sophia who was born in c.1833.

John Edward Pember Esq. a widower of St. Mary's, Lambeth married Fanny Robson, a minor, with consent of her father at St. Pancras Church, Euston Road on 9 August 1831. Fanny was the daughter of John and Deborah Robson and was baptized at St. Marylebone Church on 28 November 1810 - she was the fifth child in a family of fifteen and her siblings included Katherine (1812), Jane (1820) and Arthur (1824). Her father John Robson a gentleman was a member of the Stock Exchange (died 1848). The couple started a family and their son Edward Henry was born at Stockwell on 28 May 1832 however they were on the way up and moved to a 'mansion' on the Clapham Park estate. William M. Thackeray novelist described the area in the mid 19th century as follows: "Of all the pretty suburbs that still adorn our metropolis there are few that exceed in charm Clapham Common." (He is also connected to Merriman see Ch. 10).

In the world of building the name to conjure with was Thomas Cubitt (1788-1855). He was a master builder and speculator who bought up land in Belgravia and Pimlico and developed houses for the upper classes of society, however Sir Robert Grosvenor (1767-1845) or Viscount Belgrave was director and provided the name for the estate from Belgrave, Cheshire - his statue is at 1 Belgrave Square (see Bonsor Ch. 6). Cubitt developed a notable Classical style of columns, pediments and white stucco but all his London properties were town houses with limited or no garden space. The early F.A. members and amateur players resided in his houses, of which a large number remain, and he made an important contribution to the Capital's landscape. A bronze statue of Cubitt was erected at the junction of St. George's Drive and Denbigh Street in Pimlico near the site of his original workshop (in the latter street) and is a notable and attractive sculpture.

Thomas Cubitt had many innovative ideas and one was to build a garden suburb in Clapham, thus he purchased 229 acres of open land south east of Clapham Common from William Atkins the Lord of Clapham Manor in 1824. He then built large detached villas with extensive grounds beside wide tree-lined avenues. He purchased a further 16 acres of land at the south of the estate and some between Kings Avenue and Lyham Road in 1828. The latter area became a brickfield and enabled Cubitt to separate his houses from the less desirable Brixton, but development was slow and he still held 179 acres of land in 1842. His brother Sir William Cubitt, civil engineer, was a partner in the firm and bought Bedford Hill House in 1843 whilst Thomas lived in a mansion he built in Clarence Road. Strict covenants were laid down regarding design and there was only one terrace on the estate at the south end of Cavendish Road. St. Stephen's Church was erected in Grove Road for the gentry of Clapham Park however Cubitt refused to provide a church for the poorer people of Lyham Road - All Saints was built at the east end of New Park Road after he died. The estate itself was completed after his death and covered Loats, Kings, Clarence, Poynders, Queens, Cavendish, Atkins, Grove, Thornton, South & New Park (Roads). Cubitt built a grand estate but unlike in London only a few traces remain viz. Baptist Church in New Park Road (1842), three dated houses in Kings Avenue, coach house in Clarence Avenue and 24/58 Thornton Road - these are the best examples and are double fronted, three storey, white stucco mansions. The tree-lined avenues are still there but the remainder of Clapham Park is a modern estate and there is little trace of Pember's world. Thomas Cubitt, meanwhile, had an important link to Bonsor that is discussed in Chapter 6.

John Edward and Fanny Pember (and their son) moved into one of Cubitt's mansions at the south end of New Park Road with just one other property before the nearby fields (market gardens); indeed they were one of the first residents on the estate. Their daughter Ellen was born there and baptized at St. Matthew's, Brixton on 5 December 1833 - the church is still located in the centre of the suburb at the bottom end of Brixton Hill. Meanwhile the father Saint John Pember became sick and wrote his last will on 3 January 1835 and appointed his eldest children John and Mary Pember as executors. He left to Mary his two houses and leases in Crescent Place (and their furniture) and 'half of what I may die worth' and the remaining half to be divided amongst his other children: John, Henry, Frederick and Elizabeth. He made a few exceptions viz. his watch to grandson Edward, his green stone ring to John, his ring with his late dear Ellen's hair to John Starie, his love and any little things in the house to sister Mrs. L'Hermitte and a watch seal to sons Henry and Frederick. The witnesses were H. Pember and John Smith and he then added a codicil on the same day making a new condition - if my daughter Mary at any time should be worth an income of £100 p.a. (exclusive of what I leave) then she shall only receive the same share as the other children - witnesses John Pemberton and John Smith. Saint John Pember died a few days later at Blackfriars and was buried at St. Mary's, Lambeth with his family on 13 January 1835 age 63. William Starie builder of 11 Dorset Place, Clapham Road appeared at Doctors' Commons on 23 March 1835 and confirmed that the will was written in the hand of the deceased, whilst John Edward Pember proved the will on 7 April 1835 the like grant going to Mary Jane Pember.

The family remained at New Park Road and had four more children baptized at St. Matthew's, Brixton: Arthur (9 July 1835), Fanny (1836), Frederick (1837) and Kate (1839) and they had an affluent lifestyle.

John Edward Pember had entered the Stock Exchange by 1831 and was listed as a stockbroker from 1837, whilst Henry Pember his brother was a broker in 1837-38 but died at New Park Road and was buried at St. Mary's, Lambeth on 28 July 1838. The family's fortunes fell upon John Edward Pember and he lived at New Park Road in 1841 with wife Fanny, children Ellen, Arthur, Fanny and Kate, Elizabeth Starie (35) and daughter Sophia (8) and four servants. Mary L'Hermitte his sister a widow of 3 Vauxhall Terrace made her last will on 10 July 1841 and left £40 to Harry L'Hermitte of Leicester and a number of other small bequests, but the residue went to her niece Mary Pember for her own use. Indeed her executor Mary Jane Pember proved the will in London on 23 March 1842 and like grant went to friend Charles Rice. The family was further depleted when Elizabeth Starie died at Wandsworth in September 1843.

The father John continued to succeed at work and two more children were born at New Park Road: Howard (c.1841) and Mary Jane (1843). They were baptized at St. Matthew's, Brixton on 6 December 1843, whilst his last child George Herbert was born at Rayleigh in Essex on 2 May 1845. The family moved to "Langlands" in Kings Road, Clapham Park in 1848, which was a mansion in ½-acre of land with orchards to the rear, and was the fourth building above the junction with Atkins Road on the east side. The houses going north were Kings Road Cottage (Tudor Cottage), Waratah House (James Youl a landholder in Australia), Park Lodge School and Langlands - there is no trace other than a boundary wall of Waratah House. John E. Pember, stockbroker, lived at Kings Road in 1851 with his wife Fanny, children Edward Henry (18) undergraduate Oxford, Ellen, Arthur, Fanny, Kate, Mary Jane and George Herbert (all *scholars at home*), Kate and Jane Robson (*governesses*) and five servants - son Howard was a scholar at the Brixton Oval School on the 1851 census. The father sat on the 'Committee for General Purposes' at the Stock Exchange from 1852 and this lucrative work provided a bright future for his offspring thus three sons attended public school. The family stayed at Langlands for 14 years and John E. Pember, member of the Stock Exchange, resided there in 1861 with wife Fanny, children Edward H. (28) a chancery barrister in practice, Howard (19) clerk to a tea broker and Mary J. (17), Katherine Robson and five servants. The remaining family moved to the equally affluent Leigham Avenue in 1863, the house being at the south east end - it has not survived but some houses remain near Streatham High Road. Howard Pember, the son, apparently died in his twenties and this became a popular family name.

John and Fanny Pember lived at Leigham Avenue in 1871 with Mary Jane Pember, Katherine Robson, granddaughter Annabel Ellen Reeves (16): *see below* and three servants. The father John was a stockbroker from at least 1837-78 and represented Jones Loyd & Co (1858-65), Bank of London (1866-67) and Bank of England (1868-78) at the Stock Exchange. Fanny Pember his wife died at Loats Road, Clapham Park on 6 May 1873 and was described as 'late' of Leigham Avenue. The event was recorded in the Lyttelton Times, New Zealand on 11 July 1873 and at first glance this was an unusual entry but the reason is soon made clear. John E. Pember moved to Woodfield Cottage, Streatham near to Woodfield Avenue on the edge of Tooting Bec Common but his daughter Mary Jane died there on 16 May 1877. He made his last will on 7 November 1877 and appointed Edward Henry Pember trustee and executor and gave him his book of paintings and old silver tankard, and donated £5 to the poor of Streatham (a token gesture). He asked his executors to settle or adjust all his transactions at the Stock Exchange and bequeathed to his trustees and their assigns, "all my real estate (including), therein, all real estate to which I am entitled in New Zealand...." He made provision, in trust, for children Edward H., Ellen, Arthur, Fanny, Kate, Frederick and George H. but made special provision for the shares bequeathed to Ellen, Arthur and Frederick - he requested that Edward Henry and George Herbert should hold their shares and in the case of Arthur the income was for the benefit of his wife Alice, and in the case of Frederick Pember for the benefit of his wife Georgiana - clerks to Messrs. Druce Sons and Jackson, 10 Billiter Square were witnesses.

John Edward Ross Pember added a codicil on 20 September 1880 and left £500 to Eliza Mead, his nurse, for her un-wearying attention during his long illness and not subject to her husband's debts - witnessed Francis Ezekiel Barton and Jane Robson. He died at Woodfield Cottage, Streatham on 23 February 1881 and a brief notice of his death appeared in the South London Press on 5 March. Edward Henry Pember Q.C. of Lincoln's Inn, Alexander Devas Druce of 10 Billiter Square solicitor and Arthur Bowdler Hill of 101 Southwark Street merchant, his executors, proved his will in London on 7 April 1881, his personal estate being £16,000 - the effects of Mary Jane Pember were administered on 5 May 1881. The event was listed in the Canterbury Death Duty Register and the Index to Probate for New Zealand and one can ask - why were there special provisions for Ellen, Arthur and Frederick? The answer was that they had all emigrated and these three people are discussed shortly, however the children at home also had notable and remarkable lives.

THE CONSERVATIVE ELEMENT

Edward Henry Pember was born on 28 May 1832 and baptized at St. Matthew's, Brixton on 29 June that year then attended Harrow School in 1846-48 and Charterhouse in 1848-50 - he was in the cricket XI in 1849-50. He matriculated at Christchurch, Oxford on 23 May 1850 and was a "student" of the college gaining a B.A. in 1854 namely a 1st class degree in classical mods and in literae humaniores - with an M.A. in 1857. He had considerable literary ability and published "The Maid of Messene and other poems" (London 1855), and "Job - a dramatic poem" (1859), but his real skill was in repartee being known as "the best talker in London" and he turned his eloquence with the English language to the legal profession. He was a student at Lincoln's Inn on 2 May 1855 and qualified as a barrister on 26 January 1858 and first worked in common law practice on the Midland Circuit, but the briefs were slow in coming and he was introduced to the parliamentary bar - he was considered to be the ideal person for the job.

He was married to Fanny daughter of William Richardson M.D. in Edinburgh on 28 August 1861, she being born at Goulburn near Sydney, Australia in 1838. The couple moved to Hatfield and had sons Francis William (1862) and Howard Edward Worsley (1865) who both attended Harrow. The father had chambers at 9 New Square, Lincoln's Inn in 1862 and his home address was Hill House, Hatfield in 1871 although only Howard E. (5), Lillian (4) and five servants were there. The girl was the daughter of Arthur Pember his brother and was born in Kilburn in 1867 but there is no record of the birth with the Registrar. Her immediate family emigrated in 1868 and her uncle adopted her although the reason for this is not known - she may have been illegitimate or ill and unable to travel. Edward had chambers at 3 Brick Court, Temple in 1871-82 and was a bencher and a treasurer of Lincoln's Inn and Q.C. in 1874. Fanny a barrister's wife and Francis William undergraduate of Oxford (Trinity) and six servants lived at Vicars Hill House in the hamlet of Vicars Hill near Boldre (New Forest) above the coastal town of Lymington in 1881 - it was their home for many years. Lillian had a good upbringing and was a pupil at the "Beehive School", Osborne Road in Windsor in 1881 with a mistress, 4 governesses, 27 girls (age 11-17) and nine servants.

Edward H. Pember had chambers at 32 Great George Street near the Houses of Parliament in the 1880s-90s and debated important legal issues of the day. These included the Manchester Ship Canal debate in July 1885 when he spoke for promoters of the scheme in the face of much opposition. It was said to be one of the most effective speeches ever delivered in a parliamentary committee room. He headed a select committee that produced the *Metropolis Water Supply Bill* in 1891 and was counsel for Cecil Rhodes regarding the Jameson Raid in April 1897. He also promoted the Hull and Barnsley Railway (breaking the monopoly of the N.E. Railway Co.) and the Barry Co. line and port (allowing the export of Rhondda coal). His speeches were good examples of literary style and in general were most carefully prepared: "His fine presence, his command of flowing classical English, together with his quickness of comprehension and his readiness in repartee soon made him a prime favourite with the committees of both houses." He was a leader of such debate for at least 30 years and left papers re the House of Commons but would argue with experts and men of science, and was at times unpopular.

He was a skilled musician who studied singing under Perugini and became a prominent figure in the social and literary life of London. Charles Edward Perugini (1839-1918) was born abroad in Naples but was British in every way and was found to have talent as an artist - he was the protégé of Lord Leighton and a fine painter. Katherine Elizabeth Macready or Kate (1839-1929) was the third child of Charles Dickens and was skilled as a writer and artist. She acted in her father's theatrical group at Tavistock Square in 1855 and posed for Millais in his famous painting *The Black Brunswicker* in 1860. She married Charles Alston Collins R.A. that year but he died in 1873, and she then married 'Carlo' Perugini at St. George's Hanover Square in June 1874 (strangely there is also a record of the marriage in September 1873). They had an eminent circle of literary, artistic and musical friends who met at their house-studio in London and knew Leighton, Millais and Val Prinsep (see Merriman Ch. 10). Edward may have been amongst this group and also translated Greek and Latin verse, wrote classical plays and published several volumes of poems but only for private circulation. He was Secretary of the *Society of Dilettanti* in 1896-1911 - formed in 1732 to study ancient remains, especially of classical origin.

Fanny Pember resided at Vicars Hill House in 1901 however her husband was "away on business" and the household included niece Lillian Pember, grandsons Edward H. (3) and Raymond F. (1) and ten servants, whilst the estate also had stables and two cottages. Edward H. Pember retired from the law in 1903 and had made his mark on Victorian society thus Sir Edward Poynter R.A. painted his portrait in 1909. He died at Vicars Hill on 5 April 1911 and was buried at Boldre Church and his obituary appeared in the Times - Rev. F.H. Bowden-Smith performed the service and the mourners included G.H. Pember, F.W.

Pember, Miss Helen Hill, G. Ross Pember, John A. Druce, Francis Druce, H. Druce, Lady Gatacre, Hon A.J. Davey, Mr. Rickards K.C., E.F. Chinery (Mayor of Lymington) and several colonels and captains. His executors John Alexander Druce retired solicitor, Fanny Pember widow and Francis William Pember barrister-at-law obtained his probate in London on 11 May 1911, his effects £149,454 13s 8d. His widow moved to London and died at 21 Holland Villas, Kensington on 16 March 1925 whilst Lillian the "sister" of F.W. Pember died at the same address on 13 April 1925: Francis William Pember barrister and John Alexander Druce retired solicitor obtained joint probate on 13 May that year.

Francis William Pember was born at Hatfield on 16 August 1862. He attended Harrow from April 1875 to mid-term 1880 (Mr. Watson's) and was head of the school in 1879-80 and played for the cricket XI in 1880. He matriculated at Balliol College, Oxford on 21 October that year and was a scholar from 1880-84 and a fellow of All Souls' in 1884 - he gained his B.A. in 1884 and M.A. in 1887. He was a student at Lincoln's Inn in 1885 and became a barrister in 1889, with chambers at 9 Stone Buildings (Lincoln's Inn) and a residence at 7 Half Moon Street, Piccadilly in 1891. His brother Howard Edward Worsley Pember was born at Hatfield in December 1865 and attended Harrow from September 1879 to mid-term 1884 (Mr. Watson's). He matriculated at Balliol College on 15 October 1884 and was an exhibitioner in 1884 and gained his B.A. in 1889, however he died at Vicars Hill, Boldre on 29 November 1891 and his probate went to E.H. Pember Q.C.

Francis married the Hon. Margaret Bowen daughter of Lord Davey of Fernhurst at Midhurst, Sussex in December 1895. They had three children at Paddington: Edward Horace (December 1897), Raymond Francis (December 1899) and Katharine (June 1901) and lived at 6 Sussex Gardens in 1901 near the homes of Crake and Welch (see later). Francis had a notable career as a barrister like his father and was an honorary bencher of Lincoln's Inn, conveyancer, equity and parliamentary draughtsman and temporary assistant legal adviser to the Foreign Office. He was estates bursar for All Souls', Oxford in 1910-14, Warden of the College in 1914-32, Vice-Chancellor of Oxford University in 1926-29 and honorary fellow of All Souls' and Balliol in 1932. He lived at Broncroft Castle, Craven Arms, Shropshire, in 1929 and was a J.P. for Salop and an Officer of the Légion D'Honneur, but his most notable position was Governor of Harrow School (1910-44). For recreation he enjoyed fishing and walking and his wife Margaret died in 1942, whilst Francis died at Broncroft Castle on 19 January 1954.

His daughter Katharine Pember (1901) married Charles Galton Darwin M.C. M.A. F.R.S. at Oxford in September 1925 and they no doubt met through her father's university connections. Charles was born on 19 December 1887 and attended Trinity, Cambridge and became a university lecturer but was attached to the R.E. and R.A.F. in 1914-18. He was at Christ's College, Cambridge in 1919-22 and Edinburgh in 1923-36 and was later a member of the American Philosophical Society with honorary degrees from Bristol, Manchester, Delhi, Chicago and California. He resided at Newnham Grange, Cambridge and was awarded the K.B.E. in 1942 and died on 31 December 1962. His father Sir George Howard Darwin was born at Downe, Kent on 9 July 1845 and was son of Charles Robert Darwin (author of Origin of the Species) and Emma granddaughter of Josiah Wedgwood. He attended Trinity, Cambridge in c.1868 and was briefly a barrister in 1874 then married Maud daughter of Charles du Puy of Philadelphia in 1884. He was a learned scholar devoted to mathematical science and was President of the Royal Astronomical Society in 1899. He wrote a paper on the marriage of first cousins and produced a number of papers on tidal observations and orbit of the planets, and was no doubt familiar with J. Lubbock (see Ch. 7) - he also lived at Newnham Grange and died 7 December 1912. This was a good connection and some interesting evolution had occurred; indeed Darwin might have written on natural selection in football circles (many links are revealed later).

The Pember family can be divided into the traditional and the adventurous and a number of them remained close to their roots in Clapham. Fanny Pember was baptized at Brixton on 24 May 1836 and married Arthur Bowdler Hill at Holy Trinity, Clapham on 12 August 1858. Charles Croft Hill performed the ceremony and Charles S. Hill and Charles Druce were witnesses. Her husband was born at Aldersgate in 1828 the son of Arthur Stephen and Margaret Helen Hill, a merchant, and for an explanation of the term 'bowdlerize' see Goodwyn (Ch. 10). Arthur B. Hill a druggist merchant lived at the "Hawthorns", South Road, Clapham Park, in 1881 with his wife Fanny, children Helen, Margaret, Arthur C., Constance, Edith, Charles A. and Mary and five servants (plus some stable buildings). The couple lived with daughters Margaret and Mary at *Malwa*, Babbacombe Downs, Devon, in 1901 and Fanny died there on 11 March 1907, whilst Arthur died at the "Hawthorns", 118 Kings Avenue in Clapham Park on 18 February 1909. Arthur Croft Hill M.D. and Charles Alexander Hill wholesale druggist were executors - his estate valued at £23,001 18s 1d.

Kate Pember was baptized at Brixton on 26 June 1839 and as a minor married Alexander Devas Druce at Holy Trinity, Clapham on 2 August 1856. Arthur John Druce performed the ceremony and John E. Pember and Charles Druce the father (solicitor) were witnesses. This wealthy family had property at Dulwich Common and Alexander was born there in 1828 (see Rich Ch. 8). He also became a solicitor and lived at the "Shrubbery", Streatham High Road near St. Leonard's Church in 1881 with wife Kate, children John A., Alice, George C., Hubert A., Florence, Mary, Kate, Francis and Stephen P. and ten servants - this was a mansion and John and Hubert were students-of-law. Alexander Druce had chambers at 10 Billiter Square near Lloyd's (Fenchurch Avenue is on the site) and died at "Upper-Gatton", Merstham on 2 January 1897. His executors were Kate, John Alexander, George Claridge and Hubert Arthur (Druce) and his estate was valued at £175,476 0s 7d. Kate Druce lived at 65 Cadogan Square, Chelsea in 1901 with Hubert, Kate, Francis and Stephen and nine servants, and died there on 15 July 1921 - Thomas V. Lister K.C.M.G. the late 'Under Secretary of State' lived next door.

George Herbert Pember was born at Rayleigh, Essex on 2 May 1845 and educated at Westminster School in 1856-63. Indeed his presence there at these dates had a material effect on soccer history (see below). He was admitted to Trinity, Cambridge on 21 November 1864 and matriculated in Lent term 1865, then married Mary Louisa daughter of John Carr Badeley of Guy Harlings, Essex at Torquay, Devon in December 1869 - she was born in Chelmsford in 1844. George H. Pember a member of the Stock Exchange lived at *Launitz Villa*, Liverpool Road, Norbiton near Kingston in 1871 with wife Mary and brother-in-law Robert B. Badeley (income from mortgages). George was a stockbroker like his father and was dealing in stocks and shares from at least 1871 with offices at 19 Change Alley, London. He had children Winifred Mary M. (March 1872), Frances Evelyn (September 1874), George Ross (June 1876) and Henry Cecil (September 1879) and lived at *Meadow Bank*, Liverpool Road, in 1881, with sister-in-law Althea Badeley (44) and four servants - a fifth child Clifford Fanshawe was born on 21 October 1881. The father had offices at 62-63 Cornhill, London in 1882 and was a partner in *Pember and Boyle* who dealt at the Stock Exchange - they advertised in the Times on 20 September 1889 re bonds of the Chicago, St. Paul and Kansas City Railway.

George was successful as a stockbroker and lived at Tangier Park, Wootton near Basingstoke and was joint master (1888-93) and master (1896-1900) of the Vine Hunt, whilst his daughter Winifred Mary M. Pember was married there in December 1898. He lived with wife Mary and children Frances and George at Tangier Park, in 1901, and also had a residence at 8 Bryanston Square, Marylebone (the father and son were stockbrokers). His wife Mary Louisa died in 1908 and he married Constance Mary daughter of Sir Wyndham Spencer Portal 1st Bart. and widow of William Howley Kingsmill in 1910. George Herbert Pember died at Fair Oak Park, Eastleigh, Hants on 22 March 1921 and probate went to his executors George Ross Pember stockbroker, Francis William Pember barrister and John Alexander Druce retired solicitor on 14 June 1921 - his estate valued at £146,640 6s 1d.

His sons all had a good education and George Ross Pember attended Harrow in April 1890 (Mr. Welldon's) and was a monitor in 1893-94 then joined the family firm as a stockbroker - the third generation. He married Alice Macnabb and had a son Rawdon and daughter Felicity and lived at Docklands, Ingatestone in Essex. Indeed *Pember and Boyle* continued to trade until 1986 when they became Morgan Grenfell Government Securities, but had ceased trading in April 1989. Henry Cecil Pember attended Harrow in April 1893 (Mr. Guillemard's) then married Evelyn Mary daughter of Sir Lewis Amherst Selby Bigge in 1908 and had two sons and one daughter. Clifford Fanshawe Pember attended Winchester College in 1894 and resided at 17 Philbeach Gardens, Kensington. The families of Edward H. and George H. Pember retained traditional values and appeared in the *Armorial Families* published by Fox-Davies in 1929. They claimed a coat of arms from the old Hereford family and were aristocratic with both title and possession but there was another side to the story. Arthur, Frederick and Ellen all left England and had various motives for emigrating; indeed it is likely they had new aspirations and were attracted by the values of the 'New World'. They were not held by the traditions of the family at home and in fact spoke out against them - in no uncertain terms.

THE EMIGRANTS

A succession of Pember girls rode in a wedding carriage from Clapham Park to Holy Trinity Church and the eldest of them led the way. Ellen Pember was baptized at Brixton on 5 December 1833 and married William Reeves of Portland Place, Lambeth at Holy Trinity on 21 April 1853 the witnesses including John E. and Fanny Pember. The bridegroom was born in Clapham probably on 10 February 1825 the son of William Reeves and Jane Eliza Lamb, and was a gentleman and member of the Stock Exchange in 1852-56. The couple lived at Clapham Road in 1852-54 and 12 The Grove, Clapham in 1855-56 and had two children baptized at Holy Trinity: Annabel Ellen (25 November 1854) and Coleridge Edward (24 November 1855) *infant*. William had a financial setback at the Stock Exchange and after paying off his debt was re-admitted, but suffered some loss of credibility and with near scandal in the air immigrated to New Zealand. The British Crown and the Maori signed the Waitangi Treaty to establish the colony in 1840, but it was a controversial agreement between 'men' with a different understanding of land rights, leading to much conflict (the Maori Wars) - indeed Lord Salisbury was an outspoken critic of British policy towards the Maori. A number of settlements were started and Christchurch was established in 1850 with a grid of streets laid out on the marshlands of Canterbury Plain. There was no deep-water harbour thus vessels moored at Lyttelton across the Port Hills on Banks Peninsula, and early settlers had to take their possessions by donkey over the bridle path to reach the city - the first rail link was not built until 1867.

Lyttelton, New Zealand. The town climbs up into the Port Hills.

William, Ellen and Annabel Reeves then sailed on the "Rose of Sharon" and made the perilous three-month sea journey to arrive in Wellington on 19 January 1857. Emigrant ships sailed south down the Atlantic past the Cape de Verde Islands off Africa then east across the southern Indian Ocean, and often saw no land for over two months. The majority of immigrants travelled in squalid conditions but presumably the Reeves' had a first class passage. They did not stay in Wellington and son William Pember Reeves was born at Lyttelton on 10 February 1857. William established good connections and was a farmer at Rangiora and manager of Fernside sheep-run but returned to Christchurch as a carrier from Heathcote to Lyttelton. He remained ambitious and purchased a share in the *Lyttelton Times* from Charles Christopher Bowen in 1860 (see Ch. 7) and was the paper's manager then had seven more children: Edmund Crosbie (1858), Marion Hamilton (1860), Gertrude Mary (1861), Gilbert Edward (1864), Ellen Mary (1866), Dorothy Elizabeth (1868) *infant* and Hugh Maude (1869).

William entered politics in 1867-75 and was a minister for the South Island in 1869-72 but his main work was as proprietor of the *Lyttelton Times* from 1867 - he changed it from a staunch provincial paper to one with liberal views in the 1870s-80s. Hon. William Reeves M.L.C. J.P. lived at Gloucester Street in 1875-76 and at "Risingholme", Opawa district in 1880-81 (built 1864) but his daughter Annabel died there on 25 September 1881. He lived at Opawa South in 1885-86 but made some unwise investments (with the paper's money) and had a large mortgage on his estate. This made him virtually bankrupt and he died in Christchurch on 4 April 1891, thus his family lost control of the paper. New Zealand was the first country to give women the vote and Ellen Reeves a lady and daughter Ellen Mary of 21 Latimer Square, Christchurch were on the 'first list of women electors' in 1893. The voters at the house included Gilbert Edward insurance clerk and Hugh Maude journalist. Ellen Reeves lived at 162 Montreal Street in 1896-97 and died in Christchurch on 3 March 1919. "Risingholme" was given to the city in 1943 and is a community centre and park with oak, beech, cedar, ash, Spanish chestnut, Canadian hemlock and a rose garden by the old homestead - Reeves Road is nearby.

William Pember Reeves had a notable career and was listed in Bateman's N. Zealand Encyclopedia *1984* as, "An extraordinarily versatile man - a sportsman, politician, journalist and poet." He was educated at Christ's College, Christchurch the equivalent of a public school and lived with his family at "Risingholme", but went to England in 1874 to follow a career in the law (like his uncle Edward). He nearly attended Oxford University but his brief visit was cut short due to health problems, possibly tuberculosis, and he returned home to work as a shepherd at Ashburton. His health improved and he played cricket and rugby for Canterbury and qualified as a barrister and solicitor in 1880. His main interest was politics and he was parliamentary reporter for the *Lyttelton Times* in 1883 and editor of the weekly *Canterbury Times* in 1885. He married Magdalen Stuart Robison in Christchurch on 10 February 1885. She was the daughter of William Smoult Robison a banker in the city and was born at Mudgee, Australia on 24 December 1865. William a J.P. and solicitor resided at Hereford Street West and Opawa South in 1885-86 and had daughters Amber (1887) and Beryl (1889). He was elected to Parliament as a Liberal in 1887 and campaigned for a railway to the west coast and Nelson and became editor of the *Lyttelton Times* in 1889. He published many poems and wrote on socialism and communism, his beliefs coming from the Fabians who employed, "cautious and dilatory strategy to wear out an enemy," i.e. those who obstructed social justice. His family lost control of the paper after his father's death, however he became Minister of Education and Justice in 1891 and Minister of Labour in 1892 (the first in the Empire).

William was omitted from the electoral rolls in 1893 maybe due to his position in government however his wife Magdalen Stuart was a housewife at the Bank of New South Wales, Christchurch. William was a radical and introduced the *Industrial Conciliation and Arbitration Act* (1894) - this provided a complete code for the employer-employee relationship, and the *Factory Act* (1894) - this prevented the employment of children under 14 and limited hours for those under 16, and women, to 48 per week. Indeed he was a committed Fabian Socialist and his son was named Fabian in 1895. He was, however, too radical for some in the Liberal party especially Richard John Seddon the new leader and was sent to London as Agent-General in 1896. He had no direct influence on New Zealand politics but promoted his country abroad and was a great success in the position. He was an associate and friend of Sidney and Beatrice Webb and George Bernard Shaw all Fabians and debated the efficiency of 'Imperial control'. He continued to write thus he published *New Zealand and other Poems* and *The Long White Cloud* a detailed history of the country, in 1898, and two volumes *State Experiments in Australia and New Zealand* a scholarly survey of legislative experiments, in 1902. The position of High Commissioner replaced that of Agent-General in 1905 and he then earned more than the Prime Minister. He longed to return to New Zealand and his hopes were raised when Seddon died in 1906, but his friends advised against it. His wife known as Maud Pember Reeves was a social reformer and feminist who fought for women's suffrage in New Zealand and in England. She was on the Committee of the Fabian Society with Bernard Shaw and H.G. Wells from 1907 whilst the Fabian Women's Group was started at her London home in 1908.

Scandal, however, was in the air and his precocious daughter Amber eloped to Paris, in 1908, with H.G. Wells who was married but believed in sexual freedom. William was already an unhappy man away from his country and found he was opposed as High Commissioner and thus resigned in 1908. His friends the Webbs arranged his appointment as Director of the London School of Economics that year, whilst the Liberal leaders secured him a position as a director of the Bank of New Zealand. Meanwhile his daughter Amber had a child from her affair and married George Rivers Blanco-White at Kensington in June 1909. H.G. Wells portrayed their relationship in his novel *Ann Veronica* that year and Reeves, who was not 'liberal' in these matters, denounced the writer at every opportunity and fell out with the Fabians. His wife Maud continued her connection and did research in the poor areas of Lambeth in 1909-13 and the Fabians published, in her name, *Round about a pound a week* (1913). There was soon further heartache and son Fabian a lieutenant in the Royal Naval Air Service died in France in 1917.

The father knew the Greek Prime Minister and was involved in their affairs, and was appointed Chairman of the National Bank of New Zealand in 1917, but resigned from the L.S.E. in 1919. He then worked solely for the bank but also maintained an interest in sport and watched a rugby match - England v All Blacks, in 1925. The New Zealand team had great Maori players from as early as 1884 including fullback George Nepia in 1925 and William was inspired to poetry: "Kia toa! New Zealand see, Nepia guards the gate, a rock and house of defence is he, a tino-tangata great." Immigration to the antipodes was often a one-way journey but for some was a return trip and William visited New Zealand for the bank in 1925-26, but resigned as Chairman in 1931. Hon. William Pember Reeves died at 31 Pembroke Square, Earls Court Road, Kensington, on 15 May 1932 and widow Magdalen obtained his probate. She died at Golders Green in 1953 whilst Amber his daughter received an O.B.E.

Frederick Pember also immigrated to new lands and received influence from his relatives but his motives were different in the extreme. He was baptized at Brixton on 13 September 1837 and educated at Charterhouse School in June 1850 to August 1855 - he was in Saunderites like his brother. He also followed Edward to university and matriculated at Christchurch, Oxford on 30 May 1855 gaining a B.A. in 1859. He entered the Church and was appointed curate of Coleshill near Amersham, Bucks in 1860 and married Eliza Georgina Gibbard at St. Clement Danes, Strand on 14 October 1865 - she was born in December 1841 daughter of John Gibbard. He stayed at Coleshill however his son John Edward was born at Southampton in June 1866 and baptized at St. Clement Danes on 1 July. He was curate of Folkingham, Lincs in 1867-68 and his son Frederick Howard was born there in June 1868 but there was soon a change of direction. Bishop Harper of New Zealand contacted him, possibly through his brother-in-law William Reeves, and he was then recruited for overseas work. In fact Harper was an ardent worker in establishing the Church of England in New Zealand from 1841-68 and was described as, "A missionary par excellence, combining zeal and energy with vision and a genius for organisation." Thus a second member of the family headed for Lyttelton in New Zealand.

Edward Gibbon Wakefield organised and arranged much of the settlement of New Zealand and hoped to make a small fortune by sending immigrants to the new land. He had a notable ancestry and was descended from Edward Wakefield who married Isabella Gibbon in 1748 - a relative of Edward Gibbon the historian. Their son Edward (1750-1826) was a merchant of Gresham Street, London and married Priscilla Bell in 1771 but lost much of his money on financial gambles. She was the daughter of Daniel Bell a coal merchant of Stamford Hill and his wife Katherine Barclay of the Quaker family (bankers), whilst sister Catherine Bell married John Gurney of Earlham Hall and was the mother of Elizabeth Fry - prison reformer (see Lubbock Ch. 7). The couple's son Edward Wakefield (1774-1854) married Susanna Crush of Felsted, Essex in 1791 and was a farmer at nearby Bunham Hall but the venture failed. He moved to Shoreditch in 1814 and was a land agent at 42 Pall Mall whilst his father struggled financially thus his mother Priscilla wrote educational books for children to supplement their income and started a lying-in-charity and a frugal bank. She also helped raise the grandchildren but was committed to Whitmore House in 1812-13 and suffered at the hands of her 'jailers'. Her son Edward then became interested in the design of a humane London asylum and met James Bevans a Quaker and architect, then made plans based on Jeremy Bentham's *Panopticon* (see Reveley Ch. 20). He reported to the House of Commons Select Committee on Mad Houses in 1815 and as a land agent travelled the country and visited many asylums (see Goodwyn Ch. 10). He also attempted to set up a silk industry at Blois in France, whilst his wife Susanna died in 1816.

His son Edward Gibbon Wakefield was born London on 20 March 1796, and educated at Westminster (1808) and Edinburgh (1812). He was not satisfied with his many advantages in life and married a young heiress Eliza Susan the daughter of Captain Thomas Charles Pattle and niece of James Pattle - her cousins were Julia Margaret Cameron and Sarah Prinsep (see Merriman Ch. 10). Her father died in India in 1815 and she returned to England and married Edward in 1816, but died herself in 1820. He then set his sights on Ellen Turner a teenage schoolgirl and daughter of a wealthy manufacturer. He tricked her, saying they had her parents' consent, and persuaded her to elope to Gretna Green where they married in 1826 but the plot was discovered and her family pursued them to France - his father Edward died at this time whilst Priscilla his grandmother who raised him was much distressed (she died in 1832). Wakefield was captured and sentenced to three years in Newgate Prison (1827-30) but whilst detained made his plans - namely to buy Maori land cheaply and sell it for a large profit. He formed the South Australia Association (1833) and New Zealand Company (1837) with this in mind, but others saw a religious opportunity in the new lands. His brother William and son Edward helped to start Wellington in 1839, whilst brothers William and Arthur were agents for Nelson and other towns. John Robert Godley, meanwhile, attended Christchurch in Oxford and with some friends from the college made plans for a Christian settlement. He approached Wakefield with the idea and Christchurch was begun in 1850, although its Christian aims only lasted four years due to the arrival of many newcomers (see Bowen Ch. 7). Wakefield's obituary was in the Times on Saturday 16 August 1862 stating: "The last mail from New Zealand brings intelligence of the death of Mr. Edward Gibbon Wakefield who accomplished more for the improvement of colonisation during the last 30 years than any other man of the age."

Frederick Pember had attended Christchurch College and this may have influenced his decision to emigrate. He travelled out on the "Hydaspes" (1,655 tons) from London under the command of Captain Babot and the voyage was reported in the Lyttelton Times on 29 October 1868. The saloon passengers included Rev. F. Pember, Mrs. Pember and two children whilst the ship's cargo included cases, bales, casks and drums. This was a 'state of the art' vessel with one of Graveley's patent condensing engines for supplying fresh water. Further to this, there was a 12 horsepower steam apparatus for washing the decks with hot or cold water, hoisting up the yards, pumping the ship and heaving up the anchor - the sailors could presumably spend their time taking the sun in a deckchair! Captain Babot provided a helpful account of the voyage and noted this was her first since she became a sailing ship, having previously been a screw steamer. This was a somewhat retrogressive conversion although no comfort was apparently spared. She left Gravesend on 26 July 1868 but did not lose sight of the Lizard until 1 August - due to head winds in the Channel. She sighted Cape Finisterre near La Coruna, Spain on 4 August and sailed south under the N.E. and S.E. Trades. The winds were particularly light and in consequence of the ship being a peculiarly good 'sailer' no time was lost. The calmness of the sea gave the passengers an opportunity for sport in the way of shark fishing, however they did not catch a single shark.

Lyttelton Harbour. Ships bound for Christchurch moored here on arrival from England.

The ship passed the longitude of the Cape of Good Hope on the 26th September and the weather was remarkably fine. Soon after, they sailed within twelve miles of the Prince Edward Islands and could only just see them because of thick rain, however just for a moment the sun broke through and lit up the snow-clad peaks. In the words of Captain Babot the longitude was then run down between the parallels of 45° and 47° South. There was no ice to be seen and fine weather prevailed although the N.E. winds retarded the progress of the ship. They had soon crossed the Southern Ocean and weighed anchor at Lyttelton Harbour on 28 October 1868. The ship outstripped everything she came in sight of and was a great success for the Canterbury trade. In particular, Babot was impressed by her extreme size, numerous appliances in case of storm, and condenser providing an unlimited supply of water in the tropics. Further, she was easy to sail and protected the cargo well and he had no doubt (that) she would receive a liberal patronage. He concluded by stating that her best days work was 325 miles on 20 October.

The Pembers no doubt enjoyed the voyage but may have been less impressed when they came ashore in New Zealand, as this was still 'real' pioneer country with wooden houses, stagecoaches and gold rushes. Frederick became incumbent of All Saints, Burnham on 22 February 1869 under a temporary licence from the Waimakariri-Rakaia Diocese - this small settlement was 20 miles southwest of Christchurch on Canterbury Plain and they lived at Burnham Parsonage. A daughter Julia Theresa was born on 25 January 1870 and he baptized her there on 30 January, whilst Lucy Bethel was born on 12 November 1871 and baptized on 3 December - her sponsors or godparents being Annabel Ellen Reeves, Marion Hamilton Reeves and Richard Bethel. Indeed Annabel was living at Leigham Avenue, Streatham in April 1871 (and again the journey was not one-way). Burnham town-ship was an isolated settlement and is now best known for its army camp however Frederick Pember had grown up in Clapham Park and may have missed the greater society of others, consequently he soon returned to 'civilisation'. He was curate of Holy Trinity, Lyttelton from September 1872 to 31 March 1875 and again lived at the parsonage. His son George William Lawrence was born on 8 May 1873 and baptized at Lyttelton by Frederick on 16 May, the sponsors being Eliza Georgina Pember, William Pember Reeves and Ynyr Donald. This was, however, a harsh environment for children and Lucy Bethel died in October 1872 and George W.L. in August 1874 and both were buried at Lyttelton Cemetery. Frederick lived at Ripon Street in Lyttelton in 1875 with a view across the harbour and watched vessels arriving and departing, and indeed his work there was soon finished and he left himself - his brother Arthur may have prompted the next step (see below).

Frederick Pember sailed for London on the "Duke of Edinburgh" in 1875 and had a daughter Agnes D. that year however his stay was short and he arrived in the United States in 1876. He was initially a clergyman in the Episcopal Church and settled in Maine - his son Walter P. Ross was born there in April 1882, but then returned to the Church of England as curate of Calais, Maine in 1886-87 and rector of St. Anne's, Welshpool, Campobello, New Brunswick, in 1887-90. The latter was near to Calais but across the border in Canada, whilst Campobello Island was in the Bay of Fundy - he was funded by the Society for the Promotion of the Gospel in Campobello. He then moved south and was minister of St. John's, Arlington in 1890-92 and rector of St. Paul's, Peabody in 1892-1905 (both in Massachusetts). He lived at 197 Lowell, Peabody in 1893-94 just inland from the town of Salem and north of Boston, and with wife Eliza and son Walter at Mildham Town, Norfolk in 1900 (a citizen). He retired by 1905 and lived at 11 Hillcrest, West Roxbury in 1910 and died at Roxbury in Boston on 29 December 1914, whilst his wife Eliza Georgina died in 1920.

John Edward Pember (1866) was educated at Kennebunk, Maine and became a reporter and editor, being a feature writer for the *Boston Sunday Herald* at Washington Street and lived at 665 Tremont Street (in 1890). He married Agnes J. Cushman of Boston in 1894 and adopted a child Winifred J. then lived at 71 Albion Street in the suburb of Somerville by 1900 and was an editor in 1905. Frederick Howard Pember (1868) graduated from Tuft's College and resided at Pawtuxet, Rhode Island and was a superintendent of the American Woollen Company and married Esther Bradley of Cornish, Maine.

Julia Theresa Pember (1870) may have lived at 405 St. Nicholas Avenue, New York in 1892-93 and was a hospital attendant at St. Margaret's, Boston in 1900, then a teacher at the Sacred Heart country day school, Newton, Massachusetts. Agnes D. Pember (1875) married Frank A. Giles at Portsmouth, New Hampshire on 27 July 1896 although both lived at Peabody and later resided at Somerville (Mass.). Walter P. Ross Pember (1882) graduated from Massachusetts Institute of Technology (M.I.T.) and lived at Buffalo in New York State in 1905. He later resided at Delmar, Albany and was an architect and partner in the firm Pember and Demers. He married Amy Hewitt of Needham, Massachusetts and had children Howard, Ruth, Edna, and Edward (16 December 1909) - the latter married Lillian Bailey (1916) at New Lebanon, N.Y. on 28 February 1937.

THE SOCCER DAYS

But what of the elusive Arthur Pember - did he follow in the footsteps of his siblings? Well not exactly. He was baptized at St. Matthew's, Brixton on 9 July 1835 and grew up in Clapham Park and lived with his family at New Park Road until 1848. He did not attend public school like his brothers and was a *scholar at home* (aged 16) at "Langlands", Kings Road in 1851. He was educated with Ellen, Fanny, Kate, Mary Jane and George Herbert and their teachers were aunts Kate and Jane Robson, thus he received his education and knowledge of the world at home but missed the chance to go to university (he was surely able). Their neighbour James Arndell Youl of Waratah House was born at Cadi in New South Wales in 1811 and had children in Tasmania and was a landholder in Australia. Upon his return to England he became the Honorary Secretary of the Australian Association and was a founder of the Royal Colonial Institute. He died at Waratah House and was buried at Norwood Cemetery (5 June 1904). Maybe he told Arthur stories of foreign lands whilst his father's dealings at the Stock Exchange extended his horizons. He had a privileged background that enabled him to travel during his youth and spent time in both France and Switzerland in the late 1850s. He wrote of these adventures thus we know he visited Morlaix, Brittany on the Côte du Nord and the French and Swiss Alps; he went from Basle to Olten and to Lucerne and Grindelwald near the Eiger Mountain, as well as making more than one trip to Chamonix and Mont Blanc.

Travel and mountaineering were not his only pastimes and he also liked a game of football - but how did he become involved? It seems likely his brothers introduced him to soccer, since Edward and Frederick were at Harrow and Charterhouse whilst George Herbert was at Westminster in 1856-63. Indeed these dates are most significant since they cover the period when the first clubs were formed and games played. Arthur was either not academic (at the time) or had reasons for avoiding these institutions, thus he became a stockbroker with his father at Jones Loyd & Co. in 1857-60 (he lived at Kings Road). Arthur Pember, stockbroker of Clapham Park, married Elizabeth Hoghton at St. Mark's Church, Hamilton Terrace, Maida Vale on 13 March 1860. This was an 'in house' affair and the witnesses included John E. Pember and A.A. Hoghton. His bride was born c.1834 and was the daughter of Aubrey Alexander Hoghton who worked at the Stock Exchange from at least 1837-68 - he died at Marylebone in December 1873 age 70. The Hoghtons lived at 7 Abbey Road, St. John's Wood a house with a grand flight of stairs, arched doorway, tower style façade and castellated bay window. It still remains and is just two doors from the Abbey Road Studios. St. Mark's was of neo-Gothic design with gardens and a sweeping drive for the bride's carriage.

The marriage was most significant and had a material effect on football history as the couple moved to 26 Carlton Road, Kilburn not far from Abbey Road. This was, however, a tragic match and Elizabeth died there of complications 9 days after a miscarriage on 16 December 1860 - A.A. Hoghton was in attendance. Arthur Pember, a widower, aged 25 lived alone with three servants at 30 Carlton Road, Kilburn in 1861 however this circumstance did not last and there was soon another wedding. William Royal Grieve was born at Westminster on 25 January 1794 and was a wine merchant - gentleman who lived at St. George's Hanover Square in 1826 and Willesden by 1833. His last child Alice Mary was born at 3 Waterloo Place, Willesden in 'Kilburn Village' on 29 April 1845 but her mother Charlotte (Silver) died in June 1847, hence she was raised by her father William and step mother Eliza J. - resided 3 Waterloo Place in 1851-61. Arthur Pember a gentleman of Paddington married Alice Mary Grieve aged 17 at St. Mary's, Willesden in Neasden Lane on Wednesday 1 October 1862. The Rev. Armstrong performed the ceremony and Frederick Pember assisted him, whilst the Grieve family and Howard Pember were witnesses - details were in the Times on Saturday 4 October.

Arthur Pember left his father's firm and was a stockbroker for Kennard and Co. at the Stock Exchange in 1861-63. He remained at Carlton Road and played football for the No Names Club of Kilburn in the early 1860s. He was captain and founder and his players may have been members of the Stock Exchange, since the Civil Service and War Office had teams. There were fields just south of his house towards Edgware Road where the club may have played (re a map of 1867), and two became a cricket and football ground (and bicycle track) being known as Paddington Recreation Ground by 1893 - still there today. Arthur represented the No Names Club at the first F.A. meeting in 1863 and was President from 1863-67 and played a significant role in its early history, however his appointment was an anomaly. He did not fit the mould of contemporaries like Morley, Alcock, Marindin and Kinnaird who were sportsmen of note, yet there was Pember neither noted sportsman nor old boy heading the pack. This was indeed a quirk of history and he was just in the right place at the right time. His role cannot be over-emphasized and his place in F.A. history is guaranteed by considering his contribution further.

The founders met at the Freemasons Tavern on 26 October 1863 however the area was very different from today with narrow back streets and alleys. Great Queen Street linked Drury Lane to Lincoln's Inn Fields and was dominated by the Freemasons Hall and tavern (the Grand Lodge was formed in 1717). Why they chose this venue is not known, however those present may have had links to the freemasons or legal associations at Lincoln's Inn. The area was greatly altered after Kingsway was built in 1904-05 and a monumental Freemasons Hall was erected in 1927-33. The early F.A. meetings were held at the tavern or 3 King's Bench Walk and this only changed after the arrival of Charles Alcock in 1866 when they met at the Oval, Sportsman Newspaper and Cricket Press. The young businessmen had a specific aim when they assembled in October 1863 and wanted a code to replace existing local rules and arrangements, thereby gaining control of the sport. Arthur was elected as Chairman then the officers were appointed and some significant choices were made viz. Arthur Pember as President (proposed by Herbert T. Steward) and F.W. Campbell of Blackheath as Treasurer (proposed by A. Pember).

The Steward family had links with Westminster School for many years and their connections with both Pember and the Crusaders were most significant. Thomas Steward senior was an usher at the school and his son Thomas Francis was born at Marylebone in 1796. He attended Westminster in 1809-11 and then went to Edinburgh University and was himself an usher at the school for 46 years, and arithmetic master. He married Anne Burgoyne in 1827 and the family lived at 12 The Terrace, Dean's Yard and 15 Dean's Yard next to Westminster Abbey and three sons went to the school - the father died on 7 January 1864. Herbert Thomas Steward was born on 9 November 1838 and went to the school in 1846 and was an architect and surveyor in the firm of Hunt and Steward. He represented the Crusaders club at the first meeting and was on the F.A. Committee in 1863-65, whilst his club played football against the school at Vincent Square. His brother Francis John Steward was born in 1834 and attended the school in 1844-50; the latter was a member of the Stock Exchange in 1861 and no doubt knew Arthur Pember.

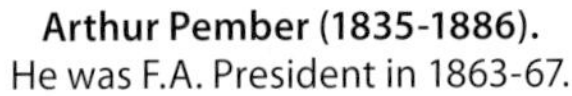

Arthur Pember (1835-1886).
He was F.A. President in 1863-67.

Eleven clubs joined the F.A. and only Charterhouse did not take up membership. G.F. Hartshorne their captain represented them and believed that the public schools should be prominent in the movement, but first wanted to ascertain the attitudes of the other schools (no other 'top' school was present) and only then would they commit to the Association. Ebenezer Morley concluded the first meeting and his last instruction was to contact the schools, then they placed an advert in *Bell's Life*, *The Field* and *Sporting Life*. The second meeting was on 10 November 1863 and the main matter of debate was the position of the public schools. Arthur Pember, the President, made an observation and said he had recently read the laws at Charterhouse and found them very simple, and believed that if two schools joined then Charterhouse would surely follow - the first set of rules were then formulated and approved. The third meeting was on 14 November 1863 and letters were received from Uppingham School and Lincoln F.C. - indeed the arrival of the latter soon created a problem and this is discussed shortly. The fourth meeting was on 17 November 1863 and the Cambridge Rules were incorporated in the existing code however this was done without the approval of all the members and there was soon trouble.

The fifth meeting took place on 1 December 1863 and was a stormy encounter with heated debate about the amendments to the rules, in particular issues of handling the ball and the practice of hacking. The family motto, "Beware of the Boot", then came into play and Mr. Pember and Mr. Lawson represented the No Names Club. Arthur Pember spoke with passion and stated: "Perhaps you will allow me to say, that I took down 'fifteen' the other day to play a match, and I was the only one who had not been at a public school and we were all dead against hacking." F.W. Campbell of Blackheath, Treasurer, took up the argument and suggested the Cambridge Rules should not have been added without all the members' agreement. Arthur Pember was most distressed by this and said, "I do not submit to the suggestion of un-gentlemanly conduct," and put forward a motion to remove both running with the ball and hacking from the game, and perversely this was 'carried'. These ideas were embodied in Rule IX - No player shall run with the ball, Rule X - Neither tripping nor hacking shall be allowed, Rule XI - A player shall not throw or pass the ball with his hands and Rule XII - No player shall take the ball from the ground with his hands. There was no ambiguity in these Laws and this was clearly a game of the boot thus soccer and rugby were separated.

The sixth and final meeting was on 8 December 1863 and a letter and postal order was received from Rev. J.C. Thring being the subscription for Uppingham. A second letter was received from Lieutenant H.C. Moore, Secretary of the Royal Engineers, Chatham and contained their subscription and comments strongly deprecating running with the ball and hacking. The rules were then printed and published and the first official committee was formed, however once all was done F.W. Campbell rose to his feet and spoke for Blackheath, saying, his club entirely approved of the objects of the Association but the Laws, as adopted, entirely destroyed the game and took away all interest in it. Thus Blackheath departed from the F.A.

Arthur Pember liked the outdoors and continued to travel after his second marriage, and his greatest fascination was with Mont Blanc (15,772 feet) on the French-Italian border near the town of Chamonix - the Matterhorn 35 miles east in Switzerland was lower at 14,692 feet. He made more than one trip to Mont Blanc and his greatest achievement was its ascent - he was so proud of the climb that he wrote about it in later life and gave talks on the subject. The first ascent was on 8 August 1786 and the British Alpine Club was formed in 1857, whilst 270 parties reached the top by 1863, of which 200 included at least one Briton. A number of people made their living from the mountain and the Coutet family had a long tradition as guides however it was a dangerous occupation and some never returned. Pember stated that most visitors did not believe it was Mont Blanc since the view from Chamonix was deceptive and it appeared lower than the other peaks, being set back across the Italian border. He added that its true height could be ascertained with a day excursion and the traveller should venture to the Mer de Glace or the Brevent (a smaller mountain on the opposite side of the valley) - from these vantage points the true nature of Mont Blanc could be seen. He called it "The Great King of the Alps" and described his expedition as follows.

His actual report was written in 1874 but we can ascertain he climbed the mountain in c.1864 since he was an "old traveller" at the time. He began: It was a beautiful August evening some years ago when he was lounging with a friend on the balcony of his hotel at Chamonix and the setting sun illuminated the peaks of the mountains - in particular he could see Mont Blanc, the Bosse du Dromedaire and Dôme du Goûter. He then truly appreciated the grandeur of Mont Blanc although he had been somewhat disappointed on previous visits to the region. He went with his friend to the *Bureau des Guides* to prepare for the next day when they would make the perilous ascent of Mont Blanc, which he believed was the ambition of all European mountain travellers. The friends returned to their hotel but soon parted company from the ladies and they went to bed early. A loud rap at the door awoke them in the morning and a French voice announced, "*Monsieur, c'est jusque cinq heures.*" Arthur Pember leapt from his bed since the expedition leader was a "thorough despot." The man in charge, Jean Philippe Coutet, declared he would only lead if he had full control since the safety of the whole expedition depended upon it!

There were strict orders to depart by six, hence the party soon assembled downstairs where the two glacier guides Coutet and (Joseph) Tissay were making final preparations. The group was completed with four porters and Tissay's dog, *Bouquet* a white French poodle who had remarkable intelligence. The porters were then loaded up with lanterns, blankets, provisions, firewood and other equipment, and the

Mont Blanc, Chamonix. From the left: The Glacier Des Bossons, The deceptive dome of Mont Blanc (4810m), Dôme Du Goûter (4304m) and Aiguille Du Goûter (3817m).

party left at 6 a.m. to a few cheers from the hotel waiters and "early" guests - the scene indeed came from "Journey to the Centre of the Earth"! The sky was cloudless, the air balmy and soft, there was little wind and the barometer was rising, which provided ideal conditions for the ascent but the guides had to slow the party who were too enthusiastic. They took a bridle path to the village of Les Pelerins where the climb would begin, and went through woodland and past the Cascades des Pelerins and the 'great' Glacier des Bossons. They took a zigzag path to the Chalet de la Para, the end of human habitation and the route then became more rugged with no trees.

They reached a huge rock boulder called the Pierre Pontue and the only way around was along a narrow ledge. The moraine of the glacier lay several hundred feet below, however they went forward despite the danger and the spirit of adventure carried them through. They descended across loose rubble to the Pierre L'Echelle and a short distance further brought them to the Glacier des Bossons - 900 feet wide and reputedly 500 feet in depth. The party stopped at this point to prepare to cross the glacier since the right clothing was essential for protection from the cold, the brightness of the sun and the roughness of the ice. The party then proceeded boldly onto the glacier although the guides were now extra-cautious and watched both Arthur Pember and his companion. At first the going seemed easy and no more difficult than the Mer de Glace, and Arthur suggested some of his lady readers might have crossed the latter. This was an inexpedient comment but it was written in Victorian times. The Glacier des Bossons, however, was far more treacherous and they had to use a ladder to cross a crevasse 10-12 feet in width. The ice became more uneven and formed numerous shapes, whilst Tissay lost his hat and a brave porter was lowered into a crevasse to retrieve it - he came out freezing due to the intense cold.

There was then a discussion between Coutet and Tissay and they decided that the party should be roped together, however the guides were not attached as they had to go ahead to mark the route - the dog Bouquet would often precede them. Arthur Pember described the scene well with its vast expanse of ice and the sapphire coloured crevasses, which lay below the summit of Mont Blanc and surrounding mountains that included the formidable Aiguille du Midi. Their progress was slow since they often had to cut steps into the ice and walk along crevasses to find a suitable crossing point, and on some occasions had to lower them-selves into a crevasse so they could reach a ledge and find a way across. Once over the guide Coutet would cut a route to the top and would raise the members of the party by rope with Tissay as anchorman. This method of crossing a crevasse involved swinging in mid-air over the chasm and was not an experience that Arthur Pember enjoyed. Nor was it dignified! One crevasse was some 40 feet wide however a fall of ice made a bridge across it, whilst others were covered with snow and on one occasion Arthur Pember fell through with his legs dangling in the air. He was soon pulled free and claimed that there was no real danger and the party laughed heartily! A different reaction might have been appropriate. Crossing the Glacier des Bossons left a great impression on Arthur Pember and he lived to tell the tale, and eventually climbed to the summit of Mont Blanc. He was also successful in the descent and the source of this detailed account is discussed further below.

Arthur Pember on Mont Blanc.
The ascent took place in c.1864.

Arthur worked for Kennard & Co. from 1861-63 however there was then a merger and they became the Consolidated Bank in 1864. He had also returned to 26 Carlton Road, Kilburn in 1864 and his son Cyril Fugion was born there on 29 January 1865 - the event was recorded in the Times on Thursday 2 February. This was an undeveloped area at the time with large semi-detached houses at the east end of Carlton Road, between Edgware and Randolph Road - south side 1-31, north side 2-32. There were some other houses further along Carlton Road however these were smaller terraced properties. The road was renamed Carlton Vale by 1893 and the only houses remaining are 1-7 and 2-12. He continued in his role as F.A. President and there were few further developments until the annual meeting at the Freemasons Tavern in 1866. A member of the No Names club complained it was hard to play under the existing rules and that they were only followed by Barnes and Crystal Palace. Indeed Lincoln F.C. were also unhappy with the rules and cancelled their membership. Arthur Pember was greatly disturbed by this action and stated, "Lincoln were strongly opposed to anything but hacking, throttling and other harsh practices." This remark by Mr. Pember caused outrage and resulted in a strong denial by the Lincoln captain in *Bell's Life* - there was a meeting at dawn and twelve paces!

A letter was received from W.J. Chesterman the Secretary of Sheffield F.C. and there was a meeting of the club captains at 3 King's Bench Walk to discuss it. The club had already joined the F.A. and suggested a contest against southern opponents, thus R.W. Willis arranged a match London v Sheffield at Battersea on 31 March 1866. This game saw a further evolution of the rules and has already been discussed however it should be noted that the London side included: Arthur Pember captain, C.M. Tebbut and A. Baker all from the No Names Club as well as C.W. Alcock, E.C. Morley and A.F. Kinnaird whilst W.J. Chesterman was captain of Sheffield. The game was an eleven-a-side contest and both sides delivered a number of hard knocks but the occasion was rounded off in the evening with, "a splendid dinner for the contestants at the Albion Hotel." These events were important in terms of football history however Arthur soon had more pressing matters at the Consolidated Bank and took a hard knock himself. The situation that unfolded is revealed in a newspaper report:

THE TIMES

TUESDAY, MAY 29, 1866

The closing of the Consolidated Bank this morning entirely checked the general recovery that had seemed certain, and the regret occasioned has been especially severe, from the fact of the disaster having been incurred by one of the most extraordinary errors ever committed by men of business entrusted with the property of others....

The history of the stoppage of the Consolidated Bank seems the most singular ever presented. This establishment was formed three years ago by a junction of the Bank of Manchester with two of the oldest private banks of London: Messrs Heywood, Kennards and Co. and Messrs Hankeys, the most experienced members of these firms maintaining their connexion with it as directors. In January last a distribution was made at the rate of 17½ per cent, a reserve of 81,808l had been accumulated, and the report to the shareholders was of a tone to indicate the exercise of that full amount of prudence which was to be looked for from bankers of such repute; and the character thus acquired was upheld through all the recent panic up to a few days back, when, by what now appears to be an impulse almost of insanity, the directors decided to take over the business of the Bank of London, without laying the slightest foundation of security for the step. At any period a negotiation with a failing concern must in the banking world be one of extreme delicacy, and not only was the present arrangement hurriedly concluded in the midst of the most disastrous crisis ever witnessed, but on terms as careless and uncertain as if they had been framed for the very purpose of inviting difficulty....

They had taken the opinion of two eminent counsel to the effect that their proceedings were not open to any objection, and upon these opinions, for the hazardous nature of which all ordinary men would have made full allowance, they permitted not only millions of property to be jeopardized, but the danger to be run of a renewal of all the financial trouble from which the entire country was happily just emerging. At length, on Saturday afternoon the injunction was granted, and still the emergency found the directors so totally unprepared that they could do nothing but decide to close their doors this morning, the sudden loss to their shareholders being no less than a million of money in the difference between the closing price of their property on Saturday afternoon and that to which it was reduced by this announcement, while to the depositors alike of their own bank and of the Bank of London the inconvenience is incalculable....

This arrangement was followed on Wednesday, the 23rd, by a petition of the Bank of London for a winding up order, and the appointment of Mr. Coleman as interim liquidator.

FRIDAY, JUNE 1, 1866

Evening additions of the Manchester papers announce that the Manchester directors of the Consolidated Bank are devising means to reorganize the Manchester business, and are anxious to mitigate the inconvenience to customers arising from the stoppage. If reorganized, the bank will be severed from the London connexion.

The following banking changes resulted from the closing of the Bank of London and the Consolidated Bank: Messrs H. Godfray Sons and Co, Old Bank, Jersey transferred their account to Messrs Smith, Payne and Smith. The Guernsey Commercial Banking Co transferred their London agency to the London and Westminster Bank. The Ceylon Co Ltd transferred their account to the National Provincial Bank of England. The Temperance Permanent Land and Building Society took their account to the Union Bank of London.

FRIDAY, JUNE 22, 1866

At a very full meeting of shareholders of the Consolidated Bank today, Mr. J.P. Heywood chair, the arrangements the directors are making with a view to the speedy resumption of business were unanimously confirmed, and it was intimated that the intention is to open the bank on Monday, 2 of July next, if no legal difficulties exist (in fact delayed)....

The directors have for a considerable time past been looking out for suitable premises near the Bank of England, but they have hitherto been unable to meet with what was required. They have now, however, as part of the arrangement with the Bank of London, secured the premises occupied by that bank in Threadneedle Street and at Charing Cross. The Threadneedle Street premises are freehold and the front portions are sublet at rents amounting to 2,100l. The Consolidated Bank is already possessed of the freehold premises in Fenchurch Street, which were purchased from Messrs Hankey at 40,000l, and the directors are assured that those premises will, even in the present depressed times, realise a large increase on their cost (this may explain the takeover).

Note: John Edward Pember - Bank of London (1866-67).

The financial crisis was over however the next year proved even more dramatic. Arthur Pember relinquished the job of F.A. President to E.C. Morley in 1867 although he was Vice-President in 1867-68. The No Names Club remained a member of the F.A. however he did not play in the county games at Battersea on 2 November 1867 and Brompton on 25 January 1868, and had moved to the sidelines. Indeed Arthur Pember was soon to end his connections with England and had good reason for emigrating after some traumatic events - he was later a writer and discussed the social climate in detail. He belonged to the great religious movement of Ritualism and stated that it was spreading in England and around the world. The practice was also known as *Sacramentalism* and was basically a form of religion that put the Holy Eucharist at the centre of worship. This was seen as a reaction to the Puritanism of the 16th century and the Ritualists believed that the English people preferred such a doctrine, since the ideas of Puritanism were alien to the country. The practice of ritual in the church was similar to the Catholic ideals however the English Church was independent and no longer 'Protestant', since its basis was not a split with Rome, but simply a belief in the sacrament of the Holy Eucharist. Arthur had some strong feelings regarding this matter and saw a religious revival, stating: "It has parted friends, it has disunited families; stormy meetings have been held advocating its suppression; bodies of rioters have sacked churches, attacked the houses of priests, and openly insulted and ill treated many inoffensive persons in the streets, simply because they were Ritualists. For many months during the year 1867 the church services were disturbed Sunday after Sunday, and the congregations were obliged to be protected by large bodies of police."

It seems certain that these accounts were of a first hand nature and were the actual experience of Arthur Pember. The matter was referred to Parliament and there was a 'Royal Commission on Ritual' that posed no less than 4,002 questions regarding the matter. The lengthy report concluded that most practices of the Ritualists were in fact legal and came within the laws of the Church of England and the *Book of Common Prayer*. This judgement gave impetus to the movement and many priests introduced ritual on the first Sunday after publication, however the Low Church took legal proceedings through the Ecclesiastical Court and tried to halt Father Mackonochie of St. Alban's, London who was one of the most advanced Ritualists of the day (a High Church near Gray's Inn, Holborn - built 1863). The prosecution totally failed to the cost of £30,000 hence the opposition actually strengthened the movement. Arthur estimated that there were 60 Ritualist churches in London and the suburbs as well as mission chapels and mission rooms. The total following in the U.K. was 1½ million and had also penetrated the Presbyterians in Scotland and Roman Catholic Ireland. The movement had spread around the world to Australia, Canada and the Bahamas as well as Calcutta, Dunedin in New Zealand, Orange Free State in Africa and the United States (under the guidance of A. Pember).

He suggested the use of more ornate worship would attract the poor and indeed the Ritualistic clergy lived entirely among them, following the example of their Catholic brethren. The Ritualists had two aims, the first was the use of ritual in church services hence they held a large number of services through the week (i.e. Matins, Litany, Evensong), the second was to help the poor. This took many forms and they provided stately churches at their own expense, hospitals, missions to fallen women, Sunday schools, savings banks, working men's clubs, libraries and clothing clubs. There were many church workers who attended to the poor however this was a dangerous business, and although they were not Catholics, there were many who saw the movement as a revival of Catholicism. One priest Father Wagner built a large church in Brighton and devoted his considerable fortune to the aid of the poor however he was often hooted through the streets of Brighton and regularly threatened, and was only saved at times by passers-by. He was even told he would receive the fate of Guy Fawkes on 5 November. The same threats occurred at the church of St. Michael's and All Angels in Shoreditch yet the people thus affronted were of a good and spiritual nature.

The spirit of devotion and self-sacrifice pervaded the whole movement and he gave special mention to the hospitals and home visits of the sisterhood. Workers were hastily despatched if a child was known to be ill and would administer the necessary medicine such as "gruel, arrowroot, tea and brandy." They would give medical help at no expense, aid families where one parent had died and also ran a day nursery service. He gave special note to the 'working men's clubs' and saw them as an important institution where men could meet away from the home and the public house. They provided a convivial atmosphere with games boards, educational books, newspapers and some refreshments (tea, coffee, bread, cheese, butter, biscuits, tobacco and pipes) with all at cost price. There was no beer or spirit allowed and the clubs were also open to wives and daughters on a monthly basis. The emphasis on these family nights was on entertainment and no "dry" subjects were allowed. Indeed, "A very small expenditure would provide an exhibition of dissolving views, a magic lantern or a conjurer. Readings from amusing books or recitations of poetry were always well received and sometimes, for a change, a series of short biographies of men of the times or descriptions of foreign travel have been tried with success (enter A.P). In fact a talk from a famous lecturer was less popular than a reading from the 'trial scene' in Pickwick."

His writings then provided some questions and answers from the Royal Commission who concluded that without the Ritualists many would have gone to the Catholic Church. He also discussed their doctrines and noted that during the Eucharist there was an emphasis on lighting, procession, singing and prayer, incense and humility before the Saviour. The Ritualists stated their case before the Archbishop of Canterbury on 30 May 1867 and laid out their doctrine and defended themselves against claims by the Low Church that they were Roman Catholic. In fact the essence of the Ritualists' belief was a spiritual presence at the time of communion, rather than the bodily presence of the Catholics. He added that the movement might eventually fail, but he thought this unlikely, since it had the potential to bring about a unification of the Christian faith. He concluded: "It is difficult to imagine that failure will attend the efforts of a system whose object is to make religion an every day practice, to promote the glory of God by a more frequent, and more reverent celebration of the Holy Eucharist, and to raise the working-man to a level of perfect equality with the rich man in the house of God." This reveals much about the social climate of the time and shows that religious belief was central to people's lives, whilst the equality he strived for came about in society rather than in the church.

Arthur Pember was clearly a man of radical belief and his other concerns went much further in terms of revolutionary change, and he stated: "Intelligent observers of the signs of the times can scarcely have failed to arrive at the conclusion that a great social and moral revolution is impending over Great Britain. That the rapid growth of liberal opinion and the gradual accumulation of liberal legislation are undermining the authoritative position, the long claimed right to govern, and the long accorded superiority over the masses, of the British aristocracy." The preceding years had seen a succession of governments after Lord Melbourne and Sir Robert Peel, namely: Lord Russell *Whig* 1846-52, Lord Derby *Cons* 1852, Lord Aberdeen *coalition* 1852-55, Lord Palmerston *Whig* 1855-58, Lord Derby *Cons* 1858-59, Lord Palmerston and Lord Russell *Whig-Liberal* 1859-66, Lord Derby and B. Disraeli *Cons* 1866-68 and W.E. Gladstone *Liberal* 1868-74. During this period the Conservatives held office for less than five years and voting patterns changed with the Reform Bills of 1832 and 1867. There were nine administrations in 1846-67 and seldom a stable majority and Lord Palmerston dictated much of the policy, but his death in 1865 was the signal for change. Middle-class ministers then replaced the old school and B. Disraeli and W.E. Gladstone dominated politics from 1867.

Arthur discussed a number of main points including his view of history and stated that the English aristocracy had three sources of power: (1) primogeniture (2) feudalism (3) hereditary titles - the first two having been practiced from the beginning of history. He revealed how the aristocracy had maintained their power over many centuries and cited the case of the Duke of Portland, a Whig leader, who refused to admit Burke and Sheridan despite their great talents since they did not belong to the right families. He added that the Reform Bill of 1832 was a major turning point and that afterwards the House of Lords had little 'real' power. He believed the British nation would no longer rely on people in power through their ancestors and that they should govern through merit. He cited three cases in the last 25 years where the common will overcame the Lords (see below) and predicted the separation of Church from State this being the will of the masses. He added, "The Church is a great and important element in the great aristocratic fabric and cannot fail in its fall to give a severe shaking to the already tottering remainder."

He was ahead of his time and had thoughts and beliefs more relevant to America than England, and stated, "While the normal duties of the aristocracy have long passed away, the privileges accorded to it for the performance of those duties are still claimed and exercised." The Lords was an anachronism but he suggested the situation would soon end, the most significant event being the creation of life peerages. The principal of such a bill was already agreed and its passing would be a direct intrusion into the sacred precincts of the hereditary aristocracy. He saw a breakdown in the law of primogeniture leading to the break up of the great estates, a change that was being promoted by social reformers who decried the present distribution of land (as in France 1789). He added, "When primogeniture, that greatest of all stays to the power and influence of the British aristocracy, shall have been removed, Great Britain will quickly become a republic in all but the name." He predicted the demise of the House of Lords and said, "They can no more stop it than Canute could stop the tide." He thought the Lords would be remodelled or even abolished and a second chamber established in the form of a senate, views that were more common in America. He concluded: "The glory of the House of Lords is departed. As it stands at present it is a mere pageant, a relic, an anachronism, an obsolete remnant of the old feudal system. The masses have taken care to render it impotent for evil, though at the same time they have rendered it impotent for good. But for a certain conservative element in the national character, it would ere this have been abolished formally, as it has for some years been abolished virtually. It has been retained in form much on that same principle which gives to men and women a tendency to preserve relics of bygone days, which, though cumbersome and useless, they have never the less not quite the heart to destroy." *Arthur Pember.*

His beliefs would not have been published in the Times and many of his ideas were, no doubt, too strong for his family and perhaps for the F.A. thus he immigrated to a land where he could voice these opinions openly. Other factors, however, may have played a part and his daughter Lillian was born at Kilburn in 1867 and adopted by her uncle Edward. The birth was not registered and she may have been illegitimate and one can ask: Did a scandal cause him to leave England? Did he fail on the Stock Exchange like his brother-in-law? The answers may never be known but he did not fit the I.D. of an emigrant, as he was neither poor nor an unattached gentleman seeking adventure. The true reason was probably his strong religious beliefs combined with his extreme views on the social order, and he may have been at odds with his family, or father, and wanted to escape the rigid confines of British Victorian society.

He continued to live at 26 Carlton Road and worked as a stockbroker at the Stock Exchange until March 1868. He was still in the employ of the Consolidated Bank who had recovered from the crisis and showed a better position in the Times on Tuesday 21 January 1868: *Report to be presented on the 23rd inst* - available total 35,451, c/f 8,188, dividend rate 5% p.a., reserves 100,000, special reserves 20,000, b/f 2,351, deposits 2,184,783, acceptances 102,414 and paid up capital 800,000. Mr. Murray Gladstone to fill the vacancy caused by the death of J.A. Turner. Arthur Pember departed from the F.A. in 1868 having played an important role in establishing the rules of the game, and most notably abolished running with the ball and hacking thus forming a game of soccer as oppose to rugby (hacking was also banned in the latter soon after). His son St. John B. Pember was born in England in 1868 but there was no time to register the birth and Arthur concluded his affairs in London, and took his wife and two sons to the United States. They set sail in 1868 at the same time as Frederick went to New Zealand. He then lived in a country where he could voice his opinions on religious and social issues, whilst his extreme views may have led to his omission from the F.A. histories written by Alcock and other officials.

THE NEW WORLD

Arthur and his family reached America and almost certainly made landfall in New York however this was a very different city from that of today. Manhattan Island had its first permanent settlement in 1625 and at the beginning of the 19th century the city of New York was still concentrated at the southern end. This changed with the Commissioners' Plan of 1811, which laid out a grid of 12 avenues, and streets from 14th to 155th. The city was rapidly developed along these lines and only Bloomingdale Road (later Broadway) cut across the grid at an angle. The state purchased 700 acres in the centre of Manhattan occupied by shanty houses and small farms, in 1853, and Central Park was opened there in 1859 although the final creation took 20 years to complete. It was not 'natural' and was based on romantic landscapes seen in England in the 18th-19th centuries. New York was still developing in the late 1860s and the Statue of Liberty was constructed in 1886 and Ellis Island was only used for immigration after 1892.

England seized several American ships during the Napoleonic Wars leading to much tension, thus Castle Clinton (a circular fort) was built at the southern tip of Manhattan in 1811. It was situated away from the shore, however never fired a shot in anger and became the 'Castle Garden' in 1824. It was then a fashionable centre for entertainment and was reached across a wooden causeway, but was joined to the land with in-fill in 1855. It then became the first official landing depot and the *New York Times* said of Castle Clinton in 1874: "It is so well known in Europe that few immigrants could be induced to sail for any other destination." 8 million newcomers entered the country through its gates in 1855-90, this being two-thirds of all immigrant arrivals in the U.S. in the period. Arthur Pember arrived in 1868 and almost certainly landed at Castle Clinton but saw an unfamiliar skyline. The first skyscraper was the Tower Building in Lower Broadway but this was not erected until 1888-89 and was demolished in 1913 and followed by many other tall buildings: Flatiron (1902), New York Times (1904), Woolworth (1913), Chrysler (1930) and Empire State (1931). These were all built long after the arrival of Arthur and his young family, whilst Battery Park is now at the southern end of Manhattan and encompasses the historic Castle Clinton.

When he stepped ashore he entered a world of immigrants and arrived in New York's Victorian society. The grid pattern allowed for the construction of cheap accommodation and this included town houses, like those in London, as well as four to five storey tenements. The family lived in New York from 1868 although their initial address is not known. There was plenty going on in the growing city with a proliferation of newspapers, therefore Arthur did not enter Wall Street (and the Stock Market) but chose a new career in journalism - he certainly had plenty to say. He was a freelance writer who worked for several papers and his article on 'lay baptism' appeared in the *New York Times* on 11 April 1869. This was of no great interest in itself however it again showed that Arthur was fervent regarding religious matters. He had read a recent article contesting the validity of lay baptism - this stated that the un-consecrated hands of a layman would "horrify" a member of the English Protestant Church. Arthur disagreed and said this was nonsense since he had seen many valid baptisms by laymen. He approved of those carried out by nonconformist clergy and revealed that when these people became Anglican they were simply "received" - there was no question of their re-baptism. He concluded, "I have seen this done frequently, and on one occasion a servant of my own was received into the Church in this manner by one of the most advanced Ritualists of the day." *Arthur Pember.*

He also produced an article called "Ritualism in England by an English Ritualist" for *Atlantic Monthly*, in 1869, a magazine of literature, science, art and politics, printed by Fields, Osgood and Co. Boston (volume XXIII) - successors to Ticknor and Fields. It was 6,500 words long and described the growth of Ritualism in England and the considerable opposition to the movement (see above). He noted its practice in America was still undeveloped and especially complained about Father Morrill, incumbent of St. Alban's, New York. This church claimed to be Ritualistic yet did not in fact practice the doctrines and he basically said they should get off the fence. This was not just a religious article but also promoted a solution to the social-ills of the world and he clearly wanted to bring these ideas to America. During this period his family travelled, possibly for his work, thus a son Roosa Herbert was born in Connecticut in November 1869.

He then wrote an article, "The Coming Revolution in England" for *Lippincott's Magazine*, in 1870, a paper of literature, science and education printed by J.B. Lippincott and Co. Philadelphia (volume V) - these were the same publishers who promoted the career of Sir Arthur Conan Doyle (see below). It was 5,000 words long and he discussed the downfall of the British aristocracy and the House of Lords and was prompted to write by further events in England (see above). W.E. Gladstone passed the Irish Church Bill on 1 March 1869 and brought about the disestablishment of the Anglican Church in Ireland. Arthur Pember believed this was a significant event in history and he cited three cases in the last 25 years where the common will had overcome the Lords, namely Jewish disabilities, paper duties and the Irish Church matter. He wrote that the abolition of a 'State Church' in Ireland was a real blow to the aristocrats and paved the way for a similar change regarding the English Church, hence he predicted the separation of Church from State. His views were revolutionary and may not have been held by everyone, but were possibly more common in America and were of interest to the readers of *Lippincott's*. He had just arrived in America when he wrote these articles and was full of passion regarding his beliefs, which no doubt prompted his immigration to America. This was a country where he was not out of place with such convictions.

1233 Third Avenue, New York. Arthur Pember lived at the left house from c.1872-77.

Arthur Pember, contributor, lived at 1233 Third Avenue, New York, in 1872 which was located to the east of Central Park in a district called the Upper East Side. The house was at the junction of Third Avenue and East 71st Street on the northeast corner, being the second going north, and was divided into apartments with two-three families living there. This had a main ground floor with three floors above and was built of brown brick with a plain façade. The house remains today, one of four on the corner of Third Avenue (1231-37), although the ground floor is converted into Grace's Market Place. Indeed the original walls of the houses can still be seen in the shop, which is a delicatessen and very "American" store selling cheese, salads, fruit pies, cakes, meat, vegetables and fish.

Arthur Pember the President of the F.A. had come a long way from Kilburn to the Upper East Side and this transformation is well illustrated by the occupation of his neighbours - the change in their composition is quite remarkable. When he lived at Carlton Road, Maida Vale the nearby houses were occupied by gentry, esquires, a fellow of the *Society of Antiquities*, a professor of music, a minister of the Church, and a school; but ten years later he lived in the Upper East Side and his neighbours were from Prussia, Austria, New York, Ireland, Germany and Hungary. Life was no less hard for the Pembers in New York and there were many trials and tragedies in the city. A son Geoffrey Francis was born at 1233 Third Avenue on 22 April 1872 and was the 'fifth' child of Alice Mary whilst the father Arthur was described as a newspaper correspondent. This confirms that Lillian, who stayed in England, was their daughter and no doubt this was a heart-breaking situation. Further to this the son Geoffrey died of enteritis and related illness on 21 July 1872.

Despite these hardships Arthur was soon involved in his most important work. He was employed by the *New York Times*, one of the premier papers in the city, and also worked for the *New York Tribune* and as stated was a freelance contributor and journalist - no doubt he wrote many articles for these newspapers. Indeed he would go to any length to get his stories and acquired the skill of disguise to aid his work and like a chameleon took on the nature of his surroundings. He then ventured forth, undetected by his closest friends, and entered the most risky of situations to obtain a good story. He developed a fascination with "people's modes of existence" and explored the lives of Americans over a number of years and wrote about his experiences in an amazing book. He was an author of some importance and produced, "The Mysteries and Miseries of the Great Metropolis, with some adventures in the country: being the disguises and surprises of a New York journalist," by 'A.P.' the amateur vagabond. It was published by D. Appleton and Company of New York in 1874 and had 462 pages and 11 plates - illustrations from photographs by Gurney. This became a historical book of some distinction and was of sufficient note to be included in Sabin's Dictionary of Books of America. This is a series of volumes of selected Americana and history that cover the period from the discovery of the country up to the present. The work by Arthur Pember is still held in the New York State Library at Albany. The preface of the book provides a good explanation of its contents, stating:

"More than one class of persons, I am inclined to think, will be apt to consider that an ordinary sense of propriety should lead me to apologise for publishing, for the benefit of one half the world, some of my varied experiences while investigating how the other half lives. There are the gamblers, prison-jailers, and keepers of disreputable houses, for instance, who will strongly object to having the light of day shed o'er *their* peculiar and very elastic mode of *earning a living*. Thieves, tramps, beggars, and curb-stone singers, too, are not likely to rub their hands gleefully at the *exposé* of their little devices for subsisting on the charity or at the expense of others. Again, there is that multitudinous class who love to isolate themselves in their own individuality and its immediate aristocratic surroundings. No, indeed! Their luxurious firesides are not to be contrasted with the so-called accommodations of the cold, damp, cellar lodging-house. They do not know and they do not care to know anything about the thousand repulsive or soul-saddening scenes which are daily, hourly, momentarily, being enacted almost within a stone's-throw of their studiously built-up throne of selfish ease and content! And, then there are those of the *dolce far niente* disposition, who will quickly exclaim, 'Write him down an ass for undergoing such very unpleasant experiences;' much in the same spirit which influenced a deaf old lady who sat in the front row of seats in

1231-37 Third Avenue, New York.
The elevated railway first came past here in 1878-79.

the Peabody Institute at Salem, Massachusetts, one evening, when I was relating my adventures 'Up and Down Mont Blanc', and who exclaimed aloud to her daughter at the conclusion of the first part - that is, when we had reached the summit of the mountain. 'Well, now, he don't look such a fool!' But to none such as these, should they happen to be remembered among my readers, do I propose to offer any thing in the way of the *amende honorable*. How could they possibly expect an apology from so hybrid an individual as an Amateur Vagabond? No! These sketches were not written for them. I respectfully dedicate them to those who, with broader views, are willing and desirous to know something of those various phases of existence, of which their occupations, their associations, or the even tenor of their far-off lives, inevitably or naturally, keep them in ignorance. That I have submitted to many inconveniences - nay, that I have undergone privations and faced dangers, while pursuing my adventures as an Amateur Vagabond, I have only a too lively remembrance. But, how could I possibly pen sketches from real life, had I not been ready to do so? My sole aim has been to describe scenes of grave or gay interest which I have actually witnessed, odd situations in which I have found myself placed, and *petites comédies* or dramas in which I have positively taken a part. I have carefully avoided putting on finishing touches of imaginative coloring or even the very thinnest coat of varnish; being convinced that a plain, unvarnished tale is, after all, the most interesting. Such as my sketches are, I commend them to the reader in his or her spells of good-nature, simply pleading for faith in their honesty and truth."

The book contained 21 sketches covering the whole range of his experiences with portraits of him in his various disguises, and showed many aspects of human life, namely: the purlieus of Water Street, the amateur beggar, diving in New York Harbour, the bogus doctor, the curb-stone singer, life on the Erie Canal, a night in the Tombs, the costermonger, down a coal mine, life in a circus, a ride on an engine, an underground lodging house, the spirit medium, the life of a tramp, a beggars banquet and the zinc miner. These all took place in New York and surrounding States however the volume concluded with a section "Up and Down Mont Blanc". This was the longest chapter being 52 pages in length and the expedition must have been close to his heart as it had a different character to the rest of the stories. In this case he was engaged in 'real' life and was not playing a part however all his adventures were 'real', and often dangerous. The preface reveals much about his character, since he was not content with the comfortable life and made strong comments regarding the privilege of the aristocracy. Indeed he may have been referring to his own family back in England. He was brought up with a deep social conscience that prompted him to investigate the 'other' side of Victorian society and showed great feeling for the people he met, thus it is worth considering his exploits in detail.

One can wonder if immigration to the United States produced a desire to understand the poverty there, as it was called the land of opportunity, yet there was great dichotomy in people's wealth. An economist would suggest that the presence of great wealth could only exist if others were poor – it was simply a by-product. Indeed those who made a fortune in New York lived in mansions along the Hudson River whilst others lived in crowded tenements on the East and West Side. The most notable character of Arthur Pember was the amateur beggar or the tramp and the *New York Times* gave him great praise for his accurate portrayal, and this is discussed further below. He was clearly amongst those who tried to understand the presence of poverty (in a civilised society) and dressed as a tramp, or the like, on a number of occasions and in particular visited the notorious Water Street district. One of his first adventures was to explore the depths of New York Bay and he went diving off the Battery where the Hudson and East Rivers meet. He confirmed that no mermaids lived in these waters but revealed they had refuse of all varieties and stated, "The content would debar me from taking a plunge in it unless I was very hard up for a wash." On another occasion he was a candidate at a medical college in Philadelphia and obtained a bogus degree of Doctor of Medicine, thus exposing the fraudulent system.

He then took a trip on the Erie Canal and joined the canal boat *Admiral* under Captain Lamoreaux at Albany, the vessel being bound for Buffalo with a cargo of stoves, fire bricks etc. However he first had to convince them he was "sea-worthy". Captain Spoor the irascible co-owner did the hiring and asked, "What are you made on? You ain't much like a boatman anyhow." The journalist managed to convince him and was employed on the strict promise that he made himself useful in an emergency, roughed it with the rest of the crew and "put on no city airs." Captain Spoor then remarked, "Hands pretty white and soft looking for boating; but I guess you wont spile nothin' aboard 'fore we git to Buffalo. Breakfast at six, dinner twelve, supper six. Where's your duds?" Arthur Pember replied that his valise was at Delavan House and the astonished captain exclaimed, "Delavan House! D--n me if I ever shipped a hand from the Delavan House afore!" Arthur was thus accepted as a passenger hand, transported his "duds" to the boat and began life as a "canawller". He described an arduous time getting through the sixteen locks between

West Troy and the aqueduct at Cohoes, known in boating parlance as the "sixteens". Captain Spoor was boiling with rage when his drivers were not available for the job, and Arthur tried to console him with a cigar but Captain Spoor stated that he only chewed. The other owner Captain Lamoreaux was more amiable and took a pipe with Arthur and discussed the weather prospects for the next day.

He then spent some time on dry land and tried his hand as a costermonger. He first approached a vendor in Chatham Square and described him as of the Milesian race (or Irish) however the man was not impressed by Arthur's plan. He thought it likely he wanted to rob him of his cart and produce and soon disappeared with his barrow across the Square, and into the Bowery. Arthur then walked down Chatham Street feeling somewhat deflated but stayed around Chatham Square, and later spied another vendor coming along East Broadway. He purchased an apple for two cents and slowly peeled it. The costermonger was rather taken by his dexterity and care and asked if he was "afeared of the cholery-morbis." Arthur amazed him by saying he had not eaten an apple for some years. The man also Irish, came from Tyrone, and was quite talkative compared to the previous gentleman, thus they were soon engaged in conversation and by coincidence Arthur had some good friends in Tyrone! The conversation went well and the costermonger obliged for the sum of around a dollar and they arranged to meet at the corner of Chambers and Pearl Street at 6 p.m. that evening, thus he donned suitable clothes and met the costermonger as agreed.

Arthur was often irritated whilst on the streets of New York and a particular annoyance was the whistling of street boys. They always had some (so-called) popular tune upon their lips and for a few months he was deluged with "down in a coal-mine." This eventually passed beyond an irritant and gave him an idea; he had never been down a coal mine! He realised he had no more knowledge of geology than the boys whistling the tune and was soon aboard a car on the Central Railroad of New Jersey. He arrived at Mauch Chunk in the Lehigh Valley after five hours, this being the principal coal-mining district in the area. The black gold there was anthracite and in his own words, he was dumped at the station. He stayed at the Mansion House Hotel in the town and revealed, "This is a place of some importance, especially in the admiring eyes of Mauch-Chunkers, the reason being that it is known as the Switzerland of America." This was clearly a subject close to his heart and he had plenty to say on the matter. He had once met a disagreeable Yankee whilst staying at St. Morlaix in France about 12 or 14 years earlier (c.1860). This was a quaint town in Brittany and was typical of those in the Côte du Nord. The American soon complained about his journey and the small streets of the town, stating, "There wasn't even room to spit!" Arthur now had his revenge and looked from his hotel window and noted there was something of the scene that reminded him of Switzerland, and in particular the lovely valleys between Basel and Olten junction - he had travelled this way en route to Lake Lucerne. The Lehigh Valley swept in a horseshoe around Bear Mountain and narrowed to a gorge just 500 feet across, and the town was squeezed in there viz. the buildings, sidewalk, river, Lehigh Canal, Lehigh and Susquehanna Railway, and Lehigh Valley Railroad. The view was attractive especially from the top of Mount Pisgah however this was not Switzerland and he stated, "The scene did not compare to the rich bright green pasturelands, wild flowers, winding paths, rustic cottages and bridges, pretty peasant girls and cows and goats of the Swiss valleys, nor was it magnificent like Chamonix and Grindelwald." He was, however, brought down to earth by the sight of canals, railroads and carts and prepared to go down a coalmine.

The Canal Boatman. Pember travelled on the Erie Canal from Albany to Buffalo.

He spent a short time in a circus and signed up at Pawtucket, this being a manufacturing town on the border of Rhode Island and Massachusetts. He was engaged by *Howes's Great London Circus and Sanger's Menagerie of Trained Animals* to appear for "positively one week only." He was not a star rider, gymnast, contortionist or merrie jester but a "supe", that is to say a humble extra. During this time he worked in the stable and was sworn at and knocked down by the proprietor for disrespect to the property but later revealed his business ability, and was trusted to collect the gate money. He even paraded down Main Street, as a knight in full armour - was this really the President of the F.A? However he soon fulfilled every boy's ambition. The whistle went and the driver announced, "Now, Sir, all aboard!" Arthur Pember was on the footplate of the 8 p.m. express from New York to Albany and joined the fireman on the platform of the engine *Constitution*. The train pulled away out of Grand Central Station and this was his first time on a locomotive. He was given a grimy soot-encrusted seat in one corner, comically referred to as "the lounge", and noted that every crack and surface was coated with fine ashes and this included the driver and fireman. He gradually came to terms with his new surroundings and the train passed slowly along Fourth Avenue, entered the Yorkville Tunnel and then went through Harlem and across the Harlem River Bridge. It curved around under High Bridge to King's Bridge and there met the junction with the old main line and the driver then "let her go".

The Model Costermonger. Pember traded on the corner of Chambers and Pearl Street, New York.

The speed was increased to forty miles an hour and he was in considerable discomfort with the noise of the wheels and the uneven movement of the engine - it was nothing like the comfort of the 'Palace' and Drawing Room coaches. Indeed it seemed as if the engine would soon escape from the train and the noise through the tunnels was almost unbearable, however there was the compensation of the moonlight on the Hudson River. The train soon passed the lights of Sing Sing prison and Arthur mused how it was better at night since the light came from within, but he was reminded of the pain and misery in the place. The train passed Peekshill ironworks, the peaks of the Highlands and the town of Newburg with its bay and steamed on to Poughkeepsie, thus making good time for Albany town-ship. He arrived shaken, blackened and bedazzled and was quite ready for bed and stated, "On my arrival in Albany, I was just in fine order to take a supe's part in the plantation dance of a minstrel troupe, without any further preparation." He then took a severe course of soap and water, to cleanse him-self, thus some time passed before he could collapse into his bed of clean white sheets. However he was lost in thought during the night, and was engaged in mental calculations to ascertain the number of weeks needed to clean an engine driver who worked for twenty years!

He also had experiences of the poorer side of life and set the following scene in Dickensian terms: "The night was drawing on apace and the booming of a distant church bell had long since proclaimed that the hour of nine was passed, when a solitary wayfarer paused for a moment on the corner of Water and Roosevelt Streets and peered wistfully around.... As the wayfarer stood in the glare of the flickering gas light, his appearance denoted the greatest poverty." This was a noisy area of New York with sailors' dance houses, lodging houses, cellar dwellings and many disreputable people - especially in Water Street. There was driving snow and piercing cold but who was the poor man idling in the street? Was this Arthur Pember in disguise? Indeed it was. He then spent a night in an underground lodging house and his wife Alice no doubt thought him mad, since he had a comfortable home not far away at 1233 Third Avenue.

On another occasion he was summoned by the managing editor of the *Tribune* and could scarcely believe what he heard as the editor announced: "A.P. I have determined to send you to prison." He was prepared to burst forth with numerous demands and protests and ask what had he done and who were his accusers? The editor soon read the expression on his face and laughed heartily, revealing his plan, this being to arrange for him to visit Ludlow Street Jail. This was not for a crime but to provide the material for a good story and indeed Arthur was 'game' to disguise himself as a poor prisoner. In a similar fashion he made a journey to Jersey City and stayed at the premises of a journalist friend, lodging in the basement of his offices. The friend being absent arranged for his clerk to meet him and at first the young man found nothing amiss in his appearance, since he had arrived properly dressed with his 'trusty valise' in hand. His countenance soon changed to astonishment as the contents of the valise were revealed and Arthur dressed in his unusual disguise and stated: "As the darkness rapidly increased, my secret devices were being artistically developed." He began by stripping to the waist and then sprinkled his face with water and had an unshaven beard of five days, however he did not wash but rubbed dust from the windowsill into his face. He then attached some dirty sticking plaster and donned the clothes of a tramp. The young clerk was incredulous, however Arthur was not out of place as he ventured onto the streets since these were 'hard times' - he then walked from the city into the countryside of Pennsylvania.

The area below the Bowery in New York was quite squalid and one of the most infamous characters was Kit Burns who owned a saloon and rat-pit at 273 Water Street. The area was well known for sailors, prostitutes, betting and drunkenness thus the clergy of New York hired his 'rooms' for an hour a day, at $150 a month, in 1868. They hoped to bring reform and Christian values to these 'hell-raisers' and had daily services whilst journalists watched with interest. They had little success and the *New York Herald* said the sermons went right over their heads, whilst Mr. Burns added: "I don't want to say a word against them preachers for they have paid me a pretty fair rent for the pit but if they ever want to reform the girls in Water Street and shut up its rum-mills they've got to do it in some other way than howling for it." The pit later became an eating saloon and Arthur Pember held a 'banquet' there for thirty of the most notorious street beggars. There were some 'fine' after dinner speeches that gave an insight into the lifestyle of the beggar, and Arthur later provided ideas for the philanthropist and social reformer, but whatever his aims this was clearly a most dangerous occupation.

He then travelled to the *Sun Hotel* in Bethlehem and stated that this was a simple building built in 1758 and a monument to the uncomfortable design of the last century. He crouched around the stove hoping it would provide a little heat and waited for the clerk who had gone to order him some supper, after his long cold ride. Bethlehem was 10 miles east of Allentown in Pennsylvania and this was an industrial area later immortalised by Billy Joel in song: "So we're living here in Allentown, and they're closing all the factories down, out in Bethlehem they're killing time, filling out forms, standing in line...." However, things were quite different in Arthur's day and there was a gentleman resting in the room of his lodgings who announced, "Been to the mines, Sir?" The question was a surprise since he certainly didn't look the part, however he soon went on another adventure as a zinc miner.

The *New York Times* reviewed Pember's book on Saturday 30 May 1874 and in the first instance attempted to correct any misconceptions about the work. There had been several other publications on the same subject but these were of an inferior nature and the paper stated: "It has no place with those other volumes, but will rank far above them, whether we regard it merely on its literary merits, or, more justly, as an able practical exemplification of certain phases of everyday life, as obtained through the courage and ingenuity of a clever journalist." Indeed the author is described as, "A man whose literary attainments and social position are such as to insure the handling of his subject in a manner far beyond the level of merely sensational writers." The paper added, "He has produced a book of the most lively interest, and one which, from a social point of view, is of exceeding value." The paper gave certain stories a special mention and that of the *Amateur Beggar* was reviewed in detail, since they believed it to be most noteworthy, however it was only later that it became far more important and if read today provides a discovery of great moment (see below).

Arthur's stories had both humour and pathos, and the paper considered one of the best to be, "A night and morning in the Tombs" - a notorious New York prison. The paper says this item was of great literary merit and promoted philosophical debate. Indeed Arthur was witness to the demise of a notorious criminal, and was much moved, and came out strongly against capital punishment, stating: "It was wrong in theory and monstrous in practice." In fact the whole book made serious statements about the condition of society. The paper then concluded: "The *Amateur Vagabond* has succeeded in the production of a work which, amongst recent publications, must be awarded a very high place for originality and intrinsic worth. It is a book which will afford a vast fund of amusement, and provoke many a hearty laugh; but it is also a book which, if rightly read, will be found to have a high social purpose, while in every page it can hardly fail to excite in the mind of the reader admiration for the personal merits of the *Amateur Vagabond* himself."

DISGUISES AND SURPRISES

Arthur's most striking character was the amateur beggar and he described the preparation of his attire in detail, and stated: "I had been prowling in search of something for nearly two hours among the shanties, the children, the goats, the cows and the dirty ducks and geese, which seem to love to congregate around the boundaries of Central Park (Rag-Town)." He was not unobserved and could have been mistaken for a poultry stealer or police officer and one Irish gentleman called him "mad as the divil." However he was not deterred and stated, "The fact is, like Don Quixote, the spirit of adventure was strong upon me. But, unlike Don Quixote, I had no faithful Sancho Panza to perform my bidding in the way of making preparations." Presumably, his wife Alice did not have time for all this and was too busy with the children. He came away with just one old boot but found another in an old ash barrel on Third Avenue, to make a pair, and picked up an old hat from the gutter. He purchased some old pantaloons and a frock coat from an old clothes store and his attire was thus complete. He placed his begging-clothes in a satchel and the next day went to the rooms of a theatrical friend who had promised to be his *valet de chambre.* Arthur donned the clothes with some much-needed guidance, whilst the friend used his green room knowledge to tone down his healthy complexion. Further to this he had not shaved for five days and soon appeared in torn and tattered clothes, toeless boots, his head bedecked with sticking plaster and wrapped in an old nightcap, his hat in one hand, the other resting on a stick and the whole figure representing woe-be-gone misery and supplication of alms.

He then merged into the streets from the kitchen of that friend's house as a city beggar. No sooner had he done so than he met an acquaintance coming along and took the opportunity of testing the merits of his disguise. He begged him for money and his friend looked him full in the face and muttered, "Sorry, he had no pennies in his pocket." The friend went on in blissful ignorance of Arthur's identity and this inspired him with confidence and he started up University Place to Union Square. It was a cold bleak wintry day as he settled in his attire to study the passers-by and he begged throughout the day until late in the evening, when he returned to his friend's lodgings. He found that $2 43c was the result of his labours, and this was not bad for less than seven hours work. The best begging walks were between Bleecker and 14th, 17th and 23rd streets and the porticos of hotels were good for 5 or 10 cents. The most hospitable people were respectable elderly ladies and young girls aged 18-25 but there was less success with gentlemen and fashionable middle-aged ladies. He had become an expert in the field and was pleased with the pecuniary benefit of his seven hours experiment, however he confessed that his sympathy for the beggar had increased and that the hardships of the life were very great, especially in winter. He added, that although professional begging was an unmanly and dishonest way of getting a living, the beggar earned every cent he received.

The Amateur Beggar.
This was Pember's most striking disguise.

This was a remarkable story in itself, however it was apparently copied and thus received even more significance. Arthur Pember, the master of disguise, was born in 1835 and was a sportsman, traveller and mountaineer being especially keen on visiting the Alps. He was also a journalist of the highest calibre and was a man of dynamic personality and considerable ability, prepared to face any danger to reveal the truth. He had a fascination with a side of life far removed from his upbringing, and was adept at reaching out to the "common" man. He could disguise himself in all ways but regretted not having a partner, and showed much interest in prison life mentioning both the Tombs and Sing Sing in his writings. He even spent time as a bogus Doctor of Medicine and also wrote for Lippincott's who were publishers in America. He published his stories of disguise and intrigue in 1874, this being a most significant date, and soon provided some notable inspiration across the Atlantic.

This brings us to a brief aside regarding the life of Arthur Conan Doyle and his creation "Sherlock Holmes" since some important similarities become apparent. Conan Doyle, the writer, was born at Picardy Place, Edinburgh on 22 May 1859 and was educated at Stonyhurst School near Preston. This was a Jesuit institution and was somewhat austere and he made no lasting friendships there, however he was a natural athlete by the age of 15 and excelled at many sports including football and cricket. He was uncertain of his career and one teacher stated, "Well Doyle, you may be an engineer, but I don't think you will ever be a civil one." He then discovered he had some literary talent and came 2nd for poetry in 1874 and edited the college magazine, whilst his uncle Richard Doyle who worked for "Punch" took him to London plays and inspired him. He then began to read all the literature he could obtain and in particular liked Thomas Babington Macaulay (the historian), Sir Walter Scott, military works and the Bible. He wrote to his relatives asking for the latest magazines and some of their favourite novels in, or about, the year 1874 and one can ask - did these relatives send him the book by Arthur Pember? Conan Doyle studied at Feldkirch College in Vorarlberg, Austria in 1875 this being a more liberal Jesuit establishment. He then went to Paris with his uncle before returning to Edinburgh as a medical student in October 1876 to August 1881 - Bachelor of Medicine.

He studied under Dr. Joseph Bell who used a skilled system of diagnosis and later adapted these skills to provide the methods of deduction used by Sherlock Holmes. During his training, Conan Doyle assisted at several practices and was working at Sheffield in 1878 and also stayed with his relatives at Clifton Gardens, Maida Vale - not far from Carlton Road (see above). The young doctor then went to a Dr. Elliot who resided at Ruyton of the Eleven Towns and he noted, "It was not big enough to make one town, far less eleven!" This famous location is mentioned later in regard to Kenyon-Slaney (see Ch. 6). Conan Doyle then went to Dr. Hoare at Birmingham and it was there that he started writing. He also developed spiritual beliefs and stated that all Christianity and the Roman Catholic religion drove him to atheism, and he became attracted to the Unitarian church and, in particular, the psychic world. He travelled as a doctor on a whaling ship to the Arctic, and went to the Ivory and Gold Coast of West Africa in 1881. He qualified as a physician in August 1881 and went to work in Bristol and Plymouth but this did not work out and he took a boat to Portsmouth in July 1882 and set up a practice in Southsea. He lived at "Bush Villa" - later renamed "Doyle House".

He had boundless energy and sport became essential thus he joined some local clubs and was captain of Portsmouth Cricket Club and played local soccer, being goalkeeper for an early Pompey side under the name A.C. Smith (in c.1883). He married Louise Hawkins at Southsea on 6 August 1885 after nursing her dying brother, and was then further attracted to psychic studies being especially interested in "mesmerism" and "spiritualism". He had few patients and little money hence he turned to writing having written short stories before his marriage. His first major success was A Study in Scarlet, the first Sherlock Holmes story, published in *Beeton's Xmas Annual* in 1887. This was especially appreciated in the United States but due to copyright problems in America he made little or no money there. The *Cornhill Magazine* arranged a dinner at the Ship Inn, Greenwich and during the meal the London agent of Lippincott's, Pennsylvania approached him, and asked for a second Sherlock Holmes story. He then attended a meeting at Langham Hotel, London with Oscar Wilde and met Joseph Marshall Stoddart - managing editor of Lippincott's. Both agreed to produce stories for the magazine and these were to be works of great significance: Oscar Wilde wrote The Picture of Dorian Gray whilst Conan Doyle wrote The Sign of Four. The contract was signed on 30 August 1889 thus the second Sherlock Holmes tale appeared in Lippincott's Magazine in February 1890. This was a tale of treachery based around the Indian Mutiny in 1857 with action in Agra, the Andaman Islands and England.

Conan Doyle left Southsea in 1890 and travelled to Vienna, arriving there on 5 January 1891, but later continued to Berlin and was engaged in a conversation on the journey that persuaded him to return to England. He then resided briefly at 23 Montague Place near the British Museum and had a practice at 2 Upper Wimpole Street however he had moved to Tennison Road, South Norwood by August 1891. He chose the latter address since it was then isolated and comfortable. He wrote several Sherlock Holmes stories during 1891, which appeared in serial form in the *Strand Magazine*, namely A Scandal in Bohemia, The Case of Identity, The Red Headed League, The Boscombe Valley Mystery and The Five Orange Pips - all were a great success. The stories included Dr. Watson from the start and introduced the famous Sherlock Holmes disguises. There is one such episode described in A Scandal in Bohemia where Dr. Watson states: "It was close upon four before the door opened, and a drunken-looking groom, ill kempt and side whiskered with an inflamed face and disreputable clothes, walked into the room. Accustomed as I was to my friend's amazing powers in the use of disguises, I had to look three times before I was certain that it was indeed he. With a nod he vanished into the bedroom, whence he emerged in five minutes tweed suited and respectable, as of old." In the words of Conan Doyle the game is afoot! However the best evidence for a new theory came soon after in August 1891 when Conan Doyle wrote "The Man With The Twisted Lip".

This is an excellent story and well worth a read, however it is the conclusion that is most pertinent to this discourse. The tale concerns the supposed murder of Mr. Neville St Clair and the man held for the crime is a poor beggar called Hugh Boone, however all was not as it seemed. Sherlock Holmes deduced the truth and revealed they were the same man! Mr. Neville St Clair then related his tale as follows: "You are the first who have ever heard my story. My father was a schoolmaster in Chesterfield, where I received an excellent education. I travelled in my youth, took to the stage, and finally became a reporter on an evening paper in London. One day my editor wished to have a series of articles upon begging in the metropolis, and I volunteered to supply them. There was the point from which all my adventures started. It was only by trying begging as an amateur that I could get the facts upon which to base my articles. When an actor I had, of course, learned all the secrets of making up, and had been famous in the green room for my skill. I took advantage now of my attainments. I painted my face, and to make myself as pitiable as possible I made a good scar and fixed one side of my lip in a twist by the aid of a small slip of flesh coloured plaster. Then with a red head of hair, and an appropriate dress, I took my station in the busiest part of the city, ostensibly as a match seller, but really as a beggar. For seven hours I plied my trade, and when I returned home in the evening I found, to my surprise, that I had received no less than twenty six shillings and four pence."

St Clair then wrote his article and thought no more of it for a few weeks, however he found himself in debt to the value of £25 and took a holiday from his employer and went begging and in ten days had the money. He then continued: "Well, you can imagine how hard it was to settle down to arduous work at two pounds a week, when I knew that I could earn as much in a day by smearing my face with a little paint, laying my cap on the ground, and sitting still. It was a long fight between my pride and the money, but the dollars won at last, and I threw up reporting, and sat day after day in the corner which I had chosen, inspiring pity by my ghastly face and filling my pockets with coppers. Only one man knew my secret. He was the keeper of a low den in which I used to lodge in Swandam Lane, where I could every morning emerge as a squalid beggar and in the evening transform myself into a well-dressed man about town. This fellow, a Lascar, was well paid by me for his rooms, so that I knew that my secret was safe in his possession." Neville St Clair made a fortune from begging and was later married, however his wife then came upon him at Swandam Lane and his secret was out. This was a good story but was it original? There are so many similarities between Conan Doyle's work and the Amateur Beggar by Arthur Pember that it cannot be a coincidence viz. a reporter on an evening paper, my editor wished to have a series of articles, begging as an amateur, when an actor I was famous in the green room for my skill, a small slip of flesh coloured plaster, for seven hours I plied my trade, twenty-six shillings and four pence, the dollars won at last, emerge as a squalid beggar.

These are almost identical lines from the two stories and give strong evidence that Conan Doyle read Arthur Pember's book and used his ideas, and especially his disguises, in the Sherlock Holmes sagas. Indeed the F.A. President died in 1886 just one year before the first Holmes story in 1887. There are many books on Conan Doyle's life and all state that Dr. Joseph Bell inspired the deductive methods of Holmes but there is no explanation of the disguises used, and they are not even alluded to in Conan Doyle's own biography! In conclusion, the disguises of the sleuth were copied from Arthur Pember and the Holmes character was, in part, based on the first President of the F.A! The evidence appears to be conclusive. The likelihood of this being correct has further support from the latter part of Conan Doyle's life, which is now discussed. He continued to live at Norwood and produced some further short stories and the first twelve, including The Man with the Twisted Lip, appeared in *The Adventures of Sherlock Holmes*, whilst eleven more stories were published under the heading *The Memoirs of Sherlock Holmes*. The last of these, The Final Problem, was published in December 1893 and Holmes met his match at the hands of Professor Moriarty. He was killed off at the Reichenbach Falls near the village of Meiringen (10 miles from Grindelwald) and Conan Doyle thought he was free of him, however it wasn't that easy - there being a public outcry. Thus, he was brought back to life and many more stories were written.

Arthur Conan Doyle travelled to Switzerland in 1893 and was then credited with introducing long distance skiing to the country (the first was in Norway). He also visited the United States and Canada in 1894 and Egypt in 1896 and then bought some land at Hindhead in Surrey and made his home there. He was involved in the South African War from 1899-1902 and wrote The Hound of the Baskervilles from August 1901 to April 1902, and it came out in book form in late 1902. He continued to use disguises in his stories and Sherlock Holmes was an Italian Priest in The Final Problem, a tourist on the moors in The Hound of the Baskervilles, and French ouvrier in The Disappearance of Lady Frances Carfax (published 1917 in *His Last Bow*). Meanwhile the profile of Conan Doyle was raised even further and he entered Parliament on two occasions, representing Central Edinburgh in 1900 and Border Burghs including Galashiels in 1905. His first wife Louise died in 1906, however he married Miss Jean Leckie of Blackheath on 18 September 1907. He solved the real crime of the Congo in 1909 and published The Lost World in 1912 and was quite a celebrity and was soon travelling again.

The *Cornhill Magazine* arranged a trip to New York and Canada and he departed Southampton on 20 May 1914, and was mobbed on his arrival in New York after making ill-advised comments regarding the suffragettes. He stayed in New York from 28 May to 1 June and visited many places, attended lectures and went to interviews. In particular he went on the skyscrapers tour, visited the Tombs Prison and met some city detectives. He also travelled to Sing Sing and Coney Island and watched a baseball game. He stayed in comfort at the *Plaza Hotel* in New York, however he noted that the Tombs in the heart of the city was a gloomy and dismal place and that Sing Sing was 20 miles up the Hudson and was built in the middle of the last century. He was stunned to find out that baseball players could earn £1,000 to £1,500 in a season! The trip then quietened down and Conan Doyle went to Canada and the Rockies. He was involved in the First War and visited the British Front, the Italian Front, the French Front and the Hindenberg Line and published "New Revelation", in 1918, a book on spiritualism. He followed this with a psychic quest to Australia and Paris in 1920, visited Canada in 1923, published his *Memories and Adventures* in June 1924 and made his last publication in the *Strand Magazine* in 1927. Sir Arthur Conan Doyle died on 7 July 1930.

He followed the steps of Arthur Pember in many ways and this included football, Switzerland and the prisons of New York. There was a great similarity in the lives of the two men and they seem to have been on the same wavelength. Doyle would have suggested a psychic connection however Pember would not have agreed since he held strong Ritualistic beliefs, nevertheless the two men were both full of disguises and surprises. However, there is yet one more twist in the tale. Charlie Chaplin was born at Walworth, London in 1889 and his first acting role was as newspaper boy Billy in *Sherlock Holmes* (1903-06). He joined the *Karno Troupe* and immigrated to America in 1912 and worked for Keystone Films in 1913. He moved to the Essanay Co. in November 1914 where he had more control over his acting and was in several shorts films from 1915 including The Tramp, The Immigrant and A Night in the Show. He then moved to Mutual in February 1916 and was in The Floorwalker, The Vagabond and The Pawnshop.

He liked to portray the poverty of the American dream and its contradictions, and poke fun at ridiculous authority and used both pathos and comedy for this purpose - his most famous character being the Little Tramp. He formed United Artists with Douglas Fairbanks and Mary Pickford and produced The Kid in 1921 and then had a trip to England where he became friends with H.G. Wells. In later years his films included: The Gold Rush (1925), The Circus (1926), City Lights (1931), Modern Times (1932), The Great Dictator (1940) and Limelight (1951). He left America after his last film and was not allowed to return by the authorities, being called a traitor and Communist. He settled at Vevey in Switzerland in 1953 and although he was later invited back to America, died abroad in 1977. His short plays have an uncanny resemblance to the short written sketches produced by Arthur Pember, and indeed the Little Tramp has the same pathos seen in the Amateur Beggar. Maybe Chaplin received inspiration from Holmes and/or from Pember and indeed they all portrayed a side of life away from the ordinary. Chaplin and Pember both aimed to expose the truth behind American society and even if their ideas were unrelated they clearly had a 'collective consciousness'.

Arthur Pember continued to live at 1233 Third Avenue however soon after his book was published his infant son Valentine was buried on 18 July 1874 - he was presumably very young since there was no record of his birth. The father continued to work as a journalist although he was also listed as an editor in 1874-75. The couple then had twin-girls Mabel and Alice Richardson who were born at 1233 Third Avenue on 27 May 1875 (listed as 7th & 8th children). However, the heat of summer and a poor water supply were an ongoing problem in the crowded tenements and both the infants died: Mabel on 20 July and Alice R. on 27 July. This was clearly a tragedy and cause of death in both cases was gastric trouble, combined with exhaustion (similar to their brother). The four infants were buried at Greenwood Cemetery on the outskirts of Brooklyn. Arthur was listed as an author, clerk and journalist in the period 1875-77 and his son Gilbert E. was born at 1233 Third Avenue on 19 November 1876 (9th child) - father aged 41.

The New York streets were completely overcrowded with horse-drawn wagons and pedestrians, in 1874, and the solution put forward was to build several elevated railways (ELS) thus the family soon witnessed major changes. The lines were constructed along Second, Third, Sixth, Eighth and Ninth Avenues and the result was pleasing since the journey from Battery to Harlem could be done in just 42 minutes. However, there was initially an outcry and legal challenges from some residents since the unattractive iron structures blocked out sunlight and caused much noise in nearby tenements. This unwelcome development went right past the Pembers' bedroom window and its impending construction prompted them to move thus they lived at 1240 Third Avenue, on the west side of the street, from 1877. Steam locomotives were used to power the first trains and the elevated line in Third Avenue was completed in 1878-79. Arthur was still described as an editor and journalist in the period 1877-79 and his last son Godfrey Churchill was born at 1240 Third Avenue on 18 March 1879 (10th child).

Arthur Pember and his family were on the American census in 1880 and were recorded as living in the 19th Ward, New York, New York, New York. The reason for this strange address was that Manhattan was still called New York, and was in New York City, in New York State - they named it thrice! Arthur's profession was listed as 'none' and he was either unemployed or retired at the time. His wife Alice M. kept house whilst his sons Cyril F. and St John B. born England were at school, and Roosa H. born Connecticut and Gilbert E. and Godfrey C. born New York were at home. Their neighbours had various occupations such as clerk, conductor, teacher, speculator, produce merchant, manufacturer and travelling agent, and several had one servant. His wife Alice Mary died of typhoid and exhaustion at 1240 Third Avenue, 19th Ward on 16 November 1881 having been resident in the city 13 years. Her children died of a similar illness and this was clearly a serious problem there in Victorian times. Her death was recorded in the *New York Times* on 18 November 1881, stating: "PEMBER On Wednesday November 16th Alice Mary wife of Arthur Pember aged 36. Funeral at St. James's Church, East 72nd Street and Lexington Avenue on Friday at 3 pm." The church was situated near their house although no longer remains, and she was buried at Marble Cemetery in the East Village district. The latter was both public and private and was located on either side of Second Avenue at the junction with 2nd and 3rd Street.

The family had suffered a dramatic change of circumstances and Arthur Pember was left with five young sons to support aged 16, 13, 11, 5 and 2 years old. He continued to live at 1240 Third Avenue from 1881-84 but it is uncertain how he supported them as no profession was listed. New York State had a considerable problem with orphans and in 1850 there were 27 orphanages and 10,000 street kids. The church worked to overcome this problem and the New York Children's Aid Society was formed in 1854 and in general the city took responsibility for the poor and orphaned. It was common practice to place children in almshouses with adults however this was banned throughout the state in 1880. At this time Herbert Spencer (1820-1903) developed the idea of *Social Darwinism* in England, from concepts of adaptation and survival of the fittest, although his theory was based more on Malthus and less on Darwin. A number of successful people in America took up these ideas and believed they had no responsibility towards the 'weak' or 'unfit', however many believed this was a misuse of Darwin and that it was their Christian duty to assist the needy - the debate also involved questions of government intervention in social issues. Yet many were philanthropic towards their fellow man and Pember supported this cause in his writings.

Arthur Pember had every intention of supporting his sons and was a man of adventure with great enthusiasm who overcame personal setbacks by looking to a new future, thus the great country of America provided him with a new opportunity in 1884. The early immigrants to America often arrived in New York and headed 'west', however the majority went to California, thus the prairie lands of the 'mid-west' were often passed by. In the late 19th century the potential of these lands was finally seen and they were opened up for cattle and wheat farming, this being facilitated by the arrival of the railroad. The Plains States were then developed and a vital factor was the building of the Northern Pacific Railway in the north of the country through North Dakota. The town of Bismarck became the State capital and was named after the 19th century German Chancellor in the hope of attracting German money to the railroad. It had reached Bismarck by 1873 but was the terminus at this point as the company went bankrupt.

This was the 'Wild West' seen in the movies and real pioneer country. The Sioux and Cheyenne Indians inhabited the area and strongly resisted the advance of the white man, although other tribes had settled in reserves by 1871. The Indians fought for their land as the settlers expanded their farms and George Armstrong Custer, the general, was stationed at Fort Abraham Lincoln near Bismarck in the early 1870s. He rode from there on two famous expeditions that have gone down in history. The first was to the Black Hills in 1874 when his troops discovered gold - this caused nothing more serious than a gold rush. The second was in 1876 and General Custer chased the Sioux Indian across the country and this ended with 'Custer's last stand' at the *Battle of Little Big Horn*. Despite this conflict the land in North Dakota was gradually settled and the railroad was extended westwards after 1879 and Bismarck became a territorial capital in 1883 - the State of North Dakota was formed in 1889.

Fargo was one of the towns that grew up along the railroad and was situated 200 miles east of Bismarck in the Red River Valley, near the Minnesota border. The railroad arrived there in 1872 and Front Street a mile long road was laid out next to the railway with Avenues at right angles, as in New York. There was a grid street pattern as in many new towns and Front Street went westwards from a loop in the Red River. There were a few wooden houses, tents, dirt tracks and 'no' trees on the flat plains in 1873, whilst the first larger buildings were the Headquarters Hotel and Court House. William G. Fargo of the Wells Fargo Express Co. put up $500 dollar to start a newspaper and the first was printed on January 1, 1874 and this became the *Fargo Times* in 1875. The Dakota Legislature passed an act to incorporate the city on 5 January 1875 and 137 voters took part in the first election whilst two other papers were started - *Republican* 1878 and *Daily Argus* 1879. The settlement developed and there was a line of brick buildings along Front Street, in 1879, with the appearance of a 'Wild West' film set, whilst a boom in wheat farming made it an important agricultural centre with rail and river links.

Northern Pacific 'rail workers' founded Jamestown in 1871 and it was located in the fertile James River Valley, halfway between Bismarck and Fargo. The first farmers arrived in 1872, whilst the James River flowed south to join the Missouri River. Judson La Moure (1839-1918) of the Territorial & State Legislature gave his name to the newly created La Moure County on 4 January 1873. This was situated about fifty miles south of Jamestown and Grand Rapids became the county seat when the area was government organised on 17 October 1881. La Moure developed after 1882 and became the regional centre in 1886 however it was always small and the population in the town remained below 1,000. The area experienced a depression in the 1870s however there was a farming boom in the 1880s and this brought new settlers. Arthur Pember was attracted by these opportunities in Dakota and with a spirit of adventure became determined to put the past behind him and headed 'west'. He left his home at 1240 Third Avenue and with his sons joined a train at Penn Station and travelled through Pennsylvania, Ohio, Indiana, Illinois, Wisconsin and Minnesota. It was a long journey - about 1,400 miles. The train eventually came to Fargo and stopped beside Front Street before continuing via the Northern Pacific to Jamestown. The six 'men' then boarded a Wells Fargo stagecoach and went south to the fledgling township of La Moure. One can ask at this point - what was the F.A. President doing in this land of cowboys and Indians? The phrase, "There's only one Arthur Pember," was surely coined for him.

Arthur did not join the local newspaper but started a new life, for a second time, and was a farmer in La Moure. This was still a dangerous place with limited medical help if one was ill, however the threat of Indian attack had receded and prosperity beckoned. Arthur Pember (50) a farmer lived in the township of La Moure with Cyril (20), St. John (17), Herbert (15), Gilbert (8) and Godfrey (6) in 1885. His neighbours were farmers, a lawyer, a real estate broker, J.P. and various labourers who came from Denmark, Sweden and Germany and other States including New York. These details are from the Dakota Territory Census of 1885 and include 132,000 people or ⅔ of the population of North Dakota. Arthur clearly had prospects for a long life and a successful future in wheat farming, however a man so important in terms of football history died in relative obscurity, and this explains his omission from official soccer histories. His obituary appeared in the *New York Times* on 4 April 1886 and stated: "Arthur Pember, formerly a writer on the New York press, died at La Moure, Dakota, yesterday morning, aged 50 years. He was an Englishman by birth. His death was the result of kidney difficulties, supplemented by blood poisoning from a carbuncle in the lumbar region." This was a sad and painful end for Arthur and there is no further record of this event since the vital statistics and death records did not start in Dakota until 1890, however his epitaph should read: "He was an Englishman by birth."

He had achieved much in his life, first as a founder of soccer and secondly as a journalist with a social conscience, however the move to North Dakota suggests that in these later years his main interest was in his sons' future, rather than his own ambition and drives. He was a man to be admired with excellent qualities that raised him above the ordinary, and played a major role in soccer history but also embarked on a remarkable career. He left some important literature there being six references to A. Pember in *Poole's Index to Periodical Literature 1802-1906* - an index of articles in prominent magazines, and two have been discussed: Atlantic Monthly, Boston (*1858-81*) and Lippincott's Magazine, Philadelphia (*1868-81*). The other four appeared in the National Review, London, one in 1883-86 and three in 1887-91. These are concerned with religious matters regarding the Church of England and children's education whilst one refers to "Patrician Pugilism" or aristocratic boxing. The latter were published posthumously.

The Pre-emption Act (1841) and Homestead Act (1862) gave rights to settlers in Dakota and they could purchase up to 160 acres of farmland, however his sons didn't see a future in farming and left La Moure soon after his decease. The eldest son Cyril Pember was a photographer at 817 Front Street, Fargo in 1887 and his four brothers may have lived with him. The property was at the west end of the town near to 14th Street and not far from the roundhouse of the Northern Pacific Railroad. There is some difficulty tracing their movements after this date as the American census for 1890 was destroyed in a fire, however the brothers then returned to their roots in New York (State). Cyril F. Pember was an artist living at 705 University Avenue, Syracuse, New York State in 1889-90 and his brothers may still have lived with him. Indeed St. John Pember remained unmarried throughout his life and may have died about this time (before 1900).

(Roosa) Herbert Pember married Mina E. McCormack in 1893. Owen and Rebecca, her parents, came from Ireland and had Mina (September 1869), William (1872), Jennie (1874) and Owen (1876) in New York but lived at Bridgeport, Fairfield, Connecticut in 1880. Her father worked in a sewing machine factory and her sister Rebecca was born there in October that year. Roosa lived in Greenwich Village in 1893-96 and had several lodgings namely 111w, 113w and 167w all in 13th Street and was described as a clerk, and had two children at this time: William H. (March 1894) and Arthur D. (May 1895). He moved to Neck Road, Brooklyn near the Boulevard in 1896-97 and was a stationer and salesman with a business at 40 Beaver Street - in the commercial district of Manhattan, and had a third son Edward V. (May 1898). Roosa H. Pember, his wife and three sons lived at Van Sicklen Street, Kings County near to Ocean Parkway, South Brooklyn on 1 June 1900. The household included sister-in-law Rebecca McCormack and the enumerator was none other than Roosa Pember himself. The family lived in New York City until at least 1935.

The younger brothers may have resided with Roosa in Brooklyn and Gilbert E. Pember married Eva J. Holsh in 1898. Her mother Ellen L. Holsh was born in England in September 1844 and came to America in 1874, her daughter Eva being born in Ohio in June that year. The three lived at 5 Maple Avenue, Richmond Borough in 1900 whilst Cyril Pember had moved to 162 New York Avenue, Richmond Borough at the time. He was still described as an artist and was a boarder with Peter and Bridget Murphy and family - he remained unmarried. Both addresses were in the Port Richmond district on the north side of Staten Island. Cyril Pember lived in New York until the 1930s whilst Gilbert Pember was rector of the Episcopal Church, Germantown, Philadelphia, and died in c.1934. Godfrey C. Pember, a streetcar conductor, was unemployed and resided at Hudson River State Hospital, Poughkeepsie, Duchess County, New York State in 1900 - 60 miles north of New York. He married Elizabeth M. Dougherty in the town on 3 October 1900 and had children Godfrey E. (1902), M. Eilene (1905), George A., Gilbert V. (1912) and Edward and was a general agent for the American Express Company. The 'five boroughs' were formed in New York in 1898: New York (Manhattan and Bronx), Queens (as before), Kings (Brooklyn) and Richmond (Staten Island) and the city had a population of 3 million - second only to London with 4 million. The family worked in journalism in Boston, New York and Christchurch but the F.A connection was then a distant memory and the other presidents still had work to do.

CHAPTER 5

All the President's Men

The F.A. had small beginnings in 1863 and with the departure of Arthur Pember the founding father E.C. Morley became President from 1867-74. He worked with three secretaries, firstly Willis and Graham his friends from Barnes F.C. and then Charles Alcock after 1870. The organisation developed and moved forward at this time especially with the advent of the F.A. Cup in 1871. With everything in order Ebenezer was able to step aside at the age of 43 and was replaced by Francis Arthur Marindin - a gentleman with a vastly different background. The latter helped guide the F.A. through the arrival of professionalism in the 1880s.

SIR FRANCIS ARTHUR MARINDIN

It would be a surprise to some that the third F.A. President and man in charge was in fact a "Frenchman", or strictly speaking a gentleman with roots in Switzerland. It is likely the details of his ancestry were not known since this was only sixty years after the days of Napoleon, although it did not set a trend, and a further century had passed when a man from Sweden joined the F.A. The Marindin family had French origins but settled in Switzerland at the time of St. Bartholomew and are traced to Pierre Marindin who resided at Congeveaux, Vallage de Movat, Switzerland in c.1590. His son Pierre Marindin (1596) became the Governor of Congeveaux and his grandson Pierre Marindin (1640) settled at Vevey town-ship on the shores of Lake Geneva in 1662 - long before the time of the Little Tramp. His son Pierre Marindin (1664) purchased the settlement of Crosier and married Madeleine Pilet of Chateau d'Oex in 1697, whilst their son Pierre Marindin (1701) married Esther Aviolat d'Aigle in 1733. He was Town Councillor of Vevey in 1742 and had four sons, and it is there that the story 'proper' begins.

The Marindin family had a coat of arms, which was traditionally a sea stag surmounted by a plume of feathers, and their motto was "Spero Meliora" translated as "Improve the World" or "I hope for better things". Their coat of arms was later a quarter shield with those of Wedderburn and Colvile - but more of this anon. Jean Philippe Marindin (1742), the third son, left the mountains of Switzerland and moved to the farmlands of Worcester-shire. He anglicised his name as John Philip and married Elizabeth Rann (1747) the daughter of Henry Rann of Hallow near Worcester. The couple had two sons who were both baptized at St. Phillip's, Birmingham namely Samuel Peter (14 October 1774) and John Philip (6 May 1777). The family continued to live at Hallow near Worcester but it seems likely their business was in the growing city of Birmingham. John Philip Marindin died on 26 January 1798, his son John Philip on 23 July 1806 and his wife Elizabeth on 5 July 1832 aged 85 (all at Hallow).

Samuel Peter Marindin married Catherine Louisa Webbe on 13 June 1805. She was baptized at Minchinhampton, Gloucester on 22 October 1782 the daughter and co-heiress of Samuel Webbe, of Henbury near Bristol, and Elizabeth his wife. The couple's first child Samuel was born at Edgbaston on 26 March 1807 and baptized there on 7 July 1807. There were three other children: John Philip (1809) baptized at Edgbaston on 5 September 1811 but died Hallow 10 September 1824, Henry Richard (1811) and Catherine Louisa (1813) born Henbury, however the mother died soon after the birth of the last child and Samuel Peter Marindin then married Eliza or Elizabeth Iddins. She was baptized at St. Phillip's, Birmingham on 15 December 1780 the daughter of John and Mary of Summerfield House, Bromsgrove, Warwick-shire. Samuel Marindin, merchant, was in business at 2 Great Charles Street, Birmingham in 1815-23 whilst Mrs. Marindin lived at 141 Great Charles Street at the time - north of St. Phillip's Cathedral and west of Snow Hill. The business was Marindin and Abick in 1821 and Samuel had a property at Perry Barr in 1821-23.

The Marindin family had succeeded in business and moved to Worfield in Shropshire by c.1835 and made a good connection - their daughter's marriage linked them to the Earls of Shrewsbury and there is now a brief aside regarding the Davenports. They are traced to Ormus de Davenport who arrived at the time of William I however the line begins with Sir Ralph Davenport, in the reign of Henry VII, and his descendant Henry Davenport esquire who married Lettice the daughter and heir of Thomas Maddocks of Bridgnorth. The couple lived at *Davenport House*, Worfield as early as 1645 and Henry Davenport, their son, married Elizabeth daughter of Sharington Talbot of Lacock Abbey on 22 October 1665. This couple's daughter Mary married Rev. Prideaux Sutton of Bredon (see below) and their son Sharington was a major general in Ireland and died in 1719, however Henry Davenport, their successor, was baptized 26 February 1677/8 and was an ancestor of Talbot of Lacock and Davenport of Worfield. Henry married on two occasions: his first wife Mary Lucy Chardin was the mother of Sharington Davenport, and his second wife Barbara was the daughter of Sir John Ivory and Anne (d. of Sir John Talbot of Lacock).

Lacock Abbey: The Sharington family purchased this property situated near Chippenham, Wilts in 1539 after the dissolution of the monasteries and converted it into a mansion house, complete with cloisters. Sir Henry Sharington left it to his daughter and co-heir Olive who had married John Talbot esquire of Salwarpe, Worcester (in the 16th century). His father Sir John Talbot was an ancestor of the present Earl of Shrewsbury - indeed Talbot is the Earl's family name and this is a complicated link that needn't be discussed here. John and Olive had a son and heir called Sharington Talbot and the estate at Lacock passed to John Ivory Talbot and his wife, who had two sons and a daughter - the son John inherited Lacock (d.1778) whilst daughter Martha married her cousin. Meanwhile Henry and Barbara Davenport (see above) had four children baptized: Henry - 11 October 1718 St. Martin in the Fields; Talbot - 4 February 1719 ditto; William - 30 May 1725 Worfield; and Barbara - 12 February 1726 ditto. The son William Davenport rector of Bredon, Worcs married cousin Martha Talbot in 1751 and had the following children baptized there: Prideaux Sutton (1752), Mary (1757), John Talbot (1759) and William (4 August 1763) and a daughter Barbara (1754) at Astley Abbots, Shropshire. The third son inherited Lacock Abbey at the age of fifteen in 1778, and changed his name to William Davenport Talbot and married Lady Elizabeth Theresa Fox Strangways in 1796. Their son William Henry Fox Talbot was born at Melbury House, Dorset on the 11 February 1800 and produced the first photographic prints at Lacock Abbey in 1833 and was honoured by the Royal Society (d.1877) - the 9th Lord Kinnaird assisted him in his work (see below). N.B. Harry Potter was later filmed there.

Davenport House: Meanwhile Sharington Davenport, son of Henry and Mary Lucy (see above), married Gratiana Rodd and had 13 children baptized at Worfield from 1733-54, and William Yelverton, the twelfth, was born on 19 February 1750 and died in 1834 when his nephew succeeded him (see below). Their last child Edward Davenport was born on 19 January 1754 and became vicar of Glazeley & Deuxhill and also of Worfield, and married Catherine daughter of Rev. Edmund Taylor of Worcester in 1776. Their son Edmund Sharington Davenport was born on 18 May 1778 and was also vicar of Worfield, and married Elizabeth Tongue on 7 August 1806, and had ten children including William Sharington born 30 July 1808 and baptized at Worfield on 24 November. The father inherited *Davenport House* from his uncle in 1834. William Sharington Davenport married Catherine Louisa Marindin at Worfield on 22 December 1835 and had five children: William Bromley (1836), Louisa Marindin (1838), Edmund Henry (1839), Vivian (1843) and Charles Talbot (1848) and inherited *Davenport House* at his own father's decease in 1842.

Meanwhile Samuel Peter Marindin, merchant, made his last will at Bridgnorth on 28 August 1839: "It is now a considerable time since I placed in Mr. Barker's hands a rough draft of memoranda for him to draw out proper for my will, this has not been done unfortunately. I am therefore very anxious to lose no further time, in my present uncertain state, to state to you my dear wife and children my wishes about the future disposition of my property and as I cannot now have this legally drawn up, I trust that my wishes will be of the same effect, and that you will all bear your parts in arranging them amicably among yourselves." He left his wife Elizabeth the household goods, horse and carriage, property at Chesterton, his portrait and his mother's jewels. He left Rev. Samuel Marindin the household goods (at his wife's decease), his pictures, portfolios and gun dogs, his farming stock and growing crops, however whilst his wife was still at Chesterton she was to have two cows and the poultry - he was clearly concerned about her diet! He also discussed financial matters and left money for Samuel to secure him against the liability for a bond of £2,000 given to his wife as a marriage settlement. The money was to be used to pay interest to her at his decease namely £1,000 at the rate of 10s. He left his son Henry Richard Marindin his house in Great Charles Street, Birmingham and German gun and pistols. He left several items to his daughter Catherine Louisa Davenport including Worcester Canal shares, her mother's picture, his and her mother's jewels, a silver coffee pot, two paintings by Roberts and, "Any drawing of mine as an affectionate remembrance which she may choose." His silver embossed cup was left to grandson Henry Colvile Marindin. Finally, he left his wife half the money in the bank and his three children the remainder of his property. He cancelled the rough draft at Mr. Barker's and made his wife Eliza and son Samuel executors and requested his funeral to be a plain one and the witnesses were C.F. Broadbent and

Mariann Vickers. He made a codicil on 30 August 1839 stating: "I leave to my eldest son the further sum of £500 as a small indemnification for the sacrifices he has made on my account."

Samuel Peter Marindin a gentleman died of stomach ulcers at the High Street, Bridgnorth on 7 September 1839 the informant being A. Turner - an "inmate" of the Crown Hotel, Bridgnorth. His will, however, was not legally written hence Mariann Vickers made an oath on 17 March 1840 and verified that the document was a true statement in front of C.F. Broadbent, commissioner. The will was proved in London on 25 March 1840 and probate was granted to Eliza Marindin widow and Rev. Samuel Marindin. The family then had a long association with Worfield and Eliza Marindin lived at Chesterton in 1841 with her niece Ann Iddins and five servants, however a larger family resided at *Davenport House*, namely E.S. Davenport (clerk), wife Elizabeth, children Edward M. (lieutenant 66th Foot), Edmund S. (fellow commoner Trinity College, Dublin), Daniel D.T. (ensign 37th Foot), Lucy S. and Catherine G. wife of Octavius E. Johnson stockbroker. There were no less than 16 servants.

Eliza Marindin (widower) a landed proprietor lived at Chesterton in 1851, with her stepdaughter Catherine Davenport and children Louisa and Charles, niece Anne Iddins (31), cousin Isabella Harbourne (50), relative Lucy Davenport (31) and eight servants including housekeeper, butler and coachman. Eliza died at 26 Grove Street, Leamington, on 20 September 1859 aged 79 and was described as, "The widow of Samuel Peter Marindin formerly a Birmingham merchant." George Horton of Bromsgrove surgeon, executor, proved her will at Birmingham on 14 November 1859 and she was stated to be formerly of Chesterton in the parish of Worfield but late of 26 Grove Street, her effects being under £5,000. Catherine Louisa Davenport died on 17 July 1865 whilst William Sharington Davenport died at *Davenport House* on 1 October 1871 and Edmund Henry Davenport, Rev. Henry Cunliffe of Shifnal and Rev. George Davenport Nicholas of Clewer, Berks (nephew), the executors, proved his will at Shrewsbury on 17 November 1871, his effects being under £20,000. Edmund Henry Davenport was then owner of *Davenport House* and died in 1890 and the family also lived at 48 Cromwell Gardens, Kensington.

Catherine was a second cousin once removed of William Henry Fox Talbot "the founder of photography" and was distantly related to the Earl of Shrewsbury - the tangled web was further weaved! The F.A. President, however, also had other notable connections (see below). Meanwhile the son Henry Richard Marindin (1811) joined the 1st or Royal Regiment of Foot and became an ensign on 11 January 1833 then a lieutenant on 18 March 1836. He married Elizabeth Jane Dartnell at St. Mary's Cathedral, Limerick on 27 October 1836 and received a number of promotions viz. captain 30 April 1841, major 20 June 1854 and regimental major 3 November 1855. He sold his commission and retired in 1858-59 however his movements are then unclear and he may have gone abroad - his last entry in the army lists being in 1878.

Samuel Marindin was born at Edgbaston on 26 March 1807 and spent his early life in Birmingham and at Hallow in Worcester. He attended Shrewsbury School in 1821-25 and may have been familiar with early soccer - the Dowling game. He then joined the army and was a cornet and sub-lieutenant in the 2nd Regiment of Life Guards on 8 August 1831. They had fought at the Peninsula and at Waterloo and their Colonel-in-Chief was the King, whilst a cornet was a fifth commissioned officer in a cavalry troop (who carried the colours). Samuel had a brief stay in the army as a cornet and left in 1834 and then entered the ministry and headed south. He married Isabella Colvile on 13 March 1834 who came from Beckenham in Kent, however the name Colvile concealed some double-barrelled ancestors and a notable Scottish family.

They are traced to Robert Wedderburn (d.1518) and his great grandson Alexander Wedderburn who was born in 1561 - he lived in Forfar-shire and accompanied James VI to England in 1603. A descendant Sir John Wedderburn was made the 1st Baronet in 1704 whilst Sir John Wedderburn, the 5th Baronet, fought as a *Jacobite* at Culloden and after being taken prisoner was executed, thus the baronetcy was forfeited in 1746. His son John Wedderburn was born on 21 February 1729 and was cornet in Lord Ogilvy's Regiment at Culloden and after his father's demise went and lived in Jamaica. This began an association with slavery that would soon haunt the family whilst the 'West India' House of Webster, Wedderburn & Co. was in London. His son David was created 1st Baronet in 1803 (at his decease) and the line went to a cousin Sir John Andrew Wedderburn-Ogilvy (born 1866) and the name was changed to Ogilvy-Wedderburn.

The son James Wedderburn was born on 28 August 1730 and went to Jamaica with his brother in 1746 and worked on the plantations as a doctor. He came back to Scotland in 1773 and bought Inveresk Lodge near Edinburgh for £1,000, and married Isabella the daughter of Andrew Blackburn and great-great niece of Robert the 3rd and last Lord Colvile of Ochiltree in March 1774. This family had a notable heritage in Scotland and James Colvile obtained Ochiltree, Ayrshire from James Hamilton in 1530 - in exchange for his property at East Wemyss, Fife. The Colviles also owned the Craigflower estate at Crombie in Fife three miles west of Dunfermline on the banks of the River Forth (see below). Isabella inherited Craigflower in May 1799 and her husband took the additional surname and arms (not by law) of Wedderburn-Colvile. The couple then had four sons at Inveresk: John (1776) who went out to Jamaica in 1794 and died there in 1799, Andrew (1779) who is treated below, Peter (1781) who took the name Wedderburn-Ogilvy - his grandson became baronet, and James (1782) who changed his name to Wedderburn - Andrew his son married Joanna Keir on 14 September 1847 and had Francis Edward K. on 11 March 1857 (see census below).

Thomas Wedderburn (1710) was brother of the 5th Baronet and his son John Wedderburn (19 August 1743) went to Jamaica in 1762 and owned several plantations. He married Mary Wisdom Bedward on 27 May 1782 and his daughter Elizabeth Susannah was born at Westmoreland on 1 January 1784. Through his wife's family he acquired the 'Spring Garden' plantation but returned to Britain in 1789 and joined the 'West India' House of Webster & Co. at 35 Leadenhall Street. He had several London residences and later resided in Clapham and became senior partner in 1801. Indeed his address was something of an irony given the work of the 'Clapham Sect'. Andrew Wedderburn-Colvile was born on 6 November 1779 and went to London in 1796, and was a salaried partner in Webster, Wedderburn & Co. in 1798. He married his second cousin Elizabeth Susannah Wedderburn on 27 December 1802 but she died at Inveresk on 22 December 1803 and there were no children. Andrew married Louisa Mary Eden at Bromley on 26 June 1806 who was born in Spain in 1788 and daughter of William, 1st Lord Auckland, whilst his father James Wedderburn-Colvile died on 14 December 1807 and left behind a family secret and 'time-bomb'.

Sir Robert Eden and his wife Mary had sons Robert (1741-84) and William (1744-1814). The first son was the Royal Governor of Maryland at the time of the American Revolution and was forced to leave the country in June 1776 (see Rich Ch. 8). His brother William was educated at Eton then called to the bar at the Middle Temple in 1769, and became a noted politician and diplomat. He was placed in charge of British intelligence on the Continent at the time of the American Revolution and married Eleanor Elliott that year, then used spies to infiltrate the American delegation to Versailles and obtained information from Benjamin Franklin and Silas Deane (see J.F. Alcock Ch. 3). He resided at Eden Farm in Beckenham and his son George was born there in 1784, but was then Ambassador to Spain in 1787 and the Netherlands in 1789. He continued to have an important role in politics after America was 'lost' and was raised to the peerage as 1st Lord Auckland in 1793. His property in Beckenham like other 'farms' nearby was 'an elegant seat' with accommodation for many guests. It was a Classical white mansion-house high on Village Way with superb gardens of oak and elm, the estate reaching to Croydon Road. His guests were reformers and evangelists and included William Pitt the younger, Henry Dundas, William Wilberforce, Vansittart and Lord Teignmouth.

William Eden, 1st Lord Auckland died at Eden Farm on 28 May 1814 and was succeeded by his son George. The latter was born on 25 August 1784 and like his father joined the bar in 1809; he was also a Whig politician and briefly 1st Lord of the Admiralty in 1834. At this time he sent William Hobson to the East Indies then became Governor General of India in 1836-42 and was created an Earl in 1838. Hobson was the Lieutenant Governor of New Zealand and negotiated the Waitangi Treaty with the Maoris in 1840 and named Auckland in his honour, but he died in 1849 and the Earldom was extinct. Andrew and Louisa Mary Colvile moved to Langley Farm, Beckenham near her father after their marriage, part of the Langley Park Estate with Eden Farm, and had thirteen children there viz. Eleanor (1808), James William (1810), John (1811), **Isabella** (24 April 1812), George (1813) *infant*, Louisa (1815), Emily (1817), Eden (1819), Jean (1820), Georgiana Mary (1822), Charlotte (1823), Isalen Mary (1825) and Caroline (1827) baptized at Beckenham Church. The property was a gentleman's home in the 19th century but was used by *Wellcome Research* and is now in a modern housing estate. Andrew took the name of Colvile in lieu of Wedderburn by *Royal Licence* on 22 June 1814 and was senior partner in Wedderburn, Colvile & Co. after John of Clapham died in 1820. He also owned the Craigflower estate after his mother died in 1821, but trouble was brewing.

Stories of promiscuity between master and slave in the West Indies are well known and indeed James Wedderburn had two 'reputed' alliances during his time there. His first association was with housekeeper and slave Rosanna and they had three sons - she was sold to Lady Douglas whilst pregnant with the third.

He then had a second liaison with Esther Trotter and had a son and daughter. Robert Wedderburn (c.1762) the youngest of the three sons grew up on the estate of Lady Douglas, and claimed his father made him and his brother James 'free' at birth. During this time he saw both his mother and grandmother whipped. He did not remain in Jamaica and became a sailor in 1778 and came to London in 1779 and worked as a tailor. He was converted to Christianity by a Wesleyan preacher and was attracted to the Unitarian Church. They believed that social evils were humanly created and their bond was anti-dogma rather than a uniform belief, and stated: "Jesus is the great exemplar which we ought to copy in order to perfect our union with God." Robert married Elizabeth Ryan at St. Katherine Creechurch on 5 November 1781 and had six children from 1786-1806.

Meanwhile Thomas Spence (one of 19 children) was born in Newcastle in 1750 and produced a pamphlet *The Real Rights of Man* and then came to London. He spoke out on many issues and in this role met Robert Wedderburn in 1812 however he died in 1814. There was then a movement called the *Society of Spencean Philanthropists* and its members were both radical and revolutionary. They arranged a mass meeting at Spa Fields near Islington on 2 December 1816 and this turned into a riot and the authorities believed that Robert Wedderburn was the ringleader, although he was not charged. He then set up a chapel at Hopkins Street, Soho and used his pulpit for religious and political aims and stated: "Lectures every Sabbath day on theology, morality, natural philosophy and politics by a self taught West Indian." He campaigned for the abolition of slavery and believed there was 'a conspiracy against the poor.' He spoke out strongly against the magistrates and yeomen regarding the 'Peterloo Massacre' in 1819 and was arrested for 'blasphemous libel'. In his defence he said, "Where, after all, is my crime. It consists merely in having spoken in the same plain and homely language which Christ and his disciples uniformly used." He was sent to Newgate Prison however his friends paid the bail and he was released. He spoke against passive radical reformers such as Henry 'Orator' Hunt, however he was against more direct action suggested by Arthur Thistlewood and other members of the Society. The latter was one of the members of the Cato Street Conspiracy, an attempt to murder the cabinet at a dinner in 1820.

Robert was not directly involved in the plot but the authorities had no more patience and he was sent to Dorchester Gaol for two years in 1820-22. William Wilberforce visited him in prison and a picture of him at the time shows him to have 'white' blood. He was released and continued to preach and wrote to *Bell's Life* regarding slavery in 1824. In this letter he said he was the son of James Wedderburn of Inveresk and that he was made free at birth, and that John (brother of Andrew) had provided a dinner for the children of his brother James, when in Jamaica. His 'brother' Andrew made a strong denial and Robert was so incensed by this that he published a pamphlet regarding the matter - this is held by the British Museum. This must have caused great discomfort to the Colvile family in their Beckenham home however the storm was soon to pass. Robert Wedderburn also known as the 'Black Preacher' was sent to Giltspur Street Prison in 1831, and maybe his day had ended, since there was change with the Reform Bill (1832) and the abolition of slavery (1833). Indeed there is no trace of Robert after this time and his preaching was over.

This was a trying time for the family and Eleanor the eldest daughter died in Beckenham on 30 November 1824 and John the second son in Eton on 17 February 1830, thus they removed to Craigflower in Scotland and had three more children: Margaret Agnes (1829), Alice Douglas (1830) and Katharine (1834) *infant*, although the second child was born in London. Samuel Marindin married Isabella, now the eldest daughter, on 13 March 1834 and Andrew Colvile of Ochiltree and of Crombie, Fife made his last will on 4 June 1834. He discussed provisions for his wife, made prior to their marriage, and a disposition dated 29 July 1823 that arranged an annuity of £400 p.a. for her at his decease - he confirmed this should stand. He left his household goods to his wife and discussed an indenture, or declaration of trust, dated 28 November 1806. An amount of £10,000 was also to be divided amongst his younger sons and unmarried daughters, the share to each son up to £3,000 and the share to each daughter up to £2,000, the interest to be paid to his wife in her lifetime and then to the children's guardians after her decease. The remainder of his estate was left to James William Colvile but if he died to Eden Colvile, or to any other son, or to his daughters. He made his wife Louisa, son James, brother Peter Wedderburn-O and brother-in-law George Lord Auckland the children's guardians and the will was witnessed at 66 Lincoln's Inn Fields. The Craigflower estate was near the village of Torryburn, one of several ports along the coast, and looked out on the River Forth and across Torry Bay towards Bo'ness. A survey of 1839 stated that Andrew Colvile was the largest landowner receiving rent of 1,640l ⅔ and that several poor children were educated at Mrs. Colvile's expense.

The family spent time in London and at Craigflower and two daughters died at the latter: Alice (1845) and Caroline (1846) who were both buried at Crombie. The father Andrew had continued to work for Wedderburn, Colvile & Co. and was a governor of the Hudson's Bay Company and a director of their subsidiary the Puget Sound Agricultural Company in the 1850s. They hoped to gain a foothold on Vancouver Island by establishing farms thus Colvile and Pelly wrote to James Douglas at Fort Victoria on 12 March 1852: "We have an arrangement with Mr. K. McKenzie of East Lothian and Mr. Skinner in Essex and request that you will select two good situations of land where farms of 500 to 1,000 acres may advantageously be established." The farms were to supply crops to Fort Victoria, the Navy at Esquimalt and export to the Russians in Alaska. The local Indians named this area near the Gorge Waterway - *Kosapsom*, however the Hudson's Bay men named it Maple Point. Kenneth McKenzie sailed to Canada on the *Norman Morison* in 1853 and the Hudson's Bay Company released four plots of land of c.600 acres on 17 May 1854. The Scot named his farm and house Craigflower in honour of Andrew Colvile and this became the name of the whole settlement. This was the most successful of the four farms and Craigflower School was built in 1854-55 and bricks were brought from Stourbridge in England. McKenzie owed a debt of $3,000 to the Hudson's Bay Company and this plagued him the rest of his life, whilst the school was used until 1911 and is now a museum.

Andrew Colvile died in London on 3 February 1856 and was buried at Holy Trinity, Brompton, and probate was granted to his widow on 12 February - like grant to his son James William and Peter Wedderburn-Ogilvy. His widow Louisa Mary Colvile died soon after on 2 December 1858 and the estates then passed to son James William Colvile. He was born on 12 January 1810 and grew up in Beckenham and had a notable career being Advocate General of Bengal Court in 1845, Judge of Bengal Supreme Court in 1848, knighted for his services in 1848 and Chief Justice in 1855. He married Frances Elinor the daughter of John Peter Grant of the Supreme Council, Calcutta on 13 April 1857 and had a son Andrew John (1859-76). He then employed David Bryce and had Craigflower re-modelled in the Scottish baronial style in 1862. It was reached across a small bridge next to Torryburn Church and a driveway went through the woods to the imposing gateposts and grand entrance. The house was of yellow and grey sandstone with round and square towers, crenellations, gables and grey slate roof. Together they created an impressive façade and the family arms and motto "Oublier Ne Puis" were displayed in several places. The house faced south towards Crombie and the River Forth, whilst nearby were several associated buildings and stables. Sir James was President of Torryburn Horticultural Society and a library was available in Craigflower schoolroom on Tuesday evening from 6-7 in 1866 - he became a member of the Judicial Committee in 1871.

Sir James William Colvile of Craigflower (Ochiltree) a member of H.M. Most Honourable Privy Council died at 8 Rutland Gate, Knightsbridge on 6 December 1880. His probate was granted to Eden Colvile of 4 Beaufort Gardens, Richard Strachey of the India Office, Whitehall (major general) and Colin Mackenzie of 28 Castle Street, Edinburgh (writer to the signet) and his estate was initially valued at £80,000 but re-sworn at £90,000. Today, there is a large corner house 2-8 Rutland Gate, which may have been altered, whilst the other houses begin with no. 10. Roland Yorke Bevan brother-in-law of A.F. Kinnaird lived at 9 Rutland Gate in 1887, which was situated immediately opposite. The four-storey property was of brown brick but had a white stucco ground floor, columned entrance and first floor window pediments. William Patrick Adam of Blair Adam, Kinross lived at 27 Rutland Gate and was M.P. for Clackmannan and Kinross in 1859-80 and his son Charles Elphinstone was born at Rutland Gate on 7 August 1859. The father was a privy councillor in 1874-80 and no doubt worked with James William Colvile, then became Governor of Madras in 1880 and died at Ootacamund in 1881. In honour of this his son

Craigflower, Scotland. Colvile and Marindin owned the baronial mansion in the 19th century.

Charles was made a baronet in 1882 and when he died, in 1922, the Blair Adam Estate went to his nephew Charles Keith Adam who married Barbara Eunice Marindin (see below). 27 Rutland Gate is a four-storey, white stucco house with columned entrance and moulded window pediments and is occupied by the Ba'hai Spiritual Association. There is a tree-lined avenue and park at the centre of these houses and all still remain in Knightsbridge - this exclusive street is opposite to Hyde Park.

Eden Colvile was born at Langley Farm on 12 February 1819 and married Anne daughter of Colonel John Maxwell of the 15th Foot on 4 December 1845. He inherited Craigflower in 1880 and also lived at 4 Beaufort Gardens, Knightsbridge - a four-storey grey brick house with white stucco ground floor, columned porch entrance, windows with white surround-pediments, and a roof cornice. He was listed at Craigflower in 1888-89 whilst Torryburn had a population of just 737 and witnessed mining in the late 19th century. Eden Colvile of Craigflower and 42 Beaufort Gardens died in the isolated village of St. Andrew's, Lustleigh in South Devon on 2 April 1893 - his sisters Emily (1889) and Jean (1895) also died there. 42 Beaufort Gardens was opposite no. 4 and had yellow-brown brick, white stucco ground floor and much Classical detail. It is now part of Parkes Hotel and all the Georgian houses remain there with a tree-lined avenue of London planes. The will of Eden Colvile was sealed in London on 8 May 1893 by the confirmation of Francis Arthur Marindin major R.E and Alexander David Martin Black (writer to the signet). He died without issue and by the terms of his father's will his sisters (including Isabella) became co-heirs to the Craigflower estate and thus it passed to the Marindin family.

Craigflower was on the outskirts of Torryburn next to Torry Bay and a large stonewall separated it from nearby cottages, whilst the Causeway went between these abodes down to the bay and a long pier ran out into the water. A track went southeast along the coast with the wall of the estate behind and a wooded bank to the rear. About a half a mile along a steep track turned inland in a cutting and rose up the hill to the old church of Crombie, whilst an ancient bridge passed over this track from the estate directly to the churchyard. The Black Friars of Dunfermline first acquired the lands and chapel of Crombie or Abercrombie in 1153 and it was gifted to Dunfermline Abbey in 1157. It became a parish church at the Reformation and was then used for worship until 1616. The parishes of Torryburn and Crombie were united in 1622 and the old 'kirk' then fell into decay whilst Crombie village was a mile to the east. There are some ancient memorials to the Colvile family (*in Latin*) within the church as well as later ones to Alice (1845), Caroline (1846), Andrew John (1876) and Sir James William (1880). There is also a memorial to Anne wife of Eden Colvile of Ochiltree died 1891, and to her husband who rests at Lustleigh who died on Easter Day 1893. Alison Cunningham was born at Craigflower in 1822 and nursed Robert Louis Stevenson (1850-94) as a child in Edinburgh. He had ill health and could not attend school whilst his father often travelled on engineering business. She became a second mother to him and read from the Bible and Scottish history, thus inspiring him and he later wrote Treasure Island, Kidnapped and Jekyll & Hyde. Alison erected a memorial at Crombie to her parents Robert Cunningham and Alison Hastie his wife.

Samuel and Isabella Marindin first lived at Worfield after their marriage and they had two sons there: Henry Colvile (1834) and Eden (1836). Samuel was then made rector of Buckhorn Weston, Dorset, in early 1837 but lived at Cucklington, Somerset a nearby village. Eden died in July 1837 and the death was registered at Wincanton just after the vital records began in England and Wales. The family were quite affluent and also took a house at Melcombe Regis near Weymouth and their son Francis Arthur was born there in 1838, whilst a son Philip Samuel was born at Cucklington in 1839. Both were baptized at Buckhorn Weston and the father was listed as rector there in 1841. Samuel Marindin a clerk aged 30 lived at Shanks House, Cucklington in 1841 with his wife Isabella, sons Henry (6), Francis (3) and Philip (1), Emily Colvile (20) and six servants. A son George Eden was born in 1841 and baptized at Buckhorn Weston and Samuel Marindin made his last will on 5 February 1842 and left his monies, stocks, funds, securities and personal estate to his dear wife Isabella, her heirs and assigns forever. He appointed his wife, Andrew Colvile of Ochiltree and Crombie and James William Colvile of Ochiltree as executors and guardians of his children. J.H. Lovett-Cameron the vicar of Fleet in Dorset and Eleanor Hobhouse spinster of Hadspen, Somerset were witnesses.

He continued as rector of Buckhorn Weston and was appointed rector of Penselwood, Somerset, in 1845 and was listed for both parishes in 1850-52. These were located on the Dorset-Somerset border, the village of Cucklington being halfway between the two, and provided him with a good living. The couple had four more children born at Cucklington and baptized at Buckhorn Weston namely: Katharine Isabella (1845), Alice Mary (1847), Eleanor Agnes (1848) and Charles Randal (1851). They followed the stereotype of the Victorian upper classes and four sons went to Eton College and then entered the army and Civil Service; indeed they helped form the backbone of the British Empire. Samuel Marindin rector of Buckhorn Weston lived at Shanks House in 1851 with his wife Isabella, children Philip, George, Katharine, Alice and Eleanor, Emily Colvile daughter of an esquire and six servants. The situation was not to last and Samuel Marindin died of gout lasting 7 weeks and exhaustion at Shanks House on 3 January 1852 aged 44, the informant J.W. Eastment of the High Street, Wincanton. His will was proved in London on 17 March 1852 and administration was granted to Andrew Colvile esquire but like grant to Isabella Marindin and Sir James William Colvile. The will was further proved in London on 15 March 1860 by the oath of Isabella Marindin with like grant to Sir James William Colvile - the two surviving executors.

Isabella Marindin had to leave Shanks House in 1852 and possibly moved in with her mother-in-law Eliza at Chesterton, Worfield, however she had certainly inherited the property by 1859 and the house was home to the family for several decades. Isabella a widow and landed proprietor resided at Chesterton in 1861 with George Eden, Charles Randal, three daughters, Jane Colvile fund holder and six servants. The residents included three Wedderburn children: Alice born India in 1853 and twins Francis and Mary born on a P&O steamer in the Mediterranean in 1857. Isabella lived at Chesterton in 1871 with daughters Katharine, Alice and Eleanor, George Eden assistant master at Eton, wife Letitia Frances and four servants. She remained at Chesterton in 1881 with three daughters, daughter-in-law Florence Cecilia a widow, grandson Francis Eden, visitor Constance Julia Davenport (captain's wife), her son Talbot and five servants.

Eleanor Agnes Marindin married Thomas John Franks J.P. of Ballyscaddane, Limerick at Worfield on 29 April 1886, whilst Isabella a landowner lived at Chesterton in 1891 with daughters Katherine and Alice, Florence Cecilia and son Philip H., Charles T. Davenport retired major and four servants. Isabella Marindin died at Chesterton on 4 August 1896 and her executors Francis Arthur Marindin and George Eden Marindin esquires obtained her probate at Shrewsbury on 23 September her effects £6,520 13s 4d. Alice Mary Marindin died at Chesterton on 3 November 1916 and George Eden Marindin attorney of Arthur and Cecil Colvile Marindin obtained her probate in London. Her sister Katharine Isabella Marindin died at Chesterton on 3 June 1923 and probate was granted to Arthur Henry Marindin (colonel commandant), whilst Eleanor Agnes Franks died on 11 March 1933. The rest of the family spent much time in the colonies and especially in India.

Henry Colvile Marindin was born at Worfield on 19 December 1834 and was educated at Eton in 1851-53. He resided at 15th house, Keats Lane, Eton in 1851 and was then a boarder with his brother Francis Arthur. He matriculated at Balliol College, Oxford on 14 March 1853 and gained a 2nd class degree in 1857, then was a barrister at Lincoln's Inn in 1860 with chambers at 3 Brick Court, Temple, London, in 1862 (see E.H. Pember). He married Mary Elizabeth daughter of John Gregory Watkins J.P. of Woodfield on 13 January 1866 and then practiced as a barrister in Calcutta. They had a daughter Mary Isabel at (Fort William) Calcutta on 16 April 1867 however she died a year later, and also had children Arthur Henry and Edith Mary, however the father succumbed like many in India and died of fever at Calcutta on 7 May 1872. Mary Elizabeth his wife later resided at Woodfield, Droitwich but died at 63 Oxford Terrace, Hyde Park on 9 August 1888 and her probate was granted to George Eden Marindin of Hillbrow, East Liss and Francis Arthur Marindin of the Board of Trade, Whitehall.

Arthur Henry Marindin was born on 18 August 1868 and went to Eton College in 1883 then New College, Oxford and Sandhurst. He married Gertrude Florence Evelyn Wilmot-Chetwode on 30 November 1899 and they had children Jean Isalen (1901), Evelyn Rachel (1903), Barbara Eunice (1905) and John Peter Erskine Colvile (1911). The father had a distinguished army career being a lieutenant in the 1st Battalion of the Black Watch (India), the A.D.C. to Sir G. White and attained the rank of lieutenant colonel commander and major general. He served in South Africa and the First War and was awarded the D.S.O (1918) and C.B (1919). He lived at Woodfield, Worcs until 1921 and was the executor of several of the family's wills but then moved to the Fordel estate just north of Glenfarg in Perthshire and may have gone there due to family connections at Craigflower. Daughter Barbara Eunice Marindin married Charles Keith Adam on 28 January 1939 - he being heir to the nearby Blair Adam Estate. The latter was home to the family of famous Scottish architects in the 18th century viz. William Adam and his sons John (who worked on Blair Adam), Robert, James and William. The most famous was Robert Adam (1728-92) who designed notable buildings and interiors i.e. Syon House, Audley End, Osterley Park, Luton Hoo, Kenwood House, The Adelphi, Saltram House and Stowe. Further to this Charles

Keith Adam was descended from his great-great grandmother Eleanora daughter of Charles 10th Lord Elphinstone. This family included William Buller Fullerton-Elphinstone lord in waiting to the Queen 1874-80 and 1885-86, (son) Sidney Herbert married Lady Mary Frances Bowes-Lyon daughter of the 14th Earl of Strathmore and (daughter) Margaret was bridesmaid to Princess Elizabeth 1947 and lady in waiting to the Queen Mother. Thus the Marindins had more notable connections. Arthur Henry Marindin died at Fordel on 28 June 1947 and his death was registered in the Arngask district whilst his will was sealed in London on 28 October 1947 and confirmed by Kenneth Murray writer to the signet and Charles Keith Adam retired captain R.N. The estate passed to his son John Marindin who sold it in 1949.

Philip Samuel Marindin was born Cucklington on 22 November 1839 and baptized at Buckhorn Weston on 5 January 1840. He went to Eton in 1853 and joined the Royal Engineers as a lieutenant on 27 August 1858, and was sent to "Boolundshuhur" or Bulandshahr, Ganges Canal, India in 1869 - 50 miles south east of Delhi. He was promoted engineer 3rd class on 1 March 1869 and captain on 12 May 1869 and married Florence Cecilia Mary daughter of Francis Hartwell Henslowe on 12 January 1870 - she was born in Tasmania in c.1845. They had sons Philip Hugh (1871) and Francis Eden (1876) at Delhi in India however the family returned to England and Philip Samuel Marindin died at 22 Endsleigh Street, Euston on 17 September 1876. The son Philip Hugh was a boarder and scholar at Clewer (Berks) in 1881 and his relative Rev. George Davenport Nicholas was also of Clewer. Francis Eden died at Wilberforce, Sierra Leone on 16 July 1901 and Philip Hugh died on 20 April 1929. Florence Cecilia Mary Marindin resided at Chesterton in 1881-91 and later at 18 Festing Road, Southsea and died in Southsea on 26 October 1929 - her probate was granted to Arthur Henry Marindin retired major general and Kathleen Mary Isabel Marindin.

George Eden Marindin was born at Cucklington on 26 October 1841 and baptized at Buckhorn Weston on 28 November 1841. He attended Eton in 1853-55 and was editor of the "Classical Review" and a fellow of King's College gaining a 1st class degree in the Classics. He married Letitia Frances daughter of George Richard Griffiths in Marylebone on 9 July 1870 - she was born at Sydney, Australia in 1844, and he was an assistant master and classical teacher at Eton in 1865-87. They had daughters Helen Cecil (1872) and Alice Isabel (1873) at Eton and the family lived at Cotton Hall, Eton College in 1881 with student boarders who included viscounts, lords and baronets. His wife Letitia died on 23 March 1925 however George lived a long life and died at the Priory, Frensham, Surrey, on 23 February 1939 aged 96 years.

Charles Randal Marindin was born Cucklington on 5 April 1851 and baptized at Buckhorn Weston on 4 May 1851. He also went to India and worked in the Civil Service and was an assistant magistrate in Bengal and a lieutenant colonel commander in North Bengal. He married Rose Cecil Drummond daughter of the Hon. Louis Jackson, High Court Judge (Calcutta) on 9 December 1876. They had children Cecil Colvile (6 July 1879), Amabel Staveley, Isabel Rose (6 January 1883) and Alice Dolores but his wife died and he then married Edith Alice daughter of Thomas Felix Pennefather Atkinson of the I.C.S. on 14 October 1893. The couple had children Philip Charles (1896), John Francis (1897), Henry Eden Allan (1899), Jocelyn de Vere (1904) and Isalen Dorothea Mercedes whilst the father Charles Randal died on 15 July 1929. Cecil Colvile Marindin (1879) was a lieutenant in the army and received the D.S.O (1918) and the C.B.E (1919) and resided at the Staff Headquarters, Lahore but died Rawalpindi on 22 October 1932. Philip Charles Marindin (1896) was educated at Clifton College and Victoria College, Jersey and had a military career serving in both World Wars. Clearly the family had many foreign connections however those of the F.A. President were to be the most interesting.

Francis Arthur Marindin was born at Melcombe Regis near Weymouth on 1 May 1838 and baptized at Buckhorn Weston on 22 July 1838. He spent his childhood in Cucklington and attended Eton College in 1851-53 being a boarder at 15th house, Keats Lane, Eton, in 1851. This was called "Dames House" and he lived there with other students including Henry his brother, whilst the head was William Evans (51), artist, and member of the 'Society of Painters in Watercolour' - he was introduced to the rigours of early football whilst at Eton. He pursued a career in the army and attended the Royal Military Academy, Woolwich then joined the Royal Engineers as a 2nd lieutenant on 28 December 1854 aged 16 years 7 months. He was promoted to 1st lieutenant on 13 January 1855 and was stationed at Chatham, Portsmouth and Woolwich in January to September 1855. He was then involved in the Crimean War and was posted to Scutari in Turkey from 15 September 1855 to 8 August 1856 a period of 328 days - he may have met Florence Nightingale. He had a months leave when the conflict had ended in August 1856 and was then at Aldershot, Chatham and Pembroke until June 1858, however he soon had a posting that would change his life.

He was stationed on the island of Mauritius in the Indian Ocean from 10 June 1858 to 2 May 1864 a total of 5 years 327 days and was also employed on special duties in Madagascar. He was appointed A.D.C. and private secretary to Sir William Stevenson the Governor in 1860-63 and connections to the Colvile family may have helped secure this eminent position, however he also had a number of qualities that aided his career. During this time he was no doubt introduced to the social life connected with the Governor's residence and soon made a most fortuitous match. He married Kathleen Mary Stevenson daughter of the Governor in Mauritius on 18 July 1860 and Rev. M.C. Adell performed the ceremony. It is not clear whether he received the appointment before or after the marriage - perhaps they went hand in hand. The Stevensons were prominent in Jamaica and Mauritius and strangely, considering the previous discourse, were also involved in the slave trade. They are now discussed since this connection had a considerable influence on the life of F.A. Marindin.

The story begins with John Lawrence who settled in Jamaica in 1675 and his will was proved in 1690. His son John Lawrence was a plantation owner of Ironshore and Running Gut and died in 1736/7 and had sons: John Lawrence (1704) who owned 5,620 acres at Ironshore and Benjamin Lawrence (1706) who owned 4,800 acres at Profitable Valley (Running Gut) - these plantations were in the north west of Jamaica in St. James parish. A third son James Lawrence of Fairfield (1709-56) was a colonel of the St. James Regiment and built Charles Square and the surrounding town later known as Montego Bay. Charles Square was more recently renamed Sam Sharpe Square and now has a fountain surrounded by a stone pavement in the shade of the bauhinia or bull-foot tree and nearby is the remains of the old 'Court House'. This is only second in size to Kingston, the capital, in the south east of the island. James Lawrence married Mary James in 1738 and had seven children from 1740-51 and their descendants play a role in a somewhat complex saga. This was a contentious episode in British history since the profits from these plantations, earned by the slaves, gave these descendants a comfortable lifestyle in England - the story of these plantations, slavery and the resulting income is already well documented.

Richard James Lawrence (4th child) was born in 1745 and was educated at Eton and Oxford and died in 1830 and had a son Charles Lawrence (1776-1853) of Mossley Hall, Liverpool. The latter's son William Frederick Lawrence was born in Liverpool in 1844 and inherited Cowesfield House near Salisbury from his uncle George Lawrence (1775-1861). Mary Lawrence (6th child) was born in 1749 and married John Robert James at St. James Parish, Jamaica on 30 March 1775. They had a daughter Mary Lawrence James at St. James on 22 May 1776 and it was she who married into the Stevenson family (discussed below). James Lawrence (7th child) was born in 1751 and was educated at Eton and St. Mary Hall, Oxford, then married Mary Brissete and had a family at Hazelymph, eight miles from Montego Bay. His daughter Emily Lawrence was born in 1783 and married Doctor Frederick Burt Zincke a gentleman at Hanover Parish in March 1811. The Zincke family also had plantation connections and owned land at Rockspring, Hanover and St. Elizabeth, and resided at Bodle's Pen near to St. Dorothy. Frederick Burt and Emily Zincke had five children viz. Frederick Burt (1813), Harp Lawrence (1815), Foster Barham (1817), William Lawrence (1819) and Mary Lawrence (1820).

William Hudson Lawrence son of James and Mary was born in London on 21 January 1793. A child of that name was baptized at St. Peter's, Cornhill on 29 July 1792 but was illegitimate and his mother Hannah - this again shows the problems faced in this kind of research. He entered the Royal Artillery as an ensign in 1810 and became a lieutenant in 1813 seeing action in the Peninsular War from April 1813 to the end in 1814 and was present at the siege of Tarragona. He became a captain in 1832 but was retired on half pay in 1840 and lived for a time in Corfu marrying a Greek lady. He spent his later years in England and resided with his nephew Rev. Foster Barham Zincke at the Vicarage, Wherstead in Suffolk in 1861 and with his niece Mary Lawrence Zincke at 4 Alma Villas, Charlcombe, Bath, in 1881 and died there on 13 March 1884. Rev. Foster Barham Zincke proved his will in Bristol and his effects were £8,654 15s 4d. Mary Lawrence Zincke had an address Alma Villas, Sion Road, Charlcombe and died on 29 June 1905. Ezekiel Charles Petgrave solicitor, William Frederick Lawrence Esq. and Francis Seymour Stevenson Esq. proved her will at Bristol on 14 August 1905. Major William Hudson Lawrence R.A. 1793-1884 and Mary Lawrence Zincke daughter of Frederick of the Island of Jamaica have a memorial in front of the chapel at Locksbrook Cemetery, Bath.

The Stevenson family, meanwhile, lived in Jamaica probably as plantation owners and William James Stevenson was born there in c.1764 and married Mary Lawrence James at Trelawny Parish, Jamaica on

5 November 1795. The couple had at least seven children viz. Thomas at Trelawny in 1797, William at Hanover on 5 September 1804, John Francis at St. James in 1808, Mary Louisa at St. James in 1810, Isabella at Kingston in 1814 and Kathleen and Arthur. They had moved to Kingston the capital by 1814 and William James Stevenson made his last will there on 24 May 1823. He stated that he had made adequate provision for his wife and continued: "I have from time to time made some little provision for all and every my dear children, according to my narrow means, by the gift of a few Negroes and by investing small sums occasionally for their respective use in the three per cent consolidated funds of the Bank of England and have made some further small provision for them by deed." Such a statement is clearly damning however it related to the period that he lived in and the barbaric practice of slavery was abolished in the Empire in 1833. There was then a move towards more enlightened times and his son made amends of his own (see below), whilst a codicil made his son William an executor on 28 August 1827 as he had now attained full age. William James Stevenson died at Hanover Street, Kingston on 16 April 1830 and Mary Lawrence Stevenson widow and relict a named executor proved his will in London by oath on 8 July 1831. She was probably living in England at this time but other family members remained in Jamaica.

The son William Stevenson married Mary Charlotte Allwood at St. Catherine's Parish near Kingston on 28 October 1839 and had two children baptized there: Kathleen Mary (12 December 1840) and William Lawrence (25 December 1844). William Stevenson was a barrister-at-law and a judge of the Supreme Court on the prison circuit in Jamaica, but his wife Mary Charlotte died after their son's birth and there was soon some match making back in England. Indeed his mother Mary Lawrence Stevenson widow of Cheltenham died at Clifton in March 1850 and her will was proved on 15 April 1850. William Stevenson prison judge from the Isles of Jamaica married Caroline Octavia Biscoe both of Barnwood House at Barnwood, Gloucester on 10 June 1852. Cathleen and Arthur Stevenson, Grattan Biscoe and Frances Stephana Hyett were witnesses. Joseph Seymour Biscoe gent and wife Stephana lived at Bletchingley, Surrey in 1800-09 and Ledbury in 1814-16 whilst their last child Caroline O. was born at Hampstead Court, Gloucester in 1820. The couple returned to Jamaica and a son was born however he died in infancy, whilst the father was soon recognized and received a call from Whitehall.

William Stevenson was appointed Governor and Commander in Chief of the island of Mauritius, hence the family sailed for the east coast of Africa in 1857 and he made a will upon his arrival dated 13 July 1857 however this was later revoked. The island itself was noted for its sugar production in the 1850s and 1860s and the capital, Port Louis, was a supply station for ships sailing to Australia. The new Governor arrived in Mauritius a year after a serious outbreak of cholera, thus he took immediate action and reformed the island's quarantine system and enforced its health laws. He was also moved by the plight of the poor peoples of the island and did much work for the island's youth. He established an orphanage for 200 Indian children, reformed the education system and increased the number of Government schools; and also secured privileges for Mauritian officials that were previously the sole preserve of the British. No doubt he implemented these reforms with the help of Lieutenant Marindin who was his private secretary, and son-in-law, in 1860-63.

There was, however, further tragedy in his personal life and a second infant son died in Mauritius. Indeed William was soon in poor health, himself, and wrote a new will on 11 February 1862 stating that he was residing but not domiciled in Mauritius. His wife Caroline had a personal fortune of £8,000 however he gave her a further £8,000 and provided all expenses for her return to England. He noted that there were no children of this marriage and made provision for his children Kathleen and William stating: "Having already given to my daughter Kathleen, on her marriage, the sum of £2,000 which has been included in her marriage settlement, I now bequeath to her the further sum of £2,000...." He left small bequests to brother Colonel (Thomas) Stevenson and sisters Louisa and Isabella and appointed wife Caroline, (second) cousin Rev. Foster Barham Zincke of Wherstead and son-in-law Francis Arthur Marindin of the Royal Engineers his executors. They were also appointed guardians of his son William until he attained 23 years of age and the will seemed to cover all his affairs. He played a significant role in the history of Mauritius and achieved much in a short space of time, and was knighted for his achievements on 23 July 1862 and was Sir William Stevenson K.C.B (Knight Commander of the Bath).

A new circumstance, however, soon developed and he made a codicil to his will on 9 January 1863 although this date is possibly inaccurate. William Stevenson may have signed the document on his deathbed and he first records that copies of his will were in the hands of his bankers and in his green despatch box. The codicil states: "In case of the birth of a child, now expected by my dear wife, I give to that child the sum of £2,000.... such child if born alive to share my residuary estate with my other children." He then continued: "I direct my wife's household expenses to be paid up to the time of her leaving Mauritius on her return to England, in case she should be detained here on account of her confinement, but I should wish her to leave the country as soon as she can make it convenient to do so. The passage of herself and of any servants she may take with her to be paid, as well as the above mentioned expenses, out of my residuary estate." The reason for this urgency is uncertain however there is a far more serious problem regarding the codicil date. The birth indexes for Mauritius state his son Francis Seymour Stevenson was born at Moka, Mauritius in 1862 and this is confirmed in Kelly's Titled and Landed Gentry (1930). This is a considerable mystery although there can be inaccuracies in the records and the will was written in French and the papers "faithfully" translated into English - thus there was a large amount of supporting paperwork.

Sir William Stevenson died at Moka in Mauritius on 9 January 1863. His will and codicil were deposited at Doctors' Commons on 23 March and Rev. Foster Barham Zincke proved the will by oath in London on 4 April 1863 - the effects £20,000. A memorial to Queen Victoria stands in the courtyard of *Government House* in Port Louis, Mauritius and a statue of Sir William Stevenson is just behind that of the Queen. This was the end of the sojourn abroad and the families of Marindin, Lawrence, Stevenson and Zincke then lived in England - the story however was to remain complex. The Rev. Foster B. Zincke of 15 Montagu Place married Caroline Octavia Stevenson of Milton Bryan in Bedford-shire next to Woburn Abbey at St. Mary's, Bryanston Square in Marylebone on 30 May 1865 - the witnesses included W. Lawrence and F.A. Marindin. This may have been a 'marriage of convenience' or at least ill advised since the parties remained separate and Foster Barham Zincke lived at Wherstead for over 40 years whilst Lady Caroline "Stevenson" kept other addresses.

Foster Barham Zincke was baptized at Hanover, Jamaica on 7 March 1817, son of Frederick Burt Zincke and Emily Lawrence. He was educated at Wadham College, Oxford and gained his B.A. in 1839 and was appointed curate of Andover in 1840 and curate of Wherstead in 1841, the latter being a village just south of Ipswich on the banks of the River Orwell. He was the vicar of Wherstead from 1847 until his death (in 1893) and was appointed chaplain in ordinary to Queen Victoria in 1858. He had little time for his marriage since in addition to his ministry was a traveller and author who wrote and published a number of books (showing his interests). He was a typical Victorian gentleman of academic leaning and prolific in his writings viz. The school of the future 1852, The duty and discipline of extemporary preaching 1867, A winter in the United States 1868, Egypt of the Pharaohs and of the Khedive 1873, A month in Switzerland 1873, Swiss Allmends and a walk to see them 1874, A walk in the Gaissons 1875, The dollar and the plough or the Englishry of a century hence 1883, and Materials for the history of Whenstone 1887. These works went on sale for 5-10 shillings (50 pence) and his publishers were in England and the United States. He kept an address with his wife at 235 Cromwell Mansions, Cromwell Road in 1890 but died at Wherstead on 23 August 1893. His probate went to Francis Seymour Stevenson Esq. and Charles Richard Steward gent his estate being valued at £50,360 14s 7d.

Francis Seymour Stevenson was born at Moka in Mauritius in 1862-63 and was educated at Harrow School from 1875-80 and attended Balliol College, Oxford. He lived as an undergraduate with his mother Lady Caroline Stevenson at "Victoria Villa", Great Malvern in 1881. He gained a B.A. in the Classics (1st class) in 1884 and was M.P. for Eye in northeast Suffolk from 1885-1906 and married Mary K. daughter of Edward Joicey of Blenkinsopp Hall at Gateshead in September 1889. He was a Suffolk J.P. in 1893, on the Parliamentary Charity Commission in 1894-95 and a Church Estates commissioner in 1906. Like his cousin he was an author and published: Robert Grosseliste Bishop of Lincoln, The History of Montenegro, and poems "conflict and quest" etc. His main residence was "Playford Mount" north of Ipswich from 1890-1930 but he also lived at 233 Cromwell Mansions in 1890 and shared 5 Ennismore Gardens, Knightsbridge with mother Lady Caroline Stevenson in 1903 - this was a Classical white stucco house and is present behind Brompton Oratory. Dame Caroline Octavia Stevenson died at Playford Mount on 30 January 1908 and probate went to Walter Hulbert and John Hulbert solicitors. Francis Seymour Stevenson died at 17 Bath Road, Felixstowe on 9 April 1938 and probate went to Edward Christian Barnes major in H.M. army - his estate was worth just £1,022 17s 4d.

Francis Arthur Marindin had married into a very extensive and well connected family and was promoted to 2nd captain on 18 October 1861, and remained in Mauritius with wife Kathleen after her father's death but left the island on 2 May 1864. He was then stationed at Aldershot from July that year and his only child Kathleen Mary Isabel was born at Farnborough, Hampshire on 1 May 1865; he also attended the wedding at Bryanston Square on 30 May 1865. Captain Marindin had some leave in January 1866 and was posted to Chatham on 1 February and made adjutant on 1 May 1866. He then played for the Engineers soccer team and was promoted to 1st captain on 22 January 1868 and spent a year in Devonport from 15 February 1868. He was posted to the School of Military Engineering, Brompton Barracks, Chatham, on 29 August 1869 and appointed Brigade Major on 1 September that year, and indeed remained at Chatham for 5 years 75 days - a posting that changed his life and the course of soccer history.

Sir Francis Arthur Marindin (1838-1900).
Royal Engineers 1854-79 and F.A. President in 1874-90.

The School of Military Engineering was formed in 1812 after a request from the Duke of Wellington and was the premier centre for engineering advance since there were no technical colleges outside the army. Over 60 years it gained a reputation for the physical and mental fitness of its officers and the Royal Engineers were soon famous for their technical ability and sporting prowess. Capt. Francis Fowke and Col. H.Y. Darracott Scott designed the Royal Albert Hall in brick, terracotta and steel using the blueprint of an ancient amphitheatre. The Royal Engineers constructed the hall from 1867-71 and developed the 'steam sapper' a traction engine that could pull trains of vehicles across the country. Major Marindin was at the forefront of these army manoeuvres and the progress of the football team, thus he developed the side that had joined the F.A. in 1863 (some say in 1869). He had a bond with his fellow officers, and the discipline and team spirit used in their work was transferred to the sports field. He had a strong football team that was extremely proficient in the game and they were also good at cricket.

Major Marindin lived at the S.M.E. Brompton Barracks in April 1871 with wife Kathleen, his daughter, a cook, parlour maid and nurse - he was an officer and a gentleman. He was a member of the F.A. Committee from 1871 and was present at the Sportsman Office on 20 July that year when the F.A. Cup competition was started by a 'unanimous' vote. He captained the Royal Engineers in the first Cup Final on 16 March 1872 although they lost 1-0 to the Wanderers. He was promoted to the full rank of major on 5 July 1872 and captained the team again in the Final on 14 March 1874 but they lost 2-0 to Oxford University. He had continued as a member of the F.A. Committee thus he was appointed President in 1874, but left Brompton Barracks on 12 November 1874 and after two weeks at Pembroke Docks arrived at Colchester later that month; he was appointed to the Eastern District, Harwich in 1875. He was then less active on the pitch but sometimes played in goal for the Old Etonians, being President of the club. He ran the line in the fourth international England v Scotland at the Oval on 6 March 1875, and Charles Alcock his colleague was captain of England. The Royal Engineers, meanwhile, had entered the Cup that season and reached the Final at the Oval on 13 March 1875, their opponents being the Old Etonians. The records state that Major Marindin watched the game from the sidelines due to a conflict of interest and thus avoided any embarrassment. It was quoted as an example of the high ideals of a Victorian gentleman, however as stated the 'Major' was in fact at Harwich at the time and unable to play. The Royal Engineers won the replay 2-0 on 16 March and this was their greatest achievement.

The army role of Major Marindin was then reduced and he was an Inspector of Railways at the Board of Trade from June 1877 to October 1879 - a duty he continued after leaving the army. He was on the temporary and reserve list at the time and retired from the army on 29 October 1879, age 41, and received a gratuity of £2,000 after 24 years 314 days service. He remained President of the F.A. and his main role on the pitch was as a referee, and he carried out this duty in the Cup Final between Clapham Rovers and Oxford University in 1880. He devoted the rest of his time to the Board of Trade his duties being: "To examine the permanent way, bridges, stations, and signals of *many* new railways and branch lines, and *subsequently* to hold inquiries on a number of accidents." His address was 5 New Street, Spring Gardens

22 Sussex Villas, Kensington.
Marindin lived here in 1882-96.

next to Trafalgar Square in 1881 (later covered by Admiralty Arch) but this was in fact his office. Francis Arthur Marindin a retired major now Inspector of Railways and wife Kathleen were visiting James Fellowes a major R.E. at New Friars, St. Nicholas's, Rochester in 1881 - their daughter may have been abroad.

Major Marindin took a permanent home at 22 Sussex Villas, Kensington from 1882 (to 1896) and made an important soccer contribution from this address. The street began life as Sussex Place and ran between Victoria Grove and Cornwall Gardens and was near to Gloucester Road. No. 22 was the last house on the west side next to Kynance Mews, being a semi-detached property with the largest garden in the street - but still somewhat limited in extent. The house, a brown brick villa with white stucco façade at the front and side, was built in the 1840s and was the largest in the street with two main storeys, a flight of steps up to a double door, a small ironwork balcony around the front window, curved side extension on two floors, a small round domed-tower above, and first floor balcony to the side (rear). The street was renamed Launceston Place in June 1905 and no. 22 is still present being a fine Victorian house with exotic plants and topiary. Not much has changed since Victorian days and the properties are now Grade II listed buildings in the *De Vere Conservation Area*.

Major Marindin led the F.A. through some difficult times and on the pitch was held in high regard being described as: "One of the very few referees who really know all the rules." He refereed the Cup Final between Blackburn Rovers and Queen's Park in 1884, and 'reputedly' cost the Scottish club victory when he disallowed two goals - he understood the offside rule better than the Scottish team! He guided the F.A. through the arrival of professionalism in 1885 and was referee for the Finals at the Oval in 1885, 1886 (replay at the Racecourse Ground, Derby) and 1887. He was on the reserve of officers in the 1880s and made his last will at 22 Sussex Villas on 8 May 1887 leaving all of his estate to Kathleen his wife whilst Eden Colvile of Craigflower and Thomas Jessop of Honley near Huddersfield were witnesses. He rendered important services to the Egyptian State Railway at this time and was thus made C.M.G. in 1887. He was referee at the Cup Final in 1888 and was involved when the League started later that year, then refereed the Final of 1889 (when Preston achieved the double) - his contact address was Board of Trade, Whitehall. He refereed the Final between Blackburn Rovers and the Wednesday at the Oval in front of 20,000 in 1890 although this was his last game. In total he officiated at nine Cup Finals but was an ardent supporter of the amateur game and could not adjust to the changes made by professional soccer - he resigned his F.A. position in 1890.

He then had a more serious role as Inspector of Railways and reported on an incident where a guard was crushed between two wagons in 1891. He discovered that many employees were over-worked and in this instance the man was in a state of physical collapse after a 22-hour stretch. He submitted a strongly worded report that led to a select committee in the House of Commons and an improvement in working conditions for railway servants. Despite these efforts there was a serious disaster at Thirsk on 2 November 1892 when two trains collided head-on in fog due to a signal fault, and it was later found that the signalman had been working 24 hours. Major Marindin declared that it was the duty of all railway companies to use mechanical and electrical appliances to make such an accident impossible, unless the driver went past fixed signals. He also encouraged the use of relief signalmen and provision of housing nearby. By plain speaking and a complete mastery of the subject he implemented several railway reforms and made the companies aware that: "The office at 8 Richmond Terrace Whitehall was not likely to allow irregularities to remain long unnoticed."

He became associated with Scotland in the 1890s and gave his contact address as Craigflower in 1892. Eden Colvile his uncle died in 1893 and he was increasingly involved with the estate and inherited Craigflower when his mother died on 4 August 1896 - she being co-heir under the will of Andrew Colvile. He established an electric lighting system in London and was appointed to the Engineer and Railway Voluntary Staff Corps on 2 January 1897, which was composed entirely of high officials connected with the railways and its administration. He became a lieutenant colonel and honorary colonel on 26 January, and was honoured for public services at home and abroad (but not India) being knighted in the Diamond Jubilee celebrations of Queen Victoria on 22 June 1897. He was then Knight Commander of St. Michael and St. George (K.C.M.G.) and appeared in Kelly's Landed Gentry in 1890-1900. He lived at 3 Hans Crescent, Knightsbridge (formerly Exeter and New Street) in 1897, part of an opulent "city mansion" on the corner with Basil Street - behind Harrods and occupied by two embassies. Francis Arthur Marindin died at 3 Hans Crescent on 21 April 1900 and his obituary was in the Times on Tuesday 24 April. His funeral was at Crombie old churchyard near Craigflower on Thursday 26 April but there was a memorial service at Holy Trinity, Sloane Street at the same time. Mourners attending the latter included the Board of Trade, major generals, Col. and Miss Fitzroy Somerset, Mr. Charles E. Hart for the F.A. and Mr. C.W. Alcock, Secretary of Surrey C.C. Dame Kathleen Mary Marindin obtained his probate on 5 June the estate worth £7,075 15s.

Lady Marindin then resided at 3 Sloane Court East just behind the Royal Hospital, Chelsea a building with eleven flats. She lived there with her daughter Kathleen and two servants in 1901 and remained at this address for the rest of her life. But what had become of Craigflower? It stayed in the family's possession in the early 20th century but may have been rented out and Thomas D. Boyd was living there in 1914, however it was then sold, and F.G. Wailes founded Craigflower Prep School in the house in 1923. Lady Marindin of 3 Sloane Square East died at Kent Lodge, Westgate on Sea, Kent, on 16 February 1939 and Kathleen Mary Isabel Marindin obtained her probate. The latter stayed unmarried and was said to be of Craigflower, Fife but died at Holcombe End, Painswick near Gloucester on 23 February 1945. She may have been allowed to live in the house despite the school. Her probate was confirmed in Scotland and granted to Arthur Henry Marindin C.B. D.S.O. and John Peter Erskine Colvile Marindin. The school was a charitable trust and made an appeal for £55-80,000 to do essential improvements in 1969 however finally closed its doors in December 1979. Craigflower became a listed building and after years of neglect was recently restored as luxury flats, and is most impressive with a good location. It is at the end of Rose Lane and there are also historic outbuildings and cottages nearby. Crombie old church did not fare so well and suffered neglect especially after the estates demise. Sir Francis A. Marindin K.C.M.G. 1838-1900, wife Kathleen Mary 1840-1939 and their daughter appear on the memorial to Eden Colvile within the church. Major Marindin was a most important figure in soccer history yet the memorial is long forgotten and sadly damaged.

LORD ARTHUR FITZGERALD KINNAIRD

The baton of office passed to 'Alfred' Kinnaird who was a notable player like his predecessor and was a great character within the game, but came from a higher level of society being a Scottish Lord. His antecedents are traced to Radalphus Rufus who was given a charter to the Barony of Kinnaird in the Carse of Gowrie, Perthshire by William the Lion, King of Scotland (1165-1214). The family obtained the nearby lands of Inchture, Perth in 1396 when Reginald de Kinnaird married Margaret the heiress of Sir John Kirkcaldy of Inchture. They had a coat of arms and motto "Patitur Qui Vincit" or "Qui Patitur Vincit" viz. "He conquers who endures". Kinnaird Castle was in the Carse of Gowrie on the way from Perth to Dundee but was eventually sold and they resided at Moncur Castle, Inchture in the late 16th century. This was an area of fertile lowland on the banks of the River Dee and was later used for strawberry growing. George Patrick Kinnaird son of Patrick of Inchture backed the Royalists in the English Civil War (1642-49) and supported claims of Charles II, being made a representative for Perth at the request of the noblemen and gentlemen of the county. He met General Monck the commander of the Republics army in Scotland at Edinburgh and Berwick in 1659 and put forward his concerns regarding the welfare of his country. The General helped secure the restoration of Charles II in 1660 whilst George Kinnaird was knighted in 1661. He represented Perth in the Scottish Parliament of 1662-63 and was raised to the peerage as 1st Lord Kinnaird of Inchture in 1682, but died in 1689.

George Kinnaird (7th Lord) was born at Dundee in 1752 and attended Pembroke College, Cambridge in November 1769. He was a banker in London and had notable connections in the Whig party and married Elizabeth Ransom at St. George's Hanover Square on 22 July 1777. Her father Griffin Ransom was a banker of New Palace Yard, Westminster now part of the precincts of the Houses of Parliament. The match was important to the Kinnaird family and the banking connections lasted until the 20th century. George was a representative peer in 1787-90 whilst Moncur Castle became a ruin and the family resided at Drimmie House north of Inchture in the 18th century. George Kinnaird and William Morland two of the partners formed the Dundee New Bank in 1802 - the London agents Ransom and Morland. Meanwhile he had six sons and two had a prominent role in society. Charles Kinnaird was born on 12 April 1780 and was educated at Eton and Edinburgh and Glasgow Universities. He was admitted to Trinity College, Cambridge on 19 May 1798, entered Lincoln's Inn in 1799, and matriculated in Easter 1800 receiving an M.A. that year. He developed refined tastes and was introduced to politics at a young age through his father's links with the Whig party and represented Leominster in the House of Commons in 1802-05. He became 8th Lord when his father died at Perth on 11 October 1805 whilst his mother died at Ballindean on 21 inst. He married Lady Olivia Letitia Catherine Fitzgerald (born 9 September 1787) daughter of 2nd Duke of Leinster at Marylebone on 8 May 1806, and was a representative peer for Scotland in 1806-07.

Drimmie House became unfashionable at the start of the 19th century and Charles began building a new home further up the hillside and away from the main road. The old village of Rossie was situated within the parkland of the estate and was half a mile from the new house, however it was too near for Charles and he had the buildings demolished and the villagers moved to a new location a mile to the west - Baledgarno was the name of the new village and the name came from Edgar son of Malcolm who once had a castle there. Meanwhile, only the village cross and church were left untouched and the latter became the Kinnaird family burial chapel - it had a Celtic cross-slab within. The new house Rossie Priory was started in 1807 and was a long low building with red ashlar stone at the front and sides, and a chapel at the centre. It had a commanding position on the hillside facing the river and was the family home for nearly 200 years. Charles had five children: George William Fox (1807), Olivia Cecilia Laura (1808), Frederica Eliza (1810), Graham Hay St. Vincent de Ros (1811) and Arthur Fitzgerald (1814). He spent much time on the Continent and secured many works that became available in the Napoleonic Wars, and had a large picture gallery at Rossie viz. works by Gainsborough and a portrait of Sheridan by Sir Joshua Reynolds. He died at Regency Square, Brighton on 12 December 1826 whilst son Graham (lieutenant R.N.) died on 14 April 1838 and Lady Olivia at Bath on 28 February 1858.

Douglas James Kinnaird, his brother, was born on 26 February 1788 and educated at Eton and Göttingen in Germany. He was admitted to Trinity, Cambridge on 21 April 1807 and Lincoln's Inn (that year) gaining his M.A. in 1811. He travelled on the Continent and was present at the Battle of Culm in 1813 but returned home from Paris in 1814 and took an active share in the Ransom and Morland Bank who then traded at Pall Mall (the will of brother Frederick John Hay of Pall Mall was proved in 1815). He had considerable literary connections and his friend Lord Byron held him in high esteem and called him: "My trusty and trustworthy trustee and banker and crown and sheet anchor." He was a friend of John Cam Hobhouse and Sheridan and joined a committee to direct the affairs of the Drury Lane Theatre in 1815, when there was much gossip about the institution and especially the role of playwright Sheridan. The committee included Lord Byron, George Lamb and Samuel Whitbread and the scandal that ensued is discussed later (Ch. 6 & 7). Douglas, meanwhile, liked to cause a stir and although he promoted the works of Lord Byron was less complimentary regarding Coleridge. The poet once read him two acts but he became bored and stated: "He had listened to enough of this nonsense," and asked the poet to hear, "A little two piece act of his own." He was also involved in politics and represented Bishop's Castle, Salop in 1819-20 and made his maiden speech on 30 November 1819. This supported Lord Althorp's motion for a select committee on *The State of the Nation* (much needed)! The partnership with Sir F.B. Morland dissolved and Douglas became chief manager of the new firm Ransom & Co. at 34 Pall Mall in 1819 and then at 1 Pall Mall East in 1829. Morland & Co. was at 57 Pall Mall (1819) and at 50 Pall Mall (1829) and Bouverie, Hon. P. Pleydell and H.S. Lefevre at 35 Craven Street, Strand (1829). Douglas was unmarried and died at 2 Pall Mall East, London on 12 March 1830 - an important address re the next generation.

George William Fox Kinnaird was born at Drimmie House on 14 April 1807 and was educated at Eton before entering the army. He became the 9th Lord Kinnaird at the decease of his father in 1826 and Baron Rossie of Rossie on the recommendation of Earl Grey in 1831. The title was in recognition of the service given by his father and grandfather to the Whig party but was exchanged for Baron Kinnaird of Rossie (in 1860). George spent much of his youth in Italy and conducted important excavations near Rome and brought back Roman antiquities to Rossie Priory, and these were added to his father's collection of art. He was a Victorian gentleman of boundless energy and was involved in every aspect of the Victorian scene (see below).

John Spencer was born on 13 May 1708 and he inherited the family estates in Beds, Northants (Althorp) and Warwicks and the property of Sarah Duchess of Marlborough his grandmother, including the newly built Wimbledon Park, in 1733-34. N.B. The Spencers purchased Althorp in 1508. His son John Spencer was born on 19 December 1734 and became a Whig politician and married the ambitious Margaret Georgiana daughter of Stephen Poyntz on 20 December 1755 and had three children: George John (1758), Georgiana and Henrietta Frances. He was a Whig M.P. for Warwick in 1756-61 and created 1st Earl Spencer and Viscount Althorp on 1 November 1765. He died on 31 October 1783 and his son George (2nd Earl) was a Whig M.P. in 1780-83, Lord of the Treasury 1782, Lord Privy Seal 1794, First Lord of the Admiralty 1794-1801 and Home Secretary 1806-07. He also built up the library at Althorp as the 'most splendid' in Europe. John Charles Spencer (1782) the 3rd Earl succeeded him and was a Whig M.P. for Okehampton 1804-06, Northants 1806-34 and also Chancellor of the Exchequer in 1830-34.

Daughter Georgiana married the 5th Duke of Devonshire on 5 June 1774 and Devonshire House then became a centre for Whig politics. This was a large property between Berkeley Street and Stratton Street, being set back from Piccadilly with a sweeping drive. There was a substantial garden to the north reaching as far as Lansdowne Row and beyond was Lansdowne House and the south side of Berkeley Square. Charles Fox and other ambitious politicians made it a base of political intrigue, gambling and secret liaisons. Henrietta Frances married Frederick Ponsonby (3rd Earl of Bessborough) on 27 November 1780 and had children: John William (1781) the 4th Earl, Frederick Cavendish (1783) Governor of Malta, Caroline (1785) and William Francis Spencer (31 July 1787) - Indeed William the 2nd Earl had married Lady Caroline Cavendish daughter of the 3rd Duke of Devonshire. Frederick received his title in 1793, whilst daughter Caroline was educated and raised at Devonshire House by her aunt Georgiana, and thus moved in the Whig social circles from a young age.

Peniston Lamb a Whig more interested in the vices of the social scene and his wife Elizabeth Milbanke lived at Melbourne House near Derby. His son William Lamb (1779-1848) married Caroline Ponsonby at St. Marylebone on 3 June 1805, and in the same year was heir (at his brother's decease) and entered Parliament as a Whig for Leominster. Lord Byron (1788-1824) also a Whig politician made his first speech regarding the Luddites in 1812 and had a four-month affair with Lady Caroline Lamb soon after. She stated that the poet was "mad, bad, and dangerous to know." This was the main subject of conversation in and out of social circles and Caroline, to her husband's consternation, pursued Byron for the next four years. In fact Byron married Anne Isabella Milbanke (a relative of his lover) on 2 January 1815 and Caroline became separated from her husband in 1825, and died in 1828. William Lamb was the Secretary for Ireland under Lord Canning (Conservative) in 1827-28 but became Lord Melbourne when his father died in 1828. He was then a Whig Prime Minister in 1834 with Lord Althorp as his Chancellor, and also in 1835-41 when he was a close *confidante* of a young Queen Victoria. Indeed the Australian city was named after him in 1835.

The brothers of Caroline were also of interest and Frederick Cavendish Ponsonby was a soldier who fought with distinction at Talavera, Salamanca and Vitoria in the Peninsular War. He was promoted to major general and wounded at Waterloo, and was Governor of Malta in 1826-35 but died in 1837. A large monument to his memory was erected on a high point of the fortifications in the northwest corner of Valletta. This had a Classical base with a large column above that could be seen for miles around and was a landmark on the island, with inscription: "Frederico Cavendish Ponsonby Melitae an. IX praefecto CIVIVM amor MDCCCXXXVIII (1838)," but today only the base survives and it also states: "The column 70 feet high erected on this base to the memory of Sir Frederick Ponsonby was destroyed by lightning in January 1864." The column was next to Hastings Gardens and nearby was Triq L-Inġinieri or Sappers Street. Sir Henry Frederick Ponsonby his son (1825-95) served in the Crimea and was private secretary to Queen Victoria until shortly before his death.

William Francis Spencer Ponsonby married Barbara Ashley-Cooper on 8 August 1814 who was co-heir of the ancient Barony of Mauley. They had two sons and a daughter Frances Anna Georgiana at Roehampton on 28 July 1817 (Caroline Lamb was her aunt). The Kinnairds as well as being politicians and bankers moved in the Whig social circles thus George William Fox Lord Kinnaird married Frances Anna

Ponsonby Memorial. He was the Governor of Malta in 1826-35.

Georgiana Ponsonby at Inchture, Perth on 14 December 1837. Her father William was created the 1st Baron de Mauley of Canford, Dorset on 10 July 1838. Both Ponsonby and Spencer were intimately associated with the Royal family and had duties of equerry and maid of honour to Queen Victoria. This continued throughout the 20th century and Lady Diana Frances Spencer (1 July 1961) was great-great-great-great granddaughter of the 1st Earl Spencer (wife of Prince Charles). The Kinnairds were associated with the Spencer family through the Whig party and the marriage secured an important connection - indeed the F.A. President was connected to the Royal family.

George Kinnaird had property at 5 'Mansion House' Albany, Piccadilly in 1829-30 and 1 Pall Mall East in 1841, whilst Lady Kinnaird his mother lived at 28 Upper Grosvenor Street in 1829-41. He had three children that died before him: Victor Alexander (1840-51), Charles Fox (1841-60), and also Olivia Barbara who married Howard Reginald Alexander Ogilvy in 1859 (10th Bart.) and died in 1871. George held a number of official Government posts and as a Whig politician in the Lords, he had considerable influence. He helped establish industrial schools throughout the country and worked for the rehabilitation of offenders as well as introducing much legislation viz. "the closing of public houses on a Sunday, the abatement of the smoke nuisance, the reform of the mint and the regulation of mines." He had close connections with free trade and supported the Anti-Corn Law League formed in Manchester in 1839. They opposed the Corn Laws on the basis that they kept prices high, restricted foreign trade and caused all kinds of social ills, and held mass meetings around the country with speeches by famous orators such as Richard Cobden and John Bright. In fact George Kinnaird was friends with both of them and thus presided at a large meeting of the League at Covent Garden Theatre. The situation came to a head with the Irish potato famine and a bad corn harvest in England, in 1845, thus Sir Robert Peel was forced to repeal the Corn Laws.

He also spent much time in the company of Mr. Fox Talbot and aided in the development of photography. Indeed D. Brewster sent a letter to W.H. Fox Talbot on 6 November 1847 and stated: "I beg to thank you for the nice little packet of Talbotypes which you sent me by post.... I expect to be at Rossie Priory in December when Lord de Mauley (father-in-law) pays his annual visit there, and I shall then deliver your remembrances. Lady Kinnaird is one of the most accomplished and interesting persons I have ever met with. She is universally worshipped; and there are few if any of our nobility who take such an interest as Lord Kinnaird does in the advancement of every benevolent and useful institution.... The Talbotype from the oil painting is singularly fine. The original cannot be more expressive of the scene." **Note** A process developed by W.H. Fox Talbot in 1840. Lord Kinnaird also had an extensive geological collection through the guidance of Sir Charles Lyell. He lived at 33 Grosvenor Street, London and Rossie Priory in 1851 and spent much time on his Scottish estate whilst his father-in-law Lord de Mauley died on 16 May 1855. He was a large landowner in the Carse of Gowrie and at the forefront of agricultural reform hence the first use of steam-ploughs and threshing machines (in Scotland) took place on his land. He was a noted philanthropist who organised evening schools for his ploughman and opened free reading rooms and libraries on his estate. He promoted the building of the East of Scotland Railway from Perth to Dundee, and since it was built across his land supervised much of the construction. He died at Rossie Priory on 8 January 1878 (without issue). Lady Frances A.G. Kinnaird died at the Knapp, Inchture on 20

March 1910 (in Longforgan) and the Right Hon. William Ashley Webb Ponsonby 3rd Baron de Mauley and Herbert Kinnaird Ogilvy writer to the signet confirmed and sealed her will in London.

Arthur Fitzgerald Kinnaird, his brother, inherited the title and estates and was the 10th Lord Kinnaird. He was born at Rossie Priory on 8 July 1814 and baptized Arthur Wellesley after his godfather the Duke of Wellington, however his father Charles became unhappy with the Duke's politics and changed the name to Arthur Fitzgerald. He went to Eton College in 1829 and was appointed to the Foreign Office, thus he was attached to the British Embassy at St. Petersburg from July 1835 to September 1837, and was private secretary to the Earl of Durham, Ambassador. He returned to Britain in 1837 and became a partner in the banking house of Ransom & Co. at Pall Mall East, London, and succeeded his uncle Douglas Kinnaird in the position. He was eventually the head of the banking firm however, like his brother George, his main interests were elsewhere and he was a tireless philanthropist. He was a member of the Whig-Liberal Party and represented Perth in the House of Commons from 1837-39: Lord Melbourne was Prime Minister. He lived at 5 Albany, Piccadilly in 1841 and married Mary Jane Hoare at Hornsey on 28 June 1843.

His wife had a notable although somewhat complex history. Gerard Noel Edwards son of Gerard Anne and Jane (Noel) was born at Tickencote, Rutland on 17 Jul 1759. Meanwhile Admiral Sir Charles Middleton (1726-1813) married Margaret Gambler and became 1st Baron Barham of *Barham Court* and left a sum of £10,000 to each of his 14 grandchildren. Gerard Noel Edwards married Diana Middleton (1762), the daughter Baroness Barham, at St. George's Hanover Square on 20 December 1780 and had several children viz. Charles Noel (1781), Louisa Elizabeth (1784) and Baptist Wriothesley (1798). Indeed the father inherited Exton Park, Rutland and changed his name to Gerard Noel Noel by *Royal Licence* on 5 May 1798. His wife Diana died in 1823 and was buried at Teston whilst Gerard died at Exton in 1838. Charles Noel was born 2 October 1781 and married his third wife Arabella Williams on 29 June 1820. He became the 3rd Baron Barham of *Barham Court* and Teston, Kent in 1823 and was made 1st Earl of Gainsborough on 16 August 1841. His daughter Lady Mary Arabella Louisa Noel (1822) married Sir Andrew Agnew 8th Bart of Lochnaw, Wigtown on 20 August 1846 - two of their children were born at Exton: son Andrew Noel (1850) and daughter Mary Alma Victoria (1854) who is treated below.

William Henry son of Henry Hoare and Lydia H. Malortie was born on 2 March 1776 and became a member of the banking family. He married Louisa Elizabeth Noel (1784) at Teston, Kent on 10 February 1807 and had five children at Kent, Battersea and Clapham in 1807-14, however Mary Jane Hoare was born at Blatherwyke Park, Northampton-shire on 14 March 1816. Her mother died soon after on 6 April whilst Mary Jane was baptized at Blatherwyke Church on 2 August. Her father William Henry was a London banker of the Grove, Mitcham however Mary Jane spent her early years with Rev. Baptist W. Noel of Hornsey (her uncle). He married Jane Baillie at Richmond on 17 October 1826 and his son Wriothesley Baptist (1827) went to Trinity, Cambridge and was a judge of the Supreme Court, Melbourne from 1854. She had a privileged childhood and was (later) the niece of the Earl of Gainsborough, but was a noted philanthropist and began such work before her marriage, forming the St. John's Training School for Domestic Servants in 1841 - with a successful branch in Brighton. As stated, she married A.F. Kinnaird in 1843.

35 Hyde Park Gardens.
A.F. Kinnaird was born here 16 February 1847.

The couple first resided at 35 Hyde Park Gardens, Paddington opposite Victoria Gate and owned by William Crake (see Ch. 7). The 'Gardens' consisted of two terraces of white stucco housing with one parallel to the road and the other located at an angle of 45°. Despite being built as terraces, these houses were Classical mansions with a desirable location and front gardens looking out across Hyde Park. The terrace parallel to the road was numbered 1-24 and the houses entered at the rear along Hyde Park Gardens Mews. The terrace at 45° to the road was numbered 25-38, however these are now 25-31, and the seven properties with their large columned porch entrances were originally divided into fourteen residences (or so it appears). The Kinnairds lived at the west end of Hyde Park Gardens on the north side of Hyde Park and the property can still be seen today. The couple then had five children: Frederica Georgiana (1845), Mary Louisa Olivia (1846) *infant*, Arthur Fitzgerald (1847), Louisa Elizabeth (1848) and Agneta Olivia (1850) all baptized at St. James's Paddington (nearby) - the mother continued her good work editing "Servants Prayers" in 1848. Arthur F. Kinnaird banker and baron's (eldest) son lived at 35 Hyde Park Gardens in 1851 with his wife Mary J., children Frederica, Arthur F. (4), Louisa, Agneta and 9 servants. He was re-elected to Parliament for Perth in 1852 and had two children at 35 Hyde Park Gardens: Gertrude Mary (1854) and Emily Cecilia (1855) both baptized at St. James's, Paddington. His wife had an association with Lady Canning and helped send nurses and aid to the wounded in Crimea in 1854-56.

He continued to represent Perth constituency until he became Lord Kinnaird and the Whig-Liberals were in power for much of this time thus he sat in Parliament under Lord Palmerston (1855-58, 1859-65), Lord Russell (1865-66) and Gladstone (1868-74). He spoke frequently on Indian matters in the House of Commons having a special knowledge of the subject, and was involved in all areas concerning the well being of the working classes. He had a special interest in the social emancipation of women, labouring on their behalf as regards homes, refuges and reformatories. He had special links with a number of institutions including the Church Missionary Society, Malta Protestant College, Lock Hospital, Dr. Barnardo's Homes, London City Mission and Aged Christian's Society. Indeed he ranked in zeal with Lord Shaftesbury and was always found at *Exeter Hall* and the 'May meetings'. He was also a fellow of the R.G.S. and a local J.P.

Ransom & Co. was at 1 Pall Mall East beside Trafalgar Square in 1851 when the partners were John Squire, Richard Williams, Frederick Squire and Hon. Arthur Kinnaird. There was then a merger and Ransom, Bouverie & Co. was at 1 Pall Mall East in 1862, whilst the Kinnairds resided at 2 Pall Mall East by c.1860. They held meetings for philanthropic and religious purposes at this address, whilst Mary founded some charitable organisations including the British Ladies' Female Emigration Society, Foreign Evangelisation Society, Calvin Memorial Hall - Geneva, Union for Prayer, Zenana Bible and Medical Mission and Young Women's Christian Association. They also had properties outside of London namely West Farm, East Barnet in 1862, Pickhurst Manor, Hayes in 1865-71 and Plaistow Lodge, Bromley from c.1874. The latter was a palatial mansion near Plaistow hamlet north of Bromley, and had extensive grounds with a long sweeping drive. The main building had a white stone ground floor, portico entrance, brown-brick at the first floor, and several columns adorning the façade. There were Classical pediments plus scrolls at the roofline, whilst the two sides had a wing and conservatory with niche statues.

Frederica Georgiana married Alfred Orlando Jones M.D. on 27 December 1870 and Agneta Olivia married Roland Yorke Bevan of Fosbury, Wilts at St. Martin in the Fields on 7 January 1874, whilst son Arthur married in 1875 (see below). Their father Arthur Kinnaird became 10th Lord when his brother died on 7 January 1878 whilst the Barony of Rossie became extinct. He was then owner of the Rossie Priory estate as well as the properties in and near London. Arthur F. Kinnaird a baron banker lived at 1-2 Pall Mall East in 1881 with his wife Mary Jane, daughters Louisa, Gertrude and Emily, grandchildren Graham Kinnaird Jones and Arthur M. Jones and fourteen servants. Arthur Fitzgerald Kinnaird of Pall Mall East and Rossie Priory, Inchture died at Pall Mall on 26 April 1887 and Arthur Fitzgerald Kinnaird of 50 South Audley Street and Roland Yorke Bevan of 9 Rutland Gate were granted probate of his will and five codicils on 1 July 1887. His personal estate in the U.K. was valued at £255,166 0s 4d but re-sworn in January 1890 at £257,235 17s 4d. It was a substantial sum and much greater than those already discussed but some even larger fortunes are revealed later. The estate and title went to his son although his five daughters were alive, whilst Mary Jane Kinnaird died soon after at Plaistow Lodge on 1 December 1888.

Arthur Fitzgerald Kinnaird was born at 35 Hyde Park Gardens on 16 February 1847 and baptized at St. James's, Paddington on 31 March that year. He grew up with his family at Hyde Park and attended Cheam Preparatory School in the late 1850s. His family moved to Pall Mall East and he was in the fifth form at Eton in 1862, but must have visited Barnet, Hayes and Rossie Priory in the holidays - he won the 350 yards race at Eton in 1864. He was admitted to Trinity College, Cambridge on 11 June 1864 and matriculated in Michaelmas 1865 but needed to find a new outlet as his family were consumed with philanthropy and the arts - he found this in sport. He had played soccer at Eton with Bonsor, Lubbock and Thompson and had "football fever" thus he formed the Old Etonians as an undergraduate in 1867. He won the 50-yard, 100-yard and half-mile swim at Cambridge in 1867, won the fives at Cambridge in 1867/68 and won the lawn tennis singles for Cambridge v Oxford in 1868/69. He gained his B.A. in 1869 (and M.A. in 1873) and then worked with his father at Ransom & Co. but clearly had time for sport. He was known as 'Alfred' Kinnaird in soccer circles and was a top early player, being noted for his skill in 'all' positions. He played for the Wanderers and the Old Etonians and was a member of the F.A. Committee in 1869. His talent was soon recognized and he captained Scotland v England in an unofficial match at the Oval in 1870. He did not play in the first Cup Final but made his mark the next year and eventually appeared in nine Finals. Charles Alcock wrote about him in the Football Annual of 1873 stating: "He was without exception the best player of the day, capable of taking any place in the field, is very fast and never loses sight of the ball, an excellent captain."

Lord Arthur Fitzgerald Kinnaird (1847-1923). He was F.A. President from 1890-1923.

He played for Scotland in a full international at the Oval on 8 March 1873 although England had a 4-2 victory, and appeared for the Wanderers in the Cup Final at Lillie Bridge on 29 March 1873. The team included five players from the first Final, whilst Kinnaird scored the second goal that clinched a 2-0 victory over Oxford University. He was a single man at this time and gave the same address as his parents (Pall Mall East). He captained the Old Etonians in the Final on 13 March 1875 however the Royal Engineers won 2-0 in a replay. This was a busy year for Arthur Kinnaird and he married Mary Alma Victoria Agnew at Leswalt, north of Stranraer, on 19 August 1875. As stated, she was born at Exton Park, Rutland on 2 September 1854 and was the daughter of Sir Andrew Agnew 8th Baronet of Lochnaw. They were second cousins and her brother Sir Andrew Noel Agnew (1850) went to Trinity in 1868. They moved to 50 South Audley Street, Mayfair, which was the last property on the west side and looked across Grosvenor Square (*the Roosevelt memorial*). South Audley Street has many historic buildings but the Kinnairds' home is gone.

Arthur captained the Old Etonians in the Final at the Oval on 11 March 1876 but lost 3-0 to the Wanderers in a replay, and his daughter Catherine Mary was born at South Audley Street on 13 June 1876. He was made a partner at Ransom, Bouverie & Co. in 1877 and his pecuniary skills meant he moved up from the F.A. Committee (1869-77) to become Treasurer in 1878. He went back to the winning side and won the F.A. Cup with the Wanderers in 1877/78 and 'scored' in both games. He was goalkeeper in the first tie but scored an own goal and a halfback in the second. He returned to the Old Etonians and won the Cup with them in 1879, whilst son Douglas Arthur (1879) was born in Perth and Kenneth Fitzgerald (1880) London. Arthur F. Kinnaird a banker lived at 50 South Audley Street in 1881 with wife Mary, children Catherine, Douglas and Kenneth and eleven servants. The amateur sides won the Cup competition through the early years however the writing was now on the wall, and the northern professional clubs started to dominate the game. Alfred Kinnaird captained the Old Etonians v Blackburn Rovers in the Final at the Oval on 25 March 1882 and the attendance for this north-south contest was 6,500. The Old Etonians won the game by a single goal and Kinnaird was overcome by the occasion - he celebrated the epic victory in style and stood on his head in front of the Oval pavilion. These antics must have caused considerable amusement and no doubt amazement in the crowd. Indeed the celebrations needed to be enjoyed since this was the last time that an amateur side won the F.A. Cup. He appeared in his last Cup Final with the Old Etonians in 1883 losing to Blackburn Olympic. They might have won in a replay but Kinnaird allowed extra time at 90 minutes, despite having one man off the field and another lame. He was clearly a gentleman and always played in white flannel trousers!

The couple had two more children at 50 South Audley Street namely Noel Andrew (1883) *infant* and Arthur Middleton (1885), whilst daughter Catherine Mary died there on 28 April 1886, this being recorded in the Times on 30 April. The greatest changes, however, came after his father died on 26 April 1887 and he became the 11th Lord Kinnaird and inherited the family estates including Rossie Priory, Plaistow Lodge and 1-2 Pall Mall East. He was F.A. Treasurer in 1878-87 but handed over this role when he became a Lord, however there was a vacancy after Marindin resigned and he was elected F.A. President in 1890. There were many banking houses in London in the 19th century including Barclay, Tritton & Bevan at 54 Lombard Street from at least 1829-62. The two banks merged as Barclay, Bevan, Tritton, Ransom, Bouverie & Co. at 54 Lombard Street & 1 Pall Mall East by 1892 thus Arthur Kinnaird was later a director of Barclay & Co.

10 St. James's Square, Piccadilly.
Lord Kinnaird lived here from 1892 to 1923.

The 11th Lord removed to a new residence at 10 St. James's Square near Piccadilly in 1892, this being laid out in the 17th century to provide fashionable homes for the aristocracy. No. 10 was a notable red brick building on the north side of the square at the corner with Duke of York Street, the latter leading up to St. James's Church (built by Sir Christopher Wren in 1684). This was a desirable residence called "Chatham House" and has an L.C.C. blue plaque that states: "Here lived three Prime Ministers, William Pitt Earl of Chatham 1708-1778, Edward Geoffrey Stanley Earl of Derby 1799-1869, William Ewart Gladstone 1809-1898." Kinnaird occupied the house after Gladstone who was there in the early 1890s and was to live there over thirty years. Today, there are few changes (outside) and the property was latterly home to the *Royal Institute of International Affairs*.

The couple had a second daughter Margaret Alma (1892) at St. James's Square whilst Alfred Kinnaird continued to play football until 1893 when many of his contemporaries had hung up their boots. During this period he was also a keen amateur cricketer. Lord Kinnaird was an honorary colonel of the Tay Division of the sub-marine miners (a coast Battalion near Dundee) and received the appointment in 1893. In fact the submarine miners were a division of his old opponents the Royal Engineers. He was F.A. President during the growth of the professional game and was involved when the Cup Final went to the Crystal Palace in 1895. He worked initially with Charles Alcock and then for many years with Frederick Wall. He decided to sell Plaistow Lodge in 1896 and was responsible for the break-up of the estate and sadly his fields were soon covered with housing (i.e. Kinnaird Avenue). The palatial family home in London Lane became *Quernmore School* and this venerable institution was present for many years. Today the gateposts of Quernmore still survive, although Plaistow Lodge is part of the Parish Primary School. His last child Patrick Charles was born at St. James's Square in 1898 whilst sons Douglas and Kenneth both attended Eton and were admitted to Trinity College, Cambridge in 1898/99.

Blue Plaque at 10 St. James's Square. Three Prime Ministers lived here before Lord Kinnaird.

Lord and Lady Kinnaird (banker) lived at 10 St. James's Square in 1901 with children Douglas, Margaret and Patrick and eleven servants. His sons Kenneth and Arthur may have been at Rossie or perhaps abroad. Lord Kinnaird had a number of interests in England and Scotland and was a J.P. for Perth, Kent and London as well as President of the Y.M.C.A. For many years he was on a committee with old school friend Quentin Hogg and established seven homes for poor or homeless boys. He was made Lord High Commissioner of the Church of Scotland in 1907-09 but football was never far from his mind and he stated: "I believe that all right-minded people have good reason to thank God for the great progress of this popular national game." He supported evangelic religion like his parents and sisters (Louisa and Emily) and once travelled in India, where he spoke on behalf of missionaries. Lord Kinnaird continued to be a character in the game and there were high jinx at New Cross in 1910. He was cordially invited to open Millwall's new ground *The Den* on 22 October 1910 however all did not go smoothly and he arrived, in error, at the Ilderton Road End of the ground. There were just seconds to go and he had to be hauled, pushed and pulled over the wall into the crowd and then rushed to the other end of the arena, where he performed a brief ceremony and led the teams on to the pitch. He was still sporting a long beard as he did in his playing days.

He was much admired in the game hence he was presented with the second F.A. Cup trophy in 1911 and certainly deserved it, having won the Cup on five occasions. There were, however, dark clouds gathering over Europe and the Kinnaird family lost two sons during the First War - Douglas Arthur (1914) and Arthur Middleton (1917) of the Scots Guards, both killed in action. This left three surviving children namely Kenneth Fitzgerald (1880), Margaret Alma (1892) and Patrick Charles (1898). Lord Kinnaird owned 11,900 acres at Rossie Priory, 10 St. James's Square and 1-2 Pall Mall East (rebuilt as "Kinnaird House" in 1922) but the winds of change were blowing. Important negotiations regarding Wembley took place after the war but he was quite old then and missed the first Final. His wife Mary Alma Victoria Kinnaird died on 19 January 1923 and this affected him deeply since he was also ill. There was then a serious report in the Times on Tuesday 30 January 1923 stating: "It was learned yesterday afternoon that the condition of Lord Kinnaird was one of grave anxiety. On inquiry later in the evening it was stated that he was a little weaker." His ancestors brought many antiquities to Britain but it is unclear if these included an Egyptian curse, since the paper also had pictures entitled: "The interior of Tutankhamen's Tomb - first photos - Lord Carnarvon and Mr. Howard Carter by the sealed doorway." There was no reprieve and Lord Kinnaird died at 10 St. James's Square on 30 January 1923.

His obituary was in the Times on Wednesday 31 January 1923 and a memorial service was held at St. Martin in the Fields the next day: "We regret to announce that Lord Kinnaird who was distinguished alike as athlete, banker and evangelical churchman, died yesterday at his house in St. James's Square, aged 75." His funeral took place at the family burial ground at Rossie Priory on Friday 2 February and Rev. J. Davidson (brother-in-law of Lady Kinnaird) took the service. He was moved on a hand carriage to the old graveyard and eight of the oldest estate workers were pallbearers. The family members present were Master and Mrs. Kinnaird, Hon. Patrick and Mrs. Kinnaird, Margaret Kinnaird, Sir Andrew Agnew, Major Charles Noel and Sir Herbert K. Ogilvy whilst many wreaths were sent including ones from the Y.M.C.A. (home and abroad), Y.W.C.A., the F.A., the Football League and other organisations. There was a further memorial service for the Y.M.C.A. at King George's Hall, Tottenham Court Road on the Sunday. Sons Kenneth and Patrick Kinnaird had probate of his estate on 24 February 1923 and it was valued at £250,000.

Kenneth Fitzgerald Kinnaird was in the Scottish Horse in the First War and became 12th Lord and Lord High Commissioner to the Church of Scotland in 1936-37. Patrick Charles Kinnaird was in the Scots Guards and fought in both wars and was a director of Barclays Bank, whilst the title went to Graham Charles Kinnaird (13th Lord) who was born 15 September 1912 but the peerage was dormant-extinct in 1997. Rossie Priory the family home then became an exclusive hotel for corporate customers. There is a family memorial to Arthur Fitzgerald Kinnaird and his wife Mary with a brief inscription beside the 'old' Rossie Church, but this is a private estate and it cannot be accessed. This was the end of an era however one more player came in at the eleventh hour and is discussed below.

SIR JOHN CHARLES CLEGG

The Cleggs were an old Sheffield family who rose through the ranks of society as well as the ranks of the Football Association. John Charles Clegg was made fifth F.A. President in 1923 at the advanced age of 73. This was a reward for years of dedicated service to soccer however his family had humble origins and like many in Sheffield made their living in the metalwork industry. The early records are incomplete with Clegg being a common name in Sheffield but they can be traced to Thomas Clegg who married Betty Buxton at St. Peters and St. Paul's, Sheffield on 7 October 1754. They had several children including Charles Clegg who was born c.1765 and baptized in Sheffield on 5 September 1766. There was also John Clegg born c.1770 who may have been his brother (or at least a relative).

Charles Clegg was a cutler and married Mary Ann Johnson at St. Peters and St. Paul's on 12 May 1795 and was buried at the church on 4 December 1842 aged 77. Charles his son was born in 1797 and was a trumpeter and music professor at 50 Barker's Pool in 1828 and 12 Cheney Row in 1845-68 - the latter being the gardens beside Sheffield Town Hall. Charles Clegg a gentleman died on 13 April 1868 and his wife Catherine at Cheney Row on 6 November 1877, whilst his son another Charles lived at Epsom, Victoria in Australia. John Clegg (1770) married Ann or Hannah Johnson at St. Peters and St. Paul's on 14 August 1795 and four children were baptized at the church: William Johnson (1797), Elizabeth (1799), Harriet (1803) and Charles (1804). The father John was a labourer, spade maker and edge tool maker whilst at the time of his son's second wedding he was 'a former file smith' (see below 1858). John Clegg was buried at the same church on 2 June 1816 aged 46 years.

St. Peters and St. Paul's, Sheffield was an historic church at the heart of the old town amongst alleys, streets and courtyards. It became Sheffield Cathedral in 1913 and henceforth is referred to in this manner. It remains today mainly in its original form with some later additions and surrounded by the same historic streets. It seems likely that the two Johnson girls were related and indeed Mary was daughter of George and Mary Johnson (brick maker). Sheffield Archives hold an agreement between the burgesses and Mary Johnson (widow of George) of 1814, referring to a plot of land in Little Sheffield near Button Lane and a further parcel of land at the back of Carver Street. A *Deed of Exchange* regarding this land of 1817 shows that the parties included, "Charles Clegg and his wife Mary (née Johnson) - child of George Johnson."

Charles Clegg was born in Sheffield on 5 December 1804 and baptized at the Cathedral on 30 December that year, whilst he married Mary Johnson at Rotherham on 7 August 1825. It seems likely this is the right marriage since Mary was born at Attercliffe in 1802, a district north east of Sheffield near Rotherham. The Sheffield directories describe Charles Clegg as a victualler of the *Mermaid*, Orchard Street in 1828. This was probably our Charles although it could be his uncle (mentioned above) who was alive at the time; however it is certain that Charles entered the profession of cutler and was quite successful in the early 19th Century. He had just one child William Johnson Clegg who was born on 23 September 1826 and baptized at the Cathedral on 23 September 1827 (one year later). This small family lived at Sylvester Street, Sheffield in 1841 near to Bramall Lane in the south of the town, and Charles was a cutler and his son William Johnson a clerk, however the lives of the two soon diverged.

Charles Clegg lived at 115 Porter Street near Sylvester Street by 1849 and resided there with wife Mary in 1851 as, "A master cutler employing 12 men," aged 46 years. He was in business as a spring knife manufacturer at nearby Earl Street in 1852 whilst his home address was 54 Hermitage Street in 1856 - the latter between London Road and Bramall Lane. There was, however, soon a change of direction and Mary died at Hermitage Street on 29 January 1858 and was buried at St. Mary's, Bramall Lane on 2 February. This was a sad loss but he spent little time grieving and Charles Clegg married Sarah Jeyes (formerly Morgan) at St. Mary's, Bramall Lane on 9 November 1858. Both parties resided at Hermitage Street and William Johnson Clegg was a witness. Sarah was the daughter of John and Elizabeth Morgan, a rope maker, and was born in Northampton in 1804. She grew up in the town and married James Jeyes mason and bricklayer in c.1825, he being born in the nearby village of Moulton in 1799.

The couple had seven children in the parish of St. Sepulchre's, Northampton and these included Sarah (1836) and Jane (1839). Her parents John and Elizabeth Morgan lived at Silver Street in 1841 whilst James and Sarah Jeyes lived there in 1841/51 and at the latter date three daughters were employed as shoe binders. Northampton had a long association with shoe making and this promoted other industry such as the tanneries on the River Nene. Here the leather was cut to shape before being made into shoes and this supported allied trades such as tool making. The town provided 1,500 pairs of shoes for Cromwell's troops in the Civil War thus the castle and town walls were destroyed by the army of Charles II, but it was no doubt quieter when James and Sarah lived there. The town was rebuilt after a disastrous fire in 1675 with new streets such as the Drapery and Silver Street around the Market Square, and the Jeyes family lived in a crowded area of town with a number of courts behind 49-53 Silver Street. James Jeyes died at Northampton in June 1856 and it is a mystery how Sarah Jeyes met Charles Clegg in Sheffield.

In fact the couple did not stay in Sheffield for long and Charles was absent from the directories in 1859, however there are often problems with this kind of research - as illustrated below. Indeed another Charles Clegg lived at *Wisewood* near Wadsley Bridge in 1861 being joint owner of Hague, Clegg and Barton saw makers &c. at the Æmilian Works, Sylvester Lane near Sylvester Street. This Charles, however, was the son of William (1798) and Sarah and was born 1830. The couple made the 80-mile journey south and Charles Clegg, cutler, lived at 53 Silver Street, Northampton in 1861 with wife Sarah and daughters-in-law Sarah and Jane Jeyes - all shoe closers. He was a shopkeeper at 53 Silver Street and 46 Crispin Street (in 1861) and remained at the former and was a cutler in 1869, and a leather cutler living with wife Sarah and daughter Jane Jeyes in 1871. He was a hardware dealer &c. at 25 Silver Street in 1874 although this may have been a printing error. He continued to work well into his seventies and was listed as a cutler at 53 Silver Street in 1877.

Charles Clegg made his last will on 23 June 1877 and left his household furniture and other household effects for the benefit of his wife Sarah and the remainder of his estate was left in trust to his son William Johnson Clegg. His trustee was required to invest the estate-money and pay the interest for the benefit of his wife during her lifetime and after her decease it was to be divided into three equal parts - one third to his son, one third to stepdaughter Jane Jeyes and one third between his wife's other children. John Charles and Mary Ellen Clegg his grandchildren witnessed the will at a solicitor's offices in Sheffield. Charles Clegg, cutler, lived with his wife Sarah and Jane Jeyes at 53 Silver Street in 1881 and died there on 3 June 1881. His son William proved his will on 8 September that year but he was not wealthy and his estate was valued at only £85 16s 9d. There was no Government pension at the time and Sarah only had a marginal provision thus a surprise entry was in an 1890 directory: "Mrs. Sarah Clegg, cutlery dealer at 53 Silver Street." She was 86 years at the time but the situation did not last long and she died at Northampton in March 1890.

William Johnson Clegg, meanwhile, was destined for greatness and became a successful and wealthy businessman in Sheffield. Mary Sykes daughter of John and Ann was born on 11 August 1826 and lived with her family at Jessop Street, Sheffield south of the Moor in 1841. Her father was a penknife cutler like Clegg and they lived next to Sylvester Street. No houses remain today but there are some signs of old industry such as *Sylvester Buildings* a warehouse. William Johnson Clegg (21) an attorney's clerk of Paradise Square married Mary Sykes at Sheffield Parish Church (Cathedral) on 3 November 1847. This may have been his place of work since it was popular with solicitors, and was a notable Georgian Square near the Cathedral. It had three-storey red brick houses on a steep slope with cobbled streets and doctors and portrait painters lived there. It was once the pulpit of John Wesley and a blue plaque records his arrival on 15 July 1779: "I preached in Paradise Square in Sheffield to the largest congregation I ever saw on a weekday." (No doubt a Wednesday). The square is little changed whilst the arrival of W.J. Clegg revealed his aspirations as a gentleman.

Mary Sykes lived at Coalpit Lane when she married and her father John was a cutler there although he was a coffeehouse keeper at 50 Coalpit Lane in 1856. Pit Lane possibly the same road is on West Street, west of Sheffield city centre. It is strange that William Johnson Clegg did not follow the profession of his forebears - the traditional occupation in Sheffield, however it was a decision that turned out to be most lucrative. The couple soon had two children: Anne Elizabeth (1849) who died that year and John Charles (1850). William J. Clegg a solicitor's managing clerk lived at 53 Broom Spring Lane, Ecclesall Bierlow in 1851 west of the city centre with his wife, John Charles (9 months) and sister-in-law Sarah Sykes (17) their servant. William Clegg had every intention of getting ahead and was a highway rate collector of 53 Broom Spring Lane in 1852 and then had children William Edwin (1852) and Albert Sykes (1854).

He was a rate collector of Cemetery Road in 1856 however the cramped courts of Sheffield were not a healthy place to live in the 19th century and the Clegg family suffered like many others. They had children Mary Ellen (1856), Frederick (1858) and Sarah Jane (1859) but three died as infants: Albert in 1857, Frederick in 1858 and Sarah Jane in 1860. William was a collector to the *Highway Board* in 1859 with a business address 40 Queen Street and a home address 127 Cemetery Road. The latter is still present west of London Road but the area is now transformed and there is no trace of the 19th century housing. There was soon a further blow and his wife Mary died at Cemetery Road on 30 September 1860 aged 34 years. His four infant children and wife were all buried at St. Mary's, Bramall Lane, which is located across John Street and in the shadow of Bramall Lane football ground. The family were sufficiently well off to erect a memorial and this remains beside the tower, despite the fact the churchyard is now grassed over. It is to the memory of his four children and wife and adds: "Also of Mary the wife of Charles Clegg and grandmother of the children who died January 29th 1858, aged 56 years." The Sykes family also have headstones but it is unclear how they are related.

Samuel and Mary Harrop lived at Hathersage near to Sheffield but were unable to think of Christian names beyond *A* and had children: Alfred (25 December 1825) baptized at Dore, Absalom (1827), Asenath (7 January 1829), Abner (1831), Amanda (1833) and Aramenta (1836) all born at Hathersage. Their son Alfred Harrop married Eliza Holland at Sheffield in September 1855 and had sons at Ecclesall: Alfred Holland (1857) and Arthur Frederic Holland (1859) and they soon played a part in the story. William Johnson Clegg widower and rate collector lived at 129 Cemetery Road in April 1861 with children John C. (10), William E. (8), Mary Ellen (4), and housekeeper Elizabeth Drake (58) from

Eckington in Derbyshire. As with his father the situation soon changed and William Johnson Clegg married Asenath Harrop at Sheffield in December 1861. He was listed as a highway rate collector at 129 Cemetery Road and an accountant and agent to the *Temperance and General Provident Institution* in 1864, being a supporter of the temperance movement - he instilled the ideas of abstinence in his children. He had two daughters Asenath Harrop (1864) and Sara Amanda (1865) in Sheffield but he was no doubt 'unpopular' as a rate collector and was soon training in the law.

Alfred Harrop his brother-in-law owed £922 13s 10d to William Johnson Clegg (law student) in 1866, which was a large sum of money, thus an agreement was drawn up between the parties: "The mortgage was in consideration of £922 13s 10d which he already owed Clegg, and as security for further sums of money which Clegg would furnish to a total of £1,200." This was secured on a property viz. "land in Orange Street with all buildings thereon and four dwelling houses built on the same site, also all the boilers and steam engines on the premises 1st December 1866." Orange Street was next to West Street not far from the Cathedral and Clegg was to take possession if the money were not repaid. He then had a son Leonard Johnson (1867) born in Sheffield and was admitted to the *Law Society* as a country solicitor on 25 September 1868. The leasehold deeds went missing but Clegg took possession and this no doubt happened after Alfred Harrop died at Ecclesall in June 1870 aged 44.

The family had improved circumstances and William J. Clegg a solicitor lived at "Alliance Villa", 22 Victoria Road, Broomhall Park in 1871 with his wife Asenath, children John C. and William E. (solicitor's articled clerks), Mary, Asenath, Sarah, Leonard and two servants - one Ellen Sykes. This was in the west of Sheffield near *Collegiate Hall* on the Ecclesall Road beyond the confines of the old town and these houses remain today. The family business was at 27 Bank Street in the old town behind the Cathedral in 1871, and the eldest sons married in 1872/73 and are discussed below. W.J. Clegg & Sons (solicitors) practiced at 57 Bank Street in 1876 whilst Mary Ellen Clegg married William Peirce Dix at Ecclesall Bierlow in June 1878. The business went from strength to strength and they moved to 14 Figtree Lane in 1878. The new chambers were just behind the Cathedral and the lane ran downhill from Hartshead (in the south) to Bank and Queen Street (in the north). The property is of much interest and W.J. Clegg & Sons practiced there until at least 1937.

There were several buildings on the west side (nos. 7-25) and they included Temple and Figtree Chambers 1881 and 19 Harold Chambers and 25 Haxworth Chambers 1901. There were three buildings on the east side including 6 Gresham Chambers and 10 Fig Tree Lane, which were the offices of accountants, solicitors and landscape and portrait painters. W.J. Clegg & Sons, "Victoria Chambers", 14 Figtree Lane (solicitors) was on the east side and was of brown sandstone with Classical pediments but had a white stucco front with columned porch. It housed the *Sheffield Hospital for Women* from 1864-78 before they moved to Jessop House and a blue plaque records this. The lane is little changed today and the red brick "Old Bank House" is next to the entrance at Hartshead near the Cathedral precincts. It is narrow and cobbled with paving and has many old properties on the west side but only Victoria Chambers, 14 Figtree Lane on the east side - the latter remains a solicitors and commissioners for oaths.

Meanwhile things were looking up. William J. Clegg "alderman and solicitor of the town of Sheffield" lived at 22 Victoria Road in 1881 with wife Asenath, children Asenath, Sarah and Leonard and sister-in-law Amanda Harrop housekeeper. William P. Dix a broker in Sheffield Stock Exchange lived at 44 Grange Crescent, Ecclesall with wife Mary, daughter Ethel and two servants. Eliza Harrop a widow and annuitant resided at 17 College Street with children Alfred (accounts clerk), Arthur (solicitor's articled clerk), Frances, Ada and Alwynne. The son Alfred died that year, but the family's social standing was on a new level and W.J. Clegg & Sons were solicitors in 1881 and agents to the *UK Temperance & General Provident Institution* in 1884. William was at 22 Victoria Road at this time but also owned a house at Bradwell (Derby) near Hathersage, whilst Charles Maples married Asenath Harrop Clegg at Sheffield in December 1885. He then moved to "Cliff Tower", 10 Whitworth Road, Ranmoor, which was in an affluent area called Upper Hallam west of Sheffield and high in the hills above the village. It was at the northeast end of Whitworth Road and looked down on the city being a two-storey, double fronted, palatial house of yellow sandstone brick with towered entrance (semi-circular columned porch). Decorative work adorned the first floor windows and it had a 'northern design' and was surrounded by extensive gardens. It is still present with Quiet Cottage to the rear but has some modern buildings in the garden area.

William Johnson Clegg, solicitor, official receiver in bankruptcy, magistrate and employer, lived at "Cliff Tower" with wife Asenath and two servants in 1891. This was an area of great significance to football history and the contribution of Sheffield and Hallam has already been discussed. Indeed "Cliff Tower" was located just below Sandygate Football Ground, which is the oldest football venue in the world, and has a picturesque setting high on a ridge in Sandygate Road (with the dales beyond). There is a sloping football pitch with white railings around it on three sides whilst a cricket pitch occupies the western side (as at Bramall Lane), and a dry-stone wall around the site confirms the rural location. There is a small covered terrace at the north end and a new 200 seat Main Stand on the east side that proudly displays: "Hallam F.C. Sandygate 1860". This is an inspiring ground in terms of football history and was so near to the Cleggs' home.

W.J. Clegg & Sons were solicitors, commissioner for oaths and official receivers in bankruptcy at Figtree Lane in 1891 whilst William Johnson Clegg esquire J.P. made his last will on 5 April 1892 and added a codicil on 10 January 1895. The papers were naturally written up at Clegg & Sons in Sheffield and the will is a complex document but can be summarised as follows. Firstly he left his furniture and household effects to his wife Asenath as well as £400, and his gold watch and chain and appendages to his son John Charles Clegg. He bequeathed all interest in his offices at Figtree Lane to sons John Charles, William Edwin and Leonard Johnson. He gave his leasehold dwelling house at 22 Victoria Road, Broomhall Park to his trustees to be held in trust, for his wife to occupy during her lifetime. He also gave £8,000 to his trustees to be invested for the benefit of his wife, then after her decease his residuary estate was to be divided as follows, that is to say in six equal parts between John Charles Clegg, William Edwin Clegg, Leonard Johnson Clegg, Mary Ellen Dix, Asenath Harrop Maples and Sara Amanda Clegg. The codicil made minor adjustments and stated that Sara Amanda Clegg was the wife of Thomas Edgar Freeston (married Ecclesall in September 1892).

William Johnson Clegg, gentleman, died at "Cliff Tower" on 15 June 1895 and his executors John Charles, William Edwin and Leonard Johnson Clegg of 14 Figtree Lane and Charles Thomas Skelton a manufacturer obtained the probate on 25 July 1895. His estate was valued at £31,827 4s 2d but re-sworn in October 1896 at £31,677 6s 2d and the adjustment may have been connected to the property he owned (re Alfred Harrop). Edwin Blyde & Co. Ltd. made cutlery and silverware at 16 Orange Street or *Orange Street Works* in a Sheffield survey dated 1896. Executors of the late W.J. Clegg assigned this to Messrs Edwin Blyde and Herbert Gamble Middleton of Sheffield, merchants and manufacturers, in consideration of a sum of £750 on 21 December 1896 namely: "The property in Orange Street with the manufacturing known as *Orange Street Works* and all other buildings." Thus ended a 30-year association with the site. Asenath Clegg died in Sheffield on 4 August 1907 and was buried with her husband at Christchurch in Fulwood on the western outskirts near to Ranmoor. There are many notable Victorian memorials in the churchyard including one to the Cleggs that would not be out of place in Westminster Abbey. It is a fine piece of stone funerary architecture with scrolls at the first level, marble columns at the second, detailed carvings, several platforms, and a flat base to the front: "In loving memory of William Johnson Clegg J.P. 1826-1895 and Asenath his widow 1829-1907," whilst John Charles and Mary, Leonard Johnson and Kate, and Charles William Clegg (wife Katie M.) are also listed.

John Charles Clegg was born at 53 Broom Spring Lane on 15 June 1850 and grew up there and at Cemetery Road and Victoria Road all west of the city. He was educated privately and lived in a town where sport and football in particular was prominent, and he made his mark as athlete and soccer player. Bramall Lane was laid out near his home in 1854 whilst Nathaniel Creswick and William Prest both former Harrovians formed Sheffield F.C. on 24 October 1857 - the first club outside the schools and universities. The Sheffield Rules (1857) stated a goal had to be kicked in open play and the ball thrown in from touch - there was a fair catch and charging and pushing were allowed, but no hacking or tripping. Other venues were established: Sandygate (1860) and the Sheaf House Ground near Bramall Lane whilst two clubs were formed: Hallam (1860) and Wednesday (1867). The Sheffield Association had a significant role and the historic meeting London v Sheffield took place on 31 March 1866 but the Cleggs did not play, as they were too young. This became a regular fixture with 2-3 meetings a year and continued until the end of the 19th century.

John Charles Clegg was soon involved in sporting activities and was an athlete from 1867-74 and won 120 prizes, held the 600-yard record and could run 100 yards in 10 seconds. Indeed the Lillie Bridge 'Riot' discussed in Ch. 12 shows that running was a serious business. John never trained but kept fit with ordinary exercise and adherence to temperance principles. He was a fast and strong forward on the soccer field and with brother William Edwin played for Sheffield F.C. and local clubs Broomhall, Albion and Wednesday. The brothers both played for Sheffield v London in c.1870 and this brought them

Sir John Charles Clegg (1850-1937).
He was F.A. President in 1923-37.

to the attention of the F.A. and they soon played for England - his most important year was 1872 aged just 22. John Charles Clegg a law student from Sheffield married Mary Sayles of Gorton at St. John's Church, Manchester on 2 September 1872. She was born at Ridgeway, Derbyshire on 1 April 1850 the daughter of John William Sayles a clerk whilst William Edwin Clegg was a witness. J.C. Clegg was admitted to the *Law Society* as a solicitor on 17 September 1872 two weeks after his marriage and became a partner in W.J. Clegg & Sons. He played in the first Sheffield v Glasgow game in 1872 and also for England v Scotland at the West of Scotland Cricket Ground on 30 November 1872 - the first international game (0-0). This was a great honour but like many Victorians he had his hand in several pies and was a skilled player, important administrator, successful businessman and a leader in Sheffield society.

The couple then had three children namely Charles William (1873), Colin (1877) and Edith Margaret (1879) and lived at 4 Wharncliffe Road, Broomhall Park by 1876, near his father in Victoria Road. John C. Clegg, solicitor and town councillor, lived at 4 Wharncliffe Road in 1881 with wife Mary and their three children, and he was at this address in 1884 but it was called "Mackenzie Place". He became involved in the game's administration being known as a clever and popular referee and was the main official for the Cup Final at the Oval on 25 March 1882. The Etonians beat Blackburn Rovers 1-0 in front of 6,500 and Alfred Kinnaird stood on his head (yellow card). He was a member of the Sheffield and Hallamshire F.A. and affiliated representative for Sheffield at the F.A. in 1885-87, being elected to the F.A. Committee in 1886 and became their Chairman in 1890 - a post he held for many years.

John Charles Clegg lived at 1 Collegiate Court in the Broomhall district in 1891 with wife Mary, daughter Edith and two servants. It was an affluent part of town and his neighbours were merchants, manufacturers, church ministers, the Chief Constable and persons living on their own means. He was a commissioner to administer oaths and 'deputy' official receiver in bankruptcy at Figtree Lane, and lived at 1 Collegiate 'Crescent'. He then refereed the last Cup Final to be played at the Oval in 1892 and had to keep his nerve since the crowd had increased to 32,810 - West Bromwich Albion beat Aston Villa 3-0. His father William died on his 45th birthday in 1895 and he then became senior partner in Clegg & Sons - he was a commissioner for oaths and official receiver in bankruptcy in 1901. Indeed his cousin Arthur Frederic Holland Harrop was a solicitor at "Harold Chambers", 19 Figtree Lane that year. He was successful in business like his father and moved to a substantial property "Clifton House", 32 Cavendish Road, Sheffield by 1901 - his home for the rest of his life. It was located in the south west of town, high on the hill above Ecclesall Road and half a mile from Broomhall. This was an affluent suburb with tree-lined avenues in Lyndhurst Road and the nearby houses date from 1860.

"Clifton House" was the last property on the southwest corner next to Chelsea Road and was two-storey plus and built of yellow sandstone brick. It had large bay windows at the side and front, a multi-gabled roof, large leafy garden and substantial coach house to the rear. The name was proudly displayed on the gatepost and was surrounded with a dry-stone wall. It was no larger than "Cliff Tower" but had a more attractive and homely appearance and it is little changed today. John Charles Clegg, solicitor, lived there in 1901 with wife Mary and children Charles W. (solicitor) and Edith M. whilst his other son Colin was a civil engineer in Battersea. There were soon three weddings two in Ecclesall and the third in Sheffield viz. Paul Edward Wilks to Edith Margaret Clegg in June 1902 (see below), Charles William Clegg to Katie May Slater in June 1903, and Colin Clegg married in June 1904.

John Charles Clegg continued to be a great servant to football and was F.A. Vice-President by 1904, President of Wednesday and United an association he didn't find "exclusive", and member of the League Appeals Committee. Charles Clegg as he was known cut a dashing figure, with handlebar moustache, and he gained a reputation as a formidable administrator with dauntingly high principles his famous saying being: "Nobody gets lost on a straight road." He was determined not to get lost 'outside' football being Chairman of Sheffield Local Employment Committee and a local J.P. from 1907. He was a lifetime abstainer who supported the *Sheffield Band of Hope Union*, and the *British Temperance League* of which he was President from 1912. He was listed as a J.P. solicitor and commissioner for oaths in 1911/21 at Figtree Lane and resided at 32 Cavendish Road. He had been the official receiver for bankruptcy since his father's death however the job passed to his brother Leonard J. Clegg in 1919. He was Chairman of the F.A. Committee until 1923 and was rewarded for his long service when he was appointed F.A. President that year (on the death of Lord Kinnaird). He worked with Frederick Joseph Wall and helped to guide the F.A. between the wars and was present at the first Wembley Cup Final in 1923. Indeed he was involved in several Cup Finals at Wembley and in a number of England tours abroad. He had come to prominence at the end of his life but had always been there and his top appointment was well deserved. He was involved in soccer for 70 years and saw it develop from its origins in Sheffield to a Wembley Final with 200,000 people.

There was also tragedy in his life and his son Charles William Clegg died on 28 January 1927 aged 53. This must have tainted events later in 1927 since John Charles Clegg was knighted for his services to the Board of Trade and Ministry of Labour. Other sources state he received the award for his services to football (he being the first). The strain of events made him ill and he was unable to attend the Cup Final in 1927 when Cardiff City beat Arsenal 1-0, however received a kind telegram from King George V. Matters were soon compounded and his other son Colin Clegg died at Kensington in September 1929 aged 51 and his wife Mary in Sheffield on 22 August 1933. He then made his last will on 7 May 1937 and left £200 to his daughters-in-law Katie May Clegg and Elizabeth Clegg and the remaining estate was put in trust to be divided into three equal parts viz. daughter Edith Margaret Wilks, grandson Derek Paul Wilks and granddaughter Valerie Enid May Wilks. He added: "I have not made any provision for my granddaughter Pauline Margaret Clegg Blades as she has been otherwise provided for," however she is something of a mystery and may have been illegitimate. He appointed brother Leonard Johnson Clegg, nephew William John Clegg and physician Cecil Andrew Swan Hamilton trustees and executors, however he was in ill health and signed with a shaky hand.

Sir John Charles Clegg died at "Clifton House" on 26 June 1937 and his obituary appeared in the Times on Monday 28 June. His death witnessed the end of an era and he was the last of the old school at the Football Association. He received tributes from Mr. S.F. Rous and Sir Frederick Wall of the F.A. whilst the Football Council sent a telegram stating: "For more than half a century he has been the outstanding personality in our game and has won the affection of all of us." Leonard Johnson Clegg and William John Clegg of 14 Figtree Lane obtained his probate on 17 August 1937 his effects £24,834 10s 2d and his epitaph stated: "In loving memory of John Charles Clegg KT 1850-1937." The president's job then went to a new generation and initially to William Pickford (1937-38), however his brothers are now considered.

William Edwin Clegg was born in Sheffield on 21 April 1852 and followed much the same path as his brother John Charles. He was educated privately and played football for Sheffield F.C., and for England v Scotland in the second international at the Oval on 8 March 1873. He married Viola (c.1852) daughter of Henry Gilles Carr of Sheffield at Camberwell in September next then worked in the family business and was admitted to the *Law Society* in 1874 and was a solicitor and commissioner for oaths and partner in Clegg & Sons. He had three children viz. Ernest William (1875), Maud Violet (1877) and Cecil Edwin (1879) and lived at Havelock Street, Broomspring Lane in 1876. He played football for Sheffield Albion and appeared for England against Wales at the Oval on 18 March 1879. This was the first game between the countries and there was a 20-minute delay before kick-off, thus they played 2 x 30 minutes, the result 2-1 to England. He lived at "Temple Villa", 34 Crescent Road, Sharrow with his wife, three children and two servants in 1879-81; then Brincliffe Rise, Osborne Road in 1884 and 6 Broomgrove Road in 1891. Cecil Edwin his son died on 7 July 1892 and was buried at Christchurch, Fulwood.

William, like his father, was greatly involved in local affairs and was an alderman in 1886-1926 and Lord Mayor of Sheffield in 1898-99. He continued as a solicitor and commissioner for oaths at Figtree Lane and his son Ernest William had joined the firm by 1901. He lived at Loxley House, Wadsley in the north of the city that year but only Viola was at home, whilst his son Ernest lived at Wadsley Lodge. William was knighted for public services in 1906 and the family moved to Anston outside of Sheffield and his wife Viola died there in September 1910. He was a Sheffield J.P. in 1912 and Chairman of the West Riding (Sheffield) Justices, and Pro-Chancellor of Sheffield University and Chairman of the Applied Science Department. Indeed he was Chairman of the Sheffield Licensing Committee and had the same aims as his father and brother, but by different means. He received the C.B.E. in 1918 and lived with his son at Bothamsall Hall near East Retford in 1921. He married Lucy A. Jonas (widow) in December 1922 who died in March 1929, whilst William Edwin Clegg died at Broomhall Place, Sheffield on 22 August 1932 and his probate was granted to Ernest William Clegg solicitor, the value £8,141 16s 1d.

Leonard Johnson Clegg was born in Sheffield in September 1867 and lived with his family at 22 Victoria Road in 1871-84 and may have resided at "Cliff Tower". He was out of the limelight but was a solicitor in the family firm and a J.P. for Sheffield. Ada Mary Wilks (1860) and Paul Edward Wilks (1876) lived with cousins at the Grange, Hazelwood, Derby, in 1881 and were children of an ironmonger. Their sister Ethel Maud Wilks (September 1867) was a pupil at a girls' school in 68 Clarkegrove Road, Ecclesall at the time. It was run by two mistresses from Petworth in Sussex and had music and French teachers and was near Broomgrove Road. Leonard Johnson Clegg worked at Clegg & Sons and married Ethel Maud Wilks at Sheffield in June 1890 whilst his niece Edith (daughter of John Charles) later married Paul Edward Wilks. The couple lived at 51 Broomgrove Road in 1891 (the same street as brother William) and had a daughter Ethel Theodora in March that year however the mother died soon after aged 23.

There was soon another connection and Kate Turton was born Ecclesall in December 1870. John Turton a steel forge and rolling mill proprietor employing 79 men and 54 boys lived at 9 Victoria Road, Ecclesall in 1881 with wife Clara, five children including Kate, sister-in-law Lucy Charlesworth and two servants. Leonard Johnson Clegg married Kate Turton at Ecclesall in September 1896 and had a son William John in December 1897. He was a solicitor living at "West Heys", Whiteley Wood Road, Sheffield, in 1901 with his wife Kate and two children. The property was later listed as no. 55 and he remained there the rest of his life, whilst a daughter Eileen Clara was born at Ecclesall in June 1901. He was a commissioner for oaths in 1911 and, as stated, became the official receiver in bankruptcy in 1919. He continued to work in the firm with his brothers and died at Hangingwater Road, Sheffield on 11 May 1939. William John Clegg solicitor and Eileen Clara Atkin (wife of Frank Roland Atkin) obtained his probate and his effects were finally valued at £29,188 14s 11d, whilst Kate Clegg died on 9 November 1947. The Cleggs made a great contribution to soccer and the F.A. and with all in order the scene was set for some great contests - the players who took part in the first Cup Final in 1872 are discussed in the following chapters.

Table 2: **PRESIDENTS OF THE F.A.**

1863-67	Arthur Pember
1867-74	Ebenezer Cobb Morley
1874-90	Major Francis Arthur Marindin
1890-1923	Lord Arthur Fitzgerald Kinnaird
1923-37	Sir John Charles Clegg

CHAPTER 6

The Eton Rifles

The Wanderers Football Club were one of the most famous amateur teams from the early period and their formation as the Forest F.C. was discussed earlier. They became the Wanderers in 1864 when they moved from Snaresbrook to the more gracious surrounds of Battersea Park. The latter was developed on land reclaimed from the Thames marshes in the 16th century and was opposite a Royal Palace and the Royal Hospital at Chelsea. It was initially known as Battersea Fields and was a venue for fairs, pigeon shooting and donkey racing, but was under the jurisdiction of H.M. Office of Works in 1846 and was drained and levelled using soil excavated from Victoria Docks (see Peto and Betts). The total site had an area of 320 acres however some was sold for housing thus Battersea Park itself covered 200 acres. There was a boating lake with cascades and Italian gardens (to the south) whilst the area by the River Thames (to the north) was reserved for cricket grounds - one for clubs, one for schools and one for matches. It was there that the Wanderers played.

The Forest F.C. featured a number of notable players before 1864 including J.F. Alcock, C.W. Alcock, W.J.C. Cutbill and C.M. Tebbut, whilst the Wanderers F.C. attracted the best footballers of the day. These players went to public school and appeared for their old boys teams being gentlemen from the higher levels of society. The Wanderers dominated the early Cup competition, although several clubs featured in the first decade of soccer and the fixtures reveal the facts. The first game to consider is London v Sheffield in 1866. There were three Wanderers players in the London side viz. C.W. Alcock, R.D. Elphinstone and Hon. A.F. Kinnaird whilst the remainder were thus: Barnes (3), Crusaders (1), No Names Club of Kilburn (3) and one unaccredited.

The next game to consider is that between Kent-Surrey and Middlesex in 1867. The Kent and Surrey side had P. Rhodes and P.M. Thornton from the Wanderers with the remainder being from Barnes (3), Civil Service (1), Clapham (2), Crystal Palace (2) and Eton College (1). The Middlesex team included C.W. Alcock and R.C. Thornton of the Wanderers, the others from Charterhouse (1), Crusaders (1), Harrow Chequers (1), No Names Club (2), Westminster School (2) and Old Westminsters (2). The third game of note had a similar pattern and was between Kent and Surrey in 1868. The Kent side had J.B. Martin of the Wanderers and Hon. A.F. Kinnaird (captain) of Trinity Cambridge, the others from Charterhouse, Crusaders, Crystal Palace (3), Old Etonians, Old Harrovians, No Names Club, St. John's Cambridge and West Kent. The Surrey side had P. Rhodes and A. Thompson of the Wanderers, the others from Barnes (4), Clapham (3), Crystal Palace (2) and Reigate Hill. These were some of the top players and their choice for the representative games gives a poll of the best teams, whilst the F.A. chose a range to avoid accusations of 'preference'. The Wanderers were well represented but were not the only team and certainly didn't have a monopoly, although J.F. and C.W. Alcock and A.F. Kinnaird kept them at the forefront and indeed two of these 'test' matches were at Battersea Park.

The Wanderers began to play at the Oval in 1869-70 and their status was further boosted when Charles Alcock became F.A. Secretary in 1870 - they were one of fifteen clubs to kick-off the first F.A. Cup tournament in 1871. The competition was no doubt fair, but the Wanderers clearly had an advantage playing at the Oval and being captained by the F.A. Secretary. The club were scheduled to play the Harrow Chequers in the first round but their opponents could not play and they received a walk over. M.P. Betts a member of Harrow Chequers then changed sides and played for the Wanderers instead, which turned out to be a most significant choice - it was within the rules since he hadn't played. The Wanderers drew Clapham Rovers, their neighbours, in the second round and proved their intentions by winning 3-1 and continued to ride their luck being drawn at home in the third round against Crystal Palace. This was a honourable 0-0 draw but with only three 'quarter-finals' both teams went into the next round. It was decided that the semi-finals should be played at a neutral venue but in the Wanderers case it made no difference. They played Queen's Park at the Oval and the game was a 0-0 draw but they were declared winners when the Scots missed the replay (they couldn't afford the fare), thus they met the Engineers in the Final and won 1-0 (see Half Time).

The Wanderers were the only team to play for, attracting all the top gentlemen players, and won the F.A. Cup on four further occasions - Oxford University 1873 (2-0), Old Etonians 1876 (3-0), Oxford University 1877 (2-1) and Royal Engineers 1878 (3-1). The times, however, were changing and the amateur sides could not compete with the northern teams who proceeded to dominate the F.A. Cup. The Wanderers folded up in about 1881 and their players returned to various old boys clubs, thus A.F. Kinnaird appeared for the Old Etonians in the Cup Finals of 1881-83. It is unclear who played for the Wanderers in the qualifying rounds but those in the Final in March 1872 are well documented. The style of play was developed in the public schools and at most of these the ball could not be passed forward. There was no midfield (as in later years) and attacking players were supported with 'backing up' viz. a player would charge at the enemy and if he lost the ball another would collect it and continue the attack. The offside rule was amended in 1867 so the ball could be passed forward thus the skill of 'middling' was added to dribbling. The strategy was to have a goalkeeper, two hard kicking backs and the rest attackers.

C.W. Alcock was captain of the Wanderers and led from the front whilst M.P. Betts (alias A.H. Chequer), A.G. Bonsor and C.H.R. Wollaston who all played for England 'backed him up' and indeed all scored important goals. The remaining forwards were E.E. Bowen, W.P. Crake, T.C. Hooman and R.W.S. Vidal, the latter two being adept at the skill of dribbling. E. Lubbock full back and A.C. Thompson halfback held the defence with some able kicking, whilst R.C. Welch was the untroubled man in goal. The captain C. W. Alcock has already been discussed in Chapter 3 thus the section commences with the other forwards.

MORTON PETO BETTS

The notable families of Peto and Betts played an important role in Victorian society being at the forefront of railway development, and the Betts family came from Charing in Kent a village near Ashford on the Pilgrims' Way. William Betts married Ann Baker at Charing on 17 November 1788 and had three children baptized there namely Susannah (1789), William (1790) and Mary (1793). The son William Betts was born on 30 August 1790 and baptized at Charing Church on 17 October that year and was an architect, surveyor, engineer and railway contractor - he then influenced the career of a famous son. Edward Ladd married Susanna Hayward at Dover on 8 August 1787 and had at least seven children - the last Elizabeth was born there on 14 November 1796 and baptized at St. Mary's, Dover the same day. Richard May Christian was baptized at the Independent Chapel, Deal on 30 April 1783 and married Mary Priest *or Philpot* Ladd (1787) sister at St. Mary's, Dover on 10 October 1805. This family appear later in the story. Indeed Elizabeth witnessed a marriage at the church on 22 July 1810 aged 14 and may have met her husband in Dover. William Betts married Elizabeth Hayward Ladd at Buckland near Dover on 17 August 1814 with parents' consent, and Edward Ladd and Mary Ann Shrewsbury were witnesses. The church was just north of Dover and (later) near to the Crabble sports venue.

William Betts was initially a millwright in the Dover area and with wife Elizabeth had eleven children, the most significant event being the birth of a son Edward Ladd Betts at Buckland on 5 June 1815 (baptized 2 July). They felt pleasure at the happy event but there was also worry since Napoleon's troops were gathering just across the Channel. Waterloo was 12 miles from Brussels and a large number of refugees poured into the city on Saturday 17 June 1815. Napoleon had returned from Elba and had an army of 70,000 French veterans; whilst in opposition were 70,000 British troops and 113,000 Prussians, with larger numbers of Austrians and Russians still arriving to the east. Wellington stated he was not concerned about his men's dress as long as they had plenty of ammunition, and being confident went to a ball given by the Duchess of Richmond in Brussels that evening. He went to bed late and the next morning engaged in battle and the French were defeated but narrowly. The cost was thousands dead and ill with disease whilst a private received a prize of just £2 11s 4d. There was celebration at home but Betts looked for a more 'profitable' way of making a living.

He remained a millwright and daughter Elizabeth Meadows was born at Dover on 2 February 1819 then baptized at St. Mary's on 18 March, and a third Mary Wicking was baptized at Southwick, Sussex on 23 January 1820, but at this point there was a change of direction. William Betts & Sons were formed as a construction company in c.1820 and may have involved father William senior. An 'association' was formed to construct the first Town Bridge at Weymouth, Dorset on 13 August 1821 and Betts received their first contract. Indeed the family moved to the town and two sons were born: William c.1822 and George 29 August 1823 - baptized at Conygar Lane Wesleyan Chapel, Weymouth on 27 September. Betts & Sons completed the bridge with a central arch in 1824 although it was rebuilt in 1880 and finally demolished in 1928.

The country was gripped by railway mania at this time and there was an important advertisement on 25 April 1829 stating: "The directors of the *Liverpool and Manchester Railway* hereby offer a premium of £500 (over and above the cost price) for a locomotive engine, which shall be a decided improvement on any hitherto constructed." The Rainhill 'trials' took place on 6 October 1829 and George Stephenson assisted by his son Robert were winners with the *Rocket* engine. The Liverpool and Manchester Railway was then opened on 15 September 1830 and the steam age had begun! - (See Rennie p. 179). The Betts family soon jumped on the wagon and became notable railway contractors, only just missing the history books. Betts & Sons secured further work in Hampshire and moved to Gosport near Portsmouth by 1829. William Betts was listed as an architect and had children Maria Reece 30 November 1828 and Richard Christian 12 March 1830 - both were baptized at Middle Street Chapel, Gosport in 1829-30. The family were Methodist at this point but they soon had a change of religion. Gosport a naval town fell within the wider parish of Alverstoke and four children were baptized in the parish church on 18 August 1832: George (1823), Maria Reece (1828), Richard Christian (1830) and Joseph Beattie born 6 July 1832. Clearly the family felt that the three earlier baptisms were not valid in the eyes of God. William was a surveyor and engineer (1832-35) and was now strictly C of E thus two children were baptized at Holy Trinity, Gosport: Ellen Rosa on 5 September 1834 and Charles Pybus Ladd (3 October) on 6 November 1835. There was also a son Frederick Betts although his birth has not been traced.

The son Edward Ladd Betts (1815) was first apprenticed to a builder named Richardson in Lincoln and showed an aptitude for mechanical pursuits by constructing a small working model of a steam engine. He was then employed to work on the Black Rock Lighthouse at Beaumaris, North Wales a job that he undertook under his father's guidance. The Stephensons were, at this time, constructing the Liverpool & Birmingham Railway and employed William Betts who took charge of the Dutton Viaduct on 5 June 1833. His son Edward aged 18 superintended some of the work. The railway was in its infancy in the 1830s however Edward had a particular flair for organising this kind of large-scale project and Dutton Viaduct was only the beginning - George Stephenson and Joseph Locke (M.P. and C.E. President) employed Betts & Sons on several occasions. The latter also worked locally and built the Royal Pier, Southampton in 1833 and H.R.H. the Duchess of Kent and Princess Victoria opened the pier - in the presence of William Betts. The family continued to work near Gosport and the Itchen Bridge Company was formed on 30 August 1833. Messrs. Hugh and James McIntosh of London were the main contractors and William Betts was the local agent and foreman. The contract involved building the floating bridge and all associated work on nearby roads and was started on 25 July 1834. It was ready for use on 23 November 1836 and indeed Floating Bridge Road still faces Portsmouth Road across the River Itchen in Southampton (not far from St. Mary's Stadium).

The company then worked on the London and Southampton Railway (1834) and this was a significant project where they met some later associates such as Brassey and Giles. A letter was received from Mr. W. Betts regarding the line on 8 February 1837 and this concerned the terms regarding Mr. McIntosh and the building of culverts. Indeed William Betts had a long association with the eminent contractor McIntosh and they worked together on the North Midland Railway linking Derby with Leeds. It was built with George and Robert Stephenson and the contractors began excavating the Clay Cross Tunnel, south of Chesterfield, on 20 January 1837. The builders realised the site had excellent mineral potential and found limestone, grit-stone and fluorspar used in steel manufacture and formed the Clay Cross Company in 1837 - Peto and Betts were company directors whilst Robert Stephenson was Chairman in 1848-51.

A floating bridge company was established in Portsmouth in 1838 whilst William Betts began work on the Gosport branch line to provide a link to the Southampton Railway, in 1839, the work being undertaken with Thomas Brassey. The floating bridge was completed on 11 May 1840 whilst Sir William Tite (architect of the Royal Exchange) designed Gosport Station with two rows of Tuscan columns, either side of a ticket office. This was completed on 7 February 1842 and the line was then opened however the journey from Portsmouth to London was notorious, as it took an hour to reach Gosport Station by ferry and foot. Queen Victoria used the station to reach Osborne and had a separate terminus at Royal Clarence Yard and some important people came through Gosport. Indeed the party in 1844 included the King of France, Prince Consort, Duke of Wellington, Duc de Montpensier and Mr. Gladstone. The long trek ended when the London to Portsmouth line was finished in June 1847 although the harbour extension was only built in 1876. The Gosport line built by Betts was closed in 1953 however the station became a listed building.

Betts & Sons also worked on the Midland Railway from Rugby to Leicester and began building the Rugby Viaduct on 2 January 1839. To facilitate the work the family moved north and lived at Regent

Street, Southfields in Leicester in 1841. The household was William Betts (50) contractor, William Betts (20) contractor, daughters Elizabeth, Mary and Ellen and niece Mary Christian (25) "independent". A number of changes took place in Leicester and son Charles Pybus Ladd Betts died there in March 1841 but there were also two weddings. George Giles married Elizabeth Meadows Betts in September 1841 and Frederick James Rowan married Mary Wicking Betts in September 1842. Both took place in Leicester and the bridegrooms were civil engineers engaged in railway projects with Betts & Sons!

George Giles was of particular note and was born at Hersham, Surrey on 15 March 1810 and apprenticed to his uncle Francis Giles of the Institute of Civil Engineers. He was engaged on the London and Southampton Railway in 1834 after the relevant Act was passed and became resident engineer on the section linking Winchester to Southampton. McIntosh and Betts then employed him to work on the southern end of the Midland Railway thus he helped construct the Rugby Viaduct and the line four miles north. Giles despite his marriage went abroad and was engineer on the Hamburg to Bergedorf Railway from 1839 until its completion in 1842. During this period the great fire of Hamburg destroyed half the city and the railway was used to transport homeless people to the country. Mr. Giles and two companions tried to stop the fire by blowing up houses with gunpowder but were nearly killed by a mob that believed they were fuelling the flames. He later received a letter of thanks and a medal from the *Senate* on 17 May 1842 and also had two children William Betts (c.1843) and Edith Maria (17 June 1846). He remained in Hamburg until 1846 and carried out William Lindley's plan for new sewers and a water supply, and built locks and bridges during the rebuilding of the city.

As a resident of Hamburg he became a member of the Institute of Civil Engineers on 30 June 1846 and William Lindley proposed him and Francis Giles and George Lowe seconded - John Rennie was Chairman. He worked on the section from Gainsborough to Peterborough as part of the Great Northern Railway in 1847 and then resided in Lincoln and had three children: Maria Grace (bapt. St. Martin's 30 November 1849), Hubert Garvey (21 December 1850) and Philip Manners (June 1852). He worked on the Paris to Marseille line from St. Rambert to Montélimart in 1850-56, which was opened early to transport French troops to the Crimea, and also on the Kaiserin Elisabeth Railway in Austria in 1856 - he built the line from Linz to Vienna with Edward Ladd Betts. His daughter Elizabeth Amy was born at Passy near Paris on 4 January 1857, however he returned to England in 1862 and retired although he continued to produce new schemes. George Giles landowner late C.E. lived at "Westfield", Bonchurch, Isle of Wight, in 1871 with wife Elizabeth, daughters Maria and Elizabeth and five servants. Mary A. Hallibrass family nurse was from Lincoln and a separate cottage housed the coachman.

The two-storey house was of grey flagstone with red banding throughout and had a colossal porch entrance on the east side. There was a 'giant' roof cornice and a semi-circular bay with large windows facing the sea, and the house now *Westfield Mansion* remains as apartments. Otto Prausnitz possibly came from Berlin and married Edith Maria Giles at Bonchurch in December 1875 whilst George Giles died there on 9 April 1877 and was buried in St. Boniface churchyard. Mrs. G. Giles then moved to the Maples, Bonchurch in 1878 and resided there with her two daughters and five servants in 1881. Hubert was then a lieutenant on the ship *Emerald* and Philip a civil engineer living at 4 Charles Street, London. Elizabeth Giles was at the Maples with two daughters and six servants in 1891 and died on 9 July 1896. There are five family memorials behind St. Boniface Church: (1) Edith Maria Prausnitz 1846-99 *German verse*, (2) Philip Manners Giles 1882, (3) George Giles 1810-77 Elizabeth Meadows Giles 1819-96, (4) *Maria* Grace Giles 1849-1940 *Elizabeth* Amy Giles 1857-1946, and (5) Hubert Garvey Giles *commander R.N.* 1850-1940. These memorials are worn with age whilst the grave of Algernon Charles Swinburne (1837-1909) the poet is near the church entrance.

Betts & Sons also worked on the South East Railway including sections from Reigate to Dover and Paddock Wood to Maidstone - one of the first lines into Kent. The company started building the Maidstone branch (and station) in 1841 whilst Edward Ladd Betts took over the Ashford section on 1 February 1842. Partners Peto and Grissell were building the line from Ashford to Folkestone at this time however Betts & Sons took over the work especially the Saltwood Tunnel just west of Folkestone in 1843 (see below). William Betts then worked with Henry Robertson and began the Glasgow to Brymbo Mineral Railway on 20 September 1842 and was a "railway contractor" living at Regent Street, South Fields, Leicester in 1843. His house was between the Midland Railway and Welford Road - near London and Oxford Road and the site of Filbert Street. The business was going well however Elizabeth Hayward Betts died of inflammation on the lungs at Regent Street on 25 January 1844 - the wife of William a railway contractor and the informant Susannah Turner of Simon Street.

The North Wales Mineral Railway Company was formed soon after, on 30 October 1844, and William Betts undertook the work however the project was delayed pending a report from Robert Stephenson. It included a section from Chester to Wrexham and to Holyhead and Anglesey and was completed under A.M. Ross and Robert Stephenson in 1846. William Betts purchased *Bevois House*, Southampton and its estate from Henry Hulton in 1844. He did much work there restoring the house and also erected the famous Stag Gates at the main entrance in 1845 - they displayed the motto "Ostendo Non Ostento" or "I show not boast". William Betts gentleman of Bevois Mount married Charlotte Bailey Arnett widow at St. Mary's Southampton on 21 August 1845. His bride was born in 1801 and her brother Rev. Kemp Bailey of St. Paul's, Hull was minister and Edward Betts, Richard Christian and M.P. Christian witnesses.

Betts & Sons "Contractors for Public Works" were dissolved by mutual agreement on 4 September 1845 and Edward Ladd Betts took over all the work and agreed to pay any outstanding debts on 19 November 1845. William Betts senior then had an advisory role and finally retired from work in 1851 and was living at Bevois House, Southampton that year. He was described as married and a landed proprietor although on the night of the census was alone in the house with his six servants. He sold the repaired property to J.H. Wolff shipping agent on 16 October 1856 but retained the land and developed housing. The Stag Gates were presented to the town as a war memorial in 1919 but demolished soon after during road widening. In this period the children of William Betts also had notable lives: William Betts junior (1822) married Delicia New Laishley at Southampton in December 1843 but she died at Stepney in March 1844, and he then married Helen Maria Watson at the Wirral in December 1845. A first child Delicia Kate Watson Betts was born at Westwell near Ashford in June 1853, however William went to Canada to work as a civil engineer and had three children there: Edward Ladd (1856), Mary Watson (1858) born Montreal and Isabel Octavia (1860) born L. Islett - there was also a son Richard Henry (1861) born at Deal. William Betts worked with his father and brother and this is discussed below.

George Betts (1823) was married at St. Saviour's, Southwark in September 1847 whilst training at a London hospital and became a member of the Royal College of Surgeons in 1849. He was stationed in Burma from 1852 and was assistant surgeon to the 45th Regiment in Rangoon, but died on the "Menasserim" when sailing there from Moulmein on 21 April 1856. Richard Christian Betts (1830) was educated by Mr. Manners at Wesley College, Yorkshire and matriculated at Trinity, Cambridge in Michaelmas 1850. He gained a B.A. in 1854 and entered the Inner Temple on 1 May 1858 and qualified as a barrister in 1864. He then lived at 3 South Square, Gray's Inn but died there on the 2 July 1870 and probate went to his widow Catherine Betts, his effects just £100. Joseph Beattie Betts (1832) a solicitor's articled clerk lived at 12 Coppen Street, Deal, in 1851 with uncle Richard May Christian. The four daughters married men of status and those to George Giles and Frederick J. Rowan have already been discussed. The other marriages were Maria Reece Betts to Robert Growse junior M.D at Eastry (near Deal) on 6 April 1853 and Ellen Rosa Betts to Thomas Smith Rowe M.D. at Eastry in December 1858.

William Betts senior left Southampton to return to his roots in c.1856 and resided at Sandown Terrace, Deal in 1858. He lived alone again with five servants at 5 Sandown on the 1861 census and was married and a house proprietor. William Betts junior a civil engineer lived next door at 3 Sandown with wife Helen, five children, Maria Pamela Rose Founier (from L. Islett) governess, six servants and a coachman. William Betts senior gentleman of Sandown made his last will on 10 January 1867, which was the longest will ever-written (20 pages)! Edward Ladd Betts and son-in-laws George Giles (civil engineer), Frederick James Rowan (civil engineer), Robert Growse M.D and Thomas Smith Rowe M.D. were executors. He confirmed an agreement and covenant to Charlotte Bailey Betts dated 25 February 1854 and gave the freehold of 5 The Terrace, Sandown to grandson Edward Peto Betts. He gave his furniture to his four daughters and his bonds in trust to Ann wife of Edward Ladd Betts, however there was a falling out with son William Betts junior and he stated: "Whereas some time since, I conveyed to my son certain valuable portions of my property, but I lament that he has since forfeited much of my confidence and affection, by an attempt to render me or my estate liable, without my authority for a large amount." Therefore he left no bequests to him but provided a trust for his son's wife and children. William Betts also owned a large amount of property around the country and left this in trust for his four daughters and families. They were to receive the rents and income as follows:

Elizabeth Giles: 13 houses Barrow Hill Terrace, 8 houses Barrow Hill Place, 19 cottages Barrow Hill Row, 2 cottages Barrow Hill Gardens, 4 houses Gravel Pit Walk (all Ashford, Kent). 30 old shares "The Southampton and Itchen Bridge and Roads Company".

Mary Wicking Rowan: 1-17 Southfield Place, Leicester.

Maria Reece Growse: Freehold land of 2 acres 2 roods 35 perches between Bevois Hill House and Garden lately sold to Captain O'Shea, Bevois Mount, messuage in Bevois Valley, Albert Nursery at Deal, 2 The Terrace Sandown, 10 cottages at Albert Place Deal, 1-2 Lower West Street Leicester, Newtown Street Leicester, messuage in Regent Street Leicester and 15 cottages at Barrow Hill Ashford.

Ellen Rosa Rowe: 3-4 The Terrace Sandown, 40 cottages at Bevois Place and 1-2 Bevois Cottages.

William also left property at Bevois Valley to his son Richard Christian Betts and left £4,000 in trust for Joseph Beattie Betts. He then made provision for his granddaughter Helen Amelia Betts the daughter of his son George, who had died many years ago in India, her guardians Edward Ladd Betts, Elizabeth Meadows Giles and Maria Reece Growse. He placed £3,000 in trust for the girl until her 27th birthday but her widowed mother was out of favour and received just £23 per annum, "On condition that she does not in any manner trouble, annoy, or interfere with any of my family, or the said Helen Amelia Betts." The will clearly revealed strained family arrangements. He bequeathed £600 to each of his grandchildren namely Edward Peto Betts, Elizabeth Peto Betts, William Betts, Delicia Kate Betts, William Betts Giles, Edith Maria Giles, William Robert Rowan, Harry Rowan, Robert Growse and William Growse. He left £500 to grandson Arthur Rowe and by default to his mother Ellen Rosa Rowe and £60 p.a. to brother Thomas Betts and £40 p.a. to sister Elizabeth West. He left his cottage at Minster and furniture to Miss Charlotte Lester, having purchased the cottage from her and then improved it, to thank her for the management of his household affairs. He left charitable bequests to the *British and Foreign Bible Society* £250, ministers and widows auxiliary fund of the *Wesley Convention* £250 and *Kent and Canterbury Hospital* £150. He also left small sums to his many friends including Henry Sampson Easty his late secretary, James Chalcott Sharp of Southampton his solicitor, George Rush his agent at Bevois Mount for 20 years, and old friend Mr. William Lankester of Southampton (see below). James Sharp junior of the same town and Edward Weller clerk of Water Street, Deal were the witnesses.

William Betts senior a gentleman aged 76 died of senile decay at "Minster Villa", Minster, Thanet on 14 August 1867 although he appeared coherent (but perhaps rambling) when he wrote the will. Indeed his demise was possibly hastened by the severe financial difficulties of his son Edward (see below). He was buried with his family at Southampton Old Cemetery and executors Edward Ladd Betts of Broome Park, Betchworth, George Giles of Westfield, Bonchurch, civil engineer, Robert Growse of Brentwood M.D. and Thomas Smith Rowe of Margate M.D. proved his will in London on 31 October 1867. His effects were valued at under £30,000 whilst widow Charlotte Bailey Betts died at Beverley, Yorkshire in June 1868. Edward Ladd Betts had been in sole control of the business since 1845 and cemented important associations thus it is now expedient to discuss these partners.

James Peto married Mary Bennett at Kirdford, Sussex near to Petworth on 30 January 1766 and had four children baptized there: James (1767), William (20 July 1768), Mary (1770) and John (1771). They then moved to Surrey and had three other children: Henry baptized East Horsley on 5 June 1774, Ann born c.1780 and Elizabeth baptized Stoke D'Abernon on 19 January 1783. Indeed the family remained in Stoke until at least 1801. There are some complicated relationships at this point however they soon connect to tell a fascinating story. Thomas Grissell married Elizabeth Sarah De La Garde at St. Clement Danes on 23 February 1777 and had a son Thomas De La Garde Grissell at Shoreditch in 1778. He married Ann Peto daughter of James at Stoke D'Abernon on 10 January 1801 and had eight children: Thomas (30 October 1801), James (1803), Charles (1805), Mary (2 August 1808), Hannah (1809), Ann (1811), Elizabeth (1813) and Henry (1815) who were mainly baptized at St. Leonard's, Shoreditch. Son Thomas with his wife Sarah had a child Thomas De La Garde Grissell baptized at St. Botolph's, Aldersgate on 14 August 1826, the church being next to Little Britain (see below).

The Alloways came from Dorking in Surrey and Ralph Alloway, son of Ralph and Elizabeth, was baptized there on 7 September 1746 and married Ann Martyr at Dorking on 31 January 1768. They had eight children in 1769-87 and these included Sophia Alloway baptized Dorking on 16 February 1783. William Peto the brother of Ann married Sophia Alloway at St. Vedast's in Foster Lane, London on 29 October 1808 and they had five children namely Samuel Morton (1809), William (1812), Sophia (1813), James (1820) and Ann (1821). The first three children were born at "Whitmore House", Sutton, Woking, whilst Ann Peto was born at Great Marlow and they lived at Cannons Farm near Cookham in 1841. William Peto 65 (?) farmer and country gentleman lived with wife Sophia, children James, Ann (20) and Sophia French, and eight servants. William Peto j. and wife Emma lived nearby at Pinkneys Farm, Cookham.

William Peto senior made his last will on 3 January 1849 and gave a legacy of £100 and his household goods to wife Sophia. He then gave his freehold property including that at Hendon in Middlesex to sons Samuel Morton Peto, William Peto junior and James Peto. The residual estate and income was to be placed in trust and any profits to go to his wife and sons, however £500 was to be paid to William Peto junior and to his daughter Sophia wife of William French. Any other residue was put in trust for his three sons and daughters Sophia French and Ann wife of Edward Ladd Betts. The will concluded with various legal details - James Taylor of Furnival's Inn a solicitor and Elizabeth Harley of North Town, Maidenhead were witnesses. William Peto gentleman died of influenza aged 80 at North Town, Cookham on 12 January 1849 and the informant was his son James Peto of North Town (Cannons Farm); Samuel Morton Peto, William Peto and James Peto his executors proved his will in London on 5 May that year. Sophia Peto died at North Town on 24 February 1869 and Sir Samuel Morton Peto of 9 Great George Street in Westminster obtained her probate on 27 March - the effects under £2,000.

The son William Peto and his wife Emma continued to live at Cannons Farm and the family owned about 380 acres. William died at Cookham on 25 June 1879 and his probate was granted to Samuel Peto (stockbroker) and William Peto (yeoman) and his estate valued at under £18,000. His wife Emma died at Cannons Farm on 15 August 1885 and probate went to Samuel Peto of 2 Crown Court, Old Broad Street stockbroker and William Peto of Cannons Farm yeoman. Samuel Peto was born at Cookham in 1846 and became a broker in the Stock Exchange and lived at Kensington in 1881. He worked for Robarts & Co. who had links with Lubbock (see Ch. 7) and for the Bank of England (1872-76), but must not to be confused with his famous uncle of the same name. William Peto the younger was born at Cookham in 1850 and died at Cannons Court Farm, Maidenhead on 5 July 1908 - his effects being £6,385 11s 10d.

Samuel Morton Peto was born at Whitmore House, Woking on 4 August 1809 and was educated at an independent boarding school in Brixton under the principal Alexander Jardine. He learnt Latin, French, Mathematics and Algebra, which were considered appropriate subjects for a business career, and showed an early talent for drawing thus he was apprenticed to uncle Henry Peto a builder of 31 Little Britain, London, in 1823. Samuel had a three-year apprenticeship in the joiners' shop, learnt all aspects of the building trade and attended a technical school after work. He trained as a builder on site, reputedly laying 800 bricks in a day, and learnt draughtsmanship from Mr. Maddox of *Furnival's Inn* and architecture from Mr. Beazley. He supervised some major building works for his uncle viz. house for Horace Twiss in Carlton Gardens and barristers' chambers, Raymond's Buildings, Gray's Inn. The latter was an extensive four-storey red brick building at the north west of the Inn and remains today with the date "1825" above the doors. Henry Peto died in 1830 hence Samuel Morton Peto inherited the business with cousin Thomas Grissell (1801).

Initially there were financial problems however the partnership of Peto and Grissell was soon to be most lucrative. Hungerford Market was first established near Charing Cross in 1680 and was named after the Hungerfords of Farleigh Castle in Somerset. The market was run down in the early 19th century and there was a meeting at the Crown and Anchor to discuss a new market. *Bell's Weekly Messenger* reported on the 28 February 1830 that a sum of 210,000*l* was required with 100,000*l* being needed for the building and the rest to purchase the site. This was to be raised in part through shares of 100*l*. There was a second report on 2 May 1830 that noted the bill was progressing through Parliament and most of the money raised, whilst the market would be one of the first to benefit from the 'new' London Bridge and the resulting improvements to navigation. The contract went to public tender and Peto and Grissell were winners - it was their first major work. The business arrangement was cemented when Samuel Morton Peto married his cousin Mary De La Garde Grissell at Lambeth on 18 May 1831 and they resided at Albany Terrace, York Road in Lambeth.

William Fowler was the architect of Hungerford Market and the foundation stone was laid on 18 June 1831. The market had three main areas viz. an upper quadrangle with colonnade, a great hall with granite columns and arches, and a lower quadrangle or fish market with a wharf beside the river. The work finished on 2 July 1833 and the market was opened, but it was of a general nature and failed to compete with Billingsgate or Covent Garden. Indeed it was not destined to last and became the site of Charing Cross Station in 1860 (see Rennie p. 179). Samuel and Mary Peto had two children during this period: Mary (1832) and Ann (1834) baptized at St. Mark's, Kennington. The partners were then attracted to the railways and had contracts with the Great Western, Great Eastern and South Eastern Railways and did work on two Birmingham stations in the 1830s. Isambard Kingdom Brunel was chief engineer of the Great Western from London to Bristol from 1833 and gave a contract to Peto and Grissell. They built the section from Hanwell to Langley including the Hanwell Viaduct but excluding the embankment in

1835. It was also known as Wharncliffe Viaduct and appears on modern maps as 'iron-bridge' whilst Wharncliffe Drive is nearby. There were payment problems over the viaduct and the resolution was arbitration or a meeting with the chief engineer. Samuel Peto chose the latter and met Brunel on many evenings after dinner and they went through the accounts together (at length). After 12 months they certified the amount claimed of £162,000 and the firm had to borrow £100,000 to carry on the work.

Another child Sophia (1837) was baptized at Kennington whilst Samuel Morton Peto became an associate of the Institute of Civil Engineers on 26 February 1839, and in his application stated he was of Lambeth and was fit to be a member because of, "his intimate acquaintance with the pursuits of the civil engineer and his competence as a builder." Joshua Field proposed him and Francis Bramah (locks-hydraulics) and George Lowe seconded him. A last child Henry (1841) was also baptized at Kennington however Mary Peto wife of Samuel and sister of Thomas Grissell died at Lambeth in June 1842, and this may have had an adverse affect on the partnership. Peto and Grissell built large parts of the South Eastern Railway including the viaduct, tunnel and martello towers from Hythe to Folkestone in 1841-43. Meanwhile Betts & Sons were building the line from Reigate to Folkestone and took over some of Peto's work in particular the Saltwood Tunnel just north of Hythe, which was started on 7 March 1843 - the families thus became acquainted through their work.

Edward Ladd Betts an engineer of Sandgate near to Folkestone married Ann Peto (1821) sister of Samuel at Cookham on 6 July 1843, the witnesses William Betts, Maria Reece Betts, William Peto and Elizabeth Grissell. The village was beside the Thames and faced the country house "Cliveden" later owned by the Astors - it attracted politicians and other notaries before the Second War (see Lubbock Ch. 7). This match was also to have benefits for the business whilst Samuel was a widower briefly and married Sarah Ainsworth Kelsall (1822) at Rochdale in September 1843 then lived mainly in London having six sons and four daughters. Peto and Grissell had contracts for some important London buildings: Conservative, Reform, Oxford and Cambridge Clubs, Lyceum, St. James and Olympic Theatres, and the Woolwich Graving Dock. They built Nelson's Column in 1843 whilst the four bronze lions at the base were by Sir Edwin Landseer (see below).

They also worked on sections of the Eastern Counties Railway from Wymondham to Dereham, Ely to Peterborough, Chatteris to St. Ives, Norwich to Brandon, and London to Cambridge and on to Ely. The work was carried out under George Stephenson and on one occasion the great engineer complained about poor work on a wooden bridge. Samuel Peto obtained the office drawings and under his own authority replaced the structure with an iron bridge. Stephenson was surprised as he had not ordered it but Peto explained it was his job to provide the utmost satisfaction! Stephenson expressed his pleasure and had great confidence in him thus the friendship lasted until Stephenson's death in 1848. Peto and Grissell however had done all they could together and the partnership ended on 2 March 1846. Thomas Grissell took on all the building work and he retained the contract for the Houses of Parliament that they began in 1840 - he lived at Norbury Park but died at Dorking in June 1874.

Samuel Morton Peto retained the railway contracts and formed a new partnership with brother-in-law Edward Ladd Betts in 1846 - the latter had taken control of the Betts & Sons contracts in late 1845. They took on further great works namely railway projects at home and abroad, which they carried out with railway 'giants' like Brassey and Crampton. Edward Ladd Betts became a member of the Institute of Civil Engineers on 26 June 1849 and resided at 29 Tavistock Square. His application stated that: "His position as an extensive contractor for public works enables him to concur with civil engineers in the advancement of preferential knowledge." William Cubitt proposed him and Robert Stephenson, George P. Bidder, Isambard Kingdom Brunel, Joseph Cubitt and Samuel Morton Peto seconded him (all from personal knowledge). Joshua Field was Chairman and indeed Edward had joined an influential and exclusive club.

Peto and Betts had built much of the S.E. Railway and worked together on several other railway projects viz. the Great Eastern (Boston to Louth), Great Northern (Peterborough to Doncaster) West Midlands (Oxford-Birmingham, Worcester-Wolverhampton) and improved the Severn Navigation under Sir William Cubitt. They had several contracts abroad including the Great Southern Buenos Ayres Railway, Dunaburg and Witepsk Russian Railway, line from Algiers to Bledah for the French Government and some Netherlands land drainage. Edward Ladd Betts was Chairman of the Eastern Counties Railway in 1851-52 and had to deal with an engine drivers' strike - he ended it successfully and thus stopped it spreading. Their most exciting work however was carried out with Thomas Brassey the ultimate Victorian entrepreneur. He was born at Buerton, Aldford in Cheshire on 7 November 1805 and was educated at Chester School then married Maria Farington Harrison daughter of Joseph Harrison of Liverpool at Birkenhead on 27 December 1831. In fact his wife encouraged him to work on the railways. He obtained a contract to build Penkridge Viaduct on the Grand Junction line from Birmingham to Liverpool under George Stephenson and Joseph Locke in 1834 - Betts & Sons were engaged on the same project (see above). He then worked on the London and Southampton Railway under Locke (another Betts' project) and employed 3,000 men whilst son Thomas was baptized at St. Mary's, Stafford on 11 February 1836.

His family moved to London that year but he continued to work on the Gosport branch line and his son Henry Arthur Brassey was born at Fareham on 14 July 1840. He then worked on the Paris-Rouen-Havre line with W. Mackenzie from 1841-45 and a third son Albert Brassey was born at Rouen on 22 February 1844. He constructed the Great Northern line in 1847-51 with over 5,000 men working on the project and then worked with Peto and Betts from 1848-63. He showed great consideration for his employees and those who worked with Brassey held him in high esteem, but the main reason was he made many of them very rich! Thomas Brassey was an associate of the Institute of Civil Engineers on 16 December 1851 being proposed by Charles May and seconded by Joseph Locke, Isambard Kingdom Brunel, George P. Bidder and Joseph Cubitt, whilst William Cubitt was Chairman. Brassey, Peto and Betts contractors then built the following:

Norwegian Grand Trunk - Christiana to Eidsvold under engineer Mr. Bidder 1851 (56 miles).

Hereford, Ross & Gloucester under Mr. Brunel 1852 (30 miles).

London - Southend under Mr. Bidder 1852 (50 miles).

Victoria Docks - warehouses London under Mr. Bidder 1852-55.

Lyon - Avignon in France agent Mr. Giles 1852 (67 miles).

Crystal Palace - South Norwood under Mr. Bidder 1853 (5 miles).

Royal Danish: Jutland and Schleswig under Mr. Bidder and G.R. Stephenson 1853 (75 miles).

East Suffolk Railway in 1855 (63 miles).

The three partners were then caught up in the public concern regarding the Crimean War and Brassey, Peto and Betts became involved in an important piece of history. The Battle of Balaklava was in October 1854 and was immortalised by "The Charge of the Light Brigade." The campaign was not going well and Queen Victoria asked Lord Palmerston to form a Government in 1855 to solve the conflict. Samuel Peto approached Lord Palmerston with plans to construct a rail link from Balaklava to Sevastopol, and thus facilitate the movement of ammunition and troops to aid the allies in the siege of Sevastopol. The railway was soon being built under the watchful eye of Edward Betts and reports state: "He took on the entire organisation of this important enterprise, and with such energy, that in a few weeks from its commencement, the line was in working order." The partners were only paid for the cost of the work and made no profit but the noble enterprise was rewarded and Samuel Peto was made a baronet on 14 February 1855. It was however a Government contract and he was obliged to resign his seat in Parliament - Betts was unlucky to receive no similar award.

Brassey, Peto and Betts continued their overseas work and built the Elizabeth-Linz Railway in Austria in 1856 - the resident engineer being M.C. Keissler and the agent George Giles (see above). One of their most notable pieces of work was the Grand Trunk Railway in Canada built from 1852-59, and in total they constructed 539 miles of track including Victoria Tubular Bridge over the St. Lawrence River at Montreal. The engineer Robert Stephenson also worked on the project whilst William Betts junior represented them in Montreal and Canada in the years 1856-60. The partnership worked in Australia in 1859-63 and built sections of the Great Northern, Great Eastern and Great Southern Railway in New South Wales and 78 miles of the Queensland Railway. Lastly they did work on the Royal Danish Railway viz. 270 miles of the Jutland line in 1860 and 75 miles of the North Schleswig line in 1863 - Mr. Rowan engineer.

Thomas Brassey "a contractor for public works" resided at 56 Lowndes Square, Knightsbridge (no plaque) however he died at St. Leonard's, Sussex on 8 December 1870. Thomas Brassey of Normanhurst Castle Battle, Henry Arthur Brassey of Preston Hall (see below) and Albert Brassey of Cahir Ireland (lieutenant 14th Regiment Hussars) were the executors. His estate was valued at a staggering £3,200,000 and he was a multi-millionaire and far richer than most of the House of Lords (put together). His wealth was divided between his sons: Thomas married Anna daughter of John Allnutt on 9 October 1860 and worked for the Admiralty, he sat for Hastings from December 1868 until he retired in 1886 and was made Baron Brassey of Bulkeley at that date. Thomas Allnutt his son married Idina Mary Nevill at Ticehurst on 28 February 1889, whilst he remarried Sybil de Vere Capel on 18 September 1890 and became Earl Brassey. He was the Governor of Victoria in 1895-1900 K.C.B. and lived at 24 Park Lane and Catsfield but died on 23 February 1918. His son died on 12 November 1919 thus the Earldom became extinct. Henry Arthur was the owner of Preston Hall and he is treated below and in Chapter 10. Albert married Matilda M.H. Bingham daughter of Baron Clanmorris on 12 January 1871 and lived with his family and twenty servants at Heythrop Mansion, Oxford in 1881 - he died 7 January 1918.

Indeed Peto and Betts also became very rich. Samuel Morton Peto built a Jacobean mansion at Somerleyton near Lowestoft in 1844 the designer John Thomas - a sculptor who had turned to architecture as a better source of income. The building had two protruding wings, central porch and Italianate tower. Samuel had three addresses in 1851: Somerleyton Hall, 47 Russell Square, London and 3 Great George Street, Westminster but lived at none of them on the census. A clerk resided in the house at Great George Street and this was no doubt his office. He built another house 12 Kensington Palace Gardens and his daughter Sophia Peto died there in June 1856 and he obtained her probate on 9 December 1856 - the effects £5,000. Samuel Peto a baronet lived at this address in 1861 with wife Sarah, son Henry, and eight children from the second marriage (one born Somerleyton and the rest London). He clearly spent most of his time in the capital and the upkeep of his large house required 16 servants. He had a number of responsibilities and was the Treasurer for the Baptist Missionary Society in 1846-67, and provided scripture readers for his workers on the Eastern Counties contract in 1846 making sure they were fed and housed. He also provided funds for the building of Bloomsbury Chapel and Regent's Park Chapel (Peto Place) but was quite a "tolerant" churchgoer and also restored the parish church at Somerleyton in Suffolk. He promoted the Great Exhibition in 1851 and gave a guarantee of £50,000 to support the project and was one of H.M. commissioners. He was a Liberal M.P. (1847-68) and represented Norwich in 1847-54 introducing "Peto's Act" in 1850, which rationalised the holding of property by religious bodies. He left Parliament after the Crimea in 1855 and then represented Finsbury in 1859-65 and Bristol in 1865-68. (N.B. Son Harold A. Peto architect employed Edwin Lutyens).

Edward Ladd Betts also enjoyed his wealth and had a family of nine children with his wife Ann (Peto). He was working on the Paddock Wood to Maidstone line in 1841 and son Edward Peto Betts was born at Wateringbury on 2 August 1844. His success meant he became quite prominent and his portrait was painted by J. Dowling in 1844 and was exhibited at the *Royal Academy*. He took a London residence 29 Tavistock Square, St. Pancras and had two children there, namely Elizabeth Peto Betts (December 1845) and Morton Peto Betts (30 August 1847). Meanwhile he wanted a more substantial home and looked in the Maidstone area. The Culpepers occupied Preston Hall near Aylesford in the 13th -18th centuries whilst Charles Milner purchased the estate and nearby Cob Tree Manor House in 1831. Charles Milner (35) of independent means lived at "Preston Hall" in 1841, however Betts had new plans for the property and purchased the house and estate from Col. Henry Robert Milner in 1848 - he set about rebuilding it. His daughter Alice Peto Betts was born at Cookham in 1849 and Ernest William Peto Betts at Aylesford on 29 October 1850, however the family lived at 29 Tavistock Square in 1851. Edward Ladd Betts was an engineer and lived there with his wife Ann, five children and eight servants.

He spent limited time at Preston Hall and a housekeeper and staff occupied the old property in 1851. He then employed J.E. Thomas the architect of Somerleyton and following the lead of his associates Brunel and Peto built a grand house in the 1850s. The finished property was certainly suitable for a country gentleman however it was probably fit for a Lord and was situated south of Aylesford, beyond the River Medway. It was an ornate "Baroque" mansion with two wings, a main one and a conservatory, whilst a central tower dominated the entrance as at Somerleyton, and the interior was equally opulent. Edward had a great interest in history, literature, drama and travel and purchased many fine items from the Stowe sale at *Christies* in 1848 and also had a group of Royal Academy pictures commissioned for the dining room as a status symbol - I.K. Brunel had a similar group done in the 1840s. He was altruistic, like many rich Victorians, and built an infants' school at Aylesford in 1853 (later St. Peter's C of E Primary School) and a school at nearby Ditton. Sir Edwin Henry Landseer painted *Scene in Braemar*, which was the most notable commission and was exhibited at the Royal Academy in 1857. The painting was 9 foot high but was not a rectangle and was curved at the upper edge to fit in the dining room. It showed a Scottish scene with a stag at the centre and came second, only, to Landseer's famous work *Monarch of the Glen*. It was mounted high on the wall in the grand dining room at Preston Hall, which was designed like the banqueting hall in a mediaeval house - the painting despite its size looked somewhat small there. Landseer asked for £600 in payment however Betts paid £800 to express "his approval of the work." This was paid to Landseer's account at Barclays, Fleet Street on 5 July 1859.

The building work and improvements were finally completed in 1857 and Edward took the coat of arms and motto used by his father: "Ostendo Non Ostento" or "I show not boast" although two other families used it. Indeed it was a good choice and reflected Betts' great engineering feats and in fact his work is still there for all to see. Perhaps it was like the epitaph to Sir Christopher Wren: "Reader, you seek my memorial, look around you." Having settled in at Preston Hall three other children were born there, namely Percy Campbell (7 January 1856), Herbert Peto (8 July 1857) and Gertrude Annie (1859). Betts progress in business meant he was a local J.P. as well as being appointed Deputy Lieutenant High Sheriff for Kent in 1858. The family owned Preston Hall "Mansion" in 1848-67 but Edward and wife Ann were not at home in 1861. The household then included Morton Peto Betts (the eldest child at home), five siblings, ten servants and a governess. Indeed five of the sons were educated at Harrow School and four went on to Trinity and Pembroke College, Cambridge.

Edward Ladd Betts (1815-72).
He built railways in England and abroad then went bankrupt.

Edward Ladd Betts shared business premises with Samuel Morton Peto at 9 Great George Street, Westminster next to Parliament Square in 1861 - only an office keeper was present. The Institute of Civil Engineers was at Great George Street from the 1840s and many of its members had offices there viz. Charles Cubitt civil engineer was at no. 3 in 1861. The Institute moved to its present address at 1-7 Great George Street in 1911-13 and inside are rooms dedicated to Brassey, Cubitt and Rennie. The only Georgian property remaining there is no. 11 and its plain red brick façade gives us a glimpse of Betts' office. The Institute of Mechanical Engineers is nearby at 1 Birdcage Walk (see Leitch). Betts' employees like those of Brassey held him in high esteem and the records of the Institute state the following: "Those only who are practically acquainted with the execution of large works, requiring constant and unremitting attention, can in any measure appreciate the amount of energy and mental labour, expended by Mr. Betts on these various enterprises. Mr. Betts was gifted with a clear judgement and a vigorous mind that grasped at once the main points of a question, and quickly decided on its merits. This almost intuitive perception of character enabled him promptly to estimate men's worth, and their capacity for any given work. That he was not often deceived in this respect, is proved by the many lifelong friendships he formed, and by the number of years his agents and employees continued to serve him with attachment and fidelity."

Peto and Betts also associated with Thomas Russell Crampton and worked together on the railway from Rustchuk to Varna in Bulgaria and on the London, Chatham and Dover Railway (1860). The latter, however, was to be their downfall. The partners had worked on Nelson's Column, the Houses of Parliament, national and world railways, and assisted in the Crimean War but there was soon to be a loss of pressure in the boiler! They completed work in Denmark and Australia in 1863 but then concentrated their efforts at home, whilst a last child Howard Evelyn Betts was born at Wantage in Berkshire on 20 August 1864. There was a serious financial crisis in the city in 1866 (see Pember Ch. 4) and the maelstrom soon affected Peto and Betts. They had liabilities of £4 million and unrealisable assets of £5 million with Crampton also implicated, thus they suspended payments to creditors on 11 May 1866. The situation was untenable and they were declared bankrupt in 1867. This was recorded in the Times on 3 March 1868 under the heading Court of Bankruptcy, Basinghall Street 2 March. A whole column reported the sorry affair and began:

IN RE. PETO BETTS AND CRAMPTON. A meeting was specially appointed for the consideration of a claim, made against the estate of the bankrupts Sir Morton Peto, Edward Ladd Betts and Thomas Russell Crampton by the London, Chatham and Dover Railway Company. Mr. Markby appeared for the assignees Mr. Lawrance for the bankrupts and Mr. Linklater for the railway company. The claim of the company is made thus:

DEBIT

Cash from the contractors to the company, and payments made by the contractors on a/c of the company	2,171,336
Works per the certificates of the company's engineers	2,993,264
Cash received from the public for Metropolitan Extension stocks and debentures taken by the contractors	4,171,450
Balance due by the contractors exclusive of interest	6,661,941
Total	**£15,997,993**

CREDIT

Cash from the company to the contractors, and payments made by the company on a/c of the contractors	4,403,44
Stocks and debentures taken or realised by the contractors	11,594,551
Total	**£15,997,993**

There were complicated arguments relating to the matter and Mr. Linklater proceeded on behalf of the London, Chatham and Dover Railway with a proof presented against the estate, at the meeting, for choice of assignees for £6,661,941 19s 1d. These were debts to make the strongest of men crumble! He summoned Sir Morton Peto for examination and noted there was a Chancery suit pending regarding the disputed amounts. The bankrupts had to produce the contracts they had entered into, whilst the matter was a question of law, since they had undertaken certain works and were to be paid in shares and debentures. The company had charged them with these, but the bankrupts said they ought not to be charged with the nominal value but only the amount realised on sale. Mr. Linklater concentrated on the Metropolitan Extension works and Eastern Section i.e. two-three contracts. The London, Chatham and Dover Railway was from Victoria-Holborn to Herne Hill, Bromley, Medway, Canterbury and Dover; the Metropolitan Extension from Herne Hill to Blackfriars and Holborn Viaduct - the latter was still under construction in 1862. Two bridges were built across the Thames and the ironwork bearing their name can still be seen at Blackfriars Bridge viz. "London, Chatham and Dover Railway 1864". The cast iron emblems that flanked the bridge and Classical columns that once carried the railway still remain.

The works of the Western Extension were performed under an agreement of August 1858 and the contract was between the East Kent Railway Company and Peto, Betts and Crampton. There was an Act of Parliament for the Metropolitan Extension in August 1860 and Mr. Betts had the principal management of these works with a proposal to undertake them on 7 September 1860. Peto stated, however, that he had no way of knowing if the capital provided by the act would be sufficient and had made no calculation of the land required and the expenses. Mr. Linklater pressed him further on this matter asking, "Was he not aware the works could not be finished?" Sir Morton Peto replied, "He was without the means of knowledge, but three or four months afterwards he certainly became aware that the amount would be insufficient, and Mr. Betts informed him that he was quite sure of it," (laughter from the gallery)! The project was under-funded in terms of its contracts from the very start. There were clearly problems brewing and at Mr. Betts' suggestion a further contract was signed on 1 October 1860 to increase the rate per mile of permanent way from £5,107 - £6,180. There were further debates in the court regarding the movement of funds, capital, shares and debentures this being no easy matter to resolve, and the hearing was adjourned until Wednesday 11th inst as the claims involved millions of pounds.

Samuel Peto was forced to resign his seat in Parliament but received tributes from Disraeli, whilst Gladstone said: "He was a man who has attained a high position in this country by the exercise of rare talents, and who has adorned that position by his great virtues." Yet, like Napoleon, he did return and continued to live well in a number of notable houses. He sold Somerleyton Hall to Sir Frank Crossley (carpets) in 1866 but continued to live at 12 Kensington Palace Gardens until 1877. He moved to Eastcote House, Eastcote Road, Pinner and resided there in 1881 being described as a baronet and J.P. The household included his wife Sarah, son Morton Kelsall Peto an artist, four other children and seven servants - the vicar of Ruislip lived next door. The family also owned Chipstead Place in Sevenoaks and the Hollands in Yeovil. Sir Samuel Morton Peto moved to Blackhurst, Tunbridge Wells in 1884 and died there on 13 November 1889, but the value of his estate is uncertain since no probate record survived. His widow Dame Sarah Ainsworth Peto remained there but died at Villa Les Vallergues, Cannes on 6 January 1892 and Sir Henry Peto baronet, Morton Kelsall Peto and William Herbert Peto Esqs. obtained her probate the value £4,880 10s 5d.

There was, however, no such comeback for Edward Ladd Betts and his last act was to contest Maidstone for the Conservative Party in 1865, but without success. He was quite spent after the trauma of the bankruptcy and financial crisis and the family were forced to leave Preston Hall. The estate of 2,810 acres was sold by auction at Tokenhouse Yard, London near the Guildhall on 17 June 1867, the auctioneers Daniel Smith, Son and Oakley of 10 Waterloo Place, Pall Mall. Indeed the property was mortgaged to Thomas Brassey thus he took possession at this time, and his son Henry Arthur (1840) went and lived in the house in 1867 and died there in 1891 (see Addison Ch. 10). Hugh William Tyrwhitt-Drake purchased Cob Tree Manor House from 'Brassey' in 1904, and Preston Hall was used for the rehabilitation of ex-servicemen after 1921 and became the Royal British Legion Village.

Edward Ladd Betts had lost his mansion but there was worse to come and his pictures and engravings were sold through Christie, Manson and Woods at 8 King Street, St. James's Square on 30 May 1868. The sale included paintings by Van Dyck, Rubens, Titian and Sir Joshua Reynolds as well as *Scene in Braemar* by Landseer. The total value of the sale was 14,473 guineas 15s however the painting by Landseer brought in the largest amount at 4,200 guineas. The second owner Henry William Ferdinand Bolckow exhibited it at the Royal Jubilee Exhibition, Manchester in 1887 although he sold it for £4,950 guineas in May 1888. The painting resurfaced at Christies on 25 March 1994 and was sold for £793,500. Edward L. Betts lived at Broome Park, Betchworth in 1867 however had moved to "The Holmwood", Bickley Park Road near Bromley, Kent in 1870. George Wythes who was also involved in the railways had built the house in the 1860s and the first owner Robert H. Alexander Esq. named it "Farrants" whilst the new name was taken in 1870. Edward had retained his status despite the bankruptcy and was a civil engineer, magistrate and Deputy-Lieutenant of Kent at the Holmwood in 1871 with his wife Ann, nine unmarried children including his sons Edward P. and Morton P. Betts civil engineers and seven servants - the property was clearly substantial.

Edward Ladd Betts had retired and took his doctor's advice in the autumn of 1871 and travelled to Egypt hoping a winter in that climate would restore his strength. However, years of unceasing labour had taken their toll and he died at Assouan, Upper Egypt on Sunday morning 21 January 1872 aged 56. Details were in the *Bromley Record* on 1 March and stated, "He died peacefully on his Dahabiah" (Nile sailing boat), whilst his remains were returned to England and interred at Aylesford in Kent. Ann Betts of Bickley widow and John Lankester of 9 Victoria Chambers, Westminster (see father's will) obtained probate in London on 7 June 1872. Edward clearly made provision for his family before his decease and his effects were £16,000, an amount that hardly compared to that of Brassey. His family remained at Bickley after his decease and daughter Alice Peto Betts married her cousin Henry Bailey Rowan at Bromley in September 1876 (son of Mary Wicking Rowan), but there was soon a further tragedy. Percy Campbell Betts (1856) was a scholar living at Preston Hall in 1861 and was educated at Harrow in 1869-73 but was at home in Bickley in 1871. He attended Trinity College, Cambridge in 1874 gaining his B.A. in 1877 but was 'accidentally' shot whilst cleaning a revolver at his mother's home in Bromley and died on 14 October 1878.

Ann Betts widow lived at the Holmwood in 1881 with Edward (civil engineer), Elizabeth, Herbert (Cambridge B.A.), Annie and four servants whilst the estate included Holmwood Lodge and a coachman's cottage. The family left the house in 1883 and the new owners changed the name back to "Farrants". It was built in mock-Tudor style with a base of red brick, half-timbered upper storey, large gables and chimneys, grey roof and conservatory at one end. It was a long rambling building and still remains today under the name Farrants Court having been converted into flats. Mrs. Edward Ladd Betts lived at "Alfred House", Easthill, Ashford, Kent, from 1887-99 and then at 11 East Hill, Ashford in 1901. The household included her daughter Alice Peto Rowan (widower), Alice R. Rowan (21), Percy S. Rowan (18) and six servants. Ann Betts died at "Oaklands", Cranleigh in Surrey on 23 January 1908 and her probate was granted to Edward Peto Betts esquire, Rev. Herbert Peto Betts and Rev. Ernest William Peto Betts - her effects £9,462 4s 7d.

Edward Peto Betts (1844) attended Trinity College, Cambridge in 1864-68 and became a civil engineer, being involved in the family business, and received a property at Sandown, Kent in his grandfather's will in 1867. He was an assistant engineer under William Hartland in 1868 during the building of the railway from Vetebsk to Nijin, Russia and made alterations to the Metropolitan and District Railways in 1869-71. He lived at home in Bickley in 1871 but was then District Government Engineer for the Cape of Good Hope in 1874-78. He resided at the Holmwood in 1881 and at Hill House, Bagshot Road, Frimley near Camberley Surrey in 1907. He died there on 24 November 1918 and his probate went to the Public

Trustee in the amount of £8,415 2s. Elizabeth Peto Betts (1846) died at 2 Oxford Terrace, Combe Down, Bath, on 1 March 1940 and her probate went to Rev. Howard Evelyn Betts.

Ernest William Peto Betts (1850) lived at Preston Hall in 1861 and was educated at Harrow in 1865-68 and Trinity, Cambridge in 1870 gaining a B.A. in 1874 and M.A. in 1877. He was curate of Wotton, Herts in 1881 and then rector of Drayton Beauchamp, Bucks from 1887-1911. He lived at Nerquis Tower, Romsey in 1925 and died at Ellerslie, Petersfield, Hants on 12 November 1932 his effects being £12,289 6s 4d. Herbert Peto Betts (1857) was educated at Harrow in 1872-75 and Pembroke, Cambridge in 1877 gaining a B.A in 1880 and M.A. in 1884. He was initially a curate then vicar of Fernhurst, Sussex in 1892-1902 and Steep, Hampshire from 1902 to at least 1925. He worked for Chichester Diocese in 1923-39 and lived at Upper Durford, Petersfield in Hants and died there on 13 August 1946. His probate went to his widow Mary Burns Betts and his estate valued at £4,626 0s 5d. Howard Evelyn Betts (1864) was educated at Harrow in 1878-82 and Trinity, Cambridge in 1882 with a B.A. in 1885 and M.A. in 1889. He was vicar of Elson, Hants in 1894-1900, N. Holmwood near Dorking in 1900-12, Todenham in 1912-19 and Hawkesbury near Badminton in 1919-29. He lived at St. Catherine's Cottage, South Terrace, Dorking, in 1938 and died on 25 March 1941 his probate to widow Helen Anne Warren Betts - £598 16s 10d. Peto and Betts, meanwhile, engineered an important football alliance.

Morton Peto Betts was born 29 Tavistock Square, St. Pancras on 30 August 1847 and lived there with his family in 1851. The square was south of Euston Station in the Bloomsbury area and near the 'new' St. Pancras Church. The house itself was located on the northwest corner and had a columned side entrance with a ground floor of white stone, and upper storeys of red brick faced with white pilasters. The property remains and with no. 30 is the School of Public Policy (*Rubin Building*) of University College, London. There is, however, no blue plaque to record Morton Peto Betts even though he holds an important place in soccer history. Morton grew up in the rural surrounds of Preston Hall near Aylesford and was living there as a scholar aged 13 in 1861. He was educated at Harrow School from 1862-65 being a member of the Headmaster's House and was good at football and cricket, as well as lawn tennis, but did not play for the Harrow eleven. He was a civil engineer aged 23 unmarried living at "The Holmwood", Bickley in 1871. He attended Harrow after the Alcocks but was involved in the early F.A. and joined the Committee in 1871-72 as a representative of West Kent and the Old Harrovians.

He was at the meeting when the F.A. Cup was established in 1871 and entered with the Harrow Chequers although, as stated, they dropped out and he then played for the Wanderers scoring the only goal in the 1872 Final. He may have played for this team at other times but was Honorary Secretary of the Old Harrovians F.C. in 1870-73. Despite his soccer prowess he spent more time playing cricket and was a good middle order batsman and wicket keeper making several county appearances. Bickley was a rural hamlet in the 1870s and was centred on Bickley Park Road with the cricket ground, parish church, rectory and the Holmwood all being adjacent. The Bickley Park Cricket Club was founded in 1868 and the club history reveals that Betts joined in March 1870 and became Honorary Secretary in February 1871. He helped to organise club dinners, the 'refreshment' tent and the appointment of a grounds-man and captained the team in 1872. He played one game for Middlesex that year, and had three innings for Kent from 1872-81 (2 matches) scoring 44 runs with a high score of 39 runs not out. He resigned his captaincy of the club in 1873 and was presented with a bat at the A.G.M. before his departure for South America - on business. He returned home in October 1876 and was soon on the ball again receiving a great honour in the game of football. He played for England v Scotland at the Oval on 3 March 1877 and represented the Old Harrovians but his side lost 3-1. He rejoined the Bickley Park Committee and continued to represent them and Bromley to 1884. He worked in Copenhagen in 1878-80 but journeyed home for his wedding during this time.

John Bouch was born at Monument Yard in 1811 and married Margaret Lowther at Islington in September 1838. Their daughter Margaret (1839) was born at St. Pancras however they moved to Dulwich and had children: John Charles (1840) *infant* baptized at the College, Frances (1841), Marion (1843), John (1844) and William (1846) two being baptized at St. Matthew's, Brixton. They then lived at Denmark Hill and had children Jane (28 July 1848), Alfred (1850) and Alice (1853) but moved to Leytonstone in the West Ham district in the late 1850s. There were soon some major changes and Margaret Bouch died at West Ham in June 1860 but this was followed with four weddings in the same area. Morell Mackenzie (1837) was born in Leytonstone and married Margaret Bouch in June 1863 and was a physician in Harley Street, whilst Edward John Luck (1833) was born near to New Kent Road and married Marion Bouch in September 1863. Edward Carey (1835) was born in Dalston and married

Frances Bouch in September 1864 then moved to Surbiton and had two children, whilst John Bouch senior married Helen Rose Carey in December 1864 - she was baptized at St. Mary's, Whitechapel on 13 March 1829 the daughter of James Edward and Rose Septima. John and Helen lived in 'West Ham' and son Ernest was born there in December 1865 but then moved to "Coombe Lea", Bickley Park not far from the Betts' and had a son Herbert Edward in June 1868, whilst two of the daughters followed their father to the area.

The Shortlands estate near to Bromley, Kent was developed in the mid-19th century and Kingswood Road was laid out with large Victorian houses. On the north side were the Gables, Woodside, Hazeldene, Oak Lodge, Ravensbourne, Oakhurst, Overdale and Mayfield whilst the south side had Kingswood House, Hillside, Ellangowan and St. Mary's Church and Vicarage. Edward Carey an underwriter to an insurance co. moved to the newly built Oak Lodge in 1869 and lived there in 1871 with his wife Frances, three children, Alfred Bouch a visitor, and four servants. The house had large gables and stood near to the road whilst the two adjacent properties were set further back: Ravensbourne or the "Castle" as it was known locally was built just to the north in 1866 and was a substantial property - Edward J. Luck lived there in 1869-75; Hazeldene was built to the south in 1874 and was white washed with half-timber features. John Bouch junior married Eliza Browne at Surbiton in June 1871 and then lived in that area of Surrey.

There was a settlement upon the marriage of Morton Peto Betts of Copenhagen and Jane Bouch of Bickley Park on 15 April 1879. This involved two life assurance policies and the trustees were John Bouch j., Surbiton gent and Reginald de Courtenay Welch, Hyde Park esq. (see Ch. 7). Morton Peto Betts married Jane Bouch at St. George's, Bickley on 17 April 1879 and Rev. Ernest W. Betts M.A. was the minister and John and Alice Bouch and Elizabeth P. and Edward P. Betts were witnesses - in the *Bromley Record* on 1 May 1879. John Bouch a retired merchant lived with his second wife Helen Rose and five servants at "Coombe Lea" in 1881. Morell Mackenzie M.D. (London) a physician lived at 19 Harley Street with his wife Margaret, three children, a visitor, a governess and eight servants. Edward Carey a merchant, wife Frances, two children and three servants lived at Oak Lodge. Edward J. Luck a timber merchant lived at 142 Cromwell Road, Kensington with wife Marion, Alice Bouch and three servants, and John Bouch a Manchester warehouseman lived at "Holmwood", South Bank, Surbiton with wife Eliza, five children and three servants. Albert B. Webb the rector of Lullingstone and his family lived at Hill Side, Granville Road, Sevenoaks with fifteen boarders and five servants - one being Herbert Bouch a scholar.

John Bouch of "Coombe Lea" made his last will on 29 July 1884 and left money and investments to his wife and children including daughters Margaret Mackenzie, Frances Carey, Marion Luck and Jane Betts. He appointed wife Helen Rose, son John Bouch and John Charleton executors and trustees but Ernest *Reithmuller* Bouch (son) replaced the latter in a codicil on 27 January 1892. Morell Mackenzie died at Marylebone in March 1892 whilst John Bouch died at Bickley on 29 March 1895 and his will was proved on 11 May - effects £34,772 17s 8d. Edward Carey lived at Oak Lodge, Shortlands in 1869-85 but died at Christchurch in March 1888 and Mrs. Carey was at the house in 1890-95. The garden area was built on in the early 1900s whilst Sydney T. Darrell lived there in 1930-39 and Darrell Court covers the site. Kingswood Road was once an area for rich Victorian gentlemen but was developed between the wars and again in more recent times. The only buildings to survive are Hazeldene, Overdale, Mayfield and the coach-house of Ravensbourne and the Gables. Indeed there is a stone tablet in memory of Arthur March Tapp and his wife Caroline who lived at Woodside (1870-78) and the Gables (1879-1914) on the wall in modern Fyfield Close.

Morton and Jane Betts also lived in the Bromley area however their daughter Marion Alice Betts was born at 19 Harley Street, Marylebone near to Cavendish Square on 14 January 1880, and named after her two aunts. Morton Peto Betts a civil engineer lived with his wife, daughter and one servant at 1 Plaistow Road, Bromley in 1881 and was a neighbour of the Kinnairds at Plaistow Lodge, but his house was somewhat smaller. He was also listed at "Beaufort Villa", 1 Plaistow Lane in 1882-83. The property was at the junction with Crescent Road (north side) and opposite St. Mary's, Plaistow, whilst the lane was much narrower then and road studs mark the former extent of the churchyard. Betts' house is still present as 88 College Road however it is much altered and better examples are at numbers 104-108. Morton Peto Betts was on the F.A. Committee again in 1881-82 and remained on the F.A. Council for some 20 years.

He did not stay in one place long and daughter Amy Margaret was born at 5 Stansfield Villas, Angles Road in Streatham on 29 November 1882; he then moved to east London and played for Essex C.C.C. before they were a first class side in 1884. Ethel Maud Liddell was born at "Sheridan House", Wanstead on 20 October 1885 and he was Secretary of Essex C.C.C. in 1887-90. He lived at the "Chestnuts", Fairlop Road in Leytonstone in 1890-91 near to Snaresbrook with Jeannie Betts, daughters Amy and Ethel, and two servants; however his wife Jane died of heart disease at 14 Montrave Road, Penge on 13 March 1892 aged 43 the informant being Morton P. Betts of the same address. He remained a civil engineer and was Secretary of the Church of England Young Men's Society at 3 St. Bride Street near Ludgate Circus in 1899-1900. This was his contact address and the offices also housed Iliffe, Sons and Sturney Ltd. (publishers).

He continued to travel for work and Morton P. Betts a widower, civil engineer and employer boarded in two rooms at 10 Oakland Terrace, Swansea in 1901. Walter Winstone a mason was head and the other occupants his daughter Louise, Emily Lloyd servant housekeeper, and lodger Benjamin W. Burton (17) civil engineer and employee. He was engaged on an engineering project and possibly worked with those in the house. Marion Betts lived at 3 Nevern Mansions on the east side of Warwick Road, Earl's Court in 1901, near Nevern Square and St. Matthias Church. This was the home of her uncle Edward John Luck but he was staying on his own means in Brighton with his wife Marion. Meanwhile Helen R. Bouch a widow lived at the "Limes", Heathfield Road, Keston between Westerham Road and Fox Hill that year with Herbert E. Bouch (32) a Manchester warehouseman, granddaughters Amy and Ethel Betts and four servants. Helen Rose Bouch died on 16 May 1902 and she was buried at West Norwood although there is a memorial to her and son Herbert Edward at Keston Church. Marion Luck and Marion Alice Betts then applied for a discharge of the residuary estate of John Bouch senior on 25 October 1902.

Morton continued to work in Swansea and was then engaged. Rev. Rees Herbert Morgan (1824) married Sarah Thomas (1827) and had children Jane Eva at Ystalfera Llanquick near Neath on 29 July 1859 and Elizabeth (1861) and William Henry (1865) both at Bedwelty in Monmouth. He died at the latter on 19 December 1869 and widow Sarah Morgan of Singleton Terrace, Swansea, administered his effects at Llandaff on 11 July 1871 - under £200. Sarah Morgan a widow on her own means lived at 28 Brynymor Crescent, Swansea in 1901 with her children Jane E., Elizabeth Haines, William Henry (copperas merchant) and one servant. The family were in a different social class and spoke Welsh although Jane herself only spoke English. Morton Peto Betts a widower and civil engineer of "Ravenswood", Oakland Terrace in Swansea married Jane Eva Morgan of "Broomford", Birdhurst Road at Croydon Register Office on 6 July 1901 (see Creswell Ch. 9) - W. Henry Morgan and Hettie Morgan were witnesses. The wedding was a quiet affair but appeared in the Times on Wednesday 10 July 1901: "BETTS-MORGAN On the 6th inst at Croydon, Morton P. Betts to Eva J. Morgan, daughter of the late Reverend Herbert Morgan of Swansea."

His mother Ann Betts died in 1908 and daughter Amy Margaret Betts married at the Strand in June 1910. He possibly received an inheritance hence he retired to Villa Massa St. Anne, Garavan, near Mentone in the Alpes Maritimes France in 1911. The district was beside the Mediterranean and next to the Italian border, near to Monaco and Monte Carlo. Morton Peto Betts died at the Villa Massa on 19 April 1914 and his will was proved in London on 5 August by executors Jane Eva Betts widow and Frank Amsden manufacturer, however his assets were abroad and his estate amounted to just £40 8s 8d. Philip M. Bendall married Ethel Maud Liddell Betts at Paddington in March 1920 whilst Jane Eva Betts died at the Aikman Eventide Home, Oakwood, Bathwick Hill, Bath on 1 March 1942 and her probate was granted to Harry Hamilton Lewis retired bank official and Gwladys Mary Lewis spinster.

ALEXANDER GEORGE BONSOR

The second forward in the Wanderers side was a member of an extremely rich family who were resident at one of the country's stately homes. The official records suggest the family came from Lincolnshire but further research found them in Nottingham. John Bonsor married Eleanor Pinder at Clarborough near East Retford on 29 May 1754 and Charles Cartwright the vicar performed the ceremony whilst they signed *John Bonsor* and *Eleanor Pinder now Bonsor* - she was clearly proud of her new name. Ellinor was baptized at East Retford on 3 December 1733 and was daughter of William Pinder who had other children in the years 1730-43. The couple had seven children at Clarborough: Elizabeth (1758), Thomas (1760), John (1763), William (1765), Joseph (1768), Susannah (1770) and Henry (1771). The story proper begins with Joseph Bonsor born at Bollam, Clarborough on 9 January 1768 and baptized there on 25 January, however he soon moved to London and amassed a small fortune as stationer and bookseller. Anthony Hartshorne, meanwhile, had eight children baptized at East Retford: George (1752), Michael (1757), Elizabeth (1760), Anthony (1763), Jane (1765), John (1767), Robert (1769) and Mary (1773). His daughter Jane Hartshorne was baptized at East Retford on 22 March 1765 but Anthony later resided at Moorgate, Clarborough and thus met the Bonsors. His son John lived at All Hallows Barking, London and married Ann Crouch at St. Martin in the Fields on 18 November 1787, and daughter Elizabeth married Musgrave Lamb at East Retford on 17 July 1788 - the latter was to be most significant (see below).

Joseph Bonsor resided at St. Anne's, Blackfriars and married Jane Hartshorne at St. Martin in the Fields on 19 March 1796. The couple signed their names and Plaxton Dickinson was the minister and George Hartshorne and Sarah Smith witnesses. His home in Blackfriars was near to Fleet Street, already a centre for publishing and books, and Dr. Samuel Johnson (1710-84) lived nearby in Gough Square - the latter was son of a bookseller and published his *Dictionary of the English Language* in 1755. The family remained on the edge of the City in the early 19th century and resided at 132 Salisbury Square in the parish of St. Bride's. The house was south of Fleet Street in the shadow of the church of St. Bride's designed by Sir Christopher Wren with its "wedding cake" tower. Salisbury Square was a small oasis in an area of narrow streets that led down to the Thames with St. Bride's Wharf and Dorset Wharf nearby. The numbers seldom went above 10 but in Salisbury Square there were numbers 1-19, 46-49 and 132-140. The reason for this oddity is uncertain.

The couple had two children at this address: Jane born 28 August 1805 and baptized 9 October, and Joseph born 15 August 1807 and baptized 8 October - both at St. Bride's Church. Their father ran a stationery business at 132 Salisbury Square and was very successful hence he soon purchased a small house in the country. Before considering this acquisition a brief digression is necessary. Richard Brinsley Sheridan was born at 12 Dorset Street, Dublin on 30 October 1751 and attended Harrow in 1762-68. He became a statesman and dramatist and had an important connection to Drury Lane Theatre. He acquired "Polsden House" and 341 acres between Great Bookham and the North Downs in Surrey in 1796 and was owner in the early 19th century - known as Polesden Lacey. Meanwhile Drury Lane Theatre burnt down on 24 February 1809 and there was a financial scandal with many hungry creditors. A committee was established to rebuild it and Samuel Whitbread was appointed Chairman with other members Lord Byron and Douglas Kinnaird. There was much discussion and Whitbread had to take a strong line and this even included a debate in the House of Commons, such was the importance of theatre before football arrived. Drury Lane was finally rebuilt and re-opened on 10 October 1812 but during this period Sheridan pursued Whitbread for £12,000. He claimed he was owed this amount by the theatre but Whitbread was not forthcoming and only gave him shares (in the theatre). The outcome was bad and Sheridan was arrested for debt at 17 Savile Row in August 1813 and after a period in prison died in 1816. Whitbread was believed to be culpable in the matter and the outcome was dire all around (see Lubbock Ch. 7). There was a son Thomas Sheridan (1775-1817) and a grandson Richard Brinsley who died in 1888.

Due to these financial problems the proposed renovations at Polesden were not carried out, and son Charles Sheridan sold the property and estate in 1818. It was commonly described as a rundown abode however the auctioneer's brochure stated: "The property is a freehold estate of 318 acres. The soil is extremely dry and healthy and the views very extensive and diversified. The only building now remaining upon the site is a stable which has been converted into a cottage and a barn and hovel, boarded and tiled." An estate map dated 1818 shows just a barn and two small buildings whilst Sheridan Road is situated in Bookham. Joseph Bonsor purchased the house and land at the auction for £10,000 and demolished the remains of Sheridan's old house, which was "in decay". He decided to rebuild Polesden and Thomas Cubitt was employed to design a new house (see Pember Ch. 4) and he soon spent a fortune there. A Regency villa was built at a cost of £7,600 in the years 1821-23 and was ready to live in by 1824, the papering and decorating costing £314, the furniture £1,641 and the china and glass £117.

The rectangular house had distinctive features, viz. an Ionic colonnade at the south front with pediment and arched windows each side, and an entrance portico with four Doric columns. The whole composition looked across a valley to Ranmore Common and Bonsor rebuilt the walled garden c.1818 and planted 20,000 trees from 1824-25. The carriage drive was along Yewtree Lane in the 1820s and came right past the house, but was re-routed as a sunken road in the 1860s; indeed the raised banking and Yew trees can still be seen to the southwest. There was further money spent on building estate lodges and stables and the area of land was increased in size from 1818-26, the total expense £47,000. The result was a landscaped estate with a Regency mansion and J.P. Neale's, "Views of the Seats of Noblemen and Gentlemen", showed it thus in 1824. The Bonsors then took up residence and enjoyed the fruits of their labours.

At this time, however, there were developments for Musgrave and Elizabeth Lamb in Reading. The couple had children George (1792), Samuel (1795), Jane (1797), Henry (9 August 1799), Charles (1802) and Thomas (2 March 1804) baptized at Broad Street Meeting House and St. Giles, Reading. Indeed Musgrave Lamb owned a sailcloth factory at Katesgrove Lane in the south of the town near St. Giles and it was quoted that: "The factory produced so much sail cloth for the Royal Navy that the Battle of Trafalgar (1805) was won in Katesgrove." The material itself was noted for its strength and whiteness whilst Musgrave and George Lamb lived at Reading in 1830. Sons Henry and Thomas worked for uncle

Joseph Bonsor in London thus Henry and Sarah Lamb lived at Shoe Lane, Fleet Street and at 132 Salisbury Square by 1832; they apparently took over the property after Joseph moved to Polesden Lacey. They had five children baptized at St. Bride's: Sarah (1825), Henry (1827), Ann (1827), Ellen (1832) and Fanny (1839). The father was a stationer and a gentleman whilst brother Charles Lamb was a solicitor at 8 Furnival's Inn in 1841.

There is now a second digression: Alexander Orme was born in Scotland in 1760 and entered the E.I.C. Service whilst his brother Cosmo Orme was born in 1781. John Fortnom married Jane Yeates at Calcutta otherwise Fort William on 3 September 1767 and had seven children there: Jane (1769), John (1770), Cordelia Ann (1771), Thomas William (1772), Hannah Mary (18 February 1774), Charlotte Elizabeth (1775) and Caroline (1778). Alexander Orme (29) married Hannah Mary Fortnom (15) at Berhampur on 14 November 1789, an inland town that was midway between Calcutta and Madras - her sisters married in Calcutta and Kanpur. Alexander Orme was made a captain on 7 January 1796 and was stationed with the 19th and 22nd Regiments of the Native Infantry in Bengal. They had children Alexander, John Thomas and Mary Jane Orme in India but returned to England in 1803 and daughter Katherine Isabella Orme was born "at sea" during the voyage. A son Malcolm was born at Marylebone in 1804 and the father was on furlough in 1804-05.

Robert Adam (1728-92) designed the south and east terraces of Fitzroy Square near to Regent's Park and Portland Place and a plaque records this fact. The Ormes arrived at Fitzroy Square in c.1806 before it was completed and had a long association with the area. They then had three further children: Margaret (1806), Cosmo Charles (1815) and Eliza Denne Orme (1818) all baptized at St. Pancras. The latter was born on 20 December 1818 and baptized on 21 April 1819 and soon enters the story. The Ormes resided at no. 39, which was part of the south terrace and had the appearance of a single building. There was a plain façade with central columns and pilasters, a white moulded stucco ground floor and round-arch windows - it remains today. The square had some early literary connections and Joanna Baillie (1762-1851) published the British Women Romantic Poets Project in 1823, a collection of manuscript poems by living authors. Longman, Hurst, Rees, Orme and Brown (London) published it and A. & R. Spottiswode, New Street Square were the printers. There was a distinguished list of subscribers many of whom are in this book: The King, Right Hon. Lady Byron, John Bowdler Esq. of Eltham, Mrs. Harriet Bowdler of Bath, James Burton Esq., N. Basevi, Thomas Coutts, Sir Humphrey Davy, William Delafield Esq., Mrs. Tyrwhitt-Drake, Mrs. Flower, S. Hoare of Ham House, Charles Hoare - Fleet Street, Sir John Lubbock Bart, Professor Muirhead Glasgow, Mrs. Orme (5 copies), Miss Orme, Miss C. Orme, A.C. Orme, Charles B. Sheridan and Mrs. Josiah Wedgwood. The last two sides of the square were added in 1825 whilst no. 29 on the west side was home to George Bernard Shaw and Virginia Woolf and meeting place of the 'Bloomsbury Group' (see Merriman Ch. 10). The square is a good example of Robert Adam's work with an attractive aspect on all four sides.

There were then some weddings in the family and Mary Jane Orme married William John Denne and daughter Mary Jane was born on 15 March 1822 and baptized at St. Marylebone on 17 March. Her brother Malcolm Orme married Jane Bonsor (1805) at Great Bookham on 28 March 1829 and this began an important association. Their daughter Jane Orme was born at Nottingham Place on 21 November 1829 and baptized at St. Marylebone on 13 January 1830, whilst sister Margaret Orme married James Alston of All Souls' at St. Pancras Church on 18 July 1835 the witnesses being A. Orme, Kate Orme, Eliza D. Orme, W.J. Denne and J. Bonsor. The connection between the three families is not certain but may have been a literary one through the stationery business or a legal one at Doctors' Commons near to St. Anne's, Blackfriars - made familiar in the writings of Dickens.

Joseph Bonsor senior of Salisbury Square and Polesden made his last will on 30 January 1834. He bequeathed £1,000 to his wife Jane Bonsor and left her, "My messuage or dwelling house at Polesden and outbuildings, garden, lawn and appurtenances." He gave his household goods, furniture and garden articles to his son Joseph however these for his wife's use during her lifetime. He bequeathed £1,000 to his daughter Jane Orme and £500 each to Henry Lamb and Thomas Lamb his assistants. He gave £5,000 in trust to son Joseph Bonsor and Malcolm Orme of Nottingham Place, the money for his granddaughter Jane Orme. He also gave an annual sum of £1,000 to his wife Jane to be paid on the quarter days and bequeathed all his real and personal estate to his son Joseph Bonsor, his executor. William Green, John Gardiner of Salisbury Square and Thomas Pursell clerk to Messrs. Green, Pemberton, Crawley and Gardiner witnessed the will. There was a codicil on 1 April 1835 and Joseph bequeathed £5,000 to his son-in-law Malcolm Orme of Nottingham Place and gave a further £500, each, to Henry Lamb and Thomas Lamb and it was witnessed by John Gardiner, James Ingram and Thomas Pursell - clerks to Messrs. Pemberton, Crawley and Gardiner. Joseph Bonsor senior died on 13 November 1835 aged 67 and was buried at St. Nicholas', Great Bookham on 20 November his son Joseph proving his will on 5 December.

Joseph Bonsor (1807) was educated at Eton College being in the fifth form in 1823 and matriculated at Exeter College, Oxford on 20 May 1825. He entered Lincoln's Inn in 1828 and gained a B.A. in 1829 and M.A. in 1832. He initially worked in the law however at his father's decease inherited Polesden Lacey and the firm at Salisbury Square and became successful in business. Indeed he was clearly a very eligible man with 'several hundred a year.' He soon entered into a marriage arrangement and there was much excitement at the prospect of the wedding and the scene came from a Jane Austen novel! The Orme family were both legal colleagues and relatives thus Joseph Bonsor of St. Bride's parish married Eliza Denne Orme at St. Pancras on 14 June 1836. The bride was a minor aged 17 and married with the consent of her father Alexander, whilst the minister was Alfred Williams and the witnesses A. Orme, Mary Jane Denne and W.J. Denne. This may have been a marriage for love however money was clearly involved and there was an indenture connected to the nuptials dated 13 June 1836, being a settlement on the marriage of £34,760 8s 10d - a considerable sum. The money had been raised by the sale of freehold, leasehold and copyhold premises and was invested in bank securities, and came in part from the Ormes (possibly £4,000 - see below). This was for the benefit of Eliza but specifically for any children from the marriage.

Alexander Orme of Fitzroy Square a major E.I.C. made his last will on 27 April 1836 and bequeathed all the provisions to his wife incl. 'the hay and corn,' and "the leasehold messuage situate in Fitzroy Square with the stables, coach-house, yards, ground and appurtenances," to brother Cosmo Orme, son Malcolm Orme and son-in-law William John Denne executors. His furniture etc. was in trust for his wife during her life or until remarriage and he left £500 to his wife, £4,000 to Katherine Isabella Orme and £4,000 to Eliza Denne Orme. He gave £40 p.a. to Mary Elizabeth Orme widow of his late son Alexander Orme whilst his residuary estate went to his executors - the money to be invested in stocks of the country but not those in Ireland. He left an annuity of £90 p.a. to John Thomas Orme at his executors' discretion and the same to Cosmo Charles Orme, whilst £1,700 of the residuary estate was given to Malcolm Orme and £4,000 to Cosmo Charles Orme. The residuary estate was for Malcolm Orme, Cosmo Charles Orme, Mary Jane wife of William John Denne, Katharine Isabella Orme, Margaret wife of James Alston and Eliza Denne Orme (in equal shares). His property was to be sold at his wife's decease and £4,000 raised from the resulting trust monies and invested for John Thomas Orme (and children), or if deceased to Alexander's other children. He finally stated that any marriage settlement to Katherine Isabella or Eliza Denne Orme was to be separate. The witnesses were John Gardiner and Arthur R. Hamilton of 20 Whitehall Place, Westminster.

He added a codicil on 24 June 1836 stating: "I hereby declare that the bond I granted to the trustees of the marriage contract executed on 13 June 1836 between Joseph Bonsor and my daughter Eliza Denne Orme, for £4,000, was in full of the bequest made to the same amount in my said will." Alexander Orme major E.I.C.S. died from 'a visitation of God' at 39 Fitzroy Square, St. Pancras on 20 December 1837 aged 77. A legal problem arose hence Peter Davison of Stratford Place and James Kiernan of Doctors' Commons confirmed they knew A. Orme for some years and stated the will and codicil were in his writing - 29 January 1838. Cosmo Orme, Malcolm Orme and William John Denne then proved the will on 1 February 1838. Jane Bonsor of Polesden made her last will on 20 January 1840 giving £2,000 in trust to Joseph Bonsor of Polesden and the like amount to Malcolm Orme of 25 Nottingham Place, London her executors. The money was to be invested and the interest paid to granddaughter Jane Orme but if she died before the legacy was paid then to her daughter Jane. She gave £100 to Anne Elizabeth Jackson who lived with her whilst George Roots of Tanfield Court, Temple and James Bosley butler of Joseph Bonsor of 'Polsden' witnessed the will.

Joseph and Eliza D. Bonsor lived in London and at Polesden after their marriage but their families stayed in the capital, hence Cosmo Orme lived with niece Katherine and five servants at 35 Fitzroy Square in 1841, whilst Mrs. Alexander Orme 'independent' and four servants resided at 39 Fitzroy Square. Malcolm Orme a proctor lived at 25 Nottingham Place, Marylebone that year with his wife Jane, mother Jane Bonsor (75) and Ann E. Jackson (40); the property itself was rebuilt in 1890. His brother Cosmo Charles Orme (1815) was educated at a private school in Surrey and matriculated at Trinity, Cambridge on 25 February 1834 then gained a B.A. in 1839. He was curate of Sleaford, Lincolnshire in 1840-41 but died at St. Pancras in June 1841. An advert that year stated: "W.J. Denne and M. Orme, proctors, 2 Great Knightrider Street, Doctors' Commons." All proctors were notaries regulated by the Court of Arches and presided over wills and estates.

Jane Bonsor died of 'paralysis' at 25 Nottingham Place on 17 September 1843 aged 78 and the informant was Ann Elizabeth Jackson. She was buried at Great Bookham in Surrey and a large memorial was erected. St. Nicholas' is an attractive church with a nave of flint, slate roof and a weather-boarded tower below the steeple. The Bonsors' memorial is located outside at the east end of the church and is the largest present thus befitting the great landowner. There is a base plinth with an architrave and cornice above and the design is of a Classical temple but incorporates both church windows and cherubs! The inscription reads: "In this vault are the bodies of JOSEPH BONSOR esqre of Polesden in this parish who died on the 13th Novr 1835 aged 67. And of JANE BONSOR wife of the above who died on the 17th of Septr 1843 aged 78." George Roots appeared in the matter of Jane Bonsor of 'Polsden' and Nottingham Place and confirmed the will was signed on the date stated with an affidavit on 20 October 1843 before John Daubeny surrogate of proctor M. Orme (public notary). Joseph Bonsor and Malcolm Orme then proved the will in London on 23 October 1843 before John Daubeny.

The family moved to Marylebone in the mid-1840s thus Cosmo Orme a fund holder and his niece Katherine lived at 15 Bryanston Square, whilst Mrs. Alexander Orme and visitor and relative Ann Lamb (23) resided at 16 Wyndham Place, Bryanston Square in 1851. Malcolm Orme a proctor was then living at 15 Sussex Square, Paddington with his wife Jane, daughter Jane and five servants. 15 Bryanston Square was a four-storey building of plain brown brick with a white stucco ground floor. 16 Wyndham Place was last on the west side next to the square, and had a similar brick and stucco façade, inset columned entrance, red brick lintel over the windows and small first floor balcony. The properties at Bryanston Square remain but Sussex Square has been rebuilt.

Jane Orme had a bright future being left money by both her Bonsor grandparents and married Archibald Little at St. James's, Piccadilly on 7 June 1854; children Archibald Cosmo (1855) and Florence Jane (1856) were baptized at St. James's, Paddington. Hannah Mary Orme widow of Alexander died at Marylebone in March 1857 whilst Cosmo Orme of Bryanston Square died at Tunbridge Wells on 12 August 1859. His probate went to Malcolm Orme of 15 Sussex Square, Hyde Park nephew and Joseph Bonsor of 6 Hill Street, Berkeley Square esq. the effects under £200,000 (a substantial sum). Malcolm Orme died at 7 Upper Belgrave Street on 21 April 1878 and his probate went to Sir Archibald Little K.C.B. lieutenant general, Archibald Cosmo Little grandson (both) of 7 Upper Belgrave Street, Henry Cosmo Orme Bonsor of 40 Belgrave Square and Alexander George Bonsor of 51 Eaton Place esq. effects under £160,000. Jane Orme (née Bonsor) died at 7 Upper Belgrave Street on 22 November 1886 and her probate went to Archibald Cosmo Little grandson a major in the 5th lancers. All these addresses were in Belgravia and were built by Thomas Cubitt.

Joseph and Eliza Denne Bonsor had a family of ten children after their marriage in 1836 and their first child Mary Josephine was born at Westminster in 1840. Despite spending much time in London they lived at 'Polsden Mansion' in 1841. Joseph Bonsor was of independent means and lived with Eliza Denne, daughter Mary Josephine and seven servants. The family then returned to London since Joseph was in business at 132 Salisbury Square and two daughters were born: Alice at Marylebone in 1843 and Ella Elizabeth at St. Mary's, Bryanston Square in 1846. In fact the Polesden Estate was rented out in 1836-47 as shown in an advert dated circa 1840:

> **"TO RENT,** a Grecian style property for a family of rank and fortune. The estate is approached along an avenue of stately beech trees. There is a capital mansion house, coach house, stables, walled garden, grapery, greenhouse, beautiful planted gardens, extensive terrace walks and orchards and paddocks. There is also a walled garden.
>
> There are two approaches one from Westhumble and the other from Bookham (the latter added by the Bonsors). There is nearby an interesting church with accommodation for a family with an extensive establishment. The property is to let for 1 or 2 years elegantly furnished or for a longer period unfurnished. It comes with a farm of 200 acres and woodland of 200 acres.
>
> The house has a notable portico entrance leading into the hall and vestibule. There is a billiard room-library, breakfast room, dining room, suite of drawing rooms, gentleman's room, schoolroom and gentleman's water closet. The principal rooms are to the south. There is a handsome staircase. The house has eight principal chambers with a large dressing room attached to four.
>
> The estate could be used for shooting or hunting. There are also facilities for a stud and horse racing takes place nearby at Epsom. There is spring water and the subsoil is chalk. Interested parties should apply to - Mr. White, auctioneer and estate agent of Dorking, or Mr. Lahee, estate and house agent of 65 Old Bond Street, London."

Polesden Lacey, Great Bookham. Once the site of Sheridan's 'rundown abode'.

Joseph Bonsor lived at Polesden permanently after 1847 and initially two children were born there: Henry Cosmo Orme (1848) and Amy Jane (1850). Joseph Bonsor owner and occupier of 670 acres employing 28 labourers lived at Polesden House in 1851 with wife Eliza, children Mary J. (10), Alice (8), Ella (4), Henry C. (2) and Amy (1), a governess, butler, housekeeper, lady's maid, nurse, schoolroom maid, coachman and footman. This was a stately home with many opulent rooms and the couple then had children Alexander George (1851) and William Joseph (1853). The father Joseph, however, was not an idle country gentleman and "Joseph Bonsor & Co." wholesale stationers traded at 132 Salisbury Square in 1841-51. He then made some major changes and closed the page on stationery and went into brewing. He sold the business at Salisbury Square to his cousin Henry Lamb in 1852 and this alone may have funded his new venture, and also tired of the country life and sold Polesden Lacey in 1853.

Henry Lamb, as stated, had lived at 132 Salisbury Square since 1832 and presumably ran the business with Joseph after his father's death in 1835. His son Henry Lamb junior of the Indian Navy was the sole resident of 132 Salisbury Square in 1851 and the business was described as "Henry Lamb & Co. (late Bonsor & Co.)", wholesale stationers, in 1862. Further to this, the business of Castle and Lamb newspaper and advertising agents were at no. 133 Salisbury Square at the latter date. Henry Lamb senior lived at the address with his daughter Fanny in 1861 and on his own in 1871, and the household had three servants in each case. He continued running the business until his decease and died at 132 Salisbury Square on 1 January 1875 - probate went to son Henry Lamb of Leatherhead and Eugene Sweny of Woolwich, his effects under £16,000.

Henry Lamb junior a retired navy officer lived at Hove in 1901, whilst the family business of Henry Lamb & Co. was at 132-34 Salisbury Square and Castle, Lamb & Starr was at no. 133-34 in 1902. The family were at Salisbury Square for over 100 years but the association was finally edited out when Henry Lamb & Co. moved to 20 Tudor Street, Blackfriars in 1906 - Iliffe & Sons Ltd. publishers also traded at this address (see Betts). However, they were "late" of 20 Tudor Street in 1911 having been incorporated with Venables, Tyler & Co. Ltd. at 17 Queenhithe in the City. The modern Salisbury Square is mainly rebuilt although no. 1 remains and is a historic town house. The narrow St. Bride's Passage is near the 'site' of 132 Salisbury Square and some old buildings are present at the entrance, namely a white-fronted property and the remains of a red brick building. The latter is partly modern but has two wings and contains the remnants of an historic house and was probably no. 132 - home of the Bonsors.

Joseph Bonsor invested the assets arising from the sale of the business into Combe, Delafield & Co., a brewers, who were then well established. John Shackley had started a brewery at Wood Yard near Covent

Garden in the mid-17th century and his son inherited the company in 1722 - it was located on Castle Street (now Shelton Street). William Gyfford purchased the brewery in 1739 and was later joined by Peter Hamond and they traded as Gyfford & Co. until 1787. Meanwhile Joseph Delafield worked for Samuel Whitbread and wrote a letter to his brother on 1 March 1786 describing the advantages of steam power. He related that last summer they used 6 horses, however these were replaced with a 10-h.p engine that did the work of 14 horses! Gyfford's sent a letter to Boulton and Watt regarding the installation of an engine at Wood Yard in April 1787. Indeed J. Delafield then became a partner at Gyfford's and his arrival coincided with the erection of an engine at Wood Yard. The application was the sixth in London and was preceded by the first at H. Goodwyn and S. Whitbread (see Ch. 7 & 10). The Combe, Delafield & Co. (partnership) was incorporated at Wood Yard on 31 July 1787 and the partners were Peter Hamond of Bloomsbury Square, Edmund Hamond of Castle Street, Harvey Christian Combe of Upper Thames Street (later M.P., Lord Mayor *1799*), Joseph Delafield formerly brewer for S. Whitbread, George Shum and William Mackes.

There were many changes and Edmund Hamond was bankrupt on 31 December 1792 thus Harvey Christian Combe of Great Russell Square, Joseph Delafield of Castle Street, George Shum of Bedford Square, George Shum younger of Gower Street and William Mackes of Charlotte Street were partners on 1 August 1797. Boulton and Watt's engine was enlarged to 20-h.p in 1798 whilst Harvey Combe the son became a partner on 6 July 1811 and the engine was raised to 26-h.p in 1817. There was then a further change in the partners and a link was established to the brewery of Henry Goodwyn, Lower East Smithfield (see Ch. 10). The basis of the company was the same with Harvey Combe of Castle Street, Joseph Delafield, Joseph Delafield younger and Edward Harvey Delafield however Sir Charles Flower Bart and James Flower (his son) joined them on 6 July 1818. They still traded under the familiar name of Combe, Delafield & Co. whilst Sir Charles Flower (merchant), father-in-law of T.W. Goodwyn, was Lord Mayor in 1808 and lived at 67 Russell Square in 1829-34. The Flowers remained with the brewery for the early part of the 19th century and a side lever 'boat type' engine of 30-h.p was erected at Wood Yard in 1833. Sir Charles Flower's will was proved on 26 September 1834 and Abraham Wilday Robarts of Lombard Street, banker and Harvey Combe of Castle Street were executors, then William George Prescott of Threadneedle Street, banker also obtained probate on 13 November. The will led to a change in the partnership and his share went to his son James Flower (of Ecclesall, Norfolk) on 24 July 1838, whilst Abraham Wilday Robarts also became a partner (see Lubbock Ch. 7). The Wood Yard premises were enlarged and extended across nearby Langley Street in 1839.

The company Bonsor joined was not without controversy and a letter was sent from 50 Fenchurch Street on 2 September 1846. It was addressed to Edward Thomas Delafield residing in Geneva and stated: "Dear Delafield, your nephew called and assured me, you were not concerned in the affair of the *Belgian Singers*. This was entirely Mr. Webster's affair and a losing concern. Despite the statement in the papers, we are assured that the business is over." This sounded like a case for Sherlock Holmes and possibly had some influence on the later story. Joseph Bonsor became a partner in Combe, Delafield & Co. in 1852 and injected £80,000 into the business the total assets being £400,000 - he owned a 16/80th share.

He then sold Polesden Lacey to Walter Rochliffe Farquhar in 1853 and only a few changes were made, namely a new entrance portico was erected and a cupola added to the roof - Cubitt's 'old' entrance was removed to the Long Walk and rests there today (above the garden terrace). The house was much the same until 1902 then Captain Ronald Greville purchased it in 1906 and it was left to Mrs. Margaret Helen Greville when he died in 1908. She made some major changes and the house was enlarged and a library added at the southeast corner. This altered the southern façade and obscured the original house although Cubitt's creation could still be seen. She totally altered the interior and a reredos from St. Matthew's, Friday Street was erected in the hall whilst Jacobean panelling and a 'copy' plaster ceiling were added to the corridor. The original 'Bonsor' living room was plain and in two sections, but it was transformed into a gilded drawing room after an acquisition from an Italian palazzo. Mrs. Greville entertained many notable people including Edward VII and Polesden was the honeymoon retreat of King George VI and Queen Elizabeth. The property was bequeathed to the National Trust in 1942 hence it is now open to the public.

Joseph Bonsor purchased a substantial house at 6 Hill Street, Berkeley Square, Mayfair, and lived there in 1853-68. The town house was on the north side near to Berkeley Square in an area developed in the 18th century on land used for a May market (*Mayfair*). It was tall and of red brick, being part of a terrace, but was individually built with bow front and imposing entrance - it remains thus today.

His son Herbert Webb, however, was born at Northill, Bedford in 1855 hence he spent some time away from London (perhaps renting). John Harvey obtained Ickwell Bury at Northill in 1680, home of the Barnardiston-Harvey family until the 20th century, whilst S. Whitbread lived nearby at Cardington and Southill Park (see Ch. 7). A company indenture and partnership agreement of 12 November 1856 stated the capital was £400,000 divided into 80th shares and shareholders: Harvey Combe (30), William Delafield (14), John William Spicer of Esher Place (14), Joseph Bonsor of Hill Street, Berkeley Square (16) and John Samuel Tanqueray of Hendon (6). Brewing was lucrative and the Bonsors had an affluent lifestyle at 6 Hill Street near St. George's Hanover Square then had two daughters there: Beatrice Eliza (1856) and Isabella Catherine (1859). Joseph Bonsor magistrate and brewer lived at 6 Hill Street in 1861 with his wife, ten children (the oldest "Cosmo" age 12) and eleven servants including butler and housekeeper who were married. The house was bustling with life as there were over twenty residents, ten being children.

6 Hill Street, Berkeley Square. The Bonsor family lived here in 1854-68.

Joseph Bonsor and the company signed an agreement in 1862 stating he would pay the regular sum of £2,200 into the joint stock of the co-partnership on 10 October each year to reach a total of £11,000 by 1866. Combe, Delafield & Co. was initially a small company but the Bonsors helped transform them into a major player. The family fortune meant that four sons were educated at Eton College in the years 1862-71, whilst two daughters married and Joseph Bonsor settled money on both of them. Alice Bonsor (1843) married William Agnew Pope in St. George's Hanover Square (district) in September 1863 and their daughter Elinor Mary was born there in June 1865, but the mother died soon after. Mary Josephine Bonsor (1840) married Florence Thomas Wethered at Hurley on 4 December 1867 the bridegroom being a widower and vicar of Hurley. The Bonsors then moved nearby to 10 Hill Street, a grey brick house of contrasting style with a white columned entrance and grand first floor rooms with ornate plaster ceilings. They lived there in 1869-71 and the house is still present but they had left Hill Street by the 1871 census. Baron de Cetto, Councillor of State for the King of Bavaria and his wife Elizabeth lived at 6 Hill Street in 1871, thus showing the status of the area. (See Addendum re Basevi).

Belgravia was a very desirable area with white stucco Regency mansions built around a number of leafy-squares; George Basevi designed Belgrave Square and old friend Thomas Cubitt built it in 1825. Joseph Bonsor moved to 1 Belgrave Square in 1872-74, which was a large property on the northeast corner next to Wilton Crescent with two main floors and white columns like a Classical temple. This was the grandest of properties and the whole square remains in its original form whilst the house is now an embassy. Joseph Bonsor of Belgrave Square made his last will on 30 April 1872 and appointed Henry Cosmo Orme and Alexander George Bonsor executors. He stated, "I am a partner in the partnership firm of Combe & Co. carrying on the business of brewers at Castle Street, Long Acre in the county of Middlesex and as such partner, I am now possessed of or entitled to nine thirty seventh shares of, and in, the capital sum of £370,000.... by the articles of the said partnership dated 7 November 1866...."

He had previously given his son Henry Cosmo a 1/37 share and now bequeathed him a further 6/37 share on condition that he paid £2,000 annually to his mother Eliza, and bequeathed to his son Alexander George Bonsor the remaining 3/37 share with the proviso that he paid £500 annually to Eliza; the total value was £100,000 as oppose to £80,000 in 1856. He divided the marriage settlement

51 Eaton Place, Belgravia.
'Upstairs-Downstairs' - the Bonsors had a real life drama.

of £34,760 8s 10d equally amongst his ten children but allowing for the fact that one daughter had died and another had married. He gave all his personal estate to his wife and his real estate and property to sons Henry Cosmo and Alexander George and lastly left £10,000 each to his six unmarried children. Joseph Bonsor died at 1 Belgrave Square on 27 November 1873 and Henry Cosmo Orme Bonsor of 5 Chesham Place and Alexander George Bonsor of 1 Belgrave Square proved the will in London on 30 December, his effects valued at under £300,000.

He left a small fortune and his widow Eliza continued to live comfortably and resided at 51 Eaton Place from 1876-88. The house was just south of Belgrave Square and another of Cubitt's creations with a white stucco front, columned porch entrance and Classical window features. The daughter Isabel Catherine Bonsor (1859) married Charles Edward Ramsbottom Isherwood at Godstone in December 1878 - he was born in Australia in 1850. Eliza Bonsor annuitant and fund-holder lived at 51 Eaton Place in 1881 with her daughters Ella, Amy and Beatrice, son William, daughter Isabella and husband Charles Isherwood and twelve servants viz. a butler, two footmen, cook, housekeeper, maids, two lady's maids and a nurse; in fact nearly two servants to each adult. The family moved just down the road to 11 Upper Belgrave Street in 1889, the house being on the corner with Wilton Street and only a short distance from St. Peter's, Eaton Square. It was a larger property than Eaton Place and was again built by Cubitt and featured Classical pilasters. Indeed the Ormes lived at no. 7 and Alfred Lord Tennyson at no. 9 (1881). The family remained at 11 Upper Belgrave Street and Eliza Bonsor was there with her three daughters in 1891 and 1901, whilst the number of servants was thirteen and eleven respectively - they provided the blueprint for the series 'Upstairs Downstairs'!

Eliza Denne Bonsor died at 11 Upper Belgrave Street on 5 March 1909 and her probate was granted to Henry Cosmo Orme Bonsor on 26 March 1909, her estate valued at £52,280 6s. Amy Jane Bonsor died at 4 Albion Villas, Folkestone on 6 July 1912, Ella Elizabeth Bonsor died at 192 Ashley Gardens, Westminster on 10 July 1928 and Beatrice Eliza Bonsor died at 4 Eccleston Square, Westminster on 18 March 1931 (all unmarried). Florence Thomas Wethered was born at Hurley near Cookham in 1840 and married Grace Emma Best at Old Alresford on 27 February 1862, however she died and he married Mary Josephine Bonsor in 1867. The couple lived at the Vicarage, Hurley in 1881 and the household included two children from the first marriage, five born at Hurley, a governess and five servants. They also lived there in 1901 and Rev. Florence Thomas Wethered died at Hurley on 17 August 1919 - effects £26,177 1s 8d. Mary Josephine Wethered died at "Priory Holme", 18 Avenue Road, Great Malvern (near the station) on 10 March 1931 and her probate went to Rev. Arthur James Wethered and Joseph Robert Wethered retired colonel. Rev. Arthur lived at Kingswood Vicarage, Tadworth and received the position from his uncle (see below) whilst wife Sydney Alice died at the Hotel Belle Vue, Bavens in Italy on 4 September 1925.

Charles Isherwood and family lived at 51 Eaton Place in 1881 and then at Bowland, Clifton Road, Southsea in 1901; at the latter date Charles was living on his own means and the household included daughters Mildred and Elsie and six servants. Charles Frank Frederic Augustus R. Isherwood died at Kilbirnie, Wellington, New Zealand on 1 August 1909 (possibly their son). Isabella Catherine R. Isherwood died at Bowland, Southsea on 15 July 1919 and Charles Edward R. Isherwood died at Warleigh, Craneswater Park, Southsea on 3 January 1934. His probate went to Lionel Charlie R. Isherwood a retired captain, his effects being £46,851 17s 3d. The sons of Joseph Bonsor, meanwhile, had every benefit that money could buy with the prospect of a successful career at the highest level of society. This came true for the eldest however there were serious problems below the surface that money (and the courts) could not solve.

Henry Cosmo Orme Bonsor was born at Polesden Lacey on 2 September 1848 and attended Eton in 1862-65 at the same time as A.F. Kinnaird. He married Emily Gertrude (1851) the daughter of James Fellowes of Kingston, Dorset in St. George's Hanover Square (district) on 18 April 1872. The couple lived at 5 Chesham Place, Belgravia in 1873-77 but the building no longer remains and a modern embassy occupies the site. There are some old properties present including 36 Chesham Place 'home of Lord John Russell 1792-1878 1st Earl and twice Prime Minister' (1846-52 and 1865-66). Cosmo, as he was known, owned Tandridge Hall, Godstone in 1877 and lived at 40 Belgrave Square in 1879-83 - a short distance from his mother at 51 Eaton Place. The couple had children Edith (1876), Mary Emily (1877), Malcolm Cosmo (1878), Reginald (1879) and Robert Cecil (1880) born in London. Cosmo Bonsor a brewer resided at 40 Belgrave Square in 1881 with wife Emily, five children, brother Herbert and eight servants. He had a son Arthur Charles but his wife Emily died on 18 July 1882 five days after the birth and he lived at 38 Belgrave Square by 1885. This was built in the grand Classical style with pilasters and pediments and was at the southeast corner adjacent to Chapel Street and near to Upper Belgrave Street - it was his London residence until his death.

11 Upper Belgrave Street. Idylls of the King - the family home from 1889-1909.

Cosmo became a partner in Combe, Delafield & Co. at his father's decease in 1873 and held a 7/37th share in the company (worth £70,000) and thus had considerable financial backing. The business was based only at Castle Street, Long Acre in 1862-71 however there were additional premises at 137 Grosvenor Road, Pimlico in 1880-91. Cosmo Bonsor was the main force behind the company's growth and being a close friend of James Watney II became a director of Watney & Co. in 1885, a brewery also based at Pimlico. He soon had his hand in many pies and was made a director of the Bank of England in 1885 and would have known Edgar Lubbock in this capacity (see Ch. 7). He was also Conservative M.P. for Wimbledon in 1885-1900, a treasurer of Guy's Hospital, a member of the Income Tax Commission and an alderman of the City. He married Mabel Grace daughter of James Brand of Sanderstead Court, Croydon at Wandsworth on 3 March 1886 and had two daughters Muriel Mary and Ethel - the former married Reginald John Thoroton Hildyard. His success continued and he purchased "Kingswood Warren" near Epsom in 1887 and he also owned the Red House, Kingswood. This began a long association with the area and he was well situated for his passion with horse racing and patron of the living at Kingswood where his nephew Rev. Wethered was vicar. His motto was "Omne Bonum Dei Donum" or "Every good is the gift of God", which came from Ecclesiastes iii 13 and meant: Enjoy good it is the gift of God.

Combe, Delafield & Co. was in a good position in the late 1880s and the Articles of Association were reconstituted on 25 June 1888. They were then described as a joint stock company and the partners were: Combe family (5 members), John E.P. Spicer, Henry Cosmo Orme Bonsor and Alexander George Bonsor. The documents were signed and sealed at 50 Old Broad Street but Alexander was absent thus he was represented by Henry Cosmo his attorney. The balance sheet revealed the financial position on 24 June 1892 and there were 12,000 shares of £100 and 80,000 5% preference shares of £10 making a total share value of £2 million. Further there was 4% debenture stock £1 million, freehold property £251,611, cash in hand £60,615, debtors £1,942,385 and creditors £97,486, which was clearly a most healthy position. The company then utilised their substantial assets and made many investments by 1895 at which time there was cash-in-hand of £81,657 and investments of £286,315. These included the Bank of England, Natal, the West Australian Government, New South Wales, Indian peninsula and shares and debentures in at least ten railway companies viz. Midland in Western Australia, London Chatham and Dover, South Eastern, Midland and Great Northern Railway - they had taken over from Betts & Sons! The business could only go forward and Cosmo negotiated a merger to create Watney, Combe and Reid on 1 July 1898. The new company was based at Brewer Street in Pimlico, Castle Street, 154-155 Grosvenor Road and Mortlake in Surrey. Indeed Combe & Co. was liquidated in January 1899 and Wood Yard closed in 1905 however the brewery buildings remain at Old Brewer's Yard near Seven Dials and Covent Garden. The warehouse buildings are clearly visible in Neal Street, Shelton Street, Earlham Street and Langley Street and their hoists evoke a different era, whilst Marks and Spencer use the old yard for deliveries.

The status of Cosmo Bonsor was being continually raised and he was Chairman of the S.E. Railway from 1898-1923 but there was also tragedy in the family. Malcolm Cosmo Bonsor (1878) the oldest son was educated at Eton in 1892 and later a captain in the Norfolk Yeomanry. He lived at the Corner House, Tadworth but died on active service in Palestine on 10 March 1918 and his probate went to Sybil Henrietta Bonsor, his widow. Sir Henry Cosmo Orme Bonsor was a baronet in 1925 and his family had received recognition after 100 years of prominence. He still lived at 38 Belgrave Square but died at the Boulevard Carabacel, Nice, France on 4 December 1929. His probate went to Sir Reginald Bonsor Bart, Robert Cecil Bonsor banker and Arthur Charles Bonsor gent - his estate being worth £717,528 1s 5d. Dame Mabel Grace Bonsor lived at Red Lodge, Tadworth and died at The Wildernesse, Seal near Sevenoaks on 11 April 1944. Her probate went to Sir Reginald John Thoroton Hildyard general and Arthur Charles Bonsor retired major - her effects £85,845 16s 2d. Sir Reginald Bonsor Bart of Liscombe, Leighton Buzzard died on 4 April 1959 and probate went to Sir Bryan Cosmo Bonsor Bart and David Victor Bonsor - the name of Cosmo went back to 1781. They also left a mark near "Kingswood Warren" with local roads Warren Drive, Warren Lodge, The Warren and Bonsor Drive.

William Joseph Bonsor the third son was baptized at Great Bookham on 18 July 1853 and attended Eton in 1868-71. He then entered New Inn Hall, Oxford and matriculated at Christchurch College on 13 October 1871 - he gained a B.A. in 1877 and M.A. in 1878. William Joseph Bonsor gentleman of 43 Curzon Street, Mayfair married Annie Mary daughter of Joseph Brown, merchant of 27 Charles Street at St. George's Hanover Square on 14 June 1884 - she was born in Newcastle in 1860. William moved to 7 Aldford Street, Park Lane (formerly Chapel Street) in 1887 and was a wholesale clothier and warehouseman in 1891, living with wife "Daisy", nephew Garnet H. Vickers and two servants. He stayed there until 1895 then moved to 72 Curzon Street, Mayfair but died at 55 Welbeck Street on 23 July 1904. His probate went to Annie Mary Bonsor widow his effects £15,246 17s 8d but re-sworn at £10,576 2s 8d. Indeed all looked well in the family at this stage however there were soon some serious developments.

Herbert Webb Bonsor youngest son was baptized at Northill, Bedford on 14 November 1855 and attended Eton in 1871 then lived at Great Cousins, Ware and was a captain in the 1st Herts Volunteers (Ware). He married Evelyn Sarah Moon at Fetcham, Surrey on 4 September 1878 and Rev. E.G. Moon performed the ceremony and H. Cosmo Bonsor, Hedworth D. Barclay, Francis S. Graham Moon and Ellen Gertrude Moon were witnesses. His bride was baptized at Fetcham on 24 August 1858 and was the daughter of Edward Graham and Ellen Moon who had eight children from 1854-67. Edward Graham Moon baronet and rector lived at the Rectory, Fetcham in 1881 with wife Ellen and children Arthur, E. Gertrude and Beatrice G. and twelve servants. Herbert Bonsor, maltster, and wife Evelyn were visitors with his brother Henry Cosmo at 40 Belgrave Square at this time. The couple had children Herbert (1881) at Ware, Alexander John (1883) at 58 Ebury Street, London and Olive B. (1887) at Worcester Park in Surrey however trouble was brewing. Evelyn Sarah Bonsor of Chessington Cottage, Worcester Park filed a petition on 6 June 1889 and stated they had co-habited at divers places since their marriage and had three children and that: "Since May 1888 her husband had habitually committed adultery with a woman known by the name of Harcourt with whom he lived as man and wife at 4 Sisters Avenue and 31 Lavendar Sweep in Clapham Junction." She requested a decree for judicial separation and custody of the children through her solicitors Stileman, Neate & Toynbee of 16 Southampton Street, Bloomsbury (see T.H. Merriman Ch. 10).

There was an affidavit to this effect dated 1 July 1889 and a petition from Mrs. Hobbs and J.M. Sturgess supporting these facts on 9 July 1889. The judge on reading the statement and affidavit ordered that personal service on respondent and citation issued against him in this case be dispensed, but that a citation and sealed copy of the petition be personally served on the mother of the respondent (Mrs. Bonsor at 11 Upper Belgrave Street). There was clearly a case to answer however the judge considered that a reprimand from his mother might put matters right. The cause was put on the reserve list on 26 November 1889 but as no one appeared, for either party, was struck out on 16 December 1890. Evelyn S. Bonsor lived at Chessington Cottage, Cuddington near Worcester Park in 1891 with her three children and two servants, however matters did not improve and her husband did not return. Her solicitors Stileman & C. filed a notice of abandonment of the previous petition, prior to taking further action, on 2 April 1895.

Evelyn Sarah Bonsor of Chessington Cottage filed a petition on 11 April 1895 and stated that: "On 9 March 1889 her husband Herbert Webb Bonsor deserted her without cause and has ever since kept and continued away from her. That for a considerable time ending in 1894 at Helena in the State of Montana U.S.A. the said husband lived and cohabited as man and wife and habitually committed adultery with a woman unknown to the petitioner under the names Mr. and Mrs. Harry Brett. The petitioner humbly prays that the marriage be dissolved and that she is given custody of the children." This was an exceptional development and had a connection to a piece of American history. Four gold miners from Georgia found the aptly named 'Last Chance Gulch' on 14 July 1864 and a gold boomtown developed with 3,000 inhabitants. It had various names until miners came from St. Helena, Minnesota and Helena then stuck. Virginia City near Bannack became the capital of Montana at the time but became a ghost town when the gold ran out. Helena was made the capital in 1875 and the North Pacific Railroad arrived from Bismarck in 1883 (see Pember Ch. 4). The town nearly lost its position as state capital to Anaconda near Bute after a close vote whilst several fires burnt the town in 1894 - when Bonsor lived there. The gold eventually ran out but its status as capital and the growth of agriculture brought new people in, and its future was secured.

Back in England the cause was undefended and the date of trial was set on 2 July 1895 and the cause set down and certificate filed on the 16th inst. There was then a hearing for the counsel of the petitioner and they were at liberty to prove the statements in paragraph 4 of the petition. They did this with an affidavit of two witnesses Derland E. Swinehart and Charles W. Wiley regarding the acts committed in America (on 22 July 1895). Lord Justice Copes dealt with the case at the Strand and issued a decree nisi on 28 October 1895: "The petition was proved and the marriage dissolved the respondent being guilty of adultery coupled with desertion of the petitioner for two years and upwards without reasonable excuse. The three children were to remain in custody of the petitioner and not removed from the court's jurisdiction." A notice was filed on 5 May 1896 and Hon. Sir John Gorell Barnes gave the final decree and dissolved the marriage on 11 May 1896 - no evidence to the contrary being provided. Evelyn S. Bonsor lived on her own means at Chessington Cottage, Cuddington in 1901 with three children and two servants. There was no trace of husband 'Herbert' and indeed all four brothers were absent from the 1901 census - they were in America, Belgium and possibly France. Herbert's death has not been found and for good reason as he went by the name of Harry Brett whilst Evelyn S. Bonsor died at Epsom in September 1928. The story is almost complete however we now come to the sporting connection.

Alexander George Bonsor was born at Polesden Lacey on 7 October 1851 and baptized at Great Bookham on 9 December that year. He spent his early life at Polesden and at 6 Hill Street, Berkeley Square and was educated at Eton College in 1865-68. He began to play soccer at this time and lived with his family at 1 Belgrave Square, London in 1872-74. He was a notable footballer in the 1870s and played in games of much significance appearing in four F.A. Cup Finals. He played for the Wanderers in the first Final in 1872 and his performance brought him to prominence thus he played for England v Scotland in the second international at the Oval on 8 March 1873. The England side included William Edwin Clegg, R.W.S. Vidal, W.S. Kenyon-Slaney and Alfred G. Goodwyn (Engineers) - the others Crystal Palace, Notts County and Uxbridge. Kenyon-Slaney scored the first ever international goal after just one minute whilst Alexander Bonsor scored on ten minutes making it 2-0 (both Wanderers). The Scots improved and levelled the game but were beaten with goals from Kenyon-Slaney on 75 minutes and Charles John Chenery (C. Palace) on 85 minutes - final score 4-2. Thus striking partners Bonsor and Kenyon-Slaney scored the first-ever international goals.

The Wanderers played their second Cup Final on 29 March 1873 and the side included five players from the earlier victory viz. A.G. Bonsor, E.E. Bowen, A.C. Thompson, R.C. Welch and C.H.R. Wollaston plus Alfred Kinnaird and William S. Kenyon-Slaney. They defeated Oxford 2-0 with goals from Kinnaird and Wollaston but, as stated, reached the Final without playing a game - they then cleaned their boots and went to watch the Boat Race. Alexander Bonsor owned shares in Combe, Delafield & Co. valued at £30,000 after his father died on 27 November 1873, however he did not play a major role in the company and had the leisurely life of a Victorian gentleman. He left the Wanderers at this stage and then played for the Old Etonians and appeared for England at the Oval on 6 March 1875. The side included C.W. Alcock and C.H.R. Wollaston of the Wanderers whilst the referee was Major Marindin and the game ended in a 2-2 draw after goals from Alcock and Wollaston. One week later he was back at the Oval and played for the Old Etonians against the Royal Engineers in the Cup Final on 13 March 1875. The Eton side included A.G. Bonsor, E. Lubbock, A.F. Kinnaird, W.S. Kenyon-Slaney and C.M. Thompson and the referee C.W. Alcock. Indeed Alexander Bonsor scored a goal and the game ended with a 1-1 draw. He also played in the replay however the Old Etonians put out a weak team, and arrived late, and the Royal Engineers won 2-0. His last major appearance was for the Old Etonians against the Wanderers in the Final on 11 March 1876. The team included Kenyon-Slaney, Kinnaird and C.M. Thompson and was a

1-1 draw but they lost the replay 3-0. Bonsor finished his career with one international and one Cup Final goal, then left the sporting limelight to take part in a far greater drama.

He lived with his family at 51 Eaton Place from 1876 and was there when he proved the will of Malcolm Orme his uncle in May 1878, but soon after spent time abroad and one wonders if the Belgian Singers had a bearing on this! He had a relationship with Maria Charlotte (a Belgian citizen) who was born in Antwerp in 1857 although they were never married. Alexander G. Bonsor, a brewer, resided at the Grand Hotel, Charing Cross in 1881 with Maria Charlotte his 'wife' and Frances Maria Miller a lady's maid from Chichester. They may have been visiting from Belgium but the relationship was not destined to last, whilst Frederick and Isabella Carver were only six rooms away and Morley's Hotel was just across the road - it's a small world (see Ch. 9). He retained his interest in Combe, Delafield & Co. and was a partner in 1888, a fact witnessed by the Articles of Association, but sold his shares and eventually took his funds abroad. Indeed the Eton College records state he was 'formerly' of Combe and Delafield in 1892. He then had a new relationship in the 1890s but it was far more traumatic than that of his younger brother.

Alexander George Bonsor (41) bachelor and gentleman of 14 Davies Street, Berkeley Square married Jeanne Marie David (24) at the Register Office, St. George's Hanover Square on 24 June 1893. His bride was born in France in 1869 and was the daughter of Maurice David gentleman and had the same London address, whilst the witnesses were A.E. Rose Hudson and Esther White. 14 Davies Street was on the east side a short distance from Berkeley Square and the present building is a four-storey bow fronted town house with roof cornice, composed of apartments and shops below - dated c.1900. The area is largely rebuilt whilst *Bourdon House* (no. 2) is a much older Queen Anne building just to the south. Indeed Bonsor was familiar with the area since Hill Street, his former home, was a short distance away on the west side of Berkeley Square. The couple initially lived at 14 Davies Street however the marriage had problems from the start and the allegations were as severe as in the case of J.F. Alcock, but the outcome was different. They then moved to a new home at 1 The Boltons and it was there that the worst problems developed.

The Boltons south of Brompton Road was originally a farm and the surrounding land market gardens. Robert Gunter sold the site in the mid-19th century and architect George Godwin designed a church and the double crescent of houses on either side - he also designed St. Jude's, Courtfield Gardens (see Addison Ch. 10). Hogarth J. Swale the perpetual curate paid most of the £6,000 cost and St. Mary's, The Boltons was consecrated on 22 October 1850. The church was built of Kentish rag capped with Bath stone and had hassock on the inside and a spire was added in 1854. There were London Plane trees in the central gardens and this was an attractive location, thus St. Mary's was called 'the country church in Kensington.' 1 The Boltons a semi-detached house was on the northeast side next to Bolton Place, near Brompton Road. It was a 'grand' white stucco three-storey mansion with columns and a balcony, flower carvings around the first floor windows, ornate iron fencing at the second floor and a roof cornice with block moulding. No expense was spared and the white stucco wall had cornice, columns and iron-gate whilst steps led up to an imposing black door with brass lamp.

Jeanne Marie Bonsor was the aggrieved party in this instance and after two years petitioned for a divorce. She stated that since the date of the marriage Alexander was continually drunk, first at 14 Davies Street and then at their new home 1 The Boltons. They stayed at the Hotel Brighton in Paris from 28 March to 10 April 1895 and he stayed out all night, then returned drunk and violent at 5-6 in the morning, and once grabbed her hair and pulled her out of bed. He swore at her and threatened her at 1 The Boltons from April to September 1895 and threw spirits and other items, and on one occasion threw a chicken at her during dinner! He threw water over her in bed and tore her nightdress in May 1895 and pushed her against a washstand and bruised her and threw her to the ground in July 1895. She had to seek refuge with the servants and was ordered to bed when ill however he banged on the door and broke a panel. He committed adultery with a woman known as Mrs. Hamilton at 1 Serpentine Road, Regent's Park from August to September 1895, and also with a woman known as Mrs. D'Este at 41 Michael's Grove, Middlesex in September 1895 (both on divers occasions).

In light of this the petitioner humbly prayed that the marriage be dissolved and that she would receive other relief on 16 October 1895. She still resided at 1 The Boltons and swore an affidavit to this effect at Lewis & Lewis, 7 Ely Place, Holborn the next day. She left London and moved to the Hotel Continental in Paris and was requested to give further details by the court after Marshall & Marshall appeared for the respondent on 8 November 1895. She replied through the Vice Consul at the British Consulate on 16 November 1895 and stated that she could give no further details of times and dates other than those in the attached schedule A. The latter had detailed description of the above events and made the case look more severe than before and was deposited on 20 November 1895. Lewis & Lewis sent a letter dated 7 December 1895 stating: "Dear Chris, It seems that although you served us with answer on the 28th ulto you did not then nor have you since filed it. Under the rules it should be filed on the day it is served. We must ask you to file it on Monday as unless this is done the case may be treated as an undefended one. If you have any difficulty please show this letter." The solicitors clearly had a more amiable relationship than that of their clients and the letter had the desired effect as Marshall & Marshall filed the answer on 9 December 1895. The court asked for this on several occasions but we shall never know what it said as it was not kept with the other papers.

The respondent was given ten days to produce all his books, vouchers and documents of income for the last 3 years so that alimony could be set on 13 January 1896. He also had to appear at the Principal Probate Registry, Somerset House, Strand at 2 o'clock Monday, 3 February 1896, to be cross examined as to income. He was ordered to pay two sums of £40 costs and there was a hearing before Sir John Gorell Barnes, Justice of the High Court, on 21 February 1896. He had little defence and the judge stated, "I have heard counsel of both parties and the petitioner has proved their case. The marriage is to be dissolved, the respondent being guilty of adultery coupled with cruelty" - (decree nisi). Indeed the same judge heard the case of his brother three months later and one wonders if this was prejudicial. Alimony was set at £150 p.a. to be paid monthly on 17 March 1896 and the two parties then took very different paths.

The divorce had caused a considerable scandal although the family had enough influence to keep the details out of the Times, whilst they had to deal with problems surrounding both Alexander and Herbert at the time. Family members such as Cosmo had high positions in society and there are suggestions that Alexander was told to 'stay away' in no uncertain terms, however there are always two sides to a story. This contributed to a family rift and being out of favour he never lived in England again. He then renewed a former connection with Belgium but was not 'cast out' on his own as one might have expected. Claire Marie Silvie Kint (Clara in English) was born in Ostende on 4 February 1872 and was the younger daughter of Jacques Edwarde Kint and Silvie Amalie Laurresières (sic). She spent her early years in Ostende and her father died there on 30 April 1895 and her mother on 26 November that same year. This was a severe blow to the family and although Claire had relatives in Brussels it seems likely she came to England to work at this time. Indeed many gentlemen had domestic servants from the Continent and the Bonsors may have employed her at 1 The Boltons. Whatever the sequence of events Alexander had a relationship with Claire, who was twenty years younger than him, and two months after the decree nisi they left London for the Continent. They went to Vilvoorde a small town five miles north of Brussels and registered there on 14 April 1896 - then lived together unmarried.

The final decree was on 16 September 1896 and he was given 7 days notice to pay £83 5s to Lewis & Lewis on 7 November, since he was defaulting, thus there was a hearing in the New Year (see below). He was now a free man again but soon entered into another marriage - clearly a triumph of hope over experience! There were several difficulties regarding his marriage in Belgium due to the fact that he was a foreigner and many details had to be supplied although in general there was much bureaucracy on the Continent: Alexandre Georges Bonsor born Polesden and without profession residing Vilvoorde divorced from Jeanne Marie David son of Joseph Bonsor of London deceased and Eliza Denne a resident of London - the British Consul in Brussels confirmed the details of the divorce and his English antecedents since word of mouth was insufficient; Claire Marie Silvie Kint born Ostende and without profession of Vilvoorde daughter of Jacques Edwarde and Silvie Amalie Kint both died at Ostende in 1895 (as above), of the other part. It was confirmed that all documents had been received regarding her parents' death and from the British Consul thus the marriage was able to proceed - dated Sunday 17 January. There was no opposition to the ceremony and the official explained the laws of a civil marriage and the two parties responded separately. Alexander George Bonsor married Claire Marie Silvie Kint in the Town Hall, Vilvoorde at 11 a.m. on 27 January 1897 before Jean Bapteles Norrès a civil officer - in Brussels district and province of Brabant. There were four witnesses to the ceremony: François Claredenes (40) a merchant of Brussels and brother-in-law of the bride, C. Brusset (36) commissioner of police, Léon Londres (32) commissioner of police a sergeant and Jean Heibbaljasen (46) Chief Clerk of the Civil Office (sic) who signed their names at the end of the document next to *A.G. Bonsor* and *C. Kint*.

They stayed in Vilvoorde for only two months after the wedding and this made the solicitors in London nervous thus Alexander was ordered to pay £15 p.m. to Jeanne Marie on 1 February 1897 for maintenance and support during their joint lives. Alexander and his young wife left Vilvoorde on 7 April that year and went to live at Knocke on the coast. The town was near the Netherlands border and not far from where she was born and they registered their arrival on 10 April. They lived at the Villa Digue de Mer at the corner of Lippenslaan and Sea Promenade although the building no longer exists. Alexander then travelled to London and as a resident of Knocke made his last will on 9 May 1897 stating: "I bequeath all my real and personal property absolutely to my wife Claire Marie Silvie and appoint her sole executrix." It was signed before W. Marshall of 3 Lincoln's Inn Fields and Ernest W. Munton of 95a Queen Victoria Street both solicitors. Meanwhile his former wife Jeanne Marie had also begun a new life.

Joseph Bonomi of Italy came to London and had two sons Ignatius (1787-1870) and Joseph (1796-1878). The first was an English architect and designed both Gothic and neo-Classical buildings. He was based in Durham and worked on Lambton Hall, Durham Cathedral and Burn Hall near Croxdale however his most significant work was as the 'first railway architect.' He provided plans for a bridge over the River Skerne on the Stockton and Darlington Railway and these were accepted on 2 July 1824. The bridge was opened on 27 September 1825 and John Dobbin did a painting of the event fifty years later from his father's sketches. The Skerne Bridge still survives after 175 years but is in the back streets of Darlington between John Street and North Road.

Sir John Soane (1753-1837) trained under George Dance and travelled to Italy in 1777-80, and was a prolific architect who produced neo-Classical designs in 1780-1831. He was appointed architect and surveyor to the Bank of England (1788) and built London churches and country houses. He was professor at the Royal Academy and began to collate his books, casts and models for his students in 1806 and designed the notable Dulwich Picture Gallery (1811-14). He rebuilt houses at Lincoln's Inn Fields no. 12 in 1792-94 and no. 13 in 1808-12 and moved into the latter. His wife died in 1815 and he concentrated on his collections and rebuilt no. 14 in 1823-24 and formed the Academy of Architecture with John Britton in 1827. He was not happy with his two sons and established a museum of architecture, painting and sculpture by Act of Parliament in 1833. The Sir John Soane Museum, 12-14 Lincoln's Inn Fields, opened after his death in 1837 and became an important library with many antiquities and documents, such as the sarcophagus of Seti I and the drawings of Willey Reveley (see Ch. 20). Joseph Bonomi (1796) travelled to Rome to study under Canova, who died before his arrival, in 1822 and he went with Robert Hay (1799-1863) on an expedition to Egypt in 1824-26. He made many sketches whilst there and became a noted sculptor and Egyptologist. James Hali-Burton (1788-1862) son of the builder James Burton (see Sealy Vidal Ch. 7) went to Italy in 1815-22 and Egypt in 1822-35 but returned to England when his father stopped his allowance.

Bonomi and he became friends and they worked together on the *Excerpta Hieroglyphica* in 1825-28 whilst the former displayed Egyptian exhibits at the British Museum in 1834 and travelled to Rome. He designed an Egyptian façade for John Marshall at Temple Mills, Leeds in 1842 and married Jessie daughter of John Martin an artist in 1845. They had four children who all died in 1852 and Isabella (1853), Cecilia Nefeeseh the Baroness de Cosson (1855), Joseph Ignatius (1857-1930) and Marion (1858). Jessie his wife died at Kensington in September 1859 and her sister Isabella Mary Martin then kept his house. Bonomi worked with Owen Jones on the Egyptian Court at Crystal Palace in 1853 and after much struggle and criticism was elected curator of the Sir John Soane Museum in 1861. With his brother he built the Camels, Wimbledon and also wrote several articles on Egypt for magazines and died at Wandsworth in March 1878. Son Joseph I. Bonomi was born at Chelsea in June 1857 and was a lieutenant at Bowerham Barracks Infantry Depot in Lancaster in 1881 and then formed a liaison. Joseph Ignatius Bonomi (40) gentleman of 35 Duke Street, St. James's married Jeanne Marie Bonsor née David (28) spinster, divorced wife of Alexander G. Bonsor, of 10 Bedford Avenue, St. Giles (father deceased) at Westminster Register Office on 12 June 1897. Jeanne Marie made it clear that she was divorced (and from whom) on her marriage certificate.

Meanwhile Alexander and Claire stayed in Knocke nine months then travelled just a few miles inland to Dudzele (now Bruges) in December 1897. They had a brief stay there and continued to her hometown Ostende where they remained for about a year. They then had a permanent move and went to 56 Rue Locquenghien, Brussels in 1899. The house was in the north west of the city in the Molenbeek district near Rue de Flandre and St. Catherine's whilst the Canal Bruxelles-Charleroi was at the west end of the street. The divorce itself did not go away and he was given seven days to pay £25 6s to Lewis & Lewis on 7 July 1899. Alexander formerly a beer merchant died at 56 Rue Locquenghien at 6-40 p.m. on 17 August 1907 being a resident there but his 'domicile' was at 11 Upper Belgrave Street in London. His death certificate said he was 55 years, 10 months, 10 days old, born at Polesden, divorced from Jeanne Marie David but married to Claire Marie Silvie Kint. Joseph Kips (35) a doctor of medicine of Brussels and Alfred Raucey (34) a 'rentier' or shareholder of Forest, Brabant were informants before Emile De Mot a civil officer on 19 August.

An affidavit was filed in London stating: "The deceased was a British subject his domicile of origin was England and his will was 'made' in Belgium." His widow Claire Marie Silvie Bonsor of 56 Rue Locquenghien proved his will in England on 12 September 1907 but it was just a formality since the gross value of his estate in Britain was £5. What had happened to the Bonsor fortune? Did he squander the money and die penniless or were the funds abroad? There is little chance of knowing due to Belgian probate laws. English wills are available to the general public but this is not the case on the Continent and there is no national register of Belgian wills and all probate is private. A lawyer would find it hard to gain access, whilst public notaries or (ministers) were private entrepreneurs who proved wills and gave the paperwork to their successors over the centuries. There are also tax details relating to the probate but it is a lengthy and expensive process to gain access with a lawyer. His widow Claire remained in the house for just one year after his death then moved to Saint-Gilles ten miles north west of Brussels on 31 August 1908. His funds remain a mystery, but he was a skilful football player from a prominent family with a life 'far removed' from English Victorian society.

WILLIAM SLANEY KENYON-SLANEY

His striking partner was somewhat stereotypical and although he did not play in the first Cup Final, holds an important place in soccer history. His family had their roots in Lancashire and North Wales and are traced to the 1st Lord, his great grandfather. Lloyd Kenyon was born at Gredington, County Flint on 5 October 1732 and was called to the bar in 1761. He married Mary daughter of George Kenyon of Peel Hall, Lancaster at Deane by Bolton on 16 October 1773 and had sons Lloyd (1775-1800), George (1776) and Thomas (1780). He was Chief Justice of Chester in 1782, Master of the Rolls in March 1784 and was made a baronet on 28 July 1784. He was Attorney General and replaced Lord Mansfield as the Lord Chief Justice of England in May 1788 and was thus raised to the peerage as 1st Baron Kenyon in June 1788 - he died in 1802. Sir Thomas Hanmer 2nd Bart (1747-1828) married Margaret Kenyon also a daughter of George Kenyon of Peel Hall at Deane by Bolton on 3 December 1779 and then had Margaret Emma. The son George Kenyon (1776) became 2nd Lord at his father's decease and married his cousin Margaret Emma Hanmer on 1 February 1803. She died in 1815 having had issue whilst Lord Kenyon lived at 9 Portman Square and Gredington Hall, Ellesmere, Flint in 1830 - he died in 1855.

Thomas Kenyon of Pradoe, Salop was born on 27 September 1780 and was Clerk of the Outlawries in the Court of King's Bench. He married Charlotte Louisa daughter of Rev. John Robert Lloyd of Aston Hall at Oswestry on 21 April 1803 (see Muirhead Ch. 8). They resided at Whittington in 1804-15 and Ruyton XI Towns in 1816-24 - the town with the unusual name was formed when 11 hamlets amalgamated in 1301. They had twelve children during this period including John Robert (1807) of Pradoe (see Graham Ch. 1), William (1815) and Arthur Richard (1818). The father died on 4 November 1851 and the mother on 11 April 1869. William Kenyon was born at Ruyton XI Towns and baptized at Whittington near Oswestry on 18 October 1815 and was a colonel in the East Indian Army. Meanwhile nearby Robert Aglionby Slaney married Elizabeth Muccleston at Hatton Grange, Shifnal on 7 February 1812. He was a gentleman of Tavistock Square (see Betts Ch. 6) and had Elizabeth Frances (1813) and Mary (1817) baptized at St. Pancras Church, Euston Road and Frances Catherine (1823) was born at Baschurch, whilst R.A. Slaney Esq. M.P. was at 16 Tavistock Square in 1830.

William Kenyon was married to Frances Catherine Slaney on 9 October 1845 and their child William Slaney Kenyon was born at Rajkote, Bombay on 24 August 1847. They returned however to England and their daughter Agnes C. (1852) was born at New Brighton. They lived at Walford near the village of Baschurch and had children: Helen Marie Elizabeth (1853), Katherine M. (1856), Francis Gerald (1858), Violet Mabel (1860) and Percy Robert (1861) - there was also a son Walter Rupert. Robert Aglionby Slaney lived at Walford Manor, Baschurch and Hatton Grange, Shifnal and was M.P. for Shrewsbury making his last will on 30 December 1857. He left his farmlands at Ryton and his *mansion house and pleasure grounds* at Hatton Grange and farms at Hatton, to his daughter(s), the income being for that daughter during her lifetime and then to her husband (thereafter to any son). N.B. Ryton is near Shifnal and is not to be confused with Ruyton. The will, however, included a vital clause and stated the inheritance was forfeited unless the husband took the surname Slaney, either alone, or in addition to his own surname. Further to this he was required to bear the family arms of Slaney at all times (thenceforth). Robert Aglionby Slaney died on 19 May 1862 and William and Frances Kenyon inherited his estate and thus applied to Queen Victoria to take the surname Slaney and to bear the arms quarterly with those of Kenyon. This was granted by *Royal Licence* at St. James's on 21 July 1862 hence the name William Slaney Kenyon-Slaney was born.

He spent his early years in India, Baschurch and Hatton Grange and was educated at Eton with H.C.O. Bonsor, A.F. Kinnaird, E. Lubbock and A.C. Thompson (all born in 1847-48). He completed his education at Christchurch, Oxford and entered the army as an ensign in 1867 being promoted to captain in 1870. He played football for England in 1873 scoring the first international goal and then played in the Cup Finals in 1873, 1875 and 1876, and was a lieutenant colonel in the Grenadier Guards in 1878. He was also a right hand batsman and played cricket for the M.C.C. in 1869-80 - 17 innings 3 not out 145 runs high 34. William and Frances Kenyon-Slaney lived at Hatton Hall, Shifnal, Shropshire, in 1881 with their son William a lieutenant in the Grenadier Guards, daughters Agnes, Katherine and Violet, brother Arthur R. Kenyon and wife Caroline, and sixteen servants. The son Walter Rupert married Kate Helen M. Schooles at Elham in September 1878 and had a son Neville Aglionby at Hythe in September 1879. The latter lived with grandmother Kate Schooles at 2 Marine Parade, Hythe in 1881. Kenyon-Slaney a dashing soldier and sportsman was attached to the Household Brigade and served with the 2nd Battalion Grenadier Guards in the Egyptian War. The Egyptian Army 'mutiny' and the Arabi Pasha revolt took place in 1881 and troops under G. Wolseley occupied the Suez Canal Zone on 4 August 1882. Kenyon-Slaney fought at the battle of Tel-el-Kebir on 13 September 1882, which took place in the desert near the Suez Canal. The name literally means 'Great Tumulus' and was next to Sweet Water Canal - he received a medal and Khedive's Star. He was a major in 1883 and father William Kenyon-Slaney died at Marylebone in December 1884 aged 69. He then left the army and entered politics as M.P. for Newport, Shropshire North in 1886 and received a pension as a colonel in 1887.

Orlando Bridgeman (1762-1825) was made 1st Earl of Bradford and married Lucy Elizabeth Byng on 29 May 1788. They had a son George Augustus F.H. Bridgeman (1789-1865) 2nd Earl who married Georgina E. Moncrieff and had children Orlando George Charles (1819-98) 3rd Earl of Bradford and John Robert Orlando (1831-97). The latter was domestic chaplain to his father and the rector of Weston under Lizard in Shropshire in 1859-97 and also appears in correspondence of Charles Darwin. Indeed Dr. Robert Waring Darwin (1766-1848) married Susannah Wedgwood who was the daughter of Josiah and moved to the Mount, Shrewsbury in 1796 and practiced there the rest of his life. He secured the position of doctor after a recommendation from father Erasmus whilst his son Charles Robert was born in Shrewsbury in 1809. John Robert Orlando Bridgeman married Marianne Caroline Clive in 1862 and had a son William Clive Bridgeman (1864-1935) who was at Eton in 1881 and played for Cambridge University in 1887-94 when he scored 361 runs. He was an eminent statesman and was Home Secretary from 25 October 1922 to 22 January 1924 - he was a Tory and served under Andrew Bonar Law and when the latter was ill under Stanley Baldwin from May 1923, however Ramsay MacDonald and his Labour Government replaced them at the end of this time. He was 1st Lord of the Admiralty and was created 1st Viscount in 1929 and resided at Leigh Manor near Minsterley in Shropshire. He was one of the first B.B.C. governors in 1933 shortly before his death.

Orlando G.C. Bridgeman 3rd Earl of Bradford married Selina Louisa Forester on 30 April 1844 and had children George Cecil Orlando (1845), Francis Charles (1846), Gerald Orlando Manners (1847), Rowland Alexander Somerset (1852), Mabel Selina (13 November 1855) and Florence Katherine (1859). The father was M.P. for Shropshire South in 1842-65 and lived at Weston Hall, Shifnal and 43 Belgrave Square near the Bonsors. He was Lord Chamberlain in 1866-68 whilst his family were visiting with the Earl of Wilton at Egerton Lodge, Melton Mowbray in 1881; the visitors Selina L. Bradford wife of the 3rd Earl, daughters Mabel (25) and Florence (22), Lieutenant Col. Laurence James Oliphant a Grenadier Guard and wife Monica, and other 'society' people. William S. Kenyon-Slaney married Mabel Selina Bridgeman at Shifnal on 22 February 1887, who was born at Wilton Crescent, Belgravia in 1855 and her sister had a link to Meysey-Thompson (see Chapter 7). The couple had a daughter Sybil Agnes born at 43 Belgrave Square on 26 January 1888 and baptized at St. Peter's, Pimlico on 25 February, and a son Robert Orlando Rodolph born at Lowndes Square on 13 January 1892.

There were soon two marriages viz. Francis Gerald at Hartley Wintney in September 1892 and Percy Robert in St. George's Hanover Square (district) in June 1895. William mainly resided at Hatton Grange, Shifnal and was M.P. for Newport, Shropshire North from 1886-1908 and member of the Privy Council.

William Kenyon-Slaney a late colonel resided at 35-36 Lowndes Street, Chelsea in 1901 with his wife Lady Mabel and children Sybil and Robert. His sisters Katherine M. and Violet M. Kenyon-Slaney were living at Assarts, Main Road in Malvern Wells. William was listed as a Shropshire J.P. of Hatton Grange, Shifnal in the titled and landed gentry of 1903 and died at Hatton Grange on 24 April 1908. Francis Gerald Kenyon-Slaney a lieutenant colonel in the army and William Clive Bridgeman esquire M.P. proved his will, the estate being valued (three times) to reach a final figure of £137,774 17s 8d. His widow Mabel Selina died on 28 January 1933 and Captain Robert O. R. Kenyon-Slaney lived at Hatton Grange and died in 1965.

CHARLES HENRY REYNOLDS WOLLASTON

The Wanderers side was full of noted strikers and none more so than C.H.R. Wollaston who made so many appearances that he was almost a "professional". He came from a religious and scholarly family however went into business and never married. His ancestors originally resided at Wollaston, Staffordshire in the reign of Edward III (14th century), however the story begins with William Wollaston born at Cotton Clanford, Staffordshire on 26 March 1659-60 the son of William a yeoman. He was educated at Lichfield and Shenstone Schools and attended Sidney Sussex, Cambridge in 1674 obtaining a B.A. in 1677-78 and an M.A. in 1681. He was a good scholar, but was at odds with the university tutors and became assistant master at a Birmingham school in 1682. He had hopes of patronage from his father's rich cousin, whilst some greedy relatives watched young William with disdain. He soon became a favourite and when the old cousin died on 19 August 1688 he inherited the noble estate of Shenton near Leicester and the motto "Ne Quid Falsi" or "Nothing False".

With great expectations he settled his affairs and looked for a wife and courted Alice Coburne however she died of smallpox on the intended day of their wedding. He then married Catharine Charlton (1670) on 26 November 1689 who was the daughter of Nicholas Charlton a draper and London merchant. The couple settled in Charterhouse Square and William never spent a night away from his new home until his death. He was a moral philosopher and wrote many learned papers the most important being *The Religion of Nature Delineated*. This provided a theory of morality and was published in 1724 selling 10,000 copies, however his wife had died in 1720 and he died on 20 October 1724 and both were buried at Great Finborough, Suffolk where the family owned an estate. The couple had several children and the third son Francis Wollaston was born at Charterhouse Square on 6 June 1694. He attended Sidney Sussex, Cambridge in 1712, gained an L.L.B. in 1717 and was a fellow of the Royal Society in 1723. He married Mary Fauquier (1702) on 19 November 1728 the eldest daughter of Dr. John Francis Fauquier and sister of Francis Fauquier, a writer on finance.

The family lived in Charterhouse Square and attended church nearby at St. Botolph's, Aldersgate a parish north of St. Paul's Cathedral. Francis and Mary Wollaston had six children baptized at St. Botolph's namely Mary (1729), **Francis** (1731), Charlton (1733), Catherine (1734), William Henry (1737) and George (1738) - the third child predicting the football connection. This was an area of some religious fervour and the evangelical conversion of Rev. Charles Wesley M.A. took place at 12 Little Britain on 21 May 1738 whilst that of Rev. John Wesley M.A. took place at 28 Aldersgate Street on 24 May 1738. There is a plaque recording these events next to St. Botolph's, Aldersgate. Mary Wollaston of Charterhouse Square died in December 1773 whilst Francis Wollaston esquire died on 27 December 1774 and was buried at St. Botolph's on 2 January 1775.

Francis Wollaston was born on 23 November 1731 and was baptized at St. Botolph's the following day and soon made his mark on the world. He was educated under Daniel Wray a private tutor and then attended Sidney Sussex, Cambridge in June 1748 and entered Lincoln's Inn on 24 November 1750. He graduated with an L.L.B. in 1754 however he had, "some moral hesitance in regard to an advocate's duties," hence he became a priest in 1754 and preached at St. Anne's, Soho in the summer of 1758. He married neighbour Althea Hyde at St. Botolph's, Aldersgate on 11 May 1758, who was born in 1738 the fifth daughter of John Hyde of Charterhouse Square, and the couple had no less than seven sons and ten daughters! Their first three children were baptized at St. Botolph's however Francis was presented with the rectory and vicarage of East Dereham, Norfolk in 1761 and the family lived there in 1761-69. He was elected fellow of the Royal Society on 13 April 1769 and the family moved to Chislehurst in Kent the same year, he being made rector of the parish. However they maintained connections with St. Botolph's and four children were baptized there in 1769-77. Francis was involved with a bill in Parliament aiming to reduce '39 articles' to a simple declaration of faith in 1772, but it was rejected with a large majority.

CHILDREN OF FRANCES AND ALTHEA WOLLASTON

1. Mary Hyde	Baptized 3 February 1760 St. Botolph Married 1803 Rev William Panchen
2. Althea Hyde	Baptized 15 December 1760 St. Botolph Married 20 December 1784 St. Botolph Thomas Heberden (Canon of Exeter)
3. Francis John Hyde	Born 13 April 1762 Bapt. St. Botolph Married 13 August 1793 Frances Hayles Died 12 October 1823 **Chemistry and Philosophy, Cambridge**
4. Charlotte Hyde	Born 1763, later of Eltham Buried 24 September 1835 Chislehurst
5. Katherine Hyde	Born 1764, later of Eltham Buried 3 December 1844 Chislehurst
6. George Hyde	Born 10 July 1765, of Clapham Common Married 23 October 1796 Mary Ann Luard
7. William Hyde	Born 6 August 1766 E. Dereham, Norfolk Died 22 December 1828, 1 Dorset Street Buried 30 December 1828 Chislehurst **Chemist and Physicist, London** **platinum and electric motor**
8. Henrietta Hyde	Born 1768, of Croom's Hill, Greenwich Buried 19 June 1840 Chislehurst
9. Anna Hyde	Baptized 14 April 1769 St. Botolph Buried 6 January 1830 Chislehurst of Greenwich
10. Frederick Hyde	Born 12 June 1770 Died September 1809 (without issue)
11.Louisa Hyde	Died as an infant in 1772
12. Charles Hyde	Born 22 November 1772 Bapt. St. Botolph Married 2 March 1795 Sarah Willett Ottley
13. Henry Hyde	Born and died in 1774
14. Amelia Hyde	Born c.1775 (Estate worth £30,000) Died 23 November 1860 - of Croom's Hill
15. Henry Septimus Hyde	Born 14 April 1776 Bapt. St. Botolph (1) Mary Ann Blankenhagen d.1805 (2) Frances Buchanan d.1827 (3) Frances Maria Monro d.1872 Died 31 January 1867 Welling **Grandfather of C.H.R. Wollaston soccer**
16. Sophia Hyde	Baptized 24 October 1777 St. Botolph Died unmarried in 1810
17. Louisa Decima Hyde	Born c.1778 Married in 1806 to Rev James Leonard Jackson of Dorset

Francis Wollaston became rector of St. Vedast's, Foster Lane in 1779 and with East Dereham and Chislehurst held all three parishes until his death in 1815. He spent his time writing articles of a religious and astronomical nature viz. *The Secret History of a Private Man*, his autobiography, which had a limited publication in 1793. This was aimed solely at his friends and a copy can be found in the British Museum. His wife Althea died on 8 June 1798 and Francis then spent his later years at Chislehurst. The church history records that the whole parish of 1,300 to 2,000 people gathered on the village green in 1814 to celebrate the signing of "The Treaty of Paris". Napoleon was almost finished thus there was great relief and Francis Wollaston entertained them all in the open air and this may have taken place in the historic cockpit - a large grass amphitheatre beside the church. Francis Wollaston died at the Rectory, Chislehurst on 31 October 1815 and was buried at St. Nicholas' on 7 November. There is a wall memorial consisting of a marble oblong surmounted by a drinking vessel to *Franciscus Wollaston* in the church. The text is written in Latin however it records his kindness, his studious nature, his zeal for life and his Christian example and that he was the son of Francis and grandson of William. Finally it states that he attended the parishioners from 1769 to 1815.

His brother Charlton Wollaston (1733) qualified as a doctor and practiced at Bury St. Edmunds, being a physician to the King and a fellow of the Royal Society. He married Phillis Byam at St. James's, Westminster in 1758 she being the daughter of Samuel Byam of Antigua. The last brother George Wollaston (1738) was educated at Charterhouse and Sidney Sussex gaining a B.A. in 1758, M.A. in 1761 and D.D. in 1774 - he attended the university with poet Thomas Gray (1716-71). He was mathematical lecturer at Sidney Sussex and became a fellow of the Royal Society on 17 February 1763. He associated with St. Mary Aldermary in 1774-90 and died at "Greenside" in Richmond on 14 February 1826.

The children of Francis Wollaston then made an even greater contribution to society. In the first case four unmarried daughters resided at Eltham and Croom's Hill, Greenwich and were buried at Chislehurst from 1830-44. Indeed Charles B. Wollaston the nephew of Katherine performed her burial service on 3 December 1844 (see below). One of the daughters was an artist and painted pictures of St. Nicholas' Church showing the old box pews and minstrels' gallery. The daughter Amelia died at Croom's Hill, Greenwich on 23 November 1860 being formerly of Charterhouse Square and Chislehurst. She was one of the last members of the family and her estate amounted to under £30,000.

Francis John Hyde Wollaston was born at Charterhouse Square on 13 April 1762 and attended Scarning School, Norfolk under Mr. Robert Potter when his family lived at East Dereham. He was educated at Charterhouse and matriculated at Sidney Sussex, Cambridge on 5 May 1779 gaining his B.A. in 1783. He was a maths lecturer and a fellow and tutor at Trinity Hall becoming the Jacksonian Professor in 1792. He lectured on chemistry and experimental philosophy and performed over 300 experiments annually. He married Frances Hayles at St. Botolph's, Cambridge on 13 August 1793 and was given the vicarage of South Weald, Essex from 1794. The couple had Althea Jane at Chesterton in 1798 and Francis Hayles at St. Benedict's, Cambridge in 1803 as well as a daughter Frances Althea. He was appointed prebendary of St. Paul's Cathedral from 1802-23 and was made Master of Sidney Sussex on 18 February 1807, however lost the position in under a year when it was revealed he was never a fellow of that college. He resigned his professorship in 1813 and was made rector of East Dereham in 1815 at the decease of his father Francis. The family had a long connection with this Norfolk parish however he usually resided at South Weald and was thus made an archdeacon of Essex - he died on 12 October 1823. Francis Hayles was born on 1 May 1803 and educated at Charterhouse and Pembroke College. He married his cousin Caroline Wollaston on 7 June 1825 and entered the ministry in 1826, being rector of East Dereham in 1827-40, but resigned his orders. Mrs. Caroline Wollaston lived at Eltham in 1839 and her husband died on 5 November 1849 and she at Eastry district in September 1877.

George Hyde Wollaston was born on 10 July 1765 and married Mary Ann daughter of William Luard Esq. of Dorset Street (see below) at Clapham on 23 October 1796. They had six children baptized at St. Mary's, Battersea namely Frederick Luard (1803), Alexander Luard (1804), Henrietta (1807), Charlotte (1808), Edward Luard (1815) and Sophia (1816) some of whom appear later in the story. Frederick Luard married Diana Harriet Sperling at Great Maplestead, Essex on 17 March 1834. Alexander Luard married Susanna Charlotte Morris at Ryde, Isle of Wight on 16 March 1837 and had children Francis Morris (1838) in Ryde, and Mary Ann (1841), Henrietta Jane (1842) and George Hyde (1844) in Kingston - the latter was assistant master at Clifton College (in 1881). They lived at Clapham Common and the father George died on 25 August 1841.

William Hyde Wollaston was born at East Dereham on 6 August 1766 and attended the private school of Mr. Williams in Lewisham for two years. He attended Charterhouse from 13 June 1774 to 24 June 1778 and matriculated at Caius College, Cambridge on 6 July 1782. He was a senior fellow in 1787 and studied astronomy thus gaining his M.D. in 1793 and was made a fellow of the Royal Society on 9 May that year. His father Francis Wollaston, his uncle William Heberden M.D., the Hon. Henry Cavendish and Sir William Herschel signed his certificate of membership. He was a physician at Huntingdon in 1789 and then at Bury St. Edmunds where his uncle Dr. Charlton had practiced. He became a fellow of the Royal College of Physicians in 1795 and then practiced at 18 Cecil Street, in the Strand, in 1797. However, he gave up medicine in 1800 when he failed to obtain an appointment at St. George's although the real reason was his sensitivity and worry about his patients. On one occasion his concerns brought him to tears and he stated, "Allow me to decline the mental flagellation called anxiety, compared with which the loss of thousands of pounds is as a fleabite." He did not have to worry about losing thousands and received a legacy at this time that enabled him to engage in chemical research and took a house at 14 Buckingham Street, Fitzroy Square and set up a laboratory (the house has not survived). He discovered important properties of platinum in the next five years, which enabled the production of a pure variety of the metal and received a Royal medal for his work. This research had considerable commercial value and brought him a small fortune of about £30,000. Wollaston published in total 56 papers covering pathology, physiology, chemistry, optics, mineralogy, crystallography, astronomy, electricity, mechanics and botany - each of which witnessed an advance in that science. He was very careful in his studies and stated that: "His predominant principal was to avoid error." (See Addendum re Heberden).

He carried out experiments with electricity from 1801-21 and established that frictional and galvanic electricity are of the same nature, in 1801. He also stated that the action of a voltaic cell (battery) was due to the oxidation of zinc, and noted that there was a "power" around a wire carrying a current. He patented the *Camera Lucida* in 1807, which led to the discoveries of William Henry Fox Talbot in 1833 (see Marindin Ch. 5) and also adopted the wave theory of light. He gave evidence regarding the imperial gallon in the House of Commons in 1814 and this measure was later adopted in the Weights and Measures Act (1824). He liked to travel during the Royal Society vacations and visited industrial areas of Manchester and France in 1814. He also served on the Board of Longitude from 1818-28. He was a personal friend of Sir Humphrey Davy and they went fly fishing together, however there was considerable competition. He was made 'acting President' of the Royal Society in 1820-21 after the death of Sir Joseph Banks who had recommended him, however he declined to take the job permanently since he understood the ambitions of Sir Humphrey Davy. He did not want a contest and stepped aside, in his favour, thus losing a more prominent place in scientific history.

He attempted to make a wire revolve on its axis during an unsuccessful experiment in April 1821, which took place in the laboratory of Sir Humphrey Davy. He was almost the 'man of the moment' however Faraday and Davy continued their work on electro-magnetism and made a wire (with current) revolve around a magnet in December 1821. It was the prototype of the electric motor and resulted in a charge of plagiarism against Michael Faraday. Despite this Wollaston stated that Faraday behaved with a kindness and liberality throughout the affair, hence the matter was amicably resolved since the charge was unfounded. He established the *Wollaston Fund* at the Geological Society in 1828 and left money to the Astronomical and Royal Society. He died at 1 Dorset Street, Marylebone on 22 December 1828 and was buried at Chislehurst on 30 December (residence of Charles Babbage mathematician 1829-71). He did not make the standard history books but was just one spark behind the likes of Faraday.

Henry Septimus Hyde Wollaston was born at Chislehurst on 14 April 1776 and baptized St. Botolph's on 29 April, and had a long life as a merchant with three wives. He first married Mary Anne Blankenhagen on 23 December 1802 and was then in business as a merchant at Clapton in East London. The couple had two children namely Henry Francis (1803) and Caroline (1805) who were baptized at St. John's Hackney. His first wife died on 25 June 1805 and his daughter Caroline married her cousin Francis. He then married Frances Buchanan (1786) at Woodmansterne in Surrey on 24 June 1813 and had six children at Clapton: George Buchanan (1814), Charles Buchanan (1816), Alfred Buchanan (1818), Charlton James (1820), Frances Buchanan (1823) and Elizabeth Buchanan (1825). They were all baptized at St. John's, Hackney but his second wife died on 26 December 1827 and was buried at Chislehurst on 3 January 1828 - she was a resident of London. There was then a change of direction and Henry moved firstly to Exeter and then to Bristol where he was in business for some years. He married for a third time to Frances Maria Monro (1794) and they had one child William Monro Wollaston born on 19 October 1831 and baptized at St. David's, Exeter on 16 November that year. Henry and his family moved to Kent and lived at Little

Danson, Welling in 1860-66. He resided there on the 1861 census and was a landed proprietor and fund holder living with wife Frances Maria, Alfred Buchanan merchant in the Cape of Good Hope, William Monro clergyman tutor of Exeter College, Oxford, sister-in-law Sophia Monro and five servants.

Henry Septimus Hyde Wollaston made his last will at Welling on 26 March 1862 but was formerly of Exeter and Bristol. He gave his land and property in Suffolk and Norfolk including freehold property at Hoxne and Wingfield to his son Charles and gave his wife his household effects including carriages, harness, horses and cows. The residue of his estate was given to his executors and this with a sum of £12,500 charged on his estate was to be divided into thirty equal shares as follows: Henry (1), Caroline (4), George (7), Charles (5), Alfred (3), Charlton (3), Elizabeth (5) and William (2). He stated that the five shares for Charles should continue as part of his estate whilst he cancelled any debts due from his children including interest paid by his son Alfred, except any amount given to them before his decease (to be deducted). He stated that £350 should be redirected from his son Charlton to daughter Caroline with regard to a debt he owes her. He made wife Frances, brother-in-law Charles Monro and nephew Frederic Luard Wollaston executors, whilst Haxman Spurrell of Belvedere and George Morley of Bexleyheath were witnesses.

He added a codicil on 28 March 1862 regarding 80 shares belonging to him and his wife. These were consolidated capital stock of the London Assurance Company and were now to form part of his residuary estate. He also left £1,000 3% Consolidated Bank annuities and their interest, in trust for his wife, and after her decease the bequest to go to William his son. Robert Webber Monro a student of Lincoln's Inn and Caroline Courtnage of Queen's Road, Norbiton witnessed the codicil. Henry Septimus Hyde Wollaston died at Welling on 31 January 1867 aged 90 years and his will was proved in London on 16 March 1867. The surviving executors were Frances Maria Wollaston and Frederick Luard Wollaston of Shirley Warren near Southampton and his effects were initially under £25,000 but were re-sworn in July 1867 at under £16,000. His widow Frances Maria died at Merton, Oxfordshire on 2 April 1872 whilst visiting her son William. He was her executor and obtained probate of her will in London on 3 June 1872. Henry had six sons from his three marriages and two had a notable career in the ministry, whilst the eldest Henry Francis (1803) died at Portsea in December 1876.

George Buchanan Wollaston (1814) married his relative Julie Adye Catharine Buchanan at All Souls', Marylebone on 7 August 1845, and lived at Bishops Well, Chislehurst in 1860-66. He died in 'Bromley' on 26 March 1899 and widow Julia Adye Catharine died at Bishops Well on 25 June 1910 aged 94 years; indeed the family were associated with Chislehurst over 140 years. Stanley George Buchanan Wollaston their son was born at Eltham in 1847 and lived with his wife and son at Derry Down, St. Mary's Cray in 1881. He was an engineer employing 25 men and 9 boys and died in 1923. Alfred Buchanan Wollaston (1818) was single for many years and married Marian Tucker (1829) at Sevenoaks in September 1878. Although married he lived alone with two servants and was in business as a woollen extractor employing 15 men, 28 women and 24 girls at Bisley, Gloucester in 1881. Both died at Hastings: Marian in December 1892 and Alfred on 28 March 1901. Charlton James Wollaston (1820) married Maria Bromley at Derby in June 1848 and had a long life like his father. He was a retired civil engineer age 80 living with wife Mary (1846) at 23 Ormiston Road, Hammersmith in 1901 - he died in c.1905.

Charles Buchanan Wollaston was born at Clapton in 1816 and was baptized at St. John's, Hackney on 5 June that year. He matriculated at Exeter College, Oxford on 29 October 1834 and gained his B.A. in 1838 and M.A. in 1841 - being awarded a 4th class degree that included mathematics and physics. He entered the church as a deacon in 1842 whilst the Bishop of London appointed him prebendary (honorary canon) in 1843. He married Eleanor the daughter of Henry R. Reynolds esquire at All Souls', Marylebone on 30 July 1846 - she was born at Marylebone in 1824. The witnesses included H.R. Reynolds, A.S.C. Reynolds, H.R. Reynolds, H. Revell Reynolds and B. Reynolds who were her grandfather, father, brother (same name) and two sisters. The antecedents of her family were as follows:

1. Henry Revell Reynolds was born at Laxton, Nottingham-shire on 26 September 1745 and was the son of John Reynolds of Gainsborough, but his father died one month before his birth. His maternal great uncle Henry Revell of Gainsborough raised him and he was educated at Beverley School and matriculated at Lincoln College, Oxford on 17 March 1763 but transferred to Trinity College, Cambridge on 3 June 1766 - he graduated M.B. in 1768. He studied medicine at Edinburgh and first practiced at Guildford and married Elizabeth Wilson there in April 1770. He continued as a practitioner and took a house at Lamb's Conduit Street, London in 1772 and gained an M.D. in 1773 and F.R.C.P. on 30 September 1774. He was a censor, registrar, lecturer and orator at the Physicians College and was elected to Middlesex Hospital in 1773-77 and St. Thomas' Hospital in 1777-83. He was in private practice and first attended George III in 1788 being made physician extraordinary in 1797 and physician in ordinary from 1806. He found that attending the King at Windsor was most exhausting and was once examined for two hours on the King's health in the House of Lords. The effort eventually broke down his strength and he died at Bedford Square on 22 October 1811 and buried at St. James's Cemetery, Hampstead Road. His son John Reynolds was an independent minister and grandson Sir John Russell Reynolds (1828-96) an eminent physician at University College Hospital. His other son:

2. Henry Revell Reynolds was born at Wembley Park in c.1775 and was educated under Mr. Newcome at Hackney and also at Clapton. He attended Trinity College, Cambridge in Michaelmas 1792 gaining a B.A. in 1796 and M.A. in 1799. He was admitted to Lincoln's Inn on 24 October 1792 and was called to the bar on 19 May 1798. He married Ann Mitford who was baptized at Bromley in Kent on 9 August 1776, daughter of John and Sarah Mitford Esq. of Bromley Common or Captain (Robert) Mitford. The couple had the following children baptized at St. Andrew's, Holborn: Henry Revell (1800), Ann (1801), Susanna Eliza (1803) and Sarah Frances (1809). He was a commissioner of bankrupts in 1806-20 and Chief Commissioner of the Insolvent Debtors Court in 1820-53. He published two reports: (i) Cases in the court for the relief of insolvent debtors (ii) Considerations on the state of the law regarding marriage with a deceased wife's sister. Henry R. Reynolds senior a commissioner in the insolvent and debtors court lived at 5 Upper Wimpole Street, Marylebone in 1851 with his wife Anne, sister Clara St. George Reynolds (65) and five servants. He had chambers at 33 Lincoln's Inn Fields at this time and died at Marylebone on 19 May 1854.

3. Henry Revell Reynolds was born in London on 16 April 1800 and was educated at Hackney School and matriculated at Trinity College, Cambridge in Michaelmas 1818 gaining his B.A in 1822 and M.A. in 1825. He was admitted to the Middle Temple on 9 May 1822 and was called to the bar on 27 January 1826. He married Mary Anne Knatchbull in 1823 whose father was Sir Edward Knatchbull baronet. The couple's first daughter **Eleanor Reynolds** was baptized at St. Marylebone Parish Church on 18 May 1824, however their next four children were baptized at All Souls' viz. Ann Susanna Charlotte (1825), Henry Revell (1827), Julia Louisa (1828) and Bertha Mitford (1833). The father Henry a barrister-at-law lived at 25 Berner Street, Marylebone in 1841 with his wife Mary, children Eleanor (15), Susan and Bertha, and four servants. His wife Mary Ann died at Marylebone in March 1843 and he married Charlotte Ann daughter of Edward W. Bullock Webster at Hendon in June 1846. The couple had four children baptized at All Souls' namely Herbert Edward (1847), Edith Mary (1848), Arthur Sutherland (1851) and Amy Beatrice (1854). Henry Revell Reynolds junior, barrister, lived at 51 Upper Harley Street, Marylebone in 1851 with wife Charlotte and three children from each marriage inc. Henry Revell Reynolds (23) and six servants. He had an address "Gwydyr House", Whitehall in 1851 and was joint solicitor to the Treasury in 1852. Henry Revell Reynolds died at 51 Upper Harley Street on 23 June 1866 and Charlotte Anne Reynolds and Henry Ray Freshfield of 5 Bank Buildings proved his will with 2 codicils. The house was 105 Harley Street in 1866 but has not survived whilst Mrs. Revell Reynolds and Herbert lived at 141 Harley Street in 1869 - this grand property remains.

4. Henry Revell Reynolds was born at Marylebone on 3 July 1827 and was educated at Eton and matriculated at Trinity College, Cambridge in Michaelmas 1846 gaining his B.A. in 1850 and M.A. in 1853. He entered the church, being at Westerham Kent 1851-56, St. Andrew's Croydon 1857-63, Markham Clinton Notts 1863-72 and St. George's Chapel Hurstpierpoint 1873-75. He lived at Southover Lodge, Lansdowne Rd, West Worthing and died at Heene on 15 September 1896. His half brother Herbert Edward Reynolds was born at Marylebone on 3 April 1847 and was educated at Eton and admitted to Trinity College, Cambridge on 1 April 1865 gaining his B.A. in 1870 and M.A. in 1873. He was curate of Oswaldkirk, Yorks in 1870-72 and a curate and chaplain in Exeter from 1872-82. He was priest vicar of Exeter Cathedral in 1873-1900 as well as Cathedral librarian - 1877-1900. He edited a number of Latin works and died at Swanage on 6 June 1910.

Charles Buchanan Wollaston made a good match with Eleanor Reynolds in 1846 and their first daughter Eleanor Annie (1847) was born in Marylebone and baptized at All Souls'. He was made vicar of Felpham near Bognor Regis, Sussex in late 1847 and indeed remained there until 1870. The couple's first son Charles Henry Reynolds Wollaston was born at Felpham in 1849 and the family lived at the Rectory, Limmards Lane, Felpham in 1851. They had four other children at Felpham viz. Clare St. George (1852), Mitford Knatchbull (1856) *infant*, Grace Mitford (1857) and Sutherland Stracey (1859). The family were not in the village in 1861 however John Smythies Greene married Eleanor Annie Wollaston there in 1867. Charles Buchanan Wollaston a resident of Felpham made his last will on 2 February 1868 soon after his father's decease and left all his estate 'unto his dear wife.' Amalie Minlas the Felpham Rectory Governess and Edmund Ibbetson a 'gardner' of Felpham were witnesses.

Charles was appointed prebendary of Chichester Cathedral in 1868-87 and after leaving Felpham was vicar of St. Mary Amport near Andover from 1870-86. He maintained connections with his former parish and Arthur Churchill Bartholomew married Clare St. George Wollaston at Felpham in 1874, whilst Ernest John Humphrey married Grace Mitford Wollaston at Brighton in 1876. As with Felpham, he was not always present in Amport and spent much time in London. He lived at 35 Westbourne Place, Sloane Square in 1881 the property owned by Jane Kimp lodging house 'keeper' and her sister Sarah a dressmaker. Charles stayed there (without) his wife and was described as the vicar of Amport, whilst his brother-in-law Henry R. Reynolds clergyman of the Church of England 'without cure of souls' was a visitor. This was a polite way of saying he was unemployed. Westbourne Place was later renamed Cliveden Place and most houses including no. 35, the last property on the north side, are still present. The Rev. Canon Charles Buchanan Wollaston died at Reading on 11 August 1887 but was described as late of 8 Bloomfield Terrace, Pimlico. His widow Eleanor renounced the probate and it was granted to her son Charles Henry Reynolds Wollaston a bank secretary of 2 Princes Street, Mansion House on 1 November 1887 - his estate came to £1,516 0s 11d. His widow Eleanor died at 8 Bloomfield Terrace on 10 December 1891 and probate was again granted to Charles H.R. Wollaston on 14 January 1892, her effects being £1,254 12s 7d - she was still listed in a local directory that year. 8 Bloomfield Terrace was a two-storey cottage for the gentry on the north side and had a notable picture window, large shutters and a plain pilaster feature. It was near St. Barnabas Church, Pimlico consecrated in 1850 and fruity Orange Square. Fields covered most of the area until the 19th century despite earlier housing that included the home of W.A. Mozart, 180 Ebury Street (1764).

William Monro Wollaston was born at Exeter on 19 October 1831 and baptized at St. David's being the only child of the third marriage. He followed a similar path to Charles, and his relative Henry Reynolds, and matriculated at Trinity College, Oxford on 11 March 1851 gaining his B.A. in 1855 and M.A. in 1857. He liked the university life and was a fellow of Exeter College, Oxford from 1855-64 and the conduct of Eton in 1863. He was the vicar of Merton, Oxfordshire in 1863-74 and married Constance Sophia MacGregor in c.1870. She was born at Woolton near Liverpool on 27 May 1841 and baptized at Childwall - the daughter of James and Jane. The couple resided at Merton Vicarage in 1871 and the household included one pupil, two servants and an agricultural labourer, whilst his mother Frances, as stated, died at Merton on 2 April 1872. He then had a long sojourn abroad and was the chaplain of St. Paul's, Cannes in France from 1874-1910. He was very involved in local affairs and sent letters to the Times in a professional capacity and three indicated his concerns, the first:

<u>Tuesday August 28, 1883</u>: *Desecration of a Cemetery at Cannes.* The French authorities have attempted to close the cemetery and remove all the memorials etc. their aim being to improve the approach to the Hôtel Continental. The cemetery was closed 11 years ago, in 1872, and there was a similar attempt at this time. The memorials can only be saved at the expense of the relatives and there will be no compensation from the French Government, therefore he urges the English Government and other citizens to protest strongly, but suggests it may already be too late.

During this period his family maintained links with England and his wife Constance Sophia late of 99 Cambridge Street, Warwick Square died at Folkestone on 29 May 1888. He then improved his situation with a Royal connection. James II of England (1633-1701) was first married to Anne Hyde (1638-71) and then Maria Beatrice de Modena (1658-1718) but it was quite permissible for the King to have a mistress. He thus formed an attachment with Arabella Churchill lady-in-waiting to Anne Hyde and older sister of John Churchill 1st Duke of Marlborough in c.1667. She was soon pregnant and had a daughter Henrietta FitzJames that same year and later three other children (by the King). Henry Waldegrave 1st Baron Waldegrave of Chewton (1661-90) married Henrietta FitzJames (1667-1730) and their descendant George Waldegrave 4th Earl was married to Elizabeth Leveson-Gower. Their son Vice Admiral William Waldegrave the 8th Earl (1788-1859) married Elizabeth Whitbread (1791-1843) on 10 August 1812 who was the daughter of Samuel Whitbread - the brewer and politician of Drury Lane fame (see Lubbock Ch. 7). William Brodie (1821-82) married daughter Maria Waldegrave (c.1820-1911) on 2 October 1844 and had a child Mary Arabella. It is not clear how they met but William Monro Wollaston married Mary Arabella Brodie on 15 April 1890 thus there was *blue blood* in the family. William then continued with his London address and was at 99 Cambridge Street, Pimlico in 1892 and voiced further concerns to the Times:

Saturday December 17, 1898 - *Letters to the Editor: The French Riviera.* Difficulties between the French and English have been settled hence the Riviera is now a friendly place to come. He speaks from experience after his 25th season as chaplain at Cannes. The weather is superb in winter and there are many bargains and a villa valued at £800 was just taken for £480 (one season). He wishes to restore confidence since there are few English visitors and this could ruin the hotels and businesses.

Wednesday January 20, 1904 - *Memorial to the late Bishop Sandford.* There was a meeting on January 15th at the Chateau de Thorenc, Cannes reference a memorial for the late Bishop of Gibraltar, whilst funds were to be raised for a Mission to Seamen in that colony. A brass was to be erected in the cathedral and all subscriptions to Messrs. Hoare, Fleet Street or W.M. Wollaston Canon of Gibraltar, hon. sec., *Villa Montboissier, Cannes.*

William M. Wollaston died at Villa Montboissier on 3 December 1910 and probate was granted to Mary Arabella Wollaston widow and Charles Henry Reynolds Wollaston esquire his executors, in London, on 18 February 1911 - his effects being £22,567 16s 3d. A memorial to him was erected in Chislehurst Church, namely a marble tablet with a brass oblong surmounted with brass cross. The inscription in red and black lettering stated: "To the glory of God, and the dear memory of WILLIAM MONRO WOLLASTON Priest M.A. Oxon Born Oct 19th 1831 fell asleep Dec 3rd 1910 r.i.p. This tablet is erected by his wife." The connection with Chislehurst presumably came through brother George and wife Julia, whilst his widow Mary Arabella died on 28 February 1921. The section concludes with a discussion of the next generation.

Eleanor Annie Wollaston was born Marylebone on 3 May 1847 and baptized at All Souls' on 1 June. Her husband John Smythies Greene son of John and Margaretha was born at Bury St. Edmunds on 15 August 1842, and they married at Felpham on 4 July 1867. The Greene family had extensive connections in the Suffolk town thus the couple lived there and had children: John W. (1870), Cecil W. (1873), Ella W. (1877), Hilda W. (1879) and Kenneth W. (1880). In fact John S. Greene solicitor lived at St. James's, Bury St. Edmunds in 1881 with the four 'youngest'. His wife Eleanor and son John W. were boarding with John Golding a lodging house 'keeper' at 19 Oriental Place, Brighton (see Muirhead Ch. 8). However both parents died at Bury when young: John on 17 October 1884 and Eleanor on 6 August 1895. The family stayed in Suffolk and John W. Greene, solicitor, lived at 10 Northgate Street, Bury in 1901 with Ella, Hilda and Kenneth (articled clerk), whilst Cecil Greene was a secretary to the 'sanitorium' at Dwygyfylchi in Caernarvon.

Clare St. George Wollaston was born Felpham on 27 January 1852 and baptized on 27 February. Her husband Arthur Churchill Bartholomew the son of Christopher C. and Fanny Teresa was baptized at Lympstone, Devon on 17 April 1846, and they were married at Felpham on 14 April 1874. He entered the profession of teacher and ran a school in Reading for many years and had two children: Clara W. (1877) and Arthur W. (1879) in the town. Arthur C. Bartholomew proprietor of school M.A. Oxon lived at Prospect Park House, Tilehurst in 1881 with wife Clara, children Clara and Arthur, and mother-in-law Eleanor Wollaston - her husband was at Sloane Square. There were 36 scholar boarders aged 9-14 and ten servants and these included William L. Napier (13), scholar, born Montreal (see Graham Ch. 1). Prospect Park was a substantial and elegant two-storey Georgian House and although plain had a colonnade of six columns at the front and two bow-fronted wings. The couple had a son Guy (1882) at Tilehurst and continued to live there with their family. Arthur still a schoolmaster was visiting Henry Ellacombe a clergyman at St. Mary's Vicarage, Bitton, Gloucester in 1901, whilst Clara and children Clara and Guy lived at Park House School, Parkside Road, Reading. There were 25 boy pupils aged 10-13 one of them being Henry R. Reynolds (11) from Hursley, Hampshire - there was also a school lodge for the gardener. They had a long life there and both died at Reading: Clara in March 1923 aged 71 and Arthur in March 1940 aged 94.

Grace Mitford Wollaston was born at Felpham on 29 December 1856 and baptized on 1 February 1857. Her husband Ernest John Humphrey was born at Wandsworth in December 1852 and they were married at Brighton in June 1876. They had children Ronan (1877) and Selwyn (1878) at Brighton whilst Ernest J. Humphrey, wharfinger, lived at Grove Road, Sutton in 1881 with his wife Grace, two sons and three servants. The family were absent from the 1901 census. Sutherland Stracey Wollaston was baptized at Felpham on 24 July 1859 and matriculated at Trinity College, Oxford on 22 November 1877. He was an undergraduate living at 55 Broad Street, Oxford in 1881 and gained a B.A./M.A. in 1886. Sutherland. S. Wollaston a school tutor lived at 134 Tilehurst Road, Reading in 1881 with Edward C. Francis also a tutor and they no doubt worked at Prospect Park. He died at 17 Pembroke Road, Kensington on 6

February 1924 and his probate was granted to Clare Wollaston Bartholomew and John Wollaston Greene solicitor. The family had made a significant contribution to the academic world and this brings us to the football connection.

Charles Henry Reynolds Wollaston was born Felpham Vicarage on 31 July 1849 and his birth was registered in West Hampnett in July-September 1849 - he was recorded as 'Male' Wollaston but was soon named after his two grandfathers. He was baptized at Felpham Church on 5 September 1849 and spent his childhood in the village, and was educated just 15 miles away at Lancing College from August 1862 to September 1868. He excelled in both sport and academic studies and was a scholar in June 1863, a prefect in 1865 and school captain in 1867. He matriculated at Trinity College, Oxford, like his uncle William, on 17 October 1868 (aged 19) and achieved a 2nd class degree B.A. in modern subjects in 1871. He then took on the work of a solicitor however was not registered at the *Law Society*.

He had made his mark on the playing fields at Lancing College and was soon one of the most prolific footballers of the 1870s, and unlike his contemporaries played only for the Wanderers. He appeared for them in the Cup Final victories of 1872, 1873, 1876 (& replay), 1877 and 1878 and played four times for England - a magnificent record. He played in the first Cup Final at the Oval on 16 March 1872, and scored a goal at Lillie Bridge on 29 March 1873 to help secure a 2-0 victory over Oxford University - the other goal from A.F. Kinnaird. He played in the third international between England and Scotland at the West of Scotland Cricket Ground, Glasgow on 7 March 1874 in front of 7,000 spectators. Indeed the games in Scotland attracted far larger crowds than those at the Oval since the Scots were most keen to defeat the 'olde enemie'. He played in the game with R.C. Welch however the Scottish side won 2-1 and also played in the next encounter at the Oval on 6 March 1875, the crowd being just 2,000. Wollaston scored his only international goal after five minutes to put England 1-0 ahead however the Scots levelled the score. Charles Alcock scored again on 70 minutes to give England a 2-1 lead but the Scots scored a second and the game finished 2-2. The contest in Scotland in 1876 did not include 'our' Wanderers players but it is worth noting that the attendance at the West of Scotland Ground was 15,000.

Charles Wollaston played in the Cup Final that year and scored in the replay on 18 March 1876 to help the Wanderers beat the Old Etonians 3-0. He then had a very busy time appearing in two Cup finals and also playing two games for England. Wollaston and M.P. Betts played for England at the Oval on 3 March 1877 in front of a crowd of only 2,000 and England lost 3-1. Meanwhile, he played against A.F. Kinnaird in 1876 but played with him in the Cup Final on 24 March 1877 and the Wanderers beat Oxford University 2-1. He also appeared with Kinnaird in the Cup Final on 23 March 1878 and the Wanderers beat the Royal Engineers 3-1. He was on the F.A. Committee from 1879-82 and during this period witnessed two epic encounters England against Scotland in 1879-80. The old opponents played at the Oval on 5 April 1879 in front of 4,500 spectators and England won this 5-4 under the watchful eye of referee C.H.R. Wollaston. The return game was at the 1st Hampden Park, Glasgow on 13 March 1880 and C.H.R. Wollaston (Wanderers) was captain of England. He led his team bravely in the game however they were up against 11 players and 12,000 tartan supporters thus the Scots gained revenge, turning the score on its head to win 5-4. This was the end of his career.

His exact occupation is unclear, however he was Assistant Secretary and Secretary for the Union Bank of London, 2 Prince's Street, Mansion House from 1878-98. He resided at 14 Coleshill Street near Sloane Square in 1881 and since this road abutted with Westbourne Place he was just a goal kick from his father. Charles was described as an unmarried solicitor and lodged with George Wheatley a lodging house (keeper) and family. No's 1-20 Coleshill Street were on the east side from Westbourne Place to Minerva Street (later Chester Row), the last being a public house. This was a four-storey Georgian property with brick façade and white stucco ground floor and the same arrangement exists today but Wollaston's abode is now 51 Eaton Terrace. These lodgings were near Battersea Park and the Oval thus he was well situated for his involvement with the Wanderers however after leaving the F.A. Committee he departed from football in 1882. He worked for the Union Bank of London and was admitted as a solicitor in 1895 but resigned as Secretary in 1898. He lived at 63 St. George's Road, Pimlico in 1900-01 and was an unmarried bank director with two servants. The house was near St. Gabriel's Church in Warwick Square (see Alcock Ch. 3) and Thomas Cubitt was the builder, whilst his uncle William lived nearby in Cambridge Street. It was a four-storey building with a white stucco finish, columned porch entrance, first floor colonnade and 'fine' moulded cornice - plus a small garden at the rear; being the first house south of the church and remains today but is combined with nos. 63-67 in St. George's Drive. A yellow brick corner house next door is unusual and is octagonal in shape.

Charles later lived at 46 Belgrave Road, Pimlico at the junction with Warwick Way and near Victoria Station. It was a four-storey corner house, on the west side, with a plain design and no rear aspect but semi-circular pediments above the first floor windows - it remains today. Whatever its merits, he did not spend much time there, and still being athletic went walking and mountaineering in Switzerland during the next twenty-five years. He wrote his last will at 46 Belgrave Road on 23 April 1926 and appointed Ella Wollaston Greene and Clare Wollaston Bartholomew, nieces, his executors, and gave them his household goods and £1,000 each. He gave his housekeeper Mrs. Laura Parsons a lifetime annuity of £100 p.a. in respect of her long service and devotion to his late sister. There was then a significant entry stating: "I leave the sum of £100 free of duty to each of my faithful guides in Switzerland, for some twenty five years, Joseph Biner and Augustin Gentinetta (both of Zermatt).... or their next of kin." He divided his estate into two equal parts, one to Ella Wollaston Greene but if she died to Kenneth Wollaston Greene, the other to Arthur Wollaston and Clare Wollaston - Bartholomew, in equal shares. Edward Pope of 1 Suffolk Street (club secretary) and A.G. Ross of 9 George Yard, Lombard Street (banking discount agent) witnessed the will. Charles H.R. Wollaston died at 46 Belgrave Road on 22 June 1926 and probate went to Ella Wollaston Greene of 61b Canfield Gardens, Hampstead and Clare Wollaston Bartholomew of 75 Tilehurst Road, Reading spinsters - his estate £22,946 18s 2d. His contribution to soccer must not be under-estimated.

THOMAS CHARLES HOOMAN

The Wanderers all played well in the 1872 Final however Vidal and Hooman attracted special notice by their skilful dribbling - this was an ability much admired at the time. The Hooman family are traced to Kidderminster in Worcestershire and had a prominent role in the town. The family included John (1755-1839), William (1756-1827) and James Hooman (c.1759-1827) who entered into the carpet 'trade'. William Pardoe, meanwhile, married Elizabeth Parker in the town on 1 December 1745 and had four children baptized: Joseph (2 February 1747), William (1750), Mary (1752) and Elizabeth (20 August 1756). The family were weavers in the mid-18th century and Joseph Pardoe and his wife Sarah had children Elizabeth (1773) and Mary (1775). He had formed the partnership of "Rouse and Pardoe" by 1776, however this was dissolved in 1780 and he then traded as Joseph Pardoe & Co. He married Mary Callow at Kidderminster on 18 March 1777 and had nine children in 1778-93 including Thomas (1783) and Charlotte (1793), plus five daughters and two infant boys. There was an important match when James Hooman married Elizabeth Pardoe at Kidderminster on 9 August 1781. The couple had ten children baptized in the town from 1782-1800 incl. James (2 May 1784), Parthenia (12 March 1787) and George (1 May 1797). The father was an attorney-at-law in 1783 but abandoned the profession to become a carpet manufacturer by c.1795, and he was no doubt attracted to the trade by his brother-in-law.

Joseph Pardoe also carpet manufacturer was then ill and made his last will on 2 January 1798. He left his wife Mary the interest on a £1,000 marriage settlement and a further £2,000 in trust for his wife and children, and Elizabeth daughter of his first wife. The latter was also to receive £100 and a further like sum from brother Thomas - on her marriage. He then left several properties to his son Thomas when he reached the age of 21 viz. dwelling and warehouse in Worcester Street, a parcel at the top of Coventry Street purchased from Thomas Rouse, small parcel at Rag Sill exchanged for one in Ourlove Field, half part in the carpet shop and factory at the bottom of Worcester Street, buildings at Pitts Lane and Bullring, and a public house at Park Gate. These were to continue in the ownership of his son but if he died they were to be sold and divided amongst his other children. The property belonging to his two friends James Hooman and Richard Jones was placed in trust for his son Thomas to be sold for the best price. He left a gold watch to both wife Mary and son Thomas and the residue for his children when Thomas reached 21 - share of daughter Charlotte likewise at 21. He appointed his wife, James Hooman and Richard Jones executors then added a codicil and stated, "I am desirous of showing some mark of esteem for James Hooman and Elizabeth his wife, my only sister, and leave each a mourning ring of 20g," dated 2 January. He then made a second codicil and left the interest on £3,000 to his wife Mary and money for the education of daughter Charlotte. Joseph Pardoe died soon after and was buried at St. Mary's, Kidderminster on 28 February 1798. James Hooman and Mary Pardoe proved his will in London on 27 October 1798 and it seems likely the trustees then ran the company since son Thomas was not 21 until 1804.

James Hooman & Co. remained in business and merged with the 'long established manufacturer' Joseph Pardoe & Co. to form "Hooman and Pardoe" in 1805. James Hooman senior was in control of both companies when the merger took place and no doubt instigated proceedings. Thomas Pardoe was the second partner, now aged 21, and married his cousin Parthenia Hooman at Kidderminster on 4 February 1806. They had a son Thomas (1807) baptized at Kidderminster but children Parthenia (1810), James (1821) and George (1831) were baptized at St. Pancras, London. The son James Hooman junior then joined the firm and they traded as "Hooman, Pardoe and Hooman" from 1809 with a main office at New Road in south Kidderminster near the River Stour. James Hooman (j) had good prospects and married Jane Carpenter (1785) at Kidderminster (or Wellington, Somerset) on 22 September 1810 and had eight children at Kidderminster viz. Jane (1811), James (bapt. 18 January 1813), Elizabeth (1815), Henry Carpenter (1816) *infant*, Ann (1817), Charles (1818), Clement (1822) and Henry (1825).

The printed records state that J. Hooman and J. Pardoe (the founders) retired in the 1820s but the facts related above clearly dispute this, although there were considerable changes at this time. St. George's, Kidderminster was consecrated in 1824 and Joseph Bowyer provided an altar cross, embellished with woven carpet work (see below). Jane Hooman wife of James junior was buried at St. George's on 18 November 1825 aged 40 and James Hooman senior was buried there on 21 February 1827 aged 68; his will was proved at the P.C.C. on 6 March (he was a carpet manufacturer). These were hard times and there was a serious strike in the town in 1828. The town's impoverished weavers had a grievance against their employers since they couldn't subsist on the meagre wages. Rev. Humphrey Price was the champion of their cause but Joseph Bowyer and most of the town's carpet manufacturers were vehemently opposed to him. Bowyer was an employer and carpet manufacturer from 1803 and showed little concern for his workers being largely indifferent to the poverty of the weavers, however he built himself a substantial house called the Copse in the mid 1820s. The strike, in 1828, posed a serious threat to Bowyer and he stood outside his house brandishing a gun whilst striking weavers marched by. They returned to stone his property whilst a new Act of Parliament compensated him two months later.

Meanwhile James Hooman junior was prepared to listen to their concerns, despite being very ill at the time, and even volunteered to be an arbitrator although his efforts came to nothing in the end. James made his last will on 22 March 1828 and requested, "to be laid by the side of my ever justly beloved wife, the much lamented mother of my children." James Hooman junior was buried at St. George's on 16 May 1829 aged 45 and his will was proved on 2 June - A recent publication confirms there are inscriptions to the family at the church. The children of James and Jane Hooman were then orphans and their upbringing was entrusted to Thomas Pardoe (1783) and George Hooman (1797). The partnership agreement was changed at this time: George Hooman succeeded his father and Thomas Pardoe (1807) son of Thomas joined his father in the company - some sources state the latter was James son of Joseph but the records do not support this. The company name was "Pardoe, Hooman and Pardoe" to reflect this in 1829. George Hooman married Mary Frances Hallen at Kidderminster on 25 August 1829 and resided at *Habberley House*.

There was severe competition in the town and a trade slump meant that Joseph Bowyer went bankrupt in 1830 and was forced to sell the Copse, although he was in business again in 1832 and moved away, dying at Caldwall Hall in 1837. This left a niche in the market for Pardoe-Hooman and they went from strength to strength and clearly knew their warps from their wefts. The firm was one of the largest in Kidderminster in 1832 and owned 130 looms in total with their main offices located in the centre of the town near Oxford Road and Vicar Street. George Hooman and his wife Mary Frances had four children baptized at Kidderminster viz. Mary Frances (1830), Eleanor Elizabeth (1832), Catharine (1833) and George James (1834). Meanwhile Elizabeth Hooman (née Pardoe) widow of James Hooman senior died nearby at Chaddesley Corbett in 1836 aged 81, and this saw the end of the older generation. The company continued to expand and had 170 looms in 1836 and George Hooman was Mayor of Kidderminster in 1837. This was a preferential position thus the company had 172 Brussels looms and 70 Kidderminster-Ingrain looms (total of 242) in 1838 - there were 360 employees. Thomas Pardoe son of Thomas was buried at St. Mary's on 4 August 1838 aged 30 and his brother James Pardoe succeeded him in the company.

The Copse was put up for sale when Joseph Bowyer went bankrupt in 1830 and was described thus: "There is a handsome entrance hall, seven bedrooms, conservatory, coach house and three acres of land.... There is a beautiful hanging wood, through which walks have been tastefully formed." This provided a perfect opportunity for the large and wealthy Hooman family who then purchased the Copse. The house was situated on a rise south of the town centre on Hoo Lane and beside Back Brook a small side channel of the River Stour. The Vicarage was just opposite the house, and across the neighbouring field was the station of the Oxford, Worcester and Wolverhampton Railway. James Hooman (1813) joined the family business in the mid-1830s and was a merchant of "The Copse". He married Mary Ann Hemming at the chapel of Great Alne on 18 September 1839 and his father was described as James Hooman a merchant "deceased" whilst the witnesses included Richard and William Hemming and George Hooman. The village of Great Alne was located just outside the town of Alcester in Warwickshire. Richard Hemming a farmer and Susannah Blakeway were married at Chaddesley Corbett on 26 May 1814; Mary Ann their daughter was baptized at Tardebigge southeast of Bromsgrove on 19 September 1815.

During this period most of the looms were located in shops and factories along Worcester Street, in the town centre, however the company built a 36-loom factory there in the 1830s and the site became the main office for a time in the 1840s. Indeed, with this kind of expansion they were the largest company in the town by 1840 having three spinning mills - one adjacent to the offices in Oxford Road, one at Caldwall and a third that they leased. With regards to the family George Hooman had a fifth child Mary Jane in 1839 but his wife Mary Frances was buried at St. George's, Kidderminster on 18 August 1841, aged 42. James and Mary Ann Hooman lived at the Copse and initially had two children there viz. Susan Henrietta (1841) and James Hemming (1845). The family had great influence in the town and George Hooman was Mayor again in 1845 but this dominance was not destined to last. The company was an innovator and one of the first to introduce tapestry carpet weaving in Kidderminster. The firm obtained a licence to use Wytock's "Tapestry-Brussels" process in 1847 and built a large factory in a narrow lane called the Sling. The factory was situated west of the town centre by the River Stour and the completed building was opened in January 1848. This was an extremely large mill dominating the town and had 110 tapestry looms and also a yarn-printing department. The building did not last and Pitts Lane Multi-Storey Car Park covers the site: 'They paved paradise and put up a parking lot,' but no doubt it was not paradise for the mill-workers.

James and Mary Ann Hooman had a daughter Mary Ann at Great Alne in 1849 and a son Thomas Charles at Kidderminster in 1850. There were also two marriages in the parish church viz. Henry Hooman to Elizabeth Chellingworth on 6 August 1850 and Mary Frances Hooman to Shadrach Chellingworth on 5 June 1851. This was the height of the company's success and James Hooman "carpet manufacturer firm of 11 employing about 700 persons 400 males 300 females" lived at the Copse in 1851 with wife Mary Ann, children Susan, James, Mary Ann and Thomas C. (3 months) and five servants - including a nurse. Their last child Frances Juliana Hooman was born at Kidderminster in 1852. This scenario of wealthy owners, workers and mills painted a post-industrial picture reminiscent of the *Rainbow* by D.H. Lawrence - however dark clouds were looming on the horizon.

This was an age of innovation and industrial modernisation and the owners realised that companies made a 'fatal mistake' when they rejected the power-loom. Consequently, the firm began an important trend in the town and applied the power-loom to the manufacture of tapestry carpets. They installed a steam engine and looms at the Sling factory and these were in operation by 1852, and the company then had 800 employees including those who worked in the spinning mills. Indeed they looked to be in a strong position and as a result concentrated on the production of tapestry carpets and sold off their Brussels handloom factories. This turned out, however, to be a fatal misjudgement regarding future trends and there was soon a reverse and the market for tapestry carpets collapsed by 1857. The company had invested heavily in the new plant and were in severe financial difficulties and the situation became progressively worse. The company was declared bankrupt the following September and the *Brierley Hill Advertiser* printed an article dated 11 September 1858:

> "We regret to announce, the eminent firm of Pardoe Hoomans and Co., Carpet Manufacturers of Kidderminster, are unable to meet their engagements. The firm and their individual members have for many years occupied the highest position in the trade, with honour to themselves and satisfaction to their connection, and the regret we feel will be shared by all ranks of the community. It is rumoured that debts amount, to from £80,000 to £100,000, part of which is secured. Their assets are very large, but in so much as they consist of trade erections, plant and machinery, it may be considered doubtful, whether means may be taken to effect a liquidation; whether the operation of the firm will be continued to the extent they have been heretofore. A meeting of creditors will be called next week by Mr. William Brinton, solicitor to the principal creditors.... the event has caused a considerable sensation in the town."

Some of the debts resulted when the firm converted to power looms and included £18,450 owed to the London Life Assurance Company. The loan was secured on life assurance policies of the four partners - George and James Hooman and Thomas and James Pardoe and by mortgages on their houses, property and factory buildings. What a mess! The outcome of the bankruptcy was closure of the Pardoe-Hooman works and a large number of people were made unemployed and the town of Kidderminster was devastated. Many of those involved in the "disaster" left the town forever and the situation was very bleak, and indeed Arthur Pember could have done a study on 'The Uncertain Life of a Mill Worker.' Those in charge, however, seem to have been prepared for the eventuality and did not lose everything as one might have assumed. Power-loom technology for the carpet industry was developed in America in about 1850 and John Crossley & Sons in Yorkshire were one of the first to take up the patent rights in England. James Pardoe became their works manager after the collapse in Kidderminster and was a director by 1864. George Hooman former Mayor stayed in the town at first and his daughter Mary Jane married John Francis Gadsden there in March 1869. Henry Hooman was a commercial traveller selling wallpaper and lived at 1 Field View Villas, Thornton Heath, Croydon in 1881 with his wife and two servants. George Hooman, annuitant, lived at 1 The Elms, West Street, Prittlewell in 1881 with his daughters Eleanor E. Grey and Mary J. Gadsden, three grandchildren, three boarders and one servant. He died in the Rochford district in September 1882 aged 85.

Kidderminster did eventually recover and the Royal Axminster power-loom was introduced to England in 1878. The firm of Tomkinson and Adam acquired the patent rights and licensed Richard Smith & Sons of Kidderminster to use the patent. The latter company were established in 1855 and erected their first looms at the Sling factory formerly owned by Pardoe-Hooman. There were fields surrounding the Copse in 1859 whilst a small factory called Longmeadow Mills was nearby however the whole area soon witnessed considerable changes. This location was a focus for manufacturing by the 1880s and several carpet factories were built around the house including Stourvale, Longmeadow and Newroad Mills - these were enlarged during the 20th century and then covered the whole area. The Copse survived as an old 'remnant' until about the 1950s and was then demolished - it was opposite to Vicarage Crescent and was a car park in 1968. The land south of the Copse was agricultural in the 19th century and centred on Aggborough Farm. A field between the Copse and the farm was laid out as a recreation ground in 1878 and was first used by the town's rugby club (Old Aggborough). Kidderminster Harriers were formed in 1886 and played their first games there, but moved across Hoo Lane to a site by the Vicarage in 1890 and the new venue was called Aggborough - the current ground.

James Hooman and his family left Kidderminster after the crisis in 1858 and moved to London. The company may have been bankrupt however they brought considerable assets with them, although the exact facts of the case are unknown. There was an element of the captain abandoning his ship, however if the firm hadn't gone bankrupt.... they would not have moved to London.... and Thomas would not have played for the Wanderers. He might have gone to Rugby instead - what a tangled web we weave! James Hooman was in business as an agent at 71 Wood Street, Cheapside in 1862 although his home address is not known. His son Thomas Charles was born at the Copse on 28 December 1850 and baptized at Kidderminster Church on 26 January 1851. He was seven years old in 1858 and would have known little of his father's bankruptcy and came to London with his family on an adventure. He was educated at Charterhouse School whilst it was still at Aldersgate and became a dayboy at the school in January 1863. He was presumably 'dropped off' there when his father went to work in the City. He was a member of *Verites* from September 1866 to December 1868 and played in the football XI and cricket XI in 1867-68. He was very good at sport and headed the batting averages at the school and took part in boxing and rifle shooting. He joined his father in business in 1868 whilst the school moved to Godalming in 1872.

6 Holly Terrace, Highgate was the home of Henry M. Ingram curate of St. Michael's, Highgate in 1861 however the Hooman family had moved there by 1871. The household included James Hooman merchant, wife Mary Ann, children Mary Ann, Thomas Charles (20) a merchant, Juliana and three servants. The father was listed in directories as a merchant of 10 Basinghall Street, City of London, in 1871, although this may have been shipping rather than the carpet trade. 6 Holly Terrace was a notable villa at the top of West Hill and was built in the Classical style favoured by Thomas Cubitt. It backed onto the street and faced across the valley towards Hampstead Heath, looking down on Holly Lodge and its extensive gardens. These houses were of white stucco with a first floor balcony, two main floors (a third in the roof) and white colonnade at roof level. The front entrances were reached through a wrought iron gate and along a path however the "main" entrances were at the rear. The entrance to no. 6 had a grand portico in white stucco with pilasters at the side and ornate black double doors. It was somewhat unusual being joined to the house by a passage - with the garden on either side. The property is now 87 Highgate West Hill and is little changed from Hooman's day although later housing spoils the view.

Thomas Charles Hooman lived at 2 Fitzroy Villas, Highgate in 1873 and his father may have been travelling at the time, whilst James Hooman lived at 7 Hampstead Lane, Highgate in 1876. In fact the two addresses were the same property and directories show 1-2 Fitzroy Villas then Park Villa, or, 6-7 Hampstead Lane then Park Villa - in each case. These three properties remain on the south side of Hampstead Lane near to The Grove. No. 1 is now 17 Hampstead Lane and is built of grey-yellow brick on three-storeys with two roof gables and a coat of arms above the door. No. 2 is now 19 Hampstead Lane and although modernised at the front has the original slate roof and old brickwork at the rear. These two properties are attached, whilst Park Villa is now divided into Park Cottage and West Cottage and is built in the Georgian style. Samuel Taylor Coleridge (1823-34) and later J.B. Priestley lived nearby at 3 The Grove.

Thomas continued to play soccer after leaving Charterhouse in 1868 and took part in some major games. The school records state he played for England v Scotland in 1870-72-73 although the official records do not show this, but we can assume he appeared in the unofficial game at the Oval in 1870. He then played for the Wanderers in the first Cup Final and there was more controversy since he later claimed to have scored the only goal (see below). He also appeared in the North v South games and for London and Middlesex in 1872-73. He was involved in many sports at school and represented England in the sprint in 1872, rowed for Kingston in the *Grand* at Henley and also played golf. William Skinner Holt and wife Marianne Ellen had children Marianne Ellen (1849), William Skinner (1851), Louisa (1854), Thomas (1857) and Charles Lisle (1859). Their second daughter Louisa was born on 9 April 1854 and baptized at St. Dunstan's, Stepney on 11 May that year. The family may have been related to William Skinner - the partner of Henry Goodwyn at the Red Lion Brewery in Lower East Smithfield (see Ch. 10). Thomas Charles Hooman a merchant of Highgate married Louisa Holt of Somerset Court, South Brent (near Weston Super Mare) at her parish church on 10 September 1879 and the witnesses included W.S. Holt esquire and Mary Ann Hooman.

Thomas C. Hooman a merchant shipbroker lived at 53 High Street, Sevenoaks, Kent, in 1881 with wife Louisa, mother-in-law Marianne Holt and two servants. William Skinner Holt a brewer resided at Mark Road, South Brent and the household included Thomas and Charles Lisle (brewers), Marianne E. Keswick his daughter, a housekeeper, five servants and a groom. Indeed the father was later an esquire of Brent Knoll. Meanwhile, Mary Ann Hooman "wife - husband travelling" lived at 6 Hermitage Villas, West Hill, Highgate in 1881 with daughters Susan and Frances and one servant. Hermitage Villas were at the bottom of West Hill next to Millfield Lane and were numbered down the hill from 1-12. Their house was a semi-detached building of yellow-brown brick with white stone at the ground floor, leaf plasterwork around the windows and moulded features at roof level. Each house had a grand stairway and path decorated with coloured mosaic. The properties are now 15-26 West Hill (the Hoomans' house being no. 21). There may have been a reversal of fortune, as the house did not compare to Holly Terrace in terms of architectural style.

James Claude son of James Webster Esq. was born in 1830 - he became a barrister-at-law and lived at 5 Pembroke Terrace, Queen's Road, St John's Wood, in 1881 with his wife Georgiana Susan H. (and two servants) however she died at Marylebone in September 1882 aged 45. James C. Webster barrister, living at St. James's, married Frances Juliana Hooman of West Hill at St. James's, Westminster on 1 December 1884 the witnesses being J. Rathbone, T.C. Hooman and Mary A. Hooman. James Claude Webster of Harcourt Lodge, Torquay died on 25 October 1908 and his widow Frances Juliana Webster obtained his probate on 3 December - estate valued at £3,840 2s. She lived at Hornyold Lodge, West Malvern but died at the Priory Nursing Home in Great Malvern on 6 December 1938.

William Ford was born at Little Rissington, Gloucester on 4 June 1812 and was the son and heir or Richard Wilbraham Ford rector of the parish. He was educated at Eton and admitted to King's College, Cambridge on 3 December 1829 gaining his B.A. in 1834 and M.A. in 1837. He was admitted as a solicitor in 1836 and became partner in the firm Ranken & Co. at 4 South Square, Gray's Inn Square in 1837. He married Fanny Thomasina Fenton at Chepstow in September 1841 and had sons William W. (1847) and Charles B.E. (1851) at Highgate. He was a member of the Council of the *Incorporated Law Society* in 1860-76 being Vice-President 1869 and President 1870-71. William Ford, solicitor, lived at Brookfield House, Millfield Lane, Highgate in 1881 with wife Fanny Thomasina, son Charles B.E. articled clerk and six servants (two nurses). William W. Ford barrister lived at 9 Spring Gardens, however wife Fanny Thomasina died at St. Pancras in June 1883 aged 65. William Ford a solicitor of Brookfield House, Millfield Lane married Susan Henrietta Hooman of 6 Hermitage Villas at St. Anne's, Highgate

Rise on 31 January 1885 and T.C. Hooman and Charles Evans were witnesses. The husband died at Majori in Italy on 10 January 1889 and probate was granted on 1 February to Arthur Ranken Ford and Charles Bell Eustace Ford solicitors, his sons - effects £43,099 9s 11d.

James Hooman was listed at 6 Hermitage Villas in 1885-86 but he may already have died by this time. The best evidence is the marriage of his daughters to elder men in quick succession (see Alcock Ch. 3). Indeed he then disappears from the scene and there was no record of his death or last will - perhaps he went travelling and just kept going? Thomas and Louisa Hooman then had two children: Eveline Maud at Sevenoaks in March 1885 and Charles Victor Lisle at Ditton on 3 October 1887. Thomas C. Hooman an employer and manufacturer of Portland cement lived at "Fernleigh", London Road, Ditton in 1891 with his wife, two children, Susannah Wheeler visitor and two servants. It was next to Bell Lane and only a short walk from Preston Hall, Aylesford (see Betts) whilst the cement industry is still there today. Thomas a retired cement manufacturer was at "Fernleigh" in 1901 with his wife Louisa, daughter Eveleen M., Susannah Wheeler the family nurse, Mary L. Fish a governess born Castle Howard and three servants. Mary Ann Hooman (85) lived at "Tedstone", Orchard Road, Malvern, this being a lodging house owned by Thomas W. and Sarah Wilden who came from Tardebigge (her birthplace) - there were four other boarders and two servants.

The family then moved to Devon and Mary Ann Hooman died at 2 Kent's Terrace, Torquay on 22 December 1904 aged 89. She was the widow of James Hooman and of independent means, whilst T.C. Hooman of "Frogmore", Torquay was the attendant and informant. Thomas and Louisa lived at "Frogmore" from at least 1904-10 the house being located in Higher Warberry Road between Ellacombe and Wellswood. Their son Charles Victor Lisle mirrored his father and went to Charterhouse, Godalming being in the school cricket XI in 1903-06 and played racket pairs for the school - he left in 1906. He attended Brasenose College, Oxford and represented the university at rackets (1907) and golf, and played in the cricket XI in 1907-10 (a blue in 1909-10). He excelled at cricket and played 15 matches for the Kent County XI and appeared in the championship side of 1910, and played golf as an amateur for England v Scotland in the Walker Cup that year - supporting the notion that sporting ability is hereditary. Charles V.L. Hooman became an American citizen and died at Palm Beach, Florida, U.S.A. in November 1969.

The couple continued to spend their retirement near the sea and lived at "Heathfield", Bingham Avenue, Parkstone near Poole in 1918 - Louisa Hooman died at Heathfield, Lilliput, Parkstone on 22 April 1923. Her husband moved to Kent and Thomas Charles Hooman died at 6 Marine Parade, Hythe on 22 September 1938 aged 87 (see Kenyon-Slaney). His obituary was in the Times on Saturday 24 September and over half the article related to the first Cup Final in 1872 and the remainder to his other sporting activities. He had obviously related this event to his family on many occasions and it stated that, "(He) scored the only goal in the first F.A. Cup Final." All the reports of the match credit M.P. Betts with the goal and he had presumably confused it with some other game, however it does leave a degree of doubt and one wonders if the ball took a deflection on the way in. Indeed he had described the match some time ago thus: "They had no referee, only a timekeeper, and the captains were the sole arbiters. The game was not stopped once for a foul. The teams changed goalkeepers several times, changed ends after scoring a goal, and played six forwards with two half-backs and two backs." It is interesting to compare this account with that in the *Sportsman Newspaper*. Charles Spencer Golding his solicitor and Eveleen Maude Hulbert (wife of Stanley F.R. Hulbert) proved his will and his effects came to £2,419 12s 7d.

Rennie - John Rennie was born at East Linton, Scotland on 7 June 1761 and like William Betts became a millwright. He went to Edinburgh University in 1780-83 and afterwards was employed by Boulton and Watt to build mills (see Muirhead Ch. 8). He worked under Watt for five years and went to the partners Albion Mills in London in 1789. This burnt down in 1791 and he then built canals viz. Lancaster (1792), Crinan (1792) and Kennet and Avon (1794). He was involved in drainage of the Norfolk Fens in 1802-10 and developed a technique for building bridges of stone and cast iron i.e. Leeds, Waterloo (1811-17) and Southwark (1815-19). He also worked on docks at Hull, Liverpool, Greenock and Leith but died when designing London Bridge in 1821. Sons John and George constructed the latter in 1824-31 and worked on the Liverpool and Manchester Railway in 1830. John was knighted for his work on the bridge, whilst George designed the foundations of Grosvenor Bridge in 1832. The latter became the Victoria Railway Bridge and the London, Chatham and Dover built the eastern side in 1858-60.

CHAPTER 7

The Harrow Chequers

It is worth considering the makeup of the first Wanderers side before continuing with these biographies. The team mainly had players from Eton and Harrow and the statistics for 1872 are as follows: Edgar Lubbock (25), Albert Childers Thompson (23) and Alexander George Bonsor (20) of Eton and Charles William Alcock (29), Morton Peto Betts (24), William Parry Crake (20) and Reginald Courtenay Welch (20) of Harrow. Edward Ernest Bowen (35), the oldest, was educated at Blackheath Proprietary and King's College Schools but was also in this group as a master of Harrow School. Thomas Charles Hooman (22) of Charterhouse, Charles Henry Reynolds Wollaston (22) of Lancing and Robert Walpole Sealy Vidal (18) of Westminster completed the side. These statistics show the dominance of Harrow in the Wanderers and in part support the claims of Alcock but the membership was not exclusive to the school. The other players are now considered and were connected to Eton, Harrow and Westminster.

ROBERT WALPOLE SEALY VIDAL

The Sportsman newspaper reported on the Final in 1872 and said that both Thomas Charles Hooman and R.W.S. Vidal attracted notice by their skilful dribbling. Indeed the latter preceded the likes of Stanley Matthews and became known as "The Prince of Dribblers". His family had an interesting if somewhat confusing history and were an old Somerset family long seated in the area. His grandfather Edward Sealy esquire gent lived at Friarn House, Bridgwater, Somerset in the early 19th century although there is no mention of the name Vidal at this point and the reason for this is discussed shortly. Edward Sealy married Elizabeth Urch Lewis at Bridgwater on 21 September 1815 who was the daughter of the Rev. William Lewis of Cannington, Somerset - a parish three miles west of Bridgwater. The witnesses included Edward Sealy senior and Ann Drake Lewis and the groom signed Ed. Sealy J. The couple had just one son Edward Urch Sealy who was born on 7 July 1816 and baptized at Bridgwater on 17 August 1816. He had "Great Expectations" and soon met a wealthy benefactor.

Edward Urch Sealy was admitted to Westminster School on 23 September 1828 and matriculated at Christchurch, Oxford on 15 May 1834 gaining his B.A. in 1838. He then trained at the Middle Temple in London and was called to the bar on 15 April 1842 and shortly afterwards practiced on the Western Circuit. It was during his time at the Middle Temple that he became acquainted with Robert Studley Vidal a gent of Cornborough House, Abbotsham in Devon. The house was in an isolated hamlet in a small parish near to Bideford and at least 50 miles west of Bridgwater. Indeed the location was obscure until Charles Kingsley's novel of 1855 gave rise to the name Westward Ho! The Vidal family had notable antecedents and are traced to Captain Robert Studley his great grandfather who married Anne King at Temple Church, London on 27 October 1692. They had six children baptized at St. Mary's, Whitechapel: Ann (1693), Robert (1694), Mary (1697), Maria (1698) Peggy (1700) and Margret (1701). Christian V of Denmark assisted him to attain his sea skills and he was made captain of the "Experiment" by Prince George of Denmark in 1707 viz. the Lord High Admiral of England and husband of Queen Anne (ruled 1702-14). He commanded the "Weymouth" in 1715 and sailed in the Baltic under Sir John Norris and then met Frederick IV King of Denmark and Norway who gave him, "a superb highly embossed silver pig tankard," at Copenhagen in 1715 - in memory of a friendship with his father Christian V. The people of Naples also presented Captain Studley with, "a two handled lava grave cup in silver," to thank him for repelling the Algerine Corsairs.

Grandfather Peter Vidal attended Westminster School and St. John's, Cambridge gaining a B.A. in 1723 and M.A. in 1729 then entered the Church. He married Mary Studley at Lincoln's Inn Chapel, Holborn on 4 May 1733 and the couple had a son Robert Studley Vidal. The latter was his father and became a solicitor in London and married Elizabeth Blinch at St. Clement Danes on 10 April 1768. His mother was daughter of William and Ann Blinch who had the following children at Buckland Brewer and Parkham in Devon: Susanna (1687), Philip (1692), Mary (1693), Philip (1695), Alice and Sarah (1698) and Elizabeth born 3 April 1706 - both parishes were near to Abbotsham. The couple's son Robert Studley Vidal junior was born in 1770 whilst the father died in Exeter on 2 January 1797. He left no will, however administration of his goods and chattels was granted to his son after his widow Elizabeth Vidal renounced the same letters, and the effects were £2,000. Robert Studley Vidal was called to the bar at the Middle Temple and, living at Cornborough, became a noted antiquarian who published a number of papers. He wrote of the local property Kenwith Castle in 1813 (see below), edited works like 'A Treatise on Copyholds' 1821 by Charles Watkins, 'Tenures' 1824 by Sir Geoffery Gilbert and Cudworth's Intellectual System, and wrote 'Christianity before Constantine' 1835. Further to this he kept a pack of hounds at his house.

Robert Vidal lived at Cornborough, Abbotsham on 7 June 1841 and was a magistrate aged 65 years. He had no family but lived with William Kelly 35 M.S., Sarah Kelly 20 F.S., Mary Kelly 15 F.S. and William Kelly 9 months as well as three other servants. He made a lengthy last will and testament on 11 November 1841, which was most illuminating and provided much of the above. He began by describing himself as late of Middle Temple now of Cornborough in the "manor or royalty of Abbotsham" and made a number of small bequests from his estate: £10 p.a. to godson Studley Vidal Smith the son of Christmas Smith late of Bideford surgeon; £10 p.a. to Lucy the wife of William Smith of Bideford M.D. an old and valued friend; £25 p.a. to William Kelly for his long service as hind at Cornborough (hind = married, skilled farm worker) and £5 p.a. to Mary Ann Kelly his 'confidential' servant. He bequeathed Langdons and Rowlesland Moors in Abbotsham to William Kelly during his lifetime and one can only wonder at some of the relations.

He gave a description of Rev. Peter Vidal and his education at Westminster and Cambridge and in memory of his grandfather established two scholarships worth £20 p.a. for the advancement of two boys to attend St. John's College. These students were to be elected from boys at Exeter Free Grammar School and to be chosen by the fellows of St. John's, the Dean of Exeter Cathedral and Mayor of Exeter. There were strenuous qualifications that included three years at the school, a certificate of education and the surname "Vidal". Indeed the last requirement made the four-year Vidalian Scholarship most exclusive! The mansion house and land at Abbotsham was given to four trustees - Charles Carter the elder, Charles Carter the younger of Bideford gents, Harry Arthur Harris of the same gent and William Castle Smith of Lawrence Pountney Place, London solicitor. It was put in trust for Edward Urch Sealy late of Christchurch College, Oxford but now of Middle Temple, but there were some important conditions:

(1) The Mansion House and Edway's farmhouse being 40 acres, to be kept whole and in good repair.

(2) He should be in residence for two months each year although the period need not be continuous.

(3) The house must be constantly occupied or inhabited.

(4) Edward Urch Sealy and his successors must use the surname and arms of Vidal.

(5) They can use no other surname and must take the name Vidal within one year by an Act of Parliament.

(6) However, if the property is let, or they do not reside there, or do not take the name, or resume their old name then the whole reverts to the trustees for the masters and fellows of St. John's, Cambridge, forever.

These were stringent conditions and were to control the life of Edward Urch Sealy since if he, or his family, broke any of the rules they would lose everything. Robert Studley Vidal, however, held him in high esteem and gave him any other property he had to be hired out at the best yearly rent, and bequeathed to him some personal items namely the Studley nautical heirlooms. He wrote about his great grandfather Captain Robert Studley and his connection with the Royal Family of Denmark and England and left to Edward, "the superb highly embossed silver pig tankard," given by Frederick IV in 1715 and, "the two handled lava grave cup in silver," presented by the people of Naples. He also left other items to Edward viz. two handled silver punch bowl, silver bread basket of antique Russian work, silver half-pint tankard with crest of Bluith, large silver salver with family arms, various silver items and a sugar basin with Studley crest. The long document was completed and Robert Vidal left his dogs, sporting apparatus and linen apparel to William Kelly and cabinet of medals, library, prints and pictures to be disposed of as was seen fit, but Edward Sealy to have first choice. Finally, he left any remaining proceeds to the Devon and Exeter Hospital for the poor of the hospital up to a limit of £2,000 and Edward Sealy to have any surplus money. John Steer reuter of Orchard Estate under R.S. Vidal and Robert Holman clerk to Messrs.

Carter & Son solicitors of Bideford were witnesses to the will. Robert Studley Vidal died on 21 November 1841 and the requirements of his will were soon carried out.

Edward Urch Sealy applied forthwith to have his name changed and Victoria R. granted this by *Royal Licence* on 12 February 1842. He was described as a kinsman of Robert Studley Vidal and became Edward Urch Vidal and moved to Cornborough House and made further plans. He became a barrister at Middle Temple in April 1842 and married Emma Harriet Eyre in a society wedding at St. Mary's, Bryanston Square, Marylebone on 19 May that year. He was a "gentleman" of Cornborough in Abbotsham parish and she a minor of 22 Bryanston Square whilst Henry S. Eyre was the officiating minister and E.C. Sealy, Alethea S.H. Eyre, Walpole Eyre and Septimus Burton (see below) witnesses. Edward Vidal proved his benefactor's will in London on 23 May 1842 and the couple then made their life at Cornborough House in Devon whilst Leigh and Sotheby sold the cabinet of medals later that year. Marylebone was laid-out as a select residential district in the 18th century and Marylebone Road was built as a new highway from Paddington to Islington in 1756. St. Mary's, Bryanston Square was built totally for effect at the far end of Wyndham Place and its semi-circular colonnade entrance was clearly visible from the square but the rear was a plain brick wall. No. 22 has gone but one can imagine the short carriage ride to the church with all the notables waiting inside.

The Eyres have a notable history and are traced to Kingsmill Eyre born at New Houses, Lancashire in 1682 who was an army man at Chelsea. He married Mary Ann Lefever at St. Martin in the Fields on 27 June 1721 and they had one child Catharine in 1722 who was baptized at the Pensioners' Army Hospital, Chelsea. He then married Susanna Atkinson and had three children baptized at Chelsea: Elizabeth (1728), Samuel (1733) and Walpole on 21 May 1734. The father Kingsmill died in 1743 and his son Walpole Eyre married Sarah Johnson then had four children: Susan Sarah (1769-74) St. James's Westminster, Henry Samuel (1770-1851) St. Marylebone, John Thomas (1771-1811) and Walpole born on 25 August 1773 both Burnham. The family had connections with Burnham near Cliveden House in Bucks and also with St. John's Wood, London whilst the father Walpole died at Burnham on 18 April 1773/75. They were the largest landowners east of Edgware Road in the early 1790s and had an ambitious plan to layout a large estate with squares and circuses. The main feature was the idea of a garden suburb with semi-detached villas rather than the usual arrangement of terraces with two rooms to a floor. Spurrier and Phipps, auctioneers, produced a plan for them in 1794 that was ahead of its time preceding later schemes for Regent's Park and St. John's Wood, but the French war intervened and the plans were shelved. Walpole Eyre married Elizabeth Annabella Johnson at Wigan on 21 October 1813 and had five children at Marylebone: Henry Samuel (1816), Frederick Edwin (1817), Elizabeth Annabella (1820), Alethea Sarah Henrietta (1822) and Emma Harriet (1824). They were all born at St. John's Wood and the first four baptized at St. Marylebone.

The Eyre family then made a connection with a builder who had antecedents of some note. Thomas Haliburton of New Mains near North Berwick married Janet Campbell and had several children baptized at Dryburgh viz. Barbara (4 March 1706), John (1707) and Robert (1718). Dryburgh and its ruined abbey were situated on the River Tweed near to Melrose in the county of Roxburgh-shire. Robert Scott (1697-1775) son of Walter Scott and Margaret Campbell lived at Sandy Knowe, Smailholm, east of Dryburgh and married Barbara Haliburton on 16 July 1728. The couple had several children at Sandy Knowe including Walter (1729-99) and Janet (1733-1805). John Haliburton a likely grandson of Thomas married Janet Scott his cousin at Minto, Roxburgh on 11 January 1751, whilst Walter Scott married Ann Rutherford at Edinburgh on 29 April 1758 (both couples had sons of great note). Walter Scott was a lawyer and lived with his wife in Edinburgh and had a large family including Walter (14 August 1771) his ninth child. The latter became a writer and popularised the romantic historical novel and some of his most famous works were Ivanhoe (1791), the Waverley series of novels (1814) including Rob Roy (1818), A Legend of Montrose (1819) and the Talisman (1825). He became Sir Walter Scott in 1820 and as well as a poet and writer was largely responsible for the development of clan tartans, as we know them. He spent much of his life at Abbotsford House near Melrose and received inspiration from the surrounding country.

He also travelled abroad on occasions and made a famous trip to Malta when the island inspired him. He stayed at the Beverley Hotel in West Street, Valletta, which was above Salvatore Bastion and looked out over Marsamxett Harbour. The Carmelite Church was behind the hotel and next door was the Auberge d'Allemagne and the Auberge Aragon of the Knights of St. John. The former was then in bad repair or a ruin and St. Paul's Anglican Cathedral replaced it in 1839-44, whilst the latter auberge was the oldest in Valletta dating from 1571. A stepped alley is located next to St. Paul's opposite Old Theatre Street and there is St. Paul's Modern Buildings (1908). The latter is of sandstone with green paintwork, and has

Valletta, Malta. Sir Walter Scott stayed in 1831 before St. Paul's was built (spire).

wooden bay windows common in the town with ornate scrolls below them. There are two inscriptions: "Erected by Gio. Dom. Debono P.A.A.," and, "On this site from the 21st November 1831 Sir Walter Scott enamoured of Valletta 'the splendid town quite like a dream' resided in the Beverley Hotel into which the Palazzo Britto had been converted." Gerolamo Lassar built St. John's co-Cathedral, Valletta with its opulent tunnel vault in 1573-77 and Sir Walter Scott visited it like many tourists since. Medina was the original settlement on Malta in 870-1090 and St. Paul's Cathedral was built there in 1697-1702. Pope Pius VII made them co-cathedrals in 1816 whilst Medina with its narrow streets was overtaken by Rabat and became 'the silent city'. Sir Walter Scott said of St. John's Cathedral, "It is the most magnificent place I ever saw in my life." He died at Abbotsford soon after on 21 September 1832 and was buried in St. Mary's aisle in the ruins of Dryburgh Abbey.

John and Janet Haliburton had a son James in c.1761 who was baptized at Wilton, Roxburgh near to Minto on 7 January 1763. James Haliburton, cousin of Sir Walter Scott, trained as a builder and moved to London with his wife Elizabeth and had children: William Ford (1784), Emma Elizabeth (1785), Eliza (1786) at *St. Andrew by the Wardrobe*, James (1788), Emily (1790) and Jane (1792) at *St. Ann Blackfriars* (the son James went to Italy and Egypt see Bonsor Ch. 6). There was a family dispute at this time and James senior changed his name to Burton and secured work, building houses in Bloomsbury. James and Elizabeth Burton then had five children baptized at St. Pancras: Septimus (1794), Octavia (1798), Decimus (1800), Alfred (1802) and Jesse (1804). The dispute was resolved and they became Haliburton again and three more children were born at St. Pancras: Elizabeth (1806), Katherine Young (1808) and Charles Drummond (1814). John Nash developed Regent's Park and approached James Burton (as he was known) in 1815 and he thus built part of Regent Street and the "Park Terraces". Decimus Burton trained as an architect under his father and together they built The Holme in Regent's Park (1818) and also Cornwall and Clarence Terrace. They lived at the former house and also at Mabledon, Tunbridge Wells.

The Eyre family then revived their plans and employed James Burton the builder-developer based on his above experience. He was called an architect, like builders such as William Adam, and developed plans with 99-year leases using a building agreement (of 1813). He designed many villas for St. John's Wood and was responsible for the first phase of development at Park Road, North and South Bank and Grove Road in 1820. This was called the Eyre Estate and is dated from Wellington Road (Waterloo 1815). James Burton also worked at Clapham Common and his designs were the basis for the new seaside town of St. Leonard's in 1828 - he died in 1837. Decimus Burton, meanwhile, designed London Zoo and its buildings (1828-37) and the arch at Hyde Park Corner. He later worked for Sir William Hooker and with his partner Richard Turner designed the Palm House at Kew (1844-48). The wrought iron technique developed by Turner was used at the Crystal Palace in 1851, whilst Burton designed the larger Temperate House at Kew and continued his father's work at St. Leonard's after 1850. The work to complete the garden suburb of St. John's Wood continued in the 1820s, and the Eyre Arms at the top of Grove End Road had assembly rooms, balloon ascents with views of the city and tried to revive jousting in the 1830s. The Eyres lived at Weybridge in Surrey but Walpole Eyre died of bronchitis at 22 Bryanston Square, Marylebone on 23 February 1856 aged 82. Alma Square was the last part of the estate to be developed in the 1860s and Eyre Court, Wellington Road, is now on the Eyre Arms' site.

Edward Urch and Emma Harriet Vidal resided at Cornborough House after they wed in 1842 and their lives were far removed from these developments in London. They soon entered into the spirit of Robert Vidal's will and helped to perpetuate the name by having fifteen children in 1843-67 most of whom became adults. Edward, however, was not comfortable with all the requirements and all his children had the name Sealy Vidal with Sealy being a Christian name viz. Edward Walpole (1843) *infant*, Emma Ann (1845), Margaret (1847), Edward (1848), Lewis (1850), Agnes (1851), Robert Walpole (1853), Henry Dashwood (1854), Eliza

Annabella (1856), Edwin Drake (1858), Alethea Harriet (1859), William (1861), George Studley (1862), Frances (1866) and Mary Katherine (1867). Cornborough House was situated at the north end of Abbotsham parish and was near to the sea and Westward Ho! Richard Attewater possessed "Hornborough" manor in 1395 whilst Thomas Kenney a merchant of Bideford bought it in 1750 and built a summer box behind the house that became known as the "watch-tower". Cornborough was in the possession of Robert Studley Vidal in the early 19th century and passed to Edward Urch Vidal in 1842. It was a two storey rugged building looking down on a lawn with woodland behind whilst the fields of the farm reached right down to the sea. There were also tall chestnut trees and a walled garden with orchards beyond. Indeed, "the property was added onto over the years to make room for a large number of children" - no doubt the Vidals.

The family were absent from Cornborough in 1851 and George Lettey coachman and two servants occupied the house, however Edward Vidal magistrate and barrister (not in practice) was there in 1861 with his wife Emma, eleven children 15 years to 5 months incl. Walpole (7), and seven servants whilst Margaret Sealy Vidal married Arthur Ruscombe Poole at Abbotsham on 29 August 1867. Edward Vidal, magistrate landowner and barrister, was also there in 1871 with his wife, seven children and eight servants whilst Edward Dansey vicar of Abbotsham lived at Kenwith not far away. There were soon two marriages there: Agnes Sealy Vidal to Frederic Gosset on 16 September 1875 and Eliza Annabella Sealy Vidal to Joseph Charles T. Smith in June 1877. Edward a magistrate in Devon and Somerset was at home in 1881 with wife Emma, children Emma, Edwin and Alethea and five servants (with a lodge nearby). Emma Anne Sealy Vidal married Philip Richard P. Braithwaite at Bridgwater in September 1882 (see below) and daughter Frances Sealy Vidal died at Abbotsham in December 1883 aged 17.

Both Sealy and Vidal had attended Westminster School and the tradition continued throughout the 19th century. The son Edward Sealy Vidal (1848) was at the school in 1861-64 and an army lieutenant in 1869. He married Beatrice Christine Hare (1851) born in Stonehouse at Stoke Damerel, Devon in December 1871. The couple had four children in Paris, Chelsea and Brighton from 1872-78 however Edward died at Brighton in March 1878 aged 29. His widow Beatrice "the widow of the late Captain E. Sealy Vidal H.M. 57th Regiment" lived at 7 Sillwood Place, Brighton in 1881 and died at Brentford in June 1903. Henry Dashwood Sealy Vidal (1854) was at Westminster in 1868-73 and was curate of St. Luke's, Jersey in 1881 and minister in the Truro Diocese (1880-87). He was unmarried and lived at 1 Peel Terrace, St. Helier with Philip R.P. Braithwaite widower (the vicar), his four children, and three servants. He was minister of St. Luke's, Liverpool, New South Wales, in 1888-89 and died at Carcoar in Australia on 1 May 1905. His widow Kate Elston Sealy Vidal died in Liverpool, New South Wales on 4 May 1929 and her probate was granted in Sydney but sealed in London.

Edwin Drake Sealy Vidal (1858) gained a B.A. at Cambridge and lived at Abbotsham in 1881 and Fremington near Barnstaple in 1901 but died at Watlington, Oxfordshire on 15 January 1937. William Sealy Vidal (1861) entered the Royal Engineers and was a lieutenant at the School for Instruction in Submarine Mining on H.M. "Hood", River Medway, Chatham in 1881 (see Kinnaird Ch. 5). He married Jane Rebecca Conington at Hagworthingham near Horncastle in December 1893. She was born there in 1866 and lived there alone 'on her own means' in 1901. George Studley Sealy Vidal (1862) lived with Godfrey B. Lee clergyman M.A. and warden of Winchester College in 1881. He was a scholar at St. Mary's College, Winchester and attended New College, Oxford being a "blue" in 1883-85. He married Constance Isabella Knox Homan at Abbotsham in September 1889 and was curate of St. Giles, Oxford and chaplain of St. John's College in 1888-92, and chaplain of New College and tutor of St. Mary Hall in 1889-92. He was then a vicar and lived at Barnsley, Gloucester in 1901 and died at the Rectory, Barnsley, Cirencester, on 18 July 1928 his probate being granted to Constance Isabella Knox Vidal widow.

Robert Walpole Sealy Vidal was born at Cornborough House on 3 September 1853 and baptized at Abbotsham Church on 9 October that year. His childhood was spent in this remote corner of Devon and his social life was limited to the local gentry and trips to Bideford, although he no doubt also went to London. He was usually referred to as Walpole being a scholar at home with his parents in 1861. He followed his father to Westminster School and was admitted there on 26 January 1867 and soon excelled at sport. He played football at nearby Vincent Square and outplayed his seniors in games against teams like the Crusaders. He was a Queen's scholar and school captain in 1871 and his talents on the football field were well known especially his skilful control of the ball, which earned him the name "The Prince of Dribblers". Indeed he was at the school when the F.A. developed the rules of soccer. He was familiar with an early home of the Wanderers and stated that he preferred Battersea to any other ground.

Robert Walpole Sealy Vidal (1853-1914).
"The Prince of Dribblers" - vicar of Abbotsham 1881-1914.

He was then chosen to play for the Wanderers and appeared in the first F.A. Cup Final on 16 March 1872 and being aged only 18 was the youngest player in the side. The match report states that after some judicious "middling" by R.W.S Vidal the Engineers' goal fell to a well-directed kick by A.H. Chequer. He was clearly held in high regard since he was also on the Committee of the F.A. for a brief period in 1872. The Final was barely over when he travelled to the country and matriculated at Christchurch, Oxford on 23 May 1872. He continued to play soccer whilst doing his studies and was selected to play for England as a representative of Oxford University in the second international on 8 March 1873. The game was at the Oval and his dribbling skills helped England beat Scotland 4-2 although this was his only appearance for his country. He then played for Oxford University against his old team the Wanderers in the Cup Final at Lillie Bridge on 29 March 1873. Oxford had an impressive march beating Crystal Palace 3-2, Clapham Rovers 3-0, Royal Engineers 1-0 and Maidenhead 4-0 (with his assistance) however they lost the Final 2-0. He played for Oxford against the Royal Engineers, who still had four players from 1872, in the Final on 14 March 1874. R.W.S. Vidal was a Cup winner for the second time since Oxford won by a 2-0 score line - this was their only Cup Final success.

He was on the F.A. Committee again in 1874 and an Oxford blue in 1874-75 and founder and first president of the university golf club and a good oarsman, but then dropped out of sport to concentrate on the spiritual life. He was a junior student at Oxford and after prolonged studies gained a B.A. in 1876 and M.A. in 1879. He attended Cuddesdon College attached to the Bishop's Palace near Oxford and was ordained in the Church of England at Salisbury in 1877. He was curate of St. Edmund's, Sarum in 1877 and Vice-Principal of Ely College in 1878-81 and curate of Holy Trinity, Ely in 1880-81, however he then secured a position that he prayed for. Edward Dansey (1810) vicar of Abbotsham lived at Kenwith House in 1871 but the post became vacant and Robert W. Barber (27), unmarried, was curate in charge at the Vicarage in 1881. Arthur Molesworth married Mary Kearney then lived in India and had children Gertrude at Madras (Fort St. George) in 1807 and Hickman Thomas on 7 August 1820. The latter married Mary Anne Lindsay who was born in Aberdeen in 1838 at St. Luke's Cheltenham on 15 April 1857. Hickman Molesworth was an officer of the Royal Artillery in India and his daughter Gertrude was born at Bangalore on 11 September 1862. Thomas Fourse Underwood was a captain in the Royal Navy and married Elizabeth Lindsay who was born at Aberdeen in 1831 at St. Mary's Portsea on 20 January 1864. Hickman Molesworth retired major general lived at Kenwith House in 1881 with his wife, seven children (three born India) and five servants. Daughter Gertrude was visiting her uncle Thomas Underwood a retired captain at 14 Athelstone Hill, Hereford and the significance of these connections is discussed shortly.

There was no sign of R.W.S. Vidal on the 1881 census and he does not appear at Ely College thus may have been abroad. Meanwhile, Lucy Christiana the daughter of Thomas Fortescue Carter master mariner and his wife Ann Holderness was born at Cowick Street, St. Thomas's Exeter on 22 December 1851. Her father later lived in Liverpool whilst she was visiting Edward C. Sherard solicitor at Cotterstock (Hall) near Oundle, Northants in 1881. The church vacancy was then filled and R.W.S. Vidal was appointed vicar of Abbotsham in 1881 - he was the only male in the family to return home and held the position for the rest of his life. He had good prospects and married Lucy Christiana Carter at Cotterstock on 2 June 1881 and the witnesses were E.C. Sherard and E.H. Vidal, whilst Henry Scott Holland of Christchurch, Oxford performed the ceremony. The couple lived at Abbotsham and had children Walpole Eyre Sealy Vidal (June 1882) and Hamilton Sealy Vidal (June 1883) however the latter child and the mother Lucy both died in June 1883. The family had scarcely recovered when Edward Urch Vidal died at Cornborough House on 18 December 1884 and his probate was granted to R.W.S. Vidal of Abbotsham, clerk. His estate was valued at £4,594 6s 1d and presumably the Vidal heirlooms went to his son.

Life, however, had to continue and Robert Walpole Sealy Vidal married Gertrude Molesworth at Abbotsham Church on 15 July 1885 the witnesses including Hickman T. Molesworth of Kenwith and E.D.S. Vidal - Rev. Roger Granville rector of Bideford carried out the ceremony since the vicar was busy at the time! The couple had three children: Avice Mary Sealy (16 October 1887), Edward Molesworth Walpole Sealy (September 1889) and Gertrude Sylvia Sealy (December 1890) and life had changed since there was once a large family of Vidals in Abbotsham, but few were remaining in 1891. Those left were Robert Walpole and Gertrude Vidal with four children and three servants at the Vicarage and Emma Harriet and Alethea Harriet Sealy Vidal with five servants at Cornborough House. There was soon a further change that affected them forever, and the stringent conditions of Robert Studley Vidal's will had been weighing down on the Sealy family for 50 years, in fact since the *Royal Licence* dated 12 February 1842. Rev. Robert Walpole Sealy Vidal may have resented this change of name, as a dishonour to his ancestors, but the more likely influence was an inheritance of some Sealy property at this time. He changed his name by deed poll on 26 May 1892 and re-assumed the surname Sealy in lieu of Vidal and dropped the middle name of Sealy. He was thereafter known as Rev. Robert Walpole Sealy and reverted to his family name almost 50 years to the day since the Vidal will was proved on 23 May 1842. Possibly there was a legal precedent allowing this without forfeiting the rights to the estate.

Indeed the family's connection with Cornborough now came to an end and Emma his mother moved to Bowood hamlet near the Vicarage, south of Abbotsham - Hickman Thomas Molesworth died on 27 January 1896 and Emma Harriet Vidal died at Bowood on 13 December 1897. The family continued to live at Abbotsham Vicarage and there was a late addition when Violet Inez was born in September 1900. The Helen Naomi Richardson Collection at Nth. Devon Record Office includes several portraits and wedding photographs of the Sealy-Vidal family, however one shows a slim Rev. Sealy winning the sprint at the local sports day - he may have been older but still had a point to prove regarding his youth. The members of the family may have changed however the photos reveal a timeless quality to life in this corner of Devon. The family were absent from the 1901 census although the son Walpole aged 18 was residing in Wiltshire. The Rev. Sealy had given his best to sport during his youth and adopted the same enthusiastic approach to life in Abbotsham. He played cricket for Devon and was a member of the Royal North Devon Golf Club. Further, he was Vice-Chairman of the local Board of Guardians, a member of Bideford R.D.C., Chairman of the Parish Council, a commissioner for income tax, a patron of Bideford Hospital, a supporter of the National Service League, member of the Devon Education Committee, member of North Devon Choral Union and Rural Dean of Hartland.

His daughter Gertrude Sylvia Sealy married Joseph Sinclair Nicholson (Civil Servant) at Abbotsham in March 1910 whilst Cornborough House and the estate were sold to the Lomas family in 1912. Robert Walpole Sealy clerk in Holy Orders wrote his last will on 5 May 1912 and left all his worldly goods to his wife Gertrude Sealy the witnesses being two domestic servants at the Vicarage. He was then given a vacant prebendal stall at Exeter Cathedral (St. Peter) but became ill and had no opportunity to use his privilege of preaching there on a Sunday afternoon. He stayed ill for some months in 1914 then seemed to recover but had a further attack and became unconscious. He died at the Vicarage on 5 November 1914 aged 61 years and the Bishop of Crediton, the Rector of Bideford and Rev. Canon Braithwaite of Winchester (brother-in-law) took the funeral at Abbotsham. The mourners were Mrs. Sealy, Rev. Walpole E. Sealy, Miss Avice Sealy, Mr. and Mrs. J.S. Nicholson, Miss Inez Sealy; Mrs. Braithwaite, Mrs. Poole and Mrs. Gosset (sisters); Mr. and Mrs. J.C.T. Heriz-Smith, Miss Vidal, Mr. Edwin S. Vidal, Rev. G. Studley S. Vidal; Mrs. J. Awdry and Miss Margaret Heriz-Smith (nieces); Mr. Charles Didham (brother-in-law), Mrs. Eyre and Mr. J. Eyre as well as Mrs. R.B. Molesworth and E.N. Molesworth-Hepworth. His son Lieutenant E.M.W. Sealy had recently left for the front. There was also a tribute to him at Exeter Cathedral and his obituary and other details appeared in the *Bideford and North Devon Weekly* on 10 November 1914. His probate was granted to his widow Gertrude Sealy at Exeter on 14 December 1914 and his effects were valued at £5,702 12s - noted in the Times 2 January 1915.

Edward Molesworth Walpole Sealy (1889) fought as a captain in the Royal Engineers in the First War. He married Caroline Balkwill at Hampstead in December 1915 (quarter) however was wounded on the Western Front and died at Mandor Isolation Hospital, Aldershot on 25 December 1915. He resided at Arnold House, Southampton Street, Farnham and his widow Caroline Sealy proved his will - fortunately his father did not witness this sad event. Violet Inez Sealy (1900) married Ernest H. Hind at Abbotsham in June 1921; whilst Alethea Harriet Sealy Vidal had left Cornborough in the 1890s and lived at 7 Taw Vale Parade, Barnstaple but died at Salford Priors, Evesham, Worcs on 22 January 1935 (see Morley Ch. 1). His widow Gertrude Sealy died at 3 Coronation Terrace, Abbotsham on 7 October 1953 aged 91 and Rev. W. E. Sealy was granted probate at £14,157 6s 11d. Walpole Eyre Sealy (1882) attended Oriel College, Oxford and gained a B.A. in 1906 and was curate of East Grinstead in 1908. He married Mary Gertrude Ashton Radcliffe at East Grinstead in June 1918 and was Headmaster of nearby Fonthill School from 1922 to at least 1948. He died at Fonthill on 13 February 1963 and probate went to Mary widow and Mary Elizabeth daughter. Avice Mary Sealy (1887) married Levy or Louis Speyer (1881) in the Surrey Mid-East in December 1941. He died at 11 Claverton Street, Westminster on 11 March 1961 and Avice at Aylesbury in March 1975. The Rev. Sealy was laid to rest at Abbotsham and many people have passed by but few know that "The Prince of Dribblers" once walked the same path.

EDWARD ERNEST BOWEN

Despite being considerably older than the other players E.E. Bowen secured his place in the Wanderers side through his keen interest in sport. The Bowen family were something of a mystery in terms of their origins since the printed records state he was born at Glenmore, County Wicklow, Ireland just south of Dublin however the I.G.I. states he was born at Hollymount, Mayo on the west coast of Ireland - the home of his antecedents. The family were Anglo-Irish gentry of Welsh origin and are traced to William Bowen and Ellen Burke whose son Christopher was born c.1775. He married Eliza Miller in Ireland in c.1800 and had eight children at Hollymount, Mayo: Christopher (1801), Croasdaile (1802), Charles (1804), Anne (1806), Eliza Louisa (1808), Robert (1810), William (1812) and Edward George (1814). The eldest son is treated below whilst Croasdaile Bowen-Miller esquire appeared on a tithe apportionment for Kilmainemore, Milford, Donegal in 1835 and was assessed on 278 acres 2 roods 36 perches at an amount of £14 0s 8d.

Charles Bowen the third brother, however, is of greater interest and was born on 15 May 1804. He married Georgiana Lambert at Crossboyne, Tuam Diocese, Galway on 19 November 1829 - she was born at Brookhill, Mayo in c.1806 the daughter of Joseph Lambert and Mary Glendining. The couple had seven children: Charles Christopher (1830), Croasdaile (1831), Joseph Lambert (1833) *infant*, Eleanor Georgiana (1834) *infant*, Elizabeth (1837), Letitia Ann Hannah (1840) and Georgiana (1843) *infant*. The story of John Robert Godley, and the settlement of New Zealand, was discussed regarding Pember (Ch. 4) however the Bowens played an important role in this process. The family may have lived at St. Leonard's, Sussex but were at Lee Park, Blackheath by 1845 and Georgiana died at Lewisham in September 1845 and Elizabeth on 9 March 1849. Indeed Letitia their only surviving daughter was baptized at St. Margaret's Lee on 1 September 1850 just prior to their departure for the colonies. Christchurch, New Zealand, a Christian settlement was begun in 1850 although some isolated farms already existed on Canterbury Plain. There were four ships that sailed that year namely the *Charlotte Jane* and *Randolph* that arrived first and the *Sir George Seymour* and *Cressy* that came soon after. Godley was there to meet them and the four vessels secured a place in history like the *Mayflower* in America, thus the names of all the settlers are recorded at Cathedral Square in Christchurch.

The *Charlotte Jane* was built in 1848 and was a 730-ton three-mast vessel being 131 feet in length and 32 feet wide. She sailed from Plymouth on 7 September 1850 with 151 passengers. The Bowens were friends of Godley and joined the ship with a spirit of adventure although their main aim was to improve their reduced fortunes. They sailed in style in the chief cabin and were listed thus: Charles Bowen (45), Georgiana (40), Letitia (10) and Anne (44) his sister. Their eldest son Charles was born at Hollymount on 29 August 1830 and educated with a private tutor in France and at Rugby where he was a good athlete. He was admitted at Caius College, Cambridge on 11 October 1849 but did not finish his degree and joined his parents on the ship in a somewhat 'casual' manner, thus the intermediate or fore cabin included Charles (20) and his brother Croasdaile (18). The vessel made the three-month journey and arrived at Lyttelton on 16 December 1850 and the settlers then climbed over the Port Hills with their belongings to reach the new settlement. There were few natural resources as the Maori had burnt much of the native woodland and everything had to arrive by ship. The family soon settled into their chosen life of building a new country and their sons were to play a prominent role.

Charles C. Bowen, the eldest, was secretary to Godley until the latter returned to England in December 1852 and also spent his time at balls, regattas and cricket matches. He was a J.P. in 1852 and Inspector of

Police and Chief Clerk in 1853 then Provincial Treasurer in 1857-59. He had romantic notions and wanted to go and fight in the Crimea although his father opposed this, whilst in his spare time he was editor and joint-owner of the *Lyttelton Times*. He strongly opposed the idea of responsible government in the new colony and made himself unpopular with other leaders in the province. William Markham was the Archbishop of York in 1777-1807 and tutor to George IV and William IV. His descendant Rev. David F. Markham married Catherine Frances Nanette Milner and had children Clements Robert (1830) at Stillingfleet and Georgina Elizabeth (1838) at Nun Appleton, Yorkshire, and the father became Canon of Windsor. His son Clements was educated at Westminster and joined the navy in 1844 and went on an expedition to the Arctic in 1850-51, but then left the service and travelled to Peru and the Andes in 1852-54.

Charles Bowen, meanwhile, liked to write poetry and published some of his verse in the *Lyttelton Times* but was not settled and travelled the world with his friend Clements from December 1859, and sold his share in the paper to William Reeves in 1860 (see Ch. 4). Indeed the friends went to Peru in 1860-61 and collected the 'chinchona' plant so that it could be taken to India. Charles Bowen married Georgina Elizabeth Markham in London on 16 July 1861 and returned to Christchurch in March 1862 and then had seven children. The friends and brothers-in-law had notable careers and were to connect again at a later date. Charles Bowen returned to the Provincial Treasury and was involved in many local social clubs including rowing and riding. He was appointed Chief Magistrate of Christchurch from 1864-74 and enjoyed being the 'judge' of others but was considered 'soft' in his judgements. His father Charles died in Christchurch on 3 April 1871 and aunt Anne in 1876. He was the member for Kaiapoi on the Legislative Council of Central Government from 1874-77 and was appointed Minister of Justice and Commissioner of Stamp Duties, but his main interest was education. Croasdaile (1831-90) was ordained a curate in 1857 and was the first vicar of St. Peter's, Riccarton, and a landscaper and architect who planted many trees in this suburb of Christchurch. He returned to England for two years in 1874 but on his return was priest of St. Barnabas, Fendalton from 1876-83 and married Annette Wyles who had a school in 1903.

Charles Bowen then lived at Middleton Grange, a large house, near to Riccarton (later a school) and continued his interest in education being on the senate of the University of New Zealand in 1881-82 and 1888-1915. He was also involved in a number of bank and trust companies and returned to the Legislative Council as a life member in 1891. His daughter Gertrude (1864) married Robert J. Scott a professor of engineering at Canterbury College and cousin of the famous explorer. George Henry Croasdaile (1867) was educated at Cheam, Bradfield College and Christ's College and matriculated at Pembroke, Cambridge in Michaelmas 1888. He was ordained in 1892 and was rector of Thrybergh, Yorkshire from 1901 and Honorary Canon of Sheffield from 1931. Charles Bowen, meanwhile, served on a Royal Commission that vetoed New Zealand joining an Australian Federation in 1901 and was Speaker of the Council in 1905. His brother-in-law Clements worked for the geographical department of the India Office and was Secretary of the Royal Geographical Society in 1863-88. During this time he went on an expedition to Abyssinia in 1867-68 and was at the storming of Magdala and also went to Greenland and the Arctic in 1874. He published many pamphlets and books on geographical subjects and was made President of the R.G.S. in 1893 a post he held for an unprecedented 12 years, and was made K.C.B. in 1896. He was then the main promoter and fund-raiser for the National Antarctic Expedition in the race to reach the South Pole. Two notable gentlemen then entered the story.

Robert Falcon Scott was born at Outlands, Stoke Damerel on 6 June 1868 and entered the navy. His career established him as a leader of men and explorer and he was chosen by Markham to take charge of the National Antarctic Expedition. He went with the Markhams to visit the explorer Nansen in Christiana (Oslo) in October 1900. The latter had just returned from the Arctic on his famous ship the *Fram*. The English party declined the ship for their own expedition it being saucer shaped and decided that a whaling vessel would be better. Ernest H. Shackleton was born at Kilkea House, Kildare, on 15 February 1874 and like the Bowens was from an Anglo-Irish family. He attended Dulwich College and joined the merchant navy in 1890 and then had many voyages between the Far East and America. He said later that during a trip from Gibraltar to New York he dreamed of going to the Poles. He signed up for the National Antarctic Expedition with Scott on 13 September 1900 and sailed on the *Discovery* for New Zealand in the summer of 1901.

The party had a warm welcome in Christchurch and Charles Bowen gave them a local base at his home Middleton Grange. The expedition lasted from 1901-04, however Shackleton had to return sick to New Zealand and arrived back in England on 12 June 1903. The race to both Poles was still on and Shackleton arranged his own expedition on the *Nimrod* in 1907-09. His headquarters were at 9 Regent Square and he first travelled to Sandefjord, Norway to look at the *Bjorn* a specialist ship owned by Mr. C. Christiansen (the town has the only whaling museum in Europe). The vessel was too expensive thus he settled on the *Nimrod* a sealer. The party sailed from Lyttelton on 23 November 1907 after Shackleton secured £5,000 from the Commonwealth and £1,000 from New Zealand. They arrived in McMurdo Sound and climbed Mount Erebus and after passing Scott's earlier attempt came within 100 miles of the Pole on 9 January 1909.

Scott then arranged a second and ill-fated expedition and left London for Christchurch with a 64-man team on 15 June 1910. The main ship was the *Terra Nova* although Scott followed later as he was still fund-raising. Charles Bowen was knighted in 1910 and the party were greeted by him and Lady Bowen and again used their house at Middleton Grange as a base. Indeed Scott trained his huskies and ponies on Quail Island in Lyttelton Harbour. The dogs were not a great success on the first trip and this time he tried ponies and motor transport although this was a complete failure and no better than the dogs. He then sailed to a base on Ross Island in McMurdo Sound. The journey began well from Hut Point on 1 November 1911 but the ponies had delayed matters and the weather became poor. The Norwegian Roald Amundsen was born near Oslo in 1872 and was also an explorer and after Peary reached the North Pole on 6 April 1909 turned his attention to the South Pole. He borrowed the *Fram* from Nansen this being the ship turned down by Scott and sailed right into Ross Sound. He reached the South Pole in December 1911 ahead of Scott who arrived there on 17 January 1912. The party included Lawrence Oates, H.R. Bowers, Edward Wilson and Edgar Evans and were no-doubt greatly disheartened when they saw the Norwegian flag. Winter was coming and they started the 800-mile trek back to the food depot. They had a series of injuries and mishaps that impeded their progress and Evans, the largest man in the party, died of malnourishment and exhaustion just 29 miles from home. Captain Oates was also exhausted with frostbite and the following morning told his companions "I am just going outside, I maybe some time." He then walked out into the blizzard and never returned. The three remaining men made camp just 11 miles from safety but were unable to move further due to a blizzard. Scott's last entry in his diary stated: "It seems a pity but I do not think I can write more.... For God's sake, look after our people." Their bodies were found eight months later and there is a statue to Scott next to Worcester Street and the River Avon (with its punts) in Christchurch, whilst his favourite line from Tennyson's *Ulysses* is inscribed upon a cross at Hut Point viz. - "To strive, to seek, to find, and not to yield."

Ernest Shackleton had a famous saying, "It's time to go south," and soon arranged the last of these great expeditions. He left London for Plymouth on 1 August 1914 and was given permission to sail on 8 August just after war broke out. He took his ship the *Endurance* to South Georgia in the Falklands and then on to the Weddell Sea. The ship was trapped for 281 days before breaking-up and the men removed to Paulet Island. They continued to walk dragging their boats and when the pack ice melted they rowed to Elephant Island. This was their first land for 16 months and most of them could go no further thus 28 men set up camp in five tents. Shackleton was determined not to lose one single man and took a small party in a boat and sailed the great distance of 800 miles to South Georgia in 14 days. They were shipwrecked 17 miles from habitation and three of the party - Shackleton, Crean and Worsley walked over the mountains and glaciers to reach the Stromness Bay Whaling Station. This was a great feat of survival. A relief ship was then sent to rescue the party on Elephant Island. As they came near the tents Shackleton called out, "Are you all well," and the answer came back, "All safe and well," he replied simply, "Thank God." Clements Markham died on 30 January 1916 and Charles Bowen was K.C.M.G. in 1914 and died at Middleton Grange on 12 December 1917. Indeed Bowen Street is to be found at Church Corner in Riccarton. Ernest Shackleton was the last of these explorers and when he returned to England in May 1917 after three years without contact he found the world much changed. Those days were over and although in ill health he planned a further expedition on the *Quest* and left St. Katherine's Dock, London on 17 September 1921. He died of a heart attack at South Georgia on 5 January 1922 and was buried there in a cemetery of Norwegian whalers.

Christopher Bowen, the eldest brother, was born at Hollymount on 12 October 1801 and educated at Trinity College, Dublin being awarded his B.A. in 1824. He entered the Church of England and gained experience in Ireland training as a minister at Killaloe near Limerick in 1825, then received an honorary M.A. from Dublin University in 1832. He married Catherine Emily the daughter of Richard Steele on 17 January 1834, who was born at Fermanagh in Ireland c.1809. The couple then had two sons and the I.G.I. states they were born at Hollymount but it is likely the census or printed records are the best indicator. Charles Synge Christopher Bowen was born at Woolaston near Chepstow on 1 January 1835 and Edward Ernest Bowen at Glenmore, Wicklow on 30 March 1836. Rev. C. Bowen had a good career and was curate of Bath Abbey in 1838-43 and perpetual curate of St. Mary Magdalen, Southwark in 1843-55, situated at the south end of Bermondsey Street in the shadow of the newly built London Bridge Station. There was a late addition to the family at this time and Francis Robert Steele Bowen was born at Charlton in 1846. Christopher Bowen incumbent of St. Mary's lived at Park Villa, Priory Lane, Lee Road, in 1850-51 with wife Catherine, sons Edward and Francis, nephew Francis Synge (13) from Ireland, the Hon. Crosby Ward (14) Viscount Bangor's son, Daniel Janverin (13) from Jersey and three servants. The older sons were educated under Rev. E.J. Selwyn at Blackheath Proprietary School at this time - the school was at the first F.A. meeting in 1863.

The father was rector of St. Thomas's, Winchester in 1855-69 the church being used as Hampshire County Record Office in the late 1970s. He retired in 1869 aged 68 years and being familiar with the rural surrounds of Ireland moved to the equally remote coast of the Isle of Wight. No doubt this reminded him of the rugged beauty and isolation of his birthplace but not so far from civilisation. Totland, at the western end of the island, was planned as the Isle of Wight Riviera in the 19th century and there was a bold scheme with opulent crescents, a spa, and ferries to France. Some large Victorian properties were built on the north coast in Freshwater parish, but the rest was but a dream. Rev. Bowen moved to Heatherwood above Totland Bay in 1869. The house had fine views of the Solent from the veranda, weather boarding and slate tiles on the wall, a slate roof with red ridge tiles, and shuttered windows and gables. It was a large property, somewhat colonial, with two rear wings but one was added later. Today four properties are situated on the drive: Highfield Lodge (25 yards), Bay Tree Cottage modern (65 yards), Glendovere 1920s (100 yards) and Heatherwood (125 yards). The former was no doubt the lodge for the original house.

Rev. Bowen owned much land in the area and was a notable benefactor who built the first temporary wooden church on land in York Road, just opposite the present church, in 1869. He was a clergyman without cure of souls and lived with Catherine and two servants at Heatherwood in 1871, but also owned Glenheadon the neighbouring property at this time. He provided land for a permanent stone church at the junction of York Road and Church Hill in 1875 and a full-time minister was appointed and a vicarage built next door in 1877: "That the legal formalities were carried through satisfactorily was mainly due to the Rev. C. Bowen M.A. a resident who most generously gave the land necessary for the church, churchyard, vicar's house and school - consecrated 14 August 1875." This was Christchurch and his house was just 30 yards away, whilst the wood for the church lych-gate came from the timbers of H.M.S "Thunderer" a 74-gun ship that fought on the *Lee Line* at Trafalgar. The old wooden church was removed to the esplanade in Totland Bay and became the Waterfront "café" and he gifted more land for Christchurch National School in 1880. He lived with his wife and two servants at Heatherwood in 1881 and no doubt had a comfortable existence there. Freshwater and Totland had long been a desirable location for the gentry and those of artistic persuasion and had a train link to Newport with ferries to the mainland. Alfred Lord Tennyson poet laureate lived at Farringford House, Freshwater in 1853-69 and wrote some of his best work there viz. "The Charge of the Light Brigade" and "Idylls of the King" - romantic poems of King Arthur that sold 10,000 copies within a month of publication. Sightseers, however, flocked to the poet's home shattering his peace thus he built a retreat at Haslemere, Surrey in 1869 (but still owned Farringford).

Rev. Bowen moved to Glenheadon a smaller property just west of his former home by 1886. This was designed in a lodge style with gables, and was a complete contrast to Heatherwood, being of yellow-brown brick with tall chimneys and had a conservatory that gave stunning views of the Solent. The property can be found in York Lane although Glenheadon Drive occupies much of its garden. Rev. Bowen remained active until late in life, travelling abroad, and died at Bordighera in Italy on 18 March 1890. His son Edward Ernest Bowen of Harrow proved his will on 9 June 1890 and his personal estate came to £36,078 4s 1d. He made a major contribution to the church and village and a white marble plaque with black mount was erected at the rear of Christchurch: "In loving remembrance of the Rev. Christopher Bowen M.A. to whose energetic and patient efforts with those of his many friends this building and consecration of this church Christchurch were mainly due - This tablet is erected by his bereaved widow to his dear memory. He was born October 16th 1801 and died in Bordighera in Italy March 18th 1890. Psalm xvi iii." Mrs. Bowen was a signatory on a testimonial to Thomas Waterhouse in Easter 1891 and this document remains on the vestry wall. His widow Catherine or Kate lived with two local servants at Glenheadon in 1891 and owned the house until her death in 1902 although she spent some time with her son at Harrow.

Charles Synge Christopher Bowen was born at Woolaston in Gloucester-shire on 1 January 1835 and was educated at Lille, Blackheath Proprietary and Rugby Schools. He matriculated at Balliol College, Oxford on 19 May 1854 and was a fellow in 1857 gaining his B.A. in 1858. He was called to the bar at Lincoln's Inn on 26 January 1861 and was a good amateur cricketer who had two innings for Hampshire C.C.C. in 1861 scoring 30 runs (when his father lived at Winchester). Charles S.C. Bowen married Emily Frances Rendel at St. John's, Hyde Park Crescent, Paddington on 7 January 1862. She was born on 31 October 1835 and baptized at the New Tabernacle or Norley Independent Chapel, Plymouth on 9 April 1836 whilst her sister Catherine Emily Rendel was born at Plymouth in December 1840 and married Clement Francis Wedgwood at St. John's on 6 November 1866 (see Leitch Ch. 16). They were the daughters of James Meadows Rendel F.R.S. who died at 10 Palace Gardens in 1856 and his wife Catharine Jane Harris who died at 18 Hyde Park Street in 1884. Charles and Emily lived at 2 Chester Place, Hyde Park Square in Kensington district and had three children: William Edward (March 1863), Maxwell Steele (22 October 1865) and Ethel Kate (23 November 1869) N.B. some records state that William was born at Milford in N.Z. on 6 October 1862. Charles Bowen became a bencher and a judge of the High Court Queen's Bench, in 1879, and lived at 1 Cornwall Gardens, Kensington in 1881 with his wife Emily, three children, a governess and eight servants, the house being near Gloucester Road and south of the High Street. He was a privy councillor and Lord Justice of Appeal in 1882 and created D.C.L. on 13 June 1883. He became Baron Bowen of Hollymount, Mayo and Colwood, Cuckfield in Sussex in August 1893 and died at Prince's Gardens, Knightsbridge on 10 April 1894. Emily Frances his widow died at 2 Queen's Gate Gardens, Kensington on 24 March 1897 aged 62 and they were both buried at Slaugham in Sussex.

William Edward Bowen (1863) was educated at Harrow School and matriculated at Balliol College, Oxford on 1 February 1882 gaining his B.A./M.A. in 1886. He was a minister in the Church of England and lived at 119 Barkston Gardens, Earl's Court in 1901. The red brick property was at the western end, part of a block 103-121, and had large bay windows looking out on the gardens. Archibald Leitch lived at no. 99 in the neighbouring block (see Ch. 17) whilst William E. Bowen died at Totland in 1938 (see below). Maxwell Steele Bowen (1865) was admitted to Trinity, Cambridge on 2 October 1884 and matriculated Michaelmas that year. He was a lieutenant in the 3rd Battalion 'Militia' Sherwood Foresters from 1898-1901. Josiah Clement the son of Clement Francis and Catherine Emily Wedgwood was born at Barlaston on 16 March 1872 and educated at Clifton and the Royal Naval College then had a notable career in politics. He married his cousin Ethel Kate Bowen (1869) at All Saints, Ennismore Gardens, London, on 3 July 1894 and then had seven children: Helen Bowen (1895) at 1 Gloucester Terrace, Rosamund (1896) & Francis Charles Bowen (1898) at 28 Burdon Terrace Newcastle, Josiah (1899) & Camilla Hildegard (1901) at Harracles Elswick, Elizabeth Julia (1907) at 4 Whitehall Street and Gloria (1909) at Maddeshall Stone. The father fought with honour in the Boer War and the First War and was M.P. for Newcastle-under-Lyme in 1906-42. There was a divorce scandal in 1918 after 24 years of marriage that damaged his career, but he survived and became a first Labour M.P. in 1919. He was a writer and published two volumes of a *History of Parliament* in 1929 but got no further. He became the 1st Baronet Wedgwood of Barlaston in 1942 and died on 26 July 1943 and Ethel Kate died in 1952. Sir Charles S.C. Bowen and his family had a high profile but brother Francis Robert Steele Bowen had a quieter life. He was born in Charlton in 1846 and matriculated at New College, Oxford, on 20 October 1865 aged 19. He was a scholar of the college and gained his B.A. in 1870 then married Frances Elizabeth Steele Graves at Mickleton Gloucester on 30 November 1871 - both were aged 25. He died on 16 July 1886.

Edward Ernest Bowen was born at Glenmore, Ireland on 30 March 1836 and was an even greater sportsman than his brother. He spent his childhood in Bath and then at Blackheath where his father lived during his time at Bermondsey (1843-55). He was educated at Blackheath Proprietary School who were a pioneer of early soccer and was thus well placed for sporting achievement. He finished his education at King's College School, London in the Strand (see Alcock Ch. 2) and matriculated at Trinity College, Cambridge on 1 February 1854. Henry VIII founded the college in 1546 by amalgamating some earlier colleges and providing a new endowment. It had first floor chambers above the great gate and it was there that Sir Isaac Newton worked on his laws of motion. Francis Bacon, Lord Byron, William Thackeray, Alfred Tennyson and Thomas Babington Macaulay were students at the college as were Arthur Fitzgerald Kinnaird and Albert Childers Thompson (both 1867). Edward excelled in his time at Trinity and was a Bell Scholar in 1855, received the Prizeman Scholarship and became President of the 'Union' in 1856. He gained a fourth class degree in the classics (B.A.) in 1858, a surprising choice of subject given his later leaning (see below). He received an honorary fellowship with his life long friend Henry Sidgwick in 1859, followed with an M.A. in 1861.

He liked the scholarly life and entered the profession of teacher becoming assistant master at Marlborough College in 1858, however he moved to Harrow School as an assistant master in 1859 and was to remain there for the rest of his life. Dr. Charles John Vaughan, Headmaster in 1845-59 gave Bowen the position and Sir George Gilbert Scott (1811-78) built the school library to the head's memory in 1861-63. The latter designed the Albert Memorial (1862) and St. Pancras (1865) and Giles Gilbert Scott (1880-1960) was his

Edward Ernest Bowen (1836-1901). He was a schoolmaster at Harrow from 1859-1901.

grandson. Edward made a versatile and unselfish contribution to the school over 42 years and took a keen interest in sports and games from the start and was described as "A pioneer of football at Harrow." He was only 23 years old when he received the appointment, not much older than the boys he taught, and arrived after the Alcocks but was well acquainted with Morton Peto Betts (1862-65), William Parry Crake (1866-70) and Reginald Courtenay Welch (1864-71). Their love of football and team spirit was cemented on the Harrow playing fields. Edward did not restrict his sporting achievements to soccer and was also an accomplished skater and mountaineer. He played cricket at Cambridge but did not make the eleven and was described as a middle order right hand batsman and occasional wicket keeper. He played amateur cricket in the summer months and had two innings with Hampshire C.C.C. in 1864 when his father lived at Winchester although he scored no runs.

He was dedicated to his students and the school and also made an important contribution to the academic side. He was a founder of the "modern side" at Harrow in 1869 whose first masters were himself, the Rev. W.D. Bushell and the Rev. R.H. Quick. He was deeply involved in this movement from 1869-93 and its upper two forms had some of the most inspiring and original masters. This was not, as it seems, a football team with sweepers but referred to modern academic subjects such as French and German. He was a "modern" man and forward thinker who played an active part in the social life of Harrow School. During his junior days he was a notable author and constant contributor to the "Saturday Review" when it was at the height of its power and reputation. He had a detailed knowledge of campaigns and battlefields and was an expert regarding Napoleon and modern history and conveyed this to his students. He took this strategy onto the sports field and his involvement in football soon paid dividends. He played for England with Charles Alcock in the unofficial international at the Oval in 1870 and for the Wanderers in their Cup Final victories of 1872/73 when he was almost 37 years old.

He made no other major appearances in the sport and then concentrated his time at Harrow School. He lived at Small House on Grove Hill from 1864-81, and the Bishop of Durham formerly held the property. Public schools did not provide rooms for their masters in the early 19th century thus they had to find some accommodation and often lived alone. They realized they could gain extra income by taking boys in as lodgers and this was the origin of the school house-system. Edward organised the 'cricket field bill' from 1879, a method of calling 500 boys names in one and a half minutes. This saved them going up the hill from the playing field to answer their names and Mr. Bowen did this every half holiday of each summer term from its inception. In addition to teaching and sport he was a keen Liberal politician and ardent reformer and thus contested Hertford against the First Lord of the Treasury in 1880, although unsuccessfully. He was an assistant master at Peterborough Road in Harrow on the Hill, in 1881, near the old buildings and playing fields. His household included nine boarders and scholars aged 14-17, a housekeeper, butler and two servants. Charles Colbeck (34) from Leamington lived next door with wife Mary and brother-in-law Francis E. Marshall (33) both assistant masters (see below). This may have been Small House and today Peterborough House with its plain grey yellow façade, Gayton House and Elmfield with portico entrance and red brick extension '1892' are on Grove Hill (behind is Peterborough Road). Edward Bowen had notable boarders in 1881 including Viscount Pears A. Vallelort (15) born London and Prince Enrich E.C. Leiningen (15) born Osborne on the Isle of Wight. Having a Prince in one's house was clearly of significance and required investigation - he was traced to Regency Britain (1810-37).

George III reigned from 1760-1820 and had a number of sons being succeeded by his first son George IV who built the Royal Pavilion at Brighton. He became an unpopular monarch ridiculed in the writings of Byron, Keats and Shelley and died in 1830 when the Times stated his death 'was little regretted.' The Duke of York had died in 1827 thus the Duke of Clarence, the third son, came to the throne. He became William IV but having spent his early years at sea was unprepared for the monarchy, and a blunt and tactless way of speaking earned him the name 'silly-billy'. Despite this he was quite astute at dealing with Parliament and helped guide the passage of the Great Reform Bill in 1832 and was King from 1830-37 at a time that could have seen revolution. Edward Duke of Kent was the fourth son of George III and his wife the Duchess of Kent had previously married Prince Charles Emich of Leiningen and had children: Prince Charles of Leiningen (1804-56) and a daughter called Fedora. Queen Victoria the daughter of the Duke and Duchess of Kent was born at Kensington in 1819 and was their half-sister. In fact the grandson Ernest Leiningen (1830-1904) was a favourite nephew of the Queen and entered the Royal Navy under her patronage. Queen Victoria, meanwhile, approached Sir Robert Peel P.M. in 1844 and asked him to find her a Royal retreat near to the sea - the result being the purchase of Osborne on the Isle of Wight. Prince Albert worked on a new plan with old friend Thomas Cubitt and redesigned and enlarged the existing house so it was suitable for a Royal household.

There were happy times at Osborne and Ernest Leiningen was made captain of the Royal Yacht in 1858 aged 28, however the tranquillity was shattered when Prince Albert died in December 1861 and Queen Victoria went into mourning. She had a strong association with her nephew Ernest that was reinforced after the death of her husband and his son Emich or Enrich E.C. Leiningen was born at Osborne in March 1866 (quarter). The Queen was an ardent admirer of Lord Tennyson, who lived at Freshwater, and may have known Rev. Christopher Bowen for philanthropy and through Island society. This might explain Leiningen's presence in Bowen's house in 1881, however the job of housemaster was at times harrowing and even Royal Princes could be a handful. In fact one story suggests that the Prince set fire to Edward Bowen's property: accidentally of course! The family, meanwhile, remained in favour and the father Ernest was made an admiral in 1887.

Edward Bowen left Small House just after the census and was living at the Grove in late 1881. He held the property for twenty years until his death and lived and worked amongst his boys. The Grove was an important house in Harrow at the end of Church Hill just beyond the Old School (1615), next to St. Mary's, and in earlier times was the vicarage. Richard Brinsley Sheridan was a pupil at Harrow in 1762-68 and liked the area so much that he came to live at the Grove in 1781-84. The old property, however, burnt down in 1833 and only part of the front and the basement survived. It was rebuilt and appears today on modern maps. This was a large Georgian house with a plain two-storey yellow stucco façade and smaller rooms with dormer windows in the slate roof. There were symmetrical chimneys and brown brick buildings to the rear and extensive gardens beyond. An old brick wall remains beside the house and a path leads downhill from the entrance to some old buildings on the left. The latter have few outer windows whilst a plaque states: "These form rooms embody the walls of Sheridan's stables" - The Foss, Grove Hill House is just opposite. Bowen altered the Grove to give all the boys single bedrooms in the 1880s, and continued his interest in politics but he could not accept *Home Rule* and had no active part after 1885 (presumably due to his background).

The Grove, Harrow. E.E. Bowen lived here from 1881-1901.

Memorial to E.E. Bowen.
Located next to St. Mary's, Harrow on the Hill.

Edward Bowen a master at Harrow School lived at the Grove in 1891 with 10 servants but no scholars on the night of the census. He was well known for Latin and English verse and especially for school songs such as "Forty Years On" many of which became classics at Harrow and elsewhere. Indeed, "There is hardly one of them that is not excellent and some show a power little short of genius." Messrs. Longman's published them in "Harrow School Songs" and one of them "Shemuel" showed a depth of religious feeling seldom seen in public, he being a most reticent man. Edward resided at the Grove in 1901 with his mother Catherine aged 94 years, 30 boarders and 14 servants. What a noise! He made an important contribution to academic life at Harrow and ruled the boys with a strictness of discipline but tempered this with gaiety, humour and sympathy. His sporting achievements were equally important and he continued to play football until the last, and half-holiday afternoons always saw him on the cricket or football field. He went on a cycling tour with Professor Bryce in 1901 and reached Moux ten miles from Saulieu, Department de la Nieme near Dijon and the Côte d'Or (golden hills) in central France. He seemed in good health but whilst mounting his bicycle became ill without warning and fell to the ground and never regained consciousness - he died on 8 April 1901.

His obituary was in the Times on Thursday 11 April 1901 and it was stated that: "The first part of the service will be in the school chapel and as space is somewhat limited those desirous of attending should apply to the Headmaster or to C. Colbeck Esq. Harrow or to Rev. Hon. W.E. Bowen of 119 Barkston Gardens." He was the senior assistant master at this time and the paper said of him: "Few men have been more consulted on important educational questions; no one ever gave more conscientious care than he did to the formation of his opinion upon all subjects concerning life and conduct. He was the truest of friends and the most generous. His gifts to the school were largely anonymous and mostly unsuspected. His death inflicts on his many friends a deep and paralysing sense of irretrievable loss, yet in its sudden closing of a busy life, lived to the full from first to last, it is probably such as he would himself have chosen." His body was returned home and he was buried at St. Mary's, Harrow beside the path he had taken each day from his house to school. The grave was near the south wall of the church, itself of flint, and first consecrated in 1094. It was secured by the kindness of the vicar Rev. F. Wayland Joyce and the Local Government Board as the churchyard had been closed for many years.

The funeral was in the chapel on Monday 15 April 1901 and a large number of Old Harrovians were present including members of his house whilst the clergy included the Headmaster Rev. Dr. Wood. A wreath from the boys of his form marked his vacant seat in the chapel. The coffin was covered with a white pall over which was laid the school cricket field flag and was taken from the chapel to the churchyard by former heads of the house. Members of the family present were Rev. Hon. W.E. and Mrs. Bowen, Hon. M.S. Bowen, Mrs. and Miss Sanders, Mr. R.A. Sanders and the Misses Synge. Other mourners included Mr. and Mrs. Bryce M.P., Earl Spencer and Dr. Walter Leaf school governors, members of the cricket and football team and a large number of masters. Rev. William Edward Bowen his nephew and Charles Colbeck Esq. of Harrow were executors and proved his will in London on 7 June 1901. The Grove passed to the Governors of Harrow at this time. Catherine Emily Bowen his mother died at Glenheadon, Totland, Isle of Wight, on 1 February 1902 but she was laid to rest with her son at Harrow. She had the same executors and her estate was valued at £10,620 18s 6d, which must have delayed her son's probate and his estate was finally valued at £68,052 0s 10d in July 1903. All three sons had died thus William Edward Bowen inherited the family estate including Glenheadon, Totland on the Isle of Wight. Indeed the Bowens owned the property for nearly seventy years and William died there on 23 July 1938. There is a plain cross memorial as he requested beside Harrow Church with bluebells in front in a stone surround: "From Strength to Strength Edward Ernest Bowen assistant master at Harrow for 42 years Died April 8: 1901 - From Faith to Faith Catherine Emily Bowen widow of Christopher Bowen Died February 1: 1902." This was a fitting tribute to a great man.

WILLIAM PARRY CRAKE

The Wanderers Cup Final side included four players from Harrow and Edward Bowen was supported in attack by his protégé William Parry Crake. The latter came from a family of merchants who were engaged in the East India trade for many years. The East India Company or colloquially John Co. was a commercial enterprise that traded in India from the 18th century, however as this trade depended greatly on the local power base they became involved in the country's administration. They controlled much of the sub-continent by the 1850s however the British Government was increasingly involved in the situation and this culminated with the Indian Mutiny and siege of Lucknow in 1857. The outcome was the demise of the E.I.C. and direct rule under the British Government from 1858-1937. India was very important to the British Empire and a large number of troops were used to secure home interests and facilitate government. There was, despite this, a large investment in the country's infrastructure and the Corps of the Royal Engineers did much of the work. The trade routes and travel to the country was enhanced with the opening of Suez in 1869. This was the stage on which families such as the Crakes made a fortune or at least had an affluent lifestyle.

The family are traced to John Crake who married Mary Crail at St. James's, Westminster on 7 June 1772 and had a son William Crake born on 16 April 1787 and baptized at St. Marylebone on 27 May. He was to become a successful property speculator in both Marylebone and Paddington although started as a builder. He may have been related to John Crake who was a chemist and druggist at 47 Chiswell Street in 1816-23 and at no. 90 in 1829 and Michael Crake statuary, surveyor and builder at 64 Portland Road, Notting Hill in 1823-29 and King's Road, Chelsea in 1835. William Mason, meanwhile, married Sarah Tuttle at St. Martin in the Fields on 15 July 1788 and had children Mary Ann (14 May, 31 May 1789), Sarah (1790), Ann (1793), William (1795), Richard (1797) and Henry (1798) all baptized at St. Marylebone Church. Indeed William Crake married Mary Ann Mason at St. Marylebone on 8 June 1809 and lived in this fashionable district of London in the early 19th century. The couple had nine children baptized at St. Marylebone: John (1811), William (1812) *infant*, Mary Ann (1814), Vandaleur Benjamin (1816), Ellen Crail (1818) Annette Sullivan (1820), Rosaline Jennet (1822), William Hamilton (1824) and Edward Neville (1826).

There was much development in this area of London at the time and architects-builders such as James Burton have already been considered under Sealy Vidal. The land between Edgware Road and Bayswater Road in the southeast corner of Paddington was a prime site for development, especially due to its location next to Hyde Park. This became known as 'Tyburnia' in the early 19th century after the local tree of that name and leases were made available for 95 years, initially to individuals. The trustees of the land hoped to maintain higher standards than if they gave the whole project to one builder such as Thomas Cubitt. In the event this proved impractical and much of the land went to speculators, namely builders who acquired plots in different streets. William Crake lived at Marylebone in 1816 and advertised as a plumber, painter & c. at 18 Old Quebec Street, Oxford Street in 1820-23. It is likely that he did work in 'Tyburnia' although regarding his advert was just a builder at this stage. Indeed he may also have worked with James Burton on the Eyre Estate since he soon accumulated some considerable funds.

William Crake did not remain in Marylebone and was living in 'Kensington' in 1824-27, although this may have been Notting Hill as it fell within that district. The church records state William was "in trade" and this no doubt referred to building and similar work. The 'Tyburnia' area was slow to develop and only 36 builders had contracted for c.570 houses in 1824 whilst one third of the site was built in 1828. St. John's, Hyde Park was constructed in 1829-32 and Gloucester Square and Sussex Square were just to the west. The Paddington Canal part of the Grand Union system was built in the early 1800s thus there was more development to the north, whilst the Great Western Railway and its London terminus arrived in the 1830s and gave a further boost to the project. This resulted in new speculative opportunities and many houses were built to compete with Belgravia, and the Crake family were part of this process. John Crake the first son was born on 25 March 1811 and baptized at St. Marylebone on 26 April and joined his father in the firm as an architect. This was a similar progression to that seen with the likes of William Adam and James Burton. William Crake was painter & c. at 18 Old Quebec Street, Portman Square in 1835 and entered into a new contract that changed the family's fortunes. He took leases on the first 'mansion houses' in Hyde Park Gardens in 1837 and acquired most of the terrace and a few houses nearby. The original plan was for a crescent and this may have become famous like in Bath, but in the end two straight terraces were built. John Crake his son was the architect of Hyde Park Gardens and these are described regarding A.F. Kinnaird in Ch. 5 as he was born at no. 35 Hyde Park Gardens in 1847. The drawings of John Crake (1811-59) are in the collection of R.I.B.A. at the British Architectural Library.

William Crake was a builder at 18 Old Quebec Street, Portman Square from 1840-43 and John Crake architect had the same address but also had offices at Carlton Chambers, 4 Regent Street. Indeed Thomas Bridges (45) clerk lived at 18 Old Quebec Street in 1841 with daughters Emma and Elizabeth both aged 15, William Mason (45) independent and one servant. William seems to have retired at this point since his ownership of most of Hyde Park Gardens was most lucrative. John Crake gave his address solely as Carlton Chambers in 1844-45 whilst Thomas Bridges took over the work and was a builder at 18 Old Quebec Street in 1845. William Crake esquire left Notting Hill in the 1840s and was a magistrate for Middlesex and Sussex living at 10 Stanhope Street, Paddington in 1851 aged 63 with his wife Mary Ann (61) and daughter Mary Ann (35) and five servants. This street was situated between St. John's Church on Southwick Crescent and Gloucester Square and may have been one of the houses that he built. The family lived in this area of Paddington for nearly eighty years and Stanhope Street was re-named Southwick Place.

William Crake also owned a property at Pelham Place, Hastings in 1851 whilst his son John Crake was at 89 Westbourne Terrace, Hyde Park and Datchet, Berkshire. The family had properties in both St. Leonard's and Hastings and may have collaborated with James Burton on the former 'new town' that was started in 1828. William Crake (73) J.P deputy lieutenant lived at 10 Stanhope Street, Paddington in 1861 with wife Mary A. (72), children Mary A. (46) and Edward Neville rector of Redbourne Warwick and curate of All Saints, Knightsbridge and six servants. He owned 7 Pelham Place, Hastings in 1861 but died at St. Leonard's on Sea on 22 November 1863 and Vandaleur Benjamin Crake of the same and Very Rev. Edward Neville Crake of Battle, clerk and dean, the sons and two of the executors, obtained his probate at the Principal Registry his effects being under £140,000. Mary Ann Crake (82) widow and 'proprietor of houses' lived at 10 Stanhope Street in 1871 with four servants. She died there on 21 May 1879 aged 90 and Vandaleur B. Crake of Highlands St. Leonard's on Sea esq., the Very Rev. Edward Neville Crake of Battle clerk and dean and William Hamilton Crake of 34 Gloucester Square Hyde Park the sons proved her will and codicil, valued at under £8,000.

Vandaleur Benjamin Crake was born at Marylebone on 31 January 1816 and baptized there on 8 June that year and was the second son of William of Notting Hill. He entered Jesus College, Cambridge on 1 May 1834 and matriculated there in Michaelmas 1834 and was admitted to Middle Temple on 7 February 1835. He gained a B.A. in 1838, was called to the bar in 1841 and received an M.A. in 1842. Vandaleur B. Crake, barrister, was at 6 King's Bench Walk in 1845 and was one of many who had chambers there viz. Morley, Meysey-Thompson, Welch and Merriman. He married Louisa Frances Browne at Chertsey in September 1849 and was at 3 Essex Court, Temple in 1851 whilst his home was at 5 Charles Street, Westbourne Terrace near to his brother John Crake. He had three children with his first wife Louisa Frances namely Winifred Constance (1850), William Vandaleur (1852) and Edward Barrington (1854) who were all baptized at St. James's, Paddington. He was then married to his second wife Mary B. and had a daughter Alice M. Crake (1860) at St. Leonard's in Sussex. Vandaleur B. Crake J.P. lived at the "Highlands", St. Leonard's in 1867. He was there in 1881 with his wife Mary B., William V. B.A. Cambs, Emmie J.V. daughter-in-law from Hanover, Alice M. and seven servants. He died at Hastings in September 1894 aged 78.

William Vandaleur Crake (1852) went to Eton and matriculated at Jesus College, Cambridge in Michaelmas 1873 and gained his B.A. in 1878. He married Emmie J.V. (1842) of Hanover a British Subject at Steyning in December 1880 and lived at St. Leonard's in 1899 and was the Honorary Secretary of Hastings Museum. He resided at Highlands, Boscobel Road in St. Leonard's on his own means in 1901 with wife Emma (59) and three servants. This was next to Essenden Road and Mary Crake (78) born Catsfield and Alice (41) also lived in the town. Edward Barrington Crake (1854) married at Battle in March 1880 and had a daughter Dorothy born at Paddington in 1883. He then married Clara Alice Woodroffe at St. George's Hanover Square in March 1894 and had children Pearl (1895) Westminster and Gladys (1897) Knightsbridge. He was a major late rifle brigade and brigade major in Portsmouth Volunteers at Chawton Parish in 1901 with wife Clara (33) born Winkfield, Ascot and three daughters. He died at Kensington in September 1910. The brother Edward Neville Crake was born in Notting Hill on 25 September 1826 and baptized at Marylebone on 6 March. He went to Kensington School under Mr. Wilkinson and was admitted to Trinity, Cambridge on 23 May 1844 and matriculated in the Michaelmas term. He gained his B.A. in 1848 and M.A in 1851 and was a deacon in 1850 and priest at London in 1851. He was the curate of Knightsbridge in 1850-61 and lived with his family at 10 Stanhope Street in 1861 and was appointed dean and vicar of Battle in 1863. He married Clara Chapman at Marylebone in September 1873 and lived at the Deanery, Battle in 1881 with his wife Clara (45) from Acton. He retired as dean and vicar in 1882 and then lived at Hans Court and died there on 21 June 1909 aged 82 (see Edgar Lubbock).

William Hamilton Crake was born at Notting Hill, Kensington on 22 May 1824 and baptized at Marylebone on 7 July that year. He may have worked with his father in the 'building' business and his prospects were good after the acquisition of Hyde Park Gardens in 1837. He moved with his family to 10 Stanhope Street in the 1840s and became a merchant in the East India trade and met his wife through these business links. William Wood married Elizabeth Cotton by licence at St. Marylebone on 27 August 1790 the witnesses George and Mabel Cotton. The couple had a son George (2 August 1793) born at Sonning then Thomas (7 June 1799), Anne (19 December 1800) and Mary (2 June 1807) at Caversham both parishes being near Reading, Berkshire. Hanger Hill House in Ealing was a three-storey property built in the 18th century to the west of Hanger Lane and not far from Park Royal (see Ch. 13). It was situated in woodland on Hanger Hill just north of Ealing and was auctioned in 1769 and the lease renewed in 1775. Richard Wood held the property from 1777 and James and Thomas Wood owned land there in the late 18th century. Indeed William and Elizabeth Wood inherited the house and their son Henry was born on 26 March 1810 and baptized at St. Mary's, Ealing on 1 May that year. William Wood the father died in 1817 and his trustees then owned the property for some years, whilst George Wood married Mary Roberts at St. James's, Paddington on 7 August 1823 and the latter held Hanger Hill as a 'tenant for life' from about 1826.

The couple had three children at Hanger Hill and baptized at St. Mary's, Ealing: Jane 3 September 1826 baptized 5 October, Katherine 30 October 1827 and Mary (born Harrow) 10 October 1828. There is also the marriage of George Wood to Mary Eliza Hamilton at St. James's, Westminster on 29 April 1829 but this may be un-related. George and Mary Wood then had three more children, George Richard 12 February 1832 at Wembley, Harrow, Edward 9 April 1833 and William 25 February 1836 at Ealing. The mother Mary Wood, however, died at Hanger Hill and was buried at St. Mary's, Ealing on 12 March 1836 aged 32 years. George was described as a gentleman or esquire and owned 501 acres at Hanger Hill in 1840 with 167 acres being leasehold. He was left with six young children although his sister Mary may have helped raise them and there were soon some family weddings although his two brothers married late in life.

Henry Wood a merchant of Craven Street, Hungerford Market son of William Wood merchant married Louisa Collett Dalgleish (1827) daughter of Robert merchant of St. George's, Bloomsbury at St. Martin in the Fields on 14 March 1850. E.W. Wood the vicar of Nazeing performed the ceremony and R.C. Dalgleish and 'John' Wood were the witnesses. William Hamilton Crake esquire of Paddington married Jane Wood the daughter of George Wood esquire by licence at Ealing Parish Church on 10 December 1850. E.W. Wood the vicar of Nazeing in Essex again performed the ceremony and George Wood, Mary Wood, William Crake, Edward Neville Crake and George Hayter were the witnesses. Indeed Sir George Hayter (1792-1871) was an English painter and his works included Henry Lascelles 2nd Earl of Harewood, the trial of Queen Caroline at the House of Lords (1820) and the coronation of Queen Victoria (1837) - see Meysey-Thompson. The Crakes then departed for the sub-continent and are treated below. Thomas Wood also a brother of George married Emma Martha Woodroffe (1807) at St. Martin in the Fields on 5 February 1852 - she was born at King's Square, Bristol.

Mary Wood daughter unmarried and annuitant lived at Hanger Hill House, Ealing in 1851 with Henry Wood a coal merchant, his wife Louisa and Isabel C. Dalgleish (the latter three visitors) and seven servants. George Wood Esq. was a magistrate at Hanger Hill in 1853 and his sister Miss Wood lived nearby at the Elms. George Wood (67) widower, magistrate and landed proprietor occupied 545 acres 32 roods at Hanger Hill House in 1861 and resided there with his daughter Mary and seven servants. He also employed 27 labourers and seven boys. Mary Wood (53) fund-holder lived next door at the Elms, Hanger Hill in 1861 with Emma Martha Wood (53), Elizabeth Cotton (14) and Mary Cotton (13) scholars from

Pilleton, Staffs all visitors, one other visitor and four servants. George Wood Esq. died at Hanger Hill on 28 January 1864 aged 70 and was buried at St. Mary's, Ealing on 4 February. Thomas Wood of Twyford Abbey in Twyford parish his brother and Francis Hamilton of Friar's Place, Acton proved his will with two codicils on 14 May 1864 his effects under £40,000. Edward Wood (1833) inherited the Hanger Hill estate however the house was uninhabited in 1871 and he moved to Shropshire in the mid-1870s. Sir Montague Nelson, Chairman of Ealing U.D.C. leased the property in 1874 and the estate comprised 560 acres in 1899. Edward died in 1904 and his son Lieutenant Colonel Charles Peevor Boileau Wood sold most of the estate to the Prudential Assurance Co. in 1906. The house itself and surrounding land was the Hanger Hill Golf Club from 1900 to at least 1935 and Victoria's County History (1911) states: "The links are on high ground above the town, there are 18 holes from 105-500 yards and the club-house is a fine old mansion situated on a hill." The house was demolished sometime in the 1930s and Hanger Hill Park is all that remains within the suburban spread.

There was a housekeeper and servants residing at the Elms, Hanger Hill in 1871 whilst Mary Wood (73) of no occupation lived there in 1881 with two visitors Bridget M. Crowther and Catherine C. Bakewell and four servants. Henry Wood (71) retired merchant was living at Woodside Lodge, Leavesden, Watford in 1881 with a large household viz. wife Louisa Collett, Major General Douglas Hamilton (62) of Sudbury, Dixon Williams Arthur and John Teage nephews and merchants from Porto, Rebecca Collett Williams sister-in-law and son Frank Dalgleish Williams, Elizabeth Collett Dalgleish sister-in-law, Cecil S.R. Butler solicitor's clerk, Ada Jane Crake great niece and five servants. Other members of the Hamilton family lived near to Ealing in 1881 and must have had a long-term connection with the Crakes (viz. William Hamilton Crake). Francis Hamilton (71) born Sudbury farmer of 200 acres employing 8 men and 3 boys resided at Willesden Road, Acton with his wife Mary from Jamaica, sons Frederick C. solicitor, Edgar G. tea merchant and daughter Katharine J. Nightingale, whilst Edward Hamilton (65) born Sudbury doctor M.D. lived at 9 Port Street, London with wife Emily and daughter Marion.

William Hamilton and Jane Crake spent a brief time in England after their marriage in 1850 and then travelled to Fort St. George, Madras on the south east coast of India. William was a merchant there however these were turbulent times and this was the period just before the Indian Mutiny. The couple had three children born in Madras during this period: William Parry (1852), George (1854) and Edith Hamilton (1855) the latter being born on 7 June 1855 and baptized at Madras on 10 October that year. The mutiny started in May 1857 when sepoys attached to the British Army rose against their officers however the mutineers were joined by thousands of rebels who aimed to drive the British out of India. They hoped to achieve this by capturing the garrison cities, which were the centre of Imperial power, thus heavy fighting took place around Delhi and Lucknow in the north. There was much fear and unease amongst the European community and it seems likely the threat of war and rebellion sent the Crakes back to England. They went to live near the Wood family and a daughter Ada Jane Crake was born at Wadham Lodge, Ealing on 28 December 1858 - her father William a merchant was the informant.

Jane Crake (34) wife and fund holder lived at Wadham Lodge, Ealing next to Uxbridge Road in 1861 with children William P. (9), George, Edith H, Ada J, Mary A. Gruggen visitor from Chichester and four servants, however William H. Crake gave his address as 7 Elgin Crescent, Notting Hill in 1862. The Indian crisis passed with the relief of Lucknow and the imposition of British rule thus the Crakes returned to Madras and had two further sons there: Arthur Hamilton (1863) and Douglas Hamilton (1865). The family returned to England on a permanent basis in c.1866 and moved to a property at 34 Gloucester Square, Paddington just around the corner from 10 Stanhope Street. The house was located at the northeast corner between Radnor Place and the open green of the 'square' and a last child Lawrence Hamilton was born there on 15 April 1868 and baptized at nearby St. James's on 13 June that year. The eldest two sons were educated at Harrow during this period viz. William Parry (1866-70) and George (1868-70) - both were in Mr. Bull's house and no doubt E.E. Bowen taught them modern subjects, languages and sport. William Hamilton Crake, East India merchant, lived at 34 Gloucester Square in 1871 with his wife Jane, children Edith, Ada, Arthur, Douglas and Lawrence, his niece Winifred Constance and nine servants.

The father William Crake died in 1863 however the family were well provided for and still owned properties in Paddington from which they received income. Indeed William's previous business relations soon influenced their future. Charles Thomas Lucas was born in London in 1820 and was a successful building contractor who did work with his brother (Sir) Thomas Lucas and perhaps with William Crake. There was an agreement dated 27 November 1852 between Charles Thomas Lucas and Thomas Lucas on the one part and Samuel Morton Peto and James Peto on the other. This related to "15 messuage or dwelling houses with another 6 lately erected" that included 7-8 Kirkley Cottages later 170-172 London Road near Lowestoft. Peto had conveyed the property to Lucas the latter being the builder, and he was subject to pay Peto £21 p.a. for life. There was also a clause stating the properties could not be converted to an inn or used for noisy or offensive trades. Samuel Morton Peto lived nearby at Somerleyton Hall and was discussed regarding Betts in Chapter 6.

Charles Thomas Lucas lived at "Sister House", Battersea Rise, on the north side of Clapham Common in the 1850s-60s and with his wife Emma had children Charles James (1852), Alfred George (1854), Frederick M. (1859) and Florence (1864). He worked with his brother Thomas and merged with John Aird M.P. a contractor who was a household name to form *Lucas and Aird*. Together they worked on the Metropolitan District Railway, the Albert Hall, the International Exhibition 1862 and that at South Kensington in 1871. Indeed John Aird & Co. also worked on the original Crystal Palace and the football ground in 1894 (see Ch. 12). Lucas was in the same mould as Edward Ladd Betts and collected art from the beginning thus as his wealth increased he moved to larger houses. He commissioned art like Betts and with J.M.W. Turner promoted the work of David Roberts. The latter was persuaded to do a series of seven paintings of the capital and the first of these was a view of the Houses of Parliament as seen from Millbank. This was painted for Charles Lucas in 1861 and exhibited at the Royal Academy the following year. Henry Tredcroft had designed Warnham Court near Horsham in 1829 with a park, gardens and pleasure grounds and Lucas purchased the estate in 1865. He kept his sculptures and paintings at Warnham and at 9 Belgrave Square in London.

His son Alfred George Lucas was born on 26 October 1854 and married Edith Hamilton Crake at Kensington in March 1877. The couple resided at Kirkley near Lowestoft and had children Eveline (1878), Sybil (1879) and Muriel (1881) whilst Alfred played for the M.C.C. in 1879. Charles Thomas Lucas (60) contract builder lived at Warnham Court Mansion in 1881 with his wife Emma, sister Anne (63), his four children born Clapham, daughter-in-law Edith and three grand children, and four visitors - a railway director, a banker and foreign subjects from Geneva and Russia. This was a vast estate and there were 20 servants in the house, a groom and coachman and five of their assistants in the stables, and four in the gardener's lodge. The obituary of Charles T. Lucas was in the Times on 6 December 1895 and Christies sold his sculptures on 13 February 1896 and his paintings on 16 May 1896. Many of the latter remained in the family and brother Thomas and son George purchased them including the Houses of Parliament by Roberts. This had several owners and price increases whilst the London Museum is the current owner. Alfred G. Lucas army colonel lived at St. James's, Westminster in 1901 whilst wife Edith H. resided at 10 Kirkley Cliff, Kirkley with children Sybil M., Muriel, Wilfred S. a 2nd lieutenant Royal Suffolk Hussars, and Alfred. The father died at Hove in June 1941 age 86. The sister Ada had a similar story and was visiting her great uncle at Watford in 1881, there being a large household. Indeed Dixon Williams Arthur Teage, visitor and relative, married Ada Jane Crake at Kensington in June 1883. He was a merchant in Portugal and the couple initially returned to Porto and a son Henry was born there in 1886, whilst Ada J. Teage lived at Haversham near to Wolverton (and Milton Keynes) in 1901 with her son Henry a scholar.

William H. Crake, East India merchant, lived at 34 Gloucester Square in 1881 with his wife Jane however all his children were away and there were seven servants including a butler, footman and lady's maid. He was listed as a partner in Crawford, Colvin & Co. merchants at 71 Old Broad Street, London in 1882 whilst his two younger sons attended Harrow at this time: Arthur Hamilton (1877-81) and Lawrence Hamilton (1882-86) both in the Headmaster's house. William Hamilton Crake a merchant of 50 Old Broad Street died at 34 Gloucester Square, Paddington on 22 November 1883 aged 59. Jane Crake widow and George Crake son of the Tamar Brewery, Devonport proved his will at an initial value of £209,825 14s 9d but re-sworn in June 1887 at £209,820 7s 10d. Jane Crake lived at 34 Gloucester Square for the rest of her life but died at Borrowstone near Aberdeen in 'North Britain' on 27 October 1895 and her death was registered in Kincardine O'Neil between Aboyne and Banchory. Her sons William Parry Crake Esq., George Crake brewer and Arthur Hamilton Crake Esq. proved her will in London on 21 December 1895 her effects being £16,469 8s. 34 Gloucester Square was once located on the corner with Radnor Place however the area is much altered and only a few old stucco buildings survive. An L.C.C. blue plaque was erected at no. 35 in 1905: "In memory of Robert Stephenson (1803-59) engineer who died here," but was moved to a new location when the property was rebuilt in 1937. This suggests that the Crakes' home was demolished just before the Second War.

George Crake was born Madras in 1854 and attended Harrow in 1868-70 at the same time as his brother William P. and after leaving school may have spent time in India. George Crake (27), brewer, was a lodger with Robert Clark a retired hotelkeeper and widower (with three children and two servants) at Carlisle House, Lowestoft in 1881, and he may have been there due to the Lucas family. He was owner of the Tamar Brewery at 12 Tamar Street, Plymouth from at least 1883-1900 and lived at Ivybridge in 1901. He died at Kensington in September 1922 aged 68 years. Arthur Hamilton Crake was born Madras in 1863 and was educated at Harrow in 1877-81. Henry M. Butler (47), married, born Gayton, Northampton the Headmaster of Harrow lived at the High Street, Harrow on the Hill in 1881 and his boarders included Arthur H. Crake (18) and Howard E. Betts (16) brother of Morton, scholars. Note: Gayton House is located on Grove Hill (see Bowen). Arthur matriculated at Pembroke College, Oxford on 10 November 1881 and gained his B.A. in 1885 and M.A. in 1889 and may have worked with his brother George since he died in Plymouth on 27 April 1897 aged 34 years.

Douglas Hamilton Crake was born Madras in 1865 and did not go to Harrow but had a private education. He was a boarder and scholar with Baron Hitchens (47) born St. Ives, married, curate of Ottershaw M.A. Oxon at Almnero House, Chertsey in 1881. This was an exclusive school and included two American visitors and only six boarders, one of these being Arthur R. Wood (17) born London. He was a pensioner at Jesus College, Cambridge on 1 October 1882 and matriculated in Michaelmas 1882 although it is unclear if he obtained a degree. He was absent from the 1901 census and died at Uxbridge in September 1929 aged 64 years. Lawrence Hamilton Crake was born at Paddington and baptized at St. James's on 13 June 1868 and attended Harrow in 1882-86. He was a member of the shooting VIII in 1885-86, captain in 1886 and also won the Spencer Cup the same year. He lived at 46 Cambridge Street, Hyde Park in 1900 near to his brother William and a former residence of the Welch family - they lived at 57 Cambridge Street in the 1880s (see below). He died at Plympton in March 1942 aged 72 years.

William Parry Crake was born in Madras on 11 February 1852 and lived with his family in India in 1852-56, and then at Ealing and Notting Hill in 1859-62. One assumes he travelled with them to India in 1863-65 before residing at 34 Gloucester Square and was educated at Harrow School in 1866-70 although he was in Mr. Bull's house (not that of Edward Bowen). He excelled at school sport being in the football XI (1868-69) and the cricket XI (1869-70) and although young was recognized as a talented player. The master E.E. Bowen presumably put his name forward and he played for England against Scotland at the Oval in 1870 (the Harrow records state 1871). This was clearly a success for William and he then played for the Wanderers in the first Cup Final in 1872, however this was his last game of note. It is likely he went to Madras to work for the family business after leaving school and this explains his absence from other major soccer games. Thomas Alexander Nicholls Chase and wife Anne Binny resided at Masulipatam (later Bandar) in the 1850s a settlement 200 miles north of Madras on the Krishna Delta. They had three children born and baptized there namely Georgiana (1855), Emily Noble (1856) and Anne Hall (1857). The middle daughter was born at Masulipatam on 29 April 1856 and baptized on 28 May her father being in the army or Civil Service. There is no record of William Parry Crake in England in 1881 and he married Emily Noble Chase in Madras in c.1882.

The picture then becomes clearer and the couple had two sons born in Madras: Ralph Hamilton Crake (13 April 1884) and Eric Hamilton Crake (25 January 1886) however the family ended their connection with India on a permanent basis and William was a merchant in London in the late 1880s. He lived at 31 Norfolk Crescent, Paddington near to his mother Jane Crake in 1892 the house looking out on a green just behind Edgware Road. The area is now completely redeveloped except for St. John's Church on Hyde Park Crescent. William retired from business in 1893 and was described as 'a late merchant in India' and then sent his two sons to Harrow School. The grand life was over and William and Emily Crake lived at 31 Norfolk Crescent in 1901 - he was a retired merchant with three servants. There were few changes although his son Eric immigrated to Kenya in 1912 and William Parry Crake died at 31 Norfolk Crescent near Hyde Park on 1 December 1921 aged 69. His widow Emily Noble Crake proved his will on 17 February 1922 and his effects came to £23,705 6s 1d and this was noted in the Times on Friday 24 February. Emily later resided at Langham Hotel, Portland Place a building with the grandest of façades opposite to All Souls', Marylebone - it is still present today. She died there on 14 April 1935 age 78 and Ralph Hamilton Crake lieutenant colonel, her surviving English relative, obtained her probate on 28 June the amount £9,205 19s 3d.

Ralph Hamilton Crake was born Madras in 1884 and educated at Harrow in 1896-1900 and was in Mr. Moss's house. Like his brother Eric he exhibited considerable sporting ability and he played in the school cricket XI in 1900 but left to join the K.O.S.B. and was a gentleman cadet aged 18 in Berkshire in 1901. He excelled at cricket and was a lower order batsman and wicket keeper playing for the M.C.C. in 1901 and was on a European tour in 1920-21. He was a lieutenant colonel in H.M. Army in 1935 and died at Dean, Edinburgh on 26 January 1952. Eric Hamilton Crake his brother was born Madras in 1886 and went to Harrow in late 1900 and resided at the school aged 14 in 1901. He was a middle order batsman for the M.C.C. in 1912 but rain stopped play and he emigrated the same year, and died at Nakuru, Kenya on 3 February 1948.

EDGAR LUBBOCK

The victory of the Wanderers in 1872 was largely due to a strong defence and their contribution was described in the "Sportsman" newspaper thus: "It was in some measure the superiority of the backs on the side of the Wanderers that tended to produce the defeat of the Sappers, as the certainty of kicking displayed by Lubbock and Thompson throughout enabled the forwards of the victors to attack without fear." Edgar Lubbock the first of these defenders came from a distinguished family whose achievements are almost endless and their ancestry is traced to Norfolk. William Lubbock married Elizabeth Cooper at Paston on the coast near to North Walsham on 26 October 1742 and was then the rector of Lamas on the River Bure ten miles from Norwich. A son John was born c.1744 and married Elizabeth Christina Commerell at St. Dunstan in the East on 12 October 1771. She was baptized at St. Thomas the Apostle, London on 2 September 1752, daughter of Frederick and Catherine. He was a successful London merchant and was created a baronet on 9 April 1806 and this was a good springboard for the family's success. William Lubbock the second son was baptized at Lamas on 6 July 1746 and married Anna in c.1772. They had four children born at Lamas with Little Hautbois: John William (1774), Charles (1777), Anna Elizabeth (1779) and Maria (1782). The will of William Lubbock of Lamas was proved at the P.C.C. on 3 December 1823.

John William Lubbock was baptized at Lamas on 26 August 1774 and joined his uncle as a merchant and banker in London, and married Mary daughter of James Entwisle Esq. of Rusholme at Manchester Cathedral on 1 August 1799. A son John William Lubbock was born at Duke Street, Piccadilly on 26 March 1803 and baptized at St. Margaret's, Westminster on 19 May that year (the only surviving son). The baptism may have taken place there since it was near New Palace Yard with its political and banking connections. The family stayed in London however due to their success purchased the High Elms Estate between Downe and Farnborough, Kent in 1808. The land was used for commercial reasons, rather than a country home, and the family engaged in sheep rearing and later mixed farming i.e. cattle and cereal crops. There were two marriages: Hugh William Brown married Anna Elizabeth Lubbock at St. Martin in the Fields on 24 September 1801 and had children at St. James's, Westminster: Eliza Maria L. (1808), Emma Christiana L. (1816), Hugh William L. (1816) and Mary L. (1818). William Jex Blake married Maria Lubbock at Lamas on 11 June 1811 and had children William (1812) *infant*, William Lubbock Jex (1817-77) and Maria Catherine (1813) - the latter two at Swanton Abbott.

Sir John Lubbock Bart of St. James's Place made his last will on 25 March 1814 with many bequests to his family. He left to his wife Lady Elizabeth Lubbock cash of £500, jewels, coach and chariot, horses and harness. Under the will of Thomas Elton of Little Gaddesden, Herts he was entitled to the interest on £8,000 and left this to his wife, then to his dear partner and nephew John William Lubbock and his dear brother William Lubbock. His wife was to retain his property at St. James's Place and his furniture and paintings, whilst his nephew was to pay his wife an annuity of £300 p.a. from a sum of £2,200 (part of the £8,000) that would rise to £500 if the house were sold. If his wife re-married the amount was reduced to £100 and his nephew J.W. Lubbock was to receive the house. He owned estates at Great Hautbois and Banningham (with advowsons and rectories), and leaseholds, and these were for his wife free of any husband. J.W. Lubbock was to dispose of his estate and deliver £5,000 to his partner John Alden Clarke as a bond to Lady Lubbock. This money was in trust for his niece Annie Eliza Brown wife of Hugh William Brown of St. James's Place. A similar £3,500 was placed in trust for niece Maria Blake wife of the Rev. William Jex Blake clerk of Lamas. There was a bond between J.W. Lubbock and his brother William Lubbock to pay an annuity of £300 and he cancelled the debts of his brother.

He also left several amounts to his family: Hugh William Brown £1,000, Rawdon Lubbock Brown and Anna E. Brown £1,000, Anna Lubbock Brown and Anna E. Brown £1,000, Anna L., Eliza L. and Emma L. Brown £500, John William Lubbock the younger £1,000, Maria Catherine Blake and Maria Blake £500. These amounts were adjusted if any of the parties married (including his wife) and he invested

£500 for William Jex Blake at his wife's decease. He purchased the above rectories on the decease of the incumbents and J.W. Lubbock was to have these and give the livings to William Jex Blake. He left £100 to John Alden Clarke for his trouble, £20 to his partners Edward Forster and Oliver Colt and to Mr. Dalton, clerk in the banking house at Mansion House Street. He left the residue to John William Lubbock and stated, "I repose the highest confidence in his honour and integrity and appoint him sole executor." He was to be buried in the family vault in the chancel of North Walsham Church or elsewhere at his executor's discretion. He added two codicils and left Banningham Rectory to Rev. William Jex Blake and further amounts to niece Maria Blake on 10 October 1814, and land he had purchased from Rev. Church to the executors of the late Mary Church on 24 September 1815. He died without any issue and the baronetcy passed to his brother's son thus Sir John W. Lubbock proved the will in London on 19 March 1816.

The second baronet became head of the banking firm Lubbock & Co. and they were listed in a trade directory of 1817 viz. Sir John Lubbock, Forster & Clarke bankers at 11 Mansion House Street, London. There was also a listing for Robarts & Curtis at 15 Lombard Street and more of this anon. Sir J.W. Lubbock Bart. M.P. lived at 25 St. James's Place (sic) and High Elms in 1820, whilst the bank was at 11 Mansion House Street in 1829. In fact there were 69 banks in London at this time and Coutts & Co. was at 59 the Strand (see below). John senior, however, then resided at High Elms hence his son came to prominence. John William Lubbock (1803) embarked on an eminent life and was educated at Eton College and matriculated at Trinity College, Cambridge in 1821 gaining a B.A. in 1825 (M.A. in 1833). He was an excellent mathematician who preferred original work to studies and after travelling briefly in 1825 entered his father's bank and engaged in a life of arduous enquiry. He was on the Committee of the *Society for the Diffusion of Useful Knowledge* from 1829 (Monty Python) and, on a more serious note, joined the Astronomical Society in 1828 and the Royal Society in 1829. He produced a number of learned papers throughout his life and his main work was on aspects of astronomy and tidal observations but he also wrote on climatic change, the banking industry and probabilities regarding life assurance.

He was made Treasurer of the Royal Society from 1830-35 and married Harriet daughter of Lieutenant Colonel George Hotham and Caroline Gee on 29 June 1833. Her parents married at St. Mary's, Hull in 1792 and lived at Beverley and South Dalton in Yorkshire - Harriet their last child was baptized at Bishop Burton, near to Beverley, on 19 August 1810. John William and Harriet Lubbock first lived at 29 Eaton Place near Belgrave Square in London and produced a family of eleven children. The house had a white stucco ground floor and red brick with white pilasters on the upper storeys - the Bonsors lived at 51 Eaton Place (see Ch. 6). The couple had six children at 29 Eaton Place: John (1834), Mary Harriet (1835), Diana Hotham (1836), Henry James (1838), Nevile (1839) and Beaumont William (1840) - all baptized at St. Peter's, Pimlico in nearby Eaton Square. Indeed the house is one of the few residences relating to this history with an L.C.C. blue plaque, it states: "Sir John Lubbock Baron Avebury 1834-1913 Born Here". There are no plaques to early soccer players in the capital and although it was not John who played the game, this was close!

John William Lubbock was variously described as a banker, merchant and gentleman at this time and was also Vice-President of the Royal Society from 1838-47 and first Vice-Chancellor of London University in 1837-42. His father John William Lubbock senior of 'Mansion House' died at High Elms, Kent on 22 October 1840 and his will was proved on 13 November, which brought about family changes. He became Sir John William Lubbock the third baronet and inherited 23 St. James's Place, Piccadilly, but mostly led a retired life at High Elms in Kent. He put much energy into developing the estate in the 1840s and the house was enlarged in the Classical Italian style. Gardens were laid out with an extensive programme of tree planting and on the business side he was an enthusiastic farmer with herds of shorthorns and 'south-downs'. He promoted the education of the local poor but also taught his children mathematics and often spent the early mornings and evenings in profound enquiries! The family lived in an Elysian paradise with landscaped grounds around a Classical mansion but were also philanthropic, being a major contributor to society who pushed back the bounds of knowledge. These could not have been the aristocrats so reviled by Arthur Pember.

The family alternated their time between Downe and London and their other children were born thus: Montagu (1842) *London*, Frederic (1844) *Downe*, Alfred (31 October 1845) *St. James's*, Edgar (22 February 1847) *St. James's* and Henrietta Harriet (1849) *Downe*. Sir John W. Lubbock guided the bank through a general commercial panic in 1847 and was one of the treasurers of the Great Exhibition in 1851. He was described as, "A banker, merchant, farmer employing 20 labourers or more," at High Elms in 1851 and the household included his wife Harriet, his eldest John, Mary and Diana and youngest Frederic, Alfred, Edgar and Henrietta and eleven servants. He was the proprietor of Lubbock, Forster & Co. at 11 Mansion House Street in 1851 with partners Edward Forster and his relative George Hotham, whilst Robarts, Curtis & Co. was at 15 Lombard Street. He continued to guide the bank with great skill through a further commercial panic in 1857, and effected the amalgamation of the two banks to form Robarts, Lubbock & Co. trading at both City addresses in 1860.

Sir J.W. Lubbock Bart, banker and merchant, lived at the High Elms Estate in 1861 and the property was fully occupied at the time. The household included wife Harriet, John and his wife, Henry and Beaumont (all bankers), Montagu merchant, Frederick solicitor, Alfred and Edgar scholars, daughter Henrietta, nieces Lucy and Caroline Nevill, Frederica Entwisle from Manchester, grandchildren Amy, John Birkbeck and Constance Lubbock born at High Elms and 19 servants plus a visiting servant. Indeed there were 38 people in the house on that night in April 1861 thus revealing the sheer scale of High Elms. Sir John William Lubbock, however, was quite ill by this time and suffered from gout and general debility and died of 'valvular' disease of the heart at High Elms on 20 June 1865. His son Sir John Lubbock baronet of the same address proved his will on 10 October 1865 at £120,000. There may have had been some distribution before his death as it seems likely the estate and property at St. James's was worth much more. The family remained at Downe and Harriet Lady Lubbock died there on 12 February 1873. The next generation had many benefits associated with wealth and all eight sons attended Eton College. Their motto was "Auctor Pretiosa Facit" or "The Giver makes them valuable" thus they were reminded their privilege was a gift of God.

The first son began life as John Lubbock (1834) became Sir John Lubbock (1865) and then became 1st Lord Avebury (1900), which was some progression! John was born at 29 Eaton Place on 30 April 1834 but grew up in Downe and was inspired by his father and Charles Darwin, the family's neighbour, who lived at Downe House (1842-82) and published 'Origin of the Species' in 1859. The famous scientist encouraged young John, persuading his father to give him a microscope and this resulted in his great love and respect for nature and science. John was educated at Eton College and entered into banking however his main interest was science and mankind. He married Ellen Frances daughter of the Rev. Peter Hordern at Altrincham in June 1856, she was born at Chorlton-cum-Hardy, Lancashire in 1834. The couple resided at High Elms and had five children there: Amey Harriet (1857), John Birkbeck (1858), Constance Mary (1860), Norman (1861) and Rolfe Arthur (1866). John Lubbock became fourth baronet in 1865 and was head of Robarts, Lubbock & Co. and sold the premises at 11 Mansion House Street. The bank then operated solely at 15 Lombard Street as in the directories of 1871-82.

He was a fellow of the Royal Society soon after his marriage in 1858 and was a fellow of the Geographical Society, a member of the Royal Academy and President of the Linnean Society. He had honorary degrees from Oxford (9 June 1875), Cambridge, Dublin, Edinburgh and Wurzburg and was Vice-Chancellor of London University in 1874-80. He was influenced by the work of Charles Darwin and wrote a large number of learned papers especially regarding plants, these included: Prehistoric Times, the Origin of Civilisation and the Primitive Condition of Man, the Origin and Metamorphoses of Insects, Fifty Years of Science and the Scenery of Switzerland. Most men would have been exhausted by these commitments however he was also a Liberal Unionist and successfully contested West Kent in 1865 and 1868 and was M.P. for Maidstone from February 1870 to April 1880 (Gladstone was P.M. 1868-74). His election manifesto was quite clear: "To promote the study of science both in secondary schools and primary schools, to quicken the repayment of the national debt and to secure some additional holidays and shorten the hours of labour in the shops." No wonder he got the vote! He was busy in Parliament and introduced several acts including a Bank Holiday Act (1871), which made him very popular since it established the August Bank Holiday - although long forgotten it was once called St. Lubbock's Day. Ellen Frances died at High Elms in December 1879 and he was then elected to represent London University in Parliament from June 1880 to January 1900, thus he was obliged to resign the post of Vice-Chancellor.

General Augustus Henry Lane Fox-Pitt-Rivers had a career in the army but established himself as an anthropologist presenting his collections to Oxford University in 1883. John Lubbock had passed the Ancient Monuments Act in 1882 and came to know the general, a skilled archaeologist, who was then appointed first "Inspector of Ancient Monuments". He also met his daughter and John Lubbock married Alice Augusta Laurentia Lane (1862) in June 1884 having several children including Ursula (1885), Irene (1886) and Harold Fox Pitt (1888) born at High Elms. Sir John passed the Shop Hours Regulation Act in 1889 limiting hours for the under 18's to 74 hours per week and also passed other Shop Acts, the

Bankers Books Evidence Act, Open Spaces Act, Wild Birds Protection Act and Public Libraries Act. He was a trustee of the British Museum in 1891 and was clearly not one of the idle-aristocracy described by Arthur Pember.

Sir John Lubbock Bart M.P., Henry James, Beaumont William and John Birkbeck Lubbock were directors of Robarts, Lubbock & Co. at 15 Lombard Street in 1892. Indeed Sir John occupied a prominent position in the banking world being the Chairman of the London Bankers, Institute of Bankers, Chamber of Commerce and London County Council (hence the plaque at Eaton Place). He was finally rewarded for his endless sense of duty and contribution to the common good and was raised to the peerage as Lord Avebury in 1900. This reflected his interest in ancient monuments the title coming from Avebury Circle in Wiltshire. He was honorary rector of St. Andrew's University and Chairman of Robarts, Lubbock & Co. a clearing bank in 1908, having homes at 48 Grosvenor Street, Mayfair and 2 St. James's Square near to Nancy Astor (4) and Lord Kinnaird (10).

Baron Avebury, Right Hon John Avebury of Wiltshire died at Kingsgate Castle, Broadstairs on 28 May 1913 and sons John Birkbeck Baron Avebury and Harold Fox Pitt Lubbock proved his will his effects being £362,877 9s 11d but re-sworn at £315,137 9s 11d. 2nd Lord Avebury and Geoffrey Lubbock were directors of Robarts, Lubbock & Co. in 1914 however the old order was about to change and the bank was amalgamated with Coutts & Co. in 1915. The directors then included 2nd Lord Avebury, Geoffrey Lubbock, Harold Fox Pitt Lubbock and members of the Robarts family - they traded at 15 Lombard Street and 440 The Strand. Harold Fox Pitt Lubbock a lieutenant in the Grenadier Guards died in France on 4 April 1918, John Birkbeck 2nd Baron Avebury died on 26 March 1929 and Lady Alice Avebury died at High Elms on 11 March 1947. The estate was the family home for over 150 years but was sold to Bromley Council in 1965 and became a nurses training centre, whilst surrounding land was designated a green belt area and used partly as a golf course. A disastrous fire at High Elms destroyed the house on August Bank Holiday 1967, St. Lubbock's Day! This was a strange fate and there is a blue plaque on the site stating: "Lord Avebury - scientist, politician, author and banker lived at High Elms."

Henry James Lubbock was born 29 Eaton Place on 7 February 1838 and was educated at Eton and boarded in the 10th house, Keats Lane, Eton in 1851 near the Marindins at the 15th house. He joined Robarts, Lubbock & Co. and married Frances Mary Turton in 1866 and they had six children at Downe and Pimlico including Geoffrey Lubbock (1873). The family lived at 90 Eaton Place in 1879 and 8 Upper Belgrave Street in 1886, which was near the Ormes - 7 in 1878-86, Alfred Tennyson (1809-92) - 9 in 1880-81 and the Bonsors - 11 in 1889-1909. Indeed Bonsor, Lubbock and Kenyon-Slaney monopolised this area of London. Henry was High Sheriff for London in 1897 and master of the West Kent Harriers hunting with them for 13 years. He was keen on sport and amongst his pursuits were cricket, racquets, tennis, golf, hunting and shooting and he died on 25 January 1910. His son Geoffrey Lubbock was High Sheriff for London in 1913.

Nevile Lubbock was born at 29 Eaton Place on 31 March 1839 and also went to Eton but then took his own route. He made his debut for the Gentlemen of Kent in 1858 and played two matches for Kent C.C.C. in 1860. He married Harriet Charlotte Wood in 1861 and resided at North Cray, Kent having six children before Harriet died in 1878. He was a widower at 6 Onslow Gardens, Kensington in 1881 and was described as a West India Merchant but married again to Constance Ann Herschel in late 1881. He held a number of important posts including President of the West India Committee, Governor of the Royal Exchange Assurance Corp., a director of the Colonial Bank and Vice-President of the Royal Colonial Institute. He became Sir Nevile Lubbock K.C.M.G. in 1899 and lived for a time at "Oakley House", Bromley Common enjoying music and golf and died on 12 September 1914. His son Charles Western Lubbock (1862) was educated at Eton and matriculated at Balliol College, Oxford on 1 February 1882 and daughter Edith Harriet Lubbock (1867) married Norman Lubbock the son of Lord Avebury in 1919.

Beaumont William Lubbock was born at 29 Eaton Place (1840) and was somewhat elusive, as he did not appear in Who's Who. He was an unmarried banker residing at Wicklow Lodge, Melton Mowbray in 1881 and the household included visitors Charles T. Praed banker, Andrew A. Brand merchant, George B. Parker no calling B.A. Cambs. and nine servants. He also gave an address at 7 Clarges Street, Mayfair a property he shared with his brother Edgar Lubbock. He was a director of Robarts, Lubbock & Co. in 1892, a banker of 15 Lombard Street in 1907 and died on 19 March 1909. Montagu Lubbock was born in London on 24 May 1842 and was educated at Eton where he was a good all rounder being in the football and cricket XI, the boating eight and a winner at running, hurdles and fives, president of the debating society and captain of walking and golf. He was captain of the 11th Kent Volunteers in 1859 and a merchant living at High Elms in 1861 but then trained as a doctor in Paris and London. He qualified as Montagu Lubbock M.D. F.R.C.P. and worked at West London and Charing Cross Hospitals. He married his relative Lora daughter of Captain George Hotham of the Royal Engineers in 1872 however she died in 1882. He married Nora daughter of Nottidge Charles MacNamara F.R.C.S. of the Lodge, Chorley Wood in 1888 and resided at 19 Grosvenor Square in 1901 and 127 Mount Street, Berkeley Square - he died on 8 April 1925.

Frederic Lubbock was born at Downe on 1 May 1844 and was also at Eton and was described as a solicitor in 1861. He married Catherine the eldest daughter of John Gurney of Earlham Hall, Norfolk in 1869. Their son Guy Lubbock was baptized at Downe in 1870 and they also had children Cecil (1872), Samuel Gurney (1873), Percy (1879), Violet C. (1881) and later Roy (1892) and Alan (1897). His wife Catherine was born in Norfolk in c.1850 and she was a member of the extensive Gurney family who were Quakers, bankers and social reformers. An earlier generation saw John Gurney marry Catherine Bell and have an extensive family including their daughter Elizabeth. She was born 21 May 1780 and married Joseph Fry cousin of J.S. Fry who started the chocolate and confectionery business. She visited the poor near Earlham and at 15 was acquainted with the *House of Correction* in Norwich and later worked for Newgate Prison, the homeless, prisons abroad and conditions of transportation. Her husband went bankrupt in 1828 but she continued as a minister for the Society of Friends and died at Ramsgate on 12 October 1845 being interred at the Friends Burial Ground in Barking. **Note** Priscilla Bell sister of Catherine married into the Wakefield family settlers of New Zealand; they were daughters of Daniel Bell and Katherine Barclay of the Quaker and banking family (see Ch. 4).

Frederic a West India merchant lived at 19 South Audley Street, Mayfair in 1881 with his wife Catherine, children Cecil, Samuel, Percy and Violet and six servants. Frederic was Chairman of the London Board of the Bank of New Zealand and was also involved with the London Merchant Bank, the London Assurance Corp. and the British Bank of South America Ltd. He later had a home at 26 Cadogan Gardens, Sloane Square and a country residence Emmetts at Ide Hill near Sevenoaks, Kent. The property was at the top of the sandstone hills and looked out across the Weald and remains today, the gardens belonging to the National Trust. Frederic Lubbock died at Emmetts on 22 June 1927 and he and his brothers had many notable properties. The family fortune was evenly distributed following the tradition of *Gavelkind* practiced in Kent for centuries. Percy Lubbock was born in London in 1879 and was educated at Eton and Cambridge. He was curate of Pepys' Library, Magdalen College in 1906-08 and did an essay on Samuel Pepys in 1909. He wrote a technical book on the skill of writing called *The Craft of Fiction* in 1921 based on the talents of Tolstoy, Flaubert and Henry James, it was later discussed by E.M. Forster during the Clark Lectures at Cambridge, 1927 (see Graham Ch. 1). His most notable work *Earlham*, written in 1922, vividly portrayed the summers of his youth spent at the Gurney estate near Norwich. He described it as, 'A beautiful old house, red and mellow, spacious, sun-bathed.' He also wrote Roman Pictures (1923), The Region Cloud (1925), Shades of Eton (1929) and Portrait of Edith Wharton (1947). He died in 1965 and the Earlham Estate was later part of East Anglia University.

Alfred Lubbock was born at St. James's on 31 October 1845 and with most options covered entered into sport in a big way. He attended Eton College from 1856-63 and was captain of the Eton XI in 1863. He played four matches comprising eight innings for Kent C.C.C. in 1863-75 and was on the Fitzgerald tour of North America in 1872 although this was not first class cricket. He was a promising young cricketer but gave the sport up for a career in banking. He was an underwriter of St. George's Hanover Square and married Louisa daughter of Hermann Wallroth merchant at St. Nicholas', Chislehurst on 1 October 1874. His bride was born in Lewisham in March 1848, and her brother Conrad Adolphus born at Lee in 1851 played cricket for Kent and Derbyshire - two innings, eight runs with the former (1872). Alfred played with his brother Edgar Lubbock, A.G. Bonsor and A. F. Kinnaird for the Old Etonians against the Engineers in the Cup Final replay on 16 March 1875 (they lost 2-0). Alfred a gentleman lived with wife Louisa and son Robin at High Road, Whetstone, Friern Barnet in 1881 and died at Kilmarth Manor, Par near St. Blazey in Cornwall on 17 July 1916. Louisa Lubbock died at Hailsham, Sussex in June 1943 aged 95 years.

Edgar Lubbock was born at 23 St. James's Place, Piccadilly on 22 February 1847 and baptized at St. James's Church on 21 March that year. The house of his birth is still present and is little altered at the rear but modernized at the front. It looks out across Green Park and is beside an historic pathway marked on old maps. Edgar grew up in the spacious surrounds of High Elms and lived there on both the 1851 and

1861 census and attended Eton College from 1859-66 - at the same time as A.F. Kinnaird. He was in the Eton XI three years and the captain in 1866 being a good middle order, right hand batsman and a noted fast under-arm bowler. He was, however, in the losing side against Harrow at Lord's during those years. He made his debut in 1st class cricket for the Gentlemen of Kent in 1866 and played two innings for Kent C.C.C. in 1871 - he scored 65 runs with a high score of 54 and bowling figures of 0 for 23.

He made his mark in the world of football and played for the Wanderers in the first Cup Final in March 1872 then went on the Fitzgerald North American tour in the summer of 1872. This was his only major game for the Wanderers and he then appeared for the Old Etonians in the Cup Finals of 1875 (both games) and 1876 (replay) although lost on both occasions. This was basically the end of his sporting career. He trained in the law but had a natural aptitude for business and changed direction to follow in the footsteps of the Bonsors. John Birkbeck Lubbock (1858), his nephew, went to Eton and matriculated at Balliol College, Oxford on 19 October 1878 and was a blue in 1881. He played for the Old Etonians v Clapham Rovers in the 1879 Final winning 1-0 and for Oxford University v the same opponents in the 1880 Final losing 1-0. John was the only family member at Oxford at the time and the records simply state that "Lubbock" played. He was an undergraduate visiting William R. Anson Bart barrister M.A. B.C.L Oxon at 'Elm Hill', Hawkhurst in Kent in 1881, and the household included two Anson sisters and four visitors from Oxford. John became a student at Lincoln's Inn in 1882, gained his B.A. and M.A. in 1885 and was then a member of Robarts, Lubbock & Co.

Edgar Lubbock became a partner in the Whitbread Brewery in 1875 (see Kinnaird Ch. 5 and Bonsor Ch. 6) and the details are worth discussing more fully. Samuel Whitbread senior came from a strict nonconformist family and inherited a small property in Bedford, but went to work at a London brewery as a young man in 1748. The brewery took premises at Chiswell Street south of Bunhill Fields and near the present day Barbican in 1750. Samuel Henry was initially a clerk but after some hard work and good fortune he owned the whole brewery, and it was the largest in the country by the end of the 18th century. He married Harriet daughter of William Hayton of Ivinghoe and their son Samuel Whitbread junior was born Cardington near Bedford in 1758. The family amassed a large fortune and purchased Cardington Manor in 1769 and commissioned John Smeaton builder of Eddystone Lighthouse (now on Plymouth Hoe) to design the village's bridge. N.B. The village later saw the maiden flight of the ill-fated R101 airship; the family also owned Bedwell Park, Essendon.

The company then approached Boulton and Watt in June 1784 regarding the erection of a 10-h.p steam engine. Whitbread did not travel to Soho but went to see Goodwyn's engine at Lower East Smithfield (see Ch. 10). The work was vital to the company's success and couldn't wait thus it took place during the brewing season in December that year. They spent a vast sum of money at Chiswell Street engaging engineers-designers John Smeaton and James Watt, the result being handsome Georgian buildings housing modern equipment: "In the years 1784 and 1785 Messrs. Boulton and Watt made several rotative engines.... one of the first of these was set up at Mr. Whitbread's brewery in Chiswell Street.... Mr. Whitbread's engine was set to work in 1785" (*The Biography of James Watt*). The brewery and its buildings were renowned and the King visited them and had a demonstration in 1787. A stone tablet commemorates the event: "Their Majesties King George III and Queen Charlotte were received in this brewery by SAMUEL WHITBREAD 24th May 1787" - Boulton and Watt were related to one of the Royal Engineers (see Ch. 8).

The family fortune was very large and they purchased Southill Park, Bedfordshire from Lord Torrington in 1795 however Samuel Whitbread senior died in 1796. His son Samuel had a strict and religious home education then attended Eton and matriculated at Christchurch, Oxford in July 1780. His progress was slow and he was transferred to St. John's College, Cambridge gaining his B.A. in 1784 and then embarked on the 'grand tour' of Europe. He returned to England in May 1786 and entered into business at the brewery and married Elizabeth Grey (daughter of Earl Grey) in 1789. He was introduced to politics and represented Bedford as a Whig from 1790 and was closely attached to the Whig leader Charles James Fox. He was constantly at odds with William Pitt and with Lord Chatham and his brother-in-law Lord Grey. He proposed an elaborate poor-law bill in 1807 that provided free education for two years, but the wearing of badges to distinguish the 'deserving poor' was criticised by Malthus and others and eventually collapsed. He had a policy of appeasement towards France, which brought him into conflict with other Whigs and he put forward a peace resolution on 29 February 1808 but Lord Grey warned him of the dangers. This caused a split in the Whig party and the outcome was the disbandment of the opposition in 1809. He was a renowned talker and, "from 1809 up to the time of his death, Whitbread spoke more frequently than any member of the House of Commons." He became a keen supporter of the Princess of Wales in 1812, championed the oppressed and stood against war up until 1815.

Samuel was involved in the rebuilding of Drury Lane Theatre in 1809 and his negotiations with Sheridan and the like caused him great anxiety and annoyance. He was a public figure, and like today, had to take much criticism thus Lord Byron said, "He was the Demosthenes of bad taste and vulgar vehemence but strong and English," whilst William Wilberforce stated, "He spoke as if he had a pot of porter to his lips and all his words came through it." To balance this out Romilly said, "He was the promoter of every liberal scheme for improving the condition of mankind." During the dispute with Sheridan there were questions asked about his mental health and he was then in a distressed state, having the belief that his public life was over. The Chiswell Street engine was enlarged to 20-h.p in 1814, but this was of little interest and he took his own life at 35 Dover Street, Mayfair on 6 July 1815 and was buried at Cardington (see Willis Ch. 1). He owned 5/8ths of the brewery at the time since his father made it compulsory for him to retain a majority of the shares, and left sons William Henry M.P. for Bedford 1818-37 (died 1867) and Samuel Charles who retained control of the business and married Julia Brand in 1824 - they had a son Samuel in 1830. The buildings at Chiswell Street were mostly unchanged but there was further innovation and a side-lever boat type engine of 30-h.p was installed in 1841.

This was the highly lucrative set-up that Edgar Lubbock joined in 1875. He was an unmarried, brother and brewer living at 7 Clarges Street, Mayfair in 1881 and Beaumont head of the house was in Melton Mowbray. Clarges Street was opposite Green Park however no. 7 is no longer present. Edgar Lubbock a brewer of Mayfair married Amy Myddelton Peacock at Greatford on 23 June 1886 the witnesses John Lubbock, William C. Higgins, Mildmay Willson and Hugh Peacock. His bride was born at Stamford in March 1862 and was the daughter of Gilbert Peacock a banker of Greatford Hall, Stamford. Her brother Horace Ogilvie Peacock was born at St. Neots on 26 September 1869 and played cricket for Lincolnshire in 1892-95 and for the M.C.C. in 1896-99. The couple had some interesting domestic arrangements in 1891. Sidney C. Cross and his wife lived at 14 Berkeley Street, Mayfair and ran lodgings that included five separate apartments. Edgar Lubbock brewer and bank director (married), John Birkbeck Lubbock banker (single), Henry W. Whitbread brewer (single) and two army gentlemen occupied the apartments each with at least three rooms. The property remains on the east side but has been altered at ground floor level. Henry W. Whitbread was born in London in 1861 and was an employer and owner of the brewery and lived at 27 Mount Street, Berkeley Square in 1892. Samuel Whitbread M.P. and Lady Isabella lived at 10 Ennismore Gardens and Southill Park in 1881-82/92 (his parents - married 1855).

Amy Myddelton Lubbock lived at 13 North Parade, Grantham in 1891 this being the family home. The Lubbocks liked to socialize and Amy had several visitors including Edward A. Skrimshaw a local magistrate, Emilie Diltman of Franstadt, Poland (a German subject), Montague Hall of the 3rd Durham Light Infantry and eight servants including a French lady's maid from Calais. Edgar divided his time between the brewery and a life in the country however he was also made a director of the Bank of England in 1891. He liked hunting as a recreation and became master of the Blankney Foxhounds who were based south of Lincoln. Edgar and Amy had three daughters although they were born several years after their marriage, the first two: Nancy Induna Frances Caroline at Taplow, Eton in December 1897 and Bridget Myfanwy Gian at Westminster in September 1901. Edgar Lubbock was a man of influence and power who moved in notable social circles and had properties at North House, Grantham and Caythorpe (a few miles north) at the turn of the century. Indeed the couple's famous connections are revealed in the 1901 census. Edgar had swapped houses at this time and resided at 13 North Parade or "North House", Little Gonerby, Grantham being a bank director, brewer and employer with five servants. Lord Avebury lived next door to Nancy Astor at St. James's Square and this may account for the fact that Waldorf Astor was one of his guests in 1901.

William Waldorf Astor was born New York in 1848 and married Mary Dahlgren Paul in 1878 and had a son Waldorf there in 1879. The father owned the "Waldorf Astoria Hotel" in that city and then resided at Hever Castle in Kent (home of Anne Boleyn) and built a Tudor Village there for his guests - he was 1st Viscount Hever. The son Waldorf Astor a naturalised British subject was educated at Eton and New College, Oxford and married Nancy Witcher Shaw in 1906. She was daughter of Chiswell Dabney Langhorne of Mirador, Greenwood, Virginia and married Robert Gould Shaw but divorced in 1903. Waldorf Astor was the M.P. for Plymouth (Sutton) in 1910-19 and was mentioned in despatches in 1917, and a major in 1918. He was parliamentary secretary to the Prime Minister in 1917-18 and was attached to the Ministry of Food in 1918 and the Ministry of Health in 1919-21. He became 2nd Viscount at his father's decease in 1919 thus sitting in the House of Lords and owned the Observer newspaper. Nancy Astor then stood for her husband's seat in Parliament and was elected for Plymouth (Sutton) in 1919 thus becoming the first woman M.P. to take up her seat. Countess Constance de Markiewcz had been elected before her, but as a member of Sinn Fein wanted an independent Ireland and would not sit in London. Nancy held the seat until 1922 and although a society lady dressed simply and said, "I want to make it possible for the humblest woman who may be elected to follow the precedent I have set." The Astors owned "Cliveden House" at Cookham before the war, a meeting place of politicians and other celebrities known as the 'Cliveden Set'. They entertained German diplomats and this led to charges of appeasement however Lady Astor helped Churchill to power in 1940.

Amy Lubbock, meanwhile, lived at "The Court", Caythorpe with Frieston, Lincolnshire, in 1901 with daughters Nancy and Gian (Bridget), father Gilbert Peacock banker, brother Hugh Peacock brewer and 20 servants. She also had several guests including Bache Edward Cunard a member of the famous shipping family who was born in New York in 1852. The Lubbocks had a further property at Hatfield and their last daughter Marigold Rosemary Stella was born there in September 1903. Edgar Lubbock of Caythorpe and Grantham and the Brewery, Chiswell Street made his last will on 25 August in 1904 - an extensive document. He gave a legacy of £1,000 to his brother Beaumont William and £500 to Edith Harriet daughter of Nevile and then left money to his butler, stud groom, second horseman, cook and helpers. To his wife he confirmed the gift of carriage, horses and equipment already in her possession at Essendon Place, Hatfield. He also gave her all his household goods and an immediate legacy of £5,000 and a lifetime annuity of £4,000 p.a. He discussed 838 ordinary shares listed in the Articles of Association of Whitbread & Co. Ltd. these being for, "the benefit of my daughters for their lives." The shares were to be placed in trust for the girls beyond the control of any husband - they could be retained or sold.

Edgar Lubbock, Frederick DuCane Godman and Whitbread & Co. Ltd. had an agreement dated 12 August 1904 stating that any dividends were to be retained for the business at the discretion of the Board of Directors. He empowered his trustees to release up to £10,000 to any of his daughters during their minority and asked them to deal with his investments, including his debenture stock in Whitbread & Co. He secured the payment of £4,000 to his wife on his freehold property at Caythorpe Court and North House in Grantham and freehold land in Welbourn Parish to the north of Caythorpe (towards Lincoln). Once the annuity was paid he left the land to any son on his attaining 21 years, or, if no son, to his daughters in order of age if they were outside of marriage. Finally, in the event of no son or unmarried daughter then the residuary estate was to be divided between the children of Nevile, Frederic and Alfred Lubbock. He witnessed the will before W.W. Hargrove solicitor and clerk at 99 Cannon Street, London. He added a first codicil and left a £2,000 annuity to Olivia Gertrude Louise Bastard of 21 Basil Street, Hans Crescent wife of John Algernon, this to be paid from the stocks and shares of Whitbread & Co. This was witnessed at Valpy, Peckham & Chaplin of 19 Lincoln's Inn Fields on 15 August 1905. He added a second codicil and revoked the immediate legacy of £5,000 to his wife and specified she should only have his household goods at Essendon Place, Hatfield. This was witnessed before A.W. Peckham and clerk at 19 Lincoln's Inn Fields on 20 June 1906.

Edgar Lubbock had risen to a prominent position and was for some time the Managing Director of Whitbread's Brewery and also a director of the Phoenix Insurance Society. Cosmo Bonsor had resigned as Deputy Governor of the Bank of England and Edgar Lubbock replaced him in the post in April 1907. He had not been trained in the preliminary offices, as was usual for such a position, but his legal education and general business knowledge meant he soon grasped the subject and had complete mastery of the difficult duties. He appeared to be in good health and was always keen on outdoor sport and was master of the Blankney Foxhounds until recent months. Edgar Lubbock died of a 'weak' heart at his flat 18 Hans Court, Knightsbridge, on 9 September 1907 aged 60 and was found by his valet who called him for his customary morning ride. His obituary appeared in the Times on Tuesday 10 September 1907 and his funeral took place at Caythorpe on the Thursday. The principal mourners included Mrs. Lubbock, Mr. H.J. Lubbock, Frederic Lubbock and Geoffrey Lubbock as well as Mr. F.A. Peacock and local dignitaries. A memorial service was held at St. Peter's, Eaton Square at the time and those present included Lord Avebury, Hon Gertrude Lubbock, Dr. Lubbock, Hon J.B. Lubbock, Mr. & Mrs. Alfred Lubbock, Mrs. Henry Lubbock, Basil Lubbock, Sir Nevile Lubbock, Beaumont Lubbock, Governor and directors of the Bank of England, Hon Hugh Boscawen, Sir Edward Birkbeck, Samuel Whitbread, H.W. Whitbread, Gordon Courage, J.R. Molyneux and employees of Whitbread & Co.

Beaumont William and John Birkbeck Lubbock bankers of 15 Lombard Street, Norman Lubbock of the Cottage, Orpington and Cecil Lubbock Esq. of Whitbread's Brewery proved his will in London on 9 November 1907, his effects £208,171 18s 10d. His wife Amy was left comfortably off but being 15 years younger was later remarried. The Trollope family can be traced to 1460 and owned 10,000 acres of land at Stamford in Rutland. John Henry Trollope (Lord Kesteven) was born 22 September 1851 and was educated at Eton and Magdalene College, Cambridge and served with the Imperial Yeomanry in South Africa in 1900. He married Amy Myddelton Lubbock at Stamford in March 1914 and they presumably moved in the same circles. They resided at Casewick Hall, Stamford but the marriage was short lived and he died at 27 Clifton Crescent, Folkestone on 23 July 1915. The estate went to his nephew Thomas Carew (Baron Kesteven) born 1891 but he died soon after at Baden Military Hospital, Oran, Algeria on 5 November 1915. Dorothy Nesta Trollope then owned the estate and married Fraude Dillon Trollope-Bellew and lived there up to 1934, whilst Sir Arthur Grant Trollope lived in Pietermaritzburg, South Africa and died at Helpston, Northants in 1937. Baroness Kesteven the Right Honourable Amy Myddelton of Shillingthorpe near Stamford died on 13 April 1941.

The Whitbread brewery at Chiswell Street was used until 1976 and the company also owned premises at 26 Wharf Road on the Grand Union Canal. The rich Georgian architecture was later restored to its former glory and became a private conference and function centre. The old brewery buildings are situated between Chiswell Street, Milton Street, Silk Street and Whitecross Street with the main entrance in Chiswell Street and to the right is a red brick Georgian house with stone plaque recording the visit of George III. There is an extensive cobbled courtyard and in the southeast corner is Watt's original two-storey engine house dated 1784, now heavily restored, whilst opposite the entrance is a clock tower building with dates 1887 and 1912. There is also a grand brick chimney that Fred Dibnah would have been proud of.

ALBERT CHILDERS THOMPSON

Edgar Lubbock's kicking partner in defence was the halfback A.C. Thompson however he proved difficult to trace. The most likely candidates on the 1881 census were Arthur C. Thompson and Alfred Cam Thompson who each had a suitable profile. The first was born at Swannington, Norfolk in 1850 and was a scripture reader and temperance agent living with his family at Egham, Surrey in 1881. The second was born at Grantham in 1846 and married Annie Doudney Densham at Lewisham in March 1874 being a bank manager at Stamford in 1881. Neither, however, quite fitted the social status of the Wanderers players and more significantly "Thompson" played for the Old Etonians. The answer was in the Eton College records since they showed that Albert Childers Meysey-Thompson was formerly A.C. Thompson.

The family came from Yorkshire and their ancestry is traced to 1066 and more recently to Jonas Thompson alive in 1460. They had several notable connections including Sir F. Fleming Master of Ordnance to Edward VI, Lord Hotham and General James Wolfe (a great grandson) who died taking Quebec in 1759. Sir Stephen Thompson was born in 1635 and succeeded by Henry Thompson born in 1677 who had the first connection with Kirby in Yorkshire, his brothers being merchants in Oporto, Portugal. The lineage continued with his sons Stephen Thompson born 1699, and then John Thompson born 1701 who married Elizabeth Croft and Mildred Childers, and by his first wife had a son Henry Thompson born 1743. The latter married Mary Spence on 30 January 1769 and their offspring included Henry whose heirs were connected to T. Croft esquire and Captain John Hotham. Their son Robert Stephen married Harriet daughter of Walbanke Childers and had offspring Childers Thompson, Harriet who married George Champney Lord Mayor of York (1828) in 1831, and Maria who married Sir James Walker the 1st Baronet of Sand Hutton. The Walker family appear later and had children Emily Mary (1848), Charlotte (1851) and Arthur (1855).

Richard John Thompson, the heir of Henry and Mary, was born at Kirby Hall on 24 January 1771 and baptized at Little Ouseburn on 25 January. He was a captain in the 4th Dragoons and a major hussar in the yeomanry residing at Kirby Hall, Little Ouseburn and the estate was north west of York. He married Elizabeth daughter of John Turton Esq. of Sugnall Hall, Staffs in 1803. Her mother Mary Meysey was daughter and co-heiress of Richard Meysey Esq. of Shakenhurst, Worcs the family being descended from the De Meyseys who came from Meysey, Brittany in 1066. These connections reveal the origins of some family names whilst the surname Hotham also appears regarding the Lubbocks. Richard John and Elizabeth Thompson lived at Kirby Hall and had ten children baptized at Little Ouseburn Church:

Eliza Mary (1804), Henrietta (1807), Richard William (1808) *infant*, Harry Stephen (1809), Caroline (1810), Thomas Charles (1811), Charlotte (1812), Amelia Frances (1815), Frederic William (1816) and Marianne (c.1818) however the mother Elizabeth died in 1840. Indeed Henry Thompson (30), Frederic (20), Caroline (30), Emily (25) and 15 servants lived at the 'Township' of Kirby Hall, Little Ouseburn in 1841 whilst a gardiner, a farmer at Aldworth Bridge and a brickyard also occupied the estate.

Harry Stephen Thompson the heir was born at Topcliffe near Thirsk on 11 August 1809 and baptized at Little Ouseburn on 15 August. He was unmarried in 1841 but this soon changed and he married Elizabeth Ann Croft at Maidstone, Kent on 26 August 1843. She was born at Thornton Watlass near Bedale, Yorkshire in 1819 but was probably baptized at Doddington in Kent her father being Sir John Croft baronet of Doddington Hall. This was a good match and the couple resided at Moat Hall near Little Ouseburn initially having the following children: Elizabeth Lucy (1844), Henry Meysey (1845), Richard Frederick (1847), Albert Childers (1848), Charles Maude (1849) and Mary Caroline (1851). Elizabeth A. Thompson resided at Moat Hall in 1851 with her six children and seven servants, however the father Richard John Thompson died in August 1853 thus the family moved to Kirby Hall and had the following children: Arthur Herbert (1852), Amelia Annie (1855), Florence Mildred (1856), Catherine Maude (1858) and Ernest Claude (1859). Harry Stephen Thompson was a local J.P. and became High Sheriff in 1856 then entered Parliament as M.P. for Whitby from 1859-65 - he replaced Robert Stephenson engineer in this post (1847 to his death in 1859). He resided at Thomas's Hotel, 25 Berkeley Square, London in 1858-61 this being a notable London hotel with an interesting history.

During his stay the residents included: Mrs. Jane Tatton, 8th Duke of Beaufort (Henry Charles Fitzroy Somerset 1824-99), Henry William Des Voeux Esq. and Lady Sophia, Lord Hatherton P.C., Viscount Hill, Hon. Rowland Clegg Hill M.P. for North Salop, Captain Washington and Mrs. Hibbert, the misses Hibbert, Earl of Bantry, Earl and Countess Bective and Lady Tyrconnell, whilst in Berkeley Square itself were Earl's, Marquis's, F.R.G.S., F.R.S., and six M.P.'s. 25 Berkeley Square was located between Jones Street and Bruton Place formerly North Bruton Mews in the north east corner, whilst Lansdowne House and its gardens occupied the southern end. The hotel itself was opened in c.1798 and was often mentioned in the annals of the Mayfair district. The Duke of Wellington called on Mrs. Porter at Berkeley Square hoping she would arrange a meeting with famous courtesan Harriette Wilson! He told his confidante: "If you have good news to communicate address a line to Thomas's Hotel." The establishment had a long life and P. Coles managed the hotel at 25-26 Berkeley Square in 1900-03 and it was described as Thomas's Hotel Ltd. in 1904, but does not appear in 1905-07 and was rebuilt at this time. The new building had 6 residents in 1908, 7 in 1909, 9 in 1910 and then 13 including Lord's in 1920-30 - Cadbury Schweppes occupy this grand white building today. The Earl of Lindsay was at no. 23 with its Victorian Classical façade in 1920-30 and Sir Herbert Kinnaird Ogilvy Bart grandson of George William Fox and Frances Anne Georgiana Kinnaird (see Ch. 5) was at no. 24 an old Georgian property still present today.

Harry Stephen Thompson could be contacted at the Travellers Club in 1860-65 and was listed at Kirby Hall from 1860. The latter was near to Thorp Underwood, Little Ouseburn village and Moat Hall and the family's life there is revealed on the 1861 census. Harry and Elizabeth lived at home and he was a deputy lieutenant magistrate, M.P. and farmer occupying 368 acres employing 10 men and 3 boys. The household included daughter Elizabeth Lucy (scholar), Henry Meysey, Richard Frederick, Albert Childers, Charles Maude and Arthur Herbert all "Etonians", Mary Caroline, Amelia Annie, Florence Mildred, Catherine Maude and Ernest Claude, Marianne Radcliff Croft born Marylebone in 1832 and 18 servants. It was a vast estate also with a carpenter, gamekeeper, farmer and farm bailiffs. Harry took a more permanent residence at 3 Mansfield Street near Portland Place and Cavendish Square in 1862-65 although the building is no longer present. He moved to 18 Mansfield Street, London in 1866-73 this being an extensive four-storey property with white stucco on all floors and a grand columned portico entrance. The Regency building remains today and notable people lived in Mansfield Street: John Loughborough Pearson and Edwin Landseer Lutyens architects (at no. 13) and Charles 3rd Earl Stanhope inventor and reformer (at no. 20). Indeed the Thompsons were at Mansfield Street from 1862-84.

Elizabeth Lucy Thompson was baptized at Little Ouseburn on 16 August 1844 and married Walter Stafford Northcote 2nd Earl of Iddesleigh on 23 September 1868. Elizabeth Anne Thompson resided at Kirby Hall in 1871 with Henry Meysey (25) magistrate and cornet to the Yorkshire Hussars, Albert Childers (22) student of law B.A., Charles Maude (21) undergraduate at Cambridge, Mary Caroline, Amelia Anne, Florence Mildred, Katherine Maude and Ernest Claude. The household also included Elizabeth Lucy and husband Walter Stafford Northcote student of law and cornet in 1st Devon yeomanry and cavalry, Stafford Henry Northcote son, Henrietta Maria E. Croft (1818) sister, Lavinia Louisa Bertie visitor daughter of Earl of Abingdon, Bertha Adolphine Kubel from Tübingen in Württemberg governess and 19 servants. There was a farm bailiff, lodge gatekeeper, gamekeeper and farmer of 120 acres on the estate, which had not diminished in any way! (See Addendum re Northcote).

The family had a notable heritage and the villages of Meysey Hampton and Marston Meysey are still present near Cirencester. They changed their surname to Meysey-Thompson in reference to these ancestors by deed poll on 19 February 1874 and the event was recorded in the Times four days later (not by Royal Licence as in other cases). Harry Stephen Meysey-Thompson became the 1st baronet on 26 March 1874 but may have invoked the curse of the Meyseys and died at Kirby Hall on 17 May 1874 - his title went to Henry Meysey Meysey-Thompson. The will with two codicils of Sir Harry Stephen Meysey-Thompson a late resident of Kirby Hall was proved at Wakefield on 13 July 1874. Rev. Thomas Charles Thompson of Ripley, Sir John Frederick Croft of Doddington Bart and William Gray of Yorkshire gent were executors his effects being valued at under £180,000. The family were entitled to a coat of arms consisting of three embattled falcons surmounted by a gauntlet and the motto was "Je Veux de Bonne Guerre", which literally means I want a good fight or feud, but a better translation is I want to see a fair fight - in keeping with the Eton traditions.

Katherine Maude Meysey-Thompson died in 1877 whilst Mary Caroline Meysey-Thompson married William Henry Bond on 2 July 1878. The son Henry resided at Kirby Hall after his father's death but was absent in 1881 and Lady Elizabeth Anne Meysey-Thompson lived at 18 Mansfield Street from 1876-84 and 45 Lennox Gardens, Pont Street, Knightsbridge by 1890. She was described as a dowager and was absent from home in 1891 but remained at Pont Street in 1892-93. The building was a red brick city mansion near St. Columba's Church and still remains today. The daughter Florence Mildred Meysey-Thompson died at Pynes House, Upton Pyne in Devon on 29 November 1893 although her usual residence was 45 Lennox Gardens and her probate went to Amelia Anne and Richard Frederick a colonel in the army. Dame Elizabeth Anne Meysey-Thompson was living at Holme Priory, Wareham, Dorset, by 1903 and died there on 28 March 1910 - her probate went to Henry Meysey Baron Knaresborough and Sir Lancelot Aubrey Fletcher Bart.

Henry Meysey Thompson was born at Moat Hall on 30 August 1845 and baptized at Little Ouseburn on 10 October that year. He attended Eton and Trinity College, Cambridge in 1863 giving his address as 18 Mansfield Street in 1873, he became 2nd baronet at his father's decease in 1874 and lived at 42 Albemarle Street, Mayfair and Kirby Hall in 1876-85. He was a Liberal Unionist and the M.P. for Knaresborough in 1880 but was absent from both addresses in 1881. He married Ethel Adeline daughter of Sir Henry Pottinger 3rd baronet in 1885 who was born at Walton on Thames in 1865. He returned to Parliament as M.P. for Brigg, Lincolnshire in 1885-86 and the couple had three children: Violet Ethel (1886), Claude Henry Meysey (1887) and Helen Winifred (1889). He was a J.P. and honorary major in the Yorkshire Hussar Yeomanry and lived at 2 Hamilton Place, London in 1890, which was near Hyde Park Corner and the Duke of Wellington's home Apsley House. No. 2 was on the west side but is no longer present whilst nos. 4-5 had a multi-columned façade on all floors and the Royal Aeronautical Society and Ambassadors Club now occupy these buildings.

Henry and Ethel Meysey-Thompson, three children and nine servants from England, Scotland and Belgium lived at Kirby Hall in 1891. Henry was M.P. for Handsworth, Staffs from 1892-1905 and his address was Kirby Hall and 2 Hamilton Place, London in 1892. He also had a property at Thorpe Green, Ouseburn but was absent from the 1901 census. He had a number of lucrative business interests being a director of the North East Railway and the Barrow Steel Co. and became 1st Baron Knaresborough. His only son Claude Henry Meysey a captain in the rifle brigade died at Bailleul, France on 17 June 1915, whilst Baroness Ethel Adeline Knaresborough of 57 Prince's Gate, Hyde Park died at Wadhurst, Sussex on 18 August 1922 - her probate went to Henry Meysey and Violet Ethel wife of Algar Henry Stafford Howard. The Right Hon. Henry Meysey Baron Knaresborough of 40 Charles Street, Berkeley Square died on 3 March 1929 and his executors included Hubert Charles Meysey-Thompson, his estate being worth £197,620 4s 11d.

Richard Frederick Thompson was born at Moat Hall on 17 April 1847 and married Charlotte Walker the youngest daughter of Sir James Walker Bart at Sand Hutton on 14 July 1879. They were second cousins and he was a major in the rifle brigade and colonel in the 4th Battalion, Prince of Wales Own West Yorkshire Regiment. They had children Violet Ileene Cassandra (1882) and Algar de Clifford Charles (1885) and Richard Frederick Meysey-Thompson died at Westwood Mount, Scarborough on

31 August 1926 and his estate was valued at £19,268 9s 11d his executrix being Violet Ileene Cassandra Knox (a widow). Charlotte his widow died at Westwood Mount on 3 March 1935 and her estate was then £68,434 7s 11d.

Charles Maude Thompson was born on 5 December 1849 and attended Eton and Cambridge (1868) and was a good football player. He was rector of Claydon, Winslow in Bucks and married Emily Mary Walker second daughter of Sir James Walker at Sand Hutton on 28 April 1874. They had a daughter Evelyn Charlotte (1875-83) and a son Harold James (1876). Charles "Thompson" played for the Old Etonians in both the initial games of the 1875 and 1876 Finals - the sides included A.G. Bonsor, A.F. Kinnaird and E. Lubbock. The couple resided at 31 Tavistock Square, Bloomsbury in 1876-77 (M.P. Betts was born at no. 29 see Ch. 6) however the family were at The Hall, Sand Hutton in 1881. James Walker (77) baronet and magistrate from York was the head and the household included son Arthur (26), Emily Mary Meysey-Thompson clergyman's wife and children Evelyn and Harold. The father Charles Maude died on 12 September 1881 and son Harold James of the 4th Battalion West Yorkshire Regiment died at The Grand Hotel, Cimiez, Nice in France, on 15 March 1926. He normally lived at Hillthorpe House, Westwood, Scarborough and his executors included Louise Georgina widow, Emily Mary widow and Edward Arthur Walker stockbroker. His widow Louise lived at Fanfarigoule, La Napoule, Alpes in France but died at Avenue du Petit, Juas near Nice on 17 August 1959.

Arthur Herbert Thompson was born on 5 October 1852 and was an engineer and lieutenant in the Yorkshire Hussars. He married Horatia Dorothy Williamson (1864) on 1 June 1896 and lived at 41 Eaton Square, Belgravia near Bonsor, Lubbock and Kenyon-Slaney. Their daughter Sylvia Dorothy was baptized at St. Peter's, Pimlico in 1897 and they had a son Guy Herbert born in 1902. Horatia Dorothy of Moorland, Hutton le Hole in Yorkshire died in Scarborough on 4 April 1949 and Arthur Herbert of 21 West Street, Scarborough died at May Lodge, Filey Road on 5 February 1950 his estate worth £26,317 4s 7d. Guy Herbert their son was a company director and engineer of 10 Church Street, Woodbridge in Suffolk and died at Ipswich Hospital on 28 May 1961.

Amelia Annie Thompson was born at Kirby Hall in 1855 and presumably lived at 45 Lennox Gardens in 1893 but was later of the Ladies Park Club, Knightsbridge and died on 29 March 1936 her executors including Hubert Charles Meysey-Thompson (see below). Ernest Claude Thompson was born on 18 February 1859 and was educated at Eton and Cambridge (1877) and was aide-de-camp to the Earl of Onslow G.C.M.G. when he was Governor of New Zealand in 1889-92. Giacomo Leoni a Venetian architect designed Clandon Park near to Guildford in Surrey (and not far from Polesden) for the 2nd Lord Onslow in c.1731. It was built in the Palladian style and Capability Brown landscaped the grounds in 1770. William Hellier Onslow was born on 7 March 1853 and became 4th Earl of Onslow in 1870 and married Hon. Florence Coulston Gardner on 3 February 1875. Mount Tarawera near Rotorua in New Zealand erupted on 10 June 1886 and this was the countries worst-ever natural disaster. 5,000 square miles of scenic land was covered with deep ash and Te Wairoa and two other villages were destroyed with the loss of 150 lives. The pink and white terraces one of the wonders of the world were gone forever. Lord Onslow was Governor soon afterwards and moved a Maori Meeting House from the site of the eruption to Clandon in 1892 and it remains today. He died on 23 October 1911. Lady Gwendolen Florence Mary his daughter married Rupert Edward Cecil Lee Guinness 2nd Lord Iveagh on 8 October 1903 (see Renny-Tailyour Ch. 8). Lady Bridgid Katherine Rachel Guinness their daughter was born 30 July 1920 and married Frederic Georg Wilhelm Christoph Prinz of Preußen (Hohenzollern) - related to Queen Victoria, Kaiser Wilhelm, Romanovs, Hanovers and later to Earl of Mornington and Arthur Wellesley (see Ch. 2).

Ernest Claude Thompson married Alice Jane Blanche (1871) daughter of Colonel John Joicey of Newton Hall, Northumberland on 1 November 1894. He was then a lieutenant in the Yorkshire Hussars Yeoman Cavalry, an M.P. for North Durham and director of Hathorn, Davy and Co. engineers in Leeds. Ernest Claude, his wife Alice and children Alice (5) and Onslow (3) lived at Rokeby in 1901 and later lived at Spellow Hill, Staveley just five miles from Kirby Hall. He represented Handsworth in Parliament from 1906-22 and died at Spellow Hill, Knaresborough on 28 February 1944 his probate being granted to Alice and his estate valued at £8,255 11s 10d. His widow Alice died at Spellow Hill on 17 July 1960 and her probate went to Onslow Victor Claude a retired colonel H.M. Army and Alice Hildegarde Eva Meysey-Thompson.

Albert Childers Thompson was born at "Kirby Hall" on 13 July 1848 and grew up in the rolling farmland of the Vale of York. He was educated at Eton College from 1862-65 and matriculated at Trinity

College, Cambridge on 14 February 1867 being at both institutions with A.F. Kinnaird. He was admitted to Lincoln's Inn on 28 January 1869 gaining his B.A. in 1871. He did not return to Yorkshire and became a London barrister but was also a good sportsman. He played in the first Cup Final on 16 March 1872 a choice possibly influenced by A.F. Kinnaird and entered the Inner Temple on 17 April 1872 being called to the bar on 6 June 1872. A player "Thompson" was in the Wanderers team in the Final on 29 March 1873 and this was almost certainly he, as these were mainly the players from the year before. One wonders if it was during these Finals that he developed the 'Meysey' run. He had chambers at 4 Paper Buildings, Temple in 1874 and was a special pleader on the Midland Circuit and North Eastern Circuit, which encompassed the North and West Riding of Yorkshire and the Leeds Borough Sessions. He took the surname of Meysey-Thompson in 1874 and practiced at 9 King's Bench Walk, Temple in 1875-76 but returned to 4 Paper Buildings from 1877-83. He lived at the family home 18 Mansfield Street with his mother from 1875-83 although Edward Lynlph Stanley a barrister of Appleton-le-Street near Malton lived there alone in 1881 - presumably a friend and colleague.

The family already had some notable ancestors however there was soon to be a significant connection. Frances Lascelles lived from 1612-67 and his son Daniel (1655) was the High Sheriff of York and died in 1734 and his grandson Henry (1690) purchased the Harewood estate north of Leeds, and ten miles south west of Kirby Hall, in 1748 but died in 1753. His son Edwin Lascelles (1712-95) became Baron Harewood and built a new house on the estate. The family had made their money from sugar plantations in Barbados and he employed John Carr (1723-1807) a northern architect to design a Palladian mansion. Whilst he was working on the stables the Baron approached Robert Adam and found himself compromised and thus had to employ both architects. The foundation stone was laid in 1759 and Carr who married into the Lascelles family designed the central façade whilst Adam was architect of the wings and the interior - this was one of his most notable works. The house was habitable by 1771 and Capability Brown landscaped the estate, however Edwin died in 1795 and the Barony became extinct. Edward Lascelles (1702-47) son of Daniel was collector of customs in Barbados and his son Edward was born in 1739 and inherited Harewood House becoming the 1st Earl of Harewood - he died in 1820. The line was continued with his son Henry Lascelles (1767-1841) and grandson Henry Lascelles (1797-1857). The latter married Lady Louisa Thynne the daughter of Sir Thomas 2nd Marquis of Bath on 5 July 1823 and had children Henry Thynne Lascelles (1824-92) 4th Earl and Rev. Hon. James Walter Lascelles (1831-1901). The second son was the rector of Goldsborough and Canon of Ripon and married Emma Clare Miles having daughters Edith Katherine (1859-1902) and Mabel Louisa (1862-1941).

Albert Childers Meysey-Thompson (34) a practicing barrister of 18 Mansfield Street married Mabel Louisa Lascelles (19) of the Rectory at Goldsborough on 9 August 1882, the church being three miles from Kirby Hall. Robert Miles was the minister and H. M. Meysey-Thompson and Edith K. Lascelles the witnesses. His bride Mabel was born at Knaresborough in December 1862 the daughter of the Hon. and Rev. James Walter Lascelles rector of Goldsborough and granddaughter of Henry 3rd Earl of Harewood. Edith K. Lascelles married Major Walter Pleydell-Bouverie on 31 October 1882, whilst Henry Ulrick Lascelles (1846-1929) 5th Earl married Lady Florence Katharine daughter of Orlando George Charles Bridgeman 3rd Earl of Bradford and wife Selina Louisa Forester. Her sister Mabel Selina Bridgeman (1855) was married to William Slaney Kenyon-Slaney in 1887 thus the latter was a cousin of A.C. Meysey-Thompson (see Ch. 6). These links were clearly high profile however there was more to come and the son Henry George Charles Viscount Lascelles (1882-1947) later 6th Earl of Harewood married Victoria Alexandra Alice Mary Windsor, Princess Royal, the daughter of George V King of England. The wedding was at Westminster Abbey on 28 February 1922 whilst a report in the Times on 28 March 1944 stated: "Harewood House, Leeds March 27 - The Princess Royal attended by Miss Kenyon-Slaney visited a factory and opened an exhibition in the West Riding this afternoon." Note: possibly Sybil Agnes (see Ch. 6).

Albert Childers and Mabel had just one son Hubert Charles on 9 June 1883 and moved to 12 Montagu Square, Marylebone in 1884 but were absent in 1891. The Georgian house had white stonework at the ground floor and a bow front and remains today on the east side of the square. Meysey-Thompson had chambers at 1 King's Bench Walk and 41 Parliament Street from 1884 the former being just two doors from those of Ebenezer Cobb Morley, John Welch special pleader and Thomas H. Merriman (see Ch. 1 and later). The last case, however, was soon closed and Albert Childers Meysey-Thompson died at 12 Montagu Square on 20 March 1894 aged 45 years. His obituary appeared in the Times on Thursday 22 March 1894 and stated: "Mr. A.C. Meysey-Thompson Q.C. the well known parliamentary counsel died on Tuesday morning. He had been in ailing health for the last two or three years, and had been compelled to spend the winter months on the west coast of America. He returned to England on Saturday with the intention of resuming his practice at the bar." He was the first of the Wanderers 1872 side to die and was described as one of Her Majesty's counsel of the Temple, London and his widow Mabel Louisa proved his will on 16 May 1894, his effects being valued at £14,618 2s 6d. Mabel Louisa Meysey-Thompson died at 52 Bayham Road, Sevenoaks, Kent, on 24 December 1941 her probate being granted to Hubert Charles Meysey-Thompson. The latter was also a barrister and died at Chestnut House, Long Melford, Sudbury, on 9 November 1956.

REGINALD COURTENAY WELCH

The last Wanderer to consider is the man between the posts or perhaps the man 'under the tape'. He had an important role in the early F.A. and came from a Lancashire family. John Welch, his grandfather, was born in 1777 and was a merchant in Lancaster who married Dorcas Walmsley (1781) in 1802 and had eleven children baptized at the High Street Chapel, Lancaster previously Mount Street Chapel - an independent or Congregational church viz. John (1803), Elizabeth (1805), Dorcas (1807), Mary (1809), Henry Walmsley (1811), Lucy (1813), Eliza (1815), William (1816), James Doveton (1819), Timothy Yeats (1822) and Catherine (1823). There was a strong tradition of nonconformity in the town and George Whitefield frequently preached at the Friends Meeting House, Lancaster in the 18th century, whilst the building itself dated from 1690.

Few records have been traced of this extensive family however the first son John Welch was born in Lancaster on 31 July 1803 and baptized at the High Street Chapel on 19 August that year. He was educated at Lancaster School and was a pensioner at Queen's College, Cambridge on 27 June 1822 and matriculated in Michaelmas that year. He was admitted to the Inner Temple on 20 September 1822 and migrated to Caius College on 25 June 1823 and gained his B.A. in 1826. He then moved to London and trained as a barrister spending his whole life as a special pleader in the courts of law. He qualified for the position in 1829 and held the post for over fifty years having a large practice and numerous pupils. Indeed one wonders if E.C. Morley trained in his 'school'. His first chambers were at 3 Hare Court, Inner Temple in 1829-30 whilst he was at 5 Hare Court in 1841 opposite to Temple Church dating from the 12th century. John was a single man at this time and concentrated on establishing his career thus he was not married until he was 41 years old.

John and Ann Sprye resided at Crediton in Devon and had six children there: Anne (1793), Henry (1794), Mary Emily (1795), Richard Samuel Mare (1798), George (1802) and William (1805). Their second son Richard Samuel Mare Sprye was born on 14 October 1798 and baptized at Crediton Church on 30 July 1800. His name suggested he would make his mark in the world and he soon travelled within the Empire working for the Civil Service. He married Henrietta Digby in c.1822 although some records suggest they were married in the Tamil Nadu district of India in c.1826. The couple sailed from England for the East Indies in 1823 and his wife was 'heavy with child' thus a daughter Henrietta Anne Ffowell Sprye was born on board ship off the Cape de Verde Islands in 1823. They arrived safely in India and their daughter, a British subject, was baptized at Madras on 25 September 1824. The family did not remain there and sailed for George Town on Penang Island in Malaya (now Malaysia) next to the Malacca Straits. They had two children there: Isabella Mary (1827) and Glanville Hele Ffowell (1828) but soon returned to India and had four more children: Reynell Richard Hele Ffowell (1829) at St. Thomas Mount in Tamil Nadu, Courtenay William Hele Ffowell (1830) in Tamil Nadu, Henry William (1831) in India and Frances Helen Hele Ffowell (1832) at Vishakhapatnam. Richard the father worked in H.M. Service or the diplomatic service in the Far East and had some notable connections but returned to England in the 1840s and then lived in London as a gentleman.

Sir Thomas Stamford Raffles was born on the "Ann" sailing off Port Morant, Jamaica on 5 July 1781 and he clearly set a trend in marine births. He was educated at Dr. Anderson's School in Hammersmith and became a representative of the East India Company being sent to Penang, Malaya in 1805 (Prince of Wales Island). He was made Lieutenant Governor of Java in 1811 but returned to England in 1817, when he was knighted, and as a keen naturalist discussed the creation of the zoological gardens with Sir Joseph Banks. He was Governor of Bencoolen (Sumatra) in 1818-23 and his most famous act was to purchase Singapore from the Sultan of Johore on 29 February 1819. He returned home again and with his knowledge of animals and plants of the East Indies helped form the London Zoological Society, but died in 1826. His main legacies were London Zoo opened to members of the society in 1828 and to the public in 1847 and also the famous Raffles Hotel in Singapore - he had no surviving children.

Thomas Raffles (1788-1863) his first cousin and an independent minister preached at Great George Street Chapel in Liverpool from 1812-62. His eldest son Thomas Stamford Raffles became a barrister and was a stipendiary magistrate of Liverpool who spent time writing his father's biography. He married Maria Cearns and their son Rev. Thomas Stamford Raffles (1853) was educated at Rugby School and Cambridge in 1877 then lived at Langham Rectory, Colchester.

John Welch a special pleader of the Inner Temple, London married Henrietta Anne Ffowell Sprye of 53 Norfolk Square, Brighton daughter of Richard Sprye a gentleman by licence at St. Nicholas' Church, Brighton on 2 November 1844. The wedding was a society affair and the bride was 20 years his junior. R.S. Smith the curate performed the ceremony and Thomas Barrow and T. Stamford Raffles were witnesses. The latter barrister was described above and his connection may have been through the law or from associations in Penang (or both). Richard Sprye a gentleman had a London address and a daughter Gertrude Helen Ffowell died at 36 Green Street, Hanover Square on 1 December 1846 aged 15 days the informant Elizabeth Chad. He then spent time back in India and his daughter Frances Helen Sprye married William Forbes there on 30 April 1858. Reynell Hele Ffowell Sprye a gentleman died of 'albuminurice' kidney disease several years and pneumonia at 18 St. George's Terrace, Kensington Town on 3 February 1867 aged 37 - the informant Ellen Moss. Indeed Henrietta Digby Sprye died of bronchitis at 1 Elgin Road, Kensington on 5 February 1875, aged 75, 'widow' of Richard a retired officer H.M.S. the informant Fanny Waller of 84 Clarendon Road, Notting Hill. The entry was unusual since Richard Samuel Mare Sprye an independent died of bronchitis at 48 Grosvenor Road, Islington on 17 November 1878 aged 80 the informant being F.H. Forbes daughter of 1 Montpelier Villas, Dover. The latter was a widow living with daughters Rachel H. and Caroline Digby at 1 Montpelier Villa, Harold Street, Dover, in 1881.

John and Henrietta Welch first lived at 6 Westbourne Place, Paddington at one end of Westbourne Terrace near the station. They had several children whilst residing there although two died in infancy and were buried at Kensal Green Cemetery also known as All Souls' Cemetery viz. Edward John Cowling (1845), Charles Bernard (1846) *infant*, Henrietta Anne (c.1848) *infant*, Arthur Wilmot (1850) and Reginald Courtenay (1851). Edward and Charles were baptized at St. James's, Paddington in 1846/47 and Henrietta and Arthur were baptized at Holy Trinity, Paddington in 1850. John Welch continued as a special pleader and moved to new chambers at 3 King's Bench Walk, Temple by 1851 and remained there until 1882. Indeed he worked there before the arrival of E.C. Morley who used these same chambers for F.A. meetings in 1866.

The Welch family moved to Lancaster Lodge, Richmond Road, Twickenham, in 1852 and lived there for over ten years the house being near a later residence of John Forster Alcock. The property was no doubt named after his birthplace and he clearly wanted to assert his allegiance since York House was directly opposite. Hopefully he did not revive the *War of the Roses* in Twickenham. The area has been described regarding J.F. Alcock (see Ch. 3) however needs some further explanation. Richmond Road arrived in Twickenham with York House on the left and Lancaster Lodge on the right whilst the circular garden of the former separated the two properties. Lancaster Lodge faced south and was situated between Oak Lane and Arragon Road, whilst Richmond Road the main thoroughfare wound into the narrow Church Street with St. Mary's Church, the River Thames and Eel Pie Island nearby.

The couple had six children at Lancaster Lodge, viz. Francis Bernard (1853), Amy Henrietta (1855), Beatrice Annie Rosa (1857), Walter Samuel (1859), Ada Dorcas (1860) and Alice Maude Jane (1862). The property included a large house, stables and outbuildings and extensive gardens to the front and rear, whilst a mode of transport could be purchased from the extensive carriage factory behind the house. John Welch certificated special pleader lived at Lancaster Lodge in 1861 with his wife Henrietta, children Reginald C. (9), Francis, Amy, Beatrice, Walter, Ada and six servants. His priority was the education of the children and three sons went to Harrow School. The first Arthur started there in September 1863 and the family moved to Harrow later that year or early in 1864. Lancaster Lodge still appeared on maps of the area but was un-named in 1894-96 and demolished in c.1914 during road widening. Church Street, the main route through the town, was very narrow thus a new road was built over Lancaster Lodge and its garden. To add insult to injury this was called York Street and a tramway ran along it. The old house stood in the middle of York Street at its junction with Cornwall Road however despite the changes York House and its outbuildings remained and are now the local council offices.

The Welch family lived at Lancaster House, College Road in Harrow from 1863/64 however there is no trace of the property as this is now one of the main shopping streets - his three sons went to the school in

1863-71. John Welch a special pleader lived at Lancaster House in 1871 with his wife Henrietta, Edward a civil engineer and his wife and son, Reginald C. (19) a scholar, Amy, Beatrice, Walter, Ada, Alice and eight servants. He worked into his seventies and retired in 1880 although he was still listed at 3 King's Bench Walk in 1882; and was a retired special pleader at "Greenhill", Parkside, Wimbledon in 1881-82 with wife Henrietta, daughters Beatrice, Ada and Alice, and Georgina L. Voight a German governess. The house also accommodated a school with five female scholars and boarders aged 9-17 years.

John Welch of 57 Cambridge Street, Edgware Road formerly a "certificated special pleader" of 3 King's Bench Walk made his last will on 9 March 1883. He was residing with his son Reginald and this was later re-named Kendal Street. He left all his estate in trust to son Reginald Courtenay Welch (otherwise Reginald de Courtenay) the money for the benefit of his wife and daughters during their lifetime then afterwards for the benefit of his son. He desired to be buried in Kensal Green Cemetery in the same grave as his deceased children the funeral to be plain and inexpensive - Duncan James Forbes, Alice Reed and Walter Samuel Welch were witnesses. He may have travelled with his wife to France and Henrietta Anne Ffowell Welch died at Cannes on 4 February 1888. He returned home to England now an old man and died at 5 Alma Terrace, Kensington on 16 May 1888. Despite a lifetime in the legal profession he did not use a solicitor to prepare his will and no executor was named, which appears to have held up his probate, although any fortune may already have been transferred to his family.

Edward John Cowling Welch was born on 11 August 1845 and baptized at St. James's, Paddington on 8 January 1846. He did not attend Harrow but qualified as a civil engineer and married Elizabeth Smith at St. Saviour in June 1870 and had a son Arthur John Digby at St. Pancras later that year. He lived with his family at Lancaster House in Harrow in 1871 and then moved back to Lancashire having daughters Constance Evelyn at Seaforth in 1873 and Mabel at Chorlton-on-Medlock in 1879. He resided at 5 Glynde Terrace, Lavendar Hill, Wandsworth Road in 1881 with his wife, three children and sister Amy Henrietta (26). Edward John C. Welch died at Kensington in September 1886 aged 41.

Arthur Wilmot Welch was born in 1850 and baptized at Holy Trinity, Paddington on 27 June 1850 and attended Harrow School from September 1863 to mid-term 1868. He spent some of this time in Monsieur Masson's house but was also a home boarder after his family moved to the area, and was in the Harrow football XI in 1867. He was admitted to Trinity Hall, Cambridge on 18 May 1868 and matriculated Michaelmas that year. He gained a B.A. '36 wrangler' in 1872 and M.A. in 1876. He was an assistant master at King Edward VI Grammar School in Bury in 1872-78 and at Harrow in 1878-80. He was the Headmaster of Brown's School living at 18 St. Paul's Street, Stamford in 1881 with a matron, assistant, seven scholars and three servants. This was also known as Stamford Grammar and he was there in 1881-82. He married Jessie Josephine the youngest daughter of Gustave Masson, librarian of Harrow School, at Harrow on 27 March 1883. He then became Headmaster of Archbishop Holgate's School, York in 1883 and was ordained as a deacon there in 1884 and became a priest in 1885. He was Headmaster in York until 1895 and then vicar of Millington with Little Givendale near York from 1896-1937. He lived there with wife Jessie (48) born Totteridge and son John (16) born York in 1901 but died in 1939. Francis Bernard Welch was born at Twickenham in 1853 and attended Harrow from November 1865 to mid-term 1869 and was a home boarder. He qualified as consulting engineer and for many years was head of Francis B. Welch & Co. based in Manchester but died there on 21 October 1890 aged 37.

Reginald Courtenay Welch was born at 6 Westbourne Place, Paddington on 17 October 1851 and Henrietta Welch his mother registered "Male" Welch on 27 November although his Christian names were added later. In fact he was the only one of the nine surviving children to be registered and his middle name was in reference to his maternal uncle. The football records usually call him Reginald de Courtenay Welch, an adjustment he made later in life. Perhaps this was done at the suggestion of a master at Harrow who suspected the name was grammatically incorrect or maybe it just sounded better. His family removed to Twickenham soon after his birth and he grew up there possibly seeing some early football at Richmond Green. He was educated at Harrow School from May 1864 to mid-term 1871, with W.P. Crake, and started there when his family moved to Lancaster House being a home boarder. He received the Whitworth Studentship in 1869-70, became a school monitor in 1870 and was joint editor of The Harrovian in 1869-71. His most notable contribution, however, was on the playing fields down Football Lane and he was in the football XI in 1870 and cricket XI in 1871. He resided with his family at Lancaster House as a scholar aged 19 in April 1871 and continued his football after leaving school.

He played in goal for the Wanderers in the first F.A. Cup Final on 16 March 1872 and also for England v Scotland in the first international at Glasgow on 30 November 1872. He again played for the

Wanderers in the Cup Final at Lillie Bridge on 29 March 1873 and finally, as Reginald de Courtenay Welch, for England v Scotland at Glasgow on 7 March 1874. He represented the Harrow Chequers on the F.A. Committee in 1873-75 and 1879-80 and was Honorary Secretary of the Harrow Chequers and Old Harrovians F.C. from 1872-84 as well as editor of various Harrow 'magazines'. He lived at Hyde Park by 1879 and was a trustee for fellow committee member M.P. Betts regarding two life assurance policies settled on his marriage (see Ch. 6). He then concentrated on his career and was "a student of the Lower Temple and tutor (at Law)," lodging at 57 Cambridge Street, Paddington in 1881. We can deduce that he was learning law but supplementing his income with teaching. His lodging was the residence of Thomas Halsey a baker his wife Esther and family, and was on the corner with Portsea Place but no longer remains. The road, as stated, is now Kendal Street and the surviving houses go up to no. 56 and have white stucco ground floors with brown brick above. William M. Thackeray (1811-63), novelist, lived nearby at 18 Albion Street (see Merriman Ch. 10).

Reginald completed his studies and was a school army tutor at 57 Cambridge Street in 1883 and his father joined him there the same year. He moved around the corner and lived at 6 Southwick Place, Paddington from 1888 opposite St. John's, Hyde Park built in Georgian times and near Gloucester Square - the road was originally Stanhope Street (see Crake). Herbert Abingdon Draper Compton and Sarah Cherry had two daughters at Cannanore north of Calicut on India's south west coast: Adeline Geraldine (1817) and Amelia Cherry (1823). Abingdon Compton a son or relative was born in the West Indies in c.1835 and married Louisa E. who was born in Trinidad and Tobago in 1833. He joined the Bombay Civil Service and Adeline Charlotte his daughter was born at Poonah 80 miles inland from Bombay in 1855. Louisa E. Compton a 'widower' lived at Porchester Lodge, Uxbridge Road in 1881 with daughter Adeline (24) and two servants. This was near Leinster Gardens and Porchester Terrace, whilst Uxbridge Road became Bayswater Road and another Lancaster House was nearby. Indeed Reginald and Adeline lived near one another.

Reginald de Courtenay Welch gentleman of 6 Southwick Place, Paddington married Adeline Charlotte Compton of Templedon House, Southsea daughter of Abingdon of the Bombay C.S. at St. Jude's Church, Portsea on 22 December 1888. Indeed his bride may have been a neighbour of Conan Doyle who lived at Bush Villa, Southsea in the 1880s and wrote stories with an Indian or colonial theme (see Pember Ch. 4). Louisa E. Compton and G.H. Willis were the witnesses to the wedding, sadly not A.C. Doyle. Strangely an Abingdon Compton (65) born in the West Indies lived on his own means at St. George's Hanover Square in 1901. The couple had just one son Walter George Frederick who was born at Paddington in March 1890. Reginald D.C. Welch a school army tutor and employer lived at 6 Southwick Place in 1891 with his wife, son and three servants. His address was 6 Southwick Place and 1 Southwick Crescent, Paddington in 1892 the two properties being near one another but only 1 Southwick Crescent in 1893. It is now renamed Hyde Park Crescent and was near to the home of William Parry Crake at 31 Norfolk Crescent - they may have found the latter this house on his return from India. He then continued as an army tutor in Paddington until 1895 when a new opportunity presented itself.

Colonel Berdoe Amherst Wilkinson (1827-95) went to the Royal Military Academy, Woolwich and was a lieutenant in the Royal Engineers in 1846 and retired from the army in 1876. During this period he spent nine years as an army tutor at Darmstadt in Germany and with this expertise established an army college at Farnham, Surrey, which he built in 1880. The college was located at Heath End near Farnham high on a hill backing onto woods, close to the road to Aldershot and Farnborough. His sons ran the college for a time but he died on 10 January 1895 and Reginald Courtenay Welch was then appointed Principal of the College and stayed there the rest of his life. He owned shares in the college, which was a limited company and this financial arrangement was possibly set up when he arrived. This appointment secured the family's future and details of their life at the college were found in local papers such as the *Surrey & Hants News* and the *Farnham Herald*. He was a busy and active man running the Army College but had several other interests and was one of the first to ski in Switzerland when the sport was introduced from Norway in 1900 (although Conan Doyle was credited with this in 1893). Reginald Welch (49) army tutor, wife Adeline (44) and son Walter (11) lived at the college in 1901 whilst sister Ada was an accountant in Kensington. Reginald Courtenay Welch army tutor was given administration (with will) of the estate of John Welch in London on 11 June 1904 and of Henrietta Welch on 16 June 1904. He was described as the residuary legatee and the effects of each parent were exactly £72 5s.

He was the driving force behind the Aldershot Command Tattoo and suggested the idea to Sir John French G.O.C. and organised the first two events at Government House before the First War. Like many

The Army College, Heath End. The college was established in 1880 - R.C. Welch principal 1895-1939.

others, however, the family's peace was shattered when Great Britain entered the war on 4 August 1914. Their only son Walter a lieutenant in the Royal Field Artillery died on the Western Front on 30 October that year. He was formerly residing at the Army College, Heath End, Farnham and his grief stricken father administered his effects on 11 February 1915. Reginald then took an active role in the First War and produced a scheme for the working class to invest savings in a War Loan, an idea initially for the residents of Hale and Heath End although it was later adopted by the War Savings Committee in Guildford and then by the Central Committee in London (F.H. 31/7/1915). He attended a recruiting rally at Farnham Picture Palace and asked for reserve forces to be sent to France to help the war effort due to the large number of casualties (S.H.N. 8/10/1915). There were similar rallies around the country however information was poor and many did not understand what the men were being sent to. Mr. Welch had no doubt received training based on 19th century tactics and was probably unfamiliar with the carnage of this kind of war. He formed the Farnham branch of the British Empire Union with the first meeting at the local corn exchange, the aim being to establish a war council "without regard to party" (F.H. 16/12/1916). He also erected a war memorial to the honour of his son in Hale with the inscription: "He was the life and soul of our little mess, a keen and good soldier" (F.H. 6/1/1917).

Reginald Courtenay Welch continued to run the college in the 1920s and 1930s and eventually trained thousands of officers for the army. He wrote his last will and testament on 17 March 1939 and although this was a lengthy document he was clearly in a lucid state of mind. His first concern was to give his birds and other belongings to Miss Emily Gunner, matron, who had served the college for forty years and had enabled it to remain open during the war. He also left a bequest to his sisters Beatrice, Ada and Alice who lived at 15 Glyn Mansions, Addison Bridge in West Kensington, which included all his belongings not the property of the Army College Ltd. and specifically pictures, books and a grandfather clock located in rooms and bedrooms 10, 11 and 12. He made provision for his sisters and Miss Gunner throughout his will although four clauses had far more significance:

> **(1)** To my wife Adeline Charlotte Welch who is already substantially provided for under our marriage settlement £300.
>
> **(2)** To my late son's old friend Mrs. Grierson (formerly Miss Nan Banister) of 1 Park Avenue, Northampton £100.
>
> **(3)** The freehold property Whitehorn, College Road, Farnham to be leased to Miss Emily Gunner as before.
>
> **(4)** The remainder of the estate was put in trust in a residuary fund and divided into two equal parts, the first for nephew John Welch and niece Madge Welch, the second for the trustees of the Royal Artillery War Commemoration Fund.

The money from the second part of the fund was to be invested and half the income used for one or more scholarships valued at £75 or under p.a. These were intended for the sons of officers of the Royal Artillery of the Regular Army, in particular, where their fathers trained at the Royal Military Academy, Woolwich or a similar institution and for boys who wished to follow a similar path to their fathers. Failing this, however, the scholarships were to be used for boys at the Royal Military College, Sandhurst or the Royal Air Force College, Cranwell. In the first instance they were available to boys at Charterhouse School, Wellington College (Berks) and Stowe School, although the restriction did not apply if the boy's father died whilst he was at school. It is strange that Harrow was excluded. Further to this the scholarships became void if: (1) the boy trained at an institution other than those stated (2) he failed in his studies (3) the family circumstances of the boy changed. The other part of the income was for non-commissioned officers and men of the Royal Artillery to assist in their children's education, the aim being to give them a fair start in life.

The monies involved were to be called: "The Walter George Frederic Welch Scholarship and Bequest," and he stated, "This trust being created to serve as a perpetual memorial of my dear and only son

Lieutenant Walter George Frederic Welch 117th Battery Royal Field Artillery who was killed in action on the evening of Friday October 30th, 1914, during the first battle of Ypres." This revealed much about Reginald Courtenay Welch since shortly before his own death his thoughts were still on the son he had lost. He finally discussed the Army College Ltd. and asked his trustees to either sell his shares or procure the winding-up of the company, or, otherwise retain the shares and continue the company by appointing a new governing director and/or principal. He referred the matter to Messrs Gabbitas Thring & Co. of 36 Sackville Street, London and Messrs Truman and Knightley Ltd. of 61 Conduit Street, London. Lieutenant Col. J.W. Hope and Col. H.E. Reinhold retired army officers witnessed the will.

Reginald Courtenay Welch of the Army College, Heath End, Farnham, died on 4 June 1939 and his will was proved in London by the Westminster Bank Ltd. on 13 September that year his effects being valued at £19,478 10s but re-sworn at £16,593 17s 10d. Meanwhile the section of the will relating to the scholarships re-opened matters concerning his son, although the Second War intervened and thus interrupted proceedings. There was a further grant regarding the effects of Walter George Frederick Welch given to the Westminster Bank Ltd. on 10 November 1944, thirty years after he died, the value being £7,142 16s 8d. It seems likely Reginald hoped the Army College would continue however it was put up for sale by auction at the Bush Hotel, Farnham on 30 June 1948, the auctioneers being Messrs Eggar & Co. of 74 Castle Street, Farnham and the solicitors Messrs Murray, Hutchins & Co. of 11 Birchin Lane, London E.C.3. The sale brochure said that the college was near the bus route from Farnham to Aldershot at an altitude of 430' above sea level and facing southeast. There were 7-8 public or reception rooms, 26 bedrooms, 6 bathrooms, staff living and bedrooms, and ample domestic offices with attractive gardens and grounds and fine level playing fields (of course), the whole area covering 5½ acres. It then went into further detail:

Lot 1 It is approached by a short road and private carriage drive (with back drive off College Road) and is of substantial red brick construction with bath stone dressing and slated roof. It was specially designed and erected some 68 years ago for use as a Private Military Academy and was thus used up until the outbreak of the late war. It would be suitable for scholastic or institutional purposes, a hostel or conversion to flats. The second floor and first floor consist mainly of bedrooms whilst the ground floor has a drawing room, library, lecture rooms, common room and dining room. The semi-basement has a scullery, pantry, servants' hall, butler's and matron's room and recreation room with a self operated electric passenger lift installed by Hammond Brothers and Champness in 1938. Outside there are further lecture rooms and a half-timbered cottage whilst the grounds have coniferous and other trees, a rose garden and a well formed holly hedge being 1¾ acres in total.

Lot 2 The house is supplemented by a level playing field of nearly 4 acres fringed by a spinney of Scots pine and comes within the Farnham building zone hence it is available for development.

Lot 3 The property includes the Army College garage previously the Presbyterian Mission Church.

The three lots were offered in vacant possession and the final summary revealed a few more facts: "The property is well known as a military training college, established and run for many years prior to the war by the late Mr. R. Courtenay Welch.... The premises have just been released from requisition by the Air Ministry and will be sold in their present condition the vendors retaining the benefit of any claim there may be for dilapidations under the Compensation (Defence) Act, 1939." The summary closes with the conditions of sale - Lot 1 is sold subject to certain covenants contained in an indenture dated 17 June 1885. Lot 2 has a covenant dated 8 June 1890 and a deed of grant relating to drainage dated 23 May 1935. Lot 3 has a conveyance of sale dated 2 May 1931. These details give a fascinating insight into life at the college however its days were numbered and the site was sold and covered by housing, whilst his widow Adeline Charlotte Welch died at Holland Court Hotel, Holland Park, London, on 5 April 1945. Thus the Wanderers were ready and booted on the Oval pitch and waited for the Royal Engineers, who are discussed in the following chapters.

CHAPTER 8

The Royal Engineers

The story of the Royal Engineers was discussed in relation to F.A. Marindin however it is worth going into some further detail. Chatham Docks were on the banks of the River Medway, north of the town, and became an important naval centre at the time of Elizabeth I being protected by strategically placed forts such as Upnor Castle. The Royal Engineers became well established at this site and the School of Military Engineering was formed at Brompton Barracks near the docks in 1812. The Corps earned a reputation as leaders in technological advance and trained their officers to a high standard of both physical and mental fitness. The records state that many officers had attended public school and, indeed, the following discussions prove this to be true with links to Brackenburys, Bruce Castle, Cheltenham, Eton, Harrow, Kensington and Marlborough.

These young men brought with them a keen interest in sports such as cricket and football, thus the Royal Engineers produced a successful football team and were involved in the F.A. from the start. H.C. Moore, Secretary of the football team, sent in their first subscription on 8 December 1863 and this was received at the sixth meeting of the F.A. when the first official Committee was formed. Captain Marindin was posted to Chatham from 1866-74 and helped make the team one of the best soccer outfits in the country. He was a member of the F.A. Committee in 1871-73 and was present when the Cup competition started on 20 July 1871, received a promotion to major on 5 July 1872 and became F.A. President in 1874-90. His colleague Captain Merriman was on the F.A. Committee in 1874-77 thus the Royal Engineers had, without doubt, a vital role in early soccer.

The sappers reached the first F.A. Cup Final in 1872 after a successful run that saw them as favourites. They received a walk over against Reigate Priory in the first round then beat Hitchin away at the 'top' field by a convincing 5-0 score in the second. They played Hampstead Heathens at home in the third winning 3-0 after their opponents had beaten Barnes F.C., and met Crystal Palace in the semi-final at the Oval with no score but humbled their opponents 3-0 in the replay. This cemented their position as favourites since

Royal Engineers Team 1872. Back - Merriman, Ord, Marindin, Addison, Mitchell.
Front - Hoskyns, Renny-Tailyour, Creswell, Goodwyn, Barker, Rich.

the Wanderers had been unable to defeat Crystal Palace in a previous round although their supremacy did not show in the Final and the rest, as they say, is history. The team reached the Final again in 1874 and fielded four players from 1872 - Addison, Marindin, Merriman and Renny-Tailyour but lost the game 2-0 to Oxford University and the skills of R.W.S. Vidal. They made it third time lucky playing the Old Etonians in the 1875 Final and with Merriman and Renny-Tailyour drew 1-1 on 13 March and won the replay 2-0 on 16 March. There was a crowd of just 3,000 to witness this historic event with one goal scored by Renny-Tailyour and the referee Charles Alcock. The Engineers played the Wanderers in their last Cup Final appearance in 1878 and lost 3-1 although they won the Amateur Cup in 1908.

Some statistics illustrate the strength of the Royal Engineers side in the 1870s: They played 86 games from 1871-75 winning 74 times and losing 3 times whilst scoring 244 goals but only conceding 21; they lost no games in the 1874-75 season when they won the F.A. Cup. These statistics could only by matched by some of today's best teams yet they tell us little about the actual players. Who were the men who took on the Wanderers in 1872? There were some difficulties tracing these players since the report in the Sportsman newspaper only gave their surnames: Captain Marindin, Captain Merriman, Addison, Bogle, Cotter, Creswell, Goodwyn, Mitchell, Muirhead, Renny-Tailyour and Rich.

They were initially found using Hart's Army List 1870-72, which recorded all officers serving during that period and gave Captain Marindin, Brigade Major, School of Military Engineering, Chatham appointed 1 September 1869 and Captain Merriman, Assistant Instructor in Field Works, Chatham promoted 31 December 1868. A list of lieutenants on p. 214 gave Adam Bogle, Royal Arsenal, Woolwich whilst the other eight players appeared on p. 215: George William Addison (leave), Hugh Mitchell, Henry Bayard Rich and Edmund William Creswell present in 1870-72; Henry Waugh Renny-Tailyour, Herbert Hugh Muirhead, Alfred George Goodwyn and Edmond William Cotter recruited 1871-72. Each lieutenant had a temporary rank and was at the School of Military Engineering, Chatham as denoted by an * beside their name. The first problem was Adam Bogle who was based at Woolwich in 1872 however he was found to be at Chatham with the others in 1870. The second problem was John Copley Addison and John Du Terreau Bogle both Royal Engineers however their service histories seem to exclude them from the team and the details are discussed later. K. Warsop has since explained that their full names appear in other match reports and confirmed these are the correct players, six of them being present at the School of Military Engineering on the census dated April 1871:

	Age	Occupation	Born
F.A. Marindin	32	Capt & Brigade Major	Weymouth
W. Merriman	33	Capt Royal Engineers	Kensington
G.W. Addison	21	Lieutenant R.E.	Bradford
H.W. Renny-Tailyour	21	"	India
H. Mitchell	21	"	Marylebone
H.B. Rich	21	"	Berbice

E.W. Cotter and H.H. Muirhead resided at the Royal Military Academy in Woolwich on the 1871 census and received their first commission with A.G. Goodwyn on 2 August 1871. A. Bogle was posted to Cork, Ireland in 1871 whilst E.W. Creswell attended the school in 1870-72 and was simply absent on that day hence the pieces of the jigsaw begin to fit and to quote the famous sleuth, "the game is afoot." The Engineers Library has a photograph of the 1872 team that includes eight players from the Cup Final side: Merriman, Marindin, Addison, Mitchell, Renny-Tailyour, Creswell, Goodwyn and Rich (see over). The picture is invaluable to the discussion and puts 'names to the faces' and Captain Merriman has the ball as in a photo from 1875.

The Royal Engineers side was more defensive than that of the Wanderers in 1872 having a goalkeeper, three backs and seven forwards. The match report states that Renny-Tailyour, Mitchell and Rich led the attack aided by was some excellent running from Muirhead, the other 'ups' being Bogle, Cotter and Creswell. The defenders were Addison and Marindin full backs and Goodwyn half back - the latter usually being in the full back position. The final defence was Merriman whom the newspaper commended for extremely efficient goal keeping. Marindin who later played in goal for the Old Etonians led the team from the rear and they continually tried to pass the backs of the enemy without success. It was hard to explain the reverse suffered however Goodwyn one of their best players was out of position whilst Creswell broke his collarbone ten minutes from the start. The side was well endowed with talent but who were the men behind the boots? Little was previously known of them yet in fact they were no different from their opponents coming from some of the most notable families. Their antecedents and careers are discussed below.

HENRY WAUGH RENNY-TAILYOUR

This first attacker was the epitome of the Royal Engineers and played both football and cricket whilst his name had the flavour of a gentleman and the British Empire. He was the Ian Botham of his day, the latter playing soccer for Scunthorpe United and cricket for England. The common soldier signed up for 21 years in the 19th century and was considered an employee, thus detailed records were kept including service and a personal description. There was, however, no such profile for officers who would have considered such revelations an insult, hence the main source regarding the Engineers was the Army Lists and service records that gave rank, postings, campaigns and some family details.

Renny-Tailyour in the tradition of Meysey-Thompson is traced to the Tailyour family who resided in Montrose on the northeast coast of Scotland. The story begins with Hercules Tailyour who possessed the manor of Borrowfield, Montrose in 1615. His son Hercules succeeded his father in 1662 and married Katherine Scott of Logie and had one daughter Elizabeth. She married her German cousin Robert Tailyour who succeeded to the estate in 1688 and eldest son Robert inherited Borrowfield at his father's decease. He married another Katherine Scott of Logie and their son Hercules Tailyour married Catherine daughter of Sir William Ogilvy Bart of Barras. Robert Tailyour their only son succeeded to the estate but he died unmarried and thus it passed to his sister Elizabeth Jean Tailyour. She married Robert Renny the grandson of Patrick Renny esquire of Usan in County Forfar in 1773. The couple had a large family namely Alexander, Hercules, Robert, Peter, Charles and seven daughters. The father Robert Renny died in 1787 whilst Hercules Renny was a lieutenant colonel in H.M. Army and Charles Renny a captain in the 40th Regiment died during the storming of Montevideo, Uruguay in 1806.

There are several old graves to the Renny-Tailyour family at the parish churchyard behind the market square in Montrose. This is the Church of Scotland or Presbyterian Church and should not be confused with the Episcopal Church near to Links Park football ground. There are three ancient graves that state: (1) Alexander Ranet burgess 9.10.1608, John Rennet son burgess, Christian Tailyour 7.1629 (2) Christian (Smith) daughter of Hercules date 1636 (3) Elisabeth Napier 1649, Hercules Tailyour of Borrowfield 1.10.1657 aged 84. These are difficult to read but give some information however that of more interest is on the other side of the path and states: "Alexander Renny 4.12.1774 3s of Robert Esq. died here 4.9.1787 aged 54 or 62 wife Mrs. Elizabeth Jean Renny died here 21.1.1806 aged 75.... his wife was heiress of Tailyour of Borrowfield so his 1s Alexander assumed Renny." The details from 3s of Robert.... were then repeated and followed by "Alexander Renny Tailyour Esq. of Borrowfield 8.2.1849 aged 74 daughter Elizabeth Bannerman Renny 1.6.1831 aged 18." There was some discrepancy in the details however the inscription does support the printed records. The town was clearly prosperous and there are many Georgian houses on the High Street, whilst the church is at the south end next to the Guildhall (extended 1820).

Alexander Renny the eldest son was born 31 January 1775 and baptized at Montrose Parish Church on 19 March that year. He succeeded to the Borrowfield estate on his mother's death in 1806 and she directed in her will that the surname Tailyour be added to that of Renny. Further to this she requested that he assume the Tailyour crest and quarter the Renny arms with those of Tailyour. The family mottoes were Renny: *Probitate Consilium Perfecitur* and Tailyour: *In Cruce Salus*. Alexander adopted the name Renny Tailyour however it seems unlikely he took all the legal steps and his son apparently used only Renny. He married Elizabeth Bannerman daughter of Sir Alexander Ramsay Bart of Balmain at Edinburgh Church on 4 April 1808 and had children: Robert (1809), Alexander Ramsay (1810), Thomas (1812), Elizabeth Bannerman (1813), William (1814), Henry (1815), Jane (1818) and Juliet (1823) whilst his wife Elizabeth died on 21 October 1825. Alexander Renny Tailyour of Borrowfield and Newmanswalls in Montrose made his last will on 21 March 1848 and this contained a deed of trust relating to lands at Borrowfield, Mile Mill, Manor Place and Howes Biggins. Indeed it stated that his descendants would forfeit the land unless they took the name Renny-Tailyour. He died on 8 February 1849 and his will was recorded in the *Book of Council and Session*, Scotland on 21 February 1849 and proved at the P.C.C. on 30 March.

Thomas Tailyour son of Alexander Renny Tailyour and his wife Elizabeth B. Ramsay was born on 18 March 1812 and baptized at Montrose Church on 26 April that year. He adopted the name Thomas Renny and as a young man entered the army as a cadet and served with the Bengal Engineers in India. Adam Atkinson

Dubton House. This was a home of Renny-Tailyour on the Borrowfield estate.

married Isabella Airey or Curry at Eglingham, Northumberland on 5 October 1780. The couple had a family baptized at Glanton Presbyterian Church from 1786-97 including Adam Atkinson born 1 May 1794 and baptized 4 May. He married Eleanor Davison at Lorbottle on 25 June 1816 and then had children Adam (1817), Isabella E.C. (1819), Eleanor (1821), Nathaniel (1822), Louisa Elizabeth (1825) and John (1829). Isabella Eliza Cook was born on 30 October 1819 and baptized at Bolam on 16 June 1820. The other baptisms were at Lorbottle and Whittingham, the villages being near Alnwick, although Bolam was a few miles to the south. Captain Thomas Renny married Isabella Eliza Cook Atkinson, daughter of Major Adam Atkinson of Lorbottle, at Montrose or St. Cuthbert's, Edinburgh on 9 June 1847. His father died in 1849 and he succeeded to the family estates in Montrose and complied with the conditions of the will.

Thomas Renny, captain in the Corps of Engineers, in service of the East India Company, Bengal, oldest surviving son and heir made an application to the *Royal Court* requesting that he and his issue could use the surname and coat armorial of Renny-Tailyour of Borrowfield. The warrant book states: "The petitioner desires to testify his grateful and affectionate respect, to the memory of his late father, and his wish to comply with the requirements of the will regarding the surname and wearing of arms.... Hence, he prays for *Royal Licence* to take the surname Tailyour in addition to Renny and to be allowed to bear both coats of arms." The request was granted by permission of Victoria R. at St. James's on 16 November 1849. Thomas Renny-Tailyour was stationed at Mussoorie near the Punjab at the time of the petition, this being 135 miles north of Delhi and 6,000' above sea level in the foothills of the Himalayas. There was a road connection to Dehra Dun and a rail link to Roorkee a military settlement 40 miles to the south. The couple had three children there: Henry Waugh (9 October 1849), Edward Ramsay (8 March 1851) and Elizabeth Lauderdale (23 August 1852). Captain Renny-Tailyour was promoted to the "local" rank of major on 28 November 1854 and was stationed in the East Indies in 1855-56. He retired from the army with the rank of lieutenant colonel in 1856 and returned to Montrose before the Indian Mutiny in 1857.

He remained in the town until his decease and, "took an active interest in every movement calculated to promote the intellectual, moral, and physical well-being of the people." The family home was Dubton House on the Borrowfield Estate two miles north of Montrose near Dubton Station and he had three children there: Louisa Isabella Sidney (22 December 1857), Charles Alexander (6 September 1860) *infant* and Thomas Francis Bruce (8 June 1863). The family had an affluent lifestyle and their three sons were educated at Cheltenham College in 1859-67 and 1876-79. Thomas supported the volunteer force at its formation and was captain of the rifle-company and later colonel of the 2nd F. Ad. Rifle Battalion. He aided the Angus and Mearns Rifle Assoc. going to their prize meetings in Montrose as a referee, and was a deputy lieutenant of Forfar-shire and J.P. for the county in 1875, whilst his daughter Elizabeth Lauderdale married William Harry Lumsden of Balmedie in 1877. He was a Whig in terms of politics and a member of the Montrose Natural History and Antiquarian Society, Montrose Asylum and Infirmary Board, County Local Authority, and County and District Road Board. Thomas Tailyour resided at Dubton House in 1881 with wife Isabella and daughter Louisa whilst local properties included Dubton Station Master's House, Dubton Company House, Hedderwick Farm House and Prettycur Cottar House and Farm.

Thomas Renny-Tailyour esquire of Borrowfield died at Dubton House near Montrose on 3 January 1885 and his will was proved before the Commissariat of Forfar on 27 March that year. Henry Waugh Renny-Tailyour of Borrowfield residing at 16 Kingswood Villas, Gillingham and William Harry Lumsden of Balmedie were executors and the will was confirmed in England on 11 April 1885. His obituary appeared in the Montrose Directory *Almanac* and stated that he was held in high respect living his life by the Scriptural maxim: "What thy hand findeth to do, do it with all thy might." He was not buried with his ancestors in Montrose but in Rosehill Cemetery on Rosehill Road one mile north of the town. There was a family plot beside the east wall with memorials both on the wall and in front. The earliest was to Robina Renny (1787-1856) daughter of Robert Renny Esq. and the next to Charles Alexander (1860-67) and Col. Thomas Renny-Tailyour (1812-85). Mrs. Isabella Renny-Tailyour, widow, continued to live at Dubton House but died at Banchory on the banks of the River Dee on 16 September 1896 and Henry Waugh Renny-Tailyour lieutenant colonel R.E. was her executor. The family remained in Montrose and Louisa Isabella Sidney Renny-Tailyour died at Dubton House on 7 May 1940 aged 82 years her probate granted to the North of Scotland Bank Ltd - the wife and daughter are also recorded at Rosehill Cemetery. The Tailyour family resided at Borrowfield for 300 years but the sons went to the corners of the British Empire.

Henry Waugh Renny-Tailyour was born at Mussoorie, India on 9 October 1849 although some records state Neemuch in the North West Province. There is also a baptism record at Montrose on 3 November 1849, which seems most unlikely, since the journey could not be accomplished in 25 days (also before the Suez Canal). Henry was in Mussoorie and India until the age of seven and returned to Montrose with his family in 1856. He was sent to Cheltenham College in the last term of 1859 at the age of 10 and was educated there with R.G. Graham (1861-62) and G.W. Addison (1863-66). He was in Beaufort House and Boyne House whilst Addison just three weeks older was also in Boyne - an association that paid great dividends in the future (see below). He played for the school cricket XI in his last year and scored 100 against Newnham College. He left the school in December 1867 and entered the Royal Military Academy, Woolwich in 1868. He joined the Royal Engineers as a lieutenant on 23 July 1870 and was posted to the School of Military Engineering, Chatham from 15 August 1870 to 10 October 1872, thus residing there on the 1871 census. He excelled at sport at public school and was soon in demand for his sporting ability. His photograph suggests he was a confident character with an amiable sense of humour and an irresistible smile. He joined Captain Marindin in the soccer team and played in the first Cup Final on 16 March 1872 helping to lead the attack - he also played rugby for his country Scotland the same year.

He received a posting to Portsmouth in December 1872 and his sporting career really took off. He played for Scotland v England at the Oval on 8 March 1873 the team including seven members of Queen's Park and Kinnaird of the Wanderers. This was the second international and Scotland lost 4-2 whilst Renny-Tailyour and A.G. Goodwyn of England were the only international players from the 1872 side. He was again posted to the School of Military Engineering from 8 May 1873 to 17 February 1876 and much happened during this time. He played with Addison, Marindin and Merriman in the Cup Final on 14 March 1874 but lost 2-0 to Oxford University; and then played a major role in the 1875 Cup Final against the Old Etonians. This was settled over two games and William Merriman and C.V. Wingfield-Stratford (see below) appeared on both occasions. The first game on 13 March 1875 was a 1-1 draw with a goal from Renny-Tailyour whilst the replay on 16 March 1875 was a 2-0 win for the Engineers with goals from Renny-Tailyour and Lieutenant W.F.H. Stafford. At least this is the official line since other sources state that Renny-Tailyour scored both the goals. He continued his cricket career during this period and played for Kent C.C.C. and the 'gentlemen' v 'players' in 1873-75. He was good in all aspects of the game being a hard hitting, middle order, right hand batsman and a right hand, fast round arm bowler and good cover point. He was an army officer and dashing sportsman thus a very eligible bachelor and he was soon introduced to Wingfield-Stratford's sister:

1. The Powerscourt Estate was situated in a magnificent location in the Wicklow Mountains having strategic importance at the time of the Normans (12th century). The Power family built a castle in the 13th century and Richard Wingfield (born before 1706) built a mansion in 1731 that had a grand north front and south front looking on to gardens. A 45-acre estate was developed in the 1740s and, nearby, the highest waterfall in Ireland flowed into the Dargle Valley. Richard was created 1st Viscount Powerscourt and died 21 October 1751 the estate passing to son Edward (1729-64). Richard Wingfield 3rd Viscount Powerscourt was baptized 24 December 1730 and married Amelia Stratford daughter of John 1st Earl of Aldborough on 7 September 1760, dying on 8 August 1788. His son Lieutenant Col. John Wingfield was born 2 August 1772 and married Francis Bartholomew 25 April 1797, having a son John in 1810 (treated below), and died 9 August 1850.

2. Clontarf Castle, two miles from Dublin, dates from 1172 and was the stronghold of King George (17th century). Sir Charles Coote a Puritan Republic General marched on the castle where King George led many rebels and took it on 15 December 1641. Oliver Cromwell gave the estate to John Blackwell who sold it to John Vernon the Quartermaster General of Cromwell's army on 14 August 1649. The family owned the castle for 300 years with the motto "Vernon Semper Viret" or "Vernon Always Flourishes".

John Vernon of Clontarf, a descendant, had a daughter Charlotte Diana (1800-35) who married General Sir John Wright Guise 3rd Baronet on 12 August 1815. The general was born 20 July 1777 and was a hero of the Peninsular War and died 1 April 1865 having had children Jane Elizabeth (1825) and John Christopher (1826). The castle was found to be unsafe in 1835 and rebuilt in 1837, but was sold by the family in 1952 then became a luxury hotel in 1998.

John Christopher Guise was born at Little Dean, Gloucester on 27 July 1826 and joined the 90th Regiment in 1845. He took part in the storming of Sevastopol in 1855 and as a major general was involved in the Indian Mutiny in 1857. He took part in the relief of Lucknow (13 November) and the storming of Secundra Bagh on 16-17 November 1857. With Sergeant S. Hill he saved the life of a captain and rescued two wounded men (whilst under fire) and acted gallantly throughout the action. He was awarded the Victoria Cross for bravery and the C.B. and commanded the 90th Regiment in 1861-64 and was lieutenant general of the Royal Leicester Regiment in 1890-95, however he took his own life and died at Gorey, County Wexford on 5 February 1895.

John Wingfield-Stratford was born at Powerscourt, Co. Wexford (or Kent) on 10 December 1810 and he married Jane Elizabeth Guise at Rendcomb south of Cheltenham on 10 December 1844. Their large family included Edward John (1849), Cecil Vernon (7 October 1853), Emily Rose (c. 6 May 1855) and Florence Mary (1858) who were all born at Addington, Kent. Indeed John a J.P. of independent means with a farm of 200 acres employing 12 men lived at Addington Park in 1881 with wife Jane, six children, brother-in-law John C. Guise and 17 servants but he died on 8 May 1881. His son Edward John Wingfield-Stratford was in the Scots Guards and a local J.P. at St. Vincent's, Addington in 1890 whilst his wife Jane E. died on 20 February 1897. Cecil Vernon Wingfield-Stratford and William Francis Howard Stafford became lieutenants at the S.M.E. Chatham on 29 October 1873 and the former played for England v Scotland at the Oval on 3 March 1877 (score 1-3). He was visiting Edward V. Bligh magistrate and clergyman, Isabel Lady Bligh, Roderick and daughter Rosalind (23) born London at Fatherwell Hall, Ryarsh in 1881. In fact Cecil married Rosalind Isabel Bligh on 12 October that year and lived at Norton, Isle of Wight (see below) - he was a brigadier general and died on 5 February 1939.

Henry Waugh Renny-Tailyour of Gillingham lieutenant R.E. married Emily Rose Wingfield-Stratford daughter of John (J.P.) at Addington, Kent on 9 September 1875. The witnesses were the two fathers and Florence Mary Wingfield-Stratford and Edward Ramsay Renny-Tailyour. Indeed there was hardly room for all the names on the marriage certificate! The father Thomas Renny-Tailyour presumably travelled there by train from Dubton Station to West Malling in Kent. Renny-Tailyour and his wife Emily had ten children in the next 22 years but it seems likely she remained at home for some of his postings. All the children were registered with the surname Tailyour but they were really Renny-Tailyour. He then had a notable appointment as aide-de-camp (A.D.C.) to the Lord Lieutenant of Ireland from 18 February to 11 December 1876 and spent this period in Dublin.

The position of Lord Lieutenant was formerly Viceroy or Lord Deputy namely the King's representative in Ireland. The Viceregal Apartments, Dublin Castle was the official residence from the 1780s between January and 17 March (St. Patrick's Day) or the 'social season' - the Viceregal Lodge, Phoenix Park was used the rest of the year. James Hamilton (1811-85) 1st Duke of Abercorn (Ireland) was educated at Harrow and Christchurch, Oxford and was Lord Lieutenant in 1866-68, when he graduated from Dublin University and was raised to the peerage. He was a Conservative politician and returned as Lord Lieutenant from 2 March 1874 to 11 December 1876. He was related to Princess Diana Spencer and his successor was John Winston Spencer Churchill 7th Duke of Marlborough who held the post from 11 December 1876 to 4 May 1880. In the mid-19th century real power was with the Chief Secretary of Ireland although the Unionists supported the Lord Lieutenant, a post that survived to the end of British rule in 1920.

Renny-Tailyour finished his posting on the same day as James Hamilton and was then sent to Gibraltar for a brief period from 18 January 1877 to 15 January 1878 (363 days) and spent the end of the month on leave. A. Bogle and H. Mitchell his team mates were both there at this time. He was ordered home in 1878 and returned to the S.M.E. Chatham from February 1878 to 31 March 1881 and was employed as Acting Instructor of Telegraphs. He continued to play cricket and was a noted batsman in military matches scoring a number of large innings, in particular 331 not out in 330 minutes against the Civil Service in 1880 - a run a minute! No doubt the Royal Engineers won and he came off to rapturous applause. His wife was at home during this period and had children: Florence Vernon (17 August 1876) Malling, Eleanor Maud (18 November 1878) Medway and John Wingfield (20 May 1881) Malling - all baptized at Addington Church.

He was made Instructor in Fortifications at the Royal Military Academy, Woolwich on 1 April 1881 and had lodgings with John and Jane Driscoll a tailor at 38 The Common, Woolwich that year. Thomas (1863) his brother was a gentleman cadet boarding at the Academy, at this time, although his wife did not appear on the 1881 census. He played further amateur games for Kent C.C.C. in 1881-83 and his career total for Kent in first class cricket was 818 runs (highest 124) and 2 wickets for 28 off 19 matches - he was aged 34. He was promoted to captain on 23 July 1882 and had two more children namely Cecil Ramsay (19 June 1882) and Eric (18 April 1884) who were baptized at the Garrison Church in Woolwich. He was the Assistant Instructor in Field Fortifications at the S.M.E. Chatham from 19 August 1884 and was residing at 16 Kingswood Villas, Gillingham in 1885. A daughter Eileen Mary (2 June 1886) was baptized at the Garrison Church, Chatham and the posting ended on 30 June 1888 but he did remain in the town in July-August that year. He continued to play cricket for the Engineers and his career lasted from 1870-88: 307 innings, 29 not out, 12,291 runs, average 44 and 52 (100s), which was an impressive record. He was posted to Gibraltar on 16 August 1888 and promoted to major on 1 December, then spent three years in the colony but did return home on occasions - the posting ended on 20 October 1891.

His daughter Rosalind Lilian was born at Braxton, Norton on the Isle of Wight on 11 September 1890. Norton hamlet was in the parish of Freshwater although the town of Yarmouth was nearer across the River Yar, and her mother Emily registered the birth with an address of 19 Dubton House, Montrose. Local directories show that Mrs. Laura Smith lived at Braxton Cottage, Norton in 1875-86 and Rev. Charles Drake at Norton Lodge in 1886. Other residents were A. Tennyson - Farringford, Miss Thackeray - The Porch, Charles A.H. and Julia M. Cameron - Dimbola, Freshwater Bay (1875); Rev. C. Bowen was at Heatherwood, Totland Bay to 1886 and his widow at Glenheadon in 1890-1902. Captain Cecil V.W. Stratford R.E. (37) lived at the Cracknells, Norton in 1891 with his wife Rosalind, children Emma C.W. and Geoffrey E.W. and four servants - Eliza White housemaid and caretaker was at Braxton Cottage across the road. Both still exist and Cracknells formerly St. John's Cottage is a stone building with large end chimneys in the trees opposite Malta Lodge (now Savoy Country Club). Braxton Cottage with its stone and whitewash walls and red tiles is on Yarmouth Road at the junction with Westhill Lane. Major Cecil V. Wingfield-Stratford R.E. lived at Norton Lodge from at least 1894-99 and Braxton may have been part of his large estate. The 'lodge' was a plain stucco house with two-storeys and bow windows and a conservatory on the east side. It was situated on a small coastal ridge and looked across the Solent and below was a boathouse. It was later a hotel and became Norton Grange a Warner complex although the old entrance and one gatepost remain. West Hill was another mansion nearby and is now part of a new housing estate - mainly bungalows.

Renny-Tailyour had avoided India however was given "special duties" in the colonial employment (local forces) at Sydney in New South Wales from 23 October 1891 to 23 October 1894, and was in fact the commander there. His wife joined him and a son Henry Frederick Thornton was born at Homebush, Sydney on 31 July 1893. He returned to England and was posted to the Thames district from October 1894 to August 1895, but was commanding the 4th Battalion (Training Division) at the S.M.E. Chatham on 6 August 1895 being promoted to lieutenant colonel on 12 August. His last two children were born at Medway - Magdalene Emily on 8 December 1895 and Stella Isabella Louisa on 5 February 1897, both baptized at Rochester Cathedral. He was given the rank of colonel on 12 August 1899 and finished at Chatham on 3 October 1899. He retired on 4 October at the age of 50 having served 29 years 73 days and was entitled to an army pension of £300 p.a.

He made some notable connections during his time in the army and none more so than the Guinness family. The tale starts with Arthur Guinness who refined the art of brewing porter in Dublin and opened St. James's Gate Brewery in 1759. His son Richard collected rents for a local bishop and converted to the Protestant faith thus they supported the Unionist cause. The Dublin brewery erected an independent engine of 10-h.p in 1808 and Benjamin Lee Guinness (1798) was sole owner in 1825 then made full use of opportunities in the British Empire. Indeed the company had a vested interest with such profitable outlets and were against Irish independence. Benjamin married Elizabeth Guinness in 1837 and was first Lord Mayor of Dublin in 1851, being the richest man in Ireland. For restoring St. Patrick's Cathedral at his own expense he was made a baronet in 1867 but died in 1868.

Edward Cecil Guinness great grandson of Arthur was born St. Anne's, Clontarf on 10 November 1847 and educated at Trinity College, Dublin. He gained sole ownership of Guinness when his brother Sir Arthur Edward (1840) became Lord Arditaun in 1880, and was the largest shareholder in the newly formed Guinness (public company) in 1886 - it was worth millions! He was made a baronet in 1885 and 1st Earl of Iveagh in 1891 purchasing the Elveden Estate from the Maharajah Duleep Singh in 1894. The estate of 23,000 acres was near Eriswell and Icklingham and the town of Thetford in Norfolk, having its own branch railway from

Barnham. Edward was a great philanthropist who contributed to many public buildings in Dublin but resided mainly in England after 1900 and did much entertaining at the Elveden Estate. He arranged many shooting parties and his guests included King Edward VII. His son Rupert Edward Cecil Lee was born at Iveagh House, Dublin on 29 March 1874 and was educated at Eton and Trinity College, Cambridge. He fought in the Boer War, married Lady Gwendolen Florence Mary Onslow on 8 October 1903 (see Meysey-Thompson Ch. 7) and was a Unionist M.P. in 1908-10 and 1912-27. He became 2nd Earl of Iveagh and Chairman upon his father's decease on 7 October 1927.

The 1st Earl of Iveagh was two years older than Renny-Tailyour and may have met him through the Lord Lieutenant in 1876. The 'old boy network' also came into play since Lieutenant Colonel G.W. Addison retired from the army on 4 October 1899, the same day as Renny-Tailyour. They were not idle for long and the Earl of Iveagh contacted both parties in 1899 and they became directors on the Guinness Board that year. Renny-Tailyour appears to have had the most active role and represented the Earl of Iveagh in Dublin, whilst Addison held the position of consultant in London. Renny-Tailyour resided at Shrewsbury House, Merion in County Dublin after his appointment and worked at the St. James's Gate Brewery. The couple spent most of their time in Ireland but did visit Dubton House in Montrose and were well known there, whilst Emily Rose died in the name Tailyour at 30 Devonshire Street, Marylebone on Friday 22 July 1904 aged 49. She was stated to be a resident of Shrewsbury House, Merion in County Dublin.

Memorial to H.W. Renny-Tailyour.
Located in Rosehill Cemetery, Montrose.

The oak coffin arrived at Montrose Station on the 9.59 a.m. east coast train on Tuesday 26 July and was covered with magnificent wreaths. A large number of mourners were waiting at the station and the cortège followed by twenty carriages went along the High Street and George Street to St. Mary's Episcopal Church. Col. H.W. Renny-Tailyour, Miss, Miss E., Mr. J. and Mr. E. Renny-Tailyour, Captain H. Wingfield-Stratford, Miss Renny-Tailyour the sister-in-law, Sir Henry and Lady Hawley of Leybourne Grange, Maidstone, Mr. and Mrs. B. Cator, Mrs. and Mr. E. Lumsden of Balmedie and Col. Dingwall-Fordyce were chief mourners. Others included Col. and Mrs. Lumsden of Langley Park, A.R. Duncan of Newmanswalls House, G. Keith of Usan, E. Millar of Rossie, R.H. Millar of Blair Castle and The Links, C. Armstrong-Smythe of Londonderry, J. Barrie Borrowfield and J. Lamb Newmanswalls - there is a memorial to her in Rosehill Cemetery with that of her husband. There was then more bad news and Cecil Ramsay his second son died in Northern Nigeria on 25 March 1911. Renny-Tailyour remained with Guinness after his wife's death and was promoted to the position of Managing Director in 1913. He had a prominent role in the company and was directly involved in decision making, thus authorising many actions. The first problem he encountered was the Dublin 'Lock Out', a strike by dockers, seamen and carters in August 1913 to February 1914. It caused severe disruption to their overseas distribution thus the company purchased its first two ships under his direction - W.M. Barkley (Nov 1913) and S.S. Carrowdore (Feb 1914). He was in charge during the First War when 800 employees went to fight, and the company paid them a half wage during this time and guaranteed them jobs on their return. He also had to deal with restrictions imposed by Lloyd George P.M. on the strength of beer. Each of these tested his managerial skills.

Henry administered his wife's effects of £369 on 14 July 1917 and retired from Guinness in early 1919. He moved permanently to Newmanswalls on the Borrowfield Estate in Montrose and his sister Louisa lived nearby at Dubton House. He only played a small role in the town and was a local J.P. and represented the landed gentry of Forfar on the Board of Directors of Montrose Royal Asylum. He resided at the house for a short time and died there on 15 June 1920 being of Borrowfield and Newmanswalls. His probate was granted to his executors Thomas Francis Bruce and John Wingfield Renny-Tailyour R.A. in Scotland however it was confirmed and sealed in London on 22 September 1920. He left two sons and six daughters and he was buried at Rosehill Cemetery with the simple inscription: "Col. Henry Waugh Renny-Tailyour of Borrowfield son of Col. Thomas born 1849 died 1920." His house Newmanswalls was left to his son John W. whilst the family remained at Dubton House until the 1960s.

The Borrowfield Estate was on the northern outskirts of town and the spire of Montrose Church could be seen two miles away on the horizon. Dubton House was on a square plot of land and was transformed from an old farmhouse into a gentleman's home. The building had two-storeys with gables, white washed walls and large chimneys. A grand bay window looked out on the garden and there were outbuildings nearby, whilst the Brechin to Dubton Railway was behind the house but was later defunct - the house remains today and is little changed from Renny-Tailyour's time. A lane beside the house continued south to a bend and there was the substantial Borrowfield Farm with three-storeys, white washed walls, a slate roof and outbuildings, plus a stream just beside it. Borrowfield Road an ancient route continued south and in those days crossed farmland to reach the main road to Montrose.

Newmanswalls was built at the southern end of the estate in the 19th century and was younger than the ancient Dubton House at the north end. The former was situated just west of North Esk Road with a lodge and tree-lined entrance in Brechin Road. It was much larger than Dubton and had an inner courtyard, extensive gardens and a northern entrance in Borrowfield Road. The house was approached from Montrose and just before it was Lochside Brewery. Today there are some old cottages on the main road dated 1869 whilst the Lochside Distillery is now derelict. This was a large building with a chateau style roof, chimneys, a coat of arms and the date 1889 upon it. Newmanswalls was demolished after the Second War and a new estate was built on the site and the roads include Newmanswalls Avenue and Renny and Tailyour Crescents. There is a stone boundary wall on the main road that delineated the 'old' estate and soon after Brechin Road there is Newhame Road on the left. The latter is a new route through the estate and a few hundred yards in on the left is Borrowfield Road. This runs parallel to Newhame Road and the old stonewall of the estate is beside it. A hundred yards along there is a break in the wall with a green behind and this was the old north entrance to Renny-Tailyour's house. Borrowfield Road then rejoins Newhame Road but veers to the left under the main railway and continues through countryside to Borrowfield Farm and Dubton House.

Henry's two brothers, meanwhile, had lives of high adventure. Edward Ramsay second son of Thomas was born at Mussoorie on 8 December 1851 and attended Cheltenham in the third term of 1863 being a member of Boyne House. He was at the school with his brother Henry and left in December 1867. He worked in a commercial office in London after leaving school and was present at Henry's wedding in Addington in 1875. Meanwhile the Dutch East India Company or V.O.C. occupied southern Africa in 1652 and held it until Napoleon invaded the Netherlands in 1795. The British as a pre-emptive move occupied V.O.C. territory in Africa, although restored it to the Batavian State in 1803 - the latter had replaced the Netherlands and was a Republic like that in France and under its 'protection'. Napoleon continued his ambitions thus the British re-occupied southern Africa and formed Cape Colony on 8 January 1806, enabling them to control trade routes to the Far East. This was always an unstable region and the Dutch and other settlers collectively known as the Boers moved north in the 1830-40s. This became known as the 'Great Trek' and they soon overcame local peoples and established the Transvaal or South African Republic north of Vaal River in 1856. The first diamonds were discovered at Orange and Vital Rivers in 1867 whilst richer deposits were found in 1871 thus Kimberley was established in 1873. Cecil Rhodes was one of the first to profit and later formed De Beers Consolidated Mines (1888).

Such wealth created more conflict in the region and the British annexed the Transvaal in 1877 followed by much unrest amongst local tribes. The Galeka people lived in Transkei region, south of Natal, beyond colonial control and they invaded Cape Colony in 1877 whilst the Gaika tribe nearby began a rebellion against the British - the answer was to send many Imperial troops to the region. Edward R. Renny-Tailyour volunteered for the army at this time and was a captain in the Gaika and Galeka War and later received a medal. This also became known as the 9th Kaffir War and was fought from August 1877 to September 1878. The Zulu War took place early the next year and began with the famous conflicts at Isandlwana and Rorke's Drift on 22-23 January 1879 but was ended at Ulundi on 4 July, whilst the Boers rebelled and claimed independence leading to the 1st Boer War in 1880-81. The largest gold fields in the world were found at Witwatersrand or the Rand in 1887 and Paul Kruger President of the Boer nation did not rejoice but predicted bloodshed.

Edward R. Renny-Tailyour saw his opportunity and moved to the Gold Fields, Barberton in the Transvaal and was in business at Port Elizabeth, then was later a gentleman of Johannesburg. He went up country to Matabeleland and made the acquaintance of King Lobengulu with whom he became a great favourite. Due to the friendship he secured a concession from the King, in return for which the Chartered Co. gave up 50 square miles of land in Mashonaland and Matabeleland and all mining rights there, the land to be chosen by

Mr. Renny-Tailyour for the syndicate. The agreement took place in 1892 and Edward returned to London in autumn 1893 to float a company to work the concession. He went out to select a territory and the work was just finishing when he was struck down with an apoplectic attack. He died at Mangwe, Matabeleland in 'South Africa' on 13 June 1894 and Henry W. Renny-Tailyour his executor and the attorney of Thomas William Chaplin administered his will in London on 24 January 1895.

Members of the Zulu tribe were forced northwards in 1847 and after suppressing local peoples formed a new tribe in Southern Rhodesia in 1850. This was the Matabeleland province and King Lobengulu ruled from 1868 when the old King died. He sealed an agreement with Cecil Rhodes in 1888 that allowed the latter to colonise the neighbouring area of Mashonaland to the east. This was placed under the governorship of Dr. Leander Starr Jameson in 1890, however the Matabele people continued their practice of raiding these lands and soon fought with the Mashonaland police. Jameson and other white pioneers launched a counter offensive and captured the head kraal of Lobengulu at Bulawayo. The King fled up the Shangani River but after meeting other tribesmen he fought the British and repelled them. Despite his agreement with Renny-Tailyour, King Lobengulu was a fugitive in the bush and died in 1893. The area lay between the Zambezi and Limpopo Rivers and was soon the scene of more action.

Cecil Rhodes asked Dr. L. Jameson to secure the Transvaal border but he took matters into his own hands and there was an incursion from 29 December 1895 to 2 January 1896. The action failed and his troops were overcome and although the British condemned what happened, the South Africa Co. were forced to pay £1 million in compensation. A second campaign took place in Matabeleland in 1896 when Lord Baden-Powell of Gilwell was involved whilst Edward Henry Pember debated the Jameson Raid in Parliament in April 1897 (see Ch. 4). This 'mistake' more than anything led to the 2nd Boer War and the Boers made a pre-emptive strike in 1899 and laid siege to Kimberley, Ladysmith and Mafeking - the latter was defended by Robert Baden-Powell. The conflict was not going well with reverses such as Spion Kop and Lord Kitchener (1850-1916) assumed control in November 1900. The Boers were defeated by May 1902 and the Transvaal and Orange Free State became part of the British Empire. The Union of South Africa a dominion was formed in 1910 and it became an independent republic in the Commonwealth in 1961.

Thomas Francis Bruce the third son was born at Montrose on 8 June 1863 and went to Cheltenham in the third term of 1876. He was also in Boyne House and left in July 1879 and attended the Royal Military Academy, Woolwich in 1880 - he was a gentleman cadet boarding there in 1881. He was a lieutenant in the Royal Engineers in 1883 and embarked on an exciting army career, and was in the Burmese War in 1885-89, went on the Chin-Lushai Expedition in 1889-90 and an expedition to the Chinese frontier with Burma in 1890-93. He was a captain in 1891, major and brevet lieutenant colonel in 1900, and was on the Sino-Burmese Boundary Commission from 1897-1900 then left China in 1901. He was a brevet colonel in 1906 and lieutenant colonel in 1907 but retired when his brother died in 1920. He lived on the family estate and died at Newmanswalls on 10 June 1937. Edward and Thomas both have memorials at Rosehill Cemetery.

Eric Renny-Tailyour (1884) was at Ely College, Cambridge in 1901 and was a resident of Chilanga, Northern Rhodesia but died in the Belgian Congo, Africa on 5 December 1922. John Wingfield Renny-Tailyour a major in H.M. Army administered his affairs. Florence (1876) and Eleanor (1878) the first two daughters lived at "Tours", The Avenue, Chobham in Surrey and died there on 14 December 1955 and 10 July 1957 respectively. John Wingfield Renny-Tailyour (1881) was in the Royal Artillery being promoted to 2nd lieutenant in 1900, lieutenant in 1901 and captain in 1910. He inherited Newmanswalls from his father in 1920 and was there as a major in 1921-25 and a colonel in 1929-30 but later moved to Dubton House (possibly after his aunt died in 1940). His wife Kate Rosalind Florence died at Dubton on 16 November 1956 and her husband D.S.O. D.L. retired colonel H.M. Army obtained her probate. John W. Renny-Tailyour died at Dubton House on 9 December 1969 and also has a memorial in Rosehill Cemetery. Montrose had several good soccer players and eight men who received Scottish caps are buried there. This was a prosperous town in the 18-20th century with sea links and a large tidal basin behind. A wooden bridge was built across the South Esk in 1792-95 and the foundation stone of a suspension bridge was laid on 10 September 1828. Montrose and Arbroath Railway had its first passengers on 1 May 1883 and old iron steps in the station state: "Craighall Ironworks, Glasgow 1910". Renny-Tailyour would have arrived there during his travels and looked out across the water with its dramatic sunsets before travelling by carriage to Dubton.

HUGH MITCHELL

The Royal Engineers had long-term connections with Gibraltar and several of the players were stationed there whilst others like Hugh Mitchell actually lived there. Indeed he fitted the common stereotype being from an army family and also from Scotland. The name Mitchell, however, is certainly a common one and this presented problems with his ancestry. His father Hugh Mitchell was born in Scotland c.1787 and was an army man who married late in life. There are two likely births - Liberton near Edinburgh on 9 December 1786 and Grahamston or Barony in Lanark on 7 January 1787, but neither of these is conclusive. Hugh Mitchell entered the army as a 2nd lieutenant or ensign on 9 July 1803 aged 16, and was promoted to 1st lieutenant on 15 August 1805. He served with the Indian Army under the E.I.C. and joined the Royal Marines division by 1820 being promoted to captain on 31 July 1826 - he was stationed for a time in Madras.

Lieutenant Colonel Sir John McCaskill (1780) was stationed in India and had children Jessie (1813) and John Charles (1817). He fought in the Sutlej Campaign - 1st Anglo-Sikh War and troops arrived at Ferozepore in late 1845 and were deployed throughout the region. There was a battle at Mudki, 25 miles away, on 18 December 1845 and the British suffered heavy losses with 872 casualties, whilst due to the nature of the conflict it was known as 'Midnight Mudki' - Lieutenant Col. Sir John McCaskill K.C.B. K.H. of the 9th Foot was killed in action. The Battle of Ferozeshah was then fought 12 miles away on 21 December 1845 (see Goodwyn Ch. 10). Jessie McCaskill was born in the East Indies in 1813-14 and John Charles McCaskill was born at the Madras 'Presidency' in 1817. He also became a lieutenant colonel in the army and as a widower married Jane Agnes Smith at St. Thomas's, Ryde on the Isle of Wight on 17 October 1867. He stated that his father was John McCaskill major general whilst his wife was born in Scotland in 1840 daughter of James Smith a clerk. They lived at Stoke near Guildford and had children: Agnes Anne (1870), John Charles Henry (1872) and Roland H.B. (1877). John Charles McCaskill retired lieutenant colonel lived at Austen Road, Stoke in 1881 with his family and two servants, but died at Bedford in December 1898 aged 78.

Hugh Mitchell (48) married Jessie McCaskill (21) in India in c.1835 but they returned to England soon after the marriage and lived at St. John's Wood. This area was mainly pasture until the end of the 18th century however the arrival of the Grand Union Canal resulted in housing for labourers in Lisson Grove. There were ambitious schemes to build large villas and these were carried out by the Eyre family and James Burton (see Ch. 7). Park Road and St. John's Wood were developed in the 1820s with separate villas unlike the terraced houses seen in Belgravia, Pimlico and Paddington. This was to be the suburb of the future. The Royal Botanical Society had gardens in Regent's Park and Edward Geo. Henderson & Son (nurserymen) owned Wellington Nursery on St. John's Wood Road in the 1850s. Thomas Lord brought cricket to the area and established a ground at Dorset Square but was forced out and moved to a new site at North Bank. The Regent's Canal Company, however, soon required the land and he moved the ground and the "turf" to a new location in St. John's Wood Road in 1814. It became Lord's Cricket Ground and home of the notable Marylebone Cricket Club (M.C.C.). The Wellington Nursery was situated at the east end resulting in the famous "Nursery End" at Lord's. During the Napoleonic Wars a military barracks was established on the site of St. John's Wood Farm and, indeed, the farm buildings still survived in the 1860s. The barracks had a gymnasium, guard room, magazine, canteen and a large parade ground whilst St. John's Wood High Street provided services for the local gentry and the military.

Hugh Mitchell came to the area in 1836 and presumably had connections with the barracks, which are still present today. He was then a major in the Madras Army and lived at 17 Wellington Terrace in St. John's Wood and his neighbour Madame Tussaud was at Wellington Road (1838-39). His son John Hugh was born on 27 December 1836 and baptized at St. Marylebone Church on 17 August 1837 but died as an infant. The family then returned to the sub-continent and daughter Jessie Camilla Mitchell was born at Cuttack, East Indies on 31 August 1839 and baptized there on 11 February 1840. The town was south west of Calcutta on the 'Mouths of the Mahanadi' delta. Hugh Mitchell was made a brevet colonel on 23 November 1841, which meant he had the rank but without corresponding pay - he gained the full rank of lieutenant colonel on 19 July 1844.

The family returned to England and resided at "West Villa", 29 Cavendish Road West in St. John's Wood from 1846-51. The property, built by the Eyre family, was situated on the north side of Lord's Cricket Ground and in those days gave a free view of games. This was a notable three-storey mansion being the last house in the street and square in design. There was a white stucco 'grand' ground floor with yellow-brown brick on the upper storeys, whilst ornate scrollwork supported a first floor balcony and similar detail was on the second floor and below the roof cornice. The building had large chimneys rising from the sidewalls and an extensive garden to the rear. The property is still present as is much of Cavendish Road and is now divided into Cavendish Avenue (3-19) and Cavendish Close (21-29). The latter is a private road (part of the Eyre Estate) and the numbering remains unchanged from the 1850s. There are eucalyptus or gum trees growing next to West Villa and in the surrounding area that may have come from the Empire. The house remains impressive but it now has a modern conservatory at the ground floor (front) and a new grandstand at Lord's obscures the view.

The couple then had two children at 29 Cavendish Road West: Mary born on 24 October 1845 and baptized at St. Marylebone on 22 April 1846, and Hugh born on 3 December 1849 and the birth registered on 8 January 1850 - the father a lieutenant colonel. Hugh Mitchell senior, aged 63, was a lieutenant colonel in the Royal Marines in 1850-51 the Corps being active in Plymouth and Gibraltar - he had a service record of 48 years Full Pay. He was a retired lieutenant colonel of the East India Company Service (age 59?) living at "West Villa", Cavendish Road, Marylebone on 30 March 1851 with his wife Jessie, children Jessie, Mary and Hugh and five servants. The neighbouring property was no. 27 and this confirmed West Villa as no. 29. Hugh Mitchell a colonel in the Royal Marines, aged 64, died of pleuro-pneumonia (12 days) at the Marine Barracks, Woolwich Dockyard on 22 May 1851. John Henry King of King Street, Woolwich was informant and the army lists state: "Colonel H. Mitchell Royal Marines deceased" in 1852-53. He left his young wife aged 38 with three children to bring up on her own however she clearly had help and ample finances. She may have resided at 19 Devonshire Terrace, Notting Hill in 1862 whilst son Hugh attended Harrow School in 1864-67.

Jessie Mitchell then lived at 87 Kensington Gardens Square, Bayswater in 1871 and the household included daughter Marie (24) and five servants, one being a lady's maid. The property was at the centre of the square and was probably speculative infill, since it obscured the view of houses at the side. The front of the house faced the road and had a façade of white stucco, being narrow and tall. There was a grand portico entrance surmounted by a window and scrolls at the first floor with an ornate cornice above. The rear was curved at the ground and first floors with pediment detail at the second, and looked out on an open lawn. The house is now part of flats numbered 86-92 and the property has clearly seen better days. The family were absent from the 1881 census but lived on the Isle of Wight by 1886. Jessie widow of Hugh Mitchell colonel in the Madras Native Infantry died after an illness lasting eight months at the Bays, Beachfield Road in Sandown on 25 March 1887 and the informant was her son Hugh Mitchell of 44 Hogarth Road, London. There was a funeral service in Sandown Church however she was buried at Kensal Green Cemetery, London, presumably with her husband and this was noted briefly in the local *County Press* on 2 April 1887. She made her will at 87 Kensington Gardens Square and Jessie Camilla Mitchell of the Bays, Sandown obtained probate at Winchester on 9 November 1887. Her estate was valued at £6,493 11s 1d but re-sworn in January 1888 at £6,552 13s 1d.

The family had several connections with the Isle of Wight and there was soon another union. Charles Wooldridge married Ann Eleanor Foot Hannington at Twyford, Hampshire on 3 December 1822 and their son William Henry Wooldridge was baptized at St. Thomas's, Winchester on 12 August 1841. He was articled to his father and was admitted a country solicitor in 1863 and married Charlotte Hearn at St. Thomas's, Ryde on the Isle of Wight on 20 August 1867 - he was a resident of St. Thomas's, Winchester son of Charles Esq. His bride was daughter of John Henry and Mary Dennett Hearn (solicitor) and was baptized at St. Thomas's, Ryde on 17 September 1843 - she lived at Couchian House. William worked with her father on the island and secured lucrative work and was also an officer in the Nunwell Company of Volunteers. There was a mortgage taken on five messuages at Bridger Street in Sandown to secure £300 (and the interest) held for 999 years at a rent of £52 10s p.a. - 20 September 1876. The agreement was made between William Higgs house agent of Fitzroy Street, Sandown in the first part and Rev. Joseph Rhodes Charlesworth of Elstead Rectory, Godalming and W.H. Wooldridge gentleman of Sandown in the second part. A building in Bridger Street used as an auction mart was the collateral security for the sum of £300.

William was clerk to the Local Board, Secretary to the I. of W. Conservative Association and the Sandown Pier Company in 1878. He was also perpetual commissioner and commissioner for oaths in 1879 with offices at Wilkes Road, Sandown and 2 St. Thomas's Street, Ryde. He was living at St. Peter's, Hill Street, Sandown, from 1878, which was the first property on the west side after Station Avenue, next to Nunwell Street and the railway refreshment room. He lived there with his wife Charlotte and one servant in 1881, however she died at St. Peter's and was buried at Christchurch, Sandown on 25

November 1885 aged 42 (there is a memorial by the path). William Henry Wooldridge married Jessie Camilla Mitchell at St. George's Hanover Square in June 1888, soon after her mother's death, and was a solicitor and clerk to the Local Board at Wilkes Road from 1888-95. He lived at St. Peter's, Hill Street with his wife Jessie and three servants in 1891 and 1901. He was briefly Wooldridge & Witton in 1899 and then took on work as clerk to the Urban District Council (U.D.C.). His business had grown and he was commissioner for oaths, clerk to I. of W. County Council, Clerk of the Peace, clerk to Sandown U.D.C., and Secretary to the Sandown Pier Extension Co. Ltd. in 1904; at County Council Offices, 20 Holyrood Street in Newport; Wilkes Road; Sandown Town Hall in Grafton Street, and Belgrave Chambers in Belgrave Road and Clarence Road (London).

He continued to live at St. Peter's, Hill Street and died there on 8 February 1907 aged 65. His obituary appeared in the *County Press* and stated that he was clerk to the local authority for some 35 years. As a mark of respect flags flew at half-mast at Newport and Sandown Town Halls, the Conservative Club and Sandown Pier. The principal mourners at his funeral were his wife Jessie, Charles Wooldridge registrar to the Diocese of Winchester, H.B. Jameson (both nephews), Mr. Nash his London agent and many local people especially from the council. Mrs. Jessie Wooldridge supported her husband and was herself President of the Primrose League and Hon. Secretary of the Soldiers and Sailors Families Assoc. and Help Society. She had a keen interest in the military people in the district and also supported the N.S.P.C.C. She died at St. Peter's on 26 February 1915 aged 75 and her obituary was in the *County Press* on 6 March stating she was the daughter of the late Colonel Hugh Mitchell H.E.I.C. Mourners at her funeral included C.S. Wooldridge and Lieut. Hugh Bellingham Jameson 2nd Cavalry, Aldershot (nephews). The latter was born in 1874 and may have been the son of Thomas and Mary Jameson (née Mitchell) who had other children born at Simla in India.

Hugh Mitchell junior did not know his father, however he had a promising career ahead of him. He was born in 1849 and lived initially at St. John's Wood and possibly Notting Hill then attended Harrow School in the third term of 1864. He would have known the master Mr. Bowen whilst his peers included Betts, Crake and Welch of the Wanderers. He represented the school shooting XI in 1867 and left in the middle term that year and almost certainly attended the Royal Military Academy, Woolwich. He became a lieutenant in the Royal Engineers on 8 January 1870, the same day as E.W. Creswell and H.B. Rich, and this led to friendships that lasted for years and were transferred to the soccer pitch. He was posted to the School of Military Engineering, Chatham from February 1870 to July 1872 and was residing there on the 1871 census. He played in the Cup Final of 1872 and no doubt learnt his soccer skills at Harrow however this was to be his only major game. He was credited with a good effort during the match and one wonders if he knew he was born in a house built by the family of R.W.S Vidal?

He was posted to Aldershot for nine months in July 1872 and was then in Bermuda from 22 February 1873 to 15 January 1875. The latter was no doubt a most desirable posting and there was probably a murmur of, "Mitchell's got Bermuda, lucky devil." He then had a significant posting to Gibraltar from 16 January 1875 to 3 March 1878, which was a popular destination for the Royal Engineers and Bogle, Cotter, Muirhead and Renny-Tailyour were all in Gibraltar in the late 1870s. In addition the Creswell family lived there for over 100 years and this soon had an affect on him (see Ch. 9). Hugh Mitchell was presumably friends with Edmund Creswell and thus was introduced to his family whilst stationed there. Creswell himself was posted to Bengal during this period but may have been in Gibraltar on leave or for his father's funeral in 1877. Whatever the series of events the outcome was romantic and Hugh was engaged to Mary Catherine Edwards Creswell, sister of Edmund, who was born in Gibraltar on 4 March 1857.

He was "ordered home" in 1878 and based at Chatham from March-June then at the R.E. Troop Depot, Aldershot from June 1878 to January 1879. His fiancé, Mary then travelled to England and they were married at White Notley, Essex on 22 August 1878 the village being located between Braintree and Witham. Hugh was described as a lieutenant R.E. of Aldershot and his bride a spinster of White Notley. This was an obscure location for the marriage but there was an explanation. William F. Fraser the vicar carried out the ceremony and was in fact Mary Creswell's uncle, on her mother's side, whilst the witnesses were H.B. Rich who was stationed at Aldershot in 1877-79 and W.R. Creswell the brother of Edmund and Mary. Indeed the friendships continued long after the last ball was kicked in the Cup Final. Hugh was at Staff College in Aldershot from February 1879 to December 1880 and after some leave finished his posting in the town in February 1881. He lived nearby at Frimley and had children

Katherine May in December 1879 and Hugh in June 1881 however they soon left Aldershot and moved nearer to London.

Hugh Mitchell a lieutenant R.E. lived at Fir Tree House, High Road, Enfield, in 1881 with wife Catherine born Gibraltar, children Katherine and Hugh, Emma Mary Creswell wife of Edmund and two servants - one being the children's nurse from Spain. Hugh had a temporary posting at the Intelligence Department of the War Office, Horse Guards from February 1881 and was promoted to captain on 8 January 1882, however he retired with a gratuity of £1,200 on 11 March that year having completed 12 years 52 days service. He then entered the legal profession and qualified as a barrister in 1884, taking chambers at 3 Elm Court, Temple, and worked on the South Wales and Chester Circuit and the Glamorgan-shire Sessions. He resided at 44 Hogarth Road near Earl's Court in 1887 and had sons Kenneth Grant (28 August 1885) and Edmund Amyot (March 1889) there whilst Philip Euen (1 May 1890) was born Wimbledon. He resided at 6 Douro Place, Victoria Road, Kensington, in 1891-92 and his wife Mary Mitchell lived there in 1891 with children Katherine, Kenneth, Edmund and Philip, and five servants, including Ana M. Duarke from Spain. 6 Douro Place was a three-storey semi-detached town house in a quiet cul-de-sac. It had a staggered plain front and flight of stairs leading up to an entrance portico with columns and cornice. It has a blue plaque to Samuel Palmer (1805-81), artist, who lived there 1851-61 but previously resided at Shoreham, Kent and did most of his work in the village. The property remains amongst several old houses at the west end of the street.

6 Douro Place, Kensington. Hugh Mitchell lived here in 1891.

The captain himself painted an interesting picture and there was soon a further twist to the tale. Mary Catherine Edwards Mitchell, his wife, died of peritonitis at 6 Douro Place, Kensington on 5 May 1892 aged 35 years. Her husband Hugh was described as a barrister whilst the informant was L. Scott of 43 Church Road, Guildford (see McCaskill). Hugh was left with four young children aged 2-13 years and it seems likely he had an offer of assistance from Gibraltar thus he had moved there by 1894. The Creswell family lived at 6 South Barrack Road, Gibraltar from 1891-1906 and the Fforde family (their relatives) lived next door at "Mount Pleasant", 7 South Barrack Road, in 1891-93 (see Ch. 9) - one mile south of the town above Rosia Bay. A large white building called Mount Pleasant, occupied by Telecom, is on the site (possibly the same property) whilst 20 South Barrack Road, opposite, is a shuttered colonial villa of 1891 occupied by the Gibraltar Broadcasting Company (G.B.C.).

ıe Plaque at 6 Douro Place. Samuel Palmer did most of his work at Shoreham in Kent.

Hugh Mitchell moved to Mount Pleasant after the Fforde family left in 1894, and then practiced as a barrister and solicitor in Gibraltar and Tangier. He was described as of the Inner Temple and had an address Cloister Chambers, Market Lane, Gibraltar, in 1897. He was concerned about the future of his young family and wrote his last will in the Registrar's Office at the Supreme Court, Gibraltar on 5 February 1903: "This is the last will of me HUGH MITCHELL of Cloister Chambers, Gibraltar. I devise and bequeath all my property, real and personal, unto and to the use of my daughter KATHARINE and I request her, but without imposing any legal obligation upon her, to apply the same at her absolute discretion, both as to capital and income, in the same way as I myself would have done if alive for her maintenance and the maintenance of my younger children, until the latter shall be in a position to maintain themselves and I appoint her sole executrix. *Hugh Mitchell.*" The will was then put in a drawer and did not surface for over 30 years.

Indeed Hugh was at Cloister Chambers for many years with an address Cloister Ramp (1902-12) and 77 Irish Town (1918-26) whilst Harrow School records listed him at Cloister Chambers in

1911, aged 62. In fact Market Lane, Cloister Ramp and Irish Town all intersect at one point near to Line Wall Road, with the Bay of Algeciras beyond. A white fronted property with traditional shutters, called Cloister Building, is only two doors from 75 Irish Town and being near Market Lane was no doubt the location of Cloister Chambers. The 'old' police station next to Cloister Ramp is just opposite and was built of red brick with marble columns and arches at the entrance - opened by General Sir William John Codrington K.C.B. Governor in 1864. Hugh would have seen the police station each day when going to work and no doubt met some of his clients there! He retired from practice in 1926 aged 77 but this was not the end of the story and he moved to Pretoria, South Africa by the 1930s, now in his eighties. The settlements of Brakpan & Benoni were 30 km east of Johannesburg in the gold mining belt the former being a gold mining centre. Hugh Mitchell died at Brakpan in the Union of South Africa on 16 August 1937 and Katherine May Mitchell his daughter registered his will at the Supreme Court, Pretoria in the Transvaal Provincial Division on 21 August. Letters of administration were issued on 6 September and duplicate papers on 25 September however the will was mostly irrelevant as his children had long been adults. Katharine's address was P.O. Box 265 Benoni or c/o the Manager's House, Government Gold Mining Areas Ltd., Brakpan and she continued to reside abroad. She employed Eustace Bernard Ames solicitor and attorney of Taylor, Willcocks & Co. 218 Strand, London as her representative and he proved the will on 18 November 1937. The effects in England came to £2,008 1s 3d and presumably his gold was in South Africa!

Katherine May Mitchell was born in December 1879 and grew up in Kensington and Gibraltar however after her time on the goldfields (1937) returned to England and lived at "Danny" near Hurstpierpoint. The latter was a country house and estate in the shadow of the South Downs dated c.1582 and was purchased by Henry and Barbara Campion in 1725, the family then owning it for seven generations. In recent times it came under the Mutual Households Association and was converted into homes but with the original form retained. Katherine May Mitchell lived in one of these properties however she died at 21 Molyneux Park Road, Tunbridge Wells on 7 January 1967 and her estate was valued at £17,778. The Country Houses Association then purchased Danny in 1984 and opened it to the public.

Cloister Ramp, Gibraltar "Old Town".
Hugh Mitchell was a solicitor here from 1894-1926.

Kenneth Grant Mitchell was born 28 August 1885 and was an assistant engineer in the Indian Service of Engineers in 1909. He married Lilian daughter of Edward Westlake of Southampton in 1911 and was executive engineer in 1917. He was a temporary captain of the Royal Engineers in India 1917-19, Under Secretary to the Punjab Government 1919, road engineer with the Indian Government 1930 and consulting engineer for Indian roads 1934-42. His wife Lilian died in 1938 and his only son was killed in Italy in 1942 thus leaving one daughter. He retired in 1946 and was created K.C.I.E. but became Chief Controller of Road Transport, India and Chief Warden of Civil Defence, West Suffolk (1953-59). Sir Kenneth Grant Mitchell K.C.I.E. then resided at St. Michael's House, Peckham Bush but died at Victoria Cottage Hospital, Tonbridge on 23 September 1966.

Philip Euen Mitchell was born 1 May 1890 and was educated privately, then at St. Paul's School and Trinity College, Oxford. He was assistant resident for Nyasaland in 1912 (Malawi from 1964) and a lieutenant, captain and adjutant in 1915-18 when he received the Military Cross. He was private secretary to the acting Governor of Nyasaland in 1918-19 and held posts regarding the Tanganyika Territory in 1919-35 marrying Margery daughter of John d'Urban Tyrwhitt-Drake in 1925. He then held senior posts and was Governor of Uganda in 1935-40, created K.C.M.G. in 1937, worked in Ethiopia and East Africa in 1940-42, Governor of Fiji and the West Pacific in 1942-44 and lastly Governor of Kenya in 1944-52. He was created G.C.M.G. in 1947 and produced a publication "African Afterthoughts" from his time on that continent, and retired to Rinoncillo, Algeciras, Spain near Gibraltar (across the Bay of Algeciras). Sir Philip Euen Mitchell died in the Royal Navy Hospital, Gibraltar on 12 October 1964 and his effects in England came to £4,734; he also had assets in Kenya thus his will was sealed there on 24 November 1965. Hugh Mitchell had many lives in one lifetime: he grew up in a Victorian villa at St. John's Wood, was a lieutenant in the Royal Engineers, worked as a barrister of the Inner Temple in Gibraltar and died on the gold fields of Africa. He had few complaints but his appearance in a single soccer match secured his place in history.

HENRY BAYARD RICH

The Rich family like both Renny-Tailyour and Mitchell had strong links with the army but not this time with Scotland. John Sampson Rich was born at Woodlands, Limerick in 1800 and married Amelia Whitfield at Manchester Cathedral on 14 April 1821. He was a captain R.A. and daughter Amelia Anne was baptized at St. Mary's Cathedral, Limerick on 2 June 1822 and son Frederick Henry was born at Woodlands, Limerick on 8 March 1824; a third child John Sampson was born in 1827. Frederick joined the Royal Engineers as ensign or 2nd lieutenant on 11 January 1843 aged 18 years 10 months and was of the Church of England. He spent the first four months of his career on leave or sick then had brief periods at Chatham, Woolwich, Dover and Devonport. He was stationed in Ireland from May 1845 and was promoted to 1st lieutenant on 1 April 1846, but was sent overseas in May 1846 where he moved in prominent circles.

He soon formed a connection with the Bayard family who had a significant role in the history of America. Their early genealogy is uncertain however they were French Huguenots and Nicholas Bayard was rector of the French Church, Antwerp at the end of the 16th century and had theological connections in Paris and with the Walloon Synod (1580). The family resided at Alphen, Holland in the early 17th century and Samuel Bayard merchant of Amsterdam married Ann Stuyvesant whilst sister Judith married Peter Stuyvesant - last Governor of New Amsterdam (New York). When Samuel died his widow Ann removed to America, in 1647, with their children Balthazar, Petrus, Nicholas and Catherine. The family had useful connections and Nicholas Bayard (1644-1707) was private secretary to Governor Stuyvesant in 1664 and also the Mayor of New York. He resided at the *Bayard Mansion* on the west side of the Bowery, which later provided land for Vauxhall Gardens and the Astor Library whilst *Bayard's Mount* became Bunker's Hill (1776). His brother Petrus Bayard died in 1690 and had a son Samuel Bayard (1675-1721) who moved to Bohemia Manor, Cecil County, Maryland in 1698. This was an area of land at the head of Chesapeake Bay provided by Cecilius Calvert, Lord Baltimore, and was initially owned by Augustine Herrman a Dutch émigré who spent 10 years mapping the area (1660-70).

A son James Bayard married Mary Asheton and they had two children of note. John Bubenheim Bayard later known as Colonel John Bayard was born at Bohemia Manor on 11 August 1738 and initially became a merchant in Philadelphia - a centre of learning and culture known as the "Athens of America". He was a leader of the movement for independence and joined the Sons of Liberty in 1766, whilst his company Hodge & Bayard supplied arms to Congress. He was colonel of a regiment raised at Philadelphia in 1775 (one of three) and was present at the battles of Brandywine, Germantown and Princeton and a member of the State Board of War when the British captured Philadelphia in 1777. He retired from business in 1788 and was later Mayor of New Brunswick, New Jersey and died there on 7 January 1807. His son Samuel Bayard was founder of the New York Historical Society in 1804 and brother Dr. James Asheton Bayard married Ann Hodge but died on 8 January 1770, leaving his children to his care.

Indeed, James Asheton Bayard was born at Philadelphia on 28 July 1767 and adopted by his uncle John, at his father's decease. He graduated from Princeton in 1784, qualified as a barrister in 1787 and married Ann daughter of Senator Richard Bassett in c.1790. He then settled at Wilmington and was in Congress as a Federalist in 1796, a member of the House of Representatives 1797-1803 and a senator 1805-13. He opposed war with Britain in 1812 and died at Wilmington 6 August 1815. James Asheton Bayard his son was senator in 1851 and 1867-69 and Thomas Francis Bayard his grandson was the fifth family member in the Senate. Richard Henry Bayard another son was born Wilmington on 23 September 1796 and graduated from Princeton in 1814 then practiced law in his native city. He married Mary Sophia Carroll, who was known as a great beauty, at Howard, Maryland in c.1824 and had a daughter Elizabeth Bayard at Delaware in c.1828 (see below). He was a Whig in the Senate from 20 June 1836 to September 1839 and Chief Justice of Delaware (and a senator) from 2 December 1839 to 3 March 1845. He was lastly *Charge D'Affaires* in Brussels from 10 December 1850 to 12 September 1853 and died at Philadelphia on 4 March 1868 - his wife Mary Sophia Carroll died in 1886.

Her ancestor Charles Carroll was a Catholic who left England after religious persecution in 1688 and his son, also Charles (1703-83), became a wealthy landowner in Annapolis, Maryland due to links with Lord Baltimore. His grandson Charles Carroll of Carrollton was born in Annapolis on 19 September 1737 and had a Jesuit education at schools in Flanders and Rheims. He then attended College Louis Le Grand in Paris, entered the law and spent several years at Temple in London but returned to America in 1765. He was on the Maryland Committee of 12 September 1775 and also the *Convention* that produced "The Association of Freemen" charter (the State constitution), their aim being to gain freedom through armed resistance and production of saltpetre. Charles voted for freedom on 28 June 1776 and was elected to the Continental Congress on 4 July taking his seat on 18 July and signing the *Declaration of Independence* on 2 August. He was the wealthiest man to sign the document and after the death of Adams and Jefferson on 4 July 1826, he was the last signatory to survive. He died at Doughoregan Manor, Baltimore on 14 November 1832 and Mary Sophia Carroll was his grand daughter.

The Royal Engineers or Royal Sappers and Miners had several 'companies' in America in the 19th century and in particular were based in Halifax (Nova Scotia), Quebec, Bermuda and Barbados. They had earlier connections with forts in Philadelphia, whilst under Lieutenant Colonel John By they built the Rideau Canal, Canada in 1826-32 and were involved in 'boundary commission' work between U.S.A. and Canada. Lieutenant Frederick Henry Rich was posted to Canada in May 1846 but after a year there was sent to the West Indies from August 1847 to January 1851. He married Elizabeth daughter of Richard Henry Bayard at St. Stephen's Church, Philadelphia on 2 August 1848 the minister being Dr. Ducachet. It is uncertain how the couple met since the U.S.A. was independent of Britain since 1783 but possibly there was a family or work connection. It is more certain, however, that Henry William Ducachet was born at Charleston, South Carolina on 17 February 1796 and had a medical practice in New York, but became an Episcopal minister in 1825. He preached at Salem and Norfolk, Virginia and was rector of St. Stephen's, 19 South Tenth Street, Philadelphia, from 1834. He held this position for the rest of his life and died in the city on 18 December 1865.

Frederick and Elizabeth Rich travelled to the West Indies after their marriage and Lieutenant Rich may have been stationed at Barbados although he also spent time in the Berbice region of British Guiana (Guyana after independence). Britain occupied the country during the Napoleonic Wars, in 1814, and purchased the districts of Berbice, Demerara and Essequibo, which were all based around rivers of the same name. The Berbice River was 300 miles long and flowed north from the Guiana Highlands to the coastal plain entering the Atlantic near New Amsterdam. The area was a British colony in 1831 and Georgetown, the capital, was formerly known as Demerara the main industry being sugar production. The labour force came from overseas resulting in a diverse population and Guyana is now the only English speaking country in South America (other than the Falklands). The couple had two children at this time: Henry Bayard Rich born at Berbice on 14 June 1849 and Charles Carroll Rich born at Portelswort Island, West Indies (sic) on 9 August 1850.

Frederick left the West Indies in January 1851 then went on leave and had a posting to Ireland in April following, which lasted for eight years. He initially resided at Athlone, Co. Westmeath in central Ireland on the banks of the River Shannon near Loch Ree (and his roots) and had three children there: Mary Emmeline (5 November 1851), Frederick St. George (14 November 1852) and Louisa Maud (1 February 1854). He was promoted to captain on 17 February 1854 and Carlisle Howard was born at Curragh, Kildare (5 November 1856) and no doubt there were fireworks. He was stationed on Malta from May 1859 to March 1861 and a daughter Agnes Blanche was born there in c.1861. He then pre-empted Major Marindin and was appointed Inspector of Railways at the Board of Trade from April-September and was permanently seconded there in October 1861.

The name Dulwich was derived in early times from a meadow where the dill once grew and soon had theatrical associations. Philip Henslowe the actor owned the Rose Theatre on Bankside near Southwark and was a rival to William Shakespeare at the Globe. He formed a partnership with Edward Alleyn (1566-1626) and established a theatre north of the City limits at Cripplegate in 1600. The Fortune Theatre as it was called was in Golding now Golden Lane and cost £500. Edward Alleyn meanwhile married Henslowe's stepdaughter and purchased the Manor of Dulwich from Sir Francis Calton in 1605. Clearly theatrics were a lucrative business since the cost of the estate was £4,900. Alleyn moved to Dulwich in 1613 and then pondered the temporal nature of life and considered the vices of the thespian: namely wine, women and song. He was a reformed man and as a penance and to save his soul he established a foundation called *The College of God's Gift* on 21 June 1619. This was a charitable institution to educate twelve poor scholars and included a chapel and almshouses. The Fortune Theatre burnt down in 1621 and was finally demolished in 1661, whilst a plaque in Fortune Street marks the site - near to Whitbread's brewery in Chiswell Street.

Alleyn's foundation flourished and his school and almshouses with chapel were built at the junction of Gallery Road and College Road, whilst Belair possibly attributed to Adam was built nearby in 1785. The area was quite remote with the nearest church being at Camberwell and highwaymen used the woods in the 1800s but things began to change. It was a desirable hamlet near to London and the property developers moved in. A number of large houses were built on Dulwich Common one example being "Glenlea" for Charles Druce date c.1804 (see Pember Ch. 4). Further building took place after enclosure in 1815 and other properties were Blew House, The Willows and Northcroft. Sir John Soane built Dulwich Picture Gallery next to the school in 1811-14 whilst the Grammar School was built opposite the almshouses in 1842 at the junction of Burbage Road and Gallery Road.

Captain F. Rich then considered his sons' education and leased "Woodlands", Dulwich Common from the College Estate in 1861, and named it after his birthplace in Limerick. This was the last house on the north side at the junction of Thurlow Park Road and College Road, with stables and four servants, whilst there were open fields and common land to the south. His four sons attended Dulwich Grammar School in the village in 1861-68 however there were soon great changes in the area. The father worked for the railways at this time and was well situated to make an ongoing inspection. Peto, Betts and Crampton were building the London, Chatham and Dover Railway from 1860 and they purchased large areas of land from the College Estates in 1863 (see Ch. 6). The enterprise brought the partners to bankruptcy in 1867, however the school profited from the transaction and Dulwich College was built to replace the old school using the funds. Sir Charles Barry junior (1823-1900) who designed the Burlington House façade of the Royal Academy was employed to do the work. 40 acres of land were set-aside south of Dulwich Common just opposite to "Woodlands" and the college was built in the neo-Baroque style with a Palladian plan. It was completed in 1866-70 for 300 pupils and the Old Alleynians include C.F.A. Voysey (1872-73), Ernest Shackleton (1887-90), C.S. Forester (1915-16) who was also at *Alleyn's* and the Rt. Hon. John Spellar (1958-66).

There was a late addition to the family when Amy Gertrude was born at "Woodlands" on 3 February 1866, whilst the father was promoted to brevet major on 24 August that year and lieutenant colonel on 8 May 1867. He ended his secondment to the railways in October 1872 then had a months leave and was at the War Office until January 1873 but retired on full pay with the rank of honorary brevet colonel on 1 February 1873. He served 30 years 21 days as an officer and received a pension of 20 shillings per-diem (day) but continued as Inspector of Railways (junior) with the Board of Trade, Whitehall. John Ruskin (1819-1900) artist, poet, scientist and philosopher moved to Coniston House in the Lake District in 1872 as he was unhappy with all the building work and development taking place in Dulwich (he should see it now). Colonel Rich followed his lead and after daughter Louisa Maud was married in Dulwich in 1875 he moved to a substantial house in London in the late 1870s. Edith Wragge and her family lived at "Woodlands" in 1881 and nearby properties included The Elms, Cypress House, Ryecotes, Allison Towers, Chestnuts, Blew House and Elm Lawn. Alexander Druce (78) born All Hallows, a copper and lead smelter and sister Ann (90) born Coleman Street 'living on property' plus six servants were at North Side, Dulwich Common at this time. Alleyn's was built as the lower school of Dulwich College in Townley Road in 1882 whilst Dulwich Park opened in 1890. There were, however, to be further connections with this area (see below).

The family were Rich by name and rich by nature thus they lived at 17 Queen's Gate Terrace, Kensington in 1881. Frederick was a retired colonel R.E. working as a railway inspector for the Board of Trade and would have known Marindin (see Ch. 5). He lived with wife Elizabeth, Howard civil and mechanical engineer, Mary, Blanche and Amy and seven servants including Richard Birchall (39) butler born Ireland. 17 Queen's Gate Terrace was a fashionable Regency house on the south side near Gore Street in the parish of St. Stephen's, Kensington. It had an imposing six-storey white stucco façade, grand portico entrance and elaborate cornice carvings above all the windows. The building was a mirror of Victorian society since the façade portrayed wealth, prosperity and respectability whilst the plain-brick rear, and the mews, was reminiscent of a city tenement - the latter showed its true nature with the stucco stripped off! The main drawback was the lack of garden and rear aspect however the buildings have survived in all their grandeur. Elizabeth Bayard Rich died at 17 Queen's Gate Terrace on 20 October 1885 and her husband administered her estate on 19 November 1886 at £500. Frederick Rich a railway inspector (junior) for the Board of Trade lived there in 1891, with Frederick commander R.N., Blanche, Amy and nine servants.

The Edict of Nantes was passed on 13 April 1598 and brought about religious liberation in France but Louis XIV the 'Sun King' revoked this on 22 October 1685 leading to renewed persecution. The Calvinist Protestants or Huguenots suffered greatly from this and many emigrated to England, Ireland and the New World. Isaac son of Pierre Olier and Genevieve Genoud de Guiberville was born at Montauban, Dauphine, France, in 1666. He was a Huguenot who suffered at the hands of the Catholics and fled to Holland, England and eventually to Dublin in Ireland. He married Martha Pilkington at Westmeath and unlike many immigrants changed his name to D'Olier so it would sound more French! He was caught up in some major political upheavals and James II of England was forced to abdicate in 1688 and set up Parliament in Dublin. William of Orange or William III married James's eldest daughter Mary II and they ruled England from 1689-1702, but he had lost lands on the Continent due to Louis XIV and supported the Protestant cause. James II rallied the Irish Catholics whilst the King of France, Louis XIV, supported the former and sent French troops to assist him. This culminated in the 'famous' Battle of the Boyne west of Drogheda on 1 Jul 1690, which was a victory for William although Ireland may have fared little better under James. Once the fighting ended the peace was secured with the Treaty of Limerick on 3 October 1691, which had two main aspects viz. military and civil. In the first instance there was a safe passage for the defeated army and 12,000 men, women and children (many Irish) boarded vessels for France. The civil part of the Treaty had far reaching consequences and secured Anglican domination and removed estates from those who fought with James and left many Catholics in poverty and ignorance for much of the 18th century. **Note** *The Edict of Tolerance was* passed on 28 November 1787 in France and resulted in renewed religious freedom.

Isaac D'Olier fought at the Battle of the Boyne and as a reward his descendants were made freemen of Dublin - he died in 1744 and was buried at St. Mary's in the town. Isaac D'Olier his son was born in 1712 and was a goldsmith and jeweller who married Joyce Keene at St. Werburgh, Dublin on 17 May 1736. His work can still be found and Bonham's the auctioneers recently sold a D'Olier marrow scoop dated '*Dublin 1768*' - he died in 1779. He had a son Isaac D'Olier (1738) at Little Forest who married Mary Keene at Finglas in 1760 and died in 1789, however it was his other son who became most famous. Jeremiah D'Olier was born at Finglas in c.1746 and married Jane Collins in 1787. He was a successful merchant in Dublin and one of the first governors of the Bank of Ireland. He was appointed City Sheriff in 1788 and was one of the Wide Street Commissioners and carried out one of the last major changes to the 'Dublin City Plan'. Indeed D'Olier Street, a well-known thoroughfare in Dublin, is named after him and has notable buildings such as D'Olier Chambers designed by J.F. Fuller, the Irish Times 'terrace' and a Gothic revival chateau on the corner of Westmoreland Street. A daughter Cecilia D'Olier was born at Finglas in 1796 whilst the will of mother Jane was proved on 8 June 1821 and that of Jeremiah D'Olier of Colleynes, Dublin on 19 October 1822 (this disputes a date for his decease of 11 October 1817 quoted elsewhere).

Philip Gowan was born in Wexford c.1779 and married Cecilia D'Olier in Dublin in 1814 and moved to Dulwich where they had a large family viz. George D'Olier Gowan (1815), Elizabeth Jane (1817), Olivia (1818), Philip Henry (1819), Frederick (1821-48), William (1822), Louisa Emily (1824)+, John Hawksly (1826)+, Francis Edward (1829) and Charles Cecil (1832) - + baptized in the college chapel. They had common ground with the Richs in Dulwich and Ireland but soon travelled to the Yankee states. The Puritans were persecuted in Virginia and fled eastwards thus they settled Annapolis on the shores of Chesapeake Bay in 1649. The county was called Anne Arundel after the wife of Cecilius Calvert 2nd Lord Baltimore and indeed to the north was Baltimore and to the south Calvert Co. This was the state capital of Maryland in 1695 and national capital at the time of the Continental Congress in November 1783 to August 1784 (see Carroll). George D'Olier Gowan was a Dulwich stockbroker but married Sarah Clementina Bowie at Anne Arundel, Maryland on 26 June 1838. A son Philip Hamilton was born on 9 May 1839 and baptized at Dulwich College chapel in the village on 11 June, and Elizabeth Hyde was born on 5 December 1840 and baptized there on 7 January 1841. They returned to America and Cecile D'Olier Gowan was born in Virginia in 1842 and Helen Jane was born on 31 May 1846 and baptized at All Hallows, Anne Arundel on 2 September. Their son Bowie Campbell was born in Dulwich in June 1852, whilst Philip Gowan the grandfather died in the village in June 1855.

Talbot County was formed on the east side of Chesapeake Bay in 1661 and faced towards Annapolis. It was named after Lady Grace Talbot sister of 2nd Lord Baltimore and wife of Sir Robert Talbot an Irish statesman. N.B. George Calvert was the 1st Lord. The county was on Eastern Bay and included mighty rivers such as the Choptank, Tuckahoe and Wye. Hunter Davidson married Mary Steele Ray at Anne Arundel on 20 July 1852 and daughter Leila was born there on 25 September 1854 and baptized on 9 November. George D'Olier Gowan died at "Woodlawn" in Dulwich on 29 December 1873 aged 58 whilst Bowie C. Gowan married Leila Davidson at Great Choptank, Cambridge in Maryland on 20 July 1875. His mother Sarah Clementina Gowan died at Dulwich in September 1877 aged 58.

Philip Gowan (41) a retired stockbroker lived at 5 Collingham Place in 1881 with his wife Eliza S. (30) born Devonport, daughter Helen D. aged one and an infant son of just four days. His sister Elizabeth H. Gowan (40) lived around the corner at 20 Courtfield Gardens with brother Bowie Campbell civil engineer his wife Leila and their children Hyde C. (2) born Sydney and George D'O (9m) born Middlesex, one visitor and five servants. Charles C. Gowan (48) a stockbroker lived at Bell House, College Road, Dulwich that year with wife Elizabeth A., four children and five servants. Charles Voysey (1828-1912) a descendant of Wesley was the founder of the Theistic Church and lived at Camden House, High Street, Dulwich in 1881 whilst his children were born at Hessle in 1856-59 and Healaugh in 1864-68 (Yorkshire). He was a minister who challenged the Church of England and his son Charles F.A. Voysey (1857-1941) was an architect who boarded at Sandy Hill Road, Duston near Northampton in 1881 and practiced the Arts and Crafts movement of William Morris - his work is at the V & A. The area had many famous residents and Sir Henry Bessemer a retired steel manufacturer FRS CEM FME lived at Denmark Hill in 1881 (see Ch. 19), whilst Charles Voysey resided at "Woodlawn", Dulwich once home to the Gowans in January 1884.

These families had much in common and probably met during their time in Dulwich, however there may have been deeper roots in Ireland or in the formation of America. Whatever the sequence of events Frederick Henry Rich a retired colonel of 17 Queen's Gate Terrace then married Cecile D'Olier Gowan of 20 Courtfield Gardens at Kensington Parish Church on 18 June 1891 and Leila Gowan and Jno. Rich were witnesses. His brother John Sampson Rich died at Plymouth in September 1900 aged 73 whilst F.H. Rich (78) a colonel retired R.E. lived at 17 Queen's Gate Terrace in 1901 with Cecile D'O (59) and six servants. These included O.C. Gasparello butler from Todera, Italy, S.H.A. Speckman cook from Oldentay, Germany and Alfred Jones coachman, wife and two children. Her brother Philip Gowan (52) a stock 'jobber' agent then lived at Godalming with Elizabeth (50) on her own means. Frederick Henry Rich lived at 17 Queen's Gate Terrace for over 25 years but died near Oare-ford, Oare, Somerset on 22 August 1904 aged 80. It was north of Exmoor near Lynton and Porlock with open moorland to the south i.e. Mill Hill, South Common and Doone Valley - made famous in R.D. Blackmore's novel "Lorna Doone". Frederick St. George Rich (captain R.N.), Howard Rich (civil engineer) and Vincent Frisby Esq. obtained his probate on 8 October the effects £89,269 6s 9d but re-sworn at £98,759 19s 6d. Philip H. Gowan died at Holsworthy near Bude in June 1906 and Cecile D'Olier Rich died at Bournemouth in December 1926 aged 84, which brings us to the next generation.

Charles Carroll Rich was born on 9 August 1850 and attended Dulwich College from 18 September 1861 to June 1868. He then went to the R.M.A. Woolwich and was a lieutenant in the Royal Artillery on 23 July 1870. He joined the Royal Horse Artillery who had formed in 1793, and sported one of the most distinguished uniforms in the army with braiding across the chest and plumes of feathers in the cap - he was a captain on 27 November 1880. Charles Carroll Rich captain R.H.A. of 17 Queen's Gate Terrace married Fanny Amelia Jessie Elliott of 2 Nightingale Terrace the daughter of Robert Poole Gabbett major R.A. at St. John's in Woolwich on 21 September 1881 and C.F. Hadden lt. R.H.A. and Blanche Rich were witnesses. They had a son Charles Bayard in India in 1883 and daughter Eileen Mary was born at Bangalore on 3 January 1885 and baptized on 12 February (parents Charles Carroll and Fanny A.J.H.E.) - there was also a second son. The father was promoted to major on 7 July 1886 and then lieutenant colonel on 1 October 1896 but resigned his commission and was absent from the army lists in 1897. Charles Bayard Rich (17) a gentleman cadet lived in London in 1901 but his father Charles Carroll Rich died at Heidelberg on 10 September 1902. The son a soldier of Hilsea, Cosham then married Audrey Marion Robertson Luxford (22) of 31 Elvaston Place at St. Paul's, Knightsbridge on 22 June 1907. Frederick S.G. Rich was a witness with her father John Stewart Odiarne Robertson Luxford a gentleman.

Frederick St. George Rich was born on 14 November 1852 and attended Dulwich College from 25 February 1862 to July 1866. He then went to H.M.S. Britannia and was a lieutenant in the Royal Navy in 1881 on board H.M.S. "Briton", a fourth rate Seren Corvette sailing off the Cape of Good Hope and the west coast of Africa. He was made a commander in 1891 and resided at 17 Queen's Gate Terrace that year whilst Mary Graham Gunner (40) lived at St. George's Hanover Square in 1901 and was daughter of Charles James Gunner of Holme Oak, Bishops Waltham. He was made a captain in 1904 and then married Mary Graham Gunner in March 1906 but had no children. He served as aide-de-camp to Edward VII in 1906-07 and retired from the navy on 20 September 1910 then became a vice-admiral in 1912. He was awarded a humane society silver medal and was a member of the Ranelagh Club. He died at "Woodlands", Chiddingfold in Surrey on 22 May 1914 and probate went to Howard Rich and Vincent Frisby Esq. his effects valued at £49,848 0s 5d.

Carlisle Howard Rich was born on 5 November 1856 but was known as Howard and attended Dulwich College in September 1865, then went to Finchley College where he trained as a civil and mechanical engineer - he lived at 17 Queen's Gate Terrace in 1881. Horatio Nelson Noble (Lt Col) army officer and his wife Sophia had two children at Agra south of Aligarh, Bengal: Edith Sophia on 5 January 1857 baptized 24 February and Montagu Mark baptized on 26 September 1862. Sophia Noble (38) widow of an officer, born Devon, lived at 30 Addison Road, Holland Park in 1881 with Edith S. (18) born Bengal and two servants. Howard Rich a civil engineer of 17 Queen's Gate Terrace married Edith Sophie Noble of 30 Addison Road at St. Barnabas, Kensington on 4 July 1885 and F.H. Rich, N. Noble, J Hills-Johnes, A. Ross and H.L. Gabbett were witnesses. They had one son Clive N. who was born in Hampshire 1887 and lived with one servant at Wimland Farm, Rusper, Sussex north of Horsham near Gardner's Farm in 1901. Howard retired from civil engineering in 1906 and worked for the Red Cross at South Mead Hospital, Bristol during the war and was a member of the Royal Dorset Yacht Club. He died at Chickerell House, Weymouth on 29 July 1933 and his effects were valued at £56,315 7s 1d.

Frederick James Crooke was born in Liverpool on 21 April 1844 and was son of Mrs. James Crooke of 3 St. Saviour's Crescent, Jersey. He was educated at Winchester College in 1858 to March 1861 and then joined Brocklebank's, Liverpool, ship owners and East India merchants. He was a good right-handed batsman and right arm (fast) round arm bowler at school and joined Liverpool C.C. and then played for Lancashire at Old Trafford in 1865. He went out to Calcutta in 1866 but returned to England on leave and stayed at Cheltenham in 1874-75. He married Louisa Maud Rich (1854) at Dulwich in March 1875 and then played cricket for Gloucester and the M.C.C. He played a game for the latter v the 'gentlemen' of Hereford-shire at Lord's on 18-19 June 1875 when he scored 121 runs and hit a six right into the grandstand. His county career figures were: 35 innings 1 not out 573 runs 56 high 16.85 average and 12 for 0 wickets. The couple returned to India in mid-1875 and their son Henry Ralph was born in Calcutta on 7 December 1875 however they came back to England in 1886. Frederick Crooke lived on his own means at 5 South Parade, Southsea in 1901 with Louisa and three servants, but died at 1 St. Ronan's Road on 6 August 1923 and was buried at Highland Road Cemetery.

His son Henry attended Fosters, Stubbington House and went to H.M.S. Britannia in 1888 (age 12) and became a midshipman in 1890. He married Lilian Ethel daughter of Col. C.E. Harman and widow of Col E.P. Smith in 1916 and was at the Battle of Jutland. He received the C.B. in 1919, retiring in 1932 and was Admiral Sir Henry Ralph Crooke (K.B.E.) in 1940. He died in 1952 but diaries and photos of his career still survive. The daughters Blanche and Amy were living at 17 Queen's Gate Terrace in 1891 but this soon changed after their father remarried. Vincent Frisby was born at Birkenhead in 1856 and married Agnes Blanche Rich (1861) at Kensington in December 1892. He was a retired army officer living at The Hoo, Great Barford near Bedford in 1901 with wife Agnes and daughter Olga (6) born Kempston. William Neill was born at Geelong near Melbourne in 1859 and married Amy Gertrude Rich (1866) at Kensington in June 1893. He was a barrister living at Benson near Abingdon in 1901 with his wife Amy and children Harry (4) and Frederick (2) born London.

Henry Bayard Rich, the eldest son, was born at Berbice, British Guiana on 14 June 1849 and grew up at Athlone in Ireland and also Malta. His family then returned to England and he lived at "Woodlands" on Dulwich Common and was educated at Dulwich College in the village from 18 September 1861 to March 1864. He did not stay there and completed his education at Marlborough College from April 1864 to December 1866. He went to the Royal Military Academy, Woolwich in 1867 and like his father joined the Royal Engineers and was a lieutenant at the School of Military Engineering on 8 January 1870 - he received his commission on the same day as H. Mitchell and E.W. Creswell. He was at the S.M.E. from 1870-72 residing there on the 1871 census and played for the Royal Engineers in the first Cup Final in 1872. The team photograph shows him to be a rather sullen individual but Lieutenant Goodwyn clearly had his eye on him - perhaps they were having a dispute or trying to keep a straight face for the photographer! Indeed Lieutenant Rich was soon going to need his dogged and determined character.

The three friends were split up soon after the Cup Final with Creswell going to Bengal and Mitchell and Rich to Aldershot. Henry Bayard Rich was posted to Aldershot in 1873 and then went overseas to Hong Kong from 1874-76. He saw some action during his time in the Far East and served with the expedition against the Malays in Perak from 2 December 1875 to 25 March 1876 - he was mentioned very favourably in despatches on 29 February 1876 receiving a medal with clasp. The Perak region centred on the Perak River, which flowed into the Malacca Straits 120 miles north of Kuala Lumpur on the Malay Peninsula. Henry was ordered home in late 1876 and arrived at Aldershot in 1877 and was in C Troop there in 1878-79. He witnessed the marriage of Hugh Mitchell to Mary C.E. Creswell at White Notley on 22 August 1878 and was no doubt the best man, since Hugh was also at Aldershot in 1878-79. Lieutenant Rich was soon travelling and went with C Troop to the Cape of Good Hope in mid-1879 - in fact the Engineers were stationed there from at least the 1830s. He was in charge of signalling in Telegraph Troop, 1st Division under 1st General Lord Chelmsford and Sir Garnet Wolseley, Commander in Chief, and saw action in the latter stages of the Zulu War in May-November 1879. For his part in this he received a medal with clasp and remained with C Troop in South Africa 'til 1880. He then returned to England and was posted to Colchester in 1881 and was re-acquainted with William Merriman - he was also betrothed and met his fiancé either in Dulwich or Malaya!

Henry Minchin Simons, son of Henry and Sarah, was born at Bradford and baptized at Pudsey on 1 January 1825. He was an East India merchant and married Caroline Melvill who was born at Islington in 1832. The couple then travelled overseas and their daughter Ada Melvill Simons was born in Singapore in 1860, whilst Henry M. Simons East India merchant lived at "Tyersall", Crescent Wood Road, Sydenham Hill, in 1881 with wife Caroline and seven servants - Ada was not at home. Henry Bayard Rich lieutenant R.E. of St. Giles, Colchester married Ada Melvill Simons of "Tyersall", Sydenham at St. Stephen's Church, South Dulwich on 3 May 1881, E.J. Selwyn rector of Pluckley near Ashford, Kent performed the ceremony and F.H. Rich and H.M. Simons (merchant) were witnesses. Henry was made a captain on 8 January 1882 exactly twelve years after his commission and remained in Colchester, but served in A troop in the Egyptian Campaign later in 1882 under Sir Garnet Wolseley - Commander in Chief. He then received a posting to India that was to be fatal, and with the risks in mind made his last will on 2 September 1882: "My last Will, I Henry Bayard Rich do hereby leave everything I have (or am likely to have) in the world, to my wife Ada Melvill Rich signed *H.B. Rich* Captain R.E."

He left Colchester and went to Roorkee, India on 7 September 1883 but travelled to Rawalpindi north of the Indus River Valley and near the North West Province and frontier (now in Pakistan). He may have been there for work or sport but soon succumbed to dangers in the region. Henry Bayard Rich died at Rawalpindi on 17 November 1884 due to an accident whilst playing polo, which was a sad end for an army man. Letters of Administration were granted to his widow Ada under section 255 of the *Indian Succession Act* at the Principal Civil Court in Rawalpindi on 10 December 1884. She agreed to make a true inventory of his property and credits and was to present this to the court within one year. His obituary was in the Times on Friday 19 December 1884 stating: "Many brother officers will regret the loss of Captain Henry Bayard Rich, whose death, the result of an accident at polo, occurred in India last month.... He was killed at Rawal Pindi on the afternoon of 17 November by a violent collision with another officer, by which captain Rich was flung to the ground and his skull fractured."

His widow Ada returned to "Tyersall", Sydenham Hill in London and administered his goods at the Principal Registry on 25 June 1885. She was described as the universal legatee there being no executor named in the will and his effects were valued at £162 16s 11d but re-sworn at £5,162 16s 11d. Francis Slater Picot was born in Victoria, Australia in 1859 the son of Philip Henry Picot gentleman and was a lieutenant adjutant of the 2nd Wiltshire Regiment. He lived at 72 Courtfield Gardens and married Ada Melvill Rich at St. Jude's Church, South Kensington on 16 July 1888. She also resided at this property (which was opposite the church) it being a four-storey town house with stucco ground floor, columned porch and elaborate cornice above, and upper storeys of yellow-brown brick - today it has apartments (see Addison Ch. 10). E.J. Selwyn rector of Pluckley, Kent performed the ceremony again and H.M. Simons and Major Gerard R.W. Macklin were witnesses. Francis S. Picot major in the 2nd Wiltshire Regiment lived at Rockley, Roundway near Devizes in 1901 with wife Ada and Gladys Violet (10) born Chippenham. The property was near Roundway Park and London Road whilst the major was no doubt at home being near a battle site (1643).

The Picot family had many relatives in St. Helier on Jersey and Ada Melvill Picot died at 24 Cadogan Court, South Kensington on 6 February 1915 and her probate was granted to Francis Slater Picot a lieutenant colonel in H.M. Army. The First War was then in its second year and Winston Churchill insisted that his troops should try and 'open' the Dardanelles. The Turkish positions were bombarded from 19 February 1915 and a major assault with 16 ships took place on 18 March that year. The hills of Gallipoli were on the port side but the result was nil although three ships and 700 men were lost. The campaign continued for the next eight months with troops from the Anzac Corp, Royal Naval Division, French and Indian Armies but without success. The Ottoman 5th Army could not be removed and the cost to both sides was many thousand deaths. This had a profound effect on the Anzac troops in particular and was one of the most futile conflicts ever fought. Indeed Philip Simons Picot of Whittington Barracks, Lichfield died at the Dardanelles on 11 July 1915 and Francis Slater Picot and James George Cotton Minchin solicitor obtained his probate in London on 19 September his effects £5,995 6s 8d but re-sworn at £6,697 9s 10d. Francis Slater Picot lived at 141 Ashley Gardens, Westminster but died at Burton on the Wolds, Loughborough on 12 October 1939.

HERBERT HUGH MUIRHEAD

The Muirhead ancestry can be traced to Scotland but unlike the previous genealogies they were not in the army and came from an academic background. They were descended from a family of that name at Lauchop and held land at Teggetsheugh, Stirling-shire for several generations but lived at Dunipace near Denny, south of Stirling - indeed the village of "Muirhead" was nearby. The line is traced to John Muirhead who was born at Dunipace in c.1687 and married Margaret Syme there on 30 December 1712. They had children: John (1713), George (1715), Patrick (1717) and Archibald (1721) - two having notable lives. George was born at Dunipace on 24 June 1715 and matriculated at Glasgow University in 1728 but graduated from Edinburgh with an M.A. in 1742. He was ordained in 1746 and appointed minister of Dysart, Fife, in 1747-52 but was elected *Professor of Oriental Languages* at Glasgow University in December 1752 and was promoted to the *Chair of Humanity* on 2 December 1754 (a post held until his death). He was described as, "An enthusiastic and accomplished classical scholar," and as *Professor of Greek* helped publish four editions of Homer and one of Virgil. He died on 31 August 1773 and John and Patrick his brothers donated £100 in his honour, in 1776, an amount that formed the basis of the "Muirhead Prizes" at Glasgow College.

Patrick Muirhead was born at Dunipace on 20 October 1717, and also entered the church replacing his brother as the minister of Dysart. The town was on the northern outskirts of Kirkcaldy and was the birthplace of Adam Smith (1723-90) the economist and Robert Adam (1728-92) the architect. Patrick married his cousin Elisabeth Muirhead at Dysart on 4 March 1761; she was born in Lanark in c.1728 the daughter of Rev. John Muirhead and Janet Bogle and was first cousin of James Watt the engineer (see below). The couple had eight children at Dysart viz. John (1762), George (1764) Lockhart (1765), William (1770), James (1771), Margaret (1773), Anne (1775) and Jean (1777). The mother Elisabeth died on 14 February 1779 and the father Patrick on 17 February 1807. Lockhart Muirhead was born at Dysart on 30 November 1765 and baptized there on 1 December then had an eminent life following in his uncle's footsteps. He was a educated man who qualified as a doctor of law (L.L.D.) and married Anna, daughter of James Campbell of Ballochlaven, at Glasgow on 19 June 1804 and had four children there - Marion (1809), Mary Elizabeth (1811), James Patrick (1813) and Anne Janet (1815). He was appointed Principal Librarian and the Regius Professor of Natural History at Glasgow University from 1809 until his death on 23 July 1829.

James Patrick Muirhead was born at The Grove, Hamilton in Lanarkshire on 26 July 1813 and attended Glasgow College from 1826-32 being awarded a number of prizes for his scholarship especially in Latin verse. He won a Snell Exhibition to Balliol College, Oxford on 3 February 1832 and matriculated there on 6 April 1832. He neglected his studies, spending his long vacations on Alpine expeditions and was distracted by an interest in the German language, thus he only achieved a 3rd class honours degree in *literae humaniores*. He gained a B.A. in 1835 and M.A. in 1838 but being a talented academic was soon engaged on his life's work. He was a second cousin (once removed) of James Watt, the engineer, and this was to be a beneficial association therefore it is worth considering this family.

Thomas Watt (1642-1734) taught mathematics, surveying and navigation at Crawfordsdyke near Greenock in Scotland. James Watt his son was born at Greenock on 5 February 1699 and with his father's help became skilled in all aspects of building, making mathematical instruments including compasses.

In addition to this he was a ship owner and merchant who was recorded thus in the Greenock town records. He married Agnes Muirhead (1702) who was the aunt of Elisabeth Muirhead (wife of Patrick) at Hamilton on 13 April 1729 and they had children: Robert (1730), Margaret (1732), Thomas (1733), **James** (1736) and John (1739). The first three died as infants whilst John born 9 September 1739 died at sea in 1763. James Watt senior was held in high esteem and was made Chief Magistrate of Greenock in 1751, whilst his wife Agnes was said to be, "A most exemplary and devoted wife and mother." She died in 1755 and her husband James in August 1782.

James Watt their surviving son was born at Greenock on 19 January 1736 and was to have a remarkable life although he was a delicate child, of ill health, and was taunted at his first school for being listless. He then showed an aptitude for geometry at 13 and attended Greenock Grammar School where he learnt Latin and Greek. During this period he spent much time in his father's shop and constructed models of great detail. He went to live with his mother's relatives in Glasgow, in 1754, and no doubt with George Muirhead of Glasgow University who was there at this time. He went south after his mother's death and was apprenticed to John Morgan of Finch Lane, Cornhill, London. He was to have further training as a mathematical instrument maker but the 'city' smog made him ill and he returned to Greenock. He tried to open a shop as a mathematical instrument maker at Glasgow, in 1757, but the local Corporation prevented him from doing this since he had not received a proper apprenticeship. Fortunately he was acquainted with John Anderson, Professor of Natural Philosophy at Glasgow University, who saved his career by securing him an appointment as mathematical instrument maker to the university. James was allowed to set up a workshop in the precincts and met learned men including Joseph Black discoverer of latent heat.

James Watt married his cousin Margaret Miller at Glasgow on 15 July 1764 and had a small family. He was given, meanwhile, a model of a Newcomen fire engine (steam) to repair in 1764, but soon realized it was in working order and only lacked power. His discovery is explained in detail elsewhere, however his methods generated much steam and the following gives a brief description. The model engine had a large boiler that failed to drive a small piston with a great loss of steam during the process, and therein lay the problem. James did not find time to attend the lectures of Joseph Black however he was familiar with his concept of latent heat and applied these ideas to the engine. As matters stood the cold water that condensed the steam was injected straight into the cylinder and since both piston and cylinder had to be warmed, to perform, there was a great loss of energy in the process viz. a large amount of steam used for a small return. Watt developed a separate condenser and pump to send condensed steam directly to the piston, without the losses due to cooling.

Steam was in fact used in the 17th century to raise water by the generation of a partial vacuum and the first 'true' steam engines with moving parts and pistons were built as early as c.1710. Thomas Newcomen developed one such engine, thus Watt did not actually invent the steam engine (as stated in some histories) but built a more efficient machine with commercial potential. His discovery was made in 1765 but the concept was not developed, as one would suppose, since he was a man of limited means who had received incorrect legal advice. He initially entered into an arrangement with John Roebuck founder of the *Carron Works* and built an engine at Kinneil near Linlithgow but this aroused little interest. The future looked bleak and Watt was heading for obscurity, whilst without income he could not make ends meet and was forced to take work making surveys and reports. The latter were in relation to canals, rivers and harbours and included the water works and harbour at Greenock where he was born. In addition he succeeded John Smeaton as engineering advisor to the Carron Foundry (see Lubbock Ch. 7).

The most significant event took place in 1767-68 when Dr. William Small, a gentleman, introduced James Watt to Matthew Boulton a fellow inventor based in Birmingham. The Boultons were also working on the steam engine at their Soho Engineering Works and since they play an intricate part in the story are discussed below. James Watt, encouraged by John Roebuck a friend of Matthew Boulton, visited the Soho Works in 1767/68 and a partnership soon emerged. Indeed the ideal circumstances existed since Watt had the invention but no funds whilst Boulton had the necessary capital to invest and the desire. Watt was slow to move but was encouraged to patent his invention in 1769 although the patent itself was based on amateur advice and the specifications were later contested. The income and success was much needed since during this period four children were born: John (1765), Margaret (1767), James (1769) and Agnes (1770) although of these a son and daughter died in infancy.

John Roebuck found that his operations were in severe difficulty in 1772, and failed, whilst Margaret Watt the wife of the inventor died in 1773. Boulton then offered to purchase a two-thirds share in Watt's engine (this being Roebuck's share) and paid a £1,200 debt owed by Roebuck in exchange for the shares. The offer was too good to miss and Watt with a family to support moved from Scotland to Birmingham in May 1774 and formed the partnership of Boulton and Watt in 1775, which heralded an exciting period in British industrial history. Watt patented his original engine for 14 years however six had expired in 1775 and Boulton approached Parliament and extended the patent for 24 years making it valid until 1800. The experimental engine was removed from Kinneil to Soho and the partners demonstrated the invention thus gaining much interest from the Cornish mines. Watt was dispatched to the South West but had a torrid time in Cornwall since he disliked the climate, the 'company' and the lack of scientific research. A number of single action engines were then installed, despite this, but solely for the pumping of water and not to drive machinery. James Watt married Ann MacGregor at Glasgow on 29 July 1776 and had a son Gregory (1777) who shared his father's interest in science and a daughter Jessie (1779).

There was, however, a slow return on the investment and initial profits were not forthcoming with capital tied-up in the machines. Watt soon wilted under the financial pressure and Boulton had to use all his energy and business talents to encourage him at this time. He did what he could to raise his spirits and wrote to him on 16 April 1781 stating: "I cannot help recommending it to you to pray morning and evening, after the manner of your countrymen (the Lord grant us a gude conceit of ourselves), for you want nothing but a good opinion and confidence in yourself and good health." This had the desired affect and Watt began to work on his invention with new vigour. At this stage it was being used to pump water or drive a water wheel, an inefficient method of working machinery, thus he developed a crank to produce a rotary motion. Unfortunately Pickard, his employee, leaked the design in 1779 and *Wasbrough and Pickard* patented a cranked steam engine in 1780. Watt was not discouraged and competed with the deception producing a number of patents from 1781-84 - including the 'sun and planet' wheel that converted reciprocating motion to rotary motion. The final result was the rotative engines built by Messrs. Boulton and Watt in 1784-85 the earliest of these being installed in London breweries viz. Henry Goodwyn, Lower East Smithfield (see Ch. 10) and Samuel Whitbread, Chiswell Street (see Ch. 7). The engine was a great success, however a number of copies were patented resulting in several court battles and Watt's only outlet was his love of science and, in particular, that of chemical science.

Matthew Boulton, Erasmus Darwin (grandfather of Charles) and John Whitehurst (clock and instrument maker) wanted to discuss and develop the practical application of science and formed the "Lunar Society", with this in mind, in c.1760. These philosophers dared to question and debate the established order and were strongly opposed by those who followed "Church and King", therefore the members met on the night of the full moon so they could travel home in safety (hence the name). Benjamin Franklin the American was in contact with the Society and it was he who introduced Dr. William Small to the group in 1765. The latter, as stated, brought Watt to Birmingham in 1767/68 and with the Society helped promote the steam engine before he died in 1775. Josiah Wedgwood and Joseph Priestley were members of this academic 'melting pot' and Erasmus Darwin one of the founders summed up their attitude saying, "A fool is a man who never tried an experiment in his life." Priestley was a dissenting churchman who joined the Society in 1780 and worked on electricity and the chemistry of gases being the first to discover oxygen, which he called 'dephlogisticated air'.

The Lunar Society provided a great atmosphere for James Watt who continued his investigations and built on the work of Priestley to discover the composition of water in 1783. He stated, "Water is dephlogisticated air deprived of part of its latent heat and united to a large dose of phlogiston.... dephlogisticated air is water deprived of its phlogiston and united to latent heat.... water has one part 'pure' or dephlogisticated air (oxygen) and two parts inflammable air or phlogiston (hydrogen) i.e. H^2O" - we all need dephlogisticated air after this debate! Watt circulated a paper at the Royal Society but Priestley was sceptical of the discovery, leading to confusion, thus a Mr. Cavendish claimed it for himself. There is little doubt, however, that Watt found the composition of water and he was made a fellow of the Royal Society, Edinburgh in 1784 and Royal Society, London in 1785. Boulton and Watt were keen to promote their product and took their proposals for steam engines to Paris in 1786, but did not release their ideas to the French because of national interest. Joseph Priestley was a radical Republican who supported the French Revolution and a mob destroyed his apparatus and documents and burnt his house in 1791. He then fled to London and thence to America.

James Watt, meanwhile, took up residence at Heathfield Hall near the Soho Works in Birmingham and continued to invent in his workshop. His competitors, as stated, patented a number of similar engines and Boulton and Watt were involved in litigation from 1792 to 1800 leading to court costs of £6,000 in 1796 to 1800. The problems arose from the vagueness of the original patent and this resulted in much stress for both Boulton and Watt. There was also some personal tragedy and his daughter Jessie died in 1793 and Margaret in 1799. The two partners retired in 1800 and the business was left to their sons James Watt junior and Matthew Robinson Boulton. After retirement Watt continued scientific research at Heathfield however his son Gregory, who assisted him, died of consumption in 1804 and left him grief stricken. Watt was a rich man and gave a library to the town of Greenock in 1816 but died at Heathfield on 25 August 1819 and was buried at St. Mary's Church, Handsworth. He was a famous man and a public meeting was held in London on 18 June 1824 to arrange a permanent monument and those present included Sir Robert Peel. As a result Chantrey, the sculptor, provided a monument for Westminster Abbey and statues for Glasgow, Greenock and Handsworth, whilst a further statue was erected in Birmingham and portraits were kept in London and Edinburgh (National Portrait Gallery). Ann Watt his wife died thirteen years later in 1832.

James Watt junior was born on 5 February 1769 and also took an interest in science going to Paris to pursue his studies in 1789. He became caught up in the revolutionary movement in France and was at first in favour with the leaders, however, after standing against their excesses was denounced by Robespierre in front of the 'Jacobin Club' and had to flee to Italy. He returned to England in 1794 and became a partner in the Soho Company taking over from his father in 1800. He purchased the 102-ton "Caledonian", in 1817, and fitted her with new engines then travelled to Holland and up the Rhine to Coblenz (this was the first steamship to leave an English port) - he later made improvements to marine engines. He lived at Aston Hall above the Lower Aston Grounds (see Ch. 20) and was engaged in writing the memoirs of his father James Watt, however this was a long and complicated business that took its toll and he became disabled by growing infirmities. He came into contact with his distant cousin James Patrick Muirhead when the latter was at university (1832-35) and being exhausted by the memoirs entrusted them to the young man. The latter was soon committed to the task and it became a life long occupation.

James Watt (72) independent and born Scotland lived at Aston Manor, Aston Park in 1841 and was the sole occupant of the large house but had seven servants. He was the last descendant of James Watt, engineer and died unmarried at Aston Hall on 2 June 1848 but did have distant relatives. James Gibson married Agnes Miller at Barony, Lanarkshire on 29 August 1826 and the couple had two children in Edinburgh: Agnes Miller (1827) and James Watt (1831) and daughter Margaret E. (1834) in England. The mother Agnes and the three children resided at Heathfield House in 1841 with four servants the property being near Soho Street, Soho Hill and Aston Villa Lane. This was the last link and Ann Grove governess ran a school there in 1851.

James Patrick Muirhead, one of the nearest relatives, received the commission from Watt and this should have been the end of the story however there was a further twist to the tale that is now discussed. John Boulton was from Northampton-shire but settled in Lichfield and his son Matthew Boulton was sent to Birmingham on business due to a decline in the family fortunes. His grandson Matthew Boulton was born in Birmingham on 3 September 1728 and spent his childhood in the growing city then entered his father's business. He soon set about improving it and was quite successful in this respect becoming the sole owner upon his father's decease in 1759. He married Anne Robinson at Lichfield in 1760 and the marriage contract included a large dowry that enabled him to invest new capital into the business and thus he established the Soho Works at Handsworth in 1762. He entered into a partnership with Mr. Fothergill and the works gained a good reputation producing wares 'far superior' to those usually found in Birmingham. In the first instance the partners improved the level of workmanship and in the second developed the artistic aspect. Boulton employed agents to find the best examples of artwork in metal, pottery and other materials and then used these ideas for his own products. He built Soho House on Soho Hill just north of Birmingham, in 1766, an elegant Classical mansion with interior to match that became the meeting place of the Lunar Society (the restored house is now open to the public).

The Soho Works was water powered and quite inefficient thus Boulton experimented with a new steam engine but was unable to make much progress and was introduced to James Watt in 1767-68. The couple, meanwhile, had two children at Handsworth: Ann baptized 10 September 1768 (died 1829) and Matthew Robinson born 1770 and baptized 9 October 1772. During this period there were further negotiations with Watt and a partnership was formed in 1775. Matthew Boulton was totally committed to the cause and employed all his capital on the project and even raised further funds to develop the steam engine. His company was taken to the verge of bankruptcy before the engine was a success and he placed his aspirations before profit, however the breakthrough came with the production of the rotative engine in

1784/85. He bolstered the flagging spirits of his depressive partner, throughout the proceedings, and Watt received a profit in 1787 whilst Boulton had to wait longer for a return due to his high investment. Thus it can be said that Watt designed the steam engine but it was Boulton's efforts that made it commercially viable. A steam press was installed at the Soho Works to produce copper coins in 1788 and the first press was patented in 1790. They made large quantities of coins for the E.I.C., foreign governments and some colonies and also produced a new copper coin for Great Britain in 1797. Boulton was acquainted with many eminent men through the Lunar Society being a fellow of the Royal Society but retired from the business in 1800. Boulton and Watt also supplied other machinery including a press to the new mint at Tower Hill in 1805 (used until 1882), whilst Matthew Boulton died at Soho House on 18 August 1809 and his will was proved on 15 September.

Matthew Robinson Boulton continued the business with James Watt junior and the Soho Works remained successful. He married Mary Ann Roul in c.1815 and had six children at Soho House who were baptized at St. Mary's, Handsworth namely Anne Robinson (1818), Katherine Elizabeth (1819), Matthew Piers Watt (1820), Hugh William (1821), Montagu (1824) and Mary Ann (1829). The family also purchased a second home called Tew Park near the village of Great Tew just north of Oxford. This became a centre of learning when Lord Falkland attracted scholars from Oxford and London in the 17th century and remains an attractive village with several cottages from that time. Matthew Robinson Boulton died in Birmingham on 16 May 1842 and his will was proved on 10 June, whilst Matthew Piers Watt Boulton a landed proprietor and wife Frances Eliza lived at Great Tew with nine servants in 1851.

James Patrick Muirhead, meanwhile, completed his university course in 1835 and then studied law but was also in contact with James Watt junior regarding the memoirs. He completed his legal studies and was admitted as an advocate at Edinburgh in 1838 and also published a legal work at this time. Mrs. Muirhead his mother lived at 26 Heriot Row, Edinburgh in 1839-40 and James P. Muirhead Esq. an advocate practiced at this address from 1840. Indeed many advocates had chambers in the street as they do today, and Robert Louis Stevenson lived at no. 17 (1857-80). The old town of Edinburgh developed along the High Street and Canongate between the castle and Holyrood House in the 16th century. This was an area of high ground but was restricted thus the tenements had many stories with narrow courts and alleys behind. The new Georgian town was laid out to the north in a grid pattern beyond Princes Street with grand houses around squares and circuses. Heriot Row was on the north side of Queen Street Gardens and was adjacent to Howe Street, and its cobbles, that led downhill to St. Stephen's Church with its multi tiered-tower. Archibald William Henry Playfair designed the latter in 1827 and in fact most of the area is unchanged from Georgian times.

James then put all his energies into the life and works of James Watt and was well suited for the job since Elisabeth Muirhead his grandmother left the family an important document - a manuscript record of Watt's youth. He obtained and translated, "The Éloge Historique de James Watt", a French work by Arago read before the Académie Des Sciences, France (8 December 1834) and travelled to Paris to do research in 1842. He was determined to settle the controversy around dephlogisticated air and phlogiston

Edinburgh: Canongate, Castle and Court. J.P. Muirhead was an advocate at 26 Heriot Row in 1840-49.

(water) and aimed to refute the claims of Henry Cavendish in favour of Watt. He spoke to acclaimed scientists such as Arago and Berzelius and made painstaking enquiries in England. He gradually prepared a case (which contained no hot air) and during this time travelled from Edinburgh to Birmingham and was given free access to the papers of Boulton and Watt. He consulted with James Watt junior at Aston Hall and Matthew Robinson Boulton at Soho House and was taken in by the academic atmosphere pervading the rooms of Soho. He became acquainted with the Boulton family and was comfortable in their society and soon became most intimate (although Matthew died in 1842).

Katherine Elizabeth Boulton was born at Soho on 5 August 1819 and baptized at St. Mary's, Handsworth on 6 September that year. She grew up in the shadow of the Lunar Society and this resulted in a keen interest in literature and classical subjects making her an ideal academic partner. James Patrick Muirhead advocate of St. Stephen's, Edinburgh married Katherine Elizabeth Boulton, spinster, at Handsworth Church on 27 January 1844. The fathers were Lockhart Muirhead, Professor of Natural History at Glasgow University and Matthew Robinson Boulton Esq. whilst M.P.W. Boulton, H.W. Boulton, Anne R. Boulton and Anne J. Muirhead were witnesses. It is interesting that his study of Watt resulted in a union with the Boultons (the object of his research) and thus the two families were united but somewhat belatedly. James continued to work as an advocate in Edinburgh and a son Lionel Boulton Campbell Lockhart was born at 26 Heriot Row in 1845. His wife Katherine, however, found the Edinburgh climate most uncongenial and pressed her husband to move back to England, thus he was forced to give up a promising career at the Scottish bar in 1846 (*National Biography*). Despite this he was listed at 26 Heriot Row until 1849.

He continued his studies and especially those regarding the debate about the composition of water. He secured conclusive evidence that Watt discovered the constituents first and set about proving his right to the accolade and published a pamphlet: "The correspondence of the late James Watt on his discovery of the Theory of the Composition of Water", in 1846, with introduction, remarks and appendix. He then submitted to his wife's wishes and moved to Haseley Court, Oxfordshire in 1847 whilst James Watt junior died in 1848. The Boulton family previously owned the property, which was at Great Haseley south east of Oxford, and was just 22 miles away from Tew Park - indeed the Muirhead family settled at Haseley Court for the next 75 years. This was a suitable environment for James to pursue his literary aspirations however the family were frequently absent and liked to travel to the sea or to a spa town. They had five children in England yet none of these were born at Haseley Court and the first three were Francis Montagu (September 1847) Leamington, Beatrix Marion (December 1849) Hastings and Herbert Hugh (December 1850) Brighton. James P. Muirhead an advocate (not practising) lived at Haseley Court near Little Haseley village in Great Haseley parish in 1851 with wife Katherine, children Lionel, Francis, Beatrix and Herbert Hugh (4 months), sisters-in-law Anne R. Boulton and Mary A. Boulton and nine servants - two from Scotland, one from Warwickshire. Robert Philip Wood married Anne Janet Muirhead in Edinburgh on 29 May 1853, whilst the former had two children: Bertram Arthur (September 1853) Brighton and Eleanor Anne (March 1855) Leamington.

The father, meanwhile, put all his energies into the biography of Watt and having amassed all the facts published three quarto volumes in 1854: (1) The Introductory Memoir of James Watt (2) Extracts from Correspondence regarding James Watt (3) The Specifications of James Watt's Patents including 34 engravings of machinery by Lowry. This was a work of great labour that provided a useful reference source for the scientific student and the learned papers came under the umbrella: "The Origin and Progress of The Mechanical Inventions of James Watt". He also had other interests and edited and published, "Winged Words on Chantrey's Woodcocks", in 1857, a collection of short poems by various writers with additional verses by Muirhead. The title came from the hunting exploits of Chantrey at Holkham, Norfolk when he killed two birds with one shot and made a sculpture of the event. This no doubt appealed to Muirhead since for leisure he enjoyed angling and shooting. The Memoirs of James Watt was his most important work and formed the basis of his later and more expansive work: "The Life of James Watt" published in 1858 with a second edition in 1859. This was an accurate study that avoided any unfounded claims and was of great importance thus providing a fitting memorial to the engineer - much of the above information came from Muirhead's work on James Watt as recorded in the *National Biography.*

His labours regarding the famous engineer were complete thus the couple concentrated on educating their children and being an affluent country family sent three sons to Eton (1859-65). They continued to travel and were absent from the 1861 census whilst Francis Montagu (B.A. Cantab) student now in law at Lincoln's Inn was the only family member at home in 1871. The father continued his writings and produced a translation of French Literature: "The Vaux de Vire of Maistre Jean Le Houx advocate of Vire" in 1875. In this work Muirhead supported Le Houx, clearly a fellow advocate, and received a complimentary letter regarding this work from Henry W. Longfellow (1807-82) the poet. Lionel Muirhead described as an artist and "drawings" lived at Haseley Court in 1881 and the household included Anne Boulton (1818) of independent income and five servants.

James was a regular contributor to "Blackwood's Magazine" from August 1882 and his work included nine original poems and twenty translations of old English-French poems into Latin and English verse. He signed with the initials J.P.M. consequently they were attributed to Professor J.P. Mahaffy, an error that had to be corrected. Katherine Elizabeth Muirhead died at Haseley Court on 23 May 1890 and her husband obtained her probate in London on 23 June the effects £826 19s 6d. James P. Muirhead M.A. D.L. advocate, retired from practice, lived on his own means at Haseley Court in 1891 with Francis Montagu a retired barrister, Eleanor and seven servants including a butler and coachman. He made his final contribution to "Blackwood's Magazine" in March that year, but still occupied himself with translations his last being a skilful work namely a free translation of Tennyson's verses into *rhyming* Latin - this arrived from the binders a few hours after his decease. James Patrick Muirhead died at Haseley Court on 15 October 1898 and Lionel and Francis (sons) and Napier George Sturt, lieutenant colonel R.E., obtained his probate in Oxford on 21 December 1898. His estate was valued at £74,227 4s but re-sworn in November 1899 at £74,979 4s 2d. He had a remarkable life being remembered mainly as the biographer of James Watt, engineer, whilst his six children all survived him.

Lionel Boulton Campbell Lockhart Muirhead was born at 26 Heriot Row on 16 January 1845 and was educated at Radley and Eton (1859-62) with Bonsor, Kinnaird, Lubbock and Thompson. He gained an M.A. at Balliol College, Oxford and liked to travel abroad however this was a risky business and the Turks took him prisoner at Palmyra, a desert town in the centre of Syria, in 1868. He had a narrow escape and retreated to the safety of Haseley Court and was an artist there in 1881 and also wrote hymns and poetry. John Henry Ashurst a J.P. in Oxon and Bucks and farmer of 200 acres lived at Waterstock Mansion, in the neighbouring village, with wife Elizabeth, four children including Grace Mary (22) and twelve servants. Lionel married Grace Mary Ashurst at Waterstock on 19 April 1887 and had children Charis Elizabeth Fosca (1888) Folkestone, Anthony John (1890) Hambleden, Buckingham and Herbert James Thomas (c.1892). He inherited Haseley Court when his father died in 1898 and lived there on his own means with wife Grace, Charis and Anthony in 1901. Lionel Muirhead died at Haseley Court on 25 January 1925 and his probate was granted to Grace Mary Muirhead widow and Anthony John Muirhead major H.M. Army his effects valued at £38,308 0s 7d, although there was a further grant to the daughter then wife of Herbert James Thomas on 15 March 1943 at £4,321 2s 6d.

Francis Montagu Muirhead was born at Leamington on 25 July 1847 and baptized there 10 August and attended Eton in 1859. He gained his B.A. at King's College, Cambridge and became a barrister at Lincoln's Inn and, as stated, lived at Haseley Court in 1871, and in 1891 when he was a retired barrister. He remained at Lincoln's Inn and died at 27 Fairholme Road, West Kensington on 15 April 1927 and Anthony John Muirhead major H.M. Army and Geoffrey Charles Napier Sturt Esq. obtained his probate the effects valued at £249,119 0s 4d (a millionaire in today's money). Bertram Arthur Muirhead was born at Brighton on 17 July 1853 and became a lieutenant in the Royal Navy. He was a lodger at 6 Great Marylebone Street, London in 1881 with Philipp Moos a 'laundress' (employing ten) British subject from Bavaria and his wife of Luxembourg. He died at St. Pancras in September 1907. Eleanor Annie Muirhead was baptized at All Saints, Leamington on 29 March 1855 and lived with her father at Haseley Court in 1891. She died on 16 December 1916. The family members up to this stage were mainly academic however others took a more active role within the Empire.

Thomas Lennox Napier Sturt married Jeanette Wilson and was a judge with the East India Company and his son Charles Sturt was born at Chunar Ghur, Bengal on 28 April 1795. The couple returned to England in c.1799 and had several children, and one of the last Evelyn Pitfield Shirley was baptized at St. Alphage's, Greenwich on 15 May 1816. Some members of the family stayed in England and included Napier Duncan Sturt (1796-1872) and Charles N. Sturt born at Marylebone in 1833 and a colonel in the Grenadier Guards. The latter lived in London and Charles Hall the attorney of H.R.H. the Prince of Wales was visiting him in 1881. They should not be confused with antipodean members of the family. Charles 'Napier' Sturt (1795) was educated at a private school in England and attended Harrow in 1810 then joined the army in 1813. He was present at the Peninsular War in Spain and went to France and

Waterloo as well as Canada and Ireland and soon came to notice. As a result he was chosen to sail to Sydney on the *Mariner* in December 1826.

Captain Sturt was a member of the 39th Regiment of Foot and arrived at Botany Bay on 25 May 1827 being assigned to convict duties. He was a favourite of the Governor Ralph Darling who appointed him Military Secretary and thus he met John Oxley and Hamilton Hume who were explorers. He went on an expedition himself up the Laughlin and Macquarie Rivers in 1828 and then covered 3,200km and discovered the Darling River and explored the Murrumbidgee River. He also found the Murray River on 10 November 1829 although Hume had previously discovered it and named it the Hume River. He was a man driven by courage, faith and prayer and always slept with a Bible under his pillow. Indeed on one occasion in the desert he threw out all his belongings including a gas lamp but kept the Holy book. He went on many expeditions facing natural dangers and conflict with Aborigines and stated: "Something more powerful than human foresight or human prudence appeared to avert the calamities and dangers with which I and my companions were so frequently threatened."

He came back to England in 1833 and published two volumes called: "Two Expeditions into the interior of Southern Australia", which influenced E.G. Wakefield and led to further colonisation of the region. Charles Sturt married Charlotte Christiana 'Sheppey' Greene at St. James the Apostle, Dover on 20 September 1834 and then sold his commission in the army and returned to New South Wales as a settler in 1835. Wakefield made plans to settle both Australia and New Zealand without penal colonies and the town of Adelaide, Southern Australia, was one of the results. The first houses and streets were built there in December 1836 and Col. William Light surgeon general named it after Queen Adelaide wife of William IV. There were difficulties, however, at first, as the settlement was self-funded and there was no money coming in. Indeed the expeditions and writings of Charles Sturt encouraged the British Colonial Office to establish Adelaide on the St. Vincent Gulf at the foot of the Mount Lofty Ranges - he was indirectly the father of Southern Australia. For his efforts he was given several thousand acres at Mittagong in New South Wales and had two sons there: Napier George (1 November 1836) and Charles Sheppey (21 September 1838). He became a cattle rancher and was one of the first to drive 400 heads across land into Adelaide. He then became familiar with an area called the Reed Beds on Port River in the Barker Inlet (named after a fellow officer in the 39th) and purchased land and built a house called the Grange. He moved to Adelaide in 1839 and was the temporary Surveyor General, Land Commissioner, Registrar General, Chairman of the Magistrates and President of the Agricultural Society. The town grew with the arrival of Lutherans from Prussia in 1839 and the population was 6,557 in 1840 with 30 satellite villages.

Charles Sturt had two more children: Evelyn Gawler (c.1840) and Charlotte Eyre (19 January 1843) and then mounted a major expedition into central Australia in August 1844. He took 16 men with him however they failed to find the mythical 'inland sea' and instead spent six months from January to July 1845 'marooned' at a waterhole. One man was lost and the rest suffered starvation and de-hydration and although they continued into the desert, Sturt had to concede defeat in November 1845. There was an element of fantasy in the idea of an inland sea since this went against all that was known about continents and their structure. He returned to England in 1847 and published: "Narrative of an Expedition into Central Australia", then travelled back to Adelaide in 1849. He was Colonial Secretary to the Legislative Council and held the post until December 1851 at which time Adelaide had a population of 14,577. Sturt decided his children's education came first and returned to England permanently in 1853 and his house the Grange later became a trust and museum.

Charles Sturt went to live in Cheltenham and was awarded the K.C.M.G. but died soon after on 16 June 1869, whilst his son Charles Sheppey Sturt married Florentina Sale at Holdenhurst on 26 August 1870. His other son Napier George Sturt entered the Royal Engineers and spent time in Calcutta and wrote a letter to Sir George Grey dated 30 May 1870. The latter was a friend of his father in Adelaide and left to be Governor of New Zealand in 1845 then spent time in England and retired to Auckland in 1870. Napier George Sturt married Beatrix Marion Muirhead at Great Haseley on 5 December 1876 - she was born at Hastings on 21 November 1849. He was a major R.E. living at 15 Victoria Park, Dover in 1881 with Beatrix his wife, Dorothy W. (1) born York Town, Katharine (1 month) born Dover and four servants. His wife sent a letter to Eva Shillington in Auckland on 7 December 1895, who had sailed there on the *Triumph* in 1883, and both letters are at Auckland City Library. Napier had retired by 1901 and lived at Llanvihangel, Monmouth with wife Beatrix and daughter Katharine but died at Abergavenny in December 1901 aged 65.

Herbert Hugh Muirhead was born at 3 Oriental Place, Brighton on 10 December 1850 and was initially educated by his parents but attended Eton College in 1865, at the same time as Alexander George Bonsor, and no doubt they played football together at the school. Herbert then embarked on an army career and in view of the families link to James Watt there was only one choice to be made. He attended the Royal Military Academy, Woolwich and resided there as a gentleman cadet on 2 April 1871 and was made a lieutenant in the Royal Engineers on 2 August 1871. He received his commission on the same day as Edmond William Cotter and Alfred George Goodwyn and the three were stationed at the School of Military Engineering, Chatham. He remained there from 1 October 1871 to 6 September 1873 and joined the successful Engineers football team and played in the 1872 Cup Final. His links with Eton no doubt ensured his place in the side but one wonders if they knew he was a relative of Boulton and Watt. He was then sent overseas and missed the Finals of 1874 and 1875.

He was posted to Ireland from 20 October 1873 to 14 October 1875 and stationed at Curragh (1874) and Cork Harbour (1875). He spent a short time back at Chatham and was then stationed in Bermuda for nearly three years from 24 January 1876 and clearly liked the overseas life. He was sent to Gibraltar on 18 November 1878 and arrived on the Rock after the departure of Mitchell and Renny-Tailyour but was there at the same time as Bogle and Cotter - no doubt they debated what might have been at the Oval. H.H. Muirhead lived at Engineer Lane, Gibraltar on the 1878 census and was a single officer in the Royal Engineers and of the Church of England. He returned to Britain on 1 June 1881 and spent six months at the Royal Military College, Aldershot before going to Curragh again on 7 November 1881 and was promoted to captain in Ireland on 2 August 1883. He was then more settled and spent the next 10 years at Woolwich in Kent working in the manufacturing department of the Royal Arsenal, Woolwich from 18 December 1883 to 31 March 1888. It is interesting to note that the Royal Arsenal F.C. was formed at the Dial Square workshop of Woolwich Arsenal in 1886 - perhaps Muirhead had a hand in this. He was 2nd assistant of building works (ordnance factories) at Royal Arsenal, Woolwich on 1 April 1888 and was promoted to major on 17 December 1889. He held this position until 31 July 1893 although spent some of the final year at Waltham Abbey.

He then went overseas again and was stationed at Esquimalt, Canada for over five years from 17 August 1893. The town was at the south tip of the 300-mile long Vancouver Island and 10 miles south west of Victoria the capital of British Colombia. Lieutenant Commander James Wood and the *Pandora* first surveyed the area in 1846 and found it to be one of the best natural harbours on the Pacific coast, whilst Vancouver Island became a Crown Colony in 1849. During the Crimean War the army was to attack Petrepavlovsk on the Russian coast and built three hospitals at Duntze Head for the wounded, in 1855, but found the Russian post abandoned soon after and these were never needed. The 'old village' and settlers' homes along Wharf Street were also built that year and the Victoria colony joined the mainland to form British Columbia in 1858. The area was soon developed and 165 Royal Engineers under Colonel R. Moody were sent to Esquimalt to survey the land and build roads. They developed the Seaport Town as a seat of Government and also built New Westminster and the Cariboo Wagon Road into Fraser Canyon.

There was a large influx of settlers after the discovery of gold with two gold rushes at the Fraser River in 1858 and the Cariboo in 1860-63. The Royal Engineers helped provide infrastructure at this time and when the unit disbanded in 1863 only 15 of their number returned to England. The remainder became settlers no doubt hoping to find gold and formed the basis of the British Columbia Reserve (20 years later). The abandoned hospital huts provided a ready-made base and the Admiralty moved the Pacific Fleet from Valparaiso in Chile to Esquimalt in 1865. During the Russo-Turkish War of 1878 the British Fleet sailed into the Black Sea and in retaliation the Russians sent ships to Victoria and Esquimalt, posing a considerable threat, thus Fort Rodd Hill was built to protect the south coast in 1883 - being there to the 1950s. The Esquimalt-Nanaimo Railway was built in 1886, a military base was established at Work Point in 1887 and those who made their wealth in Victoria erected large homes in the town. Major Muirhead was employed on special duties regarding the defence works in Esquimalt (1893-98) at these locations and was made a lieutenant colonel on 4 April 1897. The Royal Navy abandoned the site in 1905 and it was home to the Canadian Pacific Fleet from 1910, whilst the original settlement was part of the base.

Major Muirhead left Esquimalt on 17 September 1898 and was posted to Pembroke Docks seven days later on 24 September, a fact noted in the Eton College records. He lived alone with his two servants Annie and Gertrude Richards at The Elms (Coldspring), St Mary's Pembroke on the 1901 census. He was made a colonel on 4 April 1901 and finished his career at Pembroke and retired from the army on 4 April 1902 with a pension of £450 p.a. He was unmarried and then lived at 32 Seymour Street, Marylebone, a narrow four-storey town house on the north side with plain brown-brick front (just one room in width). The property is present today just west of New and Old Quebec Street (see Crake Ch. 7) and the *Edward Lear Hotel* is at no. 30 and has an L.C.C. plaque to "Edward Lear 1812-88 artist and writer". Herbert Hugh Muirhead died of pleuro-pneumonia at 32 Seymour Street on 4 March 1904 and his brother Lionel Muirhead of Haseley Court administered his effects on 15 April, which were initially valued at £16,913 7s but re-sworn at £19,001 1s. He was described as: "intestate and a bachelor without parent.... domiciled in England noted by order 9 August 1904." Thus ended a notable army career and also this discourse on the lives of Boulton and Watt.

ADAM BOGLE

The Bogle family like those already discussed had their origins in Scotland and are traced to Glasgow although this was a common name causing difficulty in the research. Archibald Bogle married Janet Cathcart at Glasgow on 6 July 1755 and had children: Robert (1756), Helen (1757), Agnes (1759), Hugh (1761), George (1762) and Margret (1775) all baptized at Glasgow. They may also have had a son Adam in the period 1762-75. Indeed their son Hugh Bogle married Agnes Bogle, a relative, at Glasgow on 16 December 1800 and had children Archibald (1801), Michael (1802), Janet Cathcart (1804), Agnes (1807) and Helen (1815). The eldest son Archibald married Janet Bogle at Old Monkland, Govan on 29 May 1825 and had a son Andrew Cathcart at Govan on 20 January 1829 who was educated at Cheltenham. He was then a lieutenant in the 78th Regiment (Infantry) and fought in the Indian Mutiny with great bravery. He led an attack on a house at Oanao on 29 July 1857, his regiment being under heavy fire and unable to advance, and was badly wounded thus he received the Victoria Cross and was promoted to major. He lived at Newland, Sherborne, Dorset, in 1881 and died on 11 December 1890.

Adam Bogle who was possibly son of Archibald married Janet Lamey at Glasgow on 19 December 1802 and had children: Jean (1805), Adam (1807), John (1808), James (1811), Janet (1813) and Elizabeth (1817) all baptized in Glasgow, the mother being Jean on the baptisms. The son John Bogle was born in Glasgow on 29 December 1808 and became a merchant in the city and formed a trading partnership, whilst Dugald John Bannatyne married Janet Bogle at Barony, Lanark on 19 June 1833 and had children: Jane (1834), Dugald (1836), Adam (1837) and Agnes (1838) - see below. John Bogle traded as Bogle, Alexander & Co. at 30 Gordon Street, Glasgow in 1834-35 and the building faced the front entrance of Central Station, although 'letters' were to be left at 100 Queen Street. Mrs. Adam Bogle his mother also lived in the centre of the city in a house at 169 West George Street that year. John Bogle found trading opportunities in the antipodes and travelled to Van Diemen's Land (or Tasmania) on business or maybe to start a new life in the late 1830s.

The Du Terreau family, meanwhile, were of French Huguenot extraction and lived in Soho and Westminster at the start of the 18th century. Jacques or James Du Terreau and wife Mary had six children viz. Benjamin (1741), Jacques (1745), Marie (1746), Anne (1748), Martha (1750) and Jean (1755). The baptisms took place in Le Temple a Huguenot chapel although Benjamin was born on 3 February 1741 and baptized at St. Anne's Soho on 18 February. He married Sarah Culverwell at the latter church on 8 April 1766 and had children Benjamin (1767), Elizabeth Winifred (1770), Mary Ann (1771), Ann (1779) and Edward (1781) - the last three at St. Marylebone. As with many immigrants they kept company with their own people and they soon had an association with another Huguenot family.

The principal watchmakers were located in the City and Soho in the 18th century and many came from France. One of the most noted was François or Francis Perigal who married Susanna and had children François (1734), Jacques (1736) and Jean (1738). He lived near Hungerford Market and the baptisms were at Castle Street, Huguenot Chapel. He founded a watchmakers business at the Royal Exchange in c.1741, which then passed to his son and grandson and was Master of the Clockmakers in 1756. Francis Perigal clockmaker and citizen of London living at Twickenham made his last will on 30 September 1765. He left his household goods, furniture, plate, jewels and linen and woollen apparel plus £50 to wife Susanna. He left the rest and residue to son Francis on trust that he paid to his wife a £150 p.a. annuity each quarter (Lady Day, Midsummer, Michaelmas and Christmas). After her death he was to pay £800 each to sons James and John plus any interest. Richard Adney of St. Mary Aldermanbury a watchmaker and John Aris of St. Olave, Old Jewry watch shagreen and case maker confirmed the will was in his writing on 24 June whilst his son proved it on 27 June 1767. Francis Perigal j. continued to run the business at the Royal Exchange and married Mary Ogier at St. Botolph's, Bishopsgate on 8 September

1763. He had a large family in 1764-86 and had children baptized at St. Bartholomew Exchange and St. Peter Le Poor in 1764-75 near to Bank and was Master of the Clockmakers in 1775. Francis Perigal & Son watchmakers advertised at 9 Royal Exchange in 1794 and 1807 and were there until c.1825 - the father died at Berry Pomeroy Devon on 8 July 1824.

Another Francis Perigal married Mary Duterreau (1746) at St. Martin in the Fields on 15 August 1765. He was a watchmaker to His Majesty King George III at 57 New Bond Street from 1770-94 and then traded as Perigal and Duterreau (watchmakers) at that address from 1794. He may have formed the partnership with his nephew Benjamin who is discussed below. They made the clock for St. Peter's, Falmouth, Trelawny in Jamaica in c.1796 whilst Francis S. Perigal j. was also watchmaker to the King and was Master of the Clockmakers in 1806. Perigal and Duterreau were likewise watchmakers to the King and traded at no. 57 in 1807 and then at 62 New Bond Street from 1811-29 (until c.1840). Francis Perigal watchmaker of New Bond Street made his last will on 13 February 1816 and left all he owned to his wife Mary absolutely the witnesses J. Latham and John Pike. His widow proved his will on 31 January 1818, whilst that of Mary Perigal of Hammersmith was proved on 10 October 1831.

John Perigal was head of the third branch of the family and was almost certainly brother of Francis Perigal of New Bond Street. He married Jane Grellier at St. James's, Westminster on 10 May 1780 and had four children baptized at the church: Mary (1781), Elizabeth (13 April 1782), Thomas (1787) and Francis (1788). John Perigal goldsmith and jeweller traded at 12 Coventry Street near Leicester Square from the 1770s until c.1800. He formed a partnership Perigal and Brown clock and watchmakers next door at no. 11 in 1794-1800. John Perigal was then a watchmaker and goldsmith at 55 Princes Street, Soho in 1807-11 whilst L. Perigal a merchant was at 'Old South Sea House'. Princes Street went north from Coventry Street and past St. Anne's, Soho but later became the south end of Wardour Street.

Edward Lloyd established a coffee house at Tower Street in 1687 and moved to larger premises at Lombard Street in 1691. He provided facilities superior to those in local taverns thus many merchants and ship owners drank there and Lloyd's list of ship movements was first produced in 1696. There were regular ship auctions regarding sailings whilst dealings also took place at the Royal Exchange. Lloyd's was a base for marine underwriters and 79 such brokers subscribed £100 to form the Society of Lloyd's in 1771. Benjamin Du Terreau (1767) worked as a watchmaker with the Perigals and may have been their partner, whilst he also did related work being an engraver of some note: The Farmer's Door & Squire's Door 1790 and Portrait of Joseph Towers 1796. He then branched out and was an insurance broker at Lloyd's Coffee House in 1807-09 but met his wife through the family business. He married Elizabeth Perigal by licence at St. Martin in the Fields on 7 May 1811 and J.H. Howlett performed the ceremony whilst J. Perigal, Mary Perigal and Sarah Moon were witnesses - the bride and groom both signed their names. Benjamin Du Terreau an insurance broker lived at 9 Buckingham Street, Charing Cross between the Adelphi designed by Robert Adam and Hungerford Market in 1813 (see Betts Ch. 6). The Victorian Embankment was not yet built and the Thames and a 'water-gate' with landing place were situated at the end of the street. A daughter Jane Sarah Du Terreau was born at Buckingham Street and baptized at St. Martin in the Fields on 9 January 1813.

Robert Hobart the British Secretary of State sent Captain David Collins to the Port Phillip region near modern day Sorrento south of Melbourne in October 1803. He was concerned that the French would establish a settlement in Victoria however Collins and the new settlement failed and the settlers and convicts moved to Van Diemen's Land in May 1804. Hobart Town was established on Sullivan's Cove and the districts of Richmond and Sorrell became profitable and exported to Sydney by 1817. Some mansions were built near Queen's Domain and a botanical gardens established whilst Battery Point provided protection in 1818 - it was not until 1834-35 that Port Phillip and Melbourne were settled. The colony provided opportunities for the adventurous thus Benjamin and his family sailed to Hobart in 1832 where he worked as an engraver. John Bogle arrived later in the 1830s and married daughter Sarah Deutereau (sic) at St. Andrew's Presbyterian Church in Hobart, Tasmania on 8 February 1838. A daughter Jane was born in the town later in 1838 but the couple returned to Glasgow by 1840.

Bogle, Alexander & Co. merchants traded at 21 Renfield Street north of Buchanan Street in Glasgow in 1840, however an advert in the *Cornwall Chronicle*, Tasmania stated: "Mrs. John Bogle of Glasgow, a son, husband in firm at Hobart of Kerr, Alexander & Co. born 1840." The child itself died as an infant but the trading links with the country continued. The Tasmanian Aborigines had a different background to those on the main continent and were forced to move there when the latter arrived from areas of India, but had a similar problem when settlers came from England in the early 19th century. George Augustus

Robinson (1788-1866) was a builder and lay preacher who arrived in Tasmania in 1824 and was made Protector of Aborigines on 22 June 1830. This was a period when there was fighting with the settlers and his job was to mend relations but also to repatriate the indigenous peoples to Flinder's Island in the Bass Strait 20km north east of Tasmania. He remained in the bush in 1830-35 and achieved his aim, which at the start was honourable towards the native people, but in the end they were betrayed. Benjamin Du Terreau had remained in Tasmania and was a colonial artist of some note who painted the Aboriginal people and made engravings. His most important work "The Conciliation" was dated 1840 and showed G.A Robinson with a group of Aborigines the mood being one of friendship and peace. This was later called the 'first' Australian history painting or the *National Picture* since it helped perpetrate a lie about the treatment of the natives. The idea that the Aborigines reached a friendly agreement with the white man lasted many years and in fact they were forcibly evicted - it was the so-called 'conciliation'. Benjamin Du Terreau died in 1851 whilst Robinson was made Chief Protector at Port Phillip in 1849-52 but returned to England on a good pension and died there in 1866.

John and Jane Sarah Bogle remained in Glasgow and then had two daughters there: Janet (1841) and Mary (1843). There was a notice in the *Teetotal Advocate* (formerly *Launceston Courier*) on 17 April 1843 stating: "Kerr, Bogle & Co. agents for 'Jane' bound for London, also 'sheep for sale' at Portland Bay." John Bogle continued to trade as a merchant in Glasgow and then had two sons viz. John Du Terreau (1845) and Adam (1848). He resided at 19 Woodside Crescent, north east of the town centre near the university whilst Bogle, Kerr & Co. merchants traded at 11 Moore Place, West George Street, both in 1849. He was successful in business and moved to the Devon Riviera in early 1850 and his family lived there 35 years. He had two more children: Benjamin William in June 1850 (died 1857) and daughter Anne who was born at "Woodside", Tormoham (the old parish name for Torquay) on 17 January 1852 - her father was described as a merchant. He was a wealthy man and had a comfortable life at "Woodside" near Braddon's Row and Higher and Lower Terrace above Torquay harbour. Woodside Drive and Upper Braddon's Road appear on modern maps near the main thoroughfare Braddon's Hill Road.

Indeed John a fundholder from Scotland lived at Woodside in 1861 with his wife Jane S., children Jane, Janet, Mary, John (15), Adam (12) and Anne, niece Agnes Bannatyne (22) and four servants - John, Adam and Anne being scholars. The profits from the business in Glasgow and Tasmania meant that his two sons attended Harrow School, John in 1860-61 and Adam in 1862-65 whilst both joined the Royal Engineers: John in 1866 and Adam in 1868. John Bogle (62) was living off his (dividend) houses etc. at Woodside, Braddon's Hill, Tormoham in 1871 with his wife Jane S., daughters Jane, Janet, Mary and Anne and four servants one of these being Mary White (57) from Scotland. There were three marriages in Devon during this period: John to Blanche Eleanora Bourchier Savile in 1869, Mary to Twynihoe William Erle in 1871 and Janet to James Richard Whyte in early 1874 (see below).

John Bogle formerly of Glasgow but now of Torquay Esq. made his last will on 18 November 1874 and revoked all former wills and in particular a will or deed of settlement, mortis causâ, dated 17 October 1849 in *Books of Council and Session* and a codicil thereto dated 8 April 1869. He bequeathed his household effects and £150 to his wife Jane Sarah Bogle, and his property and other money to his said wife, son-in-law Twynihoe William Erle of Chester Terrace, Regent's Park and sons John and Adam both Royal Engineers in trust. The money to be invested and £800 p.a. paid to his wife then after her death the money to be divided amongst his children but his daughters to receive no more than £5,000, any excess to go to his sons. The share to his son John to take into account a settlement of £11,000 for his benefit on his marriage with Blanche Eleanora Bourchier, and that for Janet wife of Rev. James Richard Whyte and Mary wife of Twynihoe William Erle to be considered their marriage settlement. The amount left to unmarried daughters Jane and Anne Bogle was to be invested and the income paid to them free of any husband and then to their children. He appointed the above executors and bequeathed to them any money or mortgages that he held in trust and asked them to pay his debts. Edward Vivian banker and R.H.D. Vivian late lieutenant R.A. were witnesses to the will. He made a codicil on 23 January 1878 and left his wife £200 p.a. in addition to the £800 and to Anne Bogle a further £5,000 unless she had a child, then for his sons. Edward Vivian of Woodfield banker and James Clancy of 1 Palk Street accountant, Torquay, were witnesses.

John Bogle died at Woodside, Torquay on 20 March 1879 aged 70 and probate of his will was granted to Twynihoe William Erle esquire of 1 Cambridge Gate, Regent's Park and Adam Bogle of Woodside a lieutenant in the Royal Engineers on 9 April 1879. He was domiciled in England and his personal estate in the United Kingdom was under £70,000 suggesting he had funds overseas. Sarah J. Bogle (sic) lived at Woodside in 1881 with daughters Jane, Anne and five servants (one Scotland, four Devon), whilst the household included John Du Terreau Bogle (captain R.E.), his wife Blanche E.B. and their son Benjamin W. The daughter Jane Bogle and son Adam Bogle were both married in 1882 but the family association with the Riviera soon ended and Jane Sarah Bogle died at Woodside, Torquay on 11 October 1885. John Du Terreau Bogle of 2 Staff Quarters, Brompton Barracks, Chatham a captain in the Royal Engineers administered her estate on 20 January 1886, which was valued at £2,480 17s 10d.

John Du Terreau Bogle was born in Glasgow on 4 June 1845 and came with his family to Torquay in 1850. He went to Harrow School in May 1860 at fifteen and was in Mr. Oxenham's House and a member of the school shooting team (first). He won the Ashburton Shield and Spencer Cup and shot at Wimbledon in 1861, but left Harrow in the third term that year. He took some time out, perhaps travelling, and entered the Royal Engineers as a lieutenant at Chatham on 17 July 1866. Bourchier Wrey Savile (1817) married Mary Elizabeth daughter of James Whyte of Pilton House, Devon in 1842 and had seven children including Blanche Eleanora Bourchier and Constance Emma Beresford (her twin) at Okehampton, Devon in March 1845. The family lived at Cleveland Place, Dawlish whilst his brother Henry Bourchier Osborne Savile (1819) was Mayor of Bristol in 1884.

Lieutenant John Du Terreau Bogle married Blanche Eleanora Bourchier Savile at Dawlish on 7 April 1869 and was posted to Portsmouth in 1870-71. His daughter Blanche "Janet" was born at Southsea on 15 January 1870 and the birth was registered thus in the Portsea district but she was later referred to as Blanche Du Terreau. John was sent to Bermuda from 11 March 1871 to 30 May 1874 a period of 3 years 81 days, which confirms his brother Adam played in the 1872 Cup Final as he was clearly abroad at the time - his son John Savile was born at Paget, Bermuda on 25 September 1872. He then returned home and was stationed at Sandhurst in 1874-76 having two children there: Constance Du Terreau in Sandhurst on 4 October 1874 registered as 'Female' Bogle in Farnham and Benjamin William born at York Town on 18 October 1875 - the Royal Military Academy was located between these two places. He was posted to Shorncliffe near Folkestone, Kent in 1877-78 and daughter Mary Eleanor was born there on 19 October 1877 and the birth registered in Elham.

John Bogle was promoted to captain on 24 January 1879 and was Assistant Instructor in Surveying at the S.M.E. Chatham in 1879-83. The family lived in Gillingham and daughter Annie was born there on 10 October 1879. Indeed Blanche J. Bogle (11) the 'head' lived at 1 Gillingham House near to Christmas Street and Church Street in the town in 1881 with four of her siblings, a governess and four servants. Captain Bogle was on leave in 1881 and resided with his wife Blanche and son Benjamin at Woodside in Torquay, whilst daughter Margaret Sybil was born in Gillingham on 8 December 1881. He returned overseas and commanded the 20th Company of the Engineers in Bermuda from 4 August 1883 to 21 November 1884, clearly a most senior position, and his son Henry Albert was born there on 28 December 1883. He was sent back to England to be Instructor in Surveying at Chatham from 1885 and lived at 2 Staff Quarters, Brompton Barracks that year. He was promoted to major on 17 July 1886 and his last child Ethel May was born at Chatham on 12 January 1888.

He was soon overseas again and was posted to Mauritius from 9 December 1889 to 9 May 1893 a period of 3 years, 152 days and was made lieutenant colonel on 1 April 1893. He was placed in command of the Engineers at Weymouth in 1894 and Blanche Du Terreau his daughter married Herbert Greenough Woolf at Weymouth in September 1894, and he lived at Aberdeen House, Esplanade in the town in 1895. There was little time to settle and he was in command of the Engineers in the Straits Settlements (Singapore) from 15 October 1895 and was made a brevet colonel on 1 April 1897. He spent 2 years 168 days in Singapore but was ordered home and retired from the army on 1 April 1898 having served 32 years 150 days - he received a pension of £450 p.a. from 14 December 1898. He then had a more settled time and like many retired army men resided in Bath, but the family were absent in 1901 apart from daughter Blanche Woolf who lived at Woking with her three children. Two daughters married in Bath: Constance Du Terreau to George Halliday Brown in June 1901 and Mary Eleanora to Ernest Hedley Davis in March 1905, whilst son Benjamin William was married at Exeter in September 1910.

He maintained London connections in this period and Harrow School records give his contact address as c/o Messrs Cox, 16 Charing Cross in 1911. It remains unclear what happened to his wife Blanche but she possibly died abroad as there is no trace of her in England. He made new associations in the early 20th century and lived at 30 Ouseley Road, Wandsworth where he made his last will on 24 March 1915. He left all moneys standing to his credit at Messrs. Cox & Company's Bank, 15 Charing Cross and with Mr. Albert H. Ward of 46 Queen Victoria Street to Madam Emmy Wisnowska of the same address, absolutely, for her own benefit. She was born on the Continent in 1875 and this clearly has 'shades' of Edith Wharton's *The Age of Innocence* - the latter book depicts New York society in the 1870s and Madam Olenska is one of the main characters.

He left to his son Major John Savile Bogle of Queen Victoria's Own Guides, Hoti Mardan, India his late father's gold watch by Breguet (no. 4783). Abraham Louis Breguet (1747-1823) was a famous watchmaker in France from 1780 and made watches for Royal and wealthy patrons and also Napoleon. He had to move to Switzerland in 1807 whilst his grandson Louis François Clement (1804-83), a watchmaker and physicist, made some of the first induction coils and helped develop electrical telegraphy. He also left his microscope to son Major Benjamin William Bogle and his cello and the residue of his personal and real estate to Emmy Wisnowska 'absolutely and beneficially'. He appointed her and David Charles Craigie of 38 Wilton Place, Belgrave executors and the latter witnessed his will with R. Jasper his clerk. John Du Terreau Bogle died at 30 Ouseley Road, Wandsworth Common, Surrey, on 17 June 1917 and his probate was granted to Emmy Wisnowska a widow on 31 August his effects £241 17s 9d. She died at Battersea in December 1933 aged 58.

The four daughters were all married although the weddings took place over a period of more than twenty years. Peter Erle baronet was born at Fifehead Magdalen, Dorset on 17 November 1796 and was a fellow of New College then a Queen's Counsel and a chief charity commissioner. He married Mary daughter of Rev. J.F. Fearon the rector of Selsey and vicar of Cuckfield. Twynihoe William his son was born Bloomsbury in 1828 and was a barrister who inherited Winterbourne Steepleton in Dorset. He lived at 12 Park Crescent, London and married Mary Bogle by licence at St. John's, Torquay on 16 May 1871. Aubrey M. Jamaica performed the ceremony and John Bogle, Jane Sarah Bogle, Janet Bogle and Constance Savile were witnesses. The couple then resided at Cuckfield and a son Christopher was born there in 1874 whilst two children were born at St. Pancras: Lilian M. (1877) and Sybil (1879). Twynihoe master of the Supreme Court of Justice lived at 1 Cambridge Gate on the east side of Regent's Park in 1879-81 with wife Mary, three children and eight servants. The father was a writer and published 'Letters from a theatrical scene painter' in 1859-62, 118 pages (J. Chisman) and then re-published it as '.... being sketches of the minor theatres of London as they were 20 years ago' in 1880, 115 pages (Mann's Ward & Co.). He had an interest in educational toys and his book 'Science in the nursery' came out in 1880. Violet Marjorie Twynihoe his daughter was baptized at Cuckfield on 29 October 1885 and he was a retired master of the Supreme Court at St. Pancras in 1901 with wife Mary and children Lilian, Sybil and Violet. He also resided at Mill Hall, Cuckfield and said to the Rev. James Cooper: "Mankind is divided into two great categories those who love Cuckfield and those who don't or do not know it," - he died 24 December 1908.

Janet Bogle married Rev. James Richard Whyte at Torquay in the Newton Abbot district in March 1874 however Janet Whyte a widow lived on dividends at Haccombe House, Exeter with three servants in 1881 and 1901. She died there on 5 November 1933 and John Savile Bogle a retired colonel H.M. Army obtained her probate. Jane Bogle married Rev. Francis Simpson at Torquay in the Newton Abbot district in June 1882 however they were not found in 1901. Rev. Francis Simpson died at Foston Rectory in Yorks near to Castle Howard on 28 July 1909 and Jane Simpson widow obtained his probate. Anne Bogle the youngest daughter married Edward Chatterton Orpen at St. Pancras, London in June 1894. He was a clergyman born in Ireland c.1831 and the couple resided at Ashcombe near Dawlish in 1901 however she became a widow and lived with her sister. Anne Orpen of Haccombe near Exeter died on 28 February 1929 and John Savile and Benjamin William Bogle retired colonels and Herbert Greenough Woolf barrister obtained her probate.

Adam Bogle was born in Glasgow on 21 June 1848 and came to Torquay with his family in 1850 and spent his childhood there. He followed his brother to Harrow School in February 1862 and was also in Mr. Oxenham's House and no doubt played soccer there before leaving in the first term of 1865. He presumably went to the Military Academy at Woolwich and then entered the Royal Engineers as a lieutenant on 15 July 1868. He was at the School of Military Engineering, Chatham from 15 August 1868 to 11 September 1870 and no doubt played with Marindin & Co. in the soccer team at the time. He had a temporary posting in Cork from 1 November 1870 to 7 August 1871, but was 'home' again at the Royal Arsenal, Woolwich on 8 August 1871 and stayed nearly three years. He was then able to rejoin the soccer team based at Chatham and played in the 1872 Cup Final.

He did a period of overseas service and was in Bermuda from 3 March 1874 (his brother John was there until 30 May) and then went to Gibraltar on 7 October 1876. He resided at Line Wall, Gibraltar in 1878 and was a single officer in the Royal Engineers and of the Church of England. A stone tablet on a building in Secretary's Lane backing onto Line Wall Road states: "Offrs Barracks No XVI", and he may have been billeted there. Indeed another historic building in Main Street near the Southport Gate also provided accommodation for officers and states "No VI". He left Gibraltar on 12 March 1879 and spent a year at Curragh, Ireland from 16 April but then received a promotion and commanded the 37th Company of Engineers at the S.M.E. Chatham from 11 May 1880 being promoted to captain on 25 November 1880. He left three months later and commanded the 25th Company of Engineers at Aldershot for a year from February 1881, and was on miscellaneous returns at Staff Quarters, Aldershot in 1881 with eight lieutenants, a vet, two grenadier guards (bachelors), Cols Howard C. Elphinstone & William B. Gossett, storekeepers, surveyors and riding master all of the R.E. Depot, Aldershot.

During this period he no doubt visited his family in Torquay and soon became acquainted with their neighbours. John J. Glossop J.P. lived at "Lunesdale", Tormoham in 1881 with his wife Harriet E., daughters Blanche, Ethel (24) born Dover and Gemma and six servants. Captain Bogle made a number of moves however the army found a position that suited him and he was appointed Instructor in Fortifications at the Royal Military College, Sandhurst on 1 February 1882. Adam Bogle married Ethel Glossop at St. Matthias, Ilsham on 20 July 1882 near to Woodside, Torquay and the Babbacombe area. He was a captain R.E. of Sandhurst and his bride of Lunesdale, her father being John James Glossop a colonel in the 3rd Battalion of the Royal Fusiliers. The marriage was by licence, and the witnesses were John J. Glossop and E.R. Henery (captain R.E.). Adam was promoted to the rank of major on 23 July 1887 and finished his posting at Sandhurst on 31 January 1889 but was overseas again in Jamaica from 21 February 1889. He spent the last two years of his army career at Dover from 7 October 1890 but had leave in early 1891, then retired as a major on 25 May 1892 after 23 years, 314 days service and received an army pension of £250 p.a.

Adam and Ethel Bogle had no children and were absent in 1901 but moved to "Collyers", Petersfield, Hampshire, by 1909. Adam Bogle made his last will there on 7 January 1909 and appointed his wife Ethel Bogle and nephews Captain John Savile Bogle and Captain Benjamin William Bogle, executors and trustees. He left his household goods, house-houses, stables and other premises to his wife as well as: "my horses and carriages and my yacht with the boats and gear and all belonging thereto or being on board thereof...." He directed that a marriage settlement dated 19 July 1882 should be divided into eight equal parts and the money distributed after his wife's decease viz. Blanche Du Terreau Woolf 1/8, John Savile Bogle 2/8, Constance Du Terreau Brown 1/8, Benjamin William Bogle 1/8, Mary Eleanor Davis 1/8 and Margaret Sybil Ingham 2/8. The remainder of his estate was put in trust and the resulting money invested for his wife, until her decease or remarriage, then paid out in three equal parts: Jane wife of Rev. Francis Simpson, Janet Whyte widow and Anne Orpen widow. After their decease the residuary trust was to be distributed, "amongst the children of my brother Colonel John Du Terreau Bogle by Blanche Eleanora his wife." He also directed that the money be invested in stocks and securities of any British colony and signed the will at Messrs. Metcalfe, Hussey and Hulbert solicitors of Lincoln's Inn. He made a codicil to the will at the London County and Westminster Bank Ltd. in Petersfield on 3 October 1910 and revoked the section regarding the residuary trust as regards nephew Captain Benjamin William Bogle but in all other respects he confirmed it.

Adam Bogle died at Collyers, Petersfield on 3 March 1915 and probate was granted to his widow Ethel Bogle on 20 May that year his estate being valued at £26,742 17s 10d but later re-sworn at £24,707 17s 10d. His widow Ethel outlived him by 30-years and died at Bramshott Chase, Bramshott in Hampshire on 27 March 1945 a village eight miles north east of Petersfield. Sir Edward Philip le Breton and John Cecil Glossop Pownall a barrister proved her will the effects £28,141 17s. This concludes the discourse on the Bogle family (not phantoms) and indeed the brothers had a significant role in the Royal Engineers especially regarding the training of officers at Chatham and Sandhurst. Both John and Adam spent periods overseas and in the next chapter the colony of Gibraltar is discussed in detail.

CHAPTER 9

The Gibraltar Connection

The Royal Engineers lost the Cup Final of 1872 however there were extenuating circumstances regarding the defeat. Lieutenant Creswell one of their best players broke his collarbone just ten minutes from the start and went off for treatment. There were no substitutes in those days and he returned to the pitch but could do little thereafter due to his injury, and the match-report states: "Too much praise cannot be accorded to him for the pluck he showed in maintaining his post although completely disabled and in severe pain until the finish." He had obviously learnt such resilience in the Royal Engineers and as a boy in Gibraltar.

The Company of Artificers was formed in Gibraltar after a *Royal Warrant* dated 6 March 1772 and the Corps of Military Artificers were established at Woolwich, Chatham, Portsmouth, Gosport, Plymouth and Channel Islands (1787). Gibraltar was incorporated in 1797 and new companies established in Malta, Nova Scotia and the West Indies in 1800. The Peninsular War caused further growth and Gibraltar had two companies in 1806 and three in 1811, whilst the School of Military Engineering, Chatham was founded in 1812 and the Corps was renamed the Royal Sappers and Miners in 1813. After Napoleon's defeat it was reduced in size to 12 companies and a *Royal Warrant* dated 30 August 1833 maintained units at Woolwich (3), Chatham, Gibraltar, Corfu, Bermuda, Halifax, Cape (and Mauritius) and three for surveying. This increased to 22 companies in 1849 whilst the Royal Sappers and Miners joined as one body with the Royal Engineer (officers) on 17 October 1856 and private soldiers then became sappers. The Corps had a long-term connection with Gibraltar and the Creswell family, who are discussed below, led the way.

TRADE AND EMPIRE

Tarik the Moorish leader landed near 'Casemates Square' in 711 thus the name Gibraltar originates from Gibel Tarik or Tarik's Hill. The Moors remained for 700 years except for the period 1309-33 and built strong defences along the coast and a castle above the town, but lost control to Spain in 1462, whilst the British captured Gibraltar from the Spanish in 1704 and the Treaty of Utrecht cemented British Sovereignty in 1713. The Moorish town was demolished in 1731 and replaced by the Casemates, an army fortification, which connected with Landport Gate - the only land entrance into the town and a large settlement developed nearby on Main Street. There were numerous sieges in the 18th century as the Spanish tried to remove the British presence and Gibraltar was 'a city under siege' with the "Great Siege" in 1779-83. The Soldiers Artificers forerunner of the Engineers dug tunnels into the limestone rock above the town, which were hundreds of yards long and punctuated by gun openings. These enabled the artillery to fire canon balls and the like onto the Spanish trenches below.

The situation was more stable in the 19th century and Gibraltar became an important centre of trade due to its pivotal position in the Mediterranean. The Fortress Felipe V protected the Spanish side of the border but was demolished at the end of hostilities (in the 19th century) and the town of La Linea de la Concepcion was begun in 1870, its full name being La Linea de Contravalacion de la Plaza de Gibraltar - now a large town just across the border. Gibraltar was a walled town, surrounded by sea and protected by battlements and had a number of gates in its walls viz. Landport, Waterport, Prince Edward's, Southport and Ragged Staff Gates. A wharf was built to provide victuals to British warships, in 1736, and Ragged Staff Gate (near Southport Gate) was constructed in the wall to connect with it although the origin of the name is not known. A further arch was cut there in the 19th century and is marked *VR* 1843 whilst the gates play a part in the story and are mentioned below. Lieutenant Charles Warren of the Engineers surveyed the peninsula under the direction of Major General Frome in 1865 and constructed a large detailed model, which can still be seen in Gibraltar Museum. The town was unchanged until dockyards were begun in 1895 and extensive land reclamation took place in the late 20th century.

The Royal Engineers had an important role in Gibraltar's history and after the "Great Siege" kept many troops on the Rock whilst Engineer Lane and Engineer Road can be found in the town. There are two memorials, the first opposite the Catholic Cathedral in Main Street states: "Presented to the people of Gibraltar by the Corps of the Royal Engineers to commemorate the continuous service given by the Corps

The Royal Engineers' Memorial. The Corps served on the Rock from 1704.

on the Rock of Gibraltar from 1704 and the formation here in 1772 of the first body of soldiers of the Corps then known as the Company of Soldiers Artificers, 26th March 1994." A similar memorial to the Engineers is on the wall of King's Chapel and is dated 27th March 1994. The basic outline of the colony is as follows: La Linea, neutral area, British lines, barracks, Engineer Lane, Main Street and town, Holy Trinity Cathedral, Governor's House, Rosia Road and Bay, Engineer Road, H.M. Dockyard and Europa Point.

A group of Franciscan monks established a friary in c.1480 and began a chapel in 1533 that was completed in 1560 (the latter date being on the building). It became the King's Chapel (C of E) when the British arrived in 1704, whilst the neighbouring convent became the Governor's residence (as it is today). Both the army and the townsfolk used the King's Chapel at first however the nave was demolished during the "Great Siege" and the building restored without the nave in 1783-88 - it was then closed during the years 1833-43. Holy Trinity church was started in 1825 and Colonel Pilkington the commanding Royal Engineer was builder although the architect is unknown. It was a rectangular building adjacent to the town walls and, surprisingly, constructed in the Moorish style being completed in 1832 and consecrated in 1838. Edward Burrow the archdeacon performed the ceremony in the presence of Dowager Queen Adelaide (widow of William IV) and it was made a cathedral in 1842. The residents of Gibraltar then used the latter, the baptisms dating from 1836, whilst the army utilised the King's Chapel of the Convent from 1843. This was an important fact to know when doing research in Gibraltar.

John Creswell the son of John was baptized at Funtington in Sussex on 5 March 1722 then married Anne and had children: Thomas (1753), John (1755) and William (1756). The son John Creswell married Esther and had six children at Funtington, namely Charles (1772), Harriet (1774), Edmund (1776), Caroline (1778), William (1780) and Juliana (1783). The story proper begins with Edmund Creswell who was baptized at Funtington on 10 March 1776 and soon formed connections in the capital. He was married at St. Mary Aldermary, London and the entry was as follows: "Edmund Creswell of the parish of Funtington in the county of Sussex, a bachelor, and Susannah Drawbridge of this parish, spinster, were married in this church by licence this 16th day of January 1802 by me John Frith A.M. Signed *Edmund Creswell*, *Ssusannah Drawbridge* in the presence of John Balcock, Phillis White and Richard White." Susannah daughter of Thomas and Elizabeth Drawbridge was born at Heathfield in c.1775 and baptized on 4 February 1787 aged 12. The church was in the business district hence only five marriages took place in 1802 - it is still present between Cheapside and 'new' Victoria Street. Harriet Creswell (1774) married Thomas Wheeler Gillham in c.1799 whilst Juliana Creswell (1783) married John Thomas Bell at All Hallows, Staining (London) on 20 March 1813 and lived in the parish of St. Mary at Hill and then Camberwell in 1823. The Gillhams and other Bell relatives appear later in the story.

Edmund and Susannah Creswell had a daughter Harriet Mary in 1808 and had moved to the small parish of Kingston near Lewes, Sussex in 1809. Their daughter Mary Creswell was born at Kingston on 25 June 1809 and baptized there on 11 August 1811. Meanwhile Thomas Wheeler Gillham, a nephew, was born at Funtington on 2 August 1801 and baptized on 12 August but also baptized at Kingston on 11 August 1811 (a family affair). He married Harriet Hurdis at St. John the Baptist, Southover between Kingston and Lewes on 1 February 1831 and resided nearby at Rodmell. He was the vicar of Lyddington, Rutland-shire and lived there with his wife Harriet, son Thomas W. and mother Harriet Gillham (née Creswell, 65) in 1841. He was vicar of Caldecott as well and lived at Lyddington with his wife, children Thomas and Anne, five visitors and three servants in 1851.

Kingston was indeed a small village and life was very quiet there with just 2 baptisms in 1810, 6 in 1811 and 2 in 1812. Most of the village was situated along The Street leading up to the South Downs and in fact little is changed today. There is a 13th century flint church with small tower dedicated to St. Pancras by the green and opposite is Hyde Manor, whilst old buildings such as Kingston Manor and Juggs Way are nearby.

There are also farm buildings, cottages and a pound with stonework taken from Southover Priory and the weather boarded 'old' post office, which was previously used as a granary store. Only a few records survive to give a picture of those times and include the overseer's accounts for Kingston - 15 April 1814. These were connected with poor relief, especially for widows, and gave the price of flour as 2s 7d for a gallon (sic) of corn with the total cost for the year £14 11s 6d. Edmund and Susannah continued to reside in Kingston and had three children baptized: Elizabeth (14 January 1812), **Edmund** (2 December 1813) and Thomas (17 October 1815) the father being a corn merchant, a most significant appellation.

Edmund Creswell then became a yeoman in the nearby parish of Falmer and had two sons baptized at St. Lawrence's Church: Charles James (25 January 1817) on 19 March 1818 and William (28 April 1821) on 16 May that year. Some further records give a flavour of those times and a militia order was presented to the churchwardens and overseers of Falmer in October 1822. The order came from John Smith, constable of Younsmere Hundred, and required them to contact all occupiers in 7 days and compile a list of persons eligible to serve in the militia in 14 days. This was to include all men aged 18-45 and those with an infirmity yet at the same time there were many classes that were exempt such as: army, navy, effective yeomanry, clergy, teachers, constables, apprentices, H.M. dockyard workers, Thames watermen, poor men with more than one child born in wedlock and persons under 5'4". The Quakers were to be listed separately and a true copy of the list attached on the door of the church or chapel including the last date for an appeal and a return sent to the deputy lieutenant on oath. Edmund was no doubt exempt since he was aged 46 years and an "effective" yeoman.

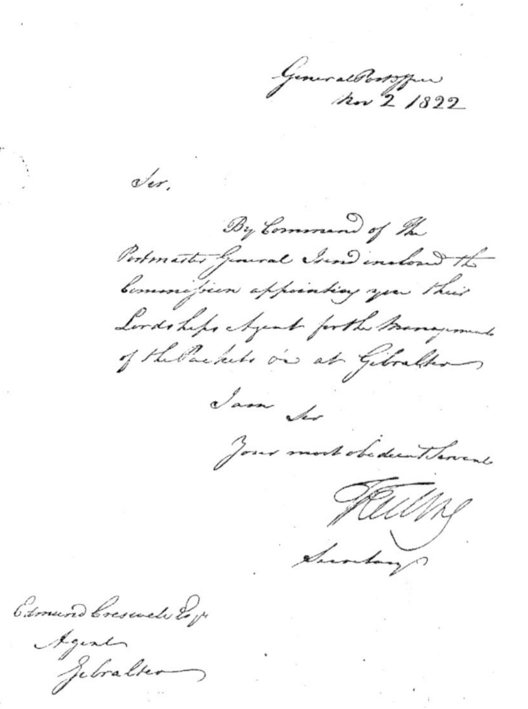
General Post Office
Nov 2 1822

Sir,

By Command of the Postmaster General I send inclosed the Commission appointing you their Lordships Agent for the management of the Packets on at Gibraltar

I am Sir
Your most obedient Servant
T Freeling
Secretary

Edmund Creswell Esq
Agent
Gibraltar

Agent for the Packets. Edmund Creswell (1776-1831) was appointed in 1822.

Edmund Creswell (corn merchant and yeoman) was clearly more than a subsistence farmer and had dealings beyond the Kingston-Falmer area - a fact supported by his London marriage. It seems likely he also had other local duties, which would have been necessary in a small village like Kingston and he may have been an agent for the postal service. Indeed Edmund probably had connections with the 'old' post office in Kingston since it was originally a store for corn and grain. The importance of the postal service and how it operated is revealed in Pigot's Directory of 1839: *John William Ferguson* was postmaster at 22 New Road, Brighton. The office was open at 7.30 a.m. in summer and at 8.00 a.m. in winter but closed at 9.30 p.m. whilst the receiving houses were at St. James Street, St. George's, Preston Street and Kemp Town. Letters to Lewes were despatched every morning at 3.30 a.m. and arrived from Lewes every morning at 7.00 a.m. *Thomas Saxby* was postmaster at 44 High Street, Lewes and there was a receiving house at 51 High Street, Cliff. Letters from Brighton, Portsmouth etc. arrived every morning at 5.00 a.m. and were despatched every evening at 8.00 p.m. The postal service was vital to local business and trade and Falmer was on the main road from Brighton to Lewes, but Kingston was off the beaten track.

Edmund Creswell had important contacts and soon left England on a permanent basis when he secured a notable job overseas. He then exchanged the rolling downs of Sussex for the 'intense' atmosphere of Gibraltar and various dates appear in the records for his departure although this can be narrowed to 1822 with two pieces of information. Gibraltar had been a colony for over 100 years when the Creswells arrived there and Edmund received a letter from the General Post Office, London on 2 November 1822 stating: "Sir, By command of the Postmaster General, I send enclosed the commission appointing you their Lordships Agent for the management of the Packets at Gibraltar, I am Sir your most obedient servant, T. Freeling Secretary."

It seems certain he had some previous experience to receive such a posting and the family departed for Gibraltar at the end of the year. Soon after their arrival there was an important marriage and the entry states: "John Longlands Cowell merchant of this garrison (bachelor) and Harriet Mary Creswell (spinster) eldest daughter of Mr. Edmund Creswell, Agent of H.M. Packets were married by licence with consent of parents in the King's Chapel on 19 April 1823 by me Rowland Grove Curtois B.D. Chaplain to the Forces." Both parties signed and Edmund Creswell, Susan Creswell, Mary Creswell and Elizabeth Creswell (the parents and two sisters) were amongst the six witnesses. This was, however, a difficult place to live with the risk of disease from foreign ships and there was a bad epidemic in 1828. Elizabeth Creswell died on 28 September 1828 age 17 and Mary Creswell on 5 October 1828 age 19, both from yellow fever, and they were buried south of the town at Sandpits Cemetery near Rosia Road (now called Withams Cemetery). This was a great loss to Edmund however he continued with his work and there were many letters to the Agent for the Packets in the 1820s regarding postal rates and lost post: "18 August 1830 - The Mediterranean packet will no longer touch Cadiz but the bag will come directly to Gibraltar for onward transport." Edmund Creswell died on 18 February 1831, age 55, and was buried at Sandpits Cemetery with his daughters whilst his duties passed to his son.

Edmund Creswell (1813) came to Gibraltar with his father in 1822 however he was educated in England before returning there in 1830. He became a notable person in Gibraltar's history and although not listed in official records had friends who held him in high esteem, thus his life was recorded in the local paper at his decease. He was appointed temporary clerk in the Ordnance Department in 1830 and transferred to the Military Secretary's Office in 1831. The "Blue Book" containing civil lists for Gibraltar recorded his advancement as follows: "Agent for the Packets: E. Creswell was appointed by the Postmaster General on 22 April 1831, salary of £50 p.a. paid by the Post Office in London. He is also 2nd clerk of the Military Secretary's Office." A letter dated 27 May 1831 confirmed the payment of £50 and was addressed to him at the Military Secretary's Office, Gibraltar.

The description, however, was misleading and he had different duties to those once attached to such an appointment being in fact the postmaster under a different name. He dealt with letters sent to England on Government sailing vessels at a cost of 2s 6d per letter and a journey time of 14-16 days. There was also an overland post under the supervision of the Colonial Secretary at a cost of 2s 4½d taking 10-12 days and clearly "time is money" did not apply. Edmund received many letters from London in the 1830s relating to postal rates and lost post and the destinations mentioned included France, Germany, Malta and Alexandria. John Williams a tailor of 368 The Strand, London posted a letter at San Roque containing a £10 bank note and the recipient should have been Mr. Power of Gibraltar, however it was lost en route thus Edmund received a letter regarding this matter on 8 April 1834 and no doubt advised them not to send cash by post. Such were the problems of an "Agent for the Packets"! There was a census in Gibraltar in 1834 and **Charles Creswell** a clerk lived at 16 Market Lane with Thomas Hassenden (20), a merchant and native of Gibraltar, however most of his family were absent on the night of the census.

The Creswells held an important position in Gibraltar and met many townsfolk and merchants through the postal service, (their) civic duties and trade thus forming associations with local families such as Cowell, Carver and Drinkwater. John Longlands Cowell, son of Edward, was born in c.1798 and came to Gibraltar in 1813 then became a merchant. He married Harriet Mary Creswell in 1823 and had five children baptized at King's Chapel namely John Hadwin (1824), Edward James (1825), *Richard Edmund* (1828), Edward Willis (1831), Henry James (1833) and Harriet Mary (1835). He was a merchant residing at 10 Irish Town near Main Street in December 1834 with wife Harriet M., children John H. (11), Richard Edmund (6) and E.W. Cowell (5), **Thomas Creswell** clerk and Edward Cowell (65) who had lived with them for six months - the adults were all Protestants from England. The couple also had three children baptized at Holy Trinity Cathedral viz. Fanny Susan (1839), James Longlands (1844) and William Glasgow (1846).

The Cowell family put regular adverts in the Gibraltar Chronicle and the "Arrow" a British schooner arrived 4 January 1845 being 13 days from Scilly with potatoes for Gibraltar - all consignments to Messrs. Longlands Cowell & Co. In addition "Eclair" a Belgian brigantine arrived 28 January 1845 being 13 days from Mogadore and in ballast for Gibraltar returning Mogadore in a few days - all consignments registered with Longlands Cowell & Co. There was a similar advert on 4 March 1845 regarding "La Belle Alliance" a 700-ton ship for London. These revealed their business activities however there were other records of the family and there were soon a number of marriages at Holy Trinity: Edward Willis Cowell married Caroline Balmelli on 24 December 1852 and they had a son Edward Willis in 1853 whilst an Edward Willis Cowell died at Valparaiso, Chile in 1881-85. This was either the father or the son and was registered in the consular returns. Harriet Mary Cowell married Alfred Mumford a merchant and citizen of London on 4 January 1860 and Richard Edmund Cowell, Edmund Creswell and Margaret Creswell were witnesses. Richard Edmund Cowell a merchant of Gibraltar married Maria Gonzales on 18 November 1867. She was born in Spain in c.1840 the daughter of Pedro A. Gonzales collector of rents and British pensioner. The witnesses to the wedding included Mary M.W. Creswell, Margaret Creswell, P. Gonzales, Isabel Gonzales, J. Cowell and W.G. Cowell. John Hadwin Cowell (widower) a merchant of Gibraltar married Eleanor Danvers Relph on 13 May 1868 and the witnesses included Edmund and Margaret S. Creswell whilst their daughter Harriet Margaret Cowell was born in 1875 - the father an esquire. It is clear that only some of these people remained in Gibraltar.

Richard and Maria Cowell lived at 22 Main Street on the corner of Tuckeys Lane from 1868-81 and Barclays Bank now occupies the site. Richard Cowell was a Protestant however his wife was a Spanish Catholic thus their children were born as Catholics. They had sons Richard Ernest P (1868) *infant* and Ernest E. Gonzales (1871) whilst the father died in the 1880s. Mrs. Richard E. Cowell a general merchant lived at the same house, now 22 Waterport Street, in 1890-91 however she died later in 1891 and was buried at North Front Cemetery. The son E. Cowell lived at Cloister Ramp in 1893-94 and may have known Hugh Mitchell who arrived at this time. There is a fascinating memorial to the family in North Front Cemetery: "John Longlands Cowell merchant died on 10 June 1859 aged 60 a resident for 45 years and Consul of Austria, Belgium and Turkey. His son William Glasgow Cowell esquire died on 10 November 1868 after a short illness aged 22 years and was His Hellenic Majesty's Consul." The "Blue Book" or civil list gives further details: J.L. Cowell Consul for Belgium 16 January 1838, Ottoman 9 August 1842 and Austria 5 March 1851 (in 1858); R.E. Cowell Consul for Belgium 23 September 1859, Turkey-Ottoman 23 January 1860 and Austria 6 June 1860 (in 1862-67); W.G. Cowell Consul for Greece 12 February 1867.

The main players in the story, however, were the Carver family who came from Leicestershire. William Carver married Ann Clark at Braunstone on 12 October 1781 and had five children baptized there namely Elizabeth (1782), *William* (1784), Martha (1785), Ann (1787), Robert (1 Sep 1788) and John (23 Jul 1790). William Carver was born at Braunstone in c.1784 but was not baptized there and married Elizabeth Simpkin at Aylestone on 26 July 1810 then settled in the small hamlet of Ingarsby. It was five miles east of Leicester and was one of the deserted villages of England after its decimation by the bubonic plague in c.1500. Ingarsby was an area of fertile farmland and was further depopulated by field enclosure in the 16th-17th centuries thus the ancient parish was incorporated with Hungarton. The remaining buildings were Ingarsby Old Hall, Ingarsby Lodge and New Ingarsby (both farms) plus a few cottages and indeed it was so small that it was absent from many maps.

William Carver was a successful farmer of great wealth with eight children baptized at Hungarton: Ann (1811), William (1813), John (1814), Elizabeth (1816), Martha (1818), Robert (1819), Benjamin (1823) & Charles (1825). He was a farmer and grazier at Ingarsby in 1841 with children Elizabeth, Martha, Robert and Benjamin and a farmer of 470 acres employing 27 labourers at Old Ingarsby in 1851 with children Anne, Robert and Charles and nine servants; he was clearly an affluent landowner. He was a farmer of 470 acres employing 19 men and 3 boys at Ingarsby in 1861 and lived with children Anne, Robert and Charles and seven servants including a carter, groom, shepherd and dairymaid, thus giving an indication of his farming practices. William Carver died soon after the census (possibly December 1861) and Ingarsby Hall was left to his children. Robert Carver a farmer of 520 acres employing 15 labourers and 5 boys owned the farm in 1871 and lived with Charles, Annie and seven servants, however the other three sons were merchants who made a fortune in the Industrial Revolution. They were based in Manchester but did much of their trade overseas, especially in Alexandria and Gibraltar.

Robert Carver was born at Braunstone in 1788 and lived with his wife Mary Ann in Queniborough and had five children: John (1826), Thomas Cave (1829), Mary Ann (1832), Benjamin (19 October 1834) and Charles (1838). Robert a farmer lived in the village in 1841 with his wife, Thomas (12), Mary (9), Benjamin (6), Charles (3) and one servant. His brother John Carver was born at Braunstone in 1790 and married Lydia, then became the first of the family to arrive in Gibraltar. He was a merchant who resided at Waterport Street in the 1820s-30s and had children Eliza (1823) and Ellen (1831) baptized at the King's Chapel although it was his nephews that played the most significant role.

William Carver junior was born at Old Ingarsby and baptized at Hungarton on 18 April 1813 although his parents were described as William Carver and his wife (Ann?) - an error in the records. He left the village and became a merchant in Manchester and joined his uncle John in Gibraltar in the 1840s. Meanwhile Emma Louisa daughter of Thomas and Emma Drinkwater was born at Flat Bastion Road,

Gibraltar (high above the town) on 7 May 1823 and baptized at King's Chapel on 4 October that year. They had three other children born at Library Ramp viz. Jane Lydia (1826), Mary (1827) and Elizabeth Anne (1832) and all lived at 38 Library Ramp on 11 December 1834. Thomas was then an ironmonger but was later a merchant and 'acting' agent for the Packet Office in 1844-45 (see below). John Drinkwater captain in the late 72nd Regiment, Royal Manchester Volunteers wrote, "A History of the Late Siege of Gibraltar" in 1785, and may have been a relative due to his association with Manchester - Drinkwater Road named after him is near the airport below the Great Siege tunnels.

William Carver married Emma Louisa Drinkwater at Holy Trinity Cathedral on 3 September 1842 - both inhabitants of the garrison. E.J. Burrow civil chaplain was minister and Thomas, Emma and Jane Drinkwater, John Longlands Cowell and Edmund Creswell were witnesses, whilst their son Edmund Drinkwater was born in Gibraltar on 3 July 1843. This brings us to an important player. James Chataway son of James and Catherine Hopkins was born in Birmingham in 1827 and went to Clare College, Cambridge in Michaelmas 1846 gaining a B.A. in 1851 (M.A. 1854). He married Elizabeth Anne Drinkwater at Holy Trinity on 3 October 1851 and Thomas Drinkwater, Jane Lydia Drinkwater, William and Emma Louisa Carver and Elizabeth Carver (sister) were witnesses. He was ordained a deacon in 1852 and son James Vincent was born at Aston on 6 September that year; he was made a prebendary at Worcs. in 1853 and daughter Ethel was baptized at Barthomley, Cheshire on 19 November 1854. He was then vicar of Wartling in 1856-66 and had two children: Mary in March 1861 and Thomas Drinkwater on 6 April 1864. He was curate of Heckfield in 1866-70 but became rector of nearby Rotherwick in 1870. He lived at the Rectory in 1881 with his wife, children Mary, George H. (10), Norman H. (9) and Olive A. (5) a governess and five servants - these two Hampshire villages have a significant role in the story. Elizabeth Anne Chataway died at Rotherwick in September 1893 and James resigned in 1895 then lived at 14 Selwyn Gardens, Cambridge where he died on 8 January 1907 - he was buried at Rotherwick.

His daughter Ethel had a notable link that is discussed below whilst his sons were adventurers. Captain John Mackay travelled north from New South Wales to find grazing land near Pioneer River in May 1860. Mackay was thus settled on the coast 500 miles north of Brisbane in 1862 and was initially a cattle-grazing area but John Spiller opened the first sugar mill in 1867 - the plantation workers or Kanakas came from the Pacific islands and were slave labour. James V. Chataway immigrated to Mackay in 1873 and 16 sugar mills were located in Pioneer Valley by 1874. Thomas D. Chataway was educated at Charterhouse and was a boarder at Sandy Lane, Godalming, in 1881 but joined his brother later that year and was a farmer on Liverpool Plains. He went to Mackay in 1882 to work as a sugar boiler in Habana Sugar Mill. His brother and W.G. Hodges purchased the *Mackay Mercury* in 1886 and he went to work at the paper then married Anna Maria Alterieth at Rockhampton, Queensland on 8 November 1890. The brothers started the *Sugar Journal and Tropical Cultivation* in 1892 and Thomas was in charge then ran both papers after 1896 - a merger with the *Chronicle* formed the *Daily Mercury* in 1905.

James was M.L.A. in Mackay from 1893 until his death on 12 April 1901, whilst Thomas was Mayor in 1904-06 then a member of the Australian Senate who was against socialism and approved the use of island labour. He had special knowledge of press, post and telegraphs and was on a select committee for press cable services in 1909. He sold the paper in 1911 then was defeated in 1913 but worked for the Federal 'leader of the opposition' in 1916 and was personal assistant to Senator E.D. Millen in 1917. He went back into journalism in Melbourne after the war but died at 6 Balmerino Avenue, Toorak on 5 March 1925. This was an opulent colonial suburb just south east of Melbourne and he was buried nearby in Brighton Cemetery. The pioneers James and Thomas Drinkwater Carver were cousins of E.W. Creswell whilst their brother-in-law had a senior role in the newspapers (see below) - Mackay a tropical city has fields of sugar cane today. Meanwhile the Carver family were related to many others Clifton, Drinkwater, Henton, Rickards and Creswell and used these as middle names for their children, whilst some remained in Gibraltar but most were temporary residents and soon returned to England.

John Carver junior was born at Old Ingarsby and baptized at Hungarton on 23 November 1814 and joined his brother William in Manchester in the 1840s. Meanwhile Charles Rickards cotton spinner married Frances Broome at Sandbach in Cheshire on 1 December 1808 then moved to Salford and had children: Thomas Broome (1811), Charles Hilditch (1812), Helen (1814), Ann (13 October 1817), William Henry (1816) and Francis Phillip (1820) - the last four were baptized at St. John's, Deansgate. John Carver a merchant of Whitmore Place, Stretford married Ann Rickards of Apsley Terrace, Stretford at Manchester Parish Church on 21 July 1842 and Charles Hilditch Rickards, Helen Rickards, W.H. Rickards, F.P. Rickards and sister Ann Carver were witnesses. The first signatory is of some considerable interest and his life is discussed later. Manchester Cathedral or parish church became a collegiate church in 1421-22 when the area was only a village and lay in the mediaeval town. Today it is opposite Chetham's Music School and Victoria Station - the latter first opened in 1844 and George Stephenson enlarged it and the façade was added in 1902. John Carver was a merchant in Carver & Nephews and his first child Frances Elizabeth was born at Chorlton in June 1843, but they soon went abroad and their journey was recorded in the Gibraltar Chronicle: "The packet ship 'Lady Mary Wood' arrived on Thursday April 4, 1844 being 7 days from Southampton and passengers included Mr. and Mrs Carver, infant, and servant."

There was a large gathering of the clan in Gibraltar then soon after a marriage that would shape history for years to come and literally start a dynasty. Edmund Creswell remained busy as Agent for the Packets and received a letter from the Admiralty regarding a packet ship of the Peninsular Steam Navigation Co. on 31 October 1838. He was advised that the ship would leave Gibraltar at "gunfire" - Hold on to your hats! He also played an important role in the community being elected Honorary Secretary of Gibraltar Public School in January 1838. His mother Susannah Creswell died on 20 August 1842 aged 67 and was buried at Sandpits Cemetery with her husband and daughters. There is no surviving memorial today however a European traveller made a transcription of one in c.1905-10. Thomas Creswell (1815) traded as a merchant and sailed on the "Great Liverpool" steam packet for Southampton on 4 July 1844 for an important engagement. Thomas Creswell a gentleman married Martha Carver (1818) at Hungarton on 27 September 1844 both residents of Ingarsby. His cousin T.W. Gillham, vicar of Lyddington, Rutland performed the ceremony and the whole family turned out for the wedding many of them travelling from Gibraltar, thus the witnesses included W. Carver, William Carver junior, Anne Carver, Robert Carver, Thomas Drinkwater, H.M. Cowell and Charles H. Rickards.

Mr. and Mrs. Creswell returned to Gibraltar on the British steam packet "Pacha" which arrived Thursday 24 October 1844, 6½ days from Southampton, 3 days from Vigo, 19 hours from Lisbon and 8 hours from Cadiz with a cargo of mails for Gibraltar. Thomas, however, did not remain for long and travelled to the Philippines hence his daughter Martha Harriet Creswell was born in Manila in 1849. The family then returned to Europe and settled in Lisbon, Portugal and soon appeared in the consular records with several children born in Lisbon, namely Frank Stenhouse in 1853 and Charles Graham and Louisa Alice between 1855-59. His daughter Eleanor Carver Creswell was born in Lisbon on 18 October 1860 and the birth registered by Thomas at the British Consulate on 6 March 1861 - the consular officer being William Smith. The Creswell family may have been in Madrid in the 1860s but maintained a connection with Lisbon for many years. James Fforde married Martha Harriet Creswell at the Consul's Office, Lisbon, on 29 January 1872 both of 136 Rua dos Tanqueiros and George Brackenbury H.M. Consul performed the ceremony and T. Creswell and Mary E. Creswell were witnesses. Her husband James son of Robert Fforde a clergyman was born in Ireland in c.1837 and became a civil engineer who lived in Ireland, South Africa, England, Gibraltar and again Ireland. The lives of Martha Harriet Fforde and Frank Stenhouse Creswell are discussed later as is the connection to George Brackenbury. A relative Phebe Emily Creswell died at 7 Rua Ribeiro, Sanches, Lisbon, on 9 November 1939 and her probate was granted to Frank Gordon Creswell a merchant in London on 2 April 1940.

The Carver family were itinerant at this time and their story is now continued. William and Emma Louisa Carver then returned to Manchester and their son Henry Clifton was born at Chorlton in March 1845. This was followed with a longer period in Gibraltar and they had four children there: Charles William (25 October 1846), Thomas Gilbert (14 November 1848), Sidney Henton (15 February 1851) and Emma Mary (27 September 1853) who were baptized at Holy Trinity (except for Thomas). The family returned to Manchester on a permanent basis in c.1857 and their address was College Road, Whalley Range, Withington, in 1858-61 this being an area south of Manchester and near to Fallowfield (see Ch. 12). They soon had two more children Walter Aspinall in June 1857 and Agnes Catherine on 2 February 1859. William Carver a merchant lived at Whalley Range in 1861 with wife Emma, all his children except for Edmund, sister Elizabeth Carver (visitor) and four servants whilst brother John was next door. Indeed Carver Brother's & Co., general merchants, traded at 7 Lower Mosley Street, Manchester from at least 1855-91.

William Carver resided at "Broomfield House" in Halliwell Lane, Cheetham in 1864 although he visited Gibraltar for a wedding in August that year. He wrote his last will on 23 January 1868 and left £20,000 to his sons Edmund Drinkwater, Henry Clifton and Charles William Carver the money to be placed in trust and the income paid to his wife Emma Louisa during her lifetime. The sons were requested to sell and convert into money all his real and personal estate not bequeathed and this would form his residuary estate with the £20,000 the total to be divided, equally, between his sons and daughters as tenants in common. The money for any daughter was to be put in trust and the interest and income paid to "her" during her lifetime free from the control of any husband. After her decease the money was to go to her children but if no child she could bequeath the money to someone of her choosing. Further she could also direct that the interests, dividends and income be paid to her husband during his lifetime. William Carver of "Broomfield", Manchester died at Heckfield on 1 February 1868 his brother-in-law being the curate there. Edmund Drinkwater Carver of Alexandria *Egyptian* merchant, Henry Clifton Carver of Broomfield engineer, Charles William Carver of Peter's Buildings Rumford Street in Liverpool cotton broker, proved his last will in Manchester on 28 May 1868 at under £50,000 but re-sworn in September 1874 at under £60,000 (see brother's decease).

Meanwhile Richard Moberly (1725-1804) married Jane Adams on 28 March 1756 and had five children baptized St. Marylebone: Edward (1759), Mary (1761), Richard (1762), Elizabeth (1765) and Thomas (1768). The son Edward was born at Knutsford on 7 October and baptized in London on 16 October 1759 then was a merchant at St. Petersburg in Russia. He married Sarah Cayley the daughter of the Consulate General on 15 July 1785 and had a large family at St. Petersburg, but moved to Ham in Surrey at the time of Napoleon due to the threat of war. He returned to Russia in 1814 when matters improved although his sons were educated in England, and he became the British Consul in 1820 and died on 26 April 1847: Henry Moberly was born on 10 February 1791 and baptized in the British Chaplaincy St. Petersburg on 5 March. He was a lieutenant colonel in the army and married Henrietta Bell (1793-1844) on 23 Jul 1821 and had a son Henry Edward in Madras on 11 December 1822 - the father died on 5 July 1852. George Moberly was born 10 October 1803 and was Headmaster of Winchester College and Bishop of Salisbury then died at the latter on 6 July 1895. Henry Edward Moberly (1822) matriculated at New College, Oxford on 6 March 1841 gaining a B.A. in 1845 and M.A. in 1849. He was a fellow, tutor, dean, bursar and sub-warder at New College then assistant master at Winchester in 1859-80. Indeed daughter Lucy Gertrude was baptized there on 2 February 1861. He was vicar of Heckfield from 1880-83 and lived there in 1881 with wife Lucy Proby Chase (1837) children Lucy G., Helen M. and Elinor M. and four servants, then rector of St. Michael's, Winchester in 1883 and died on 22 November 1907.

Heckfield was seven miles south of Reading and the Duke of Wellington was Lord of the Manor whilst Viscount Eversley lived at Heckfield Place - Speaker in the House of Commons 1839-57. The village had many connections and Frank Stenhouse Creswell was married there in 1883 (see below) whilst Rev. Chataway was curate in 1866-70 and rector at nearby Rotherwick in 1870-95. Meanwhile Thomas Bell who may have been related to Henrietta above married Elizabeth Moberly (1765) at St. Marylebone on 21 September 1789. A son Thomas Bell was baptized at the church on 29 May 1801 and was a merchant in Alexandria who married Hester Dodd in 1836. He had children in Egypt including Louisa Moberly Bell (1843) and Charles Frederic Moberly Bell (1847). He re-married Charlotte Fisher Bell (1826) on 25 November 1854 but she died in 1856 and he on 23 December 1859. Both his children appear later and are second cousins of the Moberlys of Heckfield.

John Carver junior had a short spell in Gibraltar with wife Ann and their son Charles Rickards was born there on 7 January 1845 and then baptized at Holy Trinity on 5 March that year. The family advertised in the Gibraltar Chronicle in the 19th century and for example Carver & Nephews sent goods from Liverpool to Tunis in 1844 and this no doubt referred to uncle John Carver. There was an advert on 10 January 1845 regarding a meeting on the 13th at the Public Room, New Exchange, Main Street to discuss paving, scavenging and lighting, the Committee including J. Carver and T. Drinkwater. There was another on 22 January 1845 regarding a meeting on the 20th at the Exchange Room concerning the Civil Hospital. Friends and supporters attended and the elections took place for the following year the current officers including J. Carver junior Deputy-Governor and Treasurer, and J. Glasgow and T. Drinkwater both on the Committee.

The adverts appeared on a regular basis and British schooner "Tartar" arrived on 1 February 1845 being 17 days from Liverpool with bale goods for Gibraltar the consignment to Messrs. Carver & Nephews. There was another advert on 13 March 1845 re the rates fixed on 23 December last and the Committee included T. Drinkwater and J. Carver, whilst the schooner "Mary" bound for London on 14 March 1845 had agents Carver & Nephews. There were further arrivals and M.J. Carver came from Southampton on British steam packet the "Queen" on 15 May 1845, whilst Miss Drinkwater was 10 days from Southampton on the "Royal Tar" on 8 October 1845. There were regular adverts for Carver Brothers of Irish Town, Gibraltar in the 1850s and as agents they carried goods from Liverpool, Genoa, Leghorn and Naples etc. in 1854.

John and Ann Carver, however, returned to England despite forming close family connections. They resided in Stretford and had three children there: Mary Creswell (7 September 1846), Emily (June

1848) and Frederick William (March 1850) although the births were registered in Chorlton and Barton. John Carver foreign merchant lived at Albert Terrace, Stretford New Road in 1851 with wife Ann, his four children and three servants. They had two other children Alfred John (September 1853) and Frank Henton (March 1855) and lived at 9 Albert Terrace, Stretford New Road in Old Trafford from 1855-58. John moved next door to his brother William and lived at "Sunnyside", College Road, Whalley Range in 1861 with wife Ann, children Frances, Frederick, Alfred and Frank and four servants, but only Mary C. and Alfred John (merchant's clerk) and four servants were resident in 1871. The Lancashire Independent College was next door and Alfred Newth (59) a minister and professor of philosophy and church history lived there thus the Carvers resided in genteel surroundings. The village of Evington was near to Hungarton and Henry Freeman Coleman (81) a magistrate resided at Evington Hall in 1871 with his wife and two daughters (Helen Elizabeth born there in 1845). John Carver merchant of Sunnyside died at Evington Hall on 27 February 1873 and Frederick William Carver of Whalley Range (son), Benjamin Carver of Polefield House, Prestwich (brother) and Charles William Carver of North Western Bank Buildings, Dale Street in Liverpool (nephew), merchants, proved his will in Manchester on 31 March 1873 the effects being under £120,000 - a substantial sum of money.

Frederick William Carver married Isabella Maclaren at Chorlton in March 1874. His bride was born at Oxford Road, Manchester in 1848, the daughter of James Maclaren and Lilias Bannerman. Her grandfather David Bannerman was the uncle of Sir Henry Campbell-Bannerman. Indeed Henry Campbell a son of the Lord Provost of Glasgow was born on 7 September 1836 and became Liberal M.P. for Stirling in 1868 and added his uncle's surname in 1871, being Chief Secretary of Ireland in 1886 and Leader of the House in 1898. Arthur Balfour resigned in 1905 and Edward VII asked Campbell-Bannerman to form a Government. He accepted and the Liberals won a landslide election in 1906 however he died on 22 April 1908. The Carvers, meanwhile, lived at 2 Carlton Villas, Upper Chorlton Road, Stretford although only their five children were at home in 1881. Frederick a merchant and wife Isabella were then staying at the Grand Hotel, Charing Cross in London and were just six rooms away from Alexander George Bonsor and his 'wife' Maria Charlotte - a storyline like Plaza Suite! Frederick merchant of Carver Brothers & Co. lived at "Oakhurst", Toft Road, Bexton, Knutsford in Cheshire by 1887 and was resident there in 1891. He was a general merchant and employer and the household included his wife, five daughters, son Hugh (1884) and six servants. He died at "Oakhurst" on 13 April 1922 and probate was granted to the Public Trustee and Hugh Carver merchant, his estate valued at £171,408 5s 8d. His daughter Olive Maclaren Carver (1878) was connected to the Merriman family (see Ch. 10). Mary Creswell Carver married her first cousin Charles William Carver in 1875 and the family clearly provided material for George Howard Darwin and his work on 'the marriage of first cousins' (see Ch. 4). Frank Henton Carver lived at 74 Shrewsbury Road, Oxton, Birkenhead, in 1892.

Benjamin Carver senior was born at Old Ingarsby and baptized at Hungarton on 15 April 1823 and lived with his father William at Ingarsby in 1841, however he was a merchant's clerk and lodger with Betsey Demaine (widower from Bolton) at 21 Brook Street, Hulme St. George, Manchester in 1851. He married Emily Frost at Manchester Cathedral on 4 October 1854 and now that his brothers were back in Manchester he headed for Gibraltar. The couple had seven children on the Rock namely Edith Emily (1856) *infant*, Arthur Howard (1858), Percy William (1860), Frank (1861), Frances Maude (1863), Dora Louisa (1866) and William Henton (1868) all baptized at Holy Trinity Cathedral. Benjamin was described as a merchant whilst his daughter Edith Emily died on 11 December 1857 and there is a memorial to her in North Front Cemetery. The family returned to England and Benjamin a widower and general merchant was at Polefield House, Prestwich in 1881 with his sons Arthur H. and Frank, commercial clerks, and his sister Elizabeth (1816). Benjamin was a merchant of Carver Brothers & Co. (shipping merchants) of 7 Lower Mosley Street in 1891 and had a telegram address of "Atlantic Manchester", which gave an idea of their shipping routes. He died at Polefield House on 11 July 1912 and his estate was valued at £174,894 15s 10d thus he was a wealthy man. Frank Carver was Managing Director of Cox's Brewery Ltd., Lymm, Cheshire, in 1891 and executor for Mary Scott Creswell who died Gibraltar (1921) and John Edwards Creswell who died Campamento (1928). Frank Carver died at 19 Abbey Road, Harborne in Birmingham on 15 April 1943.

Benjamin Carver junior was baptized at Queniborough on 19 October 1834, son of Robert, and was the last of the family to go to Gibraltar in the 1860s. He married Emily Leonora Jane Power at Holy Trinity on 31 August 1864 and William Carver junior and Michael and Fanny Power were witnesses. His bride was born in Gibraltar c.1838 and was the daughter of Michael Power (1808) a merchant and Roman Catholic and wife Elizabeth Frances - this family lived at 23 Irish Town in 1868. Benjamin and Emily Carver then had a family but this caused some confusion in Gibraltar in the 19th century and during the research (due to the duplication) viz. Cecil Ingram (1865), Ernest Power (1866), Herbert Benjamin (1869), Emily Mary (1872), Alice Edith (1874), Lucy (1876), Harold Power (1878) and Robert Leslie (1882) but only some were baptized at Holy Trinity the others possibly at the Catholic Cathedral nearby. They lived at 31 Castle Road in 1868-71 and 3 Arengos Lane in 1878 both addresses being high in the town near the Moorish castle. Benjamin merchant and Protestant lived at 21 Tuckeys Lane in 1881-93 with up to five servants and next door were the Cowells at 22 Main Street. He represented Carver Brothers (merchants) at Tuckeys Lane at this time and their last business entry was at Irish Town in 1894.

Benjamin Carver J.P. was recorded in the "Blue Book" and was Secretary of the Public School, trustee of the Orphan Asylum and British Poor Fund and acting Secretary of the Infant and Industrial School in 1890 and a trustee of Holy Trinity Cathedral in 1893. He lived at "Library House" from 1894 to 1907, which was on a steep hill and along a narrow path. It was a notable three storey, white fronted building with black shutters and a doorway of limestone blocks with column detail around a double door - indeed "Library House" is now 6 Library Ramp and behind the Garrison Library. Benjamin was connected with Holy Trinity Cathedral for many years and died in Gibraltar on 3 February 1907 and was buried in North Front Cemetery. He was highly respected and a gold-plated plaque with red and black lettering was erected in the cathedral: "To the glory of God and in memory of BENJAMIN CARVER Jr J.P. who was for forty five years a member of this congregation and died on February 3rd 1907 these two standard electroliers (chandelier) were erected by his sons and daughters."

AGENT FOR THE PACKETS

Meanwhile brothers Edmund and Charles James Creswell spent their whole lives in Gibraltar and Edmund in particular had a vital role in the community and continued as Agent for the Packets, a position inherited from his father in 1831. He put regular adverts in the Gibraltar Chronicle under the heading "The Packet Office - Gibraltar" and these gave the times of the 'last post' regarding the departure of packet ships: 'the mail from England for India leaves on 4 January 1844.' There was soon a further link and William Fraser was born in c.1789 and became a minister of the Church and married Mary Ward (or Way) then travelled within the British Empire. Their daughter Mary Margaret Ward Fraser was born at "Futteshur", India in 1826 the town of Futtehpoor being on a river in the Bangla district, 200 miles north of Calcutta and west of Dinajpur and 10 miles south east of Raiganj. The railway line for Delhi and Calcutta was a few miles to the north. William Fraser M.A. was appointed rector of North Waltham a remote location in the Micheldever Forest south west of Basingstoke and had four children baptized there: William Francis (31 May 1834), Frances Ann (18 April 1836), Anne Alicia (2 October 1837) and Lewis (10 February 1839) - born 27 December 1838. William Fraser a clerk aged 52 lived at North Waltham in 1841 with his daughter Mary (14), clerk George Elliott (22) and servant Elizabeth Blunden (14). Charlotte Biggs aged 76 an independent lived nearby and her household included Anne Fraser (c.45) independent and Frances Fraser (5). They travelled to Gibraltar in the early 1840s although the exact reason for their sojourn is uncertain.

Shipping records in the Gibraltar Chronicle reveal the families movements and British steam packet "Lady Mary Wood" arrived on 9 February 1844 being 7½ days from Southampton, 4 days from Vigo, 3½ days from Oporto, 2 days from Lisbon and 8 hours from Cadiz. It departed for Southampton on Monday 12 February the passengers including Mr. Creswell. Indeed this was a regular journey for the "Lady Mary Wood" and it arrived in Gibraltar on Thursday 4 April 1844 from Southampton with passengers Mr. Power, Mr. and Mrs. Carver, infant and servant. There is a print of the "Lady Mary Wood" in the entrance lobby of the Bristol Hotel, Gibraltar that shows an open topped paddle steamer assisted by sails. British steam packet "Great Liverpool" arrived in Gibraltar on Sunday 7 April 1844 being 6 days from Southampton and the passengers included the returning Mr. Creswell (either Edmund or Thomas). The ship was delivering mail for Gibraltar, Malta and Alexandria and departed the Rock for the Mediterranean on 8 April and arrived back in Gibraltar on Wednesday 3 July having taken 11 days from Alexandria and 5 days from Malta. It departed for Southampton on 4 July and Mr. (Thomas) Creswell bound for Hungarton was a passenger. The British brig "Iberia" arrived in Gibraltar on 18 July 1844 and had come from London with cotton yarn and in ballast from Cadiz the passengers including Mr. R. Cowell, whilst the British steam packet "Royal Tar" arrived from Southampton on 12 October 1844 the passengers including Mr. Mrs. and Miss Drinkwater and Mrs. and Miss Cowell.

Edmund Creswell continued to advertise in the Chronicle from July to October 1844 hence he was clearly present in Gibraltar at this time and it was his brother Thomas who travelled to England. British steam packet "Pacha" arrived in Gibraltar on Thursday 24 October 1844 being 6½ days from Southampton, 3 days from Vigo, 19 hours from Lisbon and 8 hours from Cadiz with mails for Gibraltar the passengers including both Mr. and Mrs. Creswell who returned from their wedding in Hungarton. There was an advert for the "Royal George" on Saturday 2 November 1844 that stated: "Steam between Cadiz and Genoa calling at Gibraltar, Malaga, Almeria, Cartagena, Alicante, Valencia, Tarragona, Barcelona and Marseille. The splendid 1st class British steam ship ROYAL GEORGE 500 tons 250 horsepower, Robert Cook commander, expected from Cadiz Saturday next and Sunday will proceed to above named ports. Shipping orders 4 o'clock Saturday and passage tickets 2 o'clock Sunday the 3rd November. Dated 29th October, Thomas Haire agent - The ship will be discharged on arrival and goods must be collected promptly at the wharf." These adverts included drawings for easy identification and the "Royal George" was a paddle steamer with cabins on the deck and sails above. Its movements were recorded in the Chronicle on Monday 4 November 1844, thus: the steam ship arrived on 2 November being 1 day from Cadiz and carrying wine & c. for Gibraltar, Malaga and Marseille and was cleared and departed the next day - Mr. E. Creswell was a passenger.

FOR MALAGA.

TO SAIL ON SUNDAY EVENING NEXT, THE 12TH INST.,

The British steam-ship *ROYAL GEORGE*, ROBERT COOK, Commander.

THOMAS HAIRE,

10th January. *Agent.*

Gibraltar Chronicle – Advert.
Mr. and Mrs. E. Creswell sailed on the vessel in 1845.

Captain Robert Cook greeted him with, "Welcome aboard Mr. Creswell business or pleasure?" Edmund departed on important business and his deputy Thomas Drinkwater was acting agent for the Packet Office from 7 November 1844 to 4 January 1845. The temporary packet agent put notices in the Chronicle reference closure of the mail viz. the "Oriental" on 30 December 1844 giving the last time for catching the post. Meanwhile, Edmund Creswell married Mary Margaret Ward Fraser in late 1844 but there is no record in England or Gibraltar and it may have taken place on board ship or maybe in Marseille. British steamer "Royal George" arrived in Gibraltar on Thursday 9 January 1845 under Captain R. Cook and was 8 days from Marseille, 6 days from Barcelona and 1 day from Malaga with bale-goods for Gibraltar the passengers including Mr. and Mrs. (Edmund) Creswell and departed again for Malaga on 12 January.

Edmund resumed his position as Agent for the Packets and placed his first notice in the Chronicle on 11 January 1845. He spent the rest of his life there and resided at Hargraves Parade between Town Range and Prince Edward's Gate in 1849, and soon had a large family in fact a "postman's dozen". His children were: Roderick Edmund (1845) *infant*, Margaret Susan (1847), Susan Ann (1848) *infant*, Edmund William (1849), William Rooke (1852), Henry Thomas (1854), Charles Alexander (1855), Mary Catherine Edwards (1857), Richard John (1859), Annie Jane Harriet (1861), Florence Mary (1862), John Edwards (1864) and Frederick Hugh Page (1866). The daughter Susan Ann died on 10 October 1849 and has a memorial in Sandpits Cemetery and all the children were baptized at Holy Trinity Cathedral - Rev. W.F. Fraser carried out the baptism of his nephew Richard John on 22 April 1859 (see below). This family had close connections and aunt Anne Fraser who was born in Bath in c.1791 arrived in Gibraltar just after her niece in 1845. Frances Ann Fraser died there on 16 September 1853 aged 17 and was buried at Sandpits Cemetery being described as, "the 3rd daughter of William Fraser rector of North Waltham." Her sister Anne Alicia Fraser came to Gibraltar in 1866.

There was a notice from the Packet Office on 23 January 1845 stating that the mail for Malta and the Ionian Islands was to go by H.M. steamer "Polyphemus" and the mail would be closed at the office on arrival of the packet from England. N.B. 'Letters for any part of the Mediterranean or Levant except Malta must be post paid.' Edmund Creswell had been elected Honorary Secretary of the Public School in 1838 and placed an advert in the Gibraltar Chronicle on Monday 27 January 1845 stating: "Gibraltar Public School - The A.G.M. of subscribers and friends will be holden in the Public Room of the Exchange on Wednesday next the 29th inst at 12 o'clock for the committee and treasurer's reports and to appoint a new committee for 1845 - Edmund Creswell Secretary." He held the position for the rest of his life and the post then went to relative Benjamin Carver j. but the institution did not survive to the present day.

Holy Trinity Cathedral, Gibraltar. E.W. Creswell was baptized here 11 December 1849.

There was an advert on 15 February 1845 asking for entries for the Malta Herald and Naval and Military Gazette stating that any subscribers should apply to the publisher Mr. Izzo, 93 Strada Vescovo or Mr. Muir, Strada Reale, Valletta; and a further advert from the Packet Office on 7 March 1845 stating that letters for Cadiz and Vigo must be post paid. The Post Office accounts were published on 5 July 1845 and showed that in the previous quarter the postal charges were £426 1s 6½d whilst £63 19s ¼d was carried forward. There was a despatch from Turin on 13 March 1846 regarding the British merchants in Genoa and contained a request for a regular packet service to that town. Indeed Gibraltar was an important centre for trading in the Mediterranean and the Packet Office had a pivotal position. There was correspondence regarding Turkey, Prussia and the West Indies on 22 June 1849 and also India, China and Manila on 6 November 1850. Charles James Creswell (1817) married Mary Scott Relph (1833) at Holy Trinity Cathedral on 21 January 1852 and Edmund and M.M.W. Creswell, R.J. Cowell, Harriet Cowell and J.H. Cowell were the witnesses.

Edmund Creswell was elected Treasurer of the Garrison Library in 1853, which was located at the junction of Library Ramp and Town Range. His local knowledge and experience in financial matters was invaluable to the institution and he continued in this position until his decease. He was then engaged in a most heroic act. A heavy squall struck the Bay of Algeciras on 15 February 1854 and it was 7 a.m. when the guard-boat of the "Samarang" returned to the shore but the weather was very rough and the boat was soon in difficulty. The vessel overturned and the crew clung to the keel and shouted loudly for help and the alarm was raised as Mr. Creswell passed the saluting battery on the way to town. He hastened to the Ragged Staff Gates and jumped into a boat calling for volunteers and then rowed to the assistance of the drowning men. The overturned boat was reached, although with much difficulty, and four men were saved however the boarding officer Mr. Fau and sailors Agillou and Victory were drowned. His bravery did not pass un-noticed and it was stated, "that of Mr. Creswell's good deeds this stood out in the minds of his friends."

The event was also reported in the Gibraltar Chronicle, which stated, "A dreadful hurricane blew from the north east during the night and this morning causing great damage both in town and in the south as well as in the harbour and the vane of the Upper Signal Station was blown away." The paper reported that there was a heavy squall off Wellington Front and an overturned boat was spotted from the Lower Signal Station thus the Government vessel was launched from Ragged Staff and manned by a number of seamen and some ordnance labourers. Without such an able crew no one would have been saved and there was later a collection for the widows and families of the three who drowned. Mr. Creswell was involved with the newspaper and perhaps some modesty made him withhold his name. He had other concerns at the time since the paper added, "The mail by the 'packet' has not yet been landed on account of the state of the weather.... part of the roof of the Commissary-Generals quarter has fallen in; a great number of houses have been materially injured, slates and tiles falling in all directions; terraces, chimneys and skylights blown down; trees split, felled or altogether rooted up; doors and windows smashed; sentry boxes knocked down; a great part of the scaffolding and wood work around the Presbyterian Church, which is in course of construction, has likewise been carried away and gardens' trellis work, fruit trees and plants have in many places been laid flat or destroyed. Very few persons have been able to visit the Rock from the adjoining country it being almost impossible to stem the fury with which the gale is sweeping over the isthmus and along the western beach." This report reveals the ferocity of the storm that Edmund risked his life in.

The town recovered, however, and the two Post Offices (packet and overland) were amalgamated as one establishment in 1857 and Edmund was appointed Deputy Postmaster General in 1858. A new post office was built at 7 Main Street near to Tuckeys Lane although today this is 104 (it was divided into Southport,

Church and Waterport Street). The building was officially opened on the 1 September 1858 and the Creswell family moved there from Hargraves Parade at that time. The Gibraltar Chronicle was established in 1801 and published at the Garrison Library from the 1820s and reported all movements of the mail. Edmund was appointed editor in 1862-70 but had in fact done these duties for many years previous. The journal was initially a shipping register however Edmund did much to raise it to the standard of a 'local paper' and it dealt with local subjects and incidents although had little information of births, marriages and deaths. He achieved the paper's new status through, "close attention, some enterprise and a good deal of hard work." The present day newspaper is next to the Garrison Library on Town Range and nothing has changed!

Indeed during his time as editor some of his reports provided a great public service and he reported a serious incident that took place at the port of Saffi, Morocco in 1864. The 'custom house' officer appointed by the Spanish Government died suddenly and this was attributed to poison administered by his Jewish servant. The news reached Tangier and the Spanish minister Señor Merry took some drastic action. There was no fair trial or post mortem however four Jews were condemned to death two at Tangier and two at Saffi. Edmund took the matter up in the Chronicle and brought the outrage to the attention of European Governments and this led to the mission of Sir Moses Montefiore to the Sultan, which brought about beneficial results and improved the plight of the Jewish people.

Edmund received the senior appointment of Surveyor of all Post Offices in the Mediterranean in 1867 and this included Malta, Alexandria, Cairo, Constantinople and Smyrna (Izmir). The family lived at 7 Main Street, Gibraltar (district 7) on the 1868 census and there were 17 people in the house. The format was different to that in Britain and men and women were listed separately and religion and length of residence was shown viz. Edmund (Deputy Postmaster General), wife Mary Margaret Ward, eight of their children but excluding Edmund William, William Rooke and Henry Thomas (at army college, in the navy and at school), relatives Anne and Anne Alicia Fraser (all Protestants), a labourer, a male servant and three female servants (the latter Spanish Catholics). The servants were born in San Roque, Galicia and Marbella and two were present on temporary permits since La Linea and Spain was a short walk across the border. The aunt Anne Fraser died in Gibraltar on 19 December 1873 aged 83 years and was buried at North Front Cemetery.

However life on the Rock was soon to change and good works were no protection against the vicissitudes of life. Edmund should have been wary of an advert in the Chronicle dated 20 May 1845 stating "Barbary donkey for sale by auction 26th" and presumably the animals were commonplace in Gibraltar. He was bitten by one such donkey in c.1869 and suffered a severe hand injury that developed serious symptoms thus he had four amputations in succession leaving his whole constitution weakened. Despite this he continued in his duties and was appointed Superintendent of the Gibraltar Government Telegraph on 15 November 1871. The appointment was made by the Governor and confirmed by the Secretary of State whilst the "Blue Book" revealed he was paid £700 p.a. as Postmaster General and Surveyor and £100 p.a. from local revenue for these additional duties.

There was a postal agreement between Spain and the U.K. on 21 May 1858 however a letter from London dated 14 October 1875 confirmed Gibraltar's admission to the General Postal Union on 1st January next. The contribution made by Edmund during his career as postmaster was further revealed in his obituary which stated: "Mr Creswell performed the important duties of the appointments he held with the greatest credit to himself and advantage to the public service. He was active, intelligent, well read and with a well-balanced mind had a good capacity for judging official measures and always had a clear opinion regarding his duties. He was a representative of the International Postal Congress and had a detailed knowledge of the workings of the postal service hence he made valuable suggestions to delegates in Spain and Switzerland." He was also important to the social life of Gibraltar and was praised as follows: "As a public man in our town he grudged no time or trouble to take his share in public duties and worked at them earnestly and with a hearty good will."

The amputation he had suffered, however, led to a decline in his health and his friends and family were shocked at the demise of one who was previously so strong and well. He went for a regular inspection at the end of 1875 and his condition was the reverse of satisfactory whilst the "Blue Book" reveals he was absent from work for 2½ months in 1876. He was in further pain at the start of 1877 and after suffering for a few months had further dangerous symptoms by the middle of the year and was forced to have another operation, but his strength was spent. Edmund Creswell, Deputy Postmaster General and Surveyor of the Mediterranean died at 7 Main Street, Gibraltar on 1 August 1877 aged 64 years having been resident "58" years. N.B. "40" years appeared on the 1868 census and there were clearly errors in the records; he was elsewhere described as the Post Office Surveyor. H. Stokes medical practitioner gave the cause of death as chronic nephritis lasting 14 months and general dropsy lasting 3 months (kidney disease and fluid in the body) on 6 August 1877 whilst James G. Gordon (Registrar) recorded the death and the informant was Richard John Creswell a native of Gibraltar and merchant of Waterport Street.

The demise of Edmund Creswell was recorded in the Gibraltar Chronicle (and commercial intelligence) on Thursday 2 August 1877 and the article provided much of the detail for the above discourse. It was clearly written by one of his best friends who concluded: "There have been a number of losses in the colony but none which we feel more deeply than the melancholy death of that valued Civil Servant of the Crown and our old and esteemed friend Edmund Creswell... We offer no apology for dwelling at such length on the life and character of our old friend for he has been for so long, in youth and manhood, so intimately associated with Gibraltar as to deserve more than ordinary notice. We have seen our last of him but his bright example will not soon be forgotten, we hope, in Gibraltar, but be an incentive to many of the young people among us to follow so good a leader in the path of self advancement, leading to worldly success and esteem, not however to be gained without sheer hard work and application. His sorrowing family have our fullest and most sincere sympathy and we are sure that one general feeling of painful regret will occur to all with whom he had acquaintance, not only in Gibraltar but in all parts of the world, when they hear that Edmund Creswell is no longer numbered with the living amongst us. The funeral is to take place this afternoon at 5 o'clock." This was a fitting tribute and he was buried in the family vault at North Front Cemetery in the shadow of the Rock. This was opened in c.1869 on land that had formed the battleground between the British and Spanish.

His son Edmund joined the Royal Engineers in 1870 and was initially in Chatham, but then spent several years in India, being abroad at the time of his father's funeral and may have heard of the death some days later. He had, however, introduced fellow officer Hugh Mitchell to the family and the latter was stationed on the Rock in 1875-78 thus giving support to them at a difficult time. Indeed there was constant movement to and from the Rock and William Francis Fraser (1834) may have visited Gibraltar but was educated in England and matriculated at Emmanuel, Cambridge gaining his B.A. in 1856 and M.A. in 1858. He was ordained at Rochester in 1857 and then held posts near Braintree in Essex, being curate of Coggeshall from 1857-59 although (as stated) he did visit Gibraltar in April 1859, and curate of Stisted from 1860-72. He was vicar of White Notley from 1872-83 and married Hugh Mitchell and his niece Mary Catherine Edwards Creswell in the church on 22 August 1878 (see Ch. 8). She stayed with her uncle and the witnesses were Lieutenant H.B. Rich and W.R. Creswell. He lived with his wife Mary at the Vicarage, White Notley, in 1881 but finished his career as rector of Westbere, Kent in 1887-93 and died at 92 Maison Dieu Road, Dover on 19 September 1905. His probate was granted to Herbert Meadows Frith White and Henry Thomas Creswell Esq. his effects £5,242 2s 3d.

THE CRESWELL FAMILY

Gibraltar was a mix of English and Spanish peoples sheltering under the Rock and the colony had an important strategic location and regular links to Tangier with the coast of Africa just 35 miles away. The harbour area was in continual use and in addition to the steam packets and trading vessels there were numerous naval ships moored in the bay. The post office in Main Street (or Waterport Street) was at the centre of town and nearby was The Lines, Waterfront Street, Irish Town, Market Lane, Tuckeys Lane and Commercial Square. Indeed the Creswells continued their links with the postal service. Their oldest child Margaret Susan Creswell was born in Gibraltar on 22 April 1847 and baptized at Holy Trinity on 15 May that year. She took over her father's duties at his decease and a letter was sent from the Right Honourable Earl of Carnarvon, Downing Street, to the Governor of Gibraltar on 15 September 1877 and stated: "My Lord, I have the honor to acknowledge the receipt of your despatch no. 137 of the 24th ultimo and to convey to you my approval of your having appointed Miss Creswell Postmistress of Gibraltar to be Superintendent of the Telegraph Office. I have the honor to be my Lord, your Lordships most obedient humble servant, Carnarvon." The "Blue Book" confirmed this, stating that the Governor gave her the post on 1 September 1877 and that the Secretary of State verified this at a £500 p.a. salary for the duties of postmistress and £80 p.a. from local revenue for telegraph work (these figures should be compared to those of her father).

After the demise of Edmund and the departure of his sons the family was somewhat depleted however they remained at 7 Main Street, Gibraltar in 1878 and the household included Mary M.W. Creswell aged 52 a widow, children Margaret S. (postmistress), Annie Jane H., Florence M., John Edwards and Frederic H.P., cousin William J. Harcourt Chambers and four Spanish servants of which three were in Gibraltar on a temporary permit and one on a daily ticket. The cousin William was born 10 October 1862 and was visiting from London, the son of Harcourt Chambers a barrister, Civil Servant and wine merchant and Julia Robinson from Milford in Hampshire. He had returned to England in 1881 and lived with his family at "The Sycamores", Hornsey whilst his brothers included Frederick J.H. (architect), Harcourt A.F. (clerk steam ship co.) and Francis R.C. (clerk Bank of England). The Creswells were living at "The Post Office", 7 Waterport Street in 1881 and the household included Mary Margaret Ward, her daughters Margaret (postmistress), Annie and Florence, two visitors and five servants. The men of the family had left and the only male there was grandson Edmund Fraser Creswell aged four.

The Exotic Rock of Gibraltar. The Creswells arrived in 1822 and ran the postal service for 90 years.

Margaret Susan Creswell was kept busy running the post office and a letter was received from Downing Street on 4 July 1884. This was concerning correspondence to the Earl of Derby on the 25 ultimo that discussed the (proposed) transfer of the Gibraltar P.O. to local government control. The handing over of Imperial power to the Governor was clearly resisted and the letter stated that the Gibraltar post raised little independent revenue with the only direct money from the Algeciras trade, therefore it was unlikely the service could stand alone. Henry Thomas Creswell a merchant remained in Gibraltar at this time and was married to Harriet Louisa and had five children baptized at Holy Trinity: Marjorie Ellen (1883), Ferdinand Leslie (1884), Dorothy Mary (1886) *infant*, Kate Evelyn (1887) and Harry Edmund (1889). These were the last Creswells to be born on the Rock although Henry and his family were living at Campamento in 1887.

Mrs. Edmund Creswell, Miss Margaret and H.T. Creswell lived at The Post Office, 7 Main Street in 1890 but there were soon to be changes and it was completely rebuilt on 15 August 1891 and ceased to be a family home. It was replaced with a building out of character with the surrounding area but with a certain amount of style. The 'new' post office at 104 Main Street was a notable property of brown limestone built in the Classical style with a high arched entrance and a VR and crown above it. There was a large first floor with three windows and a small second floor above and at the top was a carving stating: "Erected A.D. 1858 Lieutenant General Sir James Ferguson K.C.B. Governor," and it stood out amongst the more traditional buildings between Market Lane and Tuckeys Lane with their shop-fronts and upper storey shutters. Indeed the scene is little changed today and the post office remains at 104 Main Street and was renovated in 2002, but is clearly different to the house that the Creswells lived in.

Charles James Creswell (1817) a merchant and wife Mary Scott had no children however lived at 18 South Barrack Road with three servants in 1878, and the remainder of the family followed them there. Indeed there is a sub-post office at 18 South Barrack Road today, and this may have been connected. Charles James Creswell died in 1888 and was buried at North Front Cemetery but his wife was 16 years younger and continued to live there. Mrs. Edmund Creswell and Miss Margaret Creswell lived at 6 South Barrack Road in the Mount Pleasant area in 1891, whilst Mary M.W. and Margaret S. Creswell and Mary Scott Creswell and two servants resided there on the 1891 census. The family lived on their own means although Margaret was postmistress whilst the house was south of the town above Rosia Bay and faced towards the Spanish port of Algeciras.

James Fforde had married Martha Harriet Creswell in Lisbon in 1872 and then had two children born at Lurgan, Ireland namely Francis Creswell Fforde (1873) and "male" Fforde (1875). They had two children in South Africa: Aimée M.M. (1879) and Eveleen A.A. (1881) and four children in Kingston on Thames: Thomas Roderick (June 1882), Charles Holt (March 1884), Mabel Kathleen (December 1885) and Eric Harold (December 1887). James Fforde lived at "Mount Pleasant", 7 South Barrack Road in 1891 with his wife, six youngest children and five servants and he remained there to 1893. When he departed Hugh Mitchell moved into the house and the property itself was discussed earlier (see Ch. 8). James Fforde died at Raughlan, Lurgan, Co. Armagh on 16 October 1907 and Martha Harriet Fforde his widow, Francis Creswell Fforde (civil engineer) and Frank Stenhouse Creswell (merchant) obtained probate. The will was sealed in London on 22 January 1908 and the effects in England came to £571 10s 3d. Martha Harriet Fforde died at Raughlan on 19 February 1935 and her probate was granted to Francis Creswell Fforde (married Agnes Cicely Creswell, below). Thomas Roderick Fforde died at Bruckless, Co. Donegal on 15 November 1949 and his probate went to Frances Joan Alice Fforde widow, Aimée Mary Martha Fforde spinster and Eveleen Annie Archer Jackson widow.

Arthur Brownlow Fforde (of County Down) may have been a brother of James and was married to Mary Carver Pope who was registered at the Madras Presidency in c.1845 (clearly a relative). Arthur and Mary had three children in Bombay namely Arthur Brownlow (1872), Kate (1874) and Cecil R. (1876) however their son Herbert William was born at Wellington Road, Bollington near Macclesfield on 21 May 1878. He was assistant superintendent in the Revenue Survey but the family were absent from England in 1881, although son Arthur was a scholar at St. Aubin's School, High Street, St. Brelade, Jersey, under Headmaster John Este Vibert - the meteorological observer for the Board of Trade. Mary Carver Fforde and four children lived at 3 Glebe Road, Bedford in 1891 including her son Arthur of the Indian Civil Service whilst the Rickards lived at no. 4. She died in Bedford on 19 January 1896 and probate was granted to Arthur her son. Cecil Robert Fforde joined King's Inn as a student and was called to the Irish bar but left Ireland in December 1920 and removed to Gray's Inn being a judge of the Punjab High Court in 1922-31. He was knighted in 1930 and a judge in Bechuanaland (Botswana) and Swaziland and died in 1951. Arthur Frederic Brownlow (1900) son of Arthur attended Rugby and was a solicitor in 1925 and Headmaster of Rugby (1948-57) and B.B.C. Chairman (1957-64).

Mary Margaret Ward Creswell died at Campamento on 31 July 1892 but was only visiting the Spanish town since she still resided on the Rock. She was buried in North Front Cemetery and her probate was granted to Margaret Susan Creswell, executor, at the Supreme Court of Gibraltar and her will sealed in London on 13 April 1893 - her effects in England £1,051 10s 2d. Margaret Creswell the colonial postmistress lived at 6 South Barrack Road, Mount Pleasant in 1891 to 1906 and the archives contain many books and papers from her days there. She applied for additional ground next to the family vault at North Front Cemetery on 20 April 1904 and retired from the Post Office between 1907-12 and was awarded the Imperial Service Order (I.S.O.) for her public service. She moved to Campamento in Spain by 1918 and stayed there the rest of her life.

La Linea, as stated, was just across the border and the small village of Campamento was 2½ miles further on, whilst the road continued north to San Roque (10 miles from Gibraltar). The village could be reached by foot past the Bay of Algeciras and was a popular summer retreat for natives of Gibraltar having facilities for golf and polo and also a hotel. There were some large villas along the road from Gibraltar occupied by merchants and ex-patriots, whilst the old village centre was around Main Street and considerably older than La Linea. Margaret Creswell lived at 56 Main Street, Campamento however this is no longer present although a two-storey villa dated 1851 is opposite the Calle Benalife (Calle - street). There are old properties either side of this street that are numbered 54,48,60,48,64 etc. and those at the junction were present at the time, one being a substantial stone building. The "Calle El Polo" leads to a large open space the size of a football pitch and although now derelict was clearly once the field described in the Gibraltar Directory (1894): "Polo Club - The ground is on Campamento Common."

Mary Scott Creswell applied for a monument to her husband on 11 April 1905 however this has not survived and she resided at "Sunnyside House", South Barrack Road from at least 1890-1921 (probably no. 18). She was described as Mrs. C. Creswell whilst Mount Pleasant was opposite Sunnyside Steps and the property clearly nearby. Mary Scott Creswell died at Sunnyside, Gibraltar on 14 March 1921 and was buried in North Front Cemetery whilst her probate was granted in London to Edmund William Creswell colonel R.E. (retired) and Frank Carver esquire. Margaret Susan Creswell was forced to leave Campamento in 1936 due to the Spanish Civil War and thus died at 8 Rosia Steps, Gibraltar on 4 August 1936 (her home address Campamento). Rosia Steps was next to Rosia Parade and Rosia Ramp and not far from Mount Pleasant and Sunnyside, but no property with the no. 8 survives. Rosia Bay itself was a fortified battery and provided an anchorage for H.M.S. Victory and the body of Horatio Lord Nelson after the Battle of Trafalgar in 1805 the conflict being off Cape Trafalgar near Cadiz. There is a memorial to the event at Rosia

Bay whilst Trafalgar Cemetery (opened as Southport Ditch in 1798) is next to Southport Gate although it has just two burials from the battle. Margaret Susan Creswell was buried in North Front Cemetery and her probate granted to the Royal Bank of Scotland in London on 23 October 1936 her effects in England being £5,089 12s 5d. The family lived in Gibraltar for over 100 years but what of those on manoeuvres?

William Rooke Creswell was born in Gibraltar on 20 July 1852 and was educated at Aitkens School, Gibraltar Public School, Eastmans R.N. Academy, Southsea and H.M.S Britannia. He joined the navy in 1866 sailing on H.M.S. Phoebe in 1867 and was made a sub-lieutenant in 1871, then was specially promoted for boat action on the Laroot River in 1873. He served on H.M.S. London from 1875-78 the ship being involved in the suppression of the slave trade and received thanks from the foreign minister (Benjamin Disraeli P.M., Lord Salisbury 1878-80 Foreign Secretary - services at Zanzibar). William however was retired after being invalided in 1878 and was a witness at Hugh Mitchell's wedding in White Notley on 22 August that year. He immigrated to Australia with his brother Charles and was a successful farmer in Queensland and then took service under the South Australian Government in 1885. He married Adelaide Elizabeth (O.B.E.) the second daughter of Mr. Justice Stow judge of the Supreme Court, Southern Australia, in 1888. William Creswell is considered the 'Father of the Australian Navy' and was a commander in 1891, a post-captain in 1894, received the China Medal in 1901 and was a rear admiral in 1911. He was made C.M.G. and then K.C.M.G. in 1911 and Knight Commander of the British Empire (K.B.E.) in 1919. He was the first naval member of the Royal Australian Navy Board, a vice admiral of the Australian service and retired in August 1919 but received the Order of the Rising Sun of Japan, 2nd class, in 1920. He spent much time in offices and declared his interests as "the open air" presumably on the bridge of a ship! He lived at Ferndale, Silvan in Victoria and died on 20 April 1933.

John Edwards Creswell was born in Gibraltar on 12 March 1864 and educated at Bruce Castle School then matriculated in Michaelmas 1881 and was appointed to Cavendish, Cambridge in October that year gaining his B.A. in 1885. He was a student and house surgeon at University College Hospital, London and Senior Assistant Medical Superintendent at St. Pancras Infirmary and was M.R.C.S. and L.R.C.P. in 1889. He gained his bachelor of medicine (M.B.) and his B.C. in 1891 and married Catherine Burleigh daughter of Matthew Towgood of Ceylon. He served in the Egyptian Public Health Department and was Principal Medical Officer at Suez from 1892 to 1912 and received a C.B.E. for his services. He was an authority on tropical and epidemic diseases and did pioneer work in public health matters including malaria prevention and 'pilgrim control' in Egypt. He lived at Charmouth House, Charmouth in Dorset but died at Campamento on 25 October 1928 (whilst visiting his sister) and was buried at North Front Cemetery. Frank Carver a retired brewer and attorney of Catherine Burleigh administered his effects in Birmingham on 1 January 1929 the value £22,894 6s 11d.

Frederic Hugh Page Creswell was born in Gibraltar on 13 November 1866 and educated at Bruce Castle School and Derby (May 1882). He went to the Royal School of Mines to prepare for his future occupation and was engaged in mining in Venezuela, Asia Minor, Rhodesia and Transvaal and managed the Durban Deep Mine before the Boer War. He enrolled as a lieutenant in the Imperial Light Horse at the start of hostilities and when mining resumed after the conflict he was general manager of the Village Main Reef Mine near Johannesburg. He played a prominent part in opposing the introduction of Chinese labour to the Transvaal and resigned as manager at the end of 1903 joining a movement for the abolition of Chinese labour the actions of the group being a success. He was a member of the Union Parliament from 1910-14 and was second commander of the Rand Rifles in South West Africa during the campaign of 1914-15 and commanding officer of the 8th South African Infantry in East Africa from 1916-17. He received the D.S.O. in 1916 and rejoined the Union Parliament after the war marrying Margaret P.B. daughter of Rev. H. Boys, rector of Layer Marney, Essex in 1920 but had no children. He was Minister of Defence in 1924-33, Minister of Labour in 1924-25 & 1929-33 and presided over the Annual Conference of the International Labour Organization in Geneva in 1935. He retired from government in 1938 and died at Kuils River, Cape Province on 25 August 1948.

THE CARVER FAMILY

The discussion continues with the important connections of the Carver family and their links to trade, newspapers and education. William Carver, as stated, married Emma Louisa Drinkwater in Gibraltar on 3 September 1842 and then resided on the Rock and Manchester (dying 1868) thus his children are now considered. Edmund Drinkwater Carver was born in Gibraltar on 3 July 1843 and came to Manchester with his family but was absent from Whalley Range in 1861. He resided in Alexandria in the 1860s and was a merchant there for Carver Brothers and soon made an important connection. Thomas Bell (1801-59) discussed above was also a merchant in Alexandria and with his wife Hester had children Louisa Moberly Bell (1843) and Charles Frederic Moberly Bell (2 April 1847). Thomas continued as a merchant in Egypt however his son Charles was to have a notable career. He was educated at Wallasey under Rev. Clayton Green but returned to Egypt due to ill health in 1864 (age 17) and became a partner in Peel & Co. As a merchant he was familiar with shipping and sent details of these movements to the Times newspaper, these arriving two-three days faster than was normal, thus he became Egypt correspondent for the Times from 1865.

Meanwhile Edmund Drinkwater Carver merchant of Alexandria married Louisa Moberly Bell of the "The Cloisters", Widcombe at Widcombe, Bath on 8 May 1866. She was described as daughter of Thomas Bell merchant whilst his uncle Rev. James Chataway and G.E. Tate (vicar) performed the ceremony and the witnesses included H.C. Carver, Emma Louisa Carver and E.M. Carver. Her brother sent information to the Times about the construction of the Suez Canal (opened 17 November 1869) and then met Ethel Chataway who was the cousin of Edmund and daughter of James and Elizabeth Anne Chataway who then resided at Rotherwick near Heckfield. The outcome was that Charles Frederic Moberly Bell married Ethel Chataway on 10 August 1875 and as a result Edmund D. Carver and Charles F.M. Bell were brothers-in-law and had 'reciprocal' aunts and uncles.

Bell published 'Khedives and Pashas' in 1884 and was to have been correspondent for the Gordon Relief Expedition to Khartoum in 1885 but was injured before leaving and was left lame. He also published 'Egyptian Finance' (1887) and 'From Pharaoh to Fellah' (1889) the latter concerning the bombardment of Alexandria and the Tel-el-Kebir campaign (see Kenyon-Slaney Ch. 6). He was called back to London by the Chairman, Mr. Walter in 1890 and became Managing Director of the Times thus working on the *Times Atlas* and *Encyclopaedia Britannica* and helped establish the Times Publishing Co. Ltd. with Mr. Walter in 1908, the assets being £750,000. He died at Printing House Square whilst working on the newspaper on 5 April 1911. Edmund and Louisa Carver returned to Egypt after the marriage and had children Harry Drinkwater (1867) and Emily L. (1869) in Alexandria. They returned to England and Ethel Mary (December 1870) was born in Chorlton and William Moberly (June 1872) in Eltham (see below), but they went back to Egypt and had three more children: Gertrude M. (1874), Norman Clifton (14 January 1876) and Dorothy H. (1877). They were still abroad in 1881 and probably left Alexandria in c.1888-90 and followed their relatives to Wimbledon. Indeed their choice of a home near Worple Road was almost certainly connected to the Brackenburys as below:

John Matthew Brackenbury was born at Holme, Norfolk in 1816 the son of John a banker in Ely, and was probably related to George Brackenbury the Consul of Lisbon in 1872 (see above). John matriculated at St. John's, Cambridge in 1834 and received a B.A. in 1838 and M.A. in 1841 then was assistant master at the Collegiate School, Huddersfield in 1838-41 but was ordained in Norwich in 1841. He was appointed curate of St. Mary Magdalen, Downham, Norfolk, in 1841-43 but returned to teaching and with Dr. Wilkinson helped to start Marlborough College on 23 August 1843. He married Mary Shield at St. John the Baptist in Croydon on 3 July 1845 but Matthew John Franklin (1846) and Alice Mary (1847) were baptized at Marlborough. He was assistant master there until 1849 and then turned his attentions to Wimbledon.

The story continues with 'another' Bell family who might have been related and one Robert Bell, merchant, was a founder of the East India Company with 214 others in 1600. Due to his success he built a "fayre new howse" on family land near Wimbledon High Street in 1613 this having brick walls two feet thick, oak beams, a grand staircase and a great hall. The property left the families possession in the late 17th century and was leased to William Grenville of the House of Commons in the 1780s but was then transformed into a private school by Rev. Thomas Lancaster in 1790 (later known as Eagle House). Admiral Nelson and Lady Hamilton visited the school in 1803 and it was thereafter known as the Nelson House School and was a 'Finishing Academy for Young Gentlemen' or military academy under Orlando Mayor in 1849. John Brackenbury then came to Wimbledon and formed a partnership with 'Mayor' to run the establishment as a military school however he was such a good teacher and organizer that it had become 'Brackenburys' in 1852 and he assumed full control in 1856. Its was so successful that he decided to move the school to a location outside the village and purchased Tree and Boggy Field from Mr. Phillips in 1859, and with a mortgage of £7,000 employed Samuel Teulon an architect to design a school.

The new Wimbledon School was built between Ridgway and Worple Road (on Edge Hill) and was a substantial three-storey building of red brick with black glaze and many pointed gables. There was a long drive and imposing hall whilst the gardens were so exotic that they were opened to the public. John Brackenbury was Headmaster from 1860-82 and with assistant Rev. Charles James Wynne provided an education for c.100 pupils. The school concentrated on army examinations and prepared students age 15-

Brackenburys School. The school concentrated on military exams in 1860-87.

18 to enter Military Academies at Sandhurst and Woolwich. Meanwhile Upper Coppins a large field opposite the school was purchased in 1866 and three large mansions were built namely Ridgelands, Donhead Lodge and Charlton House all in the same style and located in Edge Hill. A further property Ivyhurst and its lodge was built next to them soon after and the four buildings first appeared on a map in 1869. John Brackenbury married his third wife Blanche Wolferstan of Darlaston Hall in 1867 and in addition to his teaching was greatly involved with his family of 'seventeen children' and local affairs. Due to such heavy commitments his health failed and he retired in 1882 and sold fields to the south to provide land for 'lower' Edge Hill and Darlaston Road in 1883. The school declined under his successor Rev. Wynne and closed in 1887, being empty five years, but the Jesuits came to serve the new Roman Catholic *Church of Sacred Heart* in Darlaston Road and thus purchased it in 1892. John Brackenbury died at Upper Norwood on 24 August 1895 whilst Wimbledon College (Jesuit) remains in Edge Hill today.

Frank Stenhouse Creswell the son of Thomas and cousin of Edmund William was born at Lisbon in 1853 and presumably knew George Brackenbury at the time of his sister's wedding in 1872. He was then a merchant in Alexandria and no doubt had business links with his cousin Edmund Drinkwater Carver thus knowing the Moberly family. Emily Scholes was born at Chorlton in December 1854 and with twin Edward were children of Joseph S. Scholes a merchant. Frank Stenhouse Creswell merchant of Alexandria married Emily Colbeck (widow) formerly Scholes at Heckfield on 8 August 1883 the bride residing in the village. The couple initially returned to Alexandria and their son Frank Gordon was born in Egypt in 1885 but moved to "Selwood", Worple Road by 1887 and had children: Thomas Scholes (March 1887) and George Hector (September 1889). They lived at "Crumpsall", 17 Darlaston Road, Wimbledon, by 1891 a name that revealed their Manchester connections - Frank general merchant and employer lived with wife Emily, children Gordon, Scholes and Hector (sic) and four servants. John Lancashire was born in January 1893 but mother Emily died at Wimbledon in December 1893 aged 39.

Ethel Maude Jerram was born in September 1865 and baptized at St. Lawrence's, Chobham on 27 March 1866 the daughter of Samuel John and Grace a clerk in Holy Orders. Frank Stenhouse Creswell a merchant of "Crumpsall" in Wimbledon married Ethel Maud Jerram at Claines St. George, Worcester on 29 August 1899. His bride was of New Baskerville, Worcester and was no doubt followed by some hounds! C. Jerram Hunt vicar of Rainbow Hill, Worcester was minister and Frank Gordon Creswell, Paul Colbeck and the Jerrams were witnesses. They had a daughter Lucy Margaret born at Wimbledon in September 1900. Frank S. Creswell a merchant on commission and employer lived at 17 Darlaston Road in 1901 with wife Ethel M., children Hector, John L. and Margaret L. and four servants. He died at "Crumpsall", 17 Darlaston Road on 8 December 1931 and Frank Gordon Creswell merchant and George Hector Creswell captain R.N. obtained probate the effects £17,885 3s 9d. This was the last house on the southwest side and no longer remains but a good example is at no. 16. Indeed there may have been two builders since the even numbers are finished in brown brick but the odd numbers in red.

William Carver had died in 1868 and his widow Emma Louisa Carver then left Manchester and moved to Eltham (probably by 1872). She lived at High Road, Mottingham hamlet near Eltham in 1881 and the household included her daughter Agnes Catherine and grandchildren Mary D. Creswell (5) born India and Margaret E. Creswell (1) born Gibraltar. However, Emma Louisa lived at 2-4 Thornton Hill, Wimbledon in 1887 near to Darlaston Road and Edge Hill. This was a tall Victorian property of three storeys-plus located high on the hill and had brown brick to the rear, yellow to the front and red corner features. This remains today and is a large property next to a VR post box. Emma Louisa Carver then lived at "Redstone", 1 Edge Hill in 1892-96 this being the second house after Darlaston Road on the north east side. The property had red brick with white banding, one main front gable and an arched doorway of red-white stone. In addition there was a flower motif and coat of arms and the date "1884" was above the door. The street was renumbered in 1900: 2-14 at the Worple Road end, 16-84 Wimbledon College and 86-90 at the Ridgway end; no. 1 was 12 Edge Hill and remains today. Emma Louisa Carver died at "Tarifa", Edge Hill on 20 August 1899 three months after her daughter (see below) and probate was granted in London to Edmund Drinkwater Carver merchant and Thomas Gilbert Carver Esq. Q.C. executors on 9 November the effects £3,984 6s 7d.

Edmund Drinkwater Carver followed his relatives to Wimbledon in 1888-90 and moved to a substantial property called Charlton House, Edge Hill and renamed it "Ingarsby" with regard to the family's roots in Leicester. The house was on the southwest side between Donhead Lodge and Ivyhurst and was built in c.1867 whilst modern flats of Oakhill Court cover the site. There were initially three properties (plus Ridgelands) on this side of Edge Hill until the lower road was developed and it was renumbered in 1900: 1-13, Ivyhurst (21), Ingarsby (29) and Donhead Lodge (33) the gaps being occupied with lodges etc. (10 properties in total). Mary Arnold the granddaughter of the Headmaster of Rugby ran a school for young ladies at Donhead Lodge in 1880-1902 and this extensive red building with portico entrance, gables and coat of arms is now Donhead Preparatory School. The only survivors on this side are lower Edge Hill (1-13) and the attractive gatehouse of Ivyhurst with its round tower, however the house itself was demolished and Edge Hill Court covers the site. Edmund Drinkwater Carver general merchant and employer lived at "Ingarsby" in 1891 with his children Emily, Ethel M. and William M. (electrical engineer) and five servants with one from France, plus a separate gardener's cottage. His niece Mary D. Creswell was a pupil at Miss Arnold's School at Donhead Lodge in 1891, whilst Edmund had business premises at Exchange Chambers, 24 St. Mary Axe in London the same year. Edmund a general produce merchant was visiting brother Charles at West Derby near Liverpool in 1901 whilst his wife Louisa was visiting son Harry and Eleanora at Alderley Edge. His daughters Emily, Ethel, Gertrude and Dorothy were at "Ingarsby" with six servants and were 'dependent on their father' a cotton merchant.

Edmund Drinkwater Carver of "Ingarsby" liked to travel and died at Buenos Aires, Argentina on 26 March 1909: Charles William Carver, William Moberly Carver engineer and Norman Clifton Carver surgeon obtained his probate the effects £113,022 3s 6d. Louisa Moberly Carver died at "Ingarsby" on 18 August 1926 thus the village name was retained for over 100 years and her probate went to William Moberly Carver and Norman Clifton Carver. Son Harry married Eleanora Constance and maintained connections with Egypt, his daughter Irene being born there in 1896, but died at Bournemouth in 1943. Norman was educated at Wellington College and King's College, Cambridge (1895) and attended St. Thomas's Hospital in 1900 becoming M.R.C.S. and L.R.C.P. in 1904. He was a surgeon-lieutenant in the Royal Navy and was mentioned in despatches in the First War and lived at 9 Lauriston Road, Wimbledon in 1939 (near Edge Hill and the Common).

Henry Clifton Carver was born at Chorlton in March 1845 and returned to Gibraltar with his family soon after birth then resided at Whalley Range in 1861. He was an engineer of "Broomfield" in 1868 and lived at Oxford Road, Manchester when he married Mary daughter of John Coates, printer at St. Mary's, Crumpsall on 8 July 1869. R.J.B. Rickards a relative and vicar of Constantine, Cornwall performed the ceremony and Charles William Carver, Emma Mary Carver and Annie Frances Coates were witnesses. They lived at 10 Park Road South, Birkenhead in 1871-72 but daughters Maude Clifton (September 1870) and Mary Glendining (June 1872) were born at Halkyn near Holywell, which was an isolated place. Their son Edmund Clifton was born at Birkenhead on 20 September 1873 whilst Robin Creswell (September 1877) and Rachel Drinkwater (June 1879) were born at Montgomery near Newtown in Central Wales. One can assume he was there on business. Henry a mechanical consulting engineer and buying agent, employer, lived at High Meadow, Pownall Fee, Wilmslow, in 1891 with Maude C., Mary G. and Rachel D., nephew Edmund F. Creswell and two servants. He was a partner in "Coates and Carver" buying agents and agents to the Maritime Insurance Co. Ltd. at Guardian Building, 3 Cross Street, Manchester in 1891 his partner being Albert Coates of Daisy Field, Alderley Edge. Their telegram address was in fact "Alberto Manchester". Henry Clifton Carver resided at Pendleton near Manchester but died at Bilbao in Spain on 6 January 1893. An event recorded in the consular returns although the town is on the north coast well away from Gibraltar. Thomas Gilbert Carver Esq. proved his will in London on 4 March 1893 the effects £5,142 17s 5d but re-sworn in July at £6,142 17s 5d. Mary Carver died at "Sunnyside", Alderley Edge, Cheshire, on 31 March 1920 and Rachel Drinkwater Fellows (wife of Frederick Macfarlane Fellows) administered her effects.

Charles William Carver was born in Gibraltar on 17 November 1846 and lived with his family at Whalley Range in 1861. He was a cotton broker for Carver & Co. and their address was Peter's Buildings, Rumford Street, Liverpool in 1868 and North Western Bank Buildings, Dale Street, Liverpool in 1873. His cousin Mary Creswell Carver (daughter of John Carver and Ann Rickards) lived next door at College Road, Whalley Range and was there until 1873 - he married her at Eltham (Lewisham) in September 1875. They had three children at West Derby: Anne Rickards (December 1876), Marjory Aspinall (September 1878) and Louisa Drinkwater (15 January 1880). Charles, Egyptian merchant lived at Holly Bank, Bankfield Road, West Derby in 1881 with his wife, children Anne R., Marjory A. and Louisa D. and brother Walter A. Carver civil engineer - he no doubt did a good line in mummies! Hester Broome (September 1882) and Joan Creswell (December 1885) were also born in West Derby.

Charles was owner of Carver Brothers & Co. cotton merchants at 7 Masons Buildings, 28 Exchange Street (east), Liverpool, in 1890 whilst his family moved to "Woodbourne", Sandfield Park, West Derby, in 1890-91. He lived there as general merchant and employer with his wife and five daughters whilst Anne Rickards Carver married Holford Harrison at West Derby in September 1899. Charles a general produce merchant and employer lived at "Woodbourne" in 1901 with wife Mary, four unmarried daughters, brother Edmund Drinkwater Carver, nieces Margaret E. Creswell and Ruth L. Creswell and six servants. Mary Creswell Carver died at "Woodbourne", Sandfield Park, West Derby, on 13 August 1915 and her probate went to her husband who was described as a cotton merchant. He continued to live at "Woodbourne" but died at the Bay Hotel, Falmouth, Cornwall, on 10 May 1922 and his probate was granted to the Public Trustee, Liverpool on 24 July 1922 his effects £106,481 18s 4d (he was also a rich man).

Thomas Gilbert Carver was born in Gibraltar on 14 November 1848 and resided at Whalley Range in 1861 but was educated at the Forest School, Snaresbrook and no doubt played soccer on the notorious common - possibly against Forest F.C. He attended St. John's College, Cambridge and was a scholar and gained his B.A. 8th wrangler in 1871 then became a barrister at Lincoln's Inn in 1873. He initially joined the Northern Circuit and practiced in Liverpool and married Frances Maud Squarey in the Wirral on 1 May 1878. She was baptized at Lower Bebington on 27 July 1856 the daughter of Andrew Tucker Squarey and Eleanor Catherine Fulton - not far from Port Sunlight. The couple had a son Gilbert Squarey Carver in September 1879 and lived at 1 Storeton Road, Oxton, Birkenhead, in 1881. They had children Catherine Fulton (c.1881), Mita Drinkwater (March 1883) and Edmund Tucker (December 1884) whilst Thomas published: "On the Law relating to the Carriage of Goods by Sea" in 1885. His families experience meant he was well qualified for this and indeed it was a success and a 4th edition came out in 1905. The couple then had children Thomas Drinkwater (September 1886 d.1940) and Phillis Maud (c.1888) whilst the father practiced at Stephenson Chambers, 25 Lord Street, Liverpool, in 1890 but left the city at the end of the year. He moved to London being at 1 Brick Court, Temple in 1892 and was a Q.C. in 1897 then a son Julian Creswell was born at Lewisham in June 1898. He was a bencher at 2 Garden Court, Temple in 1904 and for recreation enjoyed golf and cycling his home address being Yew Close, Oatlands, Weybridge in Surrey. He died at 26a Bath Street, Huddersfield on 12 May 1906 and strangely for a barrister he left no will and his administration was granted to Frances Maud Carver widow his effects £20,424 17s 2d - she died in 1937.

Emma Mary Carver was born in Gibraltar on 27 September 1853 and baptized at Holy Trinity Cathedral on 21 October that year. She returned with her family to Manchester and resided at Whalley Range in 1861 (aged 8) and after her father's decease in 1868 went with her mother Emma Louisa to Eltham (c.1872). She was then introduced to her relative Lieutenant Creswell who was in Woolwich and Chatham at the time (Thomas and Martha Creswell being their uncle and aunt) and was betrothed to the lieutenant thus following him to India in 1875 (see below). The Carvers played a significant role in the development of Gibraltar in the 19th century and there is a memorial to Thomas Drinkwater in North Front Cemetery but the writing is weathered and hard to read. Below his name there are two entries to members of his family: "In loving memory of Henry Clifton Carver grandson of the above who died at Bilbao Spain, January 6th 1893 aged 47 years." The second is even more pertinent to the above discourse and states: "In loving memory of Emma Louisa eldest daughter of the above and wife of the late William Carver of Manchester, born at Gibraltar on the 7th May 1823, died at Wimbledon on the 20th August 1899." The Carver family brought a piece of England to the peninsula and the poem of Rupert Brooke is their postscript: "If I should die think only this of me: That there's some corner of a foreign field, that is forever England...."

EDMUND WILLIAM CRESWELL

The Creswells were prominent in Gibraltar, Australia, Egypt and South Africa but were also active in India thus the discussion now moves to the football arena. Edmund William Creswell a British subject was born at Hargraves Parade, Gibraltar on 7 November 1849; a small square of houses at the south end of Town Range and just inside Prince Edward's Gate. His father was described as an 'Agent of the General Post Office' and his birth registered on 9 November. He was baptised at Holy Trinity Cathedral on 11 December that year and spent his early days on the Rock initially residing at Hargraves Parade then at the Post Office, Main Street from 1858, but received his education in England. His family had important links to the postal service and this no doubt brought them into contact with the Hill clan.

Bruce Castle at Lordship Lane, Tottenham was a manor house built in c.1626 with extensive parkland being near to All Hallows Parish Church. It was constructed on three storeys in red brick and had a central stone clock tower with cupola whilst an unusual detached tower to the north was used for falconry - indeed it had no military function. The house was enlarged at each end over the years and converted to the Georgian Classical style in the 18th century, with white stucco, but this was removed to reveal red brick once again in c.1793. Further to this crenellations and gables were removed to leave the building much as it is today, although it ceased to be a manor house and was Bruce Castle School from 1827.

Thomas Wright Hill (1763-1851) an apprentice in Birmingham was acquainted with Joseph Priestley who secured him a position at a charity school and he married Sarah Lea at St. Martin's, Birmingham on 29 July 1791. He was connected to a group of small businessmen interested in reform and after a period in Kidderminster began Hill Top School at Birmingham in 1803. He had a family of famous sons: Matthew Davenport (1792), Edwin (1793), Rowland (1795), Arthur (1798) and Frederick (1803). His third son Rowland was a student teacher at Hill Top in 1807 and with his brother Matthew became interested in educational reform and helped establish Hazelwood School at Edgbaston in 1819. That same year Matthew became a barrister at Lincoln's Inn and the brothers published a pamphlet *Public Education* (1822) that brought the school international fame and overseas students. The institution moved to Bruce Castle in 1827 and the "Hazelwood System" was introduced, which involved the abolition of corporal punishment, one afternoon's sport, science as a subject and self-government for pupils. Indeed the school was renowned for these progressive teaching methods.

The brothers all had a reforming role and Matthew (1792-1872) gained valuable experience of the law and penal system whilst a barrister. He was a member of the Society for Diffusion of Useful Knowledge (see Lubbock Ch. 7) and joined with Frederick (1803-93) who was Inspector of Prisons in Scotland and together they instigated penal reform. Rowland (1795-1879) taught at Bruce Castle until 1833 then became Secretary to the South Australian Commission and published *Post Office Reform: Its Importance and Practability* (1837). He reformed the British postal system and introduced the penny post in 1840 then became Secretary to the Postmaster General from 1846-64 and was knighted for his services in

City of GIBRALTAR

CERTIFIED COPY of an ENTRY OF BIRTH

A 48460 Pursuant to the Births and Deaths Registration Ordinance

Volume 1 Page 111
Fee: £6.50
Search Fee: --------

I, MELVYN LESLIE FARRELL --, Registrar of Births and Deaths in Gibraltar, do hereby certify that the Birth of EDMUND WILLIAM CRESWELL ----- was fully registered by HENRY MORGAN ----- on the 9th day of November 1849 as follows:—

1849 Births in the City of Gibraltar.

No.	When and Where Born.	Name (if any).	Sex.	Name and Surname of Father.	Name and Maiden Surname of Mother.	Rank or Profession of Father.	Signature, Description & Residence of Informant.	When Registered.	Signature of Registrar.	Baptismal Name if added *after* Registration of Birth.	*Insert in this Margin any Notes which appear in the original entry.*
554	7th Nov 1849	None	Male	Edmund CRESWELL A Native of England	Mary BORG Now Mary FRASER CRESWELL A Native of British East India	Agent of General Post Office	Edmund Creswell Hargraves Parade	9 Nov 1849	H Morgan	Edmund William	

WITNESS MY HAND AND SEAL this 18th day of September 2002.

CAUTION: Any person who (1) Falsifies any of the particulars on this Certificate, or (2) Uses it as true knowing it to be falsified is liable to Prosecution.

Registrar.

Edmund William Creswell. His birth certificate in Gibraltar dated 7 November 1849.

Bruce Castle School c. 1870. The Hill 'postal' family ran the school from 1827-77.

1860. He would have sent regular correspondence to Edmund Creswell in Gibraltar regarding the post, whilst his whole family became involved in the postal service as well as education a fact revealed on the Bruce Castle census for 1861.

Edwin (1793-1876) lived at the school with his wife and children and was a master as well as Supervisor of Stamps for the Inland Revenue (Somerset House). Arthur (1798-1885) was then the Headmaster of the school whilst his son Edward Bernard Lewis (1834) lived with him and was Assistant Secretary to the General Post Office. The household was completed with eleven servants and the pupils included William Glasgow Cowell from Gibraltar aged 14 (cousin of E.W. Creswell). The house was extended in the Victorian period and a three-storey school wing was added at the rear and remains today with school bell still visible. George Birkbeck Norman (1835) another son of Arthur Hill was educated at the school and was a teacher there in 1858. He succeeded his father as Headmaster in 1868-77 and like E. Bowen wrote for the *Saturday Review* and produced copious material on Dr. Samuel Johnson. William Almack married Mary Bell Gripper at Edmonton in September 1877 and took over from the Hill family at this time. He was a Headmaster, chaplain, M.A. Camb at Bruce Castle in 1881 with wife Mary, three assistant tutors, a housekeeper, eight servants and 36 students who included John Creswell (16) and Frederick Creswell (14) both boarders & scholars from Gibraltar. George Birkbeck Hill D.C.L. Oxon an author and reviewer lived at the Poplars, Burghfield, Berks, in 1881 with his wife Annie, four children all born Tottenham, two visitors and two servants. The school itself closed in 1892 then became a museum in 1906 and was later Haringey Local History and Archives.

Edmund William Creswell followed his cousin to Bruce Castle School after 1861 and, as stated, his brothers John and Frederick also went there in the late 1870s, however he then transferred to Brackenburys School at Wimbledon to prepare him for military examinations. He boarded at the school when the first houses of Edge Hill were being built (including "Ingarsby") in the late 1860s. His education prepared him for a career in the army and he went to the Royal Military Academy, Woolwich in 1868 and became a lieutenant in the Royal Engineers on 8 January 1870. He joined on the same day as H. Mitchell and H.B. Rich thus the seeds of history were sown. He was at the School of Military Engineering, Chatham from 15 February 1870 to 20 August 1872 and joined the Engineers soccer team being Secretary of the club in 1871-72. He played in the first Cup Final in 1872 and made a gallant performance with a broken collarbone and appears in the team photo with his jacket buttoned up and his woolly cap on and a bulldog expression. He looks rather cold and no doubt hoped the photographer would hurry up so he could get back to the fire - he was used to the Mediterranean not Chatham! He was a good cricketer and played in representative matches for the Engineers and visited his relatives at Eltham at this time thus meeting his cousin Emma Mary Carver, aged 18.

After some leave in August to October 1872 he travelled to a warmer climate being sent to India from 23 October 1872 to 24 February 1880 viz. 7 years and 125 days. He worked on a major canal under a Government irrigation scheme and was appointed assistant engineer 2nd grade D.P. works on 27 March 1873 and was posted to the Irrigation Branch, Bengal in 1874. His fiancée then travelled to India and Edmund married Emma Mary Carver at Christchurch, Byculla near Bombay on 30 January 1875 and Rev. A. Selehampton performed the ceremony. He lived with his young wife in the Aligarh region 80 miles south east of Delhi and in fact Emma Mary Creswell wrote her last will on 1 September 1875 only seven months after the wedding. Her bequest related to the will of her father William Carver dated 1868 and the trust and legacy of £20,000 for his children. This had stated that his daughter(s) would receive the income separate from any husband and it would then go to any grandchildren, although it was lawful for his daughters (Emma Mary and Agnes Catherine) to bequeath the money to a husband. The father had died without revoking the will and it was proved by the oaths of Edmund Drinkwater, Henry Clifton and Charles William Carver.

Under the power of her father's will she asked her executors to implement this: "Whereas I am a daughter of the said testator and a marriage was on the 30th January 1875 solemnised between myself and the said Edmund William Creswell.... from and after my death (to) pay all the interest dividends and income of the share to the interest dividends and income of which I am now or may hereafter become entitled under the trusts declared by the said will of the said William Carver deceased during my lifetime to my said husband Edmund William Creswell during his life." She also appointed her three brothers as executors and the witnesses were Duncan Alexander Johnston lieutenant Royal Engineers and Walter Philip Von der Horst civil engineer however the will remained in the Creswells' valise for many years to come. Emma was six months pregnant when she made the will and daughter Mary Drinkwater was born at Aligarh on 10 November 1875. The father was assistant engineer 2nd grade in "Khasgunj" Division in 1875-76 the town of Kasganj being 110 miles south east of Delhi in Etah region and 35 miles east of Aligarh. It was a lowland area near the River Ganges where many canals were constructed and their son Edmund Fraser was born at Aligarh (or possibly Narora) on 17 December 1876. Lt. Creswell was made assistant engineer 1st grade, Narora Division, Lower Ganges Canal, "Khasgunj" in 1877-79 and a second son Henry Duncan was born at Aligarh on 15 February 1878. Edmund finished his work in India and sailed to Gibraltar whilst on leave in February to April 1880.

He travelled by ship through the Suez Canal and Emma was heavily pregnant at the time thus his daughter Margaret Elspeth was born in Gibraltar on 15 April 1880. Lieutenant Creswell then received a posting to the School of Military Engineering, Chatham on 1 May 1880 thus his daughter was baptized at Holy Trinity on 6 May and he soon departed for England with his wife and family. He spent eleven months at Chatham however his wife returned to Gibraltar with the children in September 1880. They resided with Mary M.W. Creswell however son Henry Duncan died of double acute pneumonia (15 days) at the Post Office, Main Street on 15 March 1881 (resident six months). Benjamin Carver junior kindred of the deceased a merchant of Tuckeys Lane was informant and John N. Bryant medical practitioner registered the death on 18 March 1881. Emma sailed for England a few weeks later although her son Edmund Fraser (aged 4) remained at 7 Waterport Street and appeared there on the 1881 census.

The family were spread far and wide and lived at four locations in 1881. Edmund William Creswell married and a lieutenant R.E. (active list) boarded with Thomas and Lucy Hawkins hotelkeeper at 119 Midland Road, St. Paul's Bedford. His fellow boarder was Charles Wilkinson lieutenant R.E. and he may have been visiting the Fforde family nearby. Emma Mary wife of Lieutenant Creswell R.E. lived with Hugh Mitchell and Catherine (née Creswell) at Fir Tree House, High Road, Enfield, and was presumably recuperating from her loss. Mary D. Creswell (5) born India and Margaret E. Creswell (1) born Gibraltar lived with Emma Louisa and Agnes C. Carver at High Road, Mottingham hamlet near Eltham. There was apparently little family bonding at this point.

Edmund was sent to the Ordnance Survey for seven years on 1 April 1881 and was at Derby in 1881-82. He was a captain on 8 January 1882 and his daughter Annie Jean was born at Spondon on 15 February that year - registered in the Shardlow district. He was sent to O.S. Southampton in 1883 and his daughter

Agnes Cicely was born there on 6 July. He lived at 1a Cranbury Avenue, Newtown, Southampton, in 1884-85 and Ruth Leslie was born on 18 September 1885 whilst Edmund continued to play cricket and made appearances for the county (not 1st class). He remained with O.S. Southampton until 1888 and then had another overseas posting to the Cape of Good Hope on 19 April 1888 and became a major on 1 August that year. The family were in Cape Colony 4 years, 214 days but two children were at home: Mary Drinkwater was a scholar at Donhead Lodge, Wimbledon in 1891 whilst son Edmund Fraser resided with uncle Henry Clifton Carver at High Meadow, Pownall Fee, Wilmslow being on school holidays from Wellington College (see below). A daughter Alison was born at Wynberg in Cape Colony to the south east of Cape Town on 4 July 1891 whilst the posting ended on 18 November 1892.

Edmund remained itinerant and went to Liverpool in December 1892 and then to Shoeburyness, Essex in June 1894 where his last child John was born on 1 March 1895 - he was promoted to lieutenant colonel on 12 August that year. He then received an ill-fated posting to the sub-continent of India on 12 January 1897 and his family boarded a ship and made the journey to Bombay. They arrived in the steamy city with its unfamiliar bustle and smell of spices and boarded a train destined for Delhi. This was not a trip for the feint hearted the distance being about 750 miles in the humid Indian climate and taking about three days. They travelled up through the Gujarat Plains and the Central Indian Ranges of 600-1,500' and arrived in Delhi then changed train and made the 40-mile trip to Meerut (there was no danger as the mutiny ended in 1857). Edmund was stationed at the Military Works Department in Meerut in 1898 however he was then posted to the outskirts of the Empire.

The family travelled by train to Roorkee a journey of 70 miles and then took a local train to the terminus at Dehra Dun, which was a further 50 miles. The latter town was at 3,000 feet and the last 10 miles were by packhorse however they eventually arrived at Mussoorie in the foothills of the Himalayas at 6,000 feet. It was definitely not England and the Zaskar Mountain Range with peaks of 25,000 feet formed a backdrop. They had good company there since Renny-Tailyour was born at Mussoorie in 1849, Goodwyn was born at Roorkee in 1850, and Rich was stationed at the latter in 1884. This was, however, a dangerous place and Emma Mary Creswell died at Mussoorie, the Punjab, on 11 May 1899 - indeed the family had a double blow that year since her mother Emma Louisa died on 20 August next. Edmund D. Carver of "Ingarsby", Wimbledon and Charles W. Carver of "Woodbourne", Sandfield Park, West Derby (the surviving executors) proved her will at the Principal Registry on 22 June 1900. The gross value of her estate was £250 9s 9d and the trust money was clearly excluded.

Edmund, meanwhile, continued to serve in India after his wife's decease and was promoted to brevet colonel on 12 August 1899 and left the country on 11 August 1900 after a period of 3 years 212 days. He started his retirement on 12 August with retired pay of £450 p.a. having completed 5 years as a regimental lieutenant colonel the total being 30 years 216 days. He was a late colonel R.E. on his own means at "Spencer House", River Hill, Cobham, in Surrey in 1901 and the household included Mary D., Annie J., Agnes C., Alison and John and four servants. He then used his army skills and spent 2-3 years working for the Land Registry Department before his final retirement and continued at "Spencer House", Church Cobham in 1903-07. His daughter Agnes Cicely Creswell married her second cousin Francis Creswell Fforde at Epsom in September 1907 and died at "Lindisfarne", Broadstone in Dorset on 17 November 1925. Her husband Francis returned to Ireland and died at Raughlan on 2 September 1949 and probate went to the Northern Bank Ltd. his English effects £6,472 9s 5d.

François Justin Vulliamy was a French Huguenot and like many of his compatriots became a watchmaker in London. He married Marie and their son Benjamin was born on 27 August 1747 and baptized at Leicester Fields, Huguenot Chapel on 20 September. He married Sarah Degingins (1758) the daughter of Rodolph and Sarah at St. James's, Westminster on 17 April 1779 and they had children viz. Benjamin Lewis (1780), Mary (1781), Sarah (1783), Justin Theodore (1787) and Henry (1793,97). The father was a freeman of the City in 1781 and clockmaker to King George III and his first two sons worked in the family business - he died in 1811. Benjamin junior was a clockmaker of note who joined his father at 68 Pall Mall in c.1800 but he produced designs superior to those of his mentor and was the Master of the Worshipful Company of Clockmakers in 1821, 23, 25 and 27. He worked at the same time as Francis Perigal discussed under Bogle (see Ch. 8) and his position meant he was clockmaker to George IV, William IV and Queen Victoria. The 'old' Palace of Westminster burnt down on 16 October 1834 and Sir Charles Barry (1795-1860) was asked to plan a new building in 1837 but Augustus W.N Pugin (1812-52) designed the details. Barry approached Benjamin Vulliamy with respect to the clock tower, requiring a new clock of 30' diameter plus eight bells. A design was submitted in August 1846 but a dispute arose over this preferential approach thus the matter was put to tender; Benjamin himself was Master of the Clockmakers again in 1847. Barry and Sir George Airy the Astronomer Royal selected the design of Edward John Dent in 1852 ahead of those of Vulliamy and Whitehurst - Benjamin a gentleman and F.R.A.S. died on 8 January 1854 aged 74. His eldest son Benjamin Lewis (1816) matriculated at Merton College, Oxford on 24 March 1836 and died at Marylebone in June 1895 aged 79.

Justin Theodore Vulliamy worked with his father in London then married Elizabeth Bull. They may have had some connection with Daventry near Northampton but went to live at Nonancourt, Eure in France 50 miles west of Paris. They had several children there: Edward (1828), Justin (1832), Elizabeth (1833), Theodore (1835), Katherine (1837) and daughters Sarah and Mary. The family then re-established connections with England and J.T. Vulliamy Esq. lived at Mickleham near Dorking in 1862. Indeed Francis George Wheatcroft married Katherine at Mickleham, Surrey on 11 June 1864 and they had a daughter Rachel in France in 1869. Justin Theodore Vulliamy died in the Dorking district in September 1870 aged 83 and the Wheatcrofts returned thus Frances K. was born at Mickleham in 1871. All the family were British subjects.

Justin Vulliamy married Jeanne Emilie Labouchère who was born in 1842 and lived in France where they had several children: Agnes (1865-68), Lucie (1866), Isabel Agnes (1868), Gertrude (1872), Lionel (1874) and George (1877). His brother Theodore married Hélène Réal de Champlouis and they had children Alice (1864), Justin Theodore (1869) and Edward Owen who was born at Nonancourt on 1 January 1876. Most of the family remained abroad however Elizabeth Vulliamy an annuitant lived at Millfield, Eastbourne in 1881 with her sister Katherine Wheatcroft widow, her two children, Alice Vulliamy (16), Justin T. Vulliamy (11) and two servants. Meanwhile Justin Vulliamy a merchant moved to "Hawksview", Cobham near Mickleham in the 1890s, thus Horace Mark Gregory married his daughter Lucie at Epsom in September 1896 - they lived in Pontypridd and had children Claude Bernard (March 1898) and Maxwell Justin (June 1900). Indeed Elizabeth Vulliamy (68) lived at Tormoham on her own means in 1901 and Horace Gregory chain cable manufacturer, wife Lucie and his two sons were at Pontypridd. However, Jeanne Emilie Vulliamy died at Epsom in September 1901 aged 59.

The *French Connection* was long standing and Edward married Marie Antoinette Labouchère (1839-1915) a relative of the above and died at Nonancourt, Normandy on 5 March 1911. Theodore Vulliamy (66) lived on his own means at Ware in 1901 with Rose (55?) who was born in Switzerland. 'Amenaide' Helene of Higham Hill, Norwich wife of Theodore died on 4 February 1902 aged 57, whilst daughter Alice Vulliamy spinster of "Riversdale", Ware died at Headcorn on 27 February 1902 aged 39 and probate went to Justin Theodore Vulliamy (M.R.C.S). Rose C. Vulliamy died at Ware in March 1921 aged 95 and Theodore died there in June 1921 aged 86. Edward Owen his son was educated at Chigwell and admitted to King's, Cambridge on 1 October 1895 gaining a B.A. in 1898 (M.A. 1910). He was an assistant master at Chigwell in 1900-01 and married Katharine the daughter of Arthur Tite of Amwell House, Ware in Paddington on 21 August 1901. He was at Edinburgh Academy in 1901-09, then a captain and musketry instructor at the university and a lieutenant in Intelligence in 1914-18. After the war he was a French lecturer for modern languages at Pembroke and *Hon. Keeper of the Pictures* at the Fitzwilliam Museum - as a watercolour painter he exhibited at the English Art Club. He lived at Amwell House, Millington Road, Cambridge, in 1953 and died there on 6 January 1962 aged 86.

Edmund W. Creswell (57) colonel late R.E. living 31 Cavendish Square married Isabel Agnes Vulliamy (38) of "Hawksview" near Cobham daughter of Justin a merchant at All Souls', Marylebone on 19 October 1907; the witnesses Edmund A. Creswell, Mary D. Creswell, Justin Vulliamy, Theodore Vulliamy and Lucie Gregory. The family were British subjects and her cousin Justin Theodore married at Paddington in December 1907. Meanwhile Charles Talbot (1685) the 1st Baron Talbot of Hensol barrister M.P. and Soldier General to the Prince of Wales (1717) was descended from John Talbot of Salwarp and Olive Sharington of Lacock - the Talbot family were the Earls of Shrewsbury thus providing a link to Marindin. Very Rev. Charles Talbot (26 October 1769) became Dean of Salisbury and married Elizabeth Somerset daughter of the 5th Duke of Beaufort thus providing a link to Merriman (see Ch. 10). Sir Charles Talbot (1 November 1801) married Charlotte Georgiana Ponsonby on 11 December 1838 widow of Lieutenant Col. Stapleton and sister of 3rd Baron Ponsonby of Imokilly thus providing a link to Kinnaird. Major Francis Arthur Bouverie Talbot (27 September 1851) of the Oxfordshire Light Infantry married Alice Mary Beatrice daughter of Major General Edward Melville Lawford in 1878 and died in 1916. A son Frank Eustace George Talbot was born on 6 October 1879 and educated at Haileybury then served in China and received a medal in 1900. He married Ruth Leslie Creswell at Epsom (presumably Cobham) on 17 July 1909 then fought in the First War and was a lieutenant colonel and colonel of the 14th Sikhs. He resided at 14 Nevile Terrace, South Kensington and his wife Ruth died on 2 September 1939 and he died on 25 September 1958 leaving no children.

Edmund and Isabel resided at "Hawksview" after their marriage and had one child Michael Justin who was born at Cobham on 21 September 1909 whilst Colonel Creswell lived at "Hawks View", Fairmile, Cobham, in 1911. Meanwhile Justin T. Vulliamy died at Rugby in March that year aged 42 and father Justin Vulliamy died at Epsom on 9 April 1912 aged 80. Dark clouds were gathering and Edmund joined up for duty with the Ordnance Survey at the outbreak of war and was in Ireland and Shrewsbury. Meanwhile, Edmund Clifton Carver son of Henry Clifton Carver was born at Birkenhead on 20 September 1873 and entered the Royal Navy as a lieutenant (1894), commander (1906) and retired as captain (1912). Edmund Clifton Carver married his cousin Alison Creswell at Kingston in March 1915 and served in the war with the Royal Navy to September 1917. He was mentioned twice in despatches and thus received the D.S.O. in 1917 but joined the Royal Flying Corps in 1918. They had two sons however he married Marcella Mary daughter of William Knight a barrister at Rye in March 1931 and lived Elphicks, Charity in Burgess Hill. He died at Hurstwood Park Hospital, Haywards Heath on 30 November 1942 and John Clifton Carver lieutenant R.N. obtained his probate.

The Creswell family moved to Copse Hill, Ewhurst, Surrey, near the town of Cranleigh at the end of the war in 1918. This was a location unlike the mountains of India or the streets of Gibraltar and Pitch Hill nearby had a peak of less than 800 feet. A mere hummock! Colonel Creswell then lived quietly in his home and the Times stated: "His gentle courtesy and charm endeared him to all who came into contact with him." Indeed the family made Copse Hill their home for the next seventy years and therein lies a story. Charles Hilditch Rickards (1812) the brother of Ann Rickards was a successful paper manufacturer in Manchester and thus became an art collector. He was present at the weddings of John Carver in 1842 and Thomas Creswell in 1844 and was clearly intimate with the family. Meanwhile George Frederick Watts was born at Queen Street, Bryanston Square (now Harrowby Street) on 23 February 1817. He was the son of George and Harriet Watts a piano maker and was baptized St. Marylebone on 30 March. He became an artist of note and lived with Henry Thoby and Sara Prinsep at Holland Park from 1850. He married the young actress Ellen Terry in 1864 but the marriage only lasted a year and he painted Tennyson, Swinburne and Burne-Jones (see Ch. 10).

Charles H. Rickards became acquainted with Watts in 1865 and was his main patron buying his paintings and funding several exhibitions. His patronage lasted for many years and 21 letters that he sent to G.F. Watts survive at the National Portrait Gallery dated 1867-80. Charles Hilditch Rickards paper merchant and J.P. lived at 2 The Beeches, Seymour Grove, Stretford, in 1881 with Mary Jane Chesworth cousin and housekeeper plus three servants - he died in 1886. G.F. Watts stayed with the Prinseps at Holland Park until 1875 and then moved with them to Freshwater on the Isle of Wight, but came to live at Melbury Road in 1881. This was in fact on the site of their old house in Holland Park and he had an important gallery there. He married a designer Mary Fraser Tytler in 1886 and then built a house called Limnerslease at Compton, Guildford in 1891. The village was ten miles from Ewhurst and Watts soon explored the region with its many hills, rich woodland and rolling countryside. He no doubt passed the obelisk milepost in Cranleigh that marked the way to the village. A number of fine houses were built on Pitch Hill north of Ewhurst in 1897 and Alfred Powell a potter designed Long Copse in the style of the 'Arts and Crafts Movement'. Indeed G.F. Watts stated that Long Copse at Pitch Hill was the most beautiful house in Surrey - it seems likely that Copse Hill was nearby and in a similar style.

Watts was a modest man and was offered a baronetcy in 1885 and 1894 but turned the honour down both times. He was also a sculptor and designed a statue called *Physical Energy* in memory of Cecil John Rhodes (1853-1902) that he presented to Cape Colony in 1904. An identical cast is in Kensington Gardens. Watts supported Rhodes who was born at Bishops Stortford and made a fortune with the De Beers Co. then became Prime Minister of Cape Colony in 1890-96 and head of the British South Africa Co. that administered Rhodesia. He resigned over the Jameson Raid and indeed Creswell was in Cape Colony just prior to this period (1888-92). Watts died on 1 July 1904 and was buried at Compton whilst his sculpture to imperial vision became part of the Cecil Rhodes Memorial situated below Table Mountain in Cape Town. Sir Herbert Baker designed the composition with its eight bronze lions and Classical temple and it was built from local granite in 1906-12 - Watts' statue is at the centre.

Ann Rickards Carver the daughter of Charles William Carver married Holford Harrison in 1899 then married Edmund Fraser Creswell her cousin at Kensington in December 1920. Edmund William

Creswell of Copse Hill made his last will on 1 August 1923 and appointed his dear wife Isabel Agnes his sole executrix and bequeathed the following legacies to his daughters: Mary Drinkwater Creswell £1,000, Margaret Elspeth Waterfield £100, Agnes Cicely Fforde £100, Ruth Leslie Talbot £100 and Alison Carver £100. He left the residue to his wife Isabel Agnes and the will was witnessed at 4 Serjeant's Inn, Temple in London. He died at Copse Hill, Ewhurst on 1 May 1931 and his obituary was in the Times on Thursday 14 May stating he left 3 sons, 4 daughters, 16 grandchildren and 1 great-grandchild. His probate was granted to Isabel Agnes on 11 June his estate valued at £2,322 7s 3d but re-sworn at £2,630 6s 7d. Mrs. John Creswell lived at The Warren Cottage, Cranleigh, in 1934 before the days of broadband since the telephone number was Ewhurst 33. Isabel Agnes Creswell died at Copse Hill on 8 November 1956 and her probate was granted to Michael Justin Creswell H.M. Ambassador to Finland.

Mary Drinkwater Creswell was born at Aligarh on 10 November 1875 and lived with Emma Louisa Carver at Mottingham in 1881 and was at Donhead Lodge in 1891. Mary N. Arnold and three teachers then ran the school and there were 14 girl pupils in residence. Mary lived in Cobham in 1901 and later resided at Ashdown Park Hotel, Coulsdon but died at 11 Birdhurst Road, Croydon on 11 June 1944 and probate went to John Creswell captain R.N. Edmund Fraser Creswell was born at Aligarh on 17 December 1876 and resided at the Post Office, Gibraltar in 1881. He was educated at Wellington College from Michaelmas 1889 and attended the school at the same time as his cousin Norman Clifton Carver. He stayed with his uncle Henry at Wilmslow during the holidays in 1891 since his father was in Cape Colony and was in Lynedoch House in 1889-93 being a prefect in his last year. He attended the Royal Military Academy, Woolwich in 1893 and was a lieutenant in the Royal Artillery in 1896 and a captain in 1901. He was Assistant Superintendent of Experiments at Shoeburyness 1902-07 and Instructor in Gunnery 1st class 1908-12 being staff captain at the War Office in 1912.

He served in Belgium and France in 1914-18 and was made a major in 1915, received the D.S.O. in 1916 and was a brevet lieutenant colonel in 1918. He was commandant at the Anti-Aircraft School in 1918 and had the same position at the Chemical Warfare Experiment Station in 1920 then, as stated, married Ann Rickards Harrison (Carver) at Kensington in December 1920. He was Assistant Director of Artillery at the War Office in 1921-24 becoming a lieutenant colonel in 1921 and a colonel in 1922 and finished his career as commandant of the Anti-Aircraft Defence School in 1924, retiring from service in 1925. He lived at Pump House, Barnt Green, Birmingham and his recreations were cricket and golf whilst his club associations reflected his interests viz. United Services, M.C.C. and Royal St. George's Sandwich. He lived at 63 Grove Hall Court, Hall Road, Maida Vale but died at St. Vincent's Hospital, Eastcote, Ruislip on 5 November 1941 and probate went to the Public Trustee his effects £7,793 15s 7d.

Michael Justin Creswell was born at Cobham on 21 September 1909 and was educated at Rugby and New College, Oxford and a Laming Travelling Fellow of Queen's College in 1932. He entered the Foreign Service in 1933 and was 3rd Secretary in Berlin in 1935-38, at a difficult time. He married Elizabeth Colshorn at Surrey S.W. in June 1939 and had one son by this marriage. He was 2nd Secretary in Madrid in 1939-44 and in Athens in 1944 being with the Foreign Office in 1944-47 and a counsellor in Tehran in 1947-49 and in Singapore in 1949-51. He married Baroness Catherine M.C. Thoe Schwartzenberg En Hohenlansberg (or M.C. Montijn) at Chelsea in June 1950 and again had one son by the marriage. He was minister at the British Embassy, Cairo in 1951-54 being awarded the C.M.G. in 1952 and was Ambassador to Finland in 1954-58, then Senior Civilian Instructor at the Imperial Defence College in 1958-60. He was Sir Michael Justin Creswell K.C.M.G. in 1960 and Ambassador to Yugoslavia in 1960-64 and Argentine Republic in 1964-69 but then retired. He continued in his public duties as Chairman of the Surrey Amenity Council 1974-83 and was in Waverley D.C. 1974-85, Waverley B.C. 1985 and Surrey C.C. 1977-85. His recreations were travel and wildlife and he died at Copse Hill on 25 April 1986.

CHAPTER 10

The Empire Builders

The Royal Engineers team of 1872 and their families sailed to the four corners of the globe and helped form the backbone of the British Empire. They travelled to Barbados, Bermuda, Jamaica, British Guiana and Canada in the New World; reached Egypt, Morocco, Gold Coast (Ghana), Sierra Leone, Belgian Congo, Kenya, Rhodesia and Cape Colony on the African continent; resided in Gibraltar, Spain and Malta on the Mediterranean and reached Mauritius, Hong Kong, Malaya and New South Wales in Australia. Their main contribution, however, was in India and they were based near Delhi and Lucknow (Oudh) in towns like Aligarh, Allahabad, Boolundshuhur, Lansdowne, Mussoorie and Roorkee. They were also in Ferozepore, Rawalpindi and Afghanistan in the northwest, Calcutta and Darjeeling - West Bengal and Bangalore, Bombay, Nellore, Secunderabad and Madras in the south. This did not include the role of the Wanderers and F.A. officials who had further connections in Belgium, France, the U.S.A. and New Zealand. Who said people didn't travel far in those days? These histories are concluded with a discussion of the other four players in the Engineers side.

EDMOND WILLIAM COTTER

The last attacking player Edmond William Cotter also came from an army background and was destined for a notable career in the Engineers, travelling widely in the British Empire. The family can be traced to Edward Cotter his grandfather who was born in Youghal, Co. Cork, Ireland in c.1798 a town on the south coast between Cork and Waterford. The family were Irish Catholics and Edward was apprenticed as a tailor and came to work in London in c.1820. Meanwhile, John and Isabella Wilkie resided at White's Alley in the Liberty of the Rolls near Chancery Lane, London in the 1790s. This was an extra-parochial area located near the Law Courts and described as, "The precincts and chapel of the Master of the Rolls," and was first designated thus in c.1664. The name was derived from the Chancery and Court Rolls (i.e. rolls of legal documents) and the nearest parish church was St. Dunstan in the West. The couple had two children born at White's Alley viz. George (27 December 1795) and Isabella (31 March 1799) the latter being baptized at St. Dunstan in the West on 18 August 1799. Indeed members of the Wilkie family still resided at (Little) White's Alley in the 1830s.

Edward Cotter married Isabella Wilkie by licence at St. Martin in the Fields on 9 September 1821 both residents of the parish and John Miles was the minister and Maurice Hearn and Thomas C. Ollen witnesses. Edward was a Catholic and Isabella presumably a Protestant however only an Anglican could perform marriages in 1754-1837. The family stayed Catholic and had an association with the Sardinian Chapel in Duke Street to the west of Lincoln's Inn Fields. The registers there date from 1731 and are the oldest Catholic records in England but the chapel itself was demolished in 1904-05 during the building of Kingsway and was replaced by St. Anselm & St. Cæcilia (in Kingsway itself). John Cotter their son was born in London on 10 August 1823 and baptized thus: "Die 10 Augusti 1823 natus et die 21 Septembris 1823 baptizatus fuit Joannes filius Eduardi et Isabella Cotter olim Wilkie Conjugum Suscepere Joannes Heney et Maria Reed. A me Fred. Edgeworth Misso. Apeo."

Two other children were baptized in the chapel namely Edmund (10 November 1825) on 19 December witnesses John Virtue and John McManus and Mary (31 October 1827) born Liberty of the Rolls and baptized 2 December witnesses Bernard Murphy and Rose McManus. The couple had three other children: William (1831) at St. Pancras and Margaret (1833) and James (1838) at Liberty of the Rolls whilst their son John joined the army in 1840. Edward Cotter a tailor from Ireland lived at Little White's Alley, Liberty of the Rolls in 1841 with wife Isabella, children Mary (13), William (10), Margaret (8) and James (3) and Daniel Sullivan (15) a tailor's apprentice. Edmund Cotter pawnbroker's assistant aged 23 died of phthisis (consumption) at 12 Little White's Alley on 11 June 1848 the informant his mother Isabella. This was registered in St. Clement Danes sub-district and Strand district and he was buried at Chelsea All Souls' Catholic Cemetery on 18 June. They moved to 16 Dean Street, Fetter Lane between Chancery Lane and St. Andrew's, Holborn in 1851, which was near Plough Place but is no longer present due to the building of New Fetter Lane. Edward

Cotter a tailor lived at 16 Dean Street that year with wife Isabella, children Mary, William (apprentice brazier) and James (scholar), four lodgers and a visitor - the family were comfortable but poor.

Isabella Cotter died of chronic hepatitis and climacteric decay (ageing) at 16 Dean Street in St. Andrew's, West London (city) on 29 December 1853 aged 54, the informant being Margaret Cotter of the same address and she was buried at Chelsea All Souls' on 5 January 1854. William Cotter her son died in the Strand district in September 1856 and was also buried there on 2 September, thus the family was depleted. Edward Cotter (63) a widower and tailor lived at 16 Dean Street in 1861-62 with son James (23) a copper plate printer but were not wealthy and shared the abode with Henry Dean (46) a tailor, his wife Mary (32) a tailoress and four children born Farringdon - three other families occupied the house. Edward despite his restricted means was described as an esquire on his son's marriage certificate in 1870 and this was due to new aspirations that raised the family in society (see below). Edward retired from business and died at the Tailors Benevolent Institution, Queen's Crescent, Kentish Town, on 28 June 1875 aged 78, but an inquest was held on 30 June and established that he died of 'a fatal fainting of the heart' and 'natural causes'. Such were the medical descriptions of the time and William Hardwicke coroner for Central Middlesex was the informant.

The story of the family's rise through society is detailed below however there is considerable difficulty with this form of research and some confusion. A 'cousin' John Cotter was born at Youghal in April 1825 and was a tailor by trade. He attested for the 28th Foot Regiment at Westminster on 26 August 1843 being 5'6" in height, brown hair, hazel eyes and Irish complexion. He received 2s 6d on being attested and signed up for a bounty of £3 17s 6d then served as a private for 9 years 264 days. He was abroad in the East Indies for 3 years 2 months and received a good conduct badge however he became ill in India and was sent home and discharged as unfit at Newcastle on 16 May 1853. He was treated for 241 days for a heart problem during his time in India and at home and it was established that his illness arose due to 'the climate in India.' It was decided he was unable to serve in the army again and indeed it was a dangerous life since he now had a scar on his left shin. He was granted a further pension of 7d a day on 9 October 1855 but was refused a further pension on 24 June 1856. He may have looked similar to his London cousin but the latter had a more notable career.

John Cotter (1823) spent his early life in the confines of White's Alley near Chancery Lane and the Strand and as the eldest son may have trained as a tailor however he then joined the army. He enlisted with the 3rd Foot (1st Battalion) as a private soldier at London on 25 January 1840 aged 17 - their full title being the 3rd East Kent Regiment of Foot or "The Buffs" and nicknamed The Dragon. He was initially posted to the Chatham Depot and spent the end of 1840 at Upnor Castle on the Medway however many of his fellow-recruits then embarked for Bengal. John himself only went as far as Reading and was engaged there in recruiting from 28 December 1840 to February 1844 and was back at Chatham in March 1844. He remained there the rest of the year and spent some time on guard duty at Sheerness whilst the main Battalion was stationed at Allahabad in India. The home troops were soon on the march and were at Chichester, Gosport and Winchester in 1845-46 although John was recruiting at Kilworth north of Cork in January-July 1845 and likewise for one month in Bradford. He marched from Bristol to Winchester and received a free hot meal and was at the latter with the depot on 11 November 1845.

He was stationed at Gosport for the first nine months of 1846 and was promoted to corporal on 12 August 1846 but the 3rd Foot decamped to Dublin at the end of the year and he received three hot meals during the march. The Irish 'potato famine' took place in 1846-50 and the troops were stationed there to deal with political and social unrest. The failure of the potato crop caused an estimated one million deaths through disease and starvation whilst large numbers of people immigrated to America and there is a certain irony in the extra rations given to the troops. The 3rd Foot were stationed all over Ireland in 1846-51 being in Dublin and Naas for most of 1847. John was involved in a number of marches at this time and received extra rations going from Naas to Robertstown in August and from Dublin to Naas in September 1847 in aid of civil power (a kind of sponsored walk)! The Corps went to Belfast at the end of 1847 and John Cotter had good career prospects and was promoted to sergeant on 11 February 1848, in place of Henry Tildesley who was discharged. The 3rd Foot left Belfast at the end of July 1848 and marched south to Carrick-on-Suir near Waterford and spent three months there but moved to Limerick on 6 November 1848. John was made colour sergeant that day, replacing William Arthur who was promoted to quartermaster sergeant, then remained in Limerick to June 1850 although some of the troops were in Killaloe. They then moved north to Galway, Ballinasloe and Birr and back to Templemore in July 1850 to January 1851 but arrived in Cork in early 1851. John Cotter was married at this time as a Catholic possibly to Joanna Gibson - this is not yet traced since Protestant records began in 1845 but central Catholic records did not start until 1864.

The 3rd Foot departed Cork for the Mediterranean on 10 April 1851 and spent 24 days on board ship. They sailed on the freight ship *Athenian* under captain George Case and the passengers included the 3rd Buffs and members of the 44th Regiment. The ship arrived in Malta at 7 a.m. on 2 May 1851 and was bound for Gibraltar on 6 May. A list of passengers stated that the 3rd Buffs included: Colonel Sir J. Dennis, Captains Blair, Lobb and Maude, Lieutenants Hood and Luard, Ensigns Cowesmaker and King, Paymaster Mr. Syms, Adjutant J. Pope, Surgeon Stevenson, five ladies, 290 men, 17 women and 17 children. The *Athenian* sailed into Grand Harbour as the sun was rising with Fort Ricasoli on the port side and the ancient walled town of Valletta to starboard, and this was the first time that John Cotter had seen a foreign land.

The Knights of St. John of Jerusalem were established at the time of the first crusade in 1099 and spent 200 years in the Holy Land. They were then gradually pushed westwards and moved to Cyprus and then to Rhodes in 1310. They were happy on the island for another 200 years but Sulieman the Magnificent of the Ottoman Empire laid siege to Rhodes for six months and they were forced to leave in 1522. They were offered Malta in 1523 but initially declined since it was infertile and un-fortified and spent time in Italy and France. They accepted the offer of Malta from Charles V Holy Roman Emperor in 1530 and moved to the island, which had just two settlements - the town of Medina and village of Birgu on the coast. The Knights were divided into eight langues or countries and established themselves in Birgu and made it into a town with an auberge or 'mansion house' for each country, and also built the Inquisitor's Palace and St. Lawrence's 16th century church. There is a plaque to the German Auberge (1530-72) in the square but most of the Knights resided in Triq Hilda Tabone, whilst the Auberge d'Angleterre was nearby and is present today. The members were Catholic aristocrats who gave all their money and land to the order, and lived a secular life taking vowels of chastity, obedience and poverty. Despite these requirements the order as a whole was clearly very wealthy.

Most Mediterranean outposts seem to have had a 'Great Siege' and Malta was no different although in this case there were two. The Knights were defenders of Christendom and Sulieman sent his Turkish troops to Malta on 18 May 1565, and after taking Fort St. Elmo they laid siege to Birgu and neighbouring Senglea for four months. The Knights held out on this occasion and the Turks and their Moslem troops were decimated and fled home. Grand Master Jean Parisot de la Valette celebrated the victory in style and renamed Birgu as Vittoriosa. Despite the presence of Fort St. Elmo and Fort St. Angelo the Knights felt vulnerable and the Grand Master moved them to the new fortified city of Valletta just across the harbour upon Mount Sceberras. He laid the foundation stone himself on 18 May 1565 and streets were laid out in a grid pattern, large bastions constructed and new auberges built. There were two forts or cavaliers at the west end of the city and just one entrance that later connected to Floriana (also walled). The city was

Valletta, Malta. The walled city was founded in 1565.

Fort Ricasoli. Its seven bastions were built in 1670 (right). Lower Barracca Gardens and the Siege Bell (left).

between Marsamxett Harbour and Grand Harbour with Fort St. Elmo guarding the entrance. Pope Pius IV sent the engineer Francesco Laparelli to carry out the work but Valette died in 1568 aged 74 and they moved in under Pietro del Monte in 1571.

There were eight auberges built in the city viz. d'Allemagne now St. Paul's Cathedral, Aragon built opposite it in 1571, Castile built 1574 Baroque in 1744, Italie in Merchants Street built 1574 re-styled 1683, Provence 1575 in Republic Street, Auvergne in Republic Street bombed now the Law Courts, France in South Street bombed now social club, Palace Bali Carnar 1696 became Bavière 1784 - Anglo-Bavarian langue. With the Grand Master's Palace in the centre of the town they provided the base on which the city of Valletta was to prosper and many merchants were to trade there. Strada San Giorgio later Strada Reale was the main street and all the buildings in the city were of several storeys most with wooden bay windows supported on stone bases with scrolls. There were numerous churches throughout the city and with the old buildings and colossal walls it had a unique atmosphere, and remains thus today. The island was of great strategic importance thus Antonio Valperga, military engineer, built Fort Ricasoli with seven bastions south of Grand Harbour opposite to Fort St. Elmo in 1670. This was a huge fort capable of holding 2,000 troops and the entrance, facing Rinella Creek, had double spiral columns with an arch and plain architrave above. This was near the town of Kalkara, which only became a parish in 1897, whilst the older 'towns' of Birgu, Senglea and Cospicua were known as the three cities. The Knights overcame their vows of poverty however their comfortable days in Valletta were not to last.

Napoleon removed the Knights from the island in 1798 and a plaque on the Palazzo Parisio opposite the Auberge Italie states: "General Napoleon Bonaparte commanding an Army of the French Republic lived here during seven eventful days in the history of Malta 12 to 18 June 1798." He did not endear himself to the Maltese and damaged the auberges, plundered their wealth and worst of all put restrictions on the Catholic Church. There was a general uprising in the country and the French withdrew to Valletta and the adjacent towns. Indeed their stay was to be brief and Lord Nelson blockaded Grand Harbour and the French finally surrendered on 5 September 1800. The Maltese did not ask the Knights to return and they claimed self-government but due to its importance, perhaps in 'gunboat diplomacy', the island became a Crown Colony at the Treaty of Amiens in 1802. Thereafter many British troops were stationed in Valletta and nearby forts, whilst the Governor lived in the Grand Master's Palace and the main street was renamed Kingsway. They had considerable impact on the town with the introduction of new churches such as St. Paul's, and the Royal Engineers built the Barracca Chapel and Kingsgate the main entrance to the city - replaced by City Gate in 1964.

The later history saw the Council of Government established in 1849 whilst the island became a stronghold of the British Fleet after the Suez Canal opened in 1869. Fort Ricasoli was also expanded and the British built casements for 100 heavy guns, and new barracks that housed 700 officers and men up until 1870. Malta was of major strategic importance in the Second War and the second 'Great Siege' took place between June 1940 and 15 August 1942. The Germans bombed Valletta and the docks near Cospicua for 154 consecutive days, far longer than London, however they could not overcome the resilience of the Maltese people. A plaque on the wall of the Grand Master's Palace states: "Buckingham Palace - The Governor Malta. To honour her brave people I award the George Cross to the island fortress of Malta to bear witness to a heroism and devotion that will long be famous in history George RI April 15th 1942." The tide was turning and there was victory at El Alamein in October 1942 and the Allies invaded Sicily in 1943 and Malta was then secure. The cost to the island was great and 8,000 soldiers and civilians lost their lives whilst it took ten years to rebuild Valletta. The fact it was built of stone meant much was saved and today it is a very historic place. Malta had self-government in 1947 and was independent in 1964 and a Republic in 1974 - the main avenue was renamed Republic Street and the President occupied the Governor's residence. A ten-ton bronze siege bell was erected under a cupola beside the Lower Barracca Gardens at the entrance to Grand Harbour. This rings out across the bay for a prolonged time each day at 12-noon to remember those who perished in the siege. It is a most moving event and beside the bell is the inscription: "At the going down of the sun and in the morning, we will remember them."

John Cotter and the 3rd Foot were based at Fort Ricasoli on the south side of Grand Harbour in May-July 1851 and transferred to Fort St. Elmo at the east end of Valletta in August to September 1851. The Maltese first used the latter fort as early as 1417 but the Knights built the present structure in 1552 in preparation for the Great Siege. The design was that of a four-pointed star with a cavalier or stronghold at the seaward end and it was at the cutting edge of military design. Local white-yellow sandstone was used for the walls, which had some architectural detail with banding and notched work under the turrets. The main landward entrance was opposite Merchants Street and the gateposts had a coat of arms upon them. One angle of the fortress with its high walls and deep moat pointed towards Republic Street although this corner was altered when a modern road was built. The barracks were on the north side in the lower part of the fort, and were a distinctive three-storey building around a courtyard. The upper fort has more recently been used as a police academy, whilst the lower fort housed squatters after the war and was used for prison scenes in the film 'Midnight Express'.

The 3rd Foot remained on Malta four years and it is likely that John Cotter was billeted in the barracks of Fort St. Elmo during this time, although the officers may have stayed in the city. His son Edmond William Cotter was born in Valletta on 13 February 1852 and was named after his father's two brothers. There is no record of the birth as local registration began in 1863 whilst army chaplains on Malta only made proper returns from the mid-1860s (although they were required to do this from 1761). Since Cotter was a Catholic there may have been further problems regarding returns from his priest. Despite the large number of churches in the city there were two Catholic parishes viz. St. Paul's Shipwreck south of Merchants Street covering St. Paul Street and St. Ursula Street, and the larger parish of St. Dominic's covering the north part of the town. St. Paul was shipwrecked on Malta in A.D. 60 at which time he

Fort St. Elmo. A four pointed star guarding the entrance to Grand Harbour.

St. Elmo Entrance. Valette built the fort as part of his 'master-plan' in 1552.

stayed in a cave in Rabat and converted the island to Christianity. St. Paul's, Valletta was built in the 1570s so the cathedral could administer sacraments to the people, since the church of the Dominicans had already been declared a parish. It was rebuilt over the years and has a notable façade and interior.

St. Dominic's the original parish church was on the corner with Merchants Street and has two towers with pilasters, inset curved entrance with pediment and grand scroll doorway with statues. It was a short distance from St. Elmo's and a baptism entry states: "George Michael son of John Cotter and Joanna, married, born 8 October 1853 baptized 21 November 1853, priest Calcedoniey Dublesin, Godparents Richard and Maria Green." This is the only direct record of the family in Malta and shows they adhered to the Catholic faith although there is no later record of the child and it may have died as an infant. John Cotter colour sergeant 3rd Foot was stationed in Malta from May 1851 to April 1855 but there was soon a change of circumstances caused by world events and the Corps played a role in a far greater story. Much tension existed in Europe at this time due to the threat of Russian expansion and their army was the largest in the world. The Crimean Peninsula was annexed from the Turks in 1783 and the Russians built a formidable fortress and port at Sevastopol on the south west coast. This became the scene of a major European conflict with the Russians entrenched on one side and allies France, Great Britain, Turkey and Sardinia on the other. It had the makings of a world war with Austria, Prussia and U.S.A. waiting in the wings whilst major players included Tsar Nicholas, Napoleon III, Queen Victoria, Lord Palmerston and the Sultan of the Ottoman Empire. Indeed this was to be the first major conflict of modern warfare.

The rifle was introduced in place of the smooth bore musket and large numbers of men took part in trench warfare with new troops coming to the front to replace casualties - the same pattern was seen on a larger scale in 1914. The conflict, however, soon exposed inadequacies in the British Army and revealed a feudal hierarchy of officers and ordinary soldiers poorly trained and hired for 21 years - literally a life sentence! These British troops fell way behind the trained conscripts seen on the Continent. The conflict began in 1853-54 and the allies landed in Crimea in September 1854 and marched south. The two armies met at the Battle of Alma on 20 September 1854 and this was a success for the allies thus they gained a foothold on the peninsula and reached the fortress at Sevastopol. It was well defended on the coastal side but could be attacked from the land in the east and the main defence was the Fort Malakhov Bastion supported by the Little Redan (north) and the Great Redan (south). The first offensive was on 17 October 1854 but was inconclusive with Russian lines holding - a stalemate that started 300 days of trench warfare.

The conflict then moved south to the port at Balaklava and an infamous event occurred that exposed the outdated concepts of the British Army. The Battle of Balaklava named Kadikoi by the Russians was on 25 October 1854 - during the battle there was a breakdown of command between Lord Raglan and

Lord Cardigan and as a result 658 light cavalry were exposed to the Russian guns. This became known as "The Charge of the Light Brigade," and the Russians were astonished whilst General Bosquet of France exclaimed, "C'est magnifique, mais ce n'est pas la guerre. C'est de la folie." The charge ended with less than 200 men returning to the British lines and an inquest showed they were meant to secure guns already taken, not ride into the full force of the Russian battery. This was followed by the Battle of Inkerman east of Sevastopol at Inkerman Ridge on 5 November 1854. This was a victory for the allies however the British Army itself was overcome and only held their lines after support from the Turks and French. There were repercussions back home with a public outcry regarding the failures, but that was not all, and it emerged that troops received poor medical treatment at Scutari Hospital (opposite Constantinople) - more died of illness than of wounds.

There was a build up of troops in the region and large numbers of soldiers left Malta for the Crimea and members of the 3rd Foot sailed on the *Alipose* a tramp on 30 November 1854 with a cargo of Government stores, skillets, gunpowder, bread and clothing - they arrived in Crimea at 10 a.m. on 21 December 1854. It was a harsh winter that year and the poor links between Sevastopol and Balaklava meant supplies didn't get through and food was left to rot on the docks. The position was untenable thus Lord Aberdeen and a coalition Government 'resigned' in February 1855 and were replaced by Lord Palmerston and the Whigs who soon corrected matters. One of the main problems was poor transport to the front thus Peto, Betts and Brassey built a railway from Balaklava to Sevastopol - the first section to Kadikoi Village on 8-23 February 1855 and the final section a month later enabling the movement of supplies, troops and heavy ammunition (see Betts Ch. 6). As well as this Florence Nightingale improved conditions at Scutari. Meanwhile, some of the 3rd Foot moved to Piraeus (Greece) in January-March 1855 although others stayed in Malta, whilst John Cotter was promoted to 'acting' sergeant major on 22 March 1855 after a vacancy (until 30 September) and his pay was adjusted for 193 days. A second siege took place at Sevastopol from 9-18 April 1855 however the result of the assault was nil hence the two armies poured more troops into the region.

The 3rd Foot received their orders for the Crimea and sailed from Malta on 30 April 1855 and arrived at Balaklava on 12 May although these movements may have been staggered since their pay was adjusted for 19 days on board ship. The Corps was then stationed at Balaklava for the duration of the conflict and for a few months afterwards. There was a third siege at Sevastopol on 6 June 1855 and a fourth on 18 June however, as in the First War, there was a stalemate with both men and ammunition depleted - especially on the Russian side. The allies met on 3 September and planned a bombardment for two days later however this took place on <u>8 September 1855</u> and was a decisive attack, although assaults on the two Redans were not successful. The British had 11,000 troops and attacked the Great Redan on three occasions but were repulsed by 7,500 Russian soldiers, whilst the French took Fort Malakhov Bastion the main defence and the Russians were forced to withdraw across the river - but didn't leave the area entirely. The allies took possession of the ruined Sevastopol on 12 September 1855 and their troops remained on high alert but this was the last major conflict in the Crimea. There was a desire by most parties to end the war since troops and resources were depleted and winter was coming. John Cotter and the 3rd Foot took part in these sieges and in the decisive storming of the Great Redan and their contribution appears in the Memoranda Papers of the Commander in Chief. These letters sent by senior officers just after the conflict reveal movements of the 3rd Foot in the war and also the heroic actions of their soldiers:

<u>27 September 1855</u> - To Lieutenant General Thorn C.B. K.H. Colonel "The Buffs", from the 3rd Foot camp before Sevastopol. Sir, I am requested by Major Maude to write to you to beg in case Lieutenant and Adjutant Sidebottom be promoted to a camp, or a vacancy should occur in the Regiment, you would be pleased apply to have Colour Sergeant <u>John Cotter</u> acting Sergeant Major of the Regiment under my command promoted to the rank of ensign and in case of the promotion of Lieutenant and Adjutant Sidebottom he might succeed to the Adjutancy of the Regiment. I have the honour Sir, your most obedient and humble servant - the Captain in command of the 3rd Buffs (The letter was received on 18 October and stamped C.I.C. Office on 19 October).

<u>15 October 1855</u> - To General Yorke from Upcott House near Taunton. I wish to inform you that Lieutenant Colonel Paterson's leave will end on the 31st sub and he will then rejoin the Buffs in the Crimea or retire. He was succeeded by Major Maude who was made brevet Lieutenant Colonel and led the attack on the Redan on <u>8th ultimo</u> and was dangerously wounded. I request that Ensign Peachey be raised to the rank of lieutenant as he received a severe wound during the storming of the Redan being shot through the jaw - Yours faithfully, *N. Thorn,* Colonel 3rd Regiment or The Buffs.

18 October 1855 - To Major General Yorke at Horse Guards, London from Upcott House near Taunton. Regarding a letter from the camp before Sevastopol sent 28 September 1855. I enclose a request to lay before Field Marshall Viscount Hardinge from the officer-in-command of the Buffs in the Crimea recommending Colour Sergeant (acting Sergeant Major) John Cotton (sic) for promotion to Ensigncy in the Regiment on a vacancy without purchase. I beg leave to solicit his Lordships most favourable consideration for him to succeed Lieutenant Sidebottom in the Adjutancy of the Corps upon that officer being promoted to a company - *N. Thorn*, Lieutenant General, Colonel 3rd Regiment or The Buffs.

5 November 1855 To Major General Yorke from Upcott House. I enclose a copy of my letter dated 18 October 1855 and I send this copy in case the first letter has miscarried - Yours faithfully, *N. Thorn*, Colonel 3rd Regiment or The Buffs.

19 November 1855 From Upcott House near Taunton. My dear General Yorke, I am a long distance from London hence my letter regarding my Regiment and my officers. I forwarded to you officially a short time since a recommendation for the promotion of Sergeant Major Cotton (sic) to an Ensigncy with a view to his being ultimately appointed Adjutant of the Regiment, that recommendation I am extremely sorry to find has not been attended with success for Lieutenant Colonel Maude has informed me that in his opinion (situated as the Regiment is composed of young officers) he is the only man present with it that would keep the Adjutant's Department in its proper state. The adjutant Lieutenant Sidebottom has been sick absent since the 31 August last and the Regiment is I believe at present under the command of the 4th Captain (Major Green is also sick and the 11th Captain is acting 2nd in command). Lieutenant Colonel Paterson wrote from London on the 15th inst and he daily expects his orders to embark for the Crimea however there is no hope of poor Lieutenant Peachey's life being saved. He arrived in England in a dying state and I had the honour of seeing him and he could not talk. As I take a deep interest in everything connected with the welfare of my Regiment I have considered it necessary to make you acquainted with the circumstances under which the approach for an Ensigncy for Sergeant Major Cotton (sic) was made in order that you may bring the matter again to the notice of Lord Hardinge should you deem it advisable. The new ensigns are some fine gentlemanly young men from the Royal Military College and one is from the South Mayo Militia however will not be a success and brought only a few volunteers with him - *N. Thorn*, Colonel of the 3rd Regiment, The Buffs.

So what was the outcome of all this furious writing? Ensign H. Peachey was made a lieutenant on 4 October 1855 but was sent on leave due to his wounds and died on 15 November that year. A 'relative' Albert Peachey remained with the Regiment and was made 1st lieutenant on 23 March 1858 and captain on 19 July 1864. Leonard Sidebottom was made captain on 8 January 1856 and became adjutant at the main depot of the Battalion on 31 October that year. The most important news, however, involved Sergeant Major John Cotter since Viscount Hardinge approved his Ensigncy without purchase on 24 January 1856. The time taken may have been due to bureaucracy, but there was possibly resistance to a promotion from the 'ranks' as it might undermine the institution. He received his promotion at Balaklava aged 32, which was unusual as most officers received commissions when 21. He was a 2nd lieutenant (ensign) and Adjutant of the Corps on 1 February 1856 and the whole course of his life changed in this one decision, as did the prospects of his children. Finally the army liked to keep matters in order and a note appeared in the memoranda: "The surname of the Color Serjeant appointed to an Ensigncy without purchase and Adjutancy of the 3.Foot on the 1 February 1856, is 'Cotter', and not 'Cotton', as previously stated." **Adjutant**: "Officer who assists superior officers by communicating orders, conducting correspondence etc."

There were plans for further attacks on the Russian position in January 1856 but these came to nothing thus peace negotiations took place in Paris and the war was officially over on 29 February 1856. The Crimean War was a decisive moment in the history of the British Army since it showed the truth and revealed the flaws of the out-dated system. The best men were often those who proved themselves in the ranks rather than young inexperienced officers who purchased a commission. There were exceptions such as John Cotter but the army was slow to learn these lessons and made the same mistakes some sixty years later. Ensign John Cotter remained in the Crimea with the 3rd Foot for nine months after the fall of Sevastopol, their role being to secure the peace. The 3rd Foot left Balaklava on the "Adelaide" and "Imperador" on 10 May 1856 and sailed west to the island of Corfu (west coast of Greece) and made landfall there on 16 May.

The Venetians purchased the island of Corfu from Naples in 1402 and held it until 1797. During this period the Ottoman Turks ruled the rest of Greece and Corfu was a fortress and a haven for artists and scholars, and repository of cultural history. The French under Napoleon took the island in 1797 but an Anglo-Turkish and Russian alliance removed them after a four-month fight in 1799. Corfu became the capital of a Septinsular Republic within the Ionian State in March 1800, however the French regained control with the Treaty of Tilsit in 1807. The island came under British protection in 1814 and was the 'U.S. of Ionian Islands' under the British High Commissioner after the Treaty of Paris in 1815. The islanders supported the Greek movement against Turkish rule on the mainland but in general suffered under the British. There was a revised constitution in 1848 and some improvements in terms of roads and water supply, however the island became part of the new nation of Greece when it was formed on 21 May 1864.

John Cotter arrived on Corfu at the end of British rule and was reunited with his wife and son Edmond at this time, however life had changed and he now had one servant. A second son Francis Gibson Cotter was born in Corfu on 12 June 1857 but there is no record of his birth on the island as the records are incomplete. Indeed the archives are in the British Barracks or "Old Fortress". The 1st Battalion remained on Corfu in 1856-57 but the father transferred to the 2nd Battalion on 20 September 1857 as they were without an adjutant - a post that he could ably fill. **Note** The Regiment was formed of soldiers returning from Holland in 1665 and became Prince George of Denmark's Regiment in 1689 (see Vidal Ch. 7). They were named the 3rd East Kent Regiment of Foot or Buffs in 1782 and the 2nd Battalion was formed in 1803, disbanded 1815 and reformed at Limerick on 24 July 1857. The outfit became the Buffs East Kent Regiment in 1881 whilst Cotter always said he was of "The Buffs". He then left Corfu and was on board ship from 1-8 October 1857 and joined the 2nd Battalion at Limerick on 13 October but not for long since they transferred to Canterbury - 20-27 November. They moved to Shorncliffe Camp, Folkestone, Kent and Cotter was promoted to 1st lieutenant on 23 March 1858 and continued as adjutant - having one servant.

The depot stayed in Limerick however the rest of the Battalion left Shorncliffe and embarked on the *H.M.S. Vulcan* a large 6-gun troop ship on 16 April 1858. John Seccombe esquire was captain with 167 crewmen, and the ship stopped at Gibraltar but then left for Malta on 23 April - the voyage took five days and the *Vulcan* sailed into Grand Harbour, Valletta at 3.45 p.m. on 28 April 1858. The 2nd Battalion 3rd Foot were the only passengers as follows: Lieutenant Col. Maude C.B., Captains G. Parsons, C.M.B. Sirce, W. Stewart, F. Eleson, Lieutenants H. Parnell, S.E. Lewis, John Awhy, E.S. Cox, Hon J.W. Hewitt, A. Peachey, J. Merritt, Ensigns J. Graves and R.C. Hearn, Paymaster H. Magill, Surgeon F.D. Barker, Adjutant J. Coster (sic), 2nd Mr. G. Pittendrigh, 3 officers' wives, 8 officers' children, 3 officers' servants, 546 rank and file, 30 women and 30 children. The families no doubt included John Cotter's wife and his two sons Edmond (6) and Francis (1).

The army were concerned about education at this time as many troops were basically illiterate and G.R. Gleig Inspector General 1846-57 introduced the idea of the 'Chapel School'. It was found that no room was suitable at Fort St. Elmo thus one was built at Fort Verdala on Santa Margherita Hill in Cospicua and a second at Upper Barracca Gardens in Valletta. The gardens were on a terrace above St. Peter's Bastion and Grand Harbour and the Knights once used them for recreation. Lieutenant Col. Francis Ringler Thomson and the Royal Engineers carried out the work in 1852-55 and the cost of each school was £2,367, whilst they also improved the fortifications and built 'Porta Reale' - Kingsgate. The Barracca Chapel was located between the gardens and Piazza Regina later Castile Place, and was a plain Classical building with pilasters along each side. It had a porch with Doric columns and a large roof pediment above surmounted by a small belfry, whilst two porches at the rear led into the gardens. It was more like a Classical church than a school building and mirrored the Grecian temple to Sir Alexander Ball in the lower gardens - the Barracca Chapel School was used for teaching and for Anglican clergy i.e. army from c.1855. Lieutenant Col. J.H. Lefroy was Inspector from 1857-60 and after consultation replaced military chaplains with trained teachers. Major Proter R.E. surveyed army education in Valletta in 1858 and revealed the following: *Upper St. Elmo* - the school is in a barrack room or old chapel (late gymnasium) and is narrow and confined. *Lower St. Elmo* - the school is in a large casemated room. *Fort Ricasoli* - the school is in a storeroom. An H.M.S.O. report on education in Malta in 1859 stated that the 3rd Foot, 2nd Battalion had 121 men learning, 35 on a daily basis and also 21 children. In general 21% of troops were illiterate, whilst literacy figures were: R.E. 97%, R.A. 59% and Infantry 55%. No doubt Edmond Cotter attended the Barracca Chapel School.

During this period John Cotter received £29 11s per quarter and had to pay £1 4s income duty however did not spend all his time in Malta and embarked for England on 7 June 1860. He escorted an invalid

The Barracca Chapel. The Royal Engineers built the chapel-school in 1852-55.

home and arrived in Portsmouth on 24 June but came back via Southampton from 27 September to 6 October. He was an adjutant or acting "captain" in 1860 and had then received 4 years full pay. As an officer he may have lived in Valletta itself, however the 3rd Foot left Malta on 11 June 1862 and then sailed to Gibraltar (see below). Barracca Chapel ceased to be a garrison school in 1868 and was used by the Methodists until they moved to Floriana in 1883 and then became home of the senior chaplain to the forces (Anglican). Indeed the chapel was much cared for whilst St. Paul's Cathedral was thought 'cold and bare'. Guiseppe Cali the Maltese artist did six paintings for the chapel in 1899-1900 that were considered masterpieces. There was a dedication to St. George on 29 March 1936, which was seldom used, and after the last 200 troops left the chapel was closed in April 1950. It was briefly an army social club and then mailroom for the Post Office, whilst the Malta Stock Exchange was formed at Floriana in 1992 and moved to the renovated building in mid-1999. There is a bust of Guiseppe Cali behind the chapel and a memorial to John Bathurst Thomson M.D. 69th Regiment died 18 September 1850 age 36 (during a cholera epidemic) in the gardens. Cali's paintings were moved to the presidential palace at San Anton.

The 3rd Foot arrived on the Rock of Gibraltar on 18 June 1862 and John Cotter still received £29 11s per quarter and had one servant. He had extended leave from 7 February to 31 October 1863 (his wife may have died at this time) and then remained in Gibraltar to 12 June 1864. He then sailed for Barbados and after 24 days on board ship arrived on 10 July although some troops were at Demerara (Georgetown), Guiana in October to December 1864. He was in Barbados until 6 June 1866 but sailed for Dublin and arrived on 25 June. Indeed his life in the army took him to many places that he would only have dreamed of as a tailor. The 3rd Foot were first stationed in Dublin then moved to Belfast on 24 September 1866. They remained there in 1867 but returned to Dublin in early 1868 and were stationed at several locations in 1869: London, Devonport, Colchester, Netley and Hythe. John Cotter headed the list of lieutenants in the 3rd Foot but his army career soon ended and he was injured (or suffered a stroke) in 1869 and was afflicted with paralysis the rest of his life. His final posting may have been to Devonport and he was an adjutant with 14 years full pay in 1870. He retired as a captain on 5 January 1870 and was on the reserve list with a pension at half pay plus £10-1 January, £11-7 February and £20-10 March 1870. He then lived in Saltash and this may have been influenced by family links (see below).

Richard Northy Martyn (1807) a brewer was born at St. Austell and married Mary Ann (1816) of Landrake and they had children: Mary Ann (1840), Susan (1846) and Richard (1853) all in Saltash. John Cotter a widower and captain 3rd Foot married Mary Ann Martyn at St. Stephen's Church, Saltash in Cornwall on 23 July 1870. His father was Edward Cotter Esq. thus the whole family had been "promoted" and raised in society whilst her father was a gentleman. Both parties lived in Saltash and he signed *J. Cotter Captain The Buffs* whilst Edward Polwhele vicar performed the ceremony and Alfred Crocker, surgeon major and Ellen Williams were the witnesses (see below). This was reported to the army on 1 February 1871 and recorded at the War Office on 3 February under the *Widows Pension Regulation Act* (15 June 1855). To receive a pension the event had to be notified within six months and apparently there was one weeks allowance in this case. John Cotter a retired army captain lived at 1 Home Park Place, Saltash in 1871 with wife Mary Ann and one servant. Richard N. Martyn retired brewer, wife Mary Ann and daughter Susan Box a grocer's wife (and two children) lived next door at no. 2. There were nine houses in Home Park Place and many army and navy men lived nearby whilst Brunel Terrace was adjacent.

The couple had three children at 1 Home Park Place namely Harry John (10 September 1871), Isabella Kate (March 1873) and Bertram Wilkie (December 1877). John Cotter retired captain 3rd Foot lived at 1 Home Park Place, Saltash in 1881 with Mary Ann, three children and one servant whilst Mary A. Martyn a widow aged 64 "income from lands" and son Richard (28) a warehouse-man in drapery lived at no. 2 - with Jane Pritchard annuitant of Stoke Daml. John Cotter a major in the Royal Army died of paralysis lasting 13 years at 1 Home Park 'Terrace' on 24 July 1882 aged 58 and F.G. Cotter of the Royal Marine Barracks, Stonehouse was informant. He appeared in the Army Lists under retired pay not in reserve in 1882 and the death was recorded in 1883 (3F - majors). Mrs. Cotter lived at 1 Home Park Place in 1883 but her mother Mary Ann Martyn died at Saltash in December 1885 aged 69 and she inherited her house. She then lived with son Bertram (scholar) at 2 Home Park in 1891 and made her last will there on 31 July 1920 and Surgeon Rear Admiral Sir William Wenmoth Pryn K.B.E. C.B. of Yeoland, Yelverton (son-in-law) and Bertram Wilkie Cotter of Lloyds Bank, Bristol, cashier were executors.

She left Lieutenant Colonel Harry John Cotter her freehold at 2 Home Park, Saltash and shares viz. £200 in £2 10s (%) preferred converted ordinary Midland Railway shares, £100 "B" debentures in Alabama New Orleans Texas and Pacific Junction Railways, and £515 15s 9d invested in £5 (%) War Loans. She left daughter Isabella Kate Pryn her freehold shop and dwelling house at 106 Fore Street, Saltash and an annuity of £18 (bequeathed to her under the will of her mother from 'her' father Stephen Dyer - a perpetual annuity and first charge on Greep's Estate in Saltash), but if redeemed the money to go to her daughter. She left son Bertram Wilkie Cotter £1,150 free of duty and Minnie Deneham of 2 Home Park £25. The remainder placed in trust to be distributed equally amongst her three children, or if they died, then for the education of any grandchildren and her freehold could be rented out. Captain H.F. Smith, White Lodge, Yelverton and Ernest A. Penfold of R.N. Barracks, Devonport surgeon captain R.N. were witnesses. Mary Ann Cotter lived in Saltash on her own means in 1901 and died at 2 Home Park on 19 February 1922 whilst Sir William Wenmoth Pryn retired surgeon admiral R.N. and Bertram Wilkie Cotter bank clerk had probate - effects £4,869 8s 2d.

Edmond William Cotter was born in Valletta on 13 February 1852 but his early years are unclear. He may have stayed with his mother in Malta whilst his father fought in the Crimea, and lived in Corfu and Folkestone but returned to Malta in 1858 and went to Gibraltar in 1862. He probably received some education abroad but went to school in England when his father was posted to Barbados in 1864. He attended the Royal Military Academy, Woolwich in 1868 being a gentleman cadet there in April 1871 and became a lieutenant in the Royal Engineers on 2 August that year. He was aged 19½ and a Roman Catholic and joined up on the same day as Goodwyn and Muirhead. He went to the School of Military Engineering, Chatham on 1 October 1871 and joined the Royal Engineers soccer team thus he played in the 1872 Cup Final although this was his only major game.

The Ashanti War took place in the Gold Coast, Africa from 9 June 73 - 6 February 74 and Edmond soon played a heroic role. He was posted there on 19 November 1873 and served under the commander Major General Sir G. Wolseley - British troops were based at Cape Coast in the south of the country by the Atlantic. The Engineers built bridges and roads to aid troop movements and the 28th Company of Sappers arrived from Chatham on 10 December 1873. An expeditionary force under Wolseley crossed the River Prah and pushed northwards towards Kumasi capital of the Ashanti region (some 70 miles away) in early January - some sappers went with them whilst others protected communications on the coast. Despite some skirmishes they reached the Ashanti outpost of Eginassie on 30 January and camped out whilst Sir G. Wolseley made plans. The next day three columns attacked the stronghold at Amoaful and the 28th Company prepared roads to right and left of the central line. The advance began at 7 a.m. and the infantry moved up hill to engage the enemy - Cotter formed the rearguard of the main force at the 'Battle of Amoaful'. The Ashanti outflanked them and went to the rear then attacked the Post of Quarman - 2½ miles behind the main battle. Lieutenant Cotter and ten sappers were the only Europeans left at the post and they succeeded in defending the position until relieved by the Rifle Brigade. This gallant act preceded Rorke's Drift, which took place in the Zulu War in 1879. Nine men received the

V.C. on the latter occasion whilst Cotter was only 'present' at the defence of Quarman on 31 January and thus received a medal with clasp.

The expeditionary force resumed their advance northwards and reached Agemamue on 2 February whilst the Engineers built a bridge over the River Ordah and they secured Ordahsu without much resistance. They arrived in Kumasi on 4 February 1874 and burnt the town thus the conflict was over and they went back to Cape Coast the job being finished. Lieutenant Cotter boarded the *Himalaya* with the 28th Company and left the Gold Coast on 21 March 1874 and sailed back to Chatham - the Ashanti region was a large area within the Gold Coast colony and became Ghana in 1957. It is worth considering the life of Garnet Joseph Wolseley as he appears many times in this book. He was born at Golden Bridge, Co. Dublin on 4 June 1833 son of an army man and saw his first action in Burma and then fought with the Royal Engineers at Sevastopol. He fought with honour under Sir Colin Campbell during the relief of Lucknow and spent further time in India and Canada. He became famous during the Ashanti War and fought at Amoaful, Ordahsu and Kumasi and was then G.C.M.G., K.C.B. He went to Africa at the end of the Zulu War in 1879 and was the Governor of Natal and led a force during the Arabi Pasha revolt and fought at Tel-el-Kebir in 1882 (see below). He went to the aid of General Gordon during the relief of Khartoum in 1885 and was made 1st Viscount Cairo. He wrote some notable books viz. Life of Sir John Churchill (1894), Decline and Fall of Napoleon (1895) and The Story of a Soldier's Life (1903) although he was criticised for enjoying 'war' too much and indeed he never missed a 'game'. He died at Mentone, France in the Alpes Maritimes on 26 March 1913 (see Betts Ch. 6).

Cotter spent the remainder of that year in Chatham and Dover but was sent to Madras on 10 November 1874. He was made an assistant engineer 2nd grade D.P. works on 24 January 1875 and was also a member of the Sappers and Miners in Bangalore that year. He was based at Nellore on the coastal plain north of Madras in early 1876 but had a months leave in England on 15 July and was sent to the Northern District in August. He may have spent his period of leave with his father in Saltash and soon made an association there. Langford Frost married Ann Tyeth at Stoke Damerel, Devon on 4 December 1816 and a son Langford was born in London in c.1817. The latter was a captain in the 57th Regiment and married Mary (1823) of Stoke Damerel then moved to Saltash in c.1852 and their family included Jessie Tyeth born in June 1855. They lived at Turnpike Gate, Saltash next to Fore Street in 1861 and at 7 St. Stephens Road, Saltash in 1871 when nine children were at home including Elizabeth L.P. (21) and Jessie T. (16) - the latter was Dunheved House and they lived there 1862-83. Edmond William Cotter (24) a lieutenant R.E. of Leamington married Jessie Tyeth Frost (21) at St. Stephen's, Saltash on 11 October 1876 and Edward Polwhele was minister whilst Langford Frost, Elizabeth Louie Pollard Frost and Francis Cotter (brother) were witnesses.

Lieutenant Cotter returned to the Northern District and was in Warwick in 1876-77 and Newcastle in 1877-78 but his wife Jessie stayed with her parents in Saltash (during her confinement) and a daughter Isabella Maud was born there on 9 August 1877. The father was posted to Gibraltar on 16 January 1878 and resided at Town Range on the census that year as a married officer of the Royal Engineers, now of the "Church of England" (see above). He must have met Lieutenants Bogle and Muirhead at this time. His wife initially stayed with him on the Rock but returned home and a son Edmond Brian was born at Saltash on 11 March 1879 and registered at St. German's. He also left Gibraltar on 12 March 1880 and was sent to Portsmouth and a third child John Luis was born there on 29 October that year. Edmond Cotter a lieutenant R.E. active list lived at 2 The Laburnams, Britannia Road, Portsea in 1881 with his wife Jessie, sons Edmond and John and two servants from Cornwall. Indeed Alfred Crocker a close friend of his father also lived in the town (see below). Langford and Mary Frost lived at Dunheved House with four grown-up children and their granddaughter Isabella Maud Cotter, whilst Edward Cornish married Elizabeth Louie P. Frost at Saltash in June 1882.

Phebe Kathleen Cotter was born at Portsea on 11 August 1882 and like her two brothers was baptized at Kingston Parish Church in Portsmouth. Edmond was stationed in Ireland in February 1883 and was promoted to captain on 2 August that year then added to his credentials with distinguished service in India. He was posted to Roorkee from 28 December 1883 to 16 July 1884 but his wife Jessie remained in England and he may have met Henry B. Rich who was already stationed there. He then played a significant role in colonial history as field engineer in the Zhob Valley expedition in 1884, and commanded the 4th Company of Bengal Sappers and Miners under General Sir O. Tanner. The Zhob Valley was in the mountains between the Afghanistan border and the northeast province of Baluchistan (now a region of Pakistan). The town of Khajuri Kach was in the north and Quetta in the south whilst the valley was the shortest route from the N.W. Frontier Province to the town of Quetta - thus of great strategic importance. The Zhob region was at 10,000 feet and the valley had spectacular views with flowers and snow both at the same time but the Engineers had little time for sight seeing and were vigilant for the Pathans of the Kakar Tribe and ever-present scorpions. They were the first Europeans to go there and the expedition explored the valley and opened it up, although these forays were of a punitive nature and the British Government took control of the valley and the Gomal Pass in 1889. The Zhob region became a district in 1890 with its centre at Fort Sandemann. There was also news from back home since Jessie Mary Elsie was born at St. Stephen's, Saltash on 15 July 1884 - his wife may have joined him after the birth.

Captain Cotter was posted to Madras from 17 July 1884 to 22 February 1885 and was briefly at home in Chatham in Feb-March that year but there were soon developments in Africa. The Sudan was controlled by Egypt and Britain but an uprising occurred in February 1884, thus General Gordon was sent to Khartoum to organise a withdrawal of the troops. He failed to obey orders and the town was besieged however a relief party was not sent until October 1884 and reached Khartoum in January 1885 - two days after the death of General Gordon (see Goodwyn). The area was still unstable and Captain Cotter was posted to Egypt from 1 April to 19 October 1885 and served under Generals Lord Wolseley and Grenfell on the Nile expedition. He was the station officer at Assouan and Shellal beside the river near to the Sudan border, and also the district officer with the Nile Frontier Field Force.

He went directly to India for a third time on 20 October 1885 and stayed there 5 years 109 days. He was initially at Bangalore (as in 1875) the town being amongst the central southern hills and 170 miles west of Madras. He had some much-needed leave in 1886 but the army needed a man of his calibre and he was with the Madras Sappers and Miners at Bangalore in 1887. There was considerable tension with the rulers of Burma and with the French thus the 3rd Burma War was in 1885. The British annexed Upper Burma on 1 January 1886 and the conflict mainly involved armed resistance thus it ended by 1887. The Chin and Lushai tribes then continued to resist and the British were ambushed and shot at and telegraph lines cut. The latter tried to secure the region and improve roads etc. thus Cotter served with the Burma and Upper Burma Field Force in 1887-88. He then raised a new division the 'Burma Sappers and Miners' in 1887 and was awarded a medal with clasp for his part in the 1887-89 conflict (a rare award) - the unit was disbanded in 1929. He was sent to Secunderabad near Hyderabad in 1888-89 although there were soon further problems in Burma and 3,000 troops went south from Chittagong 200 miles east of Calcutta in late 1889. They were to meet up with a Burma force moving northwards to try and remove the rebels.

He was promoted to major on 18 January 1890 then received orders for home at the end of the year but first travelled inland to Allahabad by the Ganges in south Uttar Pradesh and completed his Indian service on 5 February 1891. He then had some leave in February to March 1891 (who needs Cooks and Thompsons)! Edmond W. Cotter major R.E. lived at 3 Winsor Terrace, Saltash in 1891 with Jessie, children Isabella, Phebe and Jessie, sister-in-law Elizabeth L.P. Cornish a farmer's wife and two servants. This property was next to Dunheved House and not far from Mary A. Cotter at 2 Home Park Place (Langford Frost died at Saltash in September 1889). Major Cotter went to Norwich in March 1891 but was stationed in Egypt from 30 September 1892 to 13 August 1897 a period of 4 years 318 days and had good memories there. He was a lieutenant colonel on 1 October 1897 then commanded the Royal Engineers at Cork from 10 October that year and was a brevet colonel on 1 October 1901. He left Cork on 30 September 1902 after 4 years 356 days and went on half pay on 1 October as an "army" lieutenant colonel - unemployed in 1904. He served 32 years 7 days (16 years 18 days abroad) and retired from the army on 12 October 1904 with a pension of £450 p.a.

He first moved to Yeovil and two daughters were married there: Jessie Mary E. to Matthew George Hodgson-Gribble in December 1906 and Phebe Kathleen to Henry George Wedd in June 1907. Edmond William Cotter a retired colonel of H.M. Corps of Royal Engineers of Kincora, Glendinning Avenue, Weymouth made his last will on 27 July 1908. He bequeathed all annuities payable by the *Sun Life Insurance Society* to his wife Jessie Tyeth Cotter and after her decease to Jessie Mary Elsie Hodgson-Gribble. The residue of his estate was left to his wife Jessie but if she died in his lifetime it went to his daughter Jessie. He appointed his wife, brother Francis Gibson Cotter colonel R.M and son-in-law Henry George Wedd executors and trustees of his will. He then resided in Bournemouth and Christchurch.

He lived at "Fair View", 40 Castlemain Avenue, Stourfield Park in 1913-16 and today there are many Victorian and Edwardian houses there with Pearce's Dairy (est. 1900) near Kimberly Road. He lived at 27 Guild Hill Road, Southbourne in 1918 a detached plain-fronted house of red brick with white above and wooden porch. Tudor Cottage (29) was next door and a water tower and park was nearby, whilst

Mrs. Cotter lived at 54 Belle Vue Road, Southbourne in 1923-25. Edmond then resided at "Esbekieh", 97 Cranleigh Road, West Southbourne in 1930 and the origin of this name is of interest. There is a Soldiers Home in the Esbekieh district and a Soldiers Club next to the Esbekieh Gardens, Cairo, thus he named his home after these (he was there in 1892-97). In fact this was rather a grand name since the property was a small semi-detached house next to Seafield Road. It had two small bays at the front and red brick with white plaster above, whilst the street was in the style of pre-war ribbon development. Edmond William Cotter died at 97 Cranleigh Road on 23 August 1934 and a brief notice appeared in *The Echo* on 25 August. Probate of his will was granted to Henry George Wedd a solicitor of Langport, Somerset on 11 October 1934 after his wife Jessie renounced the probate - his effects being £470 16s 7d. Jessie Tyeth Cotter died at Chisledene, Bourne Vale Road, Parkstone on 25 July 1937 and probate was granted to Henry George Wedd solicitor. Thus ended a remarkable life and a cross memorial (plain) was erected in East Cemetery, Boscombe: "In loving memory of Col. Edmond William Cotter *Royal Engineers* 1852-1934." Indeed King's Park and Dean Court (now Fitness First Stadium) are adjacent.

Francis Gibson Cotter was born in Corfu on 12 June 1857 and his life was recorded in the naval records. His father arrived in Saltash, by 1870, and this probably influenced his career decision since the Royal Marines (formed 1775) had three divisions at Plymouth, Portsmouth and Chatham. Francis received a direct commission as an army candidate and became a lieutenant in the Royal Marines (Light Infantry) on 1 September 1876, aged 19¼ years. He was stationed at Plymouth H.Q. his father being just across the River Tamar and passed out, receiving increased pay, on 3 December 1877. He had further initial training at Eastney near Portsmouth and passed his garrison instruction in August 1878 and was stated to be a "good draughtsman". He finished his training at Plymouth on 25 June 1879.

The "Achilles" an armour plated iron screw ship of 9,694 tons (old 6,121 tons) with 5,722 horsepower was commissioned at Devonport on 17 May 1877 - its officers from the "Resistance". Lieutenant Cotter joined H.M.S. "Achilles" on 26 June 1879 the vessel being part of the Channel Squadron (1879-80) but was re-commissioned at Devonport on 1 September 1880 in preparation for Mediterranean service. The vessel a '1st class iron clad' was moored off the neutral ground Gibraltar on 3 April 1881 and the crew included Francis Cotter a lieutenant in the Royal Marines. He left the ship at the end of the year and was at Plymouth H.Q. from 4 January 1882 and resided at the Royal Marine Barracks, Stonehouse, Plymouth, at his father's death on 24 July that year. The Khedive lost control after the mutiny of the Egyptian Army in 1881 and placed Arabi Pasha a soldier, in command, but being a nationalist this led to a revolt. Sir G. Wolseley was appointed on 4 August 1882 to take a large force to Egypt and Arabi Pasha was exiled after battles at Alexandria and Tel-el-Kebir (near the Suez). Francis joined the S.S. "Quetta" on 6 September 1882 and went on special service being stationed at the garrison at Port Said, Egypt and was involved in the surrender of Fort Ghemilers (sic).

Lieutenant Cotter returned to Plymouth H.Q. on 1 April 1883 and passed an examination for the rank of captain in January 1884 and received a special certificate - "distinguished in tactics". He embarked on the S.S. "Deccan" on 7 May 1884 and returned to the R.M. Battalion at Port Said and then, like his brother, was involved in the 1st Sudan War. He saw considerable action in Egypt and the Sudan and took part in the defence of Suakin near to Port Sudan on the Red Sea from 18 June 1884. He then went on the expedition under Sir G. Graham and was present at the actions at Hasheen (20 March 1885), MacNeill's Zariba, Tofrek (22 March 1885) and a convoy action at Tamai (24 March 1885) and thus received an Egyptian medal and clasp and bronze star. He returned to Plymouth on 17 May 1885 and was promoted to captain on 6 October and passed a course of musketry at Hythe on 8 October - 1st class certificate (score 720 out of 792). H.M.S. "Colossus", an armoured battle ship 1st class, was fitted out at Portsmouth for particular service and commissioned there on 13 April 1886. The large vessel of 9,150 tons was a steel armour plated turret ship with 7,490 horsepower (double action screw). Captain Cotter was then back at sea for a longer period and joined H.M.S. "Colossus" at Portsmouth on 13 April 1886, the day of her commission, and served on her in the Mediterranean until 20 May 1890. He returned to Plymouth again and passed a course in military equitation (horsemanship) at Canterbury in February 1891 and received a special certificate for distinguished ability in law, topography and fortification. He was then placed on recruiting service at Salisbury from 1 July 1891.

Edward and Ann Maria Crocker lived at St. Martin in the Fields, London in the early 19th century, not far from the Cotter family at the Liberty of the Rolls. They had six children baptized at the church: Anna Maria and Edward William (1815), Alfred (1818), Arthur (1819), Matilda (1824) and Rose Catherine (14 October 1825). Alfred Crocker became a surgeon general and like many army men his career took him around the world. He was married to Mary (1833) born Hanwell and had children Jessie H. (1859) Gibraltar, Sydney F. (1865), Bertram E. (1866) both West Indies, and Leonard H. (1868) Horfield, Gloucester-shire. He then lived at Stoke Damerel in Plymouth just across the River Tamar from Saltash and had two children there: Alfred G. (1870) and Herbert J. (1872). He was a friend or relative of John Cotter and was a witness at his wedding on 23 July 1870 and may have been the reason that John retired to that area of England. Indeed the latter used the name Bertram for one of his sons. Alfred Crocker retired surgeon general lived at Rugby Villa, Granada Road, Portsea, in 1881 with his wife Mary, six children and two servants. He died at Portsea in September 1888 and his brothers Edward William at Fulham in 1890 and Arthur at Wandsworth in 1894.

Anson William Henry Cartwright was born at Torquay in 1836 and gained an M.A. at Cambridge and was a minister. He married Rose Catherine Crocker at East Grinstead on 9 April 1863 and they had two children Rose Martha Anson born at Limehouse in 1865 and Katherine Anson born in the Mile End hamlet in 1867 - both at Stepney. He was a clergyman 'without cure of souls' at Brimley House, West Teignmouth, Devon, in 1881 with his wife, two daughters and three servants including Mary A. Bryant from Mile End. Francis G. Cotter met the family through his father and married Rose Martha Anson Cartwright at West Teignmouth on 19 August 1891. He was promoted to major on 6 October 1893 and had a son Francis John A. born at Alderbury (Salisbury) in March 1894. He was in Plymouth on 1 September 1894 then was Instructor of Musketry on 22 January 1895 but the position was suspended when he joined the 'senior majors list' - 29 November. He spent a month at Portsmouth in January 1896 but remained at Plymouth and his daughter Rose Katherine M. was born at East Stonehouse in March 1897. He passed a tactical test that was required to become a lieutenant colonel on 7 June 1897.

"Royal Arthur" a twin-screw cruiser 1st class (7,700 tons) was commissioned at Portsmouth on 4 November 1897 and had 10,000 natural draught power and 12,000 forced draught power. Major Cotter then went to sea for the last time and joined H.M.S. "Royal Arthur" on 4 November 1897, the day of its commission, and sailed to Australia where it replaced the "Orlando" as Flag Ship of the Fleet. He was promoted to lieutenant colonel on 1 November 1900 and finished serving on the vessel on 7 March 1901 when it lost its status as Flag Ship. He spent three years stationed at Chatham from 8 March 1901 although he was living with his wife and two children at Whitchurch near Tavistock on the 1901 census. Anson W.H. Cartwright his father-in-law died at Newton Abbot in June 1903. He became a brevet colonel on 10 February 1904 and went to the Royal Marine Depot at Deal on 24 of that month, the barracks being at Lower Walmer. He went on half pay from 1 November 1906 to 22 April 1908 but was made a colonel 2nd commandant on 23 April and having returned to full pay was at Deal until 21 February 1910. Indeed he gave his wife's address as St. Helen's, Balfour Road, Walmer.

He was made a colonel commandant on 22 February 1910 and finished his service at Portsmouth, retiring as a major general on 21 November 1910 - these later promotions being recorded in the *London Gazette*. He then resided at Woking, Surrey and received an initial pension of £175 per quarter or £700 p.a. He sent a letter from "Kilcarberry", Pembroke Road in Woking on 30 November 1913 and stated: "Dear Nicholls, In reply to your letter of the 27th inst, after due consideration I have decided not to be a candidate for the appointment at Sierra Leone. It is a great concession to have the claims of a general R.M. considered for such an appointment; and I greatly hope that one of our major generals will be selected. Yours sincerely *F. G. Cotter.*" He was held in high esteem to receive such an offer and his pension increased to £252 per quarter or £1,010 p.a. in 1920. He was officially on the retired list on 1 January 1920 and his retirement was listed in the *London Gazette* on 9 January. He then went abroad and died at "Kilcarberry", Doveton Road, Parktown West, Johannesburg, on 24 September 1928. His probate was granted to Rose Martha Anson Cotter widow in London on 26 May 1930 and his effects in England were just £38 19s 1d. Rose Martha Anson Cotter died at "Twirton", The Ridge, Woking, on 5 January 1943 and probate went to Rose Katherine Mary wife of Hugh Gordon Pritchard.

Harry John Cotter was born at Saltash on 10 September 1871 and spent his early years next to the Tamar. Meanwhile, Admiral B.M. Kelly was founder of Kelly College, Tavistock in 1877, which was a boarding school for the sons of naval officers (and gentlemen) and was situated on the edge of Dartmoor. Harry was educated there in the 1880s after his father's decease and then attended the Royal Military Academy, Woolwich in c.1887 and joined the Royal Artillery. He served in the Isazai expedition to the N.W. Frontier of India in late 1892 then married Alice Elizabeth daughter of Rev. G. Armitage at Eton in September 1902 and had one son. He received the Serbian Order of the White Eagle, 4th class, in the First War and had the rank of lieutenant colonel. A number of foreign medals were awarded to British soldiers if no suitable honour was available and the award was nominal - with no connection to the country. He later lived at Ghangora, Dehra Dun north of Roorkee in India but died at sea on 28 June 1921. Alice Elizabeth Cotter widow obtained his probate in London on 8 December that year and his effects were £867 9s 9d - He also had medals for Chitral 1895, China 1900, D.S.O. 1916 and C.I.E. 1918.

Isabella Kate Cotter was born at Saltash in March 1873 and like her father raised herself in society. William Wenmoth Pryn was born at Tredown, Saltash on 21 October 1859, the son of William Pryn (1823) of Saltash Steamboat Co. and Mary Maria Wenmoth. His education took place at College House School, Saltash and Blundells School, Tiverton (founded in 1604) and he had a career as a naval surgeon. He qualified as a gold medallist in 1880 and was house surgeon and resident obstetric at Guy's Hospital, London, then joined the Royal Navy in 1886. William Wenmoth Pryn married Isabella Kate Cotter at St. Stephen's, Saltash in September 1891 and his father William died there on 8 December that year - prob. 24 June 1919. They had children: William (1892), Amy Isabel (18 October 1893) Ascension Island - Richard Harold Cotter (March 1895), Kathleen Mary (March 1901) Saltash. The mother and children were at Saltash with Mary Pryn (77) in 1901 but the father a staff surgeon was away. He was an assistant to the Medical Director-General in 1906-10 and was Fleet Surgeon, Haslar, and Deputy Surgeon General at Chatham, Gibraltar and Plymouth Hospitals. He was Surgeon Rear-Admiral at Plymouth in 1917-19 and was awarded the C.B. in 1918 and K.B.E. in 1919 writing several articles viz. Common Infectious Diseases and the Health of the Navy (1903), Tuberculosis in the Navy 1860-1906 (1908) and Tests for Colour Vision BMJ (1910). He then lived in Sidcup with his wife although died at Red Maies, Stoke Gabriel, Devon, on 20 February 1942 and his probate went to Lloyds Bank and Lady Isabella Kate Pryn. His widow died at "Roborough", 3 Christchurch Road, Sidcup, on 3 April 1960 and probate went to Richard Harold C. Pryn retired army officer, Amy Isabel Davidson widow and Mary Greenstreet married woman.

Bertram Wilkie Cotter was born at Saltash in December 1877 and resided with his mother at 2 Home Park Place in 1891. His career was less notable than his brothers and he was a bank clerk at Langley Burrell near Chippenham in 1901 then married Margaret L. Sprawson at St. Pancras in December 1919. He was also a bank clerk at Bristol in 1920-22 however his wife died at Lymington in March 1927 aged 37 and he then married Alice H. Crowdy at Wareham in December 1931. He lived at "Pentillie", Barnes Lane, Milford on Sea, Hampshire but died at The Grove, Cornwallis Road in Milford on Sea on 30 January 1947 and his probate was granted to Alice Hilda Cotter widow and Charles Sprawson retired bank official his effects £3,302 19s. This was a remarkable story that began with Edward Cotter a humble tailor from Ireland and ended with Lady Isabella.

GEORGE WILLIAM ADDISON

Marindin and Addison the full backs and Goodwyn the half back defended the fortress of the Royal Engineers in the 1872 Cup Final and conceded just one goal in the first half. The Wanderers continued to pressure their opponents in the second and a goal by C.W. Alcock was disallowed offside. The match report states that, "on one occasion a protracted bully raged on the very edge of the Engineers' lines and once during its course the ball was absolutely driven against one of the posts." The Wanderers would no doubt have scored again, "but for the extremely efficient goal-keeping of Captain Merriman." His superior Marindin led the team and was discussed earlier thus the story turns to Addison and Goodwyn the 'backs'.

The cotton and wool industry brought considerable wealth to Lancashire and Yorkshire in the 18-19th centuries with materials and waterpower in the Pennine valleys and a large work force. Indeed the Addisons earned their wealth from wool (in particular) and had their origins in the West Riding of Yorkshire, although a fortuitous match may have influenced matters. Meltham village was located five miles south west of Huddersfield on the new road from that town to Manchester in the parish of Almondbury. There were a number of mills producing woollen cloth most of this being sold at Huddersfield market although there was also a large cotton and silk works owned by Messrs. Brooks, an iron foundry, collieries, fulling mills and dye works. William Brook married Mary Oldfield at Meltham on 30 May 1770 and had children: John (1771), Jonas (1775), Elizabeth (21 June 1777), William (1779), Mary (1783), Ann (1784), James (1786) - *Taylor Hill* and Joseph (1787). William then married Hannah Clapham at Almondbury on 4 September 1788 and had Charles (1792) and with his sons was a mill owner of some note.

William Brook & Sons were wool-staplers in Meltham and had considerable success but the father died in 1806 and the name changed to Jonas Brook & Bros. The business included William, Joseph and Charles who also helped to start a Huddersfield bank (under that name) - they must not be confused with Joseph Brook a banker in the town at the start of the 19th century. James Brook married Jane Leigh at Almondbury on 15 June 1808 and had a son William Leigh Brook at Meltham in 1809. A commercial crisis struck in 1816 and the bank suspended payments but remained successful and James and Joseph Brook agreed a 'deed' with Benjamin Wilson of the banking family in 1818. The agreement was cemented as Jonas Brook married Hannah Wilson (a sister) at Mirfield on 10 January 1820. James Brook controlled the bank in Huddersfield whilst William and Joseph handled its concerns in London and they formed the Huddersfield Banking Co. in 1827 - Joseph was a director and the other four brothers had shares. They diversified at Meltham and were manufacturers of thread and cotton warps in 1827 and sewing cotton manufacturers and silk throwsters in 1834. Richard Thornton a merchant of Hamburg owned "Thornton Lodge" in Huddersfield and rented it to James Brook in 1834 and to his son William Leigh Brook in 1840. The latter married Charlotte Armitage on 20 May 1840 then travelled abroad and made his last will at the Burgher Hospital, Cologne, Prussia on 19 September 1855. He left Meltham Hall to his son James William and the residue to his five children: James, Clara Jane and 'reputed offspring' Charles Armitage, Charlotte Amelia and Sarah Helen. William Leigh Brook died in Cologne and his executors Charles Brook and John and Edward Armitage proved his will on 4 June 1856. Joseph Brook died in 1858 and Charles Brook in 1869.

Ten miles to the north the town of Halifax was a centre for the cloth trade from the 15th century and the oldest buildings were located around St. John's Church whilst the Piece Hall, a market for cloth merchants, was built in 1779. George Wilson Addison was born in Halifax in 1788. He soon followed his ancestors into the wool trade and became acquainted with the Brook family of Meltham and travelled down to London. George Wilson Addison of Almondbury married Elizabeth Brook by licence at St. Luke's, Old Street on 3 January 1809. John Busby was the minister and John Addison and William Brook were the witnesses (the latter was in London for the bank). The couple returned to Meltham and George worked with his relatives in the cloth trade and they had three children baptized there: Martha (15 Oct 1809), Mary Ann (28 March 1813) and William Brook (1 January 1815). They then left the town and George Addison was born in Chester in 1817.

Meanwhile, Bradford had grown in the Industrial Revolution and its impressive architecture included the Town Hall and the Wool Exchange whilst worsted, one of its products, was a rough cloth composed of woollen yarn. George Wilson Addison soon went into business on his own account and became a mill owner at Bowling south of Bradford being described as a worsted spinner of Bradley Mills, Bowling Green in 1822 (Dalton). He then formed the partnership of Addison & Roper, worsted spinners, at Bowling Gate in 1828-29 and daughter Martha Addison married Joshua Healey Riley at Bradford on 10 September 1829 - they had eight children. There was a *Deed of Settlement* to the value of £10,000 dated 31 January 1834 between George W. Addison his wife Elizabeth, his four children and Joshua Healey Riley (in the first part) and Charles Brook of Healey House and William Leigh Brook of Huddersfield gent cotton spinners (in the second part). The Brook family paid the money for the benefit of wife Elizabeth during her lifetime and (then) for her four children - this was noted in his will. Addison & Roper were worsted spinners at Prospect Mill, Bowling in 1834 however the partnership was dissolved and a new company G.W. Addison & Sons, worsted spinners, was formed by 1842 - the family then lived at Hallfield.

The company were wool-staplers and worsted spinners at Hall Lane, Bowling and their residence Hall Ings in 1845 whilst son George was married in 1847 (see below). George W. Addison a worsted spinner resided at Hall Lane in 1851 with his wife Eliza, children Mary Ann, William B. (worsted spinner), grandchildren William and Fanny Riley born Berlin and three servants, although he had moved to Springbank Place in 1853. George W. Addison made his last will on 5 August 1854 and first left £100 to John Douglas merchant and his household goods and carriages etc. and £100 to wife Elizabeth, the former then to his sons. He listed the *Deed of Settlement* for £10,000 dated 31 Jan 1834 between his family and Charles Brook of Healey House cotton spinner now silk throwster and William Leigh Brook of Huddersfield gent now of Meltham Hall cotton spinner. The repayment was void if 5% interest on £5,000 was paid to them during his life and to his wife after his decease and then to his children as tenants-in-common. Daughter Martha had died on 3 September 1845 thus her share went to her husband (and eight children) whilst Mary Ann still lived with him - Charles and William Leigh Brook were to be freed from any obligation and suitably paid.

He left three amounts of £4,000 in trust to his sons and John Douglas to invest: (1) for his wife, £2,000 to go to William Brook and £2,000 to George if the interest was paid to her (2) for his grandchildren George Elizabeth Martha Ann Agnes Albert William and Fanny Riley, £2,000 after 1 year and £2,000 after 2 years (3) for his daughter Mary Ann plus £1,000 for her sole use. The residue of his estate went to his sons, in trust, and William Hirst warehouse manager and Thomas Brook of Huddersfield solicitor were witnesses (Brook, Freeman & Batley). The family remained in business at Bowling but took a house north of the city and George Wilson Addison worsted spinner died after a long illness at 8 Clifton Villas, Manningham on 25 January 1861 aged 73. His two sons and John Douglas of Prestnall Hey, Heaton Mersey, Manchester merchant proved his will at Wakefield on 28 February 1861 and his effects were under £35,000. Clifton Villas was just north of Valley Parade - home of Bradford City from the 1900s.

Elizabeth lived at 8 Clifton Villas in 1861 with Mary Ann, William B. (worsted spinner employing 360 hands), granddaughter Fanny Riley, visitor Caroline Hirst and three servants. G.W. Addison & Sons were worsted spinners at 91 Hall Lane in 1861 and 151 Hall Lane in 1863 (otherwise the *Bowling Road Works*) but had left by 1867 and were also absent in 1872. The family moved south and resided at 3 Litfield Place, Clifton near Bristol. Elizabeth Addison widow of George Wilson a gentleman died there on 19 Feb 1867 aged 90, whilst William Brook Addison retired worsted spinner from Meltham was at 3 Litfield Place in 1881 with sister Mary Ann and three servants. William B. Addison died there on 15 August 1882 and probate went to Thomas Garnett of Oakwood, Bingley and of Bradford, stuff merchant, and John Addison of Eldon Place stuff manufacturer (nephew) on 28 September - £124,113 1s 3d.

George Addison was born in Chester in 1817 and grew up at Hall Lane, Bowling then worked with his father in the worsted spinning business - being listed at Hallfield in 1842. They did not operate in isolation and raw materials and markets were around the country hence they set up a factory in Scotland. The H.E.I.C. introduced the patterned shawl to England in c.1775 and they were fashionable from 1790-1870 however the imports were very expensive and cheap copies were made at home. The handloom was adapted to make the shawls in 1812 and the Jacquard loom (with punched cards) was introduced in 1823 and the price came down further - these being made of wool. The Paisley shawl with its Kashmir pattern was sold to the mass-market in 1840-75 but once they became common they lost their appeal. Paisley was a centre for textiles and cotton in the 19th century and the leading producer of the shawls (thus taking its name). G.W. Addison & Sons were producers of raw materials in Bradford; indeed a wool-stapler grades the producer's wool and sells to the manufacturer, worsted being a rough woollen yarn. They supplied their product to the Paisley manufacturers in the 1840s and to reduce delivery costs set up their own factory in the town: G.W. Addison & Sons (spinners) at Bradford Woollen Yarn Warehouse, 15 Causeyside Street, Paisley in 1844.

The Orr family were influential and prominent in Paisley in the 18-19th century and had a large cotton mill however their history was difficult to trace, the name being very common in the town. William Orr was born in Paisley c.1762 and was a manufacturer who went to Dublin and brought back the art of printing on linen. He married Jean Maxwell in the town on 23 April 1785 and had several children from 1786-1806 including Janet baptized on 11 January 1790. Robert Orr a merchant became a partner in the newly formed Paisley Union Bank in 1788 and Orr Square was in the town. John Orr elder brother of William was also involved in the cotton industry and married Agnes Anderson at Paisley on 29 June 1782. The couple had ten children in 1783-1805 and their first son John Orr was born on 18 May 1784 and baptized at the Low Church on 26 May. The father was then a magistrate and Provost of Paisley in 1812-14 however there were soon some dramatic developments.

Indeed the family owned Underwood Cotton Mill in Paisley in the early 19th century and the son John Orr was a partner in the firm. There was trouble in the town in early 1820 when a number of mill owners reduced the workers' wages. The employees of the Underwood Mill went on strike to try and stop a similar decrease and John Orr junior was the target of much discontent and even hatred. He worked at the mill with uncle William and indeed was betrothed to Janet his daughter. In the first instance he returned home one evening and a shot was discharged at him outside his house. He was unharmed but worse was to follow. There were those who wanted direct action and Cameron and Lafferty who worked at Underwood Mill and two others met at O'Donnell's Pub in Causeyside Street in early December 1820. They made a plan and conspired to assassinate their employer at his uncle's house. One of them was to disguise himself with a greatcoat and neck-cloth, and when his partner handed a letter to Orr to distract him, would fire two pistols into his body.

The plot was to be carried out on Saturday 16 December 1820 and John Orr dined that evening at his uncle William's house in Causeyside Street. Two rough looking men came to the door and declined an invitation to go into the parlour stating their business was urgent! The housekeeper informed Orr that they wished to see him and as he reached the street door two loaded pistols were discharged. By a miracle they missed him and the plot failed thus the four conspirators ran off towards Glasgow. They decided to stop at the Paisley Tollhouse on Glasgow Road in the hope of concealing themselves in its public rooms. A maidservant took them into a backroom but was suspicious of their appearance and informed her master that, "robbers were in the house." Indeed in their haste one still had his face concealed and the pistols were seen on the table through a keyhole. They were not apprehended at this point but a reward was offered and news of the event was soon all around the town.

The family were not swayed by this threat to their lives and then made a bold statement. John Orr of this parish and Janet Orr (of the Low Church) were married in Paisley High Church on 18 December 1820, just two days after the assassination attempt. Rev. Robert Burns the minister of St. George's, High Church or Church of Scotland performed the ceremony. A reward of 20 guineas did the trick and the four conspirators were taken into custody a few days later. There was a trial at the High Court in Edinburgh and Cameron and two of the others were found guilty, although the case against Lafferty was not proved. The sentence was a public whipping through the streets of Paisley and then transportation. It was carried out in April 1821 and large crowds lined the streets of the town and the Paisley Rifle Corps guarded the jail where the three were held. The culprits were tied to a cart and with a large number of troops, sheriffs and police escorting them were taken to five places in the town and at each received fifteen lashes (75 in total). The large crowd of spectators stayed silent and with so many troops, there was no disorder. The men were taken back to jail after the gruesome ordeal and transported for life. This was a salutary warning to aggrieved mill workers, but as this was attempted murder they may have been let off 'lightly' by the authorities.

John and Janet Orr then had six children born in Paisley: John (1823), Jane (13 December 1824), William (1826), Robert (1828), Agnes (20 July 1831) and James (1833). John Orr junior & Co. were cotton spinners at Underwood Street whilst John Orr was a shawl manufacturer at 39 Causeyside Street and Mrs. John Orr was at 57 Causeyside Street - all in 1831. Indeed he held many offices of trust in the town and was a J.P. and like his father the Provost of Paisley in 1832. During his tenure in that office he held meetings regarding a scheme for a reservoir at Nethercraigs to provide 48 million cubic feet of water p.a. A letter dated 3 January 1833 stated: "The calculations have already been examined and approved by several intelligent gentlemen, but the scheme has not yet been examined by a professional engineer."

H.M. Commissioners then sent out a list of 79 questions about the employment of children in factories. John Orr replied for the company and stated: "Only cotton spinning takes place and the works were erected in 1790-92 with a small addition in 1830. Ventilation is by the windows and all upright shafts are fenced off and steam at 36 horsepower is used. Children aged under-12 are employed (he gave no reason for this). The youngest are 9-10 years and are paid by the spinning operatives and the older ones paid by the owners. The work is done at a rate of 12½ hours per day within the *Factory Hours Act*. The work continues all year except for two sacramental fast days, two days idle at New Year's Day, one on the race day, and probably two others. The cost of production is indeed enhanced by a reduction in hours. We do not work at night and believe it should be prohibited. No corporal punishment is allowed and there have been no complaints since the works came into our possession in 1810. We have one large dwelling house for 35 families that is cleaned daily and the other workers live in the town. Those trained from infancy make the best workers. The cotton mills in the area adhere to the Act but not all of the thread works. I believe the present law has been shamefully evaded in England in particular but I am not prepared to suggest a remedy and am not aware of any improper treatment of children in my works." (3 June 1833)

John Orr died during a business trip to Liverpool on 17 June 1841 however John Orr junior & Co. were still cotton spinners at Underwood Street in 1844. The Addison family then traded at 15 Causeyside Street - a cobbled road south of the station, County Square, Municipal Buildings and White Cart Water. They were acquainted with the Orr family and almost certainly did business with them supplying raw materials for the production of shawls. George Addison (31) merchant of Bradford married Jane Orr (23) of Underwood at Paisley on 15 December 1847. Banns were called three days earlier and Rev. Alexander Rennison a minister of St. George's performed the ceremony. George W. Addison & Son, yarn merchants, traded at 14 Causeyside in 1851-52 and George C. Campbell their salesman lived at 32 Glen

Street. This was the last entry for the company in Paisley and the family then concentrated their efforts in Bradford.

George Addison lived at Chestnut Cottage, Daisy Hill on the western edge of Bradford near Manningham Farm, and had sons George William (18 September 1849) and Charles (March 1851). He was described as a worsted spinner and lived there on 31 March 1851 with wife Jane (26), George Wm (1), Charles (3m), Agnes Orr (19) gentlewoman and four servants. George Addison manufacturer & spinner lived there until 1853 and Bradford Royal Infirmary is now on the site whilst cottages remain at Daisy Hill. He moved nearby to the affluent area of Calverley (Bolton) in 1854 and had children: Henry (11 June 1854), Elizabeth Janet (December 1855), John (June 1857), Jane (December 1858) and Wilson (March 1861). George Addison, worsted spinner, lived at *Bolton House*, Calverley in 1861 with his wife and seven children including George W. (11) a scholar. There were also five servants and a coachman's cottage. His father died in 1861 and son Arthur was born at Calverley in March 1864, but G.W. Addison & Sons ceased trading in c.1864-65 and like his brother he moved south.

George Addison esquire retired and lived at 1 Catherine Place, Walcot St. Swithin, Bath near to the Royal Crescent from 1865. This three-storey property of light-brown sandstone was at the southeast corner of an elegant square and had Classical window features and roof cornice, although the main door with column and pediment was at the side - Goodwyn lived at no. 14 (see below). They were affluent hence two sons went to Cheltenham College namely George W. (1863-66) and Henry (1867-70). The couples last son Robert Addison was born at Bath in September 1865. George Addison a captain of the Yeoman Cavalry lived at 1 Catherine Place in 1871 with Jane, six children and five servants (George W., Charles and John were absent). They then moved to Weston-Super-Mare for the sea air in late 1873 but they received no benefit. Henry died there on 6 January 1874 whilst George Addison gentleman died of apoplexy at 2 Atlantic Terrace West in Weston-Super-Mare on 27 August 1874 aged 57. George William Addison of Brompton Barracks was informant.

Atlantic Road and Atlantic Road South were situated between Paragon and Highbury Roads near Anchor Head; and overlooked Madeira Cove and the extensive sands of Weston Bay. The area was on the steep incline of Worlebury Hill with the long sweep of Royal Arcade below and views across the Atlantic towards Brean Down. There are some large Victorian houses on the north side of Atlantic Road next to Holy Trinity Church that may have been Atlantic Terrace West. After George's decease the family moved to 1 Madeira Villas, Atlantic Road, Weston-Super-Mare and Jane Addison "annuitant" lived there in 1881 with Jeannie, Wilson an insurance clerk and three servants. Charles Addison (1851) of 44 Portsmouth Street next Oxford Street, Manchester was named as next-of-kin in the army records of brother George but resided at Upper House Farm, Basildon in 1881. He was unmarried and a farmer of 211 acres employing 5 men and 3 boys. Arthur (17) and Robert (15) resided at Clifton House, Clifton College, Percival Road, in 1881 near their uncle's home. Arthur was at the school in 1878-81 and was a solicitor at 18 Clare Street, Bristol; Robert left in July 1882 and worked for a time at the Stock Exchange.

1 Catherine Place, Bath. Worsted wealth - The Addison home in 1865-73.

Jane Addison living on her own means remained at 1 Madeira Villas, Atlantic Road and lived there with John, Jane and Wilson and three servants in 1891 and with 'Jean' in 1901. Their family had dispersed at the latter date and Charles was a retired farmer in Hastings, Wilson on his own means in Portsmouth, Arthur a solicitor in Bristol and Robert on his own means in Westminster. Jane Addison was still at 1 Madeira Villas until 1906 and died at Weston-Super-Mare (Axbridge) in June 1916 aged 91. A 1933 directory lists Madeira Villa (18), Madeira Mansions (20) and Rockhill Mansions (22) from Hamilton Road to the corner with Highbury Road. Today, "Madeira Mansions", 20 Atlantic Road is on the corner with Highbury Road and is a 2-3 storey grey brick building with yellow detail and floral designs at the roof (semi-detached). It may have been 1 Madeira Villas or perhaps it was the next property (18), which is of a similar style.

But what was happening on the playing fields of Cheltenham? There was the small matter of the 'Battle of the Addisons' and we ask - who played in the 1872 Final? This was a problem similar to that seen regarding Bogle and Cotter. John Copley Addison the son of John was born in Glasgow on 19 August 1852 and his father later resided at Castle Hill, Maryport in Cumberland. He attended Cheltenham College in January 1866 to December 1869 and went to the Royal Military Academy, Woolwich from 1870-72, residing there as a gentleman cadet on 2 April 1871. He was an exemplary student and passed out with a 1st Engineer's Prize (Pollock) and qualified in fortification, chemistry, physics, military drawing and military history. He became a lieutenant in the Royal Engineers on 6 July 1872 and was then posted to the School of Military Engineering, Chatham from 15 August 1872 to 27 August 1874. He spent many years in Bengal from 23 October 1874 and took part in the Afghan War (1878-80) being part of the Kurum Field Force under Generals J.E. Gordon and J. Watson - gaining a medal. He was promoted to captain on 6 January 1884 and married Elizabeth Mary Ward on 9 September that year but died at Hoshangabad in India on 22 June 1887, and his widow of 46 Hamilton Terrace, St. John's Wood proved his will. This was the profile of an academic man and it seems unlikely he played in the Cup Final since he arrived at Chatham after the game was played on 16 March 1872. There was also Henry Addison who was born in Bradford on 11 June 1854 and attended Cheltenham College from August 1867 to December 1870, however he was too young and not a member of the Royal Engineers - died Weston-Super-Mare 6 January 1874. There is, thus, only one profile that fits the mould and that life is now discussed.

George William Addison was born at Chestnut Cottage, Daisy Hill on 18 September 1849 and spent his early years there and at Calverley (from 1854). He was the first of the family to go south and went to Cheltenham College from January 1863 to December 1866, his family moving to Bath in 1865. He was in Boyne House with Renny-Tailyour who was the same age and a member of the school football XI in 1866. It seems likely he played football and cricket with him and the association paid dividends in later life. He went to the Royal Military Academy, Woolwich in 1867 and was a lieutenant in the Royal Engineers on 7 July 1869. His first posting was the School of Military Engineering, Chatham from 15 August 1869 to 30 November 1871. He joined their football team and the team photo shows him to be a stoic and moustached gentleman. He had leave in late 1871 but was stationed at Brighton from 16 January 1872, with duties at Newhaven, although he played in the Final at the Oval on 16 March that year. He was posted to the S.M.E. Chatham on 23 April 1873 and joined Marindin, Merriman and Renny-Tailyour to play in the 1874 Cup Final, although they lost 2-0 to Oxford University. He did not take part in the 1875 Cup Final victory but possibly played in earlier rounds.

John Stevenson married Eliza Newcombe at St. David's, Exeter on 30 December 1809 and moved to Kenton, Devon and a son George Robert Stevenson was baptized there 11 October 1815. Not to be confused with George Robert Stephenson (1819-1905) the nephew of George and cousin of Robert - the railway family. There is also no apparent connection to Marindin. George R. Stevenson married Anna Maria Denham Cookes at St. James the Apostle, Dover on 14 February 1842 who was born Owermoigne, Dorset in c.1823. Their children were born in several places viz. Anna Harriet (1845) and George (1846) Starcross near Kenton Devon, Marianne (1847) Prestbury Gloucester, Florence (1848) Milan, Montagu (1849) Cheltenham, and Caroline Augusta (Sept 1850) Hawkhurst in Kent. George Stevenson a landed proprietor lived at "Tongs Wood", Hawkhurst near Gun Green in 1851 with his wife Anna Maria, six children, Marie Rufenacht governess of Thun, Switzerland and seven servants. They had no connection to Stephenson's "Rocket" but soon made a railway association.

Edward Ladd Betts was declared bankrupt in 1866-68 (see Ch. 6) and mortgaged Preston Hall to Thomas Brassey the railway contractor. His son Henry Arthur Brassey married Anna Harriet Stevenson at Chelsea on 24 June 1866 and the couple moved to Preston Hall, Aylesford in 1867 - they had a family of eleven children. Henry A. Brassey M.P. lived at the house in 1881 with his wife Anna, six of his children, Florence M. Stevenson sister-in-law, several visitors and 25 servants. He sat for Sandwich as a Liberal from Dec 1868 until he retired in 1885 and was Sheriff of Kent in 1890. Henry was clearly very rich however he died at Preston Hall on 13 May 1891 aged 50. His eldest son Henry Leonard C. Brassey was 1st Baron Brassey of Apethorpe whilst daughter Hilda Madeline married Charles Henry Gordon-Lennox at St. George's Hanover Square on 8 June 1893 and Evelyn Mildred married Granville Charles

The Upper Barracca Gardens.
Addison was in the Torpedo Service in 1875-77.

Gresham Leveson-Gower on 3 February 1894. His son Harold Ernest a lieutenant in the Royal Horse Guards died on 16 July 1916 whilst Edgar Hugh and Edwin Percival rose to the rank of lieutenant colonel.

George W. Addison a lieutenant R.E. of Queen's Gate Terrace was married to Caroline Augusta Stevenson of Cromwell House, Cromwell Road at St. Stephen's Church, Kensington on 30 June 1875 (see Merriman Ch. 10). Indeed the bridegroom may have lodged with the Rich family (see Ch. 8). J.H. Cookes rector of Tadmarton, Oxon performed the ceremony and G.R. Stevenson and M. Stevenson were witnesses. The attractive church with its miniature chapter house, and school-style entrance, was at the southern end of Gloucester Road. Lieutenant Addison was sent to Portsmouth on 21 August 1875 but was rocketed into a new dimension when he joined the Torpedo Service in Malta on 24 November 1875 (the island is discussed under Cotter). His wife accompanied him and a son George Henry was born in Valletta at 9 a.m. on 13 May 1876 and was baptized at Queen Adelaide's Church in the town on 30 June that year - C. Melville clerk in Holy Orders performed the baptism.

St. Paul's Anglican pro-Cathedral was built on the site of the Auberge d'Allemagne home of the German Knights in 1839-44 and looked out over Marsamxett Harbour towards Sliema. The Dowager Queen Adelaide financed its construction and William Scamp who was the architect employed the neo-Classical style. The main façade had a portico of eight Ionic columns but a Gothic spire rose to 200 feet at the west end and was a local landmark. Six Corinthian columns lined both aisles and there were pilasters in the cupola at the east end, but the ceiling was plain. In later years the organ and its pipes came from Chester whilst the altar was moved to the more spacious west end after the Second War. J. Cleugh D.D. was the minister of St. Paul's from 1844-77 and was followed by H. White M.A. in 1877-78 and E.A. Hardy M.A. in 1878-96. The church was part of the European diocese and Holy Trinity, Gibraltar was the main cathedral thus it was called a pro-Cathedral and served south and east Europe.

The 'Act of Birth' of George Henry Addison was registered at Valletta police station on 4 July 1876 before Calcedonio Bonavia and Edward Barbar (impiegato civile) who were witnesses - G.W. Addison made the declaration. A small Classical building with large roof pediment and similar features above three windows is situated at the base of St. Andrew's Bastion beside the ferry to Sliema. Inscribed within the pediment is 'Police Station' and this was the building where the registration took place although today it is a café (birth records are with the Public Registry). Lieutenant Addison spent nearly two years in Malta and presumably carried out work on the defences and other infrastructure like roads. He resided in Valletta and as an officer was probably billeted in the town rather than at Fort St. Elmo. A steep hill and steps climb up from the police station to St. John Cavalier, and in the northwest corner near the Ponsonby memorial is Triq L-Inġinieri or Sappers Street. It is only 100 yards long and the buildings three-storey with white-yellow stonework and the typical wooden bay windows seen within the city. There is a small side street called Sqaq L-Inġinieri or Sappers Lane running off on the north side and Queen Alexandra Mansion (1901) is on South Street. The eight main streets were established at the time of the Knights and Sappers Street was

St. Paul's pro-Cathedral. The Carmelite dome is to the ric

The Engineers' Quarter. Near to the Ponsonby memorial.

no doubt named after the British arrived - it may have been where Addison and other Royal Engineers lived.

His wife returned home first and a daughter Violet Florence was born at Weston-Super-Mare on 9 July 1877 although she was baptized at St. James's, Dover. Lieutenant Addison joined the Telegraph Corp on 10 August 1877 and was stationed at the P.O. Telegraph Service at Bristol in 1877-79 and at Aldershot in 1879-80. His third child Arthur Mervyn was born at the latter on 14 July 1880 and registered as 'Male' Addison at Farnham in September. He was at the War Office, Whitehall and aide-de-camp to Major General T.L.J. Gallwey Inspector General of Fortifications from 23 August 1880. George W. Addison lieutenant R.E. lived at 20 Elm Park Gardens, Fulham Road, Chelsea, in 1881 with his wife and children, George R. Stevenson J.P. Kent, Anne M.D. Stevenson, Montague C.J. Stevenson wine merchant and servant. This was a four-storey grey-brick house with a bay window at the ground floor, plaster-detail at the third floor and white roof cornice. It was an austere building on the west side and remains today but has been altered and the entrance is at no. 22. The family lived at this address for at least five years.

He was promoted to captain on 7 July 1881 and was secretary to the R.E. Committee at Chatham from 20 December 1882 but was at the G.P.O. Telegraphs, New Cross from 4 December 1884 to July 1885. His most notable position, however, was assistant private secretary to the Right Hon. W.H. Smith, Secretary of State for War, in August 1885 to February 1886. William Henry Smith (1792-1865) son of Henry Walter ran his father's newsagents at the Strand in 1812 and took advantage of the railway boom. His son William Henry Smith (1825-91) joined the business in 1846 and made the company a family name - mainly selling at railway stations. He was a Conservative M.P. in 1868, First Lord of the Admiralty in 1877 and Secretary of State for War in 1885-86 and 1886-87. Meanwhile three children were born at Chelsea: Gladys Ethel (21 March 1883), Audrey Mildred (11 May 1884) and Muriel (24 December 1885) all baptized at St. Peter's, Cranley Gardens near the Addisons' home.

The father returned to work at the G.P.O. Telegraphs, London on 1 March 1886 and was promoted to major on 1 April 1888, but left the position on 31 October and was briefly at Weymouth then had a few months at Portsmouth from December 1888. He was acting commander 'Telegraph Battalion' at the Postal Telegraphs, London on 16 September 1889 a post he held 4 years 288 days. George W. Addison major R.E. lived at 54 Courtfield Gardens, Kensington in 1891-92 with wife Caroline, five children (not Arthur M.), four servants and butler. The five-storey house was opposite to St. Jude's Church and had a columned porch entrance with white stucco ground floor and balcony, although the upper floors had yellow-brown brick with windows and pediments in white. The property still remains near Cromwell Road and the family lived in the district for the next 50 years. Indeed Ada Melvill Rich was at 72 Courtfield Gardens in 1888 and Archibald Leitch at Barkston Gardens in the 1930s. George was then appointed Inspector of Railways at the Board of Trade on 1 July 1894, his main concerns being telegraphic and general electric development, whilst he was made a lieutenant colonel on 29 March 1895. He continued in this appointment for a period of 5 years 92 days and shared these duties with Major Marindin (1877-97) and Lieutenant Colonel Rich (1861-91) but there was soon a dramatic change of direction.

Edward Cecil Guinness 1st Lord Iveagh contacted him in 1899 and asked him to be his personal assistant in England. George duly accepted the honour and became a director of Guinness on 3 August

1899, finishing at the Board of Trade on 30 September that year. It seems likely he gained this position through his old school friend Renny-Tailyour who had a similar appointment in Ireland at the time (see Ch. 8). Lieutenant Colonel Addison retired from the army on 4 October 1899 having served 30 years 89 days and had a pension of £365 p.a. - he had moved to 16 Ashburn Place, Kensington in 1901. The property was near to Courtfield Gardens and he remained there for the rest of his life, although it is no longer present. Two daughters were married at Kensington: Gladys E. to Charles B.B. Thompson in December 1913 and Muriel to Stephen A.H. Trumpler in March 1915. He then worked for Guinness in London and no doubt liased with Renny-Tailyour in Ireland especially when the latter was Managing Director in 1913-19. Indeed Addison may have consulted with Lord Iveagh at Elveden Hall, his stately mansion in Suffolk. There are, however, few records of his time at Guinness and it appears he was a non-executive 'director' with role of consultant, who kept his papers at home or in his London office - he had few dealings in Dublin. The Times suggests that Addison 'terminated his connexion with the firm of Guinness' when Lord Iveagh died in 1927, however the Guinness Archives have confirmed this to be incorrect. Indeed he corresponded with T.B. Case (Man Dir) in Dublin regarding travel arrangements etc. for board meetings there, and in London, in the 1930s and was a director until his death.

George William Addison died at 16 Ashburn Place in South Kensington on 8 November 1937 aged 88; his obituary was in the Times two days later: "He was a well-known and popular officer of the Corps, distinguished for his personal charm, professional ability, and skill at games. He chose to retire early and follow a civil career.... W.F.H. Stafford and C.V. Wingfield-Stratford (who won the Cup) are still living." He had a successful career yet his participation in the Cup (60 years earlier) was given equal merit with the other events. His funeral was at St. Jude's Church on 11 November and a large number of people attended: Mrs. G.W. Addison, Major General and Mrs. G.H. Addison, Colonel and Mrs. A.M. Addison, Miss Addison, Miss Audrey Addison, Rev C.B. and Mrs. Broughton-Thompson, Mr. and Mrs. Stephen Trumpler, the Stevenson family, Hilda Duchess of Richmond and Gordon, Sir Leonard Brassey, Lt. Col. Edgar and Edwin Brassey, Earl of Iveagh, members of the Guinness Trust, United Service Club, Trade Marks and Patents Federation, Agricultural Institute and Lister Institute, Miss May Marindin and Mrs. Pelham G von Donop (her husband R.E. played for England in 1873/75 and in the 1875 Cup Final). The burial was at Kensington Cemetery, Gunnersbury and a plain large cross memorial was erected stating: "In loving memory of George William Addison Lieut-Colonel R.E. (*dates*)."

His probate was granted to George Henry Addison retired major general, Arthur Mervyn Addison lieutenant colonel and Stephen Alfred Hermann Trumpler master Supreme Court of Judicature on 21 December, his effects being £52,549 1s 9d. Caroline Augusta Addison died at 69 Courtfield Gardens on 10 October 1938 and probate went to George Henry Addison C.B. C.M.G. D.S.O., Arthur Mervyn Addison retired and Stephen Trumpler judge. 69 Courtfield Gardens was a Regency house now apartments and was similar to no. 72 discussed in relation to Rich (see Ch. 8). G.W. Addison had a life far removed from Bradford's mills and spent most of his career in England, holding important positions at the War Office, Board of Trade and with Guinness. He was less adventurous than some of his colleagues in the Engineers, however his sons had distinguished army careers.

George Henry Addison was born in Malta on 13 May 1876 and was educated at Wellington College and R.M.A. Woolwich. He joined the Engineers in 1895, becoming a lieutenant in 1898. He served with honour in South Africa (1899-1902) and was awarded the Queen's medal 3 clasps and the King's medal 2 clasps and married Margaret Henderson in 1905, having a son and daughter. He was promoted to adjutant and major in 1914 and was highly decorated in the First War viz. D.S.O (1915), brevet lieutenant colonel, Order of St. Anne of Russia 3rd class (September 1916) and C.M.G. (1918). He received Légion d'Honneur (Chevalier), Ordre de Leopold (Officer) and Belgian Croix de Guerre in 1919 (brother Arthur M. of the Royal Artillery was badly wounded in the war). He attended King's College, Cambridge in 1920-23 and graduated with a B.A. (honours) in mechanical science and was a lieutenant colonel in 1922. He became a member of the Institute of Mechanical Engineers in 1924 and a colonel in 1926, being posted to the War Office in 1927-30. He was Chief Engineer at Aldershot in 1930-31, promoted to major general in 1931 and Engineer-in-Chief for India from 1932-36. He received the C.B. in 1933 (not confinement to barracks) and retired in 1936 however was financial adviser for Army H.Q. India in 1936-37. He rejoined from September 1939-1941 and was an honorary member of the Institute of Structural Engineers (1940) and colonel commandant R.E. (1940-46). His wife Margaret died in 1946 and he married Winifred daughter of Col. Sir William Morris and widow of Col. A.D. Legard in 1947. He died at "Lyon House", 14 Aldersey Road, Guildford, on 5 February 1964.

ALFRED GEORGE GOODWYN

The Goodwyn family had a story similar to Addison and were involved in brewing however also took part in an important piece of colonial history. Indeed A.G. Goodwyn held a notable place in football history, playing as a back, and also had an interesting army career. Henry Goodwyn was born at Great Massingham, Norfolk ten miles from King's Lynn in c.1719 and married Frances Young at Ashwicken (with Leziate) by licence on 25 January 1744, his bride being born at East Walton in c.1723. The couple moved to London and had at least four children: Henry c.1745, Frances baptized St. John Smith Square, Westminster on 5 July 1753, Robert baptized St. Paul's, Deptford on 13 May 1755 and Anna Maria c. 1760. The family settled in Deptford, Kent although it is uncertain how they made a living and Henry Goodwyn junior married Elizabeth Gray at St. Paul's, Deptford on 29 September 1766 and had four children there: Mary (1767), Elizabeth (1768), Catherine (1770), and Amelia (c.1776) who was born Greenwich. Frances Goodwyn married Rev. Julius Hutchinson at Enfield on 13 August 1773 and had a son Julius (1780) born Ware, who was a lawyer, and six children born Hatfield in 1782-93.

The Red Lion Brewery, Lower East Smithfield was started in 1492 and was between the Tower of London and Wapping beside the Thames. Several people had interests in the brewery through the centuries and Robert the Earl of Leicester was freeholder in Elizabethan times whilst Sir John Parsons owned it in the 1660s and was Lord Mayor in 1703 (died 1717). His son Humphrey Parsons succeeded him and was Lord Mayor in 1730/40 but sold the brewery to Sir John Hynde Cotton of Park Place, St. James's and Madingley, Cambridge in 1745. The latter died in 1752 and his son (of the same name and title) then owned the brewery with a Mr. Dickinson - possibly Marshe Dickinson of Dunstable, Lord Mayor 1756, whose will was proved 11 February 1765. Henry Goodwyn although based in Deptford purchased shares in the business and became a partner in the Red Lion Brewery in the 1760s - his will mentions articles dated 8 November 1766. Henry, his eldest son, was also involved in the brewery and had seven more children with his wife Elizabeth who were baptized at St. Botolph's, Aldgate: Frances (1779), Harriet (1780), Anne Delicia (1781), Charlotte (1783), Henry Robert (1784), Sophia (1785), Thomas Wildman (1788) *Greenwich* and Charles Samuel (1790). Their address was the Brew-house Lower East Smithfield and the church was only ¼-mile away from there.

Henry Goodwyn like many others learned his trade in a long established concern and even had his own malt house in 1784, although it provided only a small part of his needs. He then had plans to 'modernize' the business thus the Red Lion Brewery played a major part in Britain's industrial history. James Watt, and the development of the steam engine, was previously discussed in the sections regarding Lubbock (Ch. 7) and Muirhead (Ch. 8) however the story also plays a role here. Boulton and Watt used 'reciprocating' engines to pump-out Cornish mines until 1782 then added rotative motion to drive industrial machinery in mills. The first was installed at Bradley in late 1782 and worked a tilt hammer, whilst the second demonstrated steam milling at Soho. The porter brewers were already advanced in terms of industrial maturity thus it was no surprise that they were 'first' to take up Watt's invention. The significant development was the sun and planet gear with its parallel motion, since the brewers would not install engines for pumping alone - they also needed to replace the horse-wheel (that grinded malt) and the mill horses.

Henry Goodwyn of the Red Lion Brewery realised the potential, although Robert Barclay of Thrale & Co. Southwark was also interested, thus he visited the Soho Works and after consulting with his partners sent a firm proposal for an engine in a letter dated 17 April 1784. He laid out his requirements as follows: "It is to do the work of four strong horses regularly and constantly.... to turn the present horse wheel which now grinds the malt and pumps up the worts with that same degree of velocity it is now moved by the horses." The cost of the engine was to be £250 up front, £250 in a bond at 5% and £250 to erect an engine house (£750), thus replacing the horses that worked for fourteen hours in total. He concluded: "The house must be ready by midsummer and the engine compleated for working by the end of July therefore I entreat you Gentlemen not to lose one moment either in adjusting or prosecuting this business to a conclusion.... We flatter ourselves you will be duly sensible of the great trust and confidence we place in you respecting this business."

Boulton and Watt prepared plans for Henry Goodwyn in May 1784 and the coppersmiths who worked at the brewery were involved in the engine's construction. The brewing season, in general, finished in June and started again in August thus the engine had to be installed in the summer period and Goodwyn wrote on 16 June, "In a few days we will finish our brewing this season and in a very few weeks afterwards we will resume our occupations, which we cannot do now without your friendly assistance." There was some urgency and anxiety in this request. The base for the engine and the cistern, chimney and boiler were then prepared, whilst the engine was completed at Soho. Samuel Whitbread his competitor had placed his own order in June 1784 and Goodwyn became concerned, writing, "It will be a great disappointment to me if this Engine is not fixed by you before any other Brewing Trade, should it not, I acknowledge my *pride and vanity* will be much hurt." All parties had much confidence in the project and Goodwyn had sold half his horses within a month and the fitters had the engine running on 9 August, which was stated to be 4 horsepower as per his requirements. There was much interest in the project and plans were drawn up for other London breweries as follows: June 1784 - S. Whitbread, Chiswell Street; October 1785 - Felix Calvert, Thames Street; May 1786 - Thrale & Co, Southwark; March 1787 - J. Calvert, Whitecross Street; April 1787 - Gyfford, Long Acre (Combe, Delafield & Co). All of these had designs for 10 horsepower engines and this explains why Whitbread's engine became more prominent. Indeed King George III visited Whitbread's Brewery at Chiswell Street in 1787 to see his 'amazing new steam engine' and there was no doubt disappointment at the Red Lion Brewery.

This blow to Goodwyn's *pride and vanity* was compounded in 1788 when the brewery was devastated by fire and the victualling commissioners arranged for him to share with 'Hartshorne' on moderate terms until it was rebuilt (Clowes, Southwark had a similar fate in 1785). One wonders if a combination of coal, fire, steam and inexperience led to the disaster however people were undeterred and Boulton exclaimed that, "Britain had gone steam mill mad." Henry Goodwyn senior (now over 70) reduced his role in the 1790s and his son Henry took over his duties, thus the partners Henry Goodwyn, William Skinner and Thomas Thornton ran the business at 21 Lower East Smithfield by 1794. Indeed, there was some trouble with Watt's engine that year but in Henry Goodwyn's words, "not enough (to make it worth his while) to pay a man to come from Soho to overhaul it." Henry Goodwyn junior was an inventor himself and patented a more-simple mashing machine in 1797 and all operations were mechanical by 1800.

Henry Goodwyn of Maze Hill, Greenwich wrote his last will on 11 Aug 1801 and left a marriage settlement of £9,565 at 3% in consolidated bank annuities, purchased from the assigns of the estate of Rev. Julius Hutchinson (husband of Frances), to his executors, upon trust, for Frances his daughter. An amount of £3,427 10s arose from the sale of an estate at Marsham, Norfolk (property of his late brother Robert) and was to be invested for son Henry, then grandsons Henry Robert, Thomas Wildman and Charles. His real estate, except Bournmill in Kent occupied by Thomas Wingate, was left to Henry Goodwyn, Samuel Enderby of Croom's Hill and grandson Julius Hutchinson of Lincoln's Inn (his executors), in trust, to be sold at the best possible price. He left to his dear wife: Bournmill estate; £5,271 10s 3% investment in names of myself, herself, Julius Hutchinson and John Milles and a mortgage of £1,211 and dividends on an estate of John Milles - £700 p.a. to be paid to her, from these, in lieu of any marriage settlement. He also left her his household goods and coaches etc. and £100 for her immediate use and stated she could reside at his home in Maze Hill at an annual rent of £50. He left his daughter Anna Maria Goodwyn £360 p.a. and placed £5,000 in trust for Frances Hutchinson and £1,000 at 5% for her children, Frances to receive the £5,000 at his wife's decease. There was a similar arrangement for Henry Goodwyn (and his children). He also added a codicil at this time and left £300 to his wife per an agreement, between them, regarding articles dated 8 November 1766, and the will was signed and witnessed at Gray's Inn.

Goodwyn, Skinner and Thornton continued as brewers at 21 Lower East Smithfield however George Matthew Hoare, a son of Henry Hoare the banker, joined the partners in 1802 and brought additional funds to the company - this was a significant event in the history of the brewery and is discussed further below. Henry Goodwyn of Maze Hill died three years later and administration of his will was granted to his three executors in London on 5 August 1805. This led to a change in the articles of partnership with his son Henry taking control, thus Goodwyn, Skinner and Thornton placed their last advert in 1805, whilst Henry Goodwyn & Co. were brewers at 21 Lower East Smithfield from 1806. His son-in-law Rev. Julius Hutchinson was a clerk at Layer Bretton, Essex and his will was proved on 14 August 1811. Those familiar with the history of brewing might know of Goodwyn and his link to Watt's engine, however his connections in Greenwich are more obscure. Indeed the daughters of Henry Goodwyn junior married some important local gentlemen. (See Kinnaird Ch. 5 re Hoare).

Greenwich had Royal associations from the 15th century and the Observatory was built in 1675, thus the area attracted men of wealth who lived in roads each side of the park (Maze Hill and Croom's Hill) and also around Blackheath. This was a contrast to the adjacent town of Deptford, which was a centre for shipbuilding with the Royal Dockyard, Naval Victualling Yard and allied trades. The town first developed beside the Thames near St. Nicholas's Church and Deptford Green, but extended to the south in the 18th century between Butt Lane (High Street) and Church Street and near St. Paul's Church (consecrated 1730). This combination of wealth in Greenwich and employment in Deptford attracted many to the area, especially those with maritime aspirations. Samuel Enderby (1720-97), a ship owner in Greenwich, was the founder of Samuel Enderby & Sons - the whaling and sealing firm. Deep-sea whaling took place from 1712 with the discovery of sperm whales off the coast of North America and vessels soon sailed to Greenland and the South Atlantic, but the 'southern' fishery only extended to the Cape de Verde Islands and Brazil. This changed in the late 18th century after Captain Cook explored the coasts of New Zealand and Australia. Sir Joseph Banks (1743-1820) had a private fortune and initiated Cook's expedition to Tahiti in 1768 and persuaded the Admiralty to let him go on the voyage as a botanist, thus making landfall in Australia in 1770. He became President of the Royal Society in 1778 and held the position until his death, being prominent in matters antipodean.

The British whaling industry was curtailed after the American War of Independence (1775-83) with British ships unwelcome in coastal waters, whilst the East India Company had a charter giving them a monopoly beyond the Cape of Good Hope. Samuel Enderby (1756), son of the above, was prominent in the company and with some other 'adventurers' attended the Council Chamber, Whitehall in 1786 and stated, "I have spoken to the masters and mates of East Indiamen who have seen sperm whales in the Southern Oceans beyond the Cape." He followed this with a letter to George Chalmers on 17 January 1789 and offered to explore these claims at his own risk thus he was authorized to sail to the Pacific and report back, whilst other whalers awaited the results. The outcome was the profitable whaling industry of the late 18th and early 19th century in both the north and south, although this led to the near or total extinction of some types of whale. Enderby played a major role in the exploration of the Southern Oceans yet his name is little known (unlike that of Cook) and this scenario could be compared to the case of Betts and Brunel.

The Greenwich Rate Books reveal that the Goodwyn, 'Inderby' and Vansittart families lived at Blackheath in 1790 and the story had a further twist when Samuel Enderby married Mary Goodwyn (1767), eldest daughter of Henry, and they had children Charles, Henry, George and Elizabeth. It seems likely that Samuel and his family then lived at Croom's Hill and he was certainly there from 1801-19 (see wills). The whaling and sealing company continued to have a prominent role and helped the Third Fleet transport some early convicts to Port Jackson, near Sydney, in 1791 - the first going to Botany Bay in 1787. Joseph Banks was involved in this 'colonisation' and Samuel Enderby corresponded with him on several occasions regarding his discoveries in southern latitudes namely 25 September 1800, 29 May 1801 and 21 July 1809. Captain Abraham Bristow, master of a Samuel Enderby vessel, sailed south in 1806 and discovered the Auckland Islands, which were 390 miles south of New Zealand and included Auckland, Bristow and Enderby Islands. The will of Samuel Enderby Esq. of Blackheath was proved on 19 November 1829 and his three sons inherited the company although a *Land Tax Assessment* for 1830 lists S. Enderby Esq. at Vansittart Terrace, Greenwich.

Charles Enderby (1798-1876) took control of the company and continued to run whaling operations at St. Paul's Wharf, London and established rope and sail making at Greenwich Marsh. He built a house beside the factory with an octagonal window to look out over the Thames - it remains today beside Enderby Wharf. The company had financial difficulties and produced 'waterproof' telegraphic cabling in 1837 but this was found to leak and was a failure. He was a founder member of the Royal Geographical Society and entertained geographers and scientific friends in Greenwich however his factory burnt down in 1845 and he turned his attention to the Auckland Islands - Maoris from the Chatham Islands settled there in 1840 although the climate was cold and inhospitable. The colonisation was a fiasco however 200 settlers embarked on the "Samuel Enderby", "Brisk" and "Fancy" and sailed for the Auckland Islands in 1849. Charles was appointed Lieutenant Governor and a settlement established at Port Ross whilst the Southern Whale Fishery Co. was the means of support. The islands were too remote to be made viable and the enterprise and company collapsed in 1853, Port Ross was abandoned and the settlers returned to England. This was an ominous warning to such colonists and Samuel Enderby & Sons was wound up in 1854 and Charles died in poverty, whilst the Auckland Islands became a marine reserve (somewhat ironical). Despite this sad end they were immortalised in Herman Melville's book *Moby Dick* published in 1851, the main vessel being the "Samuel Enderby".

This might seem an ignominious end for such a notable family however they were soon raised to glory. Henry William Gordon (1786) joined the Royal Artillery in 1803, fought at Naples in 1805 and married Elizabeth *Goodwyn* the eldest daughter of Samuel Enderby, merchant and ship owner, at St. Alphage's, Greenwich on 31 May 1817. The couple had eleven children (six boys) and of these three sons achieved senior ranks in the army and all fought in the Crimea, whilst the father was a major general (died 1865). Sir Henry William Gordon K.C.B. was born at Croom's Hill in 1818 and died in 1887 whilst General Samuel Enderby Gordon was born at Woolwich in 1824 and died in 1883, however the third brother was most notable. General Charles George Gordon was born at Woolwich on 28 January 1833 and went to the Royal Military Academy in 1848 and was intended for the Royal Artillery (like his father) but joined the Engineers in 1852. He fought in the Crimea in 1854-55 and was posted to China in 1860-64 being known as Charles 'Chinese' Gordon. He had further posts in Asia and Africa then was sent to evacuate Khartoum on 18 February 1884 but decided to defend the town, going against orders. There was a public outcry and a relief force was sent under Wolseley with Kitchener as aide-de-camp. General Gordon died there on 26 January 1885 when Mahdi and his rebels stormed the town whilst the relief force came two days later. He was second cousin of A.G. Goodwyn - the football player.

Meanwhile the other children of Henry and Elizabeth Goodwyn had more connections in Deptford. William Barnard (1735-95) was a shipbuilder in Deptford who owned a 3-storey mansion on Deptford Green although his family also resided at Church Street, Greenwich in 1790. He took a lease on land used by the East India Company in 1788 and extended Deptford Dry Dock to the north and south in the late 18th century, and demolished houses south of Anchor Smith Alley to build an oval garden and plank yard. The company built both naval warships and East Indiamen there and his will was proved on 7 March 1795. William Barnard, his son, was also involved in the business and married Harriet Goodwyn having children Francis (c.1799), William Henry (1801) at Rotherhithe and Thomas (1805) St. Anne's, Blackfriars, whilst his will was proved 25 February 1805. His widow Harriet married Charles Laing at St. Alphage's on 25 August 1817 and his sons continued shipbuilding at Deptford until c.1834. There were three other marriages of note and Charlotte Goodwyn married Thomas Stokes at St. Alphage's on 8 February 1811, whilst Henry Robert Goodwyn married Laura and had children Henry (1807) at St. Botolph's, Aldgate and Eliza Amelia (1808) at St. Alphage's - the third marriage of Thomas W. Goodwyn is discussed below. Henry Goodwyn & Co. continued brewing at 21 Lower East Smithfield in 1806-23 and had links to the City regarding the Corporation.

Stephen Flower was born in London c.1720 and married Mary daughter of William and Eliza Brazier of the Minories who was baptized at St. Botolph's, Aldgate (8 July 1722). They had eleven children at the Minories in 1748-70 most of who were baptized at St. Botolph's but several died as infants. They included Charles born 18 February 1763 and baptized 3 March and brother James baptized 11 October 1764. Stephen Flower the father died at the Minories and was buried at St. Botolph's, Aldgate on 10 February 1773. Charles Flower was then a cheesemonger at 64 Minories in 1785 and a merchant at 75 Minories in 1788-91. He married Anne daughter of Joseph Squire of Plymouth and had eight children baptized at St. Botolph's, Aldgate: Ann Mary (1790), Elizabeth (30 June bapt 26 July 1791), Charles (1793), James (1794), Caroline (1796), Clarissa (1799), Maria (1800) and Jemima (1802). He traded as a merchant at 3 Crescent, Minories in 1795-1800 and became prominent being the Sheriff in 1799-1800, Master of the Framework Knitters' Company in 1801-02 and an alderman of Cornhill Ward, City of London from 1801. His wife Anne, however, died on 22 March 1803 and was buried at St. Botolph's, Aldgate on 29 March. His address was Behind the Crescent, Minories and 14 Finsbury Square in 1807-10 and he was Lord Mayor in 1808-09 then knighted in November 1809. He was familiar with Harvey Christian Combe former Lord Mayor (1799) and Henry Goodwyn through business and at St. Botolph's. His brother James married Elizabeth Rowe and had children James (1790), Charles (1793), John (1795) and Mary Ann (1797) - the latter was baptized at St. Olave, Hart Street on 25 January 1798.

Thomas Wildman Goodwyn was born on 26 April 1788 and baptized at Greenwich on 29 July then married Elizabeth Flower on 17 August 1809. The couple first resided at Tower Hill and had sons Charles Flower (1810) baptized St. Botolph's, Aldgate and Thomas Wildman (1813). The father had shares in the Red Lion Brewery and was present when an independent engine of 14-h.p was erected in 1816 to replace Watt's engine of 1784. The Hoare family were still involved with the brewery and a fifth partner joined in 1819. The couple had four more children baptized at St. Botolph's: Walter Frederick (1815),

Henry William (1817), Alfred George (1819) and Arthur John Bowdler (1821) with an address Lower East Smithfield in 1817-22, however Alfred G. was born at Mill Hill and Arthur John B. at Eltham. His brother Charles Samuel Goodwyn married Letitia Young at St. Mary's, Lewisham on 11 November 1818 and had prospects of joining the brewery thus the concern looked secure for years to come - it was not to be.

The name Bowdler was not chosen at random and indicated a prominent association. Thomas Bowdler married Elizabeth Stuart daughter of Sir John Cotton in 1742. Their son John Bowdler was born on 18 March 1746 and married Harrietta daughter of John Hanbury, Vice Consul, who had a factory in Hamburg. He was a great campaigner who wrote many wordy letters to people in authority such as the Archbishop and Lord Auckland. He sent one to John Hutchinson in 1792 about high prices stating that clergy and legal people had a negative effect on the moral and religious condition of the nation. He also produced a pamphlet 'Reform or Ruin' in 1797 and his son Thomas (1782-1856) supported him in his work whilst son John (1783-1815) joined the Clapham Sect to his great consternation. He lived at Bath and Eltham and died on 29 June 1823. His brother Dr. Thomas Bowdler was born on 11 July 1754 and received an M.D. Edinburgh in 1776 then spent four years in Europe. He did charitable work and was a member of the Royal Society and lived at St. Boniface, Isle of Wight in 1800-10 but went to Rhyddings, Swansea at the end of that time. He published "The Family Shakespeare" in 1818, which was a simplified version of the bard for public consumption and became very popular. It led to the term bowdlerize meaning to expurgate a book - he died on 24 February 1825. The Goodwyns no doubt knew the Bowdler family especially as Arthur was born in Eltham, whilst the name became popular and Arthur Bowdler Hill was born at Aldersgate in 1828 (see Pember Ch. 4).

Sir Charles Flower Bart merchant traded Behind the Crescent, Minories and lived at 14 Finsbury Square in 1811 whilst his son James Flower married Mary Jane daughter of Sir Walter Sterling Bart at St. James's, Piccadilly on 2 January 1816. Indeed their City connections brought new business interests and they both entered into brewing. Harvey Christian Combe was a founder of Combe & Co. at Wood Yard, Covent Garden in 1787 whilst new partners joined in 1797 and the Articles of Association changed (see Bonsor Ch. 6). There was an adjustment of the partners on 6 July 1818 and they became: Joseph Delafield, Sir Charles Flower Bart, James Flower, Harvey Combe, Joseph Delafield younger and Edward Harvey Delafield t/a Combe, Delafield & Co. Indeed Sir Charles Flower was very wealthy with several properties (and interests) including Behind the Crescent, Minories and 27 Finsbury Square in 1820-23. He was a director of the *Thames and Medway Canal* whose initial aim was to move military vessels from Woolwich to Chatham in a safe manner. The Gravesend to Higham section was built in 1800-01 and the more difficult tunnel to Strood in 1819-24 but it was not a commercial success and the tunnel was sold to the S.E. Railway Co. (1845). His daughter Ann Mary married the Hon. Michael H. Percival a member of the Legislative Council of Quebec. She lived up to her name and was "An amateur botanist whose specimens are among the oldest of Canadian origin kept in that countries herbaria. Many of them are cited in very important works on North American botany." His daughter Caroline married Christopher James Magnay (1793) at St. Martin Vintry on 16 October 1824 this being an ancient parish connected to St. Michael Royal (church of Dick Whittington) - the groom's father and brother were also Lord Mayor: Christopher (1821) and William (1843), however change was in the air.

Henry Goodwyn of Blackheath made his last will on 21 June 1819 and first stated, "My funeral shall be conducted in a plain manner and at a moderate expense." He gave to his executors £1032 10s 2d being the profits (of a share) in the late partnership of the Red Lion Brewery appropriated for the benefit of the family of his late son Henry Robert, but lent to Thomas Wildman to be employed in the said trade and for his younger son Charles Samuel when admitted to the trade - the interest on this amount for his daughter-in-law Laura and guardians of Henry & Eliza Goodwyn (his grandchildren). The chief part of his property was lent and advanced to Thomas Wildman Goodwyn and employed by him in the said brewing trade: Thomas having 2 shares and Charles 1 in bond and 2 in cash in the Articles of Co-Partnership. He left to Catherine (Rider) Goodwyn his daughter all of his plate, "as a token of my approbation of (her) filial attention to me during my infirm state of health for many years." He left his leasehold messuage at Blackheath where he resided to son-in-laws Samuel Enderby of Croom's Hill esq. and Thomas Stokes of Blackheath esq., in trust, to sell at auction and to form part of his personal estate. This was to be combined with all other monies, except any engaged in the brewery, to form his residuary estate and to be divided amongst his children equally - his two grandchildren to have their father's. The amount for Harriet Laing (wife of Charles) was to be placed in trust with his two sons and after her decease was to be divided amongst Francis, William and Thomas Barnard. He left Samuel Enderby and

Thomas Stokes £100 for "conjugal attention to his daughters (their wives) and their kind and obliging conduct to himself." He left 40s to his servants for each year of service and £100 to Mrs. Mary Gray of Vauxhall Bridge Road, Westminster. Samuel Enderby and Thomas Stokes (executors) were authorised to take funds from the brewery as required and the will was signed and witnessed at Messrs Forster, Cooke and Frere of Lincoln's Inn.

Henry Goodwyn & Co. remained at 21 Lower East Smithfield in 1823 but soon left the brewery trade after being in business nearly 60 years. There was a codicil to the will on 12 April 1824 stating: "Mrs. Gray to receive £20 and no more." A second on 15 May 1824 stated 'Mr. Enderby purchased a lease on his behalf from Miss Vansittart' and he bequeathed this property to his three unmarried daughters Catherine, Amelia and Anna and his son Charles Samuel for their residence. Henry Goodwyn died soon after and Samuel Enderby and Thomas Stokes proved his will in London on 8 October 1824. Indeed his death ended the family's connection with the brewery and his sons Thomas and Charles went into new trades. Hoare & Co. owned the Red Lion Brewery and their links to Hoare's Bank helped them through a trading crisis in autumn 1826 and they appeared on Stamford's London Map at Lower East Smithfield in 1862. Hoare & Co Ltd. was registered at a value of £1.6 million in July 1894 and Charrington & Co Ltd. took them over in 1933 - they ceased to brew in 1934. Hoare & Co Ltd. was liquidated in April 1938 and the Red Lion Brewery site is part of the St. Katherine's Dock development.

Thomas W. and Elizabeth Goodwyn had two other children: Julius Edmund (1824) and Elizabeth (1826) who were baptized at St. Botolph's, Aldgate on 10 May 1826 - the father a gentleman of Goodman's Yard, Minories. Thomas formed the partnership of Goodwyn & Bullock hard and soft soap makers at Goodman's Yard in 1829-31 and resided at Bernard Street, Russell Square, Bloomsbury, but died soon after and his wife Elizabeth was left with a young family. His brother Charles Samuel Goodwyn made his last will on 8 December 1819 and stated: "All I die possessed of I bequeath to my wife Letitia or otherwise my children in equal shares." He then had a family of seven children who were born at Greenwich, Kennington and Deptford in 1820-34. John Young of London and George William Young of Kennington made oath on 11 July 1838 that they were acquainted with (the late) Samuel George Goodwyn formerly of Princes Street, Lambeth starch manufacturer but late of Union Street, Deptford gent and that the will was in his writing. There was no executor and administration was granted to Letitia Goodwyn the universal legatee on 18 July. A land tax assessment for Greenwich in 1830 states that Mrs. Mason owned and Mrs. Goodwyn lived in, a property at Vansittart Terrace, whilst Henry Goodwyn (and his assigns) owned a P.H. at East Greenwich occupied by M. Preston. There was an Act in the House of Commons entitled *Amendments to the Greenwich Improvement Bill, John Roan Charity* on 7 July 1830 that included a lease indenture (25, 26 March 1824) and a release - the parties including Henry Goodwyn and Samuel Enderby (the property in the codicil). Vansittart Terrace was present in the years 1841-71 but was demolished by 1881 and 131-169 Greenwich High Road cover the site. This was the end of an era for the Goodwyns and the following generation had a completely different life.

Sir Charles Flower merchant resided at 67 Russell Square in 1829-34 whilst his premises were at 3 Crescent Mews, Minories in 1829 and at 76 Old Broad Street from 1832-34. He also had a residence Belmont House, Mill Hill that was later a preparatory school in the *Mill Hill* foundation. He wrote his last will on 26 January 1832 and was a baronet and alderman of the City of London (he represented Cornhill Ward from 1801-34). He left his freehold property in Oxford, Middlesex, Hertford and London to Abraham Wilday Robarts banker, William George Prescott of Threadneedle Street banker, Benjamin Winnell Scott of the Chamberlain's Office esq. and Harvey Combe of Castle Street, Long Acre esq. Upon trust, during the life of son James (except that in Huntingdon and his share and interest in a freehold with his partners in trade - for James) to James's children as tenants in common, Ann Mary widow of Michael Henry Percival Esq., Elizabeth widow of Thomas Wildman Goodwyn Esq., Caroline widow of Christopher Magnay Esq., Clarissa Flower and Jemima Flower (equally) or their children. James was to keep the estate in good repair viz. "mansion house, park, palings, farms, barns and outbuildings." His leasehold estate and that at the Crescent, Minories held of the Mayor and Corporation were left to his executors in trust to be invested thus: £31,000 Mary Ann Percival, £17,500 Elizabeth Goodwyn, £30,000 Caroline Magnay, £35,000 Clarissa Flower and £35,000 Jemima Flower. This could be used for their children's education whilst Maria Flower had an annuity of £400 during her lifetime. He left £500 to John Rowe Flower son of late brother James, £100 to daughter-in-law Mary Jane Flower, musical clock and organ coach and horses piano and harp to Clarissa, Jemima and Maria, gold watch and chain to James and "the gold chain used as Lord Mayor" to Ann Mary Percival. He left the 'plate picture' painted by Reinagle and other pictures and prints to James and the residue to his executors, in trust, also for his son James (and wife and children). He asked his executors to sell a number of shares and signed the will at 70 Lombard Street on the above date - Philip Reinagle (1749-1833) a landscape and portrait painter exhibited at the R.A. in 1773-85. Ramsay Richard (son) did landscapes and George Philip (g-son) maritime pictures.

He then wrote three codicils: 5 August 1833 - £1,800 p.a. could be laid out regarding some annuities; 18 September 1833 - two sums of £10,000 (indentures on his son's marriage) were to be part of the residuary estate and the trusts to be amended thus: Elizabeth Goodwyn £20,000, Caroline Magnay £20,000, Clarissa and Jemima Flower £30,000; 28 October 1833 - £500 to his son's wife was revoked and instead £5,000 to be invested. Sir Charles Flower died at *Bolton House*, Russell Square, on 15 September 1834 aged 72 and was buried at St. Botolph's, Aldgate on 22 inst. His obituary was in the *Times* and Robarts and Combe proved his will on 26 September 1834 and Prescott on 13 November whilst Scott renounced the probate. This almost concluded the story. Sir James Flower resided at Mill Hill and at 15 Wimpole Street and agreed a deed with his wife for £15,000 on 30 September 1834 and took out life assurances to the value of £32,000 in December 1834, however Dame Mary Jane died before him and (with no children) he left his estate to Mrs. Mary Lusignan a widow. He asked to be laid to rest in the chapel on his estate at Mill Hill and left his life assurances and property, in trust, to Harry John White of Broad Street and William Thomas Martrell solicitor, £10,000 being assigned to H.J. White. He also had properties at Lobb Farm, Oxford and Woodford, Essex and was the Sheriff of Norfolk in 1838. Indeed James Flower of Ecclesall, Norfolk had a share at Combe & Co. on 24 July 1838. He was a Conservative in favour of free trade and was returned for Thetford in 1841 but polled the same number of votes as the Earl of Euston. The matter went to a committee and he was duly elected and the Earl unseated. He sat in Parliament under Sir Robert Peel and retired in 1847, and his executors proved his will on 31 May 1850 and he was buried at St. Paul's, Mill Hill. Flower Lane and Goodwyn Avenue are next to Mill Hill Park although a motorway now shatters the peace.

The next generation were left in good circumstances having received an inheritance from the 'Red Lion Brewery' and also £20,000 from Sir Charles Flower (£1 million in today's money), yet spent much time in India. Henry Goodwyn (1807) - Henry IV, son of Henry Robert, joined the Royal (Bengal) Engineers and was promoted to the rank of general. He lived at Old Park, Coley Avenue, Reading in 1881 with his young daughter Faith (6) and three servants and died at Christchurch in December 1886. Rev. Charles Flower Goodwyn (1810) went to St. John's, Cambridge in 1831 and was a deacon in 1834, curate of Winfarthing, Norfolk, in 1841-50, and later resided at Hinton House, Catherington near Portsmouth. He died at "The Elms", Worthy Road in Winchester on 13 February 1888 and Thomas Wildman Goodwyn of 44 Royal York Crescent, Clifton and Arthur John Bowdler Goodwyn of Langley, Ilfracombe were executors - effects £21,134 12s 9d.

Thomas Wildman Goodwyn (1813) was born in London and joined the E.I.C.S. or Madras Civil Service after his father's death. His diaries and correspondence survive from 1832-34 and he was a Judge of the Madras Presidency but retired to Clifton in the late 1860s. He lived at 44 Royal York Crescent being of the Madras Civil Service (retired) from 1878-88 with wife Sarah E. and four servants but died at Laxton Villa, Cheltenham on 7 April 1896. Rev. Frederick Wildman Goodwyn and Henry Charles Reynolds lieutenant colonel R.E. obtained his probate - effects £16,761 6s. His son James Edward Goodwyn was born in India in 1844 and joined the 30th Regiment of Foot or Cambridgeshire Regiment. Meanwhile Charles William Jebb was born in Chesterfield in 1815 and married Eliza Yerbury at Clifton in June 1841. He was an army officer and gentleman and had daughter Frances Romana Maria (1842) baptized at the British Chaplaincy in Rome and daughter Mary Edith (1851). The eldest married at Clifton in June 1871 whilst James Edward Goodwyn a captain, 30th Regiment, of 44 York Crescent married Mary Edith Jebb of no. 30 the same at Clifton Church on 17 December 1878. Rev. F.W. Goodwyn curate of St. George's, Doncaster performed the ceremony whilst Charles William and Amy Louisa Jebb and Henry Kemble were witnesses. The 30th and 59th became the East Lancs Regiment on 7 January 1881 and James Goodwyn spent much time abroad since there is no record of him in England. He died at Bath on 5 December 1922 and has a memorial at Locksbrook Cemetery viz. "Colonel East Lancs Regiment beloved by all ranks." His wife Mary Edith died on 10 May 1931.

His brother Frederick Wildman Goodwyn was born at Calicut, Kerala (Kozhikode) on the S.E. coast of India on 20 January 1850 and was educated at Clifton College in 1863-68 then matriculated at Brasenose College, Oxford in 1868 (B.A. 1872). He lived with his father and played cricket for Gloucester in 1871-73 (69 runs, 3 innings), but took Holy Orders from Dean Vaughan at Temple in 1873 and was curate of St. Mary's, Exeter (1873-76), Doncaster (1876-78) and Kensington (1879). He was vicar of Sharrow near Sheffield in 1879 and lived at the Vicarage in 1881, then married Ethel Zoe daughter of William Thomson at York in June 1887 her father of the See of Gloucester & Bristol (1861) and Archbishop of York (1862-90). He was chaplain to his father-in-law in 1887-90 and a Canon of York from 1887-1917, whilst his daughter Zoe Eleanor was born at Bishopthorpe in March 1888. He left Sharrow to become rector of Rotherfield, Sussex in 1889 and Dorothy Zoe was born there in March 1891. He was the vicar of Eastbourne in 1898-1911 and Rural Dean for Pevensey in 1905-11 then was rector of Copgrove, Leeds (1911), Whittington, Glouc (1911) and St. Stephen's, Cheltenham (1915). He lived at 7 College Green as resident Canon of Gloucester in 1917-23 then moved to 112 Marina, St. Leonard's and his daughter Zoe E. married Thomas Jenkins there in September 1927 - he died there in 1931.

John Langdon-Davies was born at Eshowe in Zululand in 1897 the son of Guy a minister. He was educated at Tonbridge and St. John's, Oxford then lectured in the U.S.A. in 1924-36. He was a journalist and became involved in the fight against Fascism in the Spanish Civil War in 1936-38 writing many books on the subject having a special knowledge of Catalonia. He was an author of note with some eighty titles to his credit that included A Short History of the Future (1936) and Behind the Spanish Barricades (1937). He was involved with the Home Guard and Field-craft School in 1941-44 and was a humanitarian who started a scheme to foster children from the Continent. He wrote for a number of papers and retired to Holly Place, Shoreham in Kent. He gave ten volumes of papers, photographs and scrapbooks to the Borthwick Institute, York in 1969; these formed the *Goodwyn Collection* and included the diaries of Thomas W. Goodwyn and student notes of Frederick W. Goodwyn dated 1870-87 - he died in 1971.

Henry William Goodwyn (1817) was born in London and also entered the army being promoted to major. He retired to Milford Lodge, Milford, Hants, in 1881 as a widower and the household included '1st cousin' Amelia Magnay and six servants. He died at Lymington in December 1899. Alfred George Goodwyn (1819) was born at Mill Hill and is treated below. Arthur John Bowdler Goodwyn (1821) was born in Eltham and went to Clare College, Cambridge in 1841 and was a clerk in the Audit Department (Civil Service) and lived at East Bedfont near Staines in 1881 with four servants. Margaret his wife, born Scotland in 1822, was a visitor with Anne E. Prevost (86) at 18 Montpelier Terrace, Ilfracombe. He was Principal Clerk for the Exchequer and Audit Office at Somerset House in 1884 and lived at Langley near Ilfracombe in 1888. Margaret Catherine died on 24 February 1893 and Arthur J.B. at 20 St. James's Square, Bath on 17 July 1893 - his nieces Elizabeth and Teresa Constance Goodwyn obtained his probate, the effects £6,980 19s 10d. There is a memorial at Locksbrook Cemetery (see below).

Julius Edmund Goodwyn (1824) was born in London and also entered the army and married Euphemia Alexandrina Victoria Kent (1837) who was born Port Royal, Jamaica. They had a son Julius Henry in c.1859 and Norton James at Norton, Freshwater on the Isle of Wight on 7 October 1861 - the father a colonel in the 41st Regiment. He was baptized at Yarmouth Church on 17 November however the party took a ferry across the River Yar as the first bridge to Norton was only built in 1863. They had children Eliza Madeline (1863) Newcastle and Walter Meredith (1872) Ilfracombe and lived at Kersbrook, East Budleigh, Devon, in 1881 with Dora F. Goodwyn (22) visitor from Ballincrassy, Ireland, four servants and a groom. General Julius E. Goodwyn C.B. was the Colonel of the Welsh Regiment (41st, 69th Foot) from 20 January 1883 and died at Bath in March 1890 aged 66 - in some sources he was Colonel to 16 January 1894. His son Julius Henry went to Clifton College (1872-74) and R.M.C. Sandhurst and was a major in the Welsh Regiment who fought in the First War and gave an address 6 Pall Mall. Son Norton went to Clifton College in 1874 and R.M.C. Sandhurst and was half-mile army champion in 1885. He went to Burma in 1891-92, Sierra Leone in 1898-99 and was wounded at Colinso in the South African War and died May 1906.

Alfred George Goodwyn was born at Mill Hill in Hendon on 17 August 1819 and baptized at St. Botolph's, Aldgate on 14 March 1820, between Fenchurch Street and Whitechapel High Street. His father traded at Lower East Smithfield and Goodman's Yard although the family spent time at Mill Hill and Eltham in Kent. His father had died by 1832 and this may have influenced his future, thus like his cousin Henry and brothers Henry and Julius he was destined for the army life. He joined the Royal (Bengal) Engineers in India as a 2nd lieutenant or ensign on 12 June 1837 and was a 1st lieutenant on 8 January 1842. The British Government were concerned with the threat of Russian expansion at the time thus he was sent to the volatile N.W. Province near the Afghan border and Khyber Pass. He served in the 1st Afghan War (1839-42) during 1842 and may have taken part in a disastrous retreat from Kabul and he received a medal. Andrew Ross and Mary Elizabeth Kelly resided in the East Indies and had three children baptized: Maria Anne (27 October 1825) India Office Returns, Margaret Anna (1832) Meerut and Helen Frances (1834) Nussur. Indeed Alfred George Goodwyn married Maria Anne Ross in c.1844 and had a daughter Mary on 13 May 1845 (died as an infant).

Goodwyn served in the 1st Sikh War (Sutlej) in 1845-46 and took part in the Battle of Ferozeshah on 21-22 December 1845 and received a medal for his part in the campaign. The battle took place near Ferozepore and the Sutlej River in the Punjab - close to the Pakistan border. This was not the end of hostilities and troops remained in the region thus the couple had two daughters in Ferozepore - Elizabeth (7 June 1846) and Maria (bapt 16 July 1847) *infant*; a third child Emily (1848) was born at Lansdowne 45 miles east of Roorkee in the Himalayan foothills. Alfred then took part in the 2nd Sikh War (Punjab) 1848-49 this being a decisive conflict in terms of Indian history. The British Army sent a large force to engage the Sikhs at Chillianwallah on 13 January 1849, in the hill country 80 miles north of Lahore (now in Pakistan). The weather was not good and the terrain difficult thus the Engineers were sent ahead, under the cavalry's protection, to ensure that the roads and bridges were passable. There was intense fighting however the British had to retreat, despite superior numbers, and the Sikhs rested and claimed victory. This proved to be a mistake since bad weather and mud then separated the armies and the Sikhs could not finish the matter, thus the British claimed victory. They fought again at Gujerat (10 miles S.E.) on 21 February 1849 and the Sikhs were defeated and the E.I.C. secured their position in India. If they had lost at Chillianwallah their position would have been untenable but they remained and the country passed to the Crown, although this had a direct influence on attitudes and the 'Mutiny' eight years later. Alfred was at both battles and received a medal with two clasps and was promoted to brevet major.

The (Bengal) Engineers were then stationed at Roorkee and the couple had four children there: Alfred George (13 March 1850), Marian (1851), Arthur Ross (c. 31 October 1852) *infant* and Maria Catherine (9 April 1854). The settlement was 100 miles north of Delhi at 1,000 feet and had a strategic location being on a railway junction, near two canals, but there were soon further hostilities. Alfred was promoted to major on 2 August 1854 then returned to England, and son Henry Edward was born at Quay Field House, Ilfracombe on 11 October 1855 - the father was the informant and was a captain and brevet major. He was then called back to India and took part in an important piece of colonial history. The *Sepoy Rebellion* began in Meerut between Roorkee and Delhi in May 1857 - the sepoys offended by the unclean practices of the British Army (and their rule) rose against their officers. The revolt spread and local princes 'seized the moment' thus northern and central India was soon engulfed by revolution and the rebels took Delhi and laid siege to Lucknow. The Europeans were very fearful, and 1,800 men, women and children (plus 1,200 native troops) took refuge in a compound at the Commissioner's residence but were besieged by 20,000 rebels. The building had shutters, a veranda, castellated roof and round tower and they were confronted with the heat of an Indian summer, starvation, disease and constant attack - thus their morale fell to almost zero.

Sir Henry Havelock (1795-1857) was educated at Charterhouse and fought in both Sikh Wars. He was a general and broke the rebel lines at Lucknow on 25 September 1857 but his troops were exhausted and after fighting in the streets also became trapped. Sir Colin Campbell (1792-1863) fought in the Peninsular War, the Battles of Chillianwallah and Gujerat and in the Crimea. He was dispatched from England with 5,000 troops to relieve the town and began his advance from Calcutta on 9 November 1857. The news reached the garrison at Lucknow and a very heroic act soon took place. Thomas Henry Kavanagh (1822-82) a clerk and Irish postal worker volunteered to disguise himself and escape from the town although capture would mean almost certain death. This was bravery close to stupidity since he was 6-foot tall with red-gold hair and brilliant blue eyes! He left his wife and children in the compound on 9 November, went through the town and swam down a river thus reaching Campbell - he helped lead his troops through enemy lines to the garrison. They gradually captured the buildings leading to the Residency whilst Sir Henry fought a rear-guard action to assist them and Lucknow was relieved after four months on 13 November 1857. Havelock died soon after on 24 November and Campbell became Lord Clyde in 1858. Thomas Henry Kavanagh received the Victoria Cross from Queen Victoria at Windsor, being one of five civilians awarded this honour. He died at Gibraltar on 13 November 1882 aged 60 and as a postal worker may have known Creswell (see Ch. 9). He was buried in North Front Cemetery and there is a stone cross memorial to him with ivy leaf detail and long inscription regarding the V.C.

Major Goodwyn took part in the Indian Mutiny campaign and was at the relief of Lucknow under Lord Clyde in November 1857 thus received a medal with clasp, whilst the East India Company or John

Co. lost control to the British Crown. These were worrying times for the family who then resided in the east of the country and had two children: Teresa Constance (9 November 1859) in Larding, Darjeeling and Charles Flower (29 May 1861) *infant* in Calcutta. Alfred George Goodwyn had several medals and was promoted to lieutenant colonel on 18 February 1861, to colonel on 1 September 1863 and to major general on 13 October 1863, but then retired from the Bengal Engineers and went to England (to cool off). He initially lived at St. Stephen's Square, Bayswater near a garden and church (of the same name) and made his last will there on 24 July 1866. He appointed Maria Anne Goodwyn executrix and guardian of his children but she was to forfeit this right (if she married again) and was to be replaced by Arthur John B. Goodwyn Esq. of the Audit Office, Somerset House and cousin Rev. Charles James Martyn of Palgrave near Liss, Suffolk. The latter was born at Mayfair in 1836 and lived with his family at the Rectory, Long Melford in 1881. He left £400 and his personal effects and household goods to his wife and made her trustee with the two above. He placed his freehold and other property in trust - the monies to be invested in Government stocks of Great Britain, India and Canterbury (N.Z.) or any other British colony, or, in guaranteed stock, preferential shares, debentures or railway securities for the support of his wife and children. He mentioned his leaseholds (but had none at the time of probate) and signed his will at Courtenay & Croome, 2 Gracechurch Street.

The Goodwyns then moved to Bath and he added a codicil on 25 March 1869: "My eldest daughter, Elizabeth, having attained her majority and having the greatest confidence in her judgement and considering it advisable that my nearest relatives should act in the execution of the trusts of my said will, I deem it expedient to revoke the appointment of my cousin the said Charles James Martyn...." He states that Elizabeth should replace his cousin as executrix and trustee and if his wife remarries, she is to be the children's guardian (an extreme condition limiting his wife's rights) - he signed the codicil at solicitors Maule and Robertson, Bath. Major Gen. Alfred George Goodwyn R.E. lived at 27 Park Street, Bath from 1869 and was a retired major and landowner there in 1871 with his wife, daughters Elizabeth, Emily, Marian, Maria C., Terisa C. and three servants. This was a society address in a fashionable town in the Walcot St. Swithin district and John Wood junior architect built the Royal Crescent just to the south of Park Street in 1767-75 - no. 11 has a plaque: "Thomas Linley lived here and from this house his daughter Elizabeth eloped with Richard Brinsley Sheridan on the evening of the 18th March 1772." 27 Park Street was a three-storey building of light sandstone located high on a hill (east side) with arched doorway entrance, moulded blocks, grand first floor room and windows, second floor cornice and bow windows to the rear. This 'no doubt' appeared in a Jane Austen novel and was similar to no. 19 opposite although nearby houses were plainer with portico doors. Park Street ran up hill from the elegant and opulent St. James's Square - brother Arthur died at no. 20 in 1893. Years of fighting and the Indian climate, however, had taken their toll and Alfred George Goodwyn died of inflammation of the lungs (3 days) and acute mania (8 days) at Brislington House, Brislington, Somerset on 11 April 1873. Edwin Jewell of the same address was the informant although he also died in September 1876.

General Alfred George Goodwyn (1819-73).
Locksbrook Cemetery - memorials to Goodwyn and his family.

This was located south east of Bristol towards Keynsham and appeared to be a home for the gentry and to some extent it was. Dr. Edward Long Fox (1761-1835) a Cornish Quaker gained an M.D. Edinburgh and then ran an asylum at Cleve Hill near Bristol in 1794-1806. He built

Brislington House to replace it and moved there at the later date. It provided humane treatment for patients and was built with detached houses but these were later joined. It had safety features and homes for 'members of the nobility' - an up-market asylum. Edward Wakefield visited in 1815 and stated: "No coercion is used on patients, healthy occupation, amusement and exercise is employed, whilst silver pheasants and doves are found in the courtyards and greyhounds for amusement." The two sons of the doctor ran the establishment and it remained with the family for almost 150 years and closed in 1952 (lately flats). It is clear that General Goodwyn was a patient and not just a visitor who was taken ill. A brief notice appeared in the *Bath Chronicle* on Thursday April 17: "April 11 of inflammation of the lungs Major General A.G. Goodwyn retired Royal (Bengal) Engineers, 27 Park Street, Bath aged 53." Widow Maria obtained probate in London on 27 May but her status as administrator only applied during her widowhood and the effects came to under £16,000.

Alfred George Goodwyn j. the eldest son followed in his father's footsteps and was born at Roorkee on 13 March 1850. He went to England with his family in 1855 but was in India during the mutiny in 1857. He spent his early years in Darjeeling and Calcutta but may have been educated in England whilst his family were at St. Stephen's Square, Bayswater in 1866. He did not go to Bath and was at Military Academy in c.1868 and a lieutenant in the Royal Engineers on 2 August 1871 - same day as Cotter and Muirhead. He was posted to the School of Military Engineering, Chatham on 1 October 1871 and was found to be a good football player and appeared for the Royal Engineers as half back in the Cup Final on 16 March 1872 - six months after his commission. The team photo shows him to be a stocky and determined player, but was not mentioned in the match report. He usually played as a back and appeared for England with Bonsor, Vidal and W.E. Clegg in the second international at the Oval on 8 March 1873 (4-2), his opponents included Kinnaird and Renny-Tailyour. This ended his soccer career and he was at S.M.E. Chatham until 5 December 1873 and had two months leave before going to India. He was sent to Bengal on 28 January 1874 and arrived in Roorkee where he was born, but would not have remembered it. He suffered in the same way as Lt. Rich and was killed by a fall from his horse at Roorkee on 14 March 1874 having served 2 years 225 days. It was a terrible blow for his family as he died less than a year after his father and the news eventually arrived in Bath.

There has been considerable discussion of the railways in this book but what of communications. The first progress was made when Faraday and Davy experimented with electro-magnetism in the 1820s (see Ch. 6). Samuel Morse invented his code in 1836 and Cooke and Wheatstone produced the first electric telegraph in 1837. Its spread was closely connected to the growth of the railways in the 1840s whilst a cable was laid across the Channel in 1851 and Brunel's Great Eastern laid one to America in 1866. As with transport it became very important to the Empire and two overland and one maritime cable had been laid to India by 1878. Before then news must have arrived by packet or a relay system. Maria Anne Goodwyn of 27 Park Street "the only next of kin" administered his effects on 9 December 1874 at under £1,000 and his death was in the 1875 Army List - there was no indication he died in a conflict.

Mrs. Alfred G. Goodwyn lived at 27 Park Street, Bath in 1874-1901. She was "living off dividends" with her five unmarried daughters in 1881, but third daughter Marian died at Christchurch on 21 October 1894, and she lived with Elizabeth and Teresa in 1901. Henry Edward Goodwyn her son was born at Quay Field House, Ilfracombe on 11 October 1855 and joined the Engineers in 1875.

14 Catherine Place, Bath (the rear).
The Goodwyns lived in Regency elegance (1902-28).

He fought in the Afghan War (1878-80) and Egypt (1882) and received medals on both occasions, then married Margaret Mary (1855) of Ireland and had Anne Mary (1884) Secunderabad and Margaret Eileen (1885) Rangoon. He then took part in the Burma Campaign (1885-87) and was mentioned in despatches and received a medal with clasp and a D.S.O. in 1887. He had sons Alfred John (1888) India and William (1891) Bath and was a major in 1894. Indeed Major Henry E. Goodwyn R.E. resided with Margaret at Monkton Combe in 1901 whilst Alfred and William were in Bath; he gave his address as Northcroft, Combe Down in 1902. Mrs. Alfred Goodwyn and daughters went to 14 Catherine Place in 1902 near the Royal Crescent and opposite the house where the Addisons lived in 1866-74, both being similar in design. These were uncertain times and Elizabeth died on 6 November 1903 and Maria Catherine at Independence, Jackson County in Missouri on 28 October 1904 - probate going to her sister Teresa Constance. Maria Anne Goodwyn died at 14 Catherine Place on 21 January 1912 and Emily Goodwyn spinster and James Lean Esq. obtained probate on 10 February her effects £8,298 3s 2d but re-sworn at £8,649 13s 2d.

The Misses Goodwyn lived at 14 Catherine Place in 1913-28 and Emily died there on 29 January 1928. Henry Edward died on 20 January 1929 and Teresa Constance at Bosveyn, Sennen in Cornwall on 9 September 1944 - her probate to Eileen Margaret Goodwyn. The family have four cross memorials high on the hill at Locksbrook Cemetery: (1) "Sacred to the memory of Alfred George Goodwyn Major General late Royal Engineers (Bengal) died April 11th 1873 aged 53," Marian third daughter, Maria Anne wife. (2) Arthur John Bowdler Goodwyn of 'Bedfont House' and Margaret Catherine his wife, Elizabeth eldest daughter. (3) Emily second daughter, Alfred John elder son (of), "Henry E. Goodwyn D.S.O. major R.E. second son." (4) James Edward Goodwyn Col. East Lancs Regiment and Mary Edith his wife. The cemetery has several memorials to army men and notably those who received the Victoria Cross i.e. Lt. George Alexander Renny for bravery at Delhi in the Indian Mutiny on 16 September 1857. The son A.G. Goodwyn has no memorial but he is remembered for his small but important role in football history.

WILLIAM MERRIMAN

During the 1872 Cup Final the reverse suffered by the Engineers would have been far more serious, "but for the extremely efficient goalkeeping of Captain Merriman." His family have an illustrious history that is traced to Thomas Merriman inn-holder of Newbury, Berks who married Alice Russell on 15 January 1609/10 and died in 1640. John Merriman his son was baptized at Newbury on 1 May 1618 and matriculated at Trinity College, Oxford on 2 May 1634 gaining his B.A. in 1636. He was a captain in Cromwell's army under Major Colonel Riche and thus had custody of Charles I during his transfer from Carisbrooke to Hurst Castle - he married Mary Gough whose family were also allied to Cromwell and died in 1670. His youngest Nathaniel Merriman was born in 1660 and married Mary daughter of Thomas Hunt maltster of Marlborough on 14 June 1688, and became a grocer and brewer in the same town dying in 1741. Nathaniel Merriman his son was born in 1696 and inherited his father's grocery business. He acquired land at Mildenhall and Ramsbury two parishes east of Marlborough and married Elizabeth Hawkes (1697) at Preshute, Wilts on 12 April 1720, their children: Benjamin (1722), Samuel (1731), Nathaniel (1735), Elizabeth, Mary and Martha - he died in 1781.

Benjamin Merriman the eldest was born 24 September 1722 and owned a large brewery at Mildenhall. He developed scientific interests, invented machinery and wrote political essays, thus he received awards from the Society of Arts. He married his second wife Mary, daughter of William Hawkes and niece of Sir Michael Foster judge, at St. Mary's, Marlborough on 7 February 1769 and had a son Samuel (1771) who is treated below. Benjamin died in 1787 but the family were of some status and his son obtained a grant of Arms (1833) with the motto "Terar Dum Prosim" or "May I be worn out provided I do good" - most exhausting. Indeed the family pursued the motto in earnest and entered the medical profession, setting records in midwifery!

Samuel Merriman was born at Marlborough on 29 December 1731 and went to Edinburgh in 1748 and graduated M.D. in 1753. He then married Ann daughter and co-heiress of William Dance surgeon at St. George's, Mayfair on 6 December 1753. He was a physician in Bristol and Andover but moved to London and then commenced practice at Queen Street, Mayfair in April 1757 - his partner Oakley Halford was about to retire. He was apothecary and general practitioner for 20 years, and then physician, and had 14 children including William (1766-1800) who worked with him and Ann (1777) - his wife died in 1780. Indeed he was soon well qualified for all these births! Nicholas Joseph Hüllmandel (1751-1823) a native of Strasbourg and pupil of C.P.E. Bach settled in London in 1771 and became a virtuoso and music teacher who wrote and published keyboard sonatas and musical exercises. He married Camilla Aurora Ducazan and the births of their children Adelaide Charlotte Eveline (15 July 1787) and Charles (5 July 1789) were recorded at St. Mary Abbots, Kensington, although they were already baptized at the French Embassy. Mr. and Mrs. Hüllmandel lived at 17 Queen Street (Brompton) and the entries were in English, French and Latin, as they feared all record might be lost due to the *French Revolution*. The entry was certified to be a true copy of the documents in the register and Samuel Merriman M.D. of Queen Street and Barclay Square was witness. Samuel specialised as a midwife and attended more than 10,000 labours including 362 in one year but retired from practice in 1812, whilst for leisure he liked literature and Biblical studies. He died at 26 Half Moon Street, his son-in-law's house, on 17 August 1818 and was survived only by his daughter Ann.

Samuel Merriman son of Benjamin was born at Marlborough on 25 October 1771 and was educated in the town's 'free school' being head boy in 1783. He went to London in 1784 and studied medicine under uncle Samuel, but gained most knowledge from cousin William (1766-1800) and attended lectures at Westminster Lying-in Hospital. He married cousin Ann Merriman on 28 April 1799 and had children Anne (1802), Hannah Eliza (1811) and Samuel William John (1814). He wrote a pamphlet on vaccines in 1805 and published many papers throughout his life becoming a member of the Soc. of Apothecaries in 1807. He was appointed to Middlesex Hospital in 1809 and gave lectures on midwifery in 1810-25 then inherited an estate at Rodborne Cheney, Wiltshire from uncle Samuel in 1818. He went to Brook Street, Grosvenor Square in 1822 and retired from Middlesex Hospital in 1826 - his wife Ann died in 1831. He worked at the Society of Apothecaries in 1831-37 and was Treasurer of Middlesex Hospital in 1840-45. Samuel Merriman M.D. resided at 34 Lower Brook Street in 1841 and 1851 but was retired at the latter date. His house was at the junction with Davies Street and next door were the Marquis of Waterford, 56 Davies Street and Earl of Digby, 35 Lower Brook Street. The properties are renumbered and one 'corner house' remains opposite to Claridges (1898) - he died at Brook Street on 22 November 1852. Samuel W.J. Merriman was born in London on 22 October 1814 and educated at Marlborough "School" and matriculated at Caius College, Cambridge on 7 February 1831 then M.R.C.P. in 1840 and M.D. in 1841. He was a consulting physician at 34 Brook Street and 3 Charles Street, Westbourne Terrace and died "Marlborough House", Sandown, Isle of Wight, on 20 February 1873.

Nathaniel Merriman was born Marlborough on 4 May 1735 and was a cheese-factor there and married Elizabeth Baverstock at Alton on 24 June 1764 - she was baptized Alton on 17 July 1734 the daughter of Thomas and Martha. The couple had six children: Martha (1768), Nathaniel (1770), Thomas (1771), John (1774), Benjamin (1776) and James (1780). The parents were both buried at St. Peters and St Paul's Marlborough: Elizabeth 26 March 1804 and Nathaniel 16 July 1811. Most of them stayed in Marlborough and played a significant role in the town, whilst one branch also entered the medical profession and went to London. Martha Merriman married Thomas Ward a solicitor and had a daughter Elizabeth (see below) and lived until her 100th year, and Nathaniel Merriman lived at the Priory, Marlborough and died on 22 April 1825. Thomas Merriman was an attorney and banker and lived at Lockeridge House, Marlborough and married Mary Clark from Greenham, Berks on 13 November 1801. He was Town Clerk in 1795-1815 and Mayor of Marlborough in 1815-16 and 1821-22, and died on 15 May 1841. His descendants and those of brother John are treated below. Benjamin Merriman was a banker and Mayor of Marlborough and died unmarried 11 April 1847. James Merriman served in the 24th Bengal N.I. East India Co. and took part in the Bhurtpur campaign in 1804 and died 22 March 1809.

Thomas Baverstock Merriman (1802) the son of Thomas was educated at Harrow and lived at the Green in Marlborough. He married Elizabeth daughter of Thomas Ward and was a member of Ward, Merriman & Co. bankers who became the Capital and Counties Bank. He was the Mayor of Marlborough in 1842-43 and 1853-54. His brother William Clark Merriman (1805) was Mayor of the town on three occasions. Nathaniel James Merriman (1809) was educated at Winchester and Brasenose College, Oxford and was Archdeacon of Albany, South Africa in 1847. He was Canon of Cape Town in 1852-72 and Bishop of Grahamstown in 1872-82 and died 16 August 1882. Son John Xavier Merriman was the last P.M. of Cape Colony in 1908-10 before the Union of South Africa. Charles Anthony Merriman (1814) married Catherine Langshaw on 30 September 1840 and moved to Heath House, Knutsford in Cheshire and died on 30 March 1870. The couple had six sons and four daughters and Frank Merriman (1852) was educated at Sandbach Grammar School and married Mariquita daughter of John Pringle Boyd on 8 July 1879. He lived at Hollingford House in Knutsford and died 25 February 1920. His eldest son Frank Boyd Merriman was born on 28 April 1880 and was educated at Winchester and became a barrister at the Inner Temple in 1904. He served in the First War and was mentioned in despatches and received an

O.B.E. in 1918 then married Olive Maclaren Carver M.B.E. (his second wife) on 18 December 1920. She was the daughter of Frederick William Carver and Isabella Maclaren - a relative of Campbell-Bannerman the P.M. (see Ch. 9). Frank was M.P. for Rusholme in 1924-33 and knighted in 1928 and created Baron Merriman of Knutsford on 27 January 1941.

John Merriman was born at Marlborough on 26 October 1774 and came to London in 1794. He completed his medical training and was admitted a member of the Royal College of Surgeons and Society of Apothecaries and was associated with Thomas Hardwick, at Kensington, whose brother was John Hardwick of Weston under Penyard in Herefordshire. John Merriman married Jane Hardwick daughter of John at St. Mary Abbots, Kensington on 2 April 1800 and the witnesses were Thomas Hardwick (uncle) and James Merriman (H.E.I.C.S.) - his bride was born at Ross on 5 February 1770. John and Jane Merriman lived at Young Street, Kensington and had three children viz. John baptized 30 January 1801, Thomas Hardwick baptized 30 June 1802 and Jane born 30 July 1804. They then had an address Kensington Square but this may have been the same property, and James Nathaniel was born there on 21 September 1806. Thomas Hardwick widower married Sarah Stafford widow at Kensington on 8 February 1806 and the witnesses were John and Jane Merriman.

Kensington Palace and St. Mary Abbots Church dominated the town and indeed the latter is clearly visible from Hyde Park. Sir Christopher Wren rebuilt Kensington Palace for William III in 1689 and William Kent enlarged it for George I, in a more palatial style. It was the Sovereign's residence until the death of George II in 1760 although the Royal family retained the house after this date. Princess Victoria was born at Kensington in 1819 but her father died when she was eight months old and her mother the Duchess of Kent raised her at Kensington Palace. By all accounts it was a frugal existence and they soon needed a doctor for their ailments. John Merriman was general medical attendant to the Duchess of Kent in 1827 and Princess Victoria and Princess Sophia in 1828. Indeed sons John and James Nathaniel also trained as surgeons and it was a 'family business'.

There were then some weddings and most took place at St. Mary Abbots. John Merriman married Caroline Jones in c.1826. She was born at Ross in Herefordshire in 1800 the daughter of Rev. John Jones vicar of Foye a parish three miles north of Ross on Wye - Charles Gwillim Jones was her brother. Jane Merriman married Rev. Thomas Simpson Evans at Kensington on 20 December 1831 the witnesses John Merriman, Ann Hardwick, Elizabeth M. Hutchins and Hannah E. Merriman. James Nathaniel Merriman married Emily Yorke Hutchins at Kensington on 28 March 1833 and there were many witnesses including Thomas H. Merriman, Jane Merriman, Jane Evans, Sarah Yorke Hutchins, Ann Yorke Hutchins, Ann Hardwick, Elizabeth Margaret Hutchins and C. Lendon. Charles Gwillim Jones of St. George Bloomsbury married Margaret Hardwick at Kensington on 8 May 1833 and the witnesses were Charlotte Jones, John Merriman, Ann Hardwick, Emily Yorke Merriman and Margaret Hutchins. There were in fact four weddings, several baptisms and a funeral!

John Merriman surgeon and wife Caroline lived at Kensington Square and had children: John Jones (1827), Thomas Hardwick (1828), Caroline Olivia (1829), James Hardwick (1830) *infant*, Charles James (1831) and Christiana (1834). They then gave an address at 13 Young Street and had further children Septimus (1836), William (1838) and Henry Blunt (1840). His brother James Nathaniel Merriman surgeon and wife Emily Yorke resided at 11 Young Street and had children: Emily Jane (1834), Thomas Lendon (1836), Henry John (1838) *infant*, Harvey Henry (1840) and Georgiana Maria (1845). John Merriman senior continued to visit Kensington Palace and was held in good favour by the Royal girls and was appointed 'apothecary extraordinary' to H.M. Queen Victoria when she ascended to the throne in 1837. The position was a prominent one thus Newton engraved his portrait from a painting by Lucas. The honour, however, was soured as Thomas Hardwick Merriman of the 'Square' and 16 Southampton Street, Bloomsbury was buried at Kensington on 27 June 1838 aged 36.

John Merriman gentleman of Kensington was thus prompted to write out his last will on 21 December 1838. He bequeathed to his dear wife Jane Merriman: "All that my messuage or dwelling house in which I now reside situate at Kensington together with the outhouses, gardens, surgery and appurtenances thereto belonging." He also gave her his household effects and monies and confirmed to her his title in a £2,000 @ 3% annuity. This was given to her under the will of Thomas Hardwick esquire and was payable to her on the decease of the 'late' Mrs. Sarah Hardwick. He also left her a further amount bequeathed to her in the will of William Makram. He gave his sister Mrs. Martha Ward or her children £200 and his brothers Thomas and Benjamin Merriman £25 each. He confirmed settlements on his children's marriages: John Merriman £2,000, James Nathaniel Merriman £2,000 and a sum to Jane wife of Rev.

Thomas Simpson Evans. The residue went to John Merriman, James Nathaniel Merriman and Thomas Simpson Evans, in trust, to pay his debts and expenses and then to be invested for his wife's benefit until her decease. After this the money was to be divided into three equal thirds viz. John Merriman, James Nathaniel Merriman, and the trustees of Jane his daughter (the latter to be used in the same way as her £3,000 settlement). He appointed his three trustees his executors and Henrietta Gilchrist of Brompton spinster and Mary Rushbrook servant to Mr. Merriman were the witnesses. John Merriman died at Kensington Square on 17 June 1839 and was buried at St. Mary Abbots on 23 June. Henrietta Gilchrist signed an affidavit on 9 July confirming that she witnessed the will and probate was granted to the three executors in London on 11 July 1839.

The two brothers continued to practice medicine at Kensington Square and the title 'apothecary extraordinary' to the Queen was conferred on them at their father's decease. There is, however, no record of the family on the 1841 census since the returns for Kensington were lost. Local directories state that John Merriman & Co. was at 18 Young Street and John Merriman & Son at 45 Kensington Square in 1841. The two properties were adjacent and 18 Young Street may have been connected to the main house - they are now considered. 45 Kensington Square was a Georgian town house and would not have been out of place in a provincial country town. The white building was on the corner with Young Street and had just two storeys, and was 'horizontal' unlike most town houses of the era. There was a cupola style entrance with half-dome, five windows along the length of the building, small rooms in the roof space above and a leafy garden in front. There were, however, three storeys at the side of the building and a side entrance in Young Street - this had the appearance of a separate property and was no doubt the surgery at number 18. The house is present today in a complete Georgian square with each building constructed in an individual style.

Jane Merriman died at Kensington Square on 1 July 1844 aged 74 and was buried at St. Mary Abbots on 6 July but her family remained for many years. The area had some notable residents and the Merrimans soon made a famous acquaintance. William Makepeace son of Richmond and Ann Becher Thackeray was born in Calcutta in 1811. His father worked for the E.I.C. but died in 1815 and William was sent back to England to be educated. He went to Charterhouse and Trinity, Cambridge and lost a poetry contest to Tennyson at the college. He had large debts due to gambling and left without a degree in 1830 and entered the law in 1831-33, then for a brief period trained as an art student. He made some bad investments, thus his family helped him start a radical paper *The Constitution* and he went to Paris as the foreign correspondent. He married Isabella Shawe a poor Irish girl on 20 August 1836 however the paper failed and he turned to writing. His daughter Ann was born at 18 Albion Street, Paddington in 1836 and a third daughter Harriet Marion in 1840. Isabella the mother then became afflicted with mental illness and stayed in institutions the rest of her life. He wrote many articles and his first book *Barry Lynd*on was published in serial form in 1844 and he moved to 16 Young Street with his daughters in 1847. He started a friendship with the Merriman family that lasted for many years and completed *Vanity Fair*, his most famous book, in 1848.

John Merriman G.P. M.R.C.S. lived at 45 Kensington Square in 1851 with his wife Caroline, John Jones G.P., Thomas Hardwick attorney-solicitor, Caroline O., William scholar (12), Henry B., one medical assistant and four servants. James Nathaniel Merriman his brother lived with his family at 7 Kensington Square and the joint practice was at 12 Young Street (that year). The son John Jones Merriman married Frederica Anne Eliza White at Kensington in June 1852 (see below) and was both a physician and friend to Thackeray who attended the surgery. Indeed a messenger hand delivered a letter to J. Merriman Esq. at 44 Kensington Square in c.1852: "Dear Merriman, the accompanying birds were shot on the 14th and are respectfully offered to Mrs. Merriman by yours very sincerely W.M.

45 Kensington Square. The home of W.M. Thackeray is at the far right.

Thackeray." There is a copy of the letter in the Koopman Collection and it was attached to a piece he wrote called the *Sorrows of Werther*. The two were on identical paper and thus it was supposed that they were written at the same time. Thackeray was having a melancholic phase and wrote the *History of Henry Esmond* in 1852 and was suffering with unrequited love. He was without a companion and had fallen for Jane Brookfield, the wife of an old college friend. His writings at the time reflected these yearnings and it has been suggested that the 'birds' in the Merriman letter were in fact a form of satire and irony about love (due to the association with the *Sorrows of Werther*). This seems a rather speculative conclusion and no doubt they were birds he shot in Holland Park and gave to young Merriman as a gift.

Thackeray continued to write for magazines such as Punch and published *Newcomes* in 1853 but left 16 Young Street in 1854. He moved to Palace Green near Kensington Palace Gardens and sent a letter to J.J. Merriman on 15 October 1856 then published *The Virginians* in 1857. He started the Cornhill Magazine with his friend George Smith in 1859, and during this period had some notable friends. James Pattle (1775-1845) an officer in the East India Co. married Adeline de L'Etang and had a family of famous daughters viz. Julia Margaret (1815-79) who was born in Calcutta married Charles Hay Cameron, Sarah (1816-87) married Henry Thoby Prinsep and Maria (1818-92) married Dr. John Jackson. The Prinseps rented Little Holland House in the grounds of Lord Holland's estate in Kensington in 1850, which became a centre for artists and writers and in particular a meeting place of the Pre-Raphaelites such as Dante Gabriel Rossetti. Visitors to the house included Tennyson and Thackeray whilst George Frederick Watts the artist went to live there. Sarah Prinsep said of the latter, "He came to stay three days and then stayed for 30 years!" Valentine Cameron Prinsep R.A. (1838-1904) son of Thoby and Sarah was a Pre-Raphaelite artist and had encouragement from G.F. Watts. He travelled to Italy with Burne-Jones in 1859-60 and married Florence Leyland daughter of a Liverpool ship owner in 1884 and became independent, which helped finance his painting.

Tennyson moved to Farringford on the Isle of Wight in 1853 and Julia Margaret Cameron followed him in 1860. She purchased two houses overlooking Freshwater Bay and made them into one by adding a central tower. She called the new house *Dimbola* and began to experiment with photography there in 1863 (Thackeray died that same year at Palace Green). She was a main exponent of the new 'art' and her models included the young Alice Liddell and actress Ellen Terry. Indeed Rev. Dodgson or Lewis Carroll based *Alice in Wonderland* on the former and G.F. Watts married the latter. She also took photographs of her niece Julia Prinsep Jackson since she was a great beauty. Little Holland House was demolished in 1870 and Melbury Road and Napier Road now cover the site (west of Holland Park) whilst the Prinseps and G.F. Watts followed the Camerons to Freshwater Bay. Leslie Stephen (1832-1904) worked on the Cornhill Magazine and helped to start the Pall Mall Gazette with George Smith - Thackeray's old friend. The artist Edward Burne-Jones trained under Rossetti and was later a friend of William Morris and painted Julia Prinsep Jackson (1846-95) for her great beauty - she married Herbert Duckworth but became a widow. Leslie Stephen first married Harriet Marian Thackeray but she died in 1875 and he met Julia Prinsep at the house of George Smith in Hampstead. The couple were married and had children Vanessa Bell (1879-1961) painter and 'Adeline' Virginia Woolf (1882-1941) writer. Leslie Stephen was first editor of *The National Biography* (a source for this book) whilst his daughter Virginia Woolf was a member of the Bloomsbury Group. Ann Thackeray maintained links with her father's friends and lived at the Porch, Freshwater in 1875 then married cousin Richmond Thackeray Ritchie in 1877 and published *Tennyson & His Friends* in 1892. In particular she corresponded with the Merriman family and sent them several letters (see below).

James Nathaniel Merriman died at Kensington in late 1854 and his will was proved at the P.C.C. on 27 December. Brother John Merriman was then in partnership with John 'Jones' at 12 Young Street, whilst Henry Blunt died at Kensington in March 1858 aged 17. John Merriman G.P. M.R.C.S. lived at 45 Kensington Square in 1861 with wife Caroline, sons Septimus (25) and William (23) and four servants. John Jones Merriman was at 44 Kensington Square and Mrs. James Merriman was at 4 Kensington Square with her children Harvey H. and Georgiana M., some visitors from Bath and York, and three servants. Ann Thackeray sent a letter to Mrs. Merriman in 1862-64 - presumably the wife of John Jones. Today, the service entrance to Barkers Kensington is just behind 45 Kensington Square, and 18 Young Street once stood there (see above). No. 16 the adjacent property has a plaque: "William Thackeray 1811-63 novelist lived here," whilst Thackeray Street is at the southeast corner of Kensington Square. Indeed this was always an attractive and desirable area and there are two blue plaques close to the Merrimans' house on the north side: No. 40 Sir John Simon 1816-1904 pioneer of public health lived here No. 41 Sir Edward Burne-Jones 1833-98 artist lived here 1865-67. The latter was a friend of the Prinseps and an advocate of the Pre-Raphaelite movement.

John Merriman retired in the mid-1860s and moved with his wife to Bridgeman House, Teddington but his circumstances were soon to change. His daughter Christiana Merriman died at Bridgeman House on 2 October 1870 whilst his wife Caroline Merriman died on a trip to Bournemouth on 24 November 1870. He retained Bridgeman House however spent time with his son and travelled overseas. John J. Merriman surgeon resided at 45 Kensington Square in April 1871 (see below) and his father John a retired surgeon was staying with him. John Merriman made his last will at Bridgeman House on 18 December 1871 and left his household effects and personal items to his children, these to be divided at his executors' discretion. His son Thomas Hardwick Merriman had received a marriage settlement of £1,250 and he placed this, in trust, with John Jones Merriman and William Henry White Esq. The income was to be paid to his son whilst a further £1,000 was for his son's trustees (at the latter's decease). There was a settlement in contemplation of the marriage of Septimus Merriman - the amounts £2,500 and £2,000 respectively.

He added: "I devise my freehold house known as Bridgeman House with the buildings thereunto belonging, and the land surrounding the same, and my two freehold houses adjoining, all situate at Teddington, Middlesex.... to John Jones and Thomas Hardwick Merriman in trust." This was part of his residuary estate and they were to sell the property, collect his money and invest the proceeds at their discretion and divided the amount between: John Jones, Thomas Hardwick, Charles James, Septimus and William and Caroline Olivia wife of Rev. James Thomson. It was to take place after the two trusts to his sons and excluded two covenants to his daughter Caroline Olivia Thomson viz. a £1,000 Policy of Assurance, the sum and bonuses payable on his death; a £1,000 settlement for his daughter and her children payable on his death - in trust for her and her children outside the control of any husband. The will was a lengthy document and he appointed John Jones Merriman and Thomas Hardwick Merriman (solicitor) as executors. Edwin Wells a servant of Teddington and Charles Barringer a servant at the Manor House, Barnes were witnesses.

Indeed John then travelled abroad and was living in Naples, Italy in March 1872 and left all his affairs in the hands of his son Thomas Hardwick Merriman. The latter was a solicitor of Manor House, Barnes and also the lawful attorney of John Merriman. He administered the effects of Caroline Merriman for his father under the usual limitations regarding his surrogacy - value under £450. Emily Yorke Merriman continued to live at 4 Kensington Square, which was a plain fronted town house almost opposite to no. 45 (it is present today). The family were absent and two servants at home in 1871 whilst Emily Yorke Merriman died there on 31 July 1874 - John Jones Merriman surgeon of 45 Kensington Square proved the will. Thomas Lendon Merriman (1836) died at "Lencot" Herbert Road in West Bournemouth on 1 September 1901.

John then returned from Italy and resided at West Lodge, Putney and then made three codicils to his will: (1) He left £20 to his faithful servant Edwin Wells - 5 May 1874. The clerks of T.H. Merriman at Temple were witnesses. (2) He paid back to John Jones Merriman the insurance premiums his son paid regarding three life assurance policies (on his life) - 24 December 1878. George Morrison a dairyman from Putney and Edwin Wells his servant were witnesses. (3) He had loaned money to William since his marriage and received interest from him, and the latter was to be paid back to his son - 14 February 1880. James Yale surgeon of 26 Dorchester Place, Blandford Square, London and James Govringe servant were witnesses. John Merriman died at West Lodge, Putney Common on 24 March 1881 aged 80 and John Jones Merriman surgeon of 45 Kensington Square and Thomas Hardwick Merriman solicitor of 3 King's Bench Walk, Temple proved his will on 11 May 1881 - the value £25,000. John J. Merriman was given administration of the effects of Christiana Merriman on 8 August 1881 as executor of her father's will and her estate was £2,284 4s 7d, whilst John Merriman's will was re sworn in March 1882 - the value then £30,000.

John Jones Merriman was born at Kensington Square on 3 July 1827 and baptized at St. Mary Abbots on 27 July then practiced medicine from at least 1851. George White a gentleman and his wife Frederica Anne Eliza had five children in Marylebone viz. George Cosby (1825), William Henry (1826), Frederica Anne Eliza (19 January 1828), Sarah Mary (1829) and Louisa Fanny (1831) plus Alicia Elizabeth (1833) born Kensington (see below). John Jones Merriman married Frederica Anne Eliza White at Kensington in June 1852 and was friends with Thackeray and his family from that time. He initially lived at 44 Kensington Square and had children Frederica Caroline (1853), John W.C. (1855), Mary Hardwick (1857), Elizabeth (1861), Constance (1864), Emily G. (1866), George H. (1869) and Agnes Christiana (1872). He then moved to his father's house 45 Kensington Square in the 1860s and lived there in 1871 with his wife, children Frederica, Constance, Emily and George, father John, a medical assistant and seven servants. John Jones Merriman a medical practitioner also lived at no. 45 in 1881 with wife Frederica, daughters Mary H., Elizabeth and Agnes C. and five servants. Lucy A. Merriman aged 46 from Wiltshire was a visitor hence the family maintained links with Marlborough. His son John W.C. Merriman a medical practitioner lived with his wife Agnes and two children at no. 42 and John Simon a retired surgeon and his wife were at no. 40, whilst Ann Thackeray Ritchie sent further letters to J.J. Merriman in 1878-90 and on 1 May 1893. John Jones Merriman Esq. died at 13 The Steyne, Worthing on 8 September 1896 and Septimus Merriman and William John Humphrys Esq. obtained probate on 1 October 1896; his estate was worth £20,236 17s 3d but re-sworn in March 1897 at £20,598 8s 9d. Mary H. Merriman died at Holy Cross, Irene in South Africa on 16 May 1930 and William Archer Thomson solicitor and Rev. James Hamilton Charles had probate in London on 9 August - effects in England £2,645 9s 7d.

Thomas Hardwick Merriman was born at Kensington Square on 9 September 1828 and was baptized at St. Mary Abbots on 24 February 1829; he trained as an attorney and solicitor and lived with his father at 45 Kensington Square in 1851. He then resided at Petersham between Ham and Richmond and married Alicia Elizabeth White from London at Petersham on 8 February 1855. George Cosby White M.A. performed the ceremony whilst John Merriman, Charles G. Jones, Sarah M. White and William Henry White were witnesses. He was successful in his profession and lived at the "Manor House", Barnes from at least 1861-84, which was a large property beside Barnes Common at the junction of Queen's Ride and Upper Richmond Road. The house faced west with two wings at the rear and a large ornamental garden behind, whilst it was well situated for travel to London being just south of Barnes Station. He had chambers at 1 Mitre Court, Temple in 1861-68 and at 3 King's Bench Walk, Temple in 1871-81. Indeed E.C. Morley and John Welch also had chambers there whilst A.C. Meysey-Thompson was at 1 King's Bench Walk. What forces brought them there? Was it soccer or soliciting that came first?

Thomas H. Merriman solicitor lived at the Manor House, Barnes in 1871 with wife Alicia E., children Alice H. (10) and Margaret H. (8) both born in Barnes and four servants. Thomas died at the Manor House on 13 July 1884 and brothers John Jones Merriman of 45 Kensington Square and Septimus Merriman of Glenthorne, Putney Park Avenue, Putney proved his will on 19 August 1884 - his effects were initially £10,129 18s 9d but re sworn in January 1897 at £10,379 18s 9d. Alicia Elizabeth Merriman then lived at 30 Manor Road, Folkestone but died there on 22 October 1904 and probate was granted to Alice Hardwick Merriman, Margaret Hardwick Merriman and William Archer Thomson solicitor. The daughter Alice Hardwick Merriman died at the same address on 21 September 1912 and probate was granted to sister Margaret and William Archer Thomson.

Charles James Merriman was born on 10 October 1831 and baptized at St. Mary Abbots on 23 November. He attended the H.E.I.C. Military Seminary, Addiscombe, Croydon, which was the cadet school of the Honourable East India Co. (also known as Addiscombe College). He paved the way for his brother William and joined the Royal Engineers at Chatham as a 2nd lieutenant on 14 June 1850 and transferred to the Bombay Engineers in 1852. He became a 1st lieutenant on 1 August 1854 and served with the Persian expeditionary force in 1856-57 and had a major role in the campaign. He was present at the storming of Reshire on 7 December 1856, the capture of Bushire on 12 December and the battle of Koosh-Ab on 8 February 1857, and received a medal with clasp - Bushire is on the coastal plain of the Persian Gulf. He was made a captain on 27 August 1858 and married Eugenia Sybilla daughter of Col Richard Bulkley of the Bombay Army in India that year. The couple had sons Reginald Gordon (1866), Cecil (1873) and Athol Bulkley (1878) and five daughters - the first two born in Aden and Poona.

He was superintendent engineer for irrigation in Sind from 16 January 1868, this being a region north of Karachi on the Indus flood plain. He was superintendent engineer 2nd class 2nd grade on 27 April 1868, lieutenant colonel on 18 December 1869 and 2nd class 1st grade on 10 December 1870 but was listed simply as 2nd grade on 1 September 1871. Indeed he was executive engineer at Hyderabad, Karachi, Belgaum and Aden and stayed at Sind until 1872. He had a furlough in Europe in 1873 and was promoted to brevet colonel on 18 December 1874 and decorated for the famine in Bombay 'presidency' in 1876-77. He was posted to Poona 80 miles inland from Bombay in 1877-78 and was made a colonel on 24 August 1878 and received the Companion of the Star of India (C.S.I.) that same year. His promotion up the ranks continued and he was made a major general on 18 January 1882 as well as 1st Chief Engineer for Sind. He was also Government under Secretary to the Public Works and Irrigation Department in Bombay in 1880-85. He was a member of the Bombay Legislative Council and became a lieutenant general on 21 June 1884 and a general on 22 February 1887 but had retired by 1893. He lived at 79 Eaton Rise, Ealing in 1897 and with his wife and son Cecil in Dover in 1901. Charles James Merriman died at Ripley House, Castle Avenue in Dover on 4 January 1906 and his probate was granted to Eugenia Sybilla Merriman, his effects £2,615 2s 11d. Charles James Merriman outranked many of the officers in this book and one can speculate on the relationship with William his younger brother - did he have to salute him? Reginald Gordon Merriman was born at Aden on 10 November 1866 and educated at the United Services College in Westward Ho and at Woolwich. He joined the Royal Artillery in 1884 and was decorated for the expedition to Tambaku Country, West Africa in 1892 and involved in the capture of Tambi. He was a captain in Fulham in 1901 and died at "Moorlands", Minehead in Somerset on 11 October 1938.

Septimus Merriman was born at 13 Young Street on 6 April 1836 and baptized at St. Mary Abbots on 15 June. He lived at 45 Kensington Square in 1861 and married Mary Agnes daughter of Rev. William Maskelyne of Crudwell, Wilts in 1871. The couple lived at Mill Hill House, Barnes Common in 1872 and had children Beatrice (1873), Edith (1875), George Frederick M. (1877) and Eveline (1880). Septimus Merriman an underwriter in the Stock Exchange lived at "Glenthorne", Putney Park Avenue in 1881 with his wife Mary, four children and five servants then had Hugh M. (1881). He was there in 1884 but lived at Cuddington on his own means in 1901 with wife Mary, Edith and Hugh (insurance clerk). Septimus Merriman died at "Whitcomb", Worcester Park in Surrey on 6 June 1906 and probate went to William Merriman retired col. R.E., William Archer Thomson solicitor (his cousin) and George Frederick Maskelyne Merriman Esq. - effects £4,729 12s 7d.

William Merriman was born at 13 Young Street, Kensington on 2 April 1838 at 3 p.m. in the afternoon. It was a wet and windy day in Kensington as he arrived in a cruel world and as the youngest son his prospects were poor.... (Sorry that was Dickens)! He was in fact well blessed and his family already had Royal associations so it was no surprise when he married into one of the most prominent families in England. John Merriman junior a surgeon, his father, registered the birth at Kensington Town sub-district on 12 May 1838 and like his family he was baptized at St. Mary Abbots on the 25 inst. He grew up in the refined surroundings of Kensington Square and was initially educated at Kensington School (see Introspection) - he was a scholar aged 12 living with his parents in 1851. His brothers had become doctors, solicitors and army engineers and there was a tough choice however he followed Charles and attended Addiscombe College during its last days in about 1854-56.

Thomas Heron built "Addiscombe Place" at Croydon in c.1500 - it was situated between Outram and Havelock Roads. William Draper son-in-law of John Evelyn the diarist employed Sir John Vanbrugh and he completely rebuilt the house in 1702. There were several owners including Charles Talbot, Thomas Robinson the Lord Chancellor, Lord Grantham and Charles Jenkinson the 1st Earl of Liverpool. The latter died in 1808 and the house was sold to the East India Company who used it as a military college to train their cadets. The students spent 2 years there and those aged 14-16 had to be over 4' 9" and those aged 17-18 years over 5' 2". The British Government took charge of the sub-continent after the Indian Mutiny in 1857 and the role of the East India Company ended in 1858. Addiscombe College closed in 1861 and the house was demolished and the site cleared by 1863. The Victorian villas of Ashburton, Outram, Havelock, Elgin, Clyde and Canning Roads were built on the site and named after people associated with the college - indeed Lord Clyde and Sir Henry Havelock were involved in the siege of Lucknow (1857). Despite this, there are some traces of the military college still remaining viz. 137-139 Addiscombe Road otherwise "Ashleigh" and "India". A green plaque states: "1848, houses for the professors of the East India Company Military Seminary." These are on the corner with Clyde Road and there is also a gymnasium at the northeast end of Havelock Road. This is an unusual survivor of brown brick with arched windows and tiled entrance (now converted to flats) whilst a Victorian house was built in front. N.B. William E. Wilkins who designed the National Gallery was the architect of a similar institution at Haileybury near Hertford viz. The East India College (1806-58). It re-opened as Haileybury School in 1862.

William then joined the Royal (Bombay) Engineers as 2nd lieutenant (ensign) on 12 December 1856 and was promoted to 1st lieutenant on 27 August 1858, but was living with his parents at 45 Kensington Square in 1861. He was promoted to the rank of captain on 31 December 1868 and was stationed at Chatham in 1870-71. He was Assistant Instructor in Field Works at the School of Military Engineering, Brompton Barracks, Chatham, from 1 April 1871 and was recorded thus on the census dated 2 April having held the post just one day. Captain Marindin, Brigade Major was his superior officer and together they built a strong football team, whilst Fitzroy Molyneux Henry Somerset was in charge of military discipline and therein lies a story.

John of Gaunt, Duke of Lancaster and son of Edward III, ruled England in all but name during the reign of young King Richard II (1377-99). He had an illegitimate line by Catherine Swynford however the latter was made legitimate by papal decree, in 1396, and confirmed by Richard II. Their son Sir John Beaufort (1371) was created Earl of Somerset in 1396/97 and his name came from Beaufort Castle in the Champagne district of France (the family once owned it). There was soon considerable change and John of Gaunt died in 1399 and Richard II was deposed that year and Henry Bolingbroke a legitimate son of

Raglan Castle, Monmouth. This was the last castle to fall to Cromwell in 1646 after a 10-week siege.

the former seized the throne then was crowned Henry IV. The Earl of Somerset, meanwhile, lost some of his titles after the accession whilst his daughter Joan married James I of Scotland in 1423/24. They were ancestors of the Stuart dynasty who later ruled both England and Scotland, whilst granddaughter Margaret married Edmund Tudor in 1455 - the parents of Henry VII.

The Beaufort family lost the title of Duke of Somerset however Charles Somerset was created 1st Earl of Worcester in 1513/14 and Henry Somerset 1st Marquis of Worcester defended Raglan Castle when besieged by Parliament in 1646. His son Edward Somerset went on a mission to Ireland to raise troops for Charles I and was later imprisoned in the Tower but received his lands back after the Restoration. He was interested in mechanics and made experiments regarding the steam engine. His son Henry Somerset was made the 1st Duke of Beaufort in 1682 partly due to his descent from Edward III (this was a case of all change). The story proper begins with Henry Somerset (1744) 5th Duke of Beaufort who married Elizabeth daughter of Admiral the Hon. Edward Boscawen. Henry was Grandmaster of the Freemasons in 1767-72 and Master of the Horse to Queen Charlotte (1768-70) and provided many links regarding this discourse. His daughter Elizabeth Somerset married the Very Rev. Charles Talbot on 27 June 1796 and they had three sons and three daughters. Their son Charles (1801) was grandfather of Frank Eustace George Talbot who was discussed regarding E.W. Creswell (see Ch. 9). A son George Talbot (1809) was a colonel in the 43rd Regiment and his son and heir was Fitzroy Somerset Talbot (1837) - this reveals the connection to the gentleman at Chatham.

Henry Charles Somerset (1766) the first son was 6th Duke of Beaufort whilst Charles Henry Somerset (1767) the second son had descendants called Plantagenet and was father of Poulett George Henry Somerset (1822) - see below. Robert Edward Henry Somerset the third son was born on 19 December 1776 and was a cornet in the 10th Light Dragoons in 1793 and aide-de-camp to the Duke of York in 1799. He was M.P. for Monmouth Boroughs (1799-1802) and Gloucester-shire (1803-29) and was with the 4th Dragoons in Portugal from 1809. He commanded the Regiment at Talavera on 27-28 July 1809 whilst Wellesley was raised to the peerage as Viscount Wellington for his part in the battle. He commanded at Buçaco on 27 September 1810 and generally led the attack being aide-de-camp to the King at the time, and was mentioned by Wellington in despatches and made a major general in 1813. Napoleon was defeated at Toulouse on 10 April 1814 and exiled to Elba whilst Wellington was made a

Duke and Somerset thanked by Parliament for his actions in the Peninsula on 26 June. He was awarded a gold cross and K.C.B. in January next and commanded the Household Brigade Cavalry at Waterloo on 18 June 1815. He continued in this role during the occupation of France to 1818 and was later a lieutenant general and died in London on 1 September 1842.

Arthur John Henry Somerset (1780) the fourth son was married to Elizabeth Boscawen in 1808. William George Henry Somerset the fifth son was born on 2 September 1784 and entered the ministry. He married Elizabeth daughter of Lieut. Gen Sir Thomas Molyneux on 29 June 1813 and his two sons are now treated: Fitzroy Molyneux Henry Somerset was born Trenchay, Somerset on 29 December 1823 and made a cadet in the Royal Engineers on 1 January 1842. He was posted to Gibraltar on 9 May 1844 and made a 1st lieutenant on 22 April 1845 then returned home on 15 February next. He married Jemima Drummond Nairne in Edinburgh on 1 March 1849 and was sent to Canada on 20 June 1849 and whilst there had a son Fitzroy James William Henry (1850-59) and a daughter Emily Jane Anna Elizabeth in Quebec on 26 May 1851. He returned to barracks at Chatham on 7 March 1852 and was a 2nd captain on 17 February 1854 and captain on 19 June 1855. He had two children at Old Brompton - Elizabeth Frances Caroline (8 August 1854) and Arthur William Fitzroy (20 September 1855). He then had some home postings at Chatham, Woolwich, Camp Chobham, North Britain and Dover but returned to Gibraltar from 29 February 1861 to 5 January 1866. He went to Chatham and was a lieutenant colonel on 25 inst. and Officer of Military Discipline there until 31 December 1870.

During this period his daughter Emily met William Merriman but hopefully in the officers mess and not through his duties. He was sent to Aldershot on 1 January 1871, made a brevet colonel on 25 inst. and colonel on 1 June 1873. He was posted to Bermuda on 21 October 1873 however his wife died on 19 June 1874 and he was then made Commander at Colchester from 20 October 1876 to 2 October 1879. William Merriman was there at this time and Colonel Somerset was the commanding officer, which may have been a delicate situation (see below). He was appointed Commander at Aldershot and Colonel on the Staff on 3 October 1879 and retired from the army on 31 December 1881 having served 39 years 364 days. He had a deserved pension of £600 p.a. and a gratuity of £500 and married Emily Biedermann on 5 September 1882. There was then an adjustment and he reverted to half pay and was on a pension of £450 p.a. and a gratuity of £276 from 29 December 1883. He died at the Priory, Frimley on 22 February 1901 and probate was granted to William Merriman colonel R.E. and Arthur W. F. Somerset J.P., his effects £26,425 11s 6d. His brother Boscawen Thomas George Henry Somerset was born on 2 June 1833 and became the rector of Crickhowell, whilst Arthur William Fitzroy Somerset (1855) married his cousin Gwendolin Adelaide Katherine Georgiana Matilda Somerset the granddaughter of John T.H. Somerset (1787) - sixth son.

Fitzroy James Henry Somerset the seventh and youngest son was born at Badminton on 30 September 1788 and had a notable career. He was educated at Westminster and a lieutenant in the 4th Light Dragoons in 1805 and aide-de-camp to Arthur Wellesley in 1808. Indeed he fought with him at Talavera and Buçaco on the Spanish Peninsula and was appointed his military secretary in 1811 then made a lieutenant colonel in 1812 aged 24. He married Emily Harriet Wellesley-Pole daughter of 3rd Earl of Mornington on 6 August 1814. Wellington was her uncle whilst the infamous William Pole Tylney Long-Wellesley was her brother (see Alcock Ch. 2). Wellington and Somerset were confronted with the return of Napoleon and fought together at Waterloo in 1815. Somerset, however, was badly injured and lost an arm and was appointed aide-de-camp to the Prince Regent and later secretary to the Duke of Wellington. He accompanied him to St. Petersburg for the accession of Nicholas I in 1826 and was Military Secretary at Horse Guards in 1827. He held the post 25 years and was noted for his accuracy and tact in business dealings being invaluable to Wellington who described him as: "A man who couldn't tell a lie to save his life." Major Arthur William Fitzroy Somerset his elder son died of wounds at the Battle of Ferozeshah in the Sutlej campaign on 25 December 1845 (see Goodwyn). Wellington his friend and uncle died on 24 September 1852 and Henry Viscount Hardinge G.C.B. replaced him and commanded the Queen's Army from 28 September 1852. Somerset then replaced Hardinge and became Master General of the Ordnance and was raised to the peerage as Baron Raglan of Raglan, Monmouth on 12 October 1852.

He was chosen to command the troops in the Crimea in spring 1854 and was implicated in events at Balaklava on 25 October that year. Raglan stationed himself high on a hill and wrote the order: "Cavalry to advance rapidly to the front and try to prevent the enemy carrying away the guns." This was sent to Lord Lucan and punctuation may have caused an error thus he commanded a cavalry charge, which thereafter was known as "The Charge of the Light Brigade." All agreed that someone had blundered and Raglan blamed Lord Lucan in his despatch, however the order was ambiguous and referred to guns already taken and not the entrenched position of the Russian battery! Raglan was also at the Battles of Alma and Inkerman and was made Field Marshall on 5 November 1854; he continued to direct the campaign whilst his nephew Poulett George Henry Somerset (1822-75) was aide-de-camp. There was criticism of the poor condition of his troops and he felt deeply the failure of the campaign and was afflicted with dysentery - he died on 28 June 1855. His son Richard Henry Fitzroy Somerset (1817-84) was 2nd Lord Raglan.

William Merriman captain R.E. of Old Brompton married Emily Jane Anna Elizabeth Somerset (20) of 41 Elvaston Place at St. Stephen's Church, Kensington on 15 February 1872 (see G.W. Addison). Boscawen T.G.H. Somerset rector of Mitchel Troy with Cwmcarvan in Monmouth-shire performed the ceremony and John Jones Merriman, Georgiana Maria Merriman (cousin) and Colonel Fitzroy Somerset R.E. were witnesses. This was another society wedding at the attractive St. Stephen's Church, whilst Elvaston Place was two roads south of Queen's Gate Terrace (see Rich Ch. 8) and Mitchel Troy was five miles east of Raglan Castle near to Monmouth. The bride was a great granddaughter of the 5th Duke of Beaufort thus William Merriman had made a notable connection to John of Gaunt and the Kings of England. He was also related to the Creswell family and the Talbots had links to Marindin - Kinnaird. Meanwhile the Merrimans supported Cromwell whilst the Somersets were Royalists!

Captain Merriman was then Assistant Instructor in Field Works at the S.M.E. Chatham and supported Marindin in their work and on the soccer pitch. He played for the Royal Engineers in the first F.A. Cup Final on 16 March 1872 just a month after his wedding, and although he restricted the Wanderers with his 'efficient goal keeping' was unable to stop the winner. He had a daughter Ethel Fitzroy who was born at Medway in March 1873 and registered as "Female" Merriman, and continued to play in the soccer team - the following year was to be most eventful. William Merriman was made a major on 13 March 1874 and before he caught his breath played in the Cup Final the next day. The team included Marindin, Addison and Renny-Tailyour however they lost 2-0 to Oxford University. Major Marindin was appointed F.A. President in 1874 and left Brompton Barracks in November that year, whilst Major Merriman also a keen exponent of amateur soccer joined the F.A. Committee in 1874-77 - the Engineers had two representatives at the F.A. headquarters. His success was then somewhat tainted as his son William Somerset born at Medway in September 1874 died as an infant. He then took charge of the soccer team and made a strong challenge the following year, although they did play all their games at Brompton. They progressed to the semi-final after beating Marlow 3-0, Cambridge University 5-0 and Clapham Rovers 3-2 then played a tense game against Oxford University at the Oval. The first contest was a 1-1 draw but the Engineers won the replay 1-0 after extra time.

William Merriman captained the Royal Engineers in the Final at the Oval on 13 March 1875. The team included Renny-Tailyour and Wingfield-Stratford who became brothers-in-law six months later, Pelham G. von Donop a friend of the Addison family and William Francis Howard Stafford (lieutenant 29 October 1873). The 1872 team photograph shows a confident William Merriman holding the ball with Renny-Tailyour in front. There is also a team photograph of 1875 that shows Merriman holding the ball (he was the goalkeeper) and next to him Renny-Tailyour and von Donop, and behind Stafford and Wingfield-Stratford - with a regimental hat. The players were dressed in dark striped vests, trousers with striped socks pulled over them and laced boots, whilst some had woolly caps. The Etonians had a strong team including Bonsor, Kenyon-Slaney, Kinnaird, E. Lubbock and C.M. Thompson and the game was played in front of 3,000 - the referee C.W. Alcock. There was a hard contest and Bonsor and Renny-Tailyour both scored however the game ended 1-1 after extra time.

The replay took place at the Oval in front of 3,000 on 16 March 1875 and C.W. Alcock was again the referee (the crowd for a Conference game). The Engineers fielded the same side as three days earlier, being well organised, and arrived in good time for the 2 p.m. kick-off, however the Old Etonians did not turn up until just before 3 p.m. and made a number of changes to their side. Bonsor, Kinnaird, E. Lubbock and his brother A. Lubbock played in the game but they were without Thompson, Benson, Ottaway and Kenyon-Slaney and hence were not at full strength. A match record states that: "The Royal Engineers team were determined to bring the operation to some conclusion or other.... and on the whole the ball was generally about the neighbourhood of the Etonians goal." They clearly viewed their soccer as an army manoeuvre and the outcome of the sustained attack was obvious. Lieutenants Renny-Tailyour and Stafford scored and they won the Final 2-0 - it would have been an injustice to soccer history if they had not. During the game the ends were changed after each goal, however this practice was stopped thereafter. William Merriman led his team to victory in the F.A. Cup and this was their one and only triumph, despite the strength of the side.

Major Merriman was 37 at the time of the Final and this was the end of his playing career. He remained at the School of Military Engineering until 31 March 1875 and was then sent to Colchester in Essex. Fitzroy

Somerset his father-in-law was the commanding officer there from 1876-79 (see above) whilst the couple had three children in the town: Arthur Drummond Nairne (June 1876), Blanche (September 1878) and Dorothy Gladys (March 1880). William Merriman was sent abroad and served in the 1st Boer War or Basuto War from 13 September 1880 to 15 May 1881, the main conflicts in Basutoland and Transkei. Henry Bayard Rich may have been involved as he was at the Cape of Good Hope at the time. Emily Merriman lived at Military Road, Colchester in 1881 with children Ethel, Arthur, Blanche and Dorothy and three servants, but William returned and was made a brevet lieutenant colonel on 1 July 1881 - Bayard Rich was also there in 1881-82.

There was then a change of direction and he was "on leave" in early 1882 awaiting a posting to Bombay. He travelled there with his family later that year and was appointed executive engineer 1st grade D.P. Works, his main duty being the Bombay defences. Major General C.J. Merriman his brother was Chief Engineer and Government under Secretary for Public Works and Irrigation and also on the Bombay Legislative Council (1880), thus William must have worked under him. He was promoted to brevet colonel on 1 July 1885 and finally to lieutenant colonel on 9 April 1886 but had some leave in Europe in early 1888. He then returned to Bombay and was a member of the H.Q. Staff and also the superintending engineer (1st Class D.P.W.) for 'West of India' coast defences in 1889-91. He was decorated for such work in Bombay, Karachi and Aden with the Companion of the Indian Empire (C.I.E.) in 1890 and became a fellow of Bombay University. He had a large number of interests including cricket, football, hunting, shooting, rowing and golf and belonged to the East India United Service and the Byculla Club in Bombay. He took some leave in Europe in 1893 and retired from the army later that year.

William Coats Hutton (1865) married Ethel Fitzroy Merriman at Kensington in March 1893 thus they still had links with their old home, but the family went to live in Colchester where they had spent several years in the 1870s. William Merriman colonel late R.E. of Colchester, Essex made his last will on 10 March 1897 and bequeathed his household furniture, linen, wearing apparel, books, plate, pictures, china, horses, carriages, and carts, namely all his real and personal estate and money to his dear wife Emily J. A. E. Merriman the witnesses C.J. Merriman general of 79 Eaton Rise, Ealing and Septimus Merriman insurance agent of Worcester Park. William Merriman retired colonel R.E. lived at 24 Creffield Road, Colchester (St. Mary at the Wall) in 1901 with Dorothy and three servants. Arthur Drummond Nairne Merriman married Dorothy Hornby daughter of Major Frank Bradshaw of the 13th Somerset Light Infantry at Portsmouth in December 1903. He was a lieutenant colonel, officers' reserve for the Manchester Regiment and lived at Bishops Hall, Taunton. Dorothy Gladys Merriman married at Colchester in December 1904.

William Merriman a colonel C.I.E. late R.E. Bombay residence Creffield, Colchester was in *Kelly's Titled and Landed Gentry* in 1910. He died at Creffield House, Gray Road, Colchester, on 11 May 1917 and his widow Emily Merriman obtained his probate in London on 16 May 1917. His estate was valued at only £427 2s 1d thus despite Royal connections and a good career he did not have the assets of his colleagues. Emily Jane Anna Elizabeth Merriman died at the Cottage, St. Clare Road, Colchester, on 10 January 1923 and Ethel Fitzroy Hutton obtained her probate in London on 2 May 1923 the effects £1,083 2s 11d. The family had a long-term connection with the area and William Coats Hutton died at Lexden Grange, Colchester on 19 April 1926 and Ethel Fitzroy Hutton and Joshua David Casswell barrister had probate the effects £95,739 18s 1d but re-sworn on 17 March 1927 at £90,178 18s 1d (resealed Singapore). Ethel Fitzroy Hutton died at "Talcotts", Lexden Road, Colchester, on 25 September 1960 and Fitzroy Evelyn Patrick Hutton C.B. retired rear admiral R.N. and David Pelham Papillon solicitor obtained probate.

The Royal Engineers team consisted solely of officers in 1872 although they did have a variety of backgrounds. Marindin came from a religious family with roots in Birmingham and Switzerland whilst Merriman was from a medical family with roots in Wiltshire - both in the higher levels of society. The majority of the Engineers, however, had military links and Cotter, Goodwyn, Mitchell, Rich and Renny-Tailyour followed their fathers into the army. Addison and Bogle were the sons of gentlemen who were involved in the worsted mills of Yorkshire and trade in Tasmania. Creswell grew up in Gibraltar with its postal service whilst Muirhead had his roots in the academic world and steam engines of Watt. These amateurs had very different backgrounds to the players in the professional game although six of the Engineers did come from Scotland (and they weren't penalised for it). They had a better opportunity for training and played with military precision, thus were favourites for the Final on 16 March 1872 (see Half Time), then took part in confrontations on a greater stage.

The Wanderers Engineer a Win

The first Cup contest was drawing to its conclusion and the two teams assembled in the Oval pavilion to prepare for the Final. It was Saturday 16 March 1872 and the weather was bright but there was a considerable breeze and William Burrup, Secretary of the cricket club, was no doubt fretting about the wicket. The Royal Engineers were favourites to win however both sides had quality players and gentlemen of note. A fashionable crowd was present for the contest since the phenomenon of 'Cup Fever' had not yet reached the general public. Soccer was popular but remained a bit of a diversion and one wonders how many friends from school or society were present. This was a time of sportsmanship and honour on the playing field, with no room for 'foul' play.

William Ewart Gladstone *Liberal* was in power at the time and Benjamin Disraeli *Conservative* in opposition. There was a mood of change in the air and the *Reform Act* (1867) greatly extended the male vote and the *Education Act* (1871) established the first system of state education. There was exciting news in the papers and Charles Darwin published 'The Descent of Man' in 1871 - he made several astonishing assumptions and stated that men and apes were related! Edgar Lubbock his neighbour may have been somewhat perturbed by this announcement but there was no time to dwell on it as further news was breaking from Africa.

Dr. David Livingstone worked in a cotton mill when a boy but educated himself and trained as a doctor and priest. He made his first expedition across Africa in 1853-56 and during the journey discovered the Victoria Falls and followed the Zambezi River. He spent further time in Africa in 1858-64 and tried to navigate the Zambezi and find the source of the Nile and also campaigned for the abolition of slavery, however he returned there in 1866 and was lost to the world. The editor of the *New York Herald* decided to find him and sent the journalist Henry Stanley stating: "Find Livingstone if he's alive or his boots if he's dead!" Stanley spent 236 days searching and travelled 1,000 miles then arrived at the village of Ujiji by the shore of Lake Tanganyika (now in Tanzania) on 10 November 1871. He was wearing a flannel suit with newly polished boots and pushed through a crowd of Africans to find a sickly white man and uttered the immortal words, "Dr. Livingstone I presume?" The men had five months together and the doctor was a national hero whilst Stanley published his tales in England and America and found the source of both the Congo and Nile.

This was the political and social atmosphere at the time of the first Cup Final. Charles Alcock Esq. and Captain Marindin led the teams onto the pitch and the players wore the striped jerseys, socks and long trousers favoured at the time. They all came from 'society' families and would soon make their mark on the Empire, whilst the 2,000 spectators included men in top hats and ladies in long dresses. The game received several reports and one was published in the *Sportsman Newspaper* on Tuesday 19 March 1872. This provided a detailed eyewitness account and the game kicked off with cries of "Come on you Wanderers," and "Play up you Sappers." It was reported as follows:

FOOTBALL

THE ASSOCIATION CHALLENGE CUP

THE FINAL TIE

On Saturday the last of the matches which have taken place in the competition for the possession of the Challenge Cup, presented by the committee of the Football Association, took place at Kennington Oval. The two clubs left in to contend for the honour of holding the trophy for that year were the Wanderers and the Royal Engineers, and as the rivals on this occasion were certainly the two most powerful organisations supporting Association Rules, the excitement, not only among the partisans of the respective sides, but among the lovers of football generally, was intense. It may here be as well to state that during the earlier heats the Royal Engineers had defeated the Hitchin Club, the Hampstead Heathens, and the Crystal Palace, all without difficulty; while on the other hand the Wanderers had only defeated the Clapham Rovers by one goal, having drawn with the Crystal Palace, and enjoyed a walk over in their tie with the Harrow Chequers. Mainly a consequence of their easy triumph over the Crystal Palace Club on the previous Saturday, the Engineers were great favourites with the public, and that the estimation in which they were held was not unjustifiable may be gathered from the fact that for a period of two years they had never been vanquished. Moreover, the clever and effective manner in which they have always played, and still play, together, tended to produce a belief that they would be able, by better organisation and concentration, to defeat their opponents, despite the acknowledged superiority of the latter in point of individual excellence and skill. No pains, however, were spared by the Wanderers to collect their best representative eleven, and in this they succeeded admirably, as without doubt they mustered on this occasion the very best forces at their disposal, having both weight and speed forward, and certainly the two best backs in England to support the efforts of the ups.

Within a few minutes of three o'clock the ball was set in motion by the Engineers, the assemblage of spectators being very fashionable, though the numbers were hardly so large as might have been expected, owing, possibly, in some measure to an advance in the price charged for admission. The captain of the Wanderers won the toss, and thus at the outset his side gained not only the aid of the wind, but a considerable advantage in addition in having a very powerful sun at their backs. At once the Wanderers set to work with the greatest determination, and at the outset their play forward displayed more co-operation than is their custom, the backing-up being vastly superior to anything they have shown during the present season. By this means, and with the aid of faultless kicking on the part of their backs, they were able during the first quarter of an hour to besiege the Sappers closely, to the surprise of many of the spectators. Thus consistently they maintained the attack, till at length, after some judicious "middling" by R.W.S. Vidal, the goal of the Engineers fell to a well directed kick by A.H. Chequer.

Ends were now changed, but any expectations of an alteration in the state of affairs were unfulfilled, as without any diminution of energy the Wanderers, although now faced by wind and sun, continued to besiege the lines of the Engineers without allowing any opportunities to the forwards on the later side of effecting the rushes for which they are noted. Not long after the above goal the ball was again driven through the posts of the military goal by C.W. Alcock, but owing to a previous breach of the handling rule by another Wanderer, the claim was rightly disallowed. Still the game was maintained with the most remarkable animation on both sides, Renny-Tailyour, Mitchell, and Rich striving hard to pass the backs of the enemy. Once Muirhead, by an excellent run, did succeed in guiding the ball into the vicinity of the Wanderers' fortress, but A.C. Thompson interposed at the right moment, and the leather was safely removed. After this one or two chances were offered to the Wanderers, but none were realised, although more than one would doubtless have been successful but for the extremely efficient goal-keeping of Capt. Merriman.

On one occasion a protracted bully raged on the very edge of the Engineers' lines, and once during its course the ball was absolutely driven against one of the posts; but here, too, the Wanderers failed to score. During the latter part of the game it was generally imagined that the Engineers would outstay their opponents, but until the finish the play was continued as fast as ever, and soon after half-past four o'clock time was called, the Wanderers thus gaining the privilege of holding the cup for a year by one goal. It was generally admitted that the play all round was superior to anything that has been seen at the Oval. The Wanderers unquestionably surprised the spectators by the effectiveness of their play collectively, and certainly they have never shown to such advantage as in this contest. The Engineers played hard and well throughout, but they were outmatched in this instance, as they only on two occasions endangered the enemy's goal. It was in some measure the superiority of the backs on the side of the Wanderers that tended to produce the defeat of the Sappers, as the certainty of kicking displayed by Lubbock and Thompson throughout enabled the forwards of the victors to attack without fear.

In extenuation of the reverse suffered by the Engineers, it should be stated that one of their best players, Lieutenant Creswell, broke his collar-bone about ten minutes after the start, and too much praise cannot be accorded to him for the pluck he showed in maintaining his post, although completely disabled and in severe pain, until the finish. Thus ended one of the most pleasant contests in which the Wanderers have ever been engaged, the posts of umpires and referee being absolutely sinecures. On behalf of the Wanderers, though all played up throughout in fine form, R.W.S. Vidal and T.C. Hooman attracted notice by their skilful dribbling.

The umpires were J.H. Giffard (Civil Service) for the Engineers, and J. Kirkpatrick (Civil Service) for the Wanderers, A. Stair (Upton Park) acting as referee.

Sides:

Wanderers: C.W. Alcock, E.E. Bowen, A.G. Bonsor, A.H. Chequer, W.P. Crake, T.C. Hooman, E. Lubbock (back), A.C. Thompson (half-back), R.C. Welch (goal), R.W.S. Vidal, and C.H. Wollaston.

Royal Engineers: Capt. Marindin, Capt. Merriman, Addison, Mitchell, Cresswell, Renny-Tailyour, Rich, Goodwyn, Muirhead, Cotter, and Bogle.

We understand that the cup will be presented to the victors at the annual dinner of the Wanderers' Club, to be held early next month.

The Wanderers won the first Cup contest and made their mark on football history however the game was close fought and the Engineers must not be forgotten. Charles Alcock must have felt somewhat humble since he won the competition he introduced. The whole matter was a sporting and gentlemanly affair, there were no steps to climb at the end and the players left to muted applause, whilst the Cup was presented four weeks later at the Wanderers' annual dinner at Pall Mall Restaurant, Charing Cross. The majority of these players passed into obscurity however the preceding pages have made them live again. Indeed these were all amateurs who played the game for 'sport' and the following chapters discuss the early history of the professional game.

THE WANDERERS v THE ROYAL ENGINEERS

SATURDAY 16 MARCH 1872

THE WANDERERS

Goal R.C. WELCH

Full Back E. LUBBOCK

Half Back A.C. THOMPSON

Forwards C.W. ALCOCK A.G. BONSOR E.E. BOWEN

A.H. CHEQUER W.P. CRAKE T.C. HOOMAN

R.W.S. VIDAL C.H.R. WOLLASTON

Forwards A. BOGLE E.W. COTTER E.W. CRESWELL

H. MITCHELL H.H. MUIRHEAD

H.W. RENNY-TAILYOUR H.B. RICH

Half Back A.G. GOODWYN

Full Back G.W. ADDISON F.A. MARINDIN

Goal W. MERRIMAN

THE ROYAL ENGINEERS

SECTION II

The Grounds

CHAPTER 11

The Rovers and Quakers

There were two pertinent factors influencing the early days of football clubs; firstly most changed grounds on several occasions and secondly the involvement of the church in their formation. There are some good examples of the latter: Barnsley St. Peter's, Christ Church (Bolton), Fulham St. Andrew's Sunday School, St. Domingo's (Everton), Mansfield Wesleyans Boys Brigade, St. Jude's and Christchurch (Q.P.R.), St. Mary's Young Men's Assoc. (Southampton) and Bothwell Mission (Hayes). There were other varied roots including cricket, industry and speculation and some examples are Sheffield United, Manchester United and Chelsea, whilst many northern clubs grew from the professional game.

Despite shaky and uncertain beginnings the Football League was established during a meeting at the Royal Hotel, Manchester in April 1888 (already discussed). A format was laid out for the League competition at this time and was later used as a model for other national Leagues - around the world. William McGregor, as stated, put forward the idea of a League and initially consulted Aston Villa, Blackburn Rovers, Bolton Wanderers, Preston North End and West Bromwich Albion. The initial League had twelve clubs although there were only ten who laced up their boots at kick off on Saturday 8 September 1888. The highest attendance of the five games was 6,000 for that between Preston North End and Burnley, and it was at Deepdale that Jack Gordon (or maybe Fred Dewhurst) of Preston scored the first ever League goal. The first of many remarkable scores occurred in the game between Bolton Wanderers and Derby County - Bolton had a 3-0 lead after just six minutes but Derby eventually won the game 6-3!

These were, however, very different days from the present and most League members played at grounds with unfamiliar names. Yet they were League venues and are of great importance as they were the first in the world. The alphabet begins with 'A' and top of the milk adverts are Accrington F.C. who became famous in recent years for those immortal words: "Who the heck are Accrington Stanley?" For those equally bemused the town is in Lancashire and is located half way between the football giants of Blackburn and Burnley. The club Accrington F.C. formed in 1878 and played at Thorneyholme Road from 1882 - the home of Accrington Cricket Club. The 'owld' reds obviously played in red shirts and were members of the Lancashire Combination but they were soon in trouble for making illegal payments to players and came to the attention of the F.A. Committee. They were a founder member of the first Football League in 1888 but failed to make much progress and resigned (from the League) in 1893. They finished 15th just above Newton Heath and their last League game was a 1-0 defeat by Sheffield United in a *test match* at Trent Bridge. They moved to the nearby Moorhead Ground in 1894 and had two seasons in the Lancashire League but played just five games in the Combination and finally disbanded in late 1895. They were the forerunner of Accrington Stanley who began as an amateur outfit and played at Peel Park near Burnley Road - not far from the old grounds. Thus Accrington Cricket Ground, Thorneyholme Road heads the list of the twelve "most famous League grounds" - the cricketers still play there today.

The remaining eleven clubs were considerably more successful and none more so than Aston Villa who developed under the initial guidance of William McGregor. This situation mirrored that seen in the amateur game where Cup founder Charles Alcock was successful with the Wanderers. Members of the Villa Cross Wesleyan Chapel formed Aston Villa in 1874 and were known as Villa or the Villans. Indeed there is also a legend that cricketing enthusiasts formed the club after a meeting under a street corner gas lamp. Their first game was against Aston Brook St. Mary's Rugby Club, and the game had one half rugby and the other half soccer. It was played at Aston Park, which was part of Aston Hall's Deer Park or the Upper Grounds. Below Aston Hall were the Lower Grounds and these were developed into a leisure park in the 1870s-80s. Aston Villa played at the Lower Aston Grounds in 1875-76 and the sports arena was at the western end of the leisure-park and known as the Meadow. It had a Main Stand backing onto Trinity Road whilst the Villa Park site was occupied with formal gardens and an ornamental lake. A team called the Quilters also played there and were named after Mr. Quilter who laid out the leisure park. Indeed it was the presence of Villa and the Quilters that attracted W. McGregor to football.

The Lower Grounds were of some importance and saw two F.A. Cup semi-finals in 1884 and 1886, however Aston Villa required a permanent ground of their own and moved to Wellington Road, Perry

Barr in 1876. This was to the north west of Aston and roughly a mile from the present Villa Park. It was from this latter venue that the club achieved their early success in both Cup and League. They played at Wellington Road from 1876-97, however the ground was somewhat restricted and its limitations came to light soon after their arrival. A crowd of 27,000 came to watch a Cup-tie against Preston and invaded the pitch and Villa the Cup holders were disqualified from the competition. Despite this they continued there and erected a pavilion to serve as a Main Stand in 1887. This was sold to Small Heath (Birmingham City) when they departed and erected at the latter's Muntz Street ground. The venue staged F.A. Cup semi-finals in 1890 and 1896 but the club departed in 1897 and returned to their roots at Villa Park. Thus the second most famous ground is the patriotically named Wellington Road.

The pendulum now swings back towards Accrington and the next three clubs to consider are in Lancashire. Some old boys from Blackburn Grammar School formed Blackburn Rovers in November 1875 and soon became one of the strongest teams. They established their first ground in the middle of 1876 and this was a field at Oozehead or Oozebooth. This was an unsuitable venue (and certainly sounded so) thus they moved to Pleasington Cricket Ground in 1877 - Pleasington village being two miles west of Blackburn. They moved to Alexandra Meadows home of East Lancashire Cricket Club in January 1878 but the ground could be viewed from Corporation Park and was also unsuitable for large crowds. A Cup-tie against neighbours Darwen in 1880 had to be abandoned after a rowdy crowd of 10,000 attended the game. Despite this the venue staged an international England v Wales in February 1881 - the first England fixture away from the Oval.

Blackburn, however, left Alexandra Meadows two weeks after this game and moved to a nearby ground at Leamington Street, although they did play four games at Ewood Park in 1881. The ground at Leamington Street was fully enclosed with a 600-seat stand and it was from there that Blackburn entered into a very successful period in the F.A. Cup. They reached four Cup Finals before the League was formed in 1888 and in fact matched the success of the Wanderers (amateurs) - they lifted the Cup three times in 1884-86 and achieved a hat trick. Leamington Street was used for internationals in 1885/87 but despite this the club sought a new venue in 1890. The factors involved were many and varied and included an increase in rent, development of nearby housing and success on the pitch. Blackburn departed for Ewood Park and the ground was covered with housing including Rover Street. Thus Leamington Street is the third ground although Rovers were no lemmings whilst playing there.

Bolton is ten miles south of Blackburn and the former club was another with church origins, being formed as Christchurch F.C. in 1874. They initially played at the Park Recreation Ground then moved to Dick Cockle's Field on Pikes Lane in the south west of Bolton. There was a disagreement with the vicar of Christchurch who was also President of the club, in 1877, and the result was that the football club broke away from the church and renamed themselves Bolton Wanderers - due to a frequent change of H.Q. The club was one of the first to use Scottish players and moved to a more permanent ground at Pikes Lane in 1881. The venue was located south of the lane behind the Saviour's Church and had two Main Stands on the north side and three small stands on the east side - there was also a cinder track with shallow banking around it. The ground was in open country in 1890, although it was surrounded by a number of cotton mills viz. Deane, Gibraltar, Stanley and Derby Street Mills. It attracted large crowds of up to 20,000 in the late 1880s and thus the rent was increased. The land was earmarked for housing and the club approached Bolton Corporation with a request to move to wasteland on Manchester Road in 1893 - a site once intended for an extension of the town's gasworks. The club finally moved to Burnden Park in 1895 and by this time Pikes Lane was renamed Deane Road. An extension of Bankfield Street and Alice and Jessie Street covered the ground. The Pikes Lane pitch

Leamington Street, Blackburn - O.S. Map 1893. Rovers played here 1881-90.

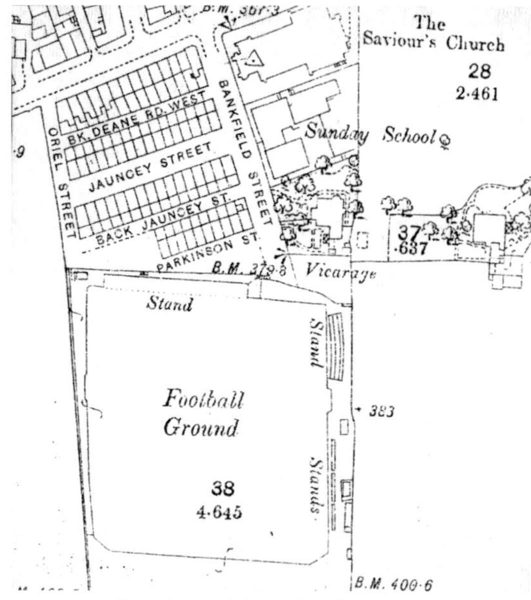

Pikes Lane, Bolton - O.S. Map 1889.
Wanderers played here 1881-95.

was renowned for becoming a bog after just a little rain however that at Burnden was initially no better - this was the nature of a top sporting venue in the 1890s. Pikes Lane is the fourth famous ground but Bolton were clearly no 'pikers'.

Our journey now takes us ten miles north to Burnley, whose team are the fourth in the country to play in the famous claret and blue, although they first played in green. They were formed as the Burnley Rovers Rugby Club in 1881 and first played at Calder Vale - named after the River Calder. They began to play soccer from May 1882 and became Burnley F.C. and moved to a new venue at Turf Moor - next to Burnley Cricket Club. This is the only ground other than Deepdale still in use from the first season of the League and is thus the second oldest League venue. There is a cricket ground still present just to the west and Turf Moor holds an important place in soccer history. The first game was a friendly against local team Rawtenstall on 17 February 1883 whilst two other grounds opened that year viz. Feethams, Darlington and Victoria Ground, Stoke but not until September 1883.

Turf Moor was simply an area of turf on the moors but the club built an 800-seat grandstand by 1885 and incorporated existing banking into the ground and built uncovered stands at each end. There was a remarkable attendance of 12,000 for a game against Padiham in the first season at Turf Moor, this being a village three miles west of Burnley, and it appears the whole population turned out for the game. Prince Albert (later Edward VII) watched part of a game against Bolton in 1886 after opening the Victoria Hospital in the town - he must have found that last turnstile! This was the first visit by a member of the Royal family to a football ground and they were nicknamed the 'Royalites' for some years. Burnley F.C. was one of six Lancashire clubs to enter the League in 1888 and the ground had a Main Stand on Brunshaw Road and the Star Stand on the other side by 1908. The latter was moved back in 1909 and extra banking erected in front of this stand, followed soon after by a cover at the Cricket Field End. In the period just before the First War the average attendance was around 22,000 and the highest crowd over 49,000. This trend continued after the war and the record attendance at Turf Moor was 54,775 on 23 February 1924 during an F.A. Cup tie against Huddersfield Town. The lower terrace of the Long Side was concreted in 1925 and later extended to the upper areas - this reached a high point in the northeast corner but the section was abandoned when a roof was erected in 1954. This roof was most substantial and covered the whole of the terrace. Turf Moor is the fifth ground from the first season and Burnley with their green jerseys could be called the "Turfers".

For the sixth club we need to move south to consider Derby County. The name of the club may be confused with the term derby, a contest between two local sides, and is in fact connected to this expression. The original *Derby* was organised by the 12th Earl of Derby in 1780 and was run annually at Epsom in Surrey - indeed 'derby' was later applied to any sporting event of equal importance. The members of Derbyshire C.C.C. formed the club in 1884 and they first wore the cricket team colours of amber, brown and pale blue. Derby had only one previous venue before a permanent home and began life at the Racecourse Ground, which was with the cricket pitch in the centre of the racecourse. This was used for F.A. Cup semi-finals in 1885/86 and later on three further occasions, and also for a Cup Final replay between Blackburn Rovers and West Bromwich Albion in 1886. It was a 2-0 victory for the Rovers and the first time the Final was settled outside of London.

There were many football clubs in the area and the team Derby Junction played in the F.A. Cup from 1884-89. Most notably they reached the semi-final in 1887-88 although they lost the game 3-0 to West Bromwich Albion. Their last F.A. Cup-tie was a 1-0 defeat away to Derby County on 2 February 1889. The sharing of sports venues often resulted in a conflict of interests and this was seen with greyhound racing at Clapton Orient and with cricket at Northampton and Notts County. The problem also occurred in Derby and horse racing would restrict the times at which they could use the ground. They were forced to play a game against

Sunderland at the Baseball Ground in March 1892 consequently they decided to move by 1895. Horse racing continued on the site until 1939 and the County Cricket Ground still remains. Francis Ley a Derby foundry owner laid out the Baseball Ground in the 1880s as a sports ground for his workers, and after visiting the U.S.A. developed the site for baseball in 1889. Derby County F.C. finished low in the League during their first few seasons but were third in 1893-94 and moved to the Baseball Ground in 1895. They brought one stand from the old ground whilst summer baseball tournaments were still played and Derby County won the contest in 1897. It is no surprise that Derby played at the Racecourse, which is the sixth venue of note.

The seventh club to consider is Everton F.C. whose early history is entwined with their neighbours Liverpool. Indeed there was a similar situation in both Nottingham and Sheffield where two clubs used one venue in their early days. Everton hold an impressive League record and have played continually in Division One since 1888 (except for 1930-31 and 1951-54). They were formed as the church team St. Domingo's in 1878 and first played at Stanley Park but changed their name to Everton F.C. in 1879 and were nicknamed the Toffees. These names relate to the local area and Everton Road and St. Domingo Road are within a mile of the ground. They first played in a black and white strip but changed to the familiar royal blue and white in 1901.

John Houlding was prominent in the town and was a councillor and later Mayor. He was Everton's main backer in the early days and provided an enclosed pitch on Priory Road in 1883-84, but this was an unsuitable venue with large crowds disturbing the peace of the area. He then offered the club a field in Anfield Road that he partly owned in 1884. Everton played the first football game at Anfield on 28 September 1884 and the contest was a friendly against Earlestown. Initially the arrangement at Anfield worked well for Houlding and the club, but after Everton entered the League in 1888 problems began to develop. Houlding had a monopoly over catering at the site and also raised the interest on his loans to Everton, which increased the yearly rental from £100 to £250. There was unrest over these arrangements, therefore after an offer of £180 was turned down the club decided to leave Anfield. George Mahon the organist of St. Domingo's secured a new venue for the club on the north side of Stanley Park. The field was a patch of wasteland in the area Mere Green and was not ideal for football being described as a howling desert as late as '1906'. The site, however, was developed and thus opened as Goodison Park on 24 August 1892. Lord Kinnaird and Frederick Wall represented the F.A. on the day and the crowd watched an athletics meeting followed by a concert and fireworks (rather than football). This was most suitable since Goodison Park was the first major football ground in England.

But what of Anfield Road which is the focus of the discussion at this point? Everton had much success in their time at Anfield and they were runners-up to the 'Old Invincibles' of Preston in 1889-90 and won the League in 1890-91. Despite this success their departure from Anfield was acrimonious with petty disputes over who owned the fittings. Houlding tried to start his own club there and wanted to call them Everton F.C. but the League would not sanction it. A few people stood by him including John McKenna later Liverpool Chairman and League President and the outcome was the formation of Liverpool F.C. although they were charged an initial rent of just £100 p.a. - this was clearly a power struggle. The ground they inherited was already a substantial venue with a capacity of around 20,000 with a main bank at the Anfield Road End and a smaller stand to the south. In addition there was a narrow cover on the east side and a main pavilion on the west side. Anfield is the seventh and most famous of the early League football grounds and is the third ground to survive from the first season (but with a different club).

The next club to consider is Notts County who were formed in 1862 and are the oldest League club - pre-dating the F.A. by one year. They were initially Nottingham or Notts F.C. and first played in the Park area of town west of Nottingham Castle. They were properly constituted in 1864 and moved to the Meadows Cricket Ground but for larger games hired Trent Bridge Cricket Ground. They moved to Notts Cricket Ground, Beeston (west of the city) in 1877 but this was a long distance from the town centre, which caused problems. They spent a season back at the Meadows Cricket Ground in 1878-79 and had one season at Trent Bridge in 1879-80, but moved to the Castle Cricket Ground across the river from Forest's Town Ground in 1880. They became Notts County in 1882 and reached the Cup semi-final in 1883 but lost 2-1 to the Old Etonians. Forest, meanwhile, played at the Meadows Cricket Ground in 1879-80 and at Trent Bridge for two seasons in 1880-82 and after they departed the latter was available for use.

Trent Bridge Cricket Ground was first laid out in 1838 and was the premier sports venue in the town. It was not ideal for soccer however Notts County made a permanent move there in 1883 and reached the F.A. Cup semi-final again in 1884 losing 1-0 to Blackburn Rovers. The club turned professional in 1885 and built a low stand on the Fox Road Side that year and used the new cricket pavilion from 1886. They were given permission to erect a temporary wooden stand on the cricket pitch whereas at other similar venues the owners only allowed wooden boards (as at Northampton). The club reached two Cup Finals at this time and lost 3-1 to Blackburn Rovers in 1891 but won 4-1 against Bolton at Goodison Park in 1894, and despite the difficulties remained at Trent Bridge for 27 years. Three Cup semi-finals were played at the ground but it struggled to hold crowds of 20,000 and was unpopular with supporters. There was a crowd of only 300 for a Second Division fixture against Crewe in 1894 and a record low attendance of 1,500 for a First Division game (mid-week) against Preston in 1901. Further, the club had to find alternative venues for games during the cricket season and played fixtures at the Town Ground in the 1890s and later the City Ground. There were complaints from other League clubs regarding the arrangement at Trent Bridge by 1905 and the cricket club did not renew the lease in 1908, thus they moved to Meadow Lane in 1910. Trent Bridge Cricket Ground is the eighth 'early' League venue and the outline of the football ground is still visible in Fox Road.

The most important ground however is Deepdale, Preston, which is the oldest surviving League venue in the country. The club's origins go back to 1863 when the North End Cricket and Rugby Club were formed. They first played cricket and moved to Moor Park (opposite Deepdale) in 1867 then became Preston North End and moved to Deepdale itself in 1875. They played rugby there in 1877 and soccer in 1879 - it was the club's only pursuit after 1881. The debate about paid players dominated football at this time and the F.A. feared a decline in the ethics of play and the loss of its high ideals (discussed in the introduction). Darwen, Blackburn Rovers and Accrington were all accused of paying their players and were dealt with accordingly, and it was footballers from Scotland who first played a professional game. Preston North End was one of the leaders in this movement and their first benefactor was William Sudell son of William and Jane who was born in Preston and baptized at St. John's, Preston on 1 September 1850. He lived at 3 St. George's Terrace with his wife and four young children in 1881 and was a cotton mill manager.

He was also manager of Preston North End F.C. and his strict regime earned him the title "Major" Sudell. He had no nonsense at the club and took on the F.A. by openly admitting to paying his players in 1884. It was his actions that hastened the arrival of the professional game in 1885. Preston North End was one of the first clubs to embrace the professional game and under William Sudell were one of the first great teams. They were already very strong when the League formed in 1888 under their captain Johnny Goodall (1863-1942). He was born in London and played in a forward position and was captain of England winning 14 caps in 1889-98. Preston won the first ever League title in 1888-89 and finished 11 points ahead of Aston Villa who presumably had been expected to win. During the season they won 18 games, drew 4 and lost none, scored 74 goals and conceded 15 and only failed to score in one game against Accrington. They also won the F.A. Cup Final at the Oval in 1889 when they defeated Wolves 3-0 and did not concede a single goal in the competition. They won the double in the first season, which was a great achievement - the next time was Aston Villa (1897) and Tottenham (1961). Preston was the first great football team in the world and became known as the 'Old Invincibles'. The club's success continued until 1893 however William Sudell then left after financial irregularities and the days of invincibility came to an end.

The surprising feature of Deepdale, given its name, was its location on a completely flat site north of the town. The ground had two stands on the west side and uncovered stands on the north and east sides in 1890, but soon fell behind others and plans were made for a new stadium. The club became a limited company in 1893 but after the departure of Sudell the planned move did not come to fruition. A new West Stand was built in 1906 with bench seats for 2,500 behind a paddock and a barrel roof supported by numerous columns that curved around at the northern end. The name for this type of wooden construction was a 'Belfast' roof and its only rivals were the Trent Bridge Stand at Notts County (1895-1978) and Gordon Road Stand at Gillingham (1899-1985). The West Stand in Preston was larger than these and became the oldest in the country being demolished in 1995. The Kop at the Fulwood End was built in 1921 and was a large structure, eventually covered by a partial roof. This terrace curved around the northeast corner and had round tunnels, with wooden cladding at the rear. A cover was built over the Town End terrace in the 1930s and a new stand called the Pavilion was built on the east side of the ground in 1934. The latter was on the halfway line and was only 40 yards long with a limited number of seats behind the terrace - it was principally the club's new offices moved from the West Stand. A new south Pavilion was added on the east side in 1936 and there were few changes until the modern Deepdale was built from 1995. This is the ninth famous League ground and now houses the *National Football Museum*.

The remaining three grounds are south of Lancashire and the first is one of two clubs in the Potteries. The date given for the formation of Stoke City must be treated with caution since there was an accepted date of 1863, which has been re-established to 1868. Either way they are one of the oldest clubs in the

Football League. Further, it was thought that they located to the Victoria Ground in 1878 but more recently the date was altered to 1883. This confirms Deepdale as the oldest League ground (for soccer) although since the move to the Britannia Stadium this debate is academic. 'Old Boys' of Charterhouse who worked for the North Staffordshire Railway Company formed Stoke Ramblers in 1868. There was another local club formed in 1863 thus the confusion. They played at unenclosed sites in Lonsdale Street north of the Victoria Ground, Glebe Street off City Road, the County Cricket Ground and Campbell Road south of the Victoria Ground.

They became Stoke F.C. in 1875 and then played at a more permanent venue known as Sweeting's Fields, which was located opposite the north end of the Victoria Ground. They merged with Stoke Victoria Athletic Club in 1878 and played at their Athletic Ground again near to Lonsdale Street. This had been a sports ground since about the 1860s and was owned by the church. Some sources state they moved to the Victoria Ground in 1878 however this was not the case. The Athletic Ground was sold for development in 1883 and Stoke F.C. moved to a new site to the south that also belonged to their landlords. It became the Victoria Ground and presumably the name derived from the associated athletic club. It soon had a familiar shape with banking on three sides and a 1,000-seat stand on Boothen Road. It also included a track since the football and athletics clubs shared the ground. The team was unsuccessful in the early days and were bottom of the League in the first two seasons. They were the first club relegated from the League and spent 1890-91 in the Alliance, but were then elected back although were relegated to Division Two in 1907-8. They had considerable debts and after a lack of support from shareholders went into liquidation and had to resign. Supporters rallied round and Stoke were re-formed however they then played in non-League football including the Southern League. They were elected to Division Two in 1919 and became Stoke City in 1925.

The Victoria Ground had a pavilion at the Boothen End beside the Main Stand in 1890 and the Butler Street Side was covered in 1904 followed by a new Main Stand in 1922. The athletics track was removed in 1930 and the Boothen End increased in size and later covered. A new Butler Street Stand was constructed in 1935 and extended around both corners in 1936. The Main Stand was replaced in stages from 1960-63 and the Stoke End terrace was re-developed with a modern two-tier stand in 1979 (upper tier 4,000 seats). The club moved to the Britannia Stadium in 1997 and the old ground was closed and all trace soon removed - the venue where Stanley Matthews showed his skills was no more. Adjacent houses remained in 1998 and a grassed area marked the site of the pitch but only earth was left where the terraces stood for 114 years. This was a sad demise to the tenth ground, which was patriotically named after Queen Victoria.

This chapter concludes in the West Midlands, firstly with West Bromwich Strollers who were formed by workers at Salter Spring Works in 1879. They became West Bromwich Albion in 1881 and their early grounds were to the east of the town in the direction of the Hawthorns. They first played at Cooper's Hill and Dartmouth Park, which were both adjacent to Herbert Street. The former was also used for cricket and this factor decided the choice of venue. They took an enclosed ground Bunn's Field just to the north in 1881 and moved to Four Acres near Park Crescent in 1882. The Earl of Dartmouth gave the latter to the town. West Bromwich (Dartmouth) Cricket Club used the ground first and initially played football in the winter months, however this activity ceased and they offered the venue to the Albion. There was a record crowd of 16,393 at Four Acres in February 1885 for an F.A. Cup tie against Blackburn Rovers. The venue could not accommodate so many spectators and the club played at Stoney Lane in 1885-90. The first game was a friendly against Scottish team Third Lanark in September 1885. A thrush was the mascot at Stoney Lane hence their nickname the Throstles, whilst the more common 'Baggies' came from wearing long shorts when out of fashion!

Stoney Lane remained a basic ground and the Main Stand was nicknamed Noah's Ark. The venue was in fact the poorest in the early League and attracted a crowd of 450 for a game against Derby in 1890. The club, however, were slow to move and played their last game at Stoney Lane in April 1900, which was an 8-0 victory over Nottingham Forest. They continued to use the ground for training until the 1980s when it was developed with housing, and this included the name Albion Field Drive. The club then found a new venue outside the town of West Bromwich on the Birmingham Road and this time chose a more suitable site with plenty of room for development. The ground was located next to the Hawthorn Estate hence the name of the Hawthorns, and the club took Noah's Ark with them and located it on the Handsworth Side. The new venue was two miles from the club's roots, and it is Stoney Lane that goes down in history as the eleventh ground.

The last ground to discuss is Dudley Road the temporary home of Wolverhampton Wanderers. A St. Luke's School team played at Windmill Field from 1877 and at John Harper's Field in 1879 - both grounds were south of the town in the Blakenhall area. This team joined with Blakenhall Wanderers Cricket Club in 1879 and formed Wolverhampton Wanderers F.C. and played at Dudley Road in 1881 - near the Wanderers Cricket Ground. Meanwhile, north of the town, the premier sporting venue was Molineux and the grounds were named after the Molineux family who lived in the nearby Molineux House (later a hotel). The house and land were sold to a Mr. McGregor in 1860 and he developed the site into pleasure gardens (similar arrangements took place at Aston Villa and the Crystal Palace). There was an athletics track at the north end of Molineux by 1880 and a rival team called Stafford Road F.C. sometimes played there in the 1880s. Wolves played one game at Molineux against Walsall Town in March 1886 but still remained at Dudley Road. They had one League season at the latter in 1888-89 and also reached the F.A. Cup Final during that year being defeated 3-0 by Preston. Dudley Road was never developed and Wolves made a permanent move to Molineux, the first game being a friendly against Aston Villa in September 1889 in front of 3,900. Wolves won the F.A. Cup in 1893 and roads near the old ground were named after the event viz. Fallowfield Terrace (from the venue) and Wanderers Avenue. There were replicas of the Cup in stone in front of these houses but none of this survives today. Thus Dudley Road (not Molineux) is the last ground and the first League kicked off at these twelve venues.

Table 3: **GROUNDS IN 1888**

FOOTBALL CLUB	GROUND
Accrington	Accrington Cricket Ground
Aston Villa	Wellington Road, Perry Barr
Blackburn Rovers	Leamington Street
Bolton Wanderers	Pikes Lane
Burnley	Turf Moor
Derby County	The Racecourse Ground
Everton	Anfield Road
Notts County	Trent Bridge Cricket Ground
Preston North End	Deepdale
Stoke	Victoria Ground
West Bromwich Albion	Stoney Lane
Wolverhampton Wand	Dudley Road

Table 4: **FOOTBALL LEAGUE 1888-89**

CLUB NAME	P	W	D	L	F	A	PTS
Preston North End	22	18	4	0	74	15	40
Aston Villa	22	12	5	5	61	43	29
Wolverhampton Wand	22	12	4	6	50	37	28
Blackburn Rovers	22	10	6	6	66	45	26
Bolton Wanderers	22	10	2	10	63	59	22
West Bromwich Albion	22	10	2	10	40	46	22
Accrington	22	6	8	8	48	48	20
Everton	22	9	2	11	35	46	20
Burnley	22	7	3	12	42	62	17
Derby County	22	7	2	13	41	61	16
Notts County	22	5	2	15	40	73	12
Stoke	22	4	4	14	26	51	12

CHAPTER 12

Up For The Cup

Today it is hard to imagine a world without soccer (although some people would like to) however there was a time not so long ago when rarely a ball was kicked. The 19th century began with the 'threat' from France and the Battle of Trafalgar (1805) and the Battle of Waterloo (1815). These were times of great economic and social change and the development of sport was closely linked to these adjustments in society. In the rural economy of the 18th century most people's lives were dictated by agriculture and the changing seasons, however there were some slack periods between ploughing and harvesting (and the like) and only at these times was there an opportunity for recreation. The most popular sports were amateur cricket and the rough game of village football however 'enclosure' and agricultural innovation changed the countryside, hence there was progressively less land available for these pursuits.

The Regency period was at the start of the 19th century and men of leisure engaged in various pastimes such as horse racing, hunting, boxing and fencing. There were also country fairs with amusements and even walking was a sport and was known as 'pedestrianism', however these days were soon numbered. The Industrial Revolution caused great changes and much of the rural population immigrated to the new towns. There were 44 official holidays recognised by the Bank of England in 1808 however only four remained in 1834 (Christmas Day, Good Friday, 1 May, 1 November). The new factories of Britain stopped for no man and there was little time for leisure, whilst there was even less room to play in the cramped urban streets. The injustices of the system, however, soon became apparent and gradually there was pressure for reform. In terms of sport cricket led the way and 'wandering circuses' of players toured the counties in the early Victorian era and promoted the game viz. William Clarke's all England XI formed 1846.

Meanwhile football survived within the public schools and their old boys helped develop the game. It was a relatively cheap form of entertainment but only progressed elsewhere after employers gave Saturday afternoon off although in Sheffield there was also a half-day Wednesday (hence Wednesday F.C.). The workers then had more spare time and soccer developed as a spectator sport in the late 19th century. Therefore soccer developed in two different environments - the public school or amateur tradition in the south and the professional game in the north. The new clubs often had a problem finding suitable land to play upon, and this meant early grounds were connected with other sporting venues i.e. cricket grounds, racecourses and pleasure grounds. As with many aspects of Victorian England the opportunity was there and it just needed someone to come forward, and in terms of the F.A. Cup competition the man was Charles Alcock. As stated he was a man of vision who realised that the knockout competition played at Harrow could work equally well at a national level.

The basis of the competition was established in 1871 and the contest then required a venue. The early rounds were to be played at local or club grounds and the semi-final and Final at a neutral venue - the Oval presented itself as the viable choice. Charles Alcock became Secretary of Surrey C.C.C. in 1872 thus the first Cup Final took place at the Oval that year (discussed earlier) and a crowd of 2,000 spectators paid the large sum of a shilling to see the game. The F.A. however was not settled on this venue and took the next Final north of the river. A county soccer match was arranged at Beaufort House in 1867 although it was played at Battersea, and a second took place at the West London Running Grounds, Brompton (Lillie Bridge) in 1868. Therefore the F.A. was familiar with the area and chose Lillie Bridge Athletic Ground for the Final on 29 March 1873, this being next to West Brompton Station and the West London Extension Railway. The area was then undeveloped and the ground was surrounded by a number of fields and orchards, whilst to the west was the rifle range and track of Beaufort House in North End Road.

There was a morning kick-off and the Wanderers continued their success there and beat Oxford University 2-0, however once the formalities were over the players went and watched the Boat Race in the afternoon. Lillie Bridge soon had competition and a field to the south was developed as Stamford Bridge Athletic Club from 1877. Indeed the whole history of soccer in the area could have been different but for dramatic events in 1887. A running contest was arranged at Lillie Bridge between Henry Gent of Darlington who had won the Sheffield handicap at Easter and Henry Hutchens who for years was a champion short distance runner. The latter had just returned from competing in Australia and normally trained in Leicester. There was much 'talk' about the event and Gent wanted a four-yard start on the 120-yard race, however fair terms were agreed and £100 stake was placed. The runners were touted like *Derby* favourites and a good attendance was expected for

Lillie Bridge Cricket Ground - O.S. Map 1874. Wanderers v Oxford University Final 1873.

the race at 5.00 pm on Monday 19 September 1887. Indeed 1,000 persons were in place at 4.30 and this had doubled by 5.00 and people were still arriving. The crowd had come from all parts of the country (especially Sheffield) and all paid 'good' gate-money to enter - ¾ were positioned in the low price area near the side road, the remainder in front of the long veranda-buildings used for dressing rooms and refreshments.

There was no sign of unrest but much betting was involved and the scene began to turn ugly. Gent had been given favourable odds to win of 3-1 however this suddenly dropped to 10-1 and there were wagers that the race would not be run. Hutchens came out and circled the ground with his trainer and was followed by Gent who appeared in perfect condition. At this point Gent's people stated that their man was unfit and had no chance, and said they would forfeit their stake to Hutchens thus saving the money they had betted - they knew they would lose their bets if the race went ahead. Hutchens and his friends were most angry and a fight between the parties was narrowly averted however they conceded to Gent and retired. There was then a serious problem since 2-3,000 people were present and they wanted their entrance money back however it had already been taken away for safety. The two runners left the arena but many spectators were unaware of events until 6.30.

Once the crowd realized they would not get their money back the whole event really 'kicked off'. Initially some of the men and lads broke down the railings before the pavilion, pulled down the flagpole and smashed chairs. Only three or four officers were on duty and once the mob realised this they took more drastic action. One group attacked the refreshment and dressing rooms on the Seagrove Road side, another the railings next to the railway and a third threw missiles at the pavilion. Many who did not want to be involved tried to escape but found their way blocked by those who attempted to find money at the turnstiles. They took an alternative route out onto the railway embankment but were stopped by railway employees and in the ensuing dispute a rail worker died of a heart attack. The rioters then set fire to the buildings and some of it was only saved through the presence of a brick wall, however those parts not burnt were ransacked in the search for money and compensation. Indeed the private lockers of club members were all torn open and a dozen bicycles (used there) were smashed. The rioters continued to pelt the police and the firemen who tried to deal with several large fires around the ground - the flames being 30-40 feet in the air. One report stated that 10,000 people were involved and many bruised or crushed whilst several policemen badly injured. The riot was quelled once reinforcements arrived and the fire brigade extinguished the flames by 10.30 and handed the ground over to the police.

A correspondent then made an inspection of the ground and stated: "Nearly every building in the grounds has been wholly or partially destroyed by fire or otherwise. The building containing the dressing rooms was standing, and its exterior bore few marks of violence. Inside, however, there was ample evidence that the place had not escaped the notice of the rioters.... the fire destroyed the large refreshment bar, smaller rooms and the stands and seats (in front) over a length of 100 feet and 20-30 feet in depth. The remainder of the stand and large gymnasium at the back were also damaged by fire and the actions of the mob." The Lillie Bridge Ground was basically destroyed and the incident received two full columns in the Times on 20 September 1887. The Athletic or Cricket Ground was on a map of 1888 however the Beaufort House track was mostly built over i.e. Seagrave, Merrington, Hildyard and St. Oswald's Road (later Ongar Road). Indeed it was not used for a Cup Final again and never recovered from the riot - due to the costs involved. The site was sold to the railways by 1895 and then became Lillie Bridge Coal Depot. Lillie Bridge Mews was once near the ground whilst Lillie Road and Lillie Yard are on present day maps. The demise of the venue paved the way for the development of Stamford Bridge in 1905 and without the riot there might have been a different story.

The Cup Final then returned to the Oval under the guidance of Charles Alcock and was played there from 1874-92 hence this was the premier venue in the early days, and comes second only to Wembley having staged 20 Finals (including the first). The Wanderers dominated the early Finals and won four times at the Oval whilst the Old Etonians had the last amateur victory there in 1882. The first northern club to win the Cup were Blackburn Olympic in 1883 and afterwards it was won at the Oval by teams from the north, all of these being founder members of the League. The attendance figures for the Finals steadily increased and had reached double figures of 14,000 in 1884 and 22,000 in 1889 - at this time Preston beat Wolves to achieve the first double. The attendance peaked at 32,810 in 1892 and the F.A. was clearly under pressure to make some new arrangements.

Surely the choice of a permanent venue for the Cup Final was of paramount importance? There was, however, indecision and uncertainty at the F.A. a situation that was mirrored 100 years later, thus four different venues were used in 1892-95. The 1893 Cup Final was played at Manchester University Athletic Ground just behind Owens Park in the Fallowfield district, south of the city centre (university area). This was the first time the Final was played outside of London (except the replay at Derby in 1886) and the only time it was played in Manchester itself - Old Trafford being a separate area. Wolves beat Everton 1-0 there in front of a record crowd of 45,000 however the country's first major football ground was being developed in Liverpool and Goodison Park opened in August 1892 with tall covered stands on three sides and a large bank on the other. The touchline was a good distance from the stands and avoided the more cramped situation found at Anfield. The first game took place at Goodison on 1 September 1892 and a crowd of 10,000 watched a friendly against Bolton. The F.A. had an easy choice and Notts County beat Bolton 4-1 there in the 1894 Final - attendance 37,000. They were the first Second Division club to win the Cup and James Logan scored three goals. He joined William Townley of Blackburn Rovers who was the first player to score a hat trick in a Final when they beat Wednesday 6-1 in 1890.

The F.A. however wanted a more permanent venue in London for this showcase event, thus the next Cup Final was taken to the Crystal Palace near Anerley. The Great Exhibition took place in Hyde Park in 1851 and was staged in the famous Crystal Palace designed by Joseph Paxton. The glass building was 1,500 feet long and covered 26 acres (three times the size of St. Paul's Cathedral) and in a period of six months the Exhibition attracted no less than 6 million visitors. The profits amounted to £186,437 and after Paxton was paid £5,000 the remainder helped to fund the building of the museums in South Kensington. The Crystal Palace was then moved to a site on Anerley Hill and was located between Anerley and Sydenham in south London. The building was officially opened on 10 June 1854 however the network of fountains, water pipes and pumping stations was not ready hence there was a second opening ceremony on 18 June 1856. The latter was in the presence of Queen Victoria and Prince Albert.

The Crystal Palace became the hub of the area and attracted hundreds of thousands of people annually, which brought great prosperity to the local shops. The transport network converged from all directions and there were two rail routes from London to the High Level and Low Level Stations and virtually every local bus and tram came to the Palace concourse. The glass structure had two large circular towers, one at each end, and extensive garden terraces below whilst at the eastern end was the lower lake - this became famous when models of prehistoric animals were erected around it in 1854. The occasion was celebrated in style and a banquet table was laid out for twenty guests inside of an Iguanadon! There was a Grand Central Walk running through the site and at the lower end were two giant fountains, each 800 feet in length. These were truly vast since a football pitch is roughly 350 feet in length. These large fountains, however, were found to be the least economic in the park and the cost of operating them was so large

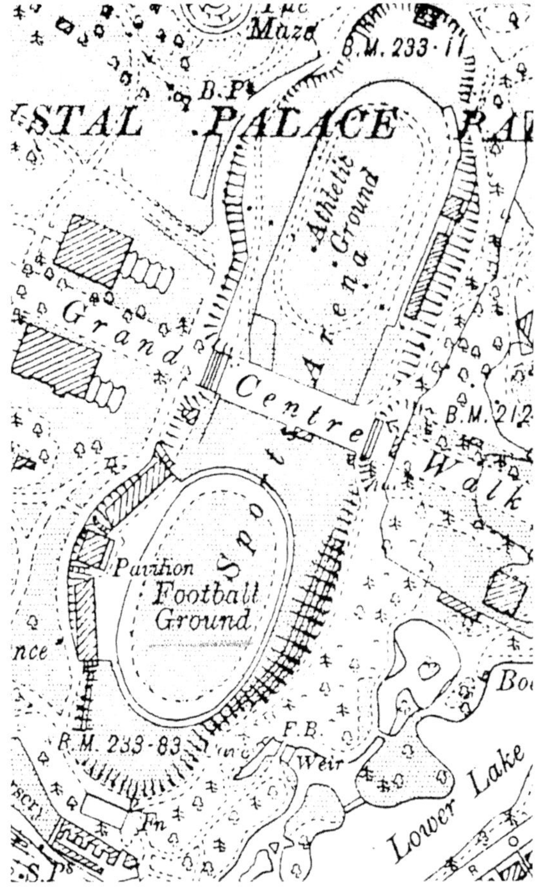

The Crystal Palace Arena - O.S. Map 1929-30.
Cup Final venue from 1895-1914.

that they were only used on special occasions. The cascades leading to them were removed in 1880 and the fountains were finally filled-in during 1894.

It was here that a sports arena was developed with an athletic ground to the north and a football ground to the south. In fact the two stadiums were fitted within the banking and outline of the original two fountains. This was the set up presented to the F.A. in 1894 and there was clearly huge potential there. Indeed what more could they ask for? There was a national landmark, good transport communications, good catering infrastructure and a site that could accommodate 100,000 spectators. There was no doubt much excitement caused by this potential and if only it were as simple today. The F.A. hesitated no longer and the ground was quickly developed thus the Crystal Palace can be considered the first national stadium. John Aird & Sons undertook the building work and were previously involved in the construction at Hyde Park. The pitch was located at the centre of an oval track and to the west was a central pavilion with forward slanting roof. This was flanked by two stands that were angled inwards towards each end of the pitch, and the shape of the fountain dictated this arrangement. The two stands were close to the original banks of the fountain and had a plain construction and provided seating for 3,000 spectators.

A team called Crystal Palace were formed as early as 1861 and were started by staff from Paxton's Crystal Palace. The club were present at the founding of the Football Association in 1863, and Walter J.C. Cutbill played for them in 1864 (see Alcock Ch. 2). They played in the first Cup contest of 1871-72 and reached the semi-final although lost 3-0 to the Royal Engineers, but faded towards the end of the 19th century - thus football took place at the Crystal Palace before the national stadium was developed. The new stadium witnessed some remarkable games as well as extraordinary club records. In the first Final of 1895 Aston Villa beat West Bromwich Albion 1-0 in front of a crowd of 42,560. One can only imagine the scene on this day with dignitaries such as Charles Alcock and Lord Alfred Kinnaird in the newly opened stand. Millwall and Southampton of the Southern League played a semi-final at Crystal Palace in 1900 and the result was 0-0 - attendance 34,760. The contest was settled in a replay at Elm Park, Reading and Saints won 3-0 in front of 10,000. They were the first non-League club to reach the Final since the League's formation in 1888 however Bury won the game 4-0.

Non-League Tottenham beat four First Division clubs on the way to the Final in 1901 and met Sheffield United at the Crystal Palace with a record crowd of 114,815 - there was a 2-2 draw. This was the first ever six-figure attendance for a football match however the replay at Burnden Park attracted only 20,470, which was the smallest attendance at a Final since 1890. There were various factors involved in the poor attendance including poor weather, but the main problem arose when the local railway company refused to provide cheap day tickets to Bolton for the game. They were rebuilding Bolton Station at the time! In the replay Spurs were 1-0 behind at half time however they came back in the second half to win 3-1 and lift the F.A. Cup. Indeed they turned out to be the only non-League winners in the 20th century. The game was mainly remembered as a commercial disaster for Bolton with severe over-catering on the day and as a consequence was known as Pie Saturday. Who ate all the pies? Bury played Derby County in the 1903 Final and the Shakers won by a record 6-0 score line in front of 63,102 spectators. This was a shock result since Derby conceded only one goal on the way to the Final, although Bury let in none in the whole competition. The venue was a success and the F.A. negotiated a five-year deal (for the Cup Final) with the Crystal Palace Co. in 1905. The three sides of terracing were then improved and two new multi-gabled stands were erected in place of the earlier ones - this raised the number of seats to 5,000. The extensive banking gave the ground a huge potential capacity.

There was another six-figure crowd in 1905 when Aston Villa beat Newcastle United 2-0 in front of 101,117 spectators. Poor old Newcastle did not enjoy their visits to the Crystal Palace and also lost the Final in 1906, 1908 and 1911 (after a replay) and then drew in 1910. The replay took place at Goodison Park and by this stage the Magpies were determined to win by any means. It was not an attractive match and Newcastle defeated "Battling" Barnsley by a 2-0 score line. Despite such good entertainment the ground was becoming dated and its days were numbered. The venue experienced financial problems as early as 1911 and was offered up for sale however there were no takers, then the F.A. declined to purchase the Crystal Palace for the nation in 1913. Despite this there was still life in the 'old girl' and the apex of the Crystal Palace came in 1913-14. Firstly Aston Villa beat Sunderland 1-0 in front of a world record crowd of 121,919 in 1913. There was then a memorable game when the reigning monarch George V attended the Final in 1914. His attendance was a great event and the whole route from Buckingham Palace to Sydenham was lined by cheering crowds. There must have been an excitable and patriotic atmosphere on the day as the Royal party reached the Crystal Palace in their carriage. Burnley beat Liverpool 1-0 in front of a smaller crowd of 72,778 and this begs the question - were the Royal family Burnley supporters?

The modern Crystal Palace F.C. were formed in the early 20th century and played at the Cup Final venue from 1905-15 before they flew to a new nest. Thus the grounds potential was fulfilled and twenty F.A. Cup Finals were played there from 1895-1914, however the sight lines were poor especially with a large crowd - 'I was there but I didn't see the game!' During the First War the ground was used as an army depot and the Cup Final was never to return there. After the war the Corinthians, a famous amateur club, took the ground over and played there from 1922-36. This team was successful in the 1920s and 1930s and had an epic F.A. Cup encounter with Millwall in 1929-30. There was a 2-2 draw at the Crystal Palace with a crowd of 32,500 followed by a 1-1 draw at the Den in front of 45,000. The match was finally settled at Stamford Bridge when Millwall won 5-1 in front of 58,775. The Crystal Palace again entertained large crowds and indeed had a further resurgence when Britain's first speedway track was laid around the football pitch in 1928. A crowd of 9,834 watched the first meeting on 19 May 1928 although the venue was little changed from 1895. The new sport went to New Cross in 1933 and the Crystal Palace itself was destroyed by fire in November 1936. This hastened the departure of the Corinthians whilst the amalgamated Corinthian-Casuals played at the Oval in 1950-63.

This was the final spectacle and "Screaming Alice" as one journalist had called it was no more. There is little remaining of these illustrious days although the present athletics stadium is on an almost identical site to the old football ground. Indeed there are remains of the old banking between the current stadium and the lake, and three turnstiles went to Gay Meadow, Shrewsbury in 1936 - made by Stevens & Sons of Southwark (1884). Meanwhile the F.A. was confronted with familiar problems in 1914: Where would they play the F.A. Cup Final? How could they find a large enough venue? Should they use a club ground or develop a purpose built national stadium? Who would fund such a development? With war looming these decisions were put on ice and the initial solution was to use club grounds again. Despite the outbreak of the First War the 1914-15 season continued to its conclusion, although many questioned whether the games should have been played. The famous Old Trafford ground was opened in 1910 and like Goodison Park before it was the most advanced stadium of its time. Hence Old Trafford was chosen as the venue for the Cup Final in 1915 and was dubbed the 'Khaki' Cup Final due to the large number of soldiers in the crowd. The contest was played in a subdued atmosphere and Sheffield United defeated Chelsea by a 3-0 score line in front of 49,557 spectators.

The Football League restarted in 1919 and the F.A. was again looking for a Cup Final venue. The London Athletics Club had laid out a new running track on a field at Stamford Bridge in April 1877. This became the club's home and was developed as a challenge to Lillie Bridge Athletic Ground, just to the north. Fred Parker was one of the founders of the athletics club and believed Stamford Bridge had great potential for development as a sports venue, and brothers Gus and Joe Mears shared his vision (see Ch. 15), hence there were many deliberations at the turn of the 19th century. For a while the future of the site was uncertain and Stamford Bridge was nearly sold to the Great Western Railway as a coal yard, but after further discussions between Fred Parker and Gus Mears there was a change of heart and developments

Wembley. The Cup Final was played here from 1923-2000.

went ahead as planned. It was on such business decisions that the future of football in the capital was decided, which was the very thing the founders of the game wanted to avoid.

Archibald Leitch had established himself at this time as the top ground designer in Scotland and also worked for Sheffield United (1902) and built Ayresome Park for Middlesbrough (1903). Mears and Parker then visited Hampden Park, Celtic Park and Ibrox Park in Scotland, which were the largest grounds at the time. Archibald Leitch developed at least two of these and after a meeting with Mears and Parker was employed to design a new ground at Stamford Bridge. Indeed soon after this Henry Norris, who would not be out done, approached him to work on Craven Cottage. A large football stadium was developed at Stamford Bridge in 1905 and consisted of a Main Stand (with gable) on the eastern-side, a large curved terrace around the other three sides and a running and cycle track around the pitch - the latter remained a prominent feature for many years to come. However Parker and Mears had an impressive new ground but no team to play there! The Mears Company was responsible for building much of Craven Cottage thus they initially approached Fulham and asked them to move to the new ground. Henry Norris, the ambitious director of Fulham, blocked this move since he wanted to retain his power. In fact Norris left Fulham for Arsenal in 1910 and it was his ambition that took the Gunners from Woolwich to Highbury in 1913 (see Ch. 13).

Thus a new team was formed to play at the venue and names such as Stamford Bridge, Kensington and London F.C. were suggested, however the name Chelsea F.C. was chosen by Fred Parker since it had more prestige. The club obtained some of the best players from other clubs i.e. William Foulkes the goalkeeper and with advanced facilities Chelsea were immediately granted a place in the Second Division. The first game at Stamford Bridge was a friendly against Liverpool on 4 September 1905 and they won by a 4-0 score line. Their first League game at Stockport was a defeat however their home debut against Hull City was a 5-1 victory. Despite small crowds at first the enterprise soon took off and 67,000 people turned up for a game against Manchester United in April 1906. The club were promoted to Division One in 1907 and with such large crowds the size of the banking was increased. This prepared the ground for a record attendance of 77,952 against Swindon in the F.A. Cup in 1911. This was a substantial modern venue therefore the F.A. staged the Cup Final at Stamford Bridge from 1920-22. There was nearly a problem in 1920 as Chelsea reached the semi-final but fortunately for the F.A. they lost 3-1 to Aston Villa. The following Cup Finals took place at Stamford Bridge during those years:

1920 - Aston Villa 1 - Huddersfield Town 0 (50,018)

1921 - Tottenham Hotspur 1 - Wolves 0 (72,805)

1922 - Huddersfield Town 1 - Preston 0 (53,000)

The two features that stand out regarding these games are the low scores and the low attendances. The former was due to the condition of the pitch, which tended to suffer when it was used for other sporting events such as athletics and baseball. The ground was not filled to capacity for these three Finals and it is possible that a neutral venue would have been more attractive, although when London club Spurs played the attendance was higher. One strange factor was that admission prices were increased to keep the numbers down - this clearly didn't help. The F.A. then really got their act together and developed a national stadium at Wembley under the guidance of (Sir) Frederick Joseph Wall. The 'most famous football stadium in the world' was originally called the Empire Stadium and later the *Venue of Legends*, and for many years playing at Wembley was the ultimate goal of clubs and their players. The initial development was as part of the British Empire Exhibition and Robert McAlpine the contractors erected the stadium in a remarkable 300 days, just in time for the Cup Final in April 1923. The safety of the ground was tested in an unusual way and a large number of workers and soldiers were employed to march up and down on the terraces!

When built it was without doubt the largest and finest stadium in the world. The main feature was the two distinctive domed towers that were connected by a balcony area. This façade provided the entrance to a dazzling white interior, whilst the terraces curved around the pitch and were reached from the outside through arched entrances. The two sides were seated and each covered by a roof, whilst the Cup was presented from the Royal Box at the top of the 'famous' flight of stairs. Bolton Wanderers beat West Ham United 2-0 in the first Final of 1923, although the game was nearly abandoned. The huge crowd spilled on to the pitch before the start of the game and a 'famous' mounted policeman rode forth. The crowd was then settled, the game went ahead and it was later dubbed the 'White Horse Final'. The first international took place in 1924 and was a 1-1 draw between England and Scotland however after the

World Cup 1966. Some people are on the pitch . . . They think it's all over . . . It is now!

Empire Exhibition there were doubts about the ground's future - these were settled when Wembley Arena was built in 1934 and the complex was further developed.

There were some famous events at Wembley including the Olympic games in 1948, the Matthews Cup Final in 1953 (when Blackpool came back to beat Bolton 4-3) and the World Cup Final in 1966. There were few later developments although the terraces were completely covered in 1963 and Wembley Way was built along the former Olympic Way. The stadium was used for every Cup Final and replay from 1923 to 2000, with the only exception in 1970, when Chelsea beat Leeds 2-1 in a replay at Old Trafford. The attendance figures for the Finals were 92-93,000 until 1938 and thereafter around 99,000. They rose to about 100,000 in the years 1950-80 before falling back to around 98,000. The stadium was all-seated in 1990 and to provide further seats the Olympic Gallery was also installed, whilst a new walkway was erected at the front of the stadium. This reduced the capacity at the Finals to 79,000 in the 1990s. In more recent years the most notable event was the European Football Championships and Final in 1996. When Charles Alcock and the F.A. began the Cup competition in 1872 they could not have dreamt of how it would grow, yet it was their actions and vision that set the ball rolling. Meanwhile early clubs built some impressive venues and there is now a discussion of these developments at the club grounds.

W.G. Grace - William Gilbert Grace was born at Downend, Bristol on 18 July 1848 and saw his first cricket match between William Clarke's All England XI and a West Gloucestershire side in 1854. He was a good all-round athlete and played first class cricket from 1865; he scored 224 runs for England v Surrey and two days later won a running race during a meeting at the Crystal Palace in 1866. He was a right hand bat who played for the Gentlemen, M.C.C. and Gloucestershire and went on R.A. Fitzgerald's tour of Canada and U.S.A. in 1872 (see Lubbock Ch. 7). He qualified as a doctor then worked in a practice at Easton in Bristol, and he only finished playing first class cricket in 1900. He was Secretary and manager of the London C.C.C. a team who played first class cricket at the Crystal Palace in 1900-04 - this left a vacancy for the football club who were formed the next year. He died on 23 October 1915.

Table 5: **FA CUP FINAL VENUES**

1872	**THE OVAL**
1873	**LILLIE BRIDGE**
1874 - 92	**THE OVAL**
Replays	1875, 1876 The Oval
	1886 The Racecourse Ground, Derby
1893	**FALLOWFIELD**
1894	**GOODISON PARK**
1895 - 1914	**CRYSTAL PALACE**
Replays	1901 Burnden Park
	1902 Crystal Palace
	1910 Goodison Park
	1911 Old Trafford
	1912 Bramall Lane
1915	**OLD TRAFFORD**
1920 - 22	**STAMFORD BRIDGE**
1923 - 2000	**WEMBLEY**
Replays	1970 Old Trafford
	1981, 1982, 1983, 1990, 1993 Wembley

CHAPTER 13

The London Connection

The F.A. had struggled to find suitable venues for the Cup Final however, despite this, the new sport of soccer had really taken off and the most successful clubs had ever-increasing crowds and needed to develop their grounds. Some were forced to relocate whilst others simply improved the old grounds - the basic principal was to have a Main Stand (for club offices, changing rooms and officials) and three sides of earth terracing and banking. It was only later that the familiar terraces were concreted and eventually roofed. The late Victorian period was a time of confidence and of Empire as a result of Britain's industrial success. This was an era of innovation when the country showed its achievements to the world with the Great Exhibition of 1851. This gave men of vision a chance to shine and none more so than George Stephenson, Isambard Kingdom Brunel and William Armstrong. Life, however, was hard for many in the new industrial cities and reform and parliamentary change was slow to come. This process began with the Great Reform Act in 1832 but most men were still unable to vote and this only changed after further Acts in 1867 and 1884. The 'Golden Jubilee' of Queen Victoria came in 1887 and Britain and the Empire celebrated its success and prosperity.

The Football League had kicked off in 1888 and the next 20 years witnessed a golden era in ground development with about sixty League clubs opening new grounds from 1890-1910. These were important sports venues and most clubs stayed at them for the next 100 years or even longer. So where did all this ground building begin? With the (temporary) loss of Accrington Stanley and Aldershot from the League the football alphabet begins with Arsenal, which is most fitting, since it was there that the history of football grounds really began. There were some early stands at Goodison Park in 1892 but it was in Kent that the most significant development took place. Arsenal Football Club was formed as Dial Square in 1886 and soon after was renamed Royal Arsenal (in reference to workshops at Woolwich). One of the founders was Fred Beardsley, formerly a Nottingham Forest player, and he arranged for his old club to donate some shirts hence the origin of Arsenal's colours. The club were renamed Woolwich Arsenal and turned professional in 1891. There was an attempt to form a League for clubs in London and the south of England in March 1892, however only Arsenal, Luton, Millwall, Swindon and West Herts attended the meeting. The outcome being that Woolwich Arsenal was elected to Division Two of the Football League in 1893 and the Southern League was formed in 1894.

The club first played on Plumstead Common however this was a poor site used for army manoeuvres thus they moved to the Sportsman's Ground at the end of 1887, which was situated on the edge of Plumstead Marshes and near to Plumstead Station. This second ground was itself often waterlogged and the club moved to an adjacent site known as the Manor Ground in 1888 (commemorated by Griffin Manor Way). The third ground was also unsuitable and had no stands whilst the spectators had to watch from carts! There was also a viewpoint beyond the ground from the banking of a sewage channel hence the club lost much needed revenue. George Weaver, a local businessman, owned the *Weaver Mineral Water Co.* and laid out the Invicta Ground just to the south. This was enclosed with a grandstand and was located off Plumstead High Street and the club moved there in 1890. It was, however, a speculative venture out of keeping with the traditions of the F.A. and when Arsenal entered the League in 1893 the rent was raised to a high level (this was a common occurrence), consequently Woolwich Arsenal moved back to the Manor Ground in 1893. Indeed the New Manor Ground (Football & Athletic) and Invicta Athletic Grounds are on a map dated 1897.

The Invicta Ground was then sold and covered by the houses of Hector and Mineral Street, whilst the remains of the terracing are still to be seen in the back gardens (on Hector Street). The team gradually improved in Division Two and were promoted in the 1903-04 season when they finished second behind Preston North End. They clearly had high aspirations, even at this early date, and their telegram address was "Forward Woolwich" which was a marked contrast to that of Leicester viz. "Fossil Leicester" (later changed to the Foxes). The Arsenal side were off to a good start at the Manor Ground and in the first season had average crowds of 6,000. Woolwich was then a bustling centre with housing on the banks of the river, shipyards to the west and the armaments factory to the east. There were, however, dark clouds gathering on the horizon and the country was engaged in the Boer War in southern Africa in 1899-

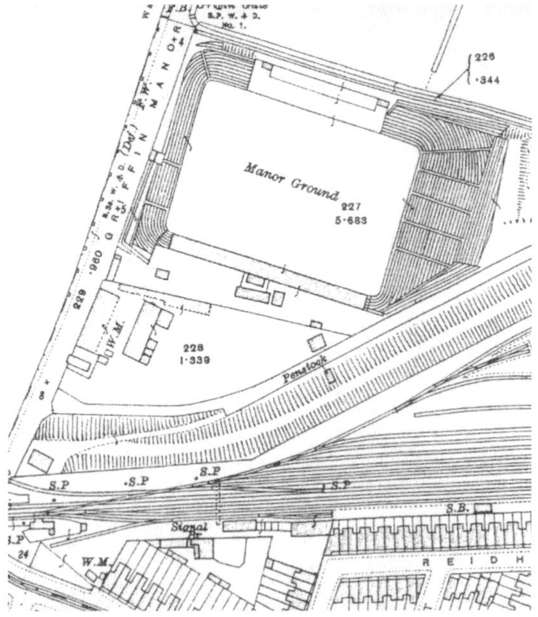

The Manor Ground, Woolwich - O.S. Map 1914.
The first Spion Kop was built 1904.

1902. The British Army fought in several 'less than successful' conflicts and one was the Battle of Spion Kop, which took place around Spion Kop Hill (an important look out point or spy hill). Indeed the British were defeated with heavy losses. The Manor Ground was being developed at this time and the club built the first large banked terrace in the country by 1904. This was located behind the goalmouth at the eastern end of the ground and provided a great lookout point for the spectators thus returning soldiers dubbed it the Spion Kop, although Liverpool F.C. have a similar claim regarding Anfield.

In terms of football grounds the main player in the capital was Henry Norris, however he was less concerned with the ideals of the beautiful game and more interested in the profits and power that he could attain - he had made much of his fortune building property in the Fulham area. He soon became attracted to the developing game of soccer and in particular to Fulham. The latter were founded as Fulham St. Andrew's Sunday School F.C. in 1879 and won the West London Amateur Cup in 1887 and the West London League in 1893. The club had a number of grounds in their early days on both sides of the River Thames at Barnes and Fulham. They first played at Star Road near to St. Andrew's Road and church and then moved to Eelbrook Common in 1883. There was then a succession of venues namely Lillie Road, Putney Lower Common and the Ranelagh Club at Barn Elms in 1888-90. The club returned to Fulham in 1891 and played briefly at Pursers Cross next to Parsons Green Station, and Eelbrook Common, then shared the Half Moon Ground of Wasps R.F.C. in Lower Richmond Road until 1894.

The house known as Craven Cottage was built in 1780 and stood on land formerly owned by Anne Boleyn. The area around it was covered by open farmland in 1885 and Stevenage Road was then called New Road and was beside Fulham Common Fields. To the north was Crabtree Farm on Crabtree Lane and the only other houses present at this time were Fulham Palace and the St. James Home. The situation changed after Craven Cottage was destroyed by fire in 1888 and Fulham F.C. took out a lease on the site in 1894. The new ground took time to prepare and the club had to spend one season at Halford Road near Stamford Bridge and should have been called Fulham Wanderers! The remains of the old house were cleared and the rubble used to form banking at the Putney End. The ground opened with uncovered terraces in 1896 whilst a small wooden stand with four roof sections was built shortly afterwards and nicknamed "The Rabbit Hutch". There must have been some amusement for the Victorian gentlemen as they squeezed into this structure in their top hats! The first game was against Minerva in a local cup contest on 10 October 1896, and the club changed their name to Fulham F.C. and became professional in 1898. Norris was on the Board and made the club a limited company in 1903 then, as stated, opposed the Mears brothers and blocked a move to Stamford Bridge in 1905.

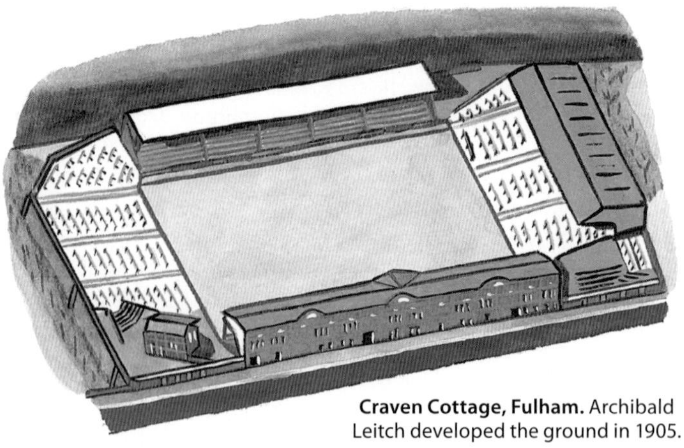
Craven Cottage, Fulham. Archibald Leitch developed the ground in 1905.

Fulham elected to stay at Craven Cottage hence they needed to develop the ground and keep up with the Jones's. The ground designer Archibald Leitch was building Stamford Bridge in early 1905 and was employed by Fulham to develop Craven Cottage. He designed the historic Main Stand there that year and this was a notable early work by Leitch. The Stevenage Road façade was built with considerable attention to architectural detail whilst inside the ground there was a distinctive gable and the famous pavilion at the south corner (see Ch. 15). Three large terraces were built at the Hammersmith and Putney Ends and also on the Riverside. It was a substantial ground, but not as large as Stamford Bridge, and was an impressive sight in 1896 on the banks of the Thames with few houses nearby. Fulham F.C. did not fulfil the potential hoped for by Norris and in some ways his ambition was thwarted. They played in Division One of the Southern League from 1903 being champions in 1906 and 1907 and were elected to Division Two of the Football League at the latter date. This success was somewhat tainted since Chelsea achieved promotion to Division One at the time. They lost a Cup semi-final to Newcastle in 1908 and came fourth in Division Two in 1907-08 then stayed in that division until the First War. The record attendance was 49,335 in 1938 for a Second Division game against Millwall.

Chelsea, however, had far more success and played in Division One in 1907-10 and 1912-15. Stamford Bridge had large crowds and there was an attendance of 77,952 in 1911 for an F.A. Cup game against Swindon (the record was 82,905 in October 1935). They also appeared in the Cup Final in 1915. Henry Norris was not happy with all this and looked for a new scheme to out-do his rivals and take him to the top, which brings us neatly back to Arsenal and the Manor Ground. The Spion Kop was completed in time for Arsenal's arrival in the First Division in 1904 and from there crowds watched games against the famous northern clubs. There were no games against southern opposition until the arrival of Bristol City in Division One in 1906-07 whilst the first London derby was against Chelsea in 1907-08. Woolwich Arsenal came sixth in Division One in 1908-09 but the Manor Ground lacked the facilities of other new venues and was difficult to reach, being a considerable distance from London.

The club just avoided relegation in 1909-10 and were forced into liquidation thus Norris saw his opportunity and intervened to save them. He initially suggested that Arsenal and Fulham should merge as a First Division team but this went the way of many such suggestions down the years and the F.A. promptly rejected it. He then tried to arrange for Arsenal to ground share at Craven Cottage however this idea also failed. Woolwich Arsenal finished mid-table in 1910-11 and 1911-12 however Henry Norris made an announcement in February 1913 that changed the course of soccer history. He decided to move the club to Highbury in north London since there were better transport communications and a large population base. The move was not popular with some and there was much opposition from local residents and neighbouring clubs Clapton Orient and Tottenham. Despite the efforts of Henry Norris the club came last in 1912-13 having won once at home all season and only three games in total. The crowds were less than those of Clapton and Millwall and the last game at the Manor Ground was on 26 April 1913. The move to Highbury was most significant regarding the future of the club and it is Henry Norris that must be thanked for this foresight.

This speculation was quite healthy for football grounds them-selves and a substantial new stadium was built. Henry Norris the owner again employed Leitch and he designed a ground with a multi-gabled Main Stand in Avenell Road and open terraces on the remaining three sides. In fact the famous North Bank terrace curved all the way into the northwest corner of the ground. The first game was played at Highbury on 6 September 1913 and was a Division Two fixture against Leicester Fosse. The club finished third in Division Two at the end of the 1913-14 season and only missed out on promotion by goal average - just behind Bradford Park Avenue. They were renamed the Arsenal in 1914 and came fifth in Division Two at the end of the 1914-15 season, however this was followed by some astonishing developments at the end of the First War. Despite their fifth place finish the club were promoted to the First Division in 1919, a decision that was tainted with controversy. The top division was expanded in number by two teams at this point and three teams had a grievance against Arsenal viz. Barnsley and Wolves who were third and fourth in Division Two and Tottenham who were bottom of Division One. The Gunners went up with Derby and Preston whilst Tottenham were relegated, despite the fact that no team had previously gone down when the League was increased in size.

There were clearly some dubious dealings and not surprisingly Henry Norris was behind them. He had become Sir Henry in 1917 and was M.P. for Fulham in 1918 and had power and influence within the game. He used this at the League's A.G.M. in 1919 and persuaded various club chairmen and members of the League Management Committee that Arsenal should be promoted, but no doubt there was dissent in some quarters. This event may have altered the history of the League since Arsenal have maintained their Division One status ever since, although Tottenham soon bounced back and were Division Two champions in 1919-20. Arsenal F.C. was a mid-table team in Division One in the early 1920s however they were nearly relegated in 1924-25 having finished in 20th place (22 clubs). Henry Norris then secured the services of manager Herbert Chapman who was previously very successful at Huddersfield Town, and the club embarked on a "golden era". Norris, however, dropped out of football soon after Chapman's arrival when financial irregularities were discovered, and his drive for success in the soccer world was finally spent. The record crowd at Highbury was 73,295 on 9 March 1935 for a First Division game against Sunderland. This period of League history saw the first Spion Kop and three impressive grounds at Stamford Bridge, Craven Cottage and Highbury, however other developments also took place in London at the time.

Thames Ironworks F.C. were formed in east London in 1895 and spent their first season at Hermit Road, Canning Town and then played at Browning Road, East Ham in 1896. The driving force behind the team was Arnold Hills who owned the Thames Ironworks Shipyard. The crowds were small at Browning Road hence the club moved to a large new arena called the Memorial Ground in 1897. This venue was developed by Arnold Hills near to 'West Ham Underground Station' and was reputed to have a large capacity. There was a West Stand backing onto Springfield Road and the pitch was surrounded by a running and cycle track and open banking. Outside the ground Memorial Avenue led from Manor Road to the arena - an arrangement like that at Wembley. Thames Ironworks joined the Southern League in 1898 and played in Division One in 1899-1900. They played against local rivals Millwall at the Memorial Ground on 23 December 1899 and this was abandoned after 69 minutes due to fog with the home side trailing 2-0. The last 21 minutes were played after the return match at East Ferry Road on 28 April 1900 although there was no further score. Such were the strange arrangements in these early days. The club became a limited company, adopted professional status and changed their name to West Ham United in 1900. There was an ongoing dispute with Arnold Hills, the owner of the Memorial Ground, over the issue of professionalism and he tried to replace them with amateurs Clapton Orient hence they moved to Upton Park in 1904. The Memorial Ground is now a recreation ground and was present as a stadium until at least the 1960s.

There were similar large-scale developments in west London and St. Jude's Institute F.C. formed in 1885 and amalgamated with Christchurch Rangers to become Queens Park Rangers in 1886. The name was chosen since most of the players lived in the Queen's Park district and they were a much-travelled club. They played at Kensal Rise Athletic Ground north of Kensal Rise Station from 1896-1901, which had a track and north pavilion and was then surrounded by fields. The club turned professional and joined the Southern League whilst at Kensal Rise but they were unable to raise sufficient funds to buy the freehold of the ground. They then moved a short distance south to Latimer Road, North Kensington in 1901 but this ground was severely tested when a crowd of 10,000 arrived for a game v Spurs. It was thus deemed unsuitable and Rangers returned to Kensal Rise Athletic Ground in 1902. The crowds greatly increased and the rent was raised accordingly but this was beyond the financial capability of the club therefore they moved west, to Park Royal, in 1904. They played on a site near the present day Cumberland Avenue that was laid out by the *Royal Agricultural Society* as a Horse Ring with an oval arena in 1902. No doubt Rangers hoped this arrangement would be permanent but unfortunately they were soon on the move again as the show grounds were sold off in 1907 - despite the additional rent received from the football team.

Rangers moved just a few hundred yards south to the "Park Royal Ground", which was on the south side of Coronation Road at its junction with Johnson Way. The Great Western Railway developed this as a speculative venture and it was certainly not amateur since the main aim was to earn an income from sporting events. It is unclear if it was built specifically for Rangers. There was a railway station immediately behind the South Stand that provided a rail connection to Paddington although not directly to Queens Park. This provided good access in one sense, however this was counteracted by the fact that the ground could only be reached along Coronation Road. There were fields to the south and the site was near to the present day Park Royal Underground Station. The venue was built in the same style as Ayresome Park, Middlesbrough but not by Leitch and had a stated capacity of 60,000. The first game was against Millwall in November 1907 with an attendance of 20,000. The result was a 3-2 victory for the visitors and despite this defeat Rangers were a strong team in the Southern League being champions in 1908 and 1912.

The Park Royal Ground could have been a great success but Rangers were forced to leave in February 1915 when the army moved in, and finished the season playing at Stamford Bridge and Kensal Rise Athletic Ground. The club were unable to stay at the latter for long as the pitch was used for allotments in 1917. The area had changed since they were last there and new streets and housing had been built around the athletics stadium. It was finally demolished in the mid-1920s and the site covered with the houses of Whitmore and Leigh Gardens. Loftus Road was first laid out in 1904 and was a basic venue with a small South Stand on the Ellerslie Road Side, and was home to Shepherd's Bush F.C. an amateur club. Rangers played two games at the White City Olympic Stadium in 1912 and soon made a permanent move to this area of London. Shepherd's Bush abandoned Loftus Road in 1917, thus Rangers moved in and their first game was in the London Cup v West Ham on 8 September 1917 - attendance 5,000. They played in the regional London Combination during the war and were founder members of Division Three in 1920.

The club began well with crowds of about 20,000 and finished third in 1920-21 but came last in 1923-24 and 1925-26, although they were third again in 1929-30. The facilities at Loftus Road remained basic consequently the club tried a larger venue (much larger). The White City Stadium was built for the Olympic games in 1908 and the buildings of the Olympic complex reached as far as the Loftus Road ground. There was a revival at the White City Stadium in the 1930s when it was used for greyhound racing and speedway, whilst its activities were further extended with the arrival of athletics from Stamford Bridge in 1932. Rangers played at the White City for two seasons in 1931-33 and the record attendance of 41,097 was set during a Cup-tie against Leeds United in January 1932 (the record at Loftus Road was 35,353 during a First Division game against Leeds in April 1974). They had a second spell there in 1962-63 but the small crowds were insignificant in such a large arena and there was no permanent move. The stadium was demolished during road building in 1984.

An important question can be asked regarding these changes - was there a design behind these developments or did they just happen by chance? The London soccer scene could have been quite different if the Memorial Ground, Park Royal or the White City had survived. Meanwhile, there is one last piece to be considered in the early jigsaw of London football grounds. The south London club Charlton Athletic were formed when several local teams merged together in 1905. The new club were near to Millwall and Woolwich Arsenal however this was not a problem at the time since their only 'ambition' was to play football. The club's first ground was Siemen's Meadow near the 'Thames Flood Barrier', however they moved to Woolwich Common in 1907 and Pound Park in 1908 - the latter on Coxmount Road just east of the current ground, then Angerstein Athletic Ground located on Horn Lane towards the Blackwall Tunnel in 1913. They moved to the site that became the Valley after the First War in 1919. The latter was a "natural" stadium site and the pitch was laid out in a hollow formed by a sand and chalk pit, whilst the main feature was the huge East Bank or "Cliff" that ran around to the south. This meant that a ground with basic facilities had the potential for very large crowds.

Charlton Athletic were still playing in local leagues in 1919 hence the Valley was prepared with the help of volunteers (a practice repeated in the 1990s) and money for the project was raised independently of any investors. The first game was played against Summerstown on 13 September 1919 in front of a crowd of just 1,000. The club soon became more ambitious and turned professional in 1920 and Edwin Radford, a director, approached the League. He tried to gain League status for the club and promoted Charlton as the next Woolwich Arsenal stating that the ground could hold crowds of 50,000. There was, however, neither terracing nor stands at this stage and the club had few funds with which to develop the ground. Despite this, Radford's arguments impressed the League and Charlton were founder members of Division Three (South) in 1921. A Main Stand was constructed on the west side by Humphreys to the design of Leitch but was only a third of the pitch in length and had four spans. The facilities remained basic and the club tried moving south to the Mount in Mountsfield Park off Brownhill Road, Catford in December 1923 - May 1924. This strange notion failed thus Charlton played at the Valley in 1924-85.

The North Terrace was roofed in 1934 and the East Bank was concreted in the 1930s, which prepared the ground for a record attendance of 75,031 on 12 February 1938 during an F.A. Cup tie against Aston Villa. The club's famous manager in the 1930s was Jimmy Seed who had plenty of ambition and nearly brought Stanley Matthews there in 1938. Charlton's finest hour came in 1947 when they won the F.A. Cup with a 1-0 victory over Burnley and the excitement was too much for some - manager Jimmy Seed dropped the trophy and broke the lid! The Valley was one of London's largest grounds and achieved the "third" highest attendance in the capital after Chelsea (82,905) and Tottenham (75,038) whilst Arsenal (73,295) was not far behind. This chapter has described some of the most interesting grounds in the capital but others were of importance and White Hart Lane is discussed under Archibald Leitch (see Ch. 16). The focus, meanwhile, turns to the rest of the country in the next chapter.

CHAPTER 14

Kop a Load of This

London was the capital and commercial centre however soccer, like Rugby League, had a considerable power base in the north and substantial grounds were built around the country. It was almost a competition to see which club could establish the largest venue and many had aspirations to build a 'Wembley of the North'. Spion Kop was first applied to the Manor Ground however the most famous Kop was at Anfield, Liverpool and the name was synonymous with both the terrace and the Liverpool supporters. Liverpool F.C. played their first game at Anfield on 1 September 1892 and this was a friendly against Rotherham Town with 1,000 spectators - the Merseyside team appeared in blue-white quarters and won 7-1. They played in the Lancashire League in their first season but joined Division Two of the Football League in 1893 with Middlesbrough Ironopolis, Newcastle United, Rotherham Town and Woolwich Arsenal - Accrington and Bootle resigned at the time. Liverpool had a flying start and they were unbeaten all season being Division Two champions in 1893-94. Their team consisted entirely of Scottish players except for their English goalkeeper Bill McOwen (who sounded Scottish)!

In the 1890s Everton was the best-supported club in the country but by the 1900s attendances at Anfield were equal to those at Everton. The club won the League title in 1901 and 1906 and the ground was ready for development. There was a cover on the Kemlyn Road Side to the east whilst a further cover was erected at the Anfield Road End in about 1903 and Liverpool approached Archibald Leitch during 1906. His work there is discussed further in Ch. 16 but can be briefly summarised and involved raising the pitch, building a new Main Stand and erecting a large earthen bank. The huge terrace constructed at the southern end was soon known as the Spion Kop and the choice of name was accredited to a local journalist Ernest Edwards. There is clearly some confusion and one can ask was it Arsenal or Liverpool who coined the famous phrase? The first game at the rebuilt Anfield was on 1 September 1906 in front of 32,000, whilst a 50' flagpole was erected south of the ground in 1906 and was formerly the topmast of S.S. Great Eastern. This vessel was built by Brunel in 1860 and was one of the first iron ships. The Kop terraces held a large number of people in some discomfort, as there was always an inadequate provision of gangways at this end of the ground. The next development was to concrete the terrace and cover the roof in 1928. Local architect Joseph Watson Cabré designed the distinctive roof and the capacity on the Kop was then a staggering 28,000. The terrace opened in August 1928 and John McKenna the League President performed the ceremony, whilst the record attendance was 61,905 on 2 February 1952 during an F.A. Cup game against Wolves.

Archibald Leitch had some exceptional schemes and his most progressive came at Villa Park. As stated Aston Villa had a brief sojourn at Wellington Road from 1876-97 and during this time the leisure park at Lower Aston Grounds went into a decline, and the ornamental gardens were turned into a basic sports ground. This area was developed into Villa Park in 1896-97 under the direction of Chairman Frederick Rinder. The initial developments that took place are discussed further in relation to Leitch however the early ground had a stand on each side and earth banking at either end. There were also features of the old pleasure park viz. the former bowling green, and Victorian buildings that were used by Villa as their club offices. It became the venue for

Villa Park. The ground in the 1950s, the Holte End held 20,000.

several Cup semi-finals after 1901, but Rinder then produced a new plan for Villa Park in 1914 to raise the ground's capacity to 104,000. These plans were put into action with the aid of Leitch however, needless to say, they never achieved this capacity. The terracing was increased in size and a new Main Stand built in 1922-24 in a style reminiscent of Aston Hall (looking down on it). There was a grand staircase, balustrade and two towers on either side as in a stately home, at the entrance, whilst inside there was a flat roof gable emblazoned in claret and blue. The Holte End was extended in 1940 and was one of the largest Kop terraces with a capacity of nearly 20,000, and there was a record attendance of 76,588 on 14 March 1946 during an F.A. Cup tie against Derby County. A roof was erected over the Holte End in 1962 however it proved impractical to fit seats to the terrace and it was finally demolished in 1994. It might appear to some that only Archibald Leitch developed grounds at this time, however this was not the case.

Rivals Birmingham City F.C. were formed at the suggestion of some cricketing enthusiasts at Trinity Church, Bordesly in 1875. They began as Small Heath Alliance and played on open ground at Arthur Street near St. Andrew's and then at Ladypool Road in Sparkbrook in 1876-77. They moved to Muntz Street off Coventry Road and played there for 29 years from 1877-1906. The ground was not developed and this restricted the size of the crowd hence the club were eventually forced to move. They changed their name to Small Heath in 1888 and Birmingham F.C. in 1905 and found a new site located in a former brick works by St. Andrew's Street. The club employed the little known Harry Pumphrey to do the job and this was a strange choice since he had no experience or qualifications! He designed St. Andrew's and it took ten months to drain and prepare the pitch. It opened in 1906 and had a large Kop and basic Main Stand designed by Pumphrey. The Kop was on the Coventry Road Side and extended around the Tilton Road End and was the largest in the country with an estimated capacity of 48,000 spectators. Developments came slowly and the rear of the Kop was covered, as was the narrow Railway End, in the late 1930s. The record crowd of 67,341 came on 11 February 1939 during an F.A. Cup tie against Everton. A two tier Main Stand was built and the Tilton Road End covered in the 1950s followed by a two-tier stand at the Railway End in 1963-64. There were few other developments and the Kop and Tilton Road End remained an awesome terrace until it was finally demolished in April 1994.

There were, meanwhile, remarkable developments in Yorkshire in the 'unlikely' soccer town of Huddersfield. The town's rugby club played at Fartown in the northern suburbs, and this was the most important sporting venue in an area dominated by rugby. The two sports seldom shared venues although there was an F.A. Cup semi-final at Fartown in 1882. There was then a meeting at the George Hotel next to the classical Huddersfield Station (built 1850), in 1895, however this was not connected with soccer and saw the formation of the Rugby League. A meeting took place at the Imperial Hotel, Huddersfield in 1906 with the aim of forming a soccer club at Fartown however the Northern Union had actively discouraged ground sharing since 1905. With this route blocked, the other option available was to develop Leeds Road Recreation Grounds, which had been used for amateur football since the end of the 19th century. This area could be reached easily by tram hence the first development of the site was undertaken in 1906. The early pitch was parallel to Leeds Road and at right angles to the later stadium and was first used for local football in March 1908 and by Huddersfield Town on 2 September 1908.

The club applied for League status in June 1910 and to support their application hired Archibald Leitch to design a new ground. This was all done very quickly and the ground was ready for League football in September 1910. It was a substantial venue with a capacity of 34,000 but attendances were low and the club had a poor start thus went into liquidation in 1912, at the same time as neighbours Leeds City. They re-started but were again in financial difficulty in 1919 and announced plans to relocate to Elland Road although this may have been a negotiating tactic. The players and supporters rallied round and in a few months the club was on a firmer footing. They were second in Division Two in 1919-20 and were promoted and also reached the Cup Final. The terracing was increased in size to achieve a capacity of 47,000 at this time, and the following season Herbert Chapman arrived at the club and this cemented their success. Huddersfield won the F.A. Cup in 1922 but this was only the beginning and they won three consecutive League titles in 1923-24, 1924-25 and 1925-26 being the first club to achieve this.

Herbert Chapman departed for Arsenal in 1925 however the impetus he had begun continued and Leeds Road was developed into a colossal ground. The capacity was raised to 60,000 in 1930 and the record attendance of 67,037 was on 27 February 1932 during an F.A. Cup tie against Arsenal (of course). The ground was also used for Cup semi-finals and a vast roof was erected over the Popular Side in 1955 however Leeds Road then declined as a venue. There were falling attendances and with a lack of money for repairs the capacity was continually reduced - 52,000 in 1962, 31,000 in 1984 and 14,000 in 1989.

The ground had really had its day and the final game took place against Blackpool on 30 April 1994 with a crowd of 16,195 - the home side lost 2-1. There were, meanwhile, some further developments 15 miles up the road in Leeds and an unusual phenomena took place in this area of West Yorkshire. The dominant sport was Rugby League or the Northern Union however when professional soccer finally arrived rugby played a major role in its growth viz.

Bradford City	Manningham Rugby Club	1903
Leeds City	Hunslet F.C.	1904
Bradford Park Avenue	Bradford Rugby Club	1907
Huddersfield Town	public meeting	1908
Halifax Town	public meeting	1911

Leeds Rugby Club first used Elland Road in 1878. The venue was some distance from the city centre, in an isolated area of old mine workings and the banking was raised using waste from local collieries. The rugby club were unable to attract a following there and under the name Yorkshire Wanderers tried a ground nearer the city centre in 1881. They returned to Elland Road in 1882 but after just one year closed down and it was then used by local teams and called the Old Peacock Sports Ground. It remained like this for the next fourteen years until Holbeck Rugby Club of the Northern Union purchased the venue in 1897. The area of Holbeck was between Elland Road and the city centre and still has several examples of quality 'back to back' housing. Indeed Leeds is one of the few places where such 19th century houses can still be seen. The first pitch was parallel to Elland Road, in common with Leeds Road, and the club built a stand along the south side and a wooden terrace on the north. The first soccer game was between Hunslet and Harrogate in the West Yorkshire Cup Final on 23 April 1898 and it was also used for local contests in 1902-03, but Holbeck Rugby Club resigned from the Northern Union in 1904 and it became vacant.

Hunslet F.C. played at Parkside home of Hunslet Rugby Club, in the south of Leeds, and then at the Nelson Ground but lost the venue in 1902 and could not play any more games. They made the important decision to take over Elland Road with the aim of achieving League status and formed Leeds City on 30 August 1904. They initially played in blue and gold and were known as the Peacocks and their first game at Elland Road was against Hull City on 15 October 1904. A limited company was established in 1905 and the club then developed the ground, erecting a stand beside Elland Road and building new terraces on the other three sides. They joined the League with Chelsea, Clapton Orient and Hull City when it was increased in size in 1905 and in their first season had crowds of 10,000, thus Elland Road was substantially developed in 1906. The club purchased land to the north of the ground and turned the pitch by 90° and built a new Main Stand on the west side with an upper tier of seating, a paddock in front and a barrel roof - it had a capacity of 8,000. New banking was built on the north and east sides of the ground and this raised the total capacity to 45,000. The ground was in fact inadequate for such large crowds and serious problems were experienced during two games: semi-final Barnsley v Everton in 1910 and a Cup (replay) Barnsley v Bradford in 1912. This was compounded by financial difficulties and the club went bankrupt at this time and sought re-election with Gainsborough Trinity in 1911-12.

There were plans to sell the club to the owners of Headingley Cricket and Rugby Ground but the situation was turned around, for the time being, when Herbert Chapman was made manager in 1912. He played for Northampton, Notts County and Tottenham from 1901 and then began his managerial career at Northampton Town. Meanwhile Leeds City came sixth in Division Two in 1912-13, fourth in 1913-14 and fifteenth in 1914-15, which saw the start of a serious decline. The army used Elland Road during the First War and the club were in serious trouble when League football resumed in 1919, being accused of making illegal payments to players before the war. The scandal was compounded when they refused to hand over their books for inspection, although Herbert Chapman denied any knowledge of illegal transactions. John McKenna the League President was going to have justice and announced: "We will have no nonsense, the football stable must be cleansed," and he came to be known as honest John. Leeds City were found guilty of "irregular practices" and expelled from the League but the football horse had already bolted, since it was common knowledge that several clubs had similar dealings. They were in fact a scapegoat and Port Vale replaced them and took on their remaining fixtures in 1919-20.

There was a 'boot sale' of Leeds City players and the football connoisseur was able to buy various fixtures and fittings from the Elland Road ground. At one point it looked as if the ground would be sold or that Huddersfield who were also ailing would move there. The situation was redressed and a new club Leeds

United was formed at Elland Road in 1919 and elected to the League in 1920. The League Committee had a certain degree of guilt over the Leeds City affair and the prompt admission of Leeds United was their attempt to make amends. They lifted a ban on Herbert Chapman in 1920 thus he went to manage Huddersfield Town. The ground was improved in the 1920s with new roofs on the Main Stand and Elland Road Stand whilst the north Kop End was increased to three times its former height. It joined the Lowfields Road Terrace at the northeast corner and a roof was erected at the rear of the latter in the late 1920s-1933. The improvements allowed for a (then) record crowd of 56,796 for a game against Arsenal in 1932 and it was chosen for three Cup semi-finals in the 1930s. The area was a real sporting Mecca and in addition to the soccer ground there was a cricket ground, greyhound stadium (1927) and speedway track (1928). The venue was little changed until the Main Stand burnt down in 1956 - the replacement was built a year later with a 10,000 capacity. The record attendance of 57,892 was on 15 March 1967 during a Cup replay v Sunderland although the ground was again found wanting when a barrier gave way - as a result the Kop End was removed and replaced by the North Stand in 1968. There were other later developments, such as moving the pitch and a second tier on the Lowfields Road Side, but the ground never reached the scale of Maine Road.

West Gorton, a church team, were formed in 1880 and played initially at Clowes Street then spent a year at Kirkmanshulme Cricket Club in Redgate Lane. They then changed their name to Gorton F.C. and moved to Clemington Park, Gorton otherwise known as 'Donkey Common' in 1882. They played at Pink Bank Lane in 1884-85 and then at Reddish Lane however moved to a permanent ground at Hyde Road in 1887. Mr. McKenzie, captain of the Gorton side, found them the new site and the club changed their name to Ardwick at this time. They were founder members of Division Two in 1892 with Bootle, Burslem Port Vale, Burton Swifts, Crewe Alexandra, Darwen, Grimsby Town, Lincoln City, Northwich Victoria, Sheffield United, Small Heath and Walsall Town Swifts. The club, however, had to seek re-election in 1893-94 and went out of business but were reformed as Manchester City - in a similar way Newton Heath became Manchester United in 1902. Facilities at Hyde Road were always basic and there was talk of leaving and moving to Belle Vue Athletics Stadium, nearby, but they decided to stay and made some basic improvements. Despite this the Main Stand burnt down in 1920 and the lease expired in 1923, hence City considered going to Old Trafford or Belle Vue but eventually chose a site two miles away in south Manchester. Their new home Maine Road was in fact a lane, and was an unusual choice being some distance from Ardwick and Gorton and two miles from Old Trafford - they moved back to their roots at the *City of Manchester Stadium* in 2003. Maine Road did have advantages though being in the densely populated area of Moss Side and with easy access.

Maine Road was developed on the site of a former clay-pit and the architect Charles Swain designed it on a grand scale. The Main Stand, to the west, was seated and built at a steep angle with a dipping roof and semi-circular gable at the front, whilst continuous terracing was banked up on three sides. There were tunnel access ways at the four corners and the Kippax Terrace, on the east side, provided the main area for standing. It was the largest English club ground with a 90,000 capacity but was not as large as Ibrox and Celtic Park in Scotland. Robert McAlpine the contractors were working on Maine Road when they completed Wembley in April 1923, thus similarities were not coincidental. There was competition amongst clubs in terms of facilities and it was similar in style to Old Trafford and nearest to the "Wembley of the North" ideal. The first game was against Sheffield United in Division One on 25 August 1923 with an attendance of 60,000, whilst the record for a club ground of 84,569 was on 3 March 1934 (Manchester City v Stoke). Despite the scale there were some problems and the pitch often became waterlogged, thus it was used for only one Cup semi-final before the Second War. A roof was erected at the Platt Lane End in 1938 and the highest League attendance of 83,260 came on 17 January 1948 (Manchester United v Arsenal). Bench seats were installed at the Platt Lane End in 1950 and a roof was erected over the Kippax Terrace in 1956. Maine Road was built after the 'great' period of construction in 1890-1910, yet was the apex of the terraces and epitomized the ambitions of the early clubs.

There were also important grounds at Newcastle, Sunderland and Middlesbrough in the North East of the country. Newcastle Rangers played at the St. James's Park site in 1880-82 and were followed by Newcastle West End in 1886-92. It was then taken over by Newcastle East End in 1892 and the club took the name Newcastle United. They joined the League when it increased in size in 1893 and were promoted to Division One in 1898 and won the championship in 1904-05, thus the club's directors visited Celtic Park and Hampden Park in Scotland. They may have been impressed but decided not to employ Leitch and had a go on their own erecting a Main West Stand in 1905 - the design was a copy of Ayresome

Molineux. The ground after 1979, the South Bank held 30,000.

Park built in 1903. The capacity was estimated to be 65,000 and there was an average attendance of 33,000 in 1906-07 when they won the League. They had a further title in 1908-09 and a record attendance of 68,386 came on 3 September 1930 during a First Division game against Chelsea. Neighbours Sunderland moved to Roker Street in 1898 and the first game had a crowd of 30,000. Leitch developed the Roker End in 1911 whilst the club built a large earth bank at the Fulwell End in 1925. The record crowd of 75,118 was on 8 March 1933 during an F.A. Cup tie against Derby County. Middlesbrough moved to Ayresome Park in 1903 and the ground was designed entirely by Leitch with a record crowd of 53,802 on 27 December 1949 during a Division One game against Newcastle. The North East grounds had large capacities and are discussed under Leitch (see Ch. 15-17).

Molineux, home of Wolves, was developed into a large venue with three distinctive features namely - the Waterloo Road Stand, the seven gabled Molineux Street Stand tapered at one end, and the huge South Bank curving around the pitch corners. The latter had a maximum capacity of 30,000 and was the largest end terrace in the country contrasting with the Holte End at Villa Park, which had no corner infill. The South Bank had numerous tunnels and entrances to the rear and would have made a good bunker for Churchill in the war! Wolves played Liverpool in the F.A. Cup on 11 February 1939 setting a record attendance of 61,315 (on the way to Wembley). Meanwhile, Burnley developed extensive terraces on the Long Side and the Bee Hole End at Turf Moor and these survived up to recent times. This was discussed in Chapter 11 and the ground had a record attendance of 54,775 on 23 February 1924 during an F.A. Cup tie with Huddersfield. Both Bramall Lane and Hillsborough in Sheffield were developed into extensive grounds however it is a complex story and is discussed more fully later (see Ch. 18). Bramall Lane had a large bank at the Shoreham Street End called the Kop and shared the venue with a cricket club and had just three sides. Despite this there was a record attendance of 68,287 on 15 February 1936 during a Cup-tie against Leeds United. Their rivals Sheffield Wednesday moved from the city centre to Owlerton in 1899 and the Spion Kop was built at the Penistone Road End in 1913. The venue was renamed Hillsborough the next year after local boundary changes and the record attendance of 72,841 was on 17 February 1934 during a Cup-tie against Manchester City.

Old Trafford was opened in 1910 and is discussed shortly in relation to Archibald Leitch (see Ch. 16) however the club record attendance of 70,504 was on 27 December 1920 during a First Division game against Aston Villa - this shows the scale of the ground at an early date. The highest attendance at Old Trafford of 76,962 came on 25 March 1939 during an F.A. Cup semi-final between Wolves and Grimsby Town however this must be put in perspective as there are now regular crowds of 67,000 at the ground. There was an all time low at Old Trafford for a game between Stockport and Leicester in May 1921. Edgeley Park was closed due to crowd trouble and only 13 paying supporters came to the game, but there was an explanation. Manchester United had played Derby County in the morning and 2,000 fans stayed on to see the second game - two for the price of one!

Other grounds had large potential capacities, although they do not stand out immediately, and in particular those of the original League members. West Bromwich Albion for instance moved to the Hawthorns in 1900 and built a large venue with high banking on the Handsworth Side and at the Smethwick End. The record attendance of 64,815 was on 6 March 1937 during a Cup-tie against Arsenal. Their rivals Bolton developed Burnden Park in 1895 and had a large terrace at the Railway End and the Burnden Stand built in 1928. The record attendance of 69,912 was on 18 February 1933 during a Cup-tie against Manchester City. To the north Blackburn Rovers had early Cup success in the 1880s and moved to Ewood Park in 1890, winning the Cup in 1890 and 1891 and the championship in 1912. This success meant that after the First War they had crowds of 28,000 and high expectations but failed to make any impact on Division One in the 1920s-30s. They won the Cup in 1928 and this resulted in a record attendance of 61,783 on 2 March 1929 during a Cup-tie against Bolton.

A number of clubs achieved a record of over 50,000 including: Stoke - Victoria Ground (1937), Hull City - Boothferry Park (1949), Portsmouth - Fratton Park (1949), Coventry City - Highfield Road (1967) and Crystal Palace - Selhurst Park (1979). There were others who came close to 50,000 and this applied to both of the grounds in Nottingham. The City Ground was the home of Forest from 1898 but there were few developments until the East Stand was built behind the terrace and the Bridgford End enlarged in 1957. This increased the capacity and the record attendance of 49,946 (or 49,045) came on 28 October 1967 during a Division One game against Manchester United - the latter were the team of the moment and won the European Cup on 29 May 1968. Their rivals Notts County arrived at Meadow Lane in 1910 and erected a stand from Trent Bridge (dated c.1895) at the Meadow Lane End - it was floated across the River Trent! The Main Stand had a barrel roof and a Kop terrace was raised at the north end, whilst the County Road Stand (with wooden terracing at the rear) was built in 1925. There was a 'golden era' with the arrival of Tommy Lawton in 1953 and the record attendance of 47,310 came on 12 March 1955 during an F.A. Cup quarter final against York City. Their opponents reached the semi-final as a Division Three side similar to Millwall in 1937.

There were other clubs who developed a Kop End on a smaller scale, such as Leicester City who moved to Filbert Street in 1891 and raised a banked terrace at the south end named the Spion Kop. The venue was always restricted thus a two-tier stand was built at that end in 1927 and the record attendance of 47,298 came on 18 February 1928 during a Cup-tie against Tottenham. The Bantams or Bradford City were successful in their early days and Valley Parade was developed in 1908 when the terrace at the Manningham End was greatly extended and called Nunn's Kop, after a city dignitary. The record attendance of 39,146 came on 11 March 1911 during a Cup game against Burnley and City went on to win the Cup (in a replay) at Old Trafford. Blackpool had a Kop terrace behind the north goal at Bloomfield Road and the 'famous' Blackpool Tower and seafront illuminations could be seen just behind, however the remaining terraces were small and narrow - the ground was squeezed-in between Blackpool Central Railway and terraced housing. The record attendance of 38,098 was on 17 September 1955 during a Division One game against Wolves. Both teams were successful at the time and Blackpool with Stanley Matthews won the Cup in 1953 and came second in the League in 1956. Wolves were also a top team under manager Stan Cullis and with captain Billy Wright won the championship in 1954, 1958 and 1959, and the Cup in 1949 and 1960.

Cardiff Arms Park and Ninian Park were the top two grounds in Wales. The former has a significant place in soccer history but is best known for Welsh Rugby Union and was, until recently, the oldest surviving international football ground still in use. Cardiff Cricket Club played nearby in 1848 and rugby was first played at Cardiff Arms Park (named after a local coaching inn) in 1876. A grandstand was erected in 1885 and Wales played England there on 3 March 1896 losing 9-1. The Welsh team continued to play there until 1910 but then had a long break and only returned to the rebuilt ground in 1989. The Millennium Stadium was opened on the site in 1999 and hosted the Rugby Union World Cup Finals the same year and with the demise of Wembley staged the F.A. Cup Finals from 2001. Riverside Cricket Club first played football at Sophia Gardens in 1899 and briefly on a rough pitch at Roath. They used the names Riverside F.C. (1899-1902) and Riverside Albion (1902-08) and tried two games at Cardiff Arms Park and one at Harlequins R.F.C. to gauge the level of support for turning professional. After promising results they became Cardiff City and moved to Ninian Park in 1910.

Sloper Road, the new venue, was on a former rubbish tip and the original plan was to call it Sloper Park however there was a financial crisis associated with building the ground. Lord Ninian Crichton Stuart provided the funds and in recognition the club named the ground after him - he kicked off the first game v Aston Villa on 1 September 1910. The Canton End was roofed in 1920 and the large Grangetown End in 1928 whilst the Main Stand on Sloper Road was rebuilt after a fire in 1937. The large terrace on the east side of the ground was called the "Bob Bank" from the days when it cost just a shilling to stand there. It was home to the Welsh national team from 1910 but the honour was shared with Swansea and Wrexham on an increasing basis from 1976 - they went to Cardiff Arms Park in 1989. The club had early success and were runners-up in Division One in 1924 and Cup winners in 1927 whilst a later revival saw an average attendance of 38,000 in 1952-53. The club record of 57,800 was during a First Division game against Arsenal in 1953, and the rear of the Bob Bank was extended and a large roof erected above it in 1958. The record attendance of 61,566 was on 14 October 1961 during a Wales v England international.

The A-Z of Spion Kops began with Arsenal in 1904 however it all came to an end as early as 1950. This did not take place in London, Liverpool or Manchester but in the unlikely setting of Port Vale. The first question one must ask with the greatest respect is where is it? The club began life as Burslem Port Vale probably in 1879 although the club emblem states 1876. The name Port Vale is familiar in the district of Burslem with a street and wharf of that name, whilst Porthill Road is nearby and the club founders met in this area. They played at various grounds in Burslem but moved to the Recreation Ground, Hanley in 1913, then with serious debts sold it back to the local Corporation in 1943. They purchased the land for Vale Park in 1944 and there was an ambitious scheme to build a 70,000 capacity "Wembley of the North". These plans did not come to fruition due to lack of funds and were clearly over-ambitious for a club often in the lower divisions. A two tier Main Stand with gable was designed, but only the paddock and tunnel were built therefore the ground opened with uncovered terracing on all four sides. The first game was against Newport in Division Three (South) on 24 August 1950 and a good crowd of 30,042 attended. For many years temporary buildings stood where the Main Stand should have been, whilst the Railway Stand was built in 1954 and the Bycars End terraced and roofed in 1959. The record attendance of c.50,000 was on 20 February 1960 during a fifth round Cup-tie against Aston Villa. The Hamil Road End was covered in 1992 when the club purchased the roof from Chester's Main Stand at the defunct Sealand Road ground.

The days of the Spion Kop, however, were numbered and only two other grounds were developed after the Second War namely Boothferry Park - Hull (1946) and Roots Hall - Southend (1955). Both theses clubs had earlier associations with the sites. Hull City played at Anlaby Road from 1906, which was the home of Hull Cricket Club and called the Circle, but had an uncertain future there thus they purchased the land for Boothferry Park in 1930. The first game was against Lincoln City in Division Three (North) on 31 August 1946 and they started well. The record attendance of 55,019 came on 26 February 1949 during a Cup game against Manchester United, and they were champions of the division in 1948-49 with average gates of 37,000 in 1950. Both club and ground then declined and the North Stand was replaced with a supermarket in 1982. They went to the impressive K.C. Stadium (Kingston Communications) with a 25,000 capacity in 2003, and had returned to their roots as this was built on the 'old' Circle at Anlaby Road. Southend played at Roots Hall in 1906-16 and after the site was altered, returned, and built a new ground in 1955-60 (see Ch. 20). The 'new' Roots Hall was the last traditional venue built and the *period of terrace building* had ended, whilst the post-war experience of these clubs showed that such grounds were now out of date. A new era arrived with the opening of Glanford Park at Scunthorpe on 14 August 1988.

Mirrlees, Watson (Ref p. 365): They started in 1840 and traded as Tait and Watson from 1868-82 although William Tait died in 1870 - then had a number of partners including William Renny Watson (1838); they became Watson Laidlaw in 1883, Mirrlees Watson in 1885, and Mirrlees Watson and Yaryan in 1889. Capt. Cook visited the island of Kauai, Hawaii to witness the transit of Venus in 1769 and another expedition came there in 1874. The whaling industry had ceased at the latter date and grazing land for cattle was then turned over to sugar cane production. Mirrlees Watson established a world reputation for cane sugar machinery and W.R. Watson leased 7,000 acres at Makaweli in western Kauai on 24 October 1889. He had an agreement with Elizabeth McHutcheson Sinclair, daughters Jane Gay and Helen Robinson and grandsons Francis Gay and Aubrey Robinson (Gay & Robinson) and together they formed the Hawaiian Sugar Company on 30 October 1889. The plantation was at Kaumakani between Waimea and Hanapepe and was the largest cane employer in 1892 with 878 workers and its own post office. W.R. Watson an engineer and bank director was knighted on 19 August 1892 whilst Leitch worked for the company in 1890-95. After he left they constructed the third diesel engine in the world in 1897 (now in the Science Museum) and worked for the Admiralty in the First War. They also had a factory in England and became Mirrlees, Blackstone in 1969 (part of Hawker Siddeley).

CHAPTER 15

Tracing Glasgow

A number of books are available that consider the development of League football grounds and these give details of the builders. There is one name, however, that continually appears and that is Archibald Leitch who could rightly be considered "The Father of Football Grounds". Indeed his name should be up there in football history with the likes of Alcock and Morley. The great period of ground building began at the end of the 19th century whilst many clubs wanted new stands at the start of the 20th century. This type of construction was a new art and the builders had to borrow from other design areas. There was no accredited person in the field thus the search was on for an expert, a man who could provide a suitable construction at the right price. Thus in modern parlance the word went out and people asked, "who you going to call," the answer came back "the ground busters!" There was only one man for the job and an ever-growing list of clubs called upon the services of Archibald Leitch. He was ultimately responsible for building two major grounds in Glasgow and 25% in England, with many of these being those of premier clubs.

Archibald Leitch appears in numerous club histories however less is known about the man himself. This omission is corrected in the following three chapters, which consider his life history and antecedents and provide a detailed insight into the background behind his work. These revelations and the following discussion of his life may reveal the answers to some searching questions: Was he a man destined for such quiet fame? Did he just apply his engineering skills to the problem put before him? Was he visionary in terms of football ground design? The history of Leitch can be compared to a broader history and like the Industrial Revolution he came from a rural background. His ancestors were rooted in the Argyll Peninsula to the west of Glasgow, an 80-mile extension of the Scottish Highlands between the Sound of Jura in the west and Loch Fyne and Kilbrennan Sound in the east. This is on average ten miles wide throughout its length. The islands of Jura and Islay are to the west and Bute and Arran to the east whilst the famous Mull of Kintyre is at the southern tip. The Leitch family lived in the northern districts of Glassary and Knapdale, a rugged land of Highland farming communities and sea lochs that seemed an unlikely source of industrial innovation. The nature of the region is best understood from a contemporary document namely "The Topographical and Historical Gazetteer of Scotland" published in 1848. This describes the area in the following terms:

Glassary is in the form of a rectangle and rises gently from both sides to the middle. It is occupied by a considerable extent of moorland covered with heath. On the banks of the River Ad the soil is a deep rich loam whilst on the shore of Loch Fyne there is black loam on limestone rock. The remains of three watchtowers are on the banks of Loch Fyne and the Crinan Canal marks the southern boundary. The church in Kilmichael Glassary was built in 1827 and the one in Lochgilphead in 1828, and there are three preaching stations at Cumlodden, Loch-Gain on Loch Fyne and at Ford on Loch Awe. The parish has two parochial schools and several private schools. **Lochgilphead** village or township was formed into a separate parish and is five miles in length and three miles in breadth, being a thriving village. It has a Baptist Chapel established 1818 and a Congregational Union Mission Station. There are daily links with Glasgow and Inverary by steamboat; these travel on Loch Fyne and also along the Crinan Canal. The parish had a population of 2,726 in 1836 with the people centred in the two villages of Lochgilphead (1,300) and Ardrishaig (300).

North Knapdale forms the coastline of the Sound of Jura and is covered by rugged mountains to the north and east. Loch Swen is at the parish centre and there are also a few small lakes. The population was 2,583 in 1831 however only 180 people lived in the two villages of Tayvallich and Ballenach (total 360). There are two parish churches at Tayvallich and Kilmichael Inverlussa that face one another across Loch Swen. **South Knapdale** extends 16 miles southward to Loch Tarbert and has two parish churches at Inverneil and Achoish. The soil is of a mossy nature and overlays a stratum of sand whilst the low ground is very loamy; there is very little arable land and most is turned over to sheep or cattle pasture. The population was 2,137 in 1831.

Recent gazetteers describe the scene further and state that Lochgilphead has a crescent of stone built houses and the nearby township of Ardrishaig has sailing boats moored in its harbour. The latter is at the southern end of the 9-mile long Crinan Canal, started by John Rennie the famous architect and builder in 1794, which saved ships the 120-mile journey around Kintyre. The town of Tayvallich is in the west on a natural harbour and is near to Carsaig Bay. The whole scene invites an image of a lone piper on a hillside his dulcet tones ringing out as the mist drifts slowly across Loch Fyne.... sorry back to the story! A dispersed rural population lived in Argyll however a large number of schools and churches were witness to a tradition of education and religious teaching in the area. There were important links to the sea and signs of pre-industrial development viz. Crinan Canal. Meanwhile, Scotland was dominated for centuries by the clan system and the Argyll region was no exception having many such allegiances regarding local families. Leitch was prominent in Glassary in the 18th century and names such as Archibald and Dugald abound. There were also marriages to the MacLachlan clan who wore a brown and yellow tartan and were present in Argyll from the 11th century and took part in the Crusades - they fought at Culloden as aides to "Bonnie" Prince Charlie.

The proliferation of Leitch in Glassary made it hard to pinpoint the family however there was a John Leitch of Monedrain born Glassary in c.1764 whose spouse was 'Mary' MacLachlan. The hamlet was a mile north of Lochgilphead and situated in the hills. The records show that John Leitch married Margaret MacLachlan at Glassary on 15 January 1789 and had four children there viz. Colin (1790), Dugald (27 September 1792), Flora (1795) and Isabell (1796). Meanwhile, Archibald MacLachlan married Mary MacArthur at Glassary on 16 January 1785 and had nine children including Anne who was baptized at Glassary on 29 December 1801. Despite some conjecture we are sure that Dugald Leitch and Anne MacLachlan were grandparents of our man and that they married at Knapdale (North or South) on 11 December 1819. Dugald had various occupations on later documents viz. labourer (1855), shepherd (1868) and fisherman (1907) and according to the births of his children was itinerant. He had sons John (1822) and Colin (1828) at Inverneil in South Knapdale, Archibald (8 March 1830) *infant* at Glassary and another Archibald (15 June 1831) at Lochgilphead but un-registered. He moved to the larger town of Dunoon on the Firth of Clyde and had two last children Dugald (1833) and Flora (1835).

The son Colin Leitch lived at 1 Forbes Place, Wemyss Bay, Inverkip just across the water from Dunoon in 1881 with his wife Mary who was born Lochgilphead. Meanwhile, Robert Robertson son of Archibald a merchant seaman was born at Lerwick in 1838 and followed his father into that trade. He married Flora Leitch a domestic servant at 36 Whitener Street, High Church, Glasgow, after banns on 27 November 1868. Both were living at 101 King Street, Tradeston and James Findlay of Camlachie Free Church was minister and Oliver Robertson and Mary Dickson witnesses. Her parents Dugald and Ann were both deceased by this time and Flora may have followed her brother to the city (see below). The couple had children Agnes McLachlan (1869) and Archibald (1872) at Tradeston and lived at 3 Cavendish Place, Govan in 1881 with lodger John Farquhar whilst Flora Robertson died at Gorbals, Glasgow in 1890. Indeed this was a time of industrial upheaval throughout the Kingdom and these movements to the town are well documented and the Leitch family did likewise.

Archibald Leitch was born at Lochgilphead on 15 June 1831 and was a blacksmith who lived at 37 Stevenston Street, Calton in Glasgow by 1855. Robert Kent a gardener and carter married Margaret McGregor at Bothwell eight miles south east of Glasgow on 17 April 1830 and had a daughter Agnes (Flint) born there on 3 December 1833. Archibald Leitch blacksmith married Agnes Kent domestic servant at Bothwell on 31 December 1855. Both gave an address 25 Canning Street, Calton but Archibald usually lived at 37 Stevenston Street and Agnes at Bothwell. The couple had six children who were all born east of Glasgow city centre: Dugald (1857) Calton, Robert Kent (1860), Margaret McGregor (1862) and Archibald (1865) High Church, Agnes McLachlan (1868) Bridgeton and Flora (1870) High Church. The family may have moved around from one tenement to another but lived at 1 Comley Park Street off Gallowgate in 1865. Indeed this was not far from the site of Celtic Park. This area is now largely rebuilt and is north of Bridgeton with its 'bandstand' clock tower and buildings dated 1900. Comley Park Street remains although all the buildings are modern whilst a few older houses are on the main road.

Archibald Leitch, the fourth child, was born at 1 Comley Park Street at 6.30 p.m. on 27 April 1865 and was destined for great things becoming the most influential person in football ground design before the Second War. He grew up in the area of Comley Park Street and Gallowgate and was exposed to his father's work as a blacksmith, which gave him some early knowledge of metal work and design. He attended Hutcheson's Grammar School at the junction of Crown Street and Rutherglen Road south of the Clyde in 1876. The architect David Hamilton designed the school in 1841 and the entrance on Crown Street had a Classical tower with dome. The building was demolished to make way for the Hutcheson E scheme (in 1969) although some of the latter is now also gone. His brother Robert Kent Leitch an apprentice calico engraver of 11 Comley Park Street married Jane Kincaid steam loom weaver at her home 90 Barrowfield Street, Camlachie on 31 October 1879 (right next to the site of Celtic Park). This

1861–1965
Extract of an entry in a REGISTER of BIRTHS
Registration of Births, Deaths and Marriages (Scotland) Act 1965

243117

No.	1 Name and surname	2 When and where born	3 Sex	4 Name, surname, and rank or profession of father, Name, and maiden surname of mother, Date and place of marriage	5 Signature and qualification of informant, and residence, if out of the house in which the birth occurred	6 When and where registered and signature of registrar
871	Archibald Leitch	1865. April Twentyseventh 6h. 30m. P.M. Comley Park St: Glasgow	M	Archibald Leitch Blacksmith, Journeyman; Agnes Leitch M.S. Kent; 1855. Dec: 31st Bothwell	Archibald Leitch Father Present	1865. May 12th at Glasgow; Peter Ferguson Asst: Registrar

Archibald Leitch. His birth certificate dated 27 April 1865.

was after banns in the Free Church and Archibald Leitch and John Kincaid (boiler maker), the fathers, were witnesses. His brother Dugald Leitch a mercantile clerk married Harriet Lawrence daughter of John a spirit merchant at 43 Finnieston Street, Anderston after banns on 26 November 1880 the witnesses Margaret Leitch and Robert Lawrence.

Indeed Archibald journeyman blacksmith then left Comley Park Street and moved the short distance to 631 Gallowgate, Glasgow where he lived with wife Agnes, children Archibald (15), Agnes and Flora in 1881. Dugald and Harriet lived at 83 Elderslie Street, Anderston west of Glasgow; Robert Kent and Jane had a son Archibald at Dennistoun in 1880 and lived at 40 Bellfield Street across the railway from Comley Park Street; and Margaret Leitch (18) lived with George Halliday and family at 21 Queen's Square, Govan. The son Archibald finished his schooling at Hutcheson's at this time and studied science at the Andersonian College for a year. He took his first steps in his chosen profession and joined Duncan Stewart & Co., London Road Iron Works, 47 Summer Street, Glasgow, in 1882, a short distance from Gallowgate and next to Bridgeton station. The iron works and all other buildings have gone and the only remnants are a few cobbles in Olympia Street (the Mile End Quarter) - Celtic Park is in the distance. The proprietor Duncan Stewart gave him this early opportunity and they were described as engineers, millwrights and boilermakers in 1887. Leitch served his time there from 1882-87 and gained experience in the pattern shop, fitting shop and drawing office of the engineering works, and in his last six months received further training as a draughtsman. He then had a complete change of course and spent the next three years at sea as an engineer and thus obtained his Board of Trade certificate. He returned home in 1890 and was re-engaged by Duncan Stewart & Co. and with new experience was made superintendent draughtsman of their marine department but remained there just eight months.

James Black a dairyman married Jane Roberts at Blythswood, Glasgow on 28 May 1858 and then had four children baptized at Torpichen: John (1859), Hendry (1861), Jessie Hardie (17 May 1866) and James (1868). Indeed the daughter Jessie was born at Blackridge, Linlithgow-shire and baptized in Torpichen. Archibald Leitch engineer's draughtsman of 631 Gallowgate married Jessie Hardie Black of 17 Wesleyan Street at Albert Hall, Bridgeton on 20 June 1890. The denomination was the Free Church - a branch of the Presbyterian Church of Scotland formed in 1843. Hugh Mair was the minister and William Thomson and Jessie McLean the witnesses. Archibald then left Duncan Stewart and entered the employ of Messrs. Mirrlees, Watson & Co. Ltd. of Glasgow in late 1890, and was placed in charge of the ordering department of their drawing office. Their Scotland Street Ironworks was at 45 Scotland Street, Tradeston and they were engineers, iron and brass founders, boilermakers and manufacturers of all kinds of machinery and apparatus for making and refining sugar in 1887-88. He was dedicated to his profession and lectured classes on machine design at the Glasgow School Board, Christian Institute and Glasgow Athenaeum in St. George's Place from 1890 (see Mirrlees, Watson p. 362).

Archibald and Jessie then moved into a four-storey tenement that ran the length of McLellan Street and just a few streets east of the 'first' Ibrox Park opened in 1887. This was a most austere building and only

97 Buchanan Street.
Leitch had his first office here in 1896.

a short distance from Scotland Street although a motorway now divides the latter in two. Indeed the area is now greatly changed although a few old buildings still exist including Scotland Street Public School. The architect Charles Rennie Mackintosh designed the school in 1903-06 and also the Willow Tea Rooms (see below). The school had 'separate' entrances, playgrounds and staircases as required at the time and was for 1,250 pupils and served the families of the local shipyards and engineering works. The south side of Scotland Street had a rope and sail works, school, subway power station, iron works, saw mill and engineering works in 1907-08 whilst many tenements occupied roads on the north side. The school is now a museum and next-door is the façade of the massive Howden's Engineering Works built in c.1910 where large turbines were built. There is a large red brick works with entrances and a decorated front at no. 39 but in general little remains. Their tenement was on the north side of McLellan Street and faced Bellahouston and Clutha Iron Works, whilst the Glasgow and Paisley Joint-Railway was adjacent and Kinning Park Station nearby (map 1907-08).

Archibald Leitch a blacksmith and wife Agnes remained at 631 Gallowgate in 1891 with daughters Margaret (factory worker), Agnes (dressmaker) and Flora (shopkeeper), and niece Agnes Robertson a visitor and factory worker - Celtic Park was opened to the south in 1892. The family showed much enterprise and daughter Agnes advertised her services as a dressmaker in local directories, whilst son Dugald remained at Anderston and Robert Kent nearby at Dennistoun. The family were well spread out and Archibald Leitch a draughtsman and his wife Jessie lived at 20 McLellan Street, Plantation, Glasgow, in 1891 with eleven other families in one tenement block. Archibald Kent, their son, was born there on 17 April 1891 the father an engineer's draughtsman (journeyman). James Barrie (30) a writer of 127 Sword Street son of William a mineral borer married Agnes McLachlan Leitch of 631 Gallowgate at the Bath Hotel, Bath Street, Blythswood in Glasgow on 30 March 1893. Her father was a foreman blacksmith and the witnesses John Coventry and sister Flora Leitch (not James M. Barrie 1860-1937).

Archibald continued to work as a mechanical draughtsman for Mirrlees, Watson & Co. Ltd. and moved a short distance south thus his daughter Jeanie Black Leitch was born at 8 South Dean Place, Mount Florida on 4 February 1894 - she died as an infant. The father had considerable experience that resulted in greater ambition and left the company after six years in late 1895, then started his own business as consulting engineer. His daughter Jane Hilda Roberts Leitch (Jeanie) was born at 12 Clincart Road, Mount Florida on 17 December 1895 and indeed the father was then a "consulting engineer". The house was at the north end of the road where it joined with Cathcart Road and a short distance southeast of the second Hampden Park. It was a terrace property of light brown stone but in a better neighbourhood and remains today, although no. 12 is hard to find and is above some shops.

The structure of his old company had changed at this time and Mirrlees, Watson and Yaryan Co. Ltd. were at Scotland Street in 1896. Archibald, meanwhile, moved into new offices and his address was 97 Buchanan Street in the centre of Glasgow that year. This was an upmarket street of shops and offices and still provides a glimpse of an opulent past, the main examples being the Clydesdale Bank (1891) of multi-coloured sandstone and the impressive Argyll Arcade (see p. 372). St. Enoch's underground station was on St. Enoch's Square at the south end of Buchanan Street and was opened in 1896. There was, however, an older history and St. Mungo's Cathedral to the east dates from the 13th century. 97 Buchanan Street remains today and the ground floor entrance is at the centre of two shops. There are three upper stories of grey stone and the windows have Classical pediments. Behind were his offices however they do not remain today and inside is a re-creation of the Willow Tea Rooms, Ingram Street. Catherine (Kate) Cranston (1849-1934) married John Cochrane of Grahamston Engineering Works and gave Charles Rennie Mackintosh his first commission and worked with him 20 years. He provided wall murals for her tearooms at 91-93 Buchanan Street and worked with Margaret Macdonald whom he married in 1900. He designed the White Dining Room or Ladies Luncheon Room (in silver) at Ingram Street that year and added the Blue-Chinese Room or Gents Tea Room in 1911. The original was dismantled in the 1970s but recreated at 97 Buchanan Street and opened by the Lord Provost on 6 August 1997.

Archibald set to work with determination and secured several general engineering contracts and was appointed the consulting engineer for Lanark-shire County Council (Middle Ward). His marine experience secured him membership of the Institute of Engineers and Shipbuilders (Scotland) but with an eye to the future he applied for associate membership of the Institute of Mechanical Engineers, 19 Victoria Street, Westminster, on 13 February 1897. This was an exclusive 'club' first established in 1847 and Sir W. Renny Watson proposed him whilst Duncan Stewart was his second (both former employers). The application was a success and he was granted associate membership after just 18 months in business on 25 March 1897. The application gave details of his early experience and was a source for some of the history above. He moved his offices a few hundred yards south of Buchanan Street to 40 St. Enoch's Square in 1897 and established a base from where he produced his greatest work i.e. in football ground design. There was considerable scope in Glasgow as the town had three major clubs namely Celtic, Rangers and Queen's Park. 40 St. Enoch's Square was on the west side and was a five-storey building with grand Classical façade. This remains today whilst no. 14 is the Institution of Electrical Engineers (est. 1871). The oldest buildings are on the south side although the east was demolished and is now the St. Enoch Shopping Centre.

Celtic F.C. who formed in 1887 had an initial ground east of Glasgow from 1888-92. They moved 200 yards to Celtic Park or Parkhead and this was opened on 20 August 1892 and the first game was played against Renton. A stadium such as this had not been seen before and one reporter called the ground "Paradise" and in fact only Goodison Park could match it at this date. Celtic Park hosted its first international in front of 45,017 on 7 April 1894 and they witnessed the scale of the venue. The club purchased the freehold in 1897 and a North Stand, pavilion, oval track and substantial banking was present in 1898. Archibald Leitch has been credited with working on Celtic Park but was not responsible for the original design as he was not in business until 1895 (the ground was clearly well developed by 1894). It then hosted five internationals between Scotland and England from 1894 to 1904 and the attendance was never below 40,000 whilst the highest was 63,000 in 1900. Rangers, their great rivals, were formed in 1872 and played in the Ibrox area of Glasgow from 1887. The club's early ground soon lagged behind Celtic Park and had one international against England with a 20,000 crowd in 1892. There was much competition thus the club moved to the "new" and present Ibrox Park with a capacity of 40,000 on 30 December 1899. This was of a similar design and had a South Stand, corner pavilion, oval track and earth banking. Leitch was more involved on this occasion but the layout was possibly suggested by Celtic Park as ground design was in its infancy.

Archibald Leitch, however, was soon involved in a controversy that might have ended his career. There was much competition to stage major matches thus Rangers developed the West Terrace of Ibrox in 1900. Leitch's company provided the design and a terracing of wooden planks on an iron framework was raised at the rear. The authorities passed this structure as safe however others were less sure of the design. Bolton and Preston built stands with wooden extensions at the rear at a later date however the problem at Ibrox was the sheer scale. Meanwhile, Jessie Hardie Leitch was born at 1110 Cathcart Road, Mount Florida on 29 March 1901 and the birth registered by Henry Hunter the registrar on 19 April. This 'tenement' house was near the junction of Cathcart Road and Bolton Drive whilst Somerville Road was opposite and led to the third Hampden Park (being built at the time). The property was four-storey and of light brown sandstone with bay window and pediments and remains today. The numbers south from Bolton Drive are 1102, 1106, 1108, 1112, 1118 and 1126 although the latter three properties are of red sandstone. Archibald Leitch 'civil engineer' (employer) lived at 1011 Cathcart Road in 1901 with wife Jessie, children Archibald, Jeanie and Jessie, Mary Skinner (14) servant from New York and Agnes Barr (61) a sick nurse. The property had five rooms with one window or more and Henry Hunter the registrar and Leónce Darligues a French subject were neighbours. The numbers may have been transposed but as the registrar lived there it seems unlikely, thus Archibald had moved across the road - still near Hampden Park.

His work at Ibrox made him a considerable amount of money and it seems likely he used some of this for his parents and the latter left the city. Archibald Leitch a retired blacksmith lived with wife Agnes, daughter Margaret their housekeeper, and grandson Hendry at 30 Wyndham Road, Rothesay on the Island of Bute in 1901. This was a newly developed area by the coast and their neighbours included

Robert F. Robertson the Superintendent of Glasgow Fire Brigade and other retired people. Dugald Leitch, mercantile clerk, lived at 3 Alexandria Terrace, Govan with wife Harriet and his large family including sons Archibald, John and Dugald, whilst Robert Kent Leitch was at Partick in 1901 and died that same year. Ibrox Park was then tested when a vast crowd attended a Scotland v England game on 5 April 1902. Some sources give the attendance at 68,114 however the I.F.F.H.S. gives a figure of 80,500 but whatever the truth it was a large crowd. The wooden terrace was saturated with heavy rain the night before and during the game there was a partial collapse and a disaster ensued with several deaths and many injuries. The game was abandoned and declared void whilst an enquiry found it hard to apportion blame - the possible reasons being design, workmanship or 'faulty' stamp of approval.

Despite this controversy Leitch emerged from the enquiry with his reputation intact and went on to greater things. Indeed he had several projects in hand at this time including Hampden Park, various factory buildings and 'new' work in England. The Victorian period had many large engineering projects and schemes and there was much competition in these developments. Glasgow led the way in terms of football grounds at the turn of the century and news of this soon reached south of the border. Leitch's company were a good prospect and his designs had innovative detail but most significantly had a competitive price. Bramall Lane, Sheffield presented a considerable challenge since a cricket pitch occupied the southern side and there was one long side against the road. The club decided they wanted to replace the existing John Street Stand even though it was erected in 1895 and the decision was hastened after a fire damaged the stand in November 1900. The Sheffield club were aware of his work at Ibrox plus his current work at Hampden, and such credentials persuaded them to speak to him. They invited him to provide a design for a new stand and his plans were promptly accepted and the building work was completed in 1902. His design was quite standard for the time with raised seating behind a terrace and a plain roof, however at the centre of the roof was a mock-Tudor gable (this became his hallmark). He also installed electric lighting and an indoor running track under the seating but despite this he did not run before he could walk. This was an early attempt at stand design and lacked the more matured features of his later work.

Archibald Leitch advertised in commercial directories during this period and was initially a consulting engineer but in later adverts was accredited as inspecting engineer and factory architect. His company did the latter work for many years and at first it was a staple source of income - in particular they designed buildings for Scottish tube works. These companies constructed the metal tubes used in boilers and for other purposes but with the demise of the steam engine the term was less familiar. Archibald Leitch consulting engineer of 40 St. Enoch's Square age 37 applied to be a full member of the Institute of Mechanical Engineers on 15 March 1902 and stated: "In business for myself as consulting engineer for 6½ years during which time I have designed and have erected and superintended important large works involving all mechanical and structural details and including the following - together with smaller works too numerous to mention." The business had clearly grown since 1897 and in his application he quoted two major football works as a reference viz. new grounds for the Rangers F.C. Ltd. at a cost of £22,000 and new (works) for the Sheffield United Cricket and F.C. Ltd. at a cost of £12,000. His work in Sheffield was his first commission in England but as this involved just one stand he clearly made a major contribution towards Ibrox Park.

His premier work, however, was for Alexander Hope Jun. & Co. and the cost of their new factory was £25,000, more than he had charged for Ibrox. They were manufacturing chemists who were based at Coatbridge Street, Port Dundas near Glasgow centre in 1896. The new premises were recorded in a directory of 1905-06 and stated: "Alexander Hope Jun. & Co, *Anchor Chemical Works*, 1005 Garngad Road, Provanmill" - a new 'out of town' location in northeast Glasgow. His second major factory work was for the Stirling Boiler Co. Ltd. at a cost of £20,000. The company were water tube boiler manufacturers at 45 Hope Street, Glasgow in 1911. Further to these Leitch also constructed new or part works as follows: Union Tube Works, Coatbridge (£12,000), Clydesdale Tube Works, Glasgow (£8,000) and Caledonian Tube Works, Coatbridge (£1,000). He then added: "I also acted as consulting mechanical engineer for Lanark-shire C.C., Renfrew-shire C.C., Ayr County Hospital, Kroonstad Corp. and engineer for several principalities in India. I employ about 30 hands in my office." James Marshall proposed him, and his application was lodged at the Institute, Storey's Gate in St. James's Park. The latter was an impressive new building and they remain there today but it is now 1 Birdcage Walk (see Willis Ch. 1). These were the credentials of a successful business and he was admitted a full member on 17 June 1902 and became M.I. Mech. Eng.

He then continued with his work in Glasgow and in particular at Hampden Park, which was only a few hundred yards from his accommodation at 1011 Cathcart Road. Queen's Park F.C. were formed in 1867 and had an important role in early soccer and took part in the first F.A. Cup in 1872, and were the core of the first Scottish national side as well as finalists in 1884 and 1885. They started at Queen's Park Recreation Ground and moved to an enclosed ground the 'first' Hampden Park in 1873. This was named after Hampden Terrace near to Cathcart and Clincart Roads. They stayed there some years but had to move when the railway from Glasgow Central was extended between Crosshill and Mount Florida and had a temporary home at Titwood Park (Clydesdale C.C.). Queen's Park hosted all international games against England at this time and these were played at the West of Scotland Cricket Ground in 1872, 1874 and 1876 and at the 1st Hampden Park in 1878, 1880 and 1882. The I.F.F.H.S. states that Scotland beat England 1-0 at Cathkin Park in the first British championships on 15 March 1884. The venue was just east of the club's first ground between Myrtle Park and Prospecthill Road. The site was developed with a brick pavilion, banking, two open stands and a cinder track and was ready as the 2nd Hampden Park in October 1884. It was used for internationals in 1886, 1888 and 1890 and the attendance at the latter date was 26,379.

The club, however, had some formidable rivals in the game of Glasgow one-upmanship and lost the internationals to Rangers in 1892 and Celtic from 1894. Despite this competition they decided to develop a substantial ground so they could compete and thus stage international games. For an amateur club the cost was prohibitive but they decided to proceed and chose a site just to the south across Prospecthill Road and next to Somerville Drive. The club purchased 12.5 acres of land and under the guidance of Leitch the 3rd Hampden Park was built there from 1900-03. He was mainly concerned with mechanical aspects of stand design but at Hampden was the architect of a colossal ground. There was oval banking around a track and pitch, and a central pavilion on the south side flanked by two stands each seating 4,000 spectators, with a capacity of about 65,000. It was similar to that built at Crystal Palace in 1895 and was apparently the Scottish version and in fact Glasgow had three of the largest grounds in the world. Celtic Park was again used in 1904 thus the terracing at Hampden was increased in size and Scotland beat England 2-1 at the new ground in front of 102,741 on 7 April 1906.

The investment had paid off and Hampden was then used in preference to Celtic Park and Ibrox Park. Indeed Scotland were undefeated against England at Hampden before the First War: 4 April 1908 1-1 (121,452), 2 April 1910 2-0 (106,205), 23 March 1912 1-1 (127,307) and 4 Apr 1914 3-1 (105,000). The pavilion at Hampden was destroyed by a fire and was replaced in 1914 whilst Queen's Park purchased extra land at the west end in 1923. They built a pitch there with grass-banked terraces on three sides and a pavilion with limited cover on the fourth. This second pitch and the pavilion stating Q.P.F.C. remains today but has only been used for reserve team games and the club still play in the national stadium. The terracing was increased in size in 1927 and 25,000 places added, thus Hampden Park was a vast uncovered amphitheatre towering over nearby houses in the 1920s-30s. The club vacated the second Hampden Park in 1903 and it became home to Third Lanark and was renamed New Cathkin Park. They played there until they folded-up in 1967 and the grass outline of the ground can still be seen today.

Leitch, meanwhile, was increasingly attracted to contracts south of the border. Middlesbrough F.C. formed in 1876 and played next to the town's cricket ground on Linthorpe Road by 1880. This was an enclosed pitch with a grandstand on the north side and backed onto the cricket ground. Some members formed a rival team 'Ironopolis' south of Linthorpe Road in 1889 and Boro who were professional in 1889-92 returned to amateur status when 'Ironopolis' entered the League. The latter disbanded in 1894 and Boro won the Amateur Cup in 1895 and 1898 but there was a football vacuum in the town, and they became professional again and were also elected to the League in 1899. They remained at Linthorpe Road however the ground had a capacity of 17,000 and they wanted to move to a new site by 1901. They obtained land that partially covered the site of the Paradise Ground (of defunct Ironopolis). There seemed to be no rush since things were going well and the club were promoted to Division One in September 1902 and top-flight football came to Linthorpe Road.

The club, however, were given notice to quit in December 1902 and gave Leitch his second commission in England. This time a complete ground was required and there was no time to waste as the venue had to be ready for September 1903. This was a landmark in Leitch's career as he produced a substantial ground at a reasonable price - these being significant criteria for cash-strapped clubs. Indeed he repeated the plan for Ayresome Park at many other grounds viz. a two-tier Main Stand with continuous terracing on three sides. There were 2,000 seats under a barrel roof with semi-circular gable at the centre, and the old Linthorpe Road stand was erected on the south side to give a capacity of 33,000. The first game completed the Scots connection and was a friendly v Celtic on 1 September 1903. The ground, however, was barely ready and the official opening was during a First Division game against Sunderland on 12 September 1903. There were few later developments at Ayresome Park however a two-tier South Stand for 9,000 spectators was built in 1936-37 (the plans may have come from Leitch's company). The ground was then largely unchanged with the barrel-roof stand although some terracing was closed or converted to seating. The final game was a crucial one against Luton Town on 30 April 1995. The club had to win to take the First Division title and did this with a 2-1 score line in front of a capacity 24,000 crowd. Leitch's ground was finally demolished later that year.

This was only the beginning for Archibald Leitch and it was in London that his career really took off. He had made a lot of money from his work at Ibrox, Hampden and the two grounds in England and moved to a new home near Kinning Park in 1903. He lived at "The Tannoch", 27 Maxwell Drive, Pollockshields, in 1903-08 just across the railway track from McLellan Street. The area, however, was completely different with large detached villas such as West Lodge at no. 56. He lived at the Tannoch with wife Jessie and children Archibald, Jeanie and Jessie - the property no doubt a substantial residence. His last child Agnes MacGregor Leitch (known as Nancy) was born at Kinning Park in 1904. He still had offices at 40 St. Enoch's Square and other businesses in the building were: American Line U.S. Mail Steamers, Central Drawing Office Co., Baptist Industrial Mission and Clyde Salvage Co. Ltd. The next developments came in 1905.

The story of Chelsea and Fulham has already been discussed in Chapters 12-13 thus here the owners are considered in more detail. Joseph Mears was born in Chelsea in 1842 and married Ann, from Basingstoke, at Chelsea in December 1863 then had sons Joseph Theophilus (September 1871) and Henry Augustus (September 1873). Joseph Mears a builder resided at 78 Queen Street, Hammersmith in 1881 with his wife Ann and children Charlotte, Beatrice, Joseph (9), Augustus (7) and Amelia. He was a builder at 76 Queen Street in 1885-86 but more significantly at Wyfold Road and Crab Tree Wharf, Crab Tree Lane in Fulham in 1894-95. His company Mears & Co. were involved in building the original Craven Cottage in 1894-96 and both premises were near the ground. There are industrial buildings at Wyfold Road today whilst the remnants of Crab Tree Wharf and associated buildings are also present. The company had both premises in 1906 but their private address was then 6 Claxton Grove, Hammersmith. This was an ordinary terraced house, which still remains, and the profits from Craven Cottage must have gone into the business.

Stamford Bridge was opened as home to the London Athletics Club on 28 April 1877. Fred Parker, one of the club's promoters, became acquainted with Joe and Gus Mears and made plans for a football ground by 1896 - no doubt prompted by Fulham. The Mears brothers were under thirty but were true entrepreneurs and, with this in mind, purchased the freehold of Stamford Bridge in 1904. The three then formed a partnership and were the driving force behind the development of the ground. Fulham were doing well in Southern League Division One in 1904-05 however their basic ground struggled to contain the large crowds. During the season the London C.C. tried to close the Main Stand also known as the "Rabbit Hutch" for safety reasons. This led to a court case in January 1905 although the matter was not reported in the local paper (*West London Press*) and may have been repressed. Fulham called a number of experts and these included Archibald Leitch and the case highlighted the need for a new ground. Fred Parker and the Mears brothers were then in discussion regarding Stamford Bridge and tried to attract Fulham F.C. to the ground however Henry Norris a director blocked the move. Their plans were almost abandoned and the site sold to the railway but after discussions between Parker and Gus Mears they went ahead.

Fred Parker and the brothers travelled to Glasgow to see the grounds built in that city and were suitably impressed and soon employed Archibald Leitch to build Stamford Bridge - indeed they wanted a ground to rival Crystal Palace. Henry Norris had similar aspirations and approached him to rebuild Craven Cottage at the same time (see below). Archibald Leitch had two large contracts in the capital and set up temporary offices at 33 Victoria Street, Westminster from 1905-07. This was near the old office of the Institute of Mechanical Engineers at no. 19 and this may have influenced his choice of location. Leitch was the designer and consulting engineer but required local builders and thus formed an association with Humphreys in 1905 that lasted for many years. Humphreys' Iron Building Works were at the junction of Buckingham Palace Road and Ebury Bridge in 1891 and backed onto Grosvenor Canal with its many wharves and barges - indeed Victoria Station was smaller than today as on a map dated 1894-95. They were at 199-205 Buckingham Palace Road in 1902 and had offices at 187-193 Knightsbridge by 1905, and Leitch must have gone there to discuss Stamford Bridge and Craven Cottage.

Stamford Bridge was to be a major venue staging football, athletics and cycling and the ground had a similar design to that seen in Glasgow. There was a track around the pitch and large banked terracing on three sides with a Main Stand on the east side. Mears & Co. built the terraces using excavations from the Kingsway tunnel and the Piccadilly line and this came along the Thames by barge to Crab Tree Wharf. Humphreys provided the materials and labour for the Main Stand, which was large scale but plain in design with raised seating for 5,000 spectators behind a terrace. The main features of the stand were a central gable or pediment and columns with criss-cross ironwork - both became Leitch hallmarks. The Mears brothers had failed to attract Fulham and, as stated, formed a new club that they called Chelsea F.C. Their debut in Division Two, however, was played at Stockport on 2 September 1905 and they lost the game 1-0.

The match report in the *West London Press* on 8 September 1905 revealed an interesting contrast to the Stamford Bridge ground: "At Stockport they were unluckily beaten by the only goal scored in a game, which for the most part was contested on one half of the pitch, and that not Chelsea's.... Stockport's ground is notoriously little better than a field on which cabbages must have grown: the disturbance of turf their growth occasioned has been allowed to remain unmolested from the attention of the roller and the machine. Its rocky surface has been the downfall of many a crack team and Chelsea is its latest victim." The reporter was no doubt biased in his statements and blamed the pitch for the only goal. William Foulkes, captain and goalkeeper, stopped a spot kick but fell on the uneven pitch and saw the ball forced into the net in the ensuing scramble. The paper stated: "I have seen it recorded that Foulkes is unreliable when dealing with ground shots," but added that the comment came from, ".... the pen of critical Mr. H.G. Norris." He was of course the director of Fulham and only too happy to discredit Chelsea who were a threat to his ambitions. N.B. Edgeley Park, Stockport was opened in 1902.

Chelsea kicked off at Stamford Bridge two days later on 4 September 1905 with a friendly against Liverpool and won 4-0 (crowd 6-7,000). The mood of the time can best be gauged from contemporary news reports and the new ground was praised in the *West London Press* on 8 September 1905. This was a total contrast with the description of Stockport and stated: "In providing London football lovers with such a magnificent arena, Mr. Mears deserves some other recognition than thanks from followers of the pastime. By an outlay

The Pavilion, Fulham. The idea of a corner pavilion came from Scotland.

The Main Stand, Fulham. No expense was spared on the ornate brickwork.

of almost colossal magnitude he has provided London with what it has been lacking for too long - a football arena worthy of the greatest city in the world. Further than this he has assisted the Chelsea F.C. in a most generous manner to get going in first class style at the very start of their career. To have an enclosure capable of giving a good sight view of a football match to 130,000 spectators (and this is what is promised for the English v Scottish League match on March 24th next) is something that cannot be equalled in any other football centre. London has had to wait a few seasons for its much-wanted great football arena but it is here at last. May the enterprise flourish in every possible way not only to the satisfaction of the promoters of the undertaking but for the healthy amusement of tens of thousands of London's toiling masses."

He was clearly carried away with the excitement of the occasion and England played at Solitude Belfast, Cardiff Arms Park and Hampden Park in February to April 1906, whilst Stamford Bridge was first used for an international on 5 April 1913 with a crowd of just 52,500. Despite this the ground developed by Leitch was much admired and only Wembley in London was its equal. The Main Stand was demolished in 1972 and made way for the famous three-tier stand, whilst the last trace of terracing was finally removed in 1997. New developments at Stamford Bridge left only the rear wall of the Shed End and there is a blue plaque to commemorate its presence - indeed this is the only plaque to football history in the capital. The Mears link with Chelsea lasted many years firstly with Joe Mears junior and then with sons Brian and David and only ended after the arrival of Ken Bates in 1982.

Henry George Norris was born in Lambeth in 1865 and was the son of John Henry Norris a warehouseman in the wool industry. He lived with his parents at 234 Blackfriars Road, Southwark in 1881 and was a solicitor's clerk but progressed well from these humble origins to become a property developer in Fulham (stated in some sources). He was a director of Fulham F.C. by 1903 and became the driving force behind the club and, as stated, employed Archibald Leitch in 1905. He wanted a ground to match his aspirations and although it was developed on a smaller scale than Stamford Bridge the architectural detail was raised to a new level. The three sides of terracing were extended and the "Rabbit Hutch" was replaced with a new Main Stand and corner pavilion. This was to be one of Leitch's most notable and enduring works. Humphreys role in the partnership was to provide ironwork and they constructed the Main Stand and pavilion at Fulham, whilst they hired labourers to extend the terraces.

Argyll Arcade, 30 Buchanan Street. Built in the Regency style 1827, façade rebuilt 1904.

The interior was of a basic design with raised seating behind a narrow paddock and a pitched roof with the club's name on a central gable. This was all fairly standard however it was the frontage on Stevenage Road that was remarkable. No expense was spared on the ornate brickwork and the style was similar to that of a London mews. There were five top pediments (later three) including a main central one and below were windows and doors throughout the length of the stand. Nothing in the design was plain and there was coursing and various brick motifs right along the front viz. Est. 1880, fFc, and 1905 with the 5 encircled by the 0. Henry Norris was no doubt very pleased with the result since this was far superior to the Main Stand built at Chelsea at the same time. The ornate cricket-style pavilion with its wrought iron balcony was at the southeast corner and this was a feature that Leitch brought from Scotland (these were not normally found at English grounds). The whole design brought an air of gentility to the ground and it was opened two days before Stamford Bridge on 2 September 1905. The first game was against Portsmouth in the Southern League and was a goalless draw in front of 20,000 spectators. The results at Craven Cottage were most satisfactory and were reported in the *West London Press* on 8 September 1905 under the heading 'Fulham's Transformed Ground' viz.

"After a threatening morning last Saturday turned out to be a beautiful afternoon, and though a trifle too warm for the 22 players who took part in the strenuous struggle between the Cottagers and Portsmouth, the conditions were ideal for the thousands of spectators who patronised the banks, stand and enclosure of the new Craven Cottage. Prior to the cheery clicking of the fifty odd turnstiles,

Fulham's new pavilion was the scene of a merry little luncheon party, which included W. Hayes Fisher Esq. M.P. - who later declared the ground open - Mr. Timothy Davies, several of the Football Association, councillors, and representatives of all the leading sporting and local newspapers." The club clearly wanted to make the most of the occasion and the paper went on to say: "Speaking later, Mr. Norris extended in the name of the Fulham Club a hearty welcome to the guests, and expressed the hope that many historic games, fought in the proper spirit, and providing plenty of enjoyment for the spectators, would be played on the enclosure hard by. Much had been done to improve the ground and its equipment now was such that they might be pardonably proud of it.... Expense at the new arena has not been spared and the result is most satisfactory for the capacity of the ground has been practically doubled and the comfort and convenience of the spectators, players and officials have been the chief considerations."

34 Argyll Chambers. Leitch had offices here in 1907-39.

There is no mention of Archibald Leitch since he was just the designer and builder and sole credit was given to those who put up the money. There were plans to develop the Riverside Terrace but they were soon shelved (not for the last time) and they are discussed later. Henry Norris went from strength to strength and moved to Arsenal in 1910 and was recorded in Kelly's Titled and Landed Gentry (1918): "Sir Henry George Norris son of the late John Norris of Wandsworth, born 1865, L.C.C. Mayor of Fulham from 1909 raised two brigades of artillery for the First War and knighted in 1917. Of Queensferry House, Richmond, Surrey." Fulham themselves remained in the lower divisions in the late 20th century thus there was no development at Craven Cottage and Leitch's stand and pavilion survived to achieve listed status. The façade was restored largely due to the efforts of supporters under the name 'Fulham 2000' in April 1999 and was then one of the last surviving examples of Leitch's work. Its future is assured in some form and with Fulham's return to Craven Cottage in 2004 it stands as a last bastion amongst the modern hi-tech stadiums. Indeed the grounds Leitch designed were high prestige and many were promptly used for internationals viz. England v Scotland at Bramall Lane 4 April 1903 (1-2) crowd 32,000; England v Ireland at Ayresome Park 25 February 1905 (1-1) crowd 25,000; England v Wales at Craven Cottage 18 March 1907 (1-1) crowd 22,000.

Leitch may not have appeared in the paper but received his own reward in terms of developments in Glasgow and future contracts. He left his offices at 40 St. Enoch's Square in 1906 and returned to where he started and had a prestigious address at 34 Argyll Arcade, 30 Buchanan Street, Glasgow, from 1907-39. The Regency arcade was first built in 1827 and ran from Buchanan Street and turned at a right angle down to Argyll Street. There were elegant shops with those on the north side being 1-34 and a glass roof lighted the arcade. The Buchanan Street façade was completely altered in 1904 and a six-storey office block erected. It was a remarkable red stone building in the Baroque style with statues, Classical columns and pediments. Above the entrance was the name of the arcade in stone and below were two mosaic apses with 1904 inscribed. 34 Argyll Chambers were on the left just inside the door and had a marble staircase with pilasters, dark wooden partitions above and marble at roof level. He shared the chambers with a number of businesses whilst the entrance must have had a positive effect on prospective clients and remains little changed today. Leitch was an innovator who kept up with new technology and his telegram address in 1911 was the intriguing "Tracing Glasgow".

CHAPTER 16

Etruscan Days

Business was looking up for Archibald Leitch with Ibrox Park, Hampden Park, Sheffield, Middlesbrough, Chelsea and Fulham under his belt and he could only go in one direction and was soon in great demand. Indeed by the First War he had worked on 15 more football grounds and this began with Blackburn Rovers, or did it? Rovers were one of the most successful early teams and moved to Ewood Park in 1890 however the ground had fallen behind others by 1905. The aptly named Laurence Cotton was Chairman of Blackburn at the time and set about improving the team and the ground. A new Main Stand was opened along Nuttall Street on 1 January 1907 and was angled towards one corner to follow the line of the street. The stand incorporated an oak-panelled boardroom whilst its plain brick exterior faced the houses on Nuttall Street. This followed Leitch's format however sources in Blackburn failed to confirm this was his work and like an unaccredited old painting it was, "In the style of Leitch." In fact he may have had little time for this as he had some had important projects elsewhere. The Riverside Stand on the east side of the ground was built in 1913 and likewise may have been his work.

Anfield Road was used for an England international in 1889 and Liverpool F.C. was established at the ground in 1892. The crowds were initially smaller than seen at Goodison Park but had become comparable by 1901, and the ground was found wanting during an international in 1905 thus the club approached Leitch in 1906. He redeveloped the ground and improved the pitch and raised it by five feet and built a new Main Stand on the west side. This was similar to his earlier designs and had 3,000 seats at the rear with paddock in front and a barrel shaped roof with curved gable at the centre - the latter had a mock-Tudor design and the name "Liverpool Football Club" upon it. The stand differed, however, from his previous work since it was constructed using reinforced concrete - a first in football stand design. Indeed the Leitch gable survived at Anfield until 1970 when a new roof was erected. A similar stand was built at St. James's Park, Newcastle in 1905 however, as stated, this was not the work of Leitch. The most important development at Anfield was the construction of a huge bank at the south end of the ground. Leitch built this at the same time as the Main Stand and it was initially called the Oakfield Road Bank but backed onto Walton Breck Road. As stated, this was renamed the Spion Kop or "Kop" at the suggestion of Ernest Edwards a local journalist in 1906. This structure alone ensured Leitch's place in football folklore and the first game at the rebuilt ground was against Stoke in the First Division on 1 September 1906 in front of 32,000. Joseph Watson Cabré a local architect designed the distinctive roof for the Kop in 1928, however like many terraces its days were eventually numbered and it made its "last stand" in April 1994 and was replaced with seating.

Leitch's reputation then went before him and he obtained new contracts by word of mouth and continued to work in the north. Indeed he only had to walk a short distance across Stanley Park to Everton and began an association in 1907 that lasted to 1938. This was the premier English ground when it opened in 1892 and had a new stand on Bullens Road and a cover on Goodison Road, by 1895, but then fell behind. The club wanted to keep up and hired him to build them two stands in 1907. His work was soon overshadowed, however, when Archibald Leitch a 'journeyman' blacksmith died of old age at Daisy Cottage, Ardbeg just north of Rothesay on 18 June 1907 age 77. The son Dugald Leitch of 3 Alexandria Terrace, Govan was the informant. The contract was finished later that year and the double-decker Main Stand with extensive uncovered terracing in front was his largest work to date and towered above the houses in Goodison Road. It had the familiar Leitch hallmarks including a pitched roof with mock-Tudor gable at the centre and criss-cross ironwork at the balcony level. Such ironwork was often seen in walkways and balconies at Victorian stations and Hammersmith Bridge, London was a good example - its significance is revealed below. This was the first time he used ironwork as an architectural tool, however the Main Stand came down in stages in 1969-70 and was replaced with "a triple-decker stand." It was for a time the largest in Britain but the Main Stand at Chelsea was demolished in 1972 and replaced with one even larger in 1974. The stand at Chelsea was a three-tier cantilevered stand with a capacity of 11,500 and looked most incongruous in Leitch's old ground and nearly took the club to bankruptcy, but later took a more suitable place in the modern Chelsea Village Development. Leitch also built a two-tiered stand at the Park End of Goodison in 1907 and this became a notable feature for many years, although of late only the front terrace was used and it was dismantled in 1994.

Leitch then secured two further contracts in Yorkshire. Bradford Park Avenue F.C. were only formed in 1907 but promptly called upon Leitch to develop their ground. He gave them a new venue at Park Avenue with two large end terraces and narrow stands on each side, the layout being determined by a cricket pitch on the south side. He erected a corner pavilion in the southeast corner at the back of the terrace - the idea coming from Scotland. A similar scheme was used at Fulham whilst an important example of a corner pavilion was built at Broomfield Park, Airdrie, also in 1907. Park Avenue were quite successful at the time and Leitch's ground soon received acclaim and was used for an England v Ireland international on 13 February 1909 - a crowd of 28,000 watched the home country win 4-0. Manningham Rugby Club formed Bradford City at Valley Parade in 1903 and there was great confidence thus they were accepted into the League that year before they even had a team! The Valley Parade ground was used for an Amateur Cup Final in 1904 however there was some uncertainty and talk of a merger with Bradford P.A. in 1907. The clubs decided against this and no sooner than Leitch had finished at Park Avenue he was asked to develop Valley Parade.

This was a particular challenge as the venue was on a steep slope thus the Main Stand was built into the hill on the west side with a double pitch roof and seating at the rear of a paddock. He also extended the Manningham End terrace to twice its previous height and, as stated, this became known as Nunn's Kop. The Midland Road Side presented the greatest problem and had a steep downward slope and backed onto the railway into Bradford Forster Square Station. The solution was to raise the stand on reinforced concrete supports although the actual structure had a wooden base and framework with three mock-Tudor gables. In retrospect this was an unsuccessful answer to the problem and was originally designed for seating but eventually left as terracing. A narrow terrace at the Bradford End incorporated the players' changing rooms. There was great success at the club at this time and they were Division Two champions in 1908 and then played in Division One. There was a good F.A. Cup-run in 1910-11 and a record attendance of 39,146 was set during a Cup game against Burnley in March that season. The club played Newcastle United in the Final at the Crystal Palace and drew 0-0 whilst a J.H. Speirs' goal won the replay at Old Trafford 1-0. There were eight Scottish players in the team and these were indeed the "glory days" for the club and ground, however they were relegated in 1921-22. Indeed the ground was ill fated and the foundations of the Midland Road Stand were found to be unsafe in 1949 and it was dismantled in 1951. The roof section was sold to Berwick Rangers and its angular shape can still be seen at Shielfield Park. Indeed an aerial view shows that the outline at Berwick exactly fitted the space on the Midland Road Side. Leitch's Main Stand burnt down at the start of a game at Valley Parade in 1985 and there was considerable loss of life. The tragedy at first heralded the end for the ground but it was rebuilt as a modern stadium.

Leitch also advised on pitch improvements at Oldham Athletic in 1908 and then turned his attention to London again. He had lived at "The Tannoch", 27 Maxwell Drive, Glasgow from 1903-08 but with much of his work south of the border decided to move to England and chose an area already familiar to him. He lived at "Inverclyde", Nicholas Road, Blundellsands on the coast, north of Liverpool, from 1909-14. His neighbours included stockbrokers, merchants, wool-cotton brokers and solicitors and Blundellsands Road west, Channel Road and the Serpentine were nearby. He maintained his offices at 34 Argyll Arcade in Glasgow but also had premises at *Prudential Assurance Buildings*, 36 Dale Street in the centre of Liverpool from 1909-14. Archibald Leitch M.I.M.E. consulting engineer and factory architect had his office on the second floor with insurance brokers, merchants and solicitors as well as R.J. Urquhart (M.I. Mech. Eng consulting engineer). Dale Street was one block north of Mathew Street and Cavern Walks and between the Royal Liver and Cunard Buildings to the west, and Liverpool Museum, St. George's Hall and Lime Street Station to the east. The Prudential (no. 30) and no. 36 were at the west end of Dale Street near the Town Hall and Water Street. They had small numbers in those days and he could be contacted on 437 Crosby and 1314 Central whilst his telegram address was none other than "Terracing".

He was then well situated for further important work. Tottenham Hotspur moved to White Hart Lane in 1899 and was one of the most successful Southern League clubs being champions in 1899-1900 and F.A. Cup winners in 1901. They were elected to Division Two of the Football League with Bradford Park Avenue in 1908 and the grounds capacity was already 40,000 at this time. They had greater aspirations and then hired Archibald Leitch to build a new stand on the west side of the ground - he soon took stand design to a new level and provided a construction larger and grander than those at Chelsea and Fulham. He worked with contractors Humphreys as was the case for much of his work in London. The new Main Stand had a pitched roof supported by columns with seats for 5,300 spectators and a paddock for 6,000 more. The main feature was a large mock-Tudor gable in the middle of the roof with the club's name in bold and it was ready at the start of the season in September 1909. This was to witness the "glory days" with Danny Blanchflower and the first modern double in 1961, however it was first to go when the ground was redeveloped and was demolished in 1980. The replacement was somewhat unusual and had two tiers with two lines of executive boxes in between. The latter was built in 1982 and was the format for the future. Leitch, however, soon returned to White Hart Lane and as with Goodison Park built most of the ground.

He was already prolific however he soon went into overdrive and built new grounds for Huddersfield, Millwall and Manchester United in 1910. Huddersfield Town like their Bradford neighbours were formed as late as 1908 and were discussed in Chapter 14. Their first game at Leeds Road was a friendly against Bradford Park Avenue in September 1908 and the club began in the Midland League. They applied to join the Football League in June 1910 and also asked Leitch to design a new ground for them and thus improve the Leeds Road venue. They used Leitch's plans to support their application and this did the trick since they were accepted into the League without a hitch. Humphreys were the contractors and work began on the ground immediately and the pitch was turned a full 90° to facilitate the scheme - it was then end-on to Leeds Road. The Main Stand on the west side of the ground followed previous designs and had 4,000 seats to the rear with a paddock in front and a single pitched roof with central gable. Banking was raised on the east and south sides and there was a cover at the Leeds Road End to give a capacity of 34,000. The work was done in a considerable hurry to prepare the ground for League football in September 1910 however John McKenna, the League President, held the official opening a year later. The club did not have a good start and crowds were under 10,000 and when it rained the pitch became a messy bog - it did not provide good football. Leitch had too many commitments at the time and the pitch did not meet his normal standards thus there was talk of the club suing him. Fortunately the problems were resolved and they were League champions in the 1920s and the capacity was raised to 67,000 making it one of the largest club grounds.

It was quite fashionable to open grounds in 1910 and no less than eight clubs took the plunge that year. Millwall Athletic were formed on the Isle of Dogs in 1885 and played in the Southern League and had a good Cup reputation thus reached the semi-finals in 1899-1900 and 1902-03. The club decided to leave their North Greenwich ground and move to New Cross in the hope of attracting greater support. They obtained a site between several railway lines, south of the Surrey Canal and next to Cold Blow Lane that once led to Cold Blow Farm. Leitch was employed to build the ground however the surrounding railway lines were a considerable constraint. Millwall were not a wealthy club and the whole ground was built at a cost of about £10,000. Humphreys were contractors however the club brought in cartloads of rubble to build up the terraces. The Main Stand on the south side was somewhat basic and seated throughout whilst several columns supported the roof and a central gable stated "Millwall F. & A. Club". A branch railway line immediately behind limited the size of the stand whilst all the terraces were open to the elements. Lord Kinnaird opened the ground on 22 October 1910 and again the prestige was revealed when the Den was chosen for an England v Wales international on 13 March 1911 in front of 22,000 (score 3-0). A bomb destroyed the north terrace during the war in April 1943 and a fire destroyed the Main Stand a week later after the London Senior Cup Final - it was not completely rebuilt until 1962 due to the restrictions of post-war austerity. The ground was little changed through the years and was demolished in May 1993 and the club moved to a new ground nearby, again between the railway lines!

Newton Heath formed in Manchester in 1878 and first played at North Road and joined the Football League in 1892 and moved to Bank Street in 1893. Like many of the early clubs they were in liquidation in 1902 but local businessman John H. Davies came to their rescue. They were reformed as Manchester United and Mr. Davies looked for a new site in 1908-09 and purchased some land in the Old Trafford area five miles from Bank Street. The early developments dictated the current shape of the ground and much of the credit goes to Archibald Leitch. There were not the constraints found at many grounds hence a uniform terrace was laid out on three sides and a Main Stand was built to the south next to the railway with a multi-span roof. He frequently used such roofs for his factory work however this was the first time such a design was used at a football ground (he later used a similar scheme at both Arsenal and Wolves). The twelve sections were at right angles to the pitch and a larger section in the centre formed the trademark gable. The stand had a "ground breaking" design with cushioned tip-up seats, magnificent changing rooms with plunge bath, massage rooms and a gymnasium, and the ground with a 80,000 capacity was hailed as the most advanced of its time. It was immediately used for an F.A. Cup semi-final and for the Cup Final itself in 1915. He had clearly improved on the designs at Sheffield and Middlesbrough however the work at Old Trafford was a team effort. Some sources give the builders as Brameld and Smith but further research showed they were a firm of architects and must have combined with Archibald Leitch on Old Trafford, as he was more concerned with engineering design and detail. Bernard William Hurt Brameld F.R.I.B.A. and John Thorley Smith (also an architect) were senior partners and they were architects and surveyors at 83 Bridge Street in 1905 and at 50-54 County Buildings, 4 Cannon Street, Manchester, in 1910.

Archibald Leitch was very busy at the time and could not have done all the work himself and his firm must have grown from the "30 hands in my office" in 1902. He may have had offices in both Manchester and Northern Ireland at this time, however they are not recorded in directories and must have been shared. Indeed they were secondary to those in Liverpool and Glasgow and his later offices in London. During this period he must have continued with factory work and certainly had ample contracts at football grounds. Indeed he continued to assist Rangers in Scotland and built up the terracing at Ibrox Park to a capacity of 63,000 by 1910. He was then called back to the northeast and commenced to work in Sunderland. The club joined the League in 1890 and had a very successful period whilst their Newcastle Road ground was used for an international in 1891. The first game at Roker Park was against Liverpool in Division One on 10 September 1898 in front of 30,000 and an international was played there in 1899. The ground needed developing and Leitch was engaged to extend the Roker End terrace. This was originally constructed of wood however the new terrace had reinforced concrete supports (as at Liverpool and Bradford) and was completed at a cost of £6,000 in 1911. The Fulwell End was increased in size on an earth bank to bring the capacity to 60,000 in 1925 but the latter was not Leitch's work. He then had prospects of a quieter year but his mother Agnes Flint Leitch died of old age at 16 Green Street, Bothwell on the evening of New Years Eve 31 December 1911 age 78. She had returned to where she was born after her husband died and Dugald Leitch her son of 35 Summerstown, Govan was informant on 1 January 1912. Regarding her family Dugald Leitch died at Cadder Western in Lanark in 1925 age 68, and Agnes McLachlan Barrie died at Newton Mearns, Renfrew in 1945 age 77.

Meanwhile Leitch, after a break from football work, secured a major contract in London and returned to work for Henry Norris who was now at Arsenal. The club were discussed in Chapter 13 and Norris purchased the struggling side when they went into voluntary liquidation in 1910. He had failed at Fulham to some extent and thus, with the future in mind, decided to move his new club away from their roots in Woolwich. Sites at both Battersea and Haringey were considered and "Football Grounds of Britain" provides a useful insight into these developments. A.G. Kearney was present at the anniversary of Highbury in 1963 and talked of the ground's development. He related how he worked at Leitch's Manchester office from 1908 and that Leitch himself visited him there in 1911 or 1912 with copious amounts of paperwork and maps showing sites on which to build a ground with a 100,000 capacity - the aim being "to provide a ground for the Cup Final to replace the Crystal Palace." This supports the notion that there was an office in Manchester although it seems unusual since the main office was clearly in Liverpool.

The Highbury site was then chosen although it was restricted on all four sides and the terraces were raised using waste from the Piccadilly line constructed nearby in 1906 - as with Stamford Bridge. Humphreys built the stand but hired workmen to do the groundwork and terracing was extended around three sides with the North Bank the main feature. The Main Stand on the east side of the ground in Avenell Road had a multi-span roof (9 sections) and 9,000 seats but lacked a central gable seen at other grounds. The first game was in September 1913 but the work was not finished and Humphreys nearly walked off the site. There was an England v Wales international there on 15 March 1920 in front of 21,180 (score 1-2) and the move was repaid in full in the 1930s when they became the strongest team in the country. The Main Stand with its multi-span roof was expensive to maintain and had a short "life span" and was replaced by that of William Binnie as early as 1936.

Archibald Leitch did further work in the Midlands before the First War and also had a contract at Hamilton Academicals F.C. in Scotland. The club were formed at the Hamilton Academy in 1874 and moved to Douglas Park in 1888 and Leitch built the Main Stand there in 1913. This was definitely one of his smaller works and had a small barrel roof with a narrow paddock in front and just 1,220 seats. The name for this type of wooden construction was a "Belfast roof" and this was similar to Preston's West Stand built in 1906. This was a complete contrast to his other projects and the stand survived until the ground was sold in 1995 (the same year as Preston's was demolished). Meanwhile, Frederick William Rinder was born in Liverpool in September 1857 and worked as a surveyor for Birmingham Corporation in the late 19th century. He joined the Aston Villa Committee in 1887 and worked with William McGregor and the club were founder members of the League in 1888. Fred Rinder was Club Chairman and rented the Lower Aston Grounds in 1896 and these were prepared as Villa Park, the first game being against Blackburn Rovers in Division One on 17 April 1897. The initial ground, as stated, had barrel roofed stands on either side. The stand in Witton Lane had three curved gables at the centre and that in Trinity Road curved around a track, whilst raised banking formed the end terraces. The club offices were in the buildings of the old pleasure park.

The club had a good start and were League champions five times from 1894-1900 and again in 1910 and also won the F.A. Cup in 1887, 1895, 1897, 1905 and 1913. This early success was under the guidance of William McGregor and Fred Rinder and the club attracted internationals at Perry Barr in 1893 and at Villa Park in 1899 and 1902 (the latter was also a popular choice for Cup semi-finals). Fred Rinder then produced a 'master plan' for Villa Park under the guidance of Leitch in 1914 with the intention of raising the capacity to 104,000. This was the blueprint for later work, and the cycle track was removed, and terracing laid in front of the Witton Lane Stand and the end terraces extended to the pitch - both in 1914. The Main Stand in Trinity Road was more elaborate than Leitch's original design and was a tribute to the aspirations of Fred Rinder. This had a familiar gable at the centre (flattened at the apex) but was not begun until 1922 and proved problematic due to escalating costs and was only completed in 1924. Fred Rinder resigned over this matter in 1925 but returned in 1936 to promote his original plans, however his efforts were short lived and he died in Birmingham in December 1938 aged 81. His scheme was continued after his death and the Holte End was extended by February 1940 and the record crowd of 76,588 was on 14 March 1946 during a Cup-tie against Derby County. Leitch also provided plans for Filbert Street in 1907-14 and these may have led to the Kop End being covered before the war, but most developments came in the 1920s.

Wednesday F.C. was formed as early as 1867 and moved to Owlerton near Sheffield in 1899 (see Ch. 18). John Charles and William Edwin Clegg were on the Board and the latter was Mayor of Sheffield in 1898-99 and kicked off the first game against Chesterfield on 2 September 1899 in front of a 12,000 crowd. The club won the Football League in 1903 and 1904 and the F.A. Cup in 1896 and 1907 and with good support developed the ground in 1913-14. In the first instance they raised a huge terrace the Spion Kop at the Penistone Road End in 1913 - this was later covered then seated and remains today. The club consulted Leitch and he provided plans for a Main Stand on the south side of the ground with an upper tier of seating for 5,600 spectators and a paddock for standing in front. It had the usual pitched roof with gable at the centre and was of a plain design, but had good facilities in the interior and with the earlier developments brought the capacity to 50,000. The Main Stand was opened at a game on 10 January 1914 however soon after on the 4 February the ground failed to cope with a crowd of just 43,000. A wall collapsed on the new Kop resulting in about 80 injuries and the ground was then further improved. There was a change of local boundaries in 1914 and it was then known as Hillsborough. The club won the League title in 1929/1930 and Leitch's stand was renovated in 1992-96. A new second tier was added consisting of 3,200 seats and a new roof erected above, however the gable was only a replica.

The story now goes off at a tangent, but for a good reason, and the craft of ball control makes way for that of the potter. Indeed this brings another innovator to the story from an earlier time. Gilbert Wedgwood was born in 1588 and lived at Dale Hall, Burslem and was founder of the Wedgwood dynasty. His son Thomas was born c.1617 and his grandson Thomas (1655-1716) was a potter of Churchyard House, Burslem. The latter had sons Thomas Wedgwood III (1687-1739) a master potter of the same address and Aaron Wedgwood (1693-1773) a potter of Hamil. It is with these gentlemen that the story begins. Thomas married Mary Stringer and their 11th child was Josiah Wedgwood (1730-95) founder of the 'Etruria' works. He developed new techniques that took the production of glazed ware from the ordinary to the extra-ordinary and made the company famous. He was appointed "potter to the Queen" in 1763 and made a 2,000-piece service for Catherine the Great of Russia, whilst his new designs were eagerly awaited viz. Queens cream-ware 1769 and Jasper ware 1775. He married his third cousin Sarah Wedgwood (1734-1815) and had several children with notable connections. His daughter Susannah (1765) married Robert W. Darwin (1766-1848) the son of Erasmus Darwin (1731-1802), the latter a poet and a member of the 'Lunar Society' with her father Josiah and others such as Matthew Boulton (see Muirhead Ch. 8). Their son Charles Robert Darwin F.R.S. (1809-82) developed the theories of evolution and married cousin Emma (see Pember Ch. 4). Thomas Wedgwood (1771-1805) was a pioneer of photography with Sir Humphrey Davy and published the pamphlet, "How to copy paintings upon glass and of making profiles by the agent of light upon silver nitrate." The method was not successful and the images quickly faded although Sir John Herschel solved the problem in 1819 (see Wollaston Ch. 6).

Josiah Wedgwood II (1769-1843) was a master potter of Maer and M.P for Stoke and married Elizabeth Allen - their children included Josiah (1795-1880), Francis (1800-88) and Emma *Darwin* (1808-96) all of whom made good matches. The son Josiah married his cousin Caroline Darwin (1800-88) and their daughter Margaret married Rev. Arthur Vaughn-Williams - their son was Ralph Vaughn-Williams (1872-1958), composer. The son Francis Wedgwood worked in the family business and married Frances Mosley in 1832 and remained a partner until 1876 - their second son Clement Francis Wedgwood was born in 1840 and became an apprentice at 'Etruria' in c.1859; he was a potter and later a partner and director. He married Emily Catherine Rendel at St. John's, Hyde Park Crescent on 6 November 1866, who was born Catherine Emily at Plymouth in December 1840 and was the daughter of James Meadows Rendel and Catharine Jane Harris. Emily Frances, her sister, was born in 1835 and married Charles Synge Christopher Bowen. The couple, meanwhile, had a child Josiah Clement Wedgwood on 16 March 1872 who married his cousin Ethel Kate Bowen and had a notable career in politics (discussed in Ch. 7). Clement F. Wedgwood a master potter lived at the Lea, Barlaston in 1881 with wife Emily C., children Josiah, Ralph, Cicely and Arthur, and seven servants. Clement died at Barlaston on 24 January 1889 whilst widow Emily and daughter Cicely lived there on their own means in 1901. Indeed Emily died at Barlaston on 6 April 1921.

We must now go back to Aaron Wedgwood who was the uncle of Josiah (founder of 'Etruria') and indeed the whole family were involved in the success. Thomas Wedgwood (1734-88) was the son of Aaron and a master potter of Burslem and 'Etruria' and the cousin and partner of Josiah Wedgwood. He married Elizabeth Taylor at Stoke on 2 July 1765 and had at least seven children the first Ralph Wedgwood baptized at Burslem on 8 May 1766. The latter had his own company Wedgwood & Co. at Hill Works, Burslem from 1785-96 and married Mary Yeomans in 1790. The couple had a daughter Mary who was baptized at the Tabernacle, Hanley on 29 April 1791 and a son Ralph born at Burslem in 1793. The father then married Sarah Taylor in 1796 and joined forces with Tomlinson & Co. at Ferrybridge, Yorks in 1796-1810. The company produced cameos, medallions and ornamental pieces however these were inferior to those produced at 'Etruria' in both body and finish. Ralph had a son Samuel at Knottingley, Yorkshire in 1800 but then married Mary Copeland and retired from business and moved to 328 Oxford Street, London by 1810. His daughter Triane was born that year and his last three children were all baptized at St. Clement Danes on 24 June 1810. His last child William Richard was born at Marylebone in 1817 and the father Ralph died in 1837.

Ralph Wedgwood junior married Hannah English (1801) who was born in Yarmouth at St. Paul's, Covent Garden on 23 March 1818 and entered into the stationery business in London - indeed he invented carbon paper. His son John Raphael Wedgwood was born at the Strand and baptized at Craven Chapel, Marshall Street, Westminster, on 14 October 1832; he also had two sons Ebenezer (1835) at Kentish Town and George Arthur (1840) at Bayswater. They moved to Barnes and Hannah Wedgwood died on 5 November 1861 and Ralph Wedgwood died at 11 Castelnau Villas on 14 October 1866. John Raphael Wedgwood then ran the stationery business in London and married Charlotte Hicks (1832) from Newton Abbot and had children Florence (1856-98) and John Percy (1859-89). They lived at "Lonsdale Lodge", Lonsdale Road otherwise 4 Park Villas in Barnes from 1867-72. The house was on the north side and the properties built in the early 1860s near Hammersmith Bridge (see Graham Ch. 1). J.R. Wedgwood a merchant lived at Lonsdale Lodge with wife Charlotte, daughter Florence, three visitors and two servants in 1871. The south side was partly developed in the 1870s with large Victorian dwellings and the last house no. 49, whilst open fields lay beyond leading to Barnes village and The Terrace.

John Raphael Wedgwood moved to 49 Lonsdale Road just after it was built in the 1870s and named it "Etruria House" after the Burslem pottery of Josiah Wedgwood. He was described as a stationer and lived at "Etruria House" next to Lowther's Farm with wife Charlotte, son J. Percy and two servants in 1881. His uncle William Richard (1817-94) married Harriet Maria Brackenbury at Heavitree, Exeter on 7 April 1859 and had four children at Exeter, Cirencester and Greyshot Hall, Headley, Hants. His wife died in 1864 (daughter of J.M. Brackenbury see Ch. 9) and William once schoolmaster and farmer lived with his four children at Fernbank, Friern Road, Camberwell, in 1881. The brother Ebenezer (1835-1902) married Huldah Brown (1845) who was born in Turnham Green at Lewisham in December 1866 and had four daughters in London and a son Joshua George English at St. Peter's Port in Guernsey in 1877. The father may have worked with brother John but was a retired draper living with his family at East Side House, Richmond in 1881. The other brother George Arthur (1840-1901) married Emma Pattison (1841) who was born in Brighton at St. Thomas's, Marylebone on 12 July 1866 and resided at "Martins", Shipbourne, Kent, in 1881. Ralph Wedgwood & Son manifold writer (manufacturer) traded at 9 Cornhill and Josiah Wedgwood & Sons potters, earthenware, china, jasper and tile manufacturers traded through an agent Charles Bachhoffner at 4-6 St. Andrew's Street, Holborn Circus, London (1882). The former were wholesale and export stationers, printers, manifold writers and *carbonic paper makers* at 145 Upper Thames Street, London in 1892.

"Etruria House" at Barnes. Leitch lived here in 1915-22.

John Raphael Wedgwood continued in business however his wife Charlotte died at Barnes on 25 August 1882 and he married Margaret Strachan at St. Stephen's in Paddington - 6 August 1885. She was born Margaret Swait the daughter of Edward and Maria (gentleman) and was possibly baptised at Richmond on 17 November 1833 although the census states she was born 1839. She married Alfred Strachan at Kingston in June 1855 but he died and she was a boarding house keeper at 2 Burton Crest near St. Pancras, London with eight boarders and one servant in 1881. John Raphael and Margaret Wedgwood lived at "Etruria House" with three servants and a groom in 1891. The house, as stated, was the last property on the south side and was also the largest, however all were substantial double-fronted detached houses. Indeed "Etruria House" was engraved on both sets of gateposts and a driveway swept past the front door and a small coach house was on the left. The central, columned porch entrance was at the top of a short flight of stairs and there were two storeys above ground level - each having large Victorian rooms. There was a moulded cornice at roof level with some large chimneys and the Wedgwoods clearly lived in considerable comfort.

John R. Wedgwood retired stationer and wife Margaret, and Ebenezer and Huldah Wedgwood and their five children all lived in Barnes in 1901. John Raphael Wedgwood died at 49 Lonsdale Road on 15 November 1902 and his widow Margaret continued to live in the house, which remained the last property until at least 1906. There was then further development between the house and Verdun Road to the west and the properties extended to 119 by 1913. Margaret Wedgwood wrote a detailed will in 1908 and added two codicils in 1911/13 and there were several significant points but four were pertinent to this discourse. She left numerous bequests and to Joshua Wedgwood: "my diamond and amethyst ring given to Mr. Ralph Wedgwood of Oxford Street (West) by the Emperor of Russia." There were further bequests to the family viz. jewellery to Huldah Wedgwood of 3 Northumberland Avenue, Barnes and to Emma Wedgwood of Feering House, Kelvedon, Essex (sister-in-laws). Charles Cook a farrier of Hammersmith married her sister Ann Maria Swait (1838) and had children Charles Edward, Arthur Rowland and Grace Bertha. They appear in the will and the daughter married Christopher Leonard Tolcher at Fulham in March 1895. Meanwhile, she left niece Grace Bertha Tolcher of 12 Hartington Villas, Hove £10,000 plus, "my diamond and amethyst pendant and my diamond and emerald bracelet and all my Wedgwood ware and wearing apparel," however her second codicil amended this to £8,000 and ".... one half of all my Wedgwood ware." The remaining half went to her executors and trustees and one wonders where this valuable heirloom went.

Clause 9 the most significant section stated: "I empower my trustees for so long a period after my death as they shall deem expedient, with a view to a sale, and until a sale of the house shall be effected, to maintain and keep up an establishment at 'Etruria House', Barnes, aforesaid, employing such person or persons and upon such terms as they shall in their sole discretion see fit, to reside therein, for the purpose of taking charge of the same. And I direct that all expenses thereof, or connected therewith, and also all expenses of keeping the said house and premises in proper repair and maintaining the garden, shall be borne by and paid out of my estate." This clause revealed the grandeur of "Etruria House" at this time but there was soon to be a change of ownership. Margaret Wedgwood died at the house on 7 October 1913 and James Leslie Sweet of 2 Bedford Row, Gray's Inn and Charles Webb of 75 Old Broad Street executors and solicitors held the property. Her will was proved in London on 4 November 1913 and her estate eventually valued at £86,553 2s 4d. The Wedgwoods were all buried at Barnes Old Cemetery - the same resting place as Morley and Willis (see Ch. 1).

Archibald Leitch grew up as a blacksmith's son in Glasgow but made large profits from his work on British football grounds and soon received rewards of a pecuniary nature. He was not born into the gentry however he was a very rich man and his success was hard earned and well deserved. He was now a businessman or professional of some status who was able to live the life of a gentleman and moved to "Etruria House", Lonsdale Road, Barnes in late 1914 or early 1915 - this made a clear statement of his new social standing. Leitch became familiar with the area when he worked on Craven Cottage and Stamford Bridge in 1905 and the City was just four miles away across Hammersmith Bridge - indeed Craven Cottage was visible in the distance from the London side. The bridge itself was a Victorian 'masterpiece' with French and Oriental influence being built across the Thames in 1887. The functional features of suspension were incorporated into the architectural design and double suspension braces on each side were held to the deck by numerous bolts and tie beams. The walkways on either side had criss-cross ironwork balconies, and there was great detail at the anchor points with elaborate scrolls and shields, and chateau style turrets above the top of the bridge. Leitch also used functional engineering in this way and one can imagine him viewing the bridge when he was working at Chelsea and Fulham in 1905, and may have received inspiration since there was a resemblance between the ironwork in his stands and that of the bridge (painted in green and gold). Barnes village was a peaceful rural suburb when Leitch moved there but he dropped the name "Etruria House" and it was then just 49 Lonsdale Road.

Leitch closed his offices in Liverpool when he moved to Barnes and advertised a temporary business address at 2 Southampton Street, Bloomsbury in 1915. There were also other changes when Victoria Station was expanded - Humphreys' Works remained on the corner of Buckingham Palace Road however the Grosvenor Canal was filled-in (for the most part) and the wharf buildings demolished (by 1913). Humphreys continued to use their offices in Knightsbridge and also owned a wharf at 9-11 Ebury Bridge Road in 1920-21 and still traded in 1928, after at least forty years. Archibald Leitch had work on his books at the start of the First War however the hostilities intervened. Heart of Midlothian or Hearts F.C. played at Tynecastle in Edinburgh from 1886 and he designed them a new Main Stand with 4,000 seats. The work began in 1914 but the construction costs doubled to £12,000 and the project was stopped due to the war and it was not completed until 1919. This was a time when many suffered great losses and success offered no protection from the vicissitudes of life, thus his daughter Jane Hilda Roberts Leitch died at Lonsdale Road on 15 June 1918 aged 22 - the father a consulting engineer was in attendance.

Dens Park, Dundee. Leitch built the Main Stand in 1919-21....

....then he built the other half of the stand.

He returned to work after the First War and was soon involved in a number of new projects in Scotland and London. The town of Dundee, in terms of soccer, had a similar story to that seen in Sheffield and Nottingham. Football was played at Clepington Park, Tannadice Street from c.1880 and was home to Dundee Wanderers in 1891 and then Dundee Hibernian in 1909 (it was then renamed Tannadice). The latter club lost their League status in 1922 and were reformed as Dundee United and were elected to the Scottish League in 1923. Meanwhile, Dundee F.C. played at Carolina Port next to the Firth of Tay from 1893 and moved to Dens Park in Dens Road in 1899. This was indeed a bold move, since the ground was very near to their rivals and backed onto Tannadice Street. The club purchased Dens Park and employed Archibald Leitch to redevelop the ground in 1919. He used the tried and trusted formula with terracing on three sides and a track around the pitch, although there was considerable banking on the south side due to the slope of the site. A two tier Main Stand was built on the north side and the balcony had decorative ironwork however the stand was angled at the centre due to the shape of Sandeman Street just behind. The rear had red brick at ground level with metal cladding above and numerous turnstiles but was rather basic, however the entrance at the eastern end had some notable features as in a 'grand house'. There were double doors with brass handles and a marble surround with D.F.C. inscribed above, whilst inside the entrance there was a moulded plaster ceiling and wooden panelling. This was a major construction and was not completed until 1921. Leitch spared no expense on this interior and it is unchanged today with red embossed wallpaper and the friendly: "Welcome to Dens Park Stadium home of the city's oldest football club." Indeed this is an impressive stadium and the blue stand is a marked contrast to the orange and black of Tannadice, just 100 yards away.

Archibald Leitch had provided another complete ground for a League club and was a man of talent and vision who matched his counterparts at the Football Association. He was committed to the business and had the energy to develop many projects, often overseeing several at the same time - he was rewarded with both prestige and satisfaction from the design of these grounds. The focus of the business, however, had shifted from Glasgow to London and although he kept Argyll Arcade he took a permanent office in London (firstly) at 3 Queen Street next to Southwark Bridge in the City from 1920-22. His company then returned to White Hart Lane and designed covers for each end of the ground viz. Paxton Road End (1921) and Park Lane End (1923). This meant that with his original Main Stand the covered capacity was about 30,000 and only Goodison Park had as much shelter at the time. This was the prelude to a busy period in London and he first worked at Charlton and soon after at Clapton Orient and Crystal Palace. Indeed Charlton Athletic moved to the Valley in 1919 but had little money for development and employed Leitch to provide a new ground in 1921.

Humphreys had a 16-year association with Leitch and built a Main Stand on the west side, however it was not innovative or progressive in its design and covered only one third of the pitch in length. The roof was constructed in four spans and looked like the 'Rabbit Hutch' built at Fulham in 1896! It was not quite so bad since Charlton's stand had a single tier of 2,500 seats whereas Fulham's had only 1,000 seats. Humphreys continued to work on the ground in 1921-22 and concreted the lower parts of the East Bank and the ground could easily hold 50,000 thus Charlton joined the Third Division (South). The Main Stand was a notable feature at the Valley for many years but the roof became unstable and was replaced in 1979. The club then faced severe problems and played at Selhurst Park and Upton Park from 1985-92 and the stand was demolished in c.1989 and replaced by a 'temporary' West Stand in 1991. Humphreys, meanwhile, did further work for Charlton and laid out a new ground called the Mount at Catford in May 1923. This was the home of Catford Southend, a local club, but the venture was not a success and Charlton played just 13 games there before returning to the Valley. Leitch then worked at Clapton Orient and Crystal Palace and these developments are discussed in the next chapter. He remained at 49 Lonsdale Road, Barnes until about 1922-23 and appeared in the electoral roll viz. Archibald Leitch, Jessie Hardy Leitch and Archibald Kent Leitch - 'voting adults' in residence (Jessie and Agnes were too young). "Etruria House" remains but has lost some of its grandeur due to a roof conversion, whilst neighbouring properties give a glimpse of how it once looked.

CHAPTER 17

For King and Country

Archibald Leitch continued to work at both English and Scottish football grounds and despite a long list of accolades managed to add some significant works to the genre. The Glyn Cricket Club in Clapton (later the Eagle C.C.) had some members who were employees of the Orient shipping line and they formed the Orient F.C. in 1888. The club played at Glyn Road and then at Whittle's Athletic Ground from 1896 and became Clapton Orient F.C. in 1898. They were elected to Division Two with Chelsea, Hull City and Leeds City and moved to a new ground at Millfields Road in 1905. The ground had a small 2,000 seat Main Stand at first and the terraces were formed of clinker from a local power station! Their best finish was fourth in Division Two in 1910-11 and 1911-12 and they contacted Archibald Leitch to develop the ground in 1923. The club laid out the large sum of £30,000 and sold the old stand to Wimbledon F.C. to recover some of the cost - it was erected at Plough Lane.

Humphreys the contractors built a substantial football ground on the site with a large Kop terrace on the north side and a Main Stand with a five-span roof on the south side - the factory style architecture again surfaced at an English football ground and it was not dissimilar to that at Charlton. The expense, however, was beyond the club and they sold the ground to Clapton Greyhound Stadium Co. in 1927 and a track was laid around the pitch and the Kop covered with another multi-span roof. They had some large crowds and there were 35,000 for a League game against Millwall on 1 September 1928 and a record of 37,615 for a Cup game against Spurs on 16 March 1929. The club, despite this, failed to make much progress and were relegated in last place at the end of 1928-29 and had problems with 'ground sharing' and were forced to leave Millfields Road in 1930. They went to Lea Bridge Road and Brisbane Road (which are discussed later) whilst the greyhound stadium was used until 1974 with Leitch's Main Stand as the central feature.

Archibald Leitch left "Etruria House" in Barnes at this time and moved to the other side of London and to a property even more palatial than the last. He resided at "Bourneside", Southgate in The Bourne (leading to Bourne Hill) from 1924-28. Next door was another large Victorian house called "The Grange" and both were built at the western end of the road in the 1860s (near the site of Southgate Underground), and appeared on a map dated 1867. Indeed each was home to a character important in Southgate's history. John Bradshaw a gentleman and philanthropist lived at "The Grange" and died there in 1939 and the house passed to Southgate Council and was demolished in the 1970s. There is a blue plaque stating: "John Bradshaw 1863-1939 benefactor of Southgate lived in a house on this site." John Miles lived nearly all his 86 years in Southgate and spent the last 50 of them at "Bourneside" until his death in 1921. He was closely associated with the public life of Southgate and his executors then sold or rented the house to Archibald Leitch. It was twice the size of "Etruria House" and had a ten-foot high wall in front with red brick gateposts and the name Bourneside engraved upon them. There was a double front of two and three storeys and a central tower and porch-veranda that extended the length of the building. The style was Victorian Gothic and might have featured in one of Hitchcock's movies. Neat lawns and grounds covering half an acre reached some distance along the border and surrounded the house, which was suitable for the well-to-do gentry. There were a number of outbuildings and stables and nearby was the country village of Southgate.

"Bourneside". Built in the 1860s - Leitch lived here from 1924-28.

"Bourneside" was the apex of his career in a time when men were measured by their wealth and standing in society, however little was previously known of him and this suggests he was a quiet and private man. Yet his influence remains in much of our football ground history and even in some of today's grounds. The house was in a rural location eight miles from London and was inaccessible at the time and he must have stayed away when he was working - his family were used to this when they lived in Scotland. Leitch also moved his offices at this time near to where they had been in 1905-07 and was at 18 Victoria Street, London from 1923-29. This was a more central location and in particular not far from the works and offices of Humphreys, his partners. Meanwhile, Crystal Palace F.C. moved to Croydon Common Athletic Ground in 1919 and renamed the venue "The Nest". The site, however, was limited with just one entrance in Selhurst Road and the club were seeking a new venue soon after their arrival. The lease on the Athletic Ground expired in 1924 and they moved nearby to Selhurst Park whilst the old ground became Selhurst Railway Depot. The club employed Leitch, and Humphreys laid out a ground in the traditional style with a Main Stand on the west side and banked terracing on the other three sides. Selhurst Park was claimed to be one of the largest grounds in London but this was just publicity and in fact a gross exaggeration. Indeed it was smaller in scale than the Valley and the Main Stand was of a basic design and fell behind his earlier work, having no ornate brickwork and not a gable in sight. The design and construction was similar to that of Chelsea and Fulham back in 1905 and the terraces had basic earth banking. The problem was a lack of finances however the ground was used for an England v Wales international in 1926. The situation was slowly remedied and the lower terrace concreted in the 1950s and the Main Stand seated and refurbished in 1979 - it survived into the new century.

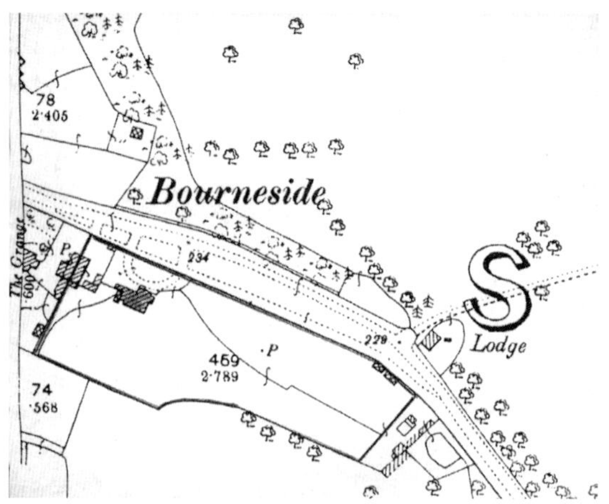

Southgate - O.S. Map 1896. The estate was similar when Leitch lived here.

The Royal Artillery was the leading club in Portsmouth in the late 19th century but they were suspended for breaking amateur regulations and played in the Southern League, Division One in 1898-99. A.J.E. Pink a local solicitor and other businessmen wanted a professional club and formed Portsmouth F.C. in 1898 and purchased some market gardens - these were laid out as Fratton Park. The initial developments were basic but the club built a mock-Tudor pavilion and entrance in Frogmore Road in 1905 and this became a notable feature of the ground. The club were champions of the Southern League in 1901-02 and 1919-20 and were founder members of Division Three in 1920. Archibald Leitch was hired to work at the ground in 1925 and Humphreys constructed a new South Stand for the club at a cost of £12,000. This was the same price as the John Street Stand, Sheffield, built in 1902 and although times had changed the stands still followed the tried and trusted formula of 20 years earlier. There was an upper tier of seating for 4,000 spectators with a paddock area below and a criss-cross ironwork balcony (first seen at Everton in 1907). The mock-Tudor entrance was pleasing to Leitch and he linked it to the new stand however unlike at Fulham the rear was plain brickwork since it backed onto houses in Carisbrook Road. There was little innovation in ground design until the 1930s (see Arsenal) and others simply followed the methods that Leitch used viz. new stand with central gable at Pittodrie, Aberdeen in 1925.

Molineux was the home of Wolves from 1889 however there was little development of the stands, which were situated around an athletics track and the situation did not change for many years. It was in need of urgent attention and Leitch was called upon to improve matters and built a new Main Stand on the west side next to Waterloo Road in 1925. This had two tiers of seating for 2,750 and a paddock area in front for 4,000 spectators. There was a basic pitched roof without gable however it was angled at the centre to follow the line of the old athletics track and was thus similar to that at Dens Park, Dundee. The stand cost £15,000 and gave the club its first proper changing rooms, which seems a remarkable fact, as Wolves were founder members of the League in 1888 and F.A. Cup winners in 1893 and 1908. John McKenna, League President was kept very busy at the time and opened the Fratton stand on 29 August 1925 and that at Molineux on 12 September 1925. Leitch and his company were on a roll and they continued north and worked at Everton and Newcastle in 1926.

Goodison Park was always one of England's premier grounds and hosted a Cup Final soon after opening in 1894. Leitch built the Main Stand and Park End Stand in 1907 and it was used for a Cup Final replay in 1910. Indeed the crowds were witness to the ground's development viz. 37,000 in 1894 and 69,000 in 1910 and it was the first visited by the ruling monarch - George V and Queen Mary went there in 1913 but did not watch a game. Leitch was employed on familiar territory to build the Bullens Road Stand in 1926 and this was a large construction (like the Main Stand) with two tiers of seating and standing in front. The price tag of £30,000 was witness to the scale and again a criss-cross balcony provided an architectural feature. The stand was built to last into the next century and Leitch had almost completed Goodison Park - just one side to go!

Newcastle East End moved to St. James's Park and changed their name to United and the first game took place against Celtic on 3 September 1892 in front of a 6,000 crowd. The club joined the League in 1893 and reached the First Division by 1898 and being very successful erected a Main Stand on the west side of the ground in 1905. The club, as stated, did not offer the work to Leitch however it had a rear tier of seating, curved roof and curved central gable and was a copy of the stand he built at Middlesbrough in 1903. Maybe Leitch could have made a claim for infringement of copyright? The ground staged internationals in 1901 and 1907 but soon fell behind many others and was in urgent need of development. This was no an easy task since the Council blocked many schemes for expansion. Despite this the Magpies asked Leitch to redevelop the ground in 1926 and he provided plans for a two-tier stand at the Gallowgate End and a low cover on the other two terraces. The scheme, however, did not come to fruition and only one cover was ever built at the Leazes Park End in 1930. In fact there were few changes until the East Stand was opened in 1973, the Main Stand demolished in 1987 and the end terraces developed after 1993. Despite these very slow beginnings the ground soon raced ahead and is now one of the largest in the country.

Archibald Kent Leitch was born in Glasgow in 1891 and may have fought in the First War and was living with his parents at 49 Lonsdale Road in 1922. He also trained as an engineer and joined his father in the business and eventually assumed full control. The father and son joined the Incorporated Association of Architects and Surveyors in 1925 and the former cited Scottish tube works and un-named football grounds in his application and they were both in the *1928-29 Yearbook*: A. Leitch, mechanical and structural engineer, A.K. Leitch, structural engineer. They were not strictly architects or surveyors and had a background of mechanical engineering and indeed the organisation became the Association of Building Engineers in 1993. They moved offices to Northampton at this time but unfortunately disposed of all early applications (including those of Leitch). The father was aged 62 in 1927 and began to look forward to his retirement although he did not relinquish control of the company at this stage. With this in mind he made his son a full partner and this was revealed in the will of his wife Jessie Hardie Leitch: "Whereas under clause 20b of Articles of Partnership dated the 30th day of December 1927 made between my late husband Archibald Leitch of the one part and my said son Archibald Kent Leitch of the other part...." Indeed this change brought new impetus and the father and son then worked together enabling the company to produce some of their greatest work.

When Archibald Leitch lived at "Bourneside" it was in a rural location and the view from the front gate was that of a tree-lined lane, however he left the property in 1927-28 and this was the end of an era for the house and the lifestyle that it evoked. It was also a time of change for Archibald Leitch as he shared duties with his son and look forward to a quieter retirement. The grand lifestyle had come to an end and he soon moved to a more convenient home in Kensington (see below). Harold John Sayer lived in the house in 1929 but the grounds were sold for housing at this time and the Piccadilly line extension was built nearby in 1931 turning the area into a London suburb. The house was part of a bygone age and was demolished in the late 1930s and new houses were built on the site - their entrances inserted through the 10' high perimeter wall. Today, only the wall and gateposts and some old trees along The Bourne still remain from his time there. Archibald Leitch reduced his role in the company he had started, in 1927-30, but still had many contracts to fulfil.

Southampton F.C. moved to the Dell in 1898 and won the Southern League in 1897, 1898, 1899, 1901, 1903 and 1904 and were the first non-League club to reach the Cup Final in 1900 (since the League began in 1888) - indeed this only happened on two other occasions: Tottenham 1901 and Southampton 1902. The club were founder members of Division Three in 1920 and were promoted as champions in 1922 then remained in Division Two for 31 years until relegated in 1953. Leitch designed a new West Stand in 1928 and Humphreys did the ironwork with an upper tier of seating for 4,500 and a paddock below for 8,500, although he also employed the Clyde Structural Company. The stand overshot the southern end of the pitch and the club offices and changing rooms were located there backing on Milton Road. This was a typical Leitch stand with criss-cross ironwork on the balcony and the east terrace was also re-profiled to raise the capacity from 20-33,000. Archibald Leitch was at the opening of the West Stand on 7 January 1928 but they soon had problems when the old East Stand burnt down in 1929. It was replaced by a new stand that was a replica of the one on the west side and both survived until the club moved to St. Mary's Stadium in 2001. In fact Southampton were the last club to give the partners a new contract and Leitch's work at British football grounds was drawing to a close - although he did return to add to his previous work.

The partnership then switched its attentions back to Glasgow however it was 25 years since he had worked on Hampden Park, in 1903, and these were very different times. The company did further work on the terraces at Ibrox Park before 1910 but now had some competition north of the border. Leitch & Co. continued as consulting and factory engineers at 34 Argyll Arcade however most of their work was outside the football arena due to a lack of opportunity. David Mills Duncan was Leitch's chief draughtsman but left the company and set up in business on his own thus the firm of Duncan & Kerr, consulting engineers, traded at 137 West Campbell Street, Glasgow in 1927-28. It should be remembered that four other clubs played in the city viz. (1) Partick Thistle who were formed in 1876 and moved to Firhill Park in 1909 (2) Clyde who were formed at Rutherglen in 1878 and moved to Shawfield beside the river in 1898. They left the ground in 1986 and spent four seasons at Firhill Park and moved to Cumbernauld in 1990 (3) Third Lanark who were founder members of the League in 1890 and moved to New Cathkin Park in 1903 - they remained there until their demise in 1967 (4) Queen's Park F.C. who were formed in 1867 have already been treated.

David Mills Duncan built the Main Stand for Partick Thistle F.C. in 1927 and this was constructed in the style of Leitch with a central angular gable whilst the remainder of the ground was an oval of open terracing. It was then used for a Scotland v Ireland international in 1928 and there was a record crowd of 54,728. Ibrox Park, meanwhile, was a huge open arena in the 1920s with a basic wooden stand on the south side and a double cover on the north side. The club approached Leitch's company in 1928 and they built a new South Stand but on a completely different scale to his other works of the period. It seems likely that his son made his mark on the company and possibly took charge of this grand project. The new stand was built on Sheildhall Road (later Edmiston Drive) and was similar in style to that of Fulham but was four times the size. The exterior was of red brick and had numerous doors and arches at the base as in a mews, a lower tier of plain windows throughout the length, tall rounded headed windows above, whilst at the top was a cornice and banding. The central section was especially grand with the name Rangers F.C. at the top (blue on white) and had a main round arch, and window pediments either side. There was a grand entrance with balcony above and inside was a mosaic floor with motifs, marble and wood panelling, and a moulded ceiling. The wings had pediment features and a gold lion (rampant) emblem on blue with a scroll motto "1873 ready 1928" - the whole being like the façade of a stately home. The stand was just as impressive inside and had seating for 10,000 spectators and the trademark criss-cross balcony and central oblong pediment stating Rangers F.C. The work was well under way when Leitch had to return to England.

John Robert Easton (1873-1959) was born at Gateshead and married Catherine Keenlyside at Tynemouth in September 1897 and had sons Robert William in March 1902 and John Keenlyside in June 1908. The family moved south and John Robert Easton a company secretary lived at 103 Fox Lane, Palmers Green from 1920-59. The house was just a short distance from "Bourneside" and there may have been a business connection. Robert William Easton bank clerk of 101 Oakley

South Stand, Ibrox Stadium. Built by Leitch - "Ready" 1928.

Street, Chelsea married Jessie Hardie Leitch of 103 Fox Lane at St. Columba's Church, Pont Street on 6 October 1928 - her father an architect. The ceremony was Church of Scotland or Presbyterian and the witnesses John R. Easton, Archibald Leitch and J. Macara Gardner (the church was rebuilt in 1950).

The Grand Façade. The entrance had mosaic, marble and wood panelling.

Archibald Leitch built a magnificent stand at Ibrox Park and it was opened soon after on 1 January 1929 and with the extensive terraces could hold very large crowds. Indeed the record League attendance at a British ground of 118,567 was set against Celtic on 2 January 1939. There was, however, always a problem with large numbers of people standing in a ground and there was a disaster at Ibrox Park in 1971. There were many deaths and the club wanted to put this behind them and cleared the old earth embankments thus the oval shape of the ground dating from the 19th century was lost. New stands were built at each end in 1978 and on the north side in 1980 however Leitch's structure with 10,000 seats and a paddock for 9,000 (standing) was central to the plan. The ground was further upgraded as Ibrox Stadium in 1990-94 and a third tier was added to Leitch's stand and new art deco stairways erected at either end. To accomplish this a beam-supported roof was raised over the structure and the ground was then all seated. The South Stand at Ibrox is a fitting monument to Leitch especially as he was born in Glasgow in 1865 and began his company there in 1895. There was much competition between the clubs, as in the early years, and Celtic did not want to get left behind. James Grant the club director built the South Stand at Celtic Park in 1898 and the remainder of the ground was a vast curving terrace. Duncan & Kerr built a new stand in the Leitch style with 4,800 seats and a central roof gable in 1929 whilst D. Mills Duncan & Co. drawing, tracing and photo-printing were at 70 Wellington Street, Glasgow in 1931-32. The record attendance at Parkhead of 83,500 (or 92,000) was during a game against Rangers on 1 January 1938 - the front terrace of the stand was converted to seating and a new roof erected in 1971 and this was the last part of the ground redeveloped after 1995.

Sunderland joined the Football League in 1890 and had much success in their early years with a number of famous players such as Charlie Buchan. They were League champions in 1892, 1893, 1895 and 1902 and Leitch built the Roker End in 1911 whilst they won the League and were Cup runners-up in 1913. The Fulwell End was extended in 1925 to give the ground a capacity of 60,000 and Leitch built a new Main Stand on the east side of the ground in 1929. The work at Rangers put the company back on track again and the stand was of an attractive design and cost the club £25,000. The constraints on space resulted in a two-tier stand with criss-cross steelwork on the balcony (the Leitch trademark) and 5,875 seats in the upper tier and two areas of terrace below. The record attendance of 75,118 was during an F.A. Cup game against Derby County in March 1933 whilst the club won the League in 1936 and the F.A. Cup in 1937. Indeed the club were only relegated to Division Two in 1957-58 after 68 years in the top flight. The Main Stand was gradually altered and the upper paddock converted to seating after the Second War and offices added to the outside, in 1966, to prepare the ground for World Cup games - executive boxes were installed in 1973. This was an atmospheric venue with the famous "Roker Roar" and the main features were Leitch's stand and the large Fulwell and Roker End terraces. The stand remained a good architectural feature at the ground until the club departed for the Stadium of Light in 1997, and Leitch's stands clearly stood the test of time.

Archibald Leitch left "Bourneside", Southgate in 1928 and there is a gap in the records until 1930 - he may have lived in a rented property or perhaps failed to register his address in a directory. Indeed he then adopted a new lifestyle and lived at 99 Barkston Gardens, Kensington opposite Earl's Court Underground Station in 1930-34. This was at the southwest corner of a London square with central lawn and was a "city mansion" popular at the time (basically an early flat built in the grand style). The residence was part of numbers 83-101 and had a notable entrance with marble columns and Classical portico forming the porch. The hallway had carved wood panelling, a moulded plaster ceiling and opulent brass handrails on the stairs - the interiors were no doubt equally plush. Archibald Leitch was aged 65 and close to retirement in 1930 and his son came to the fore and was responsible for the day-to-day affairs and later works of the partnership, with his father as a guiding influence in the background. There was a final change of offices and the business moved a short distance thus Archibald Leitch (& Partners) traded at 66 Victoria Street from 1930-55. The addition of the term 'and partners' supports a change of structure within the business, however this did not signify the end and there was still important work to do (see below). Archibald Leitch consulting engineer and architect of 99 Barkston Gardens made his last will on 4 June 1931. He had already dealt with the business under the Articles of Partnership (1927) and left all his real and personal estate to Jessie Hardie Leitch his wife. The witnesses were G.F. Braddock Civil Servant and Mary Braddock of 33 Rylett Road, Shepherd's Bush.

Archibald Leitch built the Waterloo Road Stand at Molineux in 1925 and soon after the North Terrace was re-aligned with the pitch and the massive South Bank was raised to a depth of 50-yards. Leitch was then called back to the ground in 1932 to tackle the final side that backed on to Molineux Street. This presented a considerable problem as the site tapered almost to a point at the north end, however Leitch built a stand with seven gabled roof sections that became a trademark of the Molineux ground. This was the last of his multi-span roofs and had seats for 3,450 and a paddock area for 4,500 spectators. Stands could still be built for the price of a car today and the Molineux Street Stand cost only £20,000. The company returned to Wolves in 1935 and built a new façade for the Waterloo Road Stand that gave improved access to the upper tier.

The club then had a strange story being one of the strongest teams in the country after the Second War and U.E.F.A. Cup Finalists in 1972, however the ground at Molineux became a curse and nearly brought the club to its knees. The Molineux Street Stand was found to be unsafe in 1975 and the structure failed after 43 years. It was then demolished and following some unlikely dealings at the local Council the 71 Victorian houses that stood behind were also knocked down. The John Ireland Stand replaced these and was built with the future in mind being 30-yards from the existing pitch. This was a two-tier cantilevered stand of modern materials and cost £2 million and was opened in 1979 - that's inflation for you! The four sides of the ground then stood around a "square" of grass with the pitch to one side in front of the South Bank. The club, however, then had an alarming slump and fell from Division One in 1984 to Division Four in 1986 whilst the North Bank terrace and Waterloo Road Stand were closed as unsafe in 1985. The future looked very bleak however Sir Jack Hayward saved the club in 1991 and it was only then that the rest of the ground was redeveloped and the Waterloo Road Stand was demolished in 1992 - it was still used as offices and changing rooms up to this time.

There was considerable family hardship through the years and Agnes MacGregor Leitch died of tuberculosis or consumption at 99 Barkston Gardens on 21 November 1933 aged 29 years - her father a consulting engineer. This was a common affliction at the time and A.K. Leitch her brother of 99 Barkston Gardens was the informant. Leitch returned to White Hart Lane in 1934 having already built on three sides of the ground. The East Terrace was still uncovered at this point and the club made plans to develop it. At this time Paxton Road continued south behind the terrace and the club bought up all the houses located behind and re-housed the occupants, then employed Leitch to build a colossal stand on the site. This was narrow and high at each end with an austere brick façade backing onto the road, and had two-tiers with seating for 5,100 in the upper tier and standing for 11,000 in the lower tier - the latter became a feature of the ground known as "The Shelf". There was a further paddock for 8,000 standing spectators in front of the stand making the total capacity 24,100 (today this is the capacity of a whole ground). The balcony had the familiar Leitch ironwork although in this case there were blue struts, as oppose to criss-cross, on a white background. The stand had an elongated roof gable with the club emblem on it although its main purpose was to house the press box and the total cost of the stand was £60,000. The stand was opened in September 1934 however the family loss must have diminished some of Leitch's professional satisfaction. There was not much to report at first since Tottenham were relegated to Division Two in 1935 however the record attendance of 75,038 was during an F.A. Cup game against Sunderland in March 1938. The glory days followed with the League title in 1951 and the "Double" in 1961 and the ground remained unchanged for 46 years. The Main Stand was replaced in 1980 and the East Stand was refurbished and given a new roof supported by columns in 1989 - the rear wall was not strong enough to take cantilevering. Leitch's stand then took its place in the modern White Hart Lane that was developed after 1995.

The family then left Barkston Gardens and moved back to the suburbs, again in the direction of Southgate, but this time at the end of the Piccadilly line. Cockfosters was developed after the Underground arrived in 1931 and the first houses were built in Belmont Avenue in 1932 (numbers 1-29). Archibald Leitch moved to 113 Belmont Avenue, Cockfosters, East Barnet, in 1935 when the road was just being completed. This was a brand new semi-detached property at the top of the hill and had a notable position being angled in relation to the road. Leitch called his new home "Braehead" and it was clearly meant for his retirement being quite a humble residence for a person of distinction and achievement. It is not clear if he designed the house however it would be no surprise if he did. The house was red brick with a white washed upper-storey, a bow front window and open porch, but the most notable feature was a Tudor-style gable at roof level (the Leitch trademark). His daughter Jessie and her husband R.W. Easton lived at 21 Greenwood Gardens, Palmers Green in 1929-31 but moved to "Glenview", 19 Mount Pleasant, Cockfosters, in 1935. Indeed the family remained close since the latter property was just two doors away from "Braehead".

Leitch's company continued the connection with Fulham and put forward plans to redevelop the Riverside Terrace in 1935 however the club declined - due to a lack of funds at the time. Sunderland won the League title after finishing eight points ahead of Derby County in 1936 and then invited Leitch back to the ground (he had built the Roker End in 1911 and Main Stand in 1929). The latter faced the Clock Stand terrace on the west side that was erected in 1898 and required urgent attention. Leitch replaced this with a basic pitch-roofed structure in 1936. The rear consisted of wooden steps on steel supports and had standing for 15,500 spectators, thus Leitch's company was responsible for three sides of Roker Park. There was then more work in Scotland and Leitch returned to Hampden Park where it all began back in 1900 and designed the North Stand at Hampden Park in 1937. This was built at the rear of the terrace and faced the Main Stand and was a modest structure with 4,500 seats however it brought the capacity to 150,000! The record attendance at Hampden Park was 149,415 during an international v England on 17 April 1937. This was the largest ever attendance at a British football ground and can be compared to an official 126,047 seen at Wembley in 1923, however there were often inaccuracies in these records.

Hampden Park, meanwhile, was in a poor state of repair by the 1970s and something needed to be done but it was difficult to find a way forward especially as amateurs Queen's Park owned the ground. A number of plans failed to materialize however the first stage of redevelopment began in 1981 and unlike at other venues the oval shape was retained. The North Stand was demolished and the terraces concreted in 1981-86 and the capacity was still nearly 75,000. There were plans to cover the two end terraces and install more seats but this all changed after the Taylor Report came out in 1990. The ground was then closed and there were further developments from 1992-94 and the refurbished Hampden was re-opened with a capacity of just 37,000. The ground was all seated and had new roofs on the north and east sides, but the South Stand and the west terrace with its banking still remained. The ground was dated despite much work and included the two stands built in 1903 and the replacement pavilion built in 1914 (south side). The final stage of rebuilding took place after 1995 and involved the re-roofing of the West Stand and a new South Stand. The funds for the work came from the Millennium Project Community Lottery and the South Stand includes offices of the Scottish F.A., League, Premier and Scottish Football Museum. The only trace of Leitch's old ground is banking at the east end.

The story of Archibald Leitch now draws to a close and the company's last ground construction was for Everton at Goodison Park. Leitch had built the Main and Park End Stands in 1907 and the elaborate Bullens Road Stand in 1926 and returned to the ground in 1938. His company then built a two-tier stand at the Gladwys Street End that curved around the northeast corner and joined up with the Bullens Road Stand (the two stands matched one another). This had an upper tier of seating over a terrace and again included a criss-cross ironwork balcony, however the costs had increased with time and Everton were charged £50,000 for one stand (the whole of Ayresome Park cost £11,000 in 1903). Goodison Park then had two-tier stands on all four sides of the ground and Archibald Leitch & Partners had designed and built all four of them - in some quarters it was dubbed 'Toffeeopolis'. This notable achievement was soon recognised and George VI and Queen Elizabeth visited the completed ground later in 1938 - this was a very proud moment for Archibald Leitch and the apex of his career. The club won the League in 1938-39 finishing four points ahead of Wolves and the record attendance was 78,299 against Liverpool in the First Division on 18 September 1948, whilst the ground hosted five 'World Cup' games in 1966. The Main Stand was demolished in 1969-70 however the Bullens Road Stand was re-roofed in 1972 and also the Gladwys Street End in 1986. The Park End Stand was demolished in 1994 and replaced with a modern stand and the ground was all seated however Leitch's remaining stands lasted into the new century.

Archibald Kent Leitch (47) consulting engineer of "Braehead", Belmont Avenue, Barnet married Muriel Elizabeth Nellie Ingram (31) of 30 Dysart Avenue, Kingston at Ham Parish Church on the banks of the Thames on 27 August 1938. The witnesses to the wedding were Archibald Leitch, R.W. Easton and E.R. Purchase. Indeed his father was then a consulting engineer and despite his age was still involved in the business. The bride was born at Edmonton on 18 June 1901 and was the daughter of James Alexander Ingram (deceased) a master baker and confectioner. Archibald Kent Leitch moved to some new flats at 58 Stamford Court, Goldhawk Road near Hammersmith in 1939 and remained there for the rest of his life. These changes witnessed the end of ground building for the Leitch family and also for the country in general, there being just three grounds constructed after the Second War viz. Hull City, Port Vale and Southend United. Archibald Leitch was ill by this time and died of heart disease and diabetes at "Braehead", Belmont Avenue on 25 April 1939 just two days before his 74th birthday. He died in relative obscurity and was an unsung hero of British football and his widow Jessie Hardie Leitch proved his will in Liverpool on 11 August 1939 and his estate was valued at £17,221 16s 5d - the solicitors were Cuff, Roberts & Co. of Liverpool. This was the end of an era and the offices at 34 Argyll Arcade, Glasgow were closed in 1939 and his son then operated the business in London.

Jessie Hardie Leitch continued to live at "Braehead" and wrote her last will there on 29 March 1949 and made Archibald Kent Leitch and Jessie Hardie Easton her executors. She left several legacies and to her son, "the silver salver presented to my late husband with the signatures of the donors engraved thereon," and to her sister-in-law Margaret MacGregor Leitch an annuity of £70 p.a. She then discussed the implications of Clause 20b of the Articles of Partnership (1927), which made provisions for an annuity to be paid to her daughter and herself from the business. The will was witnessed at her solicitors at 63-65 Baker Street, London. Jessie Hardie Leitch died at "Braehead" on 4 April 1950, aged 83, and probate was granted to Archibald Kent Leitch of 66 Victoria Street and Jessie Hardie Easton of "Glenview", 19 Mount Pleasant. Her son continued to run the business as "Archibald Leitch & Partners" at 66 Victoria Street, Westminster but did no further work at football grounds. The company had proposed a scheme to develop the Riverside Terrace at Fulham at a cost of £11,200 in 1935 and put forward a further plan in 1950 however the cost had escalated to £40,000. Fulham declined yet again but should have stayed with Leitch and when they built the Riverside Stand in 1971-72 the final bill was £334,000.

Archibald Kent Leitch retired in 1955 and the company was closed down and it seems unlikely that it continued in any form. Indeed Archibald Leitch and his son were the heart and soul of the business and it was in existence for exactly 60 years. The period witnessed the evolution of football grounds and the society that supported them, and indeed the Victorian world of Glasgow in 1895 was far removed from that of London in 1955. Archibald Kent Leitch died at 58 Stamford Court, Hammersmith on 2 April 1972 and as he had no children this was the end of the line. "Etruria House", Barkston Gardens and "Braehead" all exist in London today however there is no blue plaque at these locations to: "Archibald Leitch football ground designer." He came from a humble background to live in considerable style and the first of these properties epitomises his success. Only a few examples of Leitch's work still survive and since the Taylor Report in 1990 many have rapidly disappeared - the need for all seated stadiums meant they were redundant. The most recent losses include:

1902-94 John Street Stand, Sheffield United

1903-95 Ayresome Park, Middlesbrough

1905-97 Stamford Bridge terracing, Chelsea

1906-94 The Kop, Liverpool

1907-94 Park End Stand, Everton

1910-94 Leeds Road, Huddersfield

1910-93 The Den, Millwall

1911-97 Roker Park (End), Sunderland

1913-92 The North Bank, Arsenal

1925-92 Waterloo Road Stand, Wolves

1928-01 The Dell, Southampton

This was like a list of old-friends who are no longer with us but after the Hillsborough tragedy, changes were essential, and the Taylor Report highlighted how the grounds needed to be improved - crumbling terraces and ageing stands were no longer adequate in the modern age and the days of the Leitch grounds were over. Despite this a few examples of his work remain although some are altered beyond recognition. His stands were most enduring and the best examples are detailed below, but with many clubs relocating some of these may soon disappear. The Main Stand and Pavilion at Craven Cottage, Fulham were still in use at the time of writing and are a most important example of his work. They are little changed from when he built them back in 1905 and being one of his oldest works it is strange how they survived (due to the club's position in the lower Leagues and listed status). The South Stand at Ibrox Stadium is the second important example and although extended and refurbished in 1990-94 still retains the complete façade that Leitch designed in 1928 - indeed the ground regularly hosts top European football. It seems likely these two examples of his work will survive for the foreseeable future and will be his legacy to British soccer. His contribution to football history was immense yet it is un-acknowledged and most of his stands are a distant memory. Leitch, however, was not the whole story and some unusual features of early clubs and grounds are discussed in the next three chapters:

1905 Main Stand and Pavilion, Fulham (repaired 1999)
1906 Main Stand, Anfield, Liverpool (re-roofed 1970)
1914 Main Stand, Sheffield Wednesday (altered 1992-96)
1924 Main Stand, Crystal Palace (only externally altered)
1925 South Stand, Portsmouth (seated 1996)
1926 Bullens Road Stand, Everton (re-roofed 1972)
1928 South Stand, Ibrox Stadium, Glasgow (altered 1994)
1934 East Stand, Tottenham (re-roofed 1989)
1938 Gladwys Street End, Everton (re-roofed 1986)

"The Glory Days". Craven Cottage is one of the few Leitch 'survivors'.

CHAPTER 18

It's Not Cricket

It seems strange today that professional football grounds could be accommodated with cricket grounds, however this is exactly what happened in the past and it was a common practice for the newly emerging clubs to use existing cricket grounds - indeed many had their origins in cricket clubs. There are numerous examples of such ground sharing and none are more significant than the Oval, which was home to the Wanderers and used for F.A. Cup Finals. A number of clubs in the south played at cricket venues such as Brentford, Leyton Orient, Queens Park Rangers and Wimbledon in London. A local rowing club formed Brentford F.C. in 1889 and they played at Boston Park Cricket Ground in York Road in 1900 and moved to Griffin Park in 1904. The Glyn Cricket Club was formed at Homerton Theological College in 1881 and their members played football in the winter and formed the Orient in 1888. The club played at Glyn Road and changed their name to Clapton Orient in 1898 and moved to Millfields Road and to Brisbane Road in 1937 becoming Leyton Orient in 1946 (see Ch. 17). Queens Park Rangers who are discussed later played at Kilburn Cricket Ground from 1892-96. Wimbledon Old Centrals formed in 1889, then played at Malden Wanderers Cricket Ground and became Wimbledon F.C. in 1905 and moved to Plough Lane in 1912 (now Milton Keynes F.C.).

Other examples along the south coast of England are Brighton, Southampton and Torquay. Brighton United played at the Sussex County Cricket Ground from 1898 and they were in the Southern League Division One in 1898-99. Brighton and Hove Rangers replaced them in 1900 and adopted the name Brighton and Hove Albion in 1901 - they played at Home Farm, Withdean. The team also played at Sussex County Cricket Ground whilst John Clark a former director of Brighton United developed the Goldstone Ground and the club were sole occupants there by 1904. They left the Goldstone Ground in May 1997 but returned to their roots at Withdean Athletic Stadium. St. Mary's Southampton Y.M.C.A. F.C. was formed in 1885 and played next to the County Cricket Ground on Northlands Road then at Avenue Road, however this had a public footpath across it. They moved to the Antelope Cricket Ground in 1886 (home to Hampshire C.C.C. in 1863-85) whilst the County Cricket Ground was opened in 1885 and a new pavilion built in 1896. This was a well-developed venue and the football club returned to play there in 1896, became Southampton F.C. in 1897 and moved to the Dell in 1898 - they returned to their roots at St. Mary's Stadium in 2001. Old boys from Torquay and Torbay Colleges formed Torquay United whilst they listened to a band in the Princess Gardens in 1898. They played initially on Teignmouth Road and moved to Torquay Recreation Ground in 1900-05, which was used for rugby and cricket after they left. The club then played at Cricketfield Road near Teignmouth Road and the nearby Torquay Cricket Ground in 1907-10. Ellacombe F.C. merged with Torquay United in 1910 and moved up-town to Plainmoor and were renamed Torquay Town, but merged with Babbacombe F.C. to become United again in 1921.

There are several other clubs of interest in the south. Bristol had a number of professional clubs at the end of the 19th century however the town could not support them all. Bristol South End formed in 1894 and played at St. John's Lane, Bedminster but the venue was overlooked by a hill and canvas sheeting was used to obscure the view of onlookers (possibly sails from ships) - they became professional and were renamed Bristol City in 1897. The nearby team of Bedminster was formed in 1887 and played at Ashton Gate from 1896 although the venue was located to the east and a cricket pitch occupied the current ground. This was used for a Gloucester v Somerset cricket match in 1897 and the game featured an appearance by cricketer W.G. Grace. Indeed Bristol City played at Bedminster and Bedminster at Bristol City? In fact both teams played in the Southern League Division One in 1898-1900 but had merged by 1900 - it could be said that Bristol City had played against themselves. The club were elected to the League as one of the first southern teams in 1901 and only Woolwich Arsenal (1893) and Luton Town (1897) preceded them. They kept both grounds and St. John's Lane was the registered venue in 1901 but they went to Ashton Gate in 1904 and moved the pitch to its present position.

Cheltenham F.C. was founded in 1892 although there was an unofficial match v Gloucester in 1884. The club were champions of the Mid-Gloucester League in 1896-97 and played at Grafton Cricket Ground and also played friendly games on a Wednesday afternoon at a local cricket ground. They moved to

Whaddon Road in 1901 however their record attendance of 10,389 was at Cheltenham Athletic Ground during an F.A. Cup third round tie in 1934. Reading F.C. was founded in 1871 (see club crest) and thus they are the oldest League club south of Nottingham. They played at Reading Recreation Ground to the east of the town in Kings Meadow and moved nearby to Reading Cricket Ground in 1877 (and merged with Reading Hornets). They took part in the F.A. Cup as early as 1878-79 and played at Coley Park on the other side of town in 1882-89. They merged with Earley F.C. and went to Caversham Cricket Ground in 1889 but the venue could only be reached from Reading by ferry. This was not practical and there were cries of, "Hold the game the boat hasn't arrived!" The club were founder members of the Southern League in 1894 and found a new ground at Elm Park in 1896. Rev. William Pitt formed a football club as an offshoot of Spartans Cricket Club in Swindon in 1881 that merged with St. Mark's Friendly Society and became Swindon Town F.C. in 1883. They played at the Quarry Ground and Glebe Field then moved to the Croft, Devizes Road in 1884. They were founder members of the Southern League in 1894 and required an improved venue and relocated to the "first" County Ground in 1895. This was situated at the present County Cricket Ground and the current pavilion may have been there at the time - the club moved next door to their present ground in 1896.

Watford Rovers formed in 1881 and were invited to use the West Herts Sports Ground in 1890. This had been laid out on eight acres of farmland to stage various sporting events however one condition of the tenancy was to take the name West Herts F.C. The club agreed and moved there in 1891 and the ground became known as Cassio Road and had a cricket pavilion and some basic banking. There was a merger with Watford St. Mary's in 1898 and the club then became Watford F.C. and were founder members of Division Three in 1920. A crowd of 13,000 arrived to watch a derby game against Luton in 1921 and the ground was severely tested thus they moved to the more spacious Vicarage Road in 1922. There are also examples of this dual arrangement at non-League venues. For instance, Clarence Park in St. Albans is next to the cricket ground and its old pavilion and once had an 'old' oak tree growing out of the end terrace, however this was recently removed during ground 'improvements'. The Crabble in Dover is a variation on a theme and is located 1½-miles inland from the town at a place called River and is built into the side of a hill. The football pitch is situated above the cricket pitch and a number of versions of Dover F.C. have come and gone. The current club were formed in 1983 and played in the Conference, whilst Margate F.C. also used the ground.

There were similar ground arrangements in the Midlands and the north of England viz. Accrington, Blackburn and Manchester City (already discussed) however there are other good examples. Some old boys of Wyggeston School founded Leicester Fosse in a house near the Roman "Fosse Way" in 1884. The club had a number of early grounds and played some games at Aylestone Road Cricket Ground and moved to Filbert Street in 1891 and entered the League in 1894. They became Leicester City in 1919 and dropped the nickname of "The Fossils", which did not give the right image. The story in Mansfield was more complicated and a number of clubs were involved in the saga. Field Mill was built on Quarry Lane, Mansfield in 1797 and produced cotton, whilst Greenhalgh Cricket Club played at the nearby Field Mill ground from 1840 and Greenhalgh F.C. was established there in 1861. This is one of the oldest soccer venues in the world and just one year younger than Sandygate in Sheffield (1860) - home of Hallam. The Mansfield Wesleyans Boys Brigade began playing soccer in 1891 or 1897 and played at two public venues, namely Windsor Road and St. Peter's Way then moved to a ground at Newgate Lane in 1903. Mansfield Town Cricket Club used the latter from 1840-94 and then moved to Field Mill, whilst Mansfield Town F.C. formed in 1871 and played at Newgate Lane until 1894, then merged with Greenhalgh F.C. to form Mansfield F.C. and played at Stanhope Street (St. Peter's Way). The cricket club then used Field Mill but shared it with Mansfield Amateurs and later with Mansfield Mechanics from 1912. The Wesleyans, meanwhile, became the current Mansfield Town in 1910 and moved to a rough pitch "The Prairie" in 1912 and to Field Mill in 1919. They developed the ground after the cricket club departed in 1922 and won the Midland League in 1924, 1925 and 1929, and thus were elected to Division Three (South) in 1931.

The stories of the two Nottingham clubs are closely entwined and strangely Notts County play at Meadow Lane in the City and Nottingham Forest play at the City Ground in the County. This is a confusing situation that mirrors the club histories. Nottingham Forest F.C. is one of the oldest clubs in the world and they were initially based at the Forest Recreation Ground at the centre of a racecourse - site of the annual Goose Fair. Their members first played a form of hockey but became the Forest F.C. and played football from 1865. Red caps and shirts were purchased and they were known as the Garibaldi Reds after a troop of soldiers. They moved to the Meadows Cricket Ground (Queen's Walk Recreation

Ground) in 1879. The Meadows was an area of common land outside the limits of the old town and ancient laws dictated that it could not be used, leading to overcrowding in the narrow streets and alleys and great hardship for the people of Nottingham. These laws changed in the 19th century and the land was then available for the expansion of housing and also for sport. This was a successful time for the club and they reached two F.A. Cup semi-finals: 1879 - lost 2-1 to the Old Etonians; 1880 - lost 1-0 to Oxford University.

The club played at Trent Bridge Cricket Ground, which was the most developed sports venue in the town, in 1880-82, but then moved to the Lenton district on Derby Road and had two adjacent sites: Parkside (1882-85) and the Gregory Ground (1885-90). The club reached the Cup semi-final in 1885 but lost 3-0 to Queen's Park (after 1-1) and became professional and joined the Football Alliance in 1889. The Gregory Ground was an unpopular out-of-town venue thus they moved to Woodward's Field next to Trent Bridge and renamed it the Town Ground in 1890. They spent three seasons in the Football Alliance and reached the F.A. Cup semi-final for a fourth time in 1892 - they were determined to win and drew 1-1 (twice) but finally lost to West Bromwich 6-2. They were elected to Division One when it was reorganised in 1892 and won the F.A. Cup 3-1 against Derby County in 1898, and continued to play at the Town Ground but it was a limited site and they moved across the River Trent to the City Ground in 1898. Notts County were already discussed in Chapter 11 but their story is worth reiterating as the movements of Forest dictated their own. They are the oldest League club being formed in 1862 and had many cricket connections viz. Meadows Cricket Ground (1864-77), Notts Cricket Ground (1877-78), Meadows Cricket Ground (1878-79), Trent Bridge Cricket Ground (1879-80), Castle Cricket Ground (1880-83) and Trent Bridge Cricket Ground (1883-1910) - indeed where would football in Nottingham be without the help of cricket.

There are other northern clubs associated with cricket grounds and these are now considered. Crewe Alexandra is a relatively small club known as the railwaymen yet they featured in the League at an early date before the arrival of Arsenal, Liverpool and Newcastle. The Alexandra Athletic Club, Crewe was formed in 1866 and their ground was south of Earle Street between the London & North Western and Crewe & Manchester Railways. The club received its name from Princess Alexandra of Denmark who married the Prince of Wales (later Edward VII), in 1863. The main access was along Rainbow Street and there was an oval stadium with raised banking around it and a stand and pavilion on the south side. Some rail workers started to play cricket and rugby at the ground and formed a football team in 1877 and moved to Alexandra Recreation Ground on Nantwich Road - near to Gresty Road and the railway station. Aston Villa played Rangers there in an F.A. Cup semi-final in 1887 and the score was 3-1 - this was the last time a Scottish team entered the competition. Crewe F.C. reached the semi-final themselves in 1888 but lost 4-0 to Preston North End and played in the League from 1892-96. After losing their League status they played at Edleston Road and Old Sheds Field then returned to Alexandra Recreation Ground in 1897. Crewe Station was then expanded and they were forced to move to Gresty Road just to the west, in 1906, and were founder members of Division Three (North) in 1921.

Gainsborough Trinity played in the League from 1896 to 1912 and their highest position was sixth in Division Two in 1904-05. They were based at the Northolme Ground, which was also the town's cricket ground, however unlike Crewe they did not regain their League status and played non-League football since then. There was a story, meanwhile, developing in Rotherham that was reminiscent of that in Mansfield. Thornhill F.C. were formed in 1882 and played at the Red House Ground and became Rotherham County in 1905 and moved to Millmoor in 1907. Their rivals Rotherham Town played at Clifton Lane Cricket Ground next to the racecourse with its grandstand in 1882. They moved a short distance and laid out an enclosed pitch on a field south of Clifton Grove (with its houses and large gardens) and between St. James's Church and Middle Lane, in 1891. 'Clifton Grove' had one entrance in Middle Lane and a covered stand on the north side and an open stand on the east, and the club played League football there in 1893-96 however then folded up. A new club Rotherham F.C. was formed at Clifton Lane Cricket Ground in 1899 and became a new Rotherham Town in 1905. County were elected to Division Two at Millmoor in 1919 but finished bottom of Division Three (North) in 1924-25 and merged with Rotherham Town who were also struggling to form Rotherham United. There were cricket connections to the west and Heaton Norris Rovers formed in 1883 and played at Heaton Norris Wanderers Cricket Ground in 1884. The club merged with Heaton Norris F.C. in 1885 and changed venue almost every season but took an enclosed ground at Green Lane in 1889 and became Stockport County in 1890. This was in a rural area surrounded by fields and only took 4,000 spectators thus the club moved to Edgeley Park in 1902. Another case was Stoke F.C. who had a number of early sites and played at the County

Cricket Ground (see Ch. 11). Indeed most of these are long consigned to history but others such as the cricket ground next to Turf Moor are still there - Burnley C.C. played there since February 1883. Many of these examples are of considerable interest however the best five are detailed below.

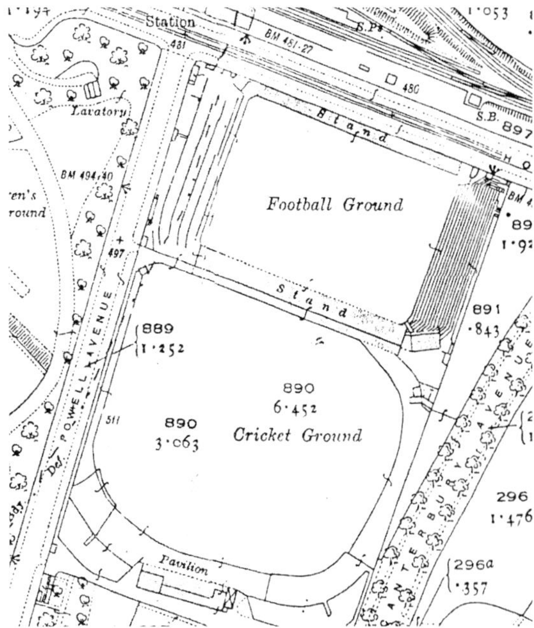

Park Avenue, Bradford - O.S. Map 1932.
League football in 1908-70.

Bradford Rugby Club formed Bradford F.C. at Park Avenue in 1907 with the aim of challenging Bradford City (formed 1903). Their ground was in the southwest of the town between Horton Park Avenue to the north and a cricket pitch and pavilion to the south. Horton Park with its lakes, bowling greens, tennis courts and bandstand was to the west and Canterbury Avenue and Horton Villa to the east. There was good access to the ground with several tramways to the north and a station of the Bradford and Holmfield L.N.E.R. line just outside the ground. Archibald Leitch, as stated, developed the venue with narrow stands on both sides and substantial banking at each end. The club played in Southern League Division One in 1907-08 however they were elected to the Football League with Tottenham Hotspur in 1908. The clubs replaced Lincoln City and Stoke (who resigned) and the latter was then admitted to the Southern League. Indeed both Bradford and Stoke were invited to join their southern opponents with the aim of raising the profile of that league, and to keep the numbers up (after all they were northern clubs). Bradford Park Avenue or the Stans finished as runners-up to Notts County in Division Two in 1913-14 and then had three seasons in Division One viz. 9th in 1914-15, 11th in 1919-20 and 22nd in 1920-21. The club were relegated to Division Three (North) in 1921-22 and became the first team to suffer two consecutive relegations.

They were champions of Division Three (North) in 1927-28 with 101 goals in the season and finished third in Division Two in 1928-29. Indeed the club were one of the strongest teams at that level in the 1930s and Len Shackleton and Ron Greenwood played for them in the 1940s (the latter was England manager in 1977-82). They were relegated again in 1949-50 and had two applicants for the manager's job in 1953 - the position went to Norman Kirkman however it was Bill Shankly who was rejected. This may have been a bad decision and the club went into a terminal decline and were playing in Division Four with Bradford City by 1963. They had to seek re-election in 1967, 1968, 1969 and 1970 and finished bottom in their last three seasons and lost their League status in 1970 - Cambridge United replaced them. The club tried to carry on and played at Valley Parade in 1973-74 but like Accrington and Third Lanark went out of existence in 1974. The Park Avenue stands were demolished in 1980 and only part of the crumbling terrace remained. When they folded-up they were one win ahead of Bradford City in League fixtures and perhaps one day the contest will resume.

Darlington Cricket Club rented a field south of the town from John Beaumont Pease a Quaker and owner of Feethams House in 1866. The new ground was called Feethams and was used for football from these early days whilst Darlington F.C. was formed at the local grammar school in 1883. The cricket pitch was next to the League football ground for well over a century and became the last surviving example of such an arrangement. The cricket pavilion was built at the northwest corner in 1906 and a notable gateway entrance with two towers and turnstiles was erected in 1913. The football ground was located to the south and the main access was via the cricket pitch itself. A Main Stand was built on the east side of the football ground in 1914-19 and a Kop terrace at the south end. These were supplemented with a small stand on the west side of the ground from 1925-27 and a low cover at the Cricket Field End in 1960. The club were initially a successful amateur side and played in the Cup as early as 1885-86 but lost 6-0 to Grimsby. They played in the Northern League from 1889 being champions in 1896 and 1900, then became professional and joined the N.E. League in 1908. They made the last sixteen of the F.A. Cup in 1910-11 and beat Sheffield United of the First Division en route and were founder members of Division Three

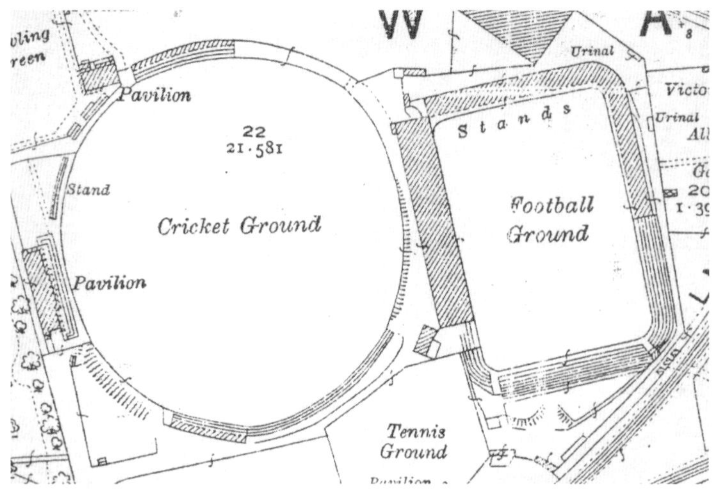

The Circle, Hull - O.S. Map 1928. League football in 1906-46 and again . . .

(North) in 1921. There were few changes except the Main Stand was replaced after a fire and it survived into the new millennium. Feethams was in a leafy suburb of Darlington next to the River Skerne, near Bank Top Station, and was a ground of yesteryear. The club moved to the purpose built George Reynolds Arena in 2003 (capacity 8,500).

Kingston upon Hull is just north of Gainsborough and this was a city where rugby was the dominant sport thus Hull City F.C. were not formed until 1904. They have a dubious record: namely the club from the largest city not to have played in the 'top' division. The club entered the F.A. Cup in 1904 and joined the League in 1905 and their first ground was the Boulevard home of Hull Rugby League Club. The arrangement did not work well and they had to play a Cup game away when the fixture coincided with a rugby match. They played a few games at Dairycoates used by amateurs Hull City in 1902-03, but then sought a more permanent venue and moved to the Circle, Anlaby Road home of Hull Cricket Club in 1906. The football ground was laid out east of the cricket pitch although they played some games back at the Boulevard until February 1907. The club then came 'very close' and were third in Division Two in 1909-10 and only missed promotion by goal difference. City developed the ground and built a 4,000 seat Main Stand next to the cricket pitch in 1914 and erected covers over the three terraces in the 1920s. It lay between the Hull & Scarborough Railway and the Anlaby Loop (L.N.E.R.), whilst to the west was the main cricket ground with two pavilions, two other cricket grounds to north and south, a bowling green, a tennis ground, and also the extensive West Park with its lake and bandstand - a real sporting Mecca. The club then had a good Cup run and the record attendance at Anlaby Road of 32,930 was in March 1930 - they reached the semi-final but lost 1-0 to Arsenal (after 2-2). The venue was restricted with the only access south of the cricket ground thus it was not suitable for large crowds. It became the site of a proposed railway in 1930 hence the club purchased some land on Boothferry Road a mile to the west and developed a ground, which they moved to in 1946 (see Ch. 14).

The stories of Bradford Park Avenue, Darlington and Hull City are fascinating however the developments in Northampton were quite extraordinary. A Colchester programme of 1993-94 stated: "One thing that always sticks in the mind about Northampton is their unusual ground." This referred to the fact that their ground had a cricket pitch on one side and with the demise of Bramall Lane (see below) this was the only example of such a League ground from 1975-94. This was definitely not a load of "cobblers" and was indeed one of the most astonishing League grounds. Northampton C.C.C. established the venue south of Abington Avenue in 1885 and some local schoolteachers formed a football club in 1897. Their nickname was the Cobblers as Northampton was an important centre for the shoe industry. There was an awkward arrangement with the cricket club from the start and no football could be played after April or before September thus all matches in August were played away (this was true right up to the last season). The club became professional and joined Kettering Town and Wellingborough in the Southern League Division One in 1901-02. Herbert Chapman began his playing career at the club in 1901 but then went to Notts County and Tottenham. The attendance figures at the County Ground in these early days were about 4,000 whilst players had to change in the cricket pavilion until a stand was built on Abington Avenue in 1907.

Records were set at the ground that year however these were of the cricketing variety. Colin Blythe of Kent took 17 wickets in a day for only 48 runs and if his nerve had held would have taken all twenty wickets - he played for Kent and England in 1899-1914. Herbert Chapman, meanwhile, returned to the club as manager from 1907-12 and they were League champions in 1908-09. They spent 19 seasons in the Southern League Division One and were founder members of the Third Division in 1920. Alfred

Cockerill a cricket enthusiast purchased the County Ground in 1923 and set up a trust that meant the cricket club paid only a nominal rent, however the terms for the football club were less preferential. A new Main Stand was built with 2,000 seats in 1924 but was repaired after fire damage in 1929 and the club then discussed relocation due to the condition of the ground and the problems associated with sharing. Various schemes were put forward and they considered moving to the site of the town's old barracks in 1938 and to a ground on Kettering Road in 1948. These plans, however, did not materialize and the wedge shaped Hotel End was roofed in 1951 - this was the traditional home end and was next to a hotel. The turnstiles were in Abington Avenue beside the Main Stand but there was also access near the cricket pavilion and patrons had to walk around the cricket pitch.

The club had limited success and remained in the Third Division (South) although they were runners-up in 1927-28 and 1949-50 and reached the fifth round of the F.A. Cup on two occasions. They were founder members of Division Four, in 1958, and then experienced a remarkable rise up the leagues that was only matched by their subsequent fall. The County Ground became the stage for top-flight football in the 1960s and the Kop End was increased in height. This formed a strange terrace in one corner whose size and shape was dictated by the adjacent cricket pitch and a bowling green. The club were promoted from Division Four in 1960-61 and were Division Three champions in 1962-63 and then runners-up to Newcastle United in Division Two, by just one point, in 1964-65. Their stay at the top was brief and they spent just one season in Division One and were relegated in 21st place with Blackburn Rovers below them. The average crowds during the season were over 18,000 and a record attendance of 24,253 was against Fulham in Division One on 23 April 1966 - indeed their London-opponents finished just two points above them.

Such crowds can only be wondered at since there were only wooden standing boards on the cricket pitch side, and who knows what the grounds-man of the cricket club suffered that season? The club then experienced one of the fastest ever slides and went from Division One in May 1966 to Division Four in August 1969. The only club to match this are Bristol City who made an even more rapid descent from 1980-82. Despite the Cobblers decline they reached the fifth round of the F.A. Cup in 1970 and played Manchester United at home. A temporary stand was erected on the cricket pitch in preparation for the game and this was the only time such a structure was allowed. Manchester United won by an 8-2 score line and George Best scored six goals to provide some suitable headlines. The club remained in the lower two divisions and when the ground was assessed in 1985 it was stated to be the worst in the League. The club had little money for repairs and decided to leave the ground by 1989 and were in dire financial straits in 1993-94, then as expected finished in last place. They were saved from Conference football when Kidderminster was denied League status on a technicality.

Northampton Borough Council put up most of the funds for a new football ground (and athletics stadium) at Sixfields, west of the town, and work was well underway in 1994. There was a last farewell to the County Ground with a crowd of 6,432 on 30 April 1994, or was it? The new ground was not ready in time for the new season and the club began 1994-95 in a familiar fashion and played five games away at Bournemouth, Doncaster, Scunthorpe, Torquay and Walsall. They also played Bournemouth, Rochdale, Hartlepool and Carlisle at the County Ground in September and October. There was then a 'final' game against Mansfield in front of 4,993 on Tuesday 11 October 1994 (score 0-1). This was the end of a remarkable ground and, when standing on the terraces, there was always the distraction of a cricket pitch and pavilion to one side. Indeed it was possible to leave the terrace and walk along the edge of the pitch, then stand on wooden boards with the linesman running next you - a most unusual League venue. Ray Warburton, the captain, led Northampton out at Sixfields just four days later on 15 October 1994 and a crowd of 7,461 watched a 1-1 draw against Barnet. All trace of football was soon removed from the County Ground and it then returned to the cricketers after 97 years.

The County Ground could be considered the prince of shared grounds however Bramall Lane in Sheffield was the 'King' and of great sporting significance over the years, although its overall status diminished in recent times. The Duke of Norfolk rented the site to several local clubs and it was laid out for cricket in 1854 - including the Wednesday Cricket Club formed in 1816 and the Sheffield Cricket Club formed in 1820. The first cricket match was played there on 30 April 1855 whilst one of the first club football matches between Sheffield F.C. and Hallam F.C. was at Bramall Lane on 29 December 1862 (see Ch. 1). The northern industrial towns were notorious in the 19th century for a lack of land and the cramped and unhygienic living conditions. There was some relief in Sheffield due to a half-day on Wednesday and the locals were free to engage in sport on that afternoon (thus Wednesday C.C.) Bramall

Lane, itself, was a good venue for cricket and after a trial match against Sussex became headquarters of Yorkshire C.C.C. in 1863. Wednesday C.C. stayed with cricket at first but some members formed the Wednesday F.C. in 1867 and their first soccer game at Bramall Lane was in 1868. The football club then hired out the venue during the next 20 years for their more important matches.

They played their regular fixtures at a pitch on London Road and moved to Myrtle Road, Heeley in 1869, then hired the Sheaf House Cricket Ground in 1877 and also played at Endcliffe west of the city, near Ecclesall Road. Bramall Lane was an extensive venue south of St. Mary's Church (see Clegg Ch. 5) between Bramall Lane in the west and Shoreham Street in the east - with terraced housing nearby. There was narrow terracing around the cricket pitch, a pavilion and a bowling green on the south side, and open land next to Shoreham Street. The circle of the Sheaf House Ground was just to the south with Cherry Street and the Anchor Brewery in between. The latter ground backed onto the brewery on the north side and faced Ebenezer Chapel to the west but was open to Shoreham Street in the east. The Sheaf House Hotel operated as the pavilion and was on the south side. Bramall Lane, meanwhile, was used for many sporting events in addition to cricket and football and had a cinder track for athletics and cycling, and tennis took place there. John Tasker of Wednesday C.C. arranged the first floodlit soccer match at Bramall Lane on 14 October 1878 between two sides specially assembled for the occasion. There was much interest as the event attracted 20,000 spectators and indeed there were only 4,500 at the Cup Final in the same year.

The professional game brought about several changes and the Wednesday Cricket Club and Football Club separated in 1883 - the former survived until 1924. The football club itself was nearly disbanded at this point when several players left to join Sheffield Rovers, a new professional team, however Wednesday F.C. then followed their lead and became professional in 1887. They found it difficult to pay the players' wages and rent the Sheaf House Ground (or Bramall Lane), and thus looked for a new ground. The club then rented a field from the Duke of Norfolk and called the venue Olive Grove. It was on some boggy land with a footpath and stream across it, next to the railway between Sheffield and Heeley Stations. A stand was erected on the railway side with 1,000 seats although there was limited banking and the first game was against the famous Blackburn Rovers on 12 September 1887. Wednesday applied to join the Football League in 1888 but had no success and they were founder members of the Football Alliance in 1889. They won the championship in the first season and finished four points ahead of Bootle and Sunderland Albion, then played Blackburn Rovers in the Cup Final in 1890 but lost the game 6-1. They continued to play in the Alliance and were elected to the Football League Division One in 1892.

Wednesday had considerable success at Olive Grove and won the F.A. Cup in 1896 when they beat Wolves 2-1 at the Crystal Palace in front of 48,836. They were, however, given notice to leave Olive Grove in October 1898 and came bottom of Division One in 1898-99. They tried to make arrangements to use Bramall Lane however a permanent move was not forthcoming and also tried to buy the Sheaf House Ground. They then considered two venues north of the town, one at Carbrook near the River Don and the other at Owlerton on the outskirts of the city. None of these plans worked out however a local gent came to their rescue. James Dixon, a wealthy silversmith, sold them some meadowland at Owlerton in 1899 and the club developed a ground there even though it was four miles north of Olive Grove. The old stand was erected on the north side and shallow banking was raised at each end and the first game was played against Chesterfield Town in Division Two on 2 September 1899. Their benefactor, meanwhile, donated his home Hillsborough Hall to the Council to be used as a library and park in 1892 and the first tram came to Owlerton in 1901. There were initial concerns that the site was beyond the city boundaries however these new transport connections gave supporters good access from the city centre. The Wednesday became a strong side and won the League championship in 1903 and 1904 and the F.A. Cup in 1907. The ground came under the Hillsborough parliamentary constituency in 1914 and took the new name, although the nickname of the Owls was to remain. The club won the League again in 1929 and 1930 and changed their name to Sheffield Wednesday at the latter date.

These proceedings in Sheffield leave us with a few strange questions. What would have happened if the Wednesday F.C. had stayed at Bramall Lane in 1887? Would they still be there now and would Sheffield United have been formed? We can, however, only deal with the version of history that survives and a vacuum was left at Bramall Lane in the late 1880s. The ground had a short cover and stand on the John Street Side by 1880 and a terrace on Bramall Lane ran around to the cricket pavilion, which was built on Cherry Street in 1881. The football ground was on the north side of the pitch, whilst there was a concentration of sports venues in the area as shown on the 1889 O.S. map viz. Bramall Lane, Sheaf

House Ground and Olive Grove all within a quarter-mile radius. There were a series of developments in the late 1880s (1) Wednesday F.C. ceased to use Bramall Lane in 1887 (2) Yorkshire C.C.C. prepared to depart for Headingley in Leeds in 1889 (3) Preston beat West Bromwich Albion 1-0 in an F.A. Cup semi-final at Bramall Lane in March 1889 with a crowd of over 22,000. The "Old Invincibles" of Preston went on the win the Cup and the double whilst the gate receipts showed that football had great potential at Bramall Lane.

The Ground Committee considered their position and formed their own team Sheffield United in September 1889. They placed advertisements in local papers to find players but this proved difficult and for a time the team consisted of just three men. They later recruited players from Scotland and their first game against Sheffield F.C. was a 3-1 defeat. They wanted to ascertain the strength of the side and the game was played in secret however the captain of Wednesday F.C. and a single reporter spied on the proceedings. Sheffield United were founder members of Division Two in 1892 and were promoted at the end of the first season and joined the Wednesday in Division One. Bramall Lane was further developed after 1889 and a stand was built on John Street with 2,000 seats in 1895 and a cover erected at the Shoreham Street End in 1897. The club became a formidable side and were runners-up to Aston Villa in 1897, then League champions ahead of Sunderland in 1898. A limited company was established that incorporated both Sheffield United Cricket and Football Clubs and they purchased Bramall Lane from the Duke of Norfolk in 1898-99. There was plenty happening at this time and the club won the F.A. Cup in 1899 and were runners-up in the League in 1900. The club played a friendly game against Rangers in Scotland in April that year and two months later had an offer from Leitch to do work at Bramall Lane, but their inclination was to decline the offer. There was then a fire in the John Street Stand in November 1900 and this changed matters and they employed Leitch to build a new stand on that side of the ground. The new John Street Stand was his first commission outside of Scotland and this important development, in 1902, was discussed in Chapter 15.

The club were runners-up to Tottenham in the F.A. Cup in 1901 and then won the Cup Final against Southampton at the Crystal Palace in 1902, whilst the ground was used for an England v Scotland international on 4 April 1903 with a crowd of 32,000. William Foulkes (1874-1916) was their most notable and well-known player and was an agile and formidable goalkeeper who once weighed 23 stone! He was attracted to Chelsea in 1905 and the London club used modern psychology, and to emphasize

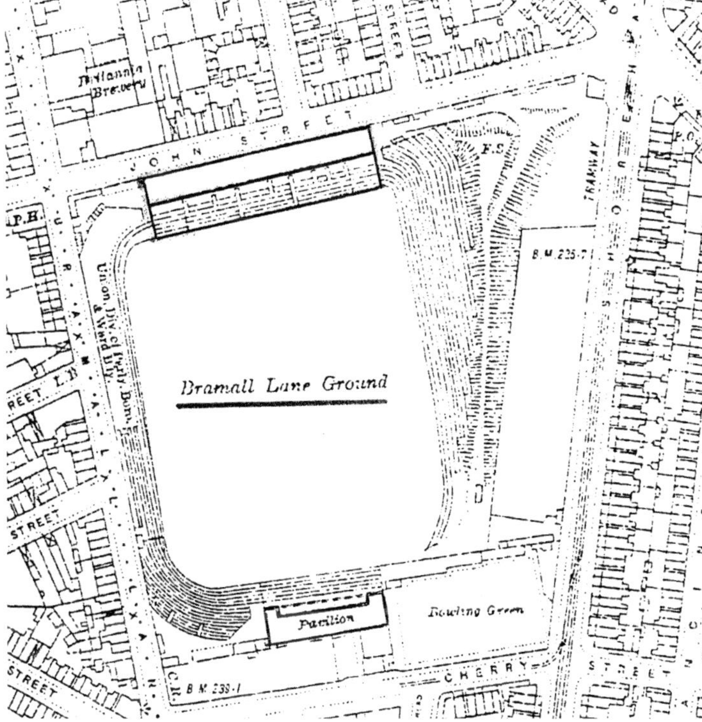

Bramall Lane, Sheffield - O.S. Map 1924. A sports venue since 1854.

his presence placed two small boys behind the goal - forerunners of the pitch side ball boys. A cover was erected at the Bramall Lane End soon after the John Street Stand was built and the two were joined with a corner extension. The cover at the Shoreham Street End was damaged by wind in 1903 and was removed and the end was enlarged and terraced before the First War. The ground then staged a Cup Final replay between Barnsley and West Bromwich in 1912 whilst the club continued to do well and won the F.A. Cup in 1915 and 1925.

Bramall Lane was an extensive venue with a large Spion Kop and it is hard to imagine such a grand football ground with just three sides. The spectators stood on the terraces and watched games with the expanse of the cricket pitch and pavilion beyond. Indeed the terracing at both the Bramall Lane End and Shoreham Street End continued to the south around the boundary of the cricket pitch and joined up in front of the pavilion on Cherry Street. This was indeed an unusual venue. A roof was added to the Shoreham Street End or Spion Kop in 1935 and the record attendance was 68,287 during a Cup game against Leeds United on 15 February 1936. During the game the terraces of both cricket and football pitches were filled with spectators, however many had a poor view and when fog descended they spilled onto the cricket pitch. Indeed the club went on to play Arsenal in the Final although they lost 1-0.

The halcyon days, however, did not continue and ten bombs hit the ground during the Second War. The John Street Stand and the Kop roof were both badly damaged as was the pitch and it took several years to repair this. The Kop received a new roof with two spans parallel to the pitch in 1948 and the John Street Stand was restored without the Leitch gable in 1954 - a roof cover joined the Kop to the John Street Stand in the high northeast corner. Five large pylons were erected as ‘permanent’ floodlights in 1955 and these became a distinctive feature of the ground. Over the years, however, the problems at Bramall Lane became apparent and as a large sporting venue it was not suitable for either sport. Indeed cricket lovers endured some considerable discomfort sitting for long periods on the hard terraces. There were various plans to relocate the football club in the 1960s but they became determined to stay and a new stand was built at the Bramall Lane End in 1966. They gave the cricket club two years notice to leave in 1971 and the last county cricket match took place at Bramall Lane on 7 August 1973 - thereafter Sheffield could no longer stage first class cricket. There was much chagrin amongst cricket lovers as this ended a 118-year association with Bramall Lane. Meanwhile Yorkshire C.C.C. then played for a few years at Abbeydale Park, Sheffield a former home of Derbyshire C.C.C. from the 1920s to c.1931.

The football club rapidly developed the fourth side of the ground and a new £1 million South Stand was opened in August 1975 bringing the capacity to just under 50,000. The cost, however, like with many clubs was crippling and they soon found themselves in a similar position to Wolves. The attendances were under 15,000 and they had reached the Fourth Division by 1981. Reg Brearley became the Chairman and injected much-needed funds into the club. The cricket pavilion on Cherry Street was demolished soon after (it became a car park) and the club offices and changing rooms were moved from John Street to the new South Stand. Indeed Leitch’s old stand became more and more dilapidated and was demolished in 1994, but no building work was done until 1997 and for three years the ground had a familiar three-sided appearance. Developments at Bramall Lane saw all trace of the shared venue disappear in the 1990s. In the case of Sheffield the cricket club were expelled whilst at Northampton the football club were removed, but it did not really matter which it was, as the shared cricket-football venue was consigned to history. Owzat!

CHAPTER 19

The Re-Election Lottery

The famous and noteworthy clubs continued on to glory however during the early years of the Football League there were many unsung heroes - some were destined to end up in the pages of football history whilst others are still with us. In some cases there was a good reason why a club failed to develop but quite often it was simply fate. There were too many teams for a single Football League in 1888 and as stated Halliwell, Nottingham Forest and the Wednesday were left out - they must have been severely disappointed at missing this epic soccer event. The outcome was the formation of the Football Alliance a year later in 1889 this being a kind of second division or feeder league. This was a bit like the Conference since it was not an official division of the League and the founder members were as follows: Birmingham St. George's, Bootle, Crewe Alexandra, Darwen, Grimsby Town, Long Eaton Rangers, Newton Heath, Nottingham Forest, Small Heath, Sunderland Albion, Walsall Town Swifts and Wednesday. The latter were champions in 1889-90 whilst Long Eaton Rangers lost their place to Stoke who became champions in 1890-91. The Football League was increased in size from 12 to 14 members and Darwen and Stoke were elected. Sunderland Albion was one of the early teams to vanish whilst Ardwick, Burton Swifts and Lincoln City were admitted to the Football Alliance.

Nottingham Forest F.C. finished as champions in 1891-92 and it then ceased to exist. There were twelve teams in the Alliance during its last season and only bottom team Birmingham St. George's failed to make it to the League. The rules of promotion were not always logical at this time and (1) Nottingham Forest, (2) Newton Heath and (4) Wednesday went into Division One whilst the remaining eight clubs formed the backbone of Division Two viz. Ardwick, Bootle, Burton Swifts, Crewe Alexandra, Grimsby Town, Lincoln City, Small Heath and Walsall Town Swifts. The other founders of the division were Darwen (relegated from one) and Burslem Port Vale, Northwich Victoria and Sheffield United. The First Division then had 16 members and the Second Division 12 members in 1892-93. The Southern League began in 1893 and was a 'third division' with only nine members in 1894-95 viz. Chatham, Clapton, Ilford, Luton Town, Millwall Athletic, Reading, Royal Ordnance, Southampton and Swindon Town. East London team Millwall helped promote the Southern League and were champions in the first two seasons whilst Southampton won six times in 1897-1904. It then grew in size and included Tottenham Hotspur (champions in 1900) and West Ham United. The League had many familiar names but also fielded Sheppey United (1896), Wolverton (1896), Chatham (1897), Bedminster, Brighton United, Royal Artillery (all 1898), Kettering Town (1900), Wellingborough (1901), Leyton (1906), Bradford (1907), Croydon Common (1909) and Stoke (1911). Twenty one teams who came from Southern League Division One formed the new Third Division in 1920 - Grimsby Town relegated from the Second Division completed the numbers.

The Football League only began in 1888 however the demise of three prospective clubs who played in the Alliance had occurred by 1892. Long Eaton Rangers were formed in 1882 and played at Long Eaton Recreation Ground and spent just one season in the Alliance in 1889-90. They were runners-up in the Midland League the next year and played in the F.A. Cup from 1883-98 and left the Midland League in 1899. Sunderland Albion, however, were more important in these early days and were closely connected to the emergence of Sunderland F.C. Jimmy Allan was a Scottish schoolmaster at Hendon Boarding School half a mile south of the town and formed Sunderland and District Teachers Association Football Club in 1879. The club first played at Blue House Fields, Hendon east of the boarding school and on the outskirts of the town, then changed the name to Sunderland Association in 1880 and to Sunderland F.C. and moved to Groves Field, Ashbrooke in 1882 (later home of Sunderland Cricket and Rugby Club). They moved north of the River Wear and played at Horatio Street in Roker in 1883 and at Abbs Field, Fulwell Road the first enclosed ground in 1884. They moved to Newcastle Road the best venue in the area (a ground they had already used) in March 1886. It belonged to the Thompson sisters whose family owned the North Sands Shipyard and was an enclosed ground with a 1,000 seat stand on the north side and fixed terraces on the remaining sides. It was a spacious venue with Eglinton Street North, Crozier Street and Newcastle Road beyond the ground, and fields to the north.

The club played the first game there against Darlington on 3 April 1886 and within a year attendances reached 8,000. Clubs such as Accrington and Preston had been penalised over the issue of professionalism and Sunderland now came under the spotlight and were expelled from the Cup in 1887-88 after fielding three ineligible Scottish players. They played Middlesbrough in the third round and won 4-2 (after a 2-2 draw) however it was their opponents who went through to the next round and reached the quarterfinals. They did not take this dispute lying down and Jimmy Allan and seven other players left the club although it is not quite clear what they meant to achieve. They formed a new team Sunderland Albion who returned to play at the Blue House Grounds and developed the site. There was a narrow stand and terrace on the east side with athletic and cycle track, and a cricket ground to the north. The coast was a few hundred yards away with two railways in-between (Sunderland & Hartlepool, Seaham & Sunderland) and the Blue House (P.H.) and a large gasworks were to the south - Valley Road School was later built on the site.

Sunderland Albion challenged Sunderland F.C. to become the top team in the town and invested heavily in their new venue, and they were founder members of the Alliance in 1889 - they came third in 1889-90 and second behind Stoke in 1890-91. During this time Richard Thompson the shipyard owner backed Sunderland F.C. and appointed Tom Watson as manager in 1889. He brought together a successful side the "Team of all Talents" who were the first elected to the Football League in 1890. They came seventh in 1890-91 but would have finished two places higher since two points were deducted for fielding an ineligible player. This was too much pressure for the Albion and despite their success in the Alliance they were forced to withdraw in 1891 - they were rapidly overtaken and folded-up in 1892. The Rokerites then became the second great team after Preston North End and won 13 matches in a row from November to April, and were League champions in 1891-92 - five points ahead of Preston. Only their captain was English and despite ineligible and 'Scottish' players the club had reached the top - thus power and influence prevailed. They won the League again in 1892-93 and reached the Cup semi-final in 1891, 1892 and 1895 whilst their success took them to Roker Park in 1898. Sunderland Albion were just left with the blues!

This was not the end of the story in the rebellious northeast and Sunderland continued to do well being League champions again in 1901-02. The team still relied heavily on Scottish players and both Ted Doig and Jimmy Millar remained there from the 1890s. Both were Scottish internationals and Millar had won two titles with both Rangers and Sunderland. The club wanted to maintain their status and signed Alf Common, who was English, from Sheffield United for £375 then finished a close third in the 1902-03 season. A sensation then broke since they sold Alf Common to Middlesbrough for the extraordinary sum of £1,000 in February 1905. He was an England inside forward however the highest transfers seen at the time were £400 and scandal was in the air. Sunderland F.C. were accused of trying to profit from these transactions whilst Boro (who were bottom of the League) had tried to buy their way out of trouble. Soccer was meant to be a honourable sport and both parties were blamed. Charles Clegg, meanwhile, who owned Sheffield United was none too pleased and felt considerably out of pocket, whilst Alf Common scored a winner at Bramall Lane to give Boro a much needed away win. The F.A. acted swiftly and introduced a ceiling on transfer fees of £350 whilst Middlesbrough were fined for making unauthorised payments to players. The idea that buying success was illegal seems strange today and indeed Trevor Francis was the first £1 million player on 9 February 1979. He went to Nottingham Forest from Birmingham City and helped them win the European Cup in 1979 and 1980 - you can't have much more success than that.

The story in Sunderland was of two teams however there was even greater proliferation in Birmingham and the city had a long list of entrants in the Cup in 1887-88 viz. Aston Shakespeare, Aston Unity, Aston Villa, Birmingham Excelsior, Birmingham Southfield, Mitchell St. George's, Small Heath Alliance, Walsall Swifts, Walsall Town, Wednesbury Old Athletic, West Bromwich Albion. There was great enthusiasm for soccer in the city and indeed West Bromwich won the Cup that season, whilst Aston was a sporting Mecca having four enclosed venues within one square mile in 1889 viz. Aston Lower Grounds, Wellington Road Perry Barr, Excelsior Cricket and Football Ground and a cricket-football pitch on Trinity Road. There was a larger cricket ground and pavilion on Wellhead Lane off Aston Lane next to the railway and near the Lion Works, which was a large ammunition factory. There were several benefactors of soccer and sport such as Mr. Quilter, William McGregor and Frederick Rinder, and the League founder lived with his son-in-law at Salisbury Road, Birchfields only a short distance from the Excelsior Ground (see Introspection). Mitchell St. George's were formed in 1875 and played at Fentham Road, Birchfields just off Trinity Road to the west of Aston Lower Grounds viz. Excelsior Cricket and Football Ground on Hampton Road just north of Fentham Road. They played in the Cup from 1881 and became Birmingham St. George's in 1889 and founder members of the Alliance that same year (Villa had already joined the League). They came 7th in 1889-90 and 4th in 1890-91 but were last in 1891-92 and were not elected into the League. They had notable players including John Devey and Dennis Hodgetts who later appeared for Aston Villa, and the former scored the winning goal for Villa in the first Cup Final at the Crystal Palace in 1895. St. George's entered the F.A. Cup from 1881-92 but due to a lack of success and too much local competition folded-up.

Accrington F.C. was the first club to lose their League status in 1893 and made a habit of this since they also left as Accrington Stanley in 1962. Their brief history was discussed in Chapter 11 however they spent five seasons in the top flight and their highest finish was 6th in 1889-90. This was a better record than some clubs although there was considerably less competition, whilst a number of northern clubs soon followed them out of the League. Bootle F.C. played at the Hawthorne Road Ground in Liverpool and first appeared in the Cup in 1887, and had three seasons in the Alliance being runners-up to Wednesday in 1889-90. They were founder members of Division Two in 1892 and briefly came behind Everton as the second team in the city. They played their last Cup game in 1892 and resigned from the League in 1893 - Liverpool (1892) joined the League when Bootle departed.

Middlesbrough Ironopolis had the longest name in the League and were formed at the Paradise Ground south of Linthorpe Road in 1889. Their rivals Middlesbrough reverted to amateur status in 1892 and as professionals they became the premier club in the town. They attracted large crowds of up to 14,000 and played one season in the Football League in 1893-94. They won eight games and finished in 11th place in Division Two however had average crowds of only 1,500 during the season and after financial losses withdrew from the League - they disbanded in 1894. Indeed when Leitch built Ayresome Park in 1903 it covered part of the site of the Paradise Ground. Northwich Victoria were formed in 1874 and played some friendly games at Stumpers Field then moved to the Drill Field - just south of the town near the River Weaver. This was quoted as being the oldest football ground in the world in continuous use by one club and was thus of great importance to soccer history. A sign at the entrance stated: "The world's oldest ground - football has been played here continuously since 1874." The trivia in many a football programme told us: "As everyone knows the Drill Field is the world's oldest ground." But was it?

Maidenhead United were formed in 1870 and with neighbours' Marlow entered the first F.A. Cup competition in 1872. The club's emblem was two footballs emblazoned with 1870, two magpies (their nickname) and the historic Maidenhead Bridge by Brunel. The club programme states: "Welcome to York Road - the home of Maidenhead United and the oldest continually used football ground in the world by the same club." There was a dispute to be settled although both had a history far longer than many League grounds (Deepdale dates from 1881). Northwich first played in the Combination and were founder members of Division Two in 1892 and finished 7th in 1892-93 but were in last place in 1893-94. They won just 3 out of 28 games and scored 30 goals whilst conceding 98 and lost their League status and returned to the Combination. They played in the Cheshire - Manchester League being champions of the latter in 1902-03 and then in the Cheshire County League after the First War. The record attendance at the Drill Field was 11,290 for a game against Witton Albion in the Cheshire League in 1949 and they were champions in 1956-57. They were founder members of the Northern Premier League in 1968 and won the 'League Cup' in 1973 and also founded the Alliance Premier League later known as the Conference in 1979. The club became concerned that they would have to leave the ground in the 1990s but funds were secured and the Dane Bank terrace was rebuilt in 1996. It had been the oldest terrace in the world and people had watched football from it for 122 years! The argument, however, was soon academic and the club left the Drill Field in 2002 and shared with Witton Albion.

There were plenty more unlikely football venues in the early days and one of these was Darwen in Lancashire just south of Blackburn - they had strong local rivals re Olympic and Rovers. Mr. J.C. Ashton and three sons of Nathaniel Walsh the owner of Orchard Mill formed Darwen F.C. from two local mill teams in 1870 - the Walsh brothers attended Harrow School. We have this club to thank for some of the most exciting score lines ever seen! The club moved to Barley Bank in 1874, a ground between rows of terraced houses with cotton mills looming large behind, and shared the ground with a cricket club whilst the players changed at the nearby Alexandra Hotel. The side adopted the Association rules in 1875 and the first game was against Turton. This was an important venue and staged a floodlit game between Darwen and members of Blackburn Rovers, Olympic and Park Road on 28 October 1878 - just two weeks after that at Bramall Lane. Darwen had some early success in the F.A. Cup at a time when southern clubs dominated and reached the quarterfinal in 1879 and took the Old Etonians to two replays. They reached the semi-final in 1881 but lost 4-1 to the Old Carthusians and did not match the Cup exploits of their neighbours - Blackburn Olympic (1883) and Blackburn Rovers (1884-86). The record attendance was 12,500 during a friendly v Blackburn Rovers on 18 March 1885 whilst the cricket team left in 1888. Jimmy Love and Fergie Suter were stars of Darwen in the 1880s and were professional players although the club denied this fact (see earlier). They played two seasons in the Alliance in 1889-91 and entered the Football League with Stoke in 1891 but spent just one season in the top flight.

Barley Bank was improved at this time and a 1,000-seat stand was erected at the Town End whilst the players changed at the Clough End. The club finished bottom of the League in 1891-92 and won only four games and conceded 112 goals, including a 12-0 defeat by West Bromwich Albion in 1892 - a record score for the First Division. The largest score, however, was when Preston North End beat Hyde 26-0 in the Cup on 15 October 1887 whilst Leicester Fosse also lost 12-0 to Nottingham Forest in 1909. They were founder members of Division Two in 1892 and came third that season then beat Notts County in a *Test Match* and returned to Division One. The Main Stand was then moved to the other end of the pitch and turnstiles erected. They were relegated in 1893-94 and then gradually declined in Division Two and set some staggering records during their last League season in 1898-99. They lost 18 games in a row and also lost 10-0 on three occasions and 9-0, 9-2, 8-0, 8-1 and 7-0. They lost all their away matches except for one draw and scored only 6 away goals while conceding 109, and in total won only two games and conceded 141 goals. Not surprisingly they failed to get re-elected and it is conjecture whether the manager survived the season - he was short of hair by the end! The club were in a poor financial position and the last League game at Barley Bank was against Newton Heath on 22 April 1899, and the final game against Burnley on 17 May. The club moved to the Anchor Ground and were champions of the Lancashire League in 1902. Hindle Street was extended across part of Barley Bank but some hoped to return until the 1930s, whilst Avondale Girls School now covers the site. The club were champions of the Lancashire Combination in 1931/32 and the record attendance at the Anchor Ground was 6,500 during a game v Chester City on 12 December 1931. The team continued to have large scores and they lost 11-1 to Arsenal in 1932.

Loughborough Town played at the Athletic Ground, which once saw an appearance by W.G. Grace the famous cricketer (during a cricket match). The club entered the F.A. Cup in 1890 and joined the Midland League in 1891 and were champions in 1894-95. They joined the Football League in 1895 in place of Walsall Town Swifts but finished near the bottom of Division Two during their five League seasons. They were in last place in 1899-1900 and won just a single game during the season having scored only 18 goals yet conceded 100. In one game they were beaten 12-0 by Woolwich Arsenal and lost their League status with Luton Town - they were replaced by Blackpool and Stockport County. The club applied to join the Midland League in 1900-01 although never competed. Blackpool, meanwhile, was a holiday resort from the mid-18th century, whilst James Atherton laid out New Brighton on the Wirral opposite to Liverpool in 1830. The aim was to have large villas and compete with existing seaside resorts thus there were grand seafront developments in the late 1890s. The resort had extensive sands along the coast however swimming was only permitted from wooden bathing machines in 1900. This was a local byelaw and there was a fine for people who bathed directly without the use of these huts. The bathers and pleasure seekers had unfamiliar attire, the men dark suits and bowler hats and the women long skirts and bonnets.

The building of a tower at New Brighton commenced in 1897 on land that formed part of the Rock Point Estate. This was a difficult undertaking and a number of workmen died in accidents during the construction. The completed tower was 562 feet high or 621 feet above sea level, and was higher than Blackpool Tower at 518 feet. There were four lifts to the top and fine views of Merseyside and the Wirral could be seen for 6d. Indeed the Tower Grounds covered 35 acres of land and had numerous attractions, reaching right to the sea front, and at night the whole area was lit by thousands of fairy lights. In addition there was a ballroom and theatre at the base of the tower and this attracted famous acts such as Harry Lauder and Dame Clara Butt. The symphony orchestra that played there was ranked as one of the finest in the country. The Tower Grounds faced across the Mersey towards Everton and Liverpool F.C. and an athletics arena was built at the south end, with a main grandstand on the north side and the popular stand on the south. There was an athletics track and first-class cycle track and the world cycling championships were held there in 1922. With the growth of football at the end of the 19th century there was clearly a commercial opportunity and this was an ideal set-up to bring football to the town.

The New Brighton Tower Company took steps to establish a football team and the club known as New Brighton Tower joined the League with Barnsley, Burslem Port Vale and Glossop in 1898 - the

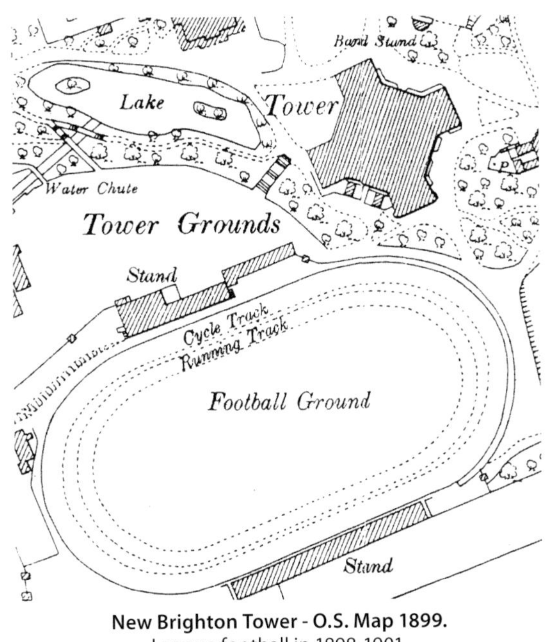

New Brighton Tower - O.S. Map 1899.
League football in 1898-1901.

League increased in size by four members. The club played at the centre of the athletics arena within the pleasure grounds and their home was known as the "Tower Athletics Ground". The choice of such a location was also seen at Aston Villa, Blackpool, Crystal Palace, Grimsby, Hull and Wolves. They finished 5th in Division Two in 1898-99 and 10th in 1899-1900 and their best finish was 4th in 1900-01. The club, however, were unable to continue at this level and despite good results resigned from the League in 1901 and this was the end of the football team. The Tower Grounds continued to be popular until the First War however the period of conflict resulted in a drop in audiences and no money was available for repairs. The tower as a result became unsafe and was dismantled in 1919-21, whilst the theatre and ballroom were in use until 1969 but were badly damaged by fire and later demolished. This however was not the end of the story in New Brighton and more of this anon.

Burton on Trent in the Midlands was one of the most famous football towns in the early years and produced no less than three League clubs! Burton Wanderers formed in 1871 and claimed to be the fourth oldest League club. They played at Derby Turn from 1871 and were developed by John Parker from 1885 and soon progressed well. They joined League Division Two with Bury and Leicester Fosse in 1894 whilst Middlesbrough Ironopolis and Northwich Victoria lost their places - the division was increased in size from 15 to 16 members. Wanderers finished 7th in 1894-95 and their best finish was 4th in 1895-96 however they lost their League status in 1896-97. They left Derby Turn in 1899 and had one season at Allsops Old Cricket Ground near the Trent Bridge. Rivals Burton Outward Star formed in 1870 and became Burton Swifts in 1883 and initially played at Shrobnall Street Cricket Ground and at Kidger's Field then moved to Peel Croft in 1891. The ground was on Lichfield Street south of New Street and had a pavilion on the north side, a cover behind the east goal, and a narrow terrace on the south side backing on to a brewery. There were railways on three sides although there was open land to the east and a grammar school across Lichfield Street. They played in the Alliance being 5th in 1891-92 and were founder members of Division Two in 1892. They had little success in the League and finished in the lower half of the table and had to seek re-election with Burton Wanderers in 1896-97. They finished last in 1900-01 and were in difficulty and merged with Burton Wanderers to form Burton United in 1901. They continued at Peel Croft in a black and maroon strip and were known as the "Crofters". The new club were immediately elected to the League in 1901-02 and finished 10th that season - their highest position. They failed to progress and had to seek re-election in 1904-05 and 1905-06 and came last in 1906-07, losing their League status and folded-up in 1910 (a rugby club then used the ground). Burton Albion F.C. formed in 1950 and play at Eton Park, Princess Way - maybe League football will return after nearly 100 years.

Gone for a Burton! O.S. Map 1901. Swifts 1891-1901, United 1901-10.

The Northolme Ground in Gainsborough was used for cricket from the 1850s and was at the north end of the town between Northolme and Back Street, east of the River Trent. The vicar of Holy Trinity formed a football team called Trinity Recreationists in 1873 that became Gainsborough Trinity and they had royal blue shirts with white trim and a nickname of the blues. Both the cricket and football club used the ground and it was in a leafy location with fields and a pinfold on the north side - there was a small pavilion on the south side. The club joined the Midland Counties League in 1889 and were champions in 1890-91 and were elected to the League with Blackpool and Walsall in 1896. They finished 7th in Division Two in 1896-97 and were then in the lower half of the table and in last place in 1901-02. Their highest finish was sixth in 1904-05 but they were again last in 1911-12 having won just five games all season. The town was too small to support League football and they lost their League status in 1912 and were replaced by Lincoln City. The club continued to play at Northolme and the ground was enclosed by 1921 and there was a new pavilion on the south side and a stand on the north side - surrounding fields were then covered with terraced housing and a gasworks. They returned to the Midland League and the record attendance was 9,760 against Scunthorpe United in the 1940s. They were founders of the Northern Premier League in 1969 and stayed there until they went in the Conference North in 2004-05. Northolme has been a sports venue for 150 years and the club spent 16 seasons in the Football League.

Glossop North End went one further and had 17 seasons in the League and played at North Road. The town was an unlikely venue for League football and was on the edge of the High Peak in the Peak District. The club were formed in 1886 and played in the North Cheshire League in 1890 then became professional in 1894. They made three applications to join the League and were admitted when the League increased in size in 1898. The pitch was located west of North Road beside the railway and there was a cricket ground with pavilion adjacent to it - they no doubt had similar problems to Northampton since there was an overlap. The club were runners-up to Manchester City in Division Two in 1898-99 and these were the first two teams to achieve automatic promotion to the First Division. Glossop then became the smallest town in the country to host First Division football however it was for just one season (1899-1900) as they finished in last place with only four wins. They came 5th in Division Two in 1900-01 and changed their name to Glossop F.C. in 1903 and had to seek re-election in 1903-04. Sir Samuel Hill-Wood a cotton baron owned the club and was later a chairman of Arsenal, whilst T.T. Fitchie an inside forward came to the club having been a top player for Woolwich Arsenal. There was a 9-2 defeat by Chelsea in the first game of the 1906-07 season and indeed the London club went on to achieve promotion. Glossop, meanwhile, finished in last place in 1914-15 having won only 6 out of 38 games. Leicester Fosse was one place above them and returned to the League in 1919 as Leicester City however Glossop failed to be re-elected and lost their League status after 17 years. They played in the Lancashire Combination and Manchester League after the war, and left North Road in 1955 and then played in local leagues at Surrey Street.

Indeed the whole social structure of the country had changed after the First War and these changes also applied to the Football League. The Southern League formed the basis of the new Third Division in 1920 and the Third Division (North) consisting of 20 clubs was added in 1921. The latter had former League members Accrington, Chesterfield, Crewe Alexandra, Lincoln City, Grimsby Town and Walsall as well as Stockport County relegated from the Second Division. There were other clubs familiar in the League today and Ashington, Barrow, Durham City, Nelson, Southport, Stalybridge Celtic and Wigan Borough who had played in regional Leagues (Birmingham, Lancashire, Manchester and Midland). Some of these did not last long and found it hard to maintain their League status. Stalybridge Celtic formed at the Bower Fold in 1909 and Herbert Rhodes a businessman developed the ground. They joined the Lancashire Combination and were professional in 1911 and played for a time in the Central League, however were runners-up to Stoke in Southern League Division Two in 1914-15. As a consequence they were founder members of Division Three (North) in 1921 and beat Chesterfield 6-0 in their first game - a record League victory for them. They came 7th in 1921-22 and had a high profile and played a first round Cup-tie against West Bromwich at the Hawthorns in front of 27,000 in 1922-23. They came 11th in 1922-23 but had insufficient backing to finance a professional club and resigned from the League in 1923 and were replaced by New Brighton. They played in the Cheshire County and North West Counties League and lost to Darlington in the 2nd round of the Cup in the 1930s, then played in the Northern Premier League in the late 1980s and reached the Conference in 1992. The Bower Fold was improved to League standard but due to relegation their plans were put on hold - for the time being.

There was a strong Welsh contingent in the Southern League Division One in the early 20th century i.e. Cardiff City (1913-14, 1914-15, 1919-20), Merthyr Town (1912-13, 1913-14, 1919-20) and Newport

County and Swansea Town (1919-20). Of these teams it was Cardiff City who emerged as the most prominent Welsh club in the 1920s. Division Three (South) was formed in 1921 and there were a number of changes: Crystal Palace F.C. came top of Division Three in 1920-21 and became the first team to be promoted from a lower division. Grimsby Town transferred to the new northern division and Aberdare Athletic and Charlton Athletic filled the two vacant spaces. Indeed Aberdare Athletic were founder members of Division Three (South) in 1921 and played at the Athletic Ground in Ynis. They came 8th in 1921-22 but had to seek re-election with Newport County in 1922-23 and the omens were not good. The club finished in last place in 1926-27 having conceded 101 goals and lost their League status to be replaced by Torquay United in 1927.

There was much football activity in this area of Wales and there was a team that played 5 miles to the east across the valleys. Merthyr Town played at Penydarren Park in Merthyr Tydfil and being in the Southern League they secured a place in the Third Division in 1920. There was an interesting structure to the league at this time and home and away games were played back-to-back in 1920-24 - perhaps to add flavour to the contest. For example Merthyr Town drew 0-0 at Millwall on 25 December 1920 in front of 26,000 then lost 0-1 to the same opponents at Penydarren Park on 27 December in front of 21,686 - the record attendance at the ground (not in 1949 as stated in some sources). The club started well and came 8th in 1920-21 but were in last place in 1924-25 and had to seek re-election again in 1927-28. They also finished last in 1929-30 and lost 27 out of 42 matches and let in a staggering 135 goals. They lost their League status and were replaced by the little known Thames F.C. in 1930. The Welsh club reformed as Merthyr Tydfil in 1945 and continued at Penydarren Park and had a successful era in the 1940s-50s.

The valleys did not have the resources or population base to support League football and the more successful teams were in the cities of Cardiff, Newport and Swansea, and Wrexham in the north. Cardiff City joined Division Two with Leeds United in 1920 and gained promotion as runners-up to Birmingham in their first season (1920-21) - they missed the Division Two title on goal average. They came 4th in Division One in 1921-22 and were runners-up to Huddersfield Town in 1923-24. Indeed they missed out on the championship on goal average and would have been top if goal difference had been used. The teams both had a goal difference of 27 however Cardiff had scored one more goal whilst they were separated by just 0-0241 of a goal. It was not until 1976 that goal difference replaced goal average as a way of separating teams on equal points (goal average = goals scored ÷ goals against). This was the only time there would have been different champions if goal difference were used in place of goal average. The club reached the semi-final of the Cup in 1921 and lost 3-1 to Wolves (in a replay) then lost the Final 1-0 to Sheffield United in 1925. They defeated Arsenal 1-0 to win the F.A. Cup in 1927 and this was the only time that it left England. There were only three Welshmen in the Cardiff side but the Arsenal keeper was Welsh, and the goal came from a speculative shot in the last 15 minutes that appeared an easy save but the keeper failed to hold it. The club then had less success and they were relegated in last place in 1928-29.

There was, meanwhile, a similar pattern in the north of England and a number of early League clubs lost their League status. The founders of Division Three (North) included Ashington, Durham City and Nelson however none lasted for more than a decade. Durham City initially played in the post-war Victory League at Garden House Park in 1918-19. They moved to the North Eastern League, which included reserve sides of League teams, and then played at Kepier Heughs near to Ferens Park. They were founder members of the Third Division (North) in 1921 and their highest finish was 11th in 1921-22 but they came last in 1922-23. They then moved to Holiday Park named after Alderman T.W. Holiday a former Mayor, near to Framwellgate. They came 21st in 1927-28 and failed to be re-elected and Carlisle United replaced them in the League. The club returned to the North Eastern League but folded in 1938 and the ground was sold. They reformed in 1950 and played at Ferens Park named after Club Chairman Alderman H.C. Ferens but it was sold for housing in 1994, and they moved to New Ferens Park at Belmont.

Ashington became affiliated to the Northumberland F.A. in 1888 and played in the Northern Football Alliance. They moved to their ground Portland Park in 1909 and were known as the "Colliers" and played in black and white stripes. They were in fact the most northerly English club to play in the League whilst the town was home to a famous family viz. Bobby Charlton, Jackie Charlton and Jackie Milburn. The club won the Northern Football Alliance and became a limited company in 1914 and joined the League in 1921 - their first home game had a crowd of 10,000. The club finished 10th in Division Three (North) in 1921-22 but had to seek re-election in 1922-23 and came as high as 8th in 1923-24. There was a record crowd of 11,837 for a Cup game v Aston Villa on 12 January 1924 but there was a gradual decline and the club came last in 1928-29 after conceding 115 goals. They lost their League status and returned to the North Eastern League whilst York City replaced them. There were hard times thus the ground was sold and used for greyhound racing in 1969, and the stand burnt down in 1971, but the club continue to play there.

Nelson began life in 1881 however the first competitive team played in the Lancashire League in 1889 and entered the Cup in 1893. They were forced to disband in 1898-99 but restarted and then played in the N.E. Lancashire League. They were promoted to the Central League after the First War and the 13 non-reserve teams became members of the Third Division (North) in 1921. The first League game was played at their Seedhill Ground in front of a record crowd of 9,000 on 27 August 1921. The club had more success than those above and were Division Three (North) champions in 1922-23, four points above Bradford Park Avenue. To celebrate the success they went on a tour of Spain and played teams like Real Madrid. They spent just one season in Division Two and they were relegated with Bristol City in 1923-24, and finished runners-up to Darlington in 1924-25 (only one team up). The team were often inconsistent and scored 104 goals in 1926-27 but finished last and conceded 136 goals in 1927-28. They finished bottom again in 1930-31 and won only six games and conceded 113 goals, and Chester replaced them in the League. The club were later reformed and played at Victoria Park whilst a motorway covered the Seedhill Ground.

There were few such stories in the "Capital" however there was one exception to this rule. West Ham United moved to Upton Park in 1904 whilst the Custom House Sports Ground was about a mile to the south off Prince Regent Lane. The latter was near to the Royal Victoria Dock (and the Custom House) and was aligned east to west and had a small pavilion on the south side and earth banking on the other three sides. The ground was reached along Bingley Road past some allotment gardens and it was present in 1919. There were considerable changes to the site in the 1920s and Nottingham Avenue was built at the end of Bingley Road - Custom House Sports Ground was demolished and replaced by the larger West Ham Greyhound Stadium and the pitch was then turned and aligned from north to south. This had covered stands on both sides and terraces around the ground and was also used for the new sport of speedway. Indeed the first track was opened at the Crystal Palace on 19 May 1928 and top riders such as Roger Frogley and Ron Johnson earned £100 per meeting at a time when top soccer players earned £8 per week. The venture was financial with income from greyhound racing and speedway and the owners decided to form a football team to increase their options (as at New Brighton). Thames F.C. joined the League in 1930 in place of Merthyr Town but lasted only two seasons. They played in the Third Division (South) but had a lack of support and only 469 spectators turned up for their home game v Luton Town in 1930; the lowest ever League crowd for a Saturday afternoon game. They came 20th in 1930-31 and 22nd in 1931-32 winning seven games and conceding 109 goals. They were not re-elected and became the only London club to lose their League status (to date), and were replaced by Newport County in 1932. The venue was present in the 1960s but the site is now covered with housing i.e. Atkinson Rd, Crooms Rd, Wilkinson Rd and Young Rd. They were the last to leave the League before the war, which brings the discussion nearer the present.

There was no League football in 1945-46 however Derby beat Charlton 4-1 in the Cup Final at Wembley. After the demise of New Brighton Tower there was a club called South Liverpool F.C. who played from 1911-21 but had to disband when their Dingle Park Ground was closed. Dr. Tom Martlew then became the main driving force behind a new club, New Brighton, who were formed after a public meeting at Egerton Street School on 28 June 1921. Some wanted to call the club Wallasey Town F.C. however it was discovered that New Brighton had already been registered. They had no link with the previous League club although Harrowby F.C. did offer them the use of the Tower Ground. They declined this since the cost was £50,000 and found a vacant site on Rake Lane in Wallasey and developed this as Sandheys Park and took the nickname the "Rakers". The ground was half a mile south of the Tower Ground between Osborne Avenue and Penkett Road. Some large semi-detached houses were near the venue although there were terraced properties across Rake Lane on Mornington Road, whilst the Welsh Presbyterian Church was to the north on the corner of Osborne Road. The club purchased the land after 20,000 ten-shilling shares were sold and the pitch was prepared, it originally having an 8-foot slope. The Lodge in Osborne Avenue was also purchased in August 1921 and was the club offices and changing rooms. There was a Main Stand on the north side and a narrow stand running the full length of the pitch to the south, and open land with trees to the east. It was quite a small ground and had a record attendance of c.15,000. The club took over South Liverpool's fixtures in the Lancashire Combination in 1921-22 and replaced Stalybridge Celtic in the Third Division (North) in 1923.

Dr. Tom and Dr. Robert Martlew were both club directors whilst their father "Old Doc Martlew" was an engineer and Chairman of the Wirral Railway. William Ralph Dean was born in Birkenhead in 1907 and as a young man played for the Wirral Railway football team. The brothers became acquainted with him and invited him to play for New Brighton however he stated he was not ready for League football. Maybe the story could have been different? Dixie Dean, as he was known, joined neighbours Tranmere Rovers in 1924 and transferred to Everton in 1925, and was one of the best centre-forwards England ever produced. George Camsell played for Middlesbrough in the Second Division and set a record of 59 League goals in 1926-27. Dixie Dean then pursued the record in 1927-28 and with one game to go had scored 57 goals. There was a crowd of 48,000 at Goodison Park to watch Everton beat Arsenal 3-1 and saw Dixie Dean score a remarkable hat trick to take the record of 60 goals. He was much sought after by other clubs and manager Herbert Chapman offered Everton, anything they wanted for him. He then moved to Notts County in 1938 and Sligo Rovers in 1939 and retired in 1940.

New Brighton started well like others and finished third behind Darlington and Nelson in 1924-25, and beat Sheffield Wednesday 2-1 at Sandheys Park in front of 12,408. They also reached the 4th round of the F.A. Cup three times however in general there was to be little glory. The club had to seek re-election in 1933 and 1936 but there was worse to come and Wallasey Corporation requisitioned Sandheys Park in 1944 and built pre-fab houses on the pitch. Of course many grounds had houses built on them at a later date, although this was by choice! The club secured the use of the Tower Ground in 1946-47 but had to seek re-election in 1948 and 1951 and on the last occasion lost their League status and Workington replaced them - they were the first club to go out after the war. They played in the Lancashire Combination but lost the tenancy of the Tower Ground and played at Castleway North, Leasowe at the expense of the Council in 1954-55. They returned to the Tower Ground the next season and had a remarkable Cup run, playing eight games to reach the 4th round, but lost 9-0 to Burnley at Turf Moor in front of 42,000. They had a loan of £8,373 from the F.A. to become owners of the Tower Ground in 1958 but declined in the 1960s and Wallasey Council purchased the site for £120,000. The club went to Hoylake six miles away and faded whilst New Brighton Rakers played in the mid-1970s.

Gateshead F.C. in the north east of England had one of the saddest football stories and matched the demise of Third Lanark in Scotland. The team South Shields Adelaide or the "Tynesiders" were formed in 1899 and entered the F.A. Cup and were runners-up in the North Eastern League in 1908-09. They became South Shields in 1910 and were champions of the same league in 1914 and 1915. They played at Horsley Hill and were elected to the Football League in 1919 and spent nine seasons in Division Two, finishing 9th in 1919-20 and 6th in 1921-22. The club, however, came last in 1927-28 and were relegated after winning only seven games and conceding 111 goals. They played in Third Division (North) however after financial problems relocated to Redheugh Park, eight miles away, and became Gateshead F.C. in 1930. This was similar to the recent change regarding Wimbledon and Milton Keynes, and the club were permitted to continue in the Third Division (North) in 1930-31. Redheugh Park was in the Low Team district of Gateshead south of the River Tyne and close to the River Team. The pitch was situated on Ropery Road opposite a hemp and wire rope works, beside the railway, and had stands on three sides and substantial terraces. Redheugh Sheet Iron & Steel Works overshadowed the ground and Team Valley Paper Mills was nearby. A tram terminus was located just at the end of Ropery Road and despite the industry there were two football grounds and a larger sports ground, just to the south.

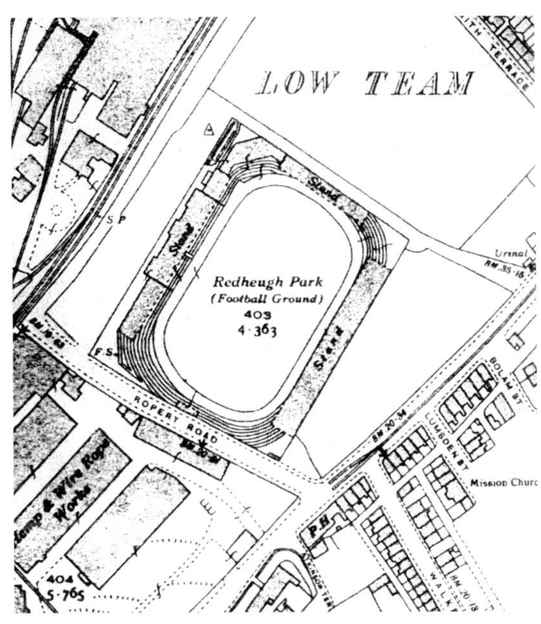

Redheugh Park, Gateshead - O.S. Map 1939.
Team leaders 1930-60.

Gateshead finished as runners-up to Lincoln City in 1931-32 and the teams were only separated by goal average - just 0-297 of a goal. They had to seek re-election in 1936-37 whilst a new South

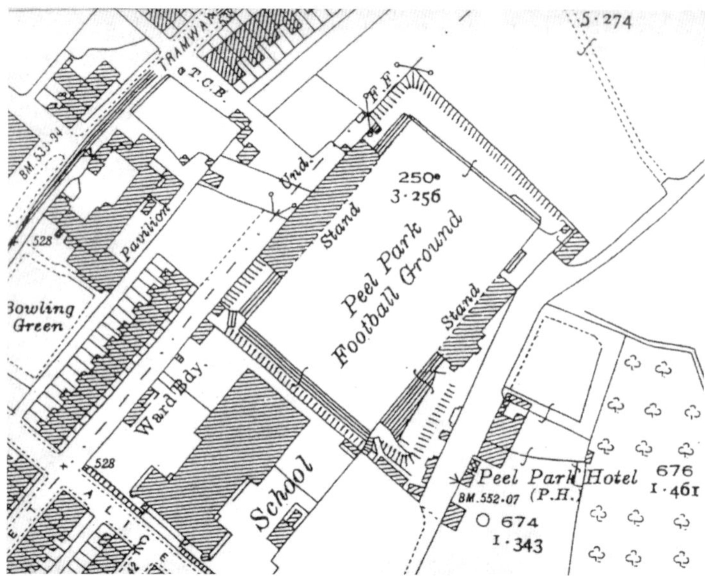

Who the heck are Accrington Stanley? O.S. Map 1931.
League football 1921-62.

Shields team joined the North Eastern League that season. Gateshead then had more success and came 4th in 1947-48, and they were runners-up to Doncaster by just two points in 1949-50. They then maintained a good position in the division whilst their greatest season was in 1952-53. They played Bolton Wanderers at Redheugh Park in the F.A. Cup quarterfinal and lost to a Nat Lofthouse goal in front of a record crowd of 17,692 - Bolton went on to reach the Final. The club were founder members of Division Four in 1958 and despite a good record finished in 22nd place in 1959-60. They had only applied for re-election on one occasion and both Oldham and Hartlepools were below them, but they lost their place in the League, which was a harsh decision considering their previous record - Peterborough United replaced them. They tried to join the Scottish League but without success, and played in regional leagues and joined the Northern Premier League in 1968, however Bradford Park Avenue took their place in 1970. They had the dubious pleasure of replacing their own reserve team in the Wearside League and after playing in the Midland League folded-up in 1973. The club then passed into history and Redheugh Park was demolished.

South Shields F.C. continued to play up until the 1970s and their ground Simonside Hall had a 20,000 capacity, whilst a new team Gateshead Town was formed and played in the Northern Combination. There was a strange repeat of history and South Shields sold their ground and amalgamated with Town to form Gateshead United. The new club played in the Northern Premier League at the Brendan Foster or International Athletics Stadium, Neilson Road but were disbanded in 1977. Gateshead F.C. was then formed and had some success and they were promoted to the Alliance Premier League in 1983, relegated in 1984-85 and reached the Conference in 1990. The ground was up to League standard and a friendly v Newcastle United resulted in a record crowd of 11,750 in 1995. The club came fifth in the Conference in 1995-96 but were relegated in 1997-98 and folded-up in 2004.

If the story of Gateshead was sad that of Accrington Stanley could bring tears to the eyes. They are the only founder member of the League to be demoted although strictly speaking it was their forerunner Accrington F.C. who had this honour viz. formed 1878, League 1888-93, disbanded in late 1895. The amateur club Stanley Villa were formed at Stanley Street in the east of the town in 1891. This was just south of Avenue Parade and the terraced houses reached the open spaces of Peel Park and Hillock Bank. They entered a district league with only seven teams in 1894-95 and became semi-professional when Accrington disbanded then played in the Lancashire League in 1895-98. They joined the Lancashire Combination in 1900, which mainly included reserve sides of League clubs, and were champions ahead of Manchester City (reserves) in 1902-03. The club was also top in 1905-06 and went to the Moorhead Ground in 1910, however the opposition weakened when the League clubs went to the Central League in 1911. The club closed down at the outbreak of war and by this time the Moorhead Ground had become dilapidated (and the rent was very high).

Sam Pilkington was the driving force behind the re-formation of Accrington Stanley in early 1919 and was a player, secretary and director at the club. With others he purchased a new ground at Peel Park for £2,500 and developed an enclosure capable of taking 20,000. The ground was off Burnley Road towards Hillock Vale in the east of Accrington. It had a large stand with a pitched roof on the north side and a further stand to the south with Peel Park Hotel behind. There was also a bowling green and pavilion behind the North Stand that suggested the site was previously used for cricket (and other sport). The east terrace had a large school next to it whilst Manor Street was then being built on the north side (it was near the old ground of Accrington F.C.). Hillock Bank overlooked the venue and in the distance was the town with its mills, works and chimneys. The club played in the Lancashire Combination in 1919-21 and they were founder members of the Third Division (North) in 1921. There was some concern that the northern clubs were not financially viable, however Accrington led the way and suggested they all paid a deposit to the League Committee. The team had limited success and crowds of 20,000 packed into Peel Park although they had to seek re-election in 1927, 1938 and 1939. They did better after the war and finished 6th in Division Three (North) in 1947-48 and had a squad formed entirely of Scottish players in the 1950s. They had to seek re-election again in 1951 and 1953 and featured on television in 1955. There was then an upturn and they finished as runners-up to Barnsley by four points in 1954-55, having scored 96 goals in the season - only Blackburn Rovers and Bristol City scored more. They came 3rd behind Grimsby and Derby in 1955-56 and also 3rd behind Derby and Hartlepools in 1956-57, and finished as runners-up to Scunthorpe in 1957-58 being founder members of the new Third Division in 1958.

The club, however, made some bad decisions and purchased a stand from the Aldershot Tattoo for £14,000 - a similar stand was erected on the Shrivenham Road Side at Swindon Town in 1958. The club soon had serious difficulties and they were relegated in last place in 1959-60 having conceded 123 goals in the season. This was the beginning of the end and the club were unable to complete the 1961-62 season. Their last game was a 1-0 defeat against Crewe at Gresty Road in a snowstorm. Indeed the storm clouds were gathering and the club owed £60,000 and had low gates and poor performances. Accrington Stanley could not meet their financial obligations and were 'forced' to resign from the League after 33 games (5 wins, 8 draws, 20 defeats, 19 goals for and 60 against). The club did not believe they had been treated fairly and Sir William Cocker the President stated: "I did think that since Accrington were among the promoters of the Football League we would have been given the breathing space we asked for to put our affairs in order. It was surely not too much to ask." The League then sold off the players and the whole matter caused considerable anger amongst supporters and Sir William considered suing 'those responsible'.

The club then entered the Lancashire Combination in 1962-63 but only in Division Two, which added insult to injury. The club was wound up in December 1963 and a new team Accrington F.C. was formed but could not use the name Stanley due to legal problems. The end was near and the last game at the neglected Peel Park was against Glossop with 50 spectators on 8 January 1966. The club was folded-up and there was soon little trace of the ground at Peel Park; the stands were torn down and the pitch became a wasteland with only a few hummocks to mark the site of nearly 50 years of League football. Accrington Stanley were reformed in 1968 and moved to the Crown Ground, Livingstone Road, Accrington, in 1970. They played in the Northern Premier League and have recently reached the Conference, and League football may soon return to Accrington (for the third time).

The story was similar after 1962 and a number of long-term members lost their League position. Bradford F.C. (Park Avenue) joined Division Two in 1908 but lost their League position in 1970 - their demise was discussed in Chapter 18. Cambridge United replaced them in 1970 and they folded-up in 1974, however re-formed as Bradford P.A. in 1988 with the aim of regaining League status. Meanwhile, Barrow F.C. or the Bluebirds were formed in September 1901 and played games at the 'Strawberry', Ainslie Street and Little Park Roose in the Lancashire Combination. They moved to their current ground Holker Street in 1909 and won the Combination in 1920-21 and were founder members of Division Three (North) in 1921. The club had little success in the League although played two notable Cup games after the Second War. They drew 2-2 with Swansea City in the third round in 1954 and there was a record crowd of 16,874 at Holker Street. They were founder members of Division Four in 1958 and played the mighty Wolves in the F.A. Cup third round in January 1959 but lost 4-2 in front of 16,340. The club came 22nd in Division Four in 1971-72 and were eight points ahead of bottom place Crewe however this was their eleventh re-election attempt, and they were voted out in favour of Hereford United (who had beaten Newcastle United 2-1 in the Cup in January 1972). They were founder members of the Alliance Premier League in 1979 and beat Leek 3-0 at Wembley to win the F.A. Trophy in 1990.

Workington on the coast of Cumbria had local iron ore and coal pits in the 18th century and thus became an industrial town with an important port - Henry Bessemer developed the 'conversion' process for making steel in the town. Workington F.C. formed in 1884 although there was no league at the time and competed in the Cumberland Cup from 1885. They were founder members of the Cumberland Association in 1890 and played in the Lancashire Combination in 1904-10, then for economic reasons spent one season in the North Eastern League, but folded-up in 1911. They were reformed as A.F.C. Workington in 1921 and re-entered the North Eastern League and their first game was against South Shields reserves. They played Preston North End in the F.A. Cup fourth round in 1933-34, but lost 2-1 at Lonsdale Park in front of 15,000. They then moved to Borough Park and joined Division Three (North) in place of New Brighton in 1951, but came last at the end of the first season. Bill Shankly was manager in 1953-56 and they played Manchester United at Borough Park in the F.A. Cup in 1958 with a record crowd of 21,000 but lost to a Dennis Violet hat trick. Their highest position was 5th in Division Three in 1965-66 however they were relegated in last place in 1966-67. Indeed the club had 13 directors at the time but even less full time players. They sought re-election in 1968, 1974, 1975, 1976 and 1977 and with gates of just 1,000 lost their League status to Wimbledon at the last attempt. They joined the Northern Premier League and after two relegations were champions of the North West Counties League in 1998-99. They won the last 14 games and this was their first major championship after 115 years!

Southport had a local rugby club in the 19th century however suffered some heavy defeats and decided to try soccer instead. Ralph L. Rylance a solicitor's managing clerk lived with his family at Carlton Villas, West Park Road, Blackburn, in 1881, and was the founding father of Southport F.C. that year. The club merged with Southport Wanderers to form Southport Central in 1888 and then played at Scarisbrook New Road in the Lancashire League. They were champions in 1903 and received promotion to the Lancashire Combination and moved to Ash Lane in 1905 - this was later renamed Haig Avenue and is their current ground. The Vulcan Motor Co. took over Southport Central in 1918 and played as Southport Vulcan for one year however the League Committee did not approve of this kind of 'sponsorship' and they reformed as Southport F.C. in 1919. The club played in black and gold and had the nickname the Sandgrounders; indeed the town certainly had some sand! They were founder members of Division Three (North) in 1921 and soon made their mark - with Exeter they were the first Division Three clubs to reach the sixth round of the F.A. Cup in 1931. The club then played Newcastle United in the fourth round of the Cup at Haig Avenue in 1932 and there was a record attendance of 20,010.

Southport had to seek re-election in 1935 and 1936, and nearly folded-up due to financial problems, and again in 1947, 1949, 1958, 1960 and 1964 - they joined Division Four in 1958. Billy Bingham became manager in 1965 and matters improved and they reached the fifth round of the F.A. Cup and were promoted. He then departed to manage Plymouth and Northern Ireland in 1968 and the club were relegated back to Division Four. They were champions of the division in 1972-73 but were relegated again and had financial problems and managerial changes. The club had to seek re-election in 1976, 1977 and 1978 and on the last occasion lost their League status by one vote (after a second round of votes). Southport F.C. was the last team to go out of the League by this process and Wigan Athletic replaced them. Haig Avenue was upgraded and the old covered terracing demolished and replaced in 1987. The club were champions of the Northern Premier League in 1993 and came third in the Conference in 1994-95 but struggled after that time.

The re-election process was now under scrutiny and there were a number of clubs who lost out; they no doubt wished that it had been abandoned long before. Southport was a 'lucky' team and continued in existence however others went to the wall upon losing their League status. The above is a comprehensive list of the teams who lost the re-election lottery, however there were several others that were forerunners of League clubs. Some of these are quite famous although others are less well known: Ardwick (1892-94), Walsall Town Swifts (1892-95), Newton Heath (1892-1902), Small Heath (1892-1905), Burslem Port Vale (1892-96, 1898-1907), Stoke (1888-90, 1891-1908), Leicester Fosse (1894-1915), Leeds City (1905-1919) and Rotherham County (1919-25). These had close links to clubs that followed them but some had more distant connections: Rotherham Town (1893-96), Chesterfield Town (1899-1909) and Wigan Borough (1921-31).

The most extraordinary story of survival, however, is the case of Hartlepool United F.C. The West Hartlepool Rugby Club laid out the Victoria Ground near to the docks in 1886 whilst a successful amateur club called West Hartlepool F.C. won the F.A. Amateur Cup in 1905. The rugby club was not a success and the ground was taken over by the newly formed Hartlepools United, in 1908, and they hoped to emulate the success of the amateur side. These plans, however, did not succeed and they were to seek re-election more times than any other club viz. 1924, 1929, 1939, 1960, 1961, 1962, 1963, 1964, 1970, 1971 and 1977. There was some limited success and they were runners-up to Derby County in Division Three (North) in 1956-57 whilst a young Brian Clough was appointed manager with assistant Peter Taylor in 1965. The club became Hartlepool United in 1977 however this made little difference and they sought re-election in 1978, 1983 and 1984. The club had applied for re-election on no less than 14 occasions, and somehow survived, whilst the system was finally abandoned in 1985-86. The last clubs to enter the lottery were Exeter City, Cambridge United, Preston North End and Torquay United - it would have been some story if Preston had followed Accrington out of the League.

Automatic promotion - relegation was introduced for one club in 1986-87 thus the bottom club was relegated into the non-League Conference. Due to this change several long-standing members soon lost their League status although other clubs that went down came back up viz. Lincoln City, Darlington, Colchester United, Halifax Town, Doncaster Rovers, Chester City and Shrewsbury Town. The rules were changed in 2002 so two teams could gain promotion and the leagues themselves were altered in 2004 - as a result it becomes more and more difficult to keep track of the changes. Lincoln City was formed in 1884 as a successor to an older club that started as early as 1861. They first played at the John Of Gaunt's Ground at the south end of the High Street behind a malt-house and stables of the same name. The site was sold in 1894 and covered by Sibthorp Street and the club then moved to Sincil Bank. They were founder members of Division Two in 1892 and then created some sort of record since they lost their League status in 1908, 1911, 1920 and 1987 but returned to the League in 1988 (and are still there).

Other clubs were less lucky. Newport County or the Ironsides formed in 1912 and played at Somerton Park on Cromwell Road just south of the railway - in the district of Somerton. The venue was just an athletic ground in 1921 but later had a stand on each side and a greyhound track around the pitch. They were founder members of the Third Division in 1920 and lost their League place from 1931-32 but were champions in 1938-39, three points ahead of Crystal Palace. They played in Division Two in 1946-47 but were relegated with 61 goals for and 133 against. They had some highs and lows, and during 1970-71 did not win one game in their first 23 matches, yet reached the quarterfinal of the European Cup Winners Cup in 1980-81. The club then had serious financial problems and finished bottom of Division Four, 19 points behind Carlisle, in 1987-88. They lost their League place after 68 years and folded-up although a new club was formed to try and regain League status.

A local newsagent helped form Aldershot F.C. in 1926 and they played at the Recreation Ground from 1927. This was unusual since it was situated in a public park and was near the railway station and below the redan, an example of a military fort (see Cotter Ch. 10). The club joined the League in 1932 and replaced Mansfield who transferred to Third Division (North) when Wigan Borough resigned. During the war some famous players were posted to the town on military service and played for the club i.e. Matt Busby, Denis Compton, Stan Cullis, Tommy Lawton, Wilf Mannion and Joe Mercer. They had severe financial difficulties in the early 1990s and resigned from the League on 20 March 1992 and went out of existence five days later. A new club Aldershot Town was formed and they were able to use the Recreation Ground and were accepted into Division Three of the Isthmian League. They had a successful rise up the pyramid to reach the Conference and may soon regain League status.

Doncaster Rovers was probably the most notable loss from the League. The club was formed in 1879 and played at various grounds until 1885 in the Belle Vue and Racecourse area of the town. They moved to the Intake Ground on Town Moor Avenue in 1885 and played in Division Two of the League from 1901-03 and 1904-05. They suffered a record 12-0 defeat against Small Heath in 1903 then during the latter season they won three games and had two draws out of a total of 34 games, which gave them just eight points at the end of the season. The club were clearly not ready for League football! They remained at the Intake Ground until 1916 when the army took it over and were then re-formed in 1920 and played at Bennetthorpe in 1920-22. They moved to Low Pastures on Bawtry Road opposite Doncaster Racecourse (with its grandstand dated 1881) in 1922, and this became Belle Vue Stadium - the current ground. The club entered the Third Division (North) when it increased in size by two members in 1923. They were not without success and won Division Three (North) in 1934-35, 1946-47 (with 33 wins out of 42 and 123 goals) and 1949-50. The ground was substantial if somewhat undeveloped and the record attendance of 37,149 was in October 1948 (as stated earlier). The club spent eight seasons in Division Two and their best finish was 11th in 1950-51 and had a number of famous managers including Lawrie McMenemy, Billy Bremner and Dave Mackay. The club and ground, however, gradually declined and they lost their League status in 1997-98 but returned stronger than before and regained their place in the 2003 play-offs.

Chester F.C. was formed in 1884 and moved to Sealand Road in 1906. The Main Stand was built there in 1931 and in the same year the club were elected to the Third Division (North). The club were renamed Chester City in 1983 and the last game at Sealand Road was in 1990. They then had a short spell at the Moss Rose Stadium in Macclesfield and moved to the Deva Stadium, near the old site of Sealand Road, in 1992. The club lost their League status in 2000 but regained their place in 2004. Shrewsbury Town was formed in 1886 and first played at the centre of Monkmoor Racecourse. They had several grounds then the local Corporation purchased Gay Meadow beside the River Severn in 1909 and the club moved there in 1910. The club played in the strong Midland League from 1938 and were champions in 1947-48 and achieved League status in 1950 - Third Division increased in size by four members **North** Scunthorpe United **South** Colchester United and Gillingham. The club spent ten years in Division Two and came 8th in 1983-84 but lost their League status briefly in 2003-04. The most recent teams to be demoted are Halifax Town and Exeter City - founder members of the Third Division, and Carlisle United (1928) and York City (1929) in 2004, whilst others that came and went are Maidstone United, Hereford United, Scarborough and Barnet. This discourse, however, is not the end of the story and for further developments - watch this space!

Table 6: **FORMER LEAGUE CLUBS**

Joined	Departed	Club Name
1888	1893	Accrington
1892	1893	Bootle
1893	1894	Middlesbrough Ironopolis
1892	1894	Northwich Victoria
1894	1897	Burton Wanderers
1891	1899	Darwen
1895	1900	Loughborough Town
1892	1901	Burton Swifts
1898	1901	New Brighton Tower
1901	1907	Burton United
1896	1912	Gainsborough Trinity
1898	1915	Glossop (North End)
1921	1923	Stalybridge Celtic
1921	1927	Aberdare Athletic
1921	1928	Durham City
1921	1929	Ashington
1920	1930	Merthyr Town
1921	1931	Nelson
1930	1932	Thames
1923	1951	New Brighton
1919	(1930)	South Shields (reformed)
(1930)	1960	as - Gateshead
1921	1962	Accrington Stanley
1908	1970	Bradford Park Avenue
1921	1972	Barrow
1951	1977	Workington
1921	1978	Southport

CHAPTER 20

Time To Make a Stand

The foregoing chapters have covered most of the significant elements of ground building in England and Scotland, and also the remarkable characters in the formative years of the game. There is, however, one more story to tell to bring the discourse to its conclusion. When visiting a League ground you could never be sure where the stands came from, or indeed, how they were built. In the case of Southend United F.C. the south terrace was, "One that I made earlier." The Roots Hall ground was first laid out on the site of an 18th century house called "Roots Hall" in 1900. Southend Athletic played there first but the newly formed Southend United replaced them in 1906. The latter stayed there until 1916 when the pitch was turned into allotments for the war effort. Southend Athletic, meanwhile, played at "The Kursaal", an amusement park named after a German health resort and near the usual sea front attractions. This became available in 1910 and Southend United moved there in 1919 and laid out a pitch and built an East Stand on Arnold Avenue.

The club were in the Southern League Division One in 1908-11, 1913-15 and 1919-20, and became founder members of Division Three in 1920. They moved to Southend Greyhound Stadium in 1934 however this was an unpopular venue with terracing a long way from the 'poor' pitch. The club were forced to stay there over 20 years and first considered a move back to Roots Hall in 1948 however this did not take place until 1955. During the forty years away from Roots Hall there were considerable changes in the landscape as a result of quarrying. A large quantity of sand was removed from the site and the new pitch was 35 feet lower than before. This was the last new ground to be built in the 'old' style and was followed by Glanford Park in 1988. The work to prepare the venue started in 1953 however it was eventually opened in 1955 with a short Main Stand on the east side, an uncovered terrace to the south, and covered terraces on the remaining two sides. Indeed the south terrace was only concreted at the front in 1955 and was gradually extended when funds were available. Sid Broomfield, the grounds-man, took charge of construction and he literally built the terrace stone by stone over five years from 1955-60. What an achievement! The record attendance of 31,090 was for an F.A. Cup tie against Liverpool in January 1979. A property developer purchased the club in the late 1980s and there were various plans to relocate. The south terrace was sold off in 1988 and 86 flats were built on the site - it had taken over five years to construct however was demolished in a few days!

In other cases stands were taken from one ground to another, like houses in Australia and New Zealand, and could be erected in just a matter of days. Aston Villa had a pavilion at Wellington Road, Perry Barr and when they left in 1897 the roof was taken to Muntz Street just off Coventry Road - home of rivals Small Heath. Other clubs took their stands with them when moving to a new ground. For example West Bromwich Albion moved the Noah's Ark Stand to the Hawthorns in 1900 and Port Vale moved the Swan Passage Stand to Vale Park in 1950. Manchester City, meanwhile, had two points of interest and became Ardwick and moved to Hyde Road in 1887. The ground was located between the Manchester-Crewe Railway in the west and terraced houses on Bennett Street in the south, with an industrial area north and east of the ground. In the first instance a railway line went across the northeast corner of the ground and was between the pitch and the terrace. The venue was always cramped with limited access (and trains going across the terrace) and after a fire in 1920 the club departed for Maine Road in 1923. The remaining stand was sold to Halifax Town and erected over the terrace at the Shay - it remained in Halifax for many years.

Some stands, meanwhile, came from other sporting venues. Accrington and Swindon purchased stands from the grounds of the Aldershot Tattoo in 1958. In the case of Accrington it brought them to bankruptcy, whilst the two-tier Shrivenham Road Stand at Swindon lasted until 1994. Mansfield Town moved to Field Mill in 1919 and the ground was slowly developed over the next few decades. The club purchased a stand from the recently closed Hurst Park Racecourse, near Hampton Court, in 1959. Due to financial constraints it was not erected until 1966 and was then re-constructed behind the old West Stand, the latter demolished and replaced by open terracing at its completion (Swindon used a similar method with their Main Stand in 1971). The Hurst Park Stand was first erected in 1937 and had rounded corners at roof level and reminded one of a date box! It was the most notable feature at the ground but was recently demolished and replaced. The practice of re-using stands went on into recent times and this happened with Chester as late as 1990. They left Sealand Road at this time and the roof of the Main Stand was sold to Port Vale and they used it to cover the Hamil Road End at Vale Park.

There were a number of oddities at League venues and some former uses have been well documented. Many grounds were literally a wasteland when the clubs first arrived and the fact football could be played was a credit to the people who prepared them. Brentford moved to Griffin Park in 1904, which was on the site of an orchard, and this must have taken more preparation than most. Southampton F.C. had an attraction to tricky grounds and their second venue at Avenue Road had a public footpath running across it. They were the most successful team in the Southern League and moved to the Dell in 1898 however when they arrived this was a swampy area with a stream running through it - the choice of name was quite descriptive! Brighton their neighbours were confronted with a different problem. John Clark lived at Goldstone House in the early 20th century near to Hove Park home of Hove F.C. He had been a director of Brighton United and his house overlooked an area known as Goldstone Bottom, and decided to develop it as a football venue. It was so named because of a large druid stone on the site and this had to be removed when the venue was prepared - put your backs into it lads! The stone was then erected in Hove Park. The ground at first had a 400-seat Main Stand and was offered to Hove F.C. and Brighton and Hove Albion used it from 1902 (they became the sole occupants when Hove departed in 1904).

There were also cases where grounds were developed on the site of a former quarry. Birmingham F.C. moved to St. Andrew's in 1906 and the ground was developed over ten months on the site of a former brick works - this involved extensive drainage of the pitch area. There were also good examples of such grounds in London. Crystal Palace moved to Selhurst Park in 1924 and the ground was prepared in a 'natural' hollow on the site of a former brickfield. Charlton Athletic moved to the Valley in 1919 and this was built on the site of a former sand and chalk pit - the large East Bank was aptly called "The Cliff". The most astonishing example, however, was to be found in Norwich. League football was slow to develop in the city although the game was played locally as early as 1868. Two local teachers formed Norwich City at the Critérion Cafe in 1902, and they first played at an enclosed ground on Newmarket Road with a wooden stand and pavilion. They were expelled from the F.A. Amateur Cup in 1904 thus they 'officially' adopted professional status in 1905, and replaced Wellingborough in Southern League Division One. They remained in the division for the next fifteen years and they were founder members of the Third Division in 1920. The ground at Newmarket Road had limitations, which were compounded when the owners imposed restrictions on when it could be used. The club then began to look for a new venue and relocated to the east of the city, and went to a site that was one of the most remarkable grounds ever seen.

Time to leave The Nest? O.S. Map 1914.
League football in Norwich 1908-35.

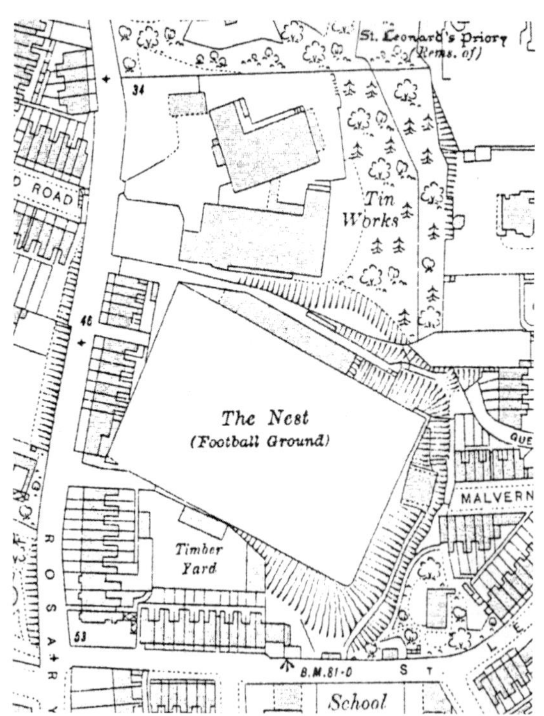

John Pyke, the Chairman, purchased a disused chalk pit on Rosary Road and moved a wooden stand there from Newmarket Road, having the ground prepared by 1908 - it was called "The Nest". Other grounds were on similar chalk pit sites however none were like this. The pitch at the Nest was up against a 30 foot cliff at the east end, and the houses of Rosary Road were close to the goal at the west end. The Newmarket Road Stand was erected on the north side and a cover the Chicken Run on the south. This was a cramped ground and, in addition to the quarry, was between a timber yard and tin works and near the local gas works and St. Matthew's Church. The ball often missed the goal and bounced onto the pitch off the cliff face, and there were even viewing points at the top. This was clearly a precarious arrangement and it was not a surprise when some barriers gave way at the top, in 1922, and it was only by good fortune that no one was killed or seriously hurt. There was an amazing record crowd of 25,037 for a Cup game against Sheffield Wednesday in February 1935, however this venue clearly couldn't last. A corner of the pitch collapsed into the old chalk workings and Norwich departed for Carrow Road in 1935 - they moved to an existing sports ground belonging to neighbouring firm Boulton and Paul. The new ground attracted George VI to a game against Millwall in October 1938. He was the first monarch to attend a Second Division game and presumably had some spare time and came down from Sandringham.

Other clubs progressed in a completely different direction and chose to locate their grounds in the centre of a racecourse. Derby County played at the Racecourse Ground from 1884-95 and this was the venue for a Cup Final replay in 1886 (discussed earlier). Indeed similar arrangements were seen elsewhere. Old boys of St. John's School formed Blackpool F.C. in 1887 and first played at Raikes Hall beside a cricket pitch and within a racecourse. The club joined the Football League in 1896 with Gainsborough Trinity and Walsall. Raikes Hall, a Victorian leisure park, had declined in popularity by the end of the 19th century and the club moved to the Athletics Ground at the centre of Whitegate Park. The football ground was at the centre of another racecourse and was behind the pavilion and trotting track. This was, however, an unpopular out of town location and now forms Stanley Park. The club returned to Raikes Hall and finished 8th in Division Two in 1896-97 and 11th in 1897-98 but had to seek re-election in 1898-99 and lost their League status along with Darwen. The club's rivals were South Shore F.C. who played at Cow Cap Lane but moved to a ground called Gamble's Field in October 1899 - beside the railway line to Blackpool Central Station. The clubs merged as a new Blackpool F.C. in December 1899 and Gamble's Field was renamed Bloomfield Road. They regained League status in 1900-01 but began poorly with a record defeat of 10-1 against Small Heath in 1901. They were no longer at the racecourse but were at the races for much of the 20th century.

Wrexham have a long history at the Racecourse Ground and horse racing was a popular sport that pre-dated professional football, thus races were first held in Wrexham in 1807. These meetings often became rowdy events and races were banned from 1858-72 and the site used solely for cricket. The cricketers formed a football club in 1872 and played on the cricket pitch within the racecourse, whilst the races were reinstated from 1873-1912. Wrexham played at Salisbury Park Road in 1872-80 and one game at nearby Aston Park in 1878 (Welsh Cup Final), and at Rhosddu Recreation Ground in 1880-83, but were expelled from the F.A. after unruly behaviour at a Cup game in 1884. Wrexham Olympic, forerunner of the present club, was formed at the Turf Hotel in 1884 and then played at the Racecourse Ground making it one of the oldest venues in the League (only Deepdale, Turf Moor, Feethams and the Victoria Ground were older). The club became Wrexham F.C. in 1887 and during these early years the club's activities were centred on the Turf Hotel. The original Main Stand was built on Mold Road in 1902 whilst the pitch was reached across the racetrack and was banked on three sides. The story of the Racecourse Ground comes in the 'strange but true' category. The last races took place in 1912 and the club were founder members of Division Three (North) in 1921 and were then able to develop the ground. A low gradient terrace was laid in front of the Main Stand and a cover erected at the Plas Coch End by 1929. The latter was joined to the Main Stand in the 1930s with an angled construction across the northwest corner - the Plas Coch Stand. The Popular Side was covered at this time whilst new changing rooms were built under the Plas Coch Stand in the 1940s.

The ground remained the same until after the Second War and the Town End or Kop was concreted in 1947, however there was soon to be a most unusual development. The club purchased 700 balcony seats from the local cinema in 1962 and erected them in the middle of the Kop End terrace! This peculiar structure was covered with a roof and received the nickname of the "Pigeon Loft". This was probably an unwelcome acquisition as most people liked watching football from a traditional terrace - cinema seats were for watching films. It certainly injected a degree of comfort for the spectators and was only previously matched by cushioned seats at Old Trafford in 1910 - anyone for the one and nines? This structure was to have a relatively long life span and the club decided to modernise in 1971 with a long-term aim of attracting more internationals. The Yale Stand was erected on the Popular Side in 1972, a new stand built at the Plas Coch End in 1978 and the Pigeon Loft demolished the same year. In fact the Kop End was only roofed in 1980. The pigeons may have flown but were soon able to find a new home in the old Main Stand on Mold Road. This dated back to the days of the racecourse and was closed as early as 1985 but was not replaced for fourteen years. The new Mold Road Stand was opened on 3 September 1999 and has a capacity of 3,500 seats.

Millwall had their origins on the Isle Of Dogs however but for a twist of fate they might never have been formed. It is uncertain how the Isle of Dogs received its name although may have been derived from 'ducks' or been a place where the King kept his hounds. Le Nôtre, designer of the park and garden at Versailles, laid out Greenwich Park for Charles II whilst Inigo Jones designed the Queen's House for Queen Anne in 1635. Sir Christopher Wren designed much of the Greenwich Hospital or Royal Naval College near the Thames in 1705. There were also Royal links in Deptford and Henry VII established a naval dockyard (1485-1869) and nearby was the Royal Victualling Yard (1745-1961). This was an area of great economic importance however the Isle of Dogs just opposite remained a marshland with few houses in the 18th century. There was a serious problem with shipping congestion in the Pool of London and John Perry built the first dock north of the Thames for East Indiamen, called Brunswick Dock, in the year 1789.

The unlikely named Willey Reveley (1760-99) was an architect who married Maria James (1770-1836) whilst in Italy. They both worked for Jeremy Bentham the political reformer and Reveley designed him a prison building called the Panopticon - a circular prison with warders at the centre. The couple had a son Henry Willey Reveley (1788-1875). It was recorded, meanwhile, that 3,663 ships entered the Pool of London in 1794 and something had to be done. Schemes were put forward to build further docks and Willey Reveley proposed an audacious plan in 1796. He noted that there was a large curve in the river around the Isle of Dogs and designed a scheme to straighten the Thames and use the curves for docks. The channel would have gone through Rotherhithe, the Isle of Dogs and Greenwich Marshes and left Ratcliffe, Greenwich and Blackwall 'islands and docks'. The plan was dismissed as too difficult an engineering feat however if it had gone ahead the geography would have completely changed and the 'isle' may never have developed. West India merchants then put up £800,000 for docks to be built however due to rival schemes this was held up and an Act finally passed in 1799. The outcome was the building of West India Dock (1802), London Dock (1805), East India Dock (1805) and Surrey Dock (1807) although Millwall Docks only filled the central area in the 1860s.

Willey Reveley moved in notable circles and was acquainted with William Godwin a radical political writer and his wife Mary Wollstonecraft who wrote *A Vindication of the Rights of Women*. The couple married in 1797 and had a daughter Mary Godwin (1797-1851) however the mother died soon after the birth. Maria Reveley nursed the child Mary for a time and after her husband died in 1799 received a marriage proposal from William Godwin in 1800. She turned this down and instead married John Gisborne and they went to live in Italy. Willey Reveley was also interested in Greek and Roman architecture and his sketches and drawings went to the Sir John Soane collection. Percy Bysshe Shelley was born in 1792 and came to hate tyranny whilst at Eton and wrote *The Necessity of Atheism* whilst at Oxford in 1811, and was promptly expelled and eloped with Harriet Westbrook aged 16. He liked the political writings of William Godwin and made his acquaintance but eloped with his daughter Mary in 1814 and went to Europe. They were both friends with Henry Willey Reveley who was an engineer and backed his scheme to run steamboats from Leghorn to Marseille, but it came to nothing. William Godwin was then reconciled with Shelley and his daughter Mary was author of *Frankenstein* in 1817. The 'Peterloo Massacre' took place whilst Shelley was abroad in 1819 and he promptly wrote *The Mask of Anarchy* blaming members of the Government for the outrage. He also published *A Call to Freedom*, which resonates in relation to this discourse (see below). Maria Gisborne became friends with Mary Shelley in Italy and on a visit to London kept Shelley's diary. The outcome was a long poem called *Letter to Maria Gisborne* written by Shelley at Leghorn on 1 July 1820. He was friendly with Leigh Hunt and Lord Byron and they published 4,000 copies of *The Liberal* in 1822 (but in Italy to avoid prosecution). Shelley was lost at sea when sailing to meet Leigh Hunt on 8 July 1822:

> Rise like lions after slumber in un-vanquishable number
>
> Shake your chains to earth like dew
>
> Which in sleep had fallen on you
>
> Ye are many they are few (*A Call to Freedom*)

Workers at the Morton & Co. jam factory formed Millwall Rovers on some waste ground in Glengall Road (now Tiller Road) in 1885. This was located on West Ferry Road on the Isle of Dogs however if Reveley's plan had been implemented would have been a channel of the Thames. Most of the team were Scottish and they moved to the rear of the 'Lord Nelson' in 1886 and became Millwall Athletic in 1889. They then had 'notice to quit' and moved to East Ferry Road in 1890. This was an enclosure capable of holding 15,000 spectators and was near to the West India and Millwall Docks south of Glengall Road and Strattondale Street. There was a small stand on the west side and a large oval of open banking around the pitch. It was the end of the Victorian age and Britain was engaged in trade around the world, thus the docks were full of vessels with tall masts and rigging. Millwall played their games at East Ferry Road with sailing ships as a backdrop and some notable teams came there including Preston North End and Sunderland in 1891. The Lions were champions of the Southern League there in 1895 and 1896, but were forced to move when the ground reverted to the dock company in 1901. They found a new venue just to the south, on a former potato field, that became known as North Greenwich. The entrance was located opposite to Chapel House Street and the spectators had to walk under a railway to reach the ground (a familiar pattern). There was a small stand on the south side, banking at either end, and wooden terracing on the north side with a rope works just behind. The ground opened with a friendly against Aston Villa in front of 5,000 in September 1901, however a Southern League game against Tottenham had a crowd of 11,000 in December 1901. The club left the Isle of Dogs and moved across the river to the Den at New Cross and the first game had 20,000 in October 1910. A map of 1916 shows the old ground on the Isle of Dogs as 'Football Ground (disused)' next to the Millwall Extension Railway and Welcome Institute.

There was, meanwhile, a similar nautical flavour in Hartlepool and the football club played at the Victoria Ground right next to the docks. These became a target during a German Zeppelin raid, in 1916, however the Germans were off target and it was the Main Stand at Hartlepool F.C. that was destroyed. Water also played an interesting part at Gay Meadow home of Shrewsbury Town. The ground was an important historical site long before the football club arrived and was an area of recreation from the 16th century. The club, as stated, arrived in 1910 however the close proximity of the River Severn was always a problem and there were severe floods in both 1948 and 1967 (on each occasion the water covered the pitch). There was also a business opportunity and for many years Fred Davies retrieved stray balls from the river in his coracle! He provided this service for a small fee until 1986. In other cases it was the stands and not the location that were unusual and West Ham F.C. had a stand the "Chicken Run" and Fulham had the "Rabbit Hutch" in the 19th century. Exeter City moved to St. James's Park in October 1894 and had several unusual names at the ground - the side terrace was known as the "Cowshed" and the end terrace as the "Big Bank". Further to this there was once a Greek market on the site of the ground and they gained the nickname of the Grecians.

Singers F.C. were formed in 1883 and became Coventry City in 1898 and moved to Highfield Road in 1899. This was a ground that was continually rebuilt and the Kop End on the eastern side was first erected in 1922. This was of irregular shape due to the curve of Swan Lane behind and the highest point in the northeast corner was called the "Crows Nest" - not a ship in sight. The club first had the nickname of the Bantams however there were major changes in 1961. Chairman Derrick Robbins brought in Jimmy Hill as manager and there was a complete image change. The club's strip was altered from blue and white stripes to sky blue, and the nickname was the "Sky Blues" (of course). The ground was also developed - a roof from Twickenham Rugby Ground erected over the west terrace in 1927 was replaced by a two tier stand at the west end in 1967. Jimmy Hill resigned in 1968 but returned as Chairman in 1975 and developed Highfield Road as the first all seated stadium - there were no new stands but just seats clamped to the terraces. This was extremely unpopular with supporters and visiting fans ripped the seats out, thus the Kop End reverted to a terrace by 1985. This all had to be changed again to seats after the Taylor Report.

There were different plans afoot in Bristol and at Ashton Gate the club had designs on moving the pitch. Bristol City came top of Division Two in 1905-06, ahead of Manchester United, and they were then runners-up in Division One in 1906-07. They reached the Cup Final in 1909 but lost 1-0 to Manchester United at the Crystal Palace in front of 71,401. The club were Division Three (South) champions in 1923 and 1927 and had hopes of returning to the glory days. With this in mind they built a cover at the Winterstoke End in 1928, which was notable for its great length. This extended way beyond the corner flags and the suggestion was that they planned to turn the pitch by 90° (although this cannot be proved). The hoped for revival did not come and City were relegated in 1932 and the ground at Ashton Gate was then left unchanged and unmoved.

There were, however, some even more exciting locations used by early League clubs namely in Victorian Pleasure Grounds. These developed as a mixture of sideshow entertainment, dance halls, exotic gardens and sporting venues. There are several good examples including Aston Villa, Blackpool, Grimsby, Hull, New Brighton Tower, Southend, Wolves and the Crystal Palace in south London. James Watt son of the famous engineer died at Aston Hall on 2 June 1848, this being an extensive property at the time. The house with its two wings stood on a hill overlooking the parish church and there were formal gardens near the house and a deer park beyond. To the north was a small lake called Dovehouse Pool that was used to supply fish to the house. This was rural at the time however the Grand Junction line was built just to the north, between Aston and Witton Stations, and there was soon terraced housing and industry covering the area. The lands of the estate were gradually sold off and the area around Dovehouse Pool was developed as a pleasure ground.

Charles Henry Quilter was born in Aston in 1856 and was the driving force behind a company that developed the Aston Lower Grounds, just north of Aston Hall. This was a triangular site with the Great Hall, a building ten times the size of Aston Hall, at the northern end. There was a cricket ground and grandstand to the west and an ornamental lake, formal gardens, smaller stand and the Holte Hotel to the east. The Great Hall was used to stage public events and there was an aquarium, restaurant, rifle range, fairground, camera obscura and various animals. The Meadow was the name of the sports ground and it was well developed with a 1,500-seat stand on Trinity Road and a track around the cricket pitch. A team referred to as the Quilters played football at the Meadow and Aston Villa used the venue for games in 1875-76. Charles Quilter married Annie Wattis in Aston in December 1878 and lived at Holte House, Lower Grounds with his wife and son, in 1881 - he being 'Manager of the Lower Grounds Company'. The household included four servants and two barmaids and it seems likely the property was the Holte Hotel. The census also shows that William and Ann Wood, coffee house keeper, lived at the Aston Park refreshment rooms with son Charles a baker, and Martin Fox (with his wife Emily) was lodge keeper at the Meadow Entrance. There were various people living in the wings of Aston Hall who were engaged in running the estate. The enterprise was run-down at the end of the century and housing covered the cricket pitch and a basic sports venue replaced the ornamental lake. Aston Villa rented the site in 1896 and a training ground was laid out where the Great Hall had stood and Villa Park opened, where the fish once swam, in 1897.

Blackpool F.C. formed in 1887 and first played at pleasure grounds called 'Raikes Hall Park, Gardens and Aquarium' or the Royal Palace Gardens. This was a few minutes walk from the sea front, and within easy reach of Blackpool Tower and the Winter Gardens, at the junction of Church Street and Park Road (with Hornby Road just to the south). The Raikes Hotel looked out over the cricket and football pitch and there was an ornamental lake nearby, with racecourse around the site. The hotel had an Indian Lounge and Ball Room attached and a theatre at the rear, whilst the grounds had numerous attractions viz. switchback railway, monkey house, skating rink, fountains, dancing platform, camera obscura, bowling green and tricycle track. Blackpool F.C. played League football in these grand surroundings in 1896-99 however after the club departed the venue declined and was eventually sold for housing. Leicester and Longton Roads cover the site and only Raikes Hall Hotel remains from these bygone days.

Grimsby Pelham formed in 1878 and they were named after the Pelhams, some local landowners. They became Grimsby Town in 1879 and took part in the F.A. Cup as early as 1882. They had three early sites, two of which were called Clee Park, however the facilities were basic and the players changed in bathing huts. People's Park was a large open space on the southern border of Grimsby with an ornamental lake, islands, fountains, swan house, refreshment rooms, bandstands, tree-lined walks and monument. It was just south of a large house called the Abbey with its fishpond, the latter built on the site of a mediaeval priory. Grimsby had to leave Clee Park as the town expanded in 1889 and rented a field immediately east of People's Park and south of Welholme Road. They spent £300 developing the site and brought the old stand from Clee Park and prepared an open ground for 10,000 spectators. The entrance lodge of the park and its flagstaff were just opposite Abbey Park, which opened in August 1889. Grimsby Town kicked off in the Football Alliance and came 4th in 1889-90 and 3rd in 1890-91 and they were founder members of Division Two in 1892. The club had a good record and never came lower than 5th from 1892-97 however Edward Heneage M.P. sold the site for housing in 1899. The club moved to Blundell Park back near the coast at Cleethorpes whilst Legsby Avenue covered the site of the old ground. The only maps surviving from the period are dated 1888 and 1908 and show the urban spread, however there is no visual record of Abbey Park. Grimsby Town came top of Division Two in 1900-01 and had two seasons in Division One although lost their League status in 1910-11. They were also in the top flight in 1929-32 and 1934-48 and Bill Shankly managed the club in 1951-53. **Note** Edward Heneage Esq. M.P. J.P. D.L. age 41 born London lived at The Hall, Hainton in 1881 with his wife, 6 children and 26 servants. The property was 15 miles south of Grimsby and Heneage Memorial Chapel still exists today.

The Tower Grounds at New Brighton are described in a guide to the Wallasey district dated 1902. This gives a good description of the Victorian Pleasure Grounds and states: "These magnificent grounds, which cost upwards of half a million pounds sterling, were opened to the public on Whit Monday 1897. The Tower, which is the highest structure in the kingdom, stands 621 feet above the sea level. From the top, which is reached by an electric lift, every few minutes, an unrivalled view is to be had of the Welsh mountains, the estuary of the Mersey and a panorama of the adjacent country. The grounds cover an area of 35 acres and are tastefully laid out. The theatre can accommodate 3,500 people and has the largest stage of any theatre in the Kingdom excepting Drury Garden. Two performances are given daily during the season and the best known variety artists engaged, and on Sundays classical concerts are held in the ballroom; most of the leading vocalists of the day are included in the programme and the orchestra numbers close on 100, the programmes comprising the works of the most celebrated composers of the past and present. A Café-Chantant conducted on Parisian lines, open free to visitors, is a popular feature, performances being given daily at 3pm and 8pm, no charge whatsoever being made for admission. The ballroom with inlaid parquetry floor, built on 2,000 carriage springs, makes one of the finest dancing floors in the country. The menagerie contains a fine collection of animals including two of the handsomest lions in Europe. The cycle track is pronounced by many professionals the best and fastest in the world."

There was no limit to what was on offer in New Brighton and the guide mentions that: "Two billiard saloons containing eight tables made by Ashcroft have been recently added. The Himalaya electric railway, water chute and Old English fair grounds add materially to the numerous other attractions, to this charming holiday resort. Whilst during the season are held band concerts, eisteddfods, musical festivals, carnivals and athletic sports, and seldom does a week pass without some special attraction being provided for the visitors." This formed an amazing backdrop in which New Brighton Tower played League football however the club could not be included in the list of attractions after 1902 (see Ch. 19). Some clubs around the country played in these spacious surrounds, but there was far more pressure on land in London and teams were forced to use grounds recently vacated.

Crystal Palace F.C. was formed in 1905 and played initially at the stadium used for the F.A. Cup Finals with the glass palace on the hill behind and numerous fairground attractions and lakes with 'dinosaurs' nearby. The club joined Division One of the Southern League in 1906 and must have found the arena rather large for contests at this level (like Q.P.R. at White City). They played local rivals Millwall on an annual basis and the crowds for the fixture were generally about 5,000. The best attendance for the visit of Millwall came in 1914-15: a crowd of 20,000 watched a 0-0 draw at the Den on Christmas Day and a further 20,000 saw Millwall win 1-0 at the Crystal Palace on Boxing Day. The club were forced to leave in 1915 after years of uncertainty concerning the future of the venue (see Ch. 12). The ground was then under the jurisdiction of the Admiralty and was used for the war effort, whilst Crystal Palace played their wartime games at Herne Hill Athletics Stadium. This was the home of amateur club West Norwood F.C. and staged the Amateur Cup Final in 1911 - near Dulwich Village and North Dulwich Station. The club was then unable to return to the Crystal Palace at the end of the war.

Croydon Common F.C. first played in Whitehorse Road on a site now covered by Henderson Road Playing Fields. They then became professional and moved to the Athletic Ground in Selhurst Road. This was laid out with a basic pavilion or stand on the north side and shallow banking around the athletics track. Selhurst Station was opposite and some open land and Norbury Brook was just behind. Croydon Common played in Division One of the Southern League in 1909-10 and 1914-15, and Crystal Palace was one of the visitors to the venue, however the former club could not continue and folded up in 1917. The Eagles saw their opportunity and took over the lease of Croydon Common Athletic Ground in 1919 and called the venue 'The Nest'. The club were founder members of the Third Division in 1920 and they were champions at the end of the season above Southampton. They then played in Division Two and teams such as Manchester United and Leeds United came to the ground, however it was limited with just one entrance and the club never intended to stay there. They moved half a mile to Selhurst Park in 1924 and the old ground reverted to the railway company and Selhurst Railway Depot covered the site - no trace of this shared venue remains.

Clapton Orient had similar problems although they were one of the first southern clubs to join the Football League in 1905 and only Woolwich Arsenal, Luton Town and Bristol City preceded them. Their time at Millfields Road has already been discussed thus this section continues with their arrival at Lea Bridge Road in 1930. The venue was opened as a speedway stadium in 1928 and was situated behind some works next to the railway and Lea Bridge Station. There was a stand on the south side and a large bank at the western end, plus a cinder track around the pitch. The club, however, had problems from the start - the main one being the width of the pitch. The League deemed that the ground was of an unsuitable standard in November 1930, and the club had to make other arrangements. Orient failed to secure a local venue at Brisbane Road or Walthamstow Avenue and played Brentford in a League game at Wembley. This seemed to be a success and it was followed with a Cup game against Luton at Highbury and a second League game against Southend at Wembley. On the latter occasion the ground receipts were too low, and matters had been resolved at Lea Bridge therefore the club went back there - the speedway company finally agreed to enlarge the pitch. These were difficulty times, however, and the club finished four places off the bottom of Division Three (South) in 1930-31. The team just below them was Thames F.C. and there was talk of a merger. Despite these problems they stayed at Lea Bridge Road and a record crowd of 20,288 (or 20,400) watched a Division Three (South) game against Millwall on 13 March 1937. The venue was not suitable for such a crowd and Orient departed a few months later, whilst the stadium was closed in 1938 after only 10 years.

Leyton F.C. formed in 1868, making them one of oldest clubs in London (Cray Wanderers date from 1860). They played in the F.A. Cup in 1874-77, their opponents including Clapham Rovers and Upton Park, and became professional in 1905. They played at Osborne Road in Leyton (later Brisbane Road) in 1905-14 and entered the Southern League, being runners-up in Division Two in 1905-06 and thus played in Division One in 1906-12. It was the equivalent of a 'Third Division' and their opponents included Brentford, Crystal Palace, Millwall and West Ham. They had a good side and the team included Charlie Buchan (1891-1960) who was later a star for Sunderland and Arsenal (under Herbert Chapman). Indeed they did well in the F.A. Cup in 1909-10 and beat Croydon Common, New Brompton and Stockport, before losing 1-0 at home to Leicester Fosse; and played both Chelsea and Liverpool in the Cup in 1910-12. The club could not continue at this level and returned to amateur status and played in the South Essex League from 1912 and left Osborne Road in 1914. The ground was then the home of the Bryant & May works team.

Leyton F.C. joined the Athenian League in 1927 and won the Amateur Cup Final in 1927 and 1928, then returned to Brisbane Road in 1929. They had a successful side and soon appeared in three more Amateur Cup Finals however they had to leave the ground, after the rent was not paid, in 1937. Clapton Orient then moved to Brisbane Road and inherited a ground with an old East Stand and terracing on three sides. Their first game was against Cardiff on 28 August 1937 and they became Leyton Orient in 1946, whilst the ground was only developed after the war. Leyton F.C. eventually found a new ground in Lea Bridge Road and continued in the Athenian League until 1975. They merged with Wingate F.C. to become Leyton Wingate in 1975 and altered their name to Leyton in 1992 - the club played in the Isthmian League. There was a merger with Walthamstow Pennant in 1995 and this resulted in a club called Leyton Pennant. There was one final twist to the story when a new club Leyton F.C. was established in 1997. They played at Wingate Stadium, Lea Bridge Road and after a dispute regarding their origins (due to the mergers) took out a High

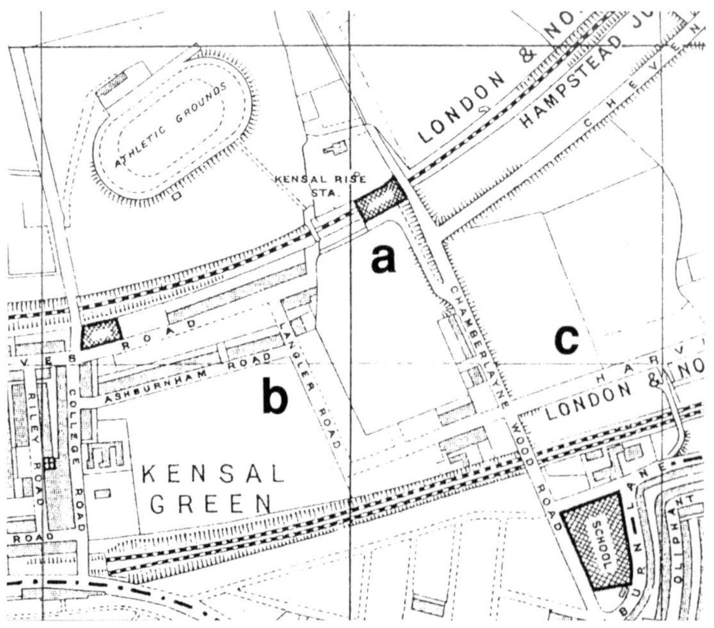

Queens Park Rangers or Rovers? O.S. Map 1894.
(a) Welford's Fields 1886-88 (b) Kensal Rise Green 1890-91
(c) Kilburn Cricket Ground 1892-96. Top - Kensal Rise Athletic Ground.

Court action on 26 July 2002. They stated that their club was the 'original' Leyton F.C. with a history back to 1868.

Queens Park Rangers (or should it be Rovers) had a similar pattern to Crystal Palace and Leyton Orient with a considerable problem finding a permanent ground, and each time they settled were forced to move again. The club hold the record for the most number of grounds having played at 13 venues, with 17 changes. The club was formed in the Queen's Park area of London in 1885 although never actually played there, and they are discussed in more detail in Chapter 13, whilst their grounds are listed below. Rangers made the final move to Loftus Road (Stadium) in 1917, former home of Shepherd's Bush F.C., but had two periods at the White City in 1931-33 and 1962-63. Kensal Rise Athletic Ground, or the National Athletics Ground, was an important early venue with a running and cycle track and small pavilion set back on the north side - the main entrance via a path from College Road. New streets were laid out around the stadium before the First War and Liddell Gardens on the north side was named after Sir Frederick F. Liddell K.C.B. local landowner. The stadium closed in the mid-1920s and housing covered the site. Eric Henry Liddell (1902-45) was born at Tientsin, China the son of Scottish missionaries. He was educated at Eltham College, Blackheath and gained a BSc at Edinburgh, then ran in the Olympic games in Paris in 1924. He became famous after refusing to run the 100m on a Sunday due to religious beliefs, although won a gold medal in the 400m - he did not expect to win and attributed the victory to God (*Chariots of Fire*). He went to China as a missionary in 1925 and his family moved to Canada for safety in 1940, but he died in a Japanese internment camp at Weishien. He was a great friend to the children in the camp and arranged athletics events for them - Liddell Gardens might have been named after him (but was not).

1886-88: Welford's Fields - south of Kensal Rise Station with entrances in Chamberlayne Wood Road and Harvist Road, today Bolton Gardens and Linden Avenue cover the site.

1888-90: London Scottish Ground, Brondesbury.

1890-91: Home Farm & Kensal Rise Green, the latter was south of Ashburnham Road and Burrows Road covers the site.

1891-92: Gun Club Ground on Wormwood Scrubs, now next to the West London Athletics Stadium.

1892-96: Kilburn Cricket Ground - opposite Welford's Fields north of Harvist Road, today Kempe Road covers the site.

1896-01: Kensal Rise Athletic Ground between Liddell Gardens and Clifford Gardens - Whitmore/ Leigh Gardens cover the site.

1901-02: Latimer Road - St. Quintin Avenue, North Kensington.

1902-04: Kensal Rise Athletic Ground.

1904-07: Park Royal Showgrounds - Royal Agricultural Society horse ring, Cumberland Avenue is on the site.

1907-15: Park Royal Ground south of Coronation Road and next to the old station, Johnson Way is on the site.

1915-17: Stamford Bridge, Kensal Rise Athletic Ground.

This discussion of ground sharing brings us to a related subject namely that of the closest grounds. The story in Nottingham and Sheffield has been well documented and in both cases the club histories are closely connected. County and Forest have always been in close proximity whilst United and Wednesday played near one another until 1899. Indeed, Meadow Lane (County) and the City Ground (Forest) are the two closest League grounds in England and face one another across the River Trent. These are, however, not the closest League venues in Britain and the honour goes to the city of Dundee. The homes of Dundee F.C. (Dens Park) and Dundee United (Tannadice) are both in Tannadice Street high on a hill above the city. There is also a modern trend for building close and the Eyrie, home ground of Bedford Town, is right next door to Bedford United. The two closest grounds in the country, however, are to be found on the south coast. Hastings F.C. play at the Pilot Field an extensive ground that once had a track around the pitch. There is a large Main Stand on the south side, earth banking on the north side and a covered terrace at the Elphinstone Road End, whilst the capacity was recently 10,000. St. Leonard's F.C. are their near neighbours and play at the Firs, which is immediately adjacent to the north side of the Pilot Field. The ground is at 90° and it is possible to look down from the rear terrace and see the Pilot Field below, whilst the two share a wall around the perimeter (built at the same time). These are surely the two closest grounds in the country and, indeed, it's a short journey to play one another away.

This chapter reveals some of the most unusual and interesting stands and is concluded by considering two of the most important developments, outside of the Leitch stable. Scunthorpe has long been a centre for the iron and steel industry and this association secures its place in football history. The Old Showground was on Doncaster Road and just north of Scunthorpe Station and had a long sporting history. It was initially used for agricultural events whilst Brumby Hall F.C. played there in 1895. This team merged with other local clubs to form Scunthorpe United in 1899 and then with North Lindsey United to form Scunthorpe and Lindsey United in 1910. The club were known as the Iron and first played in the "exclusive" Lindsey League, in 1912, then in the stronger Midland League from 1912-50. A small wooden stand with seating for 340 was erected in 1914 however burnt down in 1925 and the ground had few developments during their time in the Midland League. There was a Main Stand on the west side and a wooden stand on the east side. The club were champions of the league in 1926-27 and a cover was added at the Fox Street End in 1938. They were champions again in 1938-39 and shared the ground with Grimsby Town during the Second War - Blundell Park was in a dangerous location and could not be used for spectator events.

Scunthorpe United joined Division Three (North) in 1950 when it was increased in size from 22 to 24 members (with Shrewsbury Town). The ground was improved after the club achieved League status and the terrace at the Doncaster Road End was covered in 1954 - the name Lindsey was dropped in 1956. The club were champions in the last season of Division Three (North) in 1957-58 however there was another fire at the ground and the wooden East Stand burnt down soon after. This was replaced with the first cantilevered stand to be built at a British football ground. There had been such stands on the Continent and at other venues like racecourses since the 1930s, but this important development in construction was slow to come to football grounds - the fans had become accustomed to watching around the posts. The reason this took place in Scunthorpe is obvious, namely the proximity of the ground to the steel industry. The new stand was just 50 yards long and had bench seats for 2,200 and faced the Main Stand on the west side, and opened on 23 August 1958. The Fox Street End was re-roofed in 1959 however the ground then remained unchanged and came under scrutiny in 1985.

The club could not afford the improvements and decided to sell the ground and relocate. The last game at the Old Showground was on 18 May 1988 and the ground was soon demolished; there were attempts to relocate the cantilevered stand but this proved impractical. The club moved to Glanford Park on the outskirts of town in the neighbouring district of that name, and this was the first in a new generation of grounds. It was opened on 14 August 1988 but took a step backwards since only the Main Stand on the west side was cantilevered - the other sides had roofs supported with columns. This was similar in design to the Bescot Stadium, Walsall opened two years later. The developments in Scunthorpe came in 1958 however a new West Stand was built for Sheffield Wednesday at Hillsborough three years afterwards. This was also cantilevered but was on a totally different scale and had seats for nearly 10,000 spectators. Stanley Rous, F.A. Secretary, opened the stand on 23 August 1961 and it is now the oldest of the type in the country.

Leitch provided a basic blueprint for ground design in 1900 and his schemes were still being followed decades later. There was often little innovation and the above provides ample evidence of this. There were, however, a few who dared to be different and the architects of Highbury used a modern approach and brought the latest architectural styles to ground design. Archibald Leitch built the Main Stand with its multi-span roof on the east side in 1913. The remainder of the ground had open terracing whilst Arsenal was a mid-table team in Division One after the First War but were close to relegation in 1924-25. Herbert Chapman came to the club at the end of that season, fresh from his success with Huddersfield Town, and turned things around. He introduced new techniques of play and off-field strategies that made Arsenal the top club in the country. The club won the F.A. Cup in 1930 and their first League title, also the first for a southern club, in 1930-31. Arsenal required a stadium to match their new status and employed Claude Waterlow Ferrier an architect who had studied in Paris, and was familiar with the Art Deco style and the modern movement. Walter Gropius in Germany, Le Corbusier in France and Frank Lloyd Wright in America were the leading exponents. His first work was to extend the terraces at either end in 1931, and he then turned his attentions to the west side. He designed a stand that was in a completely different league to those that had gone before with modern style and Art Deco design. The scheme was simple with a bold white façade, horizontal and vertical lines, and some red club motifs and the total cost £50,000. The upper tier had 4,100 seats and glazing to protect spectators, and was located over the terracing below. A house was purchased to provide a new access point at the southern end and the new entrance was in the same style. The Prince of Wales (later King Edward VIII) opened the West Stand on 10 December 1932. Ground design up to this point had been lagging behind modern trends in architecture - the lack of innovation was now corrected.

Arsenal won the title in 1932-33 however Herbert Chapman was taken ill with pneumonia and died in January 1934, whilst the club won the title in 1934 and 1935. They matched Huddersfield's record from the 1920s and the largest attendance at Highbury was 73,295 in March 1935. Ferrier also designed a cover for the North Bank but died in July 1935 before the work was finished. The club continued their success and won the F.A. Cup in 1936. The Main Stand built by Leitch in 1913 had not lasted well and suffered from high maintenance costs associated with multi-span roofs - it was only 23 years old. William Binnie designed a new stand in a similar style to that on the west side, but with two tiers of seats (4,000 at each level) and a small terrace in front. The other significant difference was the price at £130,000. There was a bold façade in Avenell Road with white vertical elements and red horizontal lines, and the name Arsenal Stadium and a relief of a gun carriage. The most famous feature was a marble entrance hall with a bust of Herbert Chapman and the stand was opened on 24 October 1936. The club then won the title again in 1938. The stands at Highbury had no comparison and were the apex of ground design in the early years of the Football League.

Arsenal Stadium Mystery? The Gunners marble halls.

Highbury East Stand. Art Deco style care of Binnie dated 1936.

Retrospection

So what conclusions can be drawn from this debate; has anything been added to the much digested subject of soccer? The answer is clearly yes. Available histories give a potted account of our football heritage revealing the general story of the game without putting it in a broader context, whilst they fail to examine the character of the main players. It is hoped that this history has corrected these two omissions and exposed the development of the early game in relation to the society of the time. This was not simply a case of 'number crunching' endless facts for no reason. It was only through the use of great detail and the consideration of all the facts that new information has come to light and the truth behind early soccer shown, especially regarding the F.A. Indeed the gentlemen who started soccer are revealed as never before and have 'truly' been brought back to life. In some cases they are shown in a bad light, but no disrespect was meant, and in general they were of the highest integrity with a love of soccer and a uniting passion for the game.

The book, as stated, explores the economic and social climate in which the game of soccer developed and these influences cannot be ignored. Adam Smith (1723-90), the economist from Kirkcaldy, produced an essay entitled *The Wealth of Nations* in 1776 and explored the value of free markets and the by-product of public welfare. His basic theory was that if everyone worked for economic advancement, without intervention or controls, then the whole of society would benefit. This was written in the same year as tenders were put forward for the building of the first iron bridge at Coalbrookdale (completed 1780). The Industrial Revolution then took place in Britain and as Smith suggested it was individual ambition that drove matters forward. The creation of wealth and opportunities for personal advancement caused a change in society and a gradual erosion of the more 'feudal' ideas and institutions. Indeed these ambitions could not be contained within the limits of Great Britain and important markets were developed around the world. This caused a drive towards Empire not seen before, with external markets underpinning the economy and thus the wealth of the nation. There could be no threat to this success and many markets and trade opportunities were secured through military activity and the use of 'gunboat' diplomacy in the 19th century. The stories contained in this book are clearly part of a more general history of Empire and militarism however Adam Smith's ideas of public welfare can be debated.

The by-product of wealth creation, whether on an individual or a national basis, is the concept of winners and losers. It may be true that society in general benefited from this industrial drive and indeed the people in this book are mainly those who succeeded, however there were clearly others who lost out. Thomas Malthus (1766-1834) produced *An Essay on the Principle of Population* in 1798 and provided a counterpoint to the ideas of Smith. During this period improvements in health witnessed continual population growth in Britain and Malthus predicted that poverty and famine would be the outcome (also on a global scale). He said this was the hand of God and a decline in living standards for many, in the 19th century, supported these ideas although social reformers disliked his negativity and believed man could alleviate matters. The facts, however, at home and in the Empire suggest Malthus was correct at least in some respects. The inequality of such wealth creation and Empire is supported by examples in this book as well as by the more general aspects of history. For instance Stevenson 'put a few slaves aside for his children' in Jamaica, whilst Cotter received extra army rations as his countrymen died of starvation. These inequalities and perceived injustices led to insurrection at home and abroad thus shaping 19th century world history.

The British authorities were often insensitive to people's needs and used military and police force to repress these complaints, leaving situations that dominate society up until the present. The *Corn Laws* were introduced in Britain in 1804 to protect the larger landowners however this kept prices high and caused hardship. At the same time industry and machines destroyed people's livelihoods and resulted in the activities of the Luddites. The latter first destroyed stocking frames in Nottingham in March 1811 and shearing frames in the area of Halifax, Huddersfield, Wakefield and Leeds in February 1812. The high wheat prices resulted in starvation in Manchester and a mob of around 1,000 people went and destroyed machinery there in 1812. The calls for reform were slow to be answered and the reaction of the Government often violent and 12,000 troops were sent to the area leading to the 'Peterloo Massacre' in Manchester in 1819. The Addisons no doubt experienced such difficulties in Bradford and Huddersfield whilst the Hoomans tried to help the impoverished weavers in Kidderminster in the 1820s. Orators such as Cobden and Bright continued to press for reform of the *Corn Laws* in the 1840s and did in fact have support from the Kinnaird family. Indeed the *Corn Laws* were eventually repealed in 1846 however this failed to stop the

Irish potato famine of 1846-50 - a disaster Malthus predicted. It is unclear whether free trade or control was the cause however the selfish pursuit of wealth by nations and individuals alike perpetuated the hardship. Indeed Darwin developed his theories of *Natural Selection* after reading Malthus.

The French Revolution (1793-1801) caused much nervousness amongst the British ruling classes and the conflicts of Empire led to the Napoleonic and Peninsular Wars (1803-15), whilst reform was slow with the abolition of the slave trade in 1833, however it was during the Victorian period that such trading ambitions led to the most conflict. The people already discussed were involved in many of these wars that helped shape the world map and also attitudes towards the British nation. The list of conflicts is almost endless: 1st Afghan War (1839-42), 1st Sikh War (1845-46), 2nd Sikh War (1848-49), Crimean War (1854-55), Persian War (1856-57), Sepoy Rebellion and Lucknow (1857), Ashanti War (1873-74), Perak (1875), Arabi Pasha Revolt (1882-84), 1st Sudan War (1884-85), 3rd Burma War (1885-87), Chitral (1895) and the Boer War (1899-1902). Many of these were a direct result of colonial activity and were fuelled by resentment against domination and the presence of inequality, however this was only part of the story and the Victorians were involved in reform and brought many improvements to the world. For instance Wollaston, Watt, Boulton and Muirhead were involved in science whilst the Engineers used their skills around the world.

The individuals discussed in this book had a major role in the history of Britain, at home and abroad, and are simply a part of this history and its process. They cannot be blamed, or otherwise, for the products of Empire or the inequalities of wealth although as J.P.'s and the like they were in authority, whilst for each family in the book there were always a number of un-named servants who supported them. Victorian society had advanced from the feudal days but it remained rigid and only a few crossed these boundaries either through business success or within the army - there are several examples in this book. Despite the amount of detail the precise nature of these people can only be estimated, although in relation to soccer they had the highest of ideals. The Victorians were great innovators and took up new ideas with a passion, this certainly being true of sport. Indeed the growth of soccer could only take place with the creation of wealth and the spare time that this created - no one could kick a ball around if the table was bare. Thus the games development in the public schools and later at a popular level was tied to the economic prosperity of the country.

These discussions have revealed several facts that have lain hidden for decades and some are of particular interest - those of most significance are as follows: The story of E.C. Morley and Barnes F.C. appears in several books on the subject however his religious background and the contribution of Willis and Graham is not mentioned. The Alcock family had success both financial and social however the tale of J.F. Alcock provides an insight into the other side of Victorian society. Further to this the true origins of Forest F.C. are discussed and this questions the *versions of history* in other publications - did Alcock colour the facts? The story of F.J. Wall revealed the fragility of Victorian and Edwardian society and showed how the status of its officials could not be tainted by 'common' origins. Arthur Pember, however, was the jewel in the crown and he was certainly a man of disguises and surprises, whose role in soccer history has long been forgotten. Indeed he should always feature in the first chapter and the time of 'hand-me-down' football histories must now end.

Morley was 'The Father of Football' however Pember was the engineer and designer of the modern game and instrumental in the separation of soccer from the rugby code, yet this fact has been completely ignored and the existing histories give him no credibility at all, stating - not much is known about him. Some do not mention him at all! This serious oversight has now been corrected and the place of Arthur Pember in the history of soccer has been guaranteed. He was a man of eccentric tastes with an extraordinary history to boot and the revelations about his life are almost beyond belief, providing a discovery that rewrites a portion of British history. Arthur Pember was the original Sherlock Holmes and the facts of the case have remained hidden for over 100 years. The stories of Marindin, Kinnaird and Clegg provide an insight into a life now long gone and their biographies cement their place in football history, whilst those of the Wanderers and the Engineers are equally interesting. Their stories unfolded after detailed research and it was discovered that none of them were ordinary men, their families being involved in all aspects of British history and touching all corners of the Empire. There was a new surprise at every turn and it was hard to believe that these early players were so prominent, with so many notable associations.

Indeed the real surprise was that no one knew. How could the origins of these men have been lost? The truth lay in the nature of early football, which was an exclusive amateur game for men of rank and position with time for 'idle pursuits'. Football was taken seriously with good reports in newspapers, however it was just a pastime and the private lives of the players were not discussed. The anonymous nature of these reports meant there was nothing for the historian to find, however this omission has now been redressed and the importance of these people revealed. When the players run onto the pitch for the Cup Final they truly live again and have indeed become like old friends. There are many books on the history of football grounds and this is a fascinating subject, however the aim here was to entwine all the strands. The scene was set with the history of the early F.A. and the amateur game whilst in Section II the nature of professional football was discussed. This kicked off in the 1888-89 season and the details of the grounds, at the time, helps to provide a mental picture of that first season. The discussion of major grounds and unusual venues is not new however the book details the most interesting facts, whilst the description of 'former' League clubs is concise and complete - Ironopolis and Thames may raise eyebrows whilst New Brighton Tower are most illuminating.

Archibald Leitch played a major role in football ground history and no book on the subject is complete without him, however most existing publications give him a brief mention. This situation is also redressed and contained within is the most detailed exposé of his life available. The work he did on football grounds is well documented however little is known of his life and the facts of this are now revealed, in particular his grand homes. Despite this there is little remaining to record his achievements and most of his great football grounds have now gone. This is true of many characters in the book and this brings us to the affliction of 'plaque-itis' or the need to erect blue plaques to obscure or unknown individuals - there is a proliferation of these in London. These may have been important people in their field however they are often artists, philosophers, writers and scientists of little popular fame. Where are the blue plaques to the founders of our national game and the F.A.? The answer is none exist however this book provides some likely contenders if problems of money, planning and bureaucracy can be overcome. Surely the heroes of our national game should be rewarded in this way?

The most obvious contender for this honour is the home of E.C. Morley at 26 The Terrace, Barnes where the rules of the F.A. were formulated although 3 King's Bench Walk could also be a candidate. There are then the homes of Willis at 25 Dover Street and 5 Beverley Villas, Barnes or the site of Graham's home at St. Alban's in Hampton. For Alcock one could consider Sunnyside Lodge at Chingford, 14 Park Square East in Regent's Park, 2 Albert Villas Twickenham, Exhims at Northchurch and especially 16 Ennerdale Road at Kew. F.J. Wall the Secretary had several houses that still exist including 118 Northcote Road, Casewick House and naturally 22 Lancaster Gate. The homes of Arthur Pember at "Langlands", Kings Road and 26 Carlton Road have gone but a plaque could go on 1233 Third Avenue, New York - funds permitting. Other properties regarding the F.A. Presidents include 22 Sussex Villas, 3 Hans Crescent, 35 Hyde Park Gardens, 1-2 Pall Mall East, Plaistow Lodge and 10 St. James's Square in London but the latter would compete with one to three Prime Ministers. There are also Craigflower or Rossie in Scotland and some good candidates in Sheffield for Clegg such as Cliff Tower and Clifton House.

In terms of the Wanderers Morton Peto Betts "Scorer of the first Cup Final goal" lived at 29 Tavistock Square, Bloomsbury and The Holmwood in Bickley, whilst R.W.S. Vidal "The Prince of Dribblers" lived at Cornborough House - a bit out of the way. The Hooman family lived at 6 Holly Terrace, 2 Fitzroy Villas and 6 Hermitage Villas in Highgate which all still exist and the red carpet could be laid out there; whilst 31 Norfolk Crescent, the site of Lancaster Lodge and Heath End are available for Crake and Welch or The Grove at Harrow regarding Edward Bowen (and Sheridan). The Bonsor family provide several opportunities such as 132 Salisbury Square, 6 Hill Street, 1 and 38 Belgrave Square, 51 Eaton Place and 11 Upper Belgrave Street or maybe the Combe & Co. buildings near Covent Garden or Polesden Lacey - National Trust permitting. John Lubbock already has a plaque at 29 Eaton Place but he was not the footballer and Edgar Lubbock could be remembered at 23 St. James's Place or 14 Berkeley Street, whilst A.C. Thompson was at 12 Montagu Square and the Wollastons at 36 Westbourne Place, 14 Coleshill Street, 63 St. George's Road and 8 Bloomfield Terrace. There is also the home of Kenyon-Slaney at 43 Belgrave Square who scored the first international goal in the world - this area was saturated with early amateurs and their families but there was no Belgravia F.C.!

The Royal Engineers also provide a number of opportunities for a blue plaque and for instance 45 Kensington Square could state: "William Merriman 1838-1917 Royal Engineer and Cup Final winner lived here." Other properties or their sites include Dubton House, Norton Lodge and Woodside whilst in London there are 54 Courtfield Gardens and 29 Cavendish Road West. The latter could state: "Hugh Mitchell 1849-1937 Royal Engineer, Solicitor, Gold Miner and Cup Finalist born here." Further to this there are 6 Douro Place or Cloister Ramp and the Post Office in Gibraltar. There are several properties regarding Cotter at Bournemouth or 17 Queen's Gate Terrace, London a building with a rich heritage, whilst 32 Seymour Street, Marylebone could have a plaque thus: "Herbert Hugh Muirhead 1850-1904 relative of James Watt and Cup Finalist lived here." There are also the homes of Addison and Goodwyn at 1 Catherine Place and 27 Park Street in Bath.

Etruria House would be a good choice stating: "Archibald Leitch 1865-1939 Football Ground Designer lived here," since it would exemplify his achievements, although there are opportunities at Cathcart Road, Bourneside, Barkston Gardens and Braehead. Despite these possibilities no such memorials are in existence. Are these people not important enough? What are the criteria for funding blue plaques? Is not the worldwide sport of soccer of sufficient merit? It would appear not and two facts have been ignored. Firstly it was the British who invented the game and secondly it was the people described in this book that brought it to fruition, formed the rules and promoted it. Perhaps soccer will soon be remembered in this way as with other sports. Meanwhile the sun had set on the Empire and the Wanderers and Engineers trudged from the pitch, hanging up their boots for the last time. The Victorian and Edwardian period had finally ended with the demise of F.J. Wall and J.C. Clegg and both the world and the sport of soccer had changed. There were troubled times ahead for both, however soccer had problems even in the early days and there was crowd trouble at Blackburn in 1880 and at Aston Villa in 1888. It is no wonder that the founders of the game feared professionalism since they had developed 'a sport of gentlemen'. Soccer was to be healthy entertainment watched by enthusiastic crowds and practices such as hacking were outlawed. These men of honour could lose with equanimity and their high ideals were included in the laws of the game.

Arthur Pember epitomised the early officials when he stated, "I do not submit to the suggestion of un-gentlemanly conduct." There were some equally revealing quotes from C.W. Alcock that take us to the roots of the game: "It was the winter of 1859-60 that really saw the first game of the great football revival." Regarding the Wanderers he stated, "Great things it is said from trivial causes spring," and this could also be applied to the early F.A. Further to this Alcock also asked for, "The protection of the genuine amateur by the legalisation of professionalism." Indeed J.C. Clegg exemplified the aims of the founders when he made the all en-compassing statement: "Nobody gets lost on a straight road." These gentlemen made compliments about one another but avoided discussing their own merits and the early match reports state, "We cannot abstain from saying that the play of Mr. Morley of Barnes and Mr C. Alcock of the Forest Club elicited great applause from the spectators." Alcock wrote great things of Alfred Kinnaird and stated, "He was without exception the best player of the day capable of taking any place in the field, is very fast and never loses sight of the ball, an excellent captain." There was an equally complimentary report on Mr. Alcock who was described as, "An excellent dribbler and goal-getter and very hard to knock off the ball." He also took his turn as referee but couldn't compare to the much admired Major Marindin who was honoured as, "One of the very few referees who really know all the rules." However Sir Charles Clegg summed up the flavour of the times when he said of Sir Frederick Wall, "I would remind you that he went to matches in a top hat and frock coat." This was clearly somewhat unique even at that time.

The first F.A. officials were a product of their time and presided over a game played by their fellow gentlemen. It is hoped that the foregoing biographies have shed new light on the early history of soccer and that the 'main players' have been revealed as never before. These histories are both educational and fascinating and combined with the development of the grounds provide a unique picture of the early days. The book is based mainly on original research from a large number of archive sources and detailed work in the field, and is grounded in the facts, however as with most theories there is always room for discussion. Indeed the only embellishment is for a positive reason, that is to say, to reproduce the atmosphere of the times. The result has been most satisfying and shows that 'fact is far stranger than fiction.' The research is as accurate as possible and the book has been written walking in the boots of Arthur Pember, "The Amateur Vagabond". Without doubt he was the most fascinating character to walk the corridors of the F.A. and wrote a good postscript over 130 years ago, thus the last word goes to him: "I have carefully avoided putting on finishing touches of imaginative colouring or even the very thinnest coat of varnish, being convinced that a plain unvarnished tale is after all the most interesting. Such as my sketches are I commend them to the reader in his or her spells of good nature simply pleading for faith in their honesty and truth." A.P.

Addendum

BASEVI - George Basevi was of Italian-Jewish origin and had several children in London with his wife Bathsheba and resided at Montague Street viz. Nathaniel (1773-1824), Maria (1775-1847), James (1784) of Cheltenham, and George Elias (1794-1845). The eldest Nathaniel was a merchant and lived at 6 Billiter Square in 1794 whilst Maria had a notable connection. Isaac D'Israeli (1766-1848) was born in Enfield but his father came from Venice and like Basevi he was Jewish. He was a writer who founded the Quarterly Review and married Maria Basevi at Bloomsbury in 1802 then had a son Benjamin on 21 December 1804. Their name was changed to Disraeli and the son was baptized C. of E. in 1817 to help his prospects. This paid off since he was elected M.P. for Maidstone in 1837 and was a writer of some note who produced political works such as Sybil (1845). He was a Tory politician being Chancellor in 1852, 1858-59 and 1866-68 then Prime Minister in 1868 and 1874-80. He left the House of Commons as Earl Beaconsfield in August 1876 and died on 19 April 1881. George Elias Basevi was born on 1 April 1794 and baptized with brother Nathaniel at St. Alphage's, Greenwich in May 1811. He was a pupil of Sir John Soane and he designed Belgrave Square apart from the corner houses in 1825 and the Fitzwilliam Museum, Cambridge (completed in 1848) - he died when working at Ely on 16 October 1845. Son James Palladio Basevi (1832-71) went to Addiscombe Military College and was a lieutenant R.E. then surveyor in India but died in the Himalayas. (Reference Bonsor Ch. 6).

HEBERDEN - William Heberden was born London in August 1710 and educated at St. Saviour's Grammar School and St. John's, Cambridge in 1724. He gained a B.A. in 1728, M.A. in 1732 and M.D. in 1739 then was a M.R.C.P in 1745. He had a practice at Cecil Street and was then physician to Prince George in 1748 and fellow of the Royal Society in 1749. He married Elizabeth Martin at St. Martin on 3 June 1752 and had a son Thomas (Canon) but his wife died in 1754. He then married Mary Wollaston (1729) sister of Francis at St. Botolph's, Aldersgate on 19 January 1760 and was made physician in ordinary to Queen Charlotte the next year. He attended Dr. Samuel Johnson (1709-84) who said he was the last of the learned physicians. He had eight children including William who was baptized at St. Martin on 28 March 1767, then moved to Pall Mall in 1770 and kept a house at Datchet - he died in London on 17 May 1801 but has a memorial at Windsor. William Heberden (1767-1845) was also a physician. (Reference Wollaston Ch. 6).

NORTHCOTE - The family are traced to the 12th century in Devon but Stafford Henry Northcote was born Marylebone on 27 October 1818. He entered politics and was private secretary to Gladstone at the Board of Trade in 1843, then married Cecilia Frances Farrer (1824) of Hampstead and had sons: Walter Stafford (1845-1927), Henry Stafford (1846-1911) and John Stafford (1850-1920). The father was a secretary of the Great Exhibition in 1851 and became 8th Baronet when his father died that year. He was M.P. for Dudley (1855) and Stamford (1858) but transferred to North Devon (1866). He was a Tory despite earlier associations and was the Chancellor under Disraeli from 1874 then Leader in the Commons when the latter was made a Lord in 1876. The Tories lost power in 1880 and Northcote a privy councillor, baronet and M.P. lived 30 St. James's Place in 1881 with wife Cecilia, daughter Margaret (24) born Upton Pyne and eight servants. He was made Earl of Iddesleigh in 1885 and given a position when Lord Salisbury formed a Government in August 1886 - Lord Randolph Churchill was briefly Chancellor until January 1887. The strain of government however was too much and Northcote died at Downing Street on 13 January 1887 - he was buried at Upton Pyne near Exeter. Walter S. Northcote was born at Marylebone on 7 August 1845 and married Elizabeth Lucy Thompson at Little Ouseburn on 23 September 1868 - Stafford Henry was born there on 29 August 1869 (died 1926). Walter was a commissioner in the Inland Revenue and lived at 23 Manchester Square in 1881 with wife Elizabeth L., three daughters and six servants. He became 2nd Earl at his father's decease and died in 1927 and was buried with his wife at Upton Pyne (she died 1928). Henry S. Northcote was M.P. for Exeter in 1880 and Governor of Bombay in 1899 being made Lord Northcote; he was Gov. General of Australia in 1904-08. Rev. John S. Northcote was prebendary of St. Paul's and vicar of St. Andrew's, Westminster - his son Henry Stafford (1901) became 3rd Earl. (Reference Thompson Ch. 7).

APPENDIX 1:
Football Association Rules 1863

1. The maximum length of the ground shall be 200 yards, the maximum breadth shall be 100 yards, the length and breadth shall be marked off with flags; and the goal shall be defined by two upright posts, eight yards apart, **without** any tape or bar across them.
2. A toss for goals shall take place, and the game shall be commenced by a place kick from the centre of the ground by the side losing the toss for goals; the other side shall not approach within 10 yards of the ball until it is kicked off.
3. After a goal is won, the losing side shall be entitled to kick off, and the two sides shall change goals after each goal is won.
4. A goal shall be won when the ball passes between the goal posts or over the space between the goal posts (at whatever height), not being thrown, knocked on, or carried.
5. When the ball is in touch, the first player who touches it shall throw it from the point on the boundary line where it left the ground in a direction at right angles with the boundary line, and the ball shall not be in play until it has touched the ground.
6. When a player has kicked the ball, any one of the same side who is nearer to the opponent's goal line is out of play and may not touch the ball himself, nor in any way whatever prevent any other player from doing so, until he is in play; but no player is out of play when the ball is kicked off from behind the goal line.
7. In case the ball goes behind the goal line, if a player on the side to whom the goal belongs first touches the ball, one of his side shall be entitled to a free kick from the goal line at the point opposite the place where the ball shall be touched. If a player of the opposite side first touches the ball, one of his side shall be entitled to a free kick at the goal only from a point 15 yards outside the goal line, opposite the place where the ball is touched, the opposite side standing within their goal line until he has had his kick.
8. If a player makes a fair catch, he shall be entitled to a free kick, providing he claims it by making a mark with his heel at once; and in order to take such a kick he may go back as far as he pleases, and no player on the opposite side shall advance beyond his mark until he has kicked.
9. No player shall run with the ball.
10. Neither tripping nor hacking shall be allowed, and no player shall use his hands to hold or push his adversary.
11. A player shall not be allowed to throw the ball or pass it to another with his hands.
12. No player shall be allowed to take the ball from the ground with his hands under any pretext whatever while it is in play.
13. No player shall be allowed to wear projecting nails, iron plates, or gutta percha on the soles or heels of his boots.

N.B. Gutta percha is a tough and flexible greyish-black substance formed from the hardened juice of Malayan trees (i.e. rubber).

APPENDIX 2:
F.A. Cup Finals 1872 - 1915

Year	Winner	Runner-Up	Score	Attendance
1872	Wanderers	Royal Engineers	1-0	2,000
1873	Wanderers	Oxford University	2-0	3,000
1874	Oxford University	Royal Engineers	2-0	2,000
1875	Royal Engineers	Old Etonians	2-0 (1-1)	3,000r
1876	Wanderers	Old Etonians	3-0 (1-1)	1,500r
1877	Wanderers	Oxford University	2-1	3,000
1878	Wanderers	Royal Engineers	3-1	4,500
1879	Old Etonians	Clapham Rovers	1-0	5,000
1880	Clapham Rovers	Oxford University	1-0	6,000
1881	Old Carthusians	Old Etonians	3-0	4,500
1882	Old Etonians	Blackburn Rovers	1-0	6,500
1883	Blackburn Olympic	Old Etonians	2-1	8,000
1884	Blackburn Rovers	Queen's Park	2-1	14,000
1885	Blackburn Rovers	Queen's Park	2-0	12,500
1886	Blackburn Rovers	West Brom Albion	2-0 (0-0)	15,000r
1887	Aston Villa	West Brom Albion	2-0	15,500
1888	West Brom Albion	Preston North End	2-1	19,000
1889	Preston North End	Wolves	3-0	22,000
1890	Blackburn Rovers	The Wednesday	6-1	20,000
1891	Blackburn Rovers	Notts County	3-1	23,000
1892	West Brom Albion	Aston Villa	3-0	32,810
1893	Wolves	Everton	1-0	45,000
1894	Notts County	Bolton Wanderers	4-1	37,000
1895	Aston Villa	West Brom Albion	1-0	42,560
1896	The Wednesday	Wolves	2-1	48,836
1897	Aston Villa	Everton	3-2	65,891
1898	Nottingham Forest	Derby County	3-1	62,017
1899	Sheffield United	Derby County	4-1	73,833
1900	Bury	Southampton	4-0	68,945
1901	Tottenham Hotspur	Sheffield United	3-1 (2-2)	114,815
1902	Sheffield United	Southampton	2-1 (1-1)	76,914
1903	Bury	Derby County	6-0	63,102
1904	Manchester City	Bolton Wanderers	1-0	61,374
1905	Aston Villa	Newcastle United	2-0	101,117
1906	Everton	Newcastle United	1-0	75,609
1907	The Wednesday	Everton	2-1	84,594
1908	Wolves	Newcastle United	3-1	74,697
1909	Manchester United	Bristol City	1-0	71,401
1910	Newcastle United	Barnsley	2-0 (1-1)	77,747
1911	Bradford City	Newcastle United	1-0 (0-0)	69,098
1912	Barnsley	West Brom Albion	1-0 (0-0)	54,556
1913	Aston Villa	Sunderland	1-0	121,919
1914	Burnley	Liverpool	1-0	72,778
1915	Sheffield United	Chelsea	3-0	49,557

Attendance is for the first game unless marked r for replay.

APPENDIX 3:
League Title 1889 - 1939

Year	Champion	Pts	Runner-Up	Pts
1889	Preston North End	40	Aston Villa	29
1890	Preston North End	33	Everton	31
1891	Everton	29	Preston North End	27
1892	Sunderland	42	Preston North End	37
1893	Sunderland	48	Preston North End	37
1894	Aston Villa	44	Sunderland	38
1895	Sunderland	47	Everton	42
1896	Aston Villa	45	Derby County	41
1897	Aston Villa	47	Sheffield United	36
1898	Sheffield United	42	Sunderland	37
1899	Aston Villa	45	Liverpool	43
1900	Aston Villa	50	Sheffield United	48
1901	Liverpool	45	Sunderland	43
1902	Sunderland	44	Everton	41
1903	The Wednesday	42	Aston Villa	41
1904	The Wednesday	47	Manchester City	44
1905	Newcastle United	48	Everton	47
1906	Liverpool	51	Preston North End	47
1907	Newcastle United	51	Bristol City	48
1908	Manchester United	52	Aston Villa	43
1909	Newcastle United	53	Everton	46
1910	Aston Villa	53	Liverpool	48
1911	Manchester United	52	Aston Villa	51
1912	Blackburn Rovers	49	Everton	46
1913	Sunderland	54	Aston Villa	50
1914	Blackburn Rovers	51	Aston Villa	44
1915	Everton	46	Oldham Athletic	45
1920	West Brom Albion	60	Burnley	51
1921	Burnley	59	Manchester City	54
1922	Liverpool	57	Tottenham Hotspur	51
1923	Liverpool	60	Sunderland	54
1924	Huddersfield Town	57	Cardiff City	57
1925	Huddersfield Town	58	West Brom Albion	56
1926	Huddersfield Town	57	The Arsenal	52
1927	Newcastle United	56	Huddersfield Town	51
1928	Everton	53	Huddersfield Town	51
1929	The Wednesday	52	Leicester City	51
1930	Sheffield Wednesday	60	Derby County	50
1931	Arsenal	66	Aston Villa	59
1932	Everton	56	Arsenal	54
1933	Arsenal	58	Aston Villa	54
1934	Arsenal	59	Huddersfield Town	56
1935	Arsenal	58	Sunderland	54
1936	Sunderland	56	Derby County	48
1937	Manchester City	57	Charlton Athletic	54
1938	Arsenal	52	Wolves	51
1939	Everton	59	Wolves	55

Games played in a season:
1889 - 22, 1892 - 26, 1893 - 30, 1899 - 34, 1906 - 38, 1920 - 42

APPENDIX 4:
Ground Opening Dates

Year	Ground	Club	Description
1860	Sandygate	Hallam	oldest football ground
1870	York Road	Maidenhead	oldest with one club
1874	Drill Field	Northwich Victoria	2nd oldest one club
1881	Deepdale	Preston North End	sport from 1875
1883	Turf Moor	Burnley	
"	Feethams	Darlington	cricket from 1866
"	Victoria Ground	Stoke	
1884	Racecourse Ground	Wrexham	first football 1872
1885	Gigg Lane	Bury	
1887	Saltergate	Chesterfield Town	also 1866-70 & 1880
1888	Oakwell	Barnsley St. Peter's	
1889	Bramall Lane	Sheffield United	cricket 1855, Owls 1868
"	Molineux	Wolves	sport 1860s
1890	Ewood Park	Blackburn Rovers	
"	Aggborough	Kidderminster Harr	formed in 1886
1891	Filbert Street	Leicester Fosse	
1892	Goodison Park	Everton	
"	Anfield	Liverpool	Everton from 1884
"	St James's Park	Newcastle United	Newcastle Rangers 1880
1893	Priestfield Stadium	New Brompton	later as Gillingham
1894	St James's Park	Exeter United	later Exeter City
1895	Burnden Park	Bolton Wanderers	
"	Baseball Ground	Derby County	sport from the 1880s
"	Sincil Bank	Lincoln City	
"	Old Showground	Brumby Hall	Scunthorpe United 1899
"	Loakes Park	Wycombe Wand.	
1896	Craven Cottage	Fulham	
"	Elm Park	Reading	
"	County Ground	Swindon Town	
"	Fellows Park	Walsall	called Hillary St. to 1930
1897	Villa Park	Aston Villa	sport from 1875
"	Eastville	Bristol Rovers	
"	Moss Rose Stadium	Hallfield	Macclesfield Town 1904
"	County Ground	Northampton Town	cricket from 1885
1898	City Ground	Nottingham Forest	
"	The Dell	Southampton	
"	Roker Park	Sunderland	
1899	Bloomfield Road	South Shore	merged with Blackpool
"	Highfield Road	Coventry City	
"	Blundell Park	Grimsby Town	
"	Fratton Park	Portsmouth	
"	Hillsborough	The Wednesday	Owlerton until 1914
"	White Hart Lane	Tottenham Hotspur	
1900	The Hawthorns	West Brom. Albion	
1902	Edgeley Park	Stockport County	rugby from 1891
1903	Valley Parade	Bradford City	Manningham Rugby 1886
"	Ayresome Park	Middlesbrough	
"	Home Park	Plymouth Argyle	rugby 1894 athletics 1901
1904	Griffin Park	Brentford	
"	Goldstone Ground	Brighton & Hove A.	Hove 1901, shared 1902

"	Ashton Gate	Bristol City	cricket, Bedminster 1896
"	Boleyn Ground	West Ham United	known as Upton Park
1905	Stamford Bridge	Chelsea	athletics from 1877
"	Kenilworth Road	Luton Town	
1906	St. Andrew's	Birmingham	
"	Sealand Road	Chester	
"	Gresty Road	Crewe Alexandra	
"	Boundary Park	Oldham Athletic	football from 1896
1907	Underhill	Barnet Alston	merged with Barnet 1912
"	Portman Road	Ipswich Town	
"	Spotland	Rochdale	rugby from 1878
"	Millmoor	Rotherham County	merged with Town 1925
1908	Leeds Road	Huddersfield Town	
1909	Brunton Park	Carlisle United	
"	Layer Road	Colchester Town	United from 1937
1910	Dean Court	Boscombe	Bournemouth & Bos 1923
"	Ninian Park	Cardiff City	
"	Victoria Ground	Hartlepools United	rugby from 1886
"	Old Trafford	Manchester United	
"	The Den	Millwall Athletic	
"	Meadow Lane	Notts County	
"	Gay Meadow	Shrewsbury Town	
"	Plainmoor	Ellacombe	merged Torquay United 1910
1912	The Vetch Field	Swansea Town	sport from 1891
"	Prenton Park	Tranmere Rovers	
"	Plough Lane	Wimbledon	moved to Milton Keynes 2003
1913	Highbury	The Arsenal	
1917	Loftus Road	Queens Park Rangers	Shepherd's Bush 1904
1919	The Valley	Charlton Athletic	
"	Elland Road	Leeds United	rugby 1878, City 1904
"	Fieldmill	Mansfield Town	cricket 1840, football 1861
1920	Springfield Park	Wigan Borough	football 1897, Latics 1932
"	Huish Park (old)	Yeovil Town	
1921	The Shay	Halifax Town	
1922	Vicarage Road	Watford	
"	Belle Vue Stadium	Doncaster Rovers	
1923	Maine Road	Manchester City	
1924	Selhurst Park	Crystal Palace	
1925	Manor Ground	Headington United	became Oxford Utd 1960
1932	Abbey Stadium	Abbey United	Cambridge Utd 1951
"	Whaddon Road	Cheltenham Town	
"	Bootham Crescent	York City	
1934	London Road	Peterborough Utd	Fletton Utd c.1905
"	York Street	Boston United	
1935	Carrow Road	Norwich City	
1937	Brisbane Road	Clapton Orient	Leyton 1905, Orient 1946
1946	Boothferry Park	Hull City	purchased in 1930
1950	Vale Park	Port Vale	
1955	Roots Hall	Southend United	already used 1906-16
1994	Nene Park	Rushden & D.	formed in 1992

APPENDIX 5:

'Football Graves Walking Tour'

Those who have travelled to New York will be familiar with the famous 'Skyscrapers Walking Tour' at the southern end of Manhattan. This takes in some of the most important buildings in the city and exposes their architectural merits. This suggested a similar idea for the graves of the F.A. Secretaries since they are all in walking distance of one another. The best starting point is at West Norwood Cemetery also known as the South Metropolitan Cemetery. This was similar in status to Highgate in north London and Nunhead in south London and was the resting place of the rich and famous. The main entrance is in Norwood High Street and a path leads eastwards to a large memorial in memory of James William Gilbert esquire F.R.S. (1794-1863) who was 'engaged in the science of banking.' This has some notable pinnacles and is beside a tropical tree and the right path should be taken up the hill. The restored family memorial to **Charles William Alcock** (1842-1907) is to be found half way up on the left and is most notable with an F.A. Cup engraved upon the white marble.

There are then frequent trains from West Norwood to Wandsworth Common Station and the journey is just three stops. Come out the station which has an entrance of some architectural interest and then turn right across the common along a path called 'The Avenue' that runs between a row of ancient gnarled trees. Go across Trinity Road and behind some Victorian houses with distinctive balconies and walk to the end of Loxley Road and turn right. The main entrance of Wandsworth Cemetery is found at the end and the former is located on a hillside with views across to Wimbledon Church. Take the main path into the cemetery and walk between the two chapels and the family memorial to **Sir Frederick Joseph Wall** (1858-1944) is found on the right - just before a circular path. This is quite distinctive with its red marble face and a memorial to his parents is to the front. Leave the cemetery and turn right into Magdalen Road and make a half-mile walk to Earlsfield Station. Take a train to Clapham Junction and then catch a connection to Barnes Station (3 stops).

Walk up the steps out of the station and note the ticket office with its ornate red brick chimneys and banding and turn left into Rocks Lane and walk for about 10 minutes and go across the traffic lights. Look out for some white posts beside the road and turn right up Ranelagh Path. Note the presence of Barn Elms Park and its sports ground on the left where the first club soccer was played in 1862. Barnes Old Cemetery is found in the trees immediately on the left and is now a nature reserve and the surviving graves are found within. Skirt around the southern edge to reach a clearing at the southeast corner and the wall of Putney Cemetery is seen on the right. The family memorial to **Ebenezer Cobb Morley** (1831-1924) can be found amongst the wood and brambles - at the extreme southeast corner. Walk back along Ranelagh Path and across the main road into Ranelagh Avenue and then into Glebe Road, and Laurel Road with its distinctive red brick houses that have some amazing tile work, friezes and lion gateposts. Walk across Barnes Common where Morley first played soccer and note the site of 'Rose Cottage' home of the Willis family to the right. Continue up Barnes High Street and turn left along The Terrace beside the River Thames. The main features to note are the historic Barnes Railway Bridge, a plaque to the composer Gustav Holst at no. 10, the home of Ebenezer Cobb Morley at no. 26 with its notable conservatory, and the White Hart Inn used by the rowing fraternity.

Turn left down White Hart Lane and a short distance along see Limes Field Road on the right. It was there that Barnes F.C. played soccer against teams such as Forest and Richmond. Keep going along the road to the level crossing and then turn right down South Worple Way or alternatively continue to Upper Richmond Road (and also turn right). A short distance along is Old Mortlake Cemetery in Avenue Gardens. Take the main path into the cemetery and near to the middle find row x where the family memorial to **Robert Watson Willis** (1843-92) is to be found - a short distance in on the east side. There is also a memorial to Fanny M. Graham the mother of **Robert George Graham** (1845-1922). The latter resided some distance away at Hampton and there is a memorial to him in the local parish church. The walk combined with the short train journeys can easily be done within a day and takes in the memorials, and other points of interest, pertaining to the first five F.A. Secretaries from 1863-1934.

Bibliography, Other Sources

GENERAL BIBLIOGRAPHY

History of the Football Association published for the F.A. - Geoffrey Green (The Naldrett Press October 1953)

Association Football - A.H. Fabian and Geoffrey Green (Caxton 1960)

Association Football and the Men Who Made It - Alfred Gibson and William Pickford (Caxton Publishing Co.)

100 Years of the F.A. Cup the official centenary history - Tony Pawson (William Heinemann Ltd. 1972)

A.A. Illustrated Guide to Britain (Drive Publications Ltd. 1973)

Heritage of Britain (Readers Digest Association Ltd. 1975)

Official History of the Football Association - Bryon Butler (Macdonald Queen Anne Press 1991)

Who's Who of Cricketers - Philip Bailey (Hamlyn 1993)

Official Illustrated History of the F.A. Cup - Bryon Butler (Headline 1996)

F.A. Cup Complete Results - Tony Brown (Soccer Data Publications 1999)

London Blue Plaque Guide - N. Rennison (Sutton Stroud 1999)

International Federation of Football History & Statistics - I.F.F.H.S. (F.I.F.A. approved)

Burke's Landed Gentry, Burke's Peerage and Baronetcy, Butterworth's Dictionary of Business Biography, Crockford's Clerical Directory, 19th Century Directories (England-Scotland), Hart's Army Lists, Law Society Records, The National Biography, The Naval Lists, Oxford and Cambridge Alumni, and Who's Who - Various Editions

Eton College List, Harrow School Register, Westminster School Register

International Genealogical Index (I.G.I.) - Mormon family records

The Times Newspaper and Index

Godfrey reproduction O.S. Maps (Barnes 1867, St. John's Wood 1868 and Clapham Park & Balham 1872)

GENERAL RESEARCH

The Family Record Centre, Myddelton Street, London -

Births, Marriages and Deaths; Census Returns 1841-1901; Nonconformist Records; Wills prior to 1858 and Consular Returns

The Public Record Office, Kew -

Army Records, Naval Records, Royal Engineers' service records

The Genealogical Society, Charterhouse Buildings, London

First Avenue House, High Holborn - Wills after 1858

The Metropolitan Archives, Northampton Road, Clerkenwell

The Mormon Family Record Centre, Exhibition Road, Kensington

The Guildhall Library and Map Room, Aldermanbury, London

The Westminster Archives, St. Ann's Street, Westminster

Scottish General Register Office, New Register House, Edinburgh

The Football Association Archives, 25 Soho Square, London

Family Search (I.G.I.), Free B.M.D., G.R.O. on-line, 1901 census, P.C.C. wills and G.R.O Scotland (internet sources)

Chapter 1 - The Barnes Football Association

Local Studies, L.B. Richmond Upon Thames, Old Town Hall, Whittaker Avenue, Richmond

Ebenezer Cobb Morley

The United Reformed Church History Society, Cambridge - M. Thompson

The Congregational Yearbook 1863/64; Sources for English Nonconformity

Hull Nonconformist Records; Hull Library - Local History Section

Richmond Football Club 1861-1925 - E.J. Ereaut (Howlett & Son)

Barnes Cemetery - Barnes & Mortlake History Society (1981)

Robert Watson Willis

St. Margaret's Westminster, St. George's Hanover Square - Parish Records

Westminster Archives - rate books and directories

Local Studies Richmond - Rose Cottage

Robert George Graham

Hinxton, Cambridgeshire Parish Records; Hinxton Church History; The Life & Times of Hinxton - V. Walker

Henry Thornton, Clapham Sect, E.M. Forster (websites)

Hampton and Teddington Past - John Sheaf and Ken Howe (Historical Publications); A.H. Wood, Hampton Church, Middlesex

Winifred Graham authoress (British Library website)

Chapter 2 - From Sunderland to Snaresbrook

Durham Record Office - wills; Sunderland Library - shipping records and Bishopwearmouth O.S. Map 1855 (25")

The Merchant Seamen's Orphan Asylum: Snaresbrook viz.

L.B. of Redbridge (archives), Ilford - O.S. Map of Snaresbrook 1863; Epping Forest Then and Now - W. Ramsey (1986); and Victoria History of Essex Vol. VI (Oxford University Press)

Forest Boys' School Archives - G. Wright

Chingford Library - reference Sunnyside and O.S. Map Chingford 1914

Chapter 3 - The Movers and Shakers

John Forster Alcock

2 Albert Villas, Twickenham - Map 1894-96 (Richmond Local Studies)

Divorce Causes - Kew Record Office

Stian Bjørnø Kjendal, Matrikkel Skaatø 1905, a register (website)

Sannidal og Skåtøy Bygdebok Bind II Skåtøyboka - J. Midgaard, Utgitt Ved En Komite (Naper - Kragerø 1950) viz.

Sannidal and Skåtøy country book volume II, book from Skåtøy, published by a committee.

Edward Bancroft & George Augustus Lamb (website)

Hertfordshire Local History - Berkhamsted by Scott Hastie

NORWAY RESEARCH

Kragerø Bibliotek, Nordraaksgt 1, 3770 Kragerø

Nils and Hege Sandvik, Skjørsvik Gård, Stabbestad, Norway

Charles William Alcock

The Oval Series of Games - Charles J.B. Marriott and C.W. Alcock (Routledge & Son Ltd. 1894)

The History of Surrey County Cricket Club with a personal view by Peter May - David Lemmon (Helm Series 1989)

The Father of Modern Sport - The life and times of Charles W. Alcock - Keith Booth (Parrs Wood Press 2002)

The Lyceum Clubs 1904-2004 (website)

Sir Frederick Joseph Wall

Essex Record Office, Chelmsford - Rainham Parish Records

Chelsea Library - St. Mark's College; Chelsea from five fields to the Worlds End - R. Edmonds (1956); Chelsea Past - Barbara Denny (1996)

Balham Cricket Ground - Map 1872 (Godfrey O.S. Maps)

Sutton Library - Local History Department

Sutton and Cheam Advertiser 30th March 1944

Chapter 4 - Beware of the Boot: Arthur Pember

D.J. Brown, Bridgnorth, Shropshire - 18th century family history

Timothy Duke - Chester Herald, College of Arms, London

Metropolitan Archives - Brixton Parish Records

St. John's Wood 1868, Clapham Park 1872 (Godfrey O.S. Maps)

Lists of Stock Exchange Members (Guildhall Library)

Bureau Des Guides, Musée Alpin and Bibliotèque (ENSA) in Chamonix, France.

Bateman's New Zealand Encyclopedia (1984); The Story of New Zealand - J. Bassett, K. Sinclair and M. Stenson (Reed 1998); E. Bohan, K. & K. Sinclair, R. Fry - Dictionary of New Zealand Biography (2003)

L.J. Dangerfield - additional New Zealand research

Allan Rainey, New York State Library, Albany; Mrs. Coreen P. Hallenback researcher in Albany

Smithsonian guides to History of America

Sabine's Dictionary of Books of selected Americana: The Mysteries & Miseries of the Great Metropolis - A. Pember (D. Appleton & Co.1874)

Poole's Index to Periodical Literature - author index 1802-1906: Lippincott's Magazine and Atlantic Monthly

Greenwood Cemetery, 500 - 25th Street, Brooklyn, U.S.A.

Arthur Conan Doyle memoirs and adventures - A.C. Doyle (Crowborough 1924); Conan Doyle his life - by Michael Coren (Bloomsbury 1995)

Fargo Photographic Website and North Dakota Census 1885

NEW YORK RESEARCH

The Municipal Archives, Chambers Street - B.M.D., City Directory

The National Archives, Varick Street - Soundex census

New York Central Library - New York Times

Chapter 5 - All the President's Men

Sir Francis Arthur Marindin

Burke's Landed Gentry - Davenport and Talbot

Beckenham - E. Inman & N. Tonkin (Phillimore & Co. Ltd. 1993)

Wedderburn-Colvile family, Robert Wedderburn (website)

Beckenham, Kent; Buckhorn Weston, Somerset - parish records

Craigflower Farm, Canada (British Columbia Heritage 1998)

Genealogical Society - Lawrence of Jamaica pedigree; Guide to Mauritius

Carnegie Public Library, Abbot Street, Dunfermline - "Craigflower"

Lord Arthur Fitzgerald Kinnaird

Burke's Peerage and Baronetcy, National Biography

The Queen's Scotland (The Heartland) by Nigel Tranter - Rossie Priory

William Lamb, Lord Melbourne (website)

Correspondence of W.H. Fox Talbot 6 November 1847 (Glasgow University)

St. James's Paddington - Parish Records

Local History, Bromley Library - Plaistow Lodge

Sir John Charles Clegg

Sheffield Local Studies and Archives, 52 Shoreham Street, Sheffield

Sheffield Parish Records - The Cathedral; St. Mary's Bramall Lane

Who's Who - J.C. Clegg and W.E. Clegg

Chapter 6 - The Eton Rifles

Morton Peto Betts

Institute of Civil Engineers, 1-7 Great George Street, London

The Frank D. Smith Collection - W. Betts, E.L. Betts, G. Giles, S.M. Peto

The story of Gosport - Leonard White (Portsmouth Library)

Isle of Wight Record Office, 26 Hillside, Newport

Local History, Bromley Library - The Betts family, The Holmwood

Alexander George Bonsor

Polesden Lacey House, Surrey - National Trust

The Westminster Archives - Combe, Delafield & Co Ltd

Joseph Bonomi - Cambridge University Library (website)

Rudy Vanhalewyn, Knokke Heist Archives, Belgium

Brussels and Vilvoorde, Belgium - Population Records (Local Govt.)

William Slaney Kenyon-Slaney

Burke's Peerage and Baronetcy; Public Record Office Kew - Royal Licence

Charles Henry Reynolds Wollaston

National Biography - Wollaston; Cambridge University - Reynolds

Crockford's Clerical Directory; Lancing School Records

Thomas Charles Hooman

Local History Department, Kidderminster Library - map 1859

Carpets from Kidderminster - Legat; Kidderminster since 1800 - Tomkinson Hall; History of Kidderminster - Burton

Charterhouse School; Highgate Street Directories and Map

Chapter 7 - The Harrow Chequers

Robert Walpole Sealy Vidal

Somerset Record Office - Bridgwater Parish Records (Sealy)

North Devon Record Office, Tuly Street, Barnstaple - Senior Archivist; Helen Naomi Richardson Collection - Vidal miscellany

Public Record Office, Kew - Royal Licence

Edward Ernest Bowen

Peter J. Lineham - Dictionary of New Zealand Biography (2003)

Isle of Wight Record Office, 26 Hillside, Newport

Osborne House and Christchurch, Totland, Isle of Wight

Harrow School Archives, 5 High Street, Harrow; Cricketer's Who's Who

William Parry Crake

William Crake - Middlesex Victoria County History 1989

Ealing and St. Marylebone Parish Records; Harrow School Register

Paddington - Ealing History; Charles Thomas Lucas (websites)

Edgar Lubbock

National Biography - Lubbock, Whitbread; Who's Who

Local History Department, Bromley Library - High Elms

St. James's Piccadilly, St. Peter's Pimlico - Parish Records

History of Kent County Cricket Club - Dudley Moore

Albert Childers Meysey-Thompson

Burkes Peerage and Baronetcy; Law Society Records

Thomas's Hotel, Berkeley Square, Mayfair - map 1870 picture 1890

The Times Newspaper - Change of Name

Lascelles - Harewood House (website)

Reginald Courtenay Welch

Law Society Records; Local History Department, Twickenham Library

Richmond Local Studies - Lancaster Lodge, Twickenham O.S. Map 1863

Farnham Library - Army College, Heath End - sale June 1948 and Heath End O.S. Map 1897

Chapter 8 - The Royal Engineers

Royal Engineers Library, Brompton Barracks, Chatham - team details

Army Campaigns in the 19th century (website)

Henry Waugh Renny-Tailyour

Burke's Peerage and Baronetcy; Public Record Office, Kew - Royal Licence

Cheltenham School Register; Cricketer's Who's Who

Angus Archives, Montrose Library, 214 High Street, Montrose

Lobengulu - History of Matabeleland (website)

Powerscourt and Clontarf Castle, Ireland (websites)

Isle of Wight Record Office, 26 Hillside, Newport

Guinness Archives, St. James's Gate, Dublin

Hugh Mitchell

Hart's Army Lists; The Law Society Records; Gibraltar Archives

29 Cavendish Road West, St. John's Wood 1868 (Godfrey O.S. Maps)

Isle of Wight Record Office, 26 Hillside, Newport

Danny - The Country House Association

Henry Bayard Rich

The Bayard and Carroll families of Philadelphia - (website)

Appleton's Cyclopedia of American Biography (1887-89)

Jeremiah D'Olier, Frederick J. and Henry R. Crooke (website)

Dulwich College (D. Young) and various websites

Hart's Army List; World Gazetteer - reference British Guiana

Herbert Hugh Muirhead

National Biography - Boulton, Watt and Muirhead; Soho House Records and the Lunar Society

Charles Sturt - soldier and Australian explorer (website)

Esquimalt, Vancouver Island, Canada (website)

Adam Bogle

Francis Perigal - Middlesex Victoria County History 1911

Benjamin Du Terreau - Australian artist (website); Twynihoe William Erle barrister and writer (website); Harrow School Register

Chapter 9 - The Gibraltar Connection: Edmund William Creswell

East Sussex Record Office, Lewes - parish records and other papers

A walk up The Street, Kingston Village near Lewes

Australian Dictionary of Biography 1891-1939 Univ. Press Melbourne 1979 re Chataway; I.G.I., Times obituary and website re Moberly

Local Studies Library, Merton Civic Centre, London Road re Brackenburys School, Wimbledon

Historic Wimbledon / Two Wimbledon Roads - R. Milward

Bruce Castle Museum, Lordship Lane, London; School (various websites)

G.F. Watts and C.H. Rickards (various websites)

GIBRALTAR RESEARCH

Vital Records: Birth, Marriage and Death - 3 Secretary's Lane

Kings Chapel of the Convent next to the Governor's Residence

Gibraltar Archives - Gibraltar Chronicle, Census, Blue Lists, Post Office

Holy Trinity Cathedral, Gibraltar - Albert Langston

Chapter 10 - The Empire Builders

Edmond William Cotter

St. Anselm's Church, Kingsway, Lincoln's Inn Fields

Public Record Office, Kew - Army Service Records, Army Memorandum, Muster Rolls, Naval Records, Hart's Army Lists

Crimean War History; General Encyclopedia - the Zhob Valley (website)

Malta & Gozo AA Guide; Malta Globetrotter - B. Richards

Fort St. Elmo, Fort Ricasoli, Malta History, Corfu History (website)

Malta Family History including Barracca Chapel (website)

MALTA RESEARCH

St. Paul's Shipwreck, St. Paul Street, Valletta (Father Wilson)

St. Dominic's, Merchants Street, Valletta (Father Paul Gatt)

National Archives, Santo Spirito Hospital, Rabat - Malta

George William Addison

Huddersfield Local History and William Brook, Meltham (website)

Local Studies Library, High Street, Paisley; David Rowands - "Paisley"

Cheltenham School Register; Local Studies, Bath Public Library

Guinness Archives, St. James's Gate, Dublin

MALTA RESEARCH

St. Paul's Anglican Cathedral, West Street, Valletta (Michael Calleja)

Public Registry, 26 Old Treasury Street, Valletta (S. Bugeja)

Alfred George Goodwyn

The Brewing Industry: A Guide to Historical Records - L. Richmond & A. Turton (Manchester University Press 1990)

The Brewing Industry in England 1700-1830 - Peter Mathias (Cambridge University Press 1959 reprint Gregg Revivals 1993)

Samuel Enderby of Greenwich and whaling; William Barnard shipbuilder of Deptford (websites)

Guildhall Library, Aldermanbury, London - parish records

Local Studies, Barnet Library - R. Calder (Mill Hill Historical Society)

Hart's Army Lists; Local Studies, Bath Public Library

Isle of Wight Record Office, 26 Hillside, Newport

William Merriman

Burkes Peerage and Baronetcy - Merriman and Somerset

National Biography; St. Mary Abbots, Kensington - parish records

Thackeray, Pattle, Prinsep etc. (various websites)

The Manor House, Barnes - Map 1867 (Godfrey O.S. Maps)

Half Time - The Wanderers Engineer a Win

The Sportsman Newspaper - 19th March 1872 (Bromley Library)

FOOTBALL GROUNDS - GENERAL

Millwall a complete record 1885-1991 *fixtures* - R. Lindsay (Breedon 1991)

Breedon Book of Football League Records - G. Smailes (Breedon 1992)

Guinness Record of the F.A. Cup - semi-finals (1993)

The Cassell Soccer Companion - D. Pickering (1994)

Football Grounds from the Air - Dave Twydell (Dial House 1995)

Football Grounds of Britain *Editions 1-3* - Simon Inglis (Harper Collins 1996)

Football Grounds from the Air - Then and Now (Dial House1998)

Non-League Football 1999 - John Robinson (Soccer Books Ltd. 1998)

Rothmans Book of Football Records - J. Rollin (Headline 1998)

Rothmans Football Yearbook - J. Rollin

Sunday Times Illustrated History of Football - C. Nawrat, S. Hutchings

Cambridge Evening News - 2nd August 2002 (Parker's Piece)

Football Programmes, League & Non-League - about 500

Chapter 11 - The Rovers and Quakers

A General History of Accrington F.C. (Accrington Library)

Wellington Road, Aston Villa - O.S. 1889 (Birmingham Ref. Library)

Leamington Street, Blackburn Rovers - O.S. 1893 (Blackburn Library)

Pikes Lane, Bolton Wanderers - O.S. 1889 (Bolton Library)

The Racecourse Ground, Derby County - O.S. 1881 (Derby Library)

Meadows Cricket Ground, Town Ground and Meadow Lane (sites), Castle Cricket Ground, Trent Bridge, City Ground - O.S. 1901 (Nottingham Library)

Stoney Lane, West Bromwich - O.S. 1889 (Birmingham Ref. Library)

Chapter 12 - Up For The Cup

Kennington Oval 1888; Lillie Bridge Athletic Ground 1874; Lillie Bridge and Stamford Bridge 1888 - O.S. maps (Metropolitan Archives)

Fallowfield - Looking back at Rusholme & Fallowfield (1984)

To the Palace for The Cup - Bevan, Hibberd, Gilbert (Replay 1999)

The Crystal Palace c.1860 - Beckenham - E. Inman & N. Tonkin (Phillimore & Co. Ltd. 1993)

Map of The Crystal Palace 1929-30 (Croydon Library)

Chapter 13 - The London Connection

The New Manor Ground O.S. 1897 (Greenwich Local History)

The Manor Ground in 1914 (Godfrey O.S. Maps)

The Memorial Ground, West Ham O.S. 1916 (Newham Local History)

Kensal Rise Athletic Ground O.S. 1894, 1913 (Cricklewood Local History)

Park Royal Ground O.S. 1914-15 (Cricklewood Local History)

Chapter 14 - Kop A Load Of This

Leeds Road, Huddersfield O.S. 1932 (Huddersfield Library)

Chapter 15 - Tracing Glasgow: Archibald Leitch

Topographical & Historical Gazetteer of Scotland (1848)

Mormon Family Record Centre - Scottish Vital Records;
New Register House, Edinburgh - certificates

Institute of Mechanical & Consulting Engineers, 1 Birdcage Walk,
London - Proceedings and Memoirs 1939 volume 141

Scotland Street School Museum, Glasgow

The Story of Celtic - Official History - Gerald McNee

John Street Stand, England v Scotland 1903, Bramall Lane (I.F.F.H.S.)

Linthorpe Road, Middlesbrough O.S. 1895 (Middlesbrough Library)

West London Press, 8th September 1905 - Chelsea & Fulham

Chapter 16 - Etruscan Days: Archibald Leitch

Wedgwood - Darwin and Etruria (website)

Lonsdale Road, Barnes O.S. 1894 (Richmond Library)

Bourneside O.S. 1896 and picture (Palmers Green Archives)

Southgate: A glimpse into the past - A. Dumayne

The Bourne, Southgate - Enfield in old photographs - A. Dumayne

Chapter 17 - For King and Country: Archibald Leitch

Millfields Road, Clapton Orient O.S. 1915 (Hackney Local History)

Mrs. H. Brew, Southgate - family history

Chapter 18 - It's Not Cricket

Ashton Gate O.S. 1902; St. John's Lane O.S. 1943 (Bristol Local History)

Cassio Road, Watford O.S. 1914 (Watford Local History)

Trent Bridge Cricket Ground O.S. 1901 (Nottingham Local History)

Anlaby Road, Hull City O.S. 1928 (Hull Local History)

Bradford Park Avenue O.S 1932 (Bradford Local History)

Bramall Lane, Sheffield O.S 1889 and 1924 (Sheffield Local History)

Chapter 19 - The Re-Election Lottery

Blue House Field O.S. 1895; Newcastle Road O.S 1896 (Sunderland Local History)

The Excelsior Ground, Birmingham O.S 1889 (Birmingham Ref. Library)

History of New Brighton F.C.; Advertisement for New Brighton Tower; Local O.S. Map 1899 (Birkenhead Library)

History of Burton Football; Peel Croft, Burton O.S. 1901 (Burton Library)

Custom House Ground, Thames F.C. 1919; West Ham Greyhound Stadium c. 1930 revised (Newham Local History)

Sandheys Park, New Brighton O.S. 1926 (Birkenhead Library)

Redheugh Park, Gateshead O.S. 1939 (Gateshead Library)

Peel Park, Accrington O.S. 1931 (Accrington Library)

Chapter 20 - Time To Make A Stand

The Kursaal O.S. 1922 and The Stadium O.S. 1951 (Southend Library)

The Nest, Norwich City O.S. 1914 (Norwich Local History)

Raikes Hall O.S. 1893; Athletic Ground O.S 1912 (Blackpool Library)

East Ferry Road in 1893: Lions Through The Lens; East Ferry Road O.S. 1894 and North Greenwich O.S. 1916 (Greenwich Library)

Croydon Common Athletic Ground O.S. 1912 (Croydon Library)

Lea Bridge Road, Clapton Orient O.S. 1939 (Waltham Forest Local History)

The Old Showground O.S. 1962 (Scunthorpe Library)

Maps and Photographs

All original photographs are by J.B. Smart unless otherwise stated. The portraits of the F.A. officials are mainly from History of the Football Association (1953) and other early publications - these pictures once lined the walls of the corridor at Lancaster Gate. Every effort has been made to trace the owners of the pictures used, where possible, and the relevant permissions are listed below. The maps are 'out of copyright' and reproduced from the (date) Ordnance Survey.

Introspection - Parker's Piece, Cambridge; Freemasons Tavern, Great Queen Street, Holborn; William McGregor (1846-1911)

Ch. 1 - Richmond Green; Ebenezer Cobb Morley (1831-1924) by kind permission of Barnes and Mortlake Historical Society; 26 The Terrace, Barnes; Memorial to E.C. Morley

St. Margaret's, Westminster; Rose Cottage, Barnes by kind permission of the Local Studies Library (L.B. Richmond); 5 Beverley Villas, Barnes

Robert George Graham (1845-1922) and St. Alban's, Hampton by kind permission of the Local Studies Library (L.B. Richmond); Memorial to R.G. Graham

Ch. 2 - Druries House at Harrow; Sunnyside Lodge, Chingford

Ch. 3 - 14 Park Square East, Marylebone; "Exhims", Northchurch; A view towards Kragerø; Skjørsvik Farm; Blåbær Tjenna; Charles William Alcock (1842-1907); 16 Ennerdale Road, Kew; Memorial to C.W. Alcock

Balham 1872; Sir Frederick Joseph Wall (1858-1944); 22 Lancaster Gate, Hyde Park; Memorial to Sir F.J. Wall

Ch. 4 - Cave Calcem - "Beware of the Boot" from Fox Davies Armorial Families 1929; Lyttelton, New Zealand; Lyttelton Harbour

Arthur Pember (1835-1886) from Mysteries & Miseries of the Great Metropolis A. Pember (1874); Mont Blanc, Chamonix; Arthur Pember on Mont Blanc from Mysteries & Miseries etc.

1233 Third Avenue, New York; 1231-37 Third Avenue; The Canal Boatman, Model Costermonger and Amateur Beggar all from Mysteries & Miseries etc.

Ch. 5 - Craigflower, Scotland; Sir Francis Arthur Marindin (1838-1900); 22 Sussex Villas, Kensington

Ponsonby Memorial; 35 Hyde Park Gardens; Lord Arthur Fitzgerald Kinnaird (1847-1923); 10 St. James's Square; Blue Plaque at 10 St. James's Square

Sir John Charles Clegg (1850-1937)

Ch. 6 - Edward Ladd Betts (1815-72); Polesden Lacey, Great Bookham; 6 Hill Street, Berkeley Square; 51 Eaton Place, Belgravia; 11 Upper Belgrave Street

Ch. 7 - Valletta, Malta: Robert Walpole Sealy Vidal (1853-1914) by kind permission of B. Richardson from the Helen Naomi Richardson Collection; Edward Ernest Bowen (1836-1901) by kind permission of Harrow School Archives; The Grove, Harrow; Memorial to E.E. Bowen; The Army College, Heath End from a prospectus for sale of the college (Farnham Library)

Ch. 8 - The Royal Engineers Team 1872 by kind permission of the Royal Engineers Library, Chatham; Dubton House, Montrose; Memorial to H.W. Renny-Tailyour; 6 Douro Place, Kensington; Blue Plaque at 6 Douro Place; Cloister Ramp, Gibraltar; Edinburgh Panorama

Ch. 9 - Memorial to the Royal Engineers; Agent for the Packets letter of appointment from Gibraltar Archives; Gibraltar Chronicle - Advertisement from local newspaper; Holy Trinity Cathedral, Gibraltar

Rock of Gibraltar; Brackenburys School; E.W. Creswell birth certificate from Gibraltar Register Office; Bruce Castle School by kind permission of Bruce Castle Museum, Haringey

Ch. 10 - Valletta Panorama; Fort Ricasoli; Fort St. Elmo; Fort Entrance; Barracca Chapel; 1 Catherine Place, Bath; Upper Barracca Gardens; St. Paul's pro-Cathedral; Engineers' Quarter; Memorial to Goodwyn; 14 Catherine Place, Bath; 45 Kensington Square; Raglan Castle

Ch. 11 - Leamington Street 1893; Pikes Lane 1889

Ch. 12 - Lillie Bridge Athletic Ground 1874; Crystal Palace Stadium 1929-30; Wembley Stadium; World Cup 1966

Ch. 13 - The Manor Ground, Woolwich 1914; Craven Cottage, Fulham painting by J.B. Smart

Ch. 14 - Aston Villa - Villa Park and Wolves - Molineux both paintings by J.B. Smart

Ch. 15 - Archibald Leitch birth certificate from Scottish Register Office; 97 Buchanan Street, Glasgow; The Pavilion, Fulham; The Main Stand, Fulham; Argyll Arcade, 30 Buchanan Street; Entrance to 34 Argyll Chambers

Ch. 16 - "Etruria House", 49 Lonsdale Road, Barnes; Main Stand East and West, Dens Park, Dundee

Ch. 17 - "Bourneside" by kind permission of Palmers Green Library; Southgate 1896; South Stand, Ibrox Park; Grand Façade; "The Glory Days"

Ch. 18 - Bradford Park Avenue 1932; The Circle, Anlaby Road 1928; Bramall Lane, Sheffield 1924

Ch. 19 - The Tower Ground 1899; Peel Croft, Burton 1901; Redheugh Park 1939; Peel Park, Accrington 1931

Ch. 20 - The Nest, Norwich 1914; Kensal Rise 1894; Arsenal Stadium; East Stand, Highbury

General Index

A

B

C

D

E

F

G

H

I

J

K

L

M

N

O

P

Q

R

S

T

X, Y, Z

Names Index

A

B

C

D

E

N

O

P

Q

R

S

X, Y, Z